A-Z *of*

DOOM,
GOTHIC &
STONER METAL

GARRY SHARPE-YOUNG

www.rockdetector.com

This edition published in Great Britain
in 2003 by Cherry Red Books Ltd.,
Unit 17, 1st Floor, Elysium Gate West,
126–128 New King's Road,
London SW6 4LZ

All you need to know about the author:
Born: Münchengladbach 1964
Raised: On Judas Priest
Status: Decade of wedlock
Raising: Kerr, Krystan, Kjaric
Hair: By Vikernes

Typeset by Sarah Reed.
Printed and bound in Great Britain by
Biddles Ltd., Guildford and King's Lynn.
Cover Design by Jim Phelan at Wolf Graphics Tel: 020 8299 2342

ISBN 1-901447-14-6

Introduction

Doom, Gothic & Stoner Metal

Doom, Gothic, Stoner. All branches from a very twisted and gnarled old bit of the evolutionary Rock n' Roll tree. This book is undoubtedly the most diverse of the Rockdetector A-Zs to date, collecting together bands that would almost certainly never share stage space or audience appreciation. What they share is a sombreness and depressive bent that has taken them to the edge. Stylistically it may be a different edge these bands find themselves teetering on and the journey of discovery may have brought forth unique musical experiences, but they are all staring down into the same awning abyss.

The 'missing link' and the key that binds 90% of these artists is no palaentological puzzle. Seekers of the Doom and Stoner grail don't have to torture themselves scrabbling for mythical slabs of ancient vinyl. It is there for all to see, for the public to wonder at, the devoted to humble themselves to and Sanctuary Music to distribute. Surpassing the pyramids for sheer weight of truth, Black Sabbath rises unlike any man-made edifice before or since. If you have read this far you are an owner of a Black Sabbath album.

If, by some surreal quirk of mother nature you do not own a Sabbath album, with time travel, genetic mutation, earthquake or recent house fire being the only plausible excuses to offer, it is a prerequisite of reading further. That's right. Put the book back on the shelf and make your way to the nearest record store. There simply is no point in you persevering without the basic knowledge to understand what lies before you…

Back? You never left right? Let's deal with Doom first. All Doom bands venerate Black Sabbath. This is a universal truism that is unquestioned and heretical to even contemplate otherwise. Black Sabbath have sold over fifty million albums (yes, the equivalent of the entire population of New Zealand owning the entire Ozzy catalogue) whilst most Doom acts will be hard pressed to sell five thousand. There are no pretenders and even though it is often vacated the throne is quite safe.

In spite of the statistics governing commercial success of post Sabbath Doom bands there has been no abatement in the flow of young musicians scoring a roach, firing up a Sunn amp, striking that first detuned chord and basking in the glory of getting really down… The phrases 'Doom Metal' and 'business plan' do not occupy the same aether let alone the same language. All ye who enter are doomed.

Perversely, this is what makes Doom so appealing. There are no bands in it for the money, the fame or the stardom. There is only one reason Doom bands function and that is to make the best possible music they can. The music drives everything. Success for these artists is to release two or three albums on a cult, underground label, travel North America and Europe in conditions that would leave a Nubian slave reeling and then split up. By the time you have achieved this you will still be wearing the same clothes you started in, your gear will have been stolen and your beard will be on the floor. Oh, and you will have recorded a cover version of a Black Sabbath song for the flip side of another cult band which, when you compare it to the original, will leave you wallowing in rivers of misery. After a due period of hermit-like contemplation attempting to fathom your place on this planet, a renewed sense of purpose will take over, a means to which you can escape your mundane existence and find true fulfilment. You will start another Doom band...

That is the lot of a Doom musician, a worldwide breed but with a strange concentration in the Maryland area. Doom is so resilient that it has also seeped like a wind borne plague into other Metal strains. The obvious one is 'Stoner-Doom' but there are many Doom-Death, symphonic Doom, drone Doom, Christian Doom and Black-Doom acts too. As already stated, success and Doom do not go hand in hand. However, there are bands that have managed to claw some kind of notoriety from the flotsam & jetsam left in the wake of the S.S. Sabbath.

In England Cathedral occupies a stately position befitting its title. Leader Lee Dorrian's shadow is long and casts itself over a myriad of bands and projects. Cathedral have even supported Black Sabbath and occupied the same recording studio with the masters. In the Doom world this is on a par with sainthood for Mr. Dorrian. Musically Cathedral have struck out on their own path adding an eccentric edge courtesy of Dorrian's lyrical bent.

Chicago's Trouble exemplify Doom statesmanship. They are hallowed yet in their lifetime never attained the riches they deserved. This also applies to Saint Vitus, Pentagram and The Obsessed. A triumvirate of bands whose reputation still reverberates globally. The common factor between two of these artists – Saint Vitus and The Obsessed – is Scott Weinrich. Commonly known as Wino the man has made a huge mark upon both Doom and Stoner.

The Scandinavians naturally make an impression here. Candlemass's musical integrity matched the girth of lead vocalist Messiah Marcolin's cassock enclad stomach. Candlemass were heavy, very heavy.

Another driving force on the scene was the long defunct German Hellhound label. This bunch of Teutonic Doom worshippers gave every band with a Maryland zip code a deal and proceeded to pump out classic after classic. Naturally it was all to collapse within a very short space of time but their Spartan-like stand has become the stuff of legend. Hellhound, rather like the bumblebee that has scientifically been proven theoretically incapable of flight, defied all the laws of nature and still came up trumps.

Stoner is more controversial. Is Stoner merely another adjunct of Doom or is it is own beast? It is difficult to tell, as most bands when labelled Stoner protest vehemently. Hindsight may well afford us the benefit of being able to look at the Stoner phenomenon in its true light. I suspect it may be seen to be a rather hollow phrase rather like Grunge, a practical title for a very disparate collective of artists whose only real kinship was timing. There are a lot of Stoner tagged artists that are in fact Southern Rock bands and even plain old 80's Hard Rock acts. Where are we when The Stoner Kings just sound like Guns n' Roses?

Stoner would not exist had it not been for a bunch of Californian desert based Rockers named Kyuss. Now, of course, Kyuss likewise would still be in the gene pool if not for Black Sabbath. Kyuss have been branded in retrospect as having delivered 'perfect' music. When the band collapsed related acts such as Fu Manchu, Queens Of The Stone Age and Unida soon shot up and the spores carried far and wide. Before long a whole derivative epidemic of Kyuss-like acts were doing their thing.

The main factor that stood Stoner apart from Doom was that some of these bands were just too damn happy. Despite operating with the requisite gear, tuning down and getting utterly moroseful on occasion, Stoners revelled in vans with garish '70s paint jobs, skateboards, cool black chicks with outrageous afros, hippie-like band logos and an odd aversion to wearing black.

Europe, and in particular Sweden, lapped up Stoner and was soon re-manufacturing a whole stream of clones. Stoner's reach would extend further into Acid Rock, a realm in which a band such as Monster Magnet even managed to squeeze some very tangible commercial success out of.

As Stoner evolved it appeared that many of the bands lumped in with the first wave were in fact just good ol' Southern Rockers with more in common with Molly Hatchet and Lynyrd Skynyrd. It would soon dawn that what many of these bands were doing was delivering nothing less and nothing more than honest to goodness Rock n' Roll. Not surprising really when the genre goes under the microscope, today's bands cite their influences as '70s troopers such as Leafhound, Mountain, Black Widow, Budgie, Hawkwind, The Edgar Broughton Band and before that Blue Cheer.

Doom, Gothic, Stoner... they trip off the tongue so easily. Yet, you would not be finding fans of each tripping over each other in the concert hall. Gothic has suffered at its own hands in becoming better known outside of the clan for its fashion statements rather than its music. Gothic Metal has in fact mirrored the rise of Doom and for a while a whole crop of European and Scandinavian acts were proud to pull in the necessary soprano backing vocalist in a black wedding dress and announce themselves as Gothic Doom.

Unlike Doom and Stoner, the Gothic scene incorporates many indie elements that make a distinct mark through such sub-genres as Darkwave and Electro Goth. Other forces play an influential role here too, with The Sisters Of Mercy (much as they detest it), The Mission, The Cult and Fields Of The Nephilim being of prime importance. Groups that have carved a career for themselves include Finns Him and Paradise Lost. The latter actually a striking example of how rapidly a group can morph over each successive album to become an entirely new beast. Paradise Lost were one of the first Gothic Metal acts, adding a sense of melancholy to their formative Death Metal. My Dying Bride and Anathema, two other leaders in this field, blossomed from not only the same geographical 'bleak oop North' area but the same label Peaceville. A doff of the cap to Hammy for either recognising a pool of genius or fortuitously being in the right pub at the right time. Interestingly both My Dying Bride and Anathema would also struggle with their musical identity as time drew on.

In Europe Gothic Metal flowered into something entirely unexpected. A whole crop of bands that happened to be female fronted were quickly deemed to represent a new force in music whereas in reality bands such as Theatre Of Tragedy, Flowing Tears and The Gathering were light years apart. Premier Black Metal bands such as Dimmu Borgir and Cradle Of Filth wholeheartedly embraced Goth, the imagery and the bombasity serving them well. Both acts drew in choirs, female backing vocals and duly set themselves apart from the pack.

Of all the Rockdetector A-Zs this is the one which will prompt the question 'What on earth is that band doing in there?'. An explanation; groups have been included on grounds of fan appreciation, their influential qualities, their own words or their own music. Inspirational bands included are artists such as Leafhound, Edgar Broughton, Atomic Rooster and Blue Cheer. I could so easily have thrown in Depeche Mode, Hawkwind and Mountain the range is that vast.

Eldritch can bitch all he likes about the quality of his fan base but the fact remains that a huge proportion of his followers are proud to consider themselves Goths. It's just a label, no big deal. Soundgarden are included because, to me, they are Grunge only by default. I listen and hear Black Sabbath not Nirvana. Likewise the Melvins, Electric Frankenstein, Misfits, Prong, Danzig, Neurosis, et al. All very different, all cited as influential.

The common thread for most of these bands is that they have endeavoured to pursue a different path than the expected. What is surprising is that so many have opted to embark upon this journey in a bleak frame of mind.

My personal recommendation is to read this book listening to Saint Vitus, Tommermen, Ruin, Bottom, Slow Horse, Novembers Doom, While Heaven Wept and Flowing Tears with sufficient volume to push your local mountain range into the nearest sea.

ABOUT ROCKDETECTOR

www.rockdetector.com is the world's largest Rock devoted website. These pages are taken directly from the website. As I write it hosts information, including unique biographies and full global discographies, on over 11,800 bands. When you pick up this book tomorrow it will have even more.

We're on a mission at Rockdetector to document Rock music of all genres, persuasions and nationalities, old and new and of every persuasion.

We try to do this in a non-biased, non-opinionated manner. It matters to us that we get our facts straight and aid the promotion of all Rock artists.

We thrive on information. If you have any fact, album cover, band history or discography detail we're presently missing then contribute. If we've got anything wrong – tell us.

We are also actively looking for dedicated Rock fans with specialist knowledge of genres or territories to contribute. If you're the man who knows all the ins and outs on the Bangladeshi Emocore scene then we need to hear from you. Seriously – we're looking for quality writers.

Where do we get our information from? We're often asked this. Fortunately 15 years of journalism has helped. Very often facts are gleaned from face to face interviews with bands. Day to day stuff we get from record companies from all over the world, bands and fans.

We include ALL submissions. There is only one criteria – the band has to Rock. That covers everything in our scheme of things from AOR, Prog Rock, Classic Rock right through to Nu-Metal, Rap Metal and onto Death & Black Metal. We want it all.

Here's the address for submissions:

Musicdetector Websites Ltd,
P.O. Box 3138,
New Plymouth,
Taranaki,
New Zealand

For inclusion on the site we need one of each product format, a full biography and a high quality photo. Information regarding linking to your URLs is also of benefit to you.

If you want a record reviewing we need two copies as we send these out for review.

Here's our e-mail address: info@rockdetector.com

Bands / Labels: DON'T send us an e-mail asking for us to look at your website. We simply don't have time. Be proactive and send the stuff in. Then we'll contact you.

THANKS:

Iain McNay, Tim Wright, Jim Phelan, Adam Velasco and Sarah at Cherry Red and Karl for proof reading. Marco at Century Media, Michael (Tim), Markus & Matt at Nuclear Blast, Olly Hahn at SPV, Dig at Earache, Hammy at Peaceville, Peter Klapproth at CMM, Rob Wrong at Stonerrock.com, Deanna at Stonerrockchick.com, Doom Metal.com, Kevin & Grant at Efinity, Joshua Wood in Canada and all the bands and labels that contributed.

Hails and salutations to Goetz Kuhnemund at Rock Hard, Andy Pyke, Andy Southwell, Dave Martin, Jim Jam, Eddie & Helen Shaw, Simon & Diana Meadows, Martin Walkyier, Jayne Andrews, KK Downing, Glenn Tipton, Rob Halford, Lemmy, Bob Daisley, Martin Popoff, Brian Coles, Tim Wadzinski, Nico Wobben, Matt Sampson, Gregg Russell (where art thou?), Bernard Doe, Pete Way, Lea Hart, Stuart Ongley, Roland Hyams, David Howells, Peter, Sharon & the clan Chris, Stevie, Phillip & Lucy, Marisa & Sonia, Barry & Jane.

Without doom… Grace-Anne, Kerr, Krystan, Kjaric & me ol' Mum (we've all got 'em).

AARNI (FINLAND)
Line-Up: Master Warjomaa (vocals), Mistress Palm (vocals), Comte De Saint Germain (keyboards), Doomintroll (drums)

The melodramatic Doom act AARNI came into being during 1998 conjured up by former INEVITABLE man Markus Marjomaa. Joined by keyboard player Comte De Saint Germain and drummer Doomintroll, AARNI would be completed by Mistress Palm, oddly apparently not a real person but a computer programme.
A self-financed EP; 'Duumipiekon Paluu' ('The Return Of Doomintroll') was delivered in 2001. AARNI projected a split CD release with fellow Doom laden Finns UMBRA NIHIL for 2002 release through the Firebox label.

Singles/EPs:
MYRRYS / Lampaan Vaateissa / The Weird Of Vipunen / Transcend Humanity / Reaching Azathoth, (2001) ('Duumipiekon Paluu' EP)

ABDULLAH (Richfield, OH, USA)
Line-Up: Jeff Shirilla (vocals / drums), Alan Seibert (guitar), Chris Chiera (guitar), Ed Stephens (bass), Jim Simonian (drums)

The Doom Black duo of ex-SLOTH man Jeff Shirilla and Alan Siebert titled their project after the author of the renowned occult treatise 'Necromonicon' Abdulah Alhazad. Despite not employing a bass player and recording on primitive 4-track, ABDULLAH nevertheless engineered a near-crushing, all-enveloping quagmire Doom soundscape.
Three formative demos were issued upfront of the 1999 'Snake Lore' effort. Although only recorded on a 4-track, and still minus a bass player, ABDULLAH managed to reap praise from the Metal community with this release. The band signed to Meteor City Records offshoot People Like You for the debut album 'Abdullah', pulling in bassist Jim from BOULDER. The British Rage Of Achilles label would re-issue the 'Snake Lore' demo on CD format.
Shirilla would hook up with veteran Heavy Metal band BREAKER in January of 2002 after their singer Jim Hamar walked out unexpectedly. Shirilla maintained his position in ABDULLAH.
The band expanded for live work with the addition of SOFA KING KILLER rhythm guitarist Chris Chiera, bass player Ed Stephens and Jim Simonian of the MIKE FARLEY BAND on drums. In July of 2002 Aaron Dallison of KEELHAUL was inducted as second guitarist.

Albums:
ABDULLAH, People Like You (2000)
The Path To Enlightenment / Conundrum / Earth's Answer / Visions Of The Daughters Of Time / Now Is The Winter / Lucifer In Starlight / The Black Ones / Awakening The Colossus / Proverbs Of Hell / Journey To The Orange Island / Lotus Eaters
SNAKE LORE, Rage Of Achilles ILIAD002 (2000)
The Path To Enlightenment / Distant Lights - Sot-Weed / In The Belly Of The Beast / Firmament - Lam / The Sickness Unto Death / The Black Ones

ABIOGENESI (ITALY)
Line-Up: Tony D'Urso (vocals / guitar), Robert Piccolo (bass), Patrick Menegaldo (keyboards), Sandro Immacolato (drums)

ABIOGENESI's 2000 album 'Le Notti Di Salem' included former BLACK WIDOW man Clive Jones on flute. Also guesting were ARTI E MESTIERI's Gigi Venegoni and Marco Cimini.
ABIOGENESI also contributed to the 2000 BLACK WIDOW tribute album 'King Of The Witches'.

Albums:
ABIOGENESI, Black Widow BWR011 (1995)
Ile St. Louis / La Notte Di Ognissanti / Abiogenesi / L'oscura Tenebra / R.I.P. / Apputamento Con La Luna
IL GIOSCURO, Black Widow BWR018 (1998)
Il Giocoscuro / Sul Margine Del Bosco La Morte Libra Va La Sua Falce / Notte Da Urlare / Lunipieno / Golem
LE NOTTI DI SALEM, Black Widow BWR046 (2000)

ABLAZE MY SORROW (SWEDEN)
Line-Up: Martin Qvist (vocals), Magnus Carlsson (guitar), Roger Johansson (guitar), Anders Brorssomn (bass), Alex Bengtsson (drums)

ABLAZE MY SORROW debuted in 1993 with a line-up of vocalist Martin Qvist, guitarist Magnus Carlsson, bassist Anders Brorsson and drummer Fredrik Wenzel and soon issued a demo in early 1994 entitled 'For Bereavement We Cried'. However, Fredrik Wenzel departed in mid 1994 in favour of Alex Bengtsson.
Following recording of the debut album, 'If Emotions Still Burn', guitarist Roger Johansson made his exit. Dennis Linden

initially substituted him. ABLAZE MY SORROW promptly enlisted Kristian Lönnsjö from Death Metal act DEIFICATION as substitute

Qvist would front Black Metal act IMMEMOREAL for their 2001 debut 'Temples Of Retribution'. He would also be found as a member of DEIFICATION the same year.

Albums:
IF EMOTIONS STILL BURN, No Fashion NFR015CD (1996)
If Emotions Still Burn / The Rain That Falls / Rise Above The Storming Sea / Denial (The Way Of The Strong) / My Last Journey / As I Face The Eternity / My Revenge To Come
THE PLAGUE, No Fashion NFR026 (1998)
Dusk... / The Truth Is Sold / Into The Land Of Dreams / Mournful Serenade / The Return Of The Mighty Raven / I Will Be Your God / Plague Of Mine / As The Dove Falls Turn Apart
Suicide / ...Dawn

ABRAMIS BRAMA (SWEDEN)
Line-Up: Ulf Torkelssons (vocals), Dennis Berg (guitar), Peo (guitar), Jansson (drums)

ABRAMIS BRAMA, oddly named after a breed of particularly ugly fish, came together in November of 1994 when vocalist / guitarist Dennis Berg hooked up with drummer Jansson. Originally Jansson was slated to occupy the bass role but unable to find a drummer Jansson duly shifted position to the drum kit. Later additions had vocalist Christian and guitarist Peo entering the fold.
The debut album, a heavy Blues drenched Doom workout entitled 'Dansa Tokjävelens Vals' ('Dance The Mad Devil's Waltz'), was recorded in 1998. Uncompromisingly the band recorded all the lyrics in their native Swedish tongue.
In October of 1999, just upfront of the November release of 'Dansa Tokjävelens Vals' through the Record Heaven label, ABRANIS BRAMA added new frontman Ulf Torkelssons.
The band's second album 'När Tystnaden Lagt Sig...' ('When Silence Is Here') arrived in March of 2001. During these sessions the band recorded a cover version of NOVEMBER's 'Men Mitt Hjärta Ska Vara Gjort Av Sten' intended for future use as a single. Making it onto the album would be a rendition of the PRETTY THINGS 'Cold Stone' newly translated into Swedish and retitled 'Kall Som Sten'. ABRAMIS BRAMA would contribute to the Record Heaven CAPTAIN BEYOND tribute album with a radically reworked 'Mezmerasation Eclipse',

naturally redesignated with Swedish lyrics and so called 'Förtrollande Förmörkelse'.
In 2001 ABRAMIS BRAMA did finally relent to pressure to deliver songs with English lyrics. Unusually they would not only completely re-record earlier material with producer Per Wikström for an album 'Nothing Changes' but, unwilling to simply translate the songs the band completely re-wrote brand new words with a completely different subject matter to the Swedish originals. Only 'Svart' ('All Is Black') underwent a straight translation.

Albums:
DANSA TOKJAVELENS VALS, Record Heaven RHCD20 (1999)
Guld Och Gröna Skogar / Mamma Talar / Svarta Madam / Tunga Tankar / Dansa Tokjävelns Vals / Sömnlös / Ogräsblues / Motalaboogie / Parentesvals
NAR TYSTNADEN LAGT SIG..., Record Heaven (2001)
Abramis Brama / Kall Som Sten / Vad Jag Ser / Nålen / 100 Dagar / Svart / Kom Gör Mig Klok / Vill Inte Veta / När Alvorna Dansar / Anemone Nemorosa

ABSTRAKT ALGEBRA (SWEDEN)
Line-Up: Mats Leven (vocals), Mike Wead (guitar), Simon Johansson (guitar), Leif Edling (bass), Calle Westholm (keyboards), Jejo Perkovitch (drums)

Assembled as more of an experimental studio project by bassist Leif Edling after the demise of the critically acclaimed CANDLEMASS in 1993, the man roped in a few friends and acquaintances including ex-HEXENHAUS guitarist Mike Wead.
Whilst vocalist Mats Leven boasts an impressive pedigree, including stints with CAPRICORN, SWEDISH EROTICA and TREAT, guitarist Simon Johansson played simultaneously for FIFTH REASON. Drummer Jejo Perkovitch also had other engagements as a member of Punk rockers BRICK.
Combining classic Metallic riffs with a fairly Industrial use of sampling and keyboard work, Edling covered ground in ABSTRAKT ALGEBRA that he dare not have tried within the confines of CANDLEMASS, although the group only managed a handful of gigs in their native Sweden towards the end of 1995.
After a stint fronting EYEBALL, Leven teamed up with YNGWIE MALMSTEEN in 1997 for his 'Face The Animal' record.
Although intending to record a second ABSTRAKT ALGEBRA album, Edling felt that the new material was heading in a similar direction to CANDLEMASS, so the bassist

opted to resurrect his former band to complete the material. However, even with a full-blown CANDLEMASS re-formation underway, the pairing of Edling and Leven would reunite, forging another project band billed as KRUX and recording a debut album for 2002 release through the Mascot label. This new venture also saw contributions from the ENTOMBED rhythm section of drummer Peter Stjärnvind and bassist Jörgen Sandstrom, although the latter would switch to guitar. Other guitarists involved in the sessions included Nicko Elgstrand of TERRA FIRMA and Fredrik Åkesson from TALISMAN.

Albums:
ABSTRAKT ALGEBRA, Megarock
MRRCD024 (1994)
Stigmata / Shadowplay / Nameless /
Abstrakt Algebra / Bitter Root / April Clouds /
Vanishing Man / Who What Where When

ABYSMAL GRIEF (ITALY)
Line-Up: Labes C. Necrothytus (vocals /
keyboards), Regan Graves (guitar / drums),
Lord Alastair (bass)

ABYSMAL GRIEF are a 'Horror' Metal trio founded in 1995 by guitarist Regan Graves. The band describe, themselves as 'Misfitic' and influenced by 70s Doom with stage shows visually enhanced by "coffins, hanged dolls, blood and every sort of mourning objects". Various line-up changes in the band's formative stages saw, amongst others, the introduction of bassist Lord Alastair and lead vocalist Garian. A 1996 demo tape surfaced after which ABYSMAL GRIEF lost the services of their then drummer.
In late 1996 vocalist Labes E. Necrothytus was enrolled. A further demo, viewed by the band as their first 'official' session, 'Funereal' surfaced in late 1997. Session drummer Lord Of Fog assisted in the studio for these recordings. ABYSMAL GRIEF would also donate a new composition 'Invocation' to the Whiplash Productions compilation album 'Into The Underground Vol. 3'. The act, now

ABYSMAL GRIEF

centred on Graves and Necrothytus, would radically overhaul the line-up, bringing in three session players for a cover version of the DEATH S.S. track 'Black Mummy' for a Black Widow tribute album.

Lord Alastair made a return in November of 1999 and ABYSMAL GRIEF debuted commercially with the 'Exsequia Occulta' single, issued in May of 2000. The band signed to the Danish Horror record label for a further single, the 7" release 'Hearse' / 'Borgo Pass'. A full-length album, provisionally titled 'Cultus Lugubris', is projected for 2002 release.

Regan Graves would contribute guest lead guitar to the MALOMBRA 2002 album 'The Dissolution Age'

Singles/EPs:
Exsequia Occulta / Sepulchre Of Misfortune, Flowers Of Grave Productions FOG001 (2000)
Hearse / Borgo Pass, Horror (2002)

ACID BATH (Louisiana, USA)
Line-Up: Dax Riggs (vocals), Mike Sanchez (guitar), Sammy Duet (guitar), Audrey Petrie (bass), Jimmy Kyle (drums)

DIRTY ROTTEN IMBECILES guitarist Spike Cassidy produced ACID BATH's debut album, graced with sleeve artwork entitled 'Skull Clown' from infamous mass murderer John Wayne Gacy.

Touring America to promote the album ACID BATH guested for CANNIBAL CORPSE and Swedes ENTOMBED.

The 'Edits' mini-album is a collection of songs from the second album remixed by Cassidy. 'Paegan Terrorist Tactics' once more featured controversial artwork with the painting 'For He Is Raised' executed by the renowned "Suicide assistance" Dr. Jack Kevorkian.

The band suffered a devastating blow in January 1997 when a drunk driver killed bassist Audrie Pitrie, together with his parents.

Vocalist Dax Riggs and guitarist Mike Sanchez founded AGENTS OF OBLIVION. Guitarist Sammy Duet, also a member of heavyweights CROWBAR, forged GOATWHORE in alliance with SOILENT GREEN frontman Ben Falgoust II.

Albums:
WHEN THE KITE STRING POPS, Rotten 2095-2 (1994)
The Blue / Tranquilized / Cheap Vodka / Finger Paintings Of The Insane / Jezebel / Scream Of The Butterfly / Dr. Seuss Is Dead / Dope Fiend / Toubabo Koomi / God

Machine / The Mortician's Flame / What Color Is Death / The Bones Of Baby Dolls / Cossie Eats Cockroaches
EDITS, Rotten Records (1995)
Venus Blue (With Shit) / Diäb Soulé / Near Death Sensation / Venus Blue (With No Shit) / Bleed Me An Ocean / Dead Girl / Paegan Love Song / New Corpse / Near Death Sensation
PAEGAN TERRORIST TACTICS, Rotten (1996)
Paegan Love Song / Bleed Me An Ocean / Graveflower / Diäb Soulé / Locust Spawning / Old Skin / Near Death Sensation / Venus Blue / 13 Fingers / New Corpse / Dead Girl / The Beautiful / Downgrade

ACID KING (San Francisco, CA, USA)
Line-Up: Lori S. (vocals / guitar), Guy Pinhas (bass), Joey Osbourne (drums)

Stoner Doom power trio led by Lori S. ACID KING, titled after the nickname given to junkie murderer Ricky Kasso, evolved in 1993 after Lori S. placed an advert in a local newspaper for like-minded musicians. This call brought in bass player Peter Lucas. Drummer Joey Osbourne of ALTAMONT, the Southern rooted Stoner band fronted by Lori's husband and THE MELVINS man Dale Crover, would be found at a party.

ACID KING debuted with an eponymous 10" four track single capitalizing on this with the 1995 'Zoroaster' opus.

In 1996 Lucas bailed out to be supplanted by Dan Southwick, also of ALTAMONT. The band would release a further 10" single 'Down With The Crown' on Man's Ruin. This recording would soon after be re-released as part of a shared CD with ALTAMONT. Promotion for this release came in the form of guest slots to THE MELVINS and FU MANCHU on a West Coast run of dates.

Southwick would relinquish his position following completion of these shows with erstwhile BUZZOV.EN and SPILTH bassist Brian Hill taking the role in 1998 for the 'Busse Woods' recordings. A joint ACID KING / ALTAMONT touring spree would close with yet another vacancy in the bass role but fortunately the high profile figure of former THE OBSESSED and GOATSNAKE veteran Guy Pinhas would soon join the fold.

The 1999 Music Cartel compilation album 'In The Groove' includes an ACID KING track exclusive to this release in the form of 'Not Fragile'.

The band returned in 2001 sharing space on an album 'Free' with New Orleans act MYSTICK KREWE OF CLEARLIGHT. Both Pinhas and Osbourne would guest on the 'Experiments In Feedback' album from the

ACID KING

5

ACID KING
Photo : El Danno

newly reconstituted MEN OF PORN.

Singles/EPs:
Lead Paint / Blazing Cap / Drop / The
Midway, Sympathy For The Record Industry
SFTR 318 (1994) ('Acid King' 10" single)
Teen Dusthead / Full Reverse / Phase II,
Man's Ruin MR073 (1997) ('Down With The
Crown' 10" single)

Albums:
ZOROASTER, Sympathy For The Record
Industry SFTR 1379 (1995)
Evil Satan / If I Burn / One Ninety Six /
Vertigate No. 1 / Tank Dry Run / Fruit Cup /
Queen Of Sickness / Reload / Vertigate No. 2
DOWN WITH THE CROWN, Man's Ruin
MR088 (1997) (Split album with ALTAMONT)
Teen Dusthead / Full Reverse / Phase II
BUSSE WOODS, Man's Ruin MR104 (1999)
Electric Machine / Silent Circle / Drive Fast,
Take Chances / 39 Lashes / Carve The 5 /
Busse Woods
FREE, Man's Ruin MR 2016 (2001) (Split
album with MYSTICK KREWE OF
CLEARLIGHT)
Blaze In / Free / Four Minutes / Blaze Out

ACRIMONY (UK)
Line-Up: Dorian Walters (vocals), Lee Davies
(guitar), Stuart O'Hara (guitar), Paul Bidmead
(bass), Darren Ivy (drums)

Swansea Metallers rooted in '70's Doom with
distinct hippie overtones dating from their
inception in 1991, ACRIMONY debuted with
the 'A Sombre Thought' demo which gained
the band a deal with Belgian label Shiver.
The interest provoked by the 'Solstice
Sadness' single led to a further deal with
Italian label Godhead and the release of the
first album, 'Hymns To The Stone', which was
produced by ex-TORTOISE CORPSE
member Tim Hammill. ACRIMONY
subsequently toured with Scottish act IN
EXTREMIS in Britain on dates dubbed 'The
Celtic Invasion'.
In 1997 ACRIMONY released their second
album 'Tumuli Shroomaroom', which was
produced by former SABBAT man Andy
Sneap.
Frontman Dorrian Walters also put time into
his side project HELVIS during 1997, a band
convened by ex-members of BIVOUAC,
CONSUMED, PITCHSHIFTER and IRON
MONKEY.
ACRIMONY cut two cover tracks for

6

Peaceville Records tenth anniversary compilation album 'X', namely STATUS QUO's 'Oh Baby' and DOOM's 'Exploitation'. A split single, 'Motherslug (Mother Of All Slugs)', arrived in 1998 shared with IRON RAINBOW.

Guitarist Stuart O'Hara would form part of THE DUKES OF NOTHING, an outfit founded by ex-IRON MONKEY guitarist Dean Berry and ORANGE GOBLIN drummer Chris Turner.

Singles/EPs:
Solstice Sadness (Dance Of The Wild Flower) / For Morrow (The Last Children Of Cerriddwen), Shiver (1993)
Spaced Cat No. 7 / The Inn / Fire Dance / The Bud Song, Godhead GOD019 (1995) ('Acid Elephant' EP)
Motherslug (The Mother Of All Slugs), (1998) (Split single with IRON RAINBOW)

Albums:
HYMNS TO THE STONE, Godhead GOD010 (1994)
Leaves Of Mellow Grace / The Inn / Second Wind / Spaced Cat No. 6 / Urabalaboom / Herb / Magical Mystical Man / Whatever / Cosmic AWOL
TUMULI SHROOMAROOM, Peaceville

CDVILE 68 (1997)
Hymns To The Stone / Million Year Summer / Turn The Page / Vy / Find The Path / The Bud Song / Motherslug (The Mother Of All Slugs) / Heavy Feather / Firedance

AESMA DAEVA
(Minneapolis, MN, USA)
Line-Up: Rebecca Cords (vocals), Jon Prassos (guitar), Nick Copernicus (keyboards)

A Gothic charged Electro-Darkwave trio out of Minneapolis. AESMA DAEVA have already won heady praise for their first releases. The 2000 debut 'Here Lies Who's Name Was Written In Water' was originally issued by the German Ascension label.

Albums:
HERE LIES WHO'S NAME WAS WRITTEN IN WATER, Ascension (2000)
O Death (Rock Me Asleep) / Downvain / Stay / Disdain / Introit I / When I Have Fears That I May Cease To Be / Perpetua Luceat Eis / Introit II / Communion / Sanctus / Darkness (Stromkern)
THE EROS OF FRIGID BEAUTY, Root Of All Evil (2001)
Lysander / Devotion / In My Holy Time / The

FLOOR JANSEN of AFTER FOREVER
Photo : Nico Wobben

7

Eros Of Frigid Beauty / Overature / The
Minstrel Song / Lysander II

AFTER FOREVER (HOLLAND)

Line-Up: Floor Jansen (soprano vocals), Mark
Jansen (vocals / guitar), Sander Gommans
(vocals / guitar), Luik van Gerven (bass), Jack
Driessen (keyboards), Joep Beckers (drums)

A Gothic Doom act with a strong sense of the
majestic. AFTER FOREVER employed three
vocalists, Floor Jansen on soprano, Mark
Jansen on "screams" with Death Metal grunts
courtesy of Sander Gommans. Further vocal
enhancement came courtesy of Sharon
Janny den Adel of WITHIN TEMPTATION.

The 2002 single 'Emphasis' included two
tracks, 'Who Wants To Live Forever' and
'Imperfect Senses', that featured Damien
Wilson of British Prog Rock act THRESHOLD
on guest lead vocals.

During April of 2002 founder member Floor
Jansen decamped, his replacement swiftly
being announced as Bal Maas. Floor had
recently donated guest lead vocals to the
STAR ONE Sci-Fi concept album of AYREON
mentor Arjen Lucasson and would tour with
this project in September.

Mark Jansen, later of SAHARA DUST, was
also ensconced in the Dutch / Belgian Doom
'Supergroup' LES FAIDITS assembled by ex-
SENGIR members singer Jurgen Cobbaut
and guitarist Kris Scheerlinck.

Singles/EPs:
Follow In The Cry / Silence From Afar
(Radio edit) / Wings Of Illusion / Mea Culpa
(Acapella version), (2000)
Emphasis / Who Wants To Live Forever /
Imperfect Senses / Intrinsic, Transmission
TMS-034 (2002)

Albums:
PRISON OF DESIRE, Transmission TM-023
(2000)
Mea Culpa / Leaden Legacy / Semblance Of
Confusion / Black Tomb / Follow In The Cry /
Silence From Afar / Inimical Chimera /
Tortuous Threnody / Yield To Temptation /
Ephemeral / Beyond Me
DECIPHER, Transmission (2001)
Ex Cathedra / Monolith Of Doubt / My
Pledge Of Allegiance 1 / Emphasis / Intrinsic
/ Zenith / Estranged / Imperfect Tenses / My
Pledge Of Allegiance 2 / The Key / Forlorn
Hope

AFTERMATH (Chicago, IL, USA)

Line-Up: Charlie Tsiolis (vocals), Steve Sacco
(guitar), John Lazerty (guitar), Pat Delagarza
(bass), Ray Schmidt (drums)

Chicago based AFTERMATH formed in
October 1985, issuing the five track demo
'Killing The Future' featuring the tracks 'When
Will You Die', 'Going No Place', 'Chaos',
'Meltdown' and 'War For Freedom'. The band
added bassist John Lazerty following the
demo release but then switched Lazerty to
second guitar, recruiting Pat Delagarza on
bass. Aftermath were featured on the Metal
Forces magazine compilation 'Demolition' in
1988.

A further demo 'Words That Echo Fear'
featuring new guitarist John Lovette was
released prior to the band demoing for
Roadracer Records. Negotiations broke down
however and AFTERMATH signed to New
York's Big Chief Records. Bassist Chris
Waldron was added in 1990 and Aftermath
released a live four track demo featuring the
songs 'Eyes of Tomorrow', 'Afraid Of Time',
'The Act Of Unspoken Wisdom' and
'Reflecting Pictures'.

Albums:
THE EYES OF TOMORROW, Big Chief
(1992)

AGALLOCH (Portland, OR, USA)

Line-Up: J. Haughn, S. Breyer, L. Anderson
(guitar), J.William W. (bass)

The cold, dark mournfulness of AGALLOCH
is rooted in the 1995 Death Metal band
AEOLACHRYMAE. When this band collapsed
three bands rose up - NOTHING, AGALLOCH
and SUSURRUS IRANIS. J. Haughn and S.
Breyer created AGALLOCH, adding second
guitar player L. Anderson during mid 1996.

In this incarnation AGALLOCH weighed in
with an inaugural demo session 'From Which
Of This Oak', after which bassist J. William W.
joined the band. A further promo tape scored
the band a deal with The End Records. The
resulting album, 'Pale Folklore', was issued in
June of 1997.

A second effort, 'Of Stone, Wind And Pillor', a
collection of archive material including a cover
of the SOL INVICTUS song 'Kneel To The
Cross', was delivered in mid 2001.

Members of AGALLOCH also operate
SCULPTURED and ESPECIALLY LIKE
SLOTH.

Albums:
PALE FOLKLORE, The End TE010 (1999)
She Painted Fire Across The Skyline / The
Misshapen Steed / Hallways Of Enchanted
Ebony / Dead Winter Days / As Embers
Dress The Sky / The Melancholy Spirit
OF STONE, WIND AND PILLOR, The End
(2001)

Of Stone, Wind And Pillor / Foliorum Viridium / Haunting Birds / Kneel To The Cross / A Poem By Yeats

AGE OF HEAVEN (GERMANY)
Line-Up: Jens-Uwe Helmstedt (vocals), Erik Wolf (guitar), Torsten Sander (bass), Tom Bottcher (keyboards)

Guitarist Hendrik Gundlach took over from Erik Wolf for AGE OF HEAVEN's second album 'The Garden Of Love'.

Albums:
ARMAGEDDON, Dion Fortune (1996)
The Providence / Black Dust / Armageddon / Red Roses / Twelve O'Clock / In The Mirror / Fallen Angel / Fairy From The Moon / Over The Seven Seas
THE GARDEN OF LOVE, Age One Music (1997)
The Secret / The Garden Of Love / Broke The Chain / Time Flies / No Time To Pray / Organ / Carrie / It Comes The Night / Echoes / Behind The Walls / The Garden Of Love (Acoustic) / Reprise

AGHAST (NORWAY)

A solo project of EMPEROR member Samoth's girlfriend Nebel. AGHAST offered dark, Gothic Rock on the 1995 released debut album. In 1997 Nebel formulated a further vehicle for her endeavours titled HAGALAZ' RUNEDANCE under her real name of Andrea M. Haugen.

Albums:
HEXERI IM ZWEILICHT DER FINSTERNIS, Cold Meat Industry CMI 33 (1995)
Enthrall / Sacrifice / Enter The Hall Of Ice / Call From The Grave / Totentanz / The Darkest Desire / Das Irrlicht / Ende

AGHORA (USA)
Line-Up: Danishta Dobles (vocals), Santiago Dobles (guitar), Charlie Ekendahl (guitar), Sean Malone (bass), Sean Reinert (drums)

Female fronted Metal band AGHORA include two ex-CYNIC members in their line-up in bassist Sean Malone and drummer Sean Reinert. The latter has also been with GORDIAN KNOT.

Albums:
AGHORA, Season Of Mist (2000)
Immortal Bliss / Satya / Transfiguration / Frames / Mind's Reality / Kali Yuga / Jivatma / Existence / Anugraha

AGLAROND (MEXICO)
Albums:
THE JOURNEY'S END, American Line Productions (2001)

AGONY COLUMN (TX, USA)
Line-Up: Richie Turner (vocals), Stuart Lawrence (guitar), Pawl Willis (bass), Charlie Brownell (drums)

A quite unique fusing of Hillbilly and Metal. The 'Way Back In The Woods' album features Billy Dansfiell on bass.
Frontman Richie Turner would also head up DADDY LONGHEAD, a combo in union with Jeff Pinkus, King Coffey and Paul Leary of the BUTTHOLE SURFERS, Rey Washam of SCRATCH ACID, TAD and RAPEMAN and WASTE KING UNIVERSAL's Jim Yongue.

Singles/EPs:
Comes Alive EP - Live, Big Chief (1990)

Albums:
GOD, GUNS AND GUTS, Big Chief (1989)
God, Guns And Guts / Snakebite / 4X4 / Vicious Pack Of Lies / Fiendish Plots / 66 Six Guns / Cars, Sex And Violence / Walk The Night / Scarred For Life / Blackjack / Dead By Dawn / Bag O' Bones
BRAVE WORDS AND BLOODY KNUCKLES, Big Chief (1991)
Brave Words & Bloody Knuckles / Angel Of Def / Lord Almighty / Ultraviolent Rays / Bayou Road / No Time To Kill / Crime & Punishment / Big Two Hearted Sammy / Hellbilly Blues / Rain Comes Down / Suppertime / Hole To Hell / Mississippi Queen
WAY BACK IN THE WOODS, No Bull 34174-2 (1996)
The Spirit Rises / Way Back In The Woods / Flying Sorceress / Obey The Command / The Night Has 1000 Eyes / Silver Spoon / Whiskey Bottle / Collywog / Small Black Toad / When The Dark Clouds Return / The Devils Carnival

AION (POLAND)
Line-Up: Mariusz 'Marian' Krzyska (vocals), Dominik 'Mlody' Jokiel (guitar), Daniel Jokiel (guitar), Lukasz 'Migdal' Migdalski (keyboards), Witalis 'Milli' Jagodzinski (bass), Marcin 'Zuraw' Zurawicz (drums)

A Gothic Rock band from Poland formed in 1995. The album debut features a cover of SISTERS OF MERCY's 'Temple Of Love'.
AION toured in 1997 with THEATRE OF TRAGEDY and SAVIOUR MACHINE.

Albums:
MIDIAN, Massacre MAS PCO131 (1997)
Overture / Bleeding Heart / Land Of Dreams
/ The Anthem Of Victory / Temple Of Love /
Collapse / The Lord / Birth / The Night
NOIA, System Shock (2000)
Killing Time / Holies Unholies / Innocent
Pictures / Nightmares / Bad Place / The
Prayer / Into The Abyss / Before Dawn / O
Fortuna
RECONCILIATION, Metal Mind (2000)
R / E / C / O / N / C / I / L / I / A / T / I / O / N /
Guility 11. Days Of Fight, Days Of Hope I /
Time Of Reconciliation / Implant / Days Of
Fight, Days Of Hope II / The Meeting /
Suffering / Implant / Ten Thousand Bodies /
House Of Soul / Headless Cross / Guilty
(Video)
SYMBOL, Metal Mind (2001)
Whispers / Image / Unfulfilled Hope / Symbol
/ The Black River / The Way / As Ice /
Craving / Azure Landscape

ALABAMA THUNDERPUSSY (USA)
Line-Up: Johnny Throckmorten (vocals),
Ryan Lake (guitar), Erik Larson (guitar),
John Peters (bass), Bryan Cox Drums)

Foremost exponents of 'Moonshine' Stoner
Metal. Richmond's ALABAMA THUNDER-
PUSSY came together in 1996, founded by a
trio of guitarists Asechiah Bogdan and Erik
Larson with drummer Bryan Cox. Larson, an
ex-KILARA member, was also operating at
the time as drummer for Punk band AVAIL.
This formative version of the band even
gigged minus both bassist and vocalist.
Eventually Bill Storms filled the bass vacancy
and 'Diamond Mudgoats' the vocal role.
Before long Adrienne Droogas of San
Francisco Punk act SPITBOY assumed the
vocal mantle, a tenure that lasted precisely
one gig. Johnny Throckmorton solidified the
lead vocalist position during 1997.
The band's debut 6 track demo tape soon
secured the interest of Man's Ruin Records

ALABAMA THUNDERPUSSY
Photo : El Danno

ALABAMA THUNDERPUSSY
Photo : El Danno

and subsequently the 'Rise Again' album was launched in the summer of 1998. Shortly after Storms broke away from the band to create SUNNSHINE and ex-KILARA man Sam Krivanec was drafted as replacement. ALABAMA THUNDERPUSSY toured America in union with SOLARIZED throughout the winter of 1999.

The 'River City Revival' album followed which included a cover version of the FOUR HORSEMEN's 'Rockin' Is Ma Business'. This album prompted the band's first touring foray into Europe during 2000. Upon returning from these shows Krivanec was usurped by Bingo Tuggel for further live dates in America and the UK.

The same year ALABAMA THUNDERPUSSY cut a cover version of a CAPTAIN BEYOND track for a split single with English Doomsters ORANGE GOBLIN on the Eccentric Man label. They would also share space with New Jersey's HALFWAY TO GONE on a Game Two released split album and cut a cover track for a LYNYRD SKYNYRD tribute record. The band would contribute their version of 'Sweet Emotion' to the 2000 Small Stone Recordings AEROSMITH tribute album 'Right In The Nuts'.

American touring would recommence in the Spring of 2001 in confederation with DIXIE WITCH and SUPLECS but during the summer both Bogdan and Tuggel bade their farewells. ALABAMA THUNDERPUSSY would be brought back up to strength with the addition of guitarist Ryan Lake and bass player John Peters.

ALABAMA THUNDERPUSSY members Johnny Throckmorton and Bryan Cox also operate with side act ARS MORIENDI.

The band would feature on the 2002 Smallstone Records 'Sucking The '70s' compilation which featured covers of classic '70's tracks re-cut by modern day Rockers. ALABAMA THUNDERPUSSY weighed in with their interpretation of JETHRO TULL's 'Hymn 34'.

The band signed to the Relapse label for May 2002's Billy Anderson produced 'Staring At The Divine' album. ALABAMA THUNDER PUSSY would be confirmed for another round of American tour dates in May of 2002, old comrades ORANGE GOBLIN acting as openers. The band projected American tour dates into September in league with MASTODON and would then form a somewhat unlikely union with W.A.S.P.,

ENGINE and ex-RATT frontman STEPHEN PEARCY for a string of package dates throughout October and November.

Albums:
RISE AGAIN, Man's Ruin MR102 (1998)
Falling Behind / Victory Thrash Defeat / Folk Love / Lord's Prayer / Get Mad, Get Even / When Mercury Drops / Ivy / Speaking In Tongues / Jackass / Alto Vista / Podium / Fever 103 / Dixie
RIVER CITY REVIVAL, Man's Ruin MR154 (1999)
Dryspell / Spineless / Heathen / Mosquito / Giving Upon Living / Own Worst Enemy / Rocking Is My Business
CONSTELLATION, Man's Ruin MR177 (1999)
Crying Out Loud / Ambition / 1-4 Mile / Middle Finger Salute / 1271-31065 / 6" Shooter / Second Wind / Obsari / Foul Play / Negligence / 15 Minute Drive / Burden / Keepsake / Country Song
STARING AT THE DIVINE, Relapse (2002)
Ol Unfaithful / Motor-Ready / Shape Shifter / Whore Adore / Hunting By Echo / Beck And Call / Twilight Arrival / Esteem Fiend / S.S.D.D. / Amounts That Count

ALAS (USA)
Line-Up: Martina Hornbacher (vocals), Erik Rutan (guitar), Scott Hornik (bass), Howard Davis (drums)

Symphonic Metal band led by RIPPING CORPSE, MORBID ANGEL and HATE ETERNAL guitarist Erik Rutan. An early line-up included ex-MONSTROSITY guitarist Jason Morgan.
Morgan also created WYNJARA for a 2000 album.

ALASTIS (SWITZERLAND)
Line-Up: War D. (vocals / guitar), Nick (guitar), Raff (bass), Graven X (keyboards), Acronoise (drums)

Death Metallers ALASTIS have had a turbulent history since their inception in 1987 with vocalist Zumof, bassist Masmiseim, guitarist War D. and drummer Acronoise. The band was originally titled CRY WAR until 1988 when the 'Black Wedding' demo saw a transition to ALASTIS.
ALASTIS released two demos prior to Masmiseim's departure in 1990 to SAMAEL, shortly followed by the departure of Zumof. Endeavouring to keep the ALASTIS spirit alive War. D took over lead vocals for the 1992 album 'The Just Law' before losing bassist Eric.

A new four stringer was found in ex-MISERY man Rotten in 1993. The band added erstwhile OFFERING guitarist Nick in 1995 for their first tour as support to ANATHEMA. Further shows saw ALASTIS on a European package billing with THEATRE OF TRAGEDY and SAVIOUR MACHINE.
For the 1998 album 'Revenge' bass was now in the hands of Raff, ALASTIS also having drafted a keyboard player Graven X.

Albums:
THE JUST LAW, Head Not Found (1992)
The Just Law / Black Wedding / Illusion / Reconversion / Damned For Ever / Nightmare / The City / Faticidal Date / Messenger Of The U.W.
...AND DEATH SMILED, Adipocere AR029 (1995)
From The UW / Through Your Torpor / Let Me Die / Evil / By Thy Name / Schizophrenia (Mental Suicide) / March For Victory / Your God / Last Wishes / The Psychopath / Messenger Of The U.W. (Second Act)
THE OTHER SIDE, Nuclear Blast 77156-2 (1997)
In Darkness / Never Again / The Other Side / Out Of Time / Through The Chaos / Fight & Win / Slaves Of Rot / Remind / Under The Sign... / End Or Beginning
REVENGE, Century Media 77223-2 (1998)
Just Hate / Burnt Alive / Eternal Cycle / Sacrifice / Ecstasy / Like A Dream / Nemesis / Bring Down / Agony / Revenge
UNITY, Century Media (2001)
The Right To Die / The Elect / The Sign / Another God / Who Created The Gods / Ghastly Fancies / Existence / Antidote / To The Root Of Evil / ...And Death Smiled

ALKONOST (RUSSIA)
Line-Up: Aljona (vocals), Elk (guitar), Alex Nightbird (bass), Almira (keyboards), Anton (drums)

ALKONOST, founded by bass guitarist Elk in the Autumn of 1995, deliver a medieval Folk styled Pagan Doom Metal. Following initial demos Elk switched to lead guitar as the newly enrolled Alex Nightbird took on bass duties. ALKONOST began appearing on the live circuit and in June of 1997 issued the first official demo 'Shadows Of Timeless' with a further effort entitled 'Shadows Of Glory' arriving just weeks after.
In 1998 ALKONOST pulled drummer Vladimir Lousshin into the ranks and set about recording the album 'Songs Of The Eternal Oak'. Early the following year keyboards were added to the ALKNONOST sound courtesy of Almira. With this line-up the band participated

in a 7" compilation release 'Death Panorama'. The 'Songs Of The Eternal Oak' was finally delivered as a cassette format album in May of 2000 as a joint co-operation between the German Ketzer Productions and Latvia's Beverina label.

Promotion toward the close of the year included shooting of a promotional video for the track 'Years Of Prophecy', shortly after which female lead vocalist Aljona joined the fold. This version of the band cut the demo session 'Spirit Tending To Revolt' that December. Changes on the drum stool early in 2001 witnessed the departure of Lousshin, being substituted by Anton. The group then opted to record a Russian language demo 'Nevedomye Zemli' (Unknown Lands) in August with another video being shot for the track 'My Last Day'. Live action had ALKONOST appearing at the Kazan 'Ravnodenstvije' (Equinox) festival in October. The second album, 'Alkonsost', arrived in July of 2002.

Albums:
SONGS OF THE ETERNAL OAK, Ketzer Productions KT003 (2000) (cassette release)
ALKONOST, Ketzer Productions KCD018 (2002)
Years Of Prophecy / Sun Shine Our Land / Song Of The Smiths (Sledge Hammer) / War Is Closed By Us / Holiday Of Fathers / Rain Of Former Days (Edit) / My Last Day / Vortex Of Time / Life On Glory´s Blade

ALTAMONT (USA)
Line-Up: Dale Crover (vocals / guitar), Dan Southwick (bass), Joey Osbourne (drums)

ALTAMONT are the sinister Southern Stoner-Doom alter ego vehicle for THE MELVINS drummer Dale Crover. Both bass player Dan Southwick and drummer Joey Osbourne have operated with Crover's wife Lori S.'s retro rockers ACID KING. Osbourne also holds down a post with MEN OF PORN.

Not content with simply sharing band members ALTAMONT would share space on a 1999 split album with ACID KING.

The 1999 'Civil War Fantasy' album initially had its sleeve artwork, a photograph of gallows, censored by distributors.

The band would contribute their version of 'Make It' to the 2000 Small Stone Recordings AEROSMITH tribute album 'Right In The Nuts'.

Singles/EPs:
Pluto Washington's Introduction / Sally Greensnake / Red Jackson / Casino / Pluto Closes Shop, Man's Ruin MR072 (1998)

('Dead Or Alive' 10" single)

Albums:
ALTAMONT, Man's Ruin MR088 (1999) (Split CD with ACID KING)
CIVIL WAR FANTASY, Man's Ruin MR085 (1999)
Civil War Fantasy / Ezy Rider / Bitch Slap / Whips / My One Sin / Makers Mark / Black Tooth Powder / Up River / Down Wind / Smoke
OUR DARLING, Man's Ruin MR2020 (2001)
Saint Of All Killers / Short Eyes / Our Darling / Pirate Love / Chicken Lover / Dead Car / Swami / Peace Creep / Stripey Hole / Young Man Blues / Hell's Angel Lullaby

AMBER ASYLUM (USA)
Line-Up: Kris Force (vocals / violin / guitar), Erica Stoltz (vocals / bass), Jackie Gratz (cello), Chiyo Nukaga (drums)

Both cinematic and congruent, AMBER ASYLUM offer a quite unique proposition, delivering 'New Age' music without the naiveté and occupying a vacuum between Classical and Rock. The band transcends genres juxtaposing the modern day harshness of guitar, bass and drums with the warmth of traditional violin and cello. The act defies stereotyping to such a degree that AMBER ASYLUM find themselves with a fan base stretching from art lovers to Doom Metal fans.

Violinist Kris Force provided the catalyst for the band, which transpired following three tape workshops, credited to FROZEN IN AMBER. The formative years of AMBER ASYLUM witnessed a fluid and disparate line-up settling on Force, cellist Martha Burns, keyboard player John Oberon, pianist Michael Richards and clarinet player Heather Snider. Commercially AMBER ASYLUM debuted with the 1996 picture disc single 'Looking Glass' released by the Fireball label. The British Elfenblut label, noted for its Black Metal catalogue, picked the band up for the inaugural album 'Frozen In Amber'.

The sophomore May 1997 outing 'The Natural Philosophy Of Love' saw the band as a trio of Force, Burns and violinist Annabel Lee. Session musicians on hand included STEVE VON TILL of NEUROSIS, percussionist Timothy North and keyboard player Blaise North.

The band shifted shape to accommodate cellist Jackie Gratz, who joined in 1997, for the 'Songs Of Sex And Death' album. Once again STEVE VON TILL guested as did guitarist John Benson.

Latter additions brought in vocalist / bassist

Erica Stoltz and drummer Wendy Farina. The latter had plentiful experience with TALLOW, MOIST and TOWEL whilst also pursuing RED SHARKS and CONDOR. Stoltz operates as the leader of revered Stoner Doom band LOST GOATS.

The 2000 AMBER ASYLUM album 'The Supernatural Parlour Collection' includes a radical cover version of BLACK SABBATH's 'Black Sabbath'.

AMBER ASYLUM's Jackie Gratz and Kris Force guested on STEVE VON TILL's 'As The Crow Flies' solo album.

Farina would opt out in late 2001, her substitute being announced as Chiyo Nukaga of Doom band NOOTHGRUSH. Gratz would be found making her mark in the aftermath of the September 11th terrorist attacks, putting in a marathon fund raising bike ride from New York City to California.

Recently a whole slew of unique AMBER ASYLUM tracks has turned up on various compilation collections. 'Bounding Main' appeared on the female vocal album 'Seireneenia' issued by Projeckt Records, a remixed 'Luxuria' re-billed as 'Sopor' was included on the 'Ptolemaic Terrascope' album whilst the 'Funeral Songs' record featured 'I Saw You Fall'. The group would also donate their take on 'Leather' for a TORI AMOS tribute album 'Songs Of A Goddess' assembled by Cleopatra Records.

AMBER ASYLUM members have contributed string arrangements to no less than four NEUROSIS albums plus albums from MATMOS and TRIBES OF NEUROT.

Kris Force also busies herself with side endeavour RAPTOR, a project union with erstwhile SWANS member Jarboe and Diana Obscura.

Singles/EPs:
Looking Glass / Poppies, Fireball (1996) (Picture disc)
Avenging And Bright / I Have A Bonnet, Eishaus (1997)

Albums:
FROZEN IN AMBER, Elfenblut SAG1LP (1996)
Volcano Suite / Riviera / Black Waltz / Heckle And Jeckle / Journey To The Sleepy Water / Je Suis Le Chat La Lune / Aurora / Ave Maria / Romantic Theme
THE NATURAL PHILOSOPHY OF LOVE, Release Entertainment RR6955 (1997)
Cupid / Exodus / Looking Glass / Song Of The Spider War / Jorinda And Joringel / Looking Glass Reprise / Poppies
SONGS OF SEX AND DEATH, Release Entertainment RR6416 (1998)

Could You / Devotion / Luxuria / Everything You Touch / Vampire / Secret Ions / Dreams Of Thee / Devotion Reprise
THE SUPERNATURAL PARLOUR COLLECTION, Relapse (2000)
Black Lodge / Black Swan / Silence Of The Setting Sun / The Shepherd Remix / Disembodied Healer / Black Lodge (Reprise) / Black Sabbath

AMEN (Los Angeles, CA, USA)
Line-Up: Casey Chaos (vocals), Paul Fig (guitar), Sonny Mayo (guitar), John Fahnestock (bass), Shannon Larkin (drums)

Casey Chaos forged AMEN in 1994 upon the dissolving of his former teenage Hardcore band DISORDERLY CONDUCT. Chaos also performed a stint with renowned cult Gothic outfit CHRISTIAN DEATH. AMEN were reactivated upon the disintegration of CHRISTIAN DEATH after mentor Rozz Williams' suicide. AMEN also include erstwhile WRATHCHILD AMERICA and UGLY KID JOE drummer Shannon Larkin.

Upon the release of the 1999 self-titled debut the band toured America with COAL CHAMBER, SLIPKNOT and MACHINE HEAD. However, they became involved in a bitter war of words with the label and decamped. Live shows in 2000 found AMEN sharing the billing in America with HATEBREED and CROWBAR. Gigs in the UK had Stoke quintet CHARGER, at special invitation of Chaos, as support.

Chaos busied himself as a producer during the latter half of 2001 performing studio duties with Illinois band THE KINISON. Meantime Larkin would deputize for GLASSJAW, performing a drum session on their latest record.

Guitarist Paul Fig would decamp in November 2001 being replaced by Rich Jones of THE BLACK HALOS. Fig would later surface as a member of BLUEBIRD.

During early 2002 the AMEN pairing of Casey Chaos and Shannon Larkin in union with the QUEENS OF THE STONE AGE duo of Josh Homme and Nick Oliveri embarked on a less than expected diversion with the band project THE EAGLES OF DEATH METAL. Initially titled HEAD BAND upon initial press releases, this unit would issue the album 'Peace Love And Death Metal' through Homme's own Rekords label.

Meantime AMEN found themselves embroiled in a very public dispute with Virgin Records. A new album had been recorded but apparently shelved. The band generated a fan petition in order to get the record released but it appeared label and band were at a stalemate situation.

Come America, Roadrunner (1999)
The Price Of Reality / Motorcade Horizon, Roadrunner (2000) (7" single)
The Price Of Reality / Motorcade Horizon / In These Pills / War In Your Name / 15 + Not Alive, Roadrunner (2000) (CD single)

Albums:
AMEN, Roadrunner (1999)
Coma America / Down Human / Drive / No Cure For The Pure / When A Man Dies A Woman / Unclean / I Don't Sleep / TV Womb / Private / Everything Is Untrue / The Last Time / Fevered / Broken Design / Resignation - Naked And Violent
WE HAVE COME FOR YOUR PARENTS, Virgin (2000)
CK Killer / Refuse Amen / Justified / The Price Of Reality / May Day / Under The Robe / Waiting 18 / To Hard To Be Free / Ungrateful Dead / Piss Virus / Dead On The Bible / Take My Head / In Your Suit / Here's The Poison

AMETHYST (HOLLAND)
Line-Up: Serge (vocals), Natasja (vocals), Ayhan (guitar), Alex (guitar), Bjorn (bass), Jochem (drums)

Black Metal with female vocals and strong Gothic overtones. AMETHYST started life as a school band in 1996. Drummer Jochem is also a member of POSTMORTEM FABULAE. AMETHYST underwent numerous line up changes before the self-financed 'Dea Noctilucae' release, losing drummer Norbert and keyboard player Michael in 1999.

Albums:
DEA NOCTILUCAE, Amethyst (2000)
Withering Soul / Of Damnation In Reprise / Mistress Of Gorgon / Fear / Last Touch / My Land Beyond

AM I BLOOD (FINLAND)
Line-Up: Janne Kerminen (vocals), Pekka Kulmala (guitar), Toni Gronros (bass), Sauli Suomalainen (drums)

AM I BLOOD were previously known as ST. MUCUS upon their formation in 1990. In this guise the band issued two albums – 'Natural Mutation' in 1995 and 'Am I Blood' – on the Stupid Twins label. This latter album would be repackaged as the debut AM I BLOOD release by Germany's Nuclear Blast label.
The band all adopted anglicized surnames for later releases. Frontman Janne Kerminen became simply J. Cermine, guitarist Pekka Kulmala was known as Pexi Cornely, bass player Toni Gronros evolved into Tony

Greenrose whilst drums were handled by Gary Reini. AM I BLOOD also added second guitarist Hande Lanblade.
Both Kerminen and Gronros also operate in side act N.O. DISCIPLINE. A new AM I BLOOD EP 'Gone With You' emerged in 2000.

Singles/EPs:
Gone With You / To Enthrone Myself / Supremacy Of Failure / Emptiness, Darkside (2000) ('Gone With You' EP)

Albums:
AM I BLOOD, Nuclear Blast (1996)
Battlefreak / Disgrace / Cannot Feel / Endless Energy / Emotions / Immaterial / Frayed China / No Friend / Lust / Things You Hate / Determined Anger / Awake / Love Yourself / Ceremony To Fear
AGITATION, Nuclear Blast (1988)
Negative / Examination / The Day Will Be Executed / Segregational Holocaust / Suicidal Solution / Sorrow / Scar In My Head / The Final Scream / Stains / Suffocated Love / Eternal You
THE TRUTH INSIDE THE DYING SUN, Screaming Bannshee (2001)
Gone With You / War Of My Misery / The Truth Inside The Dying Sun / Lies Wrote Mysteries / Struggle In Disarray / The One Who Forgives / The Saddest Grief / Painful Ignorance / Nothing Realistic / Collapse Of Ritual Belief / Supremacy Of Failure

ANATHEMA (UK)
Line-Up: Darren White (vocals), Vincent Cavanagh (guitar), Daniel Cavanagh (guitar), Duncan Patterson (bass), John Douglas (drums)

Liverpool based ultra Doom Metal band exceptionally heavy in both their death fixated lyrics more akin to neo-gothic poetry than Metal and grinding riffs, ANATHEMA formed in 1990 debuting with the 'An Illiad Of Woes' demo in November of that year.
Recording a further demo, 'All Faith Is Lost', and a single ('They Die') for Swiss label Witchunt, ANATHEMA provoked the interest of Peaceville Records who signed the band in January 1992.
The Doom Metal troupe contributed the track 'Lovelorn Rhapsody' to the Peaceville 'Volume 4' compilation album before releasing their much acclaimed 'Crestfallen' EP.
The band's first full-length album, 'Serenades', again received excellent reviews, enabling the band to tour Europe with support acts CRADLE OF FILTH and Sweden's AT THE GATES before performing further shows with Germany's PYOGENESIS

and Finland's GOD FORSAKEN.

Ever the busy ones, ANATHEMA then contributed the track 'Welcome To Hell' to the VENOM tribute album before playing the 'Waldrock' festival in Belgium and the 'Vosselaar' festival in Holland. After headlining the 'Manic Depression' festival in Rumania to 5,000 fans, the band then performed dates in Brazil, headlining the 'Independent Rock' festival as well as shows in Sao Paulo and Belo Horizonte.

During 1984 the rare 'Nailed To The Cross' single was pressed in "spiritual" purple vinyl and during the latter part of 1994 ANATHEMA undertook an extensive European tour, visiting such countries as Russia, Lithuania, Sweden, Spain and Portugal.

In March 1995 ANATHEMA trimmed down to a quartet as frontman Darren White was forced out and Vincent Cavanagh assumed the role of lead vocalist. White promptly formed a new act, THE BLOOD DIVINE, with three ex-CRADLE OF FILTH members; namely guitarists Paul Allander and Paul Ryan together with keyboard player Benjamin Ryan.

Daniel Cavanagh linked up with TROUBLE front man Eric Wagner in the project band LID. An album 'In The Mushroom' resulted.

In late 1997 former SOLSTICE drummer Sean Steels was enrolled into ANATHEMA as the band's live keyboard player Les migrated to CRADLE OF FILTH.

The band laid down two obscure cover versions for Peaceville's 1998 'X' compilation album, being PINK FLOYD's 'Goodbye Cruel World' and BAD RELIGION's 'Better Off Dead'.

Patterson departed midway through a 1998 tour to be temporarily replaced with ex-DREAMWEAVER bassist Dave Pybus.

John Douglas replaced Steels in early 1999 completing a line-up comprising the Cavanagh brothers and bassist Pybus, now a full time member. MY DYING BRIDE violinist Martin Powell also contributed to the 'Judgement' album recorded in Italy and produced by Kit Woolven.

Powell joined CRADLE OF FILTH in 2000. By the summer of the following year Pybus would also be lured into CRADLE OF FILTH.

Danny Cavanagh left the band in March of 2002 to join ANTIMATTER but within weeks had retracted and opted for a return.

Singles/EPs:
They Die / Crestfallen, Witchunt (1992)
Crestfallen / ...And I Lust / The Sweet Suffering / Everwake / They Die, Peaceville VILE 36T (1992)
Nailed To The Cross / 666 / Eternal Rise Of The Sun, Peaceville Collectors CC6 (1994)

Albums:
SERENADES, Peaceville VILE 34 (1993)
Lovelorn Rhapsody' / Sweet Tears / J'ait Fait Une Promesse / They (Always) Die / Sleepless / Sleep In Sanity / Scars Of The Old Stream / Under A Veil (Of Black Lace) / Where Shadows Dance / Dreaming: The Romance
PENTECOST III, Peaceville VILE 51 (1995)
Kingdom / Mine Is Yours To Drown In (Ours Is The New Tribe) / We, The Gods / Pentecost III / Memento Mori
THE SILENT ENIGMA, Peaceville VILE 52 (1995)
Restless Oblivion / Shroud Of Frost / Untitled / Sunset Of Age / Nocturnal Emission / Cerulean Twilight / The Silent Enigma / A Dying Wish / Black Orchid
ETERNITY, Peaceville VILE 64 (1996)
Sentient / Angelica / The Beloved / Eternity (Part 1) / Eternity (Part 2) / Hope / Suicide Veil / Radiance / Far Away / Eternity (Part 3) / Cries On The Wind / Ascension
ALTERNATIVE 4, Peaceville VILE 73 (1998)
Shroud Of False / Fragile Dreams / Empty / Lost Control / Re-connect / Inner Silence / Alternative 4 / Regret / Feel / Destiny
JUDGEMENT, Music For Nations CDMFN 250 (1999)
Deep / Pitiless / Forgotten Hopes / Destiny Is Dead / One Last Goodbye / Make It Right / Parisienne Moonlight / Don't Look Too Far / Emotional Winter / Wings Of God / Judgement / Anyone, Anywhere / 2000 And Gone
A FINE DAY TO EXIT, Music For Nations CDMFN 260 (2001)
Pressure / Underworld / Leave No Trace / Breaking Down The Barriers / A Fine Day To Exit / Panic / Temporary Peace / Outside-Inside
RESONANCE VOL. 1, Peaceville CDVILE 82 (2001)
Scars Of The Old Stream / Everwake / J'fait Une Promesse / Alone / Far Away (Acoustic) / Eternity (Part 2) / Eternity (Part 3) (Acoustic) / Better Off Dead / One Of The Few / Inner Silence / Goodbye Cruel World / Destiny / The Silent Enigma (Orchestral) / Angelica (Live) / Horses / Hope (Video)

ANCIENT CEREMONY (GERMANY)
Line-Up: Christian Anderle (vocals), Patrick Meyer (guitar), Jones (bass), Christoph Rath (keyboards), Achim Mattes (drums)

A Melodic Black Death Metal band with strong Gothic "Horror" influences. ANCIENT CEREMONY's first recordings resulted in the 1993 demo 'Where Serpents Reign'. The band, founded in 1989 as ANCIENT (adding the 'CEREMONY' adjunct upon discovery of the Dutch band), was still essentially the brainchild of the founding duo vocalist Christian Anderle and guitarist F.J. Krebs. Other musicians performing on the initial demo included rhythm guitarist Dirk Wirz, bassist Frank Simon and drummer Christoph Muertes. The first self-produced mini CD recorded by the band, 'Cemetery Visions' retained the same line up as before excepting the addition of keyboard player Stefan Müller, appeared in 1995, with a full album arriving in 1997. 'Under Moonlight We Kiss', released by the British Cacophonous label, saw Ralph Gessinger on bass and Sandra Meyer augmenting the group sound with her distinctive and atmospheric backing vocals.

The heavily keyboard orientated 1999 'Fallen Angels Symphony' album found Anderle working without his founding partner for the first time. Guitars were now in the hands of Patrick Meyer and Marc Babian. Bass duties were doled out to a man who simply went under the title 'Jones'. Vocal enhancement came courtesy of Cynthia Follmann on alto and Erna Siikavirta on soprano.

ANCIENT CEREMONY would make a return in 2000 with the self-issued 'Synagoga Diabolica' opus and a completely overhauled line up. Anderle was joined by Meyer, Jones, keyboard player Christoph Rath, drummer Achim Mattes and chanteuse Cynthia Schilz. Predictably there would be a further transition in the group's line-up for the band's next album, 2002's 'The Third Testament'. Retaining Meyer, Jones and Rath ANCIENT CEREMONY also brought in Melanie Willems for 'Darkside Whispers' whilst 'Angel Chants' would be delivered by Anne Nilles

Singles/EPs:
Forsaken Gardens (Intro) / Cemetery Visions / The God And The Idol / Choir Of Immortal Queens / An Ode To The Moon, Ancient Ceremony ARCD 9501 (1995) ('Cemetery Visions' EP)

Albums:
UNDER MOONLIGHT WE KISS, Cacophonous NIHIL 21 (1997) Eternal Goddess / Her Ivory Slumber / Shadows Of The Undead / Vampyre's Birth / Thy Beauty In Candlelight / Veil Of Desire / Secrets Of Blackened Sky / Dulcet Seduction / Angel's Bloody Tears / New Eden Embraces / Pale Nocturnal Majesty / Under Moonlight We Kiss
FALLEN ANGELS SYMPHONY, Cacophonous NIHIL 32CD (1999) Death In Desire's Masquerade / Bride's Ghostly Grace / Black Roses On Her Grave / Devil's Paradise / The Tragedy Of Forsaken

Angels / Amidst Crimson Stars / Babylon Ascends / Symphoni Satani / Vampyresque Wedding Night
SYNAGOGA DIABOLICA, Alister ARCD 0900-666 (2000) Synagoga Diabolica / Forbidden Fruit Sapientia / Soul Darwinism / Choir Of Immortal Queens / Deorum Contemptor / Crowned Child / Exodus 10-28 / Creeping Death
THE THIRD TESTAMENT, Trisol (2002) Ex Insula Angelorum / Al Shaitan Mahrid / Litanies In Blood / Seed Of Evil / A Black Requiem / With Mephistophelic Egotheism / The Ultimate Nemesis / On Khaos Wings / Salute O Satana / Under Astral Tyranny / Bells Of Damnation

ANGEL ROT (USA)
Line-Up: Tom Five (vocals / guitar), Gyda Gash (bass), Stephen Kleiner (drums)

Heavy Stoner outfit founded by erstwhile WHITE ZOMBIE guitarist Tom Five (real name Tom Guay). The band is a renowned force on the American underground scene. Not only involving the man who many believe to be the real creative force behind WHITE ZOMBIE but also the illustrious figure of bassist Gyda Gash, a lady who came as near to total burn out as possible while staying alive. Gash's NYC Punk life story has been well documented. Musically she has been involved with MOTHER SUPERIOR, the TOMBOYS (releasing the "cult" single 'I Kill With My Cunt'), the transsexual fronted TRANSISTORS and MARIA EX COMMUNICATA. She has also acted out the role of WENDY O'WILLIAMS in a PLASMATICS cover band so successfully the act was invited to perform at the O'Williams tribute concert.

ANGEL ROT came about when Tom Five was fired from WHITE ZOMBIE following their 'Soulcrusher' opus. Initially bass player Mike Davis and drummer Steve Kleiner made up the numbers. Auditions were held for a vocalist but this endeavour proved fruitless so Tom Five adopted the role. Scott Octane of HIGHER OCTANE would eventually land the drummer's role.

Commercially ANGEL ROT debuted with a brace of 1991 singles – 'Screwdriver' and 'Necrostrangle', issued on Buzz Osbourne of THE MELVINS quaintly titled Fuck You Records. The 'Unlistenable Hymns Of Indulgent Damage' album, mastered by Sal Canzonieri of ELECTRIC FRANKENSTEIN, was originally recorded in 1993. Issued in limited numbers in 1995 it was picked up for re-release by Man's Ruin in 1999. The album, laced with esoteric double entendres and

17

Lovecraftian themes, has found a ready new audience in the brave new Stoner world.

With tongues firmly in cheek ANGEL ROT appease misconceptions by opening their live show with JUDAS PRIEST's 'Hell Bent For Leather'. BLACK SABBATH's 'Snowblind' often features in the set as do KISS numbers.

Singles/EPs:
Screwdriver / Monkey Rape, Fuck You (1991) (7" single)
Necrostrangle / Stayin' Alive, Fuck You (1991) (7" single)

Albums:
UNLISTENABLE HYMNS OF INDULGENT DAMAGE, Man's Ruin MR125 (1999)
Erotic Catacomb / Narcissectional Punishment / Dirt Trap / Necrostrangle / Callous Caul of Gloom / Wallow / Feotal Machine / Life-Death Strobe / Clean Disease / Screwdriver

ANGELWITCH (UK)
Line-Up: Kevin Heybourne (vocals/guitar), Kevin Riddles (bass), Dave Dufort (drums)

A band that generated a cult following among the Metalheads of the American West coast based upon the occult overtones and marked speed and heaviness of their original album, recorded with drummer Dave Hogg. Latterly the band has found appreciation amongst the Doom crowd for the acknowledged Sabbathian sounds delivered on their debut album. ANGELWITCH were founded in 1977 by guitarist Kevin Heybourne. Originally titled LUCIFER Heybourne switched to ANGELWITCH when he heard of another LUCIFER doing the rounds. The band went through numerous line-ups before the classic power trio.

The band's official debut on record was the cut 'Baphomet' on the now legendary 'Metal For Muthas' compilation in early 1980. ANGELWITCH also submitted a track 'Extermination Day' to the 1980 BBC compilation album 'Metal Explosion'. Sadly, Hogg was found to be suffering from leukemia necessitating Ex-E.F. BAND drummer Dave Dufort stepping in as replacement after the album release.

Dufort actually has a lengthy history in Rock n' Roll being an ex-member of 1965's THE VOICE, THE SCENERY and PAPER BLITZ ISSUE. All of these mid '60s acts featured latter day SAVOY BROWN, DOG SOLDIER and CHICKENSHACK guitarist MILLER ANDERSON. Dufort then moved on to EAST OF EDEN in the late '60s (he appears on the 1969 album 'Mercator Projected'), as well as being a member of KEVIN AYERS band.

At the height of their popularity ANGELWITCH ranked alongside IRON MAIDEN and SAXON at the forefront of the NWoBHM. The band's success was relatively short-lived though, as gigs became few and far between. British shows were limited to London Marquee appearances and one-off events, whilst the only date abroad was at the East German Erfurt Festival.

At one point Polydor were due to release a live album culled from a 1982 show but this never surfaced. The original band split after the debut with Riddles and Dufort going on to form TYTAN. Riddles was last spotted in a covers band with ex-ONSLAUGHT , TORINO and HIGHWIRE vocalist Tony O'Hora.

The beginning of 1982 saw Heybourne flirting briefly with DEEP MACHINE before persevering by playing the odd club gig as ANGELWITCH featuring DEEP MACHINE members, namely bassist Gerry Cunningham and drummer Micky Bruce.

ANGELWITCH became Heyborne's full-time act once more in early 1982 as Cunningham and Bruce were enticed away from DEEP MACHINE along with vocalist Roger Marsden. The line-up was merely a brief tenure, however as Heybourne eventually ended up in BLIND FURY.

Marsden joined Swedish band E.F. BAND then in 1984 forged a union with another ex-ANGELWITCH and E.F. BAND man drummer Dave Dufort to create NEVADDA FOXX.

ANGELWITCH surfaced again in 1985 with Heybourne and Gordelier splitting from BLIND FURY and enrolling original drummer Dave Hogg together with vocalist Dave Tattum. With this incarnation of the band they laid down the quite commercial edged 'Screamin And Bleedin'' album. Hogg left the band once more after its release and was replaced by former DEXYS MIDNIGHT RUNNERS drummer Spencer Hollman. Gigs were still few and far between.

Third album 'Frontal Assault' saw ANGELWITCH return to their former heaviness but Tattum left upon its completion to join NIGHTWING, leaving Heybourne to assume vocal duties.

In 1989 the band added a second guitarist Grant Dennison. A short tour of Holland followed with support act SATAN, but Heybourne eventually relocated to America where nostalgia for early ANGELWITCH reaped the reward of a live set of 'classics'. The band recorded a demo with EXODUS drummer Tom Hunting and Lee Altus of HEATHEN but failed to secure a new deal.

Although ANGELWITCH failed to live up to the legend that was created around the band early on, the band remained an influence with groups that arrived on the scene in later years with both ONSLAUGHT and TROUBLE covering the ANGELWITCH classic 'Confused'.

was renewed in the late '90s by the release of a live album on High Vaultage Records. ANGELWITCH themselves were far from dormant issuing a CD compilation of various demos including the 1987 'Psychopathic' tapes and 1999's set 'Twist Of The Knife'. The resulting album 'Resurrection' was only available via the internet.

ANGELWITCH were back in 2000 for live gigs and a projected new album. Alongside Heybourne the fresh look band comprised guitarist Keith Herzberg, bass player Richie Wicks - a former lead vocalist of SONS OF EDEN and VIOLENTLY FUNKY, and drummer Scott Higham. The band bounced back in quite spectacular style with a performance at the prestigious 'Wacken' Metal festival in Germany before setting to work on fresh studio material.

The list of bands to have covered 'Confused' increased in 2001 as Americans SIX FEET UNDER cut a grindingly heavy take for their latest album. In August of 2001 it was announced that Higham had decamped to join the highly regarded SHADOWKEEP. Ace Finchum, a former member of Glam band TIGERTAILZ, took his place.

In November the ANGELWITCH ranks splintered further with Weeks opting to resume his former role as a lead singer and opting to join fellow NWoBHM resurrectees TYGERS OF PAN TANG. Statements issued by band members in January would confirm the fact that ANGELWITCH had folded once again, Wicks resuming action with SONS OF EDEN.

However, in August a surprise official statement confirmed that Kevin Heybourne, Keith Herzberg, Richie Wicks and Scott Higham had resolved their differences and were back in action yet again.

Singles/EPs:
Sweet Danger / Flight Nineteen, EMI 5064 (1980) **75 UK**
Sweet Danger / Flight Nineteen / Hades Paradise, EMI 12 EMI 5064 (1980) (12" single)
Angelwitch / Gorgon, Bronze BRO 108 (1980)
Loser / Suffer / Dr. Phibes, Bronze BRO 121 (1981)
Goodbye / Reawakening, Killerwatt KIL 3001(1985)

Albums:
ANGELWITCH, Bronze BRON532 (1981)
Angelwitch / Atlantis / White Witch / Confused / Sorcerers / Gorgon / Sweet Danger / Free Man / Angel Of Death / Devil's Tower
SCREAMIN' AND BLEEDIN', Killerwatt KILP4001 (1985)
Who's To Blame / Child Of The Night / Evil Games / Afraid Of The Dark / Screamin' And Bleedin' / Reawakening / Waltz The Night / Goodbye / Fatal Kiss / UXB
FRONTAL ASSAULT, Killerwatt Records (1986)
Frontal Assault / Dreamworld / Rendezvous With The Blade / Religion (Born Again) / Straight From Hell / She Don't Lie / Take To The Wing / Something Wrong / Undergods
DOCTOR PHIBES, Rawpower RAWLP025 (1986)
Angelwitch / Atlantis / White Witch / Confused / Sorceress / Loser / Dr. Phibes / Gorgon / Sweet Danger / Free Man / Angel Of Death / Devil's Tower / Suffer
LIVE, Metal Blade ZORRO 1 (1990)
Angel Of Death / Sweet Danger / Confused / Sorceress / Gorgon / Baphomet / Extermination Day / Atlantis / Flight 19 / Angel Witch / White Witch
'82 REVISITED (LIVE), High Vaultage HV-1005 (1996)
Gorgon / Nowhere To Run / They Wouldn't Dare / Sorceress / Evil Games / White Witch / Angel Of Death / Angel Witch / Evil Games (Studio Version) / They Wouldn't Dare (Studio Version) / Nowhere To Run (Studio Version)
RESURRECTION, Angelwitch (1998)
Psychopathic I / Time To Die / Violence / Silent But Deadly / Twist Of The Knife / Psychopathic II / Slowly Sever / Worm / Scrape The Well / Inertia

ANTHEMON (FRANCE)

Line-Up: Nathalie Bonnaud (vocals), Sylvian Begot (guitar / keyboards), Alexandre Kohler (guitar), Marc Canlers (bass), Nicolas Joyeux (drums)

Paris based Gothic 'Sympho Doom' band convened during early 1997. ANTHEMON's self-financed 1998 debut album 'Nocturnal Contemplation' saw a line-up of vocalist Bénédicte A., guitar player / programmer Sylvain Begot and bassist Marc Canlers. Pre-ANTHEMON Begot had gained experience with Thrash acts SEARN and BLOODSTONE as well as a period with Black Metal act THE RAVENING.

In June of 1999 ANTHEMON integrated keyboard player Marina into the line-up for live work and added lead singer Joanna the month after. However, by October Joanna was out of the picture. The band suffered a further loss when rhythm guitarist Cyril also made his exit. A number of guitarists, including Andre in December of 1999 and Jeremy in January of 2000, were tried out for short periods until the band settled on Alexandre Kohler of LOARGANN.

The band, although losing the services of Bénédicte A. and undergoing numerous line-up changes, ANTHEMON, now fronted by Nathalie Bonnaud, expanded to a quintet for the September 2000 'Talvi' outing.

ANTHEMON projected a third album for early 2003 release. Guitarist Sylvian Begot also operates a Funeral Doom venture entitled MONOLITHE, recording a debut album 'Les Portes Closes Du Paradis'.

Albums:
NOCTURNAL CONTEMPLATION, (1998)
At Dusk... / Nocturnal Contemplation / Blood As A Flower / The Dark Lights / Coming Back To Life (My Third Birth)
TALVI, (2000)
Talvi / Floating Further / Shroud Of Frost / Withered Smile / Against The Emptiness / Longer Than Life / Der Todesking

ANTICHRISIS (GERMANY)
Line-Up: Sid (vocals), Dragonfly (vocals), Gnu (guitar), Waran (keyboards), Naex (uillean pipes), Kurgator (drums)

An ambitious German outfit ANTICHRISIS would be pigeonholed in the Gothic scene much to their frustration. The band actually deal in classically inspired mediaeval Folk Rock.

ANTICHRISIS made their first impression with the 'Missa Depositum Custodi' demo, which weighed in at a mighty 80 minute duration. At this juncture the band consisted of mentor Sid, going under the title 'Moonshadow', and female vocalist Willowcat. The 1997 debut, 'Cantarra Anachoretta' issued by the Ars Metalli label, would be recorded with the aid of a drum machine. Response to the album from the media placed the band squarely in the Gothic camp much to the band's annoyance.

With Willowcat parting ways with ANTICHRISIS the band employed the services of uillean pipe player Naex. This new recruit would lend a whole array of talents to the band proving adept at bodhràn, keyboards, guitars, mandolin and tin whistle A new deal was established with the Austrian Napalm label for the second effort 'A Legacy Of Love'. This outing saw session vocalist Lisa taking on vocal chores with Gnu on guitar and Waran on keyboards. Oddly press releases issued at the time stated that

'Moonshadow' had died although later his "replacement" Sid admitted they were in fact one and the same.

In the Spring of 1999 ANTICHRISIS, now fronted by female singer Dragonfly, took their show on the road as part of a Napalm package billing with Metal bands TRISTANIA, SIEBENBURGEN, THE SINS OF THE BELOVED and TRAIL OF TEARS. For these shows Naex was unavailable and ANTICHRISIS pulled in Brown Jenkin on guitar to fill out their live sound.

The group's third album 'Perfume', released in April 2000 by Napalm subsidiary Black Rose Productions, would be topped off by an adventurous cover version of LED ZEPPELIN's 'Whole Lotta Love'. Kurgator would be credited as drummer for this release.

Albums:
CANTARRA ANACHORETTA, Ars Metalli (1997)
The Endless Dance / Requiem Ex Sidhe / Goodbye To Jane / Baleias / Her Orphaned Throne / Descending Messiah
A LEGACY OF LOVE, Napalm (1998)
How Can I Live On Top Of A Mountain? (This Is My Love, Do You Like Her? (Slow Air) - The Pipe On The Hob - Will You Come Home With Me? / Nightswan - The Swans Are Rising / Trying Not To Breathe / Baleias Bailando - Toss The Feathers (Reel) / Dancing In The Midnight Sun - Snowflakes / Planet Kyrah / The Sea / Our Last Show / Forever I Ride - The Cliffs Of Moher - Lannigan's Ball / The Farewell / End Of December
PERFUME, Black Rose Productions BRP113 (2001)
Hole In My Head / Carry Me Down / We Are / The Witches / Wasteland / Like The Stars / Gates Of Paradise / Something Inside / Dragonflies / Goodbye To Jane / Whole Lotta Love

APHOTIC (Green Bay, WI, USA)

Death-Doom from erstwhile DUSK personnel.

Singles/EPs:
Livid Dread / Glide / Psychoma / A Chamee To Live / Panoramic, Aphotic (2000) ('Aphotic' EP)
Precipice / Under Veil Of Endless Grey Sky / Atmosphere / Free Me, Aphotic (2001) ('Under Veil Of Endless Dark Sky' EP)

APOLLYON SUN (SWITZERLAND)
Line-Up: Thomas Gabriel Fischer (vocals / guitar), Erol Unala (guitar), Dany Zingg

(bass), Roger Muller (keyboards), Marky Edelmann (drums),

After a lengthy hiatus former CELTIC FROST mentor Thomas Gabriel Fischer (previously known as Tom G. Warrior) announced his new project APOLLYON SUN during 1998, debuting with a startling mini album 'God Leaves And Dies' and backed by heavyweight management of Sanctuary.
Drummer Mark Edelmann is in fact former CORONER man Marquis Marky now sensibly using his real name.
By 2001 rumours of a full scale CELTIC FROST reformation, at first officially denied, would be found to bear truth.

Albums:
GOD LEAVES AND DIES, Mayan MYNCD1 (1998)
God Leaves / Reefer Boy / The Cane / Concrete Satan / Bedlam And Blind
THE NEXT LEVEL OF PROVOCATION, Sanctuary (2000)

APOTHEOSIS (GERMANY)
Line-Up: Bernd Golderer (vocals), Marcus Rembold (guitar), Udo Plieninger (guitar), Alexander Woydich (bass), Alexander Dallinger (drums / keyboards)

Formed in 1993 and issuing the 'Beyond The Grave - No Breeding Ground' demo the following year, after several live shows M.D.D. Records signed APOTHEOSIS.
Playing Death Metal with a Gothic touch, the band sing in both English and German and have, since the release of the first album, added keyboard player Marco to the ranks.

Albums:
A SHROUD OF BELIEF, M.D.D. 06 CD (1996)
Apotheosis / As Serenity Fades / A Shroud Of Belief / White Angel - Dusty God / A Landslide Called Eternity / Beyond The Grave / Stars Beyond Their Skies / No Breeding Ground / Total Silence
BLACK AND BLUE REALITY, M.D.D. 11CD (1997)
Black & Blue Reality / Exfarevanity / Pleasurefall / Horizon / Splendid / Release / Excuses / Vergangen / Innocence For Free / A Start Inside / Rain

APRIL ETHEREAL (POLAND)
Line-Up: Adrian Pe_ka (vocals), Jan Rajkow-Krzywicki (guitar), Jerzy Rajkow-Krzywicki (guitars / keyboards), Marek Gajewski (bass), Marcin Bugowski (drums)

A Dark Rock act out of Warsaw with both Gothic and Progressive inclinations. The band started out as a side concern of vocalist / drummer Jan Rajkow-Krzywicki and Jerzy Rajkow-Krzywicki handling guitar, bass and keyboards during 1996. Initially the project was entitled LEON. The Satanically minded 'Leviathan' demo surfaced in 1999, followed the same year by the 'Silva' tape. This latter effort found LEON branching out into more adventurous musical territory.
During July of 2000 the venture was re-billed as APRIL ETHEREAL. Lead vocalist Adrian Pe_ka joined the fold in January of 2001 as the group signed to the British based Conquer Records for the 'Advent' album.
APRIL ETHEREAL was brought up to strength with the addition of bass player Marek Gajewski and drummer Marcin Bugowski, both from Doom-Death act CARNAL. APRIL ETHEREAL toured the UK as openers to a NILE / BEHEMOTH package in late 2001.

Albums:
ADVENT, Conquer CD001CD (2001)
Her Silent Cry At Dawn / The First Step Into The Unknown / Departure / The Repose / Hologram / The Last Glance Into Her Eyes / Truth / Epilogue

ARCHITECT (UK)
Line-Up: Paul Mother (vocals), Tim Walker (guitar), Darren Maude (guitar), Richard Thomas (bass / keyboards), Dave Wood (drums)

Formerly known as HARLEQYN, featuring a line-up of Paul Mother, Dave Wood, Tim Walker and bassist Phil Sargeant, HARLEQYN released a three track demo in 1989. As ARCHITECT these Bradford Gothic Rockers utilized heavy freemasonic imagery and released a string of self-financed demos and vinyl efforts. Of note is the 1991 demo 'Moonage Daydream'.

Singles / EPs:
More Than Before / Castles In The Sky / Sad Cypress / Decay, Voltage VEP93 (1991)

Albums:
POETS AND THIEVES, Voltage VCD127 (1992)

ARGILE (FRANCE)
Line-Up: S.A.S de L'Argilière (vocals / guitar), Jean-Jacques Moréac (guitar / bass / drums / keyboards)

Avantgarde Doom side venture of

MISANTHROPE members S.A.S de L'Argilière and Jean-Jacques Moréac. The 2002 ARGILE album 'The Monotonous Moment Of A Monologue' includes a cover version of DARKTHRONE's 'In the Shadow Of The Horns'.
Jonathon Alonso would session on acoustic guitar.

Albums:
THE MONOTONOUS MOMENT OF A MONOLOGUE, Holy HOLY73CD (2002)
Troubled By The Storm / Satanic Music / Pandemonic Necronomicon / Pyramid Paradise / Heart Of The Celestial Empire / In the Shadow Of The Horns / Danse Macabre Mist / Organ Cries Of Iron / A Lugubrious Funeral / God's Degenerated Angel

ARTICA (ITALY)
Line-Up: Alberto Chaste (vocals / guitar), Gabriel Serafini (guitar), Michele Mariella (bass), Massimiliano Bonavita (keyboards), Stefano Marcon (drums)

Gothic "Cold Wave" Rock act ARTICA came into being during the late '80s, marking their arrival with a February 1993 demo tape 'Marea'. ARTICA's commercial debut would be with a track included on the compilation album `L'Appel De La Muse, vol. IV'.
The 'Dahlia' cassette followed a year later and a valuable spotlight in one of Mick Mercer's Gothic Rock tomes reaped further exposure across Europe. ARTICA would subsequently sign to the Stuttgart based Nyctalopia label for the album 'Ombre E Luce' ('Shadows & Light') which comprised newly recorded tracks alongside demo material.
Taking charge of their own affairs the band would self-finance the second album 'Natura' bringing in the engineering talents of Sandro Oliva, a member of the FRANK ZAPPA band. Although newly including such elements as female vocal, harpsichord and violin 'Natura' witnessed a fresh aggression in the band's sound. The record would be signed to the domestic Radio Luxor imprint for release in July 1997
ARTICA would donate their rendition of the VIRGIN PRUNES 'Caucasian Walk' to a tribute album in 1998.

Albums:
OMBRE E LUCE, Nyctalopia (1995)
Saian / Honira / Lorelei / Dahlia / Lenhia / Leila / Sarajevo / In Me / Indomita / Preqhiera MCMXCV / Ombra / Luce
NATURA, Radio Luxor RL001 (1997)
Faust / Inferno / Cenere / Boemia / Angelica / Crocifissione / Giardini / Lucrezia / Immagine

/ Tipaza

AS DIVINE GRACE (FINLAND)
Line-Up: Hanna Kalske (vocals), Ari Ala-Miekkaoja (guitar), Marko Taipole (bass), Juka Sillanpää (keyboards), Mikko Lappälainen (drums)

AS DIVINE GRACE, based in the city of Pori, would make a startling transition from their inception as a trad Death Metal band through to the 'Luno' era Doom and melancholic 'Dark Pop' swansong 'Suprematre'. The band existed in a previous guise as Death Metal band MORPHEUS. The early membership of the band comprised vocalist / bassist Jari Mäkiranta, guitarists Ari Ala-Miekkaoka and Sami Langsjö, former SYNDICATE, FUNCUNT ('F') and SCEPTICAL SCHIZO keyboard player Jukka Sillanpää and drummer Matti Tuohimaa.
The debut, 'Romantic Beatitude Of Faded Dawn', was recorded during late 1993 but not released by the German Folter label until 1996. By the time of its belated issue AS DIVINE GRACE had radically shifted their musical stance. Sillanpää would also involve himself as a member of THIS EMPTY FLOW during 1996-97.
Makiranta would relinquish the lead vocal role to Hanna Kalkes for the 'Luno' album. Makiranta would then decamp as did Tuohimaa. AS DIVINE GRACE pulled in Mikko Lappälainen of LAVRA and SCEPTICAL SCHIZO on drums and took a further musical leap with the 1999 'Suprematre' effort. Bass player Marko Taipole was later added.
Sillanpää's pursuit of side activities such as the medieval KIVIKYY and the Ambient SORB-I-TAL would eventually see the keyboard player pitching all his efforts into the latter project during mid 2000.

Albums:
ROMANTIC BEATITUDE OF FADED DAWN, Folter (1996)
Maimer Of Sleeps / Heartlessness, Lorn Pains / Garden Of Tears / Secret Winds
LUMO, Avantgarde (1997)
Perpetual / In Low Spirits / Gash / Grimstone / The Bloomsearcher / Rosy Tale / Out Of The Azure / Wave Theory
SUPREMATURE, Avantgarde (1999)
Your Julie / Morbide / Personal / Tango / Shelter / Ferocious / Be Used / The Most / Andre / Rhizome

ASEIDAD (CHILE)
Line-Up: Marcelo Vivallo (vocals), Patricio Saavedra (guitar), Marcelo Prades (guitar),

Mauricio Vivallo (bass), Luis Moya (drums)

Doomsters ASEIDAD started life as a straightforward Power Metal band during 1996 with a line-up including the Vivallo brothers, bassist Mauricio and vocalist Marcelo - the latter ex-DAMNED, guitarist Patricio Saavedra of GOLGOTAS, second guitarist Ivan Ibarra and drummer Luis Moya. Within a year ASEIDAD had shifted direction into a more Gothic / Doom stance.
Guitarist Christian Nello would fleetingly replace Ibarra before ASEIDAD were then left operating as a single guitar unit. A demo was subsequently cut with DOMINUS guitarist Jano Lizama at the controls. For the 'Autumn' album the group drafted guitar player Marcelo Prades.
ASEIDAD underwent turbulent times following the album release with a major fracturing that saw Moya, bassist Mauricio Vivallo and Prades all out of the picture. Moya joined fellow Doom merchants POEMA ARCANUS. New faces would be revealed as guitarist Juan Pablo Binimelis, ex-ASTRAL SOUL bass player Erik Birkner and drummer Mario Chacana.

Albums:
AUTUMN, (2000)
Wish / Eternal Autumn / Praise Of A Blind Child / Angel Efluvium / The Burn / Skyggerness Dal / The Ritual / Wounded / The Father's Pride / Stay By Me / Changes / Rainbow

ASHEN MORTALITY (UK)
Line-Up: Ian Arkley (vocals / guitar), Melanie Bolton (vocals/keyboards), Tim Cooper (bass), George Aytoun (drums)

West Midlands Christian Doomladen Death Metal band. ASHEN MORTALITY were created in 1993 by former SEVENTH ANGEL frontman Ian Arkley.
The original line-up comprised Arkley, vocalist and keyboard player Melanie Bolton, bassist Tim Cooper and drummer Ben Jones. ASHEN MORTALITY's debut eponymous demo was actually produced by Andy Wicket, the original singer of DURAN DURAN!
Following second demo 'Separation' Jones decamped to be replaced by Neal Harris for an appearance at the 'Greenbelt' festival and tours of Holland and Germany. To promote the debut album 'Sleepless Remorse' ASHEN MORTALITY undertook support gigs to AT THE GATES, ACRIMONY and HECATE ENTHRONED with another new face on the drum stool Neil Shivlock.
George Aytoun is the latest sticksman

appearing on second album 'Your Caress'. Arkley would guest on Australian Christian Death Metal act PARAMAECIUM's third album 'A Time To Mourn'.

Albums:
SLEEPLESS REMORSE, Forsaken (1996)
Yesterday's Gone / Faded Tapestry / Separation / Sleepless Remorse / Cast The First Stone / The Darkest Of Nights / Imprisoned
YOUR CARESS, (1999)
Broken Bonds / Your Caress / In Empty Eyes / My Reflection
From This Cage / Our Eden / Through The Vale

ASHES TO ASHES (NORWAY)
Line-Up: Kenneth Brastad (vocals), Michael Stenberg (guitars), Björn Luna (bass), Kristian Johansen (drums)

Exceptionally heavy Progressive Doom Metal band. ASHES TO ASHES was forged in 1992 by guitarist Michael Stenberg, bass player Björn Luna and drummer Kristian Johansen. Two demo tapes, 'Between The Devil And The Deep Blue Sea' and 'Temples Of Ice', set the scene for their debut 1998 album 'Shapes Of Spirits'. ASHES TO ASHES signed to Dutch label DVS Records for the 2001 outing 'Cardinal VII'.

Albums:
CARDINAL VII, DVS (2001)
New World Obscure / Embraced In Black / Among Mortals / Truth On Scaffold / Iben / Dualism / Sic Transit Gloria Mundi / Ravenous Unleashed / Behind Closed Eyes / Cardinal VII / Iben II

ASHES YOU LEAVE (CROATIA)
Line-Up: Dunja Radetic (vocals / flute), Kristijan Nilic (vocals), Breislav Poje (guitar), Neven Mendrila (guitar), Gordan Gencic (drums), Vladimir Krytuija (keyboards), Marta Batinic (violin),

Ambient Black Doom act ASHES YOU LEAVE were previously known as ICON. The group adopted the new title with the demo 'The Kingdom Before The Lies'.
Members of ASHES YOU LEAVE united with personnel from fellow Black act CASTRUM to create a new 2000 act NELDOROTH.

Albums:
THE PASSAGE BACK TO LIFE, Effigy (1997)
Salva Me / The Passage Back To Life / Thorn Of The Dead Flower / Drowning In My Dreams / Lay Down Alone / White Chains /

Tears
DESPERATE EXISTENCE, Morbid (1999)
A Wish / Never Again Alone In The Dark / Desperate Existence / Et Vidi Solem Evanere / Momentary Eclipse Of Hate / Searching For Artificial Happiness / Shadow Of Someone Else's Being / Outro
THE INHERITANCE OF SIN AND SHAME, Morbid (2000)
Tin Horns / Your Divinity / Shepherd's Song / Miles Of Worn Out Days / When Withered Flowers / And Thus You Poured Like Heaven Wept / The Inheritance Of Sin And Shame / Amber Star

ASK EMBLA (NORWAY)
Line-Up: Eivor Raudstein (vocals), Zorkham Outre (guitar / bass / programming)

A Norwegian Gothic Industrial Metal duo. ASK EMBLA, so titled after two Norse tree gods Ash and Elm, signed to the Polish Fluttering Dragon label for the 2000 debut album.

Albums:
QUESTIONS ASKED, Fluttering Dragon (2000)
Always Looked Good on Paper, Always Sounded Good in Theory / Into the Day / Savn (Til Eaivor) / Nothing Is Everything / Still Waiting / The Confined Planet / Not Pleased / Apologize / …And Another Reject / Dream

ASPHYX (HOLLAND)
Line-Up: Martin van Drunen (vocals / bass), Eric Daniels (guitar), Bob Bagchus (drums)

ASPHYX date back to 1989 when the band was formed by drummer Bob Bagchus with former member Tony Brookhuis and swiftly issued the first demo entitled 'Enter The Domain'. The band operated in the Death Metal field with a tendency to wallow in sub-Doom passages on occasion.
Frontman Martin van Drunen split from Dutch techno-thrashers PESTILENCE in late 1990 due to personality clashes within the band and, shortly after his departure, he hooked up with ASPHYX replacing former bassist / vocalist Theo Loomans.
ASPHYX went into the studio to record a projected debut album to be entitled 'Embrace The Death'. However, due to record company financial problems these tapes never saw a commercial release.
The band's second attempt, and what was to be their debut album, 'The Rack' was recorded on a minimalist budget in a deliberate attempt to achieve a deliberately primitive sound. Worldwide sales approaching 30,000 copies were boosted by a European tour alongside ENTOMBED, proving ASPHYX had chosen the right path.
'Crush The Cenotaph', issued in 1992, was a mini-album produced by Waldemar Sorychta and containing reworks of pre van Drunen era material and live tracks. Live work to promote the mini-album comprised an extensive European tour with BENEDICTION and BOLT-THROWER.
Apparently the tour was more enjoyable for van Drunen than most. Clearly impressed by each other, the bassist / vocalist joined BOLT-THROWER in 1994!
The revised line-up of ASPHYX thus emerged, comprised new vocalist / bassist Ron van Pol, guitarist Eric Daniels and drummer Sander Van Hoof.
Further ructions hit the ASPHYX line-up in 1995 as Daniels joined ETERNAL SOLSTICE and original vocalist Theo Loomanns returned. Loomanns contributed bass and guitar to the 'God Cries' album.
The 'Embrace The Death' sessions finally found a release in 1996 through Century Media with extra tracks from 'Mutilating Process'.
Despite the constant line-up changes ASPHYX continued to build on their popularity in the Death Metal market with consistent album sales. However, the band changed titles to SOULBURN for 1998's 'Feeding On Angels' album. Tragically Loomans was killed the same year in a road accident.
The 2000 album found ASPHYX, back to their former title as a mark of respect to Loomans, as a duo of Wannes Gubbles, Eric Daniel and Bog Bagchus. However, after its release ASPHYX announced their retirement.

Singles/EPs:
Mutilating Process / Streams Of Ancient Wisdom, Nuclear Blast (1990)
Crush The Cenotaph / Rite Of Shades / The Krusher / Evocation (Live) / Wasteland Of Terror (Live), Century Media 799723-2 (1992) ('Crush The Cenotaph' EP)

Albums:
THE RACK, Century Media 84 9716 (1991)
The Quest Of Absurdity / Vermin / Diabolical Existence / Evocation / Wasteland Of Terror / The Sickening Dwell / Ode To A Nameless Grave / Pages In Blood / The Rack
LAST ONE ON EARTH, Century Media (1993)
M.S. Bismarck / The Krusher / Serenade In Lead / Last One On Earth / The Incarnation Of Lust / Streams Of Ancient Wisdom / Food For The Ignorant / Asphyx (Forgotten War)

ASPHYX, Century Media CD 77063 (1994)
Prelude Of The Unhonoured Funeral /
Depths Of Eternity / Emperors Of Salvation /
'Til Death Do Us Part / Initiation Into The
Ossuary / Incarcerated Chimaeras /
Abomination Echoes / Back Into Eternity /
Valleys In Oblivion / Thoughts Of An Atheist
GOD CRIES, Century Media 77117-2 (1996)
God Cries / It Awaits / My Beloved Enemy /
Died Yesterday / Cut-Throat Urges /
Slaughtered In Sodom / Frozen Soul / Fear
My Greed / The Blood I Spilled.
EMBRACE THE DEATH, Century Media CD
77141-2 (1996)
Intro / Embrace The Death / The Sickened
Dwell / Streams Of Ancient Wisdom /
Thoughts Of An Atheist / Crush The
Cenotaph / Denying The Goat / Vault Of The
Wailing Souls / Circle Of The Secluded / To
Succubus A Whore / Eternity's Depths /
Outro / Mutilating Process / Streams Of An
Ancient Wisdom
ON THE RISING WINGS OF INFERNO,
Century Media 77263-2 (2000)
Summoning The Storm / The Scent Of
Obscurity / For They Ascend… / On The
Wings Of Inferno / 06-06-2006 / Waves Of
Fire / Indulge In Frenzy / Chaos In The Flesh
/ Marching Towards The Styx

ASTRAL RISING (FRANCE)
Line-Up: Frank Tomse (vocals / guitar),
Essem (guitar), Phillipe Guiziou (bass),
Jerome Lachaud (drums)

A French Death flavoured Doom act.
Drummer Jerome Lauchaud split after the
debut and for 1995's 'In Quest' ASTRAL
RISING drafted Eric Lauuad. The band folded
in 1996.

Singles/EPs:
Alpha State, Arckham (1992)

Albums:
ABEON AADEONA, Chaos 001 (1993)
Nocturnal Thoughts / …In Awe / Odd
Memories / Dawn In Cries / Skadia / Tactire
Tink
IN QUEST, Active AC.95-001 (1995)
In Quest / Beggar Of The New Hopes /
Wasteland / Gowns Black Viles / Anguish
Feelings / Choral Fantasy / Pray In A Garden
/ The Realm To Come / Calliope

ASTROQUEEN (SWEDEN)
Line-Up: Daniel Anghede (vocals / guitar),
Daniel Tolergard (guitar), Mattias Wester
(bass), Johan Backman (drums)

'70s infused detuned Stoner-Space Rock

replete with sideburns and afros.
ASTROQUEEN are a relatively new
development having been forged in 1998 just
outside Gothenburg. ASTROQUEEN have
supported UNIDA in their homeland.
The debut commercial outing, the 'Rufus The
Space Agent' 7" single released by the
German Monster Zero label, was limited to
500 copies.
The 'Into Submission' album was produced by
KING DIAMOND guitarist Andy LaRocque.

Singles/EPs:
Rufus The Space Agent / Asteroid Blaster
Part I, Monster Zero (2000) (7" single)

Albums:
INTO SUBMISSION, Pavement (2001)
Landslide / Out Of This World / Superhuman
God / Brain Phase Voyage / Rufus Jr. /
Planet Dust / The Sonic Ride / Soulburner / I
Go To Sleep (I'm Gone) / Serve The Sun /
Lua Vermelha

ATARAXIA (ITALY)
Line-Up: Francesca Nicoli (vocals / flute),
Vittorio Vandelli (guitar), Giovanni Pagliani
(keyboards)

Not to be confused with the Japanese act of
the same name, the Italian Black Metal act
ATARAXIA play an eclectic mix of
Progressive, Gothic and Classic styles.
Adventurously, the band delivers lyrics sung
in Latin, English, French and Italian. The track
'La Nouva Mergherita' is an Italian version of
the KATE BUSH hit 'Wuthering Heights'.
ATARAXIA vocalist Francesca Nicoli also
lends her vocals to MONUMENTUM for their
'In Absentia Christi' album.

Singles/EPs:
In Amoris Mortisque, Apollyon EFA 12165
(1995) (10" Split single with ENGELSSTAUB)

Albums:
SIMPHONIA SINE NOMINE, Apollyon EFA
12172 (1994)
Preludio / Entrata Solemne / Canzona /
Onno Corale / Fuga Trionfale / Preghiera /
Marcia Cerimoniade / Elevazione / Pastorale
/ Ode Vespertilia
AD PERPETUAM REI MEMORIUM,
Apollyon EFA 12153 (1994) (1994)
Prophetia / Anno Domini MDVLVI / Aigues
Mortes / Tu Es La Force Du Silence / Flee Et
Fabian / Nosce Te Ipsum /
Zweistimmenstäuschung / Torquemada /
Bleumarine / Vitrage / Aquarello / Emeraude
LA MALEDICTION D'ONDINE, Apollyon
EFA 12172 (1994)

Medusa / Sybil / Flora / Blanche / Annabel Lee / Astimelusa / June / Lubia / Ligeia / Ophile / Lucretia / Zela (The City Is The Sea) / Lucrecia / Ondine

THE MOON SANG ON THE APRIL CHAIR / RED DEEP DIRGES OF A NOVEMBER MOON, Apollyon EFA 12162 (1995)

A Face To Paint Tulips / Verdigis Wounds / The Tale Of The Crying Fireflies / Colouring Nocturnal Lemons / Rocking Chair Of Dreams / Satis Vixi / Lady Lazarus / Spiritus Ad Vindictum

CONCERTO No. 6: BAROQUE PLAISANTERIE, Apollyon 96029 EFA 12175-2 (1996)

Part 1: Larghetto, Passaggio Lustrale / Romanza, Scarletminded Echoes / Toccata Per Chitarra, The Winds Of Carminio / Notturno, Belle Rose Porporine / Gagliarda, Astore Serotina / Madrigale, Ticket To Ride / Arioso, La Bourgeoise Et La Noble / Gavotta, Maybe-O'-The Leaves / Forlane, Bleaumarine / Carrousel, Dulcamara / Coda, I'm The Wind / Part II: (Live) Siciliana, Lei Morra / Gavotta, Maybe-O'-The Leaves / Romanza, Scarletminded Echoes / Canticle, Wide White Wave

IL FANTASMA DELL OPERA, Avantgarde AV018 (1996)

E' Je Fantasma? (Part I) - Is It The Phantom? (Chapter One)/ E' Je Fantasma ? (Part Two) - Is It The Phantom? (Chapter Two) / La Nouva Margherita (The New Marguerite) / Je Palco N5 (The Box N5 - Chapter 5) / Le Violino Incanto (The Enchanted Violin - Chapter 6) / Faust Im Ma Sala Maldetta (Faust In A Cursed Hell - Chapter 8) / Ae Ballo Mascherato (To The Bal Masque - Chapter 13) / La Liiza Ai Apollo (Apollo's Lyre - Chapter 13) / Je Signore Delle Botole (The Lord Of The Trap-Doors - Chapter 14) / Nei Sotenanei Dell Opera (In The Opera's Vaults - Chapter 21) / Le Ore Rpsa Di Mazendezay (The Pink Hours Of Manzeneran - Chapter 25) / Fine Degli Amor' Del Mostro (End Of The Monster's Lovers - Chapter 28)

THE ATOMIC BITCHWAX (USA)

Line-Up: Chris Kosnik (vocals / bass), Ed Mundell (guitars), Keith Ackerman (drums)

THE ATOMIC BITCHWAX, fronted by Chris Kosnik of GODSPEED repute, is the side project of ex-DAISYCUTTER and present day MONSTER MAGNET guitarist Ed Mundell. The debut album included a cover of TOMMY BOLIN's 'Crazed Fandango' and CORE's 'Kiss The Sun'.

October 2000's 'Atomic Bitchwax II' album sees a guest spot for GOVT. MULE guitarist Warren Haynes. The band would contribute their version of 'Combination' to the 2000 Small Stone Recordings AEROSMITH tribute 'Right In The Nuts'.

THE ATOMIC BITCHWAX would contribute significantly to the 2001 SCENE KILLER project of 2001, featuring no less than seven tracks from the New Jersey assemblage.

The band made their live debut in the UK on the 29th of November 2001 at London's Camden Underworld.

With Ed Mundell bowing out of the band in February of 2002 it seemed as though THE ATOMIC BITCHWAX had breathed their last. The swan song Charlie Schafer produced album 'Spit Blood', released by Meteor City in March, compiled a collection of new tracks and oddities. Opening with a cover version of AC/DC's 'Dirty Deeds Done Dirt Cheap' the record included a visual documentary and a sampler of other tracks as performed by SOLACE, THE RIBEYE BROTHERS, SLAPROCKET THE MUSHROOM RIVER BAND and ORQUESTA DEL DESIERTO.

Chris Kosnik now operates BLACK NASA whilst drummer Keith Ackerman busies himself with THE CLONE OBEY, a side venture in alliance with Jason of SOLACE. Besides his priorities with MONSTER MAGNET Mundell has another band in his arsenal, GALLERY OF MITES with MONSTER MAGNET colleagues bassist Joe Calandra, drummer Jon Kleiman and Tim Cronin. Alongside the MONSTER MAGNET personnel GALLERY OF MITES boasted a nine man strong line-up including Dwayne from BLACK NASA, Stu of HALFWAY TO GONE and Mike and Jim from LORD STERLING.

Albums:

ATOMIC BITCHWAX, Tee Pee-Mia 1009-2 (1999)

Stork / Birth To The Earth / Hey Alright / Crazed Fandango / Hope You Die / Kiss The Sun / Ain't Nobody Gonna Hang Me In My Home / Last Of The V8 Interceptors / The Formula / Shitkicker

ATOMIC BITCHWAX II, Tee Pee TP 028CD (2000)

Ice Pick Freak / Forty-Five / Play The Game / Smokescreen / Cast Aside Your Masks / The Cloning Chamber / Marching On The Skulls Of The Dead / Dishing Out A Heavy Dose Of Tough Love / Solid / Liquor Queen

SPIT BLOOD, Meteor City MCY-020 (2002)

Dirty Deeds Done Dirt Cheap / Liquor Queen / Get Your Gear / Cold Day In Hell / Spit Blood / Black Trans-Am / U Want I Should / Change It (Rough mix) (MUSHROOM RIVER BAND) / Shadow Stealing (Rough mix) (ORQUESTA DEL DESIERTO) / Holy Mother Sunshine (SLAPROCKET) / Feel The Beat / Mister Ray

Charles (THE RIBEYE BROTHERS) / Loving Sickness - Burning Fuel (Rough mix) (SOLACE) / Ol' Mule Pepe

ATOMIC ROOSTER (UK)
Line-Up: John Du Cann (vocals / guitar), Vincent Crane (keyboards), Carl Palmer (drums)

Led by the extraordinary keyboard talents of Vincent Crane (né Cheeseman) ATOMIC ROOSTER purveyed a unique sound based on a hard driving Hammond organ rather than the guitar. Crane suffered from manic depression and as such the career of the band and Crane is an erratic one of unfulfilled promise.
ATOMIC ROOSTER are now being increasingly recognized by the Doom / Stoner generation as having been of great influence. Crane first came to prominence as a founder member and main lyric writer for THE CRAZY WORLD OF ARTHUR BROWN, which initially comprised Brown, Crane and drummer Drachen Theaker. Crane had played keyboards on the number one hit 'Fire' by CRAZY WORLD quitting the band in the middle of an American tour.
He formed ATOMIC ROOSTER with former CRAZY WORLD, drummer Carl Palmer and bassist Nick Graham in the early '70s. the debut album made the British charts at number 49 before dropping straight out again. 1970 saw the addition of former ANDROMEDA guitarist John Cann (he was later to change his name to John Du Cann). YES guitarist STEVE HOWE had auditioned too but Cann got the job.
Cann overdubbed guitar on the first album for its American release but before touring commenced the band lost their bass player, Graham leaving to form SKIN ALLEY and later ALIBI.
Somewhat inexplicably Crane refused a replacement and so ATOMIC ROOSTER's unique sound manifested itself with Crane performing bass parts on the lower end of his organ as the band soldiered on as a trio. Cann meanwhile had to radically change his playing style to cover for the missing bass and perform lead guitar.
Second album 'Death Walks Behind You' fared better hitting the top 20 and yielded two hit singles in 'Tomorrow Night' and 'The Devil's Answer'. After nine months of solid touring Palmer also upped and left to join form the massively successful Progressive Rock trio EMERSON LAKE AND PALMER and drum duties were entrusted to ex-HORSE man Rick Parnell. However, the new drummer's tenure was brief and before long FARM member Paul Hammond was poached into the line-up.

Parnell was to surface as part of Italian Jazz Rock outfit NOVA and much later relocated in America with ex-MC5 guitarist WAYNE KRAMER, a 1997 act BROWN RING and even as one of spoof Rockers SPINAL TAP's unfortunate drummers!
Meantime back with ATOMIC ROOSTER the early '70s also found Crane guesting for Irish Blues Rock guitarist RORY GALLAGHER.
Although successful on the surface internally ATOMIC ROOSTER were engaged in bitter in-fighting. Cann and Crane had got into a dispute regarding royalties for the second album. Although the line-up managed a third album, the top 5 'In Hearing Of...' Crane, on the eve of an American tour and toying with the idea of turning the band into a funk project, sacked Du Cann from the band. The hapless frontman found out via a job advert in the Melody Maker advertising his position! Hammond left in protest.
Crane enrolled ex-CACTUS vocalist Pete French as replacement and also pulled in guitarist Steve Bolton and a redrafted Parnell. The departing duo of Du Cann and Hammond meanwhile founded BULLET signing to DEEP PURPLE's Purple Records, a band that released one single prior to being sued by an American band of the same name and retitling themselves HARD STUFF. With this act Cann issued two albums.
Du Cann later undertook a German tour in 1973 with THIN LIZZY as guitarist but his stay in the band was purely a temporary one, filling in contracted gigs after Gary Moore had quit unexpectedly. Du Cann was later to reinvent himself as Johnny Du Cann and assembled an ad hoc band featuring STATUS QUO members Francis Rossi, Pete Kershaw and Andy Bown plus GILLAN's John McCoy on a proposed "Powerpop" project! The album, cut for Arista and to be titled 'The World's Not Big Enough' was never issued. The guitarist reverted back to his former name and gained himself a solo hit single with 'Don't Be A Dummy'.
Cann's role in ATOMIC ROOSTER was to be filled by Bill Smith. French left in 1972, later recording a solo album 'Ducks In Flight' featuring THIN LIZZY guitarist Brian Robertson, and was replaced by ex-COLOSSEUM singer CHRIS FARLOWE, a man lauded by none other than MICK JAGGER as "having the best rock voice in Britain". Farlowe was to record the 'Made in England' and 'Nice n' Greasy' albums. Bolton was supplanted by former BRAND X man Johnny Mandala (real name John Goodsall) in 1973.
Bolton formed HEADSTONE with ex-ARRIVAL bassist Phil Chen, former TRANQUILITY keyboard player Tony Lukyn

27

and a pre-RARE BIRD Mark Ashton. Bolton was to turn up again over a decade later with the 1986 project MAX & THE BROADWAY METAL CHOIR. The '90s found Bolton as guitarist for PAUL YOUNG and then in 1990 for THE WHO.

Bill Smith joined JADE WARRIOR for their 1978 Egyptian concept album 'Way Of The Sun'.

Despite releasing some excellent albums ATOMIC ROOSTER were continually dogged by line-up changes. Crane re-joined ARTHUR BROWN to record the 1978 album 'Chisholm In My Bosom' on Gull records' reuniting again in 1980 to release 'Faster Than The Speed Of Sound' on I.C. Records.

Resurrecting ATOMIC ROOSTER once more in 1980 Crane settled his differences with John Cann once more. Session man Preston Hayman was pulled in on drums for live work (he much later appeared on ASIA's 'Archiva 2' album of 1996) before none other than ex-CREAM drummer GINGER BAKER took his place. However, Baker's tenure was short and Hammond was re-enlisted to release an eponymous album on EMI Records.

The band were blighted by an horrendous piece of bad luck as the pressing plant used to manufacture their 1981 single 'Play It Again' went on strike. Calculations made afterwards revealed this had cost the band a number 15 chart placing.

Another stab at rekindling the flame arose in 1983 as Crane reassembled the band with drummer Paul Hammond once more and ex-GILLAN guitarist BERNIE TORME. This line-up toured Europe before with the release of the worthy 'Headline News' album featuring Hammond, Torme and guest musicians ex-ENERGY / OZO guitarist John Mizaroli and PINK FLOYD's guitarist DAVE GILMOUR. Torme joined OZZY OSBOURNE's band replacing Randy Rhoads on the road in America.

Crane spent his post ROOSTER time playing keyboards for DEXY'S MIDNIGHT RUNNERS live band. Another attempt to re-ignite the ATOMIC ROOSTER flame with ex-CHEVY guitarist Barry Eardley never got off the ground. Crane was also assembling some unreleased ATOMIC ROOSTER material for a projected album on the Demi Monde label titled 'Something Old, Something New - The Rooster Tapes'. Sadly Crane committed suicide in February 1989 after suffering years of depression.

The 1999 album 'The First Ten Explosive Years' adds bonus tracks re-recorded with bass from GILLAN's John McCoy.

Cann and McCoy are working on a new ATOMIC ROOSTER album. Drums are being handled by no less than original IRON MAIDEN drummer Ron Rebel.

Singles/EPs:
Friday The 13th / Banstead, B&C CB121 (1970)
Tomorrow Night / Play The Game, B&C CB 131 (1971) **11 UK**
Devil's Answer / The Rock, B&C CB 157 (1971) **4 UK**
Stand By Me / Never To Lose, Dawn DNS 1027 (1972)
Save Me / Close Your Eyes, Dawn DNS 1029 (1972)
Can't Find A Reason / Moods, Dawn (1973)
Tell Your Story (Sing A Song) / OD, Decca FR 13503 (1974)
Do You Know Who's Looking For You / Throw Your Life Away, EMI 5084 (1980)
Devil's Answer / Tomorrow Night / Can't Take No More, B&C BCS 21 (1980)
Play It Again / Start To Live, Polydor POSP 334 (1981)
Play It Again / Start To Live / Devil's Answer (Live), Polydor POSPX 334 (1981) (12" single)
End Of The Day / Living Underground, Polydor POSP 408 (1982)
End Of The Day / Living Underground / Tomorrow Night (Live), Polydor POSPX 408 (1982) (12" single)
Devil's Answer/ Tomorrow Night, Old Gold OG 9391 (1984)
Devil's Answer / , Old Gold OG 6136 (1989) (B side by HUMBLE PIE)

Albums:
ATOMIC ROOSTER, B&C CAS 1010 (1970) **49 UK**
Banstead / And So To Bed / Friday The 13th / Broken Wings / Before Tomorrow / SLY / Winter / Decline And Fall
DEATH WALKS BEHIND YOU, B&C CAS 1026 (1970) **12 UK**
Tomorrow Night / Vug / 7 Sheets / Sleeping For Years / Gershatzer / Death Walks Behind You / I Can't Take No More / Nobody Else
IN HEARING OF, Pegasus PEG 1(1971) **18 UK**
Breakthrough / Break The Ice / Decision-Indecision / A Spoonful Of Bromide Helps The Pulse Rate Go Down / Black Snake / Head In The Sky / The Rock / The Price
MADE IN ENGLAND, Dawn DNLS 3038 (1972)
Time Take My Life / Stand By Me / Little Bit Of Inner Air / Don't Know What Went Wrong / Never To Lose / Introduction / Breathless / Space Cowboy / People You Can't Trust / All In Satan's Name
NICE N' GREASY, Dawn DNLS 3049 (1973)
All Across The Country / Save Me / Voodoo

28

In You / Goodbye Planet Earth / Take One Take / Can't Find A Reason / Ear In The Snow / Satan's Wheel
ATOMIC ROOSTER, EM EMC 3341I (1982)
They Took Control Of You / She's My Woman / He Did It Again / Where's The Show? / In The Shadows / Do You Know Who's Looking For You? / Don't Lose Your Mind / Watch Out! / I Can't Stand It / Lost In Space
HEADLINE NEWS, Towerbell TOWLP 4 (1983)
Hold Your Fire / Headline News / Taking A Chance / Metal Minds / Land Of Freedom / Machine / Dance Of Death / Carnival / Time / Future Shock / Watch Out - Reaching Out
HOME TO ROOST, Rawpower RAWLP 27 (1986)
Death Walks Behind You / VUG / Seven Sheets / Sleeping For Years / I Can't Take No More / Nobody Else / Friday The 13th / And So To Bed / Broken Wings / Before Tomorrow / Banstead / Winter / Breakthrough / Decision-Indecision / Devil's Answer / Black Snake / Head In The Sky / A Spoonful Of Bromide Helps The Pulse Rate Go Down / Tomorrow Night / Break The Ice
THE BEST OF ATOMIC ROOSTER, Demi Monde DMCD 1020 (1989)
DEVIL'S ANSWER, Receiver RRCD003 (1989)
Devil's Answer / Winter / Break The Ice / Nobody Else / Friday 13th / And So To Bed / Death Walks Behind You / Can't Take No More
THE BEST AND THE REST, Action Replay CDAR 100 (1989)
THE DEVIL HITS BACK, Demi Monde DMCD 1023 (1990)
BBC LIVE IN CONCERT, Windsong WINCD 042 (1993)
SPACE COWBOY, Marble Arch CMA CD143 (1994)
Time Take My Life / Stand By Me / Little Bit Of Inner Ai r/ Don't Know What Went Wrong / Can't Find A Reason / People You Can't Trust / All In Satan's Name / Close Your Eyes / Take One Toke / Space Cowboy
IN SATAN'S NAME - THE DEFINITIVE COLLECTION, Snapper SMDCD 128 (1997)
Banstead / And So To Bed / Friday 13th / Broken Wings / Tomorrow Night / Play The Game / VUG / Sleeping For Years / Death Walks Behind You / Devil's Answer / The Rock / Breakthrough / Break The Ice / Spoonful Of Bromide / Stand By Me / Never To Lose / Don't Know What Went Wrong / Space Cowboy / People You Can't Trust / All In Satan's Name / Close Your Eyes / Save Me / Can't Find A Reason / All Across The Country / Voodoo In You / Goodbye Planet Earth / Satan's Wheel

THE FIRST TEN EXPLOSIVE YEARS, Angel Air SJPCD038 (1999)
Sleeping For Years / Seven Streets / I Can't Take No More / Taken You Over / Lost In Space / Play It Again / Devil's Answer (Live) / Rebel With A Cause / Night Living / Death Walks Behind You / It's So Unkind / When You Go To Bed / Head In The Sky / Break The Ice / Play The Game / Tomorrow Night (Live)
LIVE AND RAW 70 / 71, Angel Air SJPCD060 (2000)
Friday The 13th / Gershater / Winter / Shabaloo / Sleeping For Years / VUG / Tomorrow Night / I Can't Take No More
RARITIES, Angel Air SJPCD069 (2000)
Moonrise / Atomic Alert (U.S.A. Radio Ad) / Death Walks Behind You / V.U.G. / Broken Window / Alien Alert (U.S.A. Radio Ad) / Throw Your Life Away / Devil's Alert (U.S.A. Radio Ad) / Devil's Answer (Demo) / Do You Know Who You're Looking For? (Demo) / Don't Lose Your Mind (Demo) / He Did It Again (Demo) / Backward Forward Revealed / End Of The Day (Demo) / Lost In Space (Demo) / Hold It Through The Night / No Change By Me / Play It Again (Demo) / I Can't Take No More (Live)
THE FIRST TEN EXPLOSIVE YEARS: VOLUME 2, Angel Air SJPCD086 (2001)
Do You Know Who's Looking For You / End Of The Day / Watch Out! / Don't Lose Your Mind / V.U.G. / She's My Woman / In The Shadows / Shabaloo / Friday The 13th / Broken Window / Backward / Nobody Else / He Did It Again / A Spoonful Of Bromide / I Can't Stand It / The Rock / Where's The Show? / Gershater
HEAVY SOUL, Castle Music CMDDD364 (2001)
Banstead / Winter / Broken Wings / Friday The 13th / Tomorrow / Nobody Else / The Devil's Answer / Sleeping For Years / Death Walks Behind You / Breakthrough / Break The Ice / Black Snake / The Price / Decision–Indecision / Head In The Sky / The Rock / Close Your Eyes / Time Take My Life / Stand By Me / Breathless / People You Can't Trust / Can't Find A Reason / Save Me / Ear In The Snow / Never To Lose / Take One Take / All Across The Country / Moods / Tell Your Story / O.D.

AUTOMIND (Roxbury, MA, USA)
Line-Up: Conor Sullivan (vocals), Dang Vu (guitar), Brian Sullivan (guitar), Kevin Klein (bass), Ben Enos (drums)

Boston out of the ordinary Psych-Doomsters founded as classmates ACID WENCH during 1997. As AUTOMIND the band released a 2001 CD entitled 'Smoking Black Alien Acid God'. The band described the six track album

29

as "bottom heavy vibrate your balls and ovaries until your sperms are floating upside down and your eggs are cracked and runny". Most reviewers seemed to concur.

Albums:
SMOKING BLACK ALIEN ACID GOD, Automind (2001)
Alien Utopia / Smoking Jesus / Paingod / Biblical Acid / Black / The Great Satan

AUTUMNBLAZE (GERMANY)

AUTUMNBLAZE is led by two members of PARAGON OF BEAUTY in Eldron and Arisjel. Eldron also goes under the name of Monesol.

Albums:
DAEMMERELBEN TRAGOEDIE, (1999)
Mo(u)rningdance / Flamedoves / Äonenturm / Those Evenings We Yearned / Dreaming Moonspark Fairylands / Dryadsong / Her Golden Robe In Silence Veiled / Garden Of Slumber / The Emerald Widower / Heraldic
BLEAK, Prophecy Productions (2000)
Someone's Pictures / I Shiver / Scared / Bleak / So Close Yet So Far / Bruderseele / The Wind And The Broken Girl / Thoughts By A Weary Man's Side / ...And We Fall
MUTE BOY, SAD GIRL, Prophecy Productions (2002)
Mute Boy Sad Girl / It Never Felt Like This Before / The Nature Of Music / Can't Save Anyone / Kiss My Fear Away / I Am Water / Cold / A Crow On My Shoulder / Shells And Butterflies

AUTUMN CLAN (AUSTRIA)
Line-Up: Jens P. Hermann (vocals / guitar), Franz Baumann (guitar), Gabriel Kiri (bass), Markus Kicker (drums)

A Gothic, Black inclined Metal band formulated in 1997 by vocalist / guitarist Jens Peter Hermann, guitarist Franky Baumann, bass player Erik Kostron and drummer Christian Baumann. In 1998 AUTUMN CLAN pulled in a fresh bassist Gabriel Kiri and drummer Markus Kicker. In this incarnation the band scored a commendable second placing in a national Austrian band contest.
AUTUMN CLAN's debut demo, 'Styrian Demon', arrived in January of 2000. A second tape, produced by Boban Milunovic, was delivered shortly after. As 2001 broke Baumann made his exit, the drum stool quickly being handed over to Markus Kicker of Death Metal band BLACK PROPHECY. This line-up cut a third demo.
Signing to the new Wait And Bleed label AUTUMN CLAN recorded their debut album

'Requiem To The Sun', once again utilizing Boban Milunovic as producer.

Albums:
REQUIEM TO THE SUN, Wait And Bleed WAB005 (2002)
New Gothicism / Hollow / Requiem To The Sun / Turnin' Away / Dream Sequence / Hate Tunes / Garden Of Eden / Abuse Me / Desire / Symphony Of Sadness / Mortal / Dissonant Trip / The Lack Of Inventive Genius / Through

AUTUMN TEARS (USA)
Line-Up: Erika (vocals), Jennifer LeeAnna (vocals / keyboards), Ted (vocals / keyboards), James West (percussion)

AUTUMN TEARS

AUTUMN TEARS have carved out a unique and almost solitary niche for themselves garnering a sizable underground cult following. The band defies all Rock conventions in presenting melancholic Gothic landscapes of an ethereal quality. The band was created as a duo of keyboard player / vocalist Ted and vocalist Erika and debuted in April of 1996 with the symphonic 'Love Poems For Dying Children: Act I'. Session musicians included members of DECEMBER WOLVES. The album was limited to 2000 copies and as with all AUTUMN TEARS product, would be issued on their own Dark Symphonies imprint.

The second installment of AUTUMN TEARS vision 'Love Poems For Dying Children: Act II - The Garden Of Crystalline Dreams' arrived in May of 1997. Following this release Erika departed in order to concentrate on novel writing. Meantime the first album saw a re-issue clad in all new artwork and which included an extra track 'Intermission', the debut of new vocalist Jennifer LeeAnna.

The 12 minute 'Absolution' EP was issued in July of 1999 as a stop gap. Both Jennifer LeeAnna and Erika appeared on this release. Lyrics for the lead track 'The Absolution Of What Was' came from a poem by Claudia Lungstädt-Kukulka.

Erika returned to the fold during December of 1999 presenting AUTUMN TEARS now with two female voices. Upfront of the release of the third chapter of the 'Love Poems For Dying Children' saga Red Stream Records put out the debut in vinyl LP format. Limited to 1000 copies it was made all the more collectable with the inclusion of an exclusive track 'The Blooming'. Erika would also take time out to act as live vocalist for NOVEMBER'S DOOM.

Erika would leave the band in February of 2002.

Ted and Jennifer have also engaged with ARCANA's Peter and Ida to create the project venture PANDORA.

Singles/EPs:
The Absolution Of What Was / The Never / The Dance, Dark Symphonies DARK 4 (1999) ('Absolution' EP)

Albums:
LOVE POEMS FOR DYING CHILDREN: ACT I, Dark Symphonies DARK 1 (1996)
They Watch With Closed Eyes / Ode To My Forthcoming Winter Part 1. Spring / Ode To My Forthcoming Winter Part 2. Summer / Ode To My Forthcoming Winter Part 3. Autumn / Ode To My Forthcoming Winter Part 4. Winter / The Eloquent Sleep / And Then The Whispering / One Tender Kiss (The Lost Season) Prelude To 'The Garden Of Crystalline Dreams' / Carfax Abbey
LOVE POEMS FOR DYING CHILDREN: ACT II - CRYSTALLINE DREAMS, Dark Symphonies DARK 2 (1997)
Do They Ever Sing? / This... My Melancholic Masquerade / A Dreaming Kiss / So Sweet... The Tears / Commiseration In Mourning / The Garden of Crystalline Dreams, Act I / The Battle, Act II / The Ebony Meadow, Act III / A Shadow Painted White / Black Heaven
LOVE POEMS FOR DYING CHILDREN: ACT III - WINTER AND THE BROKEN ANGEL, Dark Symphonies DARK 8 (2000)

The Grand Celebration / The Mirror Stone / The Never / The Broken Doll / Winter's Warning - I. Prologue / Winter's Warning - II. Spring Requiem / Winter's Warning - III. Summer Requiem / Winter's Warning - IV. Autumn Requiem / Winter's Warning - V. Winter Requiem / Winter's Warning - VI. Epilogue / The Passion And The Fury / The Widowtree / The Bird Without Wings / The Eyes Of Deception

AVERNUS (Chicago, IL, USA)
Line-Up: Rick McCoy (vocals), James Genenz (guitar), Brian Whited (bass), Jeff Joseph (keyboards), Bill Hamning (drums)

Chicago Doom Metal act dating to 1993 that would give vocalist Kimberly Goss to Norway's ANCIENT and latterly her own Power Metal band SINERGY.

AVERNUS debuted with the 1993 demo tape 'A Delicate Tracery Of Red' followed by a further session 'Sadness'. Further exposure was gained with the inclusion of the track 'Godlessness' on the Metal Blade 'Metal Massacre 12' compilation. A third demo outing 'A Farewell To Eden' led to the first AVERNUS album 'Of The Fallen' for Olympic Records.

Drummer Bill Hamning deputized for ELECTRIC HELLFIRE CLUB's 2000 American dates. Recently AVERNUS added ex-EVE OF MOURNING guitarist Scott.

By mid 2002 AVERNUS, comprising vocalist Rick McCoy, guitarist James Genenz and keyboard player Jeff Joseph had reunited with drummer Rick Yifrach and were working together on material for a new studio album. Bassist Brian Whited had departed to form a union with NOVEMBERS DOOM.

Albums:
OF THE FALLEN, Olympic (1997)
Blood Gathers Frost / If I Could Exist / By Loves Will... Chaos / Renaissance / Ghost / Thousand Spirits / Beautiful Black Heart / Still Warm Ashes
WHERE THE SLEEPING SHADOWS LIE, Cursed Productions (2000)
An Endless Sea Of Evening / The Faustian Heart / Anesthesia / Ashes Of Adoration / Godlessness / Dreamburn / Disappear / Silver And Black / For Every Waking Moment / Downpour

AVIDOST (IL, USA)
Line-Up: Jennifer Gore (vocals), Oliver Homann (guitar), Joseph DeGroot (guitars), Adam Schifler (bass), Shaun C. Mackey (drums)

Female fronted avant-garde Doom act AVIDOST include guitarist Joseph DeGroot in the ranks, current day guitarist with Chicago's Death Metal unit ENFORSAKEN and ex-member of THROUGH ASHES.

AVIDOST has issued two demos to date, both in 2001. A two track affair comprising 'Claws Of Unrest' and 'A Silent Masquerade' was followed by a four track 'Official Demo'

AVRIGUS (AUSTRALIA)
Line-Up: Judy Chiara (vocals), Simon Gruer

Vowing to record the greatest Doom album ever many critics believed the Australian duo AVRIGUS may well have achieved such a feat with the desolate soundscapes portrayed on the 2001 album 'The Secret Kingdom'.

AVRIGUS have existed since 1991 but were on hold for much of the '90s as Simon Gruer fulfilled duties operating as frontman for CRUCIFORM. Upon leaving CRUCIFORM in 1995 AVRIGUS was resurrected for the 1998 EP 'The Final Wish' released on the Australian Metal label Warhead.

Gruer also divides his duties with Industrial act SUBLIMINAL CONTROL, SUBCONSCI-OUS INTERVENTION and part-time band PAIN GAME. Vocalist Judy Chiara has released a solo album and has sessioned on ELYSIUM's debut album.

Singles/EPs:
The Final Wish / As Ivy Groweth Green / Desolate / Flesh, Warhead (1998) ('The Final Wish' EP)

Albums:
THE SECRET KINGDOM, Hammerheart (2001)
Overture / Solitude And Salvation / Dark Angels Ascension / Veritas / Qliphoth / Desolate / Flesh / Til Death Do Us Unite / Shade Of My Heart / The Grail

THE AWESOME MACHINE (SWEDEN)
Line-Up: Lasse Olausson (vocals), Christian Smedström (guitar), Anders Wenander (bass), Tobbe Bövik (drums)

Stoners created in late 1996. Original drummer Peter Thorne would be replaced by Tobbe Bövik prior to the recording of a self-financed eponymous 10" vinyl album produced by Roberto Loghi. THE AWESOME MACHINE then issued the 1999 demo 'Doom, Disco, Dope, Death & Love' to high acclaim. American label Ellington Records reissued the first album on CD format adding two tracks 'Ompa Bompa' and 'God Damn Evil'. The band signed to the German concern People Like You for the 2000 album 'It's Ugly Or Nothing' produced by KING DIAMOND guitarist Andy La Rocque. The bands progress was such that a Swedish instrument manufacturer has put 'Awesome' guitars on the market!

Plans were afoot in mid 2002 to release a split 10" EP in league with German Stoners DUSTER 69.

Albums:
THE AWESOME MACHINE, The Awesome Machine (1998) (10" vinyl release)
Mula / Fortune Teller / Burning Love / Sun Don't Shine On Me / Digging
THE AWESOME MACHINE, Ellington (1999)
Mula / Fortune Teller / Burning Love / Sun Don't Shine On Me / Digging / Ompa Bompa / God Damn Evil
IT'S UGLY OR NOTHING, People Like You (2000)
Never Said I Never Fail / How Am I To Know / El Bajo / Son Of A God / Cruise Control / Supernova / Looking For Sweet Opium / Out Of Fuel / Used To Be / No Shame

BACKDRAFT (SWEDEN)

Line-Up: Jonas Ahlén (vocals), Robert Johansson (guitar), David Nordlander (guitar), Mats Rydström (bass), Niklas Matsson (drums)

Strange but true. Traditional Southern blues based Stoner Rock out of Scandinavia. BACKDRAFT was formulated by Jonas Ahlén of Thrash Metal act ANTICIPATION and left handed guitar player Robert Johansson in late 1997. They would be joined by drummer Fredrik Liefvendahl (a.k.a. 'Trizze Trash') and second guitarist David 'Snejken' Nordlander, billing themselves MORNINGWOOD. Two demos ensued and various line-up changes, including Liefvendahl journeying on to GRAND MAGUS, saw the unit evolve into BACKDRAFT with the addition of bass player Mats Rydström and drummer Niklas Matsson, both of KILLER BEE.

As BACKDRAFT the band debuted with a self-financed EP 'The Goddamn Man' issued in October of 2000. Promoting this release included a heavy gig schedule across Sweden before signing to Lunasound Recordings for the Per Wikström produced 'Here To Save You All' album. The record included a cover version of WHITESNAKE's 'Child Of Babylon' as a bonus track.

Touring would see BACKDRAFT as guests to LEADFOOT in Sweden in September of 2001 before a run of dates packaged with FIVE FIFTEEN and rounding off the year with German headline gigs. BACKDRAFT would find themselves opening for FIVE HORSE JOHNSON in Europe throughout May of 2002 then scheduled to support RAGING SLAB and FIREBIRD in Spain in September and LEADFOOT in Europe during October and November of 2002.

Albums:

HERE TO SAVE YOU ALL, Lunasound Recordings (2001)
Convoy / Wicked Man / Angels High / See You Burn / Devil's Hand / El Rancho / Goddamn Man / Original Sin / Penetration / Hillbilly Blues / Child Of Babylon

BACKDRAFT
Photo : Torbjorn Persson

33

BAD WIZARD (Brooklyn, NY, USA)
Line-Up: Curtis Brown (vocals), Eddie Lynch (guitar), Tina Gorin (guitar), Marc Tanner (bass), Scott Nutt (drums)

Retro '70s Groove Rockers originally based in Athens, Georgia. Vocalist Curtis Brown and drummer Scott Nutt, both of HARVEY MILK, relocated to Brooklyn, New York in order to create BAD WIZARD.
At one stage the band comprised Brown, Nutt, guitarist Dawg Pressman and bassist Michele Ellis. However, for recording of the August 2001 Tee Pee Records debut BAD WIZARD saw the Georgians joined by slide guitarist Tina Gorin, guitarist Eddie Lynch and bassist Marc Tanner.
The album was produced by Dean Rispler of THE BROUGHT LOW and TIGER MOUNTAIN.

Albums:
FREE N' EASY, Tee Pee (2001)
Lay Your Love On Me / Barefootin' Man / Hey Mama / Endless Lady / Keep High - Stay Low / Natural High / Tiger Tooth / Free and Easy / Come On

BEAVER (HOLLAND)
Line-Up: Roel Schoenmakers (vocals / guitar), Tos Nieuwenhuizen (guitar), Milo Beenhakker (bass), Eva Nahon (drums)

Amsterdam Stoners forged in the early '90s. The band underwent some formative line-up changes, including the departure of guitarist Tos Nieuwenhuizen and bassist Guy Pinhas to THE OBSESSED, settling in 1992 on vocalist / guitarist Roel Schoenmakers, ex-GOD guitarist Joszja de Weerdt, bass player Milo Beenhakker and drummer Eva Nahon. Early European gigs witnessed valuable supports to THE OBSESSED, QUEENS OF THE STONE AGE, the MELVINS, FUGAZI, ROLLINS BAND, FUGAZI and KYUSS.
BEAVER debuted with the March 1996 album 'B(13eaver)' for the Works label. Their excursion into the studio, with none other than QUEENS OF THE STONE AGE's Josh Homme acting as producer for the track 'Green', was included on the 'Burn One Up!' compilation of January 1997. BEAVER's rhythm section would unite with QUEENS OF THE STONE AGE for a further track '18 A.D.' reaping plenty of media attention.
BEAVER signed to the Elegy label for their sophomore outing, 'The Difference Engine', issued in September of 1997. They would further the QUEENS OF THE STONE AGE connection with a split 10" EP through Man's Ruin in 1998.

BEAVER toured Europe heavily throughout 1999, including shows with fellow Dutchmen 35007 and September dates with SPIRIT CARAVAN. Downtime in the live schedule would produce a second release for Man's Ruin 'Lodge', released in October.
A makeshift BEAVER, with early members Toz Nieuwenhuizen on guitar and Guy Pinhas on bass, debuted in America with a show at the Hollywood Troubador. Before long Nieuwenhuizen had reinstated himself, supplanting Joszja as lead guitarist. This revised version of BEAVER toured Europe and the UK extensively.
The 'Mobile' album would be recorded but got caught up in the high profile bankruptcy of the Man's Ruin label.

Singles/EPs:
Split, Man's Ruin MR-141 (1998) (Split 10" EP with QUEENS OF THE STONE AGE)

Albums:
B(13EAVER), Works (1996)
Piece Of Mind / Drown / Dolphinity / Centaur / This Room / Decisions In Time / One Eye Is King / Ripe Fruit / Snakes & Ladders / Deep Hibernation / Miss Interpreter
THE DIFFERENCE ENGINE, Elegy (1997)
On Parade / Enter The Treasury / The Reaper / Magic 7 / Friendly Planet / Green / Surrender / Supernova / A Premonition / Infinity's Blacksmith
LODGE, Man's Ruin MR-160 (1999)
Static / Tarmac / Repossessed / Interstate / I Reckon
MOBILE, Man's Ruin (2001)
Private Stash / At The Mirror Palace / End Of A Rope / Circumnavigation / Liberator / 9 Lives / Immaterialized / Hour Glass

BEDEMON (USA)
Line-Up: Bobby Liebling (vocals), Randy Palmer (guitar), Mike Matthews (bass) Geoff O'Keefe (drums)

An illustrious and revered name in American Doom folklore. BEDEMON was an offshoot of the legendary PENTAGRAM and, due to the unreleased nature of the original '70s recordings, BEDEMON's legend was elevated to the realms of the truly arcane until the issue of the 1998 collection 'Mars Hall'.
Prior to guitarist Randy Palmer officially joining the ranks of PENTAGRAM, circa 1973, he and PENTAGRAM's drummer Geoff O'Keefe and vocalist Bobby Liebling, together with mutual friend Mike Matthews committed some of Randy's compositions to tape. The project was billed as BEDEMON after a mispronunciation of two earlier title

34

suggestions 'Behemoth' and 'Demon'. These initial sessions resulted in a three song demo comprising 'Child Of Darkness', 'Serpent Venom' and 'Frozen Fear'. The enthusiasm engendered by these tracks fired off further sessions, which culminated in a whole album's worth of material. Two of these BEDEMON songs, 'Starlady' and 'Touch The Sky' would subsequently be utilized by PENTAGRAM.

Following Palmer's departure from PENTAGRAM he would reconvene with O'Keefe, Matthews and Liebling to cut further BEDEMON material during 1979. BEDEMON would evolve to find PENTAGRAM and GALACTIC 5 bassist Greg Mayne taking over from Matthews. BEDEMON, now with Palmer, O'Keefe, Mayne and guitarist Norman Lawson of SEX II, would still be recording material as late as 1986.

A recent upsurge in interest in PENTAGRAM also unearthed the existence of BEDEMON tapes and, as such, the band reunited in 2001 aiming to record new tracks under the projected title of the 'Time Bomb' EP.

BEGOTTEN (New York, NY, USA)
Line-Up: Matt Anselmo (vocals / guitar), Amanda Topaz (bass), Rob Sefcik (drums)

New York's BEGOTTEN, founded in 1997, was one of the unfortunate acts caught in the Man's Ruin Records bankruptcy. BEGOTTEN would later sell their album at gigs.

Albums:
BEGOTTEN, (2001)

BELIAL (FINLAND)
Line-Up: Jarno Antilla (vocals / guitar), Jani Lehytosaari (bass), Reima Kellokoski (drums)

BELIAL date to April 1991 and the demo 'The God Of The Pits' brought them to the attention of the Death Metal underground. At this stage the group comprised vocalist Jarno Koskinen, guitarists Jarno Antilla and Jukka Valppu, bassist Jani Lehtosaari and drummer Reima Kellokoski. However, Jukka Valppu quit to form MYTHOS in 1992. The band's earliest recordings proved to be so popular on the tape trading circuit that BELIAL's initial demos were later pressed and issued by Moribund Records.

Having participated in the recording of the 'Wisdom Of Darkness' and 'Never Again' albums, frontman Koskinen left to form ETERNITIES. Having replaced him with new singer Jarno Antilla for the much more adventurous and melancholic '3' album,

BELIAL was rocked by a further departure in early 1996 when bassist Jani Lehotosaari joined IMPALED NAZARENE.

Singles/EPs:
The Invocation / Voices Beyond / Deceased / For Them / Piece By Piece (Remix), Moribund DEAD 05 (1993) ('The Gods Of The Pit II (Paragon Below)' EP)
The Gods Of The Pit II, Moribund DEAD 05 (1993) (7" single limited edition of 1,000)
After Taste, BMTHOMP Records SHIT-1 (1994) (Limited edition of 500)
After Taste 1 1/2, E-REC 91994) (Limited edition of 50)

Albums:
WISDOM OF DARKNESS, Lethal LRC002 (1992)
Intro - The Invocation / Of Servant Of Belial / Lost Souls / Rise Of Hecate / Hypocrisy Of The God's Sons / Voices Beyond
NEVER AGAIN, Lethal LRC 666 (1993)
Firestorm / The Red One / Dragons Kiss / Swan Song / As Above So Below / The Sun / About Love / Pain-Flood / Clouds / Desires / On You
3, Witchunt WIHU 9418 (1995)
Other Channel / Mr. Blue Sky High / I Want You To Die / The End / Exit / You / Holes And Boots / One Way In And Out On Valium / Nautilus / Saturnus / One Day / Sina Inhotat Minua Rakkaani / Hate Song

BELLATOR (BELGIUM)
Line-Up: Andy Bogaert (vocals), Guy (guitar), Gunnar (guitar), Gunther Bracke (bass), Bart van Daele (keyboards), Gino (drums)

Belgian Doom protagonists BELLATOR arrived in 1995 with a line-up of singer Tom, guitarists Dimitri and Gunnar, bass player Bart, keyboard player Christophe and drummer Tony. Dimitri would not stay the course and drifted away in August of 1996 being replaced by Guy. With this line-up BELLATOR cut the 'Praise The Mighty Thor' demo.

Both Christophe and Tom disembarked the following year. BELLATOR regrouped ,enlisting vocalist David Walgrave and keyboard player Nele Stevens and issuing their debut commercial release the 'Fluxional' mini -album for Polar Bear Records.

The band would undergo another roster reshuffle when their newest members were ousted in favour of ex-FETISH keyboard man Bart van Daele and new frontman Andy Bogaert. The changes did not end there though when bass player Bart Eggermont was replaced by former TRAVACORT and

PROPHANITY man Gunther Bracke.

A further mini-album, 'Opaque Reveries' produced by Ozzy McDrake, was released in 2000 after which long-term drummer Tony broke away. The new incumbent was erstwhile DEAD MAN STAR and NIGHTVISION percussionist Gino. The line-up ructions would continue into 2001 with Gino departing in July and Kostas Panagiotou, a.k.a. 'Pan' of PANTHEIST, coming in on keyboards.

Albums:
FLUXIONAL, Polar Bear (1998)
Sensus Mortalis / The Warlord / Master Of Your Soul / The Lone Wolf
OPAQUE REVERIES, Polar Bear (2000)
A Cry To Silence / Ascension / The Centre Of Heaven / Beyond The Glacial Wall / The Ultimate Decay

BESEECH (SWEDEN)
Line-Up: Lotta Höglin (vocals), Erik Molarin (vocals), Robert Spånglund (guitar), Klas Bohlin (guitar), Daniel Elofsson (bass), Mikael Back (keyboards), Jonas Strömberg (drums)

A Swedish Gothic Metal act emanating from the town of Borås near Gothenburg. BESEECH, including former CEMETARY drummer Morgan Gredaker, was founded during November of 1992, debuting two years later with a track 'Edge Of Life' on the Belgian Shiver label's series of compilations 'Sometimes Death Is Better'.

A succession of demos, commencing with 1992's 'A Lesser Kind Of Evil' and the follow up 'Last Chapter' led to the band's third effort 'Tears' in 1995 securing the attention of We Bite Records. With contracts signed BESEECH entered the studio to lay down the debut album '...From A Bleeding Heart' with Christian Silver of SUNDOWN acting as producer. Female session vocals came courtesy of Anna Andersen. However, with the completion of the album the band learned that their label was in no position to fund its release. Finally in April of 1998 Metal Blade Records issued the record. The album received noteworthy reviews, BESEECH's symphonic Gothic style and 18th century stage apparel setting the band apart from the current crop of Scandinavian acts.

The band would then fracture with the rhythm section of bass player Andreas Wiik and drummer Morgan Gredaker going their separate way. Nicke Svensson was introduced on keyboards alongside keyboard player Micke Andersson but BESEECH splintered yet again. Vocalist Jörgen Sjöberg,

guitarists Klas Bohlin and Robert Spånglund and keyboard player Mikael Back retained the band name. The new look BESEECH shortly after inducted bass player Daniel Elofsson and drummer Jonas Strömberg.

The band also parted company with Metal Blade, signing a fresh deal with the Pavement label. BESEECH's second album 'Black Emotions' found the band, striving for a modern Gothic sound, broadening their creative scope with experimentation with new instrumental textures. The flamboyant costumes had also been consigned to the past, BESSECH now adopting the simple yet effective 'black' look. Three album tracks, 'Manmade Dreams', 'Neon Ocean' and 'Lunar Eclipse', would all feature as part of the soundtrack to the Canadian Horror movie 'Alien Agenda 5 - Alien Conspiracy'. Touring found BESEECH as opening act on a full scale European tour headed up by LACUNA COIL and THEATRE OF TRAGEDY in early 2001.

With the live work in promotion of 'Black Emotions' completed BESEECH lost the services of vocalist Jörgen Sjöberg. He was replaced by Erik Molarin.

BESEECH signed to the Austrian Napalm label for the 2002 album 'Souls Highway'. Limited editions of the record included an exclusive bonus track, a cover version of ABBA's 'Gimme, Gimme, Gimme'. Tour plans for October 2002 had BESEECH billed alongside DARKWELL and ASHES YOU LEAVE for European dates.

Guitarist Robert Spånglund also operates the Stoner band FEAR OF LIGHT.

Albums:
FROM A BLEEDING HEART, Metal Blade (1999)
Shadowscape / Rainbowman / Silverstar / Eagleheart / The Winterflame / In Her Arms / Inhuman Desire / Kiss Of November / Dimension / Moonride
BLACK EMOTIONS, Pavement PVMT32350 (2000)
Manmade Dreams / Firewalk / Little Demonchild / Ghost Story / Neon Ocean / Lunar Eclipse / Velvet Erotica / Universe / Wounded / Black Emotions
SOULS HIGHWAY, Napalm (2002)
Illusionate / Between The Lines / Souls Highway / Blinded / Endless Waters / Fiction City / Sunset 28 / A Last Farewell / A Season In Green / Beyond The Skies / Gimme Gimme Gimme

BESTIAL WARLUST (AUSTRALIA)
Line-Up: Damon Bloodstorm (vocals), K.K. Warslut (guitar), Joe Skullfucker (guitar),

Chris Corpsemolestor (bass), Markus Hellcunt (drums)

Notorious Australian Black Doom band. The unit was assembled by Damon Bloodstorm in 1990 titled CORPSE MOLESTATION, evolving into BESTIAL WARLUST in 1992 following the demo 'Descension Of A Darker Deity'.
The 1994 debut album 'Vengeance War 'Til Death' had Bloodstorm joined by guitarists K.K. Warslut and Joe Skullfucker, bassist Chris Corpsemolester and drummer Markus Hellkunt. However, Warslut would make his exit to create the equally notorious DESTROYER 666.
The band's line-up for their 'Blood And Honour' debut featured Bloodstorm, Hellcunt and Skullfucker alongside fresh recruits guitarists Battleslaughter and bass player Fiend Of The Deep.
BESTIAL WARLUST underwent a further line-up change after the second album with bassist Inferno joining but the band would fold soon after.
Damon Bloodstorm created ABOMINATOR for the 1999 album 'Damnations Prophecy'. Markus Hellcunt joined ANATOMY.

Albums:
VENGEANCE WAR 'TIL DEATH, Modern Invasion MIM 7316-2 CD (1994)
Dweller Of The Bottomless Pit / Satanic / Heathens / Hammering Down The Law Of The New Gods / Holocaust Wolves Of The Apocalypse / Storming Vengeance / At The Graveyard Of God
BLOOD AND VALOUR, Modern Invasion MIM 7321-2CD (1995)
Blood And Valour / Death Rides Out / Descention, Hellsblood / Barbaric Horde / … Til The End / Within The Storm / Legion Of Wrath / Orgy Of Souls (Hallowed Night) / I The Warrior

BETHLEHEM (GERMANY)
Line-Up: Classen (vocals), Matton (guitar), Bartsch (vocals / bass), Matton (guitar)

Bartsch and Matton, both previously with the group DARK TEMPEST, formed BETHLEHEM in order to pursue a more Death Metal direction in late 1991 than the way they had been travelling in their previous act. The pair both brought a unique set of experiences to bear on shaping BETHLEHEM's particular brand of melancholia as both had suffered from eerily alike suicides of family members, with Bartsch's girlfriend and aunt hanging themselves and Matton's father doing

likewise.
From their inception the authorities were intent on making life difficult for the band with gigs banned in Germany. Such was the level of persecution that record label Adipocere even took the step of censoring references to the devil from BETHLEHEM lyric sheets.
After several line-up changes the group released the debut 'Dark Metal' album, although the second album ('Dictius Te Necare'; translation: 'Kill You') is far more notorious with sick German lyrics.
Classen (as 'Andras'), in spite of press reports claiming he was dead, would in fact found PARAGON BELIAL for the 'Hordes Of The Dark' album and later reunite with BETHLEHEM drummer Rolf to forge DARK CREATION. He would also surface as guest lead vocalist for Swedish 'suicidal' Black Metal band SHINING on their 'Within Deep Dark Chambers' album.
PAVOR bass player Rainer Landfermann performs vocals on the second BETHLEHEM record although would be supplanted by Marco Kehran of DEINONYCHUS along with female vocals from Catharin Campen.
BETHLEHEM veered off on an industrial Metal tangent for 2001's 'Schatten Aus Der Alexander Welt'. For this opus Bartsch assembled a totally revised line-up of AARDVARKS vocalist Guido Meyer De Voltaire, guitarist Eckhardt, keyboard player and sampler Reiner Tiedemann and drummer Steve Wolz. The same year the band issued a split 7" single with Portland, Oregon act WRAITHEN on the 11:11 Kult Productions label.

Albums:
DARK METAL, Adipocere CDAR022 (1994)
The Elbereth Commandment / Apocalyptic Dance / Second Coming / Vargtimmen / 3rd Nocturnal Prayer / Funeral Owlblood / Veiled Irreligious / Gepreisen Sei Der Untergang / Supplementary Exegis / Wintermute
DICTUS TE NERARE, Red Stream RSR012 (1996)
Schatten Aus Der Alexander Welt / Die Anarchische Befreiung Der Augenzeugenreligion / Aphel - Die Schwarze Schlange / Verheißung - Du Krone Des Todeskultes / Verschleierte Irreligiösität / Tagebuch einer Totgeburt / Dorn Meiner Allmacht
SARDONISCHER UNTERGANG IN ZEICHEN IRRELIOGIÖSEN DARBIETUNG, (1998)
Durch Beflechte Berührung Meiner Nemesis / Du Sollst Dich Töten / Gestern Starb Ich Schon Heute / Teufelverrückt Gottdreizehn / Tote Weiße Marder / Nexus / Luftstehs'Ibläh / Als Ich Noch Caulerpa Taxifolia Erbrach / Tod

37

Ist Weicher Stuhlin Gar Fleischlos Gift
REFLEKTIONEN AUF'S STERBEN, (1999)
Wolfsstunde / Gestern Starb Ich schon Heute
/ Angst Atmet Mord / Du Sollst Dich Töten /
Vargtimmen / Reflektionen Auf's Sterben
PROFANE FETMILCH LENZT ELF KRANK.
Prophecy Productions (2000)
Gar Albern Es Uns Totgebar / Von
Bittersüssem Suizid
SCHATTEN AUS DER ALEXANDER WELT,
Prophecy Productions (2001)
Kapitel 1: Kapitel Radio / Kapitel 1: Das 4
Tier As Den Mutterwitz / Kapitel 1: Kapitel
Gabriel / Kapitel 1: Somnambulismus In
Maschinenzimmer 30 / Kapitel 1: Kapitel
Hummer / Kapitel 1: Mein Kuss Erstickt Im
Imperativ / Kapitel 1: Kapitel Michael /
Kapitel 1: Mary Samaels NFB 418 / Kapitel
1: Dunkle, Kalte Materie / Kapitel 2: Dunkle,
Kalte Materie / Kapitel 2: Kapitel Mensch /
Kapitel 2: Maschinensohn / Kapitel 2: Kapitel
Luzifer / Kapitel 2: Rost, Wahn & Tote Gleise
/ Kapitel 2: Kapitel Kinderzimmer / Kapitel 2:
Tod Einer Dieselkatze / Kapitel 2: Kapitel
Heimkehr / Kapitel 2: Aus Dunkler Ritze
Fruchtig Wahn

BEYOND DAWN (NORWAY)
Line-Up: Tore Gjedrm (vocals / bass), Espen

Ingierd (guitar), Petter Haavik (guitar), Einar
Sjurso (drums), Dag Midbrod (Trombone)

BEYOND DAWN display a very original,
depressive and bizarre mixture between
Doom, Psychedelic and avant-garde Rock
including the novel use of a trombonist.
Original BEYOND DAWN guitarist Sindre
Goksöyr left to found PILEDRIVER making
way for Espen Ingierd.
After one demo tape BEYOND DAWN were
able to release a four track record on
Adipocere Records before later changing
labels to Candlelight Records with whom they
released 'Pity Love' in 1996.
Drummer Einar Sjurso guess on
FLEURETY's 2000 album 'Department Of
Apocalyptic Affairs'.

Singles/EPs:
Up Through The Linear Shades, Adipocere
(1993) (7" single)

Albums:
LONGING FOR SCARLET DAYS,
Adipocere CD AR019 (1994)
Cold / Moonwomb / Chaosphere / Clouds
Swept Away The Colours
PITY LOVE, Candlelight CANDLE 012 (1996)

BEYOND DAWN

When Beauty Dies / The Penance / (Never A) Bygone Tendency / As The Evening Falters, The Dogs Howl / Embers Storm / Ripe As The Night / Daughter Sunday
REVELRY, Misanthropy AMAZON14CD (1998)
Love's (Only) True Defender / Tender / Resemblance / Stuck / Three Steps For The Chameleon (How To Seduce Modestly) / I Am A Drug / Breathe The Jackal / Life's Sweetest Reward / Chains / Phase To Phase
IN REVERIE, Eibon (1999)
Need / Rendezvous / Prey / Atmosphere / Confident As Hell / Naked / Phase-Juxtaposition / Chameleon
ELECTRIC SULKING MACHINE, Peaceville (2000)
Violence Heals / Addictions Are Private / On The Subject Of Turning Insane / Certain Qualities / Fairy Liquid / Aagae / Pop Ist Verboten / Cigarette / Pacific Blue Disorder / Hairy Liquor (Mer Kraft I Hver Draabe)

BIAS (UK)
Line-Up: Leigh Oates (vocals), Andy Stone (guitar), Joel Graham (bass), James Bottomley (drums)

A "modern, hard Stoner Rock band" from Bradford. BIAS concentrated on playing locally before the quartet recorded the 'Inertia' debut album, produced by Pat Grogan.
The album was released in February 1998.

Albums:
INERTIA, Backbone BONECD 100 (1998)
Control / Coercion / Hardcoded / Big Man / Breaking Point / Cognition / The Great Misguided / Hindsight (Luxury) / Friction / Cold Comfort

BRANT BJORK (USA)

Solo work from KYUSS and FU MANCHU drummer BRANT BJORK. The man would decamp from FU MANCHU to join QUEENS OF THE STONE AGE in late 2001 also recording a second solo venture at the same juncture. This latter effort would go under the fictional band title of BRANT BJORK AND THE OPERATORS.

Albums:
JALAMANTA, Man's Ruin (1999)
Lazy Bones / Automatic Fantastic / Cobra Jab / Too Many Chiefs... Not Enough Indians / Sun Brother / "Let's Get Chinese Eyes" / Toot / Defender Of The Oleander / Low Desert Punk / Waiting For A Coconut To Drop / Her Brown Blood / Indio

BRANT BJORK & THE OPERATORS, Music Cartel (2002)
Hinda 65 / Smarty Pants / My Ghettoblaster / Electric Lalli Land / From The Ground Up (We Just Stay The Same) / Cheap Wine / Cocoa Butter / Joey's Radio / Captain Lovestar / Hinda 65 (Return Flight)

BLACK LODGE (NORWAY)
Line-Up: Vegar Hoel (vocals), Monica Pedersen (vocals), Kim G. Andersen (guitar), Preben Z. Moller D. (guitar), Halvor Larsen (bass), Frode Gundersen (drums)

A Doom Metal act with female vocals.

Albums:
COVET, Head Not Found HNF 010 (1995)
Dissonance / Mother Urge / Cube / Tower Inertia / Travesty / Mortal (1995)

THE BLACK (ITALY)
Line-Up: Mario 'The Black' Di Donato (vocals / guitar), Enio Nicolini (bass), Gianluca Bracciale (drums)

Centred upon the enigmatic figure of Mario 'The Black' Di Donato THE BLACK deliver elaborate Progressive Doom overlaid with "Ossianic Opera" keyboard layers. The 'Refugium Peccatorum' album, which signalled the start of an ambitious trilogy based upon the death of Christ, would be issued in a limited run of 668 vinyl copies.
As well as crafting the music Di Donato paints all of THE BLACK's religiously themed album

THE BLACK

covers. A new album, 'Peccatum', would be scheduled for late 2002 release.

Albums:
REFUGIUM PECCATORUM, Black Widow BWR 008 (1994)
APOCALYPSIS, Black Widow BWR 016 (1997)
Profezie / I Sette Sigilli / Printo Et Secondo Angelo / Terzo Et Quarto Angelo / Ultimi Tre Angeli / Inutile Pentimento / Guerrain Cielo / La Bestiache Saledal Mare / Primadel Buio / La Bestiache Saledalla Terra / Apocalypsis / Il Trionfo Della Morte
GOLGOTHA, Black Widow BWRCD 036-2 (2001)
Momenti Ansiosi / Golgotha / Il Orbis (II vers) / Sospesa A Un Filo / Il Re Melograno / Ultimatum / Tormentum / Ivstitia / Il Giudizio / Coscentia Opprimi

BLACK DEBBATH (NORWAY)

Line-Up: Egil Hegerberg (vocals), Lars Lønning (guitar), Aslag Guttormsgaard (bass), Ole-Petter Andreasson (drums)

'70s styled Stoner Rock act BLACK DEBBATH ('Black Debate') confounded many international critics with their 1999 album 'Tung, Tung Politisk Rock', as the name implies a politically based record which was sung entirely in Norwegian. The band, which comprises members of GARTNERLOSJEN, LYD, AASEN, LOOPHOLE, THULSA DOOM, THE CUMSHOTS and CURTAINS OF WOOL, is fronted by Emil Hegerberg, an industrious figure holding down membership of no less than eight different bands. BLACK DEBBATH opted for English lyrics on the follow up 'Welcome To Norway'.
BLACK DEBBATH mentor 'Papa Doom' also operates Doom act THULSA DOOM. Better known as Ole-Petter Andreasson, he is renowned for his behind the desk contributions at his Caliban studios to acts such as GLUCIFER, HELLRIDE, his own 'Bonerrock' side project THE CUMSHOTS and THE WONDERFOOLS amongst many others.
None too surprisingly the group contributed a cover version of BLACK SABBATH's 'Sabbath Bloody Sabbath', albeit retitled 'Debbath Bloody Debbath', to a Duplex Records compilation.

Singles/EPs:
Mongo Norway (A Guide To Nightlife In Oslo) / Great Norwegian Comedians (Such As Oluf And Stutum) / King Of Norway / Places To Go And Things To See (Live In London), EMI (2001)
Problemer Innad I Høyre / Den Svarte Oljen Vil En Gang Ta Slutt, Men Den Hvite Oljen Vil Aldri Slutte Å Pumpe (Støtt Norsk Pornobransje) / Gjeninnfør Hatten, EMI (2001)
Martin Schanche (Radio edit) / Where To Shit And Piss In Oslo / Sightseeing In Oslo / Martin Schanche (Album version), EMI (2001)

Albums:
TUNG, TUNG POLITISK ROCK, Duplex (1999)
Dagsorden / Problemer Innad I Høyre / Reorganiser Helsevesenet! / Kultur - Og Vitenskapsdepartementet, Et Departement Med Særdeles Kort Levetid / Ikke Tukl Medelgens Habitat! / Åpent Brev Til Sporveisdirektøren / King Of Norway / Er Fenomenet Bokskred Med På Å Forringe Litteraturens Egenverdi Og Omdømme Som Sådan? Gjør Heller Fornebu Om Til Suppestasjon! / Legg Operaen Til Bøler Samfunnshus! / Eventuelt
WELCOME TO NORWAY, EMI (2001)
The Vikings (The Pioneers Of Rock) / Mongo Norway (A Guide To Nightlife In Oslo) / Martin Schanche (The Coolest Man In Norway) / Traditional Food Bunad (The National Costume) / The Four Big Ones (Essential Authors And Works) / Practical Information A Brief Guide To Norwegian (Pocket Translator) / The Leaving Of The Land Of The Midnight Sun

BLACK MOSES (UK)

Line-Up: Jim Jones (vocals), Graeme Flynn (bass), Chris Buncall (drums)

A 1999 formation of Psych fuelled groove Grungers. BLACK MOSES carried the distinction of being fronted by Jim Jones of THEE HYPNOTICS and ex-PENTHOUSE / 50 TONS OF BLACK TERROR bassist Graeme Flynn. BLACK MOSES original incarnation would be bolstered by the rhythm section of Bristol Stoners THE HEADS but a permanent resolution was found with drummer Chris Buncall, previously a member of V and LAHONDA.

Albums:
EMPEROR DEB, Lunasound Recordings LUNA007CD (2001)
Second Skin / Slow Mama / Yr Gonna Get It / Blown Away / Hot Grundies / Won't Let Go / Strange Life / Cut It Out / 20*20 / Eye On You / Yr Friend / Under The River

BLACKROCK (UK)

Line-Up: Sean (vocals), Chris (guitar), Paul

(guitar), Chris (bass), Ryszard (drums)

A Nottingham based retro Stoner outfit that debuted in late 1997. BLACKROCK issued a brace of demo CDs and had track inclusions on the compilations 'Doomed' from Dark Reign and 'The Mob's New Plan' released by Water Dragon. Their profile was raised significantly with 'The Boston Sherwood Tapes' EP shared as a split release with Massachusetts act ROADSAW, BLACKROCK donating two tracks including a rendition of BRIAN AUGER's 'Indian Ropeman'. Live dates in the UK found BLACKROCK reaping further valuable exposure as guests to UNIDA.

The 'Clutching At Straws' album emerged in February of 2002.

Singles/EPs:
Loserfuel / Indian Ropeman, (2001) ('The Boston Sherwood Tapes'. Split EP with ROADSAW)

Albums:
CLUTCHING AT STRAWS, Threeful (2002)
The Spectator / Dr. Satan's Robot (New version) / We Play For Trips / Breadhead (New version) / S.O.T.S.O.G. (New version)

BLACK SABBATH (UK)
Line-Up: Ozzy Osbourne (vocals), Tony Iommi (guitar), Geezer Butler (bass), Bill Ward (drums)

Cited by many to be THE original Heavy Metal band, BLACK SABBATH have had a massive influence on the genre and have sold countless millions of albums. BLACK SABBATH, steered into their chosen Doom / occult leanings by bassist and songwriter Geezer Butler, impose an enormous legacy upon the Heavy Metal scene. Guitarist TONY IOMMI has laid down many of the classic all-time riffs and is a versatile Blues inspired musician, revered as a guitar hero despite having lost some fingertips in a 1966 machine accident, which nearly put paid to his chosen career.

Until 1978 the band was fronted by vocalist OZZY OSBOURNE. Now renowned as one of the true legends of Metal from his BLACK SABBATH years and his subsequent massively successful solo career, Osbourne's trademark monotonous vocal style and outrageous on and off stage behaviour have gained the Brummie true Rock idol status.

Created in 1967 in the heart of industrial Birmingham, a skinhead then known as Ozzy Zig, Tony Iommi, Terry 'Geezer' Butler and BILL WARD first united, albeit briefly, under the name POLKA TULK BLUES BAND. Osbourne's first attempts at singing came just after leaving school when, together with guitarist Jimmy Phillips, he founded the short-lived act THE PROSPECTORS. Previously Iommi and Ward had been part of THE REST; a band fronted by ex-METHOD FIVE vocalist Chris Smith. The group later changed its name to MYTHOLOGY.

Osbourne and Butler, the latter a rhythm guitarist at this point, were members of RARE BREED, an act that lasted a mere two gigs. Prior to this Osbourne had stints with local bands THE BLACK PANTHERS and APPROACH as well as having served a term in jail for burglary. It was during his incarceration at her majesty's pleasure that the singer gave himself his now famous 'Ozzy' and smiley face tattoos by rubbing floor cleaning paste into his skin.

The quartet joined forces when MYTHOLOGY lost both singer and drummer. With the recruitment of Osbourne and Ward, MYTHOLOGY changed its title to MUSIC MACHINE adding saxophonist Alan Clark and Jimmy Phillips on slide guitar. Before long MUSIC MACHINE became the POLKA TULK BLUES BAND and trimmed down to a quartet, with Butler adopting a new role as bass player by taking two strings off his lead guitar. Phillips meanwhile would go onto become a keyboard player performing with PURPLE ONION, FROG and MAGIC ROUNDABOUT.

Within a short space of time the revised band had altered their moniker to the shortened to POLKA TULK before another name change was enforced, the foursome becoming EARTH.

Signing up to a management deal with Jim Simpson (who was later to manage fellow brummies JUDAS PRIEST) the band started the grind of playing the Rock and Blues clubs. Their first taste of Europe came when Simpson booked a tour of Germany. The shows included a date at Hamburg's infamous Star club (the once famous haunt of THE BEATLES), before getting the band in a four-track studio to record their first demo. This recording, featuring the tracks 'Song For Jim' and 'The Rebel' in 1969, enabled the band to gain a deal with the then 'Progressive Rock' experimental label Vertigo Records, an arm of Fontana Records.

Upon signing they were to discover that another act called EARTH had just released a single in Germany, thus necessitating a name change. According to legend it was a Dennis Wheatley novel that inspired Butler to come up with BLACK SABBATH. Despite the deal, BLACK SABBATH were financially in difficult times and it was at this point that Iommi

TONY IOMMI of BLACK SABBATH
Photo : Sean Denomey

actually left to join JETHRO TULL for all of two weeks, to replace the departed MICK ABRAHAMS.

Although Iommi's stay in JETHRO TULL was brief he did appear with the band at the legendary ROLLING STONES 'Rock n' Roll Circus' film session. However, he was soon back in the fold and BLACK SABBATH recorded their first Rodger Bain produced album for a miserly £600 on a four-track machine. (Interesting to note as an aside that the engineer for the first two albums was none other than 'Colonel' Tom Allom, himself later to find fame as a producer for JUDAS PRIEST).

The band's first product as BLACK SABBATH sunk without trace. A single, 'Wicked Woman (Don't Play Your Evil Games With Me)', a cover of THE CROWS track, had seen a release in January 1970. However, in February, the album 'Black Sabbath' emerged upon an unsuspecting world. Laden with many what are now widely regarded as all time classics; such as 'Black Sabbath', 'The Wizard' and 'N.I.B.' The latter was allegedly at the time thought to be 'Nativity In Black' but was actually a strange reference to the shape of Butler's beard! The album's almost Neanderthal bludgeoning heaviness and thick industrial riffing took Rock fans by storm. The

debut reached number 8 in the British charts with virtually no assistance from radio airplay. Live dates to promote the album saw the band once more venturing into Germany, appearing at festivals alongside RORY GALLAGHER, DEEP PURPLE, FREE, STATUS QUO and BLACK WIDOW. The band also played British shows including a support to PINK FLOYD.

Shortly after wrapping up recording for their second album, provisionally titled 'War Pigs' (again with Rodger Bain) in August 1970, BLACK SABBATH played the 10th 'Plumpton Jazz and Blues' festival alongside HUMBLE PIE and YES. Prior to the album release the record company changed the album title to 'Paranoid'. The record company objected to 'War Pigs' due to the prevailing Vietnam war and also as there was a feeling 'Paranoid' could be a possible hit. The 'War Pigs' title itself had been changed; the original composition was entitled 'Walpurgis'.

The single 'Paranoid' reached Number 4, (which still remains BLACK SABBATH's biggest hit to date), with the album reaching the dizzy heights of Number 1! The album, with the now more renowned classics such as 'Hand Of Doom', 'Fairies Wear Boots' and 'Iron Man', had BLACK SABBATH exploring a much more varied field of interests than its predecessor's predilection for the occult.

In America the second album reached Number 12 and settled in for a long chart stay, eventually clocking up a sixty five week residency. The band's first American shows also occurred, with support slots to MOUNTAIN prior to a headline tour

With the album's success came a valuable indicator to the band of the international potential of BLACK SABBATH. In a rather messy legal wrangle, BLACK SABBATH wriggled out of their management contract with Jim Simpson and signed up to Wilf Pine and Patrick Meehan, both of whom had been previously with the Arden Management company.

August 1971 saw the release of the last Rodger Bain produced BLACK SABBATH album 'Master Of Reality'. The record peaked at Number 5 in the British charts, but provided the band with a strong "out of the box" seller in America, being certified gold before its release.

The band backed up this success Stateside by a lengthy bout of touring, which by this time was beginning to take its toll both mentally and physically on the individual members. 'Volume 4' (originally to be titled 'Snowblind') gave the band another top ten British album and featured the classic ballad 'Changes', featuring YES keyboard player RICK WAKEMAN, alongside the more brutal 'Snowblind'.

Completists may wish to know that Iommi also recorded a session for FREEDOM / later SNAFU vocalist BOBBY HARRISON's solo album 'The Funkist'. FREEDOM were also part of Patrick Meehan's management stable and the band opened for BLACK SABBATH on numerous occasions. 'The Funkist' saw a release in America on the Capitol label in 1973.

The band returned to America to work on 'Volume 4's follow up but found for the first time their flow of ideas had ebbed. Relocating to rehearse in the suitably spooky setting of a Welsh castle dungeon Iommi came up with the classic riff for the track 'Sabbath Bloody Sabbath' and the creative juices started to flow once more. In late 1973 BLACK

TONY MARTIN of BLACK SABBATH
Photo : Sean Denomey

SABBATH released the renowned 'Sabbath Bloody Sabbath' album to worldwide critical acclaim.

For live work, keyboard player Gerry Woodruffe was added and BLACK SABBATH put in one of their most important American appearances at the 'California Jam' festival in 1974 alongside EMERSON LAKE & PALMER and DEEP PURPLE, playing to an audience of over quarter of a million people.

However, touring excesses and managerial nightmares had taken the band to breaking point, with Iommi and Osbourne becoming ever more confrontational. By now the band had shifted their business affairs to the notorious Don Arden. 1975's 'Sabotage' kept the flame alive and the band put in another enormous American tour supported by KISS. The 'Sabotage' album included a rarity for the band as initial copies included an unaccredited track 'Blow The Jug'. This was actually Bill Ward singing the NITTY GRITTY DIRT BAND track captured unawares by a studio engineer. Later pressings do not include this moment.

The compilation 'We Sold Our Souls For Rock n' Roll' charted well too, but many thought the 1976 experimental effort 'Technical Ecstasy' to be way below par. The album did include a first for the band though as Ward took lead vocals for the first time on the track 'It's Alright'. American dates saw the band on the road supported by the unlikely duo of REO SPEEDWAGON and THE RAMONES.

In November 1977 Osbourne announced he was bowing out from the band. Ozzy set about creating a fresh band with NECROMANDUS personnel guitarist Barry Dunnery, bass player Dennis McCarten and drummer Frank Hall but due to the chaotic circumstances prevailing at the time this project floundered. Another stab at building a solo band found Ozzy in league with former DIRTY TRICKS personnel guitarist John Frazer-Binnie, bass player Terry Horbury and drummer Andy Bierne but just as this group readied themselves for rehearsals in London Osbourne promptly rejoined BLACK SABBATH.

In the interim BLACK SABBATH had endeavoured to fill the void with ex-IDLE RACE, FLEETWOOD MAC and SAVOY BROWN vocalist David Walker.

Recordings were made with Walker for the next album, but the liaison was short-lived and, scrapping the previous songs, Osbourne was enticed back for one last album 'Never Say Die', a record featuring HIGHWAY's John Elstar on harmonica. The only track to surface from the Walker era was a version of 'Junior's Eyes' on the bootleg 'Archangel Rides Again'. The singer's public term with the band was captured on the BBC 'Look Hear' TV programme as he led the band through 'Junior's Eyes'. Walker later rejoined SAVOY BROWN.

Touring Britain in 1978, BLACK SABBATH appeared tired and uninspired; a state of affairs sharply put into focus by having the youthful VAN HALEN as guests stealing the honours throughout the tour. Upon the tour's completion OZZY OSBOURNE quit for the last time, resurfacing as a solo artist under the initial band handle of BLIZZARD OF OZZ for an immensely successful, if often shambolic, post BLACK SABBATH career.

The past reared its head with the release of a live album 'Live At Last'. Hardly the greatest sound quality and issued with no involvement from the band, the album at least gave fan's an "official" live recording of the Osbourne fronted line-up. Quite perversely 'Live At Last' charted higher in the UK than many previous efforts.

In 1980, BLACK SABBATH announced that former ELF and RAINBOW vocalist Ronnie James Dio had joined the fold. Butler also departed and for a while was supplanted by WORLD OF OZ / QUARTZ man Geoff Nichols. As Nichols shifted over to the keyboard role (a role he has occupied ever since sometimes as bona fide band member or more often than not as hired hand), ex-RAINBOW bassist Craig Gruber took the role. Apparently at this juncture the band was merely to be titled SABBATH. By the time of recording for their comeback album Butler had returned along with the full band name.

Management and legal hassles surrounded the band as the pressure was on for a farewell tour with Ozzy, but despite the adversities BLACK SABBATH came up trumps with a massively successful album entitled 'Heaven And Hell'. According to some reports many of Gruber's bass lines were left intact for the finished record but the American did not want his name to appear anywhere on the finished package.

Produced by Martin Birch, this record spawned many classics, including 'Children Of The Sea', the title track and even a hit single in 'Neon Nights', which saw BLACK SABBATH once more on the TV show 'Top Of The Pops'. Dio, a vocalist of quite awesome talents, certainly lent the epic touch of majesty Iommi needed as a foil for his increasingly monolithic riffing.

BLACK SABBATH put on a monstrous tour of America with BLUE OYSTER CULT billed as 'Black n' Blue' tour. Support came from MOLLY HATCHET and RIOT. However, shortly after the album was recorded, Ward was unceremoniously replaced midtour, as

RAY GILLAN of BLACK SABBATH
Photo : Matt Sampson

45

the years on the road finally took their toll on his health and sense of purpose with the band. Members of MOLLY HATCHET were later to claim that such was the magnitude of ill luck BLACK SABBATH were dragging around with them that at one open air show a solitary cloud deluged rain onto BLACK SABBATH on stage leaving the audience completely dry!

BLACK SABBATH drafted in ex-AXIS / BRUZER / DERRINGER drummer Vinnie Appice, who, incidentally, was asked to join OZZY OSBOURNE's new band at the same time.

Maintaining their momentum BLACK SABBATH swiftly turned out another spectacular album in 'Mob Rules' which if anything saw BLACK SABBATH getting even heavier.

The subsequent tour, kicking off with a show in Hawaii to 20,000 people, witnessed BLACK SABBATH solidifying their return to the fore. Sadly, prior to the release of a proposed double live album 'Live Evil', Dio left amidst a cloud of insults and accusations.

Bizarrely, BLACK SABBATH accused Dio of sneaking into the studio after the rest of the band had gone, to push up the vocal levels on 'Live Evil'. To cap it all Osbourne had issued a double live album 'Speak Of The Devil', chock full of BLACK SABBATH classics as performed by his band, stealing the band's fire for 'Live Evil'. The press were only too eager to fan the flames and keep the verbal feud alive, which naturally succeeded in dragging the once glorious name of BLACK SABBATH down into the mud.

Vinnie Appice was given the push along with Dio as the drummer joined the singer in forming DIO during 1983. The debut DIO album was widely regarded as a remarkable Metal album (with sales to match) and a big pointer to the direction BLACK SABBATH would have gone had Dio stayed the course.

The band's next move took the Rock world by total surprise as it was announced that BLACK SABBATH's new singer was none other than former DEEP PURPLE man Ian Gillan alongside a reinstated BILL WARD. Many GILLAN fans felt betrayed, as Gillan had, only weeks before, quit a British tour purporting to be severely affected with a throat infection that would put him out of action for months. GILLAN band members also leaked the news that an abortive attempt at putting DEEP PURPLE back together again had prompted the singer's move. When this proposed union faltered Gillan got the welcome call from BLACK SABBATH.

The ensuing album 'Born Again', featuring an incredibly garish sleeve designed by 'Kerrang!' art director Krusher Joule, was slated by critics, and the combination of Gillan and BLACK SABBATH certainly jarred with many fans. Regardless, an equal number praised this strange alliance. The record still achieved a high British chart placing and good international sales. (Someone in GUNS N' ROSES certainly had been listening. Spot the widely recognized identical riff!)

Shortly after recording 'Born Again' Ward was forced to quit due to recurring health problems and was quickly replaced by ELECTRIC LIGHT ORCHESTRA drummer Bev Bevan. Headlining the Reading festival that year BLACK SABBATH rubbed salt in the wounds by dragging out DEEP PURPLE's 'Smoke On The Water' as an encore.

Incidentally, the notorious Stonehenge stage set scene in spoof Rockumentary 'This Is Spinal Tap' was strongly rumoured to have been based on actual events surrounding the BLACK SABBATH stage design for the 'Born Again' tour, with the finished 'stones' being too big to fit into venues!

Controversy continued to follow the latest incarnation of the band wherever they roamed. At a gig in Zwolle, Holland, one insulted fan even threw a wheelchair on stage in protest at the sullying of the BLACK SABBATH legend. An American tour, with LITA FORD as opener, proved less than successful and this line-up soon fell apart, harried by the press from all quarters.

With Gillan out of the picture returning to DEEP PURPLE, Iommi and Butler geared up for a proposed new album. Initially producer Spencer Proffer was enlisted alongside former STEELER and then currently KEEL vocalist Ron Keel. Demos of four songs were cut and news of Keel's appointment was leaked to the media but the relationship was soon curtailed. Later in the year the band announced that Ward had rejoined and unveiled new vocalist, an American, David Donato, whose past credits listed various small time Californian club bands, such as HERO, HEADSHAKER and VIRGIN. The tape that secured Donato the job was recorded with ex-DEEP PURPLE bassist GLENN HUGHES and KISS guitarist Mark Norton in a band titled DALI. But within weeks Donato was out of the picture, later to emerge as frontman to ex-KISS guitarist Mark Norton's act WHITE TIGER.

The 13th July 1985 Live Aid event provided the catalyst for an impromptu reunion of the original BLACK SABBATH, but negotiations for a more permanent venture proved fruitless and Geezer Butler returned to Britain to set up a more AOR orientated act that performed a handful of club shows.

The line-up for the GEEZER BUTLER BAND included guitarist Pedro Howse, vocalist

Richie Callison and drummer John Mee. A later line-up had ex-BIRD OF PREY vocalist Kyle Michaels fronting the band, later of MASI.

It was for the initial auditions for what was originally planned as Iommi's solo album 'Seventh Star' that the American TV evangelist Jeff Fenholt actually rehearsed with the band for a short period.

Fenholt claims to have been a 'member' of the band between January and May 1985 and demos recorded with Iommi have been posted on the web.

Former ARMAGEDDON vocalist Fenholt now has his own TV show during which he regularly makes claims that he was a member of the band. Immediately after his BLACK SABBATH liaison Fenholt fronted JOSHUA for one album then DRIVER for a brief period. Strangely Fenholt apparently became involved with the widow of famed surrealist artist Salvador Dali, recording in her studio. Fenholt's parents were later announced as threatening to sue their own son for $12,000,000 in damages after he claimed they had beaten him as a child. The Fenholt

myth would only be lent further fuel when in 1996 a CD of seven studio tracks was issued. With BLACK SABBATH effectively falling apart, Iommi (who had been dating former RUNAWAYS guitarist LITA FORD) got back to business by recording a solo album entitled 'Seventh Star'. The album was originally to have featured three vocalists in Ronnie James Dio, JUDAS PRIEST's ROB HALFORD and ex-DEEP PURPLE and TRAPEZE star GLENN HUGHES. As it turned out, Hughes cut all the songs.

Persuaded by management and record company this album was eventually to see the light of day under the rather unwieldy title of BLACK SABBATH FEATURING TONY IOMMI and paradoxically was also to be one of the band's brightest moments musically.

The album gave Iommi more freedom to explore the blues-ier side of his nature and, combined with an awesome vocal display from Hughes, 'Seventh Star', produced by Jeff Glixman, is without doubt a classic album. Gordon Copley, bassist for Iommi's then girlfriend LITA FORD, provided bass.

Iommi formed a new band around this album

BLACK SABBATH

47

with Hughes, drummer Eric Singer, ex-AMERICADE and WHITE LION bassist Dave 'The Beast' Spitz and longtime keyboard player Geoff Nichols.

The American tour started out in Cleveland on March 21st with support acts W.A.S.P. and ANTHRAX, but Hughes still suffered from unreliability and alleged drug related problems. The singer claimed to have been punched the day before the debut gig by a member of BLACK SABBATH's crew and that blood was choking his throat, thus affecting his performance. Whatever the real cause the rest of the band were concerned enough to rehearse a stand-by singer, the New York ex-HARLETTE and RONDINELLI vocalist RAY GILLEN.

Upon discovering Gillen soundchecking with the band Hughes quit following a Connecticut show on March 29th, leaving Gillen to pick up the pieces. The following European tour, with support act ZENO, played to half empty houses despite the excellence of the new material and superior style of Gillen's vocals. It seemed the fans had simply had enough of constant line-up changes.

BLACK SABBATH retired to the studio, aided by producer Jeff Glixman. Unfortunately, Glixman upped and left midway through recording. His place was taken by Vic Coppersmith who lasted little longer.

Further turmoil followed as Gillen did not stick around long enough to finish recording the next album 'Eternal Idol', opting instead to join former OZZY OSBOURNE guitarist JAKE E. LEE's new act BADLANDS for two highly regarded Blues Rock outings before stints with TERRIFF and SUN RED SUN. Gillen would die tragically young in 1994 from AIDS related complications.

Singer also quit during recording to join GARY MOORE (and later KISS). Former RAINBOW, OZZY OSBOURNE and then GARY MOORE bassist Bob Daisley was enlisted to help the band out of a tight spot as producer Chris Tsangarides finally finished the album.

The band entered into discussions with former WISHBONE ASH vocalist Mervyn Spence to fill the lead vocalist's role but Spence declined, going on to cut an album with SILENT WITNESS. Daisley too was invited to join the band but declined opting to continue his alliance with GARY MOORE.

Regrouping yet again, Iommi pulled in Birmingham's Tony Martin, previously with THE ALLIANCE and TOBRUK, to fill the vacant vocal spot. 'The Eternal Idol' showcased Martin's vocal abilities, unfortunately tainted by a remarkable resemblance to Dio, but did little to stem the tide and it fared badly in the charts. However,

Gillen's stature was such already that enterprising souls leaked the original 'Eternal Idol' sessions complete with the original vocals intact.

The promotional video for 'The Shining' saw ex-HANOI ROCKS, GENERATION X and THE CLASH man Terry Chimes on the drums. Touring was erratic and a massive faux pas by the band resulting from gigs at South Africa's Sun City venue forced the band's management to issue a formal apology upon their return. BLACK SABBATH then took to the road in Europe, with ex-VIRGINIA WOLF bassist Jo Burt in the ranks. By May of 1988 Chimes was out of the picture.

In 1988 BLACK SABBATH put in a surprise low-key appearance at a local nightclub, the Oldbury Top Spot, performing for charity. A lucky handful of fans witnessed one of the strangest ever BLACK SABBATH line-ups for this one-off gig comprised Iommi, Martin, drummer Bev Bevan and keyboardist Geoff Nichols handling bass duties.

An amusing BLACK SABBATH related story emerged in April '88 when 'Kerrang!' magazine ran an 'exclusive' story related to plans for top Welsh crooner Tom Jones to join the band. The combination revealed their intention to record a concept album and undertake a tour based upon the dual subjects of bullfighting and Welsh mining. The story was, of course, a well conceived April Fool's Day hoax enjoyed by both Iommi and Tom Jones!

By this time not only had the fans stomached enough but Vertigo dropped the band shortly after 'Eternal Idol's release. Meantime original drummer BILL WARD issued his debut solo album 'Ward One - Along The Way' during 1989. Ozzy guested with lead vocals on two tracks.

Regrouping, BLACK SABBATH signed to Miles Copeland's IRS label and set about rebuilding their career with a clutch of strong album releases, kicking off with 'The Headless Cross'.

A new album naturally witnessed a further line-up shuffle, with Iommi and Martin drafting in ex-RAINBOW, WHITESNAKE and MICHAEL SCHENKER GROUP drummer COZY POWELL and little known bassist Lawrence Cottle. The latter had made his mark previously on GARY MOORE's 'After The War' album and with sessions for ERIC CLAPTON.

For live work Cottle was supplanted by former WHITESNAKE / VOW WOW bassist Neil Murray. Still, 'Headless Cross' proved a welcome return to form and saw strong sales across Europe. The album sold particularly well in Europe and Scandinavia rebuilding a great degree of BLACK SABBATH's lost

credibility. BLACK SABBATH toured Russia with Brit female Rockers GIRLSCHOOL, Europe with AXXIS as guests before American dates supported by METAL CHURCH and KINGDOM COME.

Another superbly polished BLACK SABBATH album 'Tyr', loosely based on Norse mythology - Tyr being the Viking War God, found BLACK SABBATH solidifying their return. Shows in Europe were opened by CIRCUS OF POWER.

In late 1991 the band suffered a serious setback when Powell was badly injured. The drummer's horse, Pip, suffered a heart attack and fell on Powell, fracturing his hip.

BLACK SABBATH continuously kept negotiating with OZZY OSBOURNE for his return, but in 1992, following many false starts Iommi and Butler opted finally for the next best thing by teaming up once more with Dio. Butler had jammed with DIO in America performing 'Neon Nights', after which the proposal to join forces once more was mooted. The idea was a necessary step for both parties as DIO had suffered from disastrous attendances on their American tour and BLACK SABBATH were in limbo following Ozzy's opt out of reunion plans. With Dio rejoining, TONY MARTIN pursued a solo project, releasing a 1992 album for Vertigo in Germany. He would also contribute lead vocals to two MISHA CALVIN albums.

Powell's position was taken by Vinnie Appice. The resulting album was the Mack produced 'Dehumaniser', which, despite being a heavyweight offering, failed to capture previous Dio - era glories, mainly due to a clutch of mediocre songs.

BLACK SABBATH toured Europe followed by a stint in America where Ozzy was nailing the lid on his live work by performing the supposed last two shows of his 'No More Tours' grand finale at Costa Mesa. The Oz invited BLACK SABBATH to play on the same bill then reunite for a few songs one last time following his performance. The idea was anathema to Dio, who promptly announced he was quitting once more. This was not before another ugly war of words had ensued, including a fax to journalists from the Ozzy management camp detailing the paltry attendance figures DIO the band had mustered last time they played the Costa Mesa venue. Remarkably BLACK SABBATH did play at the Ozzy shows with JUDAS PRIEST vocalist ROB HALFORD fronting the band, the singer having learnt the entire set in two days! The two gigs would be immortalized on the now famous bootleg 'When Ozzy Met The Priest - An Event In Rock History'.

During all this activity ex-members Cozy Powell and Neil Murray re-formed one of Cozy's old acts COZY POWELL's HAMMER with guitarist MARIO PARGA and singer Peter Oliver. This line-up only lasted one gig before the recruitment of another BLACK SABBATH face TONY MARTIN. The band toured Europe billed as TONY MARTIN & FRIENDS. Powell and Murray would stick together to form SAINTS AND SINNERS.

1994 saw another excellent, if overlooked, album 'Cross Purposes' surfacing. Although initially planned as an Iommi / Butler project album, akin to Iommi's 'Seventh Star', record company pressure saw its release under the BLACK SABBATH banner.

The band toured America once again, with vocalist Tony Martin and new drummer Bobby Rondinelli (ex-RAINBOW / RONDINELLI) this time, in an all British Metal package with MOTÖRHEAD, prior to a well received European jaunt with '70s BLACK SABBATH idolizing support act CATHEDRAL and Americans GODSPEED. Still, in August 1994, Rondinelli quit prior to dates in South America and his place on the drum stool was once more in the hands of original member BILL WARD.

The BLACK SABBATH 'tribute' album 'Nativity In Black' was launched at the Los Angeles Foundations Forum. Essentially a selection of up and coming, mainly American acts such as BIOHAZARD, WHITE ZOMBIE and TYPE O NEGATIVE paying homage to their heroes, the album nonetheless featured some interesting combinations; such as OZZY OSBOURNE and THERAPY?'s rendition of 'Iron Man' and MEGADETH performing 'Paranoid' . Also included was a track by the BULLRING BRUMMIES, a studio outfit consisting of JUDAS PRIEST / FIGHT vocalist ROB HALFORD, Geezer Butler, FIGHT guitarist Brian Tilse and OBSESSED / ST. VITUS guitarist Wino.

With one more original BLACK SABBATH member back in the line-up another one departed, with Butler quitting in September and going on to work on a solo album under the band handle of GZR. By the following month it was announced that the group had reinstated the 'Headless Cross' / 'Tyr' era rhythm section of Neil Murray and COZY POWELL, alongside Iommi and Martin.

Unfortunately, the resulting album, 'Forbidden', did not match the class of its predecessors, sounding rushed and lacking in terms of overall sound quality. The somewhat pedestrian production was handled by BODY COUNT guitarist Ernie C. and the album featured vocalist ICE T. guesting on the lead cut 'Illusion Of Power'.

Still, BLACK SABBATH once more set out on tour in America, co-headlining with MOTÖRHEAD for a second time. Prior to the end of these dates Powell was forced to leave to deal with personal problems and in came Bobby Rondinelli yet again. Rondinelli would join BLUE OYSTER CULT in February 1997.

In mid 1996 it appeared that Iommi was once more working with ROB HALFORD for an album project, although the former JUDAS PRIEST vocalist still had commitments to his new project TWO. These sessions were subsequently put on ice and Iommi began recording solo material with his old ally GLENN HUGHES and former TRAPEZE and JUDAS PRIEST drummer Dave Holland for a projected solo album. Interest in this project was so high that tapes for a proposed full album were leaked onto the bootleg market and issued as 'Eighth Star'.

Before this project was finalized however, and from out of the blue, BLACK SABBATH with its classic line-up relented to fan pressure and reunited.

Ozzy Osbourne had put together a touring extravaganza in America, modestly titled 'Ozzfest'. The bill included his own band together with PANTERA, COAL CHAMBER and POWERMAN 5000 to which the classic BLACK SABBATH were due to headline. Osbourne, Iommi and Butler forged the reunion, but Ward felt unable to commit himself citing health reasons, both physical and mental.

BLACK SABBATH undertook the tour, which established itself as one of the biggest draws on the American touring circuit that year, aided by OZZY OSBOURNE & FAITH NO MORE drummer Mike Bordin. The very last date of the 'Ozzfest' dates clashed with Bordin's prior commitments and former UGLY KID JOE drummer Shannon Larkin took the role for one night.

Whilst the American dates were under full steam Butler put out his second, and highly commendable, solo affair with his band now dubbed GEEZER, in the form of 'Black Science'.

The BLACK SABBATH legend was kept alive by the release of Ozzy's compilation album, 'The Ozzman Cometh'. Alongside more familiar solo Ozzy outings the CD also boasted four early unreleased BLACK SABBATH tracks with demo versions of 'Fairies Wear Boots', 'Behind The Wall Of Sleep', 'War Pigs' (in its original 'Walpurgis' format with different lyrics) and 'Black Sabbath'.

The band, fronted by Ozzy, announced two shows at the Birmingham NEC in early December '97, bringing FEAR FACTORY as support. Both shows sold out with a live album issued in 1998 titled 'Reunion'. The album was made all the more special by the inclusion of the original bands first studio recordings for two decades. However, although 'Psycho Man' features Ward the other new track 'Selling My Soul' is powered by a drum machine. 'Reunion' would be the first album since 1980's 'Heaven And Hell' to break the platinum sales marker under the BLACK SABBATH name.

With Ward's health still a subject of speculation Vinny Appice was pulled from the ranks of DIO in 1998 to occupy the drum stool. OZZY OSBOURNE keyboard player John Sinclair took over from Geoff Nichols for these dates.

SABBATH put in their last ever live gigs dubbed 'The Last Supper' at Birmingham's NEC in late December 1999 with Ward back behind the kit. Appice, after a period employed as a safety break in case Ward's health failed again, later created his own act HUNGER FARM.

2000 found Iommi busy on his solo album simply billed 'Iommi' with numerous high profile guests including Ozzy and PANTERA's Phil Anselmo. The album cut 'Who Fools Who' proved to be of keen interest to Sabbath fans including as it does both Osbourne and Ward. The guitarist did take time out to perform with impromptu club act BELCH, a band that featured his ex-BLACK SABBATH colleague friend Bev Bevan and comedian Jasper Carrott on vocals. Osbourne himself was hard at work on a further solo album.

BLACK SABBATH did reunite for a summer 2000 show although after the event they probably wished they hadn't. A surprise performance after an OZZY OSBOURNE gig at the Anaheim 'Weenie Roast' festival ended in debacle when a revolving stage snagged the band's gear resulting in a long embarrassing silence and lengthy delays.

Undaunted BLACK SABBATH would rise yet again during 2001 demonstrating renewed vigour as the main act at the California ESPN Action, Sports & Music Awards ceremony on April 7th.

This showing would provide a taster for another full-blown 'Ozzfest' global touring festival. Backing up the steadfast brummies were contemporary acts such as SLIPKNOT, TOOL, PAPA ROACH, AMEN, SOULFLY, DISTURBED and BLACK LABEL SOCIETY. MARILYN MANSON would also figure but only for the American dates. Even Geezer Butler's son got involved with his act APARTMENT 26. Also announced was that Ozzy's plans for a solo album would be put on hold whilst recording of a brand new BLACK SABBATH album was undertaken.

A warm-up show just prior to the UK Ozzfest was held at the Birmingham Academy on May 22nd with the band donating all proceeds from the gig to the homeless persons charity

St. Basil's. Another display of nostalgia came in October with the long overdue officially sanctioned release of archive live material. Divine Recordings, the label established by Sharon Osbourne, would announce the release of live tapes culled from the 'Sabotage' world tour entitled suitably 'Live in '75'. However, just after a track listing and release had been set the album was cancelled.

May of 2001 also witnessed a treat for fans when ex-BLACK SABBATH men Tony Martin and Neil Murray joined RONDINELLI, the band spearheaded by another Sabbath veteran Bobby Rondinelli. Martin also found time to tour the British clubs fronting BAILEY'S COMET as well as promote the 'Cage 2' album, his second in league with Italian guitarist Dario Mollo.

Quite surreally an Estonian outfit RONDELLUS made quite an impact upon the BLACK SABBATH faithful in March of 2002. The group of classically trained medieval folk artists reinterpreted an entire album of Sabs classics sung in operatic style, played on original medieval instruments with lyrics translated into Latin!

BLACK SABBATH would hit the music TV shows once again in the summer of 2002 courtesy of ex-member Ronnie James Dio and the video for his current single 'Push' from the DIO album 'Killing The Dragon'. A lavish Bill Schacht directed promo film would include appearances from the unlikely TENACIOUS D duo of Jack Black and Kyle Gass. TENACIOUS D had already signalled their respect for the band with the inclusion of the track 'Dio' on their current album. The video concept, in which a multitude of special effects would be employed, involved TENACIOUS D jamming BLACK SABBATH's 'Heaven And Hell' as an intro.

The Dio era BLACK SABBATH would be kept in the media too with the announcement that artist Greg Hildebrandt's 'Mob Dream', used as the cover art for the classic 1981 album 'Mob Rules' was up for sale at a cool $35,000. The previously mooted live album would also rear its head again, retitled 'Past Lives' and now set for release through Sanctuary Records. The album would comprise the 'Live At Last' album, parts of the common Paris 1970 bootleg, a February 1975 recording from Baltimore, Maryland alongside tracks from a German TV 'Beat Club' appearance.

Singles/EPs:
Evil Woman (Don't Play Your Games With Me) / Wicked World, Fontana TF 1067 (1970)
Paranoid / The Wizard, Vertigo 6059 010 (1970) **4 UK**

Tomorrow's Dream / Laguna Sunrise, Vertigo 6059 061 (1972)
Children Of The Grave (B-Side) / Roadhouse Blues (STATUS QUO) (A Side), Vertigo DJ005 (1973) (Split single with STATUS QUO - Promotional release)
Sabbath Bloody Sabbath / Changes, WWA WWS 002 (1973)
Am I Going Insane / Hole In The Sky, NEMS 6165 300 (1975)
Never Say Die / She's Gone, Vertigo SAB 001 (1978) **21 UK**
Hard Road / Symptom Of The Universe, Vertigo SAB 002 (1978) **33 UK**
Paranoid / Snowblind, NEMS NES 112 (1978) **14 UK**
Neon Knights / Children Of The Sea, Vertigo SAB 3 (1980) **22 UK**
Die Young / Heaven And Hell, Vertigo SAB 4 (1980) **41 UK**
Paranoid / Snowblind, NEMS BSS 101 (1980)
Mob Rules / Die Young, Vertigo SAB 5 (1981) **46 UK**
Turn Up The Night (Live) / Lonely Is The Word (Live), Vertigo SAB 6 (1982) **37 UK**
Paranoid / Iron Man, NEP 1 (1982) (Limited edition Picture Disc)
Trashed / Zero The Hero, Warner WEA PRO A 2102 (1983) (12" single promotional release)
Trashed (Mono) / Trashed (Stereo), Warner WEA 7 29434 (1983) (7" single promotional release)
Trashed / Stonehenge, Warner WEA 7 29434 (1986)
Heart Like A Wheel / In For The Kill / Turn To Stone, Vertigo SAB DJ 12 (1986) (12"single promotional release)
No Stranger To Love / No Stranger To Love (Edit), Warner WEA PRO A 2430 (1986) (12" single promotional release)
Danger Zone / Danger Zone, Warner WEA PRO A 2475 (1986) (12" single promotional release)
Paranoid / War Pigs / Iron Man / Black Sabbath, That's Original TOF 101 (1986)
The Shining, Vertigo (1987) (12" single promotional release)
Paranoid / Iron Man / War Pigs, Castle CD 3-5 (1988) (3" CD EP)
Headless Cross / Cloak And Dagger, IRS EIRS107 (1989) **62 UK**
Headless Cross (Extended Version) / Headless Cross / Cloak And Dagger, IRS IRS 241006-2 (1989)
Call Of The Wild / Devil And Daughter, IRS IRS (1989) (7" single)
Call Of The Wild / Devil And Daughter / When Death Calls, IRS IRS 241025-3 (1989)
Black Moon / Cloak And Dagger, IRS (1989) (Promotional release)

Devil And Daughter, IRS EIRSPD 115
(1989) (One sided)
Paranoid / Electric Funeral / Sabbath
Bloody Sabbath, Old Gold OG 6129 (1989)
The Gates Of Hell / The Gates Of Hell, IRS
(1990) (USA promotion)
Paranoid / Iron Man, Old Gold OG 9467
(1990)
Feels Good To Me / Paranoid (Live), IRS
(1991) (7" single)
Feels Good To Me / Paranoid (Live) /
Heaven And Hell (Live), IRS (1991)
TV Crimes / Letters From Earth / Paranoid
(Live), IRS (1992) **33 UK**
Black Sabbath / Blue Suede Shoes / Iron
Man / Paranoid, Burning Airlines PILOT 49
(1992) ('Black Mass' CD-ROM EP in
bloodpack)
Get A Grip, IRS CDSP111 (1995) (One
sided)
Psycho Man (Radio edit) / Psycho Man
(Danny Saber remix edit), Epic SAMPCS
5513 (1998) (Promotional release)

Albums:
BLACK SABBATH, Vertigo VO 6 (1970) **8
UK, 23 USA**
Black Sabbath / The Wizard / Behind The
Walls Of Sleep / N.I.B. / Sleeping Village /
Warning / Evil Woman (Don't Play Your
Games With Me)
PARANOID, Vertigo 6360 011 (1970) **2
GERMANY, 1 UK, 12 USA**
War Pigs / Paranoid / Planet Caravan /
Electric Funeral / Fairies Wear Boots / Iron
Man / Hand Of Doom / Rat Salad
MASTER OF REALITY, Vertigo 6360 050
(1971) **5 GERMANY, 5 UK, 8 USA**
Sweet Leaf / After Forever / Children Of The
Grave / Embryo / Lord Of This World / Into
The Void / Solitude / Orchid
VOLUME 4, Vertigo 6360 071 (1972) **8 UK,
13 USA**
Wheels Of Confusion / Tomorrow's Dream /
Snowblind / Changes / Supernaut / FX /
Laguna Sunrise / Under The Sun /
Cornucopia / St. Vitus Dance
SABBATH BLOODY SABBATH, Vertigo
WWA 005 (1973) **49 GERMANY, 4 UK, 11
USA**
A National Acrobat / Sabbath Bloody
Sabbath / Who Are You? / Killing Yourself To
Live / Spiral Architect / Fluff / Looking For
Today / Sabbra Cadabra
SABOTAGE, NEMS 9119 001 (1975) **7 UK,
28 USA**
Hole In The Sky / Don't Start (Too Late) /
Symptom Of The Universe / Megalomania /
Am I Going Insane (Radio) / The Writ /
Supertzar / Thrill Of It All
**WE SOLD OUR SOULS FOR ROCK N'
ROLL**, NEMS 6641 335 (1976)

21 SWEDEN, 35 UK, 48 USA
Black Sabbath / The Wizard / Warning /
Paranoid / Wicked World / Tomorrow's
Dream / Fairies Wear Boots / Changes /
Sweet Leaf / Children Of The Grave /
Sabbath Bloody Sabbath / Am I Going
Insane (Radio) / Laguna Sunrise / Snowblind
/ N.I.B.
TECHNICAL ECSTACY, Vertigo 9102 750
(1976) **33 SWEDEN, 13 UK**
Back Street Kids / You Won't Change Me /
Rock n' Roll Doctor / It's Alright / All Moving
Parts (Stand Still) / She's Gone / Dirty
Women / Gypsy
ATTENTION VOL. 1, Fontana 6438 057
(1975)
Paranoid / Sleeping Village / Warning / Evil
Woman / Iron Man / The Wizard / Behind
The Wall Of Sleep / N.I.B.
ATTENTION VOL. II, WWA WWA 101 (1975)
Sweet Leaf / Black Sabbath / Rat Salad /
Electric Funeral / After Forever / War Pigs /
Fairies Wear Boots
THE ORIGINAL, NEMS (1976)
Paranoid / N.I.B. / Changes / Sabbath
Bloody Sabbath / Black Sabbath / War Pigs /
Laguna Sunrise / Tomorrow's Dream
GREATEST HITS, NEMS NEL 6009 (1977)
Paranoid / N.I.B. / Changes / Sabbath
Bloody Sabbath / Iron Man / Black Sabbath /
War Pigs / Laguna Sunrise / Tomorrow's
Dream / Sweet Leaf
NEVER SAY DIE, Vertigo 9102 751 (1978)
37 SWEDEN, 12 UK
Swinging The Chain / Never Say Die / Hard
Road / Shock Wave / Johnny Blade / Junior's
Eyes / Air Dance / Break Out / Over To You
ROCK LEGENDS, Vertigo 6321 120 (1978)
(Australian release)
Backstreet Kids / Rock n' Roll Doctor / Dirty
Women / Never Say Die / Shock Wave / Air
Dance / Johnny Blade
STARGOLD, NEMS 0084.501 (197-)
Black Sabbath / Evil Woman / Warning /
N.I.B. / Changes / Sabbath Bloody Sabbath /
Laguna Sunrise / Tomorrow's Dream / Sweet
Leaf / Children Of The Grave / Lord Of This
World / Solitude / War Pigs / Paranoid /
Planet Caravan / Iron Man
LIVE AT LAST, NEMS BS001 (1980)
26 SWEDEN, 5 UK
Tomorrow's Dream / Sweet Leaf /
Cornucopia / Wicked World / Killing Yourself
To Live / Snowblind / Children Of The Grave
/ War Pigs / Paranoid / Cornucopia
HEAVEN AND HELL, Vertigo 9102 752
(1980) **25 SWEDEN, 9 UK, 28 USA**
Lonely Is The World / Heaven And Hell /
Children Of The Sea / Wishing Well / Lady
Evil / Neon Knights / Die Young / Walk Away
ROCK HEAVIES, Vertigo (1980)
Back Street Kids / Rock n' Roll Doctor / Dirty

Women / Never Say Die / Shock Wave / Air Dance / Johnny Blade
MOB RULES, Mercury 6V02119 (1981) **30 SWEDEN, 12 UK, 29 USA**
The Sign Of The Southern Cross / Mob Rules / Slipping Away / Turn Up The Night / Voodoo / Country Girl / Over And Over / Falling Off The Edge Of The World / E5150
LIVE EVIL, Vertigo SAB 10 (1983) **15 SWEDEN, 13 UK, 37 USA**
Children Of The Sea / Black Sabbath / Paranoid / Neon Knights / Iron Man / Children Of The Grave / E5150 / Heaven And Hell / Voodoo / Sign Of The Southern Cross / War Pigs / Mob Rules / N.I.B.
BORN AGAIN, Vertigo VERL 8 (1983) **7 SWEDEN, 4 UK, 39 USA**
Disturbing The Priest / Stonehenge / Zero The Hero / Trashed / The Dark / Born Again / Hot Line / Digital Bitch / Keep It Warm
BEST OF BLACK SABBATH, NEMS (1983) (Picture Disc)
30 ANOS DE MUSICA ROCK, Vertigo 8222971 (1985) (Mexican release)
Back Street Kids / You Won't Change Me / Rock n' Roll Doctor / It's Alright / All Moving Parts (Stand Still) / She's Gone / Dirty Women / Gypsy
HAND OF DOOM, Victoria JS90164 (1984) (Spanish box set release)
Black Sabbath / The Wizard / Behind The Walls Of Sleep / N.I.B. / Sleeping Village / Warning / Evil Woman (Don't Play Your Games With Me) / War Pigs / Paranoid / Planet Caravan / Electric Funeral / Fairies Wear Boots / Iron Man / Hand Of Doom / Rat Salad / Sweet Leaf / After Forever / Children Of The Grave / Embryo / Lord Of This World / Into The Void / Solitude / Orchid / Wheels Of Confusion / Tomorrow's Dream / Snowblind / Changes / Supernaut / FX / Laguna Sunrise / Under The Sun / Cornucopia / St Vitus Dance
THE BLACK SABBATH COLLECTION, Castle CCSLP 109 (1985)
Black Sabbath / The Wizard / Warning / Paranoid / War Pigs / Iron Man / Tomorrow's Dream / Fairies Wear Boots / Changes / Sweet Leaf / Children Of The Grave / Sabbath Bloody Sabbath / Laguna Sunrise / Snowblind / N.I.B.
SEVENTH STAR, Vertigo VERH 29 (1986) **11 SWEDEN, 27 UK**
In For The Kill / No Stranger To Love / Heart Like Wheel / Sphinx (the Guardian) / Turn To Stone / Angry Heart / Danger/ Seventh Star / In Memory
THE ETERNAL IDOL, Vertigo VERH 51 (1987) **66 UK**
The Shining / Ancient Warrior / Born To Lose / Lost Forever / Hard Life To Live / Scarlet Pimpernel / Glory Ride / Eternal Idol

BLACKEST SABBATH, Vertigo (1989)
Black Sabbath / Paranoid / Iron Man / Children Of The Grave / Snowblind / Sabbath Bloody Sabbath / Hole In The Sky / Rock n' Roll Doctor / Never Say Die / Lady Evil / Turn Up The Night / Sign Of The Southern Cross (Live) / Heaven And Hell (Continued) (Live) / Children Of The Sea (Live) / Digital Bitch / Trashed / Seventh Star / Born To Lose / Lost Forever
BLACKEST SABBATH, Vertigo 838 818-2 (1989) (UK version)
Black Sabbath / Paranoid / Iron Man / Snowblind / Sabbath Bloody Sabbath / Hole In The Sky / Rock n' Roll Doctor / Never Say Die / Lady Evil / Turn Up The Night / Sign Of The Southern Cross (Live) / Heaven And Hell (Continued) (Live) / Children Of The Sea (Live) / Digital Bitch / Seventh Star / Born To Lose
HEADLESS CROSS, IRS EIRSA 1002 (1990) **22 SWEDEN, 31 UK**
Gates Of Hell / Headless Cross / Devil And Daughter / When Death Calls / Kill In The Spirit World / Call Of The Wild / Black Moon / Nightwing
BACKTRACKIN', Knight (1990)
Paranoid / Iron Man / Black Sabbath / Killing Yourself To Live / Snowblind / Sweet Leaf / Into The Void / Electric Funeral / Sabra Cadabra / St. Vitus Dance / Fairies Wear Boots / Supertzar / Children Of The Grave / Sabbath Bloody Sabbath / N.I.B. / Symptom Of The Universe / Planet Caravan / War Pigs / Rat Salad / Am I Going Insane (Radio) / Megalomania / The Wizard / Cornucopia / Hole In The Sky
BACKTRACKIN', Masterpiece TRK CD 103 (1990) (UK Version)
Paranoid / Killing Yourself To Live / Snowblind / Sweet Leaf / Into The Void / Electric Funeral / Sabra Cadabra / St. Vitus Dance / Fairies Wear Boots / Sabbath Bloody Sabbath / Symptom Of The Universe / Planet Caravan / War Pigs / The Wizard / Cornucopia
THE BLACK SABBATH COLLECTION VOLUME II, Castle CCS CD 199 (1990)
TYR, IRS EIRSA 1038(1991) **12 GERMANY, 24 SWEDEN, 24 UK**
Anno Mundi / The Lawmaker / Jerusalem / The Sabbath Stones / The Battle Of Tyr / Odin's Court / Valhalla / Feels Good To Me / Heaven In Black
THE OZZY OSBOURNE YEARS, Essential ESB CD 12 (1991)
Black Sabbath / The Wizard / Behind The Wall Of Sleep / N.I.B. / Evil Woman / Sleeping Village / Warning / War Pigs / Paranoid / Planet Caravan / Iron Man / Hand Of Doom / Fairies Wear Boots / Electric Funeral / Sweet Leaf / After Forever /

Embryo / Lord Of This World / Solitude / Into The Void / Wheels Of Confusion / Tomorrow's Dream / Changes / Supernaut / Snowblind / Cornucopia / St, Vitus Dance / Under The Sun / Sabbath Bloody Sabbath / A National Acrobat / Sabbra Caddabra / Killing Yourself To Live / Who Are You / Looking For Today / Spiral Architect / Hole In The Sky / Symptom Of The Universe / Megalomania

THE OZZY OSBOURNE YEARS, Essential ESB 142 (1991) (Vinyl Version)
Black Sabbath / The Wizard / Behind The Wall Of Sleep / N.I.B. / Evil Woman / Sleeping Village / Warning / War Pigs / Paranoid / Planet Caravan / Iron Man / Hand Of Doom / Fairies Wear Boots / Electric Funeral / Sweet Leaf / After Forever / Embryo / Lord Of This World / Solitude / Into The Void / Wheels Of Confusion / Tomorrow's Dream / Changes / Supernaut / Snowblind / Cornucopia

THE MASTERS OF HEAVY METAL, Castle CHC 7022 (1991)
Paranoid / Killing Yourself To Live / Snowblind / Sweet Leaf / Sabbath Bloody Sabbath / Symptom Of The Universe / Planet Caravan / War Pigs / Into The Void / Electric Funeral / Sabbra Cadabra / St. Vitus Dance / Fairies Wear Boots / The Wizard / Cornucopia

THE BLACK SABBATH STORY, Castle CHC 7028 (1991)
Black Sabbath / N.I.B. / Paranoid / War Pigs / Iron Man / Children Of The Grave / Orchid / Lord Of This World / Snowblind / Tomorrow's Dream / Sabbath Bloody Sabbath / Sabbra Cadabra / Symptom Of The Universe / Am I Going Insane (Radio)

DEHUMANISER, IRS EIRS CD 1064 (1992)
13 GERMANY, 12 SWEDEN, 28 UK, 44 USA
Computer God / After All (The Dead) / TV Crimes / Letters From Earth / Masters Of Insanity / Time Machine / Sins Of The Father / I / Buried Alive

CROSS PURPOSES, IRS (1994)
33 GERMANY, 41 UK
I Witness / Cross Of Thorns / Psychophobia / Virtual Death / Immaculate Deception / Dying For Love / Back To Eden / The Hand That Rocks The Cradle / Cardinal Sin / Evil Eye

IRON MAN, Spectrum 550720-2 (1994)
CROSS PURPOSES LIVE, PMI 7243 491314 3 9 (1995)
Time Machine / Children Of The Grave / I Witness / Into The Void / Black Sabbath / Psychophobia / Wizard / Cross Of Thorns / Symptom Of The Universe / Headless Cross / Paranoid / Iron Man / Sabbath Bloody Sabbath

FORBIDDEN, IRS 7243 8 30620 2 7 (1995)
71 UK

Illusion Of Power / Get A Grip / Can't Get Close Enough / Shaking Off The Chains / I Won't Cry For You / Guilty As Hell / Sick And Tired / Rusty Angels / Forbidden / Kiss Of Death

1970-1983 BETWEEN HEAVEN AND HELL, Rawpower RAWCD 104 (1995)
Hole In The Sky / Into The Void / Sabbath Bloody Sabbath / N.I.B. / Paranoid / War Pigs / Iron Man / Wicked World / Supernaut / Back Street Kids / Never Say Die / Neon Knights / Mob Rules / The Dark - Zero The Hero / Black Sabbath

THE SABBATH STONES, IRS 7243 8 37532 2 2 (1996)
Headless Cross / When Death Calls / Devil And Daughter / The Sabbath Stones / The Battle Of Tyr / Odin's Court / Valhalla / TV Crimes / Virtual Death / Evil Eye / Kiss Of Death / Guilty As Hell / Loser Gets It All / Disturbing The Priest / Heart Like A Wheel / The Shining

UNDER WHEELS OF CONFUSION, Essential ESF CD 419 (1996)
Black Sabbath / The Wizard / N.I.B. / Evil Woman / Wicked World / War Pigs / Paranoid / Iron Man / Planet Caravan / Hand Of Doom / Sweet Leaf / After Forever / Children Of The Grave / Into The Void / Lord Of This World / Orchid / Supernaut / Tomorrow's Dream / Wheels Of Confusion / Changes / Snowblind / Laguna Sunrise / Cornucopia (Live) / Sabbath Bloody Sabbath / Killing Yourself To Live / Hole In The Sky / Am I Going Insane (Radio) / The Writ / Symptom Of The Universe / Dirty Women / Back Street Kids / Rock n' Roll Doctor / She's Gone / A Hard Road / Never Say Die / Neon Knights / Heaven And Hell / Die Young / Lonely Is The Word / Turn Up The Night / Sign Of The Southern Cross / Falling Off The Edge Of The World / The Mob Rules (Live) / Voodoo (Live) / Digital Bitch / Trashed / Hotline / In For The Kill / Seventh Star / Heart Like A Wheel / The Shining / Eternal Idol

CHILDREN OF THE GRAVE, Power Sound PS-SR 6011-2 (1996)
Wheels Of Confusion / Tomorrow's Dream / Changes / FX / Supernaut / Snowblind / Cornucopia / Laguna Sunrise / St. Vitus Dance / Under The Sun / Children Of The Grave (Live)

ROCK GIANTS, Spectrum 554 103-2 (1997)
Sabbath Bloody Sabbath / The Wizard / Sweet Leaf / Electric Funeral / Into The Void / Wheels Of Confusion / Paranoid / Iron Man / Am I Going Insane (Radio) / Killing Yourself To Live / Snowblind / Hole In The Sky / Laguna Sunrise / War Pigs

REUNION - LIVE, Epic 491954-9 (1998)
65 FRANCE, 11 SWEDEN, 41 UK

War Pigs / Behind The Wall Of Sleep / N.I.B. / Fairies Wear Boots / Electric Funeral / Sweet Leaf / Spiral Architect / Into The Void / Snowblind / Sabbath Bloody Sabbath / Orchid / Lord Of This World / Dirty Women / Black Sabbath / Iron Man / Children Of The Grave / Paranoid / Psycho Man (Studio) / Selling My Soul (Studio)

THE BEST OF BLACK SABBATH, Rawpower RAW DD145 (2000)

38 NEW ZEALAND, 12 SWEDEN
Black Sabbath / The Wizard / N.I.B. / Evil Woman (Don't Play Your Games With Me) / Wicked World / War Pigs / Paranoid / Planet Caravan /. Iron Man / Electric Funeral / Fairies Wear Boots / Sweet Leaf / Embryo / Children Of The Grave / Lord Of This World / Into The Void

BESTSELLER, Barracuda (2000) (Russian release)
The Gates Of Hell / Nightwing / Orchid / Changes / Snowblind / Laguna Sunrise / Sabbath Bloody Sabbath / Killing Yourself To Live / Paranoid / Children Of The Grave / Dirty Woman / She's Gone / Heaven And Hell / Lonely Is The Word / Psycho Man (Radio Edit) / Fluff / In Memory

THE SINGLES, Castle Music CMKBX002 (2001) (Box set)
Evil Woman / Wicked World / Paranoid / The Wizard / Tomorrow's Dream / Laguna Sunrise / Sabbath Bloody Sabbath / Changes / Never Say Die / She's Gone / Hard Road / Symptom Of The Universe

THE SABBATH COLLECTION, Sanctuary (2001)
Paranoid / Behind The Wall Of Sleep / Sleeping Village / Warning / After Forever / Supernaut / St. Vitus Dance / Snowblind / Killing Yourself To Live / Sabra Cadabra / The Writ

ROCK CHAMPIONS, EMI Electrola 5763722 (2001)
Heaven In Black / Anno Mundi / The Illusion Of Power / Shaking Off The Chains / Kill In The Spirit World / Guilty As Hell / The Lawmaker / Get A Grip / Jerusalem / The Gates Of Hell / Call Of The Wild / The Battle Of Tyr / I Won't Cry For You / Black Moon

MASTERS OF ROCK, EMI (2002)
Gates Of Hell / Headless Cross / Devil And Daughter / When Death Calls / Feels Good To Me / Anno Mundi / Jerusalem / The Battle Of Tyr / Odin's Court / Time Machine / TV Crimes / I / The Hand That Rocks The Cradle / Cross Of Thorns / I Won't Cry For You / Can't Get Close Enough / Forbidden

SYMPTOM OF THE UNIVERSE: THE ORIGINAL BLACK SABBATH (1970-1978), Rhino (2002)
Black Sabbath / N.I.B. / The Wizard / Warning / Evil Woman / War Pigs / Paranoid / Iron Man / Fairies Wear Boots / Sweet Leaf / Children Of The Grave / Into The Void / Lord Of This World / After Forever / Changes / Snowblind / Laguna Sunrise / Tomorrow's Dream / Supernaut / Sabbath, Bloody Sabbath / Fluff / Sabbra Cadabra / Am I Going Insane (Radio) / Symptom Of The Universe / Hole In The Sky / Rock n' Roll Doctor / Dirty Women / Never Say Die / A Hard Road

PAST LIVES, (2002)
Tomorrow's Dream / Sweet Leaf / Killing Yourself To Live / Cornucopia / Snowblind / Children Of The Grave / War Pigs / Wicked World / Paranoid / Hand Of Doom / Hole In The Sky / Symptom Of The Universe / Megalomania / Iron Man / Black Sabbath / N.I.B. / Behind The Wall / Fairies Wear Boots

BLACKSHINE (SWEDEN)
Line-Up: Anders Strokirk (vocals / guitar), Joakim Stabel (guitar), Fredrik Holmberg (bass), Anders Freimanis (drums)

Stockholm based riff hungry yet adventurous Metal band, the young Swedish act - billed as 'Goth n' Roll', started life as HETSHEADS issuing the 1995 Repulse album 'We Hail The Possessed'. The band would opt to veer away from Death Metal and rebilled themselves as BLACKSHINE, scoring a deal with the German G.U.N. label and touring in Germany prior to their debut album, 'Our Pain Is Your Pleasure' appearing in the stores. BLACKSHINE would open for U.D.O. in Europe and BRUCE DICKINSON in Scandinavia.
Switching to the SPV label BLACKSHINE parted ways with drummer Anders Freimanis, enrolling erstwhile FACE DOWN and GODBLENDER man Hakan Eriksson in his stead for the January 2001 'Soulless And Proud' album. The band put in a short run of dates supporting ENTOMBED in Sweden during November. Meantime BLACKSHINE singer Anders Strokirk would lend his vocal abilities as session guest on NECROPHOBIC's 'Bloodhymns' record.
BLACKSHINE would be allocated the support slot for the IN FLAMES tour of Germany in October of 2002.

Albums:
OUR PAIN IS YOUR PLEASURE, G.U.N. GUN 145 (1997)
My Pain Is Your Pleasure / Blow My Mind / The Dead Is The Winner / The Beast Within / Cul-De-Sac / Shade / Forever Goodbye / Lost To Eternity / My Own God / Razor Blades / Liquid Serenity

SOULLESS AND PROUD, SPV (2001)

Love Our Hell / Soulless And Proud / Sacrifice / Chocked With Feathers / Another Twist / Light The Fuse / Servants Of The Harvest / Shadowman / Blackheart Brain / Outcast / Full Moon Rising

BLACK SUN (Memphis, TN, USA)

Albums:
GEAR, Black Sun (1997)

BLACK SWAN (GERMANY)
Line-Up: Peter 'Zombie' Schmidt (vocals), Jens 'Wocke' Wockenfuss (guitar), Martin Schmidt (guitar), Gunnar (bass), Maik 'Flecky' Mark Iron (drums)

A Liepzig Gothic Metal outfit. BLACK SWAN was still active in 2000, issuing a new demo CD. Bass player Gunnar decamped in January of 2002.
Drummer Maik 'Flecky' Mark Iron is also a member of Oelsnitz Gothic Death Metal band PERSECUTION.

Albums:
THE BIRTH, Black Swan (1998)
Intro / Dibbuk / Dear Song / Seven / Black Swan / Andymion / Blood / Outro

BLACK TWILIGHT (ITALY)
Line-Up: Marco Massarenti (vocals / bass), Ivan Torelli (guitar), Roberto Bianchi (keyboards), Leo Azzali (drums)

Progressive Gothic Doom act out of Parma created in September 1995. BLACK TWILIGHT issued two demos, 1996's 'The Dark End Of A Smile' and the following years 'My Scarlet Rose' before signing to the Northern Darkness label for their September 2000 debut 'The Solitude Of Being'.
BLACK TWILIGHT members also moonlight as DEEP PURPLE cover band LILOR.

Albums:
THE SOLITUDE OF BEING, Northern Darkness (2000)

BLACK WIDOW (UK)
Line-Up: Kip Trevor (vocals), Jim Gallon (guitar), Zoot Taylor (keyboards), Bob Bond (bass), Clive Jones (saxaphone), Romeo Challenger (drums)

An occult Hard Rock band ploughing an almost identical musical furrow to contemporaries BLACK SABBATH, BLACK WIDOW formed in 1969 from the demise of soul band PESKY GEE after the release of their sole album, 'Exclamation Mark!', on Pye

Records in 1969.
BLACK WIDOW, despite performing a mock sacrifice of a nude woman onstage, put much more emphasis on their lyrical esoteric leanings than the Ozzy led BLACK SABBATH, but although the debut album charted BLACK WIDOW soon fell from favour and struggled with successive releases. Bassist Bob Bond was replaced by Frank Linx who, in turn, gave way to Geoff Griffiths. John Culley took the place of guitarist Jim Gallon prior to recording 'Three'.
Although the band toured hard album sales were falling and BLACK WIDOW were forced into self-producing their projected fourth album in August of 1972. Following recording vocalist Kip Trevor departed and the band pulled in American singer Rick E.
Demos were recorded. However, these sessions would be shelved.
Gallon joined Pop bands FOX (of 'Single Bed' fame) and YELLOW DOG then ended up working in Australia with a band titled SHERBET. Clive Jones founded the Glam band AGONY BAG, recording an album in 1979, which remained, shelved. Drummer Romeo Challenger, quite bizarrely, was to join Teddyboy hit makers SHOWADDYWADDY after the demise of BLACK WIDOW!!
Vocalist Kip Trevor would later work for Carlin Music Publishing.
The band had not entirely been forgotten though and in 1996 Swedish Black Metal act BEWITCHED covered 'Sacrifice' on their 'Encyclopedia Of Evil' EP. The following year BLACK WIDOW's fourth album, coupled with unreleased demos, finally emerged on the small Mystic label. The material was far from the 'Sacrifice' era tradition and more in keeping with ethereal lightweight Progressive Rock with not a riff in sight.
In 2000 the Italian label Black Widow Records issued a tribute album to the band titled 'King Of The Witches'. Clive Jones lent a spoken intro and Kip Trevor's act WIDOW cut a new version of 'Come To The Sabbat'. Other contributors included cult act DEATH S.S., Japan's CHURCH OF MISERY, THE BLACK, Paris based Doomsters NORTHWINDS, ETERNAL ELYSIUM, PRESENCE, MALOMBRA, and ABIOGENESI.
Jones would also contribute flute to ABIOGENESI's 'Le Notti Di Salem' 2000 album. Jones' AGONY BAG project also finally saw a release in 2001 titled 'Feelmazumba'.

Singles/EPs:
Come To The Sabbat / Way To Power, CBS 5031 (1970)
Wish You Would / Accident, CBS 7596 (1971)

Albums:
SACRIFICE, CBS 63948 (1970) **32 UK**
In Ancient Days / Way To Power / Come To
The Sacrifice / Conjuration / Seduction /
Attack Of The Demon / Sacrifice
BLACK WIDOW - MAYBE NOW, CBS
64133 (1971)
Tears And Wine / The Gypsy / Bridge
Passage / When My Mind Was Wrong / The
Journey / Poser / Mary Clark / Wait Until
Tomorrow / An Afterthought / Legend Of
Creation
THREE, CBS 64562 (1972)
The Battle / The Onslaught / If A Man
Should Die / Survival / Accident / Lonely
Man / The Sun / King Of Hearts / Old Man
IV, Mystic MYSCD 117 (1997)
Sleighride / More Than A Day / You're So
Wrong / The Waves / Part Of A New Day /
When Will You Know / Floating / Pictures In
My Head / I See You

BLIND DOG (SWEDEN)
Line-Up: Tobias Nilsson (vocals / bass),
Joakim Thell (guitar), Thomas Elenvik
(drums)

Doomsters rooted in the prior Punk band of
vocalist / bassist Tobias Nilsson and guitarist
Joakim Thell going under the formative title of
HAIRY BOTTOM (Apparently).
With drummer Thomas Elenvik onboard
BLIND DOG cut recordings for a 7" single
'10,000 Reasons' for the German Warpburner
label. The following year the band entered the
studio once more to lay down a debut album.
These tapes would be picked up by the
American Stoner specialists Meteor City and
released as 'The Last Adventures Of Captain
Dog' album.

Singles/EPs:
10,000 Reasons / Beyond My Real,
Warpburner (1999)

Albums:
**THE LAST ADVENTURES OF CAPTAIN
DOG**, Meteor City MCY-015 (2001)
Thundergroove / 10,000 Reasons / Blend /
Beyond My Reach / When I'm Finally Gone /
Feels Like My Mind... / Wish I Knew Which
Side I'm On / Damned If I Should Care /
Coming To / Back Where I've Always Been /
$%#@! / Sun / Lose

BLINDED BY FAITH (CANADA)
Line-Up: Tom Demers (Vocals), Daniel
Gingras (guitar), Pascal Cote (guitar),
Vincent Roy (bass), Tattoo (keyboards),
Hugo Pelletier (drums)

Yet another heavy act from the prolific
province of Quebec. BLINDED BY FAITH was
formed in 1996. The band play a Gothic
Doom-Death style with lyrics with a medieval
flair. After a few line-up changes and a
number of local gigs the band managed to
produce a seven-track debut release in late
1999. Guitarist Sebastian Lessard was
replaced by Pascal Cote in 2000 and the
band continues to be active and play local
gigs including the prestigious 'Polliwog'
festival.

Albums:
VEILED HIDEOUSNESS, Tuxedo
Productions (1999)
Somber Harbinger / Behind The Placid Mask
of the Starlit Cosmos / Veiled Hideousness /
My Burnt Wings / Reptilian Shudder /A
Slumber in Cobwebs / Melania
BLISS (UK)
Line-Up: Steffan Pearson (vocals / guitar),
Jay Richardson (keyboards / guitar), Luke
Roberts (bass), Paul Compson (drums /
programming)

A Gothic Rock band. BLISS originated in
1996 and first offered the 'Where The
Shadows Dance' and 'Slavonic Nights'
demos, the band actually being signed to
Massacre Records before the second tape
had even been finished!
The quartet recorded their debut album, 'Sin
To Skin', in the summer of 1997 at
Communication Studios in Frankenthal,
Germany having engaged producer Gerhard
Magin for the recording.
The 1999 album 'Re-Thought' finds the band
covering DEAD OR ALIVE's 'You Spin Me
Right Round' and FINE YOUNG CANNIBALS
'She Drives Me Crazy'.

Albums:
SIN TO SKIN, Massacre MAS CD0152 9
(1998)
Sinistre Divine / Forever Blackened Embrace
/ Eyes Dressed In Velvet / Slavonic Nights /
Moon Waltz / Another Night, Another
Darkness / The Tears, The Lust, The
Sadness / Angels Of Twilight / Death In Love
RE-THOUGHT, Massacre MASCD 0184
(1999)
Lock Down / Dark Lovers / Cage Me / You
Spin Me Round / Hidden / Body Art / Night
Skin / She Drives Me Crazy / Upon You /
Rethought

THE BLOOD DIVINE (UK)
Line-Up: Darren White (vocals), Paul Ryan
(guitar), Paul Allander (guitar), Benjamin
Ryan (keyboards), Was Sarginson (drums)

Colchester's THE BLOOD DIVINE came together in late 1995 as a vehicle for ex-ANATHEMA vocalist Darren White and features ex-CRADLE OF FILTH guitarists Paul Allander and Paul Ryan along with keyboard player Benjamin Ryan. Drummer Was Sarginson also plies his trade with DECEMBER MOON. Musically the band has opted for a Doom-laden Death Metal stance.

In support of the 'Awaken' album, dates opening for labelmates MY DYING BRIDE were undertaken in Europe prior to a batch of British headliners. Further forays into Europe saw THE BLOOD DIVINE appearing at many festivals, including the 'Rock In Madrid' show alongside BRUCE DICKINSON and NAPALM DEATH.

THE BLOOD DIVINE gave two cover tracks to Peaceville Records 1998 tenth anniversary compilation 'X' in JOY DIVISION's 'Love Will Tear Us Apart' and THE OSMONDS 'Crazy Horses'.

Sarginson enjoyed a brief spell as drummer for CRADLE OF FILTH. Allander quit to create a new act LILLITH with former ENTWINED keyboard player Mark Royce and ex-CENOBITE vocalist / guitarist Mark Giltrow. The band adopted a new name of PRIMARY SLAVE but Allander was re-enlisted into the ranks of CRADLE OF FILTH in late 1999.

Benjamin Ryan founded CROWFOOT with form WITCHFINDER GENERAL, BAJJON and LIONSHEART bassist Zakk Bajjon. This band, with the addition of ex-CRADLE OF FILTH guitarist Rishi Mehta and former INCARCERATED drummer Mark Cooper became RAINMAKER 888.

Singles/EPs:
And With The Day's Dying Light, Peaceville (1996)

Albums:
AWAKEN, Peaceville CDVILE 62 (1996)
So Serene / Moonlight Adorns / Visions (Of A Post Apocalyptic World) Part One / Wilderness / These Deepest Feelings / Aureole / Oceans Rise / Artemis / In Crimson Dreams / Heart Of Ebony / Warm Summer Rain
MYSTICA, Peaceville (1997)
Mystica / As Rapture Fades / Visions In Blue / The Passion Reigns / Leaving Me Helpless / Visions Part II: Event Horizon / I Believe / Enhanced By Your Touch / Sensual Ecstasy / Fear Of a Lonely World / Prayer

BLOOD FARMERS (Brooklyn, NY, USA)
Line-Up: Eli Brown (vocals), Dave Depraved (guitar), Matt Holt (bass), Mike Jett (drums)

Brooklyn Doom act that released a solitary classic of the genre through the illustrious German Hellhound label during 1995. Three quarters of the BLOOD FARMERS, minus guitarist Dave Depraved, evolved into M-SQUAD, issuing two Stoner infused albums to date.

Albums:
BLOODFARMERS, Hellhound H0037-2 (1995)
Albino / Bullet In My Head / Orgy Of The Rats / Theme / Y.G.B / The Holy Chalice / General Urko - I Drink In Your Blood / Twisted Brain (Part 1) / Twisted Brain (Part 2) / After The Harvest

BLOODFLOWERZ (GERMANY)
Line-Up: Kirsten Zahn (vocals), Markus Visser (guitar), Daniel Mahl (guitar), Joachim Schulz (bass), Tim Schwarz (drums)

Swabian Gothic Rockers fronted by the dreadlocked figure of Kirtsen Zahn. BLOODFLOWERZ supported ANATHEMA in Germany during December 2001. With the release of the January 2002 single 'Diabolic Angel' the band scored another valuable support tour, this time to SUBWAY TO SALLY. Headline dates would be built around the album, issued in April.

Singles/EPs:
Diabolic Angel / Lovesick / Diabolic Angel (Danger mix) / Diabolic Angel (Lucius 14 mix) / Diabolic Angel (Dark Angel mix), Silverdust (2002)

Albums:
DIABOLIC ANGEL, Silverdust (2002)
Fatal Kiss / Diabolic Angel / Lovesick / Ablaze / Sadness / One Second / Mea Culpa / Tears Of The Night / Cold Rain / Season Of Love

BLOODLET (Orlando, FL, USA)
Line-Up: Scott Angelacos (vocals), Matt Easley (guitar), Art Legere (bass), John Stewart Jr. (drums)

A distinct oddity on the scene, Florida's BLOODLET are firmly rooted in the Hardcore scene yet are freeform enough to fuel their craft with trademark Jazz pattern drums, fretless bass, obscure lyrics and enough turgid, detuned wallowing songs of immense complexity to push the band into experimental Doom territory.

Signing to the Hardcore stable at Victory Records BLOODLET assembled their previous single releases together for the 'Eclectic' release. The band's first album proper, 'Entheogen', engendered a huge wave of positive publicity for the band internationally, BLOODLET being seen by breaking the 'Metalcore' mould.

Disappointingly for the band and a fan base eager to hear a follow up 'The Seraphim Fall', issued in 1998, was seriously marred by shoddy sound quality. The band folded with drummer Charles King relocating to Berlin whilst vocalist Scott Angelacos and guitarist Art Legere transplanted themselves to Denver Colorado.

Angelacos founded HOPE & SUICIDE in alliance with bassist Tom Crowthers of BIBLE OF THE SELF and the MEASURED IN GREY trio of guitarists Sean Ryan and Bryan Raymond and drummer Kevin Ryan.

In late 2001 BLOODLET reunited for a comeback appearance at the 'Gainesville Fest' event. A new album, 'Three Humid Nights In The Cypress Trees' produced in Chicago by the esteemed Steve Albini, backed up the return in June 2002.

Albums:
ECLECTIC, Victory VR31 (1995)
Shell / Cherubim / Eucharist / Husk - The Art / One And Only / Untouchables - Litany / Undying / New Age 1993 / Sustenance / Totem / New Age 1992 / Vicious Cycle / Conditioned To The Pain / Bloodlet
ENTHEOGEN, Victory VR35 (1996)
Brainchild / Something Wicked / Annulment / One And Only / Shell / Cpai-75 / The Triumph / Eucharist / 95 / Cpai-76
THE SERAPHIM FALL, Victory VR72 (1998)
Intro / Whitney / Dogman With Horns / Sister Supreme / Stew For The Murder Minded / Shoot The Pig / Seven Hours Of Angel Food / Seraphim / Sawtooth Grin / Lamentations (In Tribute To Infamy) / Your Hours
THREE HUMID NIGHTS IN THE CYPRESS TREES, Victory VR180 (2002)

THE BLOODLINE (GERMANY)
Line-Up: Roman Schoensee (vocals / guitar), Kemi Vita (bass)

Gothic Metal act created by Roman Schoensee following his departure from PYOGENESIS in 1997. Following completion of the album Kemi Vita of Dutch band THE DREAMSIDE was enrolled.

The two musicians' roles within THE DREAMSIDE would be reversed, Vita handling lead vocals and Schoensee bass guitar.

Albums:
OPIUM HEARTS, Last Episode (2000)
Houmfor / Paralyzed / Opened Eyes Dream /

A Sacred Place
Dh'Lhya / Lost Souls In The Land Of Delight / Bloodline / Shadowflame / Left To Rot Forever

BLUE CHEER (USA)
Line-Up: Dickie Peterson (vocals, bass), Leigh Stephans (guitar), Paul Whaley (drums)

Cited by many as the band which paved the way for the Heavy Metal sound in America BLUE CHEER, named after a hallucinogenic drug, came to the fore with their high octane version of the EDDIE COCHRAN staple 'Summertime Blues' in early 1968. The band achieved such heights that one stage in their career they headlined over PINK FLOYD and shared stages with JIMI HENDRIX.

BLUE CHEER's career was steeped in tales of excess, the band pushing the limits of onstage volume as well as claiming to be managed by a Hells Angels chapter. In more recent years the band has taken special pride of place in the hearts of the Stoner community, generations of new acts finding inspiration from BLUE CHEER's distorted Fuzz Rock style.

The band were created from the sextet SAN FRANCISCO BLUES BAND. Vocalist / bassist Dickie Peterson, guitarist Leigh Stephens and drummer Paul Whaley (also an ex-member of OXFORD CIRCLE) founded BLUE CHEER - after being turned onto the proto-Rock sound being purveyed at the time.

The band's debut album 'Vincebus Eruptum' remains a classic and high sales very nearly propelled this outing into the American top ten. With heavy touring ensuing the band added keyboard player Ralph Burns Kellog for live work.

With their follow up 'Outsideinside', according to press sources so called because the album was partially recorded outside when the band blew up all the studio monitors, it was revealed that Stephens was forced to bow out owing to deafness. His replacement in BLUE CHEER was former SONS OF ADAM / OTHER HALF man Randy Holden. Strangely, despite his disability Leigh forged a solo career for himself issuing the LEIGH STEPHENS AND A CAST OF THOUSANDS project album in 1971. Stephens also teamed up with the bands PILOT and SILVER METRE.

BLUE CHEER meanwhile underwent a period of flux with Holden being supplanted in 1969 by ex-OXFORD CIRCLE / KAK guitarist Gary Yoder and Whaley losing out to former SOPWITH CAMEL man Norman Mayell on the drum kit. Within the year the band's guitarist casualty rate grew as ex-MINT TATTOO man Bruce Stephens manouvered in at Yoder's expense.

Although the act excelled themselves with 1970's 'The Original Human Beings' album the record made little commercial impact and the writing was on the wall.

BLUE CHEER finally exhausted themselves in 1971 following the 'Oh Pleasant Hope' album, which failed, to chart. The band regrouped sporadically during the '70's. Mayell re-formed SOPWITH CAMEL in 1973. CHEER struggled to maintain their standing despite a loyal cult following and were ultimately swamped by the British Hard Rock invasion. BLUE CHEER attempted a re-formation in 1975 by pulling in guitarist Rueben De Fuentes, former STEPPENWOLF man Nick St. Nicholas, ex-FLAMIN GROOVIES drummer Terry Rae and Peterson. It was short-lived. Fuentes and Rae founded HOLLYWOOD STARS for a 1977 album.

In 1978 Peterson, Whaley and Stephens re-forged BLUE CHEER with the addition of new men Gut and Abe 'Voco' Kesh.

BLUE CHEER re-formed with Peterson, Whaley and guitarist Tony Rainer in the mid '80s signing to former METALLICA manager Johnny Zazula's Megaforce label for the 'Beast Is Back' album.

For touring purposes Peterson assembled a fresh outfit of ex-SHAKIN' STREET guitarist Andrew 'Duck' McDonald and drummer David Salce. In 1985 McDonald would join SIMMONDS, the band assembled by SAVOY BROWN man Kim Simmonds. The 1987 version of BLUE CHEER comprised Peterson on bass, drummer Eric Davies and guitarist Rueben De Fuentes. De Fuentes created RENEGADE in 1989 with SUSAN LYNCH, ex-SABU bassist Rick Bozzo and former SURVIVOR drummer Marc Droubay.

BLUE CHEER's 1990 album 'Highlights And Lowlives' was produced by Jack Endino. The 1991 effort 'Dining With The Sharks' saw Peterson and Whaley joined by Dieter Saller. The album featured guests MICK JONES of FOREIGNER, GROUNDHOGS man Tony McPhee and BLODWYN PIG's Dave Anderson.

The band was still performing into the '90s, most notably in Germany and has included in its ranks former DOKKEN and GREAT WHITE drummer GARY HOLLAND. As a trio of Dickie Peterson, Andrew McDonald and Paul Whaley the group toured Japan during February of 1999. These shows would be captured on the Captain Trip live album 'Hello Tokyo, Bye Bye Osaka'. DICKIE PETERSON also had a solo album 'Tramp' issued in Japan the same month after which the guitarist hooked up with HANK DAVISON BAND members for German acoustic gigs billed as

DOS HOMBRES.

During the '90s BLUE CHEER were increasingly recognized as pioneers in the current Rock scene and in particular by the Stoner Rock generation. Acts to cover BLUE CHEER tracks include SMASHING PUMPKINS, who would regularly perform 'Out Of Focus' and MUDHONEY, who recorded 'Magnolia Caboose Babyfinger' although retitled 'Magnolia Caboose Babyshit'! The Italian Black Widow label also weighed in with a tribute album 'Blue Explosion' featuring a global collective of Stoner acts such as PENTAGRAM, NATAS, INTERNAL VOID, FIREBALL MINISTRY, DRAG PACK and SPACE PROBE TAURUS among others.

RANDY HOLDEN issued his latest solo album 'Guitar God' in 2001. That same year Dickie Peterson was still performing live with the HANK DAVISON BAND and MOTHER OCEAN.

Singles/EPs:
Summertime Blues / Out Of Focus, Phillips BF 40516 (1968) **14 USA**
Just A Little Bit / Gypsy Ball, Phillips 304 170 (1968) **92 USA**
Feathers From Your Tree / Sun Cycle, Phillips BF 1711 (1968)
The Hunter, Phillips 304 180 BF (1968)
When It All Gets Old / West Coast Child Of Sunshine, Phillips 40602 (1969)
All Night Long / Fortunes, Phillips 40651 (1969) (USA release)
Hello L.A., Bye Bye Birmingham / Natural Men, Phillips 40664 (1970) (USA release)
Fool / Ain't That The Way (Love's Supposed To Be), Phillips 605 1004 (1970)
Pilot / Babajil, Phillips 6051 010 (1971)

Albums:
VINCEBUS ERUPTUM, Phillips BL 7839 (1967) **11 USA**
Summertime Blues / Rock Me Baby / Doctor Please / Out Of Focus / Parchment Farm / Second Time Around
OUTSIDEINSIDE, Phillips SBL 78600 (1968) **90 USA**
Feathers From Your Tree / Sun Cycle / Just A Little Bit / Gypsy Ball / Come And Get It / (I Can't Get No) Satisfaction / The Hunter / Magnolia Caboose Babyfinger / Babylon
NEW! IMPROVED! BLUECHEER, Phillips SBL 7896 (1969) **84 USA**
When It All Gets Old / West Coast Child Of Sunshine / I Want My Baby Back / Aces n' Eights / As Long As I Live / It Takes A Lot Of Love, It Takes A Train To Cry / Peace Of Mind / Fruit And Icebergs / Honey Butter Love

BLUE CHEER, Phillips 6336 001 (1970)
Fool / You're Gonna Need Someone / Hello
L.A., Bye Bye Birmingham / Saturday
Freedom / Ain't That The Way (Love's
Supposed To Be) / Rock And Roll Queens /
Better When We Try / Natural Man / Lovin'
You's Easy / The Same Old Story
**BLUE CHEER 5: THE ORIGINAL HUMAN
BEINGS**, Phillips 6336 004 (1970)
Good Times Are Hard To Find / Love Of A
Woman / Make Me Laugh / Pilot / Babaji
(Twilight Raga) / Preacher / Black Sun /
Tears By My Bed / Man On The Run /
Sandwich / Rest At Ease
OH! PLEASANT HOPE, Phillips 600 350
(1971)
Highway Man / Believer / Money Troubles /
Travelling Man / Oh! Pleasant Hope / I'm The
Light / Ecological Blues / Lester The Arrester
/ Heart Full Of Soul
MOTIVE, Phillips (1972)
Summertime Blues / Feathers From Your
Tree / Sun Cycle / Just A Little Bit / Gypsy
Ball / Come And Get It / (I Can't Get No
Satisfaction) / The Hunter / Magnolia
Caboose Babyfinger / Babylon / Parchment
Farm
THE BEST OF BLUE CHEER, Phillips (1982)
THE BEAST IS BACK, Megaforce MRI 1069
(1985)
Nightmares / Summertime Blues / Ride With
Me / Girl Next Door / Babylon / Heart Of The
City / Out Of Focus / Parchment Farm
LOUDER THAN GOD, Rhino RNLP 70130
(1986)
Summertime Blues / Out Of Focus /
Parchment Farm / Feathers From Your Tree /
Just A Little Bit / Babylon / Magnolia
Caboose Babyfinger / Come And Get It /
Peace Of Mind / Fruit & Icebergs / Fool /
Hello L.A., Bye Bye Birmingham
BLITZKRIEG ON NUREMBURG (LIVE),
Thunderbolt THBL 091 (1990)
Babylon / Girl Next Door / Ride With Me /
Just A Little Bit / Summertime Blues / Out Of
Focus / Doctor Please / The Hunter / Red
House
GOODTIMES ARE HARD TO FIND, Mercury
(1990)
Summertime Blues / Out Of Focus /
Parchment Farm / Feathers From Your Tree /
The Hunter / Babylon / Peace Of Mind / Fruit
And Icebergs / Fool / Hello L.A, Bye Bye
Birmingham / Saturday Freedom / Good
Times Are Hard To Find / Pilot / Preacher /
Highway Man / I'm The Light
HIGHLIGHTS AND LOWLIVES, Nibelung
23010 413 (1990)
Urban Soldier / Hunter Of Love / Girl From
London / Blue Steel Dues / Big Trouble In
Paradise / Flight Of The Enola Gay /
Hoochie Coochie Man / Down And Dirty /

Blues Cadillac
DINING WITH SHARKS, Nibelung (1991)
Big Noise / Outrider / Sweet Child Of The
Reeperbahn / Gunfight / Audio Whore / Cut
The Costs / Sex Soldier / When Two Spirits
Touch / Pull The Trigger / Foxy Lady
**LIVE AT SAN JOSE CIVIC CENTRE &
MORE**, Captain Trip (1996)
Summertime Blues / Parchment Farm / Rock
Me Baby / Satisfaction / Out Of Focus /
Doctor Please / Summertime Blues /
Summertime Blues / Second Time Around
LIVE AND UNRELEASED '68-'74, Captain
Trip (1996)
Summertime Blues / Out Of Focus / Doctor
Please / Fighting Star / Adventures / Make It
To The Party / New Orleans / Ace In The
Hole / Punk
**HELLO TOKYO, BYE BYE OSAKA - LIVE
IN JAPAN 1999**, Captain Trip CTCD 190
(1999)
Babylon / Big Trouble In Paradise / The
Hunter / Blue Steel Dues / Urban Soldiers /
Girl Next Door / Ride With Me / Summertime
Blues / Down And Dirty / Out Of Focus /
Doctor Please

BOGEYMEN (USA)

BOGEYMEN were created by ex-MASTERS
OF REALITY men guitarist / vocalist Tim
Harrington and drummer Vinnie Lodovico.

Albums:
THERE'S NO SUCH THING AS, Delicious
Vinyl (1991)
Spiritual Beggars / Here In Paradise /
Goodbye Creator / Get On Home / Suck You
Dry (She Will) / Porkypine Chair / Killing
Ground / Dancing On Your Grave / In The
Cosmic Continuum / Damn The Safety Nets

BONGZILLA (Wisconsin, USA)
Line-Up: Mike Makela (vocals / guitar), Jeff
Schultz (guitar), Nate Dethlefsen (bass), Mike
Henry (drums)

Blues based, trudgingly lethargic Stoned out
Rockers from Wisconsin. In spite of their
obvious devotion to the weed BONGZILLA
have somehow managed to summon the
energy for extensive bouts of American
touring.
BONGZILLA initially announced their line-up
as being King Kola as 'Muleboy', The Big Bud
Man as 'The Dealer', Magma Mota as 'The
Tester' and Sensi Sparky as 'Mr. Green
Thumb'.
The band made their entrance with a 1996
demo session produced by Steve Austin of
TODAY IS THE DAY. Further tapes triggered

BONGZILLA
Photo : El Danno

the interest of Relapse Records and a deal to issue the 1997 album 'Methods For Attaining Extreme Altitudes'. A split 7" single, shared with MEATJACK, was also delivered by Pinecone Records. BONGZILLA tracks also appeared on the 'Weedstock Vol. 1' and 'Harvestfest' compilation albums. The summer of 1998 witnessed an appearance at the famous 'Milwaukee Metalfest' and Midwest tour dates billed with label mates UNSANE.
Billy Anderson would produce the 1999 effort 'Stash'.

Singles/EPs:
Bud Gun / T.H.C. /, Pinecone PC007 (1997) (Split 7" single with MEATJACK)

Albums:
METHODS FOR ATTAINING EXTREME ATTITUDES, Relapse RR 6993-2 (1998)
Melovespot / High Like A Dog / Smoke - I Love Maryjane
STASH, Relapse (1999)
Gestation / Sacred Smoke / American / Budgun-THC / Prohibition (4th Amendment) / Grog Lady / Harvest / P.O.W. / Under The Sun
APOGEE, Howling Bull (2001)
H.P. Keefmaker / Salvation / Grim Reefer / Witch Weed (Live) / Dealer McDope (Live) / Sacred Smoke (Live) / American (Live)

BORGO PASS (Baldwin, NY, USA)
Line-Up: Jimmy Tamarazzo (vocals), Tom Crane (guitar), Paul Rosado (guitar), YT (bass), Joseph Wood (drums)

A Stoner Sludge outfit dating back to 1992 when the band went under the formative title of SLOW PAINFUL DEATH. Drummer Joseph Wood was previously a member of both WINTER and NUCLEARCHY whilst guitarist Paul Rosado was with Thrash Metal band BLACK PROPHECY.
The group, then fronted by vocalist Ed Sebastian, issued the 'Invasion Of Borgo Pass' demo cassette prior to establishing their own label Loud Belly Music for the eponymous debut. During September of 2000 Sebastian announced his departure to concentrate on family life and was replaced the following June by Jimmy Tamarazzo, previously with TRANSYM and RITUAL 6.
BORGO PASS's second outing 'Powered By Sludge' was produced by SCATTERBRAIN / LUDICHRIST man Paul Nieder.

Albums:
BORGO PASS, Loud Belly Music (1999)
Waiting / Dead Lord Dorman / Nympho Barbarians On Dinosaur Hill / Crumblefuck / Dazed / Red Eye / Something / Please Don't Pet The Clowns / Banish The Light / One

63

Really Bad Day / Chocolate, Urine, Blood & Vomit
POWERED BY SLUDGE, Loud Belly Music (2001)
Meat Wallet / Afterbirth / Drunkards Doom / Off The Kings Head / Kitchen / Bellysmack / Second Story / Saloon Burn / Revelation / Beer Garden / Red Eye (Live)
SLIGHTLY DAMAGED, Loud Belly Music (2002)
I've Been Down / Shame / Camaro Crash Helmet / Razorline / Steel Blood Acid God

BORIS (JAPAN)

Psych Stoner trio BORIS are eminently collectable having released a stream of highly lauded discs in Japan prior to making waves internationally. The band arrived on the scene during 1994 contributing the track 'Water Porch' to the compilation album 'Take Care Of Scabbard Fish'.
BORIS supported THE THRONES on an American tour in 1996. A shared 10" album in collusion with BAREBONES would be later reissued on CD format with two extra live cuts. A split 7" single would be issued in alliance with Americans TOMSK the following year.
BORIS would commit their version of 'Me And The Devil Blues' to the P-Vine 2000 ROBERT JOHNSON tribute album. The 2001 international re-release of the 1996 album 'Absolutego' comprises only two songs. What would normally be considered a lengthy 'Dronedevil' clocking in at nearly 8 minutes is absolutely annihilated by the hour long title track! A Japanese release 'Flood', replete with the BORIS logo rendered in a distinctive Roger Dean BUDGIE take off, was waiting in the wings too with one goliath 70 mini track.

Singles/EPs:
Mass Mercury, Bovine BO43 (1997) (7" split single with TOMSK)

Albums:
ABSOLUTEGO, Fangs Anal Satan FAS001 (1996)
Absolutego
BORIS, Piranha PF001 (1997) (10" split album with BAREBONES)
Soul Search You Sleep / In Hush
BORIS, Piranha PF002 (1997) (Split CD with BAREBONES)
Soul Search You Sleep / In Hush / Scarebox (Live) / Mosquito (Live)
BLACK: IMPLICATION FLOODING, Inoxia IXCD 0002 (1998) (with KEIJI HAINO)
A Rise, A Moment Before Something Unexpected Is On The Verge Of Starting /

Not Knowing If It Will Be Agony Or Comfort For Us / Wonder What Colour Would Be Suitable For The Dwelling / The Decision Of A Dream Which Will Never Be Completely Red / It Should Be Matched, Not To Fail To Notice These Flashes Of An Accusation From Inside / Offer It All Up, Our Madness, That Will Be Crushed On This Land That Has Come To Be Called Chaos Unzipped / From The Distance, With Their Own Gentle Eyes Always Fixed On Us, They Are Affectionately Gazing At The Black: Implication Flooding / Don't Be Cheated By The Oozing Silt From Both Of The Accuser And The Accused Which Is Always Three, Saying "Something Have To Be Done" / The Person Who, What Is She Like, The One Who Has Been Determined And Prepared
AMPLIFIER WORSHIP, Mangrove ROOT015 (1998)
Huge / Gambou-Ki / Hama / Karumizu / Vomitself
MORE ECHOES, TOUCHING AIR LANDSCAPES, Inoxia IXCD 0003 (1999) (Split album with CHOUKOKU NO NIWA)
Kanau Parts I & II
FLOOD, Midi Creative CXCA 1076 (2001)
Flood
ABSOLUTEGO, Southern Lord SUNN10 (2001)
Absolutego / Dronedevil

BOTCH (Seattle, WA, USA)
Line-Up: David Verellen (vocals), Brian Cook (bass), Dave Knudson (guitar), Tim Latona (drums)

BOTCH was an adventurously inclined Noisecore outfit. Their technical proficiency earnt them the title of 'Mathcore'. The 1997 'Unifying Themes Of Sex, Death And Religion' album compiled the earlier 7" singles 'Faction' and 'The John Birch Conspiracy Theory' plus the track 'I Just Can't Live Without It' included on the 'Anti Death Penalty' compilation issued on Mountain Records.

Albums:
UNIFYING THEMES OF SEX, DEATH AND RELIGION, Excursion (1997)
God Vs. Science / Third Part In A Tragedy / Inch By Inch / O Fortuna / Closure / Contraction / Ebb / Stupid Me / In Spite Of This
AMERICAN NERVOSA, Hydra Head (1998)
Hutton's Great Heat Engine / John Woo / Dall's Praying Mantis / Dead For A Minute / Oma / Thank God For Worker Bees / Rejection Spoken Softly / Spitting Black / Hives
WE ARE THE ROMANS, Hydra Head (1999)

To Our Friends In The Great White North / Mondrian Was A / Transizion Was A / Swimming The C / C Thomas Howel / Saint Mathew R / Frequency Ass / I Wanna Be Ass / Man The Rampar / Electronic Race

BOTTOM (New York, NY, USA)
Line-Up: Sina (vocals / guitar), Nila (bass), Clementine (drums)

Almost a unique proposition in Stoner circles, an all female '70s Rock influenced trio from New York's lower East side. Vocalist / guitarist Sina and drummer Clementine are both erstwhile members of RACER 17. The band famously moved out of 'static' accommodation, put their gear into storage and made their touring van their home for a seemingly endless succession of shows across America.
BOTTOM self-financed their 1999 debut 'Made In Voyage' through their own Mudflap imprint. Over 300 gigs later BOTTOM signed to the Man's Ruin label for the sophomore outing 'Feels So Good When You're Gone'. The band hit troubled times during the latter half of 2001 with the collapse of their record label and a projected European tour being pulled due to the September 11th terrorist attacks. BOTTOM re-announced their European dates for 2002.

Albums:
MADE IN VOYAGE, Mudflap (1999)
25 Hawaiian / Whipping Child / The Garden / Wish You Were Mine / The Liar, The Witch & The Wardrobe / Bullseye / Here / Evil Out / OhighO / Semi-Automatic / Shine
FEELS SO GOOD WHEN YOU'RE GONE, Man's Ruin (2001)
Hell Of A Life / Forever Gone / X On Yer Hed / Love Song 2 No. 1 / Got Meth. / Deathspin / Meatbuzz / Tower: XVI / Angermeister

BOULDER (Cleveland, OH, USA)
Line-Up: Jamie Walters (vocals), Terence Hanchin (guitar), Mark Gibbs (guitar), Patrick Munn (drums)

BOULDER, whose hackneyed logo is made up of two crossed flying V's, operate in the surreal Stoner infused world of Southern Sludge style desert Rock and cliched '80s Heavy Metal, giving cause for justifiable comparisons to both KYUSS and JUDAS PRIEST! Indeed, frontman Jamie Walters has been known to arrive onstage in full leather gear, including ass-less chaps, astride a moped as his BOULDER band mates crank out 'Hell Bent For Leather'!
BOULDER's brand of avant-garde Metal

humour was first felt in 1992 when ex-PROCREATION members Walters and Gibbs united with former Hardcore exponents Munn and Hanchin from BLATANT DISREGARD.
BOULDER opened with a limited edition single 'Sac' only pressed up in 100 copies. Their 1994 demo 'Jailbreak' set the scene for what was to follow opening up with the less than subtle 'Kick The Pregnant'.
A shared 1995 single saw the band doubling up with DIMBULB. That same year the 7" 'Fist' EP would contain cover versions of BLACK SABBATH's 'Trashed' and VENOM's 'In League With Satan'. Another limited run single 'Pilzner's Bible' split with SLOTH gave the collectors something else to hunt down, again only seeing 100 copies pressed. The 1997 cover of BLACK DEATH's 'Screams Of The Iron Messiah' took BOULDER to new levels of audacity being a split 7" with no less than THIN LIZZY! The cover artwork depicting Phil Lynnot with a speech bubble stating "I gave full permission for this record". Again, another limited run of 300 only.
The 2000 'Ripping Christ' album, graced with an album cover depicting Jesus crucified upside down on a stack of Marshall amps, is a compilation of all the previous demos and singles.

Singles/EPs:
Sac / Dirt Cheap, Boulder (1993) (7" single)
Kick The Pregnant / Ming The Mercyless / **Shifty**, Lost And Found (1994) (7" single)
Anchored Down / Alley Sweeper AS015 (1995) (7" split single with DIMBULB. 500 copies)
The Eternal Quest For Edward B. Yatsko / In League With Satan / T.G.W. / Trashed, Flexovit FLX002 (1995) ('Fist' 7" EP)
Pilzner's Bible /, (1996) (7" split single with SLOTH. 100 copies)
Screams Of The Iron Messiah, (1997) (7" split single with THIN LIZZY (!) 300 copies)

Albums:
555, Flexovit FLX007 (1997)
DLR Is King / Mayhem Gook / Love Honkey / 555 / Rage With The Dead / Full Throttle
THE RAGE OF IT ALL, River On Fire ROF003 (1999)
D U Lay / The Dealer / Disrespector / Workin' For Nobody / Make And Take / Total Business / Random Hellholes / Blow Up The Fire / Who Care, Baby?
RAVAGE AND SAVAGE, Tee Pee (2000)
The Invasion / Rev It Up / Funeral Day / Southern Salvation / Heavens Ice / Ravage And Savage / Two Track Mind / Sin Goals / Fall From Graves
RIPPING CHRIST, Outlaw Recordings

BOULDER
Photo : El Danno

(2000)
DLR Is King / Mayhem Gook / Love Honkey /
555 / Rage With The Dead / Full Throttle /
Sinners Gross Beerd / Amigbro / The Power
Of 1,000 Satanic Black Moons / Anchored
Down / Kick The Pregnant / Ming The
Mercyless / Shifty / Kill The Captain / The
Eternal Quest For Edward B. Yatsko / In
League With Satan / T.G.W. / Trashed /
Pilzner's Bible / We Like No Hero
REAPED IN HALF ACT I & ACT II, Tee Pee
(2002)
Krank It Up / Live Or Dead / Ripped In Half /
Ripe And Innocent / Arrect Me / Should've
Seen Blood / Yellow Fever / Back For The
Show

THE BREATH OF LIFE (BELGIUM)
Line-Up: Isabelle Dekeyser (vocals), Philipe
Mauroy (guitar), Benoît Sokay (bass),
Giovanni Bortolin (keyboards / violin)

A highly regarded, individualistic Gothic
Darkwave act. Female vocalist Isabelle
Dekeyser had an Operatic education and this
has certainly added to THE BREATH OF
LIFE's flair for delivering Gothic and
melancholic material. The band began life as
far back as 1985, touring the Belgian club
scene on a regular basis. It was not until 1989

though, with the loss of their then drummer,
that THE BREATH OF LIFE opted to employ
a drum machine thus charting their musical
direction from that juncture onward. The band
at this point comprised vocalist Isabelle
Dekeyser, guitarist and sampler Philippe
Mauroy, keyboard player and violinist
Giovanni Bortolin and bass guitarist Benoît
Sokay.
An opening cassette release, simply titled
'The Breath Of Life', marked the band's
entrance onto the Darkwave scene in
September of 1990. February of the following
year witnessed extensive touring across
Belgium, France and Czechoslovakia. In
September of 1992 THE BREATH OF LIFE, in
a novel more established a commercial debut
with two consecutive album releases, the
studio outing 'Painful Insanity' and the 'Live In
Praha '92' album, recorded as the title
suggests live in Prague at the Bunker Club
during April that year. THE BREATH OF LIFE
had performed to a packed audience of 800
that night with the show being broadcast both
on national radio and filmed for TV. The
advent of the twin album release would be
promoted by further gigs in Czechoslovakia
and Belgium.
The Gilles Martin produced 'Taste Of Sorrow'
album, licensed to the Hall Of Sermon label,

widened the group's fan base during 1993. Touring had the band sharing stages with the likes of the COCTEAU TWINS, MIRANDA SEX GARDEN and LOVE LIKE BLOOD.

In 1995 the group toured Europe with LACRIMOSA promoting the EP 'The Shining'. Later that year a new studio album 'Lost Children' would be laid down. The band's increasing stature warranted appearances at festivals such as the 'Zillo' and 'Sommertage II' events in Germany and the domestic 'Black Eastern' show headed up by THE MISSION. Two exclusive recordings also surfaced with a remix of 'Idyll' featured on a 'Zillo' festival compilation and a reworked variant of 'Living In A Dream' donated to the compilation 'Hex Files'.

In February of 1998 THE BREATH OF LIFE maintained their momentum with the issue of the album 'Sweet Party', once again produced by Gilles Martin. Touring in Germany and the UK had the band packaged with INKUBUS SUKKUBUS and STAR INDUSTRY. Keeping up the pace 'Silver Drops' was recorded in 1999 and live work found the band playing in Italy and at the prestigious Gothic UK events the 'London Underground' and the 'Whitby' festival.

In the summer of 2000 guitarist Philippe Mauroy opted to depart. THE BREATH OF LIFE soon welcomed in a replacement in the form of Didier Czepczyk, a man whose credits include such bands as BLOODY MINDED, CANDY STRIPE and HERBERT WEST.

Singles/EPs:
Shining / Taste Of Sorrow / Kutna Hora, Third Finger 60930 (1995)

Albums:
PAINFUL INSANITY, Magic Language MLR002 (1992)
Walk In Line / Time / Misunderstood Man / Bad Race / Sacrifice / Holidays In The Mountain / Nightmare / Factory
LIVE IN PRAHA '92, Magic Language MLR003 (1992)
Factory / Walk In Line / Misunderstood Man / Dark Garden / Holidays In The Mountains / Bad Race / Young Soldier / Sacrifice / Fat Brutus / Your Tears / Living In A Dream / Nightmare / Time
TASTE OF SORROW, Third Finger 60780 (1994)
Nasty Cloud / The Sun / Go Away / Strings Of Pearls / Naureen / Shining / Down / No Way / Forgotten Trees / Gathering
LOST CHILDREN, Hall Of Sermon HOS043 (1996)
Impromptu / Noamina / Hazy Wish / Into The Flames / Nightfall / The Reason / The Last

Four Days / Thoughts / The Soul / MAIKAE / Echo / Idyll
SWEET PARTY, Hall Of Sermon HOS 7044 (1999)
Silence / Fly / Secret Grieves / Deary Daughters / Worries / A Tender Hand / Their Xanadu / Sweet / Keeping Myself / The Wind / Calling / A World Of Her Own
SILVER DROPS, Hall Of Sermon HOS 7045 (2000)
Caligan / Silver Sky / Tower / Blooming Sky / Cold Lights / The Valley / Her World / Falling Drops / Around You / Deep Mystery / Deep Blue Land

BROTHERS OF CONQUEST (USA)
Line-Up: The Rock n' Roll Outlaw (vocals), Tony Rivers (guitar), Ian Spiders (guitar), Rodney Roads (bass), ZZ Priest (drums)

BROTHERS OF CONQUEST was born out of the union of three former HOOKERS members, frontman 'The Rock n' Roll Outlaw', guitarist Ian Spiders and bassist Rodney Roads.

Pre-THE HOOKERS The Rock n' Roll Outlaw had operated as drummer for NINE POUND HAMMER and was also instrumental in founding NASHVILLE PUSSY. Roads also cites credits with PURPLE JESUS whilst Spiders was also with STARKILLER. Completing the line-up would be STARKILLER man Tony Rivers and erstwhile CRAIN drummer ZZ Priest.

BROTHERS OF CONQUEST debuted in April 2002 with the 'All The Colors Of Darkness' album through Go Kart Records.

Singles/EPs:
The Dealer / Curse Of The Witch / Sweet Little Connie, Black Lung (2002) ('Brothers Of Conquest' EP)

Albums:
ALL THE COLORS OF DARKNESS, Go Kart (2002)
Kill For Rock n' Roll / Holy Transformation / Hot Southern Nights / Curse Of The Witch / Sweet Little Connie / Evil Realized / Monster Creator / Higher / Higher / Gravel Roads / Say Goodbye

THE BROUGHT LOW
(Brooklyn, NY, USA)
Line-Up: Benjamin Howard Smith (vocals / guitar), Dean Rispler (bass), Nick Heller (drums)

THE BROUGHT LOW deliver Southern style retro roots Rock from the depths of New York. The band's lineage traces back through acts such as MURPHY'S LAW and THE VOLUPTUOUS HOUR OF KAREN BLACK with bassist Dean Rispler and SWEET DIESEL with frontman Benjamin Howard Smith. Rispler is a well known figure on the Manhattan music scene with his Punk label Go Kart Records and production credits with acts such as BAD WIZARD. He also operates with '70s melodic Rockers TIGER MOUNTAIN.

Albums:
THE BROUGHT LOW, Tee Pee (2001)
What I Found / God Damn, God Bless / Motherless Sons / Kings And Queens / Hot And Cold / City Boy / Outer Borough Dust Run / Deathbed

EDGAR BROUGHTON BAND (UK)
Line-Up: Edgar Broughton (vocals / guitar), Victor Unitt (guitar), Arthur Grant (bass), Steve Broughton (drums)

At one time on an equal paring with HAWKWIND as masters of Psychedelic Acid Rock, the EDGAR BROUGHTON BAND's momentum was stifled by constant business problems resulting in a steady decline of fortunes. The band was founded in Warwick during 1968 by brothers Edgar on vocals and guitar and drummer Steve Broughton, relocating to London upon signing to Progressive Rock label Harvest in 1970.
The line-was completed by bassist Arthur Grant and guitarist Victor Unitt. The debut 'Wasa Wasa' made quite an impression but failed to chart. Unitt opted out at this juncture to join THE PRETTY THINGS and the band persevered as a trio.
March 1970 saw the act's first hit as 'Out Demons Out' (A FUGS cover version) just grazed the top forty, the accompanying album fared better cracking the top twenty. That same year the group reaped publicity by performing at the legendary Isle Of Wight festival - not actually at the event itself but as a protest gig outside of the perimeter.
Unitt returned in time for the eponymous 1971 third album and the band's surreal version of THE SHADOWS 'Apache' gave them a further hit. The band toured relentlessly putting in gigs with the likes of STRAY, FREEDOM and THE NICE. Despite chart success though the band's fortunes took a drastic downturn and subsequent albums and singles saw a marked shift away from their previous heaviness.
In 1975 the band signed to the NEMS label bringing onboard new guitarist John Thomas for the 'Bandages' album. Further changes following the release saw guitarist Terry

Cottam being enrolled, Thomas leaving for pastures new in THE GEORGE HATCHER BAND and then cult Hard Rock act BUDGIE where he remains to this day.
The band dissolved in late 1976 having laid down a live album which was not to surface until 1978.
Edgar and Steve together with Grant Undaunted founded THE BROUGHTONS, releasing a further brace of albums. Aiding their mission were guitarists Tom Norden and Pete Tolsen and keyboard player Richard DeBastion. After the issue of 'Parlez Vous English' the band were back to a power trio once more but pulled in Norden and keyboardist Dennis Haines for 1982's 'Superchip'.
Steve Broughton journeyed to America becoming the lead vocalist for CITY BOY.
The EDGAR BROUGHTON BAND re-formed in early 1989 with the brothers reunited with Arthur Grant, now on bass, and guitarist Andrew Bristow.
By 1994 Grant had handed in his cards and in his stead came Kris Gray. He would in turn be replaced by Ian Hammond and in 1996 the EDGAR BROUGHTON BAND committed to recording new material after a 17 year hiatus out of the studio. The 1998 line-up found another generation involved as 18 year old Luke Broughton came in on keyboards.
The EDGAR BROUGHTON BAND refuse to lay down, the 'Last Supper' album being released as late as 1999. The 2000 album 'Demons At The Beeb' comprises the band's 1969 John Peel session and an 'In Concert' broadcast from 1971.

Singles/EPs:
Evil / Death Of An Electric Citizen, Harvest HAR 5001 (1969)
Out Demons Out / Momma's Reward, Harvest HAR 5015 (1970) **39 UK**
Up Yours / Officer Dan, Harvest HAR 5021 (1970)
Apache Dropout / Freedom, Harvest HAR 5032 (1970) **33 UK**
Hotel Room / Call Me A Liar, Harvest HAR 5040 (1971)
Gone Blue / Someone/ Mr. Crosby, Harvest HAR 5049 (1972)

Albums:
WASA WASA, Harvest SHVL 757 (1969)
Death Of An Electric Citizen / American Boy Soldier / Why Can't Somebody Love Me / Neptune / Evil / Crying / Love In The Rain / Dawn Crept Away
SING BROTHER SING, Harvest SHVL 772 (1970) **18 UK**
There's No Vibrations But Wait / The Moth:

a) The Moth, b) People, c) Peter / Momma's Reward (Keep Them Freaks A Rollin') / Refugee / Officer Dan / Old Gopher / Aphrodite / Granma / The Psychopath: a) The Psychopath, b) Is For Butterflies / It's Falling Away
EDGAR BROUGHTON BAND, Harvest SHVL 791 (1971) **28 UK**
Evening Over The Rooftops / The Birth / Piece Of My Own / Don't Even Know Which Day It Is / House Of Turnabout / Madhatter / Getting Hard / What Is A Woman For / Thinking Of You / For Dr. Spock
INSIDE OUT, Harvest SHTC 252 (1972)
Get Out Of Bed / There's Nobody There / Side By Side / Sister Angela / I Got Mad / They Took It Away / Home Fit For Heroes / Gone Blue / Chilly Morning Momma / The Rake / Totin' This Guitar / Double Agent / It's Not You / Rock And Roll
OORA, Harvest SHVL 810(1973)
Hurricane Man / Rock n' Roller / Roccocococooler / Eviction / Oh You Crazy Noy! / Things On My Mind / Exhibits From A New Museum: Green Lights / Face From A Window / Pretty / Hijack Boogie / Slow Down / Capers
A BUNCH OF 45'S, Harvest (1975)
BANDAGES, NEMS NEL 6006 (1976)
Get Arise / Speak Down The Wires / John Wayne / The Whale / Germany / Love Gang / One To Seven / Lady Life / Signal Injector / Fruhling Flowers / I Want To Lie
LIVE HITS HARDER, BB (1978)
There's Nobody There / Love In The Rain / One To Seven / Hotel Room / Evening Over Rooftops / Freedom/ Poppy / SignalInjector / Smokestack
PARLEZ VOUS ENGLISH?, Infinity INS 3027 (1979)
Little One / Waiting For You / Drivin' To Nowhere / Megalmaster / Didecoi / April In England / Revelations One / Anthem / Down In The Jungle / Ventasong / Young Boys / All I Want To Be
SUPERCHIP, Sheet SHEET2 (1982)
Metal Sunday / Superchip / Who Only Fade Away / Curtain / Outrageous Behaviour / Not So Funny Farm / Nighthogs / Pratfall / OD 476600 /1162 /11180 / Do You Wanna Be Immortal / Subway Information / The Last Electioneer / Goodbye Ancient Homeland / Innocent Bystanders
OUT DEMONS OUT, EMI EMS 1122 (1986)
Out Demons Out / Love In The Rain / Green Lights / I Got Mad (Soledad) / Hotel Room / Poppy / There's No Vibrations, But Wait! / Evil / Freedom / Someone / It's Not You (Unedited Version) / Call Me A Liar / Up Yours! / Mr. Crosby / Evening Over Rooftops / Apache Drop Out / The Moth a) The Moth, b) The People, c) Peter / Gone Blue / Why

Can't Somebody Love Me
AS WAS IS - THE BEST OF THE EDGAR BROUGHTON BAND, EMI CDP 790963 (1988)
Out Demons Out / Love In The Rain / Green Lights / Sister Angela / I Got Mad / Hotel Room / Thinking Of You / For Dr. Spock (Part 2) / American Boy Soldier / Call Me A Liar / Roccocococooler / Evening Over Rooftops / Momma's Reward (Keep Them Freaks A Rollin') / Refugee / Evil / House Of Turnabout / Up Yours! / Apache Drop Out (Apache Intro, Drop Out Boogie) / Homes Fit For Heroes / Things On My Mind
CLASSIC ALBUM & SINGLE TRACKS 1969-1973, Connoisseur CSAPCD 109 (1992)
Death Of An Electric Citizen / Neptune / Dawn Crept Away / Out Demons Out / Apache Dropout / Freedom / Officer Dan / Psychopath a) Psychopath, b) Is For Butterflies / Aphrodite / It's Falling Away / Poppy / Gone Blue / Mr. Crosby / Capers
THE LAST SUPPER, (1999)
DEMONS AT THE BEEB, Hux HUX 020 (2000)
For What You Are About To Receive / Why Can't Somebody Love Me? / Side By Side / Call Me A Liar / Poppy / The Rake / Gone Blue / Chilly Morning Momma / I Got Mad (Sole Dad) / And It's Not You / Out Demons Out / The Actor

BURNER (FL, USA)
Line-Up: Cliff Denny (vocals), John Paul Soars (guitar), Jason Morgan (guitar), Greg Threlkel (drums)

A Stoner Jazz-Metal combo rooted in the most unlikely of sources. Florida's BURNER, forged in September of 1999, comprise DIVINE EMPIRE and WYNJARA guitarist John Paul Soars and drummer Greg Threlkel. The band also features ex-MONSTROSITY guitarist Jason Morgan.
Founded by Soars and Threlkel in September of 1999 the duo soon enrolled guitarist Mike Puccharellie and bassist James Wellman into the fold. Prior to BURNER both six stringers had worked with each other in RAPED APE and PAINGOD. Shortly after JENGA singer Cliff Denny made up the numbers. Live work and a six track demo soon ensued. However, Puccharellie's occupation as a tattoo artist forced a career choice and the guitarist bowed out. His replacement would be Jason Morgan.

Albums:
ONE FOR THE ROAD, Arctic Music Group (2002)

American Dream / Broken / Five Pills (And A Bottle Of Whiskey) / No Regrets / Rollin' Disaster / All Alone / Six Gun / Ghost Town / At Ease / Whiskey Dick / Color / Empty

BURNING WITCH (USA)

Line-Up: Edgy 59 (vocals), Stephen O'Malley (guitar), Greg Anderson (guitar), G. Stuart Dahlquist (bass), Jamie Sykes (drums)

A "suicide Doom" outfit forged by former THORR'S HAMMER personnel Stephen O'Malley, Greg Anderson, and Englishman Jamie Sykes. Later additions included bass player G. Stuart Dahlquist and vocalist Edgy 59.

Anderson would decamp to Los Angeles, creating GOATSNAKE. This defection did not halt progress though and BURNING WITCH cut the September 1996 'Towers' album, produced by the renowned figure of Steve Albini.

Follow up 'Rift.Canyon.Dreams', with B.R.A.D. on drums, saw a slip into Drone-Doom realms. Following this release BURNING WITCH folded. Edgy 59 founded SINISSTAR whilst Dahlquist, O'Malley and Anderson conjoured up the terrifying SUNN0))). After a spell with CORVUS CORAX Sykes travelled back to his native England, joining ENCHANTED.

Singles/EPs:
The Bleeder / Communion, Hydra Head (2000) (Split single with GOATSNAKE)

Albums:
TOWERS, Slap A Ham SLAP049 (1996)
RIFT.CANYON.DREAMS, Merciless (1997)
CRIPPLED LUCIFER (SEVEN PSALMS FOR OUR LORD OF LIGHT), Southern Lord SUNN002 (1998)
Warning Signs / Stillborn / History Of Hell / Sacred Predictions / Country Doctor / Tower Place / Sea Hag

BURNOUT (USA)

Line-Up: Mark Shields (vocals), Tim (guitar), Aaron Birlson (guitar), John Hopkins (bass), Braden Peterson (drums)

Stoners founded in January of 2000. BURNOUT's inaugural live performance was as opening act to renowned female trio BOTTOM. The band expanded with the addition of second guitarist Aaron Birlson in early 2001 and with this line-up cut the debut 'Thundertits' album during the February. Reaction to live gigs and CD reviews prompted a deal from 12th Planet Music for the sequel, 'Armour Of The Gods', set for summer 2002 release.

Jeff Blain opted out though and BURNOUT duly enrolled vocalist Mark Shields and bassist John Hopkins.

Albums:
THUNDERTITS, (2000)
Speedway King / Bangzilla / Thundertits / 6 ft. Of Piss / Transmissions From The Solar Queen / Dirty Man / Out Of Control / Mudslinger / Superfuzz / Gas, Grass Or
ARMOUR OF THE GODS, 12th Planet Music (2002)

70

CALAMUS (GERMANY)
Line-Up: Ralf Burkart (vocals), Jens (guitar), Schrottie (bass), Adrian (bass)

German groove based Stoners. CALAMUS arrived brandishing a 1997 demo 'Justanothersweettrip', debuting commercially with the track 'Alone' featured on an Aberration fanzine compilation CD of 1998. Later that year an EP, 'Road Trax', was released through the small Unwucht label. The following year proved industrious for the band, issuing their 'High Drive' album and a split 7" with DUSTER 69, restricted to 333 red vinyl copies, through the Daredevil label.
Vocalist Ralf Burkart and guitarist Jens also had a side project BLACKTOP which featured on the Daredevil 'Burn The Street Vol. 1' compilation album.
CALAMUS had their second album, 'These Days', issued by the infamous I Used To Fuck People Like You In Prison label in 2001. Berserker Records would keep the momentum going with a split 7" shared with Americans SLOW HORSE, CALAMUS covering a SLOW HORSE track and vice versa.

Singles/EPs:
Road Trax EP, Unwucht (1998)
Calamus Vs. Duster 69 EP, Daredevil DD001 (1999) (Split EP with DUSTER 69)
No Sleep 'Til SHOD, Berserker (2001) (Split EP with SLOW HORSE)

Albums:
HIGHDRIVE, Daredevil DD002 (1999)
Boobtown / Speed-Queen / Cosmic Dust / Break Through / The Duke / This One / Not Tomorrow / Gasoline
THESE DAYS, I Used To Fuck People Like You In Prison (2001)
Heal All Pain / Golden Dreams / These Days / Do You Feel / In Between / Your Highway / The Blind Man / On The Run / Shitkicker! / Hold Me / Still Holding On / Under My Thumb

CALES (CZECH REPUBLIC)

A solo Pagan Doom Metal project of guitarist Peter 'Blackie' Hosek. Joining him on the sessions for the CALES 'Pass In Time' album were be a whole range of vocalists in DeSed, credited with 'screams and vocals', Skuny, Zuzha and Alesh. Additional instrumentation came courtesy of guitarist Ashok, keyboard player Tudy and drummer Evil.

Albums:
PASS IN TIME, Redblack (2001)

Wandering Phantom / Along Paths Of Return (Pagan Nostalgia) / From The Bosom Of Oblivion / Faces In The Walls / Sacrifice To Fire / Burn My Blood / The Last Winter Dance On The Way (Tribal Essence)

CANAAN (ITALY)
Line-Up: Mauro Berchi (vocals / guitar / keyboards), Matteo (guitar), Anthony Duman (bass), Luca (drums)

The Gothic Dark Wave act CANAAN was created in January 1996 by a triumvirate of erstwhile RAS ALGETHI personnel - vocalist / guitarist Mauro, guitarist Matteo and drummer Luca. With RAS ALGETHI's pedigree being almost without parallel in the Italian Doom scene from such releases as the 1994 demo 'Oblita Divinitas' and a solitary 1995 album 'Onericon - The White Hypnotic', CANAAN had a lot to live up to. As such, CANAAN's debut product, the 'Blue Fire' album, arrived in November of 1996 on the Eibon label.
In May of 1997 the band inducted Anthony Duman on bass guitar for recording of the follow up, the Paolo Sannazzaro produced 'Walk Into My Open Womb: The Apathy Manifesto', issued in September of 1998.
CANAAN would switch over to the German Prophecy Productions label for their third attempt 'Brand New Babylon'. Duman would be replaced by Nico on bass in February of 2001.

Albums:
BLUE FIRE, Eibon CAN001 (1996)
The Eleventh Shadow / Dreamsword / Thin Concentric Circles / Aranea Tedii / Incantesimo D'Autunno / Temporal Stasis / Noir (Your Coloured Soul) / Doloris Charisma / Moongod / Splendor's Bearer / Orien / The Luminous Trinity / Our Little Hidden Treasures / This Grey Enemy
WALK INTO MY OPEN WOMB: THE APATHY MANIFESTO, Eibon CAN010 (1998)
The Kanaanian Dawn / Surrounded / A Magic Farewell / The Glass Shield / The Pride Of Perdition / Aurora Consurgens / Walk Into My Open Womb / Scent Of Anguish / Remembrance / Codex Void / Left / Heaven / The Rite Of Humiliation / Roomaskin / The Orion Conspiracy / A Song For Pain / A New Beginning / Angel Nail
BRAND NEW BABYLON, Eibon CAN023 (2000)
Theta Division / In Un Cielo Di Pece / Sperm Like Honey / Disintegrate / Of Lost Desires / Shelter 1 / La Simmetria Del Dolore / For A Drowning Soul / The Circle Of Waters / 7119

71

/ The Meaning Of Solitude (Return To 9117) / Over Absolute Black / Lick My Poison / A Descent To Babylon

CANDLEMASS (SWEDEN)

Line-Up: Messiah Marcolin (vocals), Mats Bjorkman (guitar), Lasse Johansson (guitar), Leif Edling (bass), Janne Lindh (drums)

CANDLEMASS arose from the earlier NEMESIS outfit belonging to bassist Leif Edling and guitarist Christian Weberyd. Prior to the dissolving of the group NEMESIS had released the highly praised 'Day Of Retribution' album in 1984.

Debuting as CANDLEMASS on the tape trading circuit with the 'Witchcraft' demo in 1985 (featuring a line-up of Edling, Webyrd and drummer Mats Ekstrom), the band promptly signed to the French Black Dragon label. Having added former A.T.C. guitarist Mats Bjorkman the band began recording what would become the 'Epicus, Doomicus, Metallicus' debut.

During the recording of the album Christian Webyrd opted to leave and by the time it was released the group's newly acquired vocalist, Johan Lanquist and drummer Mats Ekstrom, had also departed. Still, the album considerably raised the band's profile and impressed many critics with a penchant for specializing in grandiose, Doom-laden Metal dirges that, at times, were hideously depressing but always exceptionally heavy.

Having taken well over a year to put a new line-up together (and having to pass on the offer of a tour with Black Dragon label mates HEIR APPARANT and SAVAGE GRACE) Edling, with Bjorkman still retained, settled on new drummer Jan Lindh. Also joining the fold were ex-MACBETH / HEXAGON guitarist Lars Johansonn and ex-MERCY vocalist Eddie 'Messiah' Marcolin (real name Jan Alfredo Marcolin). The latter, a rather portly chap, cut a strange figure on stage, choosing to wear a monk's habit, although his remarkable, near Operatic, vocal style quickly became the band's trademark.

Having split from Black Dragon CANDLEMASS enrolled the help of former Shades Records man Dave Constable in a management capacity and, by the end of 1987 CANDLEMASS had recorded a brand new album, 'Nightfall', which was issued through the newly established Axis label

Unfortunately, CANDLEMASS had to postpone their debut show in Britain, pulling out of a scheduled support slot to KING DIAMOND at London's Hammersmith Odeon in November 1987 due to Johannson breaking his arm. CANDLEMASS finally appeared on British shores at the end of

March the following year with a three date tour (comprising two London Marquee shows and a gig in Birmingham. CANDLEMASS had created quite a buzz with 'Nightfall' both in Britain and Europe and, following their successful appearance at the Dynamo festival later that year several record companies put in bids for their signatures. However, the band remained loyal to Axis, who changed their name to Active for legal reasons, with the albums being issued in America through Metal Blade. The group rounded out a magnificent year by supporting SLAYER in Norway and Sweden after original act NUCLEAR ASSAULT had pulled out.

The band's third album, 'Ancient Dreams', was more successful yet, even denting the American Billboard charts. To capitalize on this achievement a live show in the band's native Stockholm was recorded and released as 'Candlemass Live' in 1990. Its studio follow-up, 'Tales Of Creation' found the band working harder than ever on the live circuit with a full European tour as headliners before hitching up with KING DIAMOND to tour Europe once more.

The train came off the rails somewhat with the departure of their vocal and focal point Messiah Marcolin, although the big man was never quite able to match the profile he had in the ranks of CANDLEMASS on a journey through two albums with MEMENTO MORI and then forming STILLBORN.

After lengthy auditions ex-TALK OF THE TOWN singer Thomas Wilkström landed the job to record 'Chapter VI', but CANDLEMASS fragmented soon afterwards, with Leif Edling forming the experimental ABSTRAKT ALGEBRA with ex-TREAT / SWEDISH EROTICA vocalist Mats Leven.

Lasse Johansson teamed up with VENI DOMINE vocalist Fredrik Ohlson to form a Metal project titled ZOIC in 1995, which resulted in an album released the following year. Thomas Wikstrom, meantime, featured as guest vocalist on the 1996 album by BRAZEN ABBOT, titled 'Live And Learn'.

Strangely, in 1997 CANDLEMASS chose to return to the fray in rather odd circumstances. It transpired that Leif Edling had gone into the studio to record a projected second effort for ABSTRAKT ALGEBRA, but as recording progressed a name switch to CANDLEMASS was felt to be more the order of the day in terms of how the music was shaping. The 1997 line-up of the band thus comprised Edling alongside ex-GONE vocalist Björn Flodquist, former CARCASS / ARCH ENEMY guitarist Mike Amott (who also touted his trade with ARMADEDDON and SPIRITUAL BEGGARS), ex-BRICK guitarist Patrick and ABSTRAKT ALGEBRA's drummer Jejo

Percovich. Erstwhile EUROPE man Ian Haughland also guested on drums!

CANDLEMASS returned with the primitive sounding 'Dactys Glomerata' in 1998 after which the band pulled in guitarist Mats Stahl. The band delved even further back into the primeval '70s Rock soup for 1999 album 'From The 13th Sun', the album even including a drum solo!

The classic CANDLEMASS line-up would be tempted into a reunion invitation for the 2002 'Sweden Rocks' festival. The reunited band, which featured vocalist Messiah Marcolin, bassist Leif Edling, guitarists Mats Bjorkman and Lars Johansson with drummer Jan Lindh debuted at the 'Black Lucia' Christmas party held by 'Close Up' magazine in Stockholm on December 13th 2001.

Meantime the newly created Powerline label would re-release the first four classic CANDLEMASS albums.

The band would put in a long overdue UK performance at the London Mean Fiddler venue in Mid July, sponsored by TotalRock. The Swedes were supported by a strong cast including Martin Walkyier's RETURN TO THE SABBAT, DEVOLVED, THE DUKES OF NOTHING and expatriated Chileans CRIMINAL.

It would be learned that behind the scenes Edling had been forging another project band in league with his former ABSTRAKT ALGEBRA colleague Mats Leven. Billed as KRUX and having laid down a debut album for 2002 release through the Mascot label Edling's venture also saw contributions from the ENTOMBED rhythm section of drummer Peter Stjärnvind and bassist Jörgen Sandstrom, although the latter would switch to guitar. Other guitarists involved in the sessions included Nicko Elgstrand of TERRA FIRMA and Fredrik Åkesson from TALISMAN. Yet another CANDLEMASS spin off, C.R.A.N.K., would witness a union of guitarist Mats Bjorkman with the LIONS SHARE rhythm section of bassist Pontus Egberg and drummer Johan Koleberg as well as singer Alex Swerdh and guitarist Ulf Larsson of the KISS cover band KYSS.

Singles/EPs:

Samarithan / Solitude, Axis 7 AX1 (1988)

Samarithan / Solitude / Crystal Ball, Axis 12 AX1 (1988) (12" single)

At The Gallows End / Crystal Ball / Solitude, Metal Blade 72295-0 (1988)

Bullfest / Samling Vid Pumpen / Brollop Pa Hulda Johanssons / Tjo Och Tjilm Och Inget Annat, Megarock MRRCDS003 (1993)

Wiz, Froghouse (1998)

Albums:

EPICUS DOOMICUS METALLICUS, Black Dragon BD013 (1986)
Solitude / Demons Gate / Crystal Ball / Black Stone Wielder / Under The Oak / A Sorcerer's Pledge

NIGHTFALL, Axis LP 4 (1987)
Gothic Stone / The Well Of Souls / At The Gallows End / Samarithan / Intro / Dark Are The Veils Of Death / Mourner's Lament / Bewitched

ANCIENT DREAMS, Active LP7 (1988) **45 SWEDEN**
Mirror, Mirror / Cry From The Crypt / Darkness In Paradise / Incarnation Of Evil / Bearer Of Pain / Ancient Dreams / The Bells Of Acheron / Epistle No.81

TALES OF CREATION, Music For Nations MFN 95(1989) **48 SWEDEN**
The Prophecy / Dark Reflections / Voices In The Wind / Under The Oak / Tears / Into The Unfathomed Tower: i) Dance Of The Fay, ii) Magic/Entering The Tower, iii) Dance Of The Fay (Reprise), iv) Souls Flight, v) Towards The Unknown, vi) Choir Of Angels, vii) Outside The Gates Of Heaven / The Edge Of Heaven / Somewhere In Nowhere / Through The Infinitive Halls Of Death / Dawn / A Tale Of Creation

LIVE, Music For Nations MFN 109 (1990)
Well Of Souls / Dark Are The Veils / Bewitched / Solitude / Dark Reflections / Under The Oak / Demons Gate / Bells Of Acheron / Through The infinitive Halls Of Death / Samarithan / Mirror, Mirror / Gallow's End / Sorcerer's Pledge

CHAPTER VI, Music For Nations MFN128 (1992) **43 SWEDEN**
Dying Illusions / Julie Laughs No More / Where The Runes Still Speak / Ebony Throne / Temple Of The Dead / Aftermath / Black Eyes / The End Of Pain

THE BEST OF CANDLEMASS - AS IT IS, AS IT WAS, Music For Nations MFN 166 (1994)
Solitude / Bewitched / Dying Illusion / Demons Gate / Mirror, Mirror / Samarithan / Into The Unfathomed Tower / Bearer Of Pain / Where The Runes Still Speak / At The Gallow's End / Mourner's Lament / A Tale Of Creation / Ebony Throne / Under The Oak / Well Of Souls (Live) / Dark Are The Veils Of Death / Darkness In Paradise / The End Of Pain / Sorcerer's Pledge / Solitude' ('87 Version) / Crystal Ball ('87 Version) / Bullfest

DACTYS GLOMERATA, Music For Nations MFN 237 (1998)
Wiz / I Still See The Black / Dustflow / Cylinder / Karthago / Abstrakt Sun / Apathy / Lidocain Gold / Molotov

FROM THE 13TH SUN, Music For Nations (1999)

Droid / Tot / Elephant Star / Blumma Apt / Arx-NG 891 / Zog / Galatea / Cyclo-F / Mythos

CANDYBAR PLANET (HOLLAND)
Line-Up: Richard Plukker (vocals / bass), Murphy van Oijen (guitar), Mark Hendrickx (drums)

Niemegen Stoners CANDYBAR PLANET have been operational since 1993. The trio comprises the aptly named frontman Richard Plukker on bass and vocals, an erstwhile member of MOONSTORM and EBOMAN, ex-35007 guitarist Murphy van Oijen and drummer Mark Hendrickx.
During 2002 CANDYBAR PLANET added bass player Martin van Herpen, another former MOONSTORM man.

Singles/EPs:
Five / Billy (I'm Gonna Get That Woman) / WFO / Exposed / Sun Screamer, Drunken Maria (2000) ('Candybar Planet' 10" EP)

Albums:
32 BITCH, Suburban MRN 250399 (1999)

Hummin' / Dirttrack / Rock On / Plastic Pink / Hip / Guacamole / Powder / Candybarbarella / Red River

CANYON CREEP
(San Francisco, CA, USA)
Line-Up: Anthony Buhagiar (vocals / guitar), Dave Vasquez (bass), Jerry Rivera (drums)

A Southern style Stoner outfit founded as AMERICAN NIGHTMARE. The self-financed 'Hijack The World' album would see a reissue through the Dark Reign label. Frontman Anthony Buhagiar would from part of a 2002 side venture TORCH THE VILLAGE in alliance with Mitchell Froom of OPERATOR GENERATOR and a guitarist from WOODSHED.

Albums:
HIJACK THE WORLD, (2000)
Intro / No Brakes / Hijack The World / I Got The Shakes / Warm Beer / Black Bra / Can't Afford You / Yreka / Give Me Some

CANYON CREEP
Photo : El Danno

74

CAPTAIN BEYOND

(Los Angeles, CA, USA)
Line-Up: Rod Evans (vocals), Larry Rheinhart (guitar), Lee Dorman (bass), Bobby Caldwell (drums)

Psychedelic Hard Rock 'Supergroup' founded by ex-DEEP PURPLE vocalist Rod Evans in 1971. Joining him were former IRON BUTTERFLY men guitarist Larry 'Rhino' Rheinhart and bassist Lee Dorman. Drums were handled by former NOAH'S ARK / JOHNNY WINTER BAND member Bobby Caldwell.
Following the well received debut Caldwell departed to join DERRINGER and was replaced by Marty Rodriguez. CAPTAIN BEYOND also augmented their sound with the addition of ex-BOZ SCAGGS / PANDEMONIUM pianist Reese Wynans and percussionist Guille Garcia for 1973's Sci-Fi infused 'Sufficiently Breathless'.
Caldwell returned to the band midway through the resulting American tour but the band folded in 1974. The drummer returned to JOHNNY WINTER to complete his 'Saints And Sinners' album before forming ARMAGEDDON, the Hard Rock band led by ex-YARDBIRDS singer Keith Relf.
Evans quit in 1976 but the band persevered by drafting ex-TRUK / HUNGER frontman Willy Daffern. A third and final album ensued 'Dawn Explosion' which found Caldwell back on the drum stool. Daffern would later join Tim Bogert's PIPEDREAM and GARY MOORE's G FORCE. Latterly the singer, known most commonly as Willy Dee, fronts ZOOM LENZ and has contributed to a CAPTAIN BEYOND tribute album.
CAPTAIN BEYOND meanwhile resumed action in 1979 touring America with a line-up of Dorman, Caldwell, vocalist Robb Hanshaw and guitarist Randy. Caldwell, Hanshaw and Dorman also gigged as IRON BUTTERFLY the same year. Hanshaw quit after the tour collapsed to join GREY STAR, the band fronted by RUBY STARR.
Caldwell attempted a short-lived stab at reforming ARMAGEDDON in 1985.
CAPTAIN BEYOND reformed in 1999. Rheinhart and Caldwell were joined by former SPIRAL STARECASE vocalist Jimi Interval, ex-SAD BIRD / SUBURBAN STRATEGY / WHITE SUMMER keyboard player Dan Frye and Jeff Artabasy on bass.
This line-up cut a four track CD and resumed touring activities including a date at the Karlshamm festival in Sweden. In 1999 Lee Dorman toured Germany as part of the renewed IRON BUTTERFLY.
The 2000 tribute album included contributions from Doomsters PENTAGRAM and Swedes LOTUS and LOCOMOTIVE BREATH.

Singles/EPs:
As The Moon Speaks (Return) / Thousand Days Of Yesterdays (Time Since Come And Gone), Capricorn 0013 (1972) (USA release)
Drifting In Space / Sufficiently Breathless, Capricorn 0029 (1973) (USA release)
Gotta Move / Be As You Were / Don't Cry Over Me / Night Train Calling (Crystal Clear), Captain Beyond (1999) (CD single)

Albums:
CAPTAIN BEYOND, Capricorn K 47503 (1972)
Dancing Madly Backwards (On A Sea Of Air) / Armworth / Myopic Void / Mesmerization Eclipse / Raging River Of Fear / Frozen Over / Thousand Days Of Yesterdays (Time Since Come And Gone) / I Can't Feel Nothin' / As The Moon Speaks (To The Waves Of The Sea) / Astral Lady / As The Moon Speaks / I Can't Feel Nothin' (Part 2)
SUFFICIENTLY BREATHLESS, Capricorn CP 0115 (1973) 90 USA
Sufficiently Breathless / Bright Blue Tango / Drifting In Space / Evil Men / Starglow Energy / Distant Sun / Voyages Of Past Travellers / Everything's A Circle
DAWN EXPLOSION, Warner Bros. BS 3047 (1977)
Do Or Die / Icarus / Sweet Dreams / Fantasy / Breath Of Fire (Part 1 & 2) / If You Please / Midnight Memories / Oblivion - Space

CASKET (GERMANY)

Line-Up: Jörg Weber (vocals / guitar), Karin Trapp (vocals), Jürgen Bischoff (guitar), Marc Fischer (bass), Tobias Demel (keyboards), Steffan Klein (drums)

The Doom inclined Death Metal band CASKET were created in 1992 issuing their first demo recordings 'Voices From Beyond', the following year. A further cassette, '...But Death Comes Soon', followed in 1994 as CASKET added secondary female vocals from Karin Trapp and performed shows opening for PYOGENESIS and PANDEMONIUM.

Albums:
EMOTIONS... DREAMS OR REALITY, Serenades (1997)
Way To Happiness / Emotions... / Black Mountain / Confessions / ... Dream Or Reality / Life-Elixir / Near Heaven
TOMORROW, Serenades SR013 (1997)
A Piece Of Love / Suicide / Questions Of Life / Secrets / Last Days / No More / Feel The Fire / Tomorrow / Tears Of Sorrow

FAITHLESS, Serenades SR021 (1998)
Not Like You / A Lover In Disguise / Let Your
Hair Hang Down / Dirty Thoughts / What For
/ The Other Way Round / An Illusion / Not
Too Far / Maybe / Way To Happiness - The
Continuation

CASTLE (HOLLAND)
Line-Up: Eric (vocals), Ilja (guitar), Richard
(guitar / keyboards), Lucien (bass), Jean-
Marie (drums)

Tillburg based CASTLE offered Doom Death
Metal on their one and only release.

Albums:
CASTLE, MMI Records 009CD (1994)
The 7th Empire / The Emperor's Children /
Alter Reality / Exposed / Travelling / Castle /
Bridge Of Snow

CATHEDRAL (UK)
Line-Up: Lee Dorrian (vocals), Adam Lehan
(guitar), Gary Jennings (guitar), Griff (bass),
Mark Ramsey Wharton (drums)

Doom-laden band formed by Coventry's ex-
NAPALM DEATH frontman and Rise Above
record label driving force Lee Dorrian.
CATHEDRAL was rounded out initially by
guitarists Adam Lehan and Gary Jennings
(both ex-ACID REIGN), bassist Griff, a former
roadie for CARCASS. The first drummer was
ex-VARUCAS and SACRILEGE man Andy
Baker. The latter was replaced by former
FILTHKICK member Ben Mochrie.
The group recorded its first demo, 'In
Memorium', which included a cover of cult
American act PENTAGRAM's 'All Your Sins',
then found themselves being invited to
contribute the track 'Ebony Tears' to the 'Dark
Passages' compilation album in 1990.
The band were to tour Britain with
STORMTROOPERS OF DEATH and later ST.
VITUS before putting in more touring during
1991 appearing in Britain with SADUS and
MORBID ANGEL in March and PARADISE
LOST in Holland during April. In October
CATHEDRAL found themselves once more
on the road in Britain on a bill with YOUNG
GODS, SILVERFISH and NEW CRANES.
Drummer Mike Smail of PENANCE and
DREAM DEATH performed on the debut
'Forests Of Equilibrium' album in 1991, but
the band recruited a permanent drummer in
Mark Ramsey Wharton soon after.
Having started off very much in the retro
Doom mould with their first album the group
kicked off 1992 with British dates alongside
ANATHEMA and MY DYING BRIDE before
the they toured Europe with label mates

CARCASS, ENTOMBED and CONFESSOR
as part of the 'Gods Of Grind' tour. These
shows were rounded off by more European
dates with ST. VITUS.
The Earache package theme developed into
the teaming up of CATHEDRAL with NAPALM
DEATH, CARCASS and BRUTAL TRUTH for
the American 'Campaign For Musical
Destruction' tour before the group returned to
Europe to round off the year in Germany with
NAPALM DEATH once more along with
CROWBAR and TROUBLE.
1993 was to prove another arduous year in
the band's history, especially on the road
where CATHEDRAL found themselves
touring for a good portion of the year, opening
with European dates with SLEEP and
PENANCE before their first Japanese shows
alongside BRUTAL TRUTH and S.O.B.
Another bout of American touring followed
with dates including slots with MERCYFUL
FATE, FLOTSAM AND JETSAM, Rob
Halford's FIGHT, PENTAGRAM and
IRONMAN.
However, Griffiths departed to form YEAR
ZERO (later joining BLACKSTAR with ex-
CARCASS members) and a temporary
replacement was found in Mike Hickey of
CRONOS and VENOM. In early 1994
CATHEDRAL yet again suffered a serious
line-up shuffle when both Lehan and Wharton
left.
To promote 'The Ethereal Mirror' album (the
Japanese version boasting two extra tracks,
'Skylifter' and 'Funeral Request (Rebirth)')
CATHEDRAL toured heavily during 1994 with
guitarist Victor Griffin and drummer Joe
Hasselvander, both on loan from cult
American Death Metallists PENTAGRAM.
The band by now sported some very '70s
stage garb!
CATHEDRAL's status rose considerably
throughout Europe during the year, a highlight
of which included a prestigious opening slot
for their heroes BLACK SABBATH. Acrimony
arose however when Griffin quit before the
end of the tour quickly followed by
Hasselvander, resulting in cancellation of
scheduled British shows. The tour was
eventually rescheduled with ex-TROUBLE
drummer Barry Stern stepping into the
breach.
CATHEDRAL got back on the road for some
pre-Christmas shows with guests ELECTRIC
WIZARD and MOURN, the headliners now
with a line-up of Dorrian, Jennings, ex-
REPULSION bassist Scott Carlson and
drummer Dave Hornyak.
1995 began with European dates on a billing
with DEICIDE and BRUTAL TRUTH, although
CATHEDRAL yet again shifted personnel with
Hornyak and Carlson departing due to the

CATHEDRAL

financial constraints imposed upon them after the band had been dropped in America by Columbia Records.

No sooner had their fans got used to this latest incarnation then CATHEDRAL swiftly manoeuvered the rhythm section out and brought in ex-TRESPASS bassist Leo Smee and ex-TORINO. CAPRICE and CONTAGIOUS drummer Brian Dixon in May 1995.

CATHEDRAL promptly released 'The Carnival Bizarre' album, produced by Kit Woolven and the track 'Utopian Blaster' featured guest guitar from BLACK SABBATH's guitarist TONY IOMMI.

In order to promote the new album CATHEDRAL scheduled British headline shows with support from ANATHEMA and MOURN prior to engaging in a Euro-Scandinavian tour with MOTÖRHEAD and also made it over to Japan once more.

As former band members Hickey and Wharton resurfaced as part of the new CRONOS line-up in 1995, Dorrian was reported to have contributed lyrics and guest vocals to ex-DEATH SS guitarists PAUL CHAIN's solo album 'Alkahest', which surfaced in 1996.

The same year CATHEDRAL issued the 'Hopkins (Witchfinder General)' single, which featured a cover of the CRAZY WORLD OF ARTHUR BROWN hit 'Fire'. The studio album 'Supernatural Birth Machine' fared well and brought in steady sales. The Australian market was treated to a lavish gatefold edition compete with comic strip whilst Japanese variants added an exclusive track 'Tucker's Luck'.

Dorrian busied himself in mid 1996 on the 'Dark Passages' Doom compilation album on his Rise Above label, which featured such acts as ORANGE GOBLIN, PENTAGRAM, TROUBLE and ELECTRIC WIZARD besides CATHEDRAL themselves.

CATHEDRAL re-emerged in 1997 by performing a set at the Whitby 100th anniversary festival of Bram Stoker's 'Dracula' novel.

The 1999 'In Memorium' release is a reissue of the band's 1990 demo with live recordings from the following year. Dixon involved himself in the ARABIA side project with ex-TEN members bassist Steve McKenna and keyboard player Ged Ryland, former VON GRROVE vocalist Michael Shotton and guitarists Alan Kulke and Pete Frank.

2000 had Smee founding side project FIREBIRD with ex-CARCASS guitarist Bill Steer and SPIRITUAL BEGGERS man Ludwig Witt.

Touring to promote the 2001 'Endtyme' album saw CATHEDRAL putting in their first

American gig since 1996 when the band played the 'Metal Meltdown III' festival.

Singles/EPs:
Reaching Happiness, Touching Pain (Autumn Jade mix) / Solitude (Insobriety mix), Ultimatum (1990)
Soul Sacrifice / Autumn Twilight / Frozen Rapture / Golden Blood (Flooding), Earache MOSH40 (1992)
Statik Majik / Hypnos 164 / Midnight Mountain / Cosmic Funeral / Voyage Of The Homeless Sapien, Earache MOSH 106 CD (1994)
Mourning Of A New Day / All Your Sins / Ebony Tears / March, Rise Above RISE 9 (1994) ('In Memorium' EP)
Hopkins (Witchfinder General) / Fire / Copper Sunset / Purple Wonderland / Devil's Summit, Earache MOSH 152 CD (1996)
Gargoylian / Earth In The Grip Of A Skeletal Hand, Southern Lord (2001)

Albums:
FORESTS OF EQUILIBRIUM, Earache MOSH 43 (1991)
Picture Of Beauty And Innocence / Commiserating The Celebration / Ebony Tears / Serpent Eve / A Funeral Request / Equilibrium / Reaching Happiness, Touching Pain
THE ETHEREAL MIRROR, Earache MOSH 77 (1993)
Violet Vortex / Ride / Enter The Worms / Midnight Mountain / Fountain Of Innocence / Grim Luxuria / Jaded Entity / Ashes You Leave / Phantasmagoria / Imprisoned In Flesh
THE CARNIVAL BIZARRE, Earache MOSH 130 (1995)
Vampire Sun / Hopkins, The Witchfinder General / Night Of The Seagulls / The Carnival Bizarre / Race Of The Unicorns / Palace Of Fallen Majesty / Fangalactic Supergloria / Blue Light / Palace Of Fallen Majesty / Electric Grave
SUPERNATURAL BIRTH MACHINE, Earache MOSH156CD (1996)
Cybertron / Eternal Countdown / Vako's Conquest / Stained Glass Horizon / Cyclops Revolution / Birth Machine 2000 / Nightmare Castle / Fireball Demon / Phaser Quest / Suicide Asteroid / Dragon Ryder / Magnetic Hole
CARAVAN BEYOND REDEMPTION, Earache MOSH 211 (1999)
Voodoo Fire / The Unnatural World / Satanikus Robotikus / Freedom / Captain Clegg / Earth Messiah / The Caravan / Revolution / Kaleidoscope Of Desire / Heavy Load / The Omega Man / Dust Of Paradise

STATIK MAGICK, Earache MOSH 234 (1999)
Midnight Mountain / Hypnos / Cosmic Funeral / The Voyage Of The Homeless Sapien / Soul Sacrifice / Autumn Twilight / Frozen Rapture / Golden Blood (Flooding)
IN MEMORIUM, Rise Above RISE 21 (1999)
Mourning Of A New Day / All Your Sins / Ebony Tears / March / Commiserating The Celebration (Live) / Ebony Tears (Live) / Neophytes For The Serpent Eve (Live) / All Your Sins (Live) / Mourning Of A New Day (Live)
ENDTYME, Earache MOSH 236 (2001)
Cathedral Flames / Melancholy Emperor / Requiem For The Sun / Whores To Oblivion / Alchemist Of Sorrows / Ultra Earth / Astral Queen / Sea Serpent / Templars Arise (The Return)

CATHERINE'S CATHEDRAL
(SWEDEN)

Gothic Doom Metal band from Sweden.

Albums:
FLOWERDUST, Noxious (1993)
INTOXICATION, Noxious NOX001 (1994)
Razorius (Intoxication) / Dust Will Follow / Morpheus The Endless / For The Love Of God / Euphoria / Seeing Is Believing / Contaminate / Flowerdust / The Legacy / Metamorphos
EQUILIBRIUM, Noxious NOX004 (1995)

CAULDRON (USA)
Line-Up: Varnom Ponville (vocals), Scott Shelby (guitar), Zeb Perkins (bass), Jason Thibodeaux (drums)

The erstwhile Texan Thrash duo vocalist Varnam Ponville and guitarist Scott Shelby of GAMMACIDE relocated to Louisiana to assemble the Doom styled Thrash outfit CAULDRON. They would be joined in this endeavour by bassist Zeb Perkins and drummer Jason Thibodeaux for the ensuing 1997 Tim Kimsey produced 'For The Love Of Pain' album.

Albums:
FOR THE LOVE OF PAIN, Brainticket (1997)
Acts Of God / Mindwarp / I'll Make You Beg / Blood On The Cross / For The Love Of Pain / Theater Of The Absurd / All That I See Is Red / Too Little Too Late / Lord Have Mercy / Overcome Evil / Endless / (Earth) After Forever

CAVITY (Miami, FL, USA)
Line-Up: Rene Barge (vocals), Jason

Landrian (guitar), Ryan Weinstein (guitar), Daniel Gorostiaga (bass), Jorge Alvarez (drums)

Miami Sludgers forged in 1992 by bass player Daniel Gorostiaga and vocalist Rene Barge. Initial recruits included drummer Joey and guitarist Ralf Luna. During 1993 CAVITY sported a line-up of vocalist Rene Barge, guitarists Raf and John Bonanno, bassist Daniel Gorostiaga and drummer Jason Lederman. An inaugural three track 7" single-sold for a dollar at gigs, the first of many, arrived in 1993 after which Luna departed to join THE CRUMBS. A replacement was swiftly found in Anthony Vialon, a veteran of LOAD and FLOOR.

A string of single releases, including split singles shared with DAISYCUTTER and BONGZILLA, and extensive tour work led up to the introduction of new drummer Jorge Alvarez in 1995 as CAVITY issued the debut album, 'Human Abjection', the same year. By this stage Steve Brooks would flank Bonanno as the band's second guitarist. Released on Gorostiaga's own City Of Crime label 'Human Abjection' would be limited to a mere 500 copies. CAVITY would come to the attention of Punk artist Pushead who duly signed the band up to his own Bacteria Sour label. The 'Human Abjection' sessions plus new material and cuts taken from earlier 7" releases would be collected together for the 1996 'Drowning' release.

CAVITY's next release, 'Somewhere Between The Train Station And The Dumping Grounds', was issued via Rhetoric and included 1993 material, 1996 songs and a hidden track comprising an entire live gig recording. An EP, 'Insignificant Laid' featuring Betty Monteavaro on drums, came out in 1997 on Bacteria Sour before CAVITY signed up with Stoner specialists Man's Ruin for the high profile 1999 album 'Supercollider'. The band also put out the four track 'Wounded' EP on No! Records which included a cover version of the GERMS 'Shutdown (Annihilation Man)'. By this time the band had lost the services of Barge but pulled in Ryan Weinstein on second guitar. Vialon would take on the mantle of lead vocalist fronting a quartet of Gorostiaga, Weinstein and drummer Henry Wilson. Touring across America with Swedes THE REFUSED would culminate in the departure of both Weinstein and Vialon, the latter relocating to Switzerland.

Jason Landrian would be drafted on guitar and Barge reinstated as frontman for West Coast dates. CAVITY signed to the Hydra Head label for 2001's 'On The Lam' album. CAVITY fans who attended the 'Krazy Fest' would be in for a rare treat as a limited edition of 'On The Lam', restricted to a paltry 100 copies, would be made for sale only at this gig.

In August of 2002 CAVITY relinquished their efforts and called it quits. The erstwhile membership was quick to reveal a myriad of spin off projects. Bassist Dan Gorostiaga was collaborating with CAVITY and THE CRUMBS man John Bonnano whilst guitarist Jason Landrian formed up a fresh band project with GAMMERA's Rafael Martinez. Meantime Ryan Weinstein put together a venture with ex-MACHETE members and was rumoured to be in alliance with Aaron Turner of ISIS and OLD MAN GLOOM working up a further project.

Singles/EPs:
Scalpel / Feeling Odd / One Night's Worth Of Upheaval, City Of Crime (1993) ('Cavity' EP)
Perseverance / Crawling, Bacteria Sour (1996)
Damaged III /, Starcrunch (1996) (Split single with DAISYCUTTER)
Wounded / Burning My Eyes /, Rhetoric (1996) (Split EP with BONGZILLA)
Laid Insignificant EP, Bacteria Sour (1997)
Goin' Ann Arbor / Sometimes Sweet Susan, Rhetoric (1997)
Fuck Diablo / Snaked Side / No Deeper Than Dredgeboats In Floodwater, Arm (1998) ('Fuck Diablo' EP)
Wounded / Human Abjection / Untitled / Shutdown (Annihilation Man), No! (1999) ('Wounded' EP)

Albums:
HUMAN ABJECTION, City Of Crime (1995)
Chloride / Burning My Eyes / Chase / OTD / Intro / Drowning / Inside My Spine (Part II) / Slug
DROWNING, Bacteria Sour (1996)
The Saver / Marginal Man Blues / Butterscotch / Leech / Crawling / Perseverance / Drowning / Burning My Eyes / Chase / O.T.D / Chloride / Inside My Spine (Part 2) / Slug
SOMEWHERE BEWEEN THE TRAIN STATION AND THE DUMPING GROUNDS, Rhetoric (1996)
Goin' Ann Arbor / Your Funeral, My Time / Shake 'Em On Down / Intro Number Two / Open Transom / One Last Broken / Chloride / Inside My Spine / Drowning / Burning My Eyes / Chase
LAID INSIGNIFICANT, Bacteria Sour (1997)
The Woods / 9 Fingers On The Spider / Marginal Man / I May Go / Demon / A Bitter Cold Spell
SUPERCOLLIDER, Man's Ruin MR140CD

(1999)
Supercollider / Set In Cinders / Taint And Abandon / Inside My Spine / Threshold / Black Snake / Damaged IV / How Much Lost / Last Of The Final Goodbyes / Almost Blue
MISCELLANEOUS RECOLLECTIONS: '92-'97, Kapow! (2001)
Wounded / Big Hit Man / Sometimes Sweet Susan / Fuck Diablo / Angelrust / Spine I / Spine II / Covered Twice / The Oblivionist / Shutdown (Annihilation Man) / Perseverance / Human Abjection / Scalpel / Feeling Odd / One Night's Worth (Of Upheaval) / Slug
ON THE LAM, Hydra Head (2001)
Cult Exciter / Boxing The Hog / Sung From A Goad / Pulling Up The Stakes / Willy Williams / On The Lam / Leave Me Up / Sweat And Swagger / 9

CELESTIAL SEASON (HOLLAND)
Line-Up: Stefan Ruiters (vocals), Pim van Zanen (guitar), Robert Ruiters (guitar), Olly Smit (bass), Maaike Aarts (violin), Jiska Ter Bals (violin), Jason Kohnen (drums)

Dutch Doomsters CELESTIAL SEASON included a somewhat leftfield version of ULTRAVOX's 'Vienna' on their 'Celestial season' album and began life in 1992. The band soon released a demo, 'Promises', from which Swiss label Witchhunt Records released two tracks as the 'Flowerskin' 7".
Following the release of the debut album CELESTIAL SEASON toured Europe with NIGHTFALL and SADNESS. Further dates followed with SKYCLAD, ANATHEMA and GOREFEST.
A further 7" single was released, this time a split effort with fellow Doomsters LORDS FROM THE STONE. The band also contributed the track 'Above Azure Oceans' to the Nuclear Blast compilation album 'Death Is Just The Beginning - Volume Three'.
In 1995 the band opted to exchange their Metallic leanings for a retro styled groove Rock stance. The first real evidence of this change of tack would come with the 1997 'Orange' album. Vocalist Stefan Ruiters was latterly replaced by the enigmatically titled Cyril Crutz. CELESTIAL SEASON established their own custom imprint La Guapa for issue of the 2000 Pieter Kloos produced 'Lunchbox Dialogues'.
A four track EP, 'Songs From The Second Floor', arrived on both CD and vinyl formats in 2001. CELESTIAL SEASON called it quits in February of 2002.

Singles/EPs:
The Merciful / Surreal, Witchhunt (1993) ('Flowerskin' single)

Astral Dub / Icarus With You / Pegasus / King Lizard, Displeased D 00043 (1995) ('Sonic Orb' EP)
Black Queen Is Dynamite / Solar Child '96, Big Bloke 77.998.2 (1997)
Room 210 / Morning Theft / Watching The Fuss / Saturday (Wanna Go For A Ride?), Drunken Maria DMR-785-2 (2001) ('Songs From The Second Floor' EP)

Albums:
FOREVER SCARLET PASSION, Adipocere AR 015CD (1994)
Cherish My Pain / The Merciful / In Sweet Bitterness / Ophelia / Together In Solitude / Mother Of All Passions / Flowerskin / Afterglow / For Eternity
SOLAR LOVERS, Displeased 000038 (1995)
Decamerone / Solar Child / Body As A Canvas / Soft Embalmer Of The Till Midnight / Will You Wait For The Sun? / The Holy Snake / Dancing To A Thousand Symphonies / Vienna/ Fandango / The Scent Of Eve / A Tune From The Majestic Queens Garden
ORANGE, Big Bloke 77 999 02 (1997)
Wallaroo / Too Much Too Soon / Black Queen Is Dynamite / The Orleans Capsule / Carmensita / Salamandra / Eye Generator / Warp Speed To Vulcan / Diabolo Cruiser XL5 / 1,000 Things / Daisy's Lunch / Dive / Risin' Out Of The Loop / Diesel Reptile
LUNCHBOX DIALOGUES, La Guapa LGR 51012 (2000)
Lonely Man Burning / Sharks And Razors / Outshine / Boarding Music / Mary Meets The Sky / Body Overdrive / The Celestial Dragon / All Wrong / Comfortable Mess / From the Plains

CEMETERY OF SCREAM (POLAND)
Line-Up: Martin Kotas (vocals), Marcin Piwowarczyk (guitar), Artur Oleszkiewicz (guitar), Jacek Krolik (bass), Katharyna Rachwalik (keyboards), Grzegorz Ksiazek (drums)

Gothic Doom merchants CEMETERY OF SCREAM's debut album was initially only available on vinyl until being picked up for license by Croon Records. The band, although utilizing female backing vocals on the debut, added a permanent female member for the second effort 'Deepression' for the Serenades label in keyboard player Katharyna Rachwalik.

Albums:
MELANCHOLY, Croon CCD1 (1995)
Prologue / Melancholy / Interludium / Dolor Ante Lucem / Interludium / Gods Of Steel /

And Just The Birds... / Apocalyptic Visions (Part II) / Anxiety / Interludium / Landscape Of Sadness / Lost Flowers / Interludium / Violet Fields Of Extinction / Interludium / Epilogue / Pointa / The Shadow Of The Notre Dame Cathedral

DEEPPRESSION, Serenades SR015 (1998)
Whisper-Touch / Breeze / Episode Man / Ironic / Walkin' On Air / Reveal The Rainbow / Cruel / Float To Escape

PRELUDE TO A SENTIMENTAL JOURNEY, Hammer Muzik (2002)
Time Is Shadow / Haila / In The Cemetery Garden / The Ray Of Cry / Overcall / The Chess At The Foot Of The Mountain / Cult / A Game Of Chess / Colder Than Ever / The Hourglass / Towards To The Final Consciousness / Bridge To A Desert / Fall / When The Sun's Born Red / Radioactive Toy

CENTURIA (POLAND)

Line-Up: Anna Wojtkowiak (vocals), Jacek Baran (guitar / keyboards / programming), Daniel Kaczmarczyk (drums)

Albums:
DREAMS AND FEELINGS, Black Flames Productions BFCD 004 (2000)
Bewitched / Tristia / Forgetfulness / Fabella / Omen / Apocalypse / The Awakening / Heaven And... / Dytyramb

CEREMONIUM (Brooklyn, NY, USA)

Line-Up: Brandon Diaz (vocals / guitar), Tom Pioli (guitar), Brian Yost (bass), Chris Terederi (drums)

Underground purveyors of Doom-Death. CEREMONIUM, uniting members from former acts PUTRIFACT and FUNGUS, came together in 1992, releasing an opening 7" single 'Nightfall In Heaven' the following year. International acclaim would be heaped upon the 1995 album 'Into The Autumn Shade' but CEREMONIUM's progress was marred by constant line-up changes. In 1996 the band managed to contribute a track to the compilation album 'What's For Dinner?'
Singer Oscar Matter bailed out necessitating guitarist Brandon Diaz adding vocals to his duties. Craig Pillard of INCANTATION fame was also briefly associated with the band. Matter would later team up with Colombians DETERIORIOT as bass player.
'Azalin' and 'Laconist' (Diaz and Pioli) of CEREMONIUM would also become associated with ex-ANTHRAX, NUCLEAR ASSAULT and BRUTAL TRUTH man Dan Lilker's 1996 Black Metal side venture HEMLOCK.
The second CEREMONIUM album 'No

Longer Silent' was recorded during 1998 for the Soul Sold Music label. Subsequent disagreements between the two parties led to the establishment of CEREMONIUM's own imprint Destro Records. The 'No Longer Silent' album closes with a version of DARKTHRONE's 'Cromlech'.
Lin Recca vacated the bass position on 2000, handing the role over to Brian Yost.

Singles/EPs:
Nightfall In Heaven, Necroharmonic Productions (1993)

Albums:
INTO THE AUTUMN SHADE, Fadeless (1995)
Nightfall In Haven / Serenity / Incarnated Entity / Unveiled Tears / Our Mourning Forever Shrouds / Into The Autumn Shade
NO LONGER SILENT, Destro (1998)
No Longer Silent / Blessing Of The Flame / Forever Enthroned / Pillars Of Wisdom / Delusions Of Grandeur / Cromlech

PAUL CHAIN (ITALY)

A renaissance, not to say eccentric, figure on the Italian Doom and Gothic scene, Ancona born Paul Chain's prolific output both as an artist and for his much sought production skills has landed him the coveted position of "Italian Doomeister". Paul Chain, a dexterous talent able to handle drums, bass, keyboards and lead vocals, made his mark as a founder member of the underground, and now highly revered, Gothic Horror Metal act DEATH SS. This act, founded during 1977 fused Punk and Metal to forge a quite unique brand of 'Horror Metal' which soon rose to cult status. Chain's co-founding DEATH SS colleague Steve Sylvester made his exit in 1982 and Chain duly soldiered on with DEATH SS until April of 1984 when the group was put on ice. By September of the same year Chain had gone solo, taking the DEATH SS rhythm section of bassist Daniel Tommasini and drummer Franco Cafori, to front his own act PAUL CHAIN VIOLET THEATRE. Also during the mid '80s Chain founded the Garage band the BOOHOOS achieving notable success with the 'The Sun, The Snake And The Hoos' and 'Moonshiner' releases.
A series of four live recordings would be made available on cassette formats throughout 1992-93, albeit only to fan club members. Chain guested on his erstwhile DEATH SS comrade STEVE SYLVESTER's 1993 album 'Freeman'. It's worth noting that 1995's 'Alkahest' album featured lyrics and guest vocals from CATHEDRAL frontman Lee

Dorrian.
Chain would continue the association with STEVE SYLVESTER, appearing on both his 1997 'Broken Soul' and follow up 'Mad Messiah' album of 1998. Chain himself issued the lavish two CD set 'Emisphere' and also founded LOOSIN 'O' FREQUENCIES in 1999 for the 'Regeneration' album.

Southern Records would issue PAUL CHAIN's debut American recording, a collector's split 7" single shared with INTERNAL VOID.

Latterly Chain issues works under various handles including 'The Improviser' and 'Container'.

Singles/EPs:
Occultism / Voyage To Hell / Armageddon / 17 Day, Minotauro (1985) ('Violet Theatre: Detatching From Satan' EP)
Highway To Hell / Never Cry / The Evil The Sorrow / Way To Pain, Minotauro (1986) ('Paul Chain Violet Theatre' EP)
King Of The Dream, Minotauro (1987) (Split single with SABOTAGE)
Yellow Acid / Needful, LM Records (1997)
Solitude Man, Beyond Productions BEY015 (2000)
Sanctuary Heve, Beyond Productions BEY021 (2002)

Albums:
IN THE DARKNESS, Minotauro (1986)
Welcome To My Hell / Meat / War / Crazy / Grey Life / Woman And Knife / Mortuary Hearse / In The Darkness
VIOLET ART OF IMPROVISATION, Minotauro (1986)
Tetri Teachl In Luce Viola / Emarginante Viaggio / X-Ray / Old Way / Hypnosis / Casual Two Your Mister / Celtic Rain / Dedicated To Jesus / End By End
ASH, Minotauro (1988)
Eternal Flame / Image Down / Electroshock / I Remember A Black Mass
LIFE AND DEATH, Minotauro (1989)
Steel Breath / Antichrist / Kill Me / Ancient Caravan / My Hills / Alleluia Song / Cemetery / Oblivious
OPERA DECIMA - THE WORLD OF THE END, Minotauro (1990)
WHITED SEPULCHRES, Minotauro (1991)
Whited Sepulchres / The Fox In The Park / Traffic / Two Minutes / Are You Ready?
IN CONCERT, Labyrinth (1993)
Jumpin Jack Flash Improvisation / The Last Concert In The Summer / Black Night / Eric Lumen solo / Paul Chain Solo / Help Me / Does Improvisation
DIES IRAE, Minotauro (1994)
Years Of War / Presence Of The Soul Forest

/ Life Down / The Hope / Dies Irae / Organ Well / Red Lander / Noise In The Brain
ALKAHEST, Godhead 013 CD 022137 / WM 329 (1995)
Roses Of Winter / Living Today / Sandglass / Three Water / Reality / Voyage To Hell / Static End / Lake Without Water / Speulchra Life
EMISPHERE, Minotauro (1998)
Open (Judgment Comes From The Past) / I Want You / Transformation / Lack Of Balance / Oblivion Dimension / Gist Man / Emisphere / The Cave Of The Puppets - Part 1 / The Cave Of The Puppets - Part 2 / Easter Day / Beginning Of The End / Litany / Disease / Closed (Destiny Has Been Fulfilled)
MIRROR, Minotauro (1998)
Train Of Illusion / The Machine / Violence Of The Sun / Paradise Of The Poor / Obsession / Headroom / Sangue / Red Light / Moment Of Rage / Loveless / Luxury / Needful / Electric Funeral
THE IMPROVISER - OFFICIAL BOOTLEG, Minotauro (2000)
Intro Improvisation - Transpose I / Voyage To Hell / Transpose II Part 1 / Transpose II Part 2 / Evil Metal / Welcome To My Hell / Meat-Improvisation / Presentation Of The End Part 1
SIGN FOR SPACE, Beard Of Stars (2001)
Sign From Space Part 1 / Sign From Space Part 2 / Sign From Space Part 3 / Sign From Space Part 4
MASTER OF ALL TIMES, Andromeda Relics (2001)
Strange Philosophy Of Life / Spiritual Way / Inexplicable Inwardness / Water Of Verity / Hoping For Better Things
P.C. EX. 1. CONTAINER 47, LM Records (2001)
PARK OF REASON, Beyond Productions BEY0223 (2002)

CHALICE (AUSTRALIA)
Line-Up: Shiralee (vocals), Sean (guitar), Justin (guitar), Mark (bass), Alana (flute), Adrian (drums)

Australian Gothic Rock act CHALICE, founded in early 1997 and a band with a strong European flavour, were fronted by the sultry but still enormously vocally gifted figure of Shiralee. The concept of the band was put together by Shiralee and former TRILLIUM and BLEED guitarist Sean. Session guitars on the 'Chronicles Of Dysphoria' album were contributed by Justin Hartwig with violin from Russell. The album featured an adaptation of Edvard Grieg's 'Solvieg's Song' with lyrics from Henrik Ibsen. The lyrics to 'Requiescat' were adapted from a work by Oscar Wilde.
CHALICE would induct second guitarist Justin in late 1999 and flautist Alana, a

member of the Adelaide University Symphony Orchestra, in January of 2000. Drummer Adrian would take time out to session for Doom act MOURNFUL CONGREGATION and Industrialists INTO ETERNAL ABYSS.

A sophomore outing, 'An Illusion To The Temporary Real', emerged in 2001. During March of 2002 bass player Mark made his exit, confusingly replaced by another Mark, this one filling in from SOUL HARVEST on a temporary basis.

Albums:
CHRONICLES OF DYSPHORIA, Modern Invasion MIM7329-2CD (2000)
Solitary Waves / Requiescat / The Amber Twilight / As Powder Turns To Dust / Solvieg's Song / Interlunar Dreams / Memorial Embers
AN ILLUSION TO THE TEMPORARY REAL, Modern Invasion MIM7332-2 CD (2001)
The Jester's Banquet / An Illusion To The Temporary Real / Vista / Catalepsy In Staccato Rain / To Death Betrothed / Abyss / The Stigma of An Age

CHANT (FINLAND)

Albums:
CYNTHIA'S FIRE, Solistitium SOL032 (2000)
Tragic / By Dolores' Sword / Fever / Camouflage / Turn Away / Electric Carelia / Vertigo / Obsessive / For The Faithful / At Mr. Sherlock's Door

CHARGER (UK)
Line-Up: Tim Machin (vocals), Jay Woodruffe (guitar), Jim Palmer (guitar), Jez Leslie (bass), Paul Sandyford (drums)

A Stoke On Trent down tuned Fuzz Rock outfit. CHARGER featured on a slew of compilation albums before debuting officially with the Dave Chang November 2000 'The Foul Year Of Our Lord' album. SCORN and ex-NAPALM DEATH man Mitch Harris contributed backing vocals to this release.

The band had arrived on the scene with the 1998 'Haul Ass' demo, at that time citing a line-up of singer Mark, guitarists Jay Woodruffe and Al, bassist Jez Leslie and drummer Jon. CHARGER also featured on the Lockjaw compilations 'Helping You Back To Work' on both volumes two and three with the tracks 'Black Acid Rape' and 'Immense Mammoth' respectively.

CHARGER increased their profile by scooping the support to AMEN and RAGING SPEEDHORN's UK tour, subsequently going back out on the road with RAGING SPEEDHORN once more and VEX RED.

During June of 2001 bassist Jez Leslie opted out just upfront of a projected tour with RABIES CASTE. The band, minus a bassist, toured regardless. Tom would be drafted on bass during the August.

Guitarist Jay Woodruffe also operates the side project CRACKWHORE.

Singles/EPs:
Megatron / Immense Mammoth / Brickshithouse, Undergroove (1999) ('Fuzzbastard' EP)

Albums:
THE FOUL YEAR OF OUR LORD, Undergroove (2000)
1D / Nuance / Slope Migraine / Violent Summer / Villain Abuse / Xtab
FUZZBASTARD, (2002)
Megatron / Immense Mammoth / Brickshithouse / Sober Nerve (Demo) / Carbon Wings' (Live) / Villain Abuse / Violent Summer (Live) / Carbon Wings (Video) / Immense Mammoth (Video) / Nuance (Video) / Villain Abuse (Video) / Violent Summer

CHÉ (USA)
Line-Up: Brant Bjork (vocals / guitar), Dave Dinsmore (bass), Alfredo Hernandez (drums)

The ever industrious ex-KYUSS and present day FU MANCHU drummer BRANT BJORK switched to vocals and guitar for a 2000 project CHÉ in collusion with UNIDA's Dave Dinsmore on bass and drummer Alfredo Hernandez for the album 'Sounds Of Liberation'.

Albums:
SOUNDS OF LIBERATION, Man's Ruin MR 186 (2000)
Hydraulicks / The Knife / Pray For Rock / Sounds Of Liberation / Adelante / Blue Demon / The Day The Pirate Retired

CHORUS OF RUIN (UK)

Bradford underground Doom act CHORUS OF RUIN emerged with a 1991 demo session 'Les Miserables'. 1992's tape 'Swan Dive' preceded the 7" single 'Ocean Of Sins'.

A split EP with SORORICIDE arrived in 1994 and a promotion release 'Tragedies'.

With CHORUS OF RUIN's demise in 1996 Paul Webb forged the solo venture ANOTHER NEWBORN ZERO issuing the 'Circuit Breaker' demo in 2001. Izak would found SILVERBURN, initially being joined by CHORUS IN RUIN comrade Paul Webb and former SERENITY bassist Rob.

OFFICIUM TRISTE would cover 'Headstone' on their 1999 EP 'Roses On My Grave'.

Singles/EPs:
Ocean Of Sins / Dreaming Of Indigo, (1993)

JOHN CHRIST (USA)

Solo outing from former SAMHAIN, DANZIG and JUICE 13 guitarist JOHN CHRIST. Drums come courtesy of Stefan Svensson.
The track 'For Christ's Sake' had previously appeared on the compilation album 'Guitar's Practicing Musicians Volume III' in 1994 although a different recording including then DANZIG drummer Chuck Biscuits.
Christ produced the 1997 'Black Glue' album from former DAVID LEE ROTH guitarist MIKE HARTMAN.

Albums:
FLESH CAFFEINE, (1999)
Slow Down / One More Time / Flesh Caffeine / Talkin' Dirty / Silicone Valley / I'm Gone / Stop The World / Flesh Caffeine / For Christ's Sake

CHRISTIAN DEATH (USA)
Line-Up: Rozz Williams (vocals), Rikk Agnew (guitar), James McGearly (bass), George Belanger (drums)

Notorious Gothic Punk act centred upon vocalist Rozz William's (real name Roger Alan Painter) obsession with organized religion. Williams, born to a Southern Baptist family, came to the fore as CHRISTIAN DEATH courted controversy at every turn frequently utilizing swastikas and anti religious rhetoric. The singer, still in his mid teens, would further stoke uproar by frequently cross dressing onstage. Confusion has masked the band's career as throughout most of their career CHRISTIAN DEATH has been operating under dual identities with two groups laying claim to the band name. As many fans saw it, the 'original' American band was led by Rozz Williams, the 'imposter' band based in Europe by Valor Kand.
The band's initial 1979 Los Angeles line-up, originally known as THE UPSETTERS, included former ADOLESCENTS guitarist Rikk Agnew, bassist James McGearly and drummer George Belanger. It would be three years before CHRISTIAN DEATH debuted with an obscure EP made up of tracks from a compilation 'Hell Comes To Your House' shared with GRAVE 45 and THE SUPERHEROINES, followed by the full length 'Only Theatre Of Pain'. This outing, produced by Thom Wilson and seeing Eva O

on backing vocals, would be seen as a catalyst of the American Goth scene. Not only was the album alarmingly bleak in places but the band's formative Punk influences and undeniably Metal riffing gave the music a unique edge. Williams lyrical stance employed deliberately shocking sexual references and deliberate backwards messaging.
CHRISTIAN DEATH's appreciation in France led to a deal with the L'Invitation Au Suicide label. The debut album was reissued and a follow up mini-album 'Deathwish', actually recorded in sessions before the 'Only Theatre Of Pain' album, released in 1984. Such was the apathy in America compared to the favour afforded by Europe that Williams relocated to Paris. The singer promptly built a new version of the band comprising Australian Valor Kand on guitar, his wife and keyboard player Gitane Demone and drummer David Glass. All of these musicians were members of POMPEII 99, a band intended to back Williams on a CHRISTIAN DEATH European tour. A further French only release 'Catastrophe Ballet', recorded at Rockfield studios in Wales, ensued by which time the various members had gelled into CHRISTIAN DEATH Mk 2.
After the 1985 releases the acclaimed 'Ashes' and 'Decomposition Of Violets' live album Williams quit to concentrate on his other projects PREMATURE EJACULATION and HELTIR. The parting of the ways was initially amicable with the remaining band members intending to use the name SIN AND SACRIFICE. However, the band toured Europe minus Williams billed as CHRISTIAN DEATH and next album 'The Wind Kissed Pictures', initially only available as an Italian release, was credited to THE SIN AND SACRIFICE OF CHRISTIAN DEATH. With demand high the album would be issued in America, adding an extra track in 'Lacrima Christi' but simply credited to CHRISTIAN DEATH. A further Italian reissue included haunting instrumental outros not featured on other versions.
By the time 'Atrocities' hit the market Kand was now simply billing the band CHRISTIAN DEATH. Kand opted to persevere pulling in guitarist James Beam, flautist Sevan Kand (Valor & Gitane's son) and bassist Constance for 1987's 'The Scriptures'.
Meantime Williams founded the uncompromising SHADOW PROJECT with his wife Eva O and Jill Emery, both of THE SUPERHEROINES, and ex-CHRISTY AND THE FLESHEATERS man Tom for the 'Dreams Of A Dying' album. Also involved in both SHADOW PROJECT and CHRISTIAN DEATH was bassist Dan Canzonieri, later to found Punk band ELECTRIC

FRANKENSTEIN. Williams would also work on solo material with Gitane Demone resulting in the 'Dreamhome Heartache' album. Demone also worked with Dance act THE ALPHA PROJECT and German Goths PHALLUS DEI.

Albums throughout the '80s found the Kand version of the band unable to break out from their existing fan base and into the mainstream. By 1988 Bean and Constance had quit. The almost commercial 12" single 'Church Of No Return' witnessed the recruitment of guitarist Barry Galvin and the session bass of Johann Schumann. The follow up album 'Sex, Drugs and Jesus Christ', a distinctly heavy effort bordering on Gothic Metal, came with deliberately provocative artwork featuring the messiah injecting heroin.

In 1989 the European CHRISTIAN DEATH was down to a duo of the Kand brothers. A double set of releases 'All The Love All The Hate' saw new members Nick The Bastard on guitar, Mark Buchanan on saxophone and drummer Ian Thompson. The same year Williams, Agnew and Eva) put in a comeback CHRISTIAN DEATH tour of Canada. An album, 'The Iron Mask', was recorded for Cleopatra Records but subsequently disowned by Williams who believed unfinished master tapes had been used. William's CHRISTIAN DEATH next recorded 'The Path Of Sorrows', seen by many as one of his finest works.

1993 had only Valor Kand remaining augmented for the European CHRISTIAN DEATH 'Sexy Death God' album by Maitri on bass, Streamer on drums and Cullen and Marcel Trussell on violins and cellos.

Williams, Agnew, Eva O and a returning Belanger laid a claim to the title of CHRISTIAN DEATH. This 'original' line-up, also including Frank Agnew on guitar and bassist Casey Chaos, put out the 'Iconologica' live album, recorded at a one-off 'final' performance in Los Angeles during 1993, through Triple X as a legal battle raged between the two parties. The record's foundation was culled from the first brace of CHRISTIAN DEATH albums although it did feature the welcome addition of two new songs and a cover version of LOU REED's 'Kill Your Sons'.

Kand's CHRISTIAN DEATH signed to German Metal label Century Media for the 'Amen' album. The line-up for this release comprised Kand, guitarist Flick, Matri on bass and Steve on drums. The following year a set of William's CHRISTIAN DEATH tracks was remixed by LAIBACH among others for the 'Death In Detroit' album.

Although CHRISTIAN DEATH was by now

generating a wealth of reissues and interest in the band and various offshoots was riding a high Williams, having only just completed a further SHADOW PROJECT album, hung himself on the 1st of April of 1998. He was just 34.

Chaos has since formed AMEN in a Nu-Metal direction, releasing a 1999 debut album. Eva O issued a solo album 'Damnation' during 1999 on Massacre Records. Demone began a project with Paul Morden of THE BRICKBATS.

Kand's version of the band continues. CHRISTIAN DEATH, now including ex-CRADLE OF FILTH / BLOOD DIVINE drummer Was Sarginson toured Europe with Black Metal leaders CRADLE OF FILTH in late 2000. Various other members of CRADLE OF FILTH guested on the 2000 album 'Born Again Anti Christian'. The band would spend the latter half of 2001 working on a new studio album. Bassist Maitri also announced the arrival of a solo effort.

Singles/EPs:
Desperate Hell / Cavity / Spiritual Cramp / Romeo's Distress / Death Wish, Bemis Brain BB 127-128 (1982)
Believers Of The Unpure, Jungle JUNG 24T (1986)
Sick Of Love, Jungle JUNG 35T (1987)
Church Of No Return, Jungle JUNG 40T (1988)
What's The Verdict / This Is Not Blasphemy, Jungle JUNG 45T (1988)
I Hate You / We Fall Like Love, Jungle JUNG 055CD (1988)
Zero Sex, Jungle JUNG050T (1989)

Albums:
ONLY THEATRE OF PAIN, No Future FL 2 (1983)
Cavity - First Communion / Figurative Theatre / Burnt Offerings / Mysterious Iniquitatis / Dream For Mother / Deathwish / Romeo's Distress / Dogs / Stairs - Uncertain Journey / Spiritual Cramp / Resurrection - Sixth Communion / Prayer / Desperate Hell / Cavity
DEATHWISH, L'Invitation Au Suicide SD 4 (1984) (French release)
Deathwish / Romeo's Distress / Dogs / Desperate Hell / Spiritual Cramp / Cavity
CATASTROPHE BALLET, L'Invitation Au Suicide SD 5 (1984) (French release)
Awake At The Wall / Sleepwalk / The Drowning / The Blue Hour / Evening Falls / Andro Gynous Noise Hand Permeates / Electra Descending
THE DECOMPOSITION OF VIOLETS, R.I.O.R. A 138 (1985)

Awake The Wall / Sleepwalk / The Drowning / Theatre Of Pain / Cavity / The Blue Hour / Electra Descending / As evening Falls / Face / Cervix Couch / This Glass House / Romeo's Distress
SCRIPTURES, Jungle FREUD 18 (1987)
Prelude / Song Of Songs / Vanity / Four Horsemen / 1983 / Omega Dawn / A Ringing In Their Ears / Golden Age / Alpha Sunset / Slit Blood / Raw War / Reflections / Jezebel's Tribulation / Wraeththu
PAST AND PRESENT, Castle Showcase SHCD 163 (1987)
ANTHOLOGY OF BOOTLEGS, Nostradamus NOS 1006 CD (1988)
Awake At The Wall / Sleepwalk / Theatre Of Pain / Cavity / First Communion / The Blue Hour / When I Was Bed / Birth / Coming Forth By Day / This Glass House / The Drowning / Cervix Couch / Figura Five Theatre / Untitled (Followed By Crowd Chaos)
ASHES, Normal NORMAL 15 (1988)
Ashes (Part 1 & 2) / When I Was Bed / Lament (Over The Shadows) / Face / The Luxury Of Tears / Of The Wound
THE WIND KISSED PICTURES (PAST AND PRESENT), Supporti Fonografici SF 003 (1988) (Italian release)
Believers Of The Unpure / Ouverture / The Wind Kisses Pictures / The Lake Of Fire / Blast Of Bough / Amaterasu / The Absoloute / Lacrima Christi / Lacrima Christ (Italian version)
ATROCITIES, Normal NORMAL CD 18 (1988)
Bastinado Silhouettes / Foaming Dogs With Whips Sharp Teeth / Polished Buttons / Pelting Cadaverous Flesh / Belladonna For You Now Blue Eyes / Shuddering Following The Slice / Orgasmic Flush With Scalpel In Hand / O The Soothing / Is Such Heedless Deliverance / Worship Ye Nearing Quietus
SEX, DRUGS AND JESUS CHRIST, Jungle FREUD CD 25 (1988)
This Is Heresy / Jesus Where's The Sugar / Wretched Mankind / Tragedy / The Third Antichrist / Erection / Ten Thousand Hundred Times / Incendiary Lover / Window Pain
THE HERETICS ALIVE, Jungle FREUDCD 29 (1989)
This Is Heresy / Wretched Mankind / Sick Of Love / The Nascent Virion / Golden Age / Erection / Chimere De Si De La / Four Horsemen / Church Of No Return
THE IRON MASK, Cleopatra CLEO 57512 (1989)
Spiritual Cramp / Sleepwalk / Skeleton Kiss / Figurative Theatre / Desperate Hell / Deathwish / Luxury Of Tears / Cervix Couch / Skeleton Kiss (Death mix) / Down In The Park (Live)

PART 1: ALL THE LOVE (ALL THE LOVE, ALL THE HATE), Jungle FREUDCD 33 (1989)
Live Love Together / We Fall In Love / Love Don't Let Me Down / Suivre La Trace De Quelqu'un / Love Is Like A (B)Itchin' In My Heart / I'm Using You (For Love) / Deviate Love / Angel / Woman To Mother Earth
PART 2: ALL THE LOVE (ALL THE LOVE, ALL THE HATE), Jungle FREUDCD 34 (1989)
Born In A Womb, Died In A Tomb / Baptized In Fire / I Hate You / Children Of The Valley / Kneel Down / Climate Of Violence: Part 1 - The Relinquishment, Part 2 - The Satanic Verses (Rushdie's Lament), Part 3 - A Malice Of Prejudice / The Final Solution / Nazi Killer / Man To Father Fire
INSANUS, ULTIO, PRODITO, MISERICORDIAQUE, Jungle FREUD CD 48 (1991)
Sevan Au Rex / Malus Amor / Tragicus Conatus / Infans Vexatio / Somnium / Venenum / Mors Voluntaria / Vita Voluntaria
JESUS POINTS THE BONE AT YOU, Jungle FREUD CD 39 (1992)
Believers Of The Unpure / After The Rain / Sick Of Love / The Loving Face / Church Of No Return / Church Of No Return (Endured version) / What's The Verdict / This Is Heresy / Zero Sex / The Nascent Virion (New version) / We Fall In Love / I Hate You
LOVE AND HATE, Jungle FREUDBX 334 (1992)
LIVE IN HOLLYWOOD, Contemp CONTE 138 (1993)
TALES OF INNOCENCE: A CONTINUED ANTHOLOGY, Cleopatra CLEO 91092 (1993)
The Golden Age / Will O' The Wisp / Strange Fortune / The Wind Kissed Pictures / Between Youth / Believers Of The Unpure / Lament (Over The Shadows) / Face / Lullaby / Tales Of Innocence / Jezebel's Tribulation / Look At The Light… / Gloomy Sunday / Ventriloquist
SLEEPLESS NIGHTS LIVE 1990, Cleopatra 7209 (1993)
Cavity - First Communion / Figurative Theatre / Burnt Offerings / Do Do / Mysterium Iniquitatis / Dream for Mother / Stairs (Uncertain Journey)- Trials / Spiritual Cramp / Romeo's Distress / Resurrection - 6th Communion / Deathwish / Sleepwalk
THE RAGE OF ANGELS, Cleopatra CLEO 81252 (1994)
Trust (The Sacred And Unclean) / Lost Minds / Still Born: Still Life Part I / Sex / Her Only Sin / Bad Year / Torch Song / Still Born: Still Life, Part II (The Unknown Men) / Procession / Panic In Detroit
THE DOLL'S THEATRE - LIVE, Cleopatra

87

CLEO 62082 (1994)
Birth/Death / Cavity / Spiritual Cramp /
Desperate Hell / Deathwish / Skeleton Kiss /
Dream For Mother / Burnt Offerings /
Resurrection / Figurative Theatre / Romeo's
Distress / Dogs
SEXY DEATH GOD, Bulletproof VEST 26
(1994)
At The Threshold / Kingdom Of The Tainted
Kiss / Heresy Act Two / Damn You / Into Dust
/ Eternal Love/ The Serpent's Tail / Kingdom
Of The Solemn Kiss / Temples Of Desire /
Deeply, Deeply / Drilling The Hole / Up On
The Sea Of Blood / Eyelids Down / Invitation
Au Suicide
AMEN, Century Media CD 77107-2 (1995)
Prelude / Prologomemenon / The Nascent
Virion / Damn You / Into Dust / Sick Of Love /
Drilling The Hole / The Serpent's Trail /
Wretched Mankind / Kingdom Of The Tainted
Kiss / Children Of The Volley
**ICONOLOGIA: DREAMS, APPARITIONS
AND NIGHTMARES**, Triple X 51164-2
(1994)
Excommunicamus / Cavity - First
Communion / Figurative Theatre / Cry Baby /
Dream For Mother / Deathwish / Some Men
- The Other / Mysterium Iniquitatis / Kill Your
Sons / Stairs (Uncertain Journey) / Spiritual
Camp / Resurrection - 6th Communion /
Sleepwalk / Romeo's Distress / Dogs
THE PROPHECIES, Jungle FREUD CD 053
(1996)
Without / Is This The Will Of God / Alone /
The Great Swarm Of Bees / Into The
Shitworld / The Pig Half Man / Thunderstorm
/ The Black Ones / Black Empire / Nineteen
Ninety Nine
DEATH IN DETROIT - REMIXES, Cleopatra
CLEO 9591CD (1996)
Panic In Detroit (Numb mix) / Panic In
Detroit 1.1 (Whatever) (Rosetta Stone mix) /
Figurative Theater (Die Krupps mix) / Panic
In Detroit (Turning In His Grave) (Spahn
Ranch mix) / Venus In Furs (Claus Larsen -
Leaetherstrip mix) / Skeleton Kiss (Noise
Box mix) / Panic In Detroit (Zero Gravity mix)
/ Spiritual Cramp (Symptom Reversal)
(Joseph Biashara mix)
PORNOGRAPHIC MESSIAH, Trinity TRI
006CD (1998)
Devine Manifestations: The Great
Deception... The Corruption Of Innocence /
Devine Manifestations: The Great
Deception... The Dissention Of Faith / Devine
Manifestations: The Great Deception... The
Origin Of Man / Devine Manifestations: The
Great Deception... The Lie Behind The Truth
/ Devine Manifestations: The Great
Deception... The Millennium Unwinds /
Devine Manifestations: The Great
Deception... Weave My Spell / Dissent And

Decadence: Washing Machine / Dissent And
Decadence: Sex Dwarf / Dissent And
Decadence: Does It Hurt / Dissent And
Decadence: The Obscene Kiss / Dissent
And Decadence: Out Of Control / Philtre Of
Death: Cave Of The Unborn / Philtre Of
Death: Die With You / Philtre Of Death: She
Never Woke Up / Philtre Of Death: Pillars Of
Osiris / Philtre Of Death: Spontaneous
Human Detonation
THE PATH OF SORROWS, Cleopatra 3993
(1998)
Psalm / The Path Of Sorrows / Hour Of The
Wolf / In Absentia / Mother / The Angels /
Book Of Tears / A Widows Dream / Easter /
Venus In Furs
THE BIBLE, Candlelight 27 (2000)
Cavity - First Communion (Live) / Sleepwalk
(Live) / Ashes, Pt. 2 / Strange Fortune /
Alpha Sunset / This Is Heresy / Zero Sex
(Live) / The Nascent Virion / Malus Amor /
The Serpent's Tail / Pig Half Man / Washing
Machine
BORN AGAIN ANTI CHRISTIAN,
Candlelight CANDLE 045CD (2000)
Betrayal / Zodiac (He Is Still Out There ...) /
In Your Eyes / The Knife / Peek A Boo /
Superstition And Fear / Dead Sorry /
Malevolent Shrew / Blood Dance / Fucking In
Slow Motion / The Painted Aura / Kill Me /
Peek A Boo (Cradle Of Filth version)

CHURCH OF MISERY (JAPAN)
Line-Up: Yoshiaki Negishi (vocals), Tomohiro
Nishimura (guitar), Tatsu Mikami (bass), Junji
Narita (drums)

A respected '70s rooted Doom band founded
in 1996 by bassist Tatsu Mikami, an ex-
member of Thrash Metal band SALEM, and
guitarist Tomohiro Nishimura. Making up the
band numbers would be singer Nobukazu
Chow and drummer Hideki Shimizu.
CHURCH OF MISERY dwell lyrically almost
obsessively on the subject of serial killers but
show their obvious debt of gratitude to '70s
Rock with frequent cover versions. Apparently
the band has made a solemn vow never to
defile their 'Sanctuary' by attempting a
BLACK SABBATH cover version!
Three tracks were donated to the all
Japanese compilation album 'Doomsday
Recitation' issued by Cornucopia Records
during January of 1998. However, many fans
of the band abroad would be fooled into
purchasing 'Volume 1', a 1997 release
through Doom Records culled from a 1996
Tokyo show and including a cover of GUN's
'Race With The Devil'. The album was
projected to be an official release but then
shelved, the Doom Records version being a
bootleg.

CHURCH OF MISERY recorded a split CD with 'Born Too Late' Canadians SHEAVY, the sleeve of which depicted the notorious 'Nightstalker' killer Richard Ramirez, which reaped further international exposure. The band included their version of 'War Is Our Destiny' by ST. VITUS and the album cover artwork also spoofed BLACK SABBATH's 'Born Again'.

The same year CHURCH OF MISERY weighed in with the 'Taste The Pain' EP through Bad Acid Records. As well as three tracks chronicling the exploits of infamous serial killers - 'Room 213' Jeffrey Dahmer, 'Taste The Pain' Graham Young and 'Plainfield' Ed Gein, the band topped off the whole affair with a rendition of IRON BUTTERFLY's seminal 'In-A-Gadda-Da-Vida'. A further split release arrived in the form of a shared album with Nottingham's short-lived but influential IRON MONKEY. A split live tape also emerged, 'Live From The East' in alliance with fellow Japanese Doomsters MILLARCA. CHURCH OF MISERY contributed 'Sick Of Living (Zodiac)' to the 'Stone Deaf Forever' compilation album. The band has also laid down covers by DEATH SS, TROUBLE and BLACK WIDOW for tribute albums.

The band signed to Southern Lord Records for the February 2001 'Master Of Brutality' release, this album witnessing new members vocalist Yoshiaki Negishi and drummer Junji Narita. Another '70s cover version was naturally the order of the day for this release, CHURCH OF MISERY tackling BLUE OYSTER CULT's 'Cities On Flame'. Typically the remainder of the songs were devoted to mass murderers such as John Wayne Gacy, Herbery Mullin, Peter Sutcliffe, Ed Kemper and the Green River killer.

CHURCH OF MISERY members operate various sidelines. Both Mikami and Negishi are members of Hardcore Rock n' Roll act G.A.T.E.S. in collusion with Masahiro Futatsugi, guitarist with Crustcore band LIFE and ex-SLOGG drummer Fukawa. Another project of Mikami's is SONIC FLOWER, a '70s influenced Hard Rock band featuring BUCKET-T drummer Katarao. The bassist has also teamed up with Industrial band LONG DREAM DEAD. Negishi also busies himself with COFFINS, a side band featuring members of Sludgers DOT(.).

Singles/EPs:
Room 213 / Taste The Pain / Plainfield / In-A-Gadda-Da-Vida, Bad Acid TRIP4 (1998) ('Taste The Pain' EP)
Murder Company / Son Of A Gun, Man's Ruin MR 131 (1998) (10" single)

Albums:
BORN TOO LATE, Game Two GT-09 (1998) (Split CD with SHEAVY)
Spahn Ranch / Road To Ruin / Reverend / War Is Our Destiny
MURDER COMPANY, Man's Ruin MR 132CD (1998) (Split CD with IRON MONKEY)
Murder Company / Son Of A Gun / Where Evil Dwells
MASTER OF BRUTALITY, Southern Lord (2001)
Killfornia / Ripping Into Pieces / Megalomania / Green River / Cities On Flame / Master Of Brutality

CLENCH (ITALY)

Albums:
CLENCH (2001)
Different Worlds / Vida Perdida / Three Palms Way / Disorder / Heavy Sand / XXX Song / Rollin' / Hate / Break / Ace / Deep Inside / Slowsdonjo Song / Spacedustwave

CLOSET MONSTER (USA)
Line-Up: Jon Koopman (vocals, keyboards), Mike Dresch (guitar), Mike Pennock (guitar), Brian Masek (bass), Jeff Koller (drums)

Albums:
WHAT'S INSIDE TRIXIE'S CLOSET? Q Systems QS1A44897 (1996)
The Way It Has To Be / Wait For No One / Low / Ram It / No Time / Time Will Tell Its Tale / Running Blind / Box Of Clues / Lost / Every Roll Will Rock / Someday

CLUTCH (VA, USA)
Line-Up: Neil Fallon (vocals), Tim Sult (guitar), Dan Maines (bass), Jean-Paul Gaster (drums)

Purveyors of minimalist Stoner Rock. The highly influential CLUTCH came together in Germantown, Maryland, performing an inaugural gig during August 1991. Initially the band, just out of high school, pursued a Hardcore inclined path, evident on their 1992 debut 7" single 'Pitchfork' issued on the Inner Journey label.

Scoring a major label deal with East West Records CLUTCH released the full-length debut, Transnational Speedway League - Anthems, Anecdotes And Undeniable Truths', the following year. The eponymous 'Clutch' arrived in 1995. Touring would be prolific and included a valuable run of dates in February and March of 1997 opening for PANTERA. Although the band's promise was great a switch to another label was made to

Columbia. 1998's 'The Elephant Riders' found CLUTCH in a more reflective, rootsier mood, setting the pace for future product. CLUTCH would remain on the road for much of the year opening with a package bill in alliance with LIMP BIZKIT and SEVENDUST throughout February, March and into April dubbed the 'Ladies Night In Cambodia' tour. An interim batch of headliners led to special guest status for SLAYER and SYSTEM OF A DOWN in May and June upfront of a lengthy schedule opening for the PHUNK JUNKEEZ in July. European dates in September had the band hooked up with FEAR FACTORY and the DEFTONES and a return to the States witnessed an October four band union of CLUTCH, ULTRASPANK, SEVENDUST and STUCK MOJO

'Jam Room', a 1999 effort, would surface on the band's own River Road imprint before being picked up by the Spitfire label. Roadwork saw CLUTCH engaging in a series of U.S. headliners with DROWN as guests in February. The band would guest for IRON MAIDEN in America prior to December gigs alongside SIXTY WATT SHAMEN and support THERAPY? in Europe during 2000 prior to American dates supporting CORROSION OF CONFORMITY.

The band would elevate their status to such a renewed level that Atlantic Records duly resigned them for a 2001 Uncle Punchy produced record 'Pure Rock Fury'. The album closed with a live rendition of 'Space Grass', originally featured on their 1995 'Clutch' opus. A whole host of special guests made their presence felt including DOG EAT DOG percussionist Heartbeat, Wino of SPIRIT CARAVAN, the renowned guitarist LESLIE WEST of MOUNTAIN and personnel from SIXTY WATT SHAMEN. In by now traditional fashion CLUTCH embarked upon a gruelling series of live dates heading up a U.S. schedule in the Spring with strong support from VISION OF DISORDER, MURPHY'S LAW and TREE. The band would revisit Europe in June before returning to America for July gigs in alliance with CANDIRIA and BELLEVUE and shows the following month with SIX. By November the band would still be out on the live circuit, on tour with BIOHAZARD, CANDIRIA and PRIMER 55.

2002 would see little let up in the pace, CLUTCH co-headlining UK gigs in January with RAGING SPEEDHORN and an opening cast of CANDIRIA and LANDMINE SPRING. Support gigs to SYSTEM OF A DOWN in America then ensued upfront of summer headliners backed by GINATA PINATA, the SUPLECS and ALABAMA THUNDER PUSSY. August saw a return to the UK for just 4 gigs would be supported by THROAT. Neil

Fallon made his presence felt on the HENRY ROLLINS assembled 'West Memphis Three' benefit album 'Rise Above', lending lead vocals to a version of BLACK FLAG's 'American Waste'.

Sult, Maines and Gastor also operate the side act THE BAKERTON GROUP.

Singles/EPs:
Pitchfork, Inner Journey (1991)
Passive Restraints / Impetus / High Calibre Consecrator, Earache MOSH 074 CD (1992) ('Passive Restraints' EP)

Albums:
TRANSNATIONAL SPEEDWAY LEAGUE - ANTHEMS, ANECDOTES AND UNDENIABLE TRUTHS, East West 7567 92281-2 (1993)
A Shotgun Named Marcus / El Jefe Speaks / Binge And Purge / 12 Ounce Epilogue / Bacchanal / Milk Of Human Kindness / Rats / Earthworm / Heirloom 13 / Walking In The Great Shining Path Of Monster Trucks / Effigy
CLUTCH, Atlantic 7559 61755-2 (1995)
Big News 1 & 2 / Texan Book Of The Dead / Space Grass / Tight Like That / Droid / 7 Jam / The House That Peter Built / Tim Sult Vs. The Greys / Animal Farm / I Have The Body Of John Wilkes Booth / Escape From The Prison Planet / Rock n' Roll Outlaw
THE ELEPHANT RIDERS, Columbia (1998)
The Elephant Riders / Ship Of Gold / Eight Times Over Miss October / The Soapmakers / The Yeti / Muchas Veces / Green Buckets / Wishbone / Crackerjack / The Dragonfly
JAM ROOM, Spitfire SPTCD061 (2000)
Who Wants To Rock? / Big Fat Pig / Going To Market / One Eye Dollar / Raised By Horses / Bertha's Big Back Yard / Gnome Enthusiast / Swamp Boot Upside Down / Basket Of Eggs / Release The Kraken / Super Duper / Release The Dub
PURE ROCK FURY, Atlantic (2001)
American Sleep / Pure Rock Fury / Open Up The Border / Careful With That Mic... / Red Horse Rainbow / The Great Outdoors! / Smoke Banshee / Frankenstein / Sinkemlow / Immortal / Brazenhead / Drink To The Dead / Spacegrass (Live)

COLD MOURNING (CA, USA)
Line-Up: Matt (vocals / guitar), Angelo (guitar), Bruce (bass), U.A. (drums)

Retro Doom mongers created as far back as 1986 going under the name of CREMATION. morphing into COLD MOURNING as their music became drudgier and more sloth like in 1992. A demo cassette 'Looking Forward To

COLD MOURNING
Photo : El Danno

Reason' emerged in 1994.
A split record was issued in collusion with Dutch Doomsters OFFICIUM TRISTE. 1998 also saw a shared 7" single with WHILE HEAVEN WEPT for the Game Two label. COLD MOURNING also donated 'Boggy Creek' from their 1996 demo session to the Doom compilation 'At The Mountains Of Madness'.

Long term drummer Brad Burchell would depart the ranks although not in the upfront manner his band mates would have liked. COLD MOURNING discovered their sticksman had decamped when they saw his drum kit for sale in a local music store!

Singles/EPs:
Boggy Creek, Game Two (1998) (7" split single with WHILE HEAVEN WEPT)
Fall Of Life / In The Midst Of Stone, Weeping Willow (1998) (Split single with OFFICIUM TRISTE)

Albums:
LOWER THAN LOW, Game Two (2000)
Catacomb / Losing My Shadow / Lower Than Low / ST-321 / Seductive Embrace / The Fog / Great Bison / Possibility Of Life's Destruction / Monumental Desolation / Looking Forward / Iceland

CONFESSOR (NC, USA)
Line-Up: Scott (vocals), Stephen Shelton (drums)

North Carolina based Doom Metal band CONFESSOR emerged from a variety of high school outfits, who signed to British label Earache, releasing the 'Condemned' album after the track 'Uncontrolled' had found inclusion on British rivals Peaceville's 'Vile Vibes' compilation.
Scott would briefly front Texans WATCHTOWER during their final days in 1990.

Singles/EPs:
Condemned / Last Judgement / Endtime / Collapse... (Into Despair), Earache (1990) ('Confessor' EP)

Albums:
CONDEMNED, Earache (1991)
Alone / Prepare Yourself / Collapse Into Despair / Defining Madness / Uncontrolled / Condemned / Eve Of Salvation / The Stain / Suffer

CORE (NJ, USA)
Line-Up: Finn Ryan (vocals / guitar), Carmine Pernini (bass), Tim Ryan (drums)

Jazz based Stoners. CORE would score a deal with major label Atlantic Records for their 1996 Billy Anderson produced debut 'Revival'. Although CORE paid their dues with roadwork across America with the likes of FU MANCHU, CLUTCH and ORANGE 9MM the album would ultimately suffer from lacklustre promotion. Undaunted CORE cut a second Eric Rachel produced album, for the Tee Pee label. A further bout of touring saw CORE as part of the 'Riff Rock Railroad' tour packaged with THE ATOMIC BITCHWAX and NEBULA. CORE would contribute their version of 'Soul Shaker' to the 2000 Small Stone Recordings AEROSMITH tribute album 'Right In The Nuts'.

Bassist Carmine Pernini also performs as part of the Jazz trio LUNAR CITY.

Albums:
REVIVAL, Atlantic (1996)
Way Down / Cleargod / Kiss The Sun / Sawdust / Shift / Earth / Mosquito Song / Liquid / Blacksand / Face
THE HUSTLE IS ON, Tee Pee (1999)
The Monolith Problem / Supernumber / LD 5 / Fleetwood / Sarah's Curious Accident / No. 5 in A Series / Vacuum Life / Square and Round / Skinny Legs And All / Bicycle And Tricycle / Edge City / Blues For Gus

CORROSION OF CONFORMITY (USA)

Line-Up: Pepper Keenan (vocals / guitar), Woody Weatherman (guitar), Mike Dean (bass), Jimmy Bower (drums)

CORROSION OF CONFORMITY may well justifiably lay claim to the title of America's first Crossover act. The band effortlessly blend riffs of extreme magnitude with infectious Hardcore. Over the years CORROSION OF CONFORMITY have developed through the Thrashcore delivered on their first two albums 'Eye For An Eye' and 'Animosity' up to latter works which find the band embraced by the Stoner Sludgecore community. Originally a trio titled NO LABELS the band was forged in 1982 by vocalist / bassist Mike Dean, guitarist Woody Weatherman and drummer Reed Mullin. The band augmented their line-up with lead vocalist Eric Eyke for first album 'Eye For An Eye' in 1984, an album that was later re-released by Caroline during 1990.

With 'Animosity' in 1985 the band veered more towards straight Metal territory. However, the same year saw the departure of Dean and the band pulled in former UGLY AMERICANS singer Bob Sinister for the 'Technocracy' mini-album as the band, benefiting from the global upsurge of interest in Thrash, were now propelled to front runner status.

Sinister had left the fold by 1988 and CORROSION OF CONFORMITY were effectively put on ice until May 1989 when activity resumed with the addition of ex-SEIZURE / SCHOOL OF VIOLENCE frontman Karl Agell. During the interim a six track EP 'Six Songs With Mike Singing' was released to fulfill contractual obligations as Dean and guitarist Woody Weatherman created project band SNAKE NATION releasing an album.

Although without a contract for a lengthy period CORROSION OF CONFORMITY, now with bassist Phil Swisher, still kept up the live work touring with DIRTY ROTTEN IMBECILES, DANZIG, SOUNDGARDEN and BAD BRAINS. The band added second guitarist Pepper Keenan upfront of the 1991 album but recording of 'Blind' was delayed as Keenan recovered from a broken hip sustained whilst stagediving!

With the album release the band set about a club tour of America with support from PRONG and BULLET LAVOLTA. These dates were to trigger a world tour that would last a gruelling two years and after which vocalist Karl Agell was asked to leave following a New York show with TROUBLE, thus prompting the departure of Swisher. The departing duo would later create LEADFOOT releasing the 1997 album 'Bring It On'.

Christmas 1991 bore witness to a bout of recording between Keenan and an old friend PANTERA vocalist Phil Anselmo. The project, titled DOWN, was later to see a CD release that broke out of the usual cult appeal of side ventures into mainstream chart action.

The 1994 album 'Deliverance', with Keenan now lead vocalist, saw the return of Dean to the bass role from his interim act SPORE as the band embarked on an American tour with support from KEPONE. The band's sound had shifted once more even echoing the vintage Southern sound and twin guitar harmonies.

CORROSION OF CONFORMITY also opened the 1994 Castle Donington 'Monsters Of Rock' festival headlined by METALLICA.

Dean formed an alliance with BRUTAL TRUTH's Rich Hoak to give birth to a 1996 side project act titled NINEFINGER, an album being released the following year.

With renewed interest in the band Columbia instructed the act to adopt more commercial leanings before funding further product. The band delivered a batch of mellowed out Southern flavoured demos but found themselves dropped anyway.

CORROSION OF CONFORMITY toured America in 2000 backed up by strong support

CORROSION OF CONFORMITY
Photo : El Danno

from CLUTCH and SIXTY WATT SHAMAN. Mullin, suffering from back injuries, was replaced by EYEHATEGOD's Jimmy Bower.
As 2001 dawned it became apparent that Bower had taken the position permanently as Mullin departed to concentrate on his new career as a singer with Alternative Rock act BROWN. The band would support PANTERA on their Australian shows in April of 2001, announcing too that they had signed up with the new Sanctuary Records concern. The first results of this collaboration came in August with the issue of the band's debut live effort 'Live Volume', recorded at Harpo's Concert Theatre gig in Detroit on April 20th.
For recording of a fresh studio album in mid 2002 CORROSION OF CONFORMITY pulled in new drummer Merritt Partridge as Jimmy Bower was fully booked with projects such as DOWN, EYEHATEGOD and SUPERJOINT RITUAL. Yet another side venture also grew up during this period with Woody Weatherman, Mike Dean and Merritt Partridge involving themselves with LET' LONES.

Singles/EPs:
Eye For An Eye / Center Of The World / Citizen / Not For Me / What? / Negative Outlook, Product Inc. INCCD 002/3 (1988) ('Six songs with Mike singing' EP)

Vote With A Bullet / Condition A, Condition B / Future-Now / Break The Circle / Jim Beam And Coon Ass, Roadrunner RR 23886 (1992)

Albums:
EYE FOR AN EYE, Southern Studios (1984)
Tell Me / Minds Are Controlled / Indifferent / Broken Will / Rabid Dogs / L.S. / Redneckkk / Co-exist / Excluded / Dark Thoughts / Poison Planet / What? / Negative Outlook / Positive Outlook / No Drunk / College Town / Not Safe / Eye For An Eye / Nothing's Gonna Change
ANIMOSITY, Metal Blade ZORRO 44 (1985)
Loss For Words / Mad World / Consumed / Holier / Positive Outlook / Prayer / Intervention / Kiss Of Death / Hungry Child / Animosity
TECHNOCRACY, Metal Blade ZORRO53 (1987)
Technocrazy / Hungry Child / Happily Ever After / Crawling / Ahh Blugh
BLIND, Roadracer RO 9236-2 (1991)
These Shrouded Temples... / Damned For All Time / The Dance Of The Dead / Buried / Break The Circle / Painted Smiling Face / Mine Are The Eyes Of God / Shallow Ground / Vote With A Bullet / Great Purification / White Noise / Echoes In The Well / ....Remain

93

DELIVERANCE, Columbia 477683-2 (1994)
Heaven's Not Overflowing / Albatross / Clean My Wounds / Without Wings / Broken Man / Senor Limpio / Man De Mono / Seven Days / No. 2121313 / My Grain / Deliverance / Shale Like You / Shelter / Pearls Before Swine
WISEBLOOD, Columbia 484328-2 (1996) **43 UK**
King Of The Rotten / Longwhip - Big America / Wiseblood / Goodbye Windows / Born Again For The Last Time / Drowning In A Daydream / The Snake Has No Head / The Door / Man Or Ash / Redemption City / Wishbone (Some Tomorrow) / Fuel / Bottom Feeder (El Que Come Abajo)
AMERICA'S VOLUME DEALER, Sanctuary (2000)
Over Me / Congratulations Song / Stare Too Long / Diablo Blvd. / Doublewide / Zippo / Who's Got The Fire / Sleeping Martyr / Take What You Want / 13 Angels / Gettin' It On
LIVE VOLUME, Sanctuary (2001)
These Shrouded Temples / Diablo Blvd. / Senor Limpio / King Of The Rotten / Wiseblood / Who's Got The Fire / Albatross / My Grain / Congratulations Song / 13 Angels - 7 Days / Vote With A Bullet / Zippo / Long Whip - Big America / Shelter / Clean My Wounds

COUNT RAVEN (SWEDEN)

Line-Up: Christian Linderson (vocals), Dan Fondelius (guitar), Tommy Eriksson (bass), Christer Pettersson (drums)

Formed in 1987 as STORMVARNING, vocalist Christian Linderson would quit in 1992, having recorded the 'Storm Warning' album, to join American Doomsters ST. VITUS, necessitating COUNT RAVEN to trim down to a trio with Fondelius adopting lead vocals.
Once stabilized the Swedes recorded their second album, 'Destruction Of The Void', in 1993. The band managed to tour Britain the following summer with support from fellow Hellhound stablemates YEAR ZERO and SOLSTICE, rounding out a year in which third album 'High On Infinity' emerged, by opening for RAVEN in Germany.
Interestingly, 1995's 'Messiah Of Confusion' found COUNT RAVEN throwing caution to the wind, along with any sense of originality, by becoming complete and unashamed BLACK SABBATH soundalikes!
COUNT RAVEN folded in 1999 with Fondelius creating DOOMSDAY GOVERNMENT. Meantime Linderson re-emerged with a new act TERRA FIRMA created with ex-UNLEASHED guitarist Fredrik Lindgren. In 2001 Tommy Eriksson

emerged from retirement founding another Doom vehicle entitled SEMLAH.

Albums:
STORM WARNING, Hellhound H0009.2 (1991)
Count Raven / Inam Naudeminba / True Revelation / In The Name Of Rock n' Roll / Sometimes A Great Nation / Within The Garden Of Mirrors / Devastating Age / How Can It Be / Social Warfare
DESTRUCTION OF THE VOID, Hellhound HELL019.2 (1993)
Until Death Us Do Part / Hippies Triumph / Destruction Of The Void / Let The Dead Bury The Dead / Northern Lights / Leaving The Warzone / Angel Of Death / The Final Journey / No Ones Hero / Europa
HIGH ON INFINITY, Hellhound H0026-2 (1994)
Jen / Children's Holocaust / In Honour / Madman From Waco / Masters Of All Evil / Ode To Rebecca / High On Infinity / An Ordinary Loser / Traitor / The Dance / The Coming / Lost World / Cosmos
MESSIAH OF CONFUSION, Hellhound H0042-2 (1995)
Prediction / Shadow Box / The Loneliest One / Fallen Angels / Mountains Spirit / The Lies Of Life / P.S.I. Power / Shine / The Divided World / The Viking Sea

COVENANT (SWEDEN)

Line-Up: Eskil Simonsson (vocals / keyboards), Joakim Montelius (samples), Clas Nachmanson (keyboards)

A Helsingborg based Darkwave Electronic act that deliver droning, morose yet danceable music. COVENANT are much favoured upon the Gothic scene. The band came into being during the mid '80s, persevering through a turbulent history of line-up changes before settling on the trio of vocalist Eskil Simonsson, sampler Joakim Montelius and keyboard player Clas Nachmanson in 1991. This triumvirate issued a demo, 'Dreams From The Crotank', the same year securing a record deal. The Swedish Memento Material label asked the band to provide a track for their compilation album 'Autumn Leaves' and the resulting media appreciation afforded COVENANT's inclusion of 'Replicant' led to a full-blown album deal. The debut record, also called 'Dreams From The Cryotank', emerged in 1994.
The 'Figurehead' EP solidified their rise and album number two, 'Sequencer' released in 1996, prompted a European tour packaged with HAUJOBB and STERIL. Following these dates COVENANT issued the 'Stalker' single

which secured a lengthy grip on the club scene. 1997 witnessed headline shows in America and Europe as well as special guest slots to RAMMSTEIN in their homeland of Sweden. The 'Final Man' EP preceded a third album 'Europa' and another round of global touring across Scandinavia, Western Europe, USA and Canada. Confusion amongst distributors would then ensue as a Norwegian band, a high profile act comprising figures from leading Black Metal bands, issued an album 'Nexus Polaris' also billed as COVENANT. This act eventually adopted a new title of THE KOVENANT.

COVENANT would spend the early part of 1999 engaged in touring Germany as opening act for PROJECT PITCHFORK, prior to entering the studio for sessions resulting in the 'United States Of Mind' album. The recording schedule would be interrupted to perform at a series of summer festivals including 'Roskilde' in Denmark and the German 'Zillo' and 'Wave Gotik Treffen' events.

Singles/EPs:
Final Man / Final Man (Club version) / Control / Sample Start, Synthetic (1998)
Go Film (Hard version) / Go Film (Soft version) / Consumer / Tension (Club version) / Go Film (Disco Calculi) / Tension (Disco Calculi) / Tension (Old Skool edit), Synthetic (1998) ('Euro' EP)
Theramin EP, Metropolis (1999)
Tour De Force, (1999)
Der Leiermann (Radio edit) / Der Leiermann (Club version) / We Break Down / Like Tears In Rain, Mindbase (2000)
Dead Stars (Radio version) / Dead Stars (Club version) / We Break Down / Dead Stars (J. Cosmo Dub mix), Mindbase (2000)

Albums:
DREAMS OF A CRYOTANK, Memento Material (1994)
Theramin / Replicant / Shipwreck / Void / Hardware Requiem / Shelter / Wasteland / Voices / Edge Of Dawn / Speed / Cryotank Expansion
SEQUENCER, (1996)
Sequencer / Feedback / Stalker / Figurehead / Phoenix / Slowmotion / Tabula-Rasa / Storm / Luminal / Flux
EUROPA, (1998)
Tension / Leviathan / 2 D / Wind Of The North / Riot / I Am / Final Man (version) / Go Film / Wall Of Sound
UNITED STATES OF MIND, Mindbase (2000)
Like Tears In The Rain / No Man's Land / Afterhours / Helicopter / Tour De Force /

Unforgiven / Humility / Dead Stars (version) / One World One Sky / Still Life / You Can Make Your Own Music
SYNERGY - LIVE IN EUROPE, Mindbase (2000)
Intro / Tour De Force / Feedback / Flux / Helicopter / Dead Stars / Go Film / Tabula Rasa / I Am / One World One Sky / Der Leiermann / Wall Of Sound / Stalker / Babel

CRADLE OF FILTH (UK)
Line-Up: Dani Filth (vocals), Gian Pyres (guitar), Paul Allender (guitar), Dave Pybus (bass), Martin Powell (keyboards), Adrian Erlandsson (drums)

Probably the foremost exponents of the British Black Metal scene. CRADLE OF FILTH have built their reputation on hard gigging and inventive albums all aided by an impressive merchandising campaign with a vast range of deliberately provocative, but still highly creative, T shirt slogans. Musically and lyrically CRADLE OF FILTH operate in majestic, obviously Gothic inspired realms.
CRADLE OF FILTH was created in Suffolk during 1991 by former PDA and FEAST ON EXCREMENT vocalist Dani Filth (real name Dani Lloyd Davey), guitarist Paul Ryan, bassist Jon Richard and drummer Darren. This inaugural line-up cut the opening demo 'Invoking The Unclean' in 1992, shortly after which second guitarist Robin Graves (real name Robin Mark Eaglestone - previously with MALICIOUS INTENT) was added. Further recordings were made titled 'Black Goddess Rises'.
A further demo 'Orgiastic Pleasures' ensued after which Jon Richard departed to create HECATE ENTHRONED, the band manouevering Graves to bass to plug the gap and drafting Paul Allender on second guitar and Benjamin Ryan on keyboards. It was to be the act's third demo, 'Total Fucking Darkness' issued in December of 1993, that really set the mould for future works and scored a deal with Cacophonous Records.
Former SOLEMN drummer Was Sarginson joined but lasted a handful of gigs.
The debut album, 1994's 'The Principle Of Evil Made Flesh', found the band with yet another new face as Nicholas took over the drumstool. The ructions did not stop there though as Paul Ryan, Benjamin Ryan and Paul Allender all bailed out. This CRADLE OF FILTH triumvirate of refugees formed THE BLOOD DIVINE with ex-ANATHEMA vocalist Darren White in late 1995.
Vowing to carry on Dani quickly filled the ranks with guitarists Stuart Anstis and Jared Demeter together with Darren Gregori on keyboards. (Rumours abounded that 'Jared

Demeter' was in actually Stuart Anstis).

The band's second album 'Vempire Or Dark Faerytales In Phallustein' was produced by ex-WITCHFINDER GENERAL and LIONSHEART bassist Zakk Bajjon and, in a trend which continues to this day, found the band utilizing two female backing vocalists Sarah Jezebel Deva (Sarah Jane Ferridge) and Danielle Cneajna Cottington.

Rishi Mehta was also a guitarist for CRADLE OF FILTH during 1994 but would unite with Benjamin Ryan and Zakk Bajjon to create CROWFOOT, then RAINMAKER 888 (later re-billed as ENEMYMAKER 888).

Just as media interest peaked on the Black Metal scene CRADLE OF FILTH found themselves embroiled for most of 1995 involved in legal proceedings against their record company. With the release of the 'Vempire' album CRADLE OF FILTH quickly established themselves as the leading contenders in the Death Metal stakes and signed up to a bigger label Music For Nations replacing (?) Demeter with former SOLSTICE and SHIP OF FOOLS man Gian Pyres (real name John Piras) in the process.

The 1996 album 'Dusk And Her Dark Embrace', produced by Kit Woolven - better known for his mellower work, propelled the band into the mainstream garnering high sales globally. Sarah Jezebel Deva once again featured and would become a staple part of the band's recording and live line-up.

In outside activities Graves created the side band DECEMBER MOON with former CRADLE OF FILTH drummer Was Sarginson for a 1996 album.

American ex-BRUTALITY guitarist Brian Hipp for live work in 1996. The band toured Europe in 1997 with dates in Austria supported by Doom merchants JACK FROST. Shortly after the band's appearance at the 1997 'Milwaukee Metalfest' they announced their new keyboard player as being erstwhile ANATHEMA and SHIP OF FOOLS member Lez Smith. Hipp would later be found as a member of DIABOLIC.

Barker was to depart in early 1999 to another high profile Black Metal outfit DIMMU BORGIR and appeared as part of the highly successful LOCK UP collaboration with HYPOCRISY's Peter Tägtgren, NAPALM DEATH's Shane Embury and Jesse Pintado. The ex-drummer would also figure on the notorious 'Mexican' Death Metal band BRUJERIA's 'Brujerizmo' album.

CRADLE OF FILTH meanwhile set to work on their next album title track, and accompanying first full-length video directed by Alex Chandon of 'Pervirella' fame, with the temporary employment of THE BLOOD DIVINE and DECEMBER MOON sticksman

Wes Sargison. An even more temporary drummer was Dave Hirschheimer of INFESTATION.

By the summer of the same year the band fractured once again with both Gian Pyres and Hirschheimer departing, the drum stool now being occupied by former AT THE GATES man Adrian Erlandsson. CRADLE undertook American festival dates with a stand in session guitarist.

Allender was brought back into the ranks in late 1999 from his post THE BLOOD DIVINE act PRIMARY SLAVE as the band line-up splintered once more with Pyres returning to the fold. The turbulence was far from complete however with keyboard player Les Smith and guitarist Stuart Anstis both given their marching orders. Anstis would create the electronic act APHELION.

With all this turbulence the 'From The Cradle To Enslave' EP emerged featuring new tracks plus covers of THE MISFITS 'Death Comes Ripping' and ANATHEMA's 'Sleepless'. Former keyboard player Damien Gregori rejoined the band for these sessions. Predictably his tenure was brief, the man's work only appearing on the American Metal Blade released version of the EP.

CRADLE OF FILTH pulled in former MY DYING BRIDE keyboard player Mark De Sade (real name Mark Newby Robson) but after a handful of gigs his place was taken by another erstwhile MY DYING BRIDE man Martin Powell.

Limited edition's of 2000's 'Midian' included a cover of SABBAT's 'For Those Who Died' with guest vocal from SABBAT and SKYCLAD vocalist Martin Walkyier. CRADLE OF FILTH toured Europe in late 2000 with guests veterans Gothics CHRISTIAN DEATH. There was a huge degree of fraternization between the two bands as members of CRADLE OF FILTH including ex-drummer Was Sarginson appeared on CHRISTIAN DEATH's 2000 album 'Born Again Anti Christian'. Pyres would also guest on the EXTREME NOISE TERROR album 'Being And Nothing'.

The CRADLE OF FILTH line-up for the 'Midian' album stood at Filth, Pyres, Allender, Graves, Powell and Erlandsson. Also involved in the project was actor Doug Bradley, famed for his role as the malevolent 'Pinhead' in the 'Hellraiser' movies, donating narrative parts. Full scale European touring took the band throughout November and December.

In the summer of 2001 the band would offer up their take on New York '80s Glamsters TWISTED SISTER's 'The Fire Still Burns' to the Koch tribute album 'Twisted And Strange'. CRADLE OF FILTH would assert their independence by creating their own imprint label AbraCadaver for release of the 'Bitter

Suites To Succubi' mini-album. This interim offering saw new material, including a sequel to 'The Black Goddess Rises', alongside reworkings of vintage cuts 'The Principle Of Evil Made Flesh' and 'Summer Dying Fast'.

Live work would comprise British and Japanese shows in April but then Robin 'Graves' Eaglsetone's position was relinquished to former DREAMWEAVER and ANATHEMA bassist Dave Pybus during June for the American leg of the tour. Eaglestone was announced as joining the expatriated Chilean Death Metal band CRIMINAL. U.S. shows for CRADLE OF FILTH had rising Death Metal band NILE alongside GOD FORBID as support.

CRADLE OF FILTH, stepping into the breech left by the withdrawal of American acts after the September 11th terrorist attacks, would also appear as last minute substitutes on the massive 'Tattoo The Planet' European tour. Shortly after it would be announced that the band had signed to major label Sony for future product. Meantime Music For Nations weighed in with a lavish retrospective compilation 'Lovecraft & Witch Hearts' comprising archive material, cover versions and remixes. Also released would be a monumental DVD package 'Heavy, Left Handed & Candid' centred upon concert footage from a Nottingham Rock City gig.

The band would appear at the world famous Castle Donington venue as part of the May 2002 OZZY OSBOURNE headlined 'Ozzfest' event. CRADLE OF FILTH put in a low key club gig at the Oxford Zodiac club, supported by Martin Walkyier's RETURN TO THE SABBAT, the night before 'Ozzfest' as a warm up.

Ex-CRADLE OF FILTH guitarist Stuart Anstis unveiled his new act BASTARDSUN, a union with Ross Adams, in July. That same month CRADLE OF FILTH unveiled details of their first official live album 'Live Bait For The Dead' set for September release. The bulk of the material was recorded live at Nottingham Rock City in April 2001. The double CD set also contained two more live tracks recorded during soundchecks, alongside studio remixes of tracks from 'Bitter Suites To Succubi'. Also featured would be an alternate mix of the SISTERS OF MERCY cover track 'No Time To Cry', a cover of TWISTED SISTER's 'The Fire Still Burns', a previously unavailable remix of 'From The Cradle To Enslave' and a studio demo of 'Scorched Earth Erotica'.

CRADLE OF FILTH entered Parkgate Studios in August to commence recording of the 'Damnation And A Day' album, a 17 track affair utilizing full orchestra and choir. However, longstanding member Gian Pyres

had made a break from the band before the end of the month, apparently in an amicable split over musical differences.

Singles/EPs:
From The Cradle To Enslave / Of Blood And Fucking / Death Comes Ripping / Sleepless, Music For Nations (1999)

Albums:
THE PRINCIPLE OF EVIL MADE FLESH, Cacophonous NIHL1CD (1994)
Darkness Our Bride (Jugular Wedding) / The Principle Of Evil Made Flesh / The Forest Whispers My Name / Iscariot / The Black Goddess Rises / One Final Graven Kiss / A Crescendo Of Passion Bleeding / To Eve The Art Of Witchcraft / Of Mist And Midnight Skies / In Secret Love We Drown / A Dream Of Wolves In The Snow / Summer Dying Fast

VEMPIRE, OR DARK PHAERY TALES IN PHALLUSTEIN, Cacophonous NIHIL6CD (1996)
Ebony Dressed For Summer / The Forest Whispers My Name / Queen Of Winter / Throned / Nocturnal Supremacy / She Mourns A Lengthening Shadow / The Rape And Ruin Of Angels

DUSK AND HER DARK EMBRACE - LITANIES OF DAMNATION, DEATH AND THE DARKLY EROTIC, Music For Nations MFN 208 (1996)
Humans Inspired To Nightmare / A Gothic Romance (Red Roses For The Devil's Whore) / Haunted Shores / Dusk And Her Dark Embrace / Heaven Torn Asunder / Carmilla's Masque (Portrait Of The Dead Countess) / Beauty Slept In Sodom / The Graveyard By Moonlight / Funeral In Carpathia

CRUELTY AND THE BEAST, Music For Nations (1998) **48 UK**
Once Upon Atrocity / Thirteen Autumns And A Widow / Cruelty Brought The Orchids / Beneath The Howling Stars / Venus In Fear / Desire In Violent Overture / The Twisted Nails Of Faith / Bathory Aria / Benighted Like Usher / A Murder Of Ravens In Fugue / Eyes That Witnessed Madness / Portrait Of The Dead Countess / Lustmord And Wargasm (The Lick Of Carnivorous Winds)

MIDIAN, Music For Nations (2000)
11 FINLAND, 30 GERMANY, 63 UK
At The Gates Of Midian / Cthuhlu Dawn / Saffron's Curse / Death Magick For Adepts / Lord Abortion / Amor E Morte / Creatures Kissed In Cold Mirrors / Her Ghost In The Fog / Satanic Mantra / Tearing The Veil From Grace / Tortured Soul Asylum / For Those Who Have Died

97

BITTER SUITES TO SUCCUBI, Spitfire 5207-2 (2001) **45 GERMANY**
Sin Deep My Wicked Angel / All Hope In Eclipse / Born In A Burial Gown / Summer Dying Fast / No Time To Cry / The Principle Of Evil Made Flesh / Suicide And Other Comforts / Dinner At Deviant's Palace / The Black Goddess Rises II - Ebon Nemesis / Scorched Earth Erotica
LOVECRAFT AND WITCHEARTS, Music For Nations (2002)
Creatures That Kissed In Cold Mirrors / Dusk & Her Embrace / Beneath The Howling Stars / Her Ghost In The Fog / Funeral In Carpathia (Be Quick Or Be Dead version) / The Twisted Nails Of Faith / From The Cradle To Enslave / Saffron's Curse / Malice Through The Looking Glass / Cruelty Brought Thee Orchids / Lord Abortion / Hell Awaits / Hallowed Be Thy Name / Once Upon Atrocity / Thirteen Autumns And A Widow / For Those Who Died (Return To The Sabbat mix) / Sodomy & Lust / Twisting Further Nails (Remix) / Amor E Morte / Carmilla's Masque / Lustmord And Wargasm (The Relicking Of Cadaverous Wounds) / Dawn Of Eternity / Of Dark Blood & Fucking / Dance Macabre (Remix)
LIVE BAIT FOR THE DEAD, AbraCadaver (2002)
Intro - The Ceremony Opens / Lord Abortion / Ebony Dressed For Sunset / The Forest Whispers My Name / Cthulhu Dawn / Dusk And Her Embrace / The Principle Of Evil Made Flesh / Cruelty Brought Thee Orchids / Her Ghost In The Fog / Summer Dying Fast / Interlude - Creatures That Kissed In Cold Mirrors / From The Cradle To Enslave / Queen Of Winter Throned / Born In A Burial Gown (The Polished Coffin mix) / No Time To Cry (Sisters Of No Mercy mix) / Funeral In Carpathia (Soundcheck recording) / Deleted Scenes Of A Snuff Princess / Scorched Earth Erotica (Original Demo(n) version) / Nocturnal Supremacy (Soundcheck recording) / From The Cradle To Enslave (Under Martian Rule mix) / The Fire Still Burns / No Time To Cry (Sisters Of No Mercy video)

CREEPMIME (UK / HOLLAND)
Line-Up: Rogier Hakkaart (vocals / guitar), Andy Judd (guitar), Mark Hope (bass), Frank Brama (drums)

CREEPMIME debuted with the 1992 demo 'Anthems For A Doomed Youth' and, having gained a deal with Mascot Records appeared with the 'Shadows' album (produced by Patrick Mameli of PESTILENCE) the following year.

Albums:
SHADOWS, Mascot M7006 2 (1993)
The Fruit Of III Virtue / A Serenade For The Tragic / Suffer The Shadows / The Way Of All Flesh / Chinese Whispers / Soon Ripe, Soon Rotten / Gather The Shattered / My Soul Flayed / Bare
CHIAROSCURO, Mascot M7015-2 (1996)
The Colours Still Unwinds / Scarlet Man / In The Flesh / Clarity / Diced / Chiaroscuro / Black Widower / Fools Paradise / King Of Misrule / Gods Thoughts

CREMATORY (GERMANY)
Line-Up: Gerhard Stass (vocals), Lothar Först (guitar), Harald Heine (bass), Katrin Goger (keyboards), Markus Jüllich (drums)

Noted exponents of Gothic Metal founded in 1991 by guitarist Lothar Först and drummer Markus Jüllich. The band's inaugural line-up was completed by former REBORN ANGEL vocalist Gerhard 'Felix' Stass, bassist Marc and female keyboard player Katrin Goger. CREMATORY's debut demo of early 1992, now featuring Heinz Steinhauser on bass, scored the band a deal with Massacre Records in November of that year. Upon the 'Transmigration' album's release in May 1993 the band undertook a short batch of headlining club shows prior to supports across Europe to MY DYING BRIDE.
Harold Heine supplanted Steinhauser as CREMATORY opted in future to pursue their music with only German lyrics. The 'Just Dreaming' album broke CREMATORY out into the mainstream audiences as promotional videos for 'In My Hands' and 'Shadows Of Mine' scored valuable regular rotation on both MTV and Viva television. Finding a valuable place as part of the 'Summer Metal Meetings' festivals CREMATORY toured Europe on a strong package also comprising TIAMAT, ICED EARTH, SAVATAGE, THE GATHERING, NEVERMORE, LAKE OF TEARS and RAGE. Subsequent gigging found the band on the road with TIAMAT and ATROCITY. The 'Illusions' album, sung totally in German, capitalised on this success. In March of 1996 CREMATORY took up the prestigious position of headlining the roving 'Out Of The Dark' festivals. With THE GATHERING and MOONSPELL acting as special guests the 'Out Of The Dark' events took the band outside of Germany into Holland and Belgium. Earlier in 1995 drummer Markus Jüllich, in alliance with vocalist Michael Rohr and keyboard player Gernot Leinert, summoned up an extracurricular project dubbed CENTURY. This group arrived on the scene in August of 1995 releasing the demo 'Lost'.

Quitting Massacre Records CREMATORY took the brave step of releasing the live album on their own label CRC ('Crematory's Record Company'), a gamble which paid off handsomely as CREMATORY scored a fresh deal with Nuclear Blast Records. The 'Awake' album gave CREMATORY their first chart placing, debuting in the German national listings at number 54. From this album the group launched a notable cover of THE SISTERS OF MERCY classic 'Temple Of Love' which made a lasting impact upon the Club scene.

1999's 'Act Seven', which featured new guitarist Matthias Hechler alongside contributions from DARK's Lisa Mosinski, CENTURY's Michael Rohr and GIANTS CAUSEWAY vocalist Kalle Friedrich, also charted. The preceding single 'Fly' would also fare well on the Club circuit. Former guitarist Lothar Först decamped to found SCULPTURE in union with DARKSEED and BETRAY MY SECRETS vocalist Stefan Hertrich and SODOM bassist Hans. Jüllich's CENTURY endeavour would also debut commercially brandishing the album 'The Secret Inside'. CENTURY would act as support band for CREMATORY's German tour in May and June of 1999. The band's former label Massacre got in on the act issuing the 'Early Years' compilation, noted for its addition of recent remixes by such artists as DAS ICH's Bruno Kramm and DJ God of CAMOUFLAGE.

Gerhard Stass launched a Death Metal inclined side venture AB:NORM in 2000, issuing the 'Inside' album. CREMATORY meantime put out the 'Believe' album in September 2000 which gave the band their highest chart placing to date. A celebration of the band's tenth anniversary was marked by a headline tour of Germany in February of 2001. In a move that surprised fans, especially bearing in mind the band's status, CREMATORY announced they were to fold. The group cited "personal health and financial" reasons for their decision and bowed out with a swan song festival gig at the 'Wacken Open Air' event. The live 'Remind' album was delivered as an epitaph.

The expected new band ventures did not materialise, instead the members pursued very un-Rock n' Roll pursuits with Markus Jüllich becoming an insurance salesman, Harald Heine worked as a carpenter and Katrin Goger as an office worker.

Singles/EPs:
Ist Es Wahr / Tears Of Time / Shadows Of Mine / Eyes Of Suffering, Massacre MASS CD 096 (1996) ('Ist Es Wahr EP)

Albums:
TRANSMIGRATION, Massacre MASSCD016 (1993)
Bequest Of The Wicked / Eyes Of Suffering / Deformity / Never Forgotten Place / Hall Of Torment / Reincarnation / Victims / Through My Soul / The way Behind The Light / Bequest Of The Hallow
... JUST DREAMING, Massacre MASSCD031 (1993)
Heaven's Throat / Transmigration / Only Once In A Lifetime / Shadows Of Mine / I Saw The Angels Fly / In My Hands / The Instruction / The Prophecy / Dreams / For Those Who Believe
ILLUSIONS, Massacre MASSCD 080 (1995)
Reflexionen / Faces / Tears Of Time / My Way / Lost In Myself / An Other? / The Atmosphere / The Beginning Of The End / Sweet Solitude / Dreams of Dancing / Just Dreaming / Visions
CREMATORY, Massacre MASSCD 092 (1996)
Utopia / Das Licht In Dir / Flieg Mit Mir / Ist Es Wahr / Ewigkeit / Trugbilder / Flammen / Die Suche / Illusionen / Sehnsucht
LIVE...AT THE OUT OF THE DARK FESTIVALS, CRC IRS 992.056 (1996)
Reflexionen / Deformity / Tears Of Time / Ewigkeit / Only Once In A Lifetime / Shadows Of Mine / Out Of The Dark / Lost In Myself / Dreams / Ist Es Wahr / Eyes Of Suffering / An Other... / The Beginning Of The End / Just Dreaming / Visions
AWAKE, Nuclear Blast 27361 62692 (1997) **54 GERMANY**
Maze/ Lord Of Lies / Away / Temple Of Love / For Love / Crematory / My Last Words / The Loss / Yourself / Mirror
ACT SEVEN, Nuclear Blast NB 110525 (1999) **46 GERMANY**
Shining / I Never Die / Moonlight / Fly / Memory / The Holy One / The Game / Waiting / Awake / Tale
THE EARLY YEARS, Massacre (1999)
Tears Of Time / Dreams / Ewigkeit / The Eyes Of Suffering / Lost In Myself / Shadows Of Mine / Ist Es Wahr / Through My Soul / Medley / Dreams (Deep Growl Mix) / Ist Es Wahr (Egomania Mix) / Tears Of Time (Dance Raymix) / Through My Soul (Lost Soul Mix) / Shadows Of Mine (Eternal Darkness Mix) / Ewigkeit (Staub Mix) / Lost In Myself (Trance Raymix) / The Eyes Of Suffering (House Of Pain Mix) / Megamix / In My Hands (Video) / Es ist wahr (Video) / Shadows Of Mine (Video)
BELIEVE, Nuclear Blast NB 509-2 (2000) **34 GERMANY**
Redemption Of Faith / Endless / The Fallen / Take / Act Seven / Time For Tears / Eternal / Unspoken / Caroline / The Curse / Why /

Perils Of The Wind
REMIND, Nuclear Blast (2001)
Tears Of Time (Deutsch version) / Fly (Single
version) / Do You Know / Welcome To … /
Engulfed In Darkness (Demo) / Face The
Unknown (Demo) / Prophecies Of… (Demo)
/ Bury All Life (Demo)

CRISIS (New York, NY, USA)
Line-Up: Karyn Crisis (vocals), Afzaal
Nasirudden (guitar), Gia Chuan Wang
(bass), Fred Waring (drums)

An eclectic New York Experimental Metal unit
fronted by the visually aggressive
dreadlocked persona of Karyn Crisis.
Founder and Pakistani born guitarist Afzaal
Nasirudden would induct Karyn Crisis into the
band despite the original bass player's
protestations at the prospect of a female
singer. With Crisis duly signed up Taiwanese
Gia Chuan Wang took the bass role. CRISIS
made their first statement of intent with the
1994 album '8 Convulsions'. Signing to the
Metal Blade label for the sophomore
'Deathshead Extermination' album CRISIS
completed a two month tour of America
during mid 1996, sharing a bill with PRO-
PAIN and VOIVOD despite original drummer
Fred Waring quitting to concentrate on his
family before the dates commenced. The
band hastily pulled in NAUSEA and THORN's
Roy Mayorga for a batch of shows before
drafting ex-GORGON man Scott Bates.
European dates had the band sharing stages
with the SPUDMONSTERS and KICKBACK
before a return U.S. road trip guesting for FU
MANCHU. Mayorga later joined SOULFLY,
PALE DEMONS and even had three weeks
with OZZY OSBOURNE.
Recording the 1997 album 'The Hollowing'
was aided by studio session drummers such
as Mayorga, DEADBOLT's Chris Hamilton,
Fred Waring III and former STIGMATA and
BURNING HUMAN man Jason Bittner, the
latter taking up a full time position with the
band. ACID BATH's Sammy Pierre Duet also
contributed as did FLOODGATE's Kyle and
SWANS Norman Westberg.
Splitting from Metal Blade Records the band
took to the road in earnest. CRISIS would
feature with the track 'Captain Howdy' on DEE
SNIDER's 'Strangeland' horror movie
soundtrack album and cut a new six track
Keith Falgout produced demo. In 1999 the
band added second guitarist Jwyanza Kaloji
Hobson of TOAD EATER and Tony Costanza
of MACHINE HEAD and SALVO repute took
over the drum mantle. Costanza would later
drift off joining high profile act Sludgers
CROWBAR.
Latterly the band, pulling in drummer

Christopher J. Olivas, has retitled itself
SKULLSICK NATION. By 2002 SKULLSICK
NATION would once again be working with
Roy Mayorga on new material. As session
guests both Crisis and Nasirudden would also
lend their talents to the DEBRIS INC. debut
record, the project band of TROUBLE's Ron
Holzner and ST. VITUS man Dave Chandler.

Albums:
8 CONVULSIONS, Too Damn Hype (1994)
There Goes My Soul / Sweething / Gemini /
More Than Down / Smash To Pieces /
Drilling Me / Rotten Anyway / Keep Me From
Falling
DEATHSHEAD EXTERMINATION, Metal
Blade (1996)
Working Out The Graves / Wretched / The
Watcher / Deadfall / Methodology /
Bloodlines / Nowhere But Lost / Different
Ways Of Decay / Prisoner Scavenger /
2 Minutes Hate
THE HOLLOWING, Metal Blade (1997)
Mechanical Man / In The Shadow Of The
Sun / Fires Of Sorrow / Vision And The
Verity / Kingdom's End / After The Flood /
Sleeping The Wicked / Surviving The Siren /
Take The Low Road / Discipline Of
Degradation / Come To Light

CROWBAR (New Orleans, LA, USA)
Line-Up: Kirk Windstein (vocals / guitar),
Sammy Piere Duet (guitar), Jeff Okoneski
(bass), Tony Costanzo (drums)

Among the foremost of the NOLA ('New
Orleans, LA') exponents. The super
heavyweight, both in terms of body mass and
sheer Metal density, CROWBAR deliver
detuned, lethargic Sludged out Metal with
Hardcore and Southern elements. Frontman
Kirk Windstein and drummer Jimmy Bower
were both previously members of covers act
THE SLUGS performing renditions of JUDAS
PRIEST and IRON MAIDEN songs. Although
both created CROWBAR, Bower departed to
become guitarist for EYEHATEGOD. An early
CROWBAR guitarist, Kevin Bond, would last
roughly a year and was later to be found with
THE DEMONSEEDS.
CROWBAR's debut, the 1991 album
'Obedience Thru Suffering' found the band
citing a line-up of Kirk Windstein on vocals
and guitar, Kevin Noonan on guitar, bassist
Todd Strange and drummer Craig
Nunenmacher. Shortly after recording
Noonan was supplanted by Matt Thomas,
coming from the ranks of another Louisiana
act FALL FROM GRACE in late 1993.
Thomas paid back the debt by producing
FALL FROM GRACE's eponymous debut

101

album in 1996.

CROWBAR's line-up remained stable over the subsequent two albums, 1993's eponymous outing and 1995's 'Time Heals Nothing'. Drummer Craig Nunenmacher later joined his brother, ex-LILLIAN AXE guitarist Stevie Blaze, in NEAR LIFE EXPERIENCE as CROWBAR returned with a 1996 album 'Broken Glass' with Jimmy Bower back on drums. The band signed up to new label Mayhem Records in 1998 entitled 'Odd Fellows Rest'. The line-up boasted Windstein, "Sammysatan" Pierre Duet on guitar, T "Godcreep" Strange on bass and Wicked Crickett (Jimmy Bower) on drums.

The 2000 album 'Equilibrium' includes a completely Sludged out cover version of the 1976 GARY WRIGHT hit 'Dreamweaver and an acapella take on IRON BUTTERFLY's leviathan 'In-A-Gadda-Da-Vida'. By this juncture CROWBAR's rhythm section comprised bassist Todd Strange and drummer Sid Montz. Following completion of American dates with S.O.D. Montz decamped and former member Craig Nunemacher resumed his position.

Windstein also busies himself with side projects, the most notorious of which is DOWN in union with PANTERA's Phil Anselmo and Rex Brown, CORROSION OF CONFORMITY's Pepper Keenan and Jimmy Bower on drums. Both Anselmo and Winstein also perform as part of BODY OF BLOOD.

Guitarist Duet founded project GOATWHORE with SOILENT GREEN frontman Ben Falgout II issuing the CD 'The Eclipse Of Ages Into Black' in 2000.

CROWBAR toured America with BLACK LABEL SOCIETY and SIXTY WATT SHAMAN the same year. Drummer Craig Nunemacher was forced to deputize for headliners BLACK LABEL SOCIETY as their drummer Philth Ohnditch was taken ill. Later shows saw the band guesting for HATEBREED.

As Nunemacher made his position in BLACK LABEL SOCIETY permanent the band drafted ex-DOWNSET drummer Chris Hamilton.

Former CROWBAR man Kevin Bond would re-emerge with a plethora of PANTERA vocalist Phil Anselmo's projects including CHRIST INVERSION and SUPERJOINT RITUAL. He would also feature in SOUTHERN ISOLATION. The band, which featured Anselmo's girlfriend Stephanie Opal as lead vocalist, saw Anselmo acting as guitarist, CHRIST INVERSION keyboard player Ross Karpelman and Sid Montz on drums. A four track EP was issued in October 2001 on the Baphomet label.

For the 2001 'Sonic Excess In It's Purest Form' effort CROWBAR once more employed a new face behind the drums and on bass guitar as erstwhile SALVO, MACHINE HEAD and CRISIS man Tony Costanzo took on the percussion job and Jeff Okoneski of NEAR LIFE EXPERIENCE became the band's new four stringer.

Albums:

CROWBAR AND LIVE PLUS 1, Bulletproof VEST 5 (1994)
High Rate Extinction / All I Had (I Gave) / Will That Never Dies / Fixation / No Quarter / Self-Inflicted / Negative Pollution / Existence Is Punishment / Holding Nothing / I Have Failed / Self-Inflicted (Live) / Fixation (Live) / I Have Failed (Live) / All I Had (I Gave) (Live) / Numb Sensitive (Live)

OBEDIENCE THROUGH SUFFERING, Grindcore International 89802 (1992)
Waiting In Silence / I Despise / A Breed Apart / Obedience Thru Suffering / Vacuum / 4 Walls / Subversion/ Feeling Fear / My Agony / The Innocent

TIME HEALS NOTHING, Bulletproof VEST 51 (1995)
The Only Factor / No More Can We Crawl / Time Heals Nothing / Leave It Behind / Through The Wall Of Tears / Lack Of Tolerance / Still I Reach / Embracing Emptiness / A Perpetual Need / Numb Sensitive

BROKEN GLASS, Pavement 7243 8 22569 2 2 (1996)
Conquering / Live Broken Glass / (Can't) Turn Away From Dying / Wrath Of Time Be Judgement / Nothing / Burn Your World / I Am Forever / Above, Below And Inbetween / You Now (I'll Live Again) / Reborn Thru Me

ODDFELLOWS REST, Mayhem MAIM111162 (1998)
Intro / Planets Collide / ...And Suffer As One / 1000 Year Internal War / To Carry The Load / December's Spawn / It's All In The Gravity / Beyond The Black Horizon / New Man Born / Scattered Pieces Lay / Odd Fellows Rest / On Frozen Ground

EQUILIBRIUM, Eagle Rock (2000)
I Feel The Burning Sun / Equilibrium / Glass Full Of Liquid Pain / Command Of Myself / Down Into The Rotting Earth / To Touch The Hand Of God / Uncovering / Buried Once Again / Things You Can't Understand / Euphoria Minus One / Dream Weaver / In A Gadda Da Vida

SONIC EXCESS IN IT'S PUREST FORM, Spitfire (2001)
The Lasting Dose / To Build A Mountain / Thru The Ashes (I've Watched You Burn) / Awakening / Repulsion In It's Splendid Beauty / Counting Daze
In Times Of Sorrow / It Pours From Me /

Suffering Brings Wisdom / Failure To Delay Gratification / Empty Room
SLUDGE: HISTORY OF CROWBAR, Spitfire (2001)
All I Had (I Gave) / Existence Is Punishment / The Only Factor / Vacuum / Subversion / Waiting In Silence / High Rate Extinction / I Have Failed / Fixation (Live) / Odd Fellows Rest / Planets Collide / ...And Suffer As One / Glass Full Of Liquid Pain / Buried Once Again / Dream Weaver

CULEBRA (ARGENTINA)
Line-Up: Sebastián Centurión (vocals / guitar / drums), Trappo Verdura (guitar / keyboards), Pol Paredes (bass)

Argentinean Stoner trio forged in 1995. CULEBRA translates as 'Snake'.

Albums:
CÓFRADES DEL CREPÚSCULO, (2000)

THE CULT (UK)
Line-Up: Ian Astbury (vocals), Billy Duffy (guitar), Haggis (bass), Michael Lee (drums)

A UK Hard Rock act that made a huge impression on the Gothic Rock scene, particularly with the seminal 'She Sells Sanctuary' hit single, before concentrating their efforts on the USA. A combination of unrelenting tour work and strong songs laden with North American Indian imagery broke the band into the major arena league with the million selling 'Sonic Temple' album. Although the band line-up has fluxed the central core of vocalist Ian Astbury and guitarist Billy Duffy has remained solid.
THE CULT, originally known as SOUTHERN DEATH CULT, allegedly were formed by frontman Ian Astbury (then known as Ian Lindsay) in 1981 after the vocalist had moved into a new house in Bradford and reportedly discovered a band rehearsing in the cellar! Upon joining Astbury completed the first incarnation of this basement group alongside guitarist David Burrows, bassist Barry Jepson and drummer Haq Quereshi. SOUTHERN DEATH CULT soon saw a rapid rise to fame in the Goth revival soon became regulars on the London scene, selling out gigs promoting their debut 'Moya' single in 1982. The band then secured the support slot to BAUHAUS's British tour the following year.
Shortly after the tour ended the band folded, with Quereshi, Jepson and Burrows forming GETTING THE FEAR then INTO A CIRCLE. Astbury soon reassembled the group concept under the new guise of DEATH CULT. Meanwhile, an album of demos and live

tracks was hastily released to mark SOUTHERN DEATH CULT's legacy.
DEATH CULT comprised Astbury (now having dropped the surname Lindsay) and two members of RITUAL, bassist Jamie Stewart and drummer Ray 'The Reverend' Mondo, together with ex-NOSEBLEEDS and THEATRE OF HATE guitarist Billy Duffy. In 1983 DEATH CULT appeared at the 'Futurama' festival, although Mondo left and in came ex-SEX GANG CHILDREN and THEATRE OF HATE drummer Nigel Preston in his place. In 1984 the band shortened their name to become, simply, THE CULT.
Initial copies of the debut THE CULT album, 'Dreamtime', came with a free album of live tracks recorded at London's Lyceum. The album proved to be a huge success, with the 'Spiritwalker' single scoring the number one position in many indie charts.
BIG COUNTRY drummer Mark Brzezicki stood in for the recording of second album 'Love', following the departure of Preston (who would sadly pass away from a drugs overdose in early 1992). Further changes occurred with THE CULT adding ex-ZODIAC MINDWARP bassist Haggis (a.k.a. 'Kid Chaos'), manoeuvring Jamie Stewart onto rhythm guitar, and adding a permanent drummer in the shape of Lez Warner, whose previous credits included work with JOHNNY THUNDERS and RANDY CALIFORNIA. It would be the 'Love' album that saw the band bolstering their international standing and spawning numerous British hit singles, including the groundbreaking monster success of 'She Sells Sanctuary'.
'Love's follow-up, the 'Electric' album, was originally produced by Steve Brown but was later totally remixed with additional songs by Rick Rubin. Lack of criticism for it's unashamed LED ZEPPELIN influences only reinforced the view that the band were now of major league potential.
The group toured America in 1987 opening for BILLY IDOL, prior to headline dates with support act GUNS N' ROSES. Dates in Australia were blighted by episodes of gear trashing and upon their return to Britain THE CULT was hit with the loss of both Warner and Haggis, who quit in early 1988, the bassist forming the chaotic yet high profile band THE FOUR HORSEMEN. Warner founded the HELLFIRE CLUB with KILLING JOKE bassist Paul Raven and ex-THIN LIZZY and MOTÖRHEAD guitarist Brian Robertson.
For the comeback Bob Rock produced 'Sonic Temple' album demos had been worked up with former BLACK SABBATH drummer Eric Singer but conflicting schedules with his then act BADLANDS curtailed any further involvement. The band drafted in temporary

drummer Mickey Curry, on loan from Canadian singer / songwriter BRYAN ADAMS for the album sessions. Recorded in Vancouver, and seeing none other than IGGY POP donating backing vocals to the track 'New York City', the 'Sonic Temple' album boosted THE CULT's status further to that of an arena band. Heavy radio play in North America would be afforded to in particular to the ballad 'Edie (Ciao Baby)'. The Rockers 'Sweet Soul Sister', 'Soul Asylum' and 'Fire Woman' also crossed over to mainstream radio. A brand new permanent line-up saw the recruitment of drummer Matt Sorum (previously with JEFF PARIS and TORI AMOS' short-lived Rock band Y KANT TORI READ) and ex-ALARM and ARMOURY SHOW keyboard player Mark Taylor.

Matt Sorum was to be enticed away by a lucrative offer from GUNS N' ROSES that the drummer would've been foolish to refuse and on their next American tour THE CULT were in the bizarre position of supporting a GUNS N' ROSES line-up featuring their former drummer.

The following 'Ceremony' album was recorded with ex-KEITH RICHARDS bassist Charlie Drayton and a returning Mickey Curry. For the touring line-up Astbury and Duffy were augmented by ex-LITTLE ANGELS drummer Michael Lee and bassist Kinley Wolfe. Following a well received return to form at London's Subterranea club, THE CULT headlined to over 15,000 people at a concert in the capital's Finsbury Park.

Controversy courted the band once more when it was revealed that the parents of the native American child on the cover of the 'Ceremony' album, Eternity Crazy Bear DuBray, were ready to sue the band for $35 million for alleged abuse of the boy's religious and cultural beliefs. 'Ceremony' went on to sell three million copies worldwide, including platinum status in America.

For touring commitments in 1994 THE CULT would boast Astbury, Duffy, bassist Craig Adams, rhythm guitarist James Stevenson and drummer Scott Garrett. This latest incarnation debuted with a live appearance on 'The Word' TV show performing 'Star'. However, a planned American tour was scrapped when the album failed to sell well and Stevenson was soon to join a reformed GENE LOVES JEZEBEL.

The band were soon to fragment, Billy Duffy forming VENT with ex-WONDERSTUFF vocalist Miles Hunt and former SENSELESS THINGS bassist Morgan Nicholls, whilst Ian Astbury was to be engaged in the recording of a solo album in 1996. The vocalist along with Garrett also assembled HOLY BARBARIANS with LUCIFER WONG guitarist Patrick Sugg

for the 'Cream' album.

1999 witnessed Duffy back in the fray with his COLOURSOUND project, an album recorded with ex-ALARM frontman Mike Peters. By the time the album was issued THE CULT were back on the road with ex-STEVE JONES and SUCKERPUNCH rhythm guitarist Mike Dimkitch as well as Matt Sorum back on the drums. Support acts were AMERICAN SHAME and BIF NAKED.

2000 found the band honoured with a tribute album that included homages from various American acts such as ENUFF Z' NUFF, Jizzy Pearl of LOVE/HATE and L.A. GUNS, STEVIE RACHELLE of TUFF, ex-OZZY OSBOURNE guitarist JAKE E. LEE and ex-FAITH NO MORE guitarist JIM MARTIN.

THE CULT's 2000 single 'Painted On My Heart' was recorded for the movie soundtrack to 'Gone in 60 seconds'. The band now included former THELONIUS MONSTER and PORNO FOR PYROS man Martyn LeNoble on bass. The latter would subsequently join JANE'S ADDICTION.

Recording of a brand new album 'Beyond Good And Evil', working with noted producer Bob Rock, began in earnest during early 2001. Headline touring throughout the summer in America had MONSTER MAGNET and STABBING WESTWARD as support. THE CULT now comprised Astbury, Duffy, bassist Billy Morrison and a returning Matt Sorum on drums. The tour got a healthy boost when the band were invited to perform first single 'Rise' on prestigious 'The Tonight Show' with Jay Leno upfront of dates commencing in Reno, Nevada on June 14th. Sorum would guest on the 2001 debut HAVEN album as well as appearing as part of the BOURGEOIS PIGS project.

The new album was widely acknowledged as a return to former glories and reinstated THE CULT as a major draw. The band would perform at the annual KROQ 'Weenie Roast' festival at the massive Verizon Wireless Amphitheatre in Irvine, California on June 23rd alongside JANE'S ADDICTION, STAIND, DISTURBED, LINKIN PARK, STABBING WESTWARD, COLDPLAY, CRAZY TOWN and PAPA ROACH.

2002 would see the issue of live DVD, 'Live In Los Angeles', recorded in October of 2001. The same year Ian Astbury would be invited to perform as frontman for a concert from the legendary '60s band THE DOORS. The gig found Astbury, amongst other guests vocalists, performing with the surviving members of THE DOORS Ray Manzerek, Robby Krieger and John Densmore, on September 7th at the California Motor Speedway ground. Media conjecture hinted strongly that Astbury was in discussions to participate in a full blown resurrection of the famous '60s act. Meantime Matt Sorum had apparently reunited with former GUNS N' ROSES colleagues guitarist Slash and bassist DUFF McKAGAN in a fresh band project.

Billy Morrison, who had been working up a musical endeavour with PITCHSHIFTER frontman J.S. Clayden, revealed he had left THE CULT in August. THE CULT duly pulled in MISSION bassist Craig Adams and GOD LIVES UNDERWATER drummer Scott Garrett for a series of October West Coast dates.

Singles/EPs:

Fat Man / Moya / The Girl, Situation 2 (1982) (as SOUTHERN DEATH CULT)

Brothers Grimm / Horse Nation / Ghost Dance / Christians, Situation 2 (1983) (as DEATH CULT)

God's Zoo / These Times, Situation 2 (1983) (as DEATH CULT)

Spirit Walker / A Flower In The Desert / Bone Bag, Situation 2 SIT 33 (1984)

Go West / Sea And Sky / Brothers Grimm (Live), Beggars Banquet BEG 115 (1984)

Resurrection Joe / Resurrection Joe (Hep Cat Mix), Beggars Banquet BEG 122 (1984) **74 UK**

She Sells Sanctuary / Number 13 / The Snake / Assault Sanctuary, Beggars Banquet BEG 135 (1985) **15 UK**

Rain / Little Face / Here Comes The Rain, Beggars Banquet BEG 147 (1985) **17 UK**

Revolution / All Souls Avenue / Judith / Sunrise, Beggars Banquet BEG 152 (1985) **30 UK**

Love Removal Machine / Wolf Child's Blues / Conquistador / Groove Co, Beggars Banquet BEG 182 (1987) **18 UK**

Lil' Devil / Zap City / Bonebag (Live)/ She Sells Sanctuary (Live), Beggars Banquet BEG 188 (1987) **11 UK**

Wild Flower / Love Trooper, Beggars Banquet BEG 195 (1987)

Wild Flower / Love Trooper/ Horse Nation (Live) / She Sells Sanctuary (Live) / Outlaw (Live), Beggars Banquet BEG 195D (1987) **24 UK**

Soldier Blue, Beggars Banquet BEG 205 (1987)

Fire Woman / Automatic Blues, Beggars Banquet BEG 228 (1989) (7" single)

Fire Woman / Automatic Blues / Messin' Up The Blues, Beggars Banquet BEG 228 (1989) **15 UK, 46 USA**

Edie (Ciao Baby) / Medicine Man, Beggars Banquet BEG 230 G (1989) (7" single)

Edie (Ciao Baby) / Medicine Man / Love Removal Machine (Live), Beggars Banquet BEG 230 T (1989)

Edie (Ciao Baby) / Medicine Train / Love Removal Machine (Live) / Revolution (Live), Beggars Banquet BEG 230 CD (1989)

Edie (Ciao Baby) / Medicine Train / Love Removal Machine (Live) / Revolution (Live) / Lil' Devil (Live), Beggars Banquet BEG 230 CP (1989)

Edie (Ciao Baby) / Bleeding Heart Graffiti / Medicine Train / Love Removal Machine (Live), Beggars Banquet BEG 230 (1989) **32 UK**

Sun King / Edie (Ciao Baby) / She Sells Sanctuary, Beggars Banquet BEG 235 (1989) **39 UK**

Sun King / Edie (Ciao Baby) / She Sells Sanctuary, Beggars Banquet BEG 235 CD (1989)

Sweet Soul Sister / The River / American Horse (Live) / Soul Asylum (Live), Beggars Banquet BEG 241 (1990) **42 UK**

Wild Hearted Son / Indian / Red Jesus, Beggars Banquet (1991) **39 SWE, 40 UK**

Heart Of Soul / Earth Mofo / Edie (Ciao Baby), Beggars Banquet (1992) **51 UK**

Faith Healer / Full Tilt (Live)/ Love Removal Machine (Live), Beggars Banquet (1992) (Free with video)

Sanctuary MCMXCIII Dog Star Mix / She Sells Sanctuary (Live) / She Sells Sanctuary (Slutnostic Mix) / She Sells Sanctuary (Sundance Mix), Beggars Banquet (1993) **15 UK**

Coming Down / Gone, Beggars Banquet (1994) **50 UK**

Star / Breathing Out / The Witch, Beggars Banquet (1994) **65 UK**

Painted On My Heart, Mercury (2000)

Albums:

SOUTHERN DEATH CULT, Beggars Banquet BEGA 46 (1983) **43 UK**
The Crypt / Fat Man / Moya / False Faces / All Glory / Vivisection / Crow / Apache / The Girl

DREAMTIME, Beggars Banquet BEGA 57 (1984) **46 SWEDEN, 21 UK**
Bad Medicine Waltz / Dreamtime / Spiritwalker / Horse Nation / Gimmick / 83rd Dream / Go West / Rider In The Snow / Flower In The Desert / Butterflies

LOVE, Beggars Banquet BEGA 65 (1985) **37 NEW ZEALAND, 4 UK, 87 USA**
Nirvana / She Sells Sanctuary / Rain / Black Angel / Love / The Hollow Man / Revolution / Big Neon Glitter / The Phoenix / Brother Wolf, Sister Moon / Judith / Little Face

ELECTRIC, Beggars Banquet BEGA 80 (1987) **16 NEW ZEALAND, 24 SWEDEN, 4 UK, 38 USA**
Peace Dog / Wild Flower / Lil' Devil / Outlaw / Love Removal Machine / Born To Be Wild / Aphrodisiac Jacket / Electric Ocean / Bad

Man / King Contrary Man / Memphis
Hipshake
SONIC TEMPLE, Beggars Banquet BEGA
98 (1989) **6 NEW ZEALAND, 13 SWEDEN,
3 UK, 10 USA**
Fire Woman / Sun King / Sweet Soul Sister /
Edie (Ciao Baby) / Soul Asylum / American
Horse / Automatic Blues / Wake Up Time For
Freedom / New York City
CEREMONY, Beggars Banquet BEGA 122
(1991) **3 NEW ZEALAND, 21 SWEDEN,
9 UK, 25 USA**
Ceremony / Wild Hearted Son / Earth Mofo /
White / If / Full Tilt / Heart Of Soul /
Bangkok Rain / Indian / Sweet Salvation /
Wonderland
PURE CULT, Beggars Banquet (1993)
1 NEW ZEALAND, 28 SWEDEN, 1 UK
She Sells Sanctuary / Fire Woman / Lil' Devil
/ Spiritwalker / The Witch / Revolution / Wild
Hearted Son / Love Removal Machine / Rain
/ Edie (Ciao Baby) / Heart Of Soul / Love /
Wildflower / Go West / Resurrection Joe /
Sun King / Sweet Soul Sister / Earth Mofo
LIVE AT THE MARQUEE '91, Beggars
Banquet (1993) (Free WITH 'Pure Cult'
album')
CULT, Beggars Banquet (1994) **8 NEW
ZEALAND, 21 UK, 69 USA**
Gone / Coming Down / Real Girl / Black Sun
/ Naturally High / Joy / Star / Sacred Life /
Be Free / Universal You / Emperor's New
Horse / Saints Are Down
HIGH OCTANE CULT, Reprise 9 46047-2
(1997)
In The Clouds / She Sells Sanctuary / Fire
Woman / Lil' Devil / Spiritwalker / The Witch /
Revolution / Coming Down / Love Removal
Machine / Rain / Edie (Ciao Baby) / Heart Of
Soul / Star / Wild Flower / Resurrection Joe /
Wild Hearted Son / Sweet Soul Sister /
Beauty's On The Street
THE SINGLES 1984-1995, Beggars
Banquet BEGA 2026 CD (2000)
She Sells Sanctuary / Fire Woman / Lil' Devil
/ Spiritwalker / The Witch / Revolution / Love
Removal Machine / Rain / In The Clouds /
Coming Down / Edie (Ciao Baby) / Heart Of
Soul / Wild Flower / Star / Resurrection Joe /
Go West / Sun King / Wild Hearted Son /
Sweet Soul Sister
RARE CULT, Beggar's Banquet (2000)
Love Removal Machine (Peace remix) / Zap
City / Faith Healer / She Sells Sanctuary
(Long version) / Edie (Ciao Baby) (Acoustic)
/ Little Face / Spanish Gold / Love Trooper /
The River / Lay Down Your Gun (Version
Two) / No. 13 / Bleeding Heart Graffiti / Sea
And Sky / Go West (Crazy Spinning Circles)
(Original Mix) / Join Hands
BEYOND GOOD AND EVIL, Atlantic (2001)
21 FINLAND, 140 FRANCE, 21 GERMANY

War (The Process) / The Saint / Rise / Take
The Power / Breathe (You Bastard) / Niko /
American Gothic / Ashes And Ghosts /
Shape The Sky / Who Plays The Devil /
A True Believer / My Bridges Burn

DAKRUA (ITALY)
Line-Up: Eva Rondinelli (vocals), Alessandro Buono (guitar), Alessandro Vannicelli (guitar), William Quattrone (bass), Marco Locascio (keyboards), Davide Sangiovanni (drums)

Gothic Death Metal band DAKRUA started out titled OPERA OMNIA in September of 1995, founded by guitarists Alessandro Buono and Alessandro Vannicelli with drummer Davide Sangiovanni. Bassist William Quattrone was added in 1996 and keyboard player Marco Locascio the following year.
The band employed the temporary services of female vocalist Elena Quilici during 1998 for a promotional recording but would soon find Eva Rondinelli as a permanent fixture.
Guitarist Alessandro Vannicelli departed in 1999. Rondinelli would add guest vocals to the 2000 THY MAJESTIE album 'Lasting Power'.

Albums:
INNER WASTELANDS, Scarlet (1999)
Under The Veils / Mist / Amor, Vita, Mors / Of Chaos / The Loss / Inner Wastelands / Echoes Of… A Silent Scream / To The Sun / A New Morning
SHIFTING REALITIES, Scarlet (2001)
Ephemera / Frozen Sun / The Waiting / Deceive Me / Of Life And Will / Divine Masquerade / Dawn Ower / Seas Of Silence / Not Mine / The Outer Void / Wasted Worlds

DAMN 13 (CANADA)
Line-Up: Adam Sewell (vocals), Mike Charette (guitar), Mat Lunnen (bass)

Vocalist 'Adamn' Sewell had come to the fore with MONSTER VOODOO MACHINE. He would quit that band following their 'Ozzfest' 1998 tour to create DAMN 13 with fellow MONSTER VOODOO MACHINE drummer Dean Bentley and guitar player Paul Meyers. This unit issued the four track 'Dynamite' Gospel' EP. Bentley would join ALL SYSTEMS GO in 2000.
During early 2002 the band recorded a track 'Scarecrow Kid' with guest vocals from Canadian Dance star Simone Denny and drums courtesy of Vitor Rebello, ex-MONSTER VOODOO MACHINE drummer and MUNDANE frontman.
DAMN 13 would support GWAR in Toronto during May, pulling in original members guitar player Paul Meyers and drummer Dean Bentley for the occasion.

Singles/EPs:
The Dynamite Gospel EP, Sweet Tooth (1999)

DANSE MACABRE (BELGIUM)
Line-Up: Gunther Theys (vocals) / Jan Yrlund (guitar / programming) / Milo_ Maricevic (bass) / Merijn Mol (drums)

Electronic Gothic Metal band DANSE MACABRE was the result of a like-minded trans-European union of Gunther Theys of premier Belgian band ANCIENT RITES and Greek musicians Sotiris of SEPTIC FLESH and George Zaharopoulos, the latter a member of NECROMANTIA and erstwhile ROTTING CHRIST member. This triumvirate recorded two tracks for an intended EP release but the label that was due to handle the product went under.
Although DANSE MACABRE seemed doomed from the start by 1997 Theys had built up a new version of the band enlisting Finnish guitarist Jan 'Örkki' Yrlund, a veteran campaigner citing credits with ANCIENT RITES, LACRIMOSA, TWO WITCHES, PRESTIGE and SINMASTERS, and former ANCIENT RITES colleague Raf Corten. This unit, together with the session vocals of Antoinette of MALOCHIA, recorded the 'Totentanz' album, released by the Dutch Mascot label. The initial two shelved EP tracks would be added as bonus tracks.
The band line-up would flux as a suitable membership was found in order to perform live. In keeping with the cosmopolitan flavour of the endeavour Theys retained Yrlund and drafted Dutchman Merijn Mol on drums a Yugoslavian, Milo_ Maricevic, on the bass and an Israeli keyboard player Arik Politi. Antoinette would also perform live with the band.
During 2000 DANSE MACABRE signed to the Hammerheart label for the 'Eva' album. Antoinette would once again contribute female vocals alongside the complementary tones of Ciara. Oliver Philipps of EVERON donated his skills on the piano.
DANSE MACABRE keyboard player Davy Wouters would join Black Metal act ANCIENT RITES during October 2001. The April 2002 'Matters Of The Heart' EP would come complete with a video, shot in Finland, for the track 'Danse Macabre'. Featured as sessioneers in the footage would be Liina from TWO WITCHES on vocals and piano as well as Jani Koskela from LET ME DREAM on keyboards.

Singles/EPs:
Danse Macabre (Remastered) / Danse

Macabre (Lonely Puppet Mix) / And I Bleed / Oblivion (Addicted Heart Mix) / Trojan Horse (Hungry Ghost Mix) / Danse Macabre (Video) / The Making Of... (Video), Hammerheart (2002) ('Matters Of The Heart' EP)

Albums:
TOTENTANZ, Mascot M 7029-2 (1998)
Dust Of Centuries / Totentanz / Death In Midsummer / Gott Ist Tot (Where Science Prevailed) / Jester's Farewell (Solitude) / Decline Of Romanticism / Tristesse (Of Cardinals And Skeletons) / Ignorance Is Bliss (Di Talem Terris Avertite Pestem) / Overture To The Sun (Finsternis) / Megalomania / Psychopompos / A Dream Within A Dream
EVA, Hammerheart (2001)
Sacred / Trojan Horse / Danse Macabre / Oblivion / Burning Hills / Orchid / Grief / South Of Eden / Cypress Tree / Thick As Thieves / Bed Of Roses

DANZIG (USA)
Line-Up: Glenn Danzig (vocals), John Christ (guitar), Eerie Von (bass), Chuck Biscuits (drums)

Dubbed 'The Evil Elvis', GLENN DANZIG piloted the MISFITS and SAMHAIN before 'going solo', and venturing into, dare we say, slightly more commercial waters. His first taste of work outside of the MISFITS came with his 1981 solo single 'Who Killed Marilyn?'.
Adhering to the Henry Ford policy of "any colour so long as it's black", the darkly clad Danzig's appeal didn't just end with angry young men. More than one infatuated female has been moved enough to pay tribute to her hero by having DANZIG inspired artwork tattooed on her body somewhere or another! DANZIG's imagery is as renowned as their musical endeavours.
DANZIG's work has taken the band into almost unexplored areas of the Rock panorama by celebrating pure '50s Rock n' Roll, brooding Blues and fusing this into Glenn Danzig's mutated vision of Gothique Punk Heavy Metal.
DANZIG evolved out of Glenn Danzig's post MISFITS band SAMHAIN during 1987.
The inaugural line-up of DANZIG included former SAMHAIN members guitarist JOHN CHRIST (initially known as John Von Christ) and ex-MISFITS / ANTIDOTE drummer EERIE VON (real name Arthur Googy) now on bass guitar with drummer Chuck Biscuits. The latter had in fact journeyed his way through numerous bands including D.O.A.,

VICTORIAN PORK and Canadian acts the SUBHUMANS and POINTED STICKS. In 1982 Biscuits joined the renowned BLACK FLAG and the following year CIRCLE JERKS. The drummer was also in BROWN SOUND, very briefly a member of FEAR and RED HOT CHILI PEPPERS in 1985 and had created his own act FLOORLORDS recording the 'Black Ice Riot 2-Nite' single just previous to joining DANZIG.
Between MISFITS and DANZIG bassist Eerie Von had adopted the Hare Krishna influenced stage name of 'Bliss' whilst on Straight Edge Hardcore band ANTIDOTE.
The first outing for the band was on newly created label Def American and was credited to GLENN DANZIG AND THE POWER AND FURY ORCHESTRA with the track 'You And Me (Less Than Zero)' for the 'Less Than Zero' movie soundtrack album. The line-up for this song comprised Danzig, Christ, Biscuits and producer George Drakoulias on bass. This record also included a song recorded by ROY ORBISON but written by Danzig.
A single credited likewise was issued 'You Are My Woman'. DANZIG performed their first live show in Trenton, New Jersey in September 1988.
During 1990 Danzig took time out to produce the self-titled KINGHORSE album. Later that year DANZIG kicked off their 'Long Way Back From Hell' tour of America utilizing Rick Dittamo on keyboards.
October of 1991 found DANZIG in downbeat mood with an acoustic concert for Halloween at Riki Rachtman of MTV's club. With Biscuits, Von and Christ on acoustic guitars Danzig crooned through originals plus blues standards by the likes of MUDDY WATERS and WILLIE DIXON. The following month the band entered the studio to cut 'Danzig III: How The Gods Kill'. Blues legend WILLIE DIXON agreed to put in a guest appearance but sadly died before the sessions could be arranged.
GLENN DANZIG released the solo outing 'Black Aria' in 1992, a totally instrumental affair with female voices.
DANZIG were also seemingly thrown off a 'Monsters Of Rock' style event in Italy during 1992 headlined by IRON MAIDEN after Glenn had attempted to provoke the audience in pre-event interviews into bottling WARRANT off stage.
January of 1993 found DANZIG back in the studio to record the 'Thrall' mini-album. Christ and Biscuits would stick together to record a song 'For Christ's Sake' surfacing on a compilation album 'Guitar's Practicing Musicians Volume III' the same year.
A war of words with DEF LEPPARD at the 'Rock Am Ring' festival in Germany led to stories of fisticuffs as Glenn was reported to

have insulted Vivian Campbell's wife backstage. With journalist's present this ugly event was widely reported.

The band's world tour even took them as far as New Zealand where they came across a DANZIG covers band in Auckland and duly joined the band onstage much to the surprise of the audience.

The 1994 'Danzig IV' album saw the band again in the American charts and ALICE IN CHAINS guitarist JERRY CANTRELL guesting on three tracks. A lengthy American tour supporting METALLICA took DANZIG to the masses. Seemingly out of the blue the band's stature was raised immeasurably by the track 'Mother' actually gaining a foothold in the Billboard charts. However, in August Biscuits quit the band.

Biscuits, joining Country Punks SOCIAL DISTORTION, had been supplanted by Joey Castillo on drums.

Between DANZIG and SOCIAL DISTORTION Biscuits had formed part of a FOUR HORSEMEN re-formation for a concert in honour of his brother and FOUR HORSEMEN drummer Ken 'Dimwit' Montgomery who had died of a drug overdose in 1994. Biscuits demoed with FOUR HORSEMEN before moving on to SOCIAL DISTORTION.

In May of 1995 both Christ and Von quit DANZIG by letter. Von made way for new bassist Josh Lazie, actually already on the road with DANZIG as Castillo's drum tech.

Castillo and Lazie had previously been with CHRONIC HALITOSIS, a side project formed by MURPHY'S LAW guitarist Todd Youth. Castillo also operated with SUGARTOOTH.

Throughout this period Christ had been moonlighting performing movie soundtracks. He is credited with the music to 'Sex Freaks', 'Passion For Justice' and 'A Place For Annie'. Christ would form JUICE 13 with former OZZY OSBOURNE drummer Randy Castillo, Cheesebox from T.S.O.L. and GUNS N' ROSES bassist Krys Baratto. JUICE 13 would fold when Castillo resumed activities with OZZY OSBOURNE.

Following auditions former FIGHT guitarist Mark Chaussee was announced as Christ's replacement. However, days before the tour Chaussee bailed out. PRONG's Tommy Victor deputized for DANZIG's 1996 world tour, which kicked off with dates on the 'Ozzfest' extravaganza.

Extracurricular activities included work on Danzig's 'Prophecy II' movie, Joey Castillo guesting on ROBERT TRUJILLO's solo album the band and for Japanese act HIDE. DANZIG also recorded a proposed EP titled 'Bleed Angel'. This record would never emerge.

Following completion of the tour both Lazie and Victor decamped with the latter re-forming PRONG. Lazie undertook an abortive band project with Max Cavalera of SEPULTURA and also played for Japanese act OBLIVION DUST.

In September of 1997 SUFFER / PRONG bassist Rob Nicholson and WASTED YOUTH / ELECTRIC LOVE HOGS guitarist Dave Cushner joined the fold. However, matters were still not settled as after a special Halloween show billed under the pseudonym of BLACKACIDEVIL, which found the band treading into rare excursions into past SAMHAIN and MISFITS songs, Cushner departed.

In 1998 Danzig's movie 'Prophecy II' was released. Danzig himself portrayed the part of the angel Samayel. Meantime erstwhile 57 CROWN, PYGMY LOVE CIRCUS and SUCTION guitarist Jeff Chambers was enlisted into DANZIG. Nicholson left to join WHITE ZOMBIE under a new handle of 'Blasko'. With commitments to shows in Germany Lazie was reinstated into the band. During downtime in early 1999 Castillo performed live in Japan with ZILCH.

After a lengthy absence DANZIG returned with a new album in 1999 '6:66 Satan's Child' for German label Nuclear Blast. The album had seven songs mixed by ex-ROUGH CUTT and present day ORGY guitarist Amir Derakh. DANZIG toured Europe in late 1999 supported by Danzig's old outfit SAMHAIN, the singer fronting both bands. Alongside Castillo and Lazie DANZIG pulled in CHRONIC HALITOSIS guitarist Todd Youth for live work. Youth had an illustrious Hardcore career behind him with credits ranging from AGNOSTIC FRONT, WARZONE, MURPHY'S LAW, HOMEWRECKERS, D-GENERATION and CHROME LOCUST.

1999 saw the release of JOHN CHRIST's solo album 'Flesh Caffeine' and also found Mascot Records issuing an album by tribute band GLANZIG titled 'Danzifuge'.

Lazie departed in 2000 being replaced by in DANZIG by erstwhile D-GENERATION man Howie Pyro. Castillo found time to guest on DUFF McKAGANs 2001 ZILCH project album. DANZIG finally got around to releasing a much anticipated live album in May of 2001. 'Live On The Black Hand Side' would comprise material recorded in 1992, 1994 and 2000. However, it was widely acknowledged that the more recent recordings suffered from poor quality.

Promoting the '777: I Luciferi' album DANZIG announced touring plans to headline dates across America in the summer of 2002 with support coming from renowned Black Metal act MARDUK and Seattle's DAMNAGED. However, MARDUK's involvement would be curtailed due to immigration problems and subsequently the rejuvenated PRONG would act as special guests. The Cincinnati, Ohio date also witnessed the addition of CHIMARIA.

Ex-DANZIG drummer Joey Castillo joined leading Stoner act QUEENS OF THE STONE AGE during August of 2002.

Singles/EPs:
You Are My Woman / You & Me (Less Than Zero), Def Jam Recordings 651334 7 (1987)
Killer Wolf, Def American (1990) (USA promotion)
Mother, Def American (1990) (USA promotion)
Her Black Wings, Def American 19692 (1990) (USA promotion)
Dirty Black Summer / When Death Had No Name, Def American DEFA 17 (1992) (7" single)
Dirty Black Summer / When Death Had No Name / Bodies, Def American DEFCD 17 (1992) (CD single)
Mother / Mother (Live), Def American MOM 1 (1994) (10" single) **62 UK, 43 USA**
Mother / Mother (Live) / When Death Had No Name, Def American MOMX 1 (1994) (12" single)
Mother / Mother (Live) / When Death Had No Name / How The Gods Kill, Def American MOMDD 1 (1994) (CD single)
Sacrifice (Rust mix) / Sacrifice (Trust mix) / Sacrifice (Must mix) / Sacrifice (Crust mix) / Sacrifice (Martyr mix) / Sacrifice (Album version), Hollywood (1996)
Sacrifice (Album version) / Blackacidevil (Album version / Don't Be Afraid, Hollywood (1996) (German release)
Sacrifice (Rust mix) / Sacrifice (Trust mix) / Sacrifice (Must mix) / Sacrifice (Crust mix) / Sacrifice (Martyr mix) / Sacrifice (Album version) / Deepest (Kennedy Acid Death mix) / Deeper Still ("French Eric" Cadieaux Techno mix) / Serpentia (Winter mix), Hollywood (1996)

Albums:
DANZIG, Def American DEF 24208 (1988)
Twist Of Cain / Not Of This World / She Rides / Soul On Fire / Am I Demon / Mother / Possession / End Of Time / The Hunter / Evil Thing
DANZIG II - LUCIFUGE, Def American 8463752 (1990) **74 USA**
Long Way Back From Hell / Snakes Of Christ / Killer Wolf / Tired Of Being Alive / I'm The One / Her Black Wings / Devil's Plaything / 777 / Blood And Tears / Girl / Pain In The World
DANZIG III - HOW THE GODS KILL, Def

American 512 270-2 (1992) **24 USA**
Godless / Anything / Bodies / How The Gods Kill / Dirty Black Summer / Left Hand Black / Heart Of The Devil / Sistines / Do You Wear The Mark / When The Dying Calls
THRALL - DEMONSWEAT LIVE, Def American 514 876-2 (1993) **54 USA**
It's Coming Soon / The Violent Fire / Trouble / Snakes Of Christ / Am I Demon / Sistines / Mother
DANZIG 4, American Recordings 74321 23681 2 (1994) **29 USA**
Brand New God / Little Whip / Cantspeak / Going Down To Die / Until You Call On The Dark / Dominion / Bringer Of Death / Sadistikal / Son Of A Morning Star / I Don't Mind The Pain / Stalker Song / Let It Be Captured
DANZIG 5 - BLACKACIDDEVIL, Hollywood 162084-2 (1996) **41 USA**
7th House / Blackacidevil / See All You Were / Sacrifice / Hint Of Her Blood / Serpentia / Come To Silver / Hand Of Doom (Version) / Power Of Darkness / Ashes
6:66 SATAN'S CHILD, Nuclear Blast (1999) **31 FINLAND, 54 GERMANY, 59 SWEDEN**
Five Finger Crawl / Belly Of The Beast / Lilith / Unspeakable / Cult Without A Name / East Indian Devil (Kali's Song) / Firemass / Cold Eternal / Satan's Child / Into The Mouth Of Abandonment / Apokalips / Thirteen
LIVE ON THE BLACK HAND SIDE, Restless 73750 (2001)
Godless / Left Hand Black / How The Gods Kill / Dirty Black Summer / Pain In The World / Evil Thing / Halloween II / Not Of This World / Killer Wolf / Little Whip / Going Down To Die / Bringer Of Death / Stalker Song / Long Way Back From Hell / Satan's Child / The House / Five Finger Crawl / Unspeakable / Lilith / Her Black Wings / It's Going Down / Do You Wear The Mark / Until You Call On The Dark / Deep / Belly Of The Beast / She Rides / Twist Of Cain / Mother
777: I LUCIFERI, Spitfire 15204-2 (2002)
Unendlich / Black Mass / Wicked Pussycat / God Of Light / Liberskull / Dead Inside / Kiss The Skull / I Luciferi / Naked Witch / Angel Blake / The Coldest Sun / Halo Goddess Bone / Without Light, I Am

GLENN DANZIG (USA)

While still a member of the MISFITS frontman Glenn Danzig issued a solo single 'Who Killed Marilyn?' playing all instrumentation on the record. The record was made available in numerous coloured versions, some of which are now highly sought after by collectors.
Danzig would later split from the MISFITS to create SAMHAIN and then DANZIG.
The 1992 'Black Aria' album comprises mainly

instrumental pieces based on Milton's 'Paradise Lost' with female vocals from Janna Brown and Renee Rubach.

Danzig has written songs for artists as diverse as ROY ORBISON and JOHNNY CASH.

Singles/EPs:
Who Killed Marilyn? / Spook City U.S.A., Plan 9 PL1015 (1981)

Albums:
BLACK ARIA, Plan 9 PL9 (1992)
Overture Of The Rebel Angels / Conspiracy Dirge / Battle For Heaven / Retreat And Descent / Dirge Of Defeat / And The Angels Weep / Shifter / The Morrigu / Cwn Anwnn

DAREDEVIL (AUSTRALIA)
Line-Up: Dave Tomley (vocals), Troy Scerri (guitar), Charlie O'Neill (guitar), Jason Breitfuss (bass), Mark Mills (drums)

Sydney Stoners that have reaped high profile Australian supports to such artists as MONSTER MAGNET, NEBULA and FU MANCHU. The band was created in 1998 by a collection of seasoned musicians including guitarist Troy Scerri from renowned Thrashers MORTAL SIN. Scerri also cited credits with MURDER, STITCHFACE, WHITE TRASH and THIS THING.

DAREDEVIL's line-up comprised Scerri alongside vocalist Dave Tomley of MAMMOTH, MINDLESS, SLUT and LEOPARD SKIN LOVE, second guitarist Charlie O'Neill, bassist Jason Breitfuss of

SC5, KNUCKLEHEAD and ASYLUM and drummer Mark Mills from THIS THING and GREEN MARS.

DAREDEVIL's first album, 1999's '3rd Degree Burnout', was originally intended as a demo session although Chatterbox Records picked the tapes up for a commercial release. The 2001 'Four On The Floor' EP included a cover version of THIN LIZZY's 'Jailbreak'.

The band underwent turbulent times in December of 2001, which prompted rumours of their demise. When the dust had cleared Scerri had vacated his position, being replaced by Jay Schellhorn. However, DAREDEVIL ceased operations in May of 2002.

Singles/EPs:
Throw The Dice / 3rd Degree Burnout / Bloody Hell / Jailbreak, High Beam HBM021 (2001) ('Four On The Floor' EP)

Albums:
3RD DEGREE BURNOUT, Chatterbox (1999)
All Fucked Up / Circle Work / Jesse Custer / Geezer / Go! / Concrete
BIG BLOCK ROCK, High Beam HBM006 (2000)
Revolution 666 / Blown Away / Shadow Woman / Stone Cold Groove / Supernova / Words Fail / Scarecrow / Slow Me Down / Barely Legal / Throw The Dice

DARKEN (FRANCE)
Line-Up: Silem (vocals), Alexandre Darken (guitar), Dave Blanchard (guitar), Camille

DAREDEVIL
Photo : Helen Gorter

Preuvot (bass), Alfonso Jose (drums)

Albums:
ARCANE XIII, Kaly Productions (1998)

DARKLANDS (SWEDEN)
Line-Up: Erik Barthold (vocals), Ariel Sanga (guitar), Robert Bergius (bass), Per Walldin (drums)

Founded in 1992 this Doom Gothic Metal outfit is a side project of LEFT HAND SOLUTION drummer and songwriter Erik Barthold. DARKLANDS original drummer was Jani Erickson but the band folded before resuming action with fresh drummer Mårten Mangefors.
DARKLANDS included two of their tracks on the 1994 compilation album 'Sundsvall' and followed this up with their 'Diablerie' demo the same year.
A further session in the studio for an intended demo found the recordings unissued as DARKLANDS landed a deal with Heathendoom Records as Magnefors made way for Per Walldin.
The eponymous 1998 album saw Barthold, Bergius and Sanga joined in the studio by keyboard player Uno Helmersson and drummer Paul Wisen. 'Darklands' would be issued in cassette format through Rocris Discs in Rumania and Dagdy Music in Poland.

Singles/EPs:
Dance Her Spirit Dead / Dead But Dreaming / Doorways, Heathendoom HDMCD 002 (1996) ('Chronicles' EP)
A Memory Of You, Heathendoom (1998)

Albums:
DARKLANDS, Heathendoom HDMCD002 (1998)
Intro / Serpentkiss / The King Of Crows / Swansong / Through Your Veil / Intermission / Green Light Attraction / Of Love And Lust / A Memory Of You / Her Sinister Emanation

DARK QUARTERER (ITALY)
Line-Up: Gianni Nepi (vocals / bass), Fulberto Serena (guitar), Paolo Ninci (drums)

Technical Doom trio. Guitarist Fulberto Serena was replaced by Sandro Tersetto for the 1994 album 'War Tears'.
DARK QUARTERER would announce a comeback album, 'Violence' on the Andromeda label, for July 2002. The band now cited a line-up of Gianni Nepi on lead vocals and bass, Francesco Sozzi on guitar and drummer Paolo Ninci.

Albums:
DARK QUARTERER, Label Service (1987)
Red Hot Gloves / Colossus Of Argil / Gates Of Hell / The Ambush / The Entity / Dark Quarterer
THE ETRUSCAN PROPHECY, Cobra (1988)
Retributioner / Piercing Hail / The Etruscan Prophecy / Devil Stroke / The Last Hope / Angels Of Mire
WAR TEARS, Inline Music 8269-2 (1994)
In The Beginning / War Tears / Nightmare / Out Of Life / Lady Scolopendra / Darkness / Last Paradise / A Prayer For Mother Thereza Of Calcutta

DARK SANCTUARY (FRANCE)
Line-Up: Dame Pandora (vocals), Arkdae (guitar / keyboards), Sombre Cyr (bass), Hylgaryss (keyboards), Marguerite (violin / bagpipes), Elaine (violin),

A French Gothic Metal group, DARK SANCTUARY was originally conceived as a solo undertaking of one Arkdae (a.k.a. Fabien Pereira) during 1996. The initial steps were taken with a 45 minute ambient tempered demo session, utilizing only keyboards and guitar and billed as 'Bruises', recorded in February of that year. Only 500 copies of 'Bruises' would be distributed.
A further 20 minute demo followed for which Marquise Ermia donated vocals. The project was then elevated to band status during 1997 when Ermia, keyboard player Hylgaryss and bassist Sombre Cyr all joined the fold. These recordings would subsequently be released as the 'Funeral Cry' EP through Ancestral Craft Productions in 1998. That year also proved a critical juncture for DARK SANCTUARY, recording the debut album 'Royaume Mélancolique' and registering their first live performances in Paris.
The following year the group signed to the Wounded Love label, preparing a further album 'De Lumière Et D'Obscurité' in March of 2000. This album included a cover version of 'Summoning Of The Muse' by DEAD CAN DANCE. Shortly after Marquise Ermia made her exit to concentrate on studies. DARK SANCTUARY enlisted Sophie as replacement. A new album, 'L'être Las - L'envers Du Miroir', set for September 2002 release, would be preceded by the single 'Vie Ephémère'.
Arkdae has also involves himself with OSCULAM INFAME and as guest keyboard player with DEINONYCHUS.

Singles/EPs:
Funeral Cry EP, Ancestral Craft Productions

(1998)

Albums:
ROYAUME MELANCOLIQUE, Ancestral Craft Productions (1999)
L'Autre Monde / L'Ombre Triste / Night Rain / Le Réve De La Nymphe / Miserere / Valley Of The Pain / The Final Battle / Maze / Anathème
DE LUMIERE ET D'OBSCURIATE, Wounded Love (2000)
Preludia / De Lumiere Et D'Obscure / Le Paradis Noir / Reve Mortuaire / Cet Enfer Au Paradis / La Chute Del`Ange / Interludia / Au Milieu Des Sepultures / Ordre Et Decadence / Les Entrailles De Ce Pur Gatoire / Funerailles / Que Mon Dernier Soupir M`emporte / Summoning Of The Muse

DARKSEED (GERMANY)

Line-Up: Stefan Hertrich (vocals / guitar), Andi Wecker (guitar), Thomas Herrmann (guitar), Rico Galvagno (bass), Harald Winkler (drums)

Melodic Death Metal with a strong Gothic flavouring dating back to 1992. The band, named after the 'Darkseed' computer game and initially founded by vocalist / guitarist Stefan Hertrich and drummer Harald Winkler as a covers band, came to prominence with their 'Sharing The Grave' and 'Darksome Thoughts' demos. At this stage DARKSEED included Turkish guitarist Tarkan Duval. He in turn was superseded by Andy Wecker as the band supported ANATHEMA in their home town of Munich.

Prior to the 'Romantic Tales' EP for Invasion Records guitarist Thomas Herrmann was ousted in favour of Jacek Dworok in August of 1992. Although DARKSEED now had their commercial debut released the band would fold with Wecker and Winkler creating a more Grunge influenced outfit. Hertlich resolved himself to resurrect DARKSEED and cut a private six song demo, which soon enticed Winkler back into the fold. By November of 1995 Wecker was also re-inducted as was guitarist Thomas Hermann and bassist Rico Galvagno. This unit set about a sequel to the 'Romantic Tales' release. Although artwork was made up for what was to be 'Romantic Tales II' the project was shelved and the group signed to the Serenades label for 1996's 'Midnight Solemnly Dance' album.

DARKSEED's next step was to ink a deal with the burgeoning Nuclear Blast label. This new dawn did not exactly get off to a good start when after an industry gig at the 'Cologne Popkomm' festival alongside MOONSPELL, CREMATORY and PYOGENESIS, Wecker

was unceremoniously fired.

The band drafted guitarist Daniel Kirsten and drummer Willy Wurm for recording of their Nuclear Blast debut 'Spellcraft'. Between the studio sessions and the album's release DARKSEED put in shows supporting AMORPHIS, later captured on a live compilation video. 'Spellcraft' was issued in March of 1997 and DARKSEED set about promotion by hooking up with LACRIMOSA, SECRET DISCOVERY and THE GALLERY for a month long bout of touring. Further shows saw the act included among the ranks for the 10th anniversary Nuclear Blast festivals in Germany sharing the stage with THERION, DIMMU BORGIR, IN FLAMES and CREMATORY.

In December of 1997 Kirsten broke ranks necessitating DARKSEED employing a session guitarist for an appearance at the Austrian 'Mind Over Matter' festival. The gap was finally plugged in July of the following year when Tom Gilcher was enlisted. Unfortunately the band was struck a severe blow when they learned of the death of ex-member Andy Wecker. The young guitarist had succumbed to cancer.

A further Nuclear Blast album 'Give Me Light' ensued in March of 1999 but strangely its release was a low key affair and a subdued DARKSEED managed a mere handful of gigs that year. Before the year was out both Galvagno and Wurm were out of the picture. DARKSEED signed to major label Sony for a projected 2001 album provisionally titled 'Astral Adventure'.

Vocalist Stefan Hertrichj also operates in SCULPTURE.

Singles/EPs:
Dream Recalled On Waking / In Broken Images / Above The Edge Of Doom / A Charm For Sound Sleeping, Invasion IR 010 (1994) ('Romantic Tales' EP)

Albums:
MIDNIGHT SOLEMNLY DANCE, Serenades SR 008 (1996)
Watchful Spirit's Care / Lysander / Love's Heavy Burden / The Sealing Day / Forgetfulness / Like To A Silver Bow / Chariot Wheels / The Bolt Of Cupid Fell / Night Mislead / My Worldly Task Is Done / Winter Noon
SPELLCRAFT, Nuclear Blast NB 221-2 (1997)
Craft Her Spell / Pall Whatever Falls / Self Pity Sick / You Will Come / That Kills My Heard / Walk In Me / Spirits / Nevermight / Senca
ROMANTIC TALES, Serenades (1998)

Dream Recalled On Waking / In Broken Images / Above The Edge Of Doom / A Charm For Soul Sleeping / Last Dream / Frozen Tears / Atoned To Cries / Luctu Perditus / Atoned To Cries (Rough mix)
GIVE ME LIGHT, Nuclear Blast (1999)
Dancing With The Lion / Cold / Echoes Of Tomorrow / Cosmic Shining / Journey To The Spirit World / Give Me Light / Flying Together / Echoes Of Tomorrow (Acoustic version) / Spiral Of Mystery / Desire
DIVING INTO DARKNESS, Nuclear Blast (2000)
Forever Darkness / I Deny You / Counting Moments / Can't Find You / Autumn / Rain / Hopelessness / Left Alone / Downwards / Cold Under Water / Many Wills

DARKSIDE (AUSTRIA)

Line-Up: Wolfgang Süssenbeck (vocals / keyboards), Radek Hajda (guitar), Vlastimil Koritar (guitar), Peter Böhm (bass), Bernd Pichlbauer (drums)

Austrian atmospheric flavoured Death Metal band DARKSIDE trace their formation back to 1991, founded upon the rhythm section of bassist Peter Böhm and drummer Robert Grögler, later joined by vocalist / guitarist Peter Durst. This triumvirate cut the opening demo 'Depression'. After this first attempt keyboard player Wolfgang Süssenbeck was added to add a degree of depth to the proceedings.

For their second demo 'Herbst', Böhm was to concentrate on the lead vocal role whilst new recruit Herbert Knöchel took on the guitar duties. DARKSIDE then embarked on touring as opening act for the likes of KRABATHOR and SCABBARD. These dates established DARKSIDE a sizable fan base in the Czech republic.

The band self-financed their opening 1994 album 'Melancholia Of A Dying World'. The follow up, 1997's 'Shadowfields' saw the band signed to the Impact Records label. During this timeframe DARKSIDE gained further exposure supporting well-known acts such as THERION, SIX FEET UNDER and BAL-SAGOTH.

In April of 1998 DARKSIDE recorded 'Evolution' in the Hazienda Studio for NSM Records. DARKSIDE would then promptly resume touring putting in dates with MOONSPELL and THERION, playing 46 shows in 16 countries.

In preparation for the group's fourth album both Robert Grögler and Peter Durst left the band. To add to their woes the chosen producer apparently was none too keen on the direction of the new material or the performance of the new drummer Bernd Pichlbauer. DARKSIDE subsequently wrote new material and found a new guitarist in Vlastimil Koritar.

Although 'Cognitive Dissonance' initially had Böhm handling both bass and vocal duties it would be Süssenbeck who took the mantle of lead vocalist for live shows and the keyboard player re-recorded the vocals for the album too. DARKSIDE would also enlist the services of a second guitarist, Radek Hajda of Czech outfit SILENT STREAM OF GODLESS ELEGY. Böhm would find time to assist Black Metal band SANGUIS in the studio for their debut album 'Chaosgate Guardians'.

DARKSIDE enlisted Markus Glandecker on guitar during February of 2002. However, following the conclusion of European touring ranked alongside CARNAL FORGE and MORTICIAN, Peter Böhm, bass player and founding member of the band announced his departure.

Albums:
MELANCHOLIA OF A DYING WORLD, Darkside DARKCD001 (1995)
Deadly / To The Deceased / Prelude / Melancholia / Nemesis Of The Soul / Dying World / Shades Of Grief / Fragmental Aggression / Gedanken / Copcrusher / Pictures In Grey / A Winters Night / The Truth
SHADOWFIELDS, System Shock IR-C-093 (1997)
Intro / Of Vision And Mental Derangement / In Nomine / Shades Of Pictures In Grey / In Your Eyes / Noohoorsh / Shadowfields / The Blood On My Hands / Requiem
EVOLUTION, NSM (1998)
In The Beginning / The Gloaming / Souls Of Led Blackness / Evolution? / Traces Of Red / Spiritual Galleries / Pink Frog-Cold Smoke / Whores' Bleeding Magick / Till' (Y)our Bitter End / In Silence
COGNITIVE DISSONENCE, Season Of Mist SOM 055 (2001)
Intro / Legend Of The Gods / Hear Evil, Do Evil, Speak Evil / Cognitive Dissonance / The Fallen / Fifth / Hymn To The Chosen Ones / Mechanical Landscape / Caress Of The Sleeping Giant / Bloodbound / S.W.I.H. / Pontifex 666

DARK TRANQUILITY (SWEDEN)

Line-Up: Mikael Stanne (vocals), Niklas Sundin (guitar), Martin Henriksson (guitar), Michael Nicklasson (bass), Martin Brändström (keyboards), Anders Jivarp (drums)

A Swedish act that has managed to carve out a buoyant international fanbase with their

MIKAEL STANNE of DARK TRANQUILITY
Photo : Nico Wobben

quite unique strain of dark Metal music. The band began life in the characteristic 'Gothenburg' Death Metal style but have diversified with frightening speed with each successive release to carve out their own niche in the Metal world. Later releases employ Electronica, stark piano led pieces, orchestration, female vocal and a heady, often wholly unexpected, juxtaposition of sounds. DARK TRANQUILITY date back to 1989, but started life under the rather bizarre moniker of SCEPTIC BOILER!

Switching names to DARK TRANQUILITY, the band issued two rare 7" singles. The first of these 1992 efforts, the "Trial Of Life Decayed' EP, was limited to a thousand copies while only a mere five hundred pressings were made of the 'A Moonclad Reflection' EP. Both these recordings were re-released in Poland the following year on Carnage Records.

In the wake of the release of the 'Skydancer' debut album vocalist Anders Friden left for IN FLAMES and was replaced by Mikael Stanne for the second album 'The Gallery'. In between these albums DARK TRANQUILITY contributed a version of 'My Friend Of Misery' to the METALLICA tribute album "Metal Militia' which was released on Black Sun Records in 1994

Stanne contributed guest vocal on DENIAL's debut EP 'Rape Of The Century'. Perhaps a more significant moment in the band's history was the decision taken by Stanne and Sundin to create a tradMetal side project with former CEREMONIAL OATH drummer Jesper Strömbold and CRYSTAL AGE guitarist Oscar Dronjac titled HAMMERFALL. With the original intention of creating a non-serious, kickabout band, HAMMERFALL signed to Nuclear Blast and quite amazingly shifted over 50,000 copies of their debut album 'Glory To The Brave' in Germany alone. Unfortunately for Stanne this was after he had dropped out of the band to concentrate on DARK TRANQUILITY.

In November 1997 DARK TRANQUILITY headlined the Osmose touring extravaganza known as the 'World Domination' tour over ENSLAVED, BEWITCHED, SWORD-MASTER, DEMONIAC and DELLAMORTE.

The band, switching to the German Century Media label, toured Japan in September of 1999. The band also performed to their biggest audience the same year as part of the Italian 'Gods Of Metal' festival headlined by IRON MAIDEN. The same year Dutch band ETHEREAL SPAWN would cover 'Punish My Heaven' on their debut album.

During early 1999 second guitarist Fredrik Johansson bowed out. DARK TRANQUILITY duly shifted bassist Martin Henrikson over to the guitar role and inducted Martin Brändström on keyboards. The vacant bass role was filled by Michael Nicklasson in time for recording of 2000's 'The Haven'. During September DARK TRANQUILITY formed part of a strong Metal package bill for a lengthy European tour ranked alongside IN FLAMES, SENTENCED and TO DIE FOR. This would be followed up by a short burst of Mexican dates.

The band toured Japan for the second time in April of 2001 co-headlining with Finnish act CHILDREN OF BODOM. Returning to Europe an appearance was put in at the 'Wacken Open Air' festival in Germany. Brändström would then be lent out to TIAMAT frontman Johan Edlund's LUCYFIRE endeavour for live work upfront of DARK TRANQUILITY's first show in Istanbul, Turkey in October supported by DISHEARTEN and AFFLICTION. However, drummer Anders Jivarp injured his wrist on the eve of this jaunt and LEFAY's Robin Engström stepped into the breach at short notice.

In early 2002 Brändström would once again loan out his services - this time for TIAMAT.

DARK TRANQUILITY's momentum quickened with the 'Damage Done' album reaping worthy media praise and sales. The record would also break into the national German and Swedish album charts. Buoyed by this success an extensive run of European co-headline dates with SINERGY was organized throughout November and December. The band also cut another rendition of 'My Friend Of Misery' for a Nuclear Blast METALLICA tribute collection.

Singles/EPs:
Mid Vinter / Beyond Enlightenment / Void Of Tranquility, Guttural (1992) ('Trial Of Life Decayed' EP. Limited edition of 1000) Unfurled By Dawn / Yesterworld, Exhumed Productions CORPSE001 (1992) ('A Moonclad Reflection' EP. Limited edition of 500)
Of Chaos And Eternal Night / With The Flaming Shades Of Fall / Away, Delight, Away / Alone, Spinefarm SPI23CD (1995) ('Of Chaos And Eternal Night' EP)
Zodijackyl Light / Razorfever / Shadowlit Facade / Archetype, Osmose OPMCD 049 (1995) ('Enter Suicidal Angels' EP)

Albums:
SKYDANCER, Spinefarm SPI 16CD (1993) Nightfall By The Shore Of Time / Crimson Winds / A Bolt Of Blazing Gold / In Tears Bereaved / Skywards / Through Ebony Archways / Shadow Duet / My Faeryland Forgotten / Alone

THE GALLERY, Osmose Productions OPCD 033 (1995)
Punish My Heaven / Silence, And The Firmament Withdrew / Edenspring / The Dying Line / The Gallery / The One Brooding Warning / Midway Through Infinity / Lethe / The Emptiness From Which I Fed / Mine Is The Grandeur... And... / Of Melancholy Burning
SKYDANCER + CHAOS AND ETERNAL LIGHT, Spinefarm SP143CD (1996)
Nightfall By The Shore Of Time / Crimson Winds / A Bolt Of Blazing Gold / In Tears Bereaved / Skywards / Through Ebony Archways / Shadow Duet / My Faeryland Forgotten / Alone / Of Chaos And Eternal Night / With The Flaming Shades Of Fall / Away, Delight, Away / Alone '94
THE MIND'S I, Osmose Productions (1997)
Dreamlore Degenerate / Zodijackyl Light / Hedon / Scythe, Rage And Roses / Constant / Dissolution Factor Red / Insanity's Crescendo / Still Moving Sinews / Atom Heart 243.5 / Tidal Tantrum / Tongues / The Mind's Eye
PROJECTOR, Century Media (1999)
Freewill / Therin / Undo Control / Auctioned / To A Bitter Halt / The Sun Fired Blanks / Nether Noras / Day To End / Dobermann / On Your Time
HAVEN, Century Media 215668 (2000)
The Wonders At Your Feet / Not Built To Last / Indifferent Suns / Feasts Of Burden / Haven / The Same / Fabric / Ego Drama / Rundown / Emptier Still / At Loss For Words
DAMAGE DONE, Century Media CD 8103-2 (2002) **146 FRANCE, 83 GERMANY, 29 SWEDEN**
Final Resistance / Hours Passed In Exile / Monochromatic Stains / Single Part Of Two / The Treason Wall / Forfat C: For Cortex / Damage Done / Cathode Ray Sunshine / The Enemy / White Noise - Black Silence / Ex Nihilo

DARKWELL (AUSTRIA)
Line-Up: Alexandra Pittracher (vocals), Roman Wienicke (guitar), Roland Wurzer (bass), Christian Filip (keyboards), Moritz Neuner (drums)

Relatively new on the scene, Innsbruck dark Gothic Metal act DARKWELL have already forced a significant impact with their 'Susperia' outing. DARKWELL benefits hugely from employing the lush vocal talents of Alexandra Pittracher. The group was forged by erstwhile IMPACT and SARCASM SYNDROME bassist Roland Wurzer in league with guitarist Roman Wienicke, the latter another ex-SARCASM SYNDROME man and also live musician for EVENFALL.

Joining them would be keyboard player Christian Filip and drummer Moritz Neuner, a much in demand veteran of such acts as ABIGOR, EVENFALL, DORNENREICH and KOROVA.

With the release of 'Susperia' in September of 2000, the title track lyrically based upon a Longfellow poem, DARKWELL undertook touring with label mates SINS OF THY BELOVED and TRISTANIA. A renewed bout of touring in February of 2001 had the band sharing stages with GRAVEWORM and VINTERSORG.

However, DARKWELL would subsequently be hit by line-up problems with both Wienicke and Filip bidding their farewell. New faces would be guitar player Matthias Nussbaum and keyboard player Raphael Leposchitz.

Albums:
SUSPERIA, Napalm (2000)
Pictures Of Strive / Blackheart / Ladies' Choice / Path To Salvation / The Beginning / The Salvation / The Rejuvenation / Suspiria / Realm Of Darkness / Armageddon

DATURA (NEW ZEALAND)
Line-Up: Craig Williamson (vocals / bass), Brent Middlemiss (guitar), Jon Burnside (drums)

Eastern flavoured Psych Doomsters from New Zealand's North Island. Although DATURA have been in existence for many years the present incarnation of vocalist / bassist Craig Williamson, guitarist Brent Middlemiss and drummer 'Mad' Jon Burnside have been together since 1995.

The band debuted with the inclusion of the 'Happiness Grows' track on a Hamilton compilation album 'Atrocities One' in 1994. Two demo tapes followed during 1996 and a third the following year.

DATURA released the 'Allisone' album for Cranium Music in 1998. The record, which included an unaccredited ghost track, received praise from the global Stoner community. 'Vision Of The Celestial' would follow in 1999 although reports suggested DATURA underwent radical line-up changes since its release.

In April of 2002 Williamson re-emerged as a solo artist, taking the mystical and Psychedelic influences felt on 'Vision Of The Celestial' into mellower territory for his LAMP OF THE UNIVERSE solo project. Under this new title Williamson released 'The Cosmic Union' album, following it in June 2002 with 'Echo Of Light'.

Albums:

ALLISONE, Cranium Music (1998)
Lost In Time / Astral Man / Journey Thru Space / Man In The Moon / Phazer / Shine / Mountain
VISION OF THE CELESTIAL, Cranium Music (1999)
Magnetize / Sunshine In Purple / Reaching Out / Euphoria / Voyage / Mantra

DAWN OF DREAMS (AUSTRIA)

Line-Up: Sebastian Goralik (Vocals / guitars / programming), Ralph Ammann (keyboards / programming)

DAWN OF DREAMS, emanating from the Tyrol region of Austria, started life as the Death Metal act STABLE STENCH. The band evolved its sound into more of a Gothic Doom style in 1995 and retitled itself DAWN OF DREAMS, soon scoring a deal with English label Candlelight Records.

In February of 1998 guitarist Markus quit leaving Sebastian Goralik as solo six stringer. The band also split from Candlelight to record their third album 'Eidolon' in Poland for the Hammer Muzik label. Bruno Bassi was added on bass and DAWN OF DREAMS also utilized Robert Baum of UNDISH on drums.

DAWN OF DREAMS are commonly confused with the German band of the same name that issued the 2000 album 'Darklight Awakening'.

Albums:
AMBER, Candlelight CANDLE017CD (1996)
Like A Sundrop In The Rain / Visions / Velvet Sands / Novembre / Imprisoned Sun / Remembrance / Northwind / Wavesome / Drowning In Dreams
FRAGMENTS, Candlelight CANDLE022CD (1998)
I / II Luna / III Sunseth / Autumn / The Serpent / Scarlet / IV / Eve / V Aura / Winterveil
SONGS OF LOVE AND PAIN, Visionairre Production (2000)
Picture Of You / Written In The Wind / Benediction / Breathless / Outro
EIDOLON, Hammer Muzik (2001)
I / Lost / Eidolon / Benediction / The Wind's Bride / Do We Know / Coma / Passion / Dreamcycle / Your Eyes / Breathless

DAWN OF WINTER (GERMANY)

Line-Up: Gerrit Phillip Mutz (vocals), Jörg Michael Knittel (guitar / keyboards), Joachim 'Bolle' Schmalzried (bass), Oliver Christian Schramm (drums)

Doom Act founded by former members of GLASS CEMETARY. Bassist Joachim Schmalzried is ex-DEDE 7. The band's roots lay in the act CEMETARY which issued a 1990 demo tape 'Perfect Solitude', the line-up for these sessions being Gerrit P. Mutz on vocals, guitar and bass, drummer Oliver C. Schramm and later addition Dominic Merkt on bass guitar.

As DAWN OF WINTER the band laid down a 1991 demo 'Path Of The Worm' as a duo of Mutz and Schramm, prior to the 1993 EP 'Celebrate The Agony' which saw the band boosted to a trio with the inclusion of bassist Joachim Schmalzried. Adding guitarist Jörg Michael Knittel and new drummer Dennis Schediwy DAWN OF WINTER cut a 12 track album 'Doomcult Performance' in 1994. However, this release never saw the light of day. A 14 track live tape from the same era also bore witness to only a restricted release. The following year a demo tape 'Black Revelations' was capitalized on by a 1996 promo 'In Servitude To Destiny'. Finally a commercial release, the album 'In The Valley Of Tears', surfaced on Knittel's own Iron Glory imprint during 1998.

Both vocalist Gerrit Phillip Mutz and guitarist Jörg Michael Knittel later joined TRAGEDY DIVINE releasing a Power Metal album for Noise Records. Both musicians founded the bombastic Metal band SACRED STEEL after TRAGEDY DIVINE folded. DAWN OF WINTER's activities continued in parallel to SACRED STEEL and in 2001 the EP 'Slow Is The Suffering' arrived. The previously shelved 'Doomcult Performance' album would also be slated for a 2002 release.

Singles/EPs:
Forsaken And Forlorn / The Black Angel / Dance In Despair / Path Of The Worm / Long Forgotten Realms, Tales Of Sadness (1993) ('Celebrate The Agony' EP)
Titus Vanis / Slow Is The Suffering / Thirsty And Miserable, Iron Glory (2002) ('Slow Is The Suffering' EP)

Albums:
IN THE VALLEY OF TEARS, Iron Glory IG 1001 (1998)
Fallen Empire / Return To Forever / Ritual Magic / In The Valley Of Tears / Where Low The Ravens Fly / Carnival Of Souls / Funeral / Black Revelations / Sad Ocean / Dawn Of Winter
DOOMCULT PERFORMANCE, Iron Glory (2002)
Celebrate The Agony / Ritual Magic / Sweet Dark Misery / Dawn Of The Autumn Frost / Black Revelations / Destroy The World / Birthday Depression / Awaken In The Ashes / The Witchfinder / Elegy In Pain / The Poet Sleeps Forever

DAYLIGHT DIES (USA)
Line-Up: Guthrie Iddings (vocals), Barre Gamblings (guitar / bass), Jesse Haff (drums)

Singles/EPs:
Unending Waves / Piano Interlude One / Forfeiture of Life / Piano Interlude Two / Stronger Days, Tribunal (2000) ('Idle' EP)

DAYS OF THE NEW (Louisville, KY, USA)
Line-Up: Travis Meek (vocals / guitar), Todd Whitener (guitar), Jesse Vest (bass), Matt Taul (drums)

DAYS OF THE NEW, undeniably led by Travis Meek, have often been labelled 'post Grunge'. The DAYS OF THE NEW albums, each featuring the motif of a windswept tree design, have ploughed a progressively more melancholic, sombre path with each release. Although the 1998 Scott Litt produced debut reaped huge praise, garnered a valuable support slot to METALLICA and a platinum award for one million sales Meek, still then in his teens, set about completely dismantling the band. Meek had publicly dismissed the group members via press releases before settling their differences. Reports suggested the trio of bassist Jesse Vest, drummer Matt Taul and guitarist Todd Whitener were dumped for a second time, eventually simply stranded in Texas mid tour. The trio soon gelled into a new act billed as CARBON 14, fronted by erstwhile MERGE vocalist Hugo Ferreira

Meeks essentially became a solo artist for the follow up, simply entitled 'Days Of The New II'. When it emerged the Todd Smith produced album proved to be an acoustic driven conceptual piece with strong Eastern influences and lavish use of orchestration and choirs. For road work Meeks pulled in lead guitarist Craig Wanderm and drummer Ray Rizzo from the Louisville based JAVA MEN alongside percussionist / vocalist Nicole Scherzinger.

In 2000 Meeks struck up a partnership with surviving members of THE DOORS to re-record the classic 'The End' for a VH1 TV show. A studio version of the same would later appear on THE DOORS tribute 'Stoned Immaculate'.

The third DAYS OF THE NEW outing, untitled but generally labelled 'III'' would find Meek truly out on his own, credited for vocals, guitar, bass, percussion, drums, keyboards, production, mixing and as 'creative director'. Session musicians would be on hand to add atmospheric strings and horns.

Albums:
DAYS OF THE NEW, Outpost OPRC-A-30004 (1998)
Shelf In The Room / Touch, Peel And Stand / Face Of The Earth / Solitude / The Down Town / What's Left For Me? / Freak / Now / Whimsical / Where I Stand / How Do You Know? / Cling
DAYS OF THE NEW II, Outpost OPRC-A-30037 (1999)
Flight Response / The Real / Enemy / Weapon And The Wound / Skeleton Key / Take Me Back Then / Bring Yourself / I Think / Longfellow / / Phobics Of Tragedy / Not the Same / Provider / Last One
DAYS OF THE NEW III, Uptown 490767 (2001)
Hang On To This / Fighting With Clay / Day In Our Live / Die Born / Best Of Life / Dirty Road / Where Are You? / Never Drown / Words / Once Again / Giving In / Dancing With The Wind

DEAD END (HOLLAND)

Doom Metal act DEAD END contributed members Alwin Roes and Micha van den Ven to form WISH, colluding with THE GATHERING vocalist Bart Smits and releasing the 'Monochrome' album in 1995.

Singles/EPs:
War Time In Eden, (1995)

DEAD MEADOW (Washington D.C., USA)
Line-Up: Jason Simon (vocals / guitar), Steve Kille (bass), Mark Laughlin (drums)

Albums:
DEAD MEADOW, Tolotta (2001)
Sleepy Silver Door / Indian Bones / Dragonfly / Lady / Greensky Greenlake / Beyond The Fields We Know / At The Edge Of The Wood / Rocky Mountain High
HOWLS FROM THE HILLS, Tolotta (2002)
Drifting Down Streams / Dusty Nothing / Jusiamere Farm / The White Worm / The One I Don't Know / Everything's Going On / One and Old / The Breeze Always Blows

Albums:
DEAD ON, SBK K2 93249 (1989)
Salem Girls / Beat A Dead Horse / The Widower / The Matador's Nightmare / Full Moon / Escape / Merry Ship / Different Breed / Dead On

DEATH SS (ITALY)
Line-Up: Vampire (vocals), Death (guitar), Zombie (guitar), Mummy (bass), Werewolf (drums)

Italian Gothic horror Metal act DEATH SS date back to 1977 and have, over the years, become a cult institution, although the band has gone through various guises and titles, with the mainstay and lynchpin being founder Steve Sylvester. DEATH SS first made an impression with the 1981 demo tape 'Horned God Of The Witches'.

The first stable line-up of DEATH SS comprised vocalist Sylvester ('Vampire'), Paul Chain ('Death'), Claud Galley ('Zombie'), Danny Hughes ('Mummy') and Thomas Chaste ('Werewolf') and the group eventually debuted with a series of limited edition singles sold at gigs. Only 500 of each were pressed In 1982 DEATH SS appeared on their first compilation album, 'Gathered', with the song 'Terror' and would then add the track 'Black And Violet' to the 1983 Italian Metal compilation album 'Heavy Metal Eruption'. However, DEATH SS split later the same year with Chain forming PAUL CHAIN VIOLET THEATRE. In the interim however Chain issued the 'Chains Of Death' single under the title of DEATH SS minus Sylvester!

Sylvester himself went solo and issued an EP of his own, 'The Free Man', using the services of ex-DEATH SS members. Having since re-formed DEATH SS Sylvester now fronts the mothership act and his spin-off solo outfit SYLVESTER'S DEATH.

The 1997 album 'Do What Thou Wilt', recorded in England, saw DEATH SS with a line-up of Sylvester, guitarists Emil Bandera and Felix Moon, bassist Andrew Karloff and drummer Ross Lukather.

As a footnote, former DEATH SS drummer Mimmio Palmiotta is now a member of DOMINE appearing on their 1997 album 'Champion Eternal'.

Steve Sylvester guested on the 2000 TENEBRE album 'Mark Ov The Beast'. Chain founded LOOSIN 'O' FREQUENCIES in 1999 for the 'Regeneration' album.

DEATH SS cut their versions of 'Come To The Sabbat' and 'Ancient Days' to the BLACK WIDOW tribute album 'King Of The Witches'.

Singles/EPs:
Zombie / Terror, (198-) (Band pressing. 500 copies)
Night Of The Witch / Black Mummy (Live), (198-) (Band pressing. 500 copies)
The Profanation / Spiritualist Séance, (198-) (Band pressing. 500 copies)
In The Darkness / The Mandrake Root, (198-)
Chains Of Death / Inquisitor / Schizophrenic, Metal Eye (1983)
Kings Of Evil / Gethsemane / Murder Angel, Metalmaster MET 127 (1989)
The Cursed Singles, Avantgarde (1995)

(Limited edition. 666 copies.)
Hi Tech Jesus / Hi Tech Jesus (Digital Redemption mix) / The Devilish Meetings / Hi Tech Jesus (Virtual Messiah Ultra mix) / Jack The Ripper, Lucifer Rising (1999)

Albums:
THE STORY OF DEATH SS 1977-1984, Minotaur DEA 101 (1988)
Terror / Murder Angels / Horrible Eyes / Cursed Mania / Zombie / Violet Overture / Chains Of Death / Inquisitor / Schizophrenic / Black And Violet / The Bones And The Grave
IN DEATH OF STEVE SILVESTER, Metalmaster MET111 (1989)
Vampire / Death / Black Mummy / Zombie / Werewolf / Terror / The Hanged Ballad / Murder Angels / In Ancient Days / Come To The Sabbat (Live) / Zombie (Demo) / Black Mummy (Live 1980)
BLACK MASS, Metalmaster MET 120 (1990)
Kings Of Evil / Horrible Eyes / Cursed Mania / Buried Alive / Welcome To My Hell / Devil's Rage / In The Darkness / Black Mass
HEAVY DEMONS FEATURE, Rosemary's Babydisc 002 (1992)
Walpurgisnacht / Where Have You Gone? / Heavy Demons / Family Vault / Lilith / Peace Of Mind / Way To Power / Baphomet / Inquisitor / Templar's Revenge / All Souls' Day / Sorcerrous Valley
THE CURSED CONCERT - LIVE, Lucifer Rising (1992)
Ave Satani - Peace Of Mind / Horrible Eyes / Cursed Mama / Lilith / Vampire / Family Vault / Terror / Baphomet / Inquisitor / Templar's Revenge / Drum Solo / Where Have You Gone? / Heavy Demons / Kings Of Evil / Straight To Hell / Futilist's Lament / Heavy Demons ('92 remix) / Dog Man
FEAR OF EVIL, (199-)
THE CURSED SINGLES, Lucifer Rising (1996)
Zombie / Terror / The Night Of The Witch / Black Mummy / Profanation / Spiritualist Séance / In The Darkness / The Mandrake Root
HORROR MUSIC - THE BEST OF DEATH SS, Lucifer Rising (1996)
The Night Of The Witch / Profanation / Spiritualist Séance / Zombie / Terror / Vampire / Horrible Eyes / Cursed Mama / Kings Of Evil (Long mix version) / In The Darkness / Where Have You Gone? / Heavy Demons (Remix) / Blood And Violet ('95 version) / Chains Of Death ('95 version)
DO WHAT THOU WILT, Bossy Ogress 561 3016 20 BO (1997)
Liber I: The Awakening Of The Beast / Liber II: The Phoenix Mass / Liber III: Baron

Samedi / Liber IV: Scarlet Woman / Liber V: The Serpent Rainbow / Liber VI: Crowley's Law / Liber VII: Guardian Angel / Liber VIII: The Shrine In The Gloom / Liber IX: The Way Of The Left Hand / Liber X: Liber Samekh
PANIC, Lucifer Rising (2000)
Paraphernalia / Let The Sabbath Begin! / Hi Tech Jesus / Lady Of Babylon / Equinox Of The Gods / Ishtar / The Cannibal Queen / Rabies Is A Killer!! / Tallow Doll / Hermaphrodite / Panic / Auto Sacramental

DECEMBER (Reno, NV, USA)
Line-Up: Mark Moots (vocals), Julian Peach (guitar), Asa Dakin (bass), Jason Thomas (drums)

Reno Sludge orientated Metalcore founded in September 1994. DECEMBER, a quartet of vocalist Mark Moots, guitarist Julian Peach, bass player Asa Dakin (also a member of CRANIUM) and drummer Jason Thomas debuted with the 1996 effort 'Rise Of The Fall' on Clutchmove Records. Dakin's place would be taken by Kyle Brewer and DECEMBER also augmented their guitar sound with the addition of Jason Rickman.
 1998's 'Praying, Hoping, Nothing' would follow in 1998 through Clutchmove and would be subsequently be picked up for a remixed re-release by infamous porn movie director Matt Zane's Inzane label in 2000. The same year DECEMBER shared a split album with British Hardcore act UNITE on Blackfish Records.
The 2002 album 'The Lament Configuration', the band's first for British label Earache, was produced by DEVIN TOWNSEND. Touring in America would find DECEMBER on the road during February billed alongside PISSING RAZORS and SCAR CULTURE. By September DECEMBER would be acting as opening act for the veteran German Thrash duo KREATOR and DESTRUCTION.

Albums:
PRAYING HOPING NOTHING, Inzane INZ7110CD (2000)
Umbilical / Heaven Below / 8 Years / Monuments Collapse / Proximity - Mouthful Of Sand / Shard Intro / Shard / Hatebridge / 1 Of 2 / Lifelike (Almost)
THE NATO PROJECT, Blackfish (2000) (Split album with UNITE)
THE LAMENT CONFIGURATION, Earache (2002)
Icenine / Vertigo / Waiting For Rain / Host / Trial / The Sleeping Throne / Token Gesture / By Example / Play Dead / Quiet Cold

DECEMBER MOON (UK)
Line-Up: Robin Graves (vocals / guitar), Was Sarginson (drums)

A Doom inspired Black Metal side project by CRADLE OF FILTH's Robin Graves and EXTREME NOISE TERROR and BLOOD DIVINE drummer Was Sarginson.
Sarginson was previously a member of SOLEMN and an early incarnation of CRADLE OF FILTH.
DECEMBER MOON's debut release was released through Finnish label Spinefarm in 1996.
Sarginson joined CRADLE OF FILTH in 1999 for a short spell.

Albums:
SOURCE OF ORGIN, Spinefarm SPI32 (1996)
Exaltation Of Power / You Can't Bless The Damned / Nocturnal Transcendency / Winter Sunset / Black Millennium / The Apparition Of Mother Earth / Twinned With Destiny / An Empty Gesture

DECEMBER'S FIRE (POLAND)

Reputedly a violent Orchestral Gothic Metal project founded in 1994. Nergal of DAMNATION, HEFYSTOS and BEHEMOTH guests on the album, which is essentially a solo outing by Piotr Weltrowski who performs all instruments.

Albums:
VAE VICTIS, Last Epitaph LEP 008 (1996)
Vae Victis / Patrz, Jak Ptona Dzikie Róze... / Pragne Twej Krwi / Aniot Samotnych

DECOMPOSED (UK)
Line-Up: Harry Armstrong (vocals / bass), Pete Snasdell (guitar), James Ogawa (guitar), Tim Spear (drums)

Funeral Doom mongers DECOMPOSED debuted with a 1991 demo 'Ego Sum Lex Mundi'. The band undertook the 'Underground Titans' British club tour in 1992 alongside NIGHTLORD and GOMORRAH.

Singles/EPs:
The Funeral Obsession EP, (1992)

Albums:
HOPE FINALLY DIED, Candlelight CANDLE003CD (1994)
Inscriptions / Taste The Dying / Falling Apart / At Rest / Instrumental / Procession / (Forever) Lying In State

DECORYRAH (FINLAND)

Line-Up: Jukka Vuorinen (vocals / guitar), Jani Kakko (guitar/bass), Jonne Valtonen (keyboards), Mikko Laine (drums)

Wistful Finnish Rock charged with a grandiose Darkwave feel, strings and female backing vocals. DECORYAH, although dating back to 1989, only released their debut demo 'Whispers From The Depth' in 1992. A second demo, entitled 'Cosmos Silence', was released at the close of the year. This tape provoked attention from Switzerland's Witchunt Records prompting a 7" single release.

By the recording of their 1996 Metal Blade Records debut 'Fall Dark Waters' DECORYAH were down to a trio of Jukka Vuorinen on vocals and guitars, Jani Kakko on guitar and drummer Mikko Laine. An array of session musicians embellished the grand scale of the album with strings and female backing vocals. Contributing would be former member Jonne Valtonen sessioning on keyboards, Piritta Vainio on vocals, Maria Aspelund on viola, Sini Koivuniemi with female vocals and flute, Karolina Olin with female vocals and violin and cellist Anna Pursiheimo.

Singles/EPs:
Ebonies, Witchunt (1993)
Once Beneath The Clouded Mind / Breathing The Blue / Let The One Drown / Swinging Shapes At A Lake, Metal Blade (1997) ('Breathing The Blue' EP)

Albums:
WISDOM FLOATS, Witchunt (1994)
Astral Mirage Of Paradise / Wisdom Floats / Monolithos / Beryllos / Reaching Melancholiah / Circle Immortality / When The Echoes Start To Fade / Cosmos Silence / Intra-Mental Ecstasy / Ebonies / Infinity Awaits
FALL DARK WATERS, Metal Blade (1996)
Fall-Dark Waters / Submerged Seconds / Envisioned (-Waters?) / Some Drops Beyond The Essence / Endless Is The Stream / Gloria Absurdiah / Wintry Fluids (Portal) / She Came To Me In The Form Of Water / She Wept In The Woods

DEFUSE (FINLAND)

Line-Up: Hylzy Hyvärinen (vocals), Arzhie Ahonen (guitar), Timo Hämäläinen (guitar), Ville Tuomi (bass), Jerkko Tapaninen (drums)

Low tuned Rockers. DEFUSE was created by former ZERO CHARISMA and BLEEDING NATION members guitarist Arzhie Ahonen and singer Hylzy Hyvärinen toward the close of 2000. With the addition of second guitarist Timo Hämäläinen, AEON´s Jerkko Tapaninen on drums and bassist Ville Tuomi DEFUSE was born. The band issued a self-financed eponymous EP in 2001, following this with demo recordings produced by Janne Tolsa of TAROT repute.

Singles/EPs:
Semi-Emotional / Minus Ten Seconds / Two Species, (2001) ('Defuse' EP)

DEINONYCHUS (HOLLAND)

A prestigious keyboard orientated Doom act rooted in the Black Metal scene. Previously known as MALEFIC OATH, changing names to DEINONYCHUS (after the sickle clawed mid-Cretaceous predator) in 1993. This Dutch band, actually more of a solo project by Marco Kehren, previously known as Odin, released the 'After The Rain Falls An Empty Sky Remains' demo. Another contributing musician at this time, keyboard player Maurice Swinkels billing himself as Sephiroth, is a former member of BESTIAL SUMMONING and he also has a side band; OCCULT.

DEINONYCHUS weighed in with an eponymous demo issued in October of 1993. A subsequent rehearsal recording dubbed 'A Shining Blaze Over Darkland' secured a label deal with the British Cacophonous concern in March of 1994, the debut album 'The Silence Of December' arriving in May of the following year. The record stood proud in the welter of Black Metal releases as critics praised its fusing of both Doom and Black elements.

The follow up 'The Weeping Of A Thousand Years' introduced a more melancholic feel to the proceedings. Disagreements between the two parties forced a split between DEINONYCHUS and Cacophonous, the group signing to Supernal Records for November 1997's 'Ark Of Thought'.

DEINONYCHUS made their live debut, complete with "Vampyric Theatre By The Brides Of Dracula" in August 1997, suitably at the London Hippodrome Dracula Centenary celebrations. As it transpired this would prove to be not only the band's live inauguration but serve as their only live manifestation to date. In 1998 the Mexican Guttural label put out the mini-album 'After The Rain Falls... An Empty Sky Remains'. However, Kehren would become session lead vocalist for German Black Metal band BETHLEHEM, appearing on their April 'S.U.I.Z.I.D.' and 'Reflektionen Auf's Sterben' release in June.

DEINONYCHUS, now counting CRADLE OF FILTH, THE BLOOD DIVINE and

DECEMBER MOON drummer Will Sarginson in the ranks, signed to the Ars Metalli label out of Germany in April of 1999. An eponymous album was cut before Kehren donated vocals to a further BETHLEHEM release 'Profane Fettmilch Lenzt Elf Krank'. The 'Deinonychus' offering would be heavily delayed but when it did arrive in stores displayed a marked leaning towards more traditional Doom.

The 2000 album 'Mournument', actually recorded a year earlier than its eventual release, contained a cover version of the CANDLEMASS epic 'Ancient Dreams'. Keyboards for this outing were handled by Frenchman Arkdae (aka Fabien Pereira) of SETH, DARK SANCTUARY and OSCULAM INFAME whilst drums were once more in the capable hands of Will Sarginson.

Kehren, now a resident of Spain, also operates AK47 in alliance with Australian Shane Davidson.

Singles/EPs:
Amphetamine Machine, My Kingdom Music (2002)

Albums:
THE SILENCE OF DECEMBER,
Cacophonous NIHIL5CD (1995)
Intro - Black Sun / I, Ruler Of Paradise In Black / The Silence Of December / The Final Affliction Of Xafan / A Shining Blaze Over Darkland / Under The Autumn Tree / Here Lies My Kingdom / My Travels Through The Midnight Sky / Red Is My Blood... Cold Is My Heart / Outro - Bizarre Landscape
THE WEEPING OF A THOUSAND YEARS,
Cacophonous NIHIL13CD (1996)
The Romantic Sounds Of Death / A Gathering Of Memories / Upon The Highlands I Fought / A Last Lament / I Have Done As You Did / Lost Forever / The Awakened / The Gothic Statue
ARK OF THOUGHT, Supernal FERLY001CD (1997)
Chrysanthemums In Bloom / Revelation / My Days Until / Oceans Of Soliloquy / Serpent Of Old / Leviathan / The Fragrant Thorns Of Roses / Birth And The Eleventh Moon
AFTER THE RAIN FALLS... AN EMPTY SKY REMAINS, Guttural (1997)
Intro / A Throne On My Long Awaited Desires / A Ruler Of Paradise In Black / A Shining Blaze Over Darkland / Tears Will Flow
DEINONYCHUS, Ars Metalli ARSCD021v (1997)
You Died Before I Was Finished / Inspiring Vulnerable Thought / One Day / Moments / Building The Paradox / This, A Murder Of Crows / Balaam Wore Black / Why is it That

Angels Speak Such Evil?
MOURNUMENT, Ars Metalli ARSCD031 (2000)
Pluto's Ovoid Orbit / Salus Deceived / Odourless Alliance / Tantalised In This Labyrinth / The Crimson Tides - Oceans Of Soliloquy Pt. II / Selek From Menes / A Misleading Scenario / The Obscure Process Of Metamorphous / Arrival In Mesopotamia / Ancient Dreams / Ascension - The 40th Day After

DEMIMONDE (CZECH REPUBLIC)
Line-Up: Tanya (vocals), Kashtan (vocals / guitar), Klouzek (guitar), Ankaabrt (guitar), Pendaran (bass), D'Aven (keyboards), Ton (drums)

Prague based Black Metal act with strong Doom influences. Members of DEMIMONDE also divide their activities with the ambient Black act AFAGDDU and the album 'The Book Wanth, Rooting Out The Beast'.

Albums:
DEMIMONDE, (199-)
Sound Terror System / Where The Sun The Moon Doesn't Relieve / Shadow Symphony / Baroque Thunders / We Are Luring The Fire / Queens Pilgrimage / Empire Of Bal-Sagoth, The Chronicles

DEMON CLEANER (SWEDEN)
Line-Up: Martin Stangefelt (vocals / guitar), Kimmo (guitar), Rickard Ny (guitar), Daniel Jansson (bass), Danny Drums)

'Fuzz' Rock n' Roll act DEMON CLEANER wear their influences proud, being named after a KYUSS song. The band, fronted by Martin Stangefelt, commenced operations as an instrumental trio in May of 1996. The group debuted commercially with the track 'Kickback', included on the 'Welcome To Meteor City' compilation. During January of 1998 the band inducted vocalist / guitarist Daniel Söderholm, appearing on the 'A Fist Full Of Freebird' compilation with the track 'Pathfinder'.

However, in 1999 Söderholm decamped to pursue a career in martial arts and Stangefelt resumed his position at the lead vocal slot. In an almost unique spirit of co-operation DEMON CLEANER would share no less than three split EPs with Stoner compatriots DOZER for Stangefelt's own Molten Universe label. The pairing issued the 'Demon Cleaner Vs. Dozer' EP in 1998, 'Hawaiian Cottage' - limited to 400 orange vinyl and 100 purple vinyl copies in 1999 and the 'Domestic Dudes' EP. DEMON CLEANER's debut album, 'The

Freeflight', was also delivered by Molten Universe. The band would also feature on the 'Graven Images' MISFITS tribute album on Freebird Records donating their rendition of 'We Are 138'.

In March of 2000 Rickard "Snicken" Ny was enrolled as second guitarist and later the same year Daniel Jansson became DEMON CLEANER's new bassist. DEMON CLEANER toured Europe in a package billing with CALAMUS in 2002.

Singles/EPs:
Barracuda / Redlight /, Molten Universe MOLTEN 001 (1998) ('Demon Cleaner Vs. Dozer' split EP with DOZER)
Silverball / Riding The Machine / , Molten Universe MOLTEN 002 (1999) ('Hawaiian Cottage' EP split with DOZER)
Taurus / 45 / , Molten Universe MOLTEN 003 (2000) ('Domestic Dudes' EP split with DOZER)

Albums:
THE FREEFLIGHT, Molten Universe MOLTEN 007 (1999)
Riding High / Head Honcho / Megawheel / Green Leader / Kickback / Up In Smoke / Barracuda / Nasty Disease / Mothertrucker / Heading Home
DEMON CLEANER, Molten Universe MOLTEN 017 (2002)
Freedom's Prize / After/Before / Accelerator / Ruby / From The Ground Below / The Aftermath / All Systems Go / The Seven / Black River

DEMON WAX (GERMANY)

Singles/EPs:
Freakqueen / Demonstar / Pussy Galore / Leak, Zappatista (1999) ('Freakqueen' EP)

DERN RUTLIDGE (AUSTRALIA)
Line-Up: Craig Westwood (vocals / guitar), Jason M. (guitar), Jason P.C. (bass), Callan O'Hara (drums)

DERN RUTLIDGE, titled after two characters in a whiskey commercial, came into being with the demise of CHRISTBAIT. The band, described as Hard Rock n' Roll with tendencies toward Doom and Stoner, citing CHRISTBAIT personnel vocalist / guitarist Craig Westwood and guitarist Jason Miszewski, also includes former BLOOD DUSTER member bassist Jason P.C.
DERN RUTLIDGE made their mark with a three track demo cassette in 1997, a 7" single 'All So Lonely' also emerging the same year. A four track EP, 'High As The Sun On This

Midnight Run' arrived in 1998. The band then released a split 7" single in alliance with WARPED during 1999.
DERN RUTLIDGE received a huge boost when the 'Lines On The Table' single picked up major airplay across Australia.
Touring to promote the 'Johnny No Stars' album found DERN RUTLIDGE travelling as far afield as Switzerland. The band also performed at the Melbourne and Sydney January 2002 'Big Day Out' Australian festivals, although headline gigs in May would be postponed when guitarist Jason Miszewski injured his hand. The future of DERN RUTLIDGE would be put in some doubt with the departure of frontman Craig Westwood in June of 2002.

Singles/EPs:
All So Lonely / Lovin2HateU, International Thrash (1997)
Loaded / 7 Mile Of Highway / Silverball / Did You Ever, International Thrash (1998) ('High As The Sun On This Midnight Run' EP)
Skyblue, (1999) (Split single with WARPED)
Lines On The Table / Did You Ever / Skyblue, High Beam Music (2001)
When I'm Rockin' / Silverball / Far From The Metal (Live), High Beam Music (2001)

Albums:
JOHNNY NO STARS, High Voltage (2001)
Far From The Metal / Johnny No Stars / Lines On The Table / Smells Like Teen Pregnancy / CCR My Survival / When I'm Rockin / Loaded / On The Juice / Where Eagles Dare / Walk In The Night / Broken girl

DESERT SESSIONS (USA)
Line-Up: Josh Homme, Blag Dahlia, Nick Oliveri, Brant Bjork, Dave Catching, Fred Drake, Gene Troutman, Barrett Martin

A free form Rock co-operative of KYUSS members, various offshoot acts and friends. The albums were originally issued in 10" vinyl form before being reassembled for CD release.
Instigator Josh Homme (KYUSS / QUEENS OF THE STONE AGE) utilized the talents of SOUNDGARDEN's Ben Shepard, MONSTER MAGNET's John McBain, Chris Goss from MASTERS OF REALITY and KYUSS / FU MANCHU man Brant Bjork. Other participants included FATSO JETSON's Mario and Larry Lalli as well as Jess Hughes, Craig Armstrong, Tom Holton, Cole Leu from THE EAGLES OF DEATH METAL.
The first record, 'Desert Sessions Volume 1: Instrumental Driving Music' emerged as a 10" release on Man's Ruin during 1997 with the

second effort 'Ship's Commander Butchered' delivered the following year. With interest in the project escalating quickly these two sessions would be repackaged onto a single CD the same year.

'Desert Sessions Volume IV: Hard Walls And Little Trips' would see the inclusion of the FATSO JETSON band on three numbers. The track 'Monster In My Parasol', co-written by Josh Homme and FATSO JETSON's Mario Lalli, would reappear in a new guise recorded by the QUEENS OF THE STONE AGE for their 2000 album 'Rated R'.

'Desert Sessions Volumes 7 & 8' would be issued in a double 10" vinyl gatefold as well as the regular CD release. The vinyl version came split into black and white albums. The track 'Hanging Tree' would see lead vocals from SCREAMING TREES man Mark Lanegan. Others involved numbered Alain Johannes and Natasha Schneider of ELEVEN and the CHRIS CORNELL band, Samantha Maloney of MOTLEY CRUE and HOLE, Brendan McNichol of QUEENS OF THE STONE AGE, Nick Eldorado of LIKE HELL, Fred Drake of THE EARTHLINGS and Chris Goss.

Singles/EPs:
Girl Boy Tom / Monkey In The Middle / Cowards Way Out / Robotic Lunch, Man's Ruin (1997) ('Desert Sessions Volume I: Instrumental Driving Music' 10" EP)
Johnny The Boy / Screamin' Eagle / Cake (Who Shit On The?), Man's Ruin (1998) ('Desert Sessions Volume II: Ship's Commander Butchered' 10" EP)
Nova / At The Helm Of Hell's Ship / Avon / Sugar Rush, Man's Ruin (1998) (Desert Sessions Volume III: Set Co-ordinates For White Dwarf' 10" EP)
The Gosso King Of Crater Lake / Monsters In The Parasol / Jr. High Love / Eccentric Man / Hogleg, Man's Ruin (1999) ('Desert Sessions Volume IV: Hard Walls And Little Trips' 10" EP)
You Think I Ain't Worth A Dollar, But I Feel Like A Millionaire / Letters To Mommy / I'm Dead / Punk Rock Caveman Living In A Prehistoric Age / Goin' To A Hangin', Man's Ruin (1999) ('Desert Sessions V: Poetry For The Masses: Sea Shed Shithead By The She Sore' 10" EP)
A / A#1 / Like A Drug / Take Me To Your Leader / Teens Of Thailand / Rickshaw, Man's Ruin (1999) ('Desert Sessions VI: Poetry For The Masses: Black Anvil Ego' 10" EP)

Albums:
DESERT SESSIONS VOLUMES I & II,

Man's Ruin (1998)
Preaching / Girl Tom Boy / Monkey In The Middle / Girl Boy Tom / Cowards Way Out / Robotic, Luna (Alternative version) / Johnny The Boy / Screamin' Eagle / Cake (Who Can Shit On The?) / Man's Ruin Preach
DESERT SESSIONS VOLUMES III & IV, Man's Ruin (1998)
Nova / At The Helm Of Hells Ship / Avon / Sugar Rush / The Gosso King Of Crater Lake / Monster In The Parasol / Jr. High Love / Eccentric Man / Hogleg / You Keep On Talkin'
DESERT SESSIONS VOLUMES V & VI, Man's Ruin (1999)
You Think I Ain't Worth A Dollar, But I feel Like A Millionaire / Letters To Mommy / I'm Dead / Punk Rock Caveman Living In A Prehistoric Age / Goin' To A Hangin' / A#1 / Like A Drug / Take Me To Your Leader / Teens Of Thailand / Like A Drug
DESERT SESSIONS VOLUMES VII & VIII, Southern Lord (2001)
Don't Drink Poison / Hanging Tree / Winners / Polly Wants A Crack Rock / Up In Hell / Nenada / The Idiot's Guide / Interpretive Reading / Couvosier / Cold Sore Super Stars / Making A Cross / Ending / Piano Bench Breaks

DESIRE (PORTUGAL)
Line-Up: Tear (vocals), Mist (guitar), Eclipse (guitar), Dawn (keyboards), Flame (drums)

A Black veiled Doom outfit. Although having been a going concern for some years DESIRE have played live on only a handful of occasions. DESIRE was originally titled INCARNATED upon their foundation in 1992 by vocalist Tear and drummer Flame. Although a promo single 'Death Blessed By A God', was issued by September 1994 the band decided upon a name change to DESIRE.

The 'Infinity...' album included contributions from female vocalist Joana Pereira, bassist Jaime Souza and ex-guitarist Luis Lamelas.

Second guitarist Eclipse was added following the debut album release. Although having been a going concern for some years DESIRE have played live on only a handful of occasions.

The 1998 album 'Pentacrow' included a cover version of Doom instigators CANDLEMASS's 'Solitude'.

In early 1998 Dawn left the ranks. DESIRE pulled in two erstwhile members of WINTER WHISPERS on keyboards and bass but then Eclipse would also make the break.

INFINITY... A TIMELESS JOURNEY THROUGH AN EMOTIONAL DREAM, Skyfall SKY 85.003 (1996)
Chapter I: (Prologue) / Chapter II: (Leaving) This Land Of The Eternal Desires / Chapter III: A Ride In The Dream Crow / Chapter IV: The Purest Dreamer / Chapter V: In Delight Withy The Mermaid / Chapter VI: Forever Dreaming... (Shadow Dance) / Chapter VII: Epilogue
PENTACROW, Skyfall SKY 85.012 (1998)
A Ride In A Dream Crow / Solitude / When Sorrow Embraces My Heart - Movement I / When Sorrow Embraces My Heart - Movement II / When Sorrow Embraces My Heart - Movement III / Death Blessed By A God / The Crow Shelter
LOCUS HORRENDUS, THE NIGHT CRIES OF A SULLEN SOUL... (2002)
Preludium / Frozen Heart... Lonely Soul... / Cries Of Despair / The Weep Of A Mournful Dusk / ...An Autumnal Night Passion Movement I / ...An Autumnal Night Passion Movement II / Drama / Dark Angel Bird (A Poet Of Tragedies) / Torn Apart / (Love Is) Suicide... / Postludium

DESPAIRATION (GERMANY)

Line-Up: Sascha Blach (vocals), Martin F. Jungkunz (guitar / programming), Christoph Grunert (bass), Christian Beyer (keyboards / piano)

DESPAIRATION have made the transition through from a melodic Metal band to Gothic infused Power Metal to the present Gothic-Electro "gloomy melancholic trip rock", each evolvement bearing a revised name switch to match. The band, convened by guitarist Martin F. Jungkunz and drummer Christoph Mauer during 1994 originally went under the title of ORATORY. Evolving into DESPERATION, with a new band unit of vocalist Sascha Blach, guitarist Andreas Polig and bassist Manuel Brunner, a 1995 demo session was committed to tape but never released. Apparently this signalled the departure of Mauer.
Polig subsequently shifted over to the drum stool to fill the vacancy as DESPERATION shifted ground into a more abrasive Metal style from their former more melodic leanings. This change of emphasis became apparent on the 1996 demo 'Another Spiritworld'. Keyboard player Melanie Damm augmented the line-up in 1997, Polig reverting back to guitar as DESPERATION opted to rely on a drum computer for live gigs. In 1998 the band recorded and released the self-financed debut album 'Winter 1945', an exhibition of Power Metal with distinct Gothic touches.

Martin F. Jungkunz would also be found on the live circuit employed by Doom act GARDENS OF GEHENNA as a temporary stand in guitarist.
The following year Damm made her exit in favour of new keyboard performer Christian Beyer. For a short time ex-VANITAS drummer Chris Büching occupied the drum stool but would leave after a few rehearsals. The band splintered further when both Polig and Brunner decamped. During August, Jungkunz, Beyer and Blach morphed the band yet again, retitling the formation as DESPAIRATION and pursuing an Electro-Goth direction.
The newly renamed band signed to the Berlin based Moonstorm label for the 2000 'Scenes From A Poetic Playground' album, produced by Bruno Kramm of DAS ICH. The following year DESPAIRATION donated their rendition of 'Wolf Moon' to the Zoomica labels TYPE O NEGATIVE tribute album 'Blood, Sweat And Tears'.
DESPAIRATION added bass player Christoph Grünert for 2002's 'Songs Of Love And Redemption'

Albums:
WINTER 1945, Despairation (1998)
Overture / Children On The Threshold / Winter Solitude '45 / Horizons Above Hiroshima / Malice & Desire / The Seer's Prelude / Darkened Prophecies / Childhood's Monument / Brave New World / The Shallow Sea / Into Obscurity
SCENES FROM A POETIC PLAYGROUND, Moonstorm (2000)
Martyr / Dancing Into The Apocalyptic Sun / Catharthis III / Pentecost / Dark Mother / Perception's Bitter Shores / Anesthesia / Fragile Wonderland / Black Bird's Lullaby(e) / Returning Skywards / Les Saints Reliques
SONGS OF LOVE AND REDEMPTION, Moonstorm (2002)
Blue Haven / Magic Caravan / Subsoil Pedestrians / End Of Green / Man On The Moon / Cosmic Trigger / The Electric Shaman / Cygnet / Liquid Divine / Celestial Winter / Melissa Kissed The Sky / Transcen-Dance / VeloCity

DEVIATE DAMAEN (ITALY)

Line-Up: G. Volgar Dei Xacrestani (vocals), Blackwolf M. (guitar), Tommy (guitar), Rick A. Dunkelheit (drums)

The Roman Gothic Metal band DEVIATE DAMAEN emerged in 1992 billed as DEVIATE LADIES with the 'Crown Of Darkness' demo. 'Immorality's Colostrum' in 1993 and 'Diabolische Orgelwerke' followed in

1994. The 1997 album 'Religious As Our Methods' would see the band touting a line-up purporting to comprise vocalist G.H. Volgar, vocalist / percussionist C.L.L. Von Hadel, guitarist Ciddio, bass player Fabban and M. Auro on keyboards. The band evolved into DEVIATE DAMAEN for the Avantgarde 2001 album 'Propedeutika Ad Contritionem (Vestram!)'.

A.G. Volgar would donate backing vocals to the STORMLORD album 'At The Gates Of Utopia' and Black Metal band ABORYM's 'Kali Yuga Bizarre'.

Albums:

PROPEDEUTIKA AD CONTRITIONEM (VESTRAM!), Avantgarde AV 047 (2001) Stabat Mater 'Deviatika' a) Intro / Stabat Mater 'Deviatika' b) Il Castigo Bacia Gli Orchi Come La Maslite Il Peccator Seno Delle Loco Madri! / Stabat Mater 'Deviatika' c) Mater Delarosa / Stabat Mater 'Deviatika' d) ...Delle Rose Solo Le Spine…/ Stabat Mater 'Deviatika' e) Sanatrixieg Homeliaeil! / Stabat Mater 'Deviatika' f) Doglie Di Morte / Stabat Mater 'Deviatika' g) Vilipendiosa Ejaculatio (Pro Nobis Suavitas, Sfregio Erga Omnes) / Purgazione Canonica / S:S=Spirito:Santo / Reazione! (Autoapostolika Minzione) / Haunted By A Female Clangour (Angel From The Snow...) / I'll Teach You How To Be A Virgin! / Let Those Swallows Rape My Heart Away / Quando Non Ci Sara' Piu' Nulla... (That's The Sound Of My Tomb!

DEVILLAC (GERMANY)

Albums:

DEVILLAC VS. TRANSONIC SCIENCE, Daredevil DD010 (2001) (Split alum with TRANSONIC SCIENCE) Machinery / The Absence Of Vultures / Rebuilt / Lift Of

DIARY OF DREAMS (GERMANY)

Founded in 1989 the Dusseldorf based Gothic keyboard driven act DIARY OF DREAMS were created by ex-LOVE LIKE BLOOD man, and bass player for GARDEN OF DELIGHTS, Adrian Hates. Hates united with guitarist Alistair Kane to craft the debut 1994 album 'Cholymelan'.

Setting a trend which continues to this day, Hates established the Accession record label to release the sophomore 1996 'End Of Flowers' record.

In 1998 DIARY OF DREAMS was expanded with the addition of [Os]mium (aka Olaf Schaening) and Christian Berghoff in order to create a steady base for life performances. The resulting album, 'Psychoma?' - the band's fourth, found the group delving into more Electronic areas.

The 'Moments Of Bloom' compilation saw remixes of older songs but also included four new tracks. This outing marked DIARY OF DREAMS introduction to the North American market, being licensed to Metropolis Records. A new studio record 'One Of 18 Angels' saw the addition of another lead vocalist in Torben Wendt, a member of the Accession signed DIORAMA.

In March of 2001 female guitarist Lil' K was enrolled for German festival appearances such as 'the 'Zillo' and 'Castle Rock' events. For these gigs the band, now minus Wendt, completely re-worked some archive songs. DIARY OF DREAMS undertook German dates billed as the 'Tour Of The Cities' throughout November and December supported by ASSEMBLAGE and CUT.RATE.BOX.

Quite incredibly the 2002 album 'Freak Perfume' was delayed when master recordings stored on computer were wiped by an internet borne virus. In some more encouraging news the album taster single 'O' Brother Sleep' topped the German Alternative charts.

Singles/EPs:

O' Brother Sleep (Sleepwalker Mix) / She / O' Brother Sleep / She (Demonic Mix), Accession (2002)
Amok / Victimized (Upgrade 02) / Ex-ile (Upgrade 03) / Butterfly: Dance! (Upgrade 02), Accession (2002)

Albums:

CHOLYMELAN, (1994) Ein Wiegenlied / At The Border Of My Nation / Shattered Disguise / War On A Meadow / Holier Than Thou Approach / False Affection, False Creation / And Silence Still Remains / Phantasmogoria / To Conquer The Angel's Laugh / Cholymelan / Between The Clouds / The Stranger Remains / Bird Without Wings / Winter's Decay
END OF FLOWERS, Accession (1996) End Of Flowers / Victimized / A Fool To Blame / Scars Of Greed / Oblivion / Cold Deceit / Retaliation / Willow / Deviation / Eyesolation / Tears Of Laughter
BIRD WITHOUT WINGS, Accession (1997) Stimulation / Bird Without Wings II / Dissolution / June / Aphelion / But The Wind Was Stronger / A Sinner's Instinct / Ex-Ile / Legends / Flood Of Tears
PSYCHOMA?, Accession (1998) (ver)GiFt(et)? / Never'Freeze / Methusalem /

Luca (-Tic) / Drop Dead / Touch / E.-Dead-Motion / Never!Land / Wild / You(Das) / TranceFormation Baby / End(giFtet)?
MOMENTS OF BLOOM, Accession (1999)
Cholymelan / False Affection, False Creation III / End Of Flowers / Retaliation / But The Wind Was Stronger / Ex-Ile / Methusalem / End(giFtet)? / Moments Of Bloom / Touch II / Reality Of Mine / Predictions
ONE OF 18 ANGELS, Accession (2000)
Babylon / Butterfly: Dance! / Mankind / Winter Souls / No-body Left To Blame / Chemicals / Now This Is Human / Colorblind / People Watcher / Darker / Dead Souls Dreaming
FREAK PERFUME, Accession (2002)
Traum: A / The Curse / O'Brother Sleep / Chrysalis / Traumtänzer / Rebellion / Bastard / AmoK / She / Verdict / Play God! / She And Her / Darkness / The Curse (Freak edit) / AmoK (DJ GB Shock Mix) / Stranger Than Rebellion

DIESELHED (San Francisco, CA, USA)
Line-Up: Virgil Shaw (vocals / guitar), Zac Holtzman (guitar), Shon McAlinn (guitar), Atom Ellis (bass), Danny Heifetz (drums)

Often lumped in with the Stoner crowd DIESELHED, founded in Arcata during 1989, deliver Blues Rock with an unexpected Country flavour. DIESELHED drummer Danny Heifetz is also involved with arch pranksters MR. BUNGLE. The origins of the band are vague to say the least with band members citing a whole slew of bizarre musical projects and a supposed history involving a fund raising deep sea fishing expedition to Alaska.
The eponymous 1994 debut record, which also numbered a number of unaccredited 'hidden' tracks, would see contributions on violin from Jonathon Siegel. DIESELHED's third effort 'Shallow Water Blackout' was produced by Dusty Wakeman.
DIESELHED have become progressively mellower with each release.

Albums:
DIESLHED, Amarillo ACM 590 (1994)
Hashbrowns / Poodle's Ear / Sergio Tarus / B.A. Band / Happy Donut / Cloud Of Diesel / A-1 / 5 Shots / Hot VWs / Greyhound / Macrame Xmas Cards / Ice Chest
TALES OF A BROWN DRAGON, Amarillo ACM 601 (1995)
Brown Dragon / Butcher Boy / Wedding Song / Gravy Boat / Wipe Down The Vinyl / Pizza Box / M And M / Forklift Test / Aladdin's Lamp / Baby Song / Snowblind In The Liqueur Store

SHALLOW WATER BLACKOUT, Amarillo ACM 608 (1997)
Fog It Up / Produce Section / Yellow Kitchen / Inches Of Air / Tea Leaves / Betsy / Carving Soup / Asphalt Bib / Safety Glass / Blue Hawaiian
ELEPHANT REST HOME, Bongload BL36 (1999)
Tying Flies / Trucker's Alibi / Cold Duck / Futon Song / Lap Dance / Life Beyond Eureka / Red Chair / Twin Falls / Corrine
CHICO AND THE FLUTE, Bongload BL 49 (2001)
Prelude / Frank / Brownie / Tidepool / Froggy Con Saw / Gentle Grooming / Homemade Shoes / Marlboro Man / Starting All Over / Interlude / Bright Lights / Thick Sugary Smell / Outerlude / Tag It Up / Chico And The Flute

DILUVIAL (GERMANY)
Line-Up: Sven Buessing Loerks (vocals), Klaas van der Loo (guitar), Michael Hermsen (bass), Björn Theis (keyboards), Owoll Maternowski (drums)

DILUVIAL, from Niederrhein in the Ruhr district, blend Gothic Rock with their own brand of New Wave Metal. Whilst still in high school keyboard player Björn Theis and guitarist Klaas van de Loo operated the formative Crossover act SEWIN' COTTON. Together with drummer Nile Schmeink, vocalist Ben and temporarily van der Loo's brother handling bass duties, the duo created the first Hardcore influenced version of DILUVIAL and soon got to the task in hand, and recording the 'Disorderly Conduct' demo. In January of 1992 Denis Paul became the new bass player and shortly after Ben relocated to America. Sven Buessing Loerks, known as 'Trunks', took the vacant frontman position. As such DILUVIAL cut a further demo session billed as 'The Dwarves Quest' in 1993. The following year the band enrolled a brand new rhythm section of bass player Michael Hermsen and drummer Owoll Maternowski and issued the next promotional release 'To Sadness I Live'.
A self-financed EP, 'Seraphim', arrived in September of 1996. However, Maternowski was usurped on the drum kit by Andreas Wagner. A major splinter in the band would then witness the departure of both Michael Hermsen and Klaas van der Loo. The band persevered throughout 1997 bringing in various session musicians including Ozan Sahinbas of GOD SAID. Finally Björn Theis renamed the band CYST.

Singles/EPs:
In Emptiness / Beyond Good And Evil / As I

128

Go Insane / The Divine Light, Diluvial (1996) ('Seraphim' EP)

DIMMU BORGIR (NORWAY)
Line-Up: Shagrath (vocals), Jens-Peter (guitar), Erkejetter Silenoz (guitar), Nagash (bass), Stian (keyboards), Tjodalv (drums)

Norwegian Black Metal exponents founded in 1993. DIMMU BORGIR, who deliver bombastic Gothic driven Metal laden with choirs and effects have, with a combination of tenacity on the touring front and the undoubted maturity and increasing ambition of successive album releases quickly risen to the very top echelons of the Black Metal scene. The band now rank alongside CRADLE OF FILTH as one of the best selling Black Metal acts today. In spite of their status the band has weathered the storm of ever fluctuating line ups.

DIMMU BORGIR's vocalist Shagrath had previously been a member of FIMBULWINTER and RAGNAROK. Guitarist Erkjetter Silenoz was previously a member of NOCTURNAL BREED, going under the stage name of Ed Dominator. Drummer Åxellson Tjodalv was also an active member of OLD MAN'S CHILD and KOSMOS RØST. This initial trio soon completed the line-up with the top hat wearing keyboard player Stian Aastad and bass player Brynjard Tristian.

The band signed to Nuclear Blast Records in 1996, although they had to replace bassist Brynjard Tristan for the 'Devil's Path' EP with ex-COVENANT man Nagash (Stian Thoresen). Said EP featured two cover versions of CELTIC FROST tracks.

The band toured Europe in 1997 alongside CRADLE OF FILTH, IN FLAMES and DISSECTION touring to promote the 'Enthrone Darkness Triumphant' album. With the support of Nuclear Blast DIMMU BORGIR were to find themselves thrust to the top of the Black Metal league as their album even broke into the national German charts.

Aarstad failed to turn up for a festival performance and the band pulled in AVERNUS, THERION and ANCIENT keyboard player Kimberly Goss for these shows and the American was announced as a permanent member shortly after. Aarstad would later emerge as a member of ENTHRAL releasing albums on the Hot record label, coincidentally owned by Shagrath.

Touring saw Tjoldav, at home with a new born child, temporarily replaced by Aggressor (Carl Michael Eide) of ULVER and INFERNO infamy. In true Black Metal tradition members of DIMMU BORGIR managed to get themselves into a few scrapes, which

included Nagash being hospitalized after burning himself during a fire breathing routine and Silenoz punctured a car's tyre when a Volkswagen ran over his heavily spiked boots! In more musical related matters, Shagrath was also to appear on his countrymen RAGNAROK's album 'Arising Realm' performing keyboards.

With the album still selling in Europe DIMMU BORGIR rounded off the year as guests to KREATOR on a batch of metal festival shows. This even included an impromptu acoustic performance at a Finnish rock club.

DIMMU BORGIR's next album 'Spiritual Black Dimensions' broke the band into the mainstream with accelerated sales worldwide. Joining the band on guitar was the Australian Astennu, a member of Nagash's side project CARPE TENEBRUM, and previous to that in his homeland LORD KAOS. Goss meantime had opted out to create her own Power Metal act SINERGY.

Various members of the group continued to be prolific however and both Astennu and Nagash, together with CRADLE OF FILTH, MAYHEM and ARCTURUS members forged yet another project act COVENANT.

The 1998 mini-album includes a rather surprising cover of ACCEPT's 'Metal Heart'. DIMMU BORGIR also beefed up their sound with the addition of ex-VIDDER keyboard player Mustis (real name Øyvind Mustafarta). DIMMU BORGIR toured Britain with sell out shows. Support came from DARK FUNERAL, DØDHEIMSGARD and EVENFALL.

In a surprise move the high profile Nick Barker from the British Black Metal band CRADLE OF FILTH, probably DIMMU BORGIR's only real competitors at the time in terms of sales, was poached to join the band. Tjovald meantime re-joined his former colleagues in OLD MAN'S CHILD for their 'Revelation 666' album before creating a band project SUSPERIA with his OLD MAN'S CHILD colleagues guitarist Cyrus and bassist Memnock in 2000. Mustis would also session on the debut SUSPERIA album.

Although still very much Nagash's vehicle his main side act COVENANT adopted the new title of KOVENANT for their 2000 album 'Animatronic' and Nagash himself was renamed Lex Icon. Nagash left DIMMU BORGIR to concentrate on KOVENANT and the band drafted BORKNAGER / ex-ARCTURUS bassist Simen Hestnaes as replacement.

DIMMU BORGIR dispensed with Astennu in mid 2000 replacing him swiftly with Archon. This alliance was brief in the extreme though as within weeks it was announced that OLD MAN'S CHILD driving force Galder had taken the position. DIMMU BORGIR's grip on

Hestnaes tightened as he decamped permanently from BORKNAGER resulting in his former act having to cancel their European tour.

Barker also spread his talents to the highly successful LOCK UP collaboration with HYPOCRISY's Peter Tägtgren, NAPALM DEATH's Shane Embury and Jesse Pintado. He also figured anonymously with 'Mexican' Death Metal band BRUJERIA for their 'Brujerizmo' album.

Promoting their 2001 album 'Puritanical Euphoric Misanthropia' DIMMU BORGIR toured the European circuit heading a strong bill bolstered by IN FLAMES, SUSPERIA, NEVERMORE and LACUNA COIL.

KING DIAMOND guitarist Andy LaRocque would guest on the album performing on the Japanese bonus track 'Devil's Path'. Other notable contributors were fourteen members of the string section from the Gothenburg Orchestra.

American dates in April 2001, billed as the 'Spring Neck Break' tour, had DIMMU BORGIR headlining above running mates CANNIBAL CORPSE, THE HAUNTED and LAMB OF GOD. September saw renewed live action in the States and Canada as the band signed up for the mammoth 'Metallennium '01' touring festival package.

In November quick off the mark fans would be treated to a live mini-album 'Alive In Torment'. Produced by HYPOCRISY's mainman Peter Tägtgren the album was only made available by mail order.

Singles/EPs:

Inn I Evighetens Morke, Necromantik Gallery Productions (1994)

Master Of Disharmony / Devil's Path / Nocturnal Fear / Nocturnal Fear (Celtically Possessed), Hot SHAGRAT 006 (1996) ('Devil's Path' EP)

Albums:

FOR ALL TID, No Colours NC003 (1995) Det Nye Riket / Nader Korpenvinger / Over Bleknede Blaaer / Til Dommedag / Stien / Glittertind / For All Tid / Hunnerkongenssorgsvarte Ferd Over Steppene / Raabjoran Speiler Draugnejmenp Skodde / Den Gjente Sannhets Herpker

STORMBLAST, Cacophonous NIHIL 12CD (1996) Alt Lys Er Svunnet Hen / Broderkapets Ring / Nar Sjelen Hentes Til Helvete / Sogens Kammer / Da Den Kristne Satte Live Til / Stormblast / Dodsferd / Antikrist / Vinder Fra En Ensom Grav / Guds Fortapelse / Apenbaring Av Dommedag

ENTHRONE DARKNESS TRIUMPHANT,

Nuclear Blast NB CD 247-2 (1997) Mourning Palace / Spellbound (By The Devil) / In Death's Embrace / Relinquishment Of Spirit And Flesh / The Night Masquerade / Tormentor Of Christian Souls / Entrance / Master Of Disharmony / Prudence's Fall / A Succubus In Rapture / Raabjørn Speiler Draugheimens Skodde

GODLESS SAVAGE GARDEN, Nuclear Blast (1998) Moonchild Domain / Hunnerkongen Sorgsvarte / Ferd Over Steppene / Chaos Without Prophecy / Raabjorn Speiler Draugheimens Skodde / Metal Heart / Stormblast (Live) / Master Of Disharmony (Live) / In Death's Embrace (Live)

SPIRITUAL BLACK DIMENSIONS, Nuclear Blast NB 110521 (1999) Reptile / Behind The Curtains Of Night Phantasmagoria / Dreamside Dominions / United In Unhallowed Grace / The Promising Future Aeons / The Blazing Monoliths Of Defiance / The Insight And The Catharsis / Grotesquery Concealed (Within Measureless Magic) / Arcane Lifeforce Mysteria

PURITANICAL EUPHORIC MISANTHROPIA, Nuclear Blast NB527 (2001) **16 GERMANY** Fear And Wonder / Blessings Upon The Throne of Tyranny / Kings Of The Carnival Creation / Hybrid - Stigmata - The Apostasy / Architecture Of A Genocidal Nature / Puritania / Indoctrination / The Maelstrom Mephisto / Absolute Sole Right / Sympozium / Perfection Of Vanity / Burn In Hell

ALIVE IN TORMENT, Nuclear Blast (2001) Tormentor Of Christian Souls / The Blazing Monoliths Of Defiance / The Insight And The Catharsis / Puritania / The Maelstrom Mephisto

DISEMBOWELMENT (AUSTRALIA)

Line-Up: Renato Gallina (vocals / guitar), Jason Kells (guitar), Matt Skarajew (bass), Paul Mazziotta (drums)

A renowned Grind-Doom act. Pre-DISEMBOWELMENT bass player Matt Skarajew was a member of Thrash Metal band SANCTUM and guitarist Jason Kells with ABRAMELIN. Both vocalist / guitarist Renato Gallina and drummer Paul Mazziotti were with BACTERIA.

DISEMBOWELMENT delivered two cult demo sessions, 1990's 'Mourning September' and the 1991 follow up 'Deep Sensory Procession Into Aural Fate' before securing a deal with the American Relapse label. The band would include an alternate take of the track 'Excoriate' on the MBR Records compilation 'Pantalgia'. As a side project both Paul Mazziotti and Renato Gallina operated a

NAPALM DEATH covers band billed as SCUM.

Shortly after their one and only album 'Transcendence Into The Peripheral' DISEMBOWELMENT, having never performed live, broke up.

Jason Kells created FIREBIRD, which subsequently evolved into SOUTHERN CROSS, whilst Renato Gallina and Matt Skarajew founded ambient Folk band TRIAL OF THE BOW. Paul Mazziotti was to be found with Indie Rockers MONOCHROME.

<u>Singles/EPs:</u>
The Tree Of Life And Death / A Burial At Ornance / Cerulian Transience Of All My Imagined Shores, Relapse (1992) ('Dusk' EP)

<u>Albums:</u>
TRANSCENDENCE INTO THE PERIPHERAL, Relapse (1993)
The Tree Of Life And Death / Your Prophetic Throne Of Ivory / Excoriate / Nightside Of Eden / A Burial At Ornance / The Spirits Of The Tall Hills / Cerulean Transience Of All My Imagined Shores

DISHARMONY (GREECE)

Black Metal band DISHARMONY started life with the 1991 demo 'Day Of Doom' followed by a 1992 session 'Angels Lament'. DISHARMONY adopted the new title of THE RENAISSANCE DANCE in 1993. The band shed their Black Metal roots to become a Gothic flavoured Power Metal band.

<u>Singles/EPs:</u>
The Gate Of Deeper Sleep, Molon Lave (1993) (7" single)

DISSOLUTE PARADISE (GERMANY)
Line-Up: Roy (vocals / guitar), Pierre (guitar), Micha (bass), Eni (keyboards), Clemens (drums)

Progressive Gothic Metal band apparently in a quest to achieve not only the world's shortest album title but the longest as well. DISSOLUTE PARADISE started life as a Doom / Death act, issuing the demo tape 'Souls Of Nature' in late 1993.

<u>Albums:</u>
P, Relibu 1 (1995)
As The People Left The Earth / Human Saurian Beings / No Thanks... I Commit To Suicide / The Old Story Of The Sun / Dreams... No More / Thoughtless Verdict / P
LICHTSCHMERZKERZEMLEIDFEUER,

Relibu 2 (1996)
Exordium / Das Bild / Lichtschmerzkerzemleidfeuer / Der Komödiant / Tränen Der Gehorsamkeit / Warum / Die Komödie / Ein Bruder Der Zeit / Lebenzeit / Laßt Uns Feiern

DIXIE WITCH (Denton, TX, USA)
Line-Up: Trinidad Leal (vocals / drums), Clayton Mills (guitar), Curt Christenson (bass)

'70s influenced blues based Hard Rockers DIXIE WITCH, founded in Denton, Texas during the Autumn of 1999, fall into the Stoner camp. The group comprise a trio of lead vocalist / drummer Trinidad Leal and bass player Curt Christenson - both of Lubbock Psych Rockers LIGHT BRIGHT HIGHWAY, and guitarist Clayton Mills. Initially the three operated in late 1999 cutting their teeth on the live circuit as a BLACK SABBATH covers band called N.I.B.

DIXIE WITCH first performed live in January of 2000 at Emo's in Houston, Texas. This show provided the catalyst for a gruelling live schedule across the state. With their sound honed the band entered the recording studio in August of the same year to lay down their inaugural demo, overseen by erstwhile BUTTHOLE SURFERS man Jefferson D. Pinkus. The tape generated a worthy buzz on the band and by the close of the year DIXIE WITCH had over 75 gigs under their belts and a reputation which sparked interest from the Doom specialist Brainticket label.

The self-produced 'Into The Sun' debut album was delivered in late May of 2001. Promotion would include a nationwide coast to coast tour, achieving 43 shows in an intensive 50 day period, dubbed the 'Southern Domination' dates in alliance with ALABAMA THUNDERPUSSY and the SUPLECS.

DIXIE WITCH would strike out again on the road with the SUPLECS later that same year. DIXIE WITCH planned a split album on Meteor City Records with HALFWAY TO GONE for 2002 release.

<u>Albums:</u>
INTO THE SUN, Brainticket (2001)
Into The Sun / Throwin' Shapes / CC / Freewheel Rollin' / Thunderfoot / Makin' Time / The Bomber

DOLORIAN (FINLAND)
Line-Up: Antti Haapapuro (vocals / guitar), A. Kukkohori (bass / drums), J. Ontero (keyboards)

A multi-faceted act DOLORIAN, based in Oulu and previously entitled TEMPLES

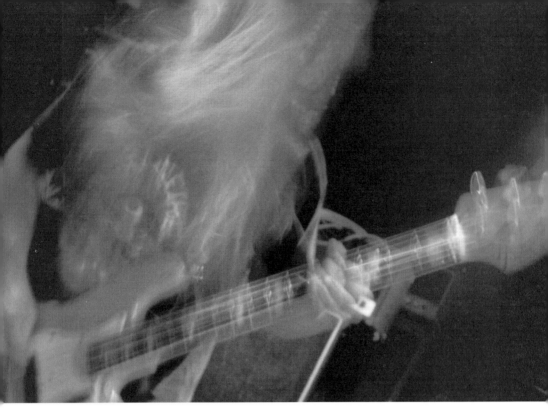

DIXIE WITCH
Photo : El Danno

BEYOND, employ elements of Black and Death Metal slowed down to labouring Doom crawl. The band themselves describe their music as leaving the listener "spiritually cramped".

Albums:
WHEN ALL LAUGHTER HAS GONE,
Wounded Love (1999)
Desolated Colours / My Weary Eyes / A Part Of Darkness / When All Laughter Has Gone / Collapsed / Fields / With Scorn I Perish

DOMINION (UK)
Line-Up: Michelle Richfield (vocals), Mass Firth (vocals / guitar), Arno Cagna (vocals / guitar), Danny North (bass), Bill Law (drums)

Starting life as Thrash influenced outfit BLASPHEMER in 1995, BLASPHEMER evolved into DOMINION over numerous demo recordings, promoting session singer and erstwhile ballet student Michelle Richfield to the lead vocalist role. However, her angelic strains still compete in the mix with the Death growls of guitarists Mass Firth and Arno Cagna.
The track 'Alive?' on the debut features MY DYING BRIDE's Ade on vocals.
DOMINION offered two bizarre cover versions to the 1998 Peaceville Records compilation album 'X' in TEARS FOR FEARS 'Shout' and the ROLLING STONES 'Paint It Black'. Michelle Richfield's presence would also be felt as backing vocalist on ANATHEMA's 1996 'Eternity' album.
Drummer Bill Law joined MY DYING BRIDE for their '34.788%... Complete' album in 1998. Michelle Richfield would also feature heavily on the same album, scoring lyrics and contributing lead vocals to the infamous 'Heroin Chic' track.
Post DOMINION Richfield and bassist Danny North forged SEAR. Utilizing the services of keyboard player Luke Pierce and guitarist Richard Kershaw SEAR cut two 2000 demos upfront of an eponymous album the same year.

Albums:
INTERFACE, Peaceville CDVILE63 (1996)
Tears From The Star / Millennium / Silhouettes / Alive? / Weaving Fear / The Voyage / Deep Into Me / Impulse / Conspire To Me / Hollowvision
BLACKOUT, Peaceville (1997)
Blackout / Release / Covet / Distortion / Ill Effect / Today's Tomorrow / Down / Prism / Threshold / Unseen / Fuelling Nothing

DOOMSWORD (ITALY)
Line-Up: Nightcomer (vocals), Deathmaster

(vocals / guitar), Dark Omen (bass),
Guardian Angel (guitar / drums)

A deliberately retro BLASPHEMER evolved
into DOMINION80s style Doom Metal band
conceived as a side project of Black Metal
band AGARTHI's Deathmaster during 1997.
Prior to AGARTHI Deathmaster had been
involved with Progressive Rock outfit ARKHE
and WARHAMMER. Initially conceived as a
medieval based venture billed as 1014 A.D.
Deathmaster, together with ex-
WARHAMMER colleague guitarist / drummer
Guardian Angel, would soon steer their
operations into classically inspired majestic
Metal and redubbed their union
DOOMSWORD.
A 5 track demo 'Sacred Metal' was cut
utilizing bassist Soldier of Fortune. However,
when AGARTHI split Deathmaster was free to
pursue DOOMSWORD as a full time
occupation and enrolled ex-AGARTHI bassist
Dark Omen into the fold. DOOMSWORD
would be completed with the addition of
vocalist Nightcomer, a member of Prog Rock
act MADRIGAL.
Session lead guitar solos for a number of
tracks on the 'Doomsword' debut came
courtesy of Gianluca Ferro of ARKHE. Other
contributing guitarists included Alex Festa
and Paco Trotta. The album included a cover
version of CIRITH UNGOL's 'Nadsokar'.
Following the album release both Guardian
Angel and Nightcomer decamped, the latter
in order to concentrate on his Progressive
band FURY AND GRACE. The band replaced
Guardian Angel with (naturally) Guardian
Angel II and Deathmaster took over the lead
vocal role.
Later in 1999 DOOMSWORD would record a
rendition of WARLORD's 'Lucifer's Hammer'
for a tribute album.
DOOMSWORD members also operate in
FIURACH.
The DOOMSWORD line-up for the June 2002
album 'Resound The Horn' stood at vocalist
Deathmaster, guitarists Guardian Angel II and
The Forger, bassist Dark Omen and drummer
Grom from cult Norwegian act ANCIENT.

Albums:
DOOMSWORD, Underground Symphony US
CD-033 (1999)
Sacred Metal / Warbringers / Helms Deep /
One Eyed God / Return To Immrryr /
Nadsokar / Swords Of Doom / On The
March
RESOUND THE HORN, Dragonheart (2002)
Shores Of Vinland / Onward The Battle / The
DoomSword / MCXIX / The Early Days Of
Finn MacCool / Resound The Horn: Odin's
Hail

DOT(.) (JAPAN)
Line-Up: Ucchy (vocals / guitar), Kohki (bass),
You (drums)

Japanese Sludge Stoners created in the
August of 1998 by erstwhile URGESNAKE
bassist Kohki and drummer Kan. DOT(.) first
performed live in September of 1999 and
issued a debut demo tape, 'Rawheavygreen'
in July of the following year. After this release
Kan would be replaced by COFFINS
drummer You.
DOT(.)'s second demo, 'Electric Weedland',
was delivered in May of 2001. The band
supported visiting Americans ATROCIOUS
MADNESS in 2002. A split EP, reportedly the
first of many such collaborations, saw DOT(.)
allying themselves with Finnish band
FLESHPRESS.
DOT(.) members are involved in Yoshiaki
Negishi of CHURCH OF MISERY's side
project COFFINS. Ucchy also operates the
solo side venture FLESHPILE.

Singles/EPs:
I Am A Monkey / Smoking Green, (2001)
('Smoking' EP)
Patchwork God / , Kult Of Nihil (2002) (Split
EP with FLESHPRESS)

DOWN (USA)
Line-Up: Phil Anselmo (vocals), Pepper
Keenan (guitar), Kirk Windstein (guitar), Todd
Strange (bass), Jim Bower (drums)

Side project of PANTERA's vocalist Phil
Anselmo and CORROSION OF
CONFORMITY guitarist Pepper Keenan.
Guitarist Kirk Windstein and bassist Todd
Strange are members of CROWBAR.
Drummer Jim Bower also plays with
EYEHATEGOD and is an founder member of
CROWBAR.
Both Bower and Anselmo also play in BODY
OF BLOOD. The duo also busy themselves
with SUPERJOINT RITUAL alongside ex-
CROWBAR guitarist Kevin Bond and
STRESSBALL drummer Joseph Fazzio.
Anselmo, billing himself as 'Anton Crowley'
would also turn up as guitarist for the 1999
reformed NECROPHAGIA for the 1999
'Holocausto De La Morte' album. 2000 found
Anselmo involved in the Black Metal 'star' side
project EIBON. With a low key track inclusion
on the 'Moonfog 2000' compilation album
EIBON consisted of SATYRICON's Satyr
Wongraven, DARKTHRONE's Fenriz, Maniac
of MAYHEM and NECROPHAGIA's Killjoy. As
if all this activity was not enough Anselmo
also performs, albeit anonymously once more
as 'Anton Crowley', with Black Metal band

VIKING CROWN.

Toward the close of 2001 Anselmo seemingly took his passion for side ventures into overdrive declaring a further two bands to his ever lengthening list of side projects. SOUTHERN ISOLATION, which featured Anselmo's girlfriend Stephanie Opal as lead vocalist, saw Anselmo acting as guitarist. The band was rounded out by CHRIST INVERSION keyboard player Ross Karpelman, Kevin Bond of CHRIST INVERSION, CROWBAR and SUPERJOINT RITUAL on bass guitar and Sid Montz on drums. A four track EP was issued in October 2001 on the Baphomet label. Also announced was another collaboration with Killjoy of NECROPHAGIA billed as ENOCH. This band also boasted the inclusion of Mirai from cult Japanese Black Metal band SIGH.

DOWN, now with Anselmo's PANTERA colleague Rex Brown on bass, would return in March of 2002 with a new album 'Down II: Bustle In Your Hedgerow'. The album debuted Billboard charts at no. 44 selling over 30,000 copies in its first week of sale. DOWN would also be a late addition to the 2002 'Ozzfest' touring festival, putting in their own headline performances along the way.

Albums:
NOLA, Elektra 7559-61830-2 (1995)
Temptation's Wings / Lifer / Pillars Of Eternity / Rehab / Hail The Leaf / Underneath Everything / Eyes Of The South / Jail / Losing All / Stone The Crow / Pray For The Locust / Swan Song
DOWN II: A BUSTLE IN YOUR HEDGEROW, Elektra (2002) **44 USA, 73 CANADA**
Lysergic Funeral Procession / There's Something On My Side / Man That Follows Hell / Stained Glass Cross / Ghosts Along The Mississippi / Learn From This Mistake / Beautifully Depressed / Where I'm Going / Doobinterlude / New Orleans Is A Dying Whore / The Seed / Lies (I Don't Know What They Say But...) / Flambeaux / Dog Tired / Wars

DOWNFALL (FRANCE)
Line-Up: Stéphane Vanstaen (vocals / guitar), Christèle Gaye (guitar), Antoine Bécot (cello), Stéphane Marquet (drums)

Gothic Dark-Folk act DOWNFALL, although French in origin, oddly sing in the German tongue.

Albums:
MEINE SELBSZERSTORUNG, Drama & Sin Company DAS003 (2000)

Mein Inneres Chaos / Ohne Ausweg / Der Anfang Vom Ende / Wie Ein Krieg In Mir / Das Gift / Mein Schmerz / Der Tod Der Menschen / Drama / Meine Selbstzerstörung

DOZER (SWEDEN)
Line-Up: Fredrik Nordin (vocals / guitar), Tommi Holappa (guitar), Johan Rockner (bass), Erik Bäckwall (drums)

Borlänge based Stoners formulated during 1995. The band's original line-up comprised vocalist / guitarist Fredrik Nordin, guitarist Tommi Holappa, bass player Magnus Larsson and drummer Erik Bäckwall. However, Larson would quit in 1997, to pursue his love of martial arts, and DOZER plugged the vacancy with Johan Rockner. This line-up of DOZER has remained solid ever since.

The band's debut was delivered by way of a split 7" single in league with DEMON CLEANER in 1998. The very first release for the Molten Universe label, the single's first edition of 300 soon sold out and a further run of 200 copies pressed onto blue vinyl came later. DOZER continued the association with DEMON CLEANER for a follow up 'Hawaiian Cottage' EP, this time offered as 100 purple and 400 orange coloured vinyls.

DOZER's split EP 'Coming Down The Mountain', issued by Meteor City in 1999, brought the band to a whole new audience courtesy of their alliance with UNIDA. Three variants of the single were issued, the CD variant including the track 'Headed For The Sun' whilst 12" vinyl copies replaced this track with 'Twilight Sleep'. Meteor City would release 1000 copies on 220 gramm red vinyl and a Subway Records co-operation - once more restricted to 1000 copies on black & white splatter effect vinyl.

Yet another collaboration with DEMON CLEANER resulted in the 2000 'Domestic Dudes' split EP. With the release of the April 2000 album 'In The Tail Of A Comet' DOZER embarked upon a European touring schedule packaged with LOWRIDER. A single, 'The Phantom', emerged to promote these dates. DOZER's second album, 'Madre De Dios', would be issued by Man's Ruin for CD and by Molten Universe on vinyl. The latter edition not only came packaged in completely different artwork but included an extra track in 'Rings Of Saturn'.

DOZER would cover the DEAD BOYS 'Sonic Reducer' for a shared 7" single with NATAS in 2002. Touring in Europe found DOZER out with road partners THE AWESOME MACHINE.

Besides his work with DOZER guitarist Tommi Holappa also brandishes a retro heavy Blues Rock side venture entitled GREENLEAF in union with Daniel of DEMON CLEANER. Both Fredrik Nordin and Johan Rockner are members of Punk band THE SICK.

Singles/EPs:
Tanglefoot / Centreline /, Molten Universe MOLTEN001 (1998) (Split single with DEMON CLEANER)
Megawheel / Heading Home, Molten Universe MOLTEN002 (1999) ('Hawaiian Cottage' split EP with DEMON CLEANER)
Headed For The Sun / Calamari Sidetrip / From Mars / Overheated, Meteor City MCY-005 (1999) ('Coming Down The Mountain' split EP with UNIDA. CD version.)
Overheated / Twilight Sleep / Calamari Sidetrip / From Mars, Meteor City MCY-005 (1999) ('Coming Down The Mountain' split EP with UNIDA. 12" vinyl version)
Octanoid / Hail The Dude, Molten Universe MOLTEN003 (2000) ('Domestic Dudes' split EP with DEMON CLEANER)
Supersoul / Lightyears Ahead / Speeder / Inside The Falcon, Man's Ruin MR135 (2000) ('In The Tail Of A Comet' 10" EP)
The Phantom / Sub Ethna, Molten Universe MOLTEN009 (2000)
Sonic Reducer, Black Juju (2002) (Split 7" single with NATAS)

Albums:
IN THE TAIL OF A COMET, Man's Ruin MR134 (2000)
Supersoul / Lightyears Ahead / Speeder / Inside The Falcon / Riding The Machine / Cupola / Grand Dragon / Captain Spaceheart / High Roller
MADRE DE DIOS, Man's Ruin MR2010 (2001)
Let The Shit Roll / Freeloader / Soulsjigh / Octanoid / Earth Yeti / Full Circle / Mono Impact / Early Grace / TX9 / Thunderbolt

DRAGONAUTA (ARGENTINA)
Line-Up: Federico Wolman (vocals), Daniel Libedinski (guitar), Martin Mendez (bass), Ariel Solito (drums)

The heavily '70s laden Buenos Aires Doom act DRAGONAUTA, titled in honour of SLEEP's 'Dragonaut' track, came into being during mid 1999. Frontman Federico Wolman and guitarist Daniel Libedinski had previously operated with Psychedelic act SUPERNALIA, Wolman then as bass player. The pair would unite with bassist Martin Mendez and drummer Ariel Solito, both of Acid Rockers PATA DE ELEFANTE to create DRAGONAUTA, reportedly to assemble a "Satanic hippie" act.
The band would share a split album release

with NATAS on the Icarus label.

Albums:
DRAGONAUTA, Icarus (2000) (Split album with NATAS)
Astroinfierno / Hombre Monstruo / Guardian Del Hongo / Profeta Del Mar

DRAGON GREEN (Allentown, PA, USA)
Line-Up: Mike Clancey (guitar), Joe America (bass), Mike Ireton, Manimal (drums)

DRAGON GREEN was forged in 2000 by former STILLWATER guitarist Mike Clancey. Unable to locate a suitable vocalist the band recorded their debut album for the Infernal Racket label 'Emissions From Green Sessions' as an entirely instrumental offering. Following the record's release DRAGON GREEN inducted erstwhile STILLWATER singer Jon Pospischil for live work but his tenure would be brief. DRAGON GREEN reverted back to an instrumental band.

Albums:
EMISSIONS FROM GREEN SESSIONS, Infernal Racket IRR 7-2 (2001)
Turning Stones / Deleted / Marker 5 / Gipsi The Amateur / Rumble Strip

DRAINED (MA, USA)
Line-Up: Bob Mendell (vocals), Neal Delongchamp (guitar), Mike Cardoso (bass), Roger Chouinard (drums)

Albums:
SUSPENSION OF DISBELIEF, Martyr Music Group MM6720200001-2 (1999)
All Will Fall / Redemption / Me Too / Take My Eyes / Next Week / Dependence / Do Something / Through It All / Brudna / Commodity / When You Give / World Of Sin

DREAD (AUSTRALIA)
Line-Up: Jason Vassallo (vocals), Jason Eames (guitar), Troy McMinn (guitar), Roger Moore (bass), Paul Toth (drums)

Melbourne Doom Stoners DREAD are fronted by former CHRISTBAIT man Jason Vassallo.

Singles/EPs:
Grunt EP, (2001)

DREADFUL SHADOWS (GERMANY)
Line-Up: Sven Friedrich (vocals / keyboards / guitar), Stefan Neubauer (guitar), Jens Reidiger (bass), Ron Thiele (drums)

Berlin's DREADFUL SHADOWS, a blend of

Psychedelic Hard Goth, were created in 1993 soon securing a deal with Sounds Of Delight Records after heavy touring.

With the release of the debut album in April 1994 DREADFUL SHADOWS performed shows in Germany alongside LOVE LIKE BLOOD, BREATH OF LIFE, CHRISTIAN DEATH and NOSFERATU.

DREADFUL SHADOWS have contributed tracks to the compilation albums 'Wave Romantics', 'Gothic Compilation' and 'Zillo Romantic Sound Sampler' as well as a cover version of the SISTERS OF MERCY track '1959' to the 'Monochrome' SISTERS OF MERCY tribute album.

Singles/EPs:
Homeless / Paradize / Dead Can Wait (Live) / Dirge (Live) / A Sea Of Tears (Piano version) / True Faith / Homeless (Cyber Edit), Sounds Of Delight (1995)
Burning The Shrouds / Burning The Shrouds (Frantic Section remix) / Ties Of Time (String version), Oblivion SPV CD 055-61873 (1997)
Twist In My Sobriety / Twist In My Sobriety (Version) / Regeneration, Oblivion (1999)
Futility / Futility (Project Pitchfork mix) / Empty Names, Oblivion (1999)

Albums:
ESTRANGEMENT, Sounds Of Delight (1994)
Resurrection / Over The Worst / Dead Can Wait / Still Alive / Through The Mirror / Funeral Procession / A Sea Of Tears / Dirge / Her Devotion / The Release / Estrangement
BURIED AGAIN, Deathwish DW0183-2 (1996)
Providence / Chains / Condemnation / Dusk / Obituary / Everlasting Words / Dissolution / Mortal Hope / The Racking Call / Buried Again
BEYOND THE MAZE, Oblivion (1998)
Crusade / Fall / The Figures Of Disguise / Ties Of Time / Craving / The Soil / The Drowning Sun / Desolated Home / Burning The Shrouds / Beyond The Maze
THE CYCLE, Oblivion (1999)
Prelude / Futility / New Day / A Better God / Intransigence / Torn Being / Courageous / The Vortex / Awakening / Vagrants In Space / Calling The Sun / Exile / The Cycle / Twist In My Sobriety

DREAM BREED (UK)
Line-Up: Dave Pybus (Vocals / guitar), Paul (bass), Gary Querns (drums)

Dave Pybus was press officer for Peaceville Records. The album features MY DYING BRIDE's Aaron on backing vocals.

Pybus later formed DREAMWEAVER and would join ANATHEMA in 1998.

Albums:
SOMETIME, Coast To Coast CTC 1CD (1995)
Sometime / To Never Know / Sleep Out / Noverna / The Very Devil / Three Worlds

DREAM INTO DUST
(New York, NY, USA)
Line-Up: Derek Rush (vocals / guitar / bass / keyboards), Bryin Dall (guitar)

A disturbingly dreary 'Dark Art' act centred upon Derek Rush. Initially the project, founded around 1997, was entitled DECEMBER, even releasing a 7" single 'Rivers Of Blood' with that title.

An exclusive song 'Somnolent' emerged on the Dragon Flight album 'The Cold, The Silent'. In keeping with their eccentric nature DREAM INTO DUST would issue a 7" single 'A Prison To Yourself' which came with a limited release cassette comprising three instrumental passages of music inspired by the '60s cult TV series 'The Prisoner'.

Following recording of 'The World We Have Lost' DREAM INTO DUST embarked upon a series of exclusive compositions for use on compilation albums. 'Stormbringer' was included on the 'Presumed Guilty' album on Misanthropy Records, 'Totestadt on Middle Pillar's 'What Is Eternal' collection, 'The Dread World Born In Sleep' on 'SOL Volume 3' for the Tursa imprint and 'Out Of Chaos Stars Are Born'. The latter song featured on 'On The Brink Of Infinity' on DREAM INTO DUST's own Chthonic Streams label. A further unique outing, 'The Chariot' would be found on the 'Major Arcana Of The Tarot' compilation released by Palace Of Worms.

DREAM INTO DUST also channels its energies into various side endeavours such as LORETTA'S DOLL, the experimental Industrial act OF UNKNOWN ORIGIN and the Electronic outfit A MURDER OF ANGELS. Guitarist Bryin Dall also operates 4TH SIGN OF THE APOCALYPSE and the 'Noise' venture URSUS NOIR. Dall, in union with the renowned figure of Genesis P-Orridge also pursues THEE MAJESTY.

Singles/EPs:
A Dance Of The Dead / Once Upon A Time, Chtonic Streams (1997) ('A Prison For Oneself' EP)
Salvations Corridor / Crystal Mirrors, World Serpent (2001) (7" Picture disc)

Albums:

NO MAN'S LAND, Chthonic Streams (1997)
The Lost Crusade / Age Of Delirium /
Dissolution / Seasons In The Mist
THE WORLD WE HAVE LOST, Elfenblut
(1999)
Maelstrom / Cross The Abyss / Mercury
Falling / Nothing But Blood / Enemy At The
Gates / Farewell To Eden / Eternal
Inquisition / The World We Have Lost / Not
Above But Apart

DREAMS OF SANITY (AUSTRIA)

Line-Up: Sandra Schleret (vocals), Christian
Marx (guitar), Andreas Wilauer (guitar),
Michael Knoflach (bass), Stefan Manges
(keyboards), Hannes Richter (drums)

A complex Austrian Gothic Rock act,
DREAMS OF SANITY was created as a trio
during April 1991 with a line-up of guitarist
Christian Marx, bass player Michael Knoflach
together with drummer Hannes Richter, the
latter an erstwhile member of
BLITZGEMETAL and HYPEN. A little over a
year later the band expanded its format
inducting frontman Gudrun Gfrerer along with
keyboard player Florian Razesberger.
By the close of 1993 ructions within the band
witnessed the departure of Richter. It would
not be the only change. Razesberger
manouevered to second guitar and Stefan
Manges took the keyboard role. Meanwhile
Gfrerer lost out to Birgit Moser. The vocal
roles would switch again when Sandra
Schleret and Martina Hornbacher assumed
the duties for the band's debut demo recorded
in May of 1994. Before the year was out
DREAMS OF SANITY lost Razesberger and
new face on second guitar turned out to be
Andreas Wilauer.
With this line-up DREAMS OF SANITY
recorded 'Komödia I' and 'Komödia II' in the Z-
Sound-Studios in Innsburck. These two tracks
emerged on the compilation album 'A
Goddamned City'.
In 1996 'Ein Liebeslied' was laid down in the
same studio and subsequently released on
the Tyrol region 'Hardboiled' sampler.
DREAMS OF SANITY hooked up with
LACRIMOSA, THE GATHERING,
SENTENCED and D-AGE for the 'Dark Winter
Nights' European tour after which a deal with
Gothic Rock specialists Hall Of Sermon was
struck.
DREAMS OF SANITY's promise was fulfilled
with the issue of the inaugural November
1997 'Komödia' album. However, further line-
up turbulence ensued with Hornbacher and
Astner departing. Hornbacher would come to
attention with contributions to THERION and
later ALAS.

Harald Obexer would replace Astner but then
Manges quit too. DREAMS OF SANITY made
up the numbers by drafting Frédéric Heil.
This variant of the band committed
themselves to recording the 1999 opus
'Masquerade' and follow up 'The Game'.
Another band casualty was Obexer, making
his exit in 2000. Patrick Schrittwieser duly
took the drum role. Heil too bade farewell and
DREAMS OF SANITY welcomed aboard
Florian Steiner.
January of 2001 would witness a period of
severe turbulence for the band. Not only did
DREAMS OF SANITY split away from Hall Of
Sermon Records but they would lose Schleret
too, the vocalist joining SIEGFRIED. Barbara
Peer would be drafted as replacement.
However, having announced a comeback
album billed provisionally as 'The End' in
January of 2002 DREAMS OF SANITY
revealed that Sandra Schleret had been
enticed back into the fold.

Albums:

KOMÖDIA, Hall Of Sermon HOS 7061
(1997)
Komödia I / Beatrice / Komödia II / Komödia
III / Komödia IV / The Prophet / Treesitter /
Blade Of Doom
MASQUERADE, Hall Of Sermon HOS 7062
(1999)
Opera / The Phantom Of The Opera /
Masquerade, Act 1 / Masquerade, Act 2 /
Masquerade, Interlude / Masquerade, Act 3 /
Masquerade, Act 4 / Within (The Dragon) /
The Maiden And The River / Lost Paradise
99
THE GAME, Hall Of Sermon HOS7063CD
(2000)
In... / The Creature That You Came To See /
Time To Set The Stones / The Beginning
That Lies / The Empress - Through The
Looking Glass (A Dream ?) / A Window To
The Sky / And So (I Walk On) / We.Ll.Sea /
The Creature That You Came To See
(Reprise) / ...Finit

DREAM WEAVER (GREECE)

Line-Up: Jim Marcou (vocals / guitar), George
Zacharoglou (guitar), Michael Kypreos (bass),
John Basimakopoulos (drums)

Doomladen Power Metal act created in May
of 1990 by guitarist George Zacharoglou and
vocalist / guitarist Jim Marcou, former
members of INFECTION. The duo would
issue the 'Infection' demo tape the following
year. DREAM WEAVER would be solidified in
mid 1992 with the enlistment of bassist
Michael Kypreos and drummer John
Basimakopoulos.

In May of 1995 DREAM WEAVER recorded the 5 track 'Dream Within A Dream' demo session. Due to members' obligations with national service it would be a full five years before DREAM WEAVER would issue their opening gambit 'Fantasy Revealed' through the Secret Port label in January 2001. Following these recordings DREAM WEAVER switched bassists, bringing in Takis Fytos. The band would support the resurrected American Heavy Metal band BROCAS HELM on their Autumn Greek shows. A 7" single, 'Soulsearching', arrived in early 2002.

Singles/EPs:
Soulsearching / Voice To Run The Miles, Eat Metal (2002)

Albums:
FANTASY REVEALED, Secret Port (20010
Destiny Dancer / Bed Of Pain / Hands On The White / Desolate Heart / Miss Another Meaning

DROWN (Orange County, CA, USA)
Line-Up: Lauren Boquette (vocals), Patrick Sprawl (guitar), Sean Demott (bass), Marco Forcone (drums)

Industrial, gloom tinged Nu-Metal act founded in 1987 as YESTERDAY'S TEAR. Switched titles to DROWN in 1989.
DROWN scored a major coup by signing to Elektra Records for their debut record 'Hold On To The Hollow' but were dropped shortly after. Bassist Rob Nicholson joined PRONG then DANZIG. He would go on to WHITE ZOMBIE and ROB ZOMBIE under the new pseudonym of 'Blasko'.
DROWN signed to Geffen but although another album was recorded and ready to go Geffen passed. The album eventually emerged on Mercury subsidiary Slipdisc.
The 1999 'Kerosene' single features ORGY's Ryan Shuck on guitar. DROWN toured America with CLUTCH to promote the record. With DROWN's eventual collapse frontman Lauren Boquette, Patrick Sprawl and Sean Demott founded FAMOUS, gaining valuable exposure on the SLAYER headlined 'Tattoo The Earth' North American tour. However, with Sprawl and Demott then opting out Boquette persevered as SIX. Ex-DROWN drummer Marco Forcone re-emerged with HUMAN LAB.

Singles/EPs:
Kerosene (Radio version) / Kerosene (Mi Vida Loca version) / Kerosene (1605 All Star version) / Kerosene (Album version) / Something To Do, Slipdisc (1998)

Albums:
HOLD ON TO THE HOLLOW, Elektra (1994)
I Owe You / Pieces Of Man / Beautiful / What It Is To Burn / Longing / Transparent / Lost / Reflection / Arms Full Of Empty / Everything
PRODUCT OF A TWO FACED WORLD, Slipdisc (1998)
You Never Listened / The Day I Walked Away / 1605 (For My Suffering) / Kerosene / Tired Of Living Like This / Alone In A Dirty World / Redial / My Private War / Need This Need / The Dirtiest Hand / Two Faced You / Monster

THE DROWNING (FRANCE)
Line-Up: Stéphane Vanstaen (vocals / guitar / drum-programming), Régis Lacoste (bass)

Albums:
WHERE IT ALL HAS TO END, Mono-Emotional 01072001-04 (2002)
My Fellowtide / Where It All Has To End / The Rain Of Endtimes / Hold You In My Harms / Down & Deeper / No One But A Silhouette / The Deeper Depths / Things That Can't Last

DRUNKHORSE (San Francisco, CA, USA)
Line-Up: Elijah Eckert (vocals / guitar), John Niles (guitar), Cyrus (bass), Cripe (drums)

Boogiefied Stoners from San Francisco. DRUNKHORSE previously operated as THE PANTS, featuring SOLID GOLD vocalist / guitarist Elijah Eckert and bassist Cyrus from BLACK FORK. As DRUNKHORSE the group debuted for the Man's Ruin label with an eponymous outing in 2000. The follow up, 'Tanning Salon / Biblical Proportions', was the fusing of two intended concept EPs, one dealing with consumerism and the other religion.
Following the second album release DRUNKHORSE issued a somewhat unexpected homage to PRINCE, covering two of the purple Pop star's tracks 'Bambi' and 'Dirty Mind' for a 7" single on Wantage USA Records. The band would also feature on the Small Stones Recording AEROSMITH tribute 'Right In The Nuts' with their take on 'Kings & Queens'.
DRUNKHORSE would team up with THE FUCKING CHAMPS and THE LAST OF THE JUANITAS for a two month nationwide American tour in May / June of 2002.

Singles/EPs:
Bambi / Dirty Mind, Wantage USA (2001)

Albums:
DRUNKHORSE, Man's Ruin (2000)
Arroyo Grande / High Score / Greazy

Moustache / Temperamental Woman / Ass
Out - Passed Out / Nocturnal Emotions /
White Lady Of The Mesa
**TANNING SALON / BIBLICAL
PROPORTIONS**, Man's Ruin MR2004
(2001)
Am/Fm Shoes / Secret Ingredient / Plastic
Doll / Intermission / In The Beginning /
Vicious & Loathes / 'lude No. 1 / Manchild /
'lude No. 2 / Is, Was... (And Ever Shall Be) /
Revelations

THE DUKES OF NOTHING (UK)

Line-Up: Tony Sylvester (vocals), Dean Berry
(guitar), Stuart O'Hara (guitar), Doug Dalziel
(bass), Chris Turner (drums)

THE DUKES OF NOTHING boast an
underground pedigree second to none, the
band including members of such esteemed
names as ACRIMONY, FABRIC, IRON
MONKEY and ORANGE GOBLIN.
The band title first came into use on IRON
MONKEY's final European tour in June of
1999. When frontman John Morrow fell
seriously ill the remaining band members
opted to fulfil tour commitments, rebilling
themselves THE DUKES OF NOTHING and
serving up a purely instrumental set.
With IRON MONKEY's demise guitarist Dean
Berry and bassist Doug Dalziel united with
ORANGE GOBLIN drummer Chris Turner
and ACRIMONY guitarist Stuart O'Hara to
reactivate the band name.
THE DUKES OF NOTHING would gain
valuable support slots to ZEN GUERILLA,
ZEKE and MOTORHEAD during April and
May of 2002.
A limited edition single, oddly of 747 copies,
arrived in August through Butcher's Hook
Records comprising 'Saxon Action' (hence
the pressing number), a cover of Country &
Western rebel DAVID ALLAN COE's 'Rock &
Roll Fever' and 'That's What I Hate'.

Singles/EPs:
Saxon Action / Rock & Roll Fever / That's
What I Hate, Butcher's Hook (2002) (Limited
edition 747 copies)

Albums:
WAR & WINE, Eccentric Man ECC003CD
(2002)
War & Wine / God V. The Nudge / 31st
Round / Miss Fortune / Don't Stop For Red /
Riding / Two Grams / White Damage

DUNKELSTORM (ARGENTINA)

Line-Up: Lucas Spattola (vocals), Matías
Otero Villagra (guitar), Augusto Miklikowski
(guitar), Julián Núñez Stolles (bass), Sergio

Núñez Stolles (keyboards / programming)

DUNKELSTORM, a 'Dark' Metal band, began
life in 1997, created by the Núñez Stolles
siblings bass player Julián and keyboard
player Sergio. In mid 1998 the band solidified
with the addition of vocalist Lucas Spátola,
Martín García Suarez on bass and Augusto
Miklikowski on guitars. Developing an
underground following, in 1999
DUNKELSTORM opted to drop drums in
favour of programming.
During mid 2001 the track 'Schicksal' was
recorded for the Furias Records compilation
'Hidden Ceremony'.

Albums:
SCHICKSAL, Furias F005 (2002)

DUSK (USA)

Line-Up: Steve Crane (vocals), Tim Beyer
(guitar), Steve Gross (guitar / keyboards),
Emily Olsen (bass), Ron Heemstra (drums)

Cult Doom Death outfit out of Wisconsin.
Drummer Ron Heemstra is an erstwhile
member of NOTHIN' SACRED and BLEED.
In 1995 DUSK would lose their vocalist Steve
Crane to a church group, the ex-Metal
musician devoting himself to a missionary in
Kenya. DUSK replaced Crane with Chad
Denslow.
Lost Disciple Records would reissue the
'Majestic Thou In Ruin' and 'Dusk' material
complete with a track from the 'Visionaries Of
The Macabre' compilation album 'Yearning
For Eternity' with Chad Denslow on vocals.
Tim Beyer subsequently joined PROFANE.

Singles/EPs:
...Majestic Thou In Ruin / Paled / Thy Bitter
Woe / The Transfiguration (And It Was So),
Requiem Productions (1995) ('Majestic Thou
In Ruin' EP)

Albums:
DUSK, Cybermusik (1994)
Envision The Terror / Element Of Symmetry /
Begotten Interlude / Dreamscape /
Consigned To Oblivion / Mourning Shadow
MOURNING... RESURRECT, Lost Disciple
(1997)
Envision The Terror / Element Of Symmetry /
Begotten Interlude / Dreamscape /
Consigned To Oblivion / Mourning Shadow /
...Majestic Thou In Ruin / Paled / Thy Bitter
Woe / The Transfiguration (And It Was So) /
Yearning For Eternity

DUSTER 69 (GERMANY)

Line-Up: Lucki Schmidt (vocals), Jochen

Böllath (guitar), Michael Fiolka (guitar), Matthias Schmidt (bass), Peter Wiesenbacher (drums)

DUSTER 69, operating in 'Fuzz Rock' Stoner-Psych territory, debuted as a trio in April of 1999 with two live in the studio recordings included on a split 7" single 'Extra Heavy' shared with fellow German Stoners CALAMUS.

Landing a deal with the Daredevil label the first album, 'Interstellar Burst' produced by Georg Graser, reaped heady praise and would soon sell out. During these album sessions DUSTER 69 cut a rendition of BLACKTOP's 'Highway', this track later finding an outlet on the 'Blood On The Streets' compilation.

Subsequent appearances would find the band including tracks on the 'Burned Down To Zero' compilation in 2000 and a new remix of 'Burn Out' to the 'New Rays From A Black Rising Sun' for the American Dirt magazine compilation the following year.

DUSTER 69's second album, released in 2001, would include a cover version of SLO BURN's 'Cactus Jumper'. Extensive European touring found DUSTER 69 acting as openers for MAMMOTH VOLUME, DOZER, KARMA TO BURN, SIXTY WATT SHAMAN, THE KRAUTS and SUNRIDE.

DUSTER 69 then added new members vocalist Lucki Schmidt and guitarist Michael Fiolka, the revised line-up putting in an inaugural showing with a track inclusion on the compilation 'A Collection Of Great Dance Tunes Volume 2'.

In mid 2002 the band unveiled plans to record tracks for a split 10" vinyl release with THE AWESOME MACHINE. Further alliances came with Norwegians GATE 9 for yet another split EP on the Underdogma Records label.

Singles/EPs:
Centretrip / Controller / , (1999) ('Extra Heavy' split 7" single with CALAMUS)

Albums:
INTERSTELLAR BURST, Daredevil DD003 (1999)
Tornado / 2nd Floor Landing / Astro-Face Man / Sound Of Ocean / Centretrip / Interstellar Burst / Spin Me Round / Signal From Mars / Controller / Grav Zero / Blue Road
DUSTER 69, Daredevil DD011 (2001)
Baby, Strip Down / Fireball / Doghouse / Monster Superblast / Burn Out / Sweetwater / Dust Crusher / Underflow / Rhino's Dance / Cactus Jumper

DYSANCHELY (SLOVALKIA)
Line-Up: Lojzo Horak (vocals), Alena Pichlerova (vocals), Nela Horvatova (vocals), Milos Kosak (guitar), Dodo Zachar (guitar), Brando Glida (bass), Milan Lux (drums)

The melancholic Doom styled Death Metal act DYSANCHELY came into being during 1995, fronted by the male vocals of Lojzo Horak and female counterpart Zuza Grujbakova. The 1996 'Messengers Of Destruction' demo announced their arrival, followed up by 'Eternal Sleep' the same year. This latter tape would see DYSANCHELY enhancing their vocal sound with the addition of Alena Pichlerova.

A deal was secured with the Czech label Leviathan but upfront of recording the debut album 'Tears' Grujbakova decided to leave. Her replacement would be Nela Horvatova, later also a member of fellow Slovakian Doom merchants THALARION.

DYSANCHELY would adopt a more Black Metal stance for a cassette album 'Songs Of Sorrow' issued by Russian label Oupiric Productions. This release featured a cover version of KISS' 'God Of Thunder', new tracks and reworked older material.

Albums:
TEARS, Leviathan (1998)
Century Of Inquisition / Return To The Hall Of Ages / Shadows Of The World / Eternal Sleep / Cruel Beauty / In The Dust Of Eternity / Tears / Instrument Of Extermination
SONGS OF SORROW, Oupiric Productions (2000)

EARTH (Olympia, WA, USA)
Line-Up: Dylan Carlson (vocals / guitar), Dave Harwell (bass), Joe Preston (vocals / percussion)

A true underground act. EARTH, with a sound reliant on long, droning passages and plentiful feedback, deliver what is commonly described as 'Ambient Metal'. EARTH came together during 1990, the idea of Dylan Carlson. The original intention had been to call the new project WORMWOOD but new members guitarist Slim Moon (Later of KILL ROCK STARS) and vocalist Greg Babior billed the act EARTH. On bass would be TDG, also involved with Carlson in the side venture THE FRAGILE SPHINCTER. Babior would soon make his exit and bassist Dave Harwell and vocalist / percussionist Joe Preston duly signed on for EARTH membership. With this line-up EARTH, with Slim Moon on vocals, performed their inaugural gig at the Blues Gallery in Portland. At the bands second show Carlson took the lead vocal mantle as EARTH ploughed through a set of cover songs by the likes of MOTORHEAD, SCORPIONS and ST. VITUS.

Mike Lastra produced EARTH's debut recordings, which witnessed a studio session from NIRVANA's Kurt Cobain on guitar. At a local show supporting L7, EARTH provoked interest from the Sub Pop label and the band's debut, 'Extra-Capsular Extraction' saw a release in 1991. Subsequent live shows, including a batch of supports to SCREAMING TREES, saw EARTH operating as a trio utilizing a drum machine. Shortly after these gigs Preston bailed out to join THE MELVINS. HELL COWS guitarist Carl Anala plugged the vacancy left by Preston albeit briefly and EARTH was reduced to a duo for recording of the second, Stewart Hallerman produced album 'Earth 2: Special Low Frequency Version'. One track from this opus 'Teeth Of Lions Rule The Divine' would later prove influential, becoming the title of a post millennium Doom-Stoner supergroup collective led by CATHEDRAL's Lee Dorrain.

Promotion of the second album for EARTH included an appearance at the 'Ultra-Fest', which caused consternation when EARTH proceeded to perform an entire set based on one 25 minute song. Dave Harwell would be the next to decamp.

Now essentially operating as a solo act EARTH nonetheless got to work on a third album, pulling in FARTZ and CRISIS PARTY guitarist Tommy Hansen on second guitar. However, these sessions would stall midway through recording as Sub Pop refused to fund the venture any further. After a lengthy hiatus

Sub Pop came back on board and EARTH resumed recording at the Soundhouse Studios with Scott Benson acting as producer and Rick Cambern on the drums. The album finally saw release in April of 1995 and reaped underground acclaim.

The Blast First label would then engage the band, now with Ian Dickson installed on bass, for recording of a live album 'Sunn Amps And Smashed Guitars' in London although Sub Pop would then re-sign the band on a three album contract. EARTH revitalized itself by pulling in new members guitarist Shawn McElligot and drummer Mike McDaniels for the 'Pentastar: In The Style Of Demons' record, EARTH's most commercially accessible album to date and one in which the band covered JIMI HENDRIX's 'Peace In Mississippi'. The group would perform at the Austrian 'Hyperstrings' festival in 1996. A live tape from this gig surfaced some years later as an obscure, and very rare limited edition one sided vinyl release. EARTH's cult status was now such that bootleg live singles were now leaking onto the market. Recordings from these bootlegs plus early demo tracks were compiled for a limited edition, clear vinyl release '10: 1990' through the Anja label in 2000.

Carlson made a fleeting appearance in the late '90s movie 'Kurt And Courtney'. The No Quarter label reissued 'Sunn Amps And Smashed Guitars' complete with four extra tracks culled from a 1990 EARTH demo.

In recent years Carlson has removed himself from the public eye.

Albums:
EXTRA CAPSULAR EXTRACTION, Sub Pop SP123 (1990)
A Bureaucratic Desire For Revenge Parts 1 & 2 / Ouroboros Is Broken
EARTH 2: SPECIAL LOW FREQUENCY VERSION, Sub Pop SP185 (1993)
Seven Angels / Teeth Of Lions Rule The Divine / Like Gold And Faceted
THRONES AND DOMINIONS, Sub Pop 292 (1995)
Harvey / Tibetan Quaaludes / Lullaby (Take 2: How Dry I Am) / Song 4 / Site Specific Carnivorous Occurrence / Phase 3: Agni Detonating Over The Thar Desert... / Thrones and Dominions / Song 6 (Chime)
SUNN AMPS AND SMASHED GUITARS, Blast First BFFP 123 (1995)
PENTASTAR: IN THE STYLE OF DEMONS, Sub Pop SPCD361 (1996)
Introduction / High Command / Crooked Axis For String Quartet / Tallahassee / Charioteer (Temple Song) / Peace In Mississippi / Sonar And Depth Charge / Coda Maestoso In F(Flat) Minor"

10.1990, Anja (2000) (Clear vinyl. Limited edition of 360)
Methadrine (Live) / German Dental Work (Live) Divine Bright Extraction / Dissolution / Bureaucratic Desire For Revenge / Orouboros (Live)
EARTH: LIVE 070796, (2001) (Limited edition 560 copies)
SUNN AMPS AND SMASHED GUITARS, No Quarter NQR001 (2001)
Ripped On Fascist Ideas / Geometry Of Murder / German Dental Work / Divine And Bright / Dissolution 1

EARTHCORPSE (UK)
Line-Up: Mark Le Page (vocals), Phil (guitar), Bob (guitar), John (bass), Daz (drums)

A Guernsey based Doom outfit that evolved from Peaceville recording artists INSURRECTION. As EARTHCORPSE the band announced their arrival in 1989 citing a line up of vocalist / drummer Mark Le Page, guitarist Jon and bassist Pete. The 'Dark Heaven' demo followed in 1991 after which Justin took on the drumming role and Matt came in on second guitar.
EARTHCORPSE's inaugural commercial outing came in 1992 with the 'Mephitis' 12" single issued by Grave Records. However guitarist Jon would depart and Paul took over from Pete on bass guitar. With this line-up EARTHCORPSE submitted the track 'Lifeless' to the Shiver Records compilation album 'Sometimes Death Is Better'. Further line-up shuffles found Bob taking the bass role and Dan enrolling as second guitarist as the debut album 'Born Bleeding' emerged through Shiver Records in 1996.
Yet again the band roster shifted, Bob filling the vacancy left by the departure of guitarist Matt and John filling the task of bassist. EARTHCORPSE's second record 'The Taste Of Sin' was issued in July of 1999. There was still more friction to come as Dan then made his exit. EARTHCORPSE's new guitarist would be named as Phil. During January of 2000 long-standing drummer Justin left the fold, supplanted by Daz. This version of the group recorded a version of BURZUM's 'Lost Wisdom' for the Cymophane compilation 'Visions'.

Albums:
BORN BLEEDING, Shiver SHR014 (1996)
Intro / Shine / On Darker Shores / Something More / Lifeless / Born Bleeding / Earthen
A TASTE OF SIN, Shiver SHR029 (1999)
Trail Of Tears / Winter /Serpents Kiss / It Is The Gods / In My Remains / Another God / The Taste Of Sin / The Life Of All Flesh / The

Suffering / Plead Forgiveness / Winter (Mentalist remix)

EARTHRIDE (MD, USA)
Line-Up: David Sherman (vocals), Kyle Van Steinberg (guitar), Joe Ruthvin (bass), Eric Little (drums)

Maryland Doomsters with pedigree. EARTHRIDE's frontman David Sherman, a veteran of such acts as WRETCHED, LOVE RAZOR and PENDULUM, also plies his trade as bassist with the high profile SPIRIT CARAVAN. Drummer Eric Little was a member of the renowned INTERNAL VOID until 1993 whilst bassist Joe Ruthvin was with CHOWDER.
EARTHRIDE debuted with an eponymous four track EP on their own Earth Brain label. The debut album, the Chris Koslowski produced 'Taming Of The Demons', was issued in June of 2002 by Southern Lord Records.

Singles/EPs:
Earthride / Black / Enter Zacfreyalz / Weak End, Earth Brain (2000)

Albums:
TAMING OF THE DEMONS, Southern Lord (2002)
Volume 10 / For Mere Remains / Train Wreck / Under A Black Cloud / Deception / Mr. Green / Taming Of The Demons

EIRA D'OR (HOLLAND)
Line-Up: Werner Kruf (vocals), Marco van Asperen (guitar), Lennart van Meegan (guitar), Matthijs van Beem (bass), Rutger van Krieken (drums)

An atmospherically charged Metal band out of Goringham, Holland. EIRA D'OR, taking their name from a Middle Earth kingdom of J.R.R. Tolkien, came together in 1998, maintaining a stable line-up to the present day.
All of EIRA D'OR's three releases are self-financed endeavours.

Singles/EPs:
King I've Never Been / The Serpents Eye / Running Through The Woods, Eira D'Or (1999) (Promotion release)
The Crimson Rose / The Black Well / Weeping In Fear / Why The Wolfs Howl, Eria D'Or (2001) ('The Black Well' EP)

Albums:
SONGS OF SORROW AND AGONY, Eira D'Or (1999)

The Serpents Eye / Running Through The Woods / King I've Never Been / Her Song Of Sorrow And Agony / Lost In Life / Ghazghkull Thraka

EISHEILIG (GERMANY)
Line-Up: Dennis Miklus (vocals), Till Maiwald (guitar), Henry Zenero (guitar), Niklas Peternek (Bass) Dominik Sapia (drums)

Little is known about this very somber Gothic Doom band. EISHEILIG remains an unknown quantity even in some Doom circles. EISHEILIG's eponymous debut included a 'secret' track of a version of THE DOORS 'Love Street'.

Albums:
EISHEILIG, Napalm NPR 090 (2001)
Die Brucken / Am Letzten Tag / Wolfzeit / Vater Unser / Sunder / Bei Dir / Mein Blut / Das Tier / Tanz Mit Mir / Das Licht / Feuerstaub / Love Street

ELBERETH (SPAIN)
Line-Up: Lola Marquinez (vocals), Asier Gonzalez (guitar), Fernando Averalo (guitar), Alvaro Castro (bass), David Diaz (drums)

Melodic Gothic Doom Metal band with not only female vocals to assert their individuality but violins, flutes and even bagpipes!

Singles/EPs:
Reminiscences From The Past, Drowned Productions (1992)

Albums:
... AND OTHER REASONS, Witchunt WIHU 9520 (1995)
From The Sea Cliff / The Idyllic Place Of Innocence / The End Of The 2nd Act / April Rain / Four Roses In My Heart / The Beautyful Short Story / Crystal World / ...And Other Reflections / So Much Affliction / Fallen Leaves / Forgotten Forever / Nostalgic Harmonies Brings The Wind / Autumn Concert

EL CACO (NORWAY)
Line-Up: Øyvind Osa (vocals / bass), Anders Gjesti (guitar), Thomas Fredriksen (drums)

Lillestrøm Stoners created in 1998. EL CACO translates as 'The Thief'. The 2000 7" single 'Cosmic' was issued as a scarce limited edition run of just 200 copies. Signing to the Black Balloon label EL CACO issued the 'Viva' debut album in May 2001. Music For Nations picked the record up for the UK and in early 2002 the band gained the valuable support slot to NEBULA's European tour.

Singles/EPs:
Cosmic / Weight, Loon (2000)

Albums:
VIVA, Music For Nations (2001)
I'll Play / Suffer / Oh You / Oh Yeah! / Shine / She-Man / Cosmic / High On A Low / Mescaline / Monster / Blue Zone / I Spill The Water

ELECTRIC FRANKENSTEIN (USA)
Line-Up: Steve Miller (vocals), Carl Porcaro (guitar), Sal Canzonieri (guitar), Dan Canzonieri (bass), Rob Sefcik (drums)

New Jersey Space-Punk band, founded in 1992, ELECTRIC FRANKENSTEIN have found favour with the Stoner Rock audience. The band's initial line-up comprised guitarist Sal Canzonieri of Space Rock band THE THING and DOOM PATROL, ex-ADRENALIN O.D. and HOLY ROLLERS guitarist Jim Foster, erstwhile KATHEDRAL, EMPIRE HIDEOUS, SHADOW PROJECT and CHRISTIAN DEATH bassist Dan Canzonieri. Original vocalist was the enigmatic Frank whose position was taken by former CRASH STREET KIDS man Steve Miller.
The band suffered frequent internal strife in the early years with former VERBAL ABUSE and CONDEMNED TO DEATH man Scott Wilkins taking lead vocals for two albums. John Caton handled drum duties during 1993 but was ousted in favour of Renee Valentine the following year. By 1995 VOICE OF DOOM and HOLESHOT drummer John Steele was on the drum stool.
ELECTRIC FRANKENSTEIN finally settled on ex-CRAWLPAPPY, FUR, UPPERCUT and MIND'S EYE drummer Rob Sifcek.
The 1996 mini-album 'Sick Songs' featured a version of the MISFITS 'Queen Wasp'. In 1997 further homages came on the 'Spare Parts' album with Wilkins on vocals included DEAD KENNEDYS 'Your Emotions' and THE DICTATORS 'Borneo Jimmy'. The same year Wilkins opted out and was superseded by original singer Steve Miller from his interim act DEAD PLANET BABIES who returned with the 1998 single 'Rocket In My veins'.
The 1999 album 'Live, Loud And Angry!' was recorded at a show in Cleveland, Ohio. Initial copies came with a free CD of rarities titled 'Recharged From The Vaults'. Further recording activity saw a split album 'Listen Up Baby!' sharing space with THE HOOKERS. The British release album 'Sod The Odds!' included cover versions of JOAN JETT's 'Bad

Reputation', 'Rock n' Roll Is Dead' by THE RUBINOOS and 'Runnin' With The Boss Sound' by GENERATION X.

Foster decamped in August of 1999 being replaced by Carl Porcaro, a veteran of UPPERCUT, BREAKDOWN and KILLING TIME.

The 1999 single 'Up From The Streets' had Steve Miller on vocals.

The 2000 album 'Don't Touch Me, I'm Electric!' was produced by MONSTER MAGNET's Phil Caivano. The record included cover versions of MOTÖRHEAD's 'We Are The Road Crew', GIRLSCHOOL's 'Not For Sale', BILL NELSON'S RED NOISE 'Don't Touch Me - I'm Electric', DEAD BOYS 'Third Generation' and CLASH's '1977'. The Victory label would issue a slightly different version of the same record but re-billed as 'Annie's Grave', substituting some of the cover tracks for video footage and a live take of 'Perfect Crime'.

ELECTRIC FRANKENSTEIN put in a short batch of British dates in December 2000 supported by DOG TOFFEE and THE CELLOPHANE SUCKERS. Signing the Victory label the band issued the Ben Elliot produced 'The Buzz Of A 1,000 Volts' in 2001, CD versions including a cover of JOHNNY CASH's 'Cocaine Blues'.

As the band celebrated its tenth anniversary in 2002 an obligatory line-up shuffle found drummer John "King of Men" Steele returning to the fold to supplant Rob Sifcek. Meantime, in lieu of the departure of Carl Porcaro, Steve Miller doubled up on guitar and vocal duties.

Singles/EPs:
Electric Frankenstein Theme / Fast And Furious, Mint Tone (1994)
Rise And Crash / We Are The Dangerous / Too Much For You / A Sweet Sickness, Demolition Derby DD020 (1994)
It's All Moving Faster / Coolest Little Monster, Punkrock PUN 005 (1995)
New Rage / Home Of The Brave, Exit EXIT 2 (1995)
Electrify Me / Just Like Your Mom, Junk JR1 (1995)
Get Off My Back / Face At The Edge Of The Crowd, Junk JR2 (1995)
Deal With It / Monster Demolisher, Sonic Swirl (1996)
Action High / Out There, Intensive Scare IS6 (1996)
Not Wit U / Pure And Simple, Get Hip GH196 (1996)
Devil Dust / Right Now!, One Foot (1996) Clockwise / Frustration, Junk (1996)
Teenage Shutdown (Live) / Demolition Joyride (Live), Reptilian (1997)
Blackout / A Singer's Blood, Victory VR61

(1997)
Imperial Void / Used To Know, Victory VR81 (1997)
Learn To Burn / Born Wild, Frank FRANK 004 (1997) (Split single with THE HELLACOPTERS)
We Are The Road Crew, Devil Doll (1997) (Split single with L.E.S. STITCHES)
Savage, Kill Yourself - Rockin' Bones (1997) (Split single with CRISPY NUTS)
Rocket In My Veins / You're So Fake, Estrus ES 7123 (1998)
Long Way Down, Frank FRANK 008 (1998) (Split single with GLUECIFER)
Monster Boots, Know (1999) (Split single with LE SHOK)
Up From The Streets / Razor Blade Touch, Cold Front CF010 (1999)
I'm Not Your (Nothing) / I Was A Punk Before You Were A Punk / Right On Target (Live), Victory VR93 (2000)
Just Can't Kick / Takin' You Down, TKO (2000)
Get Off / 3rd Generation Nation, Scooch Pooch (2000)
Tattoo Vampire / The Chain, Safety Pin (2000) (Spanish release)
Rock And Roll Is Dead, Junk (2000) (Split EP with RCR, WEAKLINGS, SPITFIRES, RC% and DRAGONS)
Porno Girl, Hangover (2000) (Split 7" single with THE STP. Italian release)
Neurotic Pleasures, Killer Release (2000) (Split 7" single with ADZ. German release)
Backs Against The Wall, Wood Productions (2000) (Split 7" single with PUSHRODS. Finnish release)
Graveyard Dragstrip, Reptilian (2000) (Split EP with CANDYSNATCHERS, B-MOVIE RATS and STREET WALKIN' CHEETAHS)
A Fistful Of Rock / Neurotic Pleasures / Blackout / Action High, Myrmecoleo (2000) ('Electric Frankenstein Meets Muddy Frankenstein' Split CD EP with MUDDY FRANKENSTEIN. Japanese release)

Albums:
THE TIME IS NOW, Nitro NITRO005 (1995) Teenage Shutdown / The Time Is Now / Superstar / Right On Target / I Want More / Demolition Joyride - Demolition Derby
CONQUERS THE WORLD, Get Hip GH 1048 (1996)
It's All Moving Faster / Electrify Me / Just Like Your Mom / New Rage / Deal With It / Home Of The Brave / Monster Demolisher / Face At The Edge Of The Crowd / Get Off My Back / Coolest Little Monster
SICK SONGS, Nesak Kado (1997)
Action High / I'll Be Standing (On My Own) / Not Wit U / Pure And Simple / Born Wild / Learn To Burn / Back At You / Clockwise /

Out There

ACTION HIGH, One Louder (1997) (UK release)

Action High / I'll Be Standing (On My Own) / Not Wit U / Pure And Simple / Born Wild / Learn To Burn / Back At You / Clockwise / Out There / Frustration

THE TIME IS NOW, Nesak Kado (1997)

Teenage Shutdown / The Time Is Now / Superstar / Right On Target / I Want More / Demolition Joyride - Demolition Derby / Electric Frankenstein Theme / Fast And Furious / Rise And Crash / We Are The Dangerous / Too Much For You / A Sweet Sickness

FRACTURED, V&V Productions (1997) (European release)

Devil Dust / Right Now! / Your Emotions / Fractured / Man's Ruin / Borneo Jimmy

SPARE PARTS, Get Hip (1997) (USA release)

Devil Dust / Right Now! / Your Emotions / Fractured / Man's Ruin / Borneo Jimmy / EF Stomp / All Moving Faster (Live) / Rise And Crash (Live) / Superstar (Live)

MONSTER, Au Go Go (1997)

Rude! / Naked Heat / Blackout / Savage / Imperial Void / Used To Know / Queen Wasp

ROCK AND ROLL MONSTER, Au Go Go (1997)

Naked Heat / Blackout / Savage / Imperial Void / Used To Know / Queen Wasp / I Got Power / Meathouse / Do The Nihil / Out There

I WAS A TEENAGE SHUTDOWN, Estrus ES1244 (1998)

Teenage Shutdown / All Moving Faster / Superstar / Rise And Cash / New Rage / I Wish I Could / EF Theme / Right On Target / Demolition Joyride

HOW I ROSE FROM THE DEAD, One Foot (1998)

Devil Dust / Blackout / Action High / Rocket In My Veins / Right Now / Deal With It / Neurotic Pleasures / The Time Is Now / Get Off My Back / EF Theme

LIVE, LOUD AND ANGRY!, Twenty Stone Blatt BAMF001CD (1999)

It's All Moving Faster / Superstar / Blackout / Action High / Rocket In My Veins / Right Now / Time Is Now / Right On Target / Neurotic Pleasures / Get Off My Back / Demolition Derby / You're So Fake / Devil Dust / Teenage Shutdown / Electric Frankenstein Theme

LISTEN UP BABY!, Man's Ruin (1999) (Split album with THE HOOKERS)

Listen Up Baby! / Neurotic Pleasures / Hostage Situation / Social Infection / Hammered / Takin' It All

HOW TO MAKE A MONSTER, Victory VR 95 (1999)

I Was A Modern Prometheus / Cut From The Inside / Speed Girl / Use Me / Friction / Feel The Burn / Don't Know How To Stop You / My World / Up From The Streets / Pretty Deadly / I'm Not Your Nothing / Something For The Pain / Phatty Boom Batty

SOD THE ODDS!, Twenty Stone Blatt (1999)

Let's Sin / Shut Your Hole / Rock n' Roll Is Dead / Runnin' With The Boss Sound / Porno Girl / Welcome To My Town / Monster Boots / Bad Reputation

DON'T TOUCH ME, I'M ELECTRIC!, Twenty Stone Blatt BAMF21 (2000)

Already Dead / Fistful Of Rock / Hate Machine / Third Generation Nation / I Just Can't Kick / Annies Grave / My Fathers Son / Not For Sale / Get Off / Graveyard Drag Race / 1977 / Takin' You Down / Backs Against The Wall / Don't Touch Me - I'm Electric / (We Are The) Road Crew

THE BUZZ OF A 1'000 VOLTS, Victory (2001)

The Mess / Dead On Beauty / Resurrection City / Prey For Me / NY Knights / Dead By Dawn / Super Sonic Nation / Bite Down On Me / Death Dealer / Can't Let Go / Finished From The Start / American Lies / Cocaine Blues

DAWN OF ELECTRIC FRANKENSTEIN, Reptilian (2002) (Vinyl release)

Electric Frankenstein Theme / Live For It All / Never Gonna Get It / Lie To Me / One Last Show / Ruin You

ELECTRIC WIZARD (UK)

Line-Up: Justin Obern (vocals / guitar), Tim Bagshaw (bass), Mark Groaning (drums)

Dorsetshire Doom mongers ELECTRIC WIZARD actually started life dubbed THY GRIEF ETERNAL before shortening this to ETERNAL. Ex-LORDS OF PUTREFACTION vocalist Justin Obern fronted the band at this point, also comprising further LORDS OF PUTREFACTION colleagues bassist Dave Pedge and drummer James Evans.

However, following the British pop charts being hit by the female quartet of the same name ETERNAL felt required to instigate a name change to ELECTRIC WIZARD. Under this handle the group has subsequently made their career. The 1998 mini-album 'Supercoven', featuring drummer Mark 'Groaning' Greening, was released only by mail order in a limited edition.

Another ex-ELECTRIC WIZARD frontman, Lee Smith, founded Doomsters SALLY in the late '90s.

The first two records were repackaged as a singles set for re-release in 1999.

Recording for ELECTRIC WIZARD's fourth album was severely delayed when Greening

145

fell off a push bike and damaged his arm. Obern was also hospitalized with alcohol poisoning. Although undertaking another round of North American touring in the summer of 2002, headlining over SONS OF OTIS and UNEARTHLY TRANCE, the band released a press statement stating that their closing gig of this run, at Philadelphia's Khyber Pass venue on June 27th, would be their final show.

Singles/EPs:
Demon Lung, Rise Above (1995)
Chrono. Naut / Nuclear Guru, Man's Ruin (1997) (Split single with ORANGE GOBLIN)
Supercoven / Burnout / Wizards Of Lore / Electric Wizard (Live), Bath Acid (1998)

Albums:
ELECTRIC WIZARD, Rise Above RISE9CD (1995)
Stone Magnet / Mourning Prayer / Mountains Of Mars / Behemoth / Devil's Bride / Black Butterfly / Electric Wizard / Wooden Pipe
COME MY FANATICS..., Rise Above RISE 14 CD (1997)
Return Trip / Wizard In Black / Doom - Mantia / Ivixor B / Phase Inducer / Son Of Nothing / Solarian 13
DOPETHRONE, Rise Above (2000)
Vinum Sabbathi / Funeralopolis / Weird Tales - Electric Frost, - Golgotha, - Altar Of Melektaus / Barbarian / I, The Witchfinder / The Hills Have Eyes / We Hate You / Dopethrone
LET US PREY, JVC Victor VICP-61781 (2002)
A Chosen Few / We, The Undead / Master Of Alchemy / House Of Whipcord / The Black Drug / The Outsider / Night Of The Shape / Princess Of Mars / Mother Of Serpents

ELEGION (AUSTRALIA)
Line-Up: Anthony Kwan, James Wallbridge

Albums:
ODYSSEY INTO DARKNESS, Candlelight CANDLE020MCD (1998)
THROUGH THE EYES OF REGRET, Modern Invasion MIM7331-2 CD (2001)
Through The Eyes Of Regret / Oration Of Indifference / Thoughts / Etiolation / A Rare Moment / Pain & Elation / Depleted / For Eternity

ELEND (AUSTRIA / FRANCE)
Line-Up: Eve Gabrielle Siskind (vocals), Renaud Tschirner (vocals / keyboards / violin) / Alexandre Iskandar (vocals / violin / keyboards)

ELEND, one of France's brightest and most innovative hopes on the current Metal scene were founded by former orchestra players Renaud Tschirner and Alexandre Iskander in 1992 adding vocalist Eve Gabrielle Siskand to complete the debut album.
ELEND's first album is a conceptual piece exploring John Milton's epic poem 'Paradise Lost'. The theme of Lucifer and the coming of pandemonium were continued for the second album. Sales were so strong for 'Les Ténebre Du Dehors', now with the additional female vocals of Nathalie Barbary, that the closing chapter of the saga promised on album number three was delayed due to significant interest being shown by the major labels. As it was the band stuck by the French label Holy Records for 1997's 'Weeping Nights'.
ELEND have a non-album 12 minute track 'Birds Of Dawn' released on the 1996 compilation album 'The Holy Bible'.

Albums:
LECONS DE TENEBRAES, Holy HOLY08CD (1994)
Lecon De Tenebres / Chanting / Into Bottomless Perdition / Deploration / Infernal Beauty / Lucifer / Eclipse / The Reign Of Chaos And The Old Night / The Emperor
LES TÉNÉBRE DU DEHORS, Holy HOLY 17 CD (1996)
Nocturne / Ethereal Journeys / The Luciferian Revolution / Eden (The Angel In The Garden) / The Silence Of Light / Antienne / Dancing Under The Closed Eyes Of Paradise / Les Ténébres Du Dehors
WEEPING NIGHTS, Holy HOLY 17 CD (1997)
Weeping Night / O Solitude / The Embrace / Nocturne / Ethereal Journeys / The Luciferion Revolution / Eden / Dancing Under The Closed Eyes Of Paradise / Les Ténèbres Du Dehors
UMBERSUN, Music For Nations CDMFN 239 (1998)
Du Tréfonds Des Ténèbres / Melpomere / Moon Of Amber / Apocalypse / Umbra / The Umbersun / In The Embrace Of Heaven / The Wake Of The Angel / Au Tréfonds Des Ténèbres

ELEPHANT BELL (FINLAND)
Line-Up: Tommy Grass (vocals / guitar), Tomi M. (guitar), Arto Ez (bass), Migis (drums)

Finnish Stoners ELEPHANT BELL, founded by the ex-SHAMOS members vocalist / guitarist Tommy Grass and guitarist Tomi M. The group debuted with the 2000 'Sunchaser' demo.

Albums:
ELEPHANT BELL, (2001)
Straight To Hell / 666 / Go / Dreamwheel /
Horse Trance Dance / Camouflage /
Sandman's Revolution

THE ELYSIAN FIELDS (GREECE)
Line-Up: Bill A., Mikhalis Katsikas, Marinos A.

ELYSIAN FIELDS is essentially a duo of
guitarist / bassist / pianist Mikhalis Katsikas
and the mysterious 'Bill'. The group actually
made its entrance in 1994 billed as
DESULPHARISE and touting a Death Metal
charged demo 'Nihilistic Era'. With the name
switch to ELYSIAN FIELDS the following year
the subsequent demo session found the pair
shifting into Doom territory.
The debut album 'Adelain', Issued by Greek
label Unisound during 1995, garnered healthy
praise in the Rock media. The group, subtly
altering the band title to THE ELYSIAN
FIELDS, would later sign to the British Wicked
World concern for the sophomore 'We… The
Enlightened'.
The band switched to the Greek label Black
Lotus and recorded a third CD '12Ablaze' in
early 1999. It finally saw the light of day in
2001
Katsikas also operates side venture
HAVORUM.

Albums:
ADELAIN, Unisound (1995)
I Of Forever / As One / Un Sentiment- I Was
Dying Once Again / Of Purity And Black /
Foredoomed Elegy / Father Forgive Them
(For They Don't Know) / Elysian Fields /
Deicide- The Auspice
WE… THE ENLIGHTENED, Wicked World
WICK02CD (1998)
Their Blood Be On Us / I Am The Unknown
Sky / Until The Night Cries Rise In Your
Heart / …And The Everdawn Faded Away /
Shall They Come Forth Unto Us / Arcana
Caelestia / The End Shall Be Tragically
Fulfilled / The Last Star Of Heaven Falls /
Wither, Oh Divine, Wither
12ABLAZE, Black Lotus BLR CD 029
(2001)
Ensheild My Hate Eternal / Of Dawns,
Perished Tranquility / Rapture And The
Mourning Virtue / Weak We Stand Before
Them / Ablazing 12 / A Serenade Like Blood
Caress / Even If I Could Forgive / The
Entreaty Unsung / As The Light Disappears

ELYSIUM (AUSTRALIA)
Line-Up: Jamie Marsh (vocals), Stuart
Prickett (vocals / guitar), Andrew Habib
(guitar), Beau Dyer (bass), Hamish Gould
(keyboards), Niel Dyer (drums)

Doomsters ELYSIUM came into being during
September of 1994, assembled by inaugural
members vocalist / guitarist Stuart Prickett
and drummer Beau Dyer, the latter also a
member of ACROSS THE SCARLET MOAT.
This pairing would soon be complemented by
bassist Robert Vickery and had undertaken
their first live work by the November. In
February 1995 the band were joined by
Hamish Gould on keyboards but shortly after
Dyer would prioritize his other act and leave
the ELYSIUM fold. The band duly pulled in
Roy Fratin as replacement and set about
gigging in earnest.
A rehearsal promotional cassette was cut in
August of 1995, capitalized on during the
October by ELYSIUM's first six track demo.
Before long Steve Pettit was added in order to
augment the band's live sound. Fratin would
then be asked to leave and Goran took over
the drum mantle but in June of 1996
ELYSIUM split with Vickery founding
DECAYED DIVINITY.
Prickett and Gould regrouped building a new
look band. Their former drummer Beau Dyer
was recruited as a bassist, LORD KAOS and
CRUCIBLE OF AGONY singer Jamie Marsh
became the new lead singer and Guy Moore
was acquired for secondary keyboards. The
experiment utilizing twin keyboards was not
deemed a success and Moore decamped.
The revised version of ELYSIUM would be
completed by LYCANTHIA drummer Lachlan
Donaldson as a fresh demo 'Shrouded In The
Veils of Dawn' was laid down.
Further line-up fluxes saw the entrance of
second guitarist in Andrew Habib in July of
1997 and Niel Dyer replacing Lachlan in
December. This incarnation of the band would
support CATHEDRAL at their 1999 Sydney
gig. A planned debut album 'Dreamscapes',
featuring guest vocals from Judy Chiara of
AVRIGUS, was recorded for the Warhead
label but this deal fell through. The De
Profundis concern soon picked the record up
for a limited edition release of 2000 copies.
The band projected a new album,
provisionally entitled 'Bird Of Stone Wings' for
2002 release.
ELYSIUM personnel spread their talents
across various bands. The Dyer siblings also
operate GRENADE and ACROSS THE
SCARLET MOAT whilst Prickett, Habib and
Gould are all involved with ARRRRGH!.
Prickett can also be found indulging in such
endeavours as DECAYED DIVINITY, OF
GRIEF EVERLASTING, CORPSICKLE and
alongside Habib in METALHEAD.

Albums:
DREAMSCAPES, De Profundis (2000)
Dark Woods And Willows Wild / Graven Bay / Elysium (Gallery Of The Fallen) / These Bleak Enshrined Emotions / Remorse At Dusk / Leafy Tendrils (Part One) / Millennia Gone

ELYSIUM (POLAND)

Line-Up: Maciej Miskiewicz (vocals), Michal Maryniak (guitar), Jakub Jasic (guitar), Roman Felczynski (bass), Kola (keyboards), Mariusz Bogacz (drums)

ELYSIUM is an atmospheric Doom styled Death Metal act, not to be confused with the Australian Doom act of the same band name and a coincidentally similar album title. The band came together in 1996, building up an underground following on the Polish club scene. In January of 1998 the group lost the services of bassist Marcin but added second guitarist Kuba Jasic for recording of the 'Dreamlands' album. Prior to entering the studio in April of 1999 keyboard player Tomasz decamped. The band inducted Maciej Kopias-Czekay as replacement, the new member being inaugurated with a gig supporting CHRIST AGONY and LUX OCCULTA.

Albums:
DREAMLANDS, Morbid Noizz (2000)
Six Cold Days / Sister Moon / Dreamlands / Swallow Her / Suicidal Angels / Edenfall / Starguardians / Our Love Is Eternal / Farewell / April Rainy Night

EMBRAZE (FINLAND)

Line-Up: Lauri Tuohimaa (vocals / guitar), Olli-Pekka Karvonen (guitar), Sami Siekkinen (bass), Heidi Maatta (keyboards), Ilkka Leskela (drums)

EMBRAZE, an atmospheric Gothically charged Death Metal outfit out of Kiiminki, were formed in late 1994 by frontman Lauri Tuohimaa (ex-CREATURE and KALLISTA KAKKAA) and drummer Ilka Leskela. The latter, also a 'veteran' of KALLISTA KAKKAA, was a mere 12 years old upon the bands formation!
Making up the inaugural unit would be female keyboard player Heidi Maatta, bassist Petri Henell and guitarist Juka Rytkonen. A succession of well received demo tapes, commencing with May 1995's 'Allotria', and consistent gigging would lead eventually to a coveted overall winner award at the Finnish Rock Championships. The group would also add two second places in the same competitions to their tally. An original billing of EMBRACE would soon give way to EMBRAZE
April 1998 saw EMBRAZE committed to commercial recording with the issue of debut album 'Laeh' for Mastervox Records with videos being shot for 'Amid Peals' and 'Charm Of The Wilderness'. The album caught the attention, not withstanding its fusing of Dark Wave and Death Metal but for its inspired cover version of the KISS '70s Disco classic 'I Was Made For Lovin' You'. Before the close of the year work ensued on a second album and a cover of SLAYER's 'Chemical Warfare' was donated to the 'Straight To Hell' tribute record. Headline touring in Finland billed as the 'Dark Side Of Laeh' dates had AFTERWORLD as running mates.
In January 1999 in the midst of recording sessions both guitarists Janne Regelin and Janne Räsänen exited the ranks. The latter, who as well as acting as bassist for EMBRAZE was holding down guitar duties in ROOSTER, would team up with GRINSTER - as a drummer!
However, the band persevered and 1999 would see the band sharing the stage at the 'Nummirock' festival sharing the stage with countrymen CHILDREN OF BODOM and STRATOVARIUS and international artists such as DREAM THEATER, SLAYER and PANTERA. 1999 also brought the April release of the single 'Sin, Love And The Devil' and further recording sessions resulting in their second full-length album entitled 'Intense'.
Requested to return to the 'Nummirock' event once more EMBRAZE rubbed shoulders with bands such as MOTÖRHEAD, SCORPIONS, DANZIG and HAMMERFALL. They then headed for the 'Liosaarirock' festival to share the stage with ANATHEMA, HENRY ROLLINS and PARADISE LOST. Further line-up shuffles would see both bassist Tony Kaiso and guitar player Markus Uusital decamping. Fresh blood came in the form of the NORMAL FIGURES duo of Sami Siekkinen on four string duties and guitarist Olli-Pekka Karvonen.
In May 2000 'Endless Journey' would garner valuable international media praise. The record would see global releases by MTM Metal in Germany, NEH Records in America and in Brazil on the Moria imprint.
During March of 2002 Lauri Tuohimaa was announced as part of the formation of a Finnish 'Gothic Metal supergroup' dubbed FOR MY PAIN. Joining him in this endeavour would be the ETERNAL TEARS OF SORROW triumvirate of bassist Altti Veteläinen, guitarist Olli-Pekka Törrö and drummer Petri Sankala, keyboard player

Tuomas Holopainen of NIGHTWISH and fronted by REFLECTION vocalist Juha Kylmänen.

The bulk of EMBRAZE also co-exist as side project MAPLE CROSS.

Albums:
LAEH, Mastervox (1998)
Charm Of The Wilderness / Dead Spring / Fragments Of Life / Autumn Child / Close My Stage / Mystic / I Was Made For Lovin' You / This Moment / Amid Peals / Sweet Hate / Stream Of Emptiness / Little Reaction
INTENSE, Mastervox (1999)
Sin, Love And The Devil (Single edit) / This Cold Day / Rain And Moon / Endless Journey / Passion / One Moon, One Star / Shame / Sin, Love And The Devil (Album version) / Looking Ahead Into The Embrace Of Hell
ENDLESS JOURNEY, MTM Metal 1704-7 (2001)
Whispers / Lost / Endless Journey / Robot Stud / Passion / Tenderness / One Moon One Star / This Cold Day / Lethal Dance / Looking Ahead To The Embrace Of Hell

EMINENZ (GERMANY)
Line-Up: Leviathan (vocals), Darkman (guitar), Karsten Breitung (guitar), Butcher (bass), Henry Kuhnert (drums)

EMINENZ, led by the fire breathing vocalist Leviathan, were a union of ex-Death Metal musicians, the previous influences plainly audible on the two albums. The group first came together during early 1989 with a line-up of Leviathan on vocals, guitarists Zwerg and Butcher, bassist Darkman and drummer Iten. The band pulled off a huge coup of gaining the support slot to MAYHEM on their 1990 European dates and followed this feat the following year by issuing a brace of demo sessions in 'Slayer Of My Daughter' and 'Necromonicon Exmortis'.
During 1992 EMINENZ guested for a visiting CARCASS and delivered further demos 'Ghost', 'Preacher Of Darkness' and 'Blasphemy Live'. The band had by now been augmented by keyboard player Benedict Kern. The group's debut album 'Exorial' arrived via the Lethal label in 1994. However, shortly after its release both Kern and Zwerg made their exit. By 1995 the gap in the ranks had been plugged by keyboard player Lorenzo and bassist Black Abyss, Darkman having manoeuvred over to the guitar role.
'The Heretic' album ensued capitalized on by support gigs to MAYHEM once again and MARDUK. EMINENZ would then switch labels to the Last Episode label for 1998's

'Anti- Genesis'. Further line-up shuffles found Iten out and Heretic coming in on drums. This latest recruit would depart too though after laying down drums on the 'Blackest Dimension' album. EMINENZ duly drafted Illeies on drums as well as Micha, the latter boosting EMINENZ up to a three guitar compliment.
Early demos were collected together for the 2001 vinyl release 'Deathfall', limited to 500 copies.
Guitarist Karsten Breitung also operates BELMEZ.

Albums:
EXORIAL, Lethal LRC9666 (1994)
Introduction Black Thoughts / Jesus Wept Nevermore / Demons From The Black Abyss / Angel Rip Angel / The Unholy (Preachers Of Darkness) / Blasphemy / Ghost / Demons Awake / Only Flesh / Dark Millennium / Exorial / Outro
THE HERETIC, Lethal LRC24 (1996)
Demons Cross The Fiery Path / Bloodred Nights / Day Of Battle, Night Of Thunder / Lucifers Return / Thousand Blasphemies / The Gate / Necronomicon Exmortis / The Heretic / Lucifers Return
ANTI GENESIS, (1998)
Nocturnal Horizon / God's Downfall / Praise The Death / Army Of Immortals / Apocalypse / Triumph Of The Nightforces / Grey Souls / Conspiracy Of The Witches / Anti Genesis
THE BLACKEST DIMENSION, Last Episode LEP 045 (2000)
Exorials Return / Voices / Diabolical Majesty / Darkness Come Over Us / Seraph's Flight / Sink In Oblivion / Warriors / Demons Warpath / Sentenced To Victory
DEATHFALL, (2001)
Intro / Beware Your Head / Slayer Of My Daughter / Black Crusade / Death Fall / Stenched Carcass / Pleasure And Glory / Intro / Suffocate In Blood / Mutilated Mutant / Rotting Process / Necronomicon Exmortis / The Ruin Of The House Usher / Outro

ENCHANTMENT (UK)
Line-Up: Paul Jones (vocals), Marc (guitar), Steve (guitar), Mark (bass), Chris (drums)

A volatile mixture of Gothic, Thrash and Death Metal ENCHANTMENT's debut recording, the demo tape 'A Tear For The Young Eloquence', was produced by Peaceville Records boss Hammy. The group was later snapped up by the German label Century Media.

Albums:
DANCE THE MARBLE NAKED, Century

149

Media (1994)
Kneading With Honey / My Oceans Vast / The Touch Of A Crown / Carve Me In Sand / Summer For The Dames / God Send / Of Acorns That Gather / Meadows

END ZONE (RUSSIA)
Line-Up: Igor Lobanov (vocals / guitar), Oleg Mishin (guitar / keyboards), Roman Senkin (bass), Valeri Dedov (drums)

Moscow based Gothic Metal band END ZONE was created in 1993 by frontman Igor Lobanov, with bass guitarist Roman Senkin and drummer Valery Dedov joining up shortly after. This trio took over a year in locating a suitable lead guitarist, finally settling on Oleg Mishin. END ZONE employ flute, keyboards and female backing vocals on their increasingly adventurous catalogue.
END ZONE's debut album 'First Bequest' arrived in 1995, released on cassette by the Russian Aria label, and found the band in distinct Thrash-Death territory. Extensive gigging across Russia culminated in an appearance at the Polish 'Shark Attack 7' festival.
During February of 1996 the Metal Agen imprint re-issued 'First Bequest' on CD format. That same year END ZONE inducted keyboardist Alexander Dronov and drummer Oleg Milovanov into the ranks. This version of the band commenced recording a Evgeny Trushin produced entirely instrumental album entitled 'Thalatta Et Thanatos' for Metal Agen. Amongst the compositions would be Metal classic reworkings of masters such as Handel, Grieg and Tchaikovsky.
A third album, 'Eclectica' comprised four new tracks, a cover version of SEPULTURA's 'Refuse/Resist' and an ambitious interpretation of Mussorgsky`s 'Khovanschina'.

Albums:
END BEQUEST, Metal Agen (1995)
From The Distance / Conqueror Night / Dangerous Gift / Ulterior Solitude / Oblivion Flow / S.O.D. / The Edge Of String / Questions With No Answer / Remember The Fallen / Candlestick Of Parcass / Last Hope Of Suffered Soul / The Castle Of Woman Of Mine / Rock n' Roll
THALLETA ET THANATOS, Metal Agen (1996)
Overture / Thalatta / End Zone / Baba-Yaga / Roma / Elements / Death Of Tsar (Dedicated To Russian Emperor Pavel I) / Passacagli / The Edge Of String (Turbo version) / Parkinson's Ballet / Castle Of Woman Of Mine / Cobalt / Night Of The Sun / Dance Of

The Lore / Outflow
ECLECTICA, Matal Agen (1998)
Alpha / The Vortex Of Reality / Hovanchina (Final) / Dual Infinity / The Remedy / Refuse / Resist / Afterwards

ENERTIA (Albany, NY, USA)
Line-Up: Scott Featherstone (vocals), Dave Stafford (guitar), Roman Singleton (guitar), Joe Paciolla (bass), Jeff Daily (drums)

Albums:
LAW OF THREE, Enertia (1996)
The Mirror / Child Now Lost / I Know Your Demons / Same Old Story / If I Were You
MOMENTUM, Enertia (1998)
Ripped Out / Dear God / And So You Fall / Six Weeks / Weight Of The World / You Know / Sever The Wicked / Walls

ENSOPH (ITALY)
Line-Up: Nicola (vocals), Giuliano (guitar), Massimo (bass), Leonardo (keyboards), Anna (flute), Zenone (drums)

Venice based ENSOPH began life in 1998 as a Doom / Gothic hybrid, evident on their 'Les Confessions Du Mat' mini-album debut for No Brain Records. The group, which includes drummer Zenone of Black Metal band THE SECOND COMING and also holds its roots in the Death Metal band ENDYMINION, subsequently evolved into more Industrial landscapes for the second effort 'Bleeding Womb Of Ananke'.
The members of ENSOPH virtually all hold down side ventures. Most significant are the Industrial Metal act DIE WUNDE, featuring vocalist Nicola, guitarist Guiliano and Zenone. Flautist Anna is also a member of Progressive Rock act FALANGE, Nicola boasts membership of DEATH DIES whilst bass player Massimo also holds down a position in BURIAL PALACE.

Albums:
LES CONFESSIONS DU MAT, No Brain (1999)
BLEEDING WOMB OF ANANKE, Beyond Productions (2001)
Shattered Void / The Spyral Stigmata / I (Be & Will Be) / Tanz der Erinnerung / In The Blossom Of Inertness / Aletheia / Amber Shrine / The Ivory Ouroboros / The Bleeding Womb Of Ananke / 7 Volte 3 (E'Un Sole Ermetico)

ENTOMBED (SWEDEN)
Line-Up: Lars Göran Petrov (vocals), Uffe Cedarlund (guitar), Alex Hellid (guitar), Jorgen Sandström (bass), Nicke

Andersson (drums)

In the plethora of Death Metal bands to have emerged ENTOMBED have proven themselves as ranking among the elite. Never less than skull crushingly heavy, the band have carved their own niche in the market with deft musicianship and a unique perspective generating a 'Death-Doom' style. The band's 1993 album 'Wolverine Blues' is generally acknowledged to be a masterpiece of the genre.

Originally known as NIHILIST, under which name they recorded the 'Drowned', 'But Life Goes On' and 'Premature Autopsy' demos. Both vocalist Lars-Göran Petrov and guitarist Ulf Cederlund had previously made their mark with MORBID, the band that featured a pre-MAYHEM Per 'Dead' Ohlin. With bassist Johnny Hedlund forming UNLEASHED, NIHILST duly folded only to reunite a matter of days later retitled ENTOMBED.

The first demo the band recorded as ENTOMBED was titled 'Only Shreds Remain' and following the release of the 'Left Hand Path' debut album in 1990 (with both guitarists handling bass duties in the studio) ENTOMBED recruited a permanent bass player in CARBONISED / MONASTARY man Lars Rosenberg.

1991 was a quite eventful year for the Swedish outfit. Vocalist Göran Petrov was fired in July after personal clashes within the band and was replaced by ex-CARNAGE vocalist Johnny Dordevic. However, the 'Crawl' single was recorded with vocalist Orvar Safstrom of NIRVANA 2002 stepping in on a temporary basis following the split with Petrov.

In the Autumn the band toured America alongside fellow Swedes UNLEASHED and headliners MORBID ANGEL, although by the middle of the following year Johnny Dordevic had left to have his position filled by the reinstated Goran Petrov. In his sabbatical from ENTOMBED the vocalist had recorded with both COMECON and MORBID.

In 1994 ENTOMBED, promoting the landmark 'Wolverine Blues' album released in 1993, toured Europe heavily as guests to NAPALM DEATH. General opinion was that ENTOMBED consistently stole the show from a flagging headliner. Subsequent American dates were only marred by the band having to play as a trio in Canada minus Goran Petrov and Sandström losing their passports when ENTOMBED's tour van was stolen in Cleveland. ENTOMBED persevered with a show in Toronto utilizing guitarist Uffe Cederlund as lead vocalist. Further chaos was to impinge itself though when, for the second show in Montreal, Cederlund lost his

voice completely, prompting the band to invite audience members to participate to plug the gap!

Aside from 'The Singles Compilation' album released by Earache the only other ENTOMBED product to see release during 1994 was the 'Out Of Hand' 7" single, which saw the band covering tracks by such diverse influences as KISS and REPULSION.

Midway through 1995 bassist Rosenberg opted to join THERION, having filled in on a temporary basis for live work. ENTOMBED would add ex-GRAVE bassist Jörgen Sandström in his place and would part company with Earache Records in 1996 to sign with major label East West. However, despite finalizing recording of a projected album the band found themselves embroiled in record company politics and the album was shelved. Luckily, a deal was hastily negotiated between East West and leading independent Music For Nations in order for 'To Ride, Shoot Straight And Speak The Truth' to be released in 1997.

Digipack versions of the album came with a free 'Family Favourites' EP which saw ENTOMBED ripping through BLACK SABBATH's 'Under The Sun', VENOM's 'Bursting Out', KING CRIMSON's '21st Century Schizoid Man' and MC5's 'Kick Out The Jams'.

Aside from ENTOMBED drummer Nicke Andersson also began to dabble with a side Punk project known as THE HELLACOPTERS with Dick Hakansson (a.k.a. Dregan) from BACKYARD BABIES. Andersson issued his first full-length album for THE HELLACOPTERS in late 1996 to laudatory reviews. The band received such acclaim, even being requested to support KISS on their Scandinavian dates, that Andersson felt obliged to quit his parent act to concentrate fully on THE HELLACOPTERS.

In 1996 Cederlund and Andersson released the 'Seven Deadly Sins' album together with KONKHRA's vocalist Anders Lundemark under the band name of DAEMON. Incidentally, Uffe Cederlund also dabbled with a Punk crew titled HAYSTACK together with BACKYARD BABIES bassist Johan Blomqvist, the band releasing a 1998 album 'Slave Me'.

ENTOMBED, now with MERCILESS, FACE DOWN, REGURGITATE and LOUD PIPES drummer Peter 'Flinta' Stjärnwind, put in an American tour to kick off 1998.

The following year both Petrov and Hellid would make their presence felt as session guests to the 'Wasting The Dawn' album from Finnish vampire Rockers THE 69 EYES.

Opting for a complete rethink after the artistic failure of 'Same Difference' ENTOMBED went back to the very basics. The 2000 album 'Uprising', costing a miserly £4,000, being deliberately under-produced and harking back to past glories. Not only was the old logo revived but the album cover was in fact the artwork from their original 'But Life Goes On' demo tape. If that was not enough ENTOMBED reworked the title track from 'Left Hand Path' retitling it 'Say It In Slugs'. With ENTOMBED's star in the ascension once again former label Earache issued a set of live tapes culled from a 1992 London Astoria show for the 'Monkey Puss - Live In London' album.

2000 also saw Cederlund and Stjärnvind in collusion with DISMEMBER's Matti Karki and Richard Cabeza for their MURDER SQUAD project album 'Unsane, Insane And Mentally Damaged'. Another ENTOMBED offshoot, the Thrash band BORN OF FIRE, would see Stjarnvind and Cabeza in alliance with Dimman and ex-UNLEASHED and present day LOUD PIPES and TERRA FIRMA man Fredda Lindgren. Sandström would also engage publicly with his new act, the Gothic-Electro Death Metal unit THE PROJECT HATE.

ENTOMBED would stretch their creativity during February and March of 2002 with a series of ambitious concert performances at the Royal Opera Hall in Stockholm. Billed as the 'Unreal Estate' these gigs witnessed a 45 minute ENTOMBED set complimented by a ten year old actor and a ballet troupe!

Bassist Jörgen Sandstrom, acting as a guitarist, and drummer Peter Stjärnvind would announce the formation of a new side venture entitled KRUX, featuring such prominent players as Leif Edling of CANDLEMASS, guitarist Michael Amott of ARCH ENEMY and vocalist Tomas Person. KRUX signed up to Mascot Records for their debut, although a line-up change saw erstwhile YNGWIE MALMSTEEN and ABSTRAKT ALGEBRA frontman Mats Leven assuming the mantle of lead vocalist. Uffe Cederlund would embark on another high profile side concern entitled WASHOE in alliance with the MISERY LOVES CO. trio of Vocalist Patrick Wiren, bass player Patrick Thorngren and drummer Olle Dahlstedt.

Music For Nations released a compilation of ENTOMBED archive cover versions and B sides in 2002 billed as 'Sons Of Satan - Praise The Lord'.

ENTOMBED

ENTROPY (HOLLAND)

Line-Up: Maaike Breijman (vocals), Esther Ladiges (vocals), Erik van Duin (guitar), Tom Kuilboer (guitar), Martin Stoop (bass), Stephan Stoop (keyboards), Daniel From (drums)

A complex, self styled "cortex Metal" band founded in 1989. ENTROPY blend Gothic and Progressive threads in a quest to produce a unique sound.

The group arrived with the demo 'It's Time' which led in turn to a deal with the German Gorgon label for the 1995 album 'Become A God'. After these recordings original keyboard player Casper made way for his replacement Stephen Stoop, a former member of CONCUSSION.

ENTROPY's next step was to issue the three track 'Perception' EP through the Xymphonia label. A lengthy period of inactivity would ensue before the band's comeback with 'Echoes In The Past', which introduced former SANGAMO vocalist Esther Ladiges to the band.

Both vocalists, Maaike Breijman and Esther Ladiges also operate IXION.

Singles/EPs:
Mouths In War / Foe He Who Walks Among Us / Descend, Xymphonia (1998)
('Perceptions' EP)

Albums:
BECOME A GOD, Gorgon (1995)
Through The Ashes Of Creation / When To Die / Race Between Races / The Guard's Eye / Become A God / Dreamrun / The Nightmare Chase / Red Lines / Phantoms Domain / Burn Out Or Fade Away
ECHOES IN THE PAST, Xymphonia (2001)
Phases Of Being / Shapes That Won't Fit / Withheld / Crossroads (Deathbed Regrets) / Mouths In War / Luna / Masquerade / After This / Theatre Of Repression / For He Who Walks Among Us / An Eye For An Eye

ENTWINE (FINLAND)
Line-Up: Miika Tauriainen (vocals), Tom Mikkola (guitar), Jani Miettinen (bass), Riita Heikkonen (keyboards), Aki Hanttu (drums)

Although ENTWINE have found commercial success with their brand of melodic dark flavoured Gothic Metal, the group was rooted in a Death Metal prototype set up by vocalist / guitarist Tom Mikkola, drummer Aki Hanttu and bassist T. Taipole during late '1995. As time drew on this band shed its aggression and steadily became lighter. P. Willman would be inducted to add second guitar and take over the lead vocal chores from Mikkolla.

The first evidence of this shift in direction came in 1997 with the demo 'Divine Infinity'. Keyboard player Riita Heikkonen was drafted and first live performances came in February of 1998.

ENTWINE signed to the domestic Spikefarm label for the inaugural album 'The Treasures Within Hearts' which novelly included a cover version of DEPECHE MODE's 'Enjoy The Silence'. However, in April of 2000 Willman broke ranks. This period of flux saw ENTWINE replacing Willman with Miika Tauriainen and also recruiting a new bassist, Jani Miettinen.

2001 proved to be ENTWINE's year with both the single 'New Dawn' and album 'Gone' charting in their homeland. The group recruited Jaani Kähkönen as a session guitarist for live work but would soon announce the new man as a fully enrolled member. 2002 would bode well for the band too with an announcement of a European tour in alliance with THEATRE OF TRAGEDY and RAM-ZET announced for the Spring and the single 'The Pit' entering the national Finnish single charts at no. 6.

Outside of Finland ENTWINE are licensed to Century Media for European and American releases.

Singles/EPs:
New Dawn / Closer (Not Love), Spikefarm NAULA 011 (2001) 10 FINLAND

Albums:
THE TREASURES WITHIN HEARTS, Spikefarm NAULA 002 (1999)
Into The... / Thy Guiding Light / Deliverance / In The Frame Of Wilderness / My Mistress / Enjoy The Silence / Veiled Woman / Don't Let This Night Be Over
GONE, Spikefarm NAULA 013 (2001)
18 FINLAND
Losing The Ground / Snow White Suicide / Closer (My Love) / New Dawn / Grace / Silence Is Killing Me / Thru The Darkness / Blood Of Your Soul
TIME OF DESPAIR, Spikefarm NUALA 028 (2002)
Stream Of Life / The Pit / Nothing Left To Say / Safe In A Dream / Burden / Falling Apart / Until The End / Learn To Let Go / Time Of Despair

ENTWINED (UK)
Line-Up: Stephen John Tovey (vocals), Lee James (guitar), Simon (bass), James Southgate (drums)

ENTWINED feature erstwhile ESTRANGED members vocalist Stephen John Tovey, bassist Simon and drummer James Southgate. Guitarist Lee James has credits with MORTAL TIDE and METAL STORM. As ENTWINED the band bowed in with the demos 'XIII' and 'Hot Cherished Mask'. ENTWINED supported MORBID ANGEL on

their 1998 European tour promoting the 'Dancing Under Glass' album but would fold shortly after.
Former ENTWINED keyboard player Mark Royce joined PRIMARY SLAVE and then the expatriated Chilean Death Metal band CRIMINAL in March of 2002.

Albums:
DANCING UNDER GLASS, Earache (1998)
The Sound Of Her Wings / Shed Nightward Beauty / Under A Killing Moon / The Forgotten / A Moments Sadness / The Sacrifice Of Spring / Red Winter / Heaven Rise / XIII

ESOTERIC (UK)
Line-Up: Greg Chandler (vocals), Steve Peters (guitar) (guitar), Gordan Bickwell (guitar), Bryan Beck (bass), Keith York (drums)

A Birmingham based ultra Sludge Black Doom band founded in 1992. ESOTERIC debuted in 1994 with an 82 minute long demo tape! The debut album 'Epistemological Despondency' was recorded with drummer Darren although he quit shortly after recording. ESOTERIC employed the services of a drum machine for the highly praised follow up 'The Pernicious Enigma'.
The 'Metamorphogenesis' EP includes Tom Kvalskoll of Norwegian act PARADIGMA on guest vocals.
ESOTERIC is a rare sight on the live scene only having completed a handful of gigs.

Singles/EPs:
Dissident / The Secret Of The Secret / Psychotropic Transgression, Eibon (1999) ('Metamorphogenesis' EP)

Albums:
EPISTEMOLOGICAL DESPONDENCY, Aesthetic Death (1995)
Bereft / Only Hate (Baresark) / The Name Of Despair / Lamented Despondency / Edadification (Of Thorns) / Awaiting My Death
THE PERNICIOUS ENIGMA, Aesthetic Death (1997)
Creation Through Destruction / Dominion Of Slaves / Allegiance / Nox: BC 9701040 / Sinistrous / At War With The Race / A Worthless Dream / Stygeon Narcosis / Passing Through Matter

ESTATIC FEAR (AUSTRIA)
Line-Up: Beowulf (vocals / bass), Stauff (guitar), Calix Miseriae (guitar / keyboards), Astaroth Magus (drums)

This Doom / Death / Black / Gothic Metal band was formed in 1993 and has featured a stable line-up since 1994.
On the debut album, which features strong medieval themes, the band was assisted by female vocalist Marion and the flute playing of Petra Hölzl.
Drummer Astaroth Magus ('Milan Dejak') also operates in ASTAROTH, THIRD MOON and SEPTIC CEMETARY.

Albums:
SOMNIUM OBMUTUM, CCP 100151-2 (1996)
Des Nachtens Suss' Gedone / Somnium Obmutum / As Autumn Calls / Ode To Solitude
A SOMBRE DANCE, CCP 100197-2 (199-)
Intro (Unisomo Lute Instrumental) / Chapter I / Chapter II / Chapter III / Chapter IV / Chapter V / Chapter VI / Chapter VII / Chapter VIII / Chapter IX

ESTUARY OF CALAMITY
(Cincinnati, OH, USA)
Line-Up: Ash Thomas (vocals / bass), Adam Ellis (guitar), Brad Howard (guitar), Leslie Anderson (keyboards), Jesse Wilson (drums)

Ohio act founded in October of 1992, originally billed as NECROLATRY, describing themselves as "Grinding Doom Death". As a trio of vocalist / bassist Ash Thomas, guitarist Adam Ellis and drummer Jesse Wilson a Death Metal influenced demo arrived in 1993. By May of that same year though, wishing to distance themselves from a plethora of acts of similar name, the band became ESTUARY OF CALAMITY, adding second guitarist Brad Howard at the same juncture. As a newly billed quartet recorded the demo 'Losing Myself In The Cryptic Breeze'.
Although suffering from an obvious lack of financial input 'Losing Myself In The Cryptic Breeze' engendered favourable press reports. Wishing to duplicate the more experimental music displayed on the demo the band inducted keyboard player Leslie Anderson. However, by 1995 the group had folded with Thomas and Anderson forging ahead with THORNS OF THE CARRION.
ESTUARY OF CALAMITY lay dormant until October of 1997 when Thomas, Ellis and Anderson resurrected the band. For this revised version Thomas switched to guitar whilst Ellis became bass player. The track 'Unheard In The Storm' would be shopped as a promotional tool as well as cutting 'Mansions In Darkness' for the KING DIAMOND tribute album 'Church Of The Devil'.

The full-length album 'The Sentencing' was delivered in May of 2000.

Albums:
THE SENTENCING, (2000)
A Grain Of Sand, A Breath Of Life / At The Dreamscape Ruins / The Spiritual Beheading / The Sentencing / Nightsky Awakening / Unheard In The Storm / Summoned At Daybreak

ETERNAL (COLOMBIA)

Line-Up: Jorge Munox (vocals / drums), Susanna Correa (vocals), Ivan Rios (guitar), Gabriel Sanchez (guitar), Camilo Barrera (bass), Miguel Gongora (keyboards)

Medellin based Gothic Death Metal act created during 1995. ETERNAL, who seemingly have a penchant for wearing sinister monk's cassocks, issued the demo tape 'Dreamworld' in 1997, the band's membership at this time consisting of Jorge Munox on lead vocals and drums, guitarists Ivan Rios and Gabriel Sanchez, soprano vocalist Maria Carolina Echeverry, bassist Jairo Hurtado and keyboard player Hammell Atehortua.

By the time of recording the debut album 'Gothic Dreams' ETERNAL had undergone line-up changes with new faces being bass player Camilo Barrera, keyboard player Miguel Gongora and the striking Susanna Correra on vocals.

Gongora would bow out in August of 2001, being replaced on the ivories by Juan Carlos Gomez. The band supported THERION on their Colombian dates.

Albums:
GOTHIC DREAMS, (2000)
Gothic Dreams / Slaves Of Concrete / Garden Of Souls / Freezing Winds / Dark Shine / Princess / Misregard For Fear / Last Day / Broken Promises / Cold Woman

ETERNAL AUTUMN (SWEDEN)

Line-Up: John Carlsson (vocals / guitar), Thomas Ahlgren (guitar), Sami Nieminen (bass), Ola Sundström (drums)

Founded in 1993 ETERNAL AUTUMN underwent numerous line-up changes until the introduction of drummer Andreas Tullson provided some much needed stability. However, the band hired a bass player in quick succession then shortly after vocalist and founder member Daniel quit. The band issued an inaugural demo recording in 1994 before Daniel was to re-enter the fold, although this time taking up the duties of bass player. A 1996 demo was issued after which Daniel made his exit again and Tullson decamped too.

A third effort, the six track 'Moonscape' cassette, witnessed a revised line-up comprising vocalist / rhythm guitarist John Carlsson, Thomas Ahlgren on lead guitar, Tobias Vipeklev on bass and drummer Ola Sundström. This last session led to a deal with the Black Diamond label for the 1998 album 'The Storm'. In the midst of laying down the debut Vipeklev was asked to leave necessitating the two guitarists sharing the bass duties. Musically the album was firmly entrenched in traditional Heavy Metal territory although, by the band's admission, the whole affair was liberally injected with a degree of Gothicism.

ETERNAL AUTUMN, now with Sami Nieminen on bass, would cut their version of 'Return Of The Vampire' for the MERCYFUL FATE tribute album 'The Unholy Sounds Of The Demon Bells'. Although a new album '...From The Eastern Forest' was announced for release through the Japanese Soundholic label ETERNAL AUTUMN folded in the summer of 2001.

Albums:
THE STORM, Black Diamond BDP005 (1998)
The Storm / Autumn Fire / In My Recent Shape / As The Last Leaf Fell / Moonscape / Autumn Opus, No 1 / Floating... / In A Land Dawn Never Reached
...FROM THE EASTERN FORESTS, Soundholic SHCD1-0037 (2000)

ETERNAL CONSPIRACY (HOLLAND)

A female fronted Gothic Black Metal band from Kampen, founded in 1997 and boasting the inclusion of guitarist Michiel Dekker of DEAD HEAD in the ranks. Originally Kristen would take on the role of singer but she would later be replaced by Karen.

ETERNAL CONSPIRACY members Martijn Moes and Michiel Dekker would unite with former EXPOSING INNARDS guitarist Corvin Keurhorst, EXPOSING INNARDS and SLAYNE vocalist Robin Kok alongside drummer Sjoerd Visch of ALTAR and ELYSIUM to found the harsh Death Metal band MONOLITH in March of 2002

Singles/EPs:
Serenades Of Dark Angels / Reborn In Moonlight / Existence / Words Of Despair, (1997) ('Serenades Of Dark Angels' EP)
Albums:
DARK PERVERSITIES AT FUNERAL GROUNDS, Happy Holochrist HHCR 66602

(1999)
Walpurgis Night / The Platitude Of Bestial Slavery / Serenades Of Dark Angels / Abhory Of Sunset / Woods Of Despair / The Vampiric Graveyard Ouverture / A Funeral Banquet At Dawn / Clasp In Dark Embrace / Eclipse Of The Crescent Moon

ETERNAL DARKNESS (SWEDEN)
Line-Up: Janne (vocals), Jompa (guitar), Tony (guitar), Tero Viljanen (bass), Make Pesonen (drums)

Singles/EPs:
Doomed / Psycopath, Distorted Harmony DH006 (1992)

ETERNAL ELYSIUM (JAPAN)
Line-Up: Yukito Okazaki (vocals / guitar), Toshiaki Umemura (bass), Tom Huskinson (drums)

'Spiritualized' Doomsters ETERNAL ELYSIUM, a power trio centred upon former RAN-JA man Yukito Okazaki, were founded during 1991 and have undergone a constantly shifting line-up over three albums to date. The original assemblage of the band saw Okazaki joined by his fellow RAN-JA comrade Atsutoshi Tachimoto on bass and drummer Jiro Murakami. A succession of demos led up to recording of the 'Faithful' album sessions. Guitarist Mitsuru Kondoh would guest on two tracks.
In January of 1994 both Tachimoto and Murakami made their exit. ETERNAL ELYSIUM was soon built back up to strength by enlisting a fresh rhythm section of bass player Jun Kawasaki and drummer Yashuhiro Okada as the group entered into negotiation for an album release through the German Black Mark label. However, the band eventually terminated these talks and in March of 1995 Kawasaki and Okada decamped. By May ETERNAL ELYSIUM sported a revised line-up of Okazaki, bassist Eiichi Okuyama and Takashi Kuroda on the drums. The band would be put on hold though as Okazaki fell ill, necessitating the cancellation of touring plans.
Okazaki had recuperated enough by February of 1997 in order for the band to resume activities. ETERNAL ELYSIUM made appearances on a whole slew of Doom compilation records including the track 'Easygoin'' to the 'At The Mountains Of Madness' album from the British Miskatonik Foundation label, the Japanese Cornucopia 'Doomsday Recitation' album and Meteor City's 'I Am Vengeance'. The group also released a further demo, the live recording

'Spiritual Conclusion'.
Signing to the American Stoner Doom specialists Meteor City ETERNAL ELYSIUM's 2000 album 'Spiritualized D' features a cover version of IRON MAIDEN's 'Innocent Exile', also included on the tribute offering 'Slave To The Power'. Further line-up changes witnessed the departure of Okuyama in April of 2000, his replacement Toshiaki Umemura entering the fold a few weeks later. The group then set about a laying down a series of special tracks including 'Godzilla' for a Sci-Fi inspired album set for release by the Italian Black Widow label as well as covers of WITCHFINDER GENERAL's 'Burning A Sinner' and the ST. VITUS song 'Just A Friend'.
Takashi Kuroda left in February of 2002 shortly before recording of the third ETERNAL ELYSIUM album 'Share'. Although Rio Okuya would record percussion parts for the album, new man Tom Huskinson was subsequently positioned on drums and would feature on one track on the album, 'Movements And Vibes'.

Albums:
FAITHFUL, Cornucopia ECR-04CR (1995)
Sunrise Again / Doomsday Recitation / Suffer / Rest In Peace / With Zero / Pasttime Is Endtime / Ancestral Message / Faithful
SPIRITUALISED D, Meteor City MCY-011 (2000)
W.T.G.B. / Splendid, Selfish Woman / Floating Downer / Trick Or Steal / What A Difference A Day Makes / Stone Wedge / Easygoin' / Innocent Exile / Faithful '99
SHARE, Meteor City MCY-019 (2002)
Schizy / Feel The Beat / Movements And Vibes / Waiting For The Sun / Machine / No Answer / Love Is All / Dogma / Fairies Never Sleep

ETERNAL MOURNING (SPAIN)
Line-Up: Mário Pereira (vocals), Rita Gamito (vocals), Mini (guitar), José Meninas (guitar), Marco Faria (bass / keyboards), Nuno Costa (drums)

Albums:
DELUSION AND DEMENTIA, Goimusic (2001)
Cry Of The Damned / The Strange Forms Of Universe / Final Lament - Part I (Into Unconsciousness) / Dreams Of Desiring Lust / Sombras Do Desconhecido / Final Lament - Part II (Supremum Male Dicere) / A Shameless Smile / Sowing Threads / The Calling

ETERNAL OATH (SWEDEN)
Line-Up: Joni Maensivu (vocals), Peter Nagy (guitar / drums), Petri Tarvainen (guitar), Peter Wendin (bass), Par Almquist (keyboards), Ted Jonsson (drums)

ETERNAL OATH guitarist Peter Nagy also has credits with HYPOCRITE, WYVERN and MÖRK GRYNING. The band came together during 1991 citing an inaugural line-up comprising vocalist Joni Mäensivu, guitarist Petri Tarvainen bass player Ted Lundström and drummer Ted Jonsson. A later addition saw the ranks swelled with the introduction of second guitarist Daniel Dziuba. This formation cut an opening three track demo in the December of 1992. However, shortly after Lundström took leave to join up with AMON AMARTH and a replacement on bass was found in Martin Wiklander. Because of this line-up shuffle the demo remained consigned to the vaults.
A full year later the band set about recording a second demo, a five track session entitled 'Art Of Darkness'. This new material demonstrated ETERNAL OATH's drift away from the basic Death Metal approach. Peter Nagy took Dziuba's position that same year. In February of 1994 a further demo was laid down, prompting the interest of Rat Pack Records and resulting in recording of songs for the mini-album 'So Silent'. The album never emerged on Rat Pack though, ETERNAL OATH severing ties with the label and industriously releasing the record under their own steam in June of 1996.
Wiklander lost interest and decamped and ETERNAL OATH pulled in Peter Wendin as substitute for the debut full length album 'Through The Eyes Of Hatred', issued by the Singapore based Pulverized label. The 2002 ETERNAL OATH outing 'Righteous', released by the Greater Arts label, would include a cover version of PARADISE LOST's 'Eternal'.

Albums:
SO SILENT, N Wrapped Media NWM01 (1996)
The Dawn / Harmonic Souls Departed / So Silent / Insanity / Eternal Rest / Dream Of Rising
THROUGH THE EYES OF HATRED, Pulverized (1999)
Beyond Forgiveness / Without Tears / Angel Of Deception / When The Dreams Die / The Funeral Winds / Lost Somewhere Between / Through The Eyes Of Hatred / The Secret Flame / Soulpoem
RIGHTEOUS, Greater Art (2002)
Preserve The Emotions / Into The Dreamscape / Dreams Of The Silent / Righteous / The Destiny Forsaken / Crown

Of Emptiness / And I Close My Eyes / Eternal / Undeceived World / The Tears For Time

ETERNAL PASSION (GERMANY)
Line-Up: Jürgen Hofmann (vocals), Armin Binder (guitar), Günther Rascher (guitar), Bernhard Atzesberger (bass), Dieter Kasberger (keyboards), Freddy Pongratz (drums)

A Doom / Death Metal act.

Albums:
THE SLEEPING RIVER, Gin Phonic GIN001 (1995)
The Past Is Like The Future / Yearning / Land Of Melancholy / Awake / Darkside / Waiting For Death (Live Studio Track)

ETERNAL SADNESS (GERMANY)
Line-Up: Wolfgang Lutsch (vocals / guitar), Alex Hagenauer (vocals / guitar), Jörg Mensche (bass), Timo Lechner (keyboards), Helmuth Welther (drums)

This five-piece band mixes Death Metal with Gothic Metal and Techno Thrash. ETERNAL SADNESS have played with BOLT-THROWER in their time and received some glowing press coverage. The group, founded in January of 1994 as a trio of vocalist / guitarist Wolfgang Lutsch, guitarist Alex Hagenauer and drummer Tom Hemmerlein was brought up to full strength with the addition of bassist Jörg Mensche and Timo Lechner on keyboards the following year. In this incarnation the band proceeded to lay down the opening demo 'Autumn'.
The 'Elation' album marked the arrival of ETERNAL SADNESS commercially. Hemmerlein would leave the fold during 1998 to be replaced by Helmuth Welther as the band set about recording a new album 'Celebrate...', released in July of 1999. A mini-album, 'Set My Soul On Fire', arrived in January of 2001.
The band has now folded.

Albums:
ELATION, Eternal Sadness (1996)
Elation / Shadows From The Past / Autumn / Descending Glances / Drowned Fate / Like A Mourner / Your Beauty / Dance Of The Dawn
CELEBRATE..., Eternal Sadness (1999)
No More To Live For / Black Magic / Eyes Of Horror / The Nightside / Someone's Dead Forever / My Domain / Death Black Life / So We Danced / Tomorrow Never Knows / Your Beauty / Rain / Follow Me
SET MY SOUL ON FIRE, Eternal Sadness

(2001)
Set My Soul On Fire / When The Night Comes / Sweet Romance / As I Lay / Not Worth Fighting For

ETERNE (UK)
Line-Up: David Dando (vocals / guitar / bass / programming), Martyn Lear (keyboards / programming)

Welsh duo ETERNE offer Avant-garde Doom.

Singles/EPs:
As The Silence Fades / Lament, (1993)
A Certain Kind Of Bitterness / Epilogue / Thanatos, Candlelight (1995)

Albums:
STILL DREAMING, Candlelight 009CD (1995)
Flesh Made World / Divine / The Crawling Chaos / Scarlet Field / Marionette / The Endless / Forever / A Certain Kind Of Bitterness / Epilogue / Thanatos / Still Dreaming / In Retrospect
DEAD AUTHOR, Candlelight 016CD (1997)
Bleed / Pandora / Jyhad / Naked / Complicity / Heal / Delirium / Lexicon / Numb / Deadauthor

ETHERIAL WINDS (HOLLAND)
Line-up: Henri (vocals / keyboards), Bert (guitar), Freddy (bass), Micha (drums)

Previously known as EMBITTER, this Dutch band became ETHERIAL WINDS in 1992. They supply a mixture of Doom and Death Metal.

Albums:
SAVED, MMI 008 (1995)
Calmed (Intro) / Into The Serene / Winter / Benevolence Of The Opaque / In Depression / Endless (Outro)
FIND THE WAY... TOGETHER, Massacre MASS CD059 (1995)
Together / Entrance / Hymne Of Gladness / Elements Of Sorrow / Wish / Hunger / Can't You Sleep / Tragedy

EVENFALL (ITALY)
Line-Up: Roberta Staccuneddu (vocals), Ansgar Zöschg (vocals), Ivan D'Alia (guitar), Jones Adang (guitar), Mark Stagni (bass), Max Boi (keyboards)

A bombastic Gothic Black Metal outfit out of Italy centred upon mentor and prime motivator guitarist Ivan D'Alia. EVENFALL emanated from the Doom Death cult act RESURRECTURIS. Initially EVENFALL was intended as a side embarkation. Vocalist Ansgar Zöschg would front the project for the 1993 demo tape 'My Cross'. In 1994 the

EVENFALL

159

whole scheme was re-billed as CONSPECTU MORTIS, issuing a further promotional session 'Sepolcrum'. The following year tracks would surface on the Metal Horse compilation 'Dawn Of Gods'.

The venture became EVENFALL in 1996, issuing an opening 5 track eponymous EP the following year. Alongside D'Alia and Zöschg would be guitarist Eric Treffel. The band's rhythm section for this record would comprise bassist Cris Espen and acclaimed Austrian drummer Moritz Neuner, a man whose credits include ABIGOR, DARKWELL, SIEGFRIED and DORNENREICH among many others. The full-length album 'Still In The Grey Dying', which included new keyboard player Max Boi and drummer Viktor Ivanovic, arrived during 1999.

Promoting this release EVENFALL were chosen to accompany DIMMU BORGIR and DARK FUNERAL on a 45 date tour of mainland Europe. The band's touring rhythm section for these shows included Neuner once again plus his DARKWELL colleague Roland Wurzer on bass. However, soon after these dates D'Alia opted to completely restructure the band.

During March of 2001 female singer Roberta Staccuneddu would be inducted. New bassist Mark Stagni was enrolled in September with guitarist Jones Adang the following month. Guesting on the 2002 release 'Cumbersome' would be Devon Graves of PSYCHOTIC WALTZ, going under the nom de guerre of 'Buddy Lackey' for his session on the cover version of HEROES DEL SILENCIO's 'Entre Dos Tierras'.

Albums:
EVENFALL, (1996)
Conspectu Mortis / Fear / Opus XIII / Into The Crypt / Shadows
STILL IN THE GREY DYING, Century Media (1999)
Forbidden Tales / Black Bloody Roses / Garden Of Sadness / Still In The Grey Dying / Fallen From Grace / Frozen Mystery / Evenfall / Sales Of Charon / Dark Is The Season / In Between Days
CUMBERSOME, Century Media (2002)
Rawish / Frontloader / Dogma / Entre Dos Tierras / In Absentia Christi / Overcast Sky / Cumbersome / Vangelis Mundi / Unworshipped / Conspectu Mortis II

EVEREVE (GERMANY)
Line-Up: Tom Sedotschenko (vocals), Thorsten Weißenberger (guitar), Stephan Kiefer (guitar), Stefan Müller (bass), MZ Eve 51 (keyboards), Marc Werner (drums)

EVEREVE made quite an impact with their Nuclear Blast debut album 'Seasons'. However, a second effort 'Stormbirds' saw progress stalling despite roadwork in Europe with CREMATORY.

1999 would see former VERMILION FIELDS singer Benjamin Richter take Tom Sedotschenko's position. Tragically the troubled Sedotschenko would commit suicide on May 1st.

Although not charting in Europe the 'Regrets' album would achieve the dubious distinction of being number one on the Lebanese independent radio charts for a three week run! In September of 1999 EVEREVE put in European dates on a package billing with HYPOCRISY and COVENANT.

In January of 2000 drummer Marc Werner departed making way for the mysterious MC Wifebeater, actually Martin Claas. Signing to Massacre Records for the 2001 album 'E-Mania' EVEREVE would dispense with Richter's services as keyboard player MX Eve 51 (real name Michael Zeissl) took over the role.

EVEREVE now operate in self-aggrandized 'Cyber Gothic Metal' territory.

Singles/EPs:
Intro / Darkmere / Salvation / Stormbirds / Autumn Child, Promo-Split-CD (1995)
(Promotional Split CD with PARRACIDE)

Albums:
SEASONS, Nuclear Blast NB222-2 (1996)
Prologue: The Bride Wears Black / A New Winter / The Phoenix, Spring / The Dancer, Under A Summer Sky / Twilight / Autumn Leaves / Untergehen Und Auferstehen / To Learn Silent Oblivion / A Winternight Depression / Epilogue
STORMBIRDS, Nuclear Blast (1998)
Embittered / Fields Of Ashes / Escape / On Lucid Wings / Martyrium / The Failure / The Downfall / Dedications / Stormbirds / As I Breathe The Dawn / Spleen / Universe / A Past For You / Valse Bizarre
REGRETS, Nuclear Blast (1999)
Misery's Dawn / Fall Into Oblivion / Holyman / Redemption / House Of The Rising Sun / The Eclipse Of The Seventh Sun / Passion And Demise / Dies Irae (Grave New World) / Where No Shadows Fall / House Of The Rising Sun (Club edition)
E-MANIA, Massacre MAS CD0270 (2001)
K.M. (Most Terrible God) / Pilgrimage / The Flesh Divine / Someday / This Is Not ... / Suzanne / Demons / Ligeia / See The Truth / T.O O.ur D.Enial / Fade To Grey / 515151

EVIL BARDS (ITALY)

Line-Up: Arwen (vocals), Alexi (guitar), Rhae (bass), Hamish (keyboards), Rig (drums)

EVIL BARDS is a Triuggio based Gothic Metal outfit, founded in February 1998. Over the next three years the band would undergo so many line-up fluxes that drummer Rig stood as the sole surviving founder member. The band put in extensive live work in early 1998 billed as the 'Total Evil' tour and debuted with a November eponymous demo session. For this tape EVIL BARDS was citing a line-up of vocalist Dusk, guitar players Mael and Whisper, bassist Forest and Rig on drums.

Initially EVIL BARDS ploughed a Death / Thrash furrow, matured into an admitted Scandinavian melodic Death Metal style and subsequently, with the addition of vocalist / violinist Syn and keyboard player Vidharr, adopted distinct Gothic leanings. At this juncture guitars were in the hands of Asgardh and Mimir and bassist Bolthorn succeeded to the role of lead vocalist.

The 'Prelude To Sadness' album followed, a record which found EVIL BARDS lyrically pursuing themes of Northern sagas and "romantic tales of the XIX century". By the recording stage Agnehorr had supplanted Asgardh and shortly after release Midgard was pulled in to fulfill bass duties, freeing Bolthorn to concentrate on his duties as frontman.

In February of 2001 Vidharr decamped and the next month EVIL BARD's line-up was further dented when Syn opted out for health reasons. Some stability was enabled with the induction of keyboard player Helgi. Further tribulation occurred in October as Midgard bade his farewell. Worse was to come though as the entire band unit split away from Rig to found a fresh project leaving the drummer standing on his own.

A rejuvenated EVIL BARDS was assembled featuring vocalist / guitarist Alexi, guitarist Jack, bass player Rhae and keyboard player Hamish. Of these members Rig, Alexi and Rhae also operated the side venture BLOODEW. Jack's tenure in EVIL BARDS was brief, the guitarist breaking free in December of 2001. EVIL BARDS would enroll a new member though in female vocalist, and member of BLOODEW, Arwen.

Albums:
PRELUDE TO SADNESS, (2000)
Prelude / Demon's Cry / Don't Follow My Way / Mimir's Tale / Bards March / Evil Bard / Lost God / Cloud /Waiting for Walhalla

EXHORDER (New Orleans, LA, USA)

Line-Up: Kyle Thomas (vocals), Vinnie La Bella (guitar), Jay Ceravollo (bass), Chris Nail (drums)

Following the debut album release EXHORDER lost bassist Andy Villaferra, bringing in replacement Frank Sparcello. EXHORDER's 1992 album 'The Law' included a cover version of BLACK SABBATH's 'Into The Void'.

EXHORDER split in 1994 with vocalist Kyle Thomas creating PENALTY and bass guitarist Jay Ceravolo joining FALL FROM GRACE as replacement for departing Matt Thomas who had jumped over to CROWBAR. Thomas later fronted Chicago Doomsters TROUBLE and created FLOODGATE.

In the summer of 2002 Kyle Thomas revealed the details of a brand new band project entitled JONES'S LOUNGE. His compatriots in this endeavour comprised Dax Thieler of GREEN LEAF CULT, Jimmy Bower of DOWN, CORROSION OF CONFORMITY, SUPERJOINT RITUAL and EYEHATEGOD as well as Jason Portera from PITS VS. PREPS. A debut JONES'S LOUNGE album would see production handled by former UGLY KID JOE guitarist Dave Fortman.

Albums:
SLAUGHTER IN THE VATICAN, Roadracer RO 93632 (1990)
Death In Vain / Homicide / Desecrator / Exhorder / The Tragic Period / Legions Of Death / Anal Lust / Slaughter In The Vatican
THE LAW, Roadracer RO 92342 (1993)
Soul Search Me / Unforgiven / I Am The Cross / Un-Born Again / Into The Void / The Truth / The Law / Incontinence / (Cadence Of) The Dirge

EYEHATEGOD (Harvey, LA, USA)

Line-Up: Michael Williams (vocals), Brian Patton, Jim Bower (guitar), Vince LaBlanc, Michael Williams, Joseph LaCaze (drums)

Revered outfit EYEHATEGOD are one of the very few artists who can lay genuine claim to originating a style - in this case New Orleans Hardcore edged Sludge. The band has trod a turbulent career, apparently on the edge of disintegration on numerous occasions. EYEHATEGOD was formed in 1988 by ex-CROWBAR drummer Jimmy Bower taking up guitar to create EYEHATEGOD. Both Bower and CROWBAR frontman Kirk Windstein had been members of covers act THE SLUGS. The band made an immediate impact with a relentless touring schedule and shows that saw EYEHATEGOD delivering a quite unique

EYEHATEGOD

brand of detuned violent Metal. Over the years the group, despite an ever fluxing line up, has gained respect for a no compromise approach to their art backed up with over a dozen nationwide tours of America as well as forays into both Europe and Asia. EYEHATEGOD's line-up for the 1992 'In The Name Of Suffering' album was vocalist Mike Williams, guitarists Jim Bower and Marc Schultz, bassist Steve Dale and drummer Joey LaCaze.

Bower keeps himself occupied outside of EYEHATEGOD with numerous projects, the most well known being DOWN with Windstein, CORROSION OF CONFORMITY's Pepper Keenan and PANTERA's Phil Anselmo and Rex Brown. Bower also occupies the drum stool with SUPERJOINT RITUAL, again with Anselmo, ex-CROWBAR guitarist Kevin Bond and former STRESSBALL drummer Joe Fazzio. Bower has yet another band CLEARLIGHT. Brian Patton divides his duties between EYEHATEGOD and SOILENT GREEN.

During 1997 the band enrolled former MALIGNANT MINDS and SUPLECS bassist Danny Nick, this latest recruit's tenure lasting until 2000 when he re-joined the SUPLECS. 2000's 'Southern Discomfort' album is a collection of early demos. The same year found Bower performing drum duties with CORROSION OF CONFORMITY for touring purposes deputizing for an injured Reed Mullins. Bower also supported for some dates

on the tour with his side band CLEARLIGHT. EYEHATEGOD would still be going strong as 2002 drew in, citing a line-up of vocalist Mike Williams, guitarist Jimmy Bower, Joe LaCaze on drums and newest recruit Gary Mader on bass guitar. The band would feature two tracks, '30 $ Bag' and 'Jack Ass In The Will Of God' recorded at the Hollywood Roxy in September of 2001, included on the Century Media tenth anniversary DVD release.

EYEHATEGOD would gain the distinction of being the debut release for Ben Falgoust of GOATWHORE and SOILENT GREEN and Jay Branch of SKINCRAWL's new label Incision Records with a limited edition split 7" affair in alliance with SOILENT GREEN. Restricted to just 2,000 pieces the record was made even more collectable by the fact that 500 of these would be in either clear or coloured swirl vinyl.

EYEHATEGOD would participate in a tribute concert to the late Johnny Morrow of IRON MONKEY at the Nottingham Rock City venue in the UK during August, building a series of club gigs, supported by MYWAR and LABRAT, around the event. Cited as Morrow's favourite act EYEHATEGOD reportedly bore their own travel costs in order to fulfil these shows. With Jimmy Bower already committed to tour work in North America with DOWN the band pulled in ex-HAWG JAW guitarist Gary Mader and Marvin of the VARUKERS and CHAOS UK to handle bass. Vocalist Mike Williams would arrive in the UK upfront of the main EYEHATEGOD contingent to lay down vocal tracks on a MYWAR album project that was originally to have included Morrow.

A further union with SOILENT GREEN had the band committing the track 'The Age Of Bootcamp' to a split 7" single through Incision Records.

The summer of 2002 would also bring confirmation that Jimmy Bower was involved in a heavyweight brand new band project entitled JONES'S LOUNGE. His compatriots in this endeavour comprised EXHORDER and FLOODGATE frontman Kyle Thomas, Dax Thieler of GREEN LEAF CULT as well as Jason Portera from PITS VS. PREPS. A debut JONES'S LOUNGE album would see production handled by former UGLY KID JOE guitarist Dave Fortman.

Singles/EPs:
Ruptured Heart Theory / Story Of The Eye / Blank-Shoplift (LIVE), Bovine (1994)
Southern Discomfort, Slap A Ham SAH 24 (1996) (Split single with 13)
Serving Time In The Middle Of Nowhere / Lack Of Almost Everything, Ax/tion (1996) (Split EP with 13)
Sabbath Jam (Cornicopia - Hand Of Doom - Behind The Wall Of Sleep), Hydra Head (1997) (Split 7" with ANAL CUNT)

Albums:
IN THE NAME OF SUFFERING, Century Media 77-9738-2 (1992)
Depress / Man Is Too Ignorant Too Exist / Shinobi / Pigs / Run It Into The Ground / Godsong / Children Of God / Left To Starve / Hostility Dose
TAKE AS NEEDED FOR PAIN, Century Media 77052-2 (1993)
Blank / Sister Fucker (Part 1) / Shop Lift / White Nigger / 30 $ Bag / Disturbance / Take As Needed For Pain / Sister Fucker (Part 2) / Crimes Against Skin / Kill Your Boss / Who Gave Her The Roses / Laugh It Off
DOPESICK, Century Media 77114-2 (1996)
My Name Is God (I Hate You) / Dogs Holy Life / Masters Of Legalized Confusion / Dixie Whiskey / Ruptured Heart Theory / Non Conductive Negative Reasoning / Lack Of All Most Everything / Zero Nowhere / Methamphetimine / Peace Thru War (Thru Peace And War) / Broken Down But Not Locked Up/ Anxiety Hangover
SOUTHERN DISCOMFORT, Century Media (2000)
Ruptured Heart Theory / Story Of The Eye / Blank-Shoplift / Southern Discomfort / Serving Time In The Middle Of Nowhere / Lack Of Almost Everything
Peace Thru War (Thru Peace And War) /

Depress / Dopesick Jam
CONFEDERACY OF RUINED LIVES, Century Media 77308-2 (2000)
Revelation-Revolution / Blood Money / Jack Ass In The Will Of God / Self Medication Blues / The Concussion Machine Process / Inferior And Full Of Anxiety / .001% / 99 Miles Of Bad Road / Last Year (She Wanted A Doll House) / Corruption Scheme
10 YEARS OF ABUSE (AND STILL BROKE), Century Media (2001)
Left To Starve (Demo) / Hit A Girl (Demo) / Depress (Demo) / Children Of God (Demo) / White Nigger (Live KXLU session) / Depress (Live KXLU session) / Take As Needed For Pain (Live KXLU session) / My Name Is God (I Hate You) (Live KXLU session) / Lack Of Almost Everything (Live) / Blood Money (Live) / Children Of God (Live) / Sister Fucker (Part I) & Sister Fucker (Part II) (Live) / 30$ Bag (Live) / Zero Nowhere (Live) / Methamphetamine (Live)

EYES OF LIGEIA (Atlanta, GA, USA)

EYES OF LIGIEA is a one man Doom venture of Toby Chappell, an erstwhile member of Atlanta, Georgia Thrash act SKIPTOE. The act, fuelled by an appreciation of the work of writer Edgar Allan Poe, bowed in with the 1999 recording 'A Dirge For The Most Lovely Dead', three songs bleakly spanning a sombre half hour of music. 'The Night's Plutonian Shore' followed in June 2001. Chappell also operates ambient project WITHOUT A SHADOW and, billing himself as 'Beelphazoar', the completely instrumental Progressive keyboard laden AMPHIGORY.

Albums:
A DIRGE FOR THE MOST LOVELY DEAD, Unsung Heroes UHR032 (1999)
Watcher In The Water / And Yet You Stare / To Drown Beyond The Sunset - Perhaps Someday Softer Rains Will Come
THE NIGHT'S PLUTONIAN SHORE, Unsung Heroes UHR042 (2001)
As The Twilight Fades Away / To Drown Beyond The Sunset / Nevermore / Khephra In Thy Hiding / In The Place Where There Is No Darkness / Seraphs Uplifted With The Sun

FAITH (SWEDEN)
Line-Up: Roger Berndtsson (vocals), Roger Johansson (guitar), Christer Nilsson (bass), Peter Svensson (drums)

Prior to the release of the debut single, 'Hymn Of The Summer', Swedish Metal Doom mongers FAITH were known as STORMBRINGER.
Sometime after the 45's release frontman Roger Berndtsson decamped necessitating bassist Christer Nilsson to take on the additional role of frontman. But, whilst the group continued as a trio for a period, FAITH splintered and drummer Peter Svensson joined the much more slothsome MERCY and later joined GLOBE.
Johansson and Nilsson have apparently since been reunited with Svensson and have been reported to have commenced writing and recording together, although it is unclear as to whether any material will emerge under the FAITH banner.

Singles/EPs:
Hymn Of The Summer / Possessed, Hellrec HSP 2060 (1986)

FALL FROM GRACE (Metairie, LA, USA)
Line-Up: Wil Buras (vocals), Jay Ceravollo (guitar), Marc Hernandez (bass), Eric Stierwald (drums)

FALL FROM GRACE came into being in 1992 after bassist Wil Buras and guitarist Matt Thomas opted to break away from their then band RAZOR WHITE, an act that at the time included future PANTERA vocalist Phil Anselmo. Drummer Eric Stierwald and bassist Marc Hernandez (Buras now on lead vocals) augmented the duo soon after and the band toured the Louisiana clubs under the title of BUTT UGLY.
By late 1993 Thomas succumbed to an offer to join CROWBAR as BUTT UGLY trimmed down to a trio for a while. Eventually erstwhile EXHORDER guitarist Jay Cerevello brought the band back up to strength and with it a new name FALL FROM GRACE.
A five track 1996 demo cultivated worthy press, which led swiftly to a deal with the Futurist Label group, and a self-titled debut produced by old colleague Matt Thomas.

Albums:
FALL FROM GRACE, Music For Nations MFN 217 (1997)
Snake Eyed Saviour / Seven Shades Of Grey / Feel / Never / Before It Grows / It Ain't Like That / Gone / Hero Zero / Open Arms

And Broken Hands / Violent Truth / Sin (Takes Over)

FALL OF THE LEAFE (FINLAND)
Line-Up: Tuomas Tuominen (vocals), T. Hatakka (guitar), Juha Kouhi (bass), Petri Hannuniemi (keyboards), Marko Hyytiä (drums)

A highly rated Finnish atmospheric Black inclined outfit. FALL OF THE LEAFE's first release, the demo 'Storm Of The Autumnfall', included early members vocalist Jani Lindstrom and guitarist Kaj Gustafson.
Following the recording of the 'Evanescent, Everfading' album singer Jani Lindstrom parted ways with the group, being replaced by Tuomas Tuominen. Gustafson would later bail out to be supplanted by M. Rostedt. T. Hatakka displaced him in turn.
Longstanding bassist Juha Kouhi exited in 2000 with his place being filled by P. Santola then P. Burka. However, Kouhi was to return to the fold the following year. For their third album the band signed with the Argentinean Icarus concern.
Members of FALL OF THE LEAFE also operate in UNHOLA. Tuominen also fronts Gothic Rock artists SARANTH.

Albums:
STORM OF THE AUTUMNFALL, Northern Sound (1996)
Into The Autumnsphere / Storm Of The Autumnfall / The Garden Of The Shoreless Sea / Starfire / Upon The Verdant Vales Of North
EVANESCENT EVERFADING, Defiled DLF 4724-2 (1998)
The Celestial Keeper / …And My Heavens Fall / The Garden By The Shoreless Sea / Wings Of My Desire Untamed / My Weeping Goddess / With Each Fall Of The Leafe / Within The Everfrozen Winternight / Evanescent, Everfading
AUGUST WERNICKE, Icarus ICARUS07 (2000)
Into The Autumnsphere / Deference, Diminuend / Platinum / A Feather To The juniper / Machina Mimesis (In The Corner Café) / Lectured By The Demons Of Dreams / Wonder Clouds Rain / Effloresce Black And White / In Morning Mood And Utopia Revelation / Bleak Picture, August
FERMINA, (2002)
Counterfeit Bloom / Feather Duster Premiere / Stumbling Stone / Blind Carbon Copies / Chameleon Loop / Flamenco Scheme / Fermination, Smooth And Fine / Soul Bay Beat / Signatures, Baby Bomb

FATSO JETSON (USA)

Line-Up: Mario Lalli (vocals / guitar), Larry Lalli (bass), Tony Tornay (drums)

Southern Californian Desert dwelling, highly individual Stoners. FATSO JETSON, a band with deserved cult status, had been forged during 1994 by the Lalli siblings - vocalist / guitarist Mario Lalli and bassist Larry, together with former SOLAR FEAST drummer Tony Tornay. Mario Lalli's musical journey had seen him journey through school acts such as DEAD ISSUE and ACROSS THE RIVER.

Alongside Lalli both future KYUSS personnel bassist Scott Reeder and drummer Alfredo Hernandez had cut their teeth with school Punk band DEAD ISSUE, an outfit that also featured vocalist / guitarist Herb Lineau and guitarist Mario Lalli. With Lineau's departure DEAD ISSUE evolved into ACROSS THE RIVER. Reeder would then decamp and Hernandez and Lalli, adding Larry Lalli on bass and Gary Arce on guitar, became ENGLENOOK in 1987. This band too shifted shape into YAWNING MAN. As the Lalli brothers later created FATSO JETSON Hernandez and Reeder reunited to found KYUSS.

YAWNING MAN would make an imprint on Stoner history when their track 'Catamaran' was recorded by Stoner legends KYUSS on their 1995 record 'And The Circus Leaves Town'. Mario Lalli had also written the track 'N.O.' which appears - with Lalli contributing guitar, on the 1994 KYUSS album 'Sky Valley'.

The band debuted live in September 1994, opening a show for former BLACK FLAG guitarist Greg Ginn. So impressed was the headliner that a deal was immediately extended for FATSO JETSON to join Ginn's S.S.T. label. Subsequently the inaugural 'Stinky Little Gods' album arrived in August of 1995 and a follow up, 'Power Of Three', in November of 1997.

FATSO JETSON's 1998 split single shared with FU MANCHU would see BRANT BJORK aiding on rhythm guitar. Bjork would also figure on a further split single that same year, 'Accelerator General', shared with THE BLOODSHOT and the song 'Procrastination Process' included on the compilation 'Welcome To Meteor City'.

The band added second guitarist Gary Arce, from their formative ENGLENOOK days, in August 1998 for the Man's Ruin 'Flames For All' album. Touring to promote this record found FATSO JETSON paired up with QUEENS OF THE STONE AGE on West Coast dates. During 1999 FATSO JETSON donated their take on 'Devil's Whorehouse' to

the Freebird Records MISFITS tribute album 'Graven Images'. Both Lalli siblings would be included on 'The Desert Sessions Volume 4 - Hard Walls and Little Trips' collection, part of the ongoing loose jam sessions organized by QUEENS OF THE STONE AGE frontman Josh Homme. The band members appear on the songs 'Monster In The Parasol', 'Jr. High Love' and 'Eccentric Man'. Mario Lalli would also participate in 'The Desert Sessions Volume 5 - Poetry For The Masses' vocalising on the track 'You Think I Ain't Worth A Dollar, But I Feel Like A Millionaire'. Both Mario Lalli and Gary Arce showed up at the sessions for BRANT BJORK's solo record 'Jalomantra'.

The 'Desert Sessions' track 'Monster In My Parasol', co-written by Josh Homme and Mario Lalli, would reappear in a new guise recorded by the QUEENS OF THE STONE AGE for their 2000 album 'Rated R'.

Chris Goss of MASTERS OF REALITY produced the 'Toasted' album, released by the Bongload label. Gary Arce undertook European touring with the band, including a showing at the Dutch 'Dynamo Open Air' festival in 1999, before making his exit in April of 2000. FATSO JETSON continued as a three piece announcing a new deal with Josh Homme's own Rekords label. The band hooked up with QUEENS OF THE STONE AGE once more to lay down a collaborative version of the CIRCLE JERKS song 'Coup De Taut' for a tribute record to aid the ailing Keith Morris.

FATSO JETSON made a return with the 2002 album 'Cruel & Delicious'. The record would include a cover version of DEVO's 'Ton O' Love'.

Singles/EPs:
Swollen Offering /, Sessions (1998) (Split 7" single with FU MANCHU)
Accelerator General, Miracle (1998) (Split 7" single with THE BLOODSHOT)
King Faduke, Cattle Productions (1999) (Split 7" single with FIREBALL MINISTRY)

Albums:
STINKY LITTLE GODS, S.S.T. (1995)
Kettles Of Doom / Joke Shop / Von Deuce / Captain Evil / Pressure For Posture / Nightmares Are Essential / Gargle / Salt Chunk Mary's / Highway 86 / Corn On The Macabre
POWER OF THREE, S.S.T. (1997)
Builders & Collectors / Ugly Man, Ugly Name / Mummified / Orgy Porgy / El Taurino / Phil The Hole / Phantom Of The Opry / Handgun / Sandy The Clock Farmer / Bored Stiff / Itchy Brother / Drones Pills.
FLAMES FOR ALL, Man's Ruin MR143CD

(1998)
The Untimely Death Of The Keyboard Player / Vatos Of The Astral Plane / Fucked Up & Famous / Flames For All / Icon To Excon / Let's Clone / August In Lawndale / Graffiti In Space / Deaf Conducter
FLAMES FOR ALL, Man's Ruin MR143 (1998) (10" vinyl)
The Untimely Death Of The Keyboard Player / Vatos Of The Astral Plane / Fucked Up & Famous / Flames For All / Icon To Excon
TOASTED, Bongload Custon (1999)
New Age Android / Magma / I've Got The Shame / She's So Borg / Swollen Offering / Tutta Dorma / Rail Job / Procrastination Process / Too Many Skullz
CRUEL AND DELICIOUS, Rekords (2002)

FESTER (NORWAY)
Line-Up: Rolf Tommy Simonsen (vocals / guitar), Tiger Mathisen (vocals / guitar), Jörgen Skjolden (bass), Jan Skjolden (drums)

This Norwegian outfit combine Doom and Death Metal with a brand of Black Metal that, on the 'Silence' album incorporates mainly whispered vocals!

Albums:
WINTER OF SIN, No Fashion NFR 002 (1994)
Winter Of Sin / Senses Are The True You / The Ancient Gods Wore Black / Entering... / Victory!!! / Liberation / As The Swords Clinch The Air / A Dogfight Leaves A Trace / The Commitments That Shattered
SILENCE, Lethal LRC 756 (1995)
Dream / Silent Is The Raven / Frustrations / The Maze / The Conformists / Voices From The Woods / Elisabeta In My World Of Thoughts / Growing Thirst / Nar Noen Dor

FIELDS OF THE NEPHILIM (UK)
Line-Up: Carl McCoy (vocals), Paul Wright (guitar), Peter Yates (guitar), Tony Pettitt (bass), Nod Wright (drums)

A highly influential band that has amassed a sizable cult following in Gothic Rock circles, particularly in Germany. The band, based in Hertfordshire, first emerged in 1984 citing a line up of vocalist Carl McCoy, guitarist Paul Wright, bass player Tony Pettit, saxophonist Gary Whisker and drummer Nod Wright. The band's mystic stance would be exemplified by their name, the Nephilim being biblical angels attributed with delivering arcane secrets to mankind. Musically the band managed to attain that rarest of tangibles - a unique sound. Lyrically McCoy also strove for originality infusing the songs with teasing tidbits of arcana and ancient lore.

An intensive run of gigging across the UK was broken by the issue of the 'Burning The Fields' EP. Initially pressed in a run of just 500 the record was subsequently re-manufactured to cope with demand. Shortly after this release, and signing to the Beggars Banquet label, Whisker departed. FIELDS OF THE NEPHILIM pulled in guitarist Peter Yates to round out their sound in time for the inaugural Beggars Banquet product the single 'Power'. A second single, 'Preacher Man', was delivered in 1986 and backed by an evocative video short by Richard Stanley, director of the 'Hardware' movie in which McCoy performed a cameo part. The accompanying album 'Dawnrazor' elicited strong media and fan support with the 1988 single 'Moonchild' topping the indie charts and marking the pinnacle of achievement in the UK for the band.

The 1990 'Elyzium' album and follow up live affair 'Earth Inferno' solidified their fan base internationally. However, as the band's career was still in ascendancy they stunned fans by announcing the 'Fire Festivals' at London's Town and Country Club were to be the swan song gigs for the band.

McCoy bailed out in October 1991 taking the rights to the band name with him. He would build a fresh venture succinctly billed NEFILIM. The remaining members regrouped as RUBICON drafting vocalist Andy Delaney. In this new guise and with a toughened up sound RUBICON achieved quite considerable success in mainland Europe commencing with the 1992 album 'What Starts, Ends'.

After an absence of ten years FIELDS OF THE NEPHILIM marked their return with a single made up of reworked songs from their debut 1985 EP 'Burning The Fields'.

The band became simply NEPHILIM in 1996 constituting McCoy, guitarist Paul Miles, bassist Cian Houchin and drummer Simon Rippin for the 'Zoon' album, somewhat based upon the occult legend of the descent of Inanna. The preceding single 'Penetration' received markedly opposing views from critics. A tour was embarked upon but curtailed after just a few shows.

In 1997 reports that McCoy and the other erstwhile FIELDS OF THE NEPHILIM band members were to reunite were confirmed.

Oddly, FIELDS OF THE NEPHILIM would mark their return in 2000 with the inclusion of 'Trees 98' / 'Trees AD' on a hard to get hold of compilation album issued only in South Africa. Jungle Records would officially mark the resurrection with the May single 'One More Nightmare (Trees Come Down AD)' / 'Darkcell AD'. The Wright siblings would also

166

FIELDS OF NEPHILIM
Photo : Julian Calverley

debut their LAST RITES project, announcing an album release through Dreamcatcher Records.

Upfront of a new album FIELDS OF THE NEPHILIM pencilled in dates for June 2001 at the German 'Zillo' and 'Wave-Gothik-Treffen' festivals. However, with the recording process taking longer than expected these shows would be nixed. During the interim the German SPV label issued a compilation of rarities entitled 'From Here To Gehenna'. This outing comprised material recorded in 1985-86, including the original versions of the songs the band remade for the 'One More Nightmare' single as well as an early version of their first single for Beggars Banquet,

'Power', and different versions of 'Laura'.

Singles/EPs:
Back In The Gehenna / Trees Come Down / Dark Cell / Laura, Tower N1 (1985) ('Burning The Fields' EP)
Power / Secrets / The Tower, Situation 2 SIT 42T (1986) (12" single)
Preacher Man / Laura II, Situation 2 SIT 46 (1987) (7" single)
Preacher Man / Laura II / Preacher Man (Contaminated version), Situation 2 SIT 46T (1987) (12" single)
Blue Water / In Every Dream Home A Heartache, Situation 2 SIT 48 (1987) **75 UK** (7" single)
Blue Water / In Every Dream Home A Heartache / Blue Water (Electrostatic mix) / Blue Water (Hot Wire version), Situation 2 SIT 48T (1987) (12" single)
Moonchild (First Seal) / Shiva, Situation 2 SIT 52 (1988) **28 UK** (7" single)
Moonchild (First Seal) / Shiva / Moonchild (Longevity version), Situation 2 SIT 52T (1988) (12" single)
Moonchild (First Seal) / Shiva / Power (Live) / Vet For The Insane (Live), Situation 2 SIT 52TR (1988) (12" single)
Psychonaut (Lib.II) / Celebrate (Second Seal), Situation 2 SIT 57 (1989) 35 UK (7" single)
Psychonaut (Lib.II) / Psychonaut (Lib. III) / Psychonaut (Lib. I) / Psychonaut Lib. IV), Situation 2 SIT 57T (1989) (12" single)
Psychonaut (Lib.II) / Celebrate (Second Seal) / Psychonaut (Lib.IV), Situation 2 SIT 57CD (1989) (CD single)
For Her Light / Submission, Beggars Banquet BEG 244 (1990) **54 UK** (7" single)
For Her Light (Extended version) / Submission (Extended version), Beggars Banquet BEG 244T (1990) (12" single)
Sumerland (Dreamed) / The Watchmen (Live), Beggars Banquet BEG 250 (1990) **37 UK** (7" single)
Sumerland (Dreamed) / The Watchmen (Live) / Blue Water (Live) / Phobia (Live), Beggars Banquet BEG 250T (1990) (12" single)
One More Nightmare (Trees Come Down A.D.) / Dark Cell A.D., Jungle (2000)

Albums:
DAWNRAZOR, Situation 2 SITU 18CD (1987) **62 UK**
Intro (The Harmonica Man) / Slow Kill / Volcane (Mr. Jealousy Has Returned) / Vet For The Insane / Dust / Reanimator / Dawnrazor / The Sequel / Power / Laura II / Secrets / The Tower
THE NEPHILIM, Situation 2 SITU22CD

(1988) **14 UK**
Endemoniada / The Watchman / Phobia / Moonchild / Chord Of Souls / Shiva / Celebrate / Love Under Will / Last Exit For The Lost
RETURN TO GEHENNA, Supporti Fonograph SF008 (1988)
Power (New version) / Laura (New version) / Secrets / The Tower / Returning To Gehenna (New version)
ELIZIUM, Beggars Banquet BEGA 115CD (1990) **22 UK**
(Dead But Dreaming) For Her Light (At The Gates Of Silent Memory) Paradise Regained / Submission / Sumerland (What Dreams May Come) / Wail Of Summer / And There Will Your Heart Be Also
EARTH INFERNO: LIVE, Beggars Banquet BEGA120CD (1991) **39 UK**
Intro (Dead But Dreaming) For Her Light (At The Gates Of Silent Memory) Paradise Regained / Moonchild / Submission / Preacher Man / Love Under Will / Sumerland / Last Exit For The Lost / Psychonaut / Dawnrazor
BBC RADIO ONE LIVE IN CONCERT, Windsong WINCD023 (1992)
Endemoniada / Love Under Will / Moonchild / Blue Water / Chord Of Souls
REVELATIONS, Beggars Banquet BEGA 137CD (1993)
Moonchild / Chord Of Souls / Last Exit For The Lost / Preacher Man / Love Under Will / Power / Psychonaut (Lib. II) / For Her Light / Blue Water / Vet For The Insane / The Watchman / Dawnrazor
BURNING THE FIELDS, Nostadamus MOO 1CD (1993)
FROM HERE TO GEHENNA, SPV 085-148072 CD (2001)
Trees Come Down / Back In Gehenna / Darkcell / Laura / Power / Laura 2 / Secrets / The Tower / Returning To Gehenna

FIFTH REASON (SWEDEN)
Line-up: Kristian Andren (vocals), Marco A. Nicosia (guitar), Simon Johansson (guitar), Oscar Tillman (bass), Martin Larsson (drums)

FIFTH REASON can boast ex-members of ABSTRAKT ALGEBRA, HEXENHAUS and MEMENTO MORI. The band came together in 1992, created by guitarist Simon Johansson and Niklas Oreland, offering a demo tape titled 'Stranded'.
Progress was halted when Johansson was enticed away to ABSTRAKT ALGEBRA to record their self-titled debut, although after leaving ABSTRAKT ALGEBRA in late 1996 Johansson had a brief flirtation with MEMORY GARDEN prior to resurrecting FIFTH REASON, pulling in former TAD

MOROSE / MEMONTO MORI vocalist Kristian Andren.

With the addition of bassist Oscar Tillman and drummer Martin Larsson FIFTH REASON were soon up and running, securing a deal with Heathendoom Records. Second guitarist Marco A. Nocosia, previously with HEXENHAUS, joined in time for recording.

The debut album, entitled 'Psychotic', was produced by MERCYFUL FATE / MEMENTO MORI guitarist Mike Wead.

Albums:
PSYCHOTIC, Heathendoom HDMCD004 (1997)
Psychotic / My Friend / This Journey Of Mine / Above, Below And Beyond / A Shadow Remains / Strange Intimation / In Between / A Final Wish
WITHIN OR WITHOUT, Scarlet (2002)

FISTULA (USA)

Singles/EPs:
Hybrid / Goatskin / El Amor De La Gorilla, (2001) (Split EP with SOFA KING KILLER)

Albums:
HYMNS OF SLUMBER, (2001)

5IVE (Boston, MA, USA)
Line-Up: Ben Carr (guitar), Charlie Harrold (drums)

Although titled exactly the same as the British Pop Boyband this 5IVE out of Boston are a Psychedelic Doomcore duo consisting solely of guitarist Ben Carr and drummer Charlie Harrold. The eponymous album arrived first on heavyweight 180 gramm vinyl before being picked up for CD release, with differing cover artwork, by Tortuga Records. 5IVE drafted MILLIGRAM vocalist Jonah J. Jenkins in to add guest vocals to their second 2001 outing, 'Telestic Disfracture'.

Albums:
5IVE, Tortuga (2001)
Burning Season / Orange / The Baron / Jules Vernes' Dream / Bicycle Rider / Cerrado
TELESTIC DISFRACTURE, Tortuga (2001)
Stockholm Blues / Nitinol / Shark Dreams / Synapse X 3 ...a) Sleep For The Larsen B Shelf ...b) Telluric In Transudate ...c) Comae

500 FT. OF PIPE (Detroit, MI, USA)
Line-Up: Ross Westerbur (vocals / keyboards), Kevin Edwards (guitar), Mick Stone (drums)

Detroit's 500 FT. OF PIPE, dating back to

1996, got their unique bass-less sound and distinctive band name in one fell swoop. Previously employing a bassist cum day job plumber, the four stringer's constant complaints about having to lay 500 feet of piping forced his dismissal and gave the act a new band name. From that point vocalist / keyboard player Ross Westerbur - a celebrated figure in Detroit, being a maths teacher at Wayne State University well known for his Acid Rock side venture, took on the lower end sound spectrums with a Micromoog.

500 FT. OF PIPE debuted with a self-financed 1997 album 'Better Living Through Alchemy' issued on their own High Clopse Music label. Their industry would extend to a further well received effort, 'The Electrifying Church Of The New Light', during 1998.

The 'Dope Deal' album includes a cover version of DONOVAN's Psychedelic sixties hit 'Sunshine Superman'.

Singles/EPs:
So Good / Your Heart Is Angry (But Your Mind Is Stoned), Stolen (2000) (7" single)

Albums:
BETTER LIVING THROUGH ALCHEMY, High Clopse Music (1997)
Full On Baby / Graffenberg Decision / Down Syndrome / Alice / Supercharger / Egyptian Lust / You See, Oh Nexus
THE ELECTRIFYING CHURCH OF THE NEW LIGHT, High Clopse Music (1998)
Turn Me On, Baby / Marshmallow / Skynet / Molotov Cocktail / Automation / Century 21 / Open The Pod Bay Doors, HAL / Sonic Nutrition / The Electrifying Church Of The New Light
DOPE DEAL, Beard Of Stars (2001)
Detroit City (Never Done Me No Good) / '77 Burnout / Nout Your Mule / Dope Deal / 420 To Go / Big Brother / D.E.A. / Sunshine Superman / Wear It Out / We Blew The Whole Thing Up

FLOODLAND (AUSTRIA)
Line-Up: Christian Meyer (vocals), Bernhard Wieser (guitar), Harald Schmid (bass / keyboards / programming), Markus Schmid (drums)

Neo Gothic outfit FLOODLAND came into being during 1995, staking their claim with the demo session 'Chapter One'. A four track EP, 'Seasons', was delivered in April of 1997, produced by Michael Piesch, with a full-length effort entitled 'The Now And Here Is Never' arriving in October of 1998 via the Viennese label Serpent Qui Danse. Second guitarist

169

Martin Svoboda then departed.
A further demo CD, 'Coming Home Tonight', led up to a run of gigs in their homeland as support to THE GATHERING, CHRISTIAN DEATH and LETZTE INSTANZ. The 2002 album release 'Ocean Of The Lost' was produced by Milos 'Dodo' Dolezal of VITACID fame for the brand new Wait And Bleed label. The record proved a more mature outing than previous efforts, finding the band stretching away from the obvious creative associations their name implies. Guests included vocalist Zuzana from SILENT STREAM OF GODLESS ELEGY and New York Orchestra of Modern Art alto sax player Ivan Myslikovian. FLOODLAND would not rest on their laurels, preparing for another album provisionally entitled 'Decay'.

Singles/EPs:
Graves Of Winter´s End / Eternity / And We Fall / The Crow, Floodland (1997) ('Seasons' EP)

Albums:
THE NOW AND HERE IS NEVER, Serpent Qui Danse SQD4 (1998)
The Now And Here Is Never / War In My Head / Digital Heaven / Sister Of Mercy / Talking To My Radio / Trust, Believe & Die / Shepherd Death / Marionette / The Plague / Black Rain / Neon Dreams / Too Late / Behind The Unicorn
OCEAN OF THE LOST, Wait And Bleed WAB004 (2002)
White Skin, Black Soul / Ocean Of The Lost / Crepusculum / Never / I Standing Fall / Always On The Wrong Side / The Dawn (Version) / Remembering Tomorrow / Coming Home Tonight / Mist Of Time / Sea Of Light / Prague / 1648 / The Camp / Coming Home Tonight (Reprise)

FLOWING TEARS (GERMANY)
Line-Up: Stefanie Duchêne (vocals), Benjamin Buss (guitar / keyboards), Frederic Lesny (bass), Stefan Gemballa (drums)

An inventive and hugely talented song based Dark Rock act. Previously known as FLOWING TEARS AND WITHERED BEAUTY issuing the 1996 debut album 'Swansongs'. Under their previous incarnation the band also released 1998's 'Joy Parade', which witnessed the induction of lead vocalist Stefanie Duchêne, and 1999's

FLOWING TEARS
Photo : Volker Beushausen

'Swallow' mini-album. Under their truncated title FLOWING TEARS debut 2000 album 'Jade' was produced by GRIP INC. guitarist Waldemar Sorychta. Following this album the band underwent a radical overhaul of membership with guitarist Manfred Bersin, keyboard player Mike Volz and drummer Eric Hilt all departing.

FLOWING TEARS' January 2002 opus, the quite superb 'Serpentine', saw drums supplied by Stefan Gemballa, previously with RED AIM. The band would support the record with a lengthy European tour in March alongside label mates TIAMAT and MOONSPELL. During June Gemballa would set about recording a solo album in alliance with ANGEL DUST's Dirk Thurisch and TIAMAT's Anders Iwers.

Both guitarist Benjamin Buss and drummer Stefan Gemballa have also made themselves a name operating the less than serious Stoner Rock outfit RED AIM.

Albums:
JADE, Century Media 77273-2 (2000)
Godless / Sistersun / Swallow / Lovesong For A Dead Child / Under The Red / Turpentine / The One I Drowned / Vanity / Radio Heroine / Coma Garden / Jade / White Horses
SERPENTINE, Century Media 8070-2 (2002)
Intro / Starfish Ride (For A Million Dollar Handshake) / Serpentine / Children Of The Sun / The Marching Sane / Breach / Portsall (Departure Song) / Justine / The Carnage People / Merlin / Cupid Of The Carrion Kind / For Tonight

FLOWING TEARS AND WITHERED BEAUTY (GERMANY)
Line-Up: Manfred Bersin (vocals), Benjamin Buss (guitar / keyboards), Frederic Lesny (bass), Christian Zimmer (drums)

'Dark Wave' Rock act FLOWING TEARS AND WITHERED FLOWERS were assembled in 1994 issuing their first recordings in February the following year in the form of the 'Bijou' demo.

Several line-up shuffles ensued prior to a follow up tape 'Flowers In The Rain' preceding the 1996 debut album 'Swansongs'. Promotion for this release found the band making great inroads as support to THE 3RD AND THE MORTAL on their 1997 European dates. The 1998 'Joy Parade' offering witnessed the induction of lead vocalist Stefanie Duchêne and drummer Eric Hilt replacing previous incumbent Christian Zimmer. An EP, 'Swallow' which included a

revamp of the melancholy NEW ORDER classic 'Love Will Tear Us Apart', surfaced in 1999.

By 2000 the band were simply known as FLOWING TEARS releasing the 'Jade' album through Century Media.

Singles/EPs:
Swallow / Love Will Tear Us Apart / Purple Red Soil / Odium, Seven Art (1999) ('Swallow' EP)

Albums:
SWANSONGS, Seven Art Music SA CD 001 (1996)
Flowers In The Rain / Waterbride / Fallen Leaves / Arion / Crystal Dance / Flowing Tears & Withered Flowers / ...Along A Dreamin' Ocean... / ...And I Drown...
JOY PARADE, Seven Art (1998)
Purple Red Soil / Gerion / Joy Parade / Bluefield / Odium / Trust / Sundrops / Spirals Meet The Sea / Rainswept / The Day You Took My Breath

FOREST OF SOULS (FRANCE)
Line-Up: Jerome Deres (vocals / guitar), Denis Barjettas (bass / keyboards), George Noguerira (keyboards), Wilfrid Rodel (drums)

FOREST OF SOULS mix a heady brew of Doom Metal and Gothic overtones. For the 1998 album the band added guitarist Fred Mariotti.

Albums:
WAR AND POETRY, Adipocere ADS CD 001 (1995)
War And Poetry – Act I: The Ritual / The Anthem Of Eternity / War And Poetry – Act II: The Curse / Into The Infinity Sorrow Of My Mind / The Time Of Broken Gates
CONTES ET LEGENDES D'EFEANDAYL, Adipocere CD AR 041 (1998)
The Discreet Korrigan's Presence / Esmahilv / Deliverance / Dream's Challenger / ...When They Watch Out / Watcher's Line / Song For The Autumn Lady / A Strange Family / Two Disturbing Souls / The Time Of Broken Gates – Part II / La Venue Du Grand Brouillard / Le Marin Des Mers De L'Ouest

FOREVER (Chicago, IL, USA)
Line-Up: Jack Emrick (vocals), Steve McCarley (guitar), Ray Burke (bass), Kevin Tanner (drums)

A Doom laden Metal band Chicago's FOREVER actually originated in Dayton, Ohio and formed by guitarist Steve McCarley in 1984. The band also issued product the same year billed as FOREPLAY.

Having relocated to Chicago, the band's manager, Jack Manis, took a demo tape with him to the Cannes Music Festival in France a year or so later. The recording impressed the Wolverhampton based Heavy Metal label who promptly signed FOREVER to its Heavy Metal America imprint.

Bassist Ray Burke featured on IMPELLITERRI vocalist ROB ROCK's 2000 solo album and is a member of Metal act WARRIOR.

Albums:
FOREVER... AND EVER, Heavy Metal America (1986)

FORGOTTEN SILENCE
(CZECH REPUBLIC)
Line-Up: Hanka Nogolova (vocals), Alexander Novacek (vocals / bass), Pavel Urbanek (guitar), Jan Friedman (keyboards), Miloslav Nahodil (drums)

Moravian Doom Metal band FORGOTTEN SILENCE, forged in late 1993, made their entrance in 1994 with the cassette 'The Nameless Forever... The Last Remembrance'. Previously the various members had operated with the Doom band REMEMBRANCE and Thrashers SAX. The 'Thots' album arrived, on cassette format via Obscene Productions, in 1995 followed by the inclusion of tracks on the 'Sometimes Death Is Better' series of compilation albums put out by the Belgian Shiver label.

A split 7" single 'Clara - The Clairvoyant', shared with DISSOLVING OF PRODIGY, was delivered in 1996 as 'Thots' also saw a CD release through Metal Age. A further split single 'The Hills Of Senyaan Part II' found the band in collaboration with AGONY. This release served as a taster for the 'Senyaan' album which came in both CD and cassette variants with differing cover artwork on the Redblack label.

In 1999 FORGOTTEN SILENCE would share their third split release, the 555 edition 7" EP 'Hathor's Place', with NOTRE DAME, the track being recorded live on a joint tour of Transylvania. That same year the band would contribute to a tribute album in honour of the cult underground Czech Black Metal band MASTERS HAMMER. By this juncture the band was citing a line-up of singer Hanka Nogolova, guitarist Medved, bassist Krusty and drummer Chrobis.

FORGOTTEN SILENCE guitarist Medved pursues a Thrash Metal side project billed as CHATEAU, comprising guitarist Zoro, bassist Smetol and drummer Milon. Vocalist Hanka embarked upon an Electronic based venture in union with the erstwhile HYPNOS, XYZ and MONASTERY man Iggy. This alliance, with Krusty on bass, produced a cover version of 'Lucifer Sam' for the tribute album 'The Electronic Tribute To Pink Floyd Volume II' released by the American Vitamin imprint.

Released by the Czech Redblack label in 2000 the 'Ka Ba Ach' album found the band operating without keyboards for the first time. Second guitarist Biggles was introduced to the line-up but midway through recording Chrobis vacated, the band hastily drafting Milon as replacement. 'Ka Ba Ach' was released in cassette format in Yugoslavia by the Rock Express label in June of 2002.

Singles/EPs:
Clara - The Clairvoyant, Obscene Productions (1996) (Split 7" single with DISSOLVING OF PRODIGY)
The Hills Of Senyaan Part II, Obscene Productions (1997) (Split 7" single with AGONY)
Hathor's Place, (1999) (Split 7" single with NOTRE DAME)

Albums:
THOTS, Metal Age MA 0008-2-331 (1996)
Clara Writes.../ Rosa The Beauty / Tres Marias Part I / Tres Marias Part II / Clara The Clairvoyant / A Night At 'Christabel Colon' / Blanca The Endless Desire / The Awakening / Alba The Little Girl / The Evenings / The Old Memories 'The House Of The Spirits' / ... And You Read
SENYAAN, Redblack MBR002 (1999)
Once Upon A Time (The Beginning Of An Eternal Winter): Chapter I - The Oldest Sanctuary, Chapter II - The White Oceans (Days, Weeks, Months...) / It's Getting Dark... / Once Upon A Time (The Beginning Of An Eternal Winter): Chapter III - The Ancient Forest / The Loneliness / (Interlude) / Diamonds Of The Night / Once Upon A Time (The Beginning Of An Eternal Winter): Chapter IV. - The Snowscreams / The Snowflakes / Once Upon A Time (The Beginning Of An Eternal Winter): Chapter V. - The Hills Of Senyaan Pt.II / The Moonshine / The White Roses / Once Upon A Time (The Beginning Of An Eternal Winter): Chapter VI. - (In) The Marble Halls III / Once Upon A Time (The Beginning Of An Eternal Winter): Chapter VII. - The Strange Being / We, The Strange Beings...
KA BA ACH, Redblack MBR010 (2000)
Red Paiom / Rostau / Al Qáhir / Saqqára / FL2C / Vaset / Memnon / Ipet Isut / Dendara / Idfu / Syene / As Suwais

FORGOTTEN SUNRISE (ESTONIA)
Line-Up: Anders Meltz (vocals), Margus Gustavson (guitar), Jan Talts (bass), Tarvo Valkm (drums)

A band from Tallinn formed in 1993, after the debut demo ('Behind The Abysmal Sky') appeared FORGOTTEN SUNRISE signed to the Finnish label Rising Realm.
The band's debut CD highlighted their melodic Death Metal laced with plentiful Doom influences to nice effect; the group utilizing violin, flute, keyboards and female backing vocals in the mix.

Albums:
FOREVER SLEEPING GRAVESTONES, Rising Realm REALM 003 (1994)
Unknown Land Of Silence / Ode To The Depressive Timedance / Enjoyment Of Sunrise / In Your Eyes

FREEDOM BLEEDER (SWEDEN)
Line-Up: Henrik Renstrom (vocals), Johan Haag (guitar), Gustav Grusell (bass), Peter Hedberg (drums)

FREEDOM BLEEDER are Uppsala based Psych-Sludge Stoners founded during 1995. The initial line-up comprised vocalist Henrik Renstrom, guitarist Johan Haag and bass player Gustav Grusell guitars, Henrik Renstrom, vocals and Gustav Grusell. An acquaintance of the band, Kim Nordberg, assisted in laying down drums on their first demo session.
Further recordings saw the employment of Johan Hedman on the drum stool, later replaced by Andreas Wiil. A 1997 7" single, shared as a split release with MUGWUMPS, arrived in 1997 on the Supercharger label. The following year the band donated the sing 'Freerider' to the 'Fistful Of Freebird' compilation. FREEDOM BLEEDER's efforts would signal the attentions of the London based Yperano label in 1999 for a projected two album deal. However, this arrangement fell through. Toward the close of the year Peter Hedberg was drafted as the band's new drummer.
In 2000 FREEDOM BLEEDER contributed their version of the MISFITS 'Ghouls Night Out' to the Freebird tribute album 'Graven Images'.
FREEDOM BLEEDER issued the single 'Breathing' for the Molten Universe label in January of 2001. 'Breathing' scored well in the Rock media, even being chosen as 'single of the week' by 'Kerrang' magazine in the UK. A full-length album, provisionally entitled 'Ten Out Of Ten', was scheduled for 2002 issue.

Singles/EPs:
Third Day / Frazzle, Supercharger FRV 974 (1997) (Split 7" single with MUGWUMPS)
Breathing / Redemption / Away From The Sun, Molten Universe MOLTEN 010 (2001)

FROWN (SLOVALKIA)
Line-Up: Marian Drac (vocals), Jan Kolesar (guitar), Jan Kavulic (bass), Martin Porubsky (keyboards), Frantisek Zeleznik (drums)

Presov based modern Gothic Metal act founded in the Autumn of 1997. FROWN debuted with the 'Falsehood' demo followed by a second effort 'The Gift Of Suffering' in December 1998.

Albums:
FEATURES AND CAUSES OF THE FROZEN ORIGIN, Moonstorm (2002)
Unnatural Notion Of Love / Dawning (For A Sweet Girl) / Features And Causes Of The Frozen Origin / Enslaved Hope / Breath For Dead / Purged By The God / Dreadful Moon / Dark Side Of The Bark / Skyline (Demo 1998) / I'm Haunted (Demo 1998

FUCKEMOS (Austin, TX, USA)
Line-Up: Russell Porter (vocals), Edward Rancourt (guitar), Mike Belyea (bass), Sean Powell (drums)

Exponents of 'Cum Rock', actually a bizarre amalgam of '80s trad Metal and (s)avant-garde Stoner. The FUCKEMOS apparently evolved out of WARTHOG, a club band that comprised Edward 'Creepy' Rancourt on guitar, Joseppi on bass and Russell 'Rusty' Porter on lead vocals and drums. With the induction of 'Cheesy' Sean Powell on drums, leaving Porter to concentrate on singing, the WARTHOGS became the FUCKEMOS. According to legend Porter had written the words 'Fuck Emos' (Emos being a night club he was aggrieved with) on his bass drum and from that moment the new band name stuck. A succession of bassists followed before the arrival of Mike Belyea afforded some degree of stability.
The band's debut album, 'Fuckemos Can Kill You', saw issue in 1994 through the Rise label. It would be followed by 'Lifestyles Of The Drugged And Homeless' in 1995 and 'Hi, What Stupid Band Are You In?' the following year. FUCKEMOS signed to Frank Kozik's Man's Ruin imprint for 1998's 'Celebration', the album as label tradition dictated being made available in both 10" vinyl and CD formats with different track listings. Recording line-up for this outing had Porter and Powell joined by ex-CHERUBS drummer Brent

173

Prager on bass and guitarist Brian McGee. Man's Ruin Records would reissue the first and third albums in 1998 with differing sleeve artwork, excising the track 'Barf Baby' and pointedly retitling the 1996 effort as 'Black Helicopters'.

The band has shared numerous split singles including collaborations with the MOTARDS, CHERUBS and CHAINDRIVE. Their 1994 alliance with CHERUBS found FUCKEMOS covering the CHERUBS track 'Shoofly' whilst conversely their vinyl partners took on the FUCKEMOS own 'Do You Wanna Dance?' The FUCKEMOS have also donated their version of 'Thunderstruck' to the 1999 Reptilian Records AC/DC tribute collection 'Hell Ain't A Bad Place To Be'.

Russell Porter and Brian McGee also operate USS FRIENDSHIP.

Singles/EPs:
Berlin. 45, 6 Inch Doylie (1993) (Split EP with CHAINDRIVE)
Shoofly, Unclean UR-026 (1994) (Split single with CHERUBS)
Conspiracy, No Lie (1995) (Mexican clear vinyl one sided release)
The Eastern Side / The Cavity, Little Deputy LD-7009 (1995) (Split EP with MOTARDS)

Albums:
CAN KILL YOU, Rise RR124 (1994)
The Screams Of The Wild Women / Do You Wanna Dance? / I Can't Smell Joseppi / 2 Punk 2 Fuck / Work / 80 Gay Sailors / Berlin '45 / Your Lies / Fuck Emos / Putrid Human Waste / Pedophile / Opus Russ / Fuck Emos Play At Parties
LIFESTYLES OF THE DRUGGED AND HOMELESS, No Lie NL007 (1995)
Ed The Creep / Hurtin' / Lingerie Dreams / Tokyo / Ready To Drop / Dancin' Queen / Be Nice Don't Be Mean / Pro Choice (Life Is Murder) / Vietnambla / Mexico / Speedo / Print Your Own Damn Single Covers / Toby The Nueter / Wet My Bed Boo Boo / Love Is Like Oxygen / Pretty Flowers / Fuckemos Smoke Cigarettes / Bela Lugosi / Hail Satan / Three Winecoolers (By Anal Pope)
HI, WHAT STUPID BAND ARE YOU IN?, IFA IFA-020 (1996)
Black Helicopters / Frank's Bicycle / Rockstar / My Face Your Butt / Barf Baby / This Land Is Your Land / Please Police Me / Be Nice Don't Be Mean / Turn To Stone / Whale / I Gotta Go / Pussies Ride In Planes / White Sunshine
CELEBRATION, Man's Ruin MR79 (1998) (10" vinyl version)
Celebration / Who Is My Shaman / Bladder Control / Vague & Mysterious / Birdies /

Wimpy Band / New Mexico / Leslie Ann
CELEBRATION, Man's Ruin MR80 (1998) (CD version)
Celebration / Love 40 / Wimpy Band / Leslie Ann / Smoke / Who Is My Shaman / Vague & Mysterious / New Mexico / Birdies / Bladder Control / Woolly Mammoth / Birdies (Reprise)
BLACK HELICOPTERS, Man's Ruin MR128 (1998)
Black Helicopters / Frank's Bicycle / Rockstar / My Face Your Butt / This Land Is Your Land / Please Police Me / Be Nice Don't Be Mean / Turn To Stone / I Gotta Go / Pussies Ride In Planes / White Sunshine
AIRSHOW 2000, Man's Ruin MR181 (2000)
Something Stinky This Way Comes (Pee You) / Toss It Salad (Yum) / Amputeen (Rotten Cheese) / Airshow (Flock Of Emos) / Klepto Maniac (Attack) / Someday (Mmm) / Stuckemos (Oh No) / S.F.L.M. (Eddieddieddie) / C.U.C. Me (Foe) / Yer Family (Ruff) / Lame That Tune (?) / Sex Body (Ugh) / Metal Gods (Gmotgpp) / Honky In The Sky (Sorry)

FU MANCHU (Orange County, CA, USA)
Line-Up: Scott Hill (vocals), Bob Balch (guitar), Brad Davis (bass), Brant Bjork (drums)

Orange County retro mongers FU MANCHU, founded during 1988, are notorious for their love of all things '70s (in particular Chevy vans). FU MANCHU's initial line-up for the 1990 Slap-A-Ham 7" single 'Kept Between The Trees' comprised vocalist Glen Chivens, guitarist Scott Hill, bass player Greg McCaughey and drummer Ruben Romano. Some two years later the 'Senioritis' single emerged on the German Zuma label, FU MANCHU having morphed into a new look band with Scott Hill handling both guitar and lead vocals, Scott Vatow on guitar, Mark Abshire on bass and Romano retained on the drums. This same unit cut two further follow up 7"s 'Pick Up Summer' and 'Don't Bother Knockin' (If This Van's Rockin'), both served up on Elastic Records.

The debut album 'No One Rides For Free' witnessed the recruitment of ex-ALL OF ONE guitarist Eddie Glass. Following the band's second album, 1995's 'Daredevil', Abshire was replaced by Brad Davis.

Touring Europe in support of the 'In Search Of...' album it became obvious that FU MANCHU were in serious difficulties and after an American trek with CLUTCH the band fragmented in half with Hill and Davis retaining the name. The new look FU MANCHU bowed in during 1997 rather unconventionally through Man's Ruin

174

175

Records, with a 10" single version of BLUE OYSTER CULT's mighty '70s classic 'Godzilla'.

Glass and Romano were to team up with ex-KYUSS bassist Scott Reeder to create NEBULA. Reeder was to quit NEBULA prior to recording of the 1998 album 'Let It Burn' and, keeping it in the family, NEBULA pulled in their ex-FU MANCHU colleague Mark Abshire on bass for recording.

FU MANCHU meantime pulled in ex-KYUSS drummer Brant Bjork for recording of their fourth album. As an aside Bkork put together an almost hippie jam session for an album release during 1998. Joining him on the DESERT SESSIONS album 'Volume I & II' were ex-SOUNDGARDEN bassist Ben Shepherd and QUEENS OF THE STONE AGE guitarist Josh Homme.

Although the 1998 album 'The Action Is Go', produced by WHITE ZOMBIE guitarist J. Yeunger and closing out with a cover of S.S.D.'s 'Nothing's Done', appeared on the seemingly smalltime label Mammoth it is in fact part of the massive Polygram conglomerate. FU MANCHU undertook an extensive headline tour of Europe in early 1998 supported by Swedes SPIRITUAL BEGGARS and KINGS OF INFINITE SPACE. BRANT BJORK issued a solo album 'Jalamanta' in 1999.

Backing up the album 'King Of The Road', which included a cover version of DEVO's 'Freedom Of Choice', FU MANCHU undertook their first tour of Japan in mid 2000. The same year found the band executing a number of cover versions for various tribute albums including CIRCLE JERKS and TWISTED SISTER's 'Ride To Live (Live To Ride)'.

The ever industrious Bjork switched to vocals and guitar for a 2000 project CHÉ in collusion with UNIDA's Dave Dinsmore on bass and drummer Alfredo Hernandez for the album 'Sounds Of Liberation'. In November of 2001 Bjork jumped ship to join QUEENS OF THE STONE AGE. The erstwhile drummer would also issue a second solo outing, credited to the fictional band BRANT BJORK AND THE OPERATORS.

FU MANCHU got to grips with a nationwide tour in early 2002, preceded by extensive radio play of the single 'Squash That Fly', to promote the 'California Crossing' album. Fans picking up the album at Best Buy stores would be rewarded with a bonus two track disc featuring 'Planet Of The Ape Hangers' and 'Breathing Fire'.

FU MANCHU tagged up with SPEEDEALER and BRAND NEW SIN for headline American dates in the summer commencing July 30th in San Francisco.

Singles/EPs:
Kept Between Trees / Bouillabaisse / Jr. High School Ring (7 Karat), Slap A Ham (1990)
Senioritis / Pinbuster / El Don, Zuma (1992) Pick Up Summer / Vankhana (Rollin' Rooms), Elastic ELS 005 (1992) (USA release)
Don't Bother Knockin' (If This Van's Rockin) / Space Sucker, Elastic ELS 007 (1992)
Asphalt Risin' / Chevy Van, Mammoth MR 139-7 (1996)
Missing Link / Ojo Rojo, Mammoth MR 157-7 (1996)
Godzilla / Module Overload / Living Legend, Mammoth MR 048 (1997) (USA release)
Jailbreak, Sessions (1998) (Split single with FATSO JETSON)
Jailbreak / Urethane / Coyote Duster (Live), Mammoth (1998)

Albums:
NO ONE RIDES FOR FREE, Bongload BL10 (1994)
Time To Fly / Ojo Rojo / Show And Shine / Mega Bumpers / Free And Easy (Summer Girls) / Superbird / Shine It On / Snakebellies
DAREDEVIL, Bongload BL19 (1995)
Trapeze Freak / Tilt / Gathering Speed / Coyote Duster / Travel Agent / Sleesteak / Space Farm / Lug / Egor / Wurkin' / Push Button Magic
IN SEARCH OF..., Mammoth MR 0134-2 (1996)
Regal Begal / Missing Link / Asphalt Risin' / Neptune's Convoy / Redline / Cyclone Launch / Strato-Streak / Solid Hex / The Falcon Has Landed / Seahag / The Bargain / Supershooter
EARLY RECORDINGS, Elastic ELS014 (1997)
THE ACTION IS GO, Mammoth 35498 0173-2 (1998)
Evil Eye / Urethane / The Action Is Go / Burning Road / Guardrail / Anodizer / Trackside Hoax / Unknown World / Laserblast! / Hogwash / Grendel, Snowman / Strolling Astronomer / Saturn III / Nothing Done
RETURN TO EARTH 91-93, Elastic (1998)
Don't Bother Knockin' (If This Van's Rockin') / Senioritis / Pick-Up Summer / El Don / Ojo Rojo / Simco / Space Sucker / Pinbuster / Vankhana (Rollin' Rooms)
EATIN' DUST, Man's Ruin (1998)
Godzilla / Module Overload / Living Legend / Eatin' Dust / Shift Kicker / Orbiter / Mongoose / Pigeon Toe
KING OF THE ROAD, Mammoth (1999)
Hell On Wheels / Over The Edge / Boogie

Van / King Of The Road / No Dice / Blue Tile Fever / Grasschopper / Weird Beard / Drive / Hotdoggin' / Freedom Of Choice
CALIFORNIA CROSSING, Warner Bros. (2001) 59 SWEDEN
Separate Kingdom / Hang On / Mongoose / Thinkin' Out Loud / California Crossing / Wiz Kid / Squash That Fly / Ampin' / Bultaco / Downtown In Dogtown / The Wasteoid

FUNERAL (NORWAY)
Line-Up: Toril Snyen (vocals), Thomas Angell (guitar), Christian Loos (guitar), Einar Fredriksen (bass), Anders Eek (drums)

A Melodic Doom Metal band with a penchant for lengthy songs and high female vocalizing, FUNERAL feature a rhythm section of bassist Einar Fredriksen of MYSTICUM and PARADIGMA and drummer Anders Eek that also plies its trade in THE FLESH, ODIUM and MYRSKOG.
The band signed to the Italian Nocturnal Music label for the March 2002 album 'In Fields of Pestilent Grief'. FUNERAL at this juncture featured a completely overhauled line-up of vocalist Hanne, Einar Fredriksen on bass, guitarists Christian Loos and 1349 man Idar, DISIPLIN keyboard player Kjelil and drummer Anders Eek.

Albums:
TRISTESSE, Wild Rags (1995)
Thoughts Of Tranquillity / A Poem For The Dead / Yearning For Heaven
TRAGEDIES, Arctic Serenades SERE 003 (1996)
Taarene / Under Ebony Shades / Demise / When Nightfall Daspys / Moment In Black
IN FIELDS OF PESTILENT GRIEF, Nocturnal Music (2002)

FURBOWL (SWEDEN)
Line-Up: Johan Axelsson (vocals / guitar), Nicke Stenemo (guitar / keyboards), Johan Liiva (bass), Max Thornell (drums)

A Växjö based Death Goth Metal band formed in 1991 by ex-CARNAGE man Johan Axelsson and former JESUS EXERCISE drummer Max Thornell, FURBOWL's first demo, 'The Nightfall Of Your Heart' featured the ever busy ex-CARCASS guitarist Mike Amott making a guest appearance.
Bassist Johan Liiva would join Amott in his late '90s act ARCH ENEMY.
Subsequent to the release of debut album 'Those Shredded Dreams', Axelsson left to be superseded by Per Jungberger and after 'The Autumn Years' album emerged in 1994 the band have, more recently, adopted the new name WONDERFLOW.

Albums:
THOSE SHREDDED DREAMS, Step One SOROO4 (1992)
Damage Done / Nothing Forever / Razorblades / Desertion / Sharkheaven / Those Shredded Dreams
THE AUTUMN YEARS, Black Mark BMCD47 (1994)
Bury The Hatchet / Cold World / Dead And Gone / The Needle / Is This Dignity / Weakend / Baby Burn / Stabbed / Road Less Travelled / Still Breathing

GALADRIEL (SLOVAKIA)
Line-Up: Sona Witch Kozakova (vocals), Dodo Datel (vocals / bass), Tomax Gabris (guitar), Gabriel Holenka (guitar), Lubomir J.S. Kozina Kozak (keyboards), Dr. Victor (drums)

GALADRIEL, founded in 1995, not to be confused with the Spanish Progressive Rock act of the same title, are a Slovak Doom Metal band that saw their first three albums released by the English Unknown Territory label. In their home country GALADRIEL albums are available in cassette format.

The group was forged by two former TROJAN WARRIOR members vocalist / bassist Dodo Datel and drummer Dr. Victor. Joining them would be lead guitarist Voloda Zadropa, rhythm guitarist Chulo Malachovsky and, in 1996, female lead singer Sona 'Witch' Kozakova. The debut album, 1997's 'Empire Of Emptiness', saw a guest keyboard session from LUNATIC GODS man Ivan 'King' Kral. Shortly after recording Zadrapa departed, his place being taken by the 16 year old Tomax Gabris, already a veteran of VICTIM and NEURASTENIA.

1999's 'The Mirror Of Ages' would see Erik

Schmeer on keyboards. A third album, 'Oblivion', had Malachovsky's place taken by Gabriel Holenka and Lubomir J.S. Kozina Kozak took the keyboard role.

GALADRIEL would switch to the domestic Metal Ages Productions for a fourth album 'From Ashes To Dust', set for April 2002 release.

Albums:
EMPIRE OF EMPTINESS, Unknown Territory (1997)
Empire Of Emptiness / Solitude / Sad Leaves Of The Dying Rose / One Lost Child / Kingdom Under The Ocean / Silence And Screams / Immortal Visions / Dreaming Memories / Tears Of Emptiness
THE MIRROR OF AGES, Unknown Territory (1999)
The Forest Lullaby / The Flower And The Dark Butterfly / Fear In Their Eyes / Twilight Time / In The Garden Of Lost Shades / 1848 / Vampirian Love / Lost Paths Of Unicorns / The Battle By Wogastisburg / Solitude
OBLIVION, Unknown Territory (2000)
On The Wings Of Gwaihir / Strokes Of Desire / As Your Body Burns / Blindness / Lavondyss / The Evening ... And Then Came The Night / My December / It Ends / When

GAMMERA
Photo : El Danno

178

The Moon Loses Its Face / Rivers Of Oblivion / Dowina / Acheron
FROM ASHES TO DUST, Metal Ages Productions (2002)

GAMMERA (San Francisco, CA, USA)
Line-Up: Scott Selfridge (vocals / guitar), Rafael Martinez (guitar), Clint Ragsdale (bass), Vadim Canby (drums)

San Franciscan Sludgers. Following the issue of the six track 'Angelburner' EP for Meteor City, GAMMERA added second guitarist Rafael Martinez, debuting their new line-up with a support gig to ROADSAW and NEBULA in July of 1999.
By mid 2002 Martinez was working up a side project band with guitarist Jason Landrian from the recently folded CAVITY.

Singles/EPs:
Caterpillar Man / Angelburner / Rust / Zangy Tizzle / Juniper Queen / Lucifer's Secret 3:AM, Meteor City (1999) ('Angelburner' EP)

Albums:
SMOKE AND MIRRORS, (2001)
Angelburner / Today Is Tomorrow / Almond Eye / Trail To Baghdad / Stalefish / Henry Chinaski Likes 'Em Thick / Smoke And Mirrors / El Franco Diablo / Sidewinder

GARDENS OF GEHENNA (GERMANY)
Line-Up: Andreas Opel (vocals / guitar), Christian Wachter (guitar), Bastian Rosner (guitar), Birgit Lages (bass), Michael Schöner (keyboards)

Death-Doom outfit GARDENS OF GEHENNA, comprising frontman Andreas Opel (who also operates as singer for Power Metal band ANACONDA), bass player Birgit Lages, guitarist Holger Fiedler, drummer Thomas Drechsel and keyboard player Michaela Marek, came into being during 1995. Although a regular on the live circuit throughout Germany, since losing the services of Dreschel GARDENS OF GEHENNA have utilized a drum machine on stage for many years. Two demo sessions were delivered during 1996 and the band garnered extra exposure by a track inclusion on the Belgian Shiver label series of compilation albums 'Sometimes Death Is Better'. The group reaped valuable live exposure performing as opening act on select dates of the 'Heaven Shall Burn' MARDUK, GEHENNA and MYSTICUM tour as well as shows supporting DAS ICH.
The debut album, 'Mortem Saluta' produced

by DAS ICH member Bruno Kramm, was recorded in January of 1997 and subsequently issued by the Shiver label in February of 1998. Despite this progress the group underwent serious line-up changes which eventually saw only Opel and Lages remaining. Temporarily Martin F. Jungkunz of DESPAIRATION was employed as live guitarist. GARDENS OF GEHENNA was brought back up to strength with the addition of guitarist Christian Wachter and keyboard player Michael Schöner. This new formation signed to the Last Episode label for a second album 'Dead Body Music' once again produced by Bruno Kramm, released in July of 2000.
Upfront of the third album 'The Mechanism Masochism' the band included their version of 'A Prelude To Agony' on a TYPE O NEGATIVE tribute album in 2001.
GARDENS OF GEHENNA added second guitarist Bastian Rosner from Black Metal band ETERNAL SILENCE in 2002.

Albums:
MORTEM SALUTA, Shiver (1998)
Nebelmond / Beyond The Gates Of Dusk / Blood / Those Who Walk The Shadows / Mortem Saluta / Iconoclasm / Prophecy / Nebelmond (DAS ICH remix)
DEAD BODY MUSIC, Last Episode (2000)
Requiem / Iesaiah 14:12 / Tod Und Teufel / Gethsemane / Beautiful Blackness / Lacrimae Rerum / From A Silent Yearning Dark / Dust Of Life

GASCOINE (GERMANY)
Line-Up: Jentz L. (vocals), Michael G. (guitar), Oliver Klasen (bass), Volker S. (drums)

Singles/EPs:
Something Sweet / The Voodoopriest / Poundy Bedtime Stories / All Worn Out / Spacetrain / California, Loudsprecher (2002) (10" 'Storiesofmajortroubledirtyfingernailsand menwhoshouldknowbetter' EP)

GAS GIANT (DENMARK)
Line-Up: Jesper Valentin (vocals), Stefan Krey (guitar), Thomas Carstensen (bass), Pete Hellhammer (drums)

Copenhagen Space Rockers. GAS GIANT previously operated as BLIND MAN BUFF, issuing a 1997 four track EP 'Alien Frequency' under that title. The 'Live Series' release was an ambitious box set compiling five live discs 'The Heavy Ones', 'Spaced Out', 'The Fast Ones', 'The Jams' and 'The Slow Ones'. GAS GIANT would bring onboard a new drummer, Kjeld', for recording of their split album shared with WE 'Riding The Red Horse To The Last Stronghold Of The Freaks'. However, Kjeld would bow out shortly after these sessions were completed.

The band's show at the Copenhagen 'Spacerock' festival was recorded, the 13 minute track 'Creeping' making it onto the compilation subsequent album.

Albums:
PORTALS OF NOTHINGNESS, (1999)
Never Leave This Way / Grow / Back On The Headless Track / Under The Tree / Senses / Super Sun Trigger / Firetrigger / Embrace
PLEASANT JOURNEY IN HEAVY TUNES, Burnthehippie (2000)
Too Stoned (New version) / Sit Down / Down The Highway / All Creatures / Super Sun Trigger / Desert Call / Freak Sensation / Storm Of My Enemies / Holy Walker
LIVE SERIES, (2001)
Tripping Away / Storm Of My Enemies / Sit Down / Too Stoned / Back On The Headless Track / Moonshake / Clowner Spaced Out / Never Leave This Way / Super Sun Trigger / Down The Highway / Walk The Monsterline / Firetripper / Reach You - Jam For Scott / Intro Jam / Storm Of My Enemies - Jam / Holy Walker / Clowner / Alien Frequency / Ride The Red Horse / Embrace
RIDING THE RED HORSE TO THE LAST STRONGHOLD OF THE FREAKS, Burnthehippie (2001) (Split album with WE)
Fire Tripper / Never Leave This Way / Ride The Red Horse
MANA, (2002)
There´s One / Dragonscave / Moonshake / M A N A / Green Valley / Phantom Tanker / Safehaven / Notaman / Orange Fender / Back On The Headless Track / New Day Rising

GATE 9 (NORWAY)
Line-Up: Jan Mikael Sørensen (vocals / bass), Are Bransted (guitar), Jon Amund Magnæs (drums)

Norwegian Doom inclined Stoners. Guitarist Are Bransted had previously been a member of COWSHED BOYS, SALAD DAYS and a tribute band to THE RAMONES entitled THROMBONES. Both frontman Jan Mikael Sørensen and drummer Jon Amund Magnæs are ex-ALTER EGO and TORSO.

GATE 9's 2001 three track demo 'Dwarves Of Might' secured a deal with the American Underdogma label for release of a debut album 'Moon Ranger Gone Evil'.

Plans would be afoot in mid 2002 to record a split EP in union with German Stoners DUSTER 69.

Albums:
MOON RANGER GONE EVIL, Underdogma (2002)
Dwarves Of Might / Autodirect / Queen Of Hades / La Strada Astra / Empress Of Andromeda / Master Of Doom / Vivid Void / Slaves Of Tide / Transmission Overload

GENEROUS MARIA (SWEDEN)
Line-Up: Goran Florstrom (vocals), Dan Johansen (guitar), Ulrik Nilsson (guitar), Jeppe Klarqvist (bass), Mats Ohlsson (drums)

Gothenburg Stoners leaning more toward a more Rock n' Roll approach than the familiar Sabbathisms. The group was founded in 1998 with a line- up comprising of vocalist Goran Florstrom, guitarists Ulrik Nilsson and Mikael Bodling, bassist Jesper Klarqvist and drummer Johan Gadler. Line-up changes saw Gadler replaced by Mats Ohlsson. GENEROUS MARIA issued a demo 'Strict Nurse' in July of 1999 then signed to the Spanish Alone label for a split album in alliance with SKUA, this album being licensed to Custom Heavy for an American release. The track 'Strict Nurse' would also turn up on the Mexican 'Sacred Groove' compilation issued by the Monstruo De Gila label. In 2000 FINAL BENSON man George Winnberg took the guitar role from Bodling.

'Command Of The New Rock', GENEROUS MARIA's debut full-length album recorded with Dan Johansen taking Winnberg's place, arrived in early 2002 through Lunasound Recordings.

Albums:
GENEROUS MARIA, Alone AR-002 (2000) (Split album with SKUA)
Strict Nurse / Like A Dog With A Frisbee / Lack Of Faith / Brother Pain
COMMAND OF THE NEW ROCK, Lunasound (2002)
Big Shiny Limo / A Bed At The Edge Of The Universe / All Units Are Out / Anchorage & Quito / Soulflight / Ashram Of The Absolute / All Good Things (Must Come To An End) / DumDum Bullet / Firebug / Bridge Out Of Time

GIANTS CAUSEWAY (GERMANY)
Line-Up: Kalle Friedrich (vocals), Barbara Rippe (vocals / flute), Erich Lutz (guitar), Heiko Wallauer (guitar), Guido Holzmann (bass), Jorg Klomann (drums)

Vocalist Kalle Friedrich would act as guest vocalist on CREMATORY's 'Act Seven' album. GIANT'S CAUSEWAY bass guitarist Guido

Holzmann would later join Dark Wave outfit CENTURY.

Albums:
IS THERE ANYWAY?, Swan Lake MASSCD070 (1995)
Pain / Something / Lost / Careless / Is There Any Way / Falling / View From The Inside / Altered States / Withering / Deprivation
NEW LIGHT, Swan Lake MASSCD113 (1996)
Reversion / Doubt / New Light / Gift Of Life / Stripped / Death / Attraction / Seven Years / Forever / Land's End / Last Train
DESTINATION INSECURE, Serenades SR016 (1998)
Turned / Again / Summary / No One / Flicker / Destination: Insecure / Eclipsed / Alice / Enchanted / Here Today… / Gone Tomorrow?

GILAH MONSTER (SPAIN)
Line-Up: Eriz (vocals), JuanPa (guitar), Txetxu (bass), Alex (drums)

Bilbao's Psyched Stoners GILAH MONSTER have their roots in LOVERCRAFT. Bass player Txetxu has a tradition stretching back through the '80s Punk bands KOME DE AKI and LA SECTA. The latter band undertook extensive gigging backed by numerous release. By 1996 Txetxu had forged an alliance with former LIE ME NOT vocalist Eriz for several projects including THEE PRANKSTERS and THE PHANTABULOUS & FURRY. Eventually some solidity was found with LOVERCRAFT during 1998 comprising Eriz, Txetxu, LA SECTA's Pat and guitarist Iñigo and drummer Conte, both erstwhile personnel from THE DRELLAS.
With Pat's departure from the band LOVERCRAFT evolved into GILAH MONSTER and professed to move into a more Metal cum Desert Rock direction.

THE GLASSPACK (Louisville, KY, USA)
Line-Up: 'Dirty' Dave Johnson (vocals / guitar), Marcus Moody (guitar), Chris 'The Hitman' Matthews (bass), Matt Tucker (drums)

Bluegrass state fuzzed out Stoners THE GLASSPACK, titled after a hot rod muffler, came into being during 1999. The band would debut with the highly praised 2001 album 'American Exhaust', issued on frontman 'Dirty' Dave Johnson's own Riverock label. Prior to forging THE GLASSPACK Johnson, a figure well known for setting fire to his more intimate body parts onstage, had led BLACKLISTED.

Johnson's initial line-up comprised a trio featuring bassist Chris Matthews and BODYHAMMER drummer Brian Foor. For the 'American Exhaust' album second Andy Garrett, bassist Zack Dorsette and drummer Ben Holzscaw would be enlisted although the lead track, 'Hall Of The Mountain Speedlab' – a homage to HAWKWIND, featured the Matthews / Foor rhythm axis.
The membership of THE GLASSPACK is credited on the 2002 "Powderkeg" album as Dirty Dave ("'Free speech infringement and pick wielding"), Lil Bucky ("Amplified arson with distortive behaviour"), Bobby Nova ("Low frequency levels of catastrophic nature"), Reverend ("High time on the keys of death") and The Capn ("Assault with intent to commit assault").
The band delivered a version of THE STOOGES 'TV Eye' for a Small Stone Recordings compilation 'Sucking In The 70s'.

Albums:
AMERICAN EXHAUST, Riverock (2001)
Hall Of The Mountain Speedlab / Smut / Whiskey House / Shut Up & Ride / Powerbait One / Kentucky Night / Jim Beam And Good Green / Sunday Afternoon
POWDERKEG, Small Stone Recordings SS-029 (2002)
The Glasspack Song / Shut Up & Ride / Mrs. Satan / Whiskey House / Sleeping Pills / Mopar Fire Paint / The Heebeegeebees / Back Seat Whore / Demolition Derby / Jim Beam And Good Green

GNOME (JAPAN)

A one man venture into aural insanity strictly not for the faint hearted. Doom of the most laboriously heavy nature spiked with histrionic screaming make GNOME a quite unique if terrifying proposition. The 1999 album 'Story - Legendary Japanese Wolves' is a split effort with NYARLATHOTEP.

Albums:
STORY- LEGENDARY JAPANESE WOLVES, Weird Truth Productions WT001 (1999) (Split album with NYARLATHOTEP)
Canis Lupis Holphialax / 1905 (W.O.Y.N.) / Forever…

GOATHORN (CANADA)
Line-Up: Jason Decay (vocals / bass), Brandon Wars (vocals / guitar), Steelrider (drums)

These three Canadian Doomsters formed GOATHORN in late 1999. As long-time friends songs were quickly written and gigs

THE GLASSPACK
Photo : El Danno

were played around the Ottawa Valley before drummer Steelrider moved to Toronto. During the absence of Steelrider, Wars and Decay put together a 5 song demo in Wars' basement, later being dispatched to Steelrider to sample.

In February of 2001 the band journeyed to Toronto to record the 'Voyage To Nowhere' debut album. All the tracks had to be blasted out in one day due to GOATHORN being in a studio they could barely afford.   As of September 2001, the entire band relocated to Toronto to promote the band and album.

Albums:
VOYAGE TO NOWHERE, (2001)
Goat Horn / Alcoholic Faith / Eternal Quest For Eternal Happiness / Shattered Dream / Voyage To Nowhere / Wasted Warrior / Doom March

GOATSNAKE (USA)
Line-Up: Pete Stahl (vocals), Greg Anderson (guitar), Stephen O' Malley (guitar), Stuart Dahlquist (bass), Greg Rogers (drums)

Founded by the former THE OBSESSED rhythm section of bassist Guy Pinhas and drummer Greg Rogers. Prior to his enrollment in THE OBSESSED Pinhas was a member of Dutch Stoners BEAVER, an outfit he would share stages with in later years too. GOATSNAKE are fronted by ex-WOOL / THE SCREAM vocalist Pete Stahl, a man who also

divides his time between GOATSNAKE and Josh Homme's 'Desert Sessions'.

Guitarists Stephen O' Malley and Greg Anderson together with bassist Stuart Dahlquist are all ex-BURNING WITCH. Anderson was also with KID ENGINE. The band's 1999 British tour saw Pinhas replaced by another ex-THE OBSESSED man, and KYUSS member, Scott Reeder, later to join UNIDA, when Pinhas was unable to get the necessary work permit.

GOATSNAKE toured Britain in 2000, with their ex-BURNING WITCH colleague bassist Stuart Dahlquist on bass, as guests to ORANGE GOBLIN. Pinhas had opted out, putting in a showing on the 1999 FIREBALL MINISTRY album 'Ou Est La Rock?' and then joining ACID KING.

Anderson, O' Malley and Dahlquist are also members of SUNN0))).

O'Malley created another offshoot with BURNING WITCH's Greg Anderson - THORR'S HAMMER - releasing an album 'Dommedagsnatt' in 2000.

O'Malley and Anderson would also figure in the 2001 unit TEETH OF LIONS RULE DIVINE, a bona fide Stoner Rock 'supergroup' fronted by CATHEDRAL mainman Lee Dorrian on vocals and featuring erstwhile IRON MONKEY member Justin Greaves.

During 2002 Pinhas and Rogers founded a one-off band for a tongue in cheek tribute to SIR LORD BALTIMORE courtesy of the 'Sucking In The 70s' album issued by Smallstone   Records.   SIR   LORD

BALTIMORE's 'Woman Tamer' was covered the GOATSNAKE rhythm section plus FIREBALL MINISTRY's Reverend James T. Rota II and erstwhile WHITE ZOMBIE guitarist J. Yuenger.

Singles/EPs:
The Orphan / Long Gone / Heartbreaker / Raw Curtains / Man Of Light, Southern Lord (2000) ('Dog Days' EP)

Albums:
GOATSNAKE, (1999)
Slippin The Stealth / Innocent / What Love Remains / IV / Mower / Dog Catcher / Lord Of Los Feliz / Trower
FLOWER OF DISEASE, Rise Above (2000)
A Truckload Of Mamma's Muffins / Easy Greasy / El Coyote Manigote / Flower Of Disease / Live To Die / Prayer For A Dying / The Dealer / The River

GODEATGOD (IL, USA)

GODEATGOD was started in 1999 by vocalist and multi-talented instrumentalist Scott Myers who had left SCARSIX with some instrumental tracks which eventually became the Doom orientated promotional release 'Demo For The Sick'. In 2000 Myers wrote some 15 new tracks, 5 of which were later dropped and entered the recording studio once again for 'The Sawblade Demo's'.
Towards the end of 2001 GODEATGOD recorded 4 new tracks and repackaged them with the previous two demos in order to create 'The Evolution of Revolution' release.
GODEATGOD re-entered the studio in 2002. Myers also involved himself with SOULDIVIDER bassist Mattias Nilsson's side project THE SATANIC ALL STARS along with vocalist Sick Royale and HIBERNUS MORTIS drummer Caesar Placeres.

Albums:
THE EVOLUTION OF REVOLUTION, (2001)
The War Wage On... / 12 Step Program Jesus / Addictive / Dead Snake Smile / Only Son / Give / Defile... Destroy... Deny / Torn Apart / Lockjaw / Victim / Gaddamn / Goddamn Blindfold / Self-Replicating Virus / Wither / Empty (2000 version) / Chamber / Crawl / Gethsemane / Empty (1999 version)

GODSEND (NORWAY)

Line-Up: Per Morten Kjöl (vocals), Gunder Audun Dragsten (guitar), Tom Wahl (guitar), Tommy Halseth (bass), Henrik Pettersen (drums)

Initially a one man Doom project pioneered by

erstwhile ATROX guitarist Gunder Audun Dragsten, GODSEND issued a three song demo in 1992 featuring drummer / vocalist Dan Swano of EDGE OF SANITY for the tracks 'Starfall', 'Slaydream' and 'Silence Of Time'. 'Slaydream' later appeared on the compilation album 'Against All Gods'.
For the debut album, 'As The Shadows Fall', released by the French Holy Records label in November of 1993, Dragsten drafted in Swano once more plus another EDGE OF SANITY member, drummer Benny Larsson.
For the second outing 'Into The Electric Mist' Dragsten succeeded in building a full band compliment of lead vocalist Per Morten Kjöl, second guitarist Tom Wahl, bass player Tommy Halseth and Henrik Pettersen on drums.
A completely new band was assembled for 1998's 'A Wayfarer's Tears'. Coming back into the fold would be Dan Swano and Benny Larsson alongside guitarist Tomas Steinscherer and NIGHTINGALE bassist Erik Oskarsson.

Albums:
AS THE SHADOWS FALL, Holy HOLY03 (1993)
Slaydream / As The Shadows Fall / With The Wind Comes The Rain / Autumn Leaves / Spiritual Loneliness / Beyond The Mist Of Memories / My Lost Love / Walking The Roads Of The Unbeheld / Silence Of Time
INTO THE ELECTRIC MIST, Holy HOLY15CD (1995)
Down Upon You / Nobody Home / Life Must Go On / In The Bitter Waters / Clarion Call / Voyage In Oblivion / The Sun Will Shine Again / Lost / Under Silver Linings / Tranquility / Thoughts And Shadows
A WAYFARER'S TEARS, (1998)
Delusions Of Grandeur / Sermon / Galactic Galleon / Eidolon / A Wayfarer's Tears Part I / A Wayfarer's Tears Part II / A Wayfarer's Tears Part III / A Wayfarer's Tears Part IV / A Wayfarer's Tears Part V / Starfall / Slaydream / Silence Of Time

GODS TOWER (BELARUS)

Line-Up: Lesley Knife (vocals), Alexander Urakoff (guitar / keyboards), Yuri Sivtsoff (bass), Dmitry Ovchinnikoff (keyboards), Vladislav Saltsevich (drums)

An innovative Belarus Folk-Gothic Metal band formed in 1989 as CHEMICAL WARFARE by guitarist Alexander Urakoff and vocalist Lesley Knife. During its formative stages the line-up of CHEMICAL WARFARE, operating in Death-Thrash territory initially, was fluid. Some stability was afforded in the summer of

1992 with the introduction of bass player Yuri Sivtsoff and drummer Vladislaw Saltsevich. With this roster GODS TOWER cut the 'Demolition Tape' demo session in August that same year. By the close of 1992 CHEMICAL WARFARE had evolved into GODS TOWER due to a shift in musical styles. Now utilizing session keyboard players the band had shifted over to a Pagan influenced Doom Metal stance, liberally laced with mythicism and Belarusian Folk.

As GODS TOWER the group debuted with 'The Eerie' demo in mid 1993. Response to this tape generated an offer from the Moscow based Final Holocaust Records and in September the band cut two tracks in a Moscow studio for an EP 'Beyond Praying'. Incredibly Final Holocaust mislaid the master tape and the planned EP never materialized. As some consolation GODS TOWER put in extensive live work with the likes of ZHELEZNY POTOK, THRASHER, CORPSE and KRABATHOR among others.

During 1994 second guitarist Al. J. Eristoff was added to the ranks and a promotional video shot for the track 'Beyond Praying'. The next recording, an experimental demo entitled 'Canticles', witnessed Psychedelic and ritual influences creeping into the band sound. Shortly after these sessions GODS TOWER performed outside of Russia for the first time, appearing in the Czech Republic alongside PURGATORY, CANNIBAL CORPSE, SAMAEL and DESULTORY. Gigs back in Belarus and the Ukraine saw live action with BRAINSTORM and DEATH VOMIT. In May of 1995 Dmitry Ovchinnikoff secured the permanent keyboard position although GODS TOWER then suffered the loss of Eristoff.

The act signed to the Metal Agen label having their debut album issued on cassette format in early 1997. In May and June GODS TOWER re-recorded 'The Eerie' compositions for CD release.

The 2001 'Abandon All Hope' album, which now saw Valery Novoseltsev on bass guitar and Sergey Sergeichikoff on keyboards, was a collection of rarities comprising covers of BLACK SABBATH's 'Iron Man', EUROPE's 'Final Countdown' and ARIA's 'Power & Reason' alongside new tracks, remixes and the 'Beyond Praying' video.

Albums:
THE TURNS, Metal Agen MARCD 024 97 (1996)
Intro / The Turns / I Am The Raven / Seven Rains Of Fire / Twilight Sun / An Eye For An Eye / Rising Arrows / Blood / Mysterious
THE EERIE, Metal Agen MARCD 036 97 (1997)
Reign Of Silence / When Life Ends / Inis

Afalon / Til Death Do Us Part / The Eerie / Beyond Praying
EBONY BIRDS, Sturmesflugel (1999)
Seven Rains Of Fire / An Eye For An Eye / Rising Arrows / Tilt Death Do Us Part / The Eerie / Beyond Praying / Twilight Sun / Blood / Mysterious
ABANDON ALL HOPE, Metal Agen (2001)
Civilization / Abandon All Hope / Iron Man / Final Countdown / Power & Reason / When Life Ends (7" EP version) / Reign Of Silence (Oversun edit) / Civilization (Last World War mix) / Beyond Praying (Video)

GOLGOTHA (SPAIN)
Line-Up: Amon Lopez (vocals), Vicente J. Paya (guitar), Ivan Ramos (guitar), Toni Soler (bass), Jose Nunez (keyboards), Ruben Alarcon (drums)

More of a project than an actual band, Spain's GOLGOTHA was the brainchild of UNBOUNDED TERROR's Vicente J. Paya, who felt he needed a vehicle for songs that he'd written that didn't fit the concept of his main outfit.

The debut GOLGOTHA release, the 'Caves Of Mind' mini-album, which included a cover version of BLACK SABBATH's 'Snowblind' and was recorded with a line-up of Paya, Gustavo Garcialo, David Garcialo and vocalist Amon Lopez.

It received glowing reviews in Europe and this gave Paya the incentive to put something a little bit more permanent together, adding DEHUMANIZED members Ivan Ramos and Ruben Alarcon amongst others. The 1995 outing 'Melancholy' featured the female vocals of Carmen Jaime.

GOLGOTHA are believed to be one of the few Spanish acts to truly have what it takes to break on an international scale.

Singles/EPs:
The Way Of Confusion / Embrace Me / Snowblind, Repulse (1997)

Albums:
CAVES OF MIND, Repulse (1994)
Lake Of Memories / Calachos Julisbol (Memories) / Embrace Me (Into The Cold Darkness) / Immaterial Deceptions / Snowblind
MELANCHOLY, Repulse RPS011 (1995)
Lonely / Lake Of Memories / Nothing / Raceflections / Lost / Immaterial Deceptions / Stillness / Virtualis Demens / Caves Of Mind
EMOTIONAL CHAPTERS, Repulse (1998)
Emotionless / Dark Tears / The Way Of Confusion / The Wood In Me / Lifetrappers /

Answers / Save Me, Kiss Me / The Proverb /
Internal Fight / Love Gun / Elemental
Changes

GOLGOTHA (USA)
Line-Up: Karl Foster, Mark James

UNMAKER OF WORLDS, Communiqué
CMGCD 003 (1990)
Counter State Directive / Unmaker Of Worlds
/ Another Sunny Christmas / Raining On Still
Waters
SYMPHONY IN EXTREMIUS, Communiqué
CMGCD 009 (1993)
Symphony In Extremis- To Will One Thing /
Holocaust In A Minor - The Burning / The
Cunning Of Reason - The Thin Blue Line /
Enter The Nightmare - Silence Is Your Savior

GORDIAN KNOT (USA)
Line-Up: Ron Jarzombek (guitar), Trey Gunn
(guitar), Glenn Snelwar (guitar), Sean
Malone (bass), John Myung (keyboards),
Sean Reinert (drums)

GORDIAN KNOT's 1998 debut, fronted by ex-
CYNIC man Sean Malone, is an all
instrumental heavy Jazz Rock affair which
sees contributions from guitarists Ron
Jarzombek of WATCHTOWER and SPASTIC
INK, Glenn Snelwar alongside Trey Gunn
from KING CRIMSON. Even DREAM
THEATER's John Myung contributes
percussion. Drums are in the hands of Sean
Reinert.
Malone and Reinert joined AGHORA in 2000.
Malone would session on SPASTIC INK
recordings in 2001. During May of 2002 it
would be revealed that Malone was
entrenched in a new Prog Rock 'supergroup'
mentored by DREAM THEATER drummer
Mike Portnoy. The impressive cast list for this
venture also cited such esteemed figures as
PAIN OF SALVATION frontman Daniel
Gildenlöw, erstwhile DREAM THEATER and
presently CHROMA KEY keyboard player
Kevin Moore and FATES WARNING guitarist
JIM MATHEOS.

Albums:
GORDIAN KNOT, Sensory SR3005 (1998)
Galois / Code-Anticode / Reflections /
Megrez / Singularity / Redemption's Way /
Komm Susser Tod, Komm Sel'ge / Rivers
Dancing / Srikara Tal / [Grace]

GORESLEEPS (RUSSIA)

Albums:
AND THE VOICE FROM LEGEND WILL

PROCLAIM, MetalAgen (1995)
FAR AWAY FROM ANYWHERE ELSE.
MetalAgen (1997)
Avalon Dreams (The Voice From Legend) /
The Old Sea-King / Mary / Raging Wind /
Byarmia Land / The Realm Of The Lost /
Song Of Wandering / Stone Of Grey

GORILLA (UK)
Line-Up: John Redfern (vocals / guitar), Sarah
Russell (bass), Richard Guppy (drums)

Retro power trio Stoners founded in the
summer of 1998.

Albums:
GORILLA, Lunasound LUNA005CD (2001)
Good Time Rockin' / Coxsackie / Roachend
Salad / She's Got A Car / Buzzard /
Nowhere To Go But Down / Acorn Brain /
Forty Winks / Day Blindness / Iron Ball

GOTHIC (FRANCE)
Line-up: Goth (vocals / guitar), The Xela
(bass), Wax (drums)

Parisian Gothic (!) Rockers GOTHIC first
came together in 1992 as a quartet of bassist
The Xela (apparently only 11 years old at the
time!), guitarist / vocalist Goth, Demetus and
drummer Rony. The following year GOTHIC,
all still teenagers at this stage, recorded the
'Pain Before Insane' demo cassette with
second guitarist Wolf now on board.
Before the band could play live both Wolf and
Demetus departed. This did not affect the
group's progress however and subsequent
gigs generated the second demo, a live
recording titled 'Pleasures Of Brutality',
limited to 100 copies.
1995 saw their efforts coming to fruition with
the self-financed mini-album, 'Brutal
Conditions Of Extreme Alchemy'.
Rony was to leave the fold in advance of
GOTHIC recording a second album, titled
'Prelude To Killing'. GOTHIC drafted a new
sticksman in the form of Wax.
GOTHIC band members are also active in
FAST FORWARD, a project band involving
TREPONOM PAL drummer D.

Albums:
**BRUTAL CONDITIONS FOR EXTREME
ALCHEMY**, Gothic (1995)
PRELUDE TO KILLING, Gothic (1997)
CRIMINAL ART MOTIVATION, (1999)

GOTHICA (ITALY)
Line-Up: Alessandra Santovito (vocals),
Roberto Del Vecchio (vocals), Carmine
Giagiacomo (guitar), Laura Vinciguerra

(violin), Daniele Prosperi (oboe), Luigi
Pagano (percussion), Marco Bacceli (drums)

GOTHICA emerged with a self-titled 1995
demo. Adding violinist Laura Vinciguerra the
band contributed the track 'Nothingness' to
the 1996 Italian compilation album 'Screams
From Italy'.
GOTHICA's first album was released on the
Cruel Moon label, a sub division of Sweden's
Cold Meat Industry concern.

Albums:
NIGHT THOUGHT, Cruel Moon (2000)
Stagione Oscura / Nothingness / Medusa /
Spirits Of The Dead / Proserpina / Spirit
Dance / The Land Under The Waves /
Penelope / The Pure Nymph / The Grave /
Lost In Reverie / Sepulchres

GOTHIC SEX (SPAIN)
Line-Up: Lord Gothic (vocals / guitar /
programming), Lady Gothic (vocals / bass /
programming)

Gothic Metal band infused with heavy S&M
and bondage imagery. The group, which
featured former members of NOTRE DAME
and CADAVARES ATERCIOPELADOS,
debuted a year after their formation with the
1989 7" single 'El Frenesi'. This would be
followed up in 1992 by a novel conceptual
video which included live footage. The
'Ritualis Mortis' album would be a split affair
shared with another Spanish act.
'Ritualis Mortis' saw the band with a line-up of
Lord Gothic on vocals and guitar, Lady Gothic
on vocals and drums and keyboard player
Madame Morgue. The follow up 'Divided We
Fall' introduced Averno on bass and had
GOTHIC SEX acting as support to
Germany's UMBRA ET IMAGO for dates in
Belgium. The band's succinctly titled 'Death'
tour that year would provoke strong media
response as GOTHIC SEX re-enacted
scenes of flagellation, sado-masochism and
bondage onstage. The outrage did not end
there though as the stages would be awash
with genuine blood, entrails and animal
heads.
Following 1996's 'Moonrise' record GOTHIC
SEX went on tour with Lord and Lady Gothic
aided by guitarist Metal Storm and bassist Dr.
Van Hellsing. Further tour work, to promote
the 1997 offering 'Laments', had Lord & Lady
Gothic joined by guitarist Metal Storm once
again with Paimon on drums.
The 'Rarities' album included a cover version
of W.A.S.P.'s 'Wild Child'.

Albums:
RITUALIS MORTIS, (1993)
Phantom / Enigma / New Goths / Requiem I
/ Promise In The Dark / Promise In The Dark
(Hard mix) / Epilogue
DIVIDED WE FALL, (1994)
Divided We Fall / Someone Gone Die /
Nosferatu / Psychosis / Divided We Fall
(Intro Orchestral) / Fuck 'Em All /
Condemnation / The Wind In Death House /
Hysteria / Sangre An La Arena / El Vacio
(Female Voice) / Divided We Fall (Church
mix)
MOONRISE, Ausfahrt (1996)
Moonrise / I Lost My Faith / Necronomicon /
The Frenzy-Loving The Vampire / Old
Wizzard / Voodoo Dolly / What Do You Want
From Me / Abyss Of Glory / My Preacher Of
The Iron Mask / Dust To Dust / The Frenzy -
Love Never Dies
LAMENTS, Ausfahrt EFA 06343 (1997)
The Night Scream / Laments / Nightbreed In
Midian / Bloody Love / Alone In The Dark /
Scream / Ashes To Ashes / Silence Lifts /
The New Christ / I'd Like To Feel
RARITIES, (1999)
The Book Of Shadows / And Again / Chants
Or Invocations / I Lost My Faith / Abyss Of
Glory / Moonrise / Nightbreed In Midian /
Alone In The Dark / Silence Lifts / Voodoo
Dolly / Wild Child

GRAND MAGUS (SWEDEN)
Line-Up: Janne Christoffersson (vocals /
guitar), Foxy (bass), Trisse (drums)

Blues based Doomsters unit fronted by
former SUPERMOUTH and CARDINAL
FANG vocalist Janne Christoffersson. Bassist
Foxy is another CARDINAL FANG veteran.
The Stockholm act has its roots in SMACK,
the need for a new drummer with the
departure of former incumbent Iggy
prompting a change in direction and name
change to GRAND MAGUS. The band would
locate their new sticksman, erstwhile
MORNING WOOD man Trisse (a.k.a. Fredrik
Liefvendahl), at an anniversary screening of
DEEP PURPLE's 'California Jam' film. A three
track demo led on to a split 7" single with
SPIRITUAL BEGGARS entitled 'Twilight Train'
for the Southern Lord label. The eponymous
debut album was produced by Fred Estby of
DISMEMBER.
Christoffersson would later join SPIRITUAL
BEGGARS.

Singles/EPs:
Twilight Train, Southern Lord (2000) (Split
single with SPIRITUAL BEGGARS)

Albums:
GRAND MAGUS, Rise Above (2001)
Gauntlet / Legion / Never Learned / Black /
Hound Of Vengeance / Coat Of Arms /
Generator / Wheel Of Time / Lodbrock /
Black Hole / Mountain Of Power

GRASSHARP (GERMANY)
Line-Up: Gero (vocals), Fritz (guitar), Bo
(guitar), Murgl (bass), Andy (drums)

Parading a blend of retro styled Hard Rock
and Doom Metal with forceful vocals German
outfit GRASSHARP arrived with the
'Cosmodrome' EP in 1994 and followed it up
with 1995's 'Orphans Of Infinity' release.
The latter record was pressed up as a green
vinyl 10" affair issued as a split release with
touring mates INTO THE ABYSS, whose
'Dragon Snake' cut could be found on the flip
of GRASS HARP's thirteen minute epic
'Orphans...'. Only 300 copies were pressed.

Singles/EPs:
Mushroom Circus / Golden Spangles / Too
Dizzy, Moonbeam CD 004 (1994)
('Cosmodrome' EP)
Orphans Of Infinity, Moonbeam 005 (1995)

(10" single, split with INTO THE ABYSS)

GRAVE (SWEDEN)
Line-Up: Jörgen Sandström (vocals / guitar),
Ola Lindgren (guitar), Jonas Torndal (bass),
Jensa Paulsson (drums)

GRAVE are one of the founders of the
Swedish Death / Doom Metal scene releasing
their first demo, 'Sick Disgust Eternal', in 1987
following a name change from CORPSE. Two
further demos, 1988's 'Sexual Mutilation' and
1989's 'Anatomia Corporis Humanum' gained
the band an enviable cult status. The latter
demo was also to be issued as a four track
EP.
The band toured Europe as guests to Florida
thrashers MALEVOLENT CREATION in
September 1991 shortly followed by dates
opening for ENTOMBED.
In 1992 bassist Jonas Torndal quit and
frontman Jörgen Sandström took over four
string duties. Following the release of 1994's
'Soulless' GRAVE toured America in a
headlining capacity prior to hooking up with
the CANNIBAL CORPSE and SAMAEL tour
as support. Further dates had the band
putting in an appearance on the 'Full Of Hate'

GRAVE

187

festivals and acting as openers for MORBID ANGEL.

Following this bout of activity Sandström wound up joining ENTOMBED in 1995. GRAVE persevered as a duo with Lindgren now responsible for vocals for the 1996 Tomas Skogsberg produced 'Hating Life' record.

GRAVE, centred upon vocalist / guitarist Ola Lindgren and bassist turned guitarist Jonas Torndal, reconvened in September of 2001. New members would transpire to be THERION bassist Fredrik Isaksson and drummer Jensa Paulsson. This unit set to work on the Tomas Skogsberg produced 'Back From The Grave'. Subsequent European live dates would bear witness to the introduction of COERCION drummer Pelle Ekegren into the fold, regular skinsman Jensa Paulsson being temporarily out of action.

Singles/EPs:
Extremely Rotten Flesh / Brutally Deceased / Septic Excrements / Reborned Miscarriage, M.B.R. (1989)
...And Here I Die... Satisfied / I Need You / Black Dawn / Tremendous Pain / Day Of Mourning / Inhuman, Century Media 77066-2 (1993) (...And Here I Die... Satisfied' EP)

<u>Albums:</u>
GRAVE, Prophecy SRT 91L2878 (1991) (Split LP with DEVOLUTION)
INTO THE GRAVE, Century Media 84 9721 (1992)
Deformed / In Love / For Your God / Obscure Infinity / Hating Life / Into The Grave / Extremely Rotten Flesh / Haunted / Day Of Mourning / Inhuman / Banished To Live
SOULESS, Century Media CD 77070 (1994)
Turning Black / Soulless / I Need You / Bullets Are Mine / Bloodshed / Judas / Unknown / And Here I Die / Genocide / Rain / Scars
YOU'LL NEVER SEE, Century Media CD 9733 (1995)
You'll Never See / Now And Forever / Morbid Way To Die / Obsessed / Grief / Severing Flesh / Brutally Deceased / Christi(ns)anity
HATING LIFE, Century Media 77106-2 (1996)
Worth The Wait / Restrained / Winternight / Two Of Me / Beauty Within / Lovesong / Sorrowfilled Moon / Harvest Day / Redress / Still Hating Life
EXTREMELY ROTTEN LIVE, Century Media (1997)
Extremely Rotten Flesh / Turning Black / Restrained / Winternight / Haunted / Two Of Me / Hating Life / You'll Never See / Lovesong / Sorrowfilled Moon / Rain /

Soulless / And Here I Die... / Into The Grave / Reborn Miscarriage

GRAVE FLOWERS (SWEDEN)

GRAVE FLOWERS is the Doom side project of GODGORY front man Matte Andersson. Prior to the 'Solace Me' album GRAVE FLOWERS had tested the waters with the 1997 demo "Gamonbozia".

<u>Albums:</u>
SOLACE ME, Last Episode CD 5 2030 20 561 (2000)
Insomnia / Mentally Exposed / No More Winters / Wistful Whispering / Voluntary Silence / Dayexchange / Different Moods

GRAVEYARD RODEO
(New Orleans, LA, USA)
Line-Up: Mark Brignac (vocals), Jay Gracianette (guitar), Gary Gennaro (guitar), Tommy Scanlon (bass), Gary Hebert (drums)

New Orleans Hardcore Sludge. GRAVEYARD RODEO's first recording line-up was built around bassist Tommy 'Mescalin' Scanlon and comprised lead vocalist Perry McAuley, guitarists Gary Gennaro and Brad Christian and drummer Wayne Fabre.

The band dated back to 1980 and had first made an impression with the demo tape 'Realms Of The Undead'. A second session, 'Sowing Discord In The Haunts Of Man' found CORROSION OF CONFORMITY's Pepper Keenan aiding on guitar.

After a European tour to promote the debut album 'Sowing Discord In The Haunts Of Men' the group splintered. Scanlon enrolled a whole new cast for the 1994 'On The Verge' record including former BILE and NEW RELIGION vocalist Mark Brignac and another ex-NEW RELIGION man drummer Gary Hebert.

Post GRAVEYARD RODEO Jay Gracianette became bassist and Wayne Fabra vocalist for the renowned CHRIST INVERSION project of PANTERA mainman Phil Anselmo.

<u>Albums:</u>
SOWING DISCORD IN THE HAUNTS OF MEN, Century Media (1993)
Behind Enemy Lines / My God / Marduk / Internal Damage / Bad Seed / Cell XIII / The Truth Is In The Gas Chamber / Future Of The Carcass / Kommon Knowledge / Graveyard Rodeo
ON THE VERGE, Century Media CM 77069-2 (1994)
Self Holyness / Freedom Is Peace / Black Stone / Choices / Burn Out / The Turning /

GREENHOUSE EFFECT

GREENHOUSE EFFECT
Photo : El Danno

Thoughts Of The Past / Taught Well / Roaches / Nothing To Say

GRAYSCALE (FINLAND)
Line-Up: Lasse Harma (vocals), Miika Partonen (guitar), Matti Hamalainen (guitar), Matti Reinola (bass), Jenni Hytonen (keyboards), Janne Jukarainen (drums)

GRAYSCALE previously operated under the title of FOUR BITCHES.

Albums:
WHEN THE GHOSTS ARE GONE, Sound Riot (2002)
The World Today / A Dead Season / Gray Singer / Squeeze / The Fire Inside Me / Absent / Shape In The Shadows / Cast Aside / When The Ghosts Are Gone

GREENHOUSE EFFECT
(Oakland, CA, USA)
Line-Up: Eric Hagen (vocals / guitar), Jason James (guitar), Mike Brumley (bass), Craig Sitter (drums)

Fuzz infused Oakland Rockers founded in 1999. GREENHOUSE EFFECT, having debuted in April 2000 in Concord, California as openers for MERRICK and GROWTH OF ALLIANCE, built up a solid fan base from extensive live work prior to issuing the 2001 album 'Blast Shield Down'.
Released on the Purple Astronaut label the record delivered a heady mixture of retro '60s style Jazz inspired Space Rock laden with modern walls of sound.
The band parted ways with bass player Mike Brumley during mid 2002. A replacement was soon announced in ex-WAKEMAN'S CAPE man Gregg Emley.

Albums:
BLAST SHIELD DOWN, Purple Astronaut GE2530 (2001)
Zapruder / The Mayor / Iraq 69 / Lando / Palm Tree Metropolis / Gildor / Outro…

GREENWOOD (CANADA)
Line-Up: Mark Faulkner (vocals), Greg Nelson (guitar), Gary Kowal (bass), Steve Nunnaro (drums)

Toronto based Psych-Rockers GREEN-WOOD came together during 1998. Although firmly in the 'Riff Rock' camp many reviewers have likened the band to more modern Alt-Metal acts due to the distinctive nature of singer Mark Faulkner's vocal delivery. Their 2001 EP 'Seas Of Another World' would prompt a deal from the 12th Planet Music

label.

Singles/EPs:
Seas Of Another World EP, (2001)

Albums:
HORUS ON THE HORIZON, 12th Planet Music (2002)
Morphine / Dirty Bob / Cosmic Rebirth / Deep Green Hollow / Supra Song / Horus On The Horizon / Seas Of Another World

GRIEF (Boston, MA, USA)
Line-Up: Jeff Hayward (vocals / guitar), Terry Savastano (guitar), Eric Harrison (bass), Rick Johnson (drums)

An ultra ponderous Sludge Doom outfit out of New England fuelled by utter lyrical despondency. GRIEF was formulated during 1991 by erstwhile DISRUPT guitarist Terry Savastano. The band made their entrance with an eponymous 7" single on their own Grievance label, following this up with the 'Dismal' 12". Thereafter a whole slew of shared singles ensued witnessing GRIEF allied with DYSTOPIA, 16, SOILENT GREEN, SUPPRESSION and Japanese Stoners CORRUPTED.
1994's 'Come To Grief' album would emerge on the German Century Media label before GRIEF switched to the Pessimiser concern of fan Chris Elder for future outings. During 1995 a compilation album 'He Is No Good To Me Dead' would include rare GRIEF demos, tracks from DISRUPT as well as CHICKEN CHEST AND THE BIRD BOYS, the side venture of Hayward and DISRUPT guitarist Jay.
The drum stool position within GRIEF would remain fluid. Both Peter Cassin of THE McVEIGHS and Chuck Conlan, the latter appearing on the 2000 album 'And Man Will Become The Hunted', held terms but former drummer Rick Johnson would rejoin during January of 2000.
There was talk of the band switching titles to that of EMPTY but GRIEF would finally draw to a halt in 2001 with Hayward, Savastano and Harrison vowing to create a fresh project. Both Savastano and Hayward also operate in the Punk act THE SQWAGS.

Singles/EPs:
Grief EP, Grievance (1991)
Dismal EP, Grievance (1992) (12" single)
Split, Theologian T-35 (1994) (Split 7" single with 16)
Pessimiser, Pessimiser PESS24 (1995) (Split 7" single with 16)
No Choice, Bovine (1995) (Split 7" single

with SUPRESSION)
Green Vegetable Matter, Pessimiser (1996)
(Split 10" single with SOILENT GREEN)
My Dilemma, H.G. Fact (1996) (Split 7"
single with CORRUPTED)

Albums:
DISMAL, Common Cause (1993)
Rhinoceros / Isolation / Coma / Shoot Me... /
Fucked Upstairs / Depression / Virus /
Fleshpress / The Drone
COME TO GRIEF, Century Media 77087-2
(1994)
Earthworm / Hate Grows Stronger / World
Of Hurt / I Hate You / Ruined / Fed Up /
Stricken / Come To Grief
MISERABLY EVER AFTER, Pessimiser
(1996)
One Of Those Days / Low Life / Nuisance /
Angry Man / Miserably Ever After / Straight-
Edge Closed Mind / Why Should You Care? /
I Hate The Human Race / Trust
TORSO, Pessimiser PESS 23 (1997)
I Hate Lucy / Polluted / Amorphous / Life
Can Be / To Serve and Neglect / Beyond
Waste / Tar
AND MAN WILL BECOME THE HUNTED,
Pessimiser PESS33 (2000)
Predator / I Won't Come Back / If The World
Was Flat / Ostrich / Hurricane Jello / Down
In The Dumps Again / No Escape / When
Rotten Ideas Break Free

GREY SKIES FALLEN (New York, USA)
Line-Up: Rich Habeeb (vocals / guitar), Joe
Sanci (guitar), Jimmy White (bass), Craig
Rossi (keyboards), Sal Gregory (drums)

A dark yet melodic New York Metal act
founded during 1997 by the trio of vocalist /
guitarist Rick Habeeb, guitarist Joe D'Angelo
and bass player Chris Montalbano. Previously
the band had operated as EVE OF
MOURNING. Shortly after their formation
GREY SKIES FALLEN was joined by
keyboard player Craig Rossi and drummer
Aaron Wiliams and with this line-up cut the
self-financed debut 'The Fate Of Angels'. The
band pressed up 1000 copies after which
Nightfall Records took on distribution.
During late 1998 Williams made his exit,
replaced by Sal Gregory. The following year
the group inducted guitarist Kevin Spinner
and bassist Ryan Lipinski, the latter replaced
in turn by Frank Caninno. The bass position
would change again with the arrival of Jimmy
White. GREY SKIES FALLEN would record
their sophomore effort, 'Tomorrow's In Doubt',
for the Canadian Maelstrom Music label.
D'Angelo would decamp in December of
2001 to concentrate on his project

SYNESTHESIA and GREY SKIES FALLEN
duly welcomed replacement guitarist Joe
Sanci into the fold.
Both Habeeb and Gregory operate the Grind
side project DISCOLORED TAINT.

Albums:
THE FATE OF ANGELS, Nightfall (1999)
The Purest Form / The Great Fall / Spiral
Dreams / This Burden I Bear / Drawn To The
Earth / Dawn / When The Rains Come /
Athena / Shadowburn / Walk This Bloody
Path / The Fate Of Angels
TOMORROW'S IN DOUBT, Maelstrom
Music (2002)
Intro / Essence Of Motion / Dream The Day
Away / Tomorrow's In Doubt / Let Me Breath
/ Silent Cry / Fragments

GROMS (NORWAY)
Line-Up: Øyvind Haugland (vocals / guitar),
Hans Dalen (guitar), Haakon Johannesson
(bass), Petter Gordon Jensen (drums)

Kristiansand based Christian Death-Doom
Metal outfit GROMS ('God Rules Over My
Soul') date back to 1992. The group toured
Poland in 1993 and issued the 'Ascension'
album two years later. There were reports of a
further album 'I Beseech Thee'.

Albums:
ASCENSION, Arctic Serenades SERE 002
(1995)
Ascension / From Dust To Dust / True
Wisdom / The Riddle / Truth Misunderstood /
Noone / The End Of The Age / The Voice Of
Righteousness / The Just Shall Live By Faith

GRUNTRUCK (Seattle, WA, USA)
Line-Up: Ben McMillan (vocals), Tom
Niemeyer (guitar), Alex Sibbald (bass), Josh
Sinder (drums)

A Seattle bottom end, Sabbathian stanced no
frills Rock unit caught up in the Grunge
movement and later to be held in high esteem
by the following wave of Stoners.
GRUNTRUCK frontman Ben McMillan had
been with SKIN YARD. Bassist Tim Paul was
very briefly a member of Portland Punks
POISON IDEA in 1987. Guitarist Tom
Niemeyer had been pivotal in the notorious
act THE ACCUSSED.
GRUNTRUCK issued two highly rated albums
through the Roadrunner label, the second
outing in particular, 1992's Gary King and
Jack Endino produced 'Push' bolstered with
heavy airplay afforded to the lead track 'Tribe',
being hailed by many as an underground
classic. The band line-up at this juncture

comprised McMillan, Niemayer, bassist Tim Paul and drummer Scott McCullum.

The band then got embroiled in protracted disagreements with their label. A 1996 EP arrived entitled 'Shot', once again produced by Gary King and Jack Endino and witnessing a fresh rhythm section pulled from THE ACCUSSED of bass player Alex Sibbald and drummer Josh Sinder. Sibbald had also been a member of numerous now notorious Punk acts such as MAGGOT BRAINS, ITCHY BROTHER and CHEATING DEATH. Sinder was also with heavyweights TAD. After a 1997 demo outing emerged GRUNTRUCK subsequently folded.

Sibbald and Sinders created RED HOT LUNATIC. Niemeyer, after a spell with HELLCAT, would go on to form part of LYE together with Paul and ex-MY SISTERS MACHINE drummer Chris Grohde.

McMillan, Niemeyer and McCullum joined MONA DIESEL.

Singles/EPs:
Shot / Illusion / New God, (1996) ('Shot' EP)

Albums:
INSIDE YOURS, Roadrunner RO 92602 (1991)
Not A Lot To Save / Crucifunkin' / Paint / Eyes Of Stone / So Long / Buried / Flesh Fever / Inside Yours / Move In Silence / Melt / Broken
PUSH, Roadrunner RR 91302 (1992)
Tribe / Machine Action / Racked / Crazy Love / Above Me / Gotta Believe / Break / Slow Scorch / Follow / Body Farm / Lose / Push

HAGGARD (GERMANY)
Line-Up: Asis Nasseri (vocals / guitar), Markus Reisinger (vocals / guitar), Taki Saile (vocals / piano), Andreas Nad (bass), Vera Hoffman (violin), Katherina Quast (cello), Luz Marsen (drums)

HAGGARD were founded in late 1991 and released their first demo, 'Introduction', the following year. The band toured heavily supporting the likes of DEICIDE, BIOHAZARD, AGRESSOR, ANATHEMA and PYOGENESIS. During these formative years HAGGARD would evolve from a straightforward melodic Death Metal combo into a full-blown 16-piece Metal orchestra.
1993 saw HAGGARD's first self-financed mini-album 'Progressive' and in 1994 they toured Europe as support to AMORPHIS and DESULTORY.
In 1995 the group issued the 'Once… Upon A December's Dawn' promo tape touring with Danes ILLDISPOSED and DISGUST. By now the group had inducted a violinist, cellist, soprano vocalist and pianist and for the first time HAGGARD took a line-up roster out on the road comprising 16 musicians.
The follow up album 'And Thou Shalt Trust… The Seer' proved to be an ambitious affair with German, English and Latin lyrics atop a heady mix of Metal, Classical and mediaeval music.
HAGGARD toured alongside RAGE in 1997 and ATROCITY in February of 1998. Later that same year HAGGARD had elevated themselves to headliner status undertaking a September batch of European dates with guests SOLEFALD and TRISTANIA. The group's debut live album 'Awaking The Gods', culled from headline shows in Mexico, would arrive in August of 2001.

Albums:
PROGRESSIVE, Progressive (1993)
Charity Absurd / Mind Mutilation / Incapsuled / Progressive / Daddy Was Her First Man
AND THOU SHALT TRUST… THE SEER, Serenades SR011 (1997)
Chapter 1: The Day As Heaven Wept / Chapter 2: Origin Of A Crystal Soul / Chapter 3: In A Pale Moon's Shadow / Chapter 4: De La Morte Noire / Chapter 5: Lost (Robin's Song) / Chapter 6: A Midnight Gathering
AWAKEN THE CENTURIES, Drakkar (2000)
Rachmaninov: Choir / Pestilencia / Heavenly Damnation / The Final Victory / Saltorella La Manuelina / Awaking The Centuries / Statement Zur Lage Der Musica / In A Fullmoon Procession / Menuett (I) Prophecy

Fulfilled / Menuett (II) And The Dark Night Entered / Courante / Rachmaninov: Choir
AWAKING THE GODS - LIVE IN MEXICO, Drakkar (2001)
Intro - Rachmaninov Choir / Mediaeval Part / Lost / Prophecy Fulfilled - And The Dark Night Entered / Menuett / Origin Of A Chrystal 50 VI / Awakening The Centuries / Courante / In A Full Moon Procession / Final Victory / In A Pale Moon's Shadow

HALF MAN (SWEDEN)
Line-Up: Janne Bengtsson (vocals / guitar), Peter Lilja (guitar), Patric Carlsson (bass), Roger Bengtsson (drums)

'70s fuelled Riff Rockers HALF MAN first came together during the mid '80s but after a few years folded. The band would be reconstituted with a line-up comprising original personnel vocalist / guitarist Janne Bengtsson and bassist Patric Carlsson along with guitarist Peter Lilja and drummer Roger Bengtsson. A demo arrived in 1994 but it would not be until 1998 that recordings took place for the full-length debut, 'The Complete Field Guide For Cynics'. The album was at first released independently by the band and restricted to 500 copies. The Border label later picked the album up for international distribution.
HALF MAN contributed their version of 'Round And Round' to the Small Stone Recordings 2000 AEROSMITH tribute 'Right In The Nuts'.
The February 2002 album 'Red Herring' was delivered via the Italian Beard Of Stars label in two formats, CD and vinyl, the latter issued some two months later and enclosed in a lavish gatefold sleeve with completely different artwork and a bonus track.

Singles/EPs:
Red Herring / Acid Park, (1999) ('Half Man Vs. Mothercake' Split EP with MOTHERCAKE)

Albums:
THE COMPLETE FIELD GUIDE FOR CYNICS, Border (1999)
Blues Ain't Nothin' (But A Botheration On Your Mind) / Insane / Home For Two / Nowhere Leading Road (Parts 1 & 2) / When The Train Comes Back / Ain't Ya Coming Home, Babe? / Two Perverted Men In The Swamp (Parts 1 & 2) / Hardly Wait / Searching For A Woman / Two Drinks Of Wine / Rodney's Song / Shake That Thing
RED HERRING, Beard Of Stars (2002)
Repulsion / Too Late / Pigs In Space / Sunday Morning Is Coming Down / Willy The Pimp /

Sugar Mama / Departed Souls / Same Thing On My Mind / Grass Stains / Journey Into Darkness / Hard Road / No Title

HALFWAY TO GONE (NJ, USA)
Line-Up: Lou Gorra (vocals / bass), Lee Stuart (guitar), Chuck Dukehart III (drums)

Although based in New Jersey HALFWAY TO GONE deliver Stoner Rock with a distinct Southern flavour. The band was created by two former members of SOLARIZED, vocalist / bassist Lou Gorra and guitarist Lee Stuart. Drummer Danny Golin would appear on the debut split EP with ALABAMA THUNDERPUSSY and the full-length 'High Five' album. However, Gollin would make his exit in March of 2001. HALFWAY TO GONE duly enrolled Chuck Dukehart III, erstwhile of SIXTY WATT SHAMAN. . Touring in October of that year had the band paired with FIVE HORSE JOHNSON.

By the time of recording the 2002 'Second Season' album Kenny Wagner, yet another erstwhile SIXTY WATT SHAMAN man, had taken the drum stool. The band were back on the road in North America for an extensive run of shows throughout March and April, teaming up with the SUPLECS prior to June gigs with NASHVILLE PUSSY and NEBULA, rounded off with a batch of shows supporting CLUTCH.

Singles/EPs:
Darktown Strutter / Thee Song, Game Two (2000) (Split EP with ALABAMA THUNDERPUSSY)

Albums:
HIGH FIVE, Small Stone Recordings SS-020 (2000)
Holiday in Altamont / The Big W / Devil Spit (The Van Zant Shuffle) / Kind Words For The Southern Gentlemen / King Snake / Story Of My Life / Green Mountain Hotshot / Limb From Limb / Blues For Burnt Fly Bog / Stingin' / Stormy Day / Being It
SECOND SEASON, Small Stone Recordings SS-020 (2002)
Great American Scumbag / Already Gone / Black Coffy / Escape From Earth / Thee Song (A Slight Return) / Whiskey Train / Brocktoons Wake / Outta Smokes / Lone Star Breakout / Never Comin Home / Trytophan

HANGNAIL (UK)
Line-Up: Harry Armstrong (vocals / guitar), Graham Smith (guitar), Jim Ogawa (guitar), Paul Elphick (bass), Mark Cronin (drums)

South London band signed to CATHEDRAL mainman Lee Dorrian's Rise Above label. Founded back in 1993 HANGNAIL underwent numerous line-up shuffles prior to settling in 1997 upon frontman Harry Armstrong, guitarist Jim Ogawa, sole surviving founder member bass player Paul Elphick and erstwhile MOURN drummer Mark Cronin. Both Armstrong and Ogawa were members of Progressive Death Metal band COLLAPSE, having recorded a demo 'From Another Place' during 1995. At the same juncture Armstrong would be undertaking bass duties in HANGNAIL and MOURN.

Solid progress commenced with the recording of a 1997 demo session 'Charge The Vibe' which found its way into the hands of Frank Kozik and Man's Ruin Records. The subsequent 'One Million Layers BC' EP garnered laudatory reviews for HANGNAIL's distinctive brand of Seventies imbibed sounds. The band also released a limited edition white vinyl single of 'Charge The Vibe' through the Gamp label, restricted to just 500 copies.

The August 1999 'Ten Days Before Summer' album, produced by Dave Chang, saw female vocal accompaniment from Katty Heath. Promotion included UK support dates with ANATHEMA.

Sophomore release 'Clouds In The Head', issued in April of 2001, found ORANGE GOBLIN's Ben Ward guesting on the track 'That There Soul'.

In early 2002 the band re-inducted rhythm guitarist Graham Smith, a band member back in HANGNAIL's formative years, back into the band to allow Armstrong to concentrate on his frontman role. HANGNAIL cut two LED ZEPPELIN cover versions during that same year. Their take of 'Friends' appeared on the acoustic 'Mary Jane's Kitchen Party' EP whilst a rendition of 'Bron-Y-Aur Stomp' was donated to the Smallstone Records 'Sucking The 70s' compilation.

Armstrong, as bassist, also operates avant-garde Rockers THE WINCHESTER CLUB, so titled after the famous London drinking establishment from the cult TV series 'Minder'. THE WINCHESTER CLUB also comprises members of DECOMPOSED and CHINESE BURN.

Not to be confused with the Wisconsin Christian Nu-Punk HANGNAIL who have also issued two albums to date.

Singles/EPs:
Charge The Vibe / The View / Side-Slide / One Million Layers BC, Man's Ruin MR 116 (1998) ('One Million Layers B.C.' EP)
Charge The Vibe / The Name Escapes Me, Gamp GAMP004 (1999)

Albums:
TEN DAYS BEFORE SUMMER, Rise Above
CDRISE 23 (1999)
Overhang / Side-Slide / Keep On / Summer
Rain / Visit My World / Sun Quake / 4:28 /
One Million Layers BC / Easy Tiger
CLOUDS IN THE HEAD, Rise Above
CDRISE32 (2001)
Slowhead / Third Time Around / Clouds In
The Head / Martyr Youthair / Release / Into
The Ether / Gone / That There Soul / The
Watcher / Riffmeister Jesus

HARDWARE (UK)
Line-Up: Greg David (vocals), Paul Solynskyj
(guitar), Martin Hawthorn (bass), Andrew
Hoult (keyboards), Aynsley Dickinson (drums)

A British Gothic Metal act that included in its
ranks former EXCALIBUR guitarist Paul
Solynskyj and ex-LOUD and P.A.D.D. bassist
Martin Hawthorn. HARDWARE toured
Germany but ultimately to no avail. Solynskyj
is now a guitar roadie for American act
PIST.ON.

Singles/EPs:
What Race? / Piece Of Mind / Back To You /
Faith Fall Down / Military Hardware, Bullet
Proof IRS 993. 622 (1996) ('Race Religion &
Hate' EP)

HARLEQYN (UK)
Line-Up: Paul Mother (vocals), Titus Walker
(guitar), Phil Sargeant (bass), Dave D. Wood
(drums)

Bradford based HARLEQYN later adopted
the name ARCHITECT and released more
self-financed records.

Singles/EPs:.
Burn, Starlight ST001 (1988)

Albums:
THE ORDER OF THE GOLDEN DAWN,
Voltage VLP 14 (1989)

HATEBALL (SWEDEN)

Albums:
DOUBLE DELUXE, Daredevil DD014 (2001)
(Split album with RICKSHAW)
Coockies / Lightyears Away / Seven Hours /
Let's Have A Riot Here / Shine / Trash Of The
Century / Soul Rotten To The Core

THE HEADS (UK)
Line-Up: Simon Price (vocals / guitar), Paul R.
A. Allen (guitar), Huge Morgan (bass), Wayne
C. Maskell (drums)

Avon based Acid Stoners. THE HEADS draw
their influences from late sixties Psychedelia
but employ enough distorted heaviness to
have been embraced by the Stoner crowd.
The band debuted live as opening act for
BABES IN TOYLAND in Bristol during 1990,
pulling in drummer Wayne C. Maskell
following this gig. A number of guitarists came
and went prior to Paul R.A. Allen enrolling and
THE HEADS cutting the 1991 'Quad'
sessions.
Despite solid progress afforded by the debut
album 'Relaxing With...' and the Man's Ruin
label issued collection of singles 'The Time Is
Now' in 1998, THE HEADS went into
retirement for much of 1999 with frontman
Simon Price attending college and the band's
rhythm section working up a band project with
members of THEE HYPNOTICS. Finally the
band reassembled for a new studio album for
the Sweet Nothing label.
THE HEADS toured North America for the
first time alongside NEBULA for West Coast
dates during 2000 promoting the 'Everybody
Knows We Got Nowhere' album. For this
record, compiled mainly from material dating
back two years earlier, the group re-recorded
earlier tracks 'Legavaan Satellite' and 'Dirty
Water'.
The Rocket 'Sessions 02' album of
unreleased material featured guitarist Paul
R.A. Allen on lead vocals for opening cut
'Filler', the 16 minute 'Planet Suite No. 3'and
the original unedited recording of 'Long
Gone'. The release inspired fan fervour, being
limited to just 1000 copies of which 100 came
manufactured in blue vinyl. To add to demand
the initial 100 pressings also came with a free
7" single. Just 70 of these would also come
with a unique band photo.

Singles/EPs:
Quad, Rooster HH7-01 (1994)
Coogan's Bluff, Rooster (1995)
Television, Headhunter (1996)
Gnu / Demonizer 48-48 / Looking At You /
Jellystoned Park, Headhunter HH7-01
(1996) ('Gnu' EP)
Delwyn's Conkers / Snake Pit / Spliff Riff
(Roached Out), Man's Ruin MR41 (1996)
('The Heads' EP)
Mao Tinitus / Legevaan Satellite, Man's
Ruin MR78 (1998)
Dirty Water, Butcher's Hook 003 (1998)
(Split with MAGIC DIRT)
Split EP, Rocket (1999) (Split single with
LILYDAMWHITE)
Spliff Riff (Conga'd Out...) / #75 (All Of It),
Rocket LAUNCH 008 (2000)
Disappear Into Concrete / Jellystone
(Remix loop edit), Rocket (2002) (Free
limited edition single. 100 copies)

RELAXING WITH…, Headhunter HUK01 (1996)
Quad / Don't Know Yet / Chipped / Slow Down / U33 / Television / Woke Up / Widowmaker / Taken Too Much / Coogan's Bluff
THE TIME IS NOW, Man's Ruin MR97 (1998)
Delwyn's Conkers / Snake Pit / Spliff Riff / Dirty Water / Mao Tinitus / Legevaan Satellite / You Can Lean Back Sometimes
EVERYBODY KNOWS WE GOT NOWHERE, Sweet Nothing SNCD007 (2000)
Legavaan Satellite / Thumbs / Fuego / Kraut Byrds / Could Be... / # '75 / Wobble / Barcoded / Song No 1 / My My / Stab Railroad / Chrome Plated / Motorjam / Dirty Water / Pill Jam / Long Gone
UNDER SIDED, Sweet Nothing SNCD0011 (2002)
Dissonant / VBM / Canlike / Bedminster / False Heavy / Vibrating Digit / Energy / Heavy Sea
SESSIONS 02, Rocket LAUNCH 05 (2002) (Limited edition 1000 copies)
Filler / Planet Suite No. 3 / Long Gone (Part One) / K.R.T.5-1

HEAVEN GREY (LATVIA)

Line-Up: Ansis Melders (vocals), Vyacheslav Nikitin (guitar), Sigvard Blazhevich (guitar), Vladislav Kalinin (bass), Ernests Libietis (cello), Ervin Ozolinsh (drums)

HEAVEN GREY are a Riga based Doom Metal band borne out of Thrash and Death roots. Unusually the band employs the use of a cellist on stage. The group came together during 1993 in the wake of the dissolution of the Death Metal unit SCAFFOLD and Grindcore mongers DISGORGED. Both guitarist Vyacheslav Nikitin and bass player Vladislav Kalinin had been SCAFFOLD members with second guitarist Janis and drummer Ervin Ozolinsh had been with DISGORGED. Andris, previously bassist for GRINDMASTER DEAD, the band that would evolve into SKYFORGER, completed the line-up by adopting a new role as lead vocalist.
Initially HEAVEN GREY took on a distinct Death cum Grindcore direction as expected but slowly Doom elements began to creep in. The group let Ansis go due to personal problems in 1994 and Ansis Melders, also the band manager, took on the duties as frontman. The group also augmented their sound with the addition of cellist Ernests Libietis. With this new formation HEAVEN GREY, also utilizing female session lead vocals, laid down their first demo recordings 'Under The Grey Clouds'.
Toward the close of 1994 the track 'Broken

Mirror' was recorded for a radio show but shortly after Janis decamped. The vacancy on second guitar was soon filled by Sigvard Blazhevich, previously with Thrash Metal band MYSTERY. Their debut album 'Memory River' was issued in cassette format by Mapl Music, promoted by extensive touring which would include gigs outside of Latvia.
In January of 1998 the band recorded a further album's worth of atmospheric Doom material billed as 'Northwind'. A video would be shot for the track 'Zemes Elpa (The Breath Of Earth)' and aired on Latvian TV.

Albums:
MEMORY RIVER, Mapl Music (1996) (Cassette release)
Storm Of The Souls / Dreams / Shadows In Rain / Instrumental / The Beat Of Heart / Upe / From The Depth Of Heart / Under The Grey Clouds / Broken Mirror

HELDEN RUNE (ITALY)

Line-Up: Mercy (vocals / bass), Tony Tears (guitar), Claudio Dondo (keyboards), Franz Ekurn (piano)

HELDEN RUNE is an offshoot project of MALOMBRA members vocalist Mercy and pianist Franz Ekurn.

Albums:
THE WISDOM THROUGH THE FEAR, Black Widow BWR 048-2 (2002)
La Maison Dieu / A Love Against The Age / Loving And Sterile / We Were The Young Blades / The House Of Good Return Part I / The House Of Good Return Part II / Arlequinade / Mirror Mirror / St. Martin's Summer Garden Party / The Hanged Man / Baroque Boredom / Pestilence / Blood And Soil / Black Abbey Tune / The Early Night Of Frost

HER ENCHANTMENT (HOLLAND)

Line-Up: Richard (vocals), Marije (vocals), Teun (guitar), Dave (guitar), John (bass), Elwin (drums)

An Arnhem melancholic Doom style act that started life in a Death Metal incarnation during 1994 originally billed as CRUCIFIED CORPSE. The group's first line-up consisted of a quartet of vocalist / guitarist Richard, guitarist Nick, bass player John and LAND'S END drummer Elwin. In late 1994 they would be joined by female lead vocalist Marije and subsequently laid down an opening demo tape 'Reflections From The Other Side', released in November.
The following year Nick was usurped by new

guitarist Dave. CRUCIFIED CORPSE recorded a second promotion cassette, 'Servile To The Serene', and had their track 'Devour Thy Soul' included on the Shiver Records compilation 'Sometimes Death Is Better Vol. 3'. 1996 saw the introduction of Jasper on guitar as Richard opted to concentrate solely on vocals. However, Marije then departed, having her position filled by Nienke. In 1998 the band, having directed themselves into a Gothic imbued stance, retitled themselves HER ENCHANTMENT, releasing the album 'Sagas'.

Nienke left in 1999 allowing a return for Marije to her original position in the September. In 2001 Jasper was supplanted by Teun, guitarist with Death Metal band MORTAL FORM. HER ENCHANTMENT members Marije, John and Elwin, in union with CERBERUS guitarist Reamon, would announce the formation of a Symphonic Metal side project ARMS OF VALOUR in February of 2002. June witnessed a further casualty in the HER ENCHANTMENT ranks as mainstay Richard bade his farewell. By July the band had inducted former WE, THE GODS frontman Richard Noordzij as substitute.

Albums:
SAGAS, (1998)
Frozen In Dark / The Conqueror Awaits Thee / Prodigiously Doleful / Awakening Of A Goddess / Morpheus / The Gate Keeper / Penetrating Testimony / Defiance Within

HERMANO (USA)

All star Stoner assemblage led by the esteemed figure of KYUSS, UNIDA and SLO BURN vocalist John Garcia. HERMANO's 'Only A Suggestion' album was delivered in 2002 but recorded some three years earlier. The HERMANO sessions also included Mike Callahan of DISENGAGE, David Angstrom of BLACK CAT BONE and SUPAFUZZ, Steve Earle of the AFGHAN WHIGS and Dandy Brown from ORQUSTA DEL DESIERTO.

Albums:
ONLY A SUGGESTION, Tee Pee (2002)
The Bottle / Alone Jeffe / Manager's Special / Señor Moreno's Introduction / Senor Moreno's Plan / Landetta (Motherload) / 5 To 5 / Nick's Yea

HERMH (POLAND)
Line-Up: Bart (vocals), Kris (guitar), Tom (guitar), Marcel (bass), Mark (keyboards), Mark (drums)

Self-styled Depressive Metal act HERMH convened with their 1994 demo 'Oremus Peccatum (Refaim)'. A second tape arrived in 1995 dubbed 'Crying Crowns Of Trees' selling over 2,000 copies. The enterprising Italian label Entropy Productions cobbled together both demos to make up the 'Echo' CD.

HERMH signed to German label Last Episode for their official debut 'Taran'. Guests on this album included female vocalist Justine of DECADES and Rafat Salmanowicz on acoustic guitar.

Although the band were far from happy with the finished sound of the album nevertheless HERMH went on the road to promote it, supporting the likes of VADER, BEHEMOTH and LAKE OF TEARS.

In late 1996 HERMH signed to domestic label Pagan Moon records for their 'Angeldemon' outing. A further studio album, projected to be entitled 'Eden's Fire', was in the works but the band collapsed. HERMH members subsequently went onto join bands such as CHRIST AGONY, UNKNOWN DIMENSIONS and MOON.

Albums:
ECHO, Entropy Productions (1995)
Chapter I - Oremus Peccatum - Refaim / Fallen Ancient Babiloon / Neverending War / The Burning Bush / Troubled Outlines Chapter II - Crying Crowns Of Trees / Crying Crowns Of Trees / Hermh
TARAN, Last Episode (1995)
Blackness I / Voyage Of The Beauty Land / The Hour Of The Witching Dance / Golden Sea / Blackness II / Rising Tears / Blackness III / In The Shadow Of The Trees / Blackness IV / Atmosphere Of The Passing Years / First Knight Of Nothingness / Last Blackness / Crying Crowns Of Trees
ANGELDEMON, Pagan Moon CD 009 (1997)
Intro - Wonderlust / The Silent Touch Of Bloody Rain / Dreamdeath Lover / Winged Emptiness / Years Of Dying / Wolfish Flower / Vampire The Angeldemon / Streak From Kozmoz / Immortalize - Outro

HEXENHAUS (SWEDEN)
Line-Up: Tommie Agrippa (vocals), Mike Wead (guitar), Rick Meister (guitar), Jan Blomqvist (bass), Ralph Raideen (drums)

HEXENHAUS were originally titled MANNINYA BLADE, under which name they released one album. Having adopted the new name in 1987, the band's line-up for the debut album ('A Tribute To Insanity') comprised vocalist Nicklas Johansson, ex-CANDLEMASS guitarist Mike Wead (real name Mikael Vikström), second guitarist ex-

DAMIEN man Rick Meister (real name Andreas Palm), bassist Jan Blomqvist and drummer Ralph 'Raideeen' Ryden.
In early 1989 Niclas Johansson left, to be superseded by ex-DAMIEN vocalist Tommie Agrippa (real name Thomas Lundin). 1990's 'The Edge Of Eternity' album also features a fresh bassist in former NAGASAKI, DAMIEN and MANNYINA BLADE man Mårten Marteen (real name Mårten Sandberg).
MANNINYA BLADE reformed in 1990 with Rutström, Leif Eriksson, Blomqvist and drummer Johan Eriksson, although Leif was to leave after the band cut a new demo tape in 1995.
For the third HEXENHAUS album, 'Awakening', only Wead and Lundlin remained with the band's new members being guitarist Marco A. Nicosia, ex-MEZZROW bassist Conny Welen and ex-PARASITE drummer John Billerhag.
After the album emerged Mike Wead created MEMENTO MORI then formed ABSTRAKT ALGEBRA with his old buddy, ex-CANDLEMASS bassist Lief Edling.
Marco Nicosia appeared on the 1997 'Psychotic' album by FIFTH REASON, a band founded by refugees from TAD MOROSE, ABSTRAKT ALGEBRA and MEMORY GARDEN.
Marteen joined MEMENTO MORI.

Albums:
A TRIBUTE TO INSANITY, Active ACTLP 6 (1988)
It / Eaten Alive / Delirious / As Darkness Falls: 1st Movement. a) Shades Of An Obscure Dream, b) A Fatal Attraction, c) In The Spiders Web. 2nd Movement. a) The Possession, b) The Damnation, 3rd Movement. a) On The Threshold Of Insanity, b) Behind Closed Doors, c) The Fall From Grace / Incubus / Death Walks Among Us / Memento Morie - The Dead Are Restless / Requiem
THE EDGE OF ETERNITY, Active ATVLP13 (1990)
Prelude / Toxic Threat / Prime Evil / Home Sweet Home / The House Of Lies / A Temple For The Soul / The Eternal Nightmare / At The Edge Of Eternity
AWAKENING, Active ATV19 (1991)
Shadows Of Sleep / Awakening / Betrayed (By Justice) / Necromonicon Ex Mortis / Code 29 / The Forthcoming Fall / Sea Of Blood / Paradise Of Pain / The Eternal Nightmare Act III / Incubus
DÉJÀ VOODOO, Black Mark BMCD 98 (1997)
Dies Irae - Vreden's Dag / Reborn (At The Back Of Beyond) / Phobia / Nocturnal Rites / Dejavoodoo / From The Cradle To The Grave

/ Rise Babylon Rise

HIGH ON FIRE (San Francisco, CA, USA)
Line-Up: Matt Pike (vocals / guitar), George Rice (bass), Des Kensel (drums)

Exceptionally heavy, Metal edged Stoner. Frontman and HIGH ON FIRE founder Matt Pike was previously a founder member of premier underground Doom merchants SLEEP. As SLEEP dissolved during 1997, after London Records put the brakes on releasing the 52 minute track 'Jerusalem' – now regarded a Stoner classic, Pike set about formulating a fresh act, emerging with HIGH ON FIRE in 1999. The proto band reportedly went through a few members before settling on the trio of Pike, bassist George Rice and drummer Des Kensel.
HIGH ON FIRE's debut release would be an eponymous three track EP, the first product to be issued by the newly established 12th Records. Promoting the 2000 Billy Anderson produced album 'The Art Of Self Defense' HIGH ON FIRE toured Europe alongside ALABAMA THUNDER PUSSY before touring North America packaged with CLEARLIGHT. A further round of gigs would see the band heading out as headliners.
With the demise of Man's Ruin Records the Tee Pee label would reissue 'The Art Of Self Defence' in 2002 complete with two extra tracks 'Steel Shoe' and 'The Usurper'. Fresh product, in the form of the May 2002 'Surrounded By Thieves' record for new label Relapse, would once again see production duties delegated to Billy Anderson. Subsequent road dates had HIGH ON FIRE sharing stages in the USA with GODFLESH.

Singles/EPs:
Blood Of Zion / 10,000 Years / Master Of Fists, 12th Records (1999) ('High On Fire' EP)

Albums:
THE ART OF SELF DEFENSE, Man's Ruin (2000)
Baghdad / 10,000 Years / Blood From Zion / Last / Fireface / Master Of Fists
SURROUNDED BY THIEVES, Relapse RLP6529 (2002)
Eyes & Teeth / Hung, Drawn And Quartered / Speedwolf / The Yeti / Nemesis / Thraft Of Caanan / Surrounded By Thieves / Razor Hoof

HIEROPHANT (USA)

HIEROPHANT is the funeral Death-Doom endeavour of sole member John Del Russi,

198

199

also owner of Black Beyonds Music & Autumn Dusk Productions. An EP, simply billed as 'Hierophant', marked the band's entrance in 1999. Two recordings plus the lengthy 'The Weight Of Winter' would be collected together for a later EP, the two earlier tracks remastered by Dario Derna, keyboard player with EVOKEN. Derna and Russi had previously shared an alliance in a Black Metal side project.

New HIEROPHANT compositions were delivered in 2002 in the form of the 'Autumn Dark' demo. Besides HIEROPHANT Russi also operates the primitive Black Metal venture SECT.

Singles/EPs:
Forever Dying / Where No Light Hath Shone… (But For That Of The Moon), (1999) ('Hierophant' EP)
Forever Dying / Where No Light Hath Shone… (But For That Of The Moon) / The Weight Of Winter, Black Beyonds Music (2001) ('The Weight Of Winter' EP)

HIM (FINLAND)
Line-Up: Valo Hermanni Ville (vocals), Daniel Lioneye (guitar), Michael Eros (bass), Emerson Burton (keyboards), Buddha Cognac (drums)

A massively successful Gothic Rock act led by the charismatic heart throb figure of frontman Valo Ville. HIM have not only dominated the charts in their native Finland but also across Europe and in particular Germany. HIM (abbreviated HIS INFERNAL MAJESTY) are managed by Seppo Vesteriren, the mastermind behind Finland's only other commercially bankable Rock export HANOI ROCKS.

The original incarnation of HIM saw Ville, a former member of BLOOD and KEMOTERAPIA, handling both bass and vocals. Guitars came from Mikko Lindstrom ('Lily Lazer' or 'Daniel Lioneye'), Ville's BLOOD and KEMOTERAPIA compatriot, with drums from Juhana Rantala and keyboards delegated to Antto Melasniemi. Before long Mikko Paananen (a.k.a. 'Michael Eros' or 'Mige Amour') of BULLSHIT ASS took over the bass role leaving Ville free to concentrate on lead vocals. HIM's second demo tape, which included a cover version of CHRIS ISAAK's 'Wicked Game', scored the band a deal with the major label BMG. With Melasniemi making his exit ex-MARY ANN man Zoltan Pluto was the new face behind the keyboards.

The 'Razorblade Romance' album broke new boundaries for the band, selling over a million copies. However, line-up shuffles saw Rantala departing after the album release, being replaced by erstwhile KYYRIA and DEMENTIA man Mika Kristian Kappinen, better known as 'Buddha Cognac' or 'Gas Lipstick'. Zoltan Pluto put in his final gig with HIM on New Year's Eve 2000, later founding NEW DAWN FOUNDATION. HIM subsequently drafted 'Emerson Burton' (Jani Purttinen) on keyboards. Purttinen previously cited membership of SUB-URBAN TRIBE, TORPEDO and COSMOS TANGO.

The esteemed production team of John Fryer and Kevin Shirley would take command in the studio for the 2001 'Deep Shadows And Brilliant Highlights' album. A later German edition came repackaged complete with extra tracks and video cuts.

The band encountered an unexpected obstacle in mid 2002 when it was revealed that a Chicago act had already registered the band title HIM for the United States. In the face of less than savoury remarks from the American HIM the Finns wryly serviced their single, 'Join Me', to US radio stations under the assumed title of HER.

Singles/EPs:
Wicked Game / For You / Our Diabolikal Rapture / Wicked Game, G.U.N. (1998)
When Love And Death Embrace (Radio edit) / When Love And Death Embrace (AOR Radio mix) / When Love And Death Embrace (Original Single edit) / When Love And Death Embrace (Album version), G.U.N. (1999)
Join Me In Death / It's All Tears (Unplugged version) / Rebel Yell (Live) / Dark Sekret Love, G.U.N. (1999)
Your Sweet 666, BMG (2000)
Right Here In My Arms (Radio edit) / I've Crossed Oceans Of Wine To Find You / Sigillum Diaboli, G.U.N. (2000)
Poison Girl / Right Here In My Arms / It's All Tears, G.U.N. (2000)
Gone With The Sin (Radio Edit) / Gone With The Sin (Orchestra Version) / For You (Acoustic Version) / Bury Me Deep Inside Your Heart (Live) / Gone With The Sin (Album version), G.U.N. (2000)
Pretending (John Fryer mix) / Pretending (The Cosmic Pope Jam version) / Pretending / Please Don't Let It Go (Acoustic version) / Lose You Tonight (Caravan version), G.U.N. (2001)
In Joy And Sorrow (Radio edit) / Again / In Joy And Sorrow (String version) / Salt In Our Wounds (Thulsa Doom version) / Beautiful (Rock version), G.U.N. (2001)
Heartache Every Moment / Close To The Flame / Salt In Our Wounds, G.U.N. (2002)

GREATEST LOVE SONGS VOLUME 666, BMG (1999)
Your Sweet Six Six Six / Wicked Game / The Heartless / Our Diabolikal Rapture / It's All Tears (Drown In This Love) / When Love And Death Embrace / The Beginning Of The End / (Don't Fear) The Reaper / For You / 666
RAZORBLADE ROMANCE, RCA 74321 75034 2 (2000)
Your Sweet 666 / Poison Girl / Join Me In Death / Right Here In My Arms / Bury Me Deep Inside Your Heart / Wicked Game / I Love You / Gone With The Sin / Razorblade Kiss / Resurrection / Death Is In Love With Us / Heaven Tonight
DEEP SHADOWS AND BRILIANT HIGHLIGHTS, BMG (2001)
Salt In Our Wounds / Heartache Every Moment / Lose You Tonight / In Joy And Sorrow / Pretending / Close To The Flame / Please Don't Let It Go / Beautiful / Don't Close Your Heart / Love You Like I Do
DEEP SHADOWS AND BRILLIANT HIGHLIGHTS - LIMITED EDITION, G.U.N. (2001)
Salt In Our Wounds / Heartache Every Moment / Lose You Tonight / In Joy And Sorrow / Pretending / Close To The Flame / Please Don't Let it Go / Beautiful / Don't Close Your Heart / Love You Like I Do / Pretending / Again / In Joy And Sorrow (String version) / Pretending (Cosmic Pope Jam version) / Pretending (Video) / In Joy And Sorrow (Video)

HØEK (GERMANY)
Line-Up: Robin Christopher Graff (vocals / guitar), Martin Godowski (bass), Alessandro Paglialonga (drums)

German self styled "Overdrive session Rock" act. HØEK began life as a quartet but had trimmed down to trio status for their opening 2000 EP, a release shared with BIJOLA. During 2000 the band supported LEADFOOT for a nationwide German tour before uniting with CELESTIAL SEASON and MUSHROOM RIVER BAND for further dates.
Promoting the 2002 'Alt. 157' album HØEK formed part of a European touring package billed with MUSHROOM RIVER BAND, Norway's PAWNSHOP and Swedes THE AWESOME MACHINE.

Singles/EPs:
Inner State / Sonic Rollercoaster / From Beyond / Another Ride / Pain Is Gone, (2000) ('HØEK Meets Bijola' EP)

Albums:

HØEK, (1998)
Icarus / Hey / Senseless / One And Only / Endophilia – The Trip To… / Yield (Live) / The Only Way Out (Live)
ALT. 157, Cargo (2002)
Your Ocean / Not Me / Don't Push / CMS Martyr / Too Much But Not Enough / Amazing Dick-Tator / My Way / Changes / ACC.ASC. / The Way To Tim Buktu

HOGWASH (ITALY)
Line-Up: Enrico (vocals / guitar), Max (bass), Roberto (drums)

'70s revering Riff Rockers. HOGWASH emerged in public view during 1995 brandishing an 11 track demo tape '21 Inches Sun'. 1999 found the HOGWASH track 'Hide' within the grooves of the Red Sun compilation 'Stone Deaf Forever'. The group also combined forces with ACAJOU, VORTICE CREMISI and THAT'S ALL FOLKS! for a four way split EP entitled 'Cookery Course - Part One Step By Step Guide To Super Cooking', HOGWASH contributing 'Rip Roarin'.
The band donated their rendition of 'Mantra Caboose Babyfinger' to the 2000 Black Widow Records tribute to BLUE CHEER 'Blue Explosion'.
Roberto, Enrico and Max would all be involved in the 2002 COLT 38 album 'Freaky Experiment Through 99th Dimension' through the Magic Vinyl 3 label. This project, recorded during 2000, allied the HOGWASH members with personnel from acts such as THAT'S ALL FOLKS!, ACAJOU, VERDENA, GEA and VORTICE CREMISI.

Albums:
FUNGUS FANTASIA, Lucifer Rising (1997)
Fungus Fantasia / Spiral Walls / The Spine / 21 Inches Sun / Willie The Rebel / Short Stupid Sad Song / The Bait / Bloodgrim / 5 Poles Field / Limpid / Rosemary Tree / 2nd Hand Dreams / Season Wrap - Florilegium
TAILORING, Red Sun (2000)
Snapshot / Ginger Queen / Darkjoy / Ladybird / Chronic / Just A Little Bit / hsawgoH / Twelfth / Snapshot Reprise

HONCHO (NORWAY)
Line-Up: Trond Skog (vocals), Jorgen Berggraf (guitar), Haakon Eng (guitar), Steinar Knapstad (bass), Kenneth Andersson (drums)

Desert Rock from the icy climes of Oslo, Norway. The group was founded in November of 1999 comprising vocalist Trond Skog, bass player Steinar Knapstad, guitarist Mathias Ingvarsson and drummer Kenneth

Andersson. The 2001 'Evil Women' EP led in turn to the self-released 'Sun Sessions' opus. HONCHO contributed two tracks 'Murmansk' and 'Industrial Lane', to the Water Dragon 'Greatest Hits Volume 1' compilation.

Ingvarsson would then relocate to his native Sweden and HONCHO duly filled the gap with two six stringers, Jorgen Berggraf and Haakon Eng.

Singles/EPs:
Hypnolpilot / Industrial Lane / Synthetic Depression / Powerlock, (2000) ('Evil Women' EP)

Albums:
SUN SESSIONS, (2001)
Snake Eyes / Guardian / Demon / In The Woods / There Is Something Going On Out There / Peyote / Realize
CORPORATE ROCK, Water Dragon (2002)
Grebo Mentor / In The Woods / Frontside Disaster / Peyote / Industrial Lane / Loco Steam / Dark Tunnel Of Love / Hide Behind / Hypnolpilot / Messy Ferguson / Snake Eyes

HONKY (Austin, TX, USA)
Line-Up: Jeff Pinkus (vocals / bass), Bobby Landgraf (guitar), Lance Farley (drums)

Southern Stoned Rock from Jeff Pinkus of the notorious BUTTHOLE SURFERS. Besides their pursuit of honest Riff Rock and a seemingly unquenchable thirst for life on the road, the band has made a name for itself by delivering such song titles as 'Your Bottom Is At The Top Of My List', 'Saline Mountains' dedicated to the joys of breast implants and the ode to ex-wives 'Don't Shoot Me Baby I Love You'.

Having decamped from the BUTTHOLE SURFERS in 1994 Pinkus teamed up with DADDY LONGHEAD before a stint with SKINNY LYNERD, the latter act including former DOUBLE PENETRATION and future HONKY guitarist Carson Vester. Gelling together as HONKY, the trio of Vester, Pinkus and drummer Lance Farley debuted on Frank Kozik's Man's Ruin cult label in 1997 with the 'Ten Inches' EP. An eponymous full-length album surfaced on Pinkus's own Honest Abe's Custom label in 1998.

Vester departed and HONKY drew in replacement guitarist Gable Barber from Punk band THE BULEMICS. Barber's tenure lasted just over eight months before Bobby Landgraf of GODZILLA MOTOR COMPANY stepped in.

The band's live album 'Attacked By Lesbians In A Chicago Bowling Alley' was so titled after a real life encounter when the band was indeed attacked onstage by lesbians at a show supporting L7.

HONKY would contribute their take on AEROSMITH's 'Adam's Apple' to the Small Stone Recordings 'Right In The Nuts' homage as well as AC/DC's 'Dirty Deeds' to the Reptilian Records tribute offering 'Hell Ain't A Bad Place To Be'. They also had a stab at VAN HALEN's 'Beautiful Girls' for a split 7" with IRONBOSS on Thick Records.

Greg Main joined the band for summer 2002 touring billed with NASHVILLE PUSSY and REVEREND HORTON HEAT.

Singles/EPs:
Deezy / Strange / Comes A Time / What She Needs, Man's Ruin (1997) ('Ten Inches' EP)
Beautiful Girls, Thick (1998) (Split picture disc EP with IRONBOSS)

Albums:
HONKY, Honest Abe's Custom Records (1998)
Smokin' Weed With Helios Creed / Mellow Larry / Deezy / Honky Jam / Nice And Tastee / Toy Story / Comes A Time / What She Needs / Strange / Ticket Holder / Mandingdong / Sancha / Honkadelic
ATTACKED BY LESBIANS IN A CHICAGO BOWLING ALLEY, Eat At The Y (1999)
Badfoot / What She Needs / Deezy / The Pleaser / Saline Mountains / Don't Shoot Baby I Love You / Tense Moment #1 / Smokin Weed With Helios Creed / Tense Moment #2 / A Man Who Is Simple / Heartbreaker Commentary
HOUSE OF GOOD TIRES, Hall Of Records (2001)
Don't Shoot Baby I Love You / Your Bottom's At the Top Of My List / Badfoot / The Pleaser / Sweet Honey Country Girl / House Of Seven / Bavarian Goggles / I Might Just Shoot Somebody / St. Melanne / Lung Punch / She's Mad

HORRIFIED (GREECE)
Line-Up: Gore (vocals), Stavros (guitar), Thanos (bass), Stelios (drums)

Lethargic, laboured medieval flavoured Death Metal. HORRIFIED came into being during 1989 as a quartet of vocalist Gore, guitarist Timos, bassist Kostas and drummer Stelios. The 'Prophecy Of Gore' demo was summoned up in 1990 after which Kostas was supplanted by Bill who, in turn, was shortly after replaced by Thanos.

In this incarnation HORRIFIED signed to the Black Power label. The first fruits of this relationship would be the 1991 12" single 'Eternal God' for which Spiros was inducted as rhythm guitarist. However, Timos would decamp thereafter and in came Stavros for 'The Ancient Whisper Of Wisdom' 7" release. Promoting this release HORRIFIED put in numerous support shows to bands such as ROTTING CHRIST and SEPTIC DEATH.

The full-length album 'In The Garden Of Unearthly Delights' would herald the introduction of Mina as female backing vocalist. In spite of the obvious forward momentum HORRIFIED split.

HORRIFIED reunited in 1998, signing to the Black Lotus label for the 'Animal' outing.

Singles/EPs:
Eternal God, Black Power (1991) (12" single)
The Ancient Whisper Of Wisdom, Black Power (1991)

Albums:
IN THE GARDEN OF THE UNEARTHLY DELIGHTS, Black Power BPR008 (1991)
The Awakening / Elisaph / Early Dawn Enraged / Crawling Silence / Down At The Valley Of The Great Encounter / Dying Forest / Baptized In Venereal Blood / Poetry Of War / Unbridled God / Dancing Next To Dying Souls
ANIMAL, Black Lotus BLRCD 004 (1998)
Hypnos / Forbidden Knowledge / Ghost / Redemption / Davolja Varos / Under The Roots / Evol Morena / Empty Moment / Funny Man

HYBERNOID (UK)
Line-Up: Dunk Goodenough (vocals), Paula Smith (vocals), Dave Evans (guitar), Andy Bennett (guitar), Andy J. Bennett (bass), Andy Slater (keyboards), Paul Stansfield (drums)

HYBERNOID debuted with the 'Opthaphobia' demo before signing to Displeased Records following a second demo entitled 'Well Of Grief'. This tape was backed up by an ambitious accompanying surreal video and duly landed the band a deal. The 'Technology' single was only released in America.

HYBERNOID's debut album 'The Last Day Begins?' pulled in strong media support and was licensed to Massacre Records for German release. Despite heady praise heaped upon the Doom styled 1996 album 'Today's Tomorrow Yesterday' HYBERNOID subsequently underwent a radical musical shift. The band would leave Displeased Records when the Dutch label disagreed with HYBERNOID's new electronic based stance of demo material. Keyboard player Andy Slater and guitarist Andy Bennett spent time working up a proposed project venture which ultimately transformed itself into a fresh and

near guitar absent 1998 HYBERNOID album 'Advanced Technology' for the German Visage label.

HYBERNOID disbanded during 1999. Andy Slater subsequently would industriously pursue a swathe of other musical projects such as ELECTRO DIESEL, SENSORIA and "Viking re-enactment" musical venture MUNIN'S WING.

Singles/EPs:
Dust In The Wind / Mind / Liberty, Displeased D-00026 (1993)
Technology / Regressions / Akeldama, Psycho Slaughter PS008 (1993)
World Of Ruin / Sear, Displeased D-00036 (1994)

Albums:
THE LAST DAY BEGINS?, Displeased D-00028 (1994)
Revery / Reality Wave / World Of Ruin / Ash In The Sky / Permafrost / Life Fade / Akeldema / Skin / Mind-Liberty
TODAY'S TOMORROW YESTERDAY, Displeased D-00042 (1996)
Dread The Time / Today's Tomorrow Yesterday / Menali / Strive To Convert / Skin III / Akelkama / Dust In The Wind / Mind-Liberty / World Of Ruin / Sear / When Two Lives
ADVANCED TECHNOLOGY, Visage (1998)
Prologue / Trapped / Recoil / Kullu / Eyewall / Chimera / Sentient Beings / Hideaway / Fiat Lux / Creed

HYPONIC (HONG KONG)
Line-Up: Roy (vocals / guitar), Kin (guitar), Mei Funn (bass)

Doom Death uniquely from Hong Kong. Frontman Roy performed drums on the self-financed May 2001 'Black Sun' album excepting 'The Last Track' credited to Kit.

Albums:
BLACK SUN, Hyponic (2001)
Labyrinth Of Ignorance / A False Legend / The Last Divine / Third / Vile / Black Sun / The Last Track

I FOUND GOD
(Los Angeles, CA, USA)
Line-Up: Christy Gerhart (vocals), Stress (guitar), Devin Kramer (bass), Todd Wyatt (drums)

The supremely heavy I FOUND GOD, commonly known simply as I.F.G., was assembled sometime during 1992, initially as a trio comprising guitarist Stress, vocalist Christy Gerhart and bassist Christian. Stress was also operating another act in parallel entitled DEAD GIRLFRIEND. The proposed drummer for this band, Todd Wyatt, would be enrolled into I FOUND GOD. Christian would then be asked to leave and a session man was brought in for demos. Soon after Devin Kramer, a member of yet another of Stress' side acts TEMPORARY INSANITY, took on bass duties.

A six song cassette dubbed 'Migraine', produced by Michael Ciravolo of CONGREGATION, arrived in 1993. Constructing their own record label with the Outcast imprint I FOUND GOD issued the debut album 'Lure' in 1995. This inaugural outing, displaying the band's thick Psychedelic Middle Eastern infused Sludge, reaped ecstatic reviews across Europe. During recording of a second album, 'Before He Turned The Gun On Himself', Devin Kramer decamped, performing his last gig with the band in August of 1996. Stress duly took on the bass mantle for the album sessions. Rich Florio would assume the four string role for recording of a 7" single 'Satan Claus'.

1998 brought about a radical series of line-up shuffles for I FOUND GOD. Todd Wyatt bowed out and Steve Markowitz would fill in on drums for a take of BLONDIE's 'Call Me' donated to the Cleopatra 'New Wave Goes To Hell' tribute record. Markowitz would also briefly gig with the band before permanent replacement Chris Morgeson was inducted. Florio was then ejected. This situation resolved itself eventually in Stress opting to take on bass full-time and new recruit Alan Brieder coming in on guitar.

A third album 'What Now?' was recorded, being licensed to the German Dream Circle label. However, this label subsequently went under and in this time of adversity Morgeson bailed out. Jeff Edwards became the band's latest drummer as I FOUND GOD signed to the Italian Adrenaline label. First product of this union was a cover version of U2's 'Hold Me, Thrill Me, Kiss Me Kill Me' for the homage album 'Pride'. Unfortunately further delays would result in the release date for 'What Now?' being pushed back no less than three times in succession. It eventually surfaced in 2001.

In an odd move I FOUND GOD contributed a swing piece to the blockbuster movie 'The Grinch'. Although included in the movie the track mysteriously failed to make the official soundtrack album.

A second 7" single was delivered in the form of 'Junkie Sex Monkey' in 2001 on the Deep Six label. This release paired the track 'Satellite' with a rendition of BLACK SABBATH's 'Symptom Of The Universe'. That year the group decided upon a subtle name switch to IFOUNDGOD.

2002 found the band occupied in crafting a fresh studio album provisionally billed as 'Hellhound On My Trail'.

Singles/EPs:
Blue Christmas / Just As Well, Outcast (1997) ('Satan Claus' EP)
Satellite / Symptom Of The Universe, Deep Six (2001) ('Junkie Sex Monkey' EP)

Albums:
LURE, Outcast OC CD001 (1995)
Glad I'm Not You / Disconnected / Sister / Junkie / On The Bottom / The Last Time / Take It / No More / Penny / Cryin' / Slow Crumble / Go To Hell / Nothing Works / Junkie (O.D. mix)
BEFORE HE TURNED THE GUN ON HIMSELF, Outcast OC 50002 (1996)
Find A Way (Benny's Song) / Bring You Down / I Don't Mind / Don't You Want To Hear / Seems To Me / Conspiracy / I Die / What You Wanted / Fade Away / Follow / Break You / Drowning / Reason / Soul Collector
WHAT NOW?, Adrenaline (2001)
Downtown Burning / Not Enough / Drive / Same As Ever / Never Come Down / Wake Up / Cannot Stop The Feelin' / Struggle / Come On / Crawl / Disarray / Summer's Gone / Just Another Day

INKUBUS SUKKUBUS (UK)
Line-Up: Candia Riley (vocals), Tony McKormack (guitar), Bob (bass)

Gloucestershire Gothic esoteric Folk Metallers with an enviable reputation for high quality albums infused with Wiccan and Paganist themes. The band was founded in 1989 as a trio of vocalist Candia Riley, guitarist Tony McKormack and Adam Henderson. Originally titled after a local ancient monument BELAS KNAP the band soon evolved into INCUBUS SUCCUBUS releasing the 7" single 'Beltaine'. Despite the high profile nature of this release the band splintered with Riley and McKormack

continuing as CHILDREN OF THE MOON.
By late 1991 the duo had resurrected
INCUBUS SUCCUBUS with the addition of
drummer Bob. Early material from the
CHILDREN OF THE MOON sessions was
issued as the debut INCUBUS SUCCUBUS
album 'Beltaine'. The band toured Britain
heavily promoting this and further releases
such as 1993's 'Belladonna And Aconite'
including dates with artists as diverse as
NOSFERATU, ZODIAC MINDWARP, THE
DAMNED and CLAWFINGER. The 1994
album 'Wytches', released on the Pagan
Media label, saw a distinct shift in musical
style. The album would quickly become a
much sought after rarity.
Promoting the 'Heartbeat Of The Earth' album
the band toured as guests to DANZIG and the
GENITORTURERS before dates at major
festivals in Germany. By 1995 the group
changed both their name, subtly to 'INKUBUS
SUKKUBUS', and their format to manouevre
Bob to bass to accommodate the inclusion of
a drum machine.
1996 had INKUBUS SUKKUBUS further
enhancing their status with showings on
British TV and further European touring. The
band also cut a version of 'Spellbound' for a
SIOUXSIE AND THE BANSHEES tribute
album.
Latterly INKUBUS SUKKUBUS have put in
their inaugural American shows and are
regulars at established Gothic festivals and
the Whitby Dracula events. INKUBUS
SUKKUBUS toured Britain with CRADLE OF
FILTH in 1999. The 2001 'Supernature' album,
the band's eighth, was promoted with
showings at the 'Gotham' festival in London
and the Reading 'Goth' event as headliners
and acting as support to MARILYN MANSON
at the 'M'era Luna' festival. Evidence of
continued growth in the band's fan base was
confirmed as 'Belladonna And Aconite' went
into its twelfth pressing to cope with demand
and the MP3.com exclusive track 'Vampirella'
witnessed massive download activity.

Albums:
BELLADONNA AND ACONITE,
Resurrection ABCD 7 (1993)
Beltaine / Midnight Queen / Trinity /
Belladonna And Aconite / Soul Inside / Song
Of The Siren / Vampyres / Eternity / Incubus
/ All The Devil's Men / I Am The One / Old
Hornie / Vlad / Samhain
WYTCHES, Pagan Media PMR CD7 (1994)
Wytches / Queen Of The May / Pagan Born /
Gypsy Lament / Leveller / Call Out My Name
/ Conquistadors / Burning Times / Song To
Pan / Enchantment / Catherine / Church Of
Madness / The Rape Of Maude Bowen /
Dark Mother / Devils

HEARTBEAT OF THE EARTH, Resurrection
ABCD 5 (1995)
Heartbeat Of The Earth / Young Lovers /
Underworld / Prince Of Shadows / Craft Of
The Wise / Corn King / Witch Hunt / Fire Of
Love / Love Spell / Song For Our Age /
Intercourse With The Vampire / Sabrina /
Catherine / Take My Hunger
BELTAINE, Resurrection ABCD 11 (1996)
Beltaine / Wytches I / Pagan Born / Song To
Pan / Goblin Jig / Midnight Queen / Trinity / I
Am The One / Vampyre Kiss / Wytches II /
Burning Times / The Leveller / Church Of
Madness / Wytches (Chant)
VAMPRYE EROTICA, Resurrection ABCD
17 (1997)
Heart Of Lilith / Woman To Hare / Hail The
Holly King / Wake Of The Christian Knights /
Paint It Black / All Along The Crooked Way /
The Witch Of Berkeley / Danse Vampyr /
Vampyre Erotica / Wild Hunt / Sweet
Morpheus / Hell-Fire / Whore Of Babylon
AWAY WITH THE FAERIES, Resurrection
ABCD 21 (1998)
Wytches Chant '98 / Away With The Faeries
/ Come To Me (Song Of The Water Nymph) /
Turnera / Starchild / Io Pan / Woman To Hare
/ Paint It Black / Craft Of The Wise /
Heartbeat Of The Earth / Witch Hunt /
Queen Of The May / Take My Hunger /
Vampyre Erotica / Belladonna And Aconite
WILD, Resurrection ABCD 24 (1999)
Rune / Wounded / Kiss Of Hades /
Struwwlpeter / Bright Star / Lord Of The
Flame / Aradia / Storm / Smile Of Torment /
Reptile / Nymphomania / Lammas Song /
Wild / Delilah
SUPERNATURE, Resurrection ABCD 26
(2001)
Supernature / Lucifer Rising / Take The Kiss
/ Fey / Hang Around / Concubine / Vermilion
Rush / Whore Of Heaven / Wings Of Desire
/ We Belong With The Dead / Preacher Man
/ Gypsies, Tramps & Thieves

INNER SHRINE (ITALY)
Line-Up: Luca Liotti (vocals / guitar), Cecilia
Boninsegni (vocals), Anna Vignozzi (vocals),
Leonardo Moretti (bass), Claudio Tovagli
(drums)

Gothic Metal from Florence featuring the
operatic singing of Cecilia Boninsegni and the
"mystic voices" of Anna Vignozzi.

Albums:
**NOCTURNAL RHYMES ENTANGLED IN
SILENCE**, Dragonheart (1997)
Fatum (Intro) / Dream On / The Last Breath /
Bleeding Tears By Candlelight (The Illusion
Of Hope Act I) / Awaiting The Solar

Awakening (The Illusion Of Hope Act II) /
Soliloqium In Darkness (The Illusion Of
Hope Act III) / Enveloped By A Conquest's
Shadow / Subsidence / Breaking The Mortal
Shell Of Love
FALLEN BEAUTY, Dragonheart (2000)
Sanguis Vitae / In The Garden Of Sadness /
Angelic Visions / Free In Emptiness /
Enlightened By Splendour / Symphony Of
The Absolute Bulwark / Passage To Eternity
/ The Inner Research Of The Shrine

INSANITY REIGNS SUPREME
(BELGIUM)
Line-Up: Criz Jamers (vocals), Ron Cotar
(guitar), Howard, Omer (bass), Christof,
Edward Jacobs (drums)

INSANITY REIGNS SUPREME issued a
1991 Death Metal flavoured promotion tape
but by the 1996 demo 'Our Path Is Dark And
Lonely' the band had adopted a definite
Doom Metal stance.
Drummer Edward Jacobs was previously with
TYPHOON.

Albums:
**...AND DARKNESS DROWNED THE LAND
DIVINE**, Teutonic (1997)
Trauma Paradise / The Bitter Kiss Of Death /
Finsternis / The Pain Eternal / In The Arms
Of Solitude / La Tristesse Eternelle / Burn
The Flame Of Sadness

INSIDER (ITALY)
Line-Up: Eugene Mucci (vocals), Marco
Ranalli (guitar), Pero Ranalli (bass /
keyboards), Giuseppe Miccoli (drums)

Psychedelic Stoners INSIDER started up in
1991 as a trio of CITY SEVEN SYSTEM men
Marco and Pero Ranalli and REQUIEM and
THE BLACK drummer Giuseppe Miccoli. The
latter would decamp shortly after recording
debut product, 1998's 'Land Of Crystals'. For
the Beard Of Stars 2000 EP 'Jammin' For A
Smiling God' EP the band drafted vocalist
Andrea Sestri whilst Pero Ranalli took over
programmed drum duties.

Singles/EPs:
Divine Breath / Falling Down / Blind And
Bloody Quietness / Jammin' For A Smiling
God, Beard Of Stars (2000) ('Jammin' For A
Smiling God' EP)

Albums:
LAND OF CRYSTALS, Dolmen Productions
(1998)

INTERNAL VOID (Frederick, MD, USA)
Line-Up: J.D. Williams (vocals), Kelly
Carmichael (guitar), Adam Heinzmann
(bass), Ronnie Kalimon (drums)

INTERNAL VOID, founded in August of 1987
and debuting with the demo recordings
'Smokestack' in 1989 and 'Voyage' in 1991,
first made their presence felt with two tracks
'Internal Void' and 'Nothing But Misery'
included on the 'What The Hell' compilation
issued by German Doom specialists
Hellhound. INTERNAL VOID subsequently
signed to Hellhound for the masterly 1992
album 'Standing On The Sun'. Nationwide
touring followed in league with the revered
SAINT VITUS before the demise of their label
signalled a lull in activity. Eric Little broke
ranks in the Autumn of 1993 and would later
re-emerge as part of Doomsters
EARTHRIDE, the band led by SPIRIT
CARAVAN's David Sherman.
Soldiering on with a plethora of short-term
sticksmen the band finally found a solid
replacement in 1995 when they drafted
Ronnie Kalimon, a veteran of
UNORTHODOX, ASYLUM and IRON MAN.
The band made a spirited return with the
Chris Kozlowski produced 'Unearthed' album
for Southern Lord in 2000. The record
included a cover version of 'After The Storm'
originally recorded by British Boogie
merchants STRAY.
The 1996 track 'Window To Hell' emerged as
a split single release with Italian cult icon
PAUL CHAIN.

Singles/EPs:
Window To Hell, Southern Lord (2000) (Split
single with PAUL CHAIN)

Albums:
STANDING ON THE SUN, Hellhound (1992)
Warhorse / Take A Look / The Peace Song /
Utopia Of Daze / Standing On The Sun /
Unclean Spirit / Devil In Drag / Eclipsed /
Line In The Sand / Desolate Cemetery
UNEARTHED, Southern Lord SUNN008
(2000)
With Apache Blood / Beyond Anger / Too Far
Gone / Pint Of Love / Seek The Truth /
Thoughts of Misconception / In A Bit Of Jam
/ Blindside / After the Storm / Closure /
Chapter 9

IN THE COLONNADES (SWEDEN)
Line-Up: Johan Petersson (vocals / bass),
Magnus Gehlin (guitar), Ingemar Sollgard
(guitar), Olle Borg (keyboards), Okke
Petersson (drums)

207

IN THE COLONNADES, Gothic Doom Rockers from Stockholm, were created in 1984 by ex-PLAST guitarist Magnus Gehlin and keyboard player Olle Borg. Lead vocalist Ulf Lennemann quit in 1993 necessitating bassist Johan Petersson taking over his duties.

IN THE COLONNADES contributed their cover version of BLACK SABBATH's 'Sabbath Bloody Sabbath' to the 1990 compilation album 'The Legacy'.

Singles/EPs:
Talk For An Hour / Black Soul / Beating / Kill The Sun / Fox Hill / Total Destruction, Joker ITC 610 (1986)
Wheels / Sort Of Heaven, Joker JOKE 712 (1987)
Fry day / War / REPO, Pale & Common PCR001 (1989)

Albums:
IN THE COLONNADES, Yellow (1989)
SCRAP METAL VALUE, CBR CBRCD 127 (1991)
N.D.E. / Fryday / Sexgun / Grind 'Em Down / Funeral Pyre / Pig After Pig / Birth Of A Nation / Sabbath Bloody Sabbath / This n' That
REST AND RECREATION, Accelerating Blue Fish ACC CD 25 (1995)
Time And Space / Chemical Hangman / Point Blank / No Remorse / A Citizens Lament / Red Sun Black Moon / Inside The Circle / Sick Is How I Feel / Rest And Recreation

IN THE WOODS (NORWAY)
Line-Up: Jan Ovl Svithjod (vocals), Oddvar A.M. (guitar), Christer C.H. Botteri (guitar), X. Botteri (bass), Anders Kobro (drums)

IN THE WOODS formed in 1992. Despite showing obvious quirks of originality even in their formative stage the group was often lumped in with the Black Metal crowd. The group's first commercially available demo, 'Isle Of Men', released the following year, gained a deal with British label Misanthropy Records. The band also re-released the band's demo in CD format. The band's debut single was a version of the '60s JEFFERSON AIRPLANE druggie classic 'White Rabbit'.

The Autumn of 1996 saw IN THE WOODS on the road in Europe with support from KATATONIA and VOICE OF DESTRUCTION. For the 1997 album 'Omnio' the band introduced a new guitarist in Bjoern Harstad. Vocalist Jan Ovl 'Overlord' Svithjod and guitarist Christer guested on the 1999 DRAWN album 'A New World'.

Drummer Anders Kobro also moonlights with CARPATHIAN FOREST and features as part of SCARIOT for their 2000 album 'Deathforlorn'.

IN THE WOODS twins guitarist Christer C.H. Botteri and bassist X. Botteri also feature on the GREEN CARNATION album 'Journey To The End Of Night'. The compilation 'Three Times Seven On A Pilgrimage' would mark the beginning of the end. IN THE WOODS performed their farewell gig in their hometown of Kristiansand on 29th of December 2000.

X BOTTERI issued a solo album 'Raining Gold'.

Singles/EPs:
White Rabbit / Mourning The Death Of Aase, Misanthropy (1996)

Albums:
HEART OF THE AGES, Misanthropy AMAZON 004 (1995)
Yearning The Seeds Of A New Dimension / (HE) Art Of The Ages / ...In The Woods / Mourning The Death Of Aase / Wotan's Return / Pigeon / The Divinity Of Wisdom
A RETURN TO THE ISLE OF MEN, Hammerheart HHR 007 (1996)
The Wings Of My Dreamland / Tell De Dode / In The Woods... / Creations Of An Ancient Shape / Wotan's Return / Heart Of The Ages / ... And All This... (Child Of Universal Tongue)
OMNIO, Misanthropy AMAZON 011 (1997)
299 796 kms / I Am Your Flesh / Kairos! / Weeping Willow / Omnio? (Pre- Bardo- Post)
THREE TIMES SEVEN ON A PILGRIMAGE, Prophecy Productions (2000)
Seed Of Sound / Karmakosmic / Epitaph / Empty Room / Let There Be More Light / Child Of Universal Tongue / Soundtrax For Cycoz (1st Ed) / White Rabbit / Mourning The Death Of Aase / If It's In You

INTO THE ABYSS (GERMANY)
Line-Up: Janis Kalifatidis (vocals / guitar), Kostas Tzeras (bass), Jens Gellner (drums)

A band from Darmstadt mixing Gothic and Progressive Rock with Heavy Metal, frontman Janis Kalifatidis is one of the leading players in the German Rock scene and is the publisher of the fanzine 'Fight Amnesia'.

Singles/EPs:
Dragon's Snake (The Crimson Version), Moonbean 10" 005 (1995)

Albums:
MARTYRIUM, Spectre 084-25232 (1993)
Martyrs / Banner Of The Fray / Just Another

IRON BOSS

Voice... / (War) Against Their Will / Research Without Conscience / Dumb Crutches / Madman / Swingin' Scythe
THE FEATHERED SNAKE, Glasnost GLASS 33 (1995)
Whirl Of The Aeons / Resignation To The Void / Crimes In Advance / The Eternal Heat / La Sceur D'Icare / Captivity / Dragon Snake / Flight Of Quetzalcoatl / Carousel

INTRA-VENUS (UK)
Line-Up: Apollos (vocals), Mark Tansley (guitar)

Gothic act INTRA-VENUS was created by former SUSPERIA guitarist Mark Tansley.

Singles/EPs:
Martyrs EP, Nightbreed (2000)

IRONBOSS (Baltimore, MD, USA)
Line-Up: Chris Roten (vocals / guitar), Metal Mark Crocco (guitar), Dave Waugh (bass), Patrick Kennedy (drums)

Thundering Doom from the foot of the Catoctin and Allegheny mountains. IRONBOSS are led by the daunting figure of professional moto cross driver Chris Roten, a man who proudly wears the scars of over 50 bone breakages and plays guitar despite losing part of a finger. Bassist Dave Waugh is an internationally renowned tattoo artist whilst guitarist 'Metal' Mark Crocco is rarely seen without a retro '70s Heavy Metal T shirt.
IRONBOSS debuted with a track 'Turning' on the 'Hot Rock Action Volume 2' compilation single alongside STINKING LIZAVETA, DEADFALL and MOTOCASTER. Next release was 7" single 'Bullethole', which naturally, included a real bullet hole in the picture sleeve. The 'Age Of Gasoline' album, released in Europe through V&V Productions followed and the following year a novel split 7" record shared with the notorious Texan outfit HONKY, actually a side venture of BUTTHOLE SURFERS man Jeff Pinkus. For this release both bands contribute takes on classic VAN HALEN tunes, IRONBOSS delivering 'Everybody Wants Some'. IRONBOSS donated their version of AC/DC's seminal 'Whole Lotta Rosie' to the 1999 tribute album 'Hell Ain't A Bad Place To Be' and that of 'Train Kept A Rollin' to the Smallstone Records 2000 AEROSMITH tribute collection 'Right In The Nuts'.
The 2000 album 'Ironboss Rides Again' piqued the interest of collectors with a total of three different territorial sleeve designs. Releases in North America through Reptilian, Europe via Twenty Stone Blatt and Australia

on Out Of The Loop were all clad in alternate sleeves. The Australian version also came packaged with a free 'Live In Belgium' bonus disc. The Reptilian Records 2001 re-release of 'Ironboss Rides Again' included three extra tracks, a live version of the CACTUS classic 'Rumblin' Man', an acoustic version of 'Angus' dubbed 'Malcolm' and 'Sunshine On My Knife'.
The 2002 compilation 'Roll Out The Rock' proved of note for the inclusion of rare singles tracks, demos and unreleased material.
IRONBOSS established their own label, Iron Empire Worldwide', for projected live bootleg releases. Quite surreally as well as promoting their music IRONBOSS offer both tattooing services and furniture constructed from car parts!

Singles/EPs:
Bullethole / Movin' To Texas, Reptilian REP 017 (1997)
Everybody Wants Some, Thick THK-059 (1998) (Split 7" picture disc with HONKY)
Motorcycle Man / Thinkin' Problem, Underdogma (2000) (Red vinyl)

Albums:
AGE OF GASOLINE, V&V Productions (1997)
Outlaw / No Revolution / Last Inning / New Song / Walk / Eyes Fer Killin' / Edge Of Life / One Man / Goat / Bleedin' Heart / Get Outta My Way / Age Of Gasoline
IRONBOSS RIDES AGAIN, Twenty Stone Blatt (2000)
Motherfucker / Give Me The Rose / Run Fast, Jump High & Die / My Jesus / Hot Shoe / Angus / Brass Pin / Eco Freak's Nightmare / Ride Again / Baja / Hell Ride
GUNS DON'T KILL PEOPLE - IRONBOSS DOES, Underdogma IE-02 (2001)
Theme From Ironboss / Foghat / Motherfucker / Chrome And Gold / Run Fast, Jump High And Die / Pussy On The Corner / Hung Like Horses / Low Man / Bad Motherfuckers / Motorcycle Man
ROLL OUT THE ROCK - SINGLES 1995 - 2001, Underdogma (2002)
Intro / Bad Motherfuckers / Movin' To Texas / Rumblin' Man / Sunshine On My Knife / Whole Lotta Rosie / Turnin' / Crocco Vs. Schenker / Motorcycle Man / Thinkin' Problem / Motherfucker / Dirty Rotten Stinkin' Fuck / My Jesus / Everybody Wants Some / Give Me The Rose / Bullethole / Train Kept A' Rollin' / Ironboss / Go, Go, Go / Eyes For Killin' / Roll Out The Rock

IRON GIANT (CANADA)
Line-Up: Chris Lewis (vocals), Derek

Robichaud (guitar), Patrick Dunphy (bass), John Flanagan (drums)

Toronto Stoners IRON GIANT, founded in 2000, include two former members of THE MONOXIDES.

Albums:
NO LONGER SLEEPING, 12th Planet Music (2002)
Take Her Down / Mississippi / Road To Nowhere / Blown Away / On And On / Sexist Cliché / Long / Way Back From Heaven / Battle Never Ending / Buzzkiller / In Shadows

IRON KIND (Centennial, CO, USA)
Line-Up: Conan Hultgren (vocals), Jeff Montoya (guitar), Keith Sanchez (guitar), Tony Comulada (bass), Haraldo Mardones (drums)

Colorado Boogie-Doom band IRON KIND is fronted by Conan Hultgren, known for his endeavours with the specialist Doom label Game Two. IRON KIND, comprising former members of BEREAVEMENT, CATHETER and REFORM CONTROL amongst others, issued a live recorded four track demo during 2001.

IRON LUNG (NJ, USA)

Although a Metal band in the Retro-Doom tradition IRON LUNG are in fact an evolvement from Hardcore outfit SOCIAL DISEASE. Bassist and founder Josh Barohn is an ex-member of both SUFFOCATION and AUTOPSY.

Albums:
CHASING SALVATION, Progress (1997)
Far To Late / Jinx / Chasing Salvation / Tolerance / Dying / Reality Check / Sunblock / Birdman

IRON MAN (Maryland, USA)
Line-Up: Rob Levey (vocals), Al Morris III (guitar), Larry Brown (bass), Gary Isom (drums)

BLACK SABBATH fixated multi-racial band of high repute. Initially founded in as FORCE, releasing a 4 track EP, in 1988 band members decided to operate purely as a BLACK SABBATH tribute band. Some five years of touring across America led to the realization that there was a market for an album of Sabbath inspired originals. IRON MAN recorded for the cult yet ill-fated German Doom label Hellhound Records. The debut March 1993 'Black Night' album featured vocalist Rob Levey, guitarist Al Morris III, bassist Larry Brown and drummer Ron Kalimon. Promotion included a West Coast tour in alliance with CATHEDRAL and PENTEGRAM.

With 'Black Night' having generated enthusiastic media and fan response demos were cut for a second album but Hellhound rejected them, insisting the band obtain a new vocalist. Levey was supplanted by New Yorker Dan Michalek for the October 1995 sophomore effort 'The Passage' which also witnessed Gary Isom as the band's new drummer. The rhythm section underwent another overhaul prior to the third album 'Generation Void', released by the Brainticket label in 1999. New recruits this time were female bassist Ginger and drummer Vic Tomaso.

Gary Isom joined SPIRIT CARAVAN, led by former ST. VITUS and THE OBSESSED man Wino. Ron Kalimon journeyed through ASYLUM and UNORTHODOX before teaming up with INTERNAL VOID in 1995.

Rob Levey is well respected on the scene as the driving force behind the 'Stoner Hands Of Doom' festivals.

Albums:
BLACK NIGHT, Hellhound (1993)
Choices / The Liar / Black Night / Leaving Town / Life After Death / Life's Toll / A Child's Future / Vampires / Time For Change / Why Can't You See Me?
THE PASSAGE, Hellhound (1995)
The Fury / Unjust Reform / The Gargoyle / Harvest Of Earth / The Passage / Iron Warrior / Freedom Fighters / Waiting For Tomorrow / Time Of Indecision / Tony Stark / End Of The World
GENERATION VOID, Brainticket (1999)
On The Mountain / Boston Strangler / Survivor / King Of Kings / Winds Of Change / Generation Void / As The Gods Have Spoken / Ironica Blue / Forever Yours / Shadows Of Darkness / Juggernaut

IRON MONKEY (UK)
Line-up: Johnny Morrow (vocals), Jim Rushby (guitar), Dean Berry (guitar), Doug Dalziel (bass), Justin Greaves (drums)

Short-lived Nottingham controversial Sludgecore exponents named after an Asian mythical martial arts hero. Not only did the band push all known parameters musically but also Johnny Morrow's 'vocal' style proved uniquely disturbing. IRON MONKEY drew massive media attention by way of their 1998 'Iron Monkey' mini-album. Originally released by the Union Mill label the record, which saw

Steve Watson on guitar, was later reissued by Earache.

The full length 'Our Problem' album arrived via Earache Records in 1999 and had Watson substituted by Dean Berry. Both releases would be produced by erstwhile SABBAT and GODSEND guitarist Andy Sneap. The latter, which opened up with a mind numbing twenty minute track, caused furore over its grossly obscene cover art by Mike Diana. According to reports Diana's work had attracted itself to the band when they had learned the artist had served time for the lurid nature of previous paintings.

During the course of their brief existence guitarist Jim Rushby would be replaced by Stuart O'Hara. After a swan song 10" EP for the Man's Ruin label the group imploded. During a tour of Europe in June of 1999 vocalist John Morrow fell seriously ill. The remainder of the band persevered, completing the tour as a purely instrumental combo and re-dubbing themselves THE DUKES OF NOTHING. The full line-up of IRON MONKEY bowed out with a farewell gig at Nottingham Rock City in September of 1999.

Former IRON MONKEY man bassist Steve Watson created a new act, HELVIS, in 1997 together with ex-ACRIMONY member Dorian Walters on vocals, former PITCHSHIFTER guitarist Stewart Toolin, ex-BIVOUAC guitarist Matthew Grundy and ex-CONSUMED drummer Chris Billam.

Guitarist Dean Berry and bass player Doug Dalziel teamed up with ORANGE GOBLIN's Chris Turner and ex-ACRIMONY and FABRIC members for live gigs reactivating the band title of THE DUKES OF NOTHING. This outfit released the 'War & Wine' debut album in February of 2002.

Ex-IRON MONKEY men vocalist Johnny Morrow, guitarist Jim Rushby and drummer Justin Greaves forged ARMOUR OF GOD in league with Sean of HARD TO SWALLOW (a unit which also figured Greaves and Rushby) and Marvin from the VARUKERS and CHAOS UK.

Greaves would also figure in the 2001 combo TEETH OF LIONS RULE DIVINE, a bona fide Stoner Rock 'supergroup' fronted by CATHEDRAL mainman Lee Dorrian on vocals along with BURNING WITCH's Steve O'Malley and GOATSNAKE's Greg Anderson. During December vocalist John Morrow had announced his new act MURDER ONE, a confederation between erstwhile MEDULLA NOCTE, LABRAT and CHARGER personnel. However, tragically Morrow died from kidney complications at the age of 28 in June of 2002. The singer had been on dialysis and awaiting a kidney transplant.

Singles/EPs:
Arsonaut / Kiss Of Death / Sleep To Win, Man's Ruin (1999) ('We've Leaned Nothing' EP)

Albums:
IRON MONKEY, Earache (1997)
Fink Dial / Web Of Piss / Big Loader / 666 Pack / Black Aspirin / Shrimp Fist
OUR PROBLEM, Earache MOSH207 (1999)
Bad Year / Supaorganizer / Boss Keloid / I.R.M.S. / House Anxiety / 2 Golden Rules / 9 Joint Spiritual Whip

IRONSIDE (UK)
Line-Up: Richard Armitage (vocals), James Rushby (guitar), Clive Hughes (guitar), Douglas Dalziel (bass), Sean Steels (drums)

Bradford based Doom Metallers. Drummer Sean Steels joined SOLSTICE in early 1995.

Singles/EPs:
Fragments Of The Last Judgement, Subjugation (1993)
A Woman / The House Will Perish, Stormstrike SSR003 (1994)

ISIS (Boston, MA, USA)
Line-Up: Cliff Meyer (vocals / programming), Aaron Turner (guitar), Mike Gallagher), Jeff Caxide (bass), Aaron Harris (drums)

Firmly in the Sabbathian Doom camp Boston's ISIS, mentored by Aaron Turner also responsible for the esteemed Hydrahead label, impressed mightily with the crushing 'Celestial' outing. The band, which included erstwhile members of LOGA, CABLE and UNION SUIT, had gelled in 1997 around Turner and a rhythm section comprising bassist Jeff Caxide and drummer Aaron Harris. Later Personnel came in the form of second guitarist Mike Gallagher and vocalist Cliff Meyer.

The group made a forcible entry upon the scene with the 1998 'Mosquito Control' EP. Electronics for this release would be supplied by Chris Merechuk. A follow up EP 'Red Sea' boasted keyboards courtesy of AGORAPHOBIC NOSEBLEED's Jay Randall.

The 'Celestial' album made for disconcerting listening fracturing monolithic slabs of twin guitar Doom hung together with eerie 'SGNL' drone passages. The double vinyl version of 'Celestial' would come lavishly packaged with an elaborate gatefold sleeve complete with multiple inserts. The records themselves would come pressed in red and beige marbled heavyweight vinyl.

Turner and other ISIS members also became embroiled in the HOUSE OF LOW CULTURE project in 2000. Resulting in an album 'Submarine Immersion Techniques' for the Crowd Control Activities label, HOUSE OF LOW CULTURE also involved James Plotkin and Stephen O'Malley of ATOMSMASHER and Jay Randall from AGORAPHOBIC NOSEBLEED. ISIS musicians also figure in a further side venture dubbed OLD MAN GLOOM in collaboration with CAVE IN and CONVERGE members. OLD MAN GLOOM's output includes the 'Seminar II: The Holy Rites Of Primitivism Regressionism' and 'Seminar III: Zozobra' albums.

The 2001 ISIS EP 'SGNL>05', which found ISIS drifting into more melancholic and even ambient pastures, included a remix of 'Celestial (Signal Fills The Void)' by Justin Broadrick of GODFLESH. The EP would see CD variants on the Neurot label with vinyl delivered through the Tortuga imprint. Promotion on the road came with North American June 2001 dates allied with SOILENT GREEN and further August shows with Swiss band KNUT.

ISIS has also issued ultra scarce releases in the form of a split EP with PIG DESTROYER and a Tortuga Recordings EP of BLACK SABBATH and GODFLESH covers.

During 2002 ISIS signed to the Ipecac label, owned by former FAITH NO MORE frontman Mike Patton and Greg Werckman of Alternative Tentacles repute, for a new studio album 'Oceanic'. That same year Turner was working up a fresh band project with former CAVITY guitarist Ryan Weinstein.

Singles/EPs:
Poison Eggs / Life Under the Swatter / Hive Destruction / Relocation Swarm, Escape Artist (1998) ('Mosquito Control' EP)
Charmicarmicat Shines To Earth / The Minus Times / Red Sea, Second Nature (1999) ('Red Sea' EP)
Streetcleaner, Relapse (2000) (Split EP with PIG DESTROYER)
SGNL>05 (Final Transmission) / Divine Mother (The Tower Crumbles) / Beneath Below / Constructing Towers / Celestial (Signal Fills The Void) (Justin K. Broadrick remix), Neurot (2001) ('SGNL>05' EP)

Albums:
CELESTIAL, Escape Artist (2000)
SGNL>1 / Celestial (The Tower) / Glisten / Swarm Reigns (Down) / SGNL>2 / Deconstructing Towers / SGNL>3 Collapse And Crush / CFT (New Circuitry and Continued Evolution) / Gentle Time / SGNL>4 (End Transmission)

OCEANIC, Ipecac (2002)
The Beginning And The End / The Other / False Light / Carry / - / Maritime / Weight / From Sinking / Hym

JACK FROST (AUSTRIA)
Line-Up: Phred Phinster (vocals / bass), Mournful Morales (guitar), Gary Gloom (guitar), Collossos Rossos (drums)

Doom-laden triumvirate, noted not only for their depressingly dirgeful music but their ability to imbibe huge quantities of alcohol, forged in Linz during 1992. Earlier vocalist Manfred Klahre and guitarist Robert Hackl had assembled a band during 1989. However, the first rehearsal was made all the more memorable when afterward Klahre, in an acknowledged drunken state, was pulled up by the police and duly lost his driving license!
In 1993 drummer Martin Kollross and a "nameless" bass player joined the group. With the anonymous four stringer's departure later that same year Klahre took on bass duties as the band then titled itself JACK FROST. Following a brace of demos 'Wish' and 1995's 'Maelstrom' JACK FROST signed with CCP Records for the debut 'Eden' album, recorded in a mere 5 days. The band put in a release party for the record in the city of Linz, sharing the evening with Japanese act ZENI GERA. A later support gig to American Doom vets SOLITUDE AETURNUS would turn in the band's favour as John Perez from the headline act offered to distribute JACK FROST albums through his own Brainticket Records.
1996 found JACK FROST putting in a showing at the Bietingham 'German Doom' festival. Unfortunately for the band their set was less than their best, being obviously drunk and then to make matters worse released as a commercial video! Better news came with the release of second album 'Elsewhere', an album which completely sold out of its pressing.
Touring throughout 1997 saw JACK FROST as guests to CRADLE OF FILTH's Austrian dates. The band would also appear at the Linz 'Autumn Twilight' festival alongside NAEVUS,

END OF GREEN and MIRROR OF DECEPTION. A short tour in alliance with MIRROR OF DECEPTION would then ensue. A third album 'Glow Of A Dying Sun' arrived in 1999, their last for CCP Records.
For the 2000 album, 'Gloom Rock Asylum', released by Last Episode Records and mastered by ATROCITY's Alex Krull, JACK FROST members all adopted stage names. Drummer Martin Kollross became 'Collossos Rossos', whilst the rest of the band comprised 'Phred Phinster' on vocals and bass with guitarists 'Mournful Morales' and 'Gary Gloom', the latter a new inductee pulled from Austrian Hardcore veterans STAND TO FALL.
2001 saw further road action as in March JACK FROST toured in league with British Doomsters WARNING and in November alongside LEGACY OF HATE. A new deal was then struck with Napalm Records offshoot label Wait & Bleed for a projected June 2002 album billed as 'Self Abusing Uglysex Ungod'.

Albums:
EDEN, CCP 100140-2 (1995)
Bleed / Into Oblivion / My Silent Brother / I Descent / Doomride / Room Of Light / False Gods / Exit… To Eden
ELSEWHERE, CCP 100158-2 (1997)
Rise / Embedded / Shadowplay / Sentenced / Sleepless / Nightfall / Elsewhere / …And Our Faces Wither
GLOW OF A DYING SUN, CCP 100194-2 (1999)
Dark Ages / Crawl / Undying / Black Veil Torn / Queen Jack / Dive / Everstoned / Lady In Black
GLOOM ROCK ASYLUM, Serenades SR024 (2000)
Sober / You Are The Cancer / How Will I Sleep / In Gloom / Psychodrome / Sink / California Dreamin' / Beyond The Rubicon
SELF ABUSING UGLYSEX UNGOD, Wait & Bleed WAB006 (2002)
Mother Mary Sleeps With Me / One Hundred Percent Pain / Unseen Insane I / The Dance / Some You / Last Monday / It All Means Nothing To Me / El Funeral Del Dictator

J.J. PARADISE PLAYERS CLUB
(Brooklyn, NY, USA)
Line-Up: Dave Curran (vocals / bass), Joel Hamilton (guitar), Eric Cooper (guitar), James Paradise (drums)

A Brooklyn based Riff Rock amalgam of members culled from acts such as KISS IT GOODBYE, UNSANE, KILL VAN KULL, GLAZED BABY and SHINER. The group was

JACK FROST
Photo : Markus Vehle

214

formulated in early 2000 by ex-UNSANE vocalist / bassist Dave Curran, guitarist Joel Hamilton of GLAZED BABY, second guitarist Eric Cooper from KISS IT GOODBYE and KILL VAN KULL sticksman James Paradise. The limited edition 7" single 'Teddy Salad' sees a B side cover version of 'Never In My Life', originally by MOUNTAIN.

Singles/EPs:
Teddy Salad / Never In My Life, Tee Pee (2001)
Beware The Ides Of Moose / House Of Torment / No / The Smeller, Tee Pee (2001)

Albums:
WINE COOLER BLOWOUT, Tee Pee (2001) Stash Panties / Teddy Salad / Beware The Ides Of Moose / Rubber Inner-Tubes / Toppler / Robot Shaft In Acid Canyon / House Of Torment / Wine Cooler Blowout / B-Boy Rib / Linden Bulletvard / Spoiler vs. Trailblazer

JONES LOUNGE (USA)

In the summer of 2002 Kyle Thomas, frontman for DRIP, EXHORDER and FLOODGATE, revealed the details of a brand new band project entitled JONES'S LOUNGE. His compatriots in this endeavour comprised Dax Thieler of GREEN LEAF CULT, Jimmy Bower of DOWN, CORROSION OF CONFORMITY, SUPERJOINT RITUAL and EYEHATEGOD as well as Jason Portera from PITS VS. PREPS. A debut JONES'S LOUNGE album would see production handled by former UGLY KID JOE guitarist Dave Fortman.
In August the band would be joined by SOILENT GREEN drummer Tommy Buckley, a former comrade of Thomas's in the mid '90s act DRIP.

JOSIAH (UK)
Line-Up: Matt (vocals / guitar), Sie (bass), Chris (drums)

Singles/EPs:
Head On / Malpaso / Spacequake / Sweet Smoke / Black Maria, Cargo (2001) ('Out Of The First Rays' EP)

JPT SCARE BAND (USA)
Line-Up: Terry Swope (vocals / guitar), Paul Grigsby (bass), Jeff Littrell (drums)

A '70s power combo whose early jam recordings are now held in high regard. The 'Past Is Prologue' album comprises tracks spanning three decades including a brand new 2001 recording.

Albums:
SLEEPING SICKNESS, Monster (2000) Sleeping Sickness / Slow Sick Shuffle / King Rat / It's Too Late / Acid Acetate Excursion / I've Been Waiting / Time To Cry
PAST IS PROLOGUE, Electric House Music (2001)
Burn in Hell / I've Been Waiting / Wino / Sleeping Sickness / Time to Cry / Titan's Sirens / Jerry's Blues / It's Too Late

JUGGERNAUT (MN, USA)
Line-Up: Mark Stone (vocals), Danny Wistrcill (guitar), Eric Fratzke (bass), Dan Haney (drums)

Minnesota's JUGGERNAUT delivered an album of prime Stoner years before its time. Bassist Eric Fratzke was later spotted as a member of the avant-garde AUTO BODY EXPERIENCE and Jazz act HAPPY APPLE.

Singles/EPs:
Deliverance / Bitter / The Gift / The Vibe, (1993)

Albums:
BLACK PAGODA, Noise N 0215-2 (1994) Shedding / Bitter / Decide / Difference / Green Lightning / I.Q. / Reality Easel / Whisper / Make It So Hard / Machine / Cry Me A River / Master Of Pricks / Searching For A Better High

KAPTAIN SUN (SWEDEN)
Line-Up: Anders Håkansson (vocals / guitar), Andreas Svensson (guitar), Rickard Gustafsson (bass), Marcus Hamrin (drums)

Karlsham's KAPTAIN SUN made their first impressions billed as CLANDESTINE, an act that was created in 1993 with a line-up comprising vocalist / guitarist Anders Håkansson, guitarist Martin Lindholm, bass player Rickard Gustafsson and drummer Marcus 'Mackie' Hamrin. With a progression of line-up changes CLANDESTINE's musical approach began to shift away from earlier Doom influences into more '70s vibes.

Lindholm bade his farewell in late 1997, being replaced by Martin Fairbanks the following January. This latest recruit's tenure lasted until November of that year when Andreas Svensson took on the role. Around this juncture the band opted for a fresh title of KAPTAIN SUN and laid down demo recordings in 1999. The opening 'Trip To Vortex' album, praised for its union of trad Metal riffs and Stoner infusions, was culled from the earlier demo tapes and issued by the British Rage Of Achilles label.

Further demo sessions, billed as 'Back From The Vortex', surfaced in 2001. KAPTAIN SUN made a new track 'Cosmic Magic From The Doomed Planets Below' available for internet download in 2002.

Albums:
TRIP TO VORTEX, Rage Of Achilles ILIAD004 (2000)
Trip To Vortex / Restless Case / Kaptain Sun / Hypnotical Kiss / Final Fantasy / Marmalade Sky

KARI (NORWAY)

Adopting simply her first name for her first solo release, THE 3RD AND THE MORTAL vocalist Kari Rueslåtten quit the Norwegian outfit after recording the 'Sorrow' and 'Tears Laid In Earth' albums to pursue a solo career with roots lying somewhere in her Norwegian Folk influences.

Her first 1995 album 'Demo Recordings' was produced with the help of Swedish based Megarock Records, but released on Kari's own label and available through mail order. With Kari's later success this album would be reissued by the Sycamore label in 1997.

Flame haired Kari was also involved in the Folk project STORM. For the 'Nordavind' album KARI would work with some of Norway's premier Black Metal musicians

including Gylve Nagel, a.k.a. 'Fenriz' of DARKTHRONE, and Sigurd Wongraven, better known as 'Satyr' of SATYRICON.

The singer would land a deal with the major Sony Music label in March of 1996. The first fruits of this liaison would be the well received 'Spindelsinn' ("Fully") opus of January 1997. 'Mesmerized', recorded in English language, followed in October of 1998. KARI's touring band for 1998 comprised guitarist Geir Sundstøl, bass player Malika Rasmussen and drummer Trond Augland.

A new album, 'Pilot', emerged through the Peach Music label in 2002.

Albums:
DEMO RECORDINGS 1995, KR PR CD1 (1995)
The Homecoming Song / Vakenatt / The Gathering / Rapunsel / Forsaken / The Shadowchant / In Here / Dead / In A Day
SPINDELSINN, Columbia COL 487304-2 (1997)
I Månens Favn / Spindelsinn / Skogens Kjole / Agatha / Trollferd / Vintersol / Jeg Kommer Inn / Hør Min Sang / Som Av Meg / Nordnatt
MEZMERISED, Columbia COL 492596-2 (1998)
My Lover / All You Had In Me / Different Angle / Balcony Boulevard / Happy. Amused / Cinderella / Make Me A Stone / Borrowing You / «Little Low» / Images Of You / Paint My Wings
PILOT, Peach Music (2002)
Calling You / River / Never Fly Away / Denial / Snow / Exile / Pilot / Smile In Your Sleep / Leaving / Beautiful Morning / Love I Gave / Butterfly-Milk

KARMA TO BURN (WV, USA)
Line-Up: William Mecum (vocals / guitar), Rich Mullins (bass), Rob Oswald (drums)

West Virginians KARMA TO BURN's career, although high profile and certainly delivering musically, has been blighted by line-up problems. Frontman William Mecum had made his first forays into the world of Rock n' Roll with the band ADMIRAL, an outfit that included in its ranks future CROWHATE RUIN and HOOVER man Joseph McRedmond. ADMIRAL issued a solitary 7" three track single 'Brother Can You Spare A Dime?' in 1990.

Mecum would become the guitarist for RED OAK SOCIAL CLUB, an act also comprising frontman J.C. Belial, bassist Orville Weal and drummer Nathan Limbaugh. Substituting Belial for singer Curtis Duhn the band evolved into RED OAK CONSPIRACY, recording the demo tape 'Twelve Songs Amounting To

Nothing'.
Subsequently Mecum and Limbaugh, together with bassist Rich Mullins, founded KARMA TO BURN. Early stages of the band briefly saw the inclusion of a second guitar player Jim Davison. Former LEECH vocalist Karim Chatila joined up in 1994 but only lasted a matter of months before opting out and going on to found LEBHEAD. Undaunted, KARMA TO BURN cut a demo in 1995, already using the soon to be familiar numbers as song titles, and signed to the Roadrunner label, recording an entirely instrumental album. The label refused to release it until the band located a singer. During 1997 the band pulled in KYUSS man John Garcia but his tenure lasted a mere twelve gigs, the group concerned that Garcia's influence was too Metal orientated. Reportedly erstwhile guitarist Jim Davison was invited to record vocal tracks for the album but this projected union also evaporated. Eventually the eponymous debut was recorded using singer Jason 'J.J.' Jarosz. The record featured a twisted version of JOY DIVISION's '24 hours'. Just before 'Karma To Burn's' release the band switched drummers, drafting Chuck Nicholas of CHUM. This revised unit fronted by Jarosz actually performed a run of gigs before the singer was given his marching orders. Tour dates in Europe ensued, including an appearance at the Dutch 'Dynamo' festival where John Garcia, there with his new act SLO BURN, put in an impromptu vocal spot. Throughout August and September KARMA TO BURN was on the road in the USA opening for CORROSION OF CONFORMITY, DRAIN and CLUTCH.
Rumours abounded as the band split away from Roadrunner Records. Press reports suggested a fresh album billed as 'Nino Brown' with John Garcia on vocals. Nicholas broke away and Rob Oswald took on the drumming responsibilities. Although the mooted union with Garcia failed to materialize the band undertook further instrumental shows, selling an exclusive self-financed EP at gigs. February of 1999 had the band backing QUEENS OF THE STONE AGE on Midwest dates.
The sophomore album 'Wild, Wonderful... Purgatory' would unpatriotically take its title as a pun on the West Virginia state motto 'Wild, Wonderful West Virginia'. KARMA TO BURN's British shows in late 1999 were supported by RAGING SPEEDHORN.
Upfront of the release of the 'Almost Heathen' album, released by the Spitfire label, reprised the group's wry sense of humour when it came to their home state, this time spoofing another well known State motto 'Almost

Heaven'. The summer found the band criss-crossing North America with CORROSION OF CONFORMITY and SPEEDEALER before support shows to both ANTHRAX and CLUTCH. KARMA TO BURN then paired up with SIXTY WATT SHAMAN for European gigs in December of 2001.
The band announced plans to cut a new album for Spitfire during 2002, mooting the prospect of utilizing guest vocalists. Apparently those that had offered their services include CORROSION OF CONFORMITY's Pepper Keenan and Burton C. Bell of FEAR FACTORY. Founder member Rich Mullins joined SPEEDEALER in April casting doubt on the tenability of KARMA TO BURN's future.

Singles/EPs:
1 / 3 / 7 / 8, (1996) ('Wild, Wonderful & Apocalyptic' EP)
Ma Petite Mort / Bobbi, Bobbi, Bobbi - I'm Not God / Twenty Four Hours, Roadrunner RR 215 (1997) (Promotional release)

Albums:
KARMA TO BURN, Roadrunner RR 8862-2 (1997)
Waltz Of The Playboy Pallbearers / Bobbi, Bobbi, Bobbi... I'm Not God / Patty Hearst's Closet Mantra / Mt. Penetrator / Eight / Apalachian Woman / 24 Hours / Six Gun Sucker Punch / Thirteen Six / Ma Petite Mort / Twin Sisters And A Half Bottle Of Bourbon
WILD, WONDERFUL... PURGATORY, Roadrunner (1999)
Twenty / Twenty Eight / Thirty / Thirty One / Twenty Nine / Thirty Two / Twenty Five / Twenty Six / One / Three / Seven / Eight
ALMOST HEATHEN, Spitfire 5203-2 (2001)
Nineteen / Thirty Eight / Thirty Four / Thirty Seven / Thirty Nine / Thirty Six / Thirty Three / Thirty Five / Five / Forty

KATATONIA (SWEDEN)
Line-Up: Sombreius Blackheim (vocals / guitar), Israphel Wing (bass), Lord Seth (drums)

Celebrated propagators of ambitious melancholic Doom-Death. KATATONIA started life as a duo of guitar Sombreius Blackheim (real name Anders Nyström) and vocalist / drummer Lord Seth (real name Jonas Renske) in 1987. The group issued the 1992 demo 'JHVA Elohim Meth' which was later released in CD form by Dutch label Vic Records.
In late 1992 KATATONIA added bassist Israphael Wing (real name Guillaume Le Hucke) signing to No Fashion Records.

KATATONIA
Photo : Harry Vallmaki

218

In addition to the material listed below the band have also contributed two tracks ('Black Erotica' and 'Love Of The Swan') to the Wrong Again Records compilation album 'W.A.R.' in 1995. Further recordings of interest included a split 7" EP with PRIMORDIAL the following year.

Blackheim also has a side project band titled BEWITCHED releasing the 'Diabolical Desecration' album on Osmose Records in 1996. Seth would also be working on his OCTOBER TIDE project.

KATATONIA performed a short British tour in late 1996 with support acts IN THE WOODS and VOICE OF DESTRUCTION.

Blackheim and Seth also pursue another Death Metal project titled DIABOLICAL MASQUERADE. In 2000 the pair forged Black Metal project act BLOODBATH with EDGE OF SANITY's industrious Dan Swanö and OPETH's Mikael Akerfeldt.

The 2001 KATATONIA 'Teargas' EP, whilst holding only three tracks would prove deceptive as the final track 'March' boasted a duration of no less than 45 minutes.

The 2002 KATATONIA line-up comprised vocalist Jonas Renske, guitarist Anders Nyström and UNCANNY, FULMINATION and OCTOBER TIDE man Fredrik Norrman, ex-DELLAMORTE bassist Mattias Norrman and SUBDIVE and WICKED drummer Daniel Liljekvist.

Singles/EPs:
Midvinter Gates (Prologue) / Without God / Palace Of Frost / The Northern Silence / Crimson Tales, Vic VIC 1 (1994) ('Jhva Elohim Meth...The Revival' EP)
Funeral Wedding / Shades Of Emerald Fields / For Funerals To Come... / Epistal, Avantgarde AV 009 (1995) ('For Funerals To Come' EP)
Scarlet Heavens EP, Misanthropy (1996) (Split EP with PRIMORDIAL)
Nowhere / At Last / Inside The Fall, Avantgarde (1997) ('Sounds Of Decay' EP)
Saw You Drown / Scarlet Heavens, Avantgarde (1997)
Teargas / Sulfur / March, Peaceville (2001)
Tonight's Music / Help Me Disappear / O How I Enjoy The Light, Peaceville (2001)

Albums:
DANCE OF THE DECEMBER SOULS, No Fashion 005 (1995)
Seven Dreaming Souls / Gateways Of Bereavement / In Silence Enshrined / Without God / Elohim Meth / Velvet Thorns (Of Drynwhyl) / Tomb Of Insomnia / Dancing December
BRAVE MURDER DAY, Avantgarde AV022

(1996)
Brave / Murder / Day / Rainroom / 12 / Endtime
DISCOURAGE ONES, Avantgarde AV 029 (1998)
I Break / Stalemate / Deadhouse / Relention / Cold Ways / Gone / Last Resort / Nerve / Saw You Drown / Instrumental / Distrust
TONIGHT'S DECISION, Peaceville (1999)
For My Demons / I Am Nothing / In Death, A Song / Had To (Leave) / This Punishment / Right Into The Bliss / No Good Can Come Of This / Strained / A Darkness Coming / Nightmares By The Sea / Black Session
SINGLES COLLECTION, (2000)
Midvinter Gates (Prologue) / Without God / Palace Of Frost / The Northern Silence / Crimson Tears (Epilogue) / Funeral Wedding / Shades Of Emerald Fields / For Funerals To Come... / Epistal / Nowhere / At Last / Inside The Fall
LAST FAIR DEAL GONE DOWN, Peaceville (2001)
Dispossession / Chrome / We Will Bury You / Teargas / I Transpire / Tonight's Music / Clean Today / The Future Of Speech / Passing Bird / Sweet Nurse / Don't Tell A Soul

KEELHAUL (Cleveland, OH, USA)
Line-Up: Aaron Dallison (vocals / bass), Chris Smith (vocals / guitar), Dana Embrose (guitar), Will Scharf (drums)

Cleveland Hardcore edged Riff Rockers forged in late 1997 with a line-up comprising vocalist / bassist Aaron Dallison, guitarists Chris Smith and Dana Embrose and drummer Will Scharf. Embrose previously operated with Boston's LA GRITONA whilst Scharf maintains membership of both KEELHAUL and CRAW. Other members cite credits with INTEGRITY, ESCALATION ANGER and the INMATES.

In a spirit of self endeavour KEELHAUL financed their debut Bill Korecky produced recordings in 1998, released on their own imprint Cambodia Records, and soon set about touring. This spate of live action attracted the attention of the Escape Artist label who subsequently reissued the album. Hydra Head Records also weighed in with a contract for a new album and single 'Ornamental Iron', the song title being the band's own attempt to describe their musical style. Much of 1999 was spent by KEELHAUL on the road in North America, sharing stages with label mates ELVIS '77 and BOTCH.

Bill Korecky once again assumed responsibilities behind the desk for the 'Keelhaul II' album issued in late 2001.

Upfront of the release KEELHAUL toured nationwide, billed with EYEHATEGOD and Baltimore's MEATJACK.

KEELHAUL united with Boston's ANODYNE for a split 7" single 'De Omnibus Dubitandum Est' in 2002. The track featured a guesting McTigh of CRAW on vocals. In July KEELHAUL's Aaron Dallison was inducted as second guitarist for Stoners ABDULLAH.

Singles/EPs:
Ornamental Iron / Human / Self Helped Hell, Hydra Head (2000)
De Omnibus Dubitandum Est, Chainsaw Safety (2002) (Split single with ANODYNE)

Albums:
KEELHAUL, Escape Artists (2000)
Tuco / 3X3 Eyes / Cleanser / Khmir / Corrugated Blacklung / Fuimus / Unleaded / Enervate / Leveling Mechanism / ESP
KEELHAUL II, Hydra Head (2001)
360 / Some Day Some Other Place / New Void / Unwound / Practicing / 39F / Lackadaisical Chinese Tubesocks / LWM

KELTGAR (BELGIUM)
Line-Up: Evy (vocals), Nikolaas (vocals / guitar), Maarten (guitar), Ken (bass), Jeroen (keyboards), Jenny (keyboards / piano), Kristoff (drums)

Young Gothic Metal act KELTGAR was founded during the summer of 1998 as a trio of guitarist and "Deathgrunter" Nikolaas, bassist Bert and keyboard player Jeroen. In late December of the same year drummer Kristof augmented the line-up and as a quartet cut the opening March 1999 demo tape 'Moriath'. Lead vocalist Evy teamed up with KELTGAR just prior to recording of the EP 'In Shadows They Live' for the Uxicon label.

In the summer of 2000 KELTGAR added erstwhile PANCHRYSIA guitarist Maarten before recording the full-length album 'Wintermist', released by Uxicon in February 2001. Bert would decamp but new recruit Ken filled the vacancy quickly. The group also enlisted a second keyboard player Jenny.

Singles/EPs:
Nightly Liberation / Sioban / In Shadow They Live, Uxicon (2001) ('In Shadow They Live' EP)
Break Of Dawn / Scars Of A Poisoned Dream, (2002)

Albums:
WINTERMIST, Uxicon (2001)
Intro / As They Walk Away / Wintermist /

Solitude By Damnation / The Gates To My Fantasy / My Kingdom / Nightly Liberation / Sioban / In Shadow They Live

KHANATE (New York, NY, USA)
Line-Up: Alan Dubin (vocals), Stephan O'Malley (guitar), James Plotkin (bass), Tim Wyskida (drums)

An NYC Doom band of quite awesome pedigree. KHANATE was assembled by bassist James Plotkin, a veteran of such esteemed acts as OLD, SCORN, REGURGITATION and ATOMSMASH and guitarist Stephen O'Malley, the latter citing credits with such influential outfits as SUNN O)))), BURNING WITCH and THORR'S HAMMER.
KHANATE was rounded off by OLD vocalist Alan Dubin and Tim Wyskida on drums from BLIND IDIOT GOD and MANBYRD.

Albums:
KHANATE, Southern Lord (2001)
Pieces Of Quiet / Skincoat / Torching Koroviev / Under Rotting Sky / No Joy

KHANG (UK)
Line-Up: Bryan Outlaw (vocals), Rich Savage (guitar), Lee Baines (guitar), Bri (bass), Rick Miah (drums)

A British Doom band with pedigree. Formed in April of 1998 KHANG came into being when the remnants of fabled Doom mongers SERENITY, guitarists Lee Baines and Rich Savage together with drummer Gary Riley opted to persevere in a new unit. Before long the band was being fronted by singer Bryan Outlaw and joined by former DOOM bassist Bri. However, Riley would be forced out due to personal commitments and Rick Miah, previously with premier act MY DYING BRIDE stabilized the line-up.
KHANG got into gear at last performing a run of UK support gigs to acts such as UNIDA, HANGNAIL, SALLY, ORANGE GOBLIN and SPIRIT CARAVAN. Baines would also be inducted into the ranks of MY DYING BRIDE. On Halloween 1999 the band recorded the 'Premeditated' debut album which included an inspired cover version of LEAFHOUND's 'Stagnant Pools'. A 2002 follow up, 'Worship The Evil', is projected for 2002.

Albums:
PREMEDITATED, (1999)
Evening Rain / 25 Or 64T / Premeditated / Airlock / Gypsy / Intelligent Stimulation / Who Knows Part 10 / Stagnant Pool
WORSHIP THE EVIL, Bionic Conker (2002)

The Creator Has A Master Plan / Death Instinct / (You Make Me Feel So) God Damn Heavy / Evilhead / Got To Love It / If All The Gods Are Dead

KILLING JOKE (UK)
Line-Up: Jaz Coleman (vocals), Geordie (guitar), Youth (bass), Paul Ferguson (drums)

London act KILLING JOKE proved themselves to be a hugely influential force almost immediately from their inception. Not only could the band's live shows and sheer sonic delivery give most Heavy Metal bands a run for their money but the whole package was imbued with vocalist Jaz Coleman's rages against the weakness of his kind and portents of impending doom. Musically KILLING JOKE employ mantra like bass driven riffing atop mournful keyboard washes. KILLING JOKE first emerged in 1979 when Coleman united with guitarist Geordie (Walker), former RAGE bassist Youth (real name Martin Glover) and drummer Paul Ferguson. The band took out a loan to finance the inaugural 'Turn To Red' EP and its impact soon secured a deal with Island Records for a further single release.

1982 saw Youth decamping to forge BRILLIANT and have his position filled by Guy Pratt for the 'Revelations' album. Later the same year ex-BRILLIANT and NEON HEARTS man Paul Raven took Pratt's place as the latter joined Australian Electro Pop act ICEHOUSE.

Surprisingly KILLING JOKE broke the British charts with undoubtedly their most commercial release to date the Chris Kimsey produced 'Night Time' album. The main single 'Love Like Blood' would win them whole new legions of fans.

The late '80s found the band splintering. Convinced of the coming apocalypse Coleman relocated to Iceland. The vocalist believed, in an echo of myths of Thuringia, that "an island at the end of the earth" would be saved from the deluge. The singer took this belief further by moving to New Zealand where he would become involved at a high level in the national Symphony Orchestra.

Raven quit to join American noisemongers PRONG. Geordie had discussions with FAITH NO MORE toward being a possible replacement for JIM MARTIN although this union never transpired.

In 1990 Coleman would produce the debut album for Leeds Rock act LOUD entitled 'D Generation'.

Coleman regrouped with Geordie for a new look KILLING JOKE drafting erstwhile PUBLIC IMAGE LTD. drummer Martin Atkins and former SMITHS bassist Andy Rourke.

The latter was soon to make way for Taff. However, later in 1990 the Coleman, Geordie and Atkins axis had been bolstered by the return of Raven for the 'Extremities, Dirt And Various Repressed Emotions' album for the German Noise label.

1991 had Youth returning to the fore with the ZODIAC YOUTH project in alliance with ZODIAC MINDWARP. Although tracks for a proposed single 'Fast Forward The Future' were recorded the release was shelved and the unit splintered.

Jaz Coleman gained credits for the production of the New Zealand newcomers SHIHAD's 'Churn' debut. The album, released in July of 1993 and heavily imbued with the trademark Coleman sound, shot SHIHAD to star status in their homeland. Debut single 'I Only Said' gained a top five placing and the band embarked on a twelve month Australasian tour. Larkin's services were requested for KILLING JOKE's 'Pandemonium' album. The cult British band would ask for Larkin's commitment to European touring but the sticksman opted to stay the course with SHIHAD.

In 1993 Atkins decamped from KILLING JOKE to PIGFACE and was replaced by former ART OF NOISE drummer Geoff Dugmore.

KILLING JOKE's star was ascending once again and the mid '90s saw a renaissance in their appeal. The rise of Grunge only served to highlight KILLING JOKE's influence but in an unexpected way. By far Grunge's fastest rising star NIRVANA found themselves landed with a lawsuit by Geordie over 'similarities' between NIRVANA's hit single 'Come As You Are' and KILLING JOKE's 'Eighties'. A casual listener to both would be hard pressed to distinguish between the two song's core riffs. During the lull between albums Youth found himself a new niche in the Dance world quickly establishing himself as an in demand producer.

Paul Ferguson contributed drums to 1994's 'Pandemonium' but did not tour with the band. METALLICA gave the band's international status a boost by covering 'The Wait'. One of Germany's leading Gothic Rock acts LOVE LIKE BLOOD not only named themselves after the KILLING JOKE track but covered the same song for a 1998 single.

KILLING JOKE would announce a re-formation during 2001 with Coleman and Geordie reforging ties with Paul Raven. The bassist would also bring into the fold his erstwhile PRONG colleague Ted Parsons on drums. Chris Vrenna, noted for his high profile membership of NINE INCH NAILS would also form part of the new line-up which ambitiously set out to record a new album in such far flung

221

locations as Los Angles, Prague and Morocco.

In addition their activities as part of KILLING JOKE Raven and Parsons would embark on a whole series of side activities. Both would tour as members of GODFLESH as well as recording with Parsons former SWANS colleagues Norman Westberg and Algis Kizys.

Not content with all this activity the bass player would also found a Los Angeles based side endeavour SOCIETY ONE in union with ex-WHITE ZOMBIE drummer Ivan DePrume. Parsons too had other cards up his sleeves, working with ex-MASTERS OF REALITY guitarist Brendan McNichol in Ambient duo DRONE and also with the New York act TELEDUBGNOSIS.

KILLING JOKE would set to work on new material during 2002 despite Coleman being engaged in Classical works with commitments stretching until 2003.

Singles/EPs:

Are You Receiving Me / Turn To Red / Nervous System, Malicious Damage MD 410 (1979) (10" single)

Nervous System / Turn To Red, Island WIP 6550 (1979) (7" single)

Nervous System / Turn To Red / Almost Red / Are You Receiving Me, Island 12WIP 6550 (1979) (12" single)

Wardance / Psyche, Malicious Damage MD 540 (1980) (7" single)

Requiem / Change, EG EGMD 100 (1980) (7" single)

Requiem / Change / Requiem 434 / Change (version), EG EGMX 100 (1980) (12" single)

Follow The Leaders / Tension, EG EGMDS 101 (1981) **55 UK** (7" single)

Follow The Leaders / Tension / Follow The Leaders (Dub), EG EGMDX 1010 (1981) **55 UK** (10" single)

Empire Song / Brilliant, EG EGO 4 (1982) **43 UK** (7" single)

Chop Chop / Good Samaritan, EG EGO 7 (1982) (7" single)

Birds Of A Feather / Flock The B Side, EG EGO 10 (1982) **64 UK** (7" single)

Birds Of A Feather / Flock The B Side / Sun Goes Down, EG EGOX 10 (1982) (12" single)

Let's All Go (To The Fire Dances) / Dominator (version), EG EGO 11 (1983) 51 UK (7" single)

Let's All Go (To The Fire Dances) / Dominator (version) / The Fall Of Because (Live), EG EGOX 11 (1983) (12" single)

Me Or You? / Wilful Days, EG EGOD 14 (1983) **57 UK** (7" single)

Me Or You? / Feast Of Blaze, EG KILL 1-2 (1983) (Free 7" with 'Me Or You?' single)

Me Or You? / Let's All Go (To The Fire Dances) / The Fall Of Because (Live) / Dominator (Version), EG EGOXD 14 (1983) (12" single)

Eighties / Eighties (Coming mix), EG EGO 16 (1984) **60 UK** (7" single)

Eighties / Eighties (Coming mix) / Eighties (Serious Dance mix), EG EGO 16 (1984) (12" single)

A New Day / Dance Day, EG EGO 17 (1984) **56 UK** (7" single)

A New Day / Dance Day / A New Day (Dub), EG EGOX 17 (1984) (12" single)

Love Like Blood / Blue Feather, EG EGO 20 (1985) **16 UK** (7" single)

Love Like Blood / Blue Feather / Love Like Blood (Gestalt mix), EG EGOY 20 (1985) (12" single)

Love Like Blood / Blue Feather / Love Like Blood (Gestalt mix) / Love Like Blood (Instrumental), EG EGOX 20 (1985) (12" single)

Kings And Queens / The Madding Crowd, EG EGO 21 (1985) **58 UK** (7" single)

Kings And Queens / The Madding Crowd / Kings And Queens (Right Royal mix), EG EGOX 21 (1985) (12" single)

Kings And Queens / The Madding Crowd / Kings And Queens (Knave mix), EG EGO 21 (1985) (12" single)

Adorations / Exile, EG EGO 27 (1986) **42 UK** (7" single)

Adorations / Exile / Ecstasy / Adorations (Instrumental), EG EGOD 27 (1986) (Double 7" single)

Sanity / Goodbye To The Village, EG EGO 30 (1986) **70 UK** (7" single)

Sanity / Goodbye To The Village / Victory, EG EGOX 30 (1986) (12" single)

America / Jihad (Beyrouth edit), EG EGO 40 (1988) (7" single)

America / Jihad (Beyrouth edit) / America (Extended version), EG EGOX 40 (1988) (12" single)

America / Jihad (Beyrouth edit) / America (Extended version) / Change (1980 mix), EG EGOCD 40 (1988) (CD single)

My Love Of This Land / Darkness Before Dawn, EG EGO 43 (1988) (7" single)

My Love Of This Land / Darkness Before Dawn / Follow The Leaders (Dub) / Psyche, EG EGOX 43 (1988) (12" single)

My Love Of This Land / Darkness Before Dawn / Follow The Leaders (Dub) / Sun Goes Down, EG EGOCD 43 (1988) (CD single)

Money Is Not Our God / North Of The Border, Noise International AG 054-6 (1991) (12" single)

Change / Requiem, Virgin VST 1432 (1992) (12" single)

Change / Change (Spiral Tribe mix) /

Change (Trash Greg Hunter mix), Virgin VSCDT 1432 (1992) (CD single)
Change / Change (A Youth mix) / Change (B Youth mix), Virgin VSCDX (1992) (CD single)
Exorcism / Exorcism (Live) / Exorcism (German mix) / Whiteout (Ugly mix) / **Another Cult Goes Down (mix)** / Exorcism (Bictonic revenge mix), Butterfly BFL T 11 (1994) (10" single)
Millennium / Millennium (Cybersank remix), Butterfly BFL 12 (1994) 34 UK (7" single)
Millennium / Millennium (Cybersank remix) / Millennium (Drum Club remix) / Millennium (Juno Reactor mix), Butterfly BFLT 12 (1994) (12" single)
Pandemonium / Pandemonium (mix), Butterfly BFL T 17 (1994) 28 UK (12" single)
Jana (Youth remix) / Jana (Dragonfly mix) / Love Like Blood (Live) / Whiteout, Butterfly BFLDA 21 (1995) 54 UK (CD single)
Jana (Youth remix) / Jana (Dragonfly mix) / Jana (Live) / Wardance (Live) / Exorcism (Live) / Kings And Queens (Live), Butterfly BFLT 21 (1995) (12" single)
Democracy / Democracy (Rooster Carcass remix) / Mass, Butterfly BFLDA 33 (1996) **39 UK** (CD single)
Democracy (United Nations mix) / Democracy (Russian Tundra mix) / Democracy (Hallucinogen mix), Butterfly BFLDB 33 (1996) (CD single)
Love Like Blood / Intellect, Dragonfly 48 (1998) (USA release)

Albums:
KILLING JOKE, EG EGMD 545 (1980) **39 UK**
Requiem / Wardance / Tomorrow's World / Bloodsport / The Wait / Complications / S.O. 36 / Primitive
WHAT'S THIS FOR…!, EG EGMD 550 (1981) **42 UK**
The Fall Of Because / Tension / Unspeakable / Butcher / Follow The Leaders / Madness / Who Told You How? / Exit
REVELATIONS, EG EGMD3 (1982)
The Hum / Empire Song / We Have Joy / Chop Chop / The Pandys Are Coming / Chapter III / Have A Nice Day / Land Of Milk And Honey / Good Samaritan / Dregs
HA - KILLING JOKE LIVE, EG EGMD T 4 (1982) **66 UK**
Psyche / Sun Goes Down / The Pandys Are Coming / Take Take Take / Unspeakable / Wardance
FIRE DANCES, EG EGMD 5 (1983) **29 UK**
The Gathering / Fun And Games / Rejuvenation / Frenzy / Harlequin / Feast Of Blaze / Song And Dance / Dominator / Let's All Go (To The Fire Dances) / Lust Almighty
NIGHT TIME, EG EGMD 6 (1985)
50 SWEDEN, 11 UK

Night Time / Darkness Before Dawn / Love Like Blood / Kings And Queens / Tabazan / Multitudes / Europe / Eighties
BRIGHTER THAN A THOUSAND SUNS, EG EGCD 66 (1986) **54 UK**
Adorations / Sanity / Chessboards / Twilight Of The Mortal / Love Of The Masses / A Southern Sky / Wintergardens / Rubicon / Goodbye To The Village / Victory
OUTSIDE THE GATE, EG EGCD 73 (1988) **92 UK**
America / My Love Of This Land / Stay One Jump Ahead / Unto The Ends Of The Earth / The Calling / Obsession / Tiahuanaco / Outside The Gate / America (Extended version) / Stay One Jump Ahead (Extended version)
LAUGH? I NEARLY BOUGHT ONE!, Caroline CDV 2693 (1992)
Turn To Red / Psyche / Requiem / Wardance / Follow The Leaders / Unspeakable / Butcher / Exit / The Hum / Empire Song / Chop Chop / Sun Goes Down / Eighties / Darkness Before Dawn / Love Like Blood / Wintergardens / Age Of Greed
EXTREMITIES, DIRT AND VARIOUS REPRESSED EMOTIONS, Noise International AGR 054-2 (1990)
Money Is Not Our God / Age Of Greed / Beautiful Dead / Extremities / Inside The Termite Mound / Intravenus / Solitude / North Of The Border / Slipstream / Kalijuga Struggle
THE COURTHOLD TALKS, Invisible INV 004 (1993)
PANDEMONIUM, Butterfly BFL CD 9 (1994) **16 UK**
Pandemonium / Exorcism / Millennium / Communion / Black Moon / Labyrinth / Jana / Whiteout / Pleasures Of The Flesh / Mathematics Of Chaos
WILFUL DAYS: REMIXES, Caroline CDOVD 440 (1995)
Are You Receiving? / Follow The Leaders (Dub) / Sun Goes Down / Dominator (Extended) / Me Or You / Wilful Days / Eighties (Serious Dance mix) / A New Day / Love Like Blood (Gestalt mix) / The Madding Crowd / Ecstasy (Extended mix) / America (Extended) / Change (Re-Evolution mix)
BBC LIVE IN CONCERT, Windsong WINCD 068 (1995)
Twilight Of The Mortals / Chessboards / Kings & Queens / Darkness Before Dawn / Love Like Blood / Sanity / Love Of The Masses / Requiem / Complications / Wardance / Tabazan / Tension / Pssyche
ALCHEMY - THE REMIXES, Zomba (1996)
Requiem / Stations Of The Sun / Pandemonium / Drug / Millennium / Exorcism / Pandemonium / Democracy
DEMOCRACY, Butterfly BFL CD 17 (1996)

223

71 UK
Savage Freedom / Democracy / Prozac People / Lanterns / Aeon / Pilgrimage / Intellect / Medicine Wheel / Absent Friends / Another Bloody Election
WAR DANCE: REMIXS, Imprint 114151 (1998)
Love Like Blood (Deedrah remix) / Savage Freedom (UX remix) / Democracy (NIN remix) / Four Stations Of The Sun (Hallucinogen remix) / Pandemonium (Man With No Name remix) / Jana (Hallucinogenic) / Black Moon California Sunshine / Interllect (Johan remix) / White Out (Johan remix)
NO WAY OUT BUT FORWARD GO (LIVE 1985), NMC (2001)
The Hum / Darkness Before Dawn / Requiem / Empire Song / Tabazan / Night Time / Kings & Queens / The Good Samaritan / Love Like Blood / Blood Sport / Complications / The Wait / Pssyche / Eighties / Wardance / Adorations / Chessboards

KILLING MIRANDA (UK)
Line-Up: Richard Pyne (vocals / guitar), Alien Dave (guitar), Irish Dave (bass), Belle (drums)

Middlesex based Gothic Rock band with a Metal edge. KILLING MIRANDA first product, the 1998 'Burn Sinister' EP, was actually conceived as a solo venture by frontman Richard Pyne. After the release a band unit was assembled comprising guitarists Alien Dave and Irish Dave, bassist Chris and drummer Belle, individual members citing experience with prior acts such as RESTORATION II, PROPHECY, CATHEDRAL LUNG, NOSFERATU and ONE TRACK MIND.
The debut album, 'Blessed Deviant' released by Nightbreed, pulled in an extra degree of media exposure due to its graphic sleeve photograph. Chris left after this release and Irish Dave took on bass duties for the tougher 'Transgression By Numbers' album.

Singles/EPs:
Does This Mean Anything? / Touched By Jesus / Taking Over / Fade To Shadows (Sex In The Toilets version), Eclipse (1998) ('Burn Sinister' EP)

Albums:
BLESSED DEVIANT, Nightbreed (1999)
H8red / Burn Sinister / Pray / Kelly Told Me / The Game / Nailed / Veil Of Seduction / Whipping Boy / Blackeyed / Send In The Clowns / The Ballad Of Torrens St. /

Dreaming / Touched By Jesus (Intra Venus mix)
TRANSGRESSION BY NUMBERS, (2002)
Discotheque Necronomicon / Spit / Angelfly / Salome / Blessed Deviant / Meat / Teenage Vampire / Blood-Seed / See You In Disneyland / Transgression By Numbers

KINCH (GERMANY)
Line-Up: Haris (vocals / guitar), Zacki (vocals / bass), Malte (drums)

Munich Stoner trio dating back to April of 1999. KINCH's debut was served up by the Daredevil label as a split release with fellow Germans SHARD. Both vocalist / guitarist Haris and bass player Zacki are members of side act SCOFF.

Albums:
KINCH VS. SHARD, Daredevil DD007 (2000) (Split album with SHARD)
Man & Buduh / N.L.W. / Hula / Safie / Barn / Cadu

KOHLLLAPSE (AUSTRALIA)
Line-Up: Ro Edwards (vocals / guitar), Matt Aitchison (drums)

Christian Doom act KOHLLAPSE was centred upon the duo of vocalist / guitarist Ro Edwards and drummer Matt Aitchison. Session bass player Bevan would be employed for the 1996 eponymous debut record although Gavin took over for live work. Following recording of the 'Distant Mind Alternative' album of 1999 Aitchison made his exit and KOHLLAPSE duly… collapsed.

Albums:
KOHLLLAPSE, (1996)
Path / Tell Me Your Fears / Never / Towards / Take Me Away / My Child / An End To Pain / Self Infliction / Serenity
DISTANT MIND ALTERNATIVE, (1999)
Thorn / Real Man In Quicksand / Seven / Gravitation / Ghost Storm / Eclipse / Contort / Deep Blue / Insight / Untitled

KORPSE (UK)
Line-Up: Fluff (vocals / bass), Sid (guitar), Taff (drums)

Scottish Sabbath inspired Death n' Groove Metal.

Singles/EPs:
X, (1995)

Albums:
PULL THE FLOOD, Candlelight (1994)

Rusted / The Smell Of Broken Glass / Three / Illegal Music / Pull The Flood / X / Stomp / Neg / From The Heart
REVIRGIN, Candlelight CANDLE014 (1996)
Octochoosy / Milk And Two Salts / Tilt / The Only Way Out Is Dead / No Exit / Mirrordistance / 19 Dyce / To Be Continued... / Vitamin F / International 1001 / Revirgin / Mirrordistance

LIV KRISTINE (NORWAY)

Solo work by THEATRE OF TRAGEDY vocalist Liv Kristine. Nick Holmes, vocalist with PARADISE LOST, puts in a guest appearance.
Kristine toured to promote the record as guest to ATROCITY.

Singles/EPs:
3AM (Club mix) / 3 AM (single edit) / Huldra Part III / Good Vibes, Bad Vibes (Dance On The Ocean), Swan Lake MAS CD 0151 (1998)

Albums:
DEUS EX MACHINA, Swan Lake MAS CD0154 (1998)
Requiem / Deus Et Machina / In The Heart Of Juliet / I Am / Waves Of Green / Take Good Care / Huldra / Portrait: Ei Tulle Med Oyne Bla / Good Vibes, Bad Vibes / Outro

KUNG PAO (New York, NY, USA)
Line-Up: Chovie D (vocals / guitar), T.B. (bass), Davey D (drums)

Self styled "Hard ass denim Rock" out of New York. This power trio tour the land in the "Crack van" in pursuit of America's finest toilets. During the 'Sheboygan' album sessions Chovie D, Davey D.-Drums and 'PeaceBear' cut tracks as PEACEBEAR, releasing these on a scarce CD single restricted to just 50 copies.

Albums:
BOGATA, Maduro (2001)
We Got Limo / Drop Wolfbait / D Is For Denim / Poppin' Wheelies / Iron Lung / Hootie World / Nakoma / Below / River Huber / Freezerburn / Sex Attack
SHEBOYGAN, Maduro (2002)
Hotpockets / Freeballin' USA / Honk / Go Frenchie Go! / Truckstop / Dewsicle / Braces / Dolby Surround / Like Leprechaun / Anti-Wovy Machine / Miss Ice Cream Cool

KYUSS (Palm Springs, CA, USA)
Line-Up: John Garcia (vocals), Josh Homme (guitar), Nick Oliveri (bass), John Brant Bjork (drums)

Influential and revered exponents of Stoner Rock. KYUSS was the first in a line of Doom influenced acts that introduced a trippy 'Desert' groove to their sound. The amalgam of Grunge attitude, '60s Garage, '70s Heavy Rock and B movie imagery allied to Doom roots almost single handed invented the phrase 'Stoner Rock'. They achieved this by tuning way down and summoning up a subterranean, organic sound designed for equal impact upon both the brain and the bowels. Although never truly commercially successful during the active life span of the band the KYUSS legacy has weighed heavy on the Stoner scene.
The band's original line-up included vocalist John Garcia, guitarist Josh Homme, bassist Scott Reeder of THE OBSESSED and drummer Alfredo Hernandez. Both Reeder and Hernandez had cut their teeth with school Punk band DEAD ISSUE, an outfit that also featured vocalist / guitarist Herb Lineau and guitarist Mario Lalli. With Lineau's departure DEAD ISSUE evolved into ACROSS THE RIVER. Reeder would then decamp and Hernandez and Lalli, adding Larry Lalli on bass and Gary Arce on guitar became ENGLENOOK in 1987. This band then shifted shape into YAWNING MAN. As the Lalli brothers later created FATSO JETSON Hernandez and Reeder reunited to found KYUSS. Chris Cockrell, later of SOLAR FEAST, would actually earn the distinction of being the first KYUSS bassist if only for a short period.
KYUSS debuted with 1991's 'Wretch' album, an under-produced basic Punk Rock offering that generally went unnoticed. The band transformed their sound for their breakthrough 'Blues For The Red Sun' album, produced by Chris Goss Of MASTERS OF REALITY. Heavy on instrumentals 'Blues For The Red Sun' was the first album to capture the KYUSS brand and included perennials such as 'Thumb', the staccato 'Thong Song', the numbing trance inducing 'Mondo Generator' and 'Green Machine', the latter hedonistic enough to boast a bass solo. Poignantly, such was the influence of the album that later generations of Stoner fledglings would take these song titles as band names.
With the fragmentation of the Dali-Chameleon label KYUSS were duly snapped up by a perceptive Elektra label for 1994's 'Welcome To Sky Valley'. This album saw the inclusion of 'N.O.', an archive ACROSS THE RIVER track complete with a guesting guitar slot from co-writer Mario Lalli. Critically praised KYUSS were ahead of their time and

album sales failed to match expectations. Notwithstanding, 'Welcome To Sky Valley', which came with listener instructions "Listen without distraction" and with tracks divided into suites and sequenced minus pauses so as to discourage skipping, is widely regarded now as a seminal Rock release worthy of classic distinction.

A further set, 1995's '...And The Circus Leaves Town' again had the media in raptures. This album included the track 'Catamaran', originally an early YAWNING MAN composition. Unable to make headway KYUSS folded in 1995.

Garcia put together SLO BURN following the band's break up. Homme, after touring as a member of SCREAMING TREES for nearly two years, founded QUEENS OF THE STONE AGE, an act that one time SOUNDGARDEN drummer Matt Cameron aided in the live situation but later included original KYUSS drummer Alfredo Hernandez. Former DWARVES bassist Nick Oliveri (adopting the pseudonym of 'Mondo Generator') would later join the fold to boost the ex-KYUSS contingent. The Man's Ruin label weighed in on Homme's behalf by issuing the KYUSS album 'Queens Of The Stone Age' collecting together KYUSS rarities with three new tracks from Homme's brand new outfit.

Drummer Brant Bjork teamed up with FATSO JETSON as rhythm guitarist appearing on a brace of split 7" singles before opting out to concentrate on his priority act FU MANCHU in late 1997 for their 'The Action Is Go' album. John Garcia was found fronting KARMA TO BURN in 1997 although his employment with the famed West Virginians lasted a mere twelve gigs. Studio recordings were commenced but shelved. The two parties attempted a fresh union, KARMA TO BURN even releasing press releases regarding a new album billed as 'Nino Brown', but once again the alliance faltered.

Both Bjork and Homme laid down the DESERT SESSIONS album 'Volume I & II' during 1998. More 'Desert Sessions' albums were to follow.

By 1999 Garcia had created UNIDA for the 'Coping With The Urban Coyote' album. After recording another ex-KYUSS man, bassist Scott Reeder, who had been touring with GOATSNAKE, joined the band for live work.

Singles/EPs:
Demon Cleaner / Freedom Run (Live), Elektra EKR 192 (1994) (Blue vinyl 7" single)
Demon Cleaner / Day One (To Dave & Chris) / El Rodeo / Hurricane, Elektra EKR 192CD1 (1994) (CD single)
Demon Cleaner / Gardenia (Live) / Thumb (Live) / Conan Trout Man (Live), Elektra EKR 192CD2 (1994) (CD single)
Gardenia / U.N. Sandpiper, Elektra EKR 197CD (1995) (CD single)
Into The Void / Fatso Forgetso, Man's Ruin MR 015 (1997)

Albums:
WRETCH, Dali (1991)
(Begining Of What's About To Happen) Hwy… / Love Has Passed Me By / Son Of A Bitch / Black Widow / Katzenjammer / Deadly Kiss / The Law / Isolation / I'm Not / Big Bikes / Stage III
BLUES FOR THE RED SUN, Dali Chameleon PRCS 61340-4 (1992)
Thumb / Green Machine / Molten Universe / 50 Million Years Trip / (Downside Up) / Thong Song / Apothecaries Weight / Caterpillar March / Freedom Run / 800 / Writhe / Capsized / Allen's Wrench / Mondo Generator / Yeah
WELCOME TO SKY VALLEY, Elektra 7559-61571-2 (1994)
Gardenia / Asteroid / Supa Scoopa And Mighty Scoop / 100 / Space Cadet / Demon Cleaner / Odyssey / Conan Troutman / N.O. / Whitewater
...AND THE CIRCUS LEAVES TOWN, Elektra 7559-61811-2 (1995)
Hurricane / One Inch Man / Thee Ol' Boozeronny / Gloria Lewis / Phototropic / El Rodeo / Jumbo Blimp Jumbo / Tangy Zizzle / Size Queen / Catamaran / Spaceship Landing
QUEENS OF THE STONE AGE, Man's Ruin MR 063 (1998)
Into The Void / Fatso Forgotso / Fatso Forgotso Phase 2 / If Only Everything / Born To Hula / Spiders And Vinegaroons
MUCHAS GRACIAS: THE BEST OF, Elektra 7559 62571-2 (2000)
Un Sandpiper / Shine / 50 Million Year Trip (Downside Up) / Mudfly / Demon Cleaner / A Day Early And A Dollar Extra I'm Not / Hurricane / Flip The Phase / Fatso Forgotso / El Rodeo / Gardenia (Live) / Thumb (Live) / Conan Troutman (Live) / Freedom Run (Live)

LACRIMOSA (GERMANY)

Line-Up: Tilo Wolff (vocals), Anne Nurmi (vocals), Jan Yrlund (guitar), Sebastian Hausmann (guitar), A.C. (drums)

Probably the leading Darkwave Rock project in Germany. The band's career kicked off with a 1990 demo entitled 'Clamor'. Originally thought out as a solo project by Tilo Wolff in 1994 erstwhile TWO WITCHES vocalist Anne Nurmi was added along with guitarist Yrlund of PRESTIGE and drummer A.C. of RUNNING WILD.

LACRIMOSA are at the forefront of the Gothic Rock revival in Germany, making it into the national charts with their 1995 album 'Inferno'.

Singles/EPs:

Alles Lüge / Alles Lüge (Sanguis Mix) / Diener Eines Geistes (Dirus Mix) / Ruin, Hall Of Sermon DW 084-2/27361 60432 (1993) ('Alles Lüge' EP)

Schakal (Edit Version) / Schakal (Piano Version) / Schakal (Akustik Version) / Schakal (Metus Mix), Hall Of Sermon 27361 68812 (1994) ('Schakal' EP)

Stolzes Herz (Edit Version) / Ich Bin Der Brennende Komet / Mutatio Spiritus / Stolzes Herz (Piano Version), Hall Of Sermon HOS 771 (1996) ('Stolzes Herz' EP)

Albums:

ANGST, Hall Of Sermon DW 083/27361 60342 (1992)
Seele In Not / Requiem / Lacrima Mosa / Der Ketzer / Der Letze Hilfeschrei / Tränen Der Existenzlosigkeit

EINSAMKEIT, Hall Of Sermon DW 082-2/27361 60592 (1992)
Tränen Der Sehnsucht (Part I & II) / Reissende Blicke / Einsamkeit / Diener Eines Geistes / Loblied Auf Die Zweisamkeit / Bresso

SATURA, Hall Of Sermon HOS 741 / DW 086 27361 60852 (1993)
Satura / Erinnerung / Crucifixio / Versuchung / Das Schweigen / Flamme Im Wind

INFERNO, Hall Of Sermon HOS 761 DW 088 27361 69682 (1995)
Intro / Kabinett Der Sinne / Versiegelt Glanzumströmt / No Blind Eyes Can See / Schakal / Vermächtnis Der Sonne / Copycat / Der Kelch Des Lebens

STILLE, Hall Of Sermon HOS 781 (1997)
Der erste Tag / Not Every Pain Hurts / Siehst Du Mich Im Licht / Deine Nähe / Stolzes Herz / Mein zweites Herz / Die Strasse der Zeit

LIVE, Hall Of Sermon HOS 7791 (1998)

Lacrimosa Theme / Ich Bin Der Brennende Komet / Vermächtnis Der Sonne / Deine Nähe / Tränen Der Sehnsucht / Siehst Du Mich Im Licht / Not Every Pain Hurts / Schakal / Seele in Not / Kabinett der Sinne / Make It End / Satura / Stolzes Herz / Versiegelt Glanzumströmt / Versuchung / Copycat / Alles Lüge

ELODIA, Hall Of Sermon HOS 7820 (1999)
Am Ende Der Stille / Alleine Zu Zweit / Halt Mich / The Turning Point / Ich Verlasse Heut Dein Herz / Dich Zu Toten Fiel Mir Schwer / Sanctus / Am Ende Stehen Wir Zwei

FASSADE, Nuclear Blast NB 780-2 (2001)
Fassade – Act 1 Act / Der Morgen Danach / Senses / Warum So Tief? / Fassade - Act 2 / Liebesspiel / Stumme Worte / Fassade - Act 3

LACUNA COIL (ITALY)

Line-Up: Cristina (vocals), Andrea (vocals), Raffaele (guitar), Claudio (guitar), Marco (bass), Leonardo (drums)

Slowly building up a ground roots following for themselves, Italian outfit LACUNA COIL were founded in 1994, although then known as SLEEP OF RIGHT. In recent years LACUNA COIL, blessed with the photogenic Cristina Scabbia, have made serious headway into the European Rock market.

Line-up changes saw the band reduced to a trio of guitarist Claudio Leo, vocalist Cristina and drummer Leonardo and another name change to ETHEREAL. A resulting two track demo in May of 1996 inspired a deal with Germany's Century Media label before another, final title shift to LACUNA COIL.

Upon the release of the debut mini-album, produced by GRIP INC.'s Waldemar Sorychta, LACUNA COIL were tagged unkindly as "Gothic Doom Bon Jovi with female vocals"!! The band themselves describe their music as "Darkly dreamy"! The record, issued in October of 1997 was promoted by a support tour in Europe to Portuguese act MOONSPELL. However, just three gigs into the run Zagaria, Leo and Leonardo decamped en masse. Undaunted LACUNA COIL persevered pulling in Anders Iwers from TIAMAT and CEMETARY on guitar and Markus of KREATOR on drums.

The band regrouped in January of 1998 by enlisting THY NATURE's Cristiano Migliore on guitar and TIME MACHINE's Cristiano Mozzati on drums. This revised formation embarked on European touring throughout April in alliance with THE GATHERING and SIEGMEN. Additional personnel utilized for live work would be NODE's Steve Minelli on guitar and keyboard player Alice Chiarelli. LACUNA COIL put in an inaugural showing at the August 1998 German 'Wacken' festival

LACUNA COIL

before gearing up for recording of the 'In A Reverie' album. As 1999 opened the band was brought up to strength with the addition of guitarist Marco Biazzi and soon after engaged in European mainland touring once more in alliance with England's SKYCLAD. On the back of these gigs LACUNA COIL jumped onboard the May 'Into The Darkness' package alongside running mates SAMAEL, MY INSANITY and GRIP INC. Returning to their homeland the act put in a showing at the 'Gods Of Metal' festival headlined by METALLICA. Before the year was out a further schedule was put in place as the band guested for LACRIMOSA in Germany during October. These dates would be marred when Biazzi broke some ribs when falling down stairs.

The millennium witnessed LACUNA COIL back in action with the 'Halflife' EP, a collection that oddly included a DUB STAR cover version. The band's status was such now that a series of headline shows in Europe was undertaken in April. The group would perform for the first time in Mexico during December and as the new year broke would hook up with THEATRE OF TRAGEDY and BESEECH for a further round of European dates. This activity was capitalized on by their inclusion in the high profile March 'Metal Odyssey' touring package of DIMMU

BORGIR, NEVERMORE, IN FLAMES and SUSPERIA. May would see headline gigs back in Italy.

During 2001 a Gothic Metal band CAYNE was forged by LACUNA COIL founding guitarists Claudio Leo and Raffaele Zagaria. An inaugural album 'Old Faded Pictures' saw a November release through Scarlet Records. The band would act as guests for MOONSPELL's December American tour.

During late 2001 live keyboard player Alice Chiarelli announced a new Doom Metal band project ALICE IN DARKLAND, issuing 'The Evil's Entrails' album through Nocturnal Music in March of 2002. LACUNA COIL themselves announced a month's worth of North American dates commencing in San Francisco on September 16th backing up headliners IN FLAMES and SENTENCED with support from KILLSWITCH ENGAGE. However, with the release date for a new studio album entitled 'Comalies' being pushed back the band later withdrew from these shows. An extensive European tour scheduled as guests to SENTENCED would take the band through October.

Albums:
LACUNA COIL, Century Media CD 77201-2 (1998)
No Need To Explain / The Secret... / This Is

CRISTINA SCABBIA of LACUNA COIL
Photo : Nico Wobben

229

My Dream / Soul Into Hades / Falling / Un Fantasma Tra Moi (A Ghost Between Us)
IN A REVERIE, Century Media 77234-2 (1999)
Circle / Stately Lover / Honeymoon Suite / My Wings / To Myself & Turned / Cold / Reverie / Veins Of Glass / Falling Again
HALF LIFE, Century Media 77239-2 (2000)
Halflife / Trance Awake / Senzafine / Hyperfast / Stars
UNLEASHED MEMORIES, Century Media 77360-2 (2001)
Heir Of A Dying Day / To Live Is To Hide / Purify / Senzafine / When A Dead Man Walks / 1:19 / Cold Heritage / Distant Sun / A Current Obsession / Wave Of Anguish

LAKE OF TEARS (SWEDEN)

Line-Up: Daniel Brennare (vocals / guitar), Jonas Eriksson (guitar), Mikael Larsson (bass), Johan Ouidhuls (drums)

LAKE OF TEARS have created their own niche in the European Gothic Rock scene with their blend of psychedelic Dark Metal.

The Borås based group was assembled in May of 1992 with a fusion of talents from various Death Metal bands, vocalist / guitarist Daniel Brennare, guitarist Jonas Eriksson and bass player Michael Larsson coming from CARNAL ERUPTION whilst drummer Johan Oudhuis had previously been with FORSAKEN GRIEF. A demo cut in 1993 soon secured a five album contract with the Black Mark label.

The 1994 debut album 'Greater Art' was recorded at the world famous Sunlight Studios and produced by CEMETERY's Matthias Lodmalm and ENTOMBED's Tomas Skogsberg, the latter also adding guitar and keyboard touches. In March of 1995 LAKE OF TEARS entered the recording studio again for a second effort, 'Headstones', engineered by Ulf Pettersson.

The band toured hard throughout 1996, opening for such acts as TIAMAT, EDGE OF SANITY and RAGE, but guitarist Jonas Eriksson had departed by the 1997 album and his duties were handled by guesting musicians in the form of DISMEMBER guitarist Magnus Sahlgren and keyboard player / guitarist Ronny Lahti. The track lifted for the single 'Lady Rosenred' featured a lead guest vocal by Jenny Tebler. Following completion of the record LAKE OF TEARS inducted guitarist Ulrik Lindblom.

Touring to promote 'A Crimson Cosmos' was extensive. The first round of European dates had the band packaged with THEATRE OF TRAGEDY and HEAVENWOOD before summer dates which included an appearance at the German 'Wacken Open Air' festival. The

LAKE OF TEARS

group then formed part of the billing for the 'Out Of The Dark' touring festivals sharing the stage with CREMATORY, THERION, DARK and GRAVEWORM. However, Lindblom bowed out after these shows to take care of his family life.

'Forever Autumn', acknowledged by the band to be a more morose affair than previous efforts, was delivered for a German release in June of 1999. The group added keyboard player Christian Saarinen to fill out their newly acquired atmospheric direction. Magnus Sahlgren also weighed in with a guest guitar solo once again.

LAKE OF TEARS returned in April of 2002 with the Ulf Wahnberg produced 'Neonai' album. Jenny Tebler was used once again for female vocal parts.

Singles/EPs:
Lady Rosenred / Devil's Diner / A Crimson Cosmos, Black Mark BMCD 106 (1997)

Albums:
GREATER ART, Black Mark BMCD 49 (1994)
Under The Crescent / Eyes Of The Sky / Upon The Highest Mountain / As Daylight Yields / Greater Art / Evil Inside / Netherworld / Tears
HEADSTONES, Black Mark BMCD 72 (1995)
A Foreign Road / Raven Land / Dreamdemons / Sweetwater / Life's But A Dream / Headstones / Twilight / Burn Fire Burn / The Path Of The Gods (Upon The Highest Mountain Part II)
A CRIMSON COSMOS, Black Mark BMCD 97 (1997)
Boogie Bubble / Cosmic Weed / When My Sun Comes Down / Devil's Diner / The Four Strings Of Mourning / To Die Is To Wake / Lady Rosenred / Raistlin And The Rose / A Crimson Cosmos
FOREVER AUTUMN, Black Mark BMCD 132 (1999)
So Fell Autumn Rain / Hold On Tight /

Forever Autumn / Pagan Wish / Otherwheres / The Homecoming / Come Night I Reign / Demon You - Lily Anne / To Blossom Blue
THE NEONAI, Black Mark (2002)
Return Of Ravens / The Shadowshires / Solitude / Leave A Room / Sorcerers / Can Die No More / Nathalie And The Fireflies / Let Us Go As They Do / Down The Nile

LAMB OF GOD (Richmond, VA, USA)
Line-Up: Randy Blythe (vocals), Will Adler (guitar), Mark Morton (guitar), John Campbell (bass), Chris Adler (drums)

LAMB OF GOD were previously known as BURN THE PRIEST. LAMB OF GOD teamed up with SHADOW'S FALL, SCISSORFIGHT, , DARKEST HOUR, FROM AUTUMN TO ASHES and UNEARTH for a series of American East Coast dates in May of 2002. The band scheduled recording of a second album for November of 2002, bringing in the highly respected DEVIN TOWNSEND to act as co-producer.

LAMB OF GOD

Albums:
NEW AMERICAN GOSPEL, Prosthetic 3984143452 (2000)
Black Label / A Warning / In The Absence Of The Sacred / Letter To The Unborn / The Black Dahlia / Terror And Hubris In The House Of Frank Pollard / The Subtle Art Of Murder And Persuasion / Pariah / Confessional / O.D.H.G.A.B.F.E.

LAMP OF THE UNIVERSE
(NEW ZEALAND)

Having released two highly praised albums fronting Stoners DATURA, Craig Williamson struck out on the solo path billing himself LAMP OF THE UNIVERSE. With this new project Williamson pursued the Eastern mystic flavours evident of DATURA's last outing 'Vision Of The Celestial' but took the whole trip into mellower and more adventurously Psychedelic territory with the opening April 2001 'The Cosmic Union' album.
A second LAMP OF THE UNIVERSE album 'Echo In Light', which included the 17 minute trance inducing 'Dream Sequence', arrived in June 2002.

Albums:
THE COSMIC UNION, Cranium Music CR005 (2001)
Born In The Rays Of The Third Eye / Lotus Of A Thousand Petals / In The Mystic Light / Give Yourself To Love / Freedom In Your Mind / Her Cosmic Light / What Love Can Bring / Tantra Asana.
ECHO IN LIGHT, Cranium Music (2002)
Freedom To Godliness / Resonance / Our Celestial Flow / Love / Pyramids Of Sun / Dream Sequence

L'ARME IMMORTALE (AUSTRIA)
Line-Up: Thomas Rainer (vocals), Sonja Kraushofer (vocals), Hannes Medwenitsch

An Austrian Gothic Electronic Rock act. Session musicians utilized for the 2001 'Denn Habe Ich Umsonst Gelebt' album included guitarists Alen Markulin and Jochen Schibertz, bassist Robert Bayer and drummer Simon T. Ostheim.

Albums:
DENN HABE ICH UMSONST GELEBT, Trisol (2001)
Erinnerung / Judgement / Epitaph / Rearranging / Slut / Umsonst Gelebt ? / Licht Und Schatten / Voiceless / Was Halt Mich Noch Hier / Forgive Me / Leaving / Dead Actor's Requiem / Life Will Never Be The Same Again

LAS CRUCES (TX, USA)
Line-Up: Mark Zamarron (vocals / bass), George Trevino (guitar), Mark Lopez (guitar), Steve Martinez (drums)

LAS CRUCES was one of the early signing of the Brainticket label founded by John Perez of SOLITUDE AETURNUS. Like SOLITUDE AETURNUS, the Doom band was based in Texas and they even used Perez to produce their debut 1996 album, S.O.L. ('Solitude Of Lunacy')
LAS CRUCES consist of ex-PASSAGE TEMPLE and WICKED ANGEL vocalist / bassist Mark Zamarron and the twin guitars of former MERCYNARY man George Trevino and erstwhile SWEETLEAF member Mark Lopez. The album features drums by Michael

Hosman although he was subsequently superseded by Steve Martinez.

Prior to scoring their deal with Brainticket Records LAS CRUCES had opened for both SOLITUDE AETURNUS and MERCYFUL FATE.

Just upfront of recording for the sophomore release 'Ringmaster' guitarist Mark Lopez announced his departure. Lopez would bow out after having recorded guitar parts for the album which emerged in January of 1999. 'Ringmaster' would bear witness to a further change in line-up with Ben Regio Montana taking over the drum stool.

LAS CRUCES regrouped for a self-financed EP's worth of material 'Lowest End' in 2001. Featured would be two new guitarists, Dana Hawkins and Mando Tovar, along with new drummer Paul DeLeon.

Singles/EPs:
Lowest End EP, (2001)

Albums:
S.O.L., Brainticket BTR 2139 (1996)
Skin Chamber / Valley Of Unrest / Eve In Sorrow / Silence / Sophia / Shotgun / D.I.G. / Jed's White Owl / Heroine
RINGMASTER, Brainticket (1999)
Behemoth / Killer Kane / Black Waters / Pigz / Cascades Of Phantoms / Doomed / Ringmaster / Human Form / This Time / Lazy Drag

LAST CHAPTER (Arlington, TX, USA)
Line-Up: Shawn Green (vocals), Darrin Davis (guitar), Cody Griffith (guitar), Terry Pritchard (bass), Chris Clifford (drums)

Pure, unadulterated Christian Texan Doom with a strong eschatological lyrical theme. LAST CHAPTER was conceived in Arlington during 1989 as BRICK WINDOW, a trio comprising guitarist Darrin Davis, bassist Terri Pritchard and drummer Jason Spradlin. With the recruitment of second guitarist Cody Griffith the band, still minus a vocalist at this point in time, switched title to LAST CHAPTER.

By 1993 the group's search for a singer had still not yielded results so Robert Lowe of the cult act SOLITUDE AETURNUS stepped into the breach for demo recordings. Although the tape served them well the lack of a suitable singer remained such an obstacle that the group actually disbanded. Whilst on hiatus from LAST CHAPTER the Spradlin / Pritchard rhythm axis loaned themselves out to SOLITUDE AETURNUS guitarist John Perez, sessioning on his 1996 experimental album credited to THE LIQUID SUNDAY COMPANY

'Exploring The Psychedelic'. Perez in turn persuaded LAST CHAPTER to regroup and record an album for his Brainticket label.

Once again Robert Lowe was hired in for 'The Living Waters' debut, recorded in early 1997 and issued in the June. Bill Pohl also donated his services on synth guitar.

A mammoth five year gap then dragged out before arrival of a follow up. 2002's 'Paths To Always' would see Shawn Green taking command of the microphone whilst Chris Clifford took over the drum stool.

Albums:
THE LIVING WATERS, Brainticket (1997)
H Sequence / Thorn Of Creation / Coma Crowd / The Belated / The Living Waters / In The Wake Of Delusion / Dimensions / A Warning Never Heard / Things To Come
PATHS TO ALWAYS, Brainticket (2002)
Paths To Always / A Little Slumber / Three, Two, One... / Dead End Ride / In Time / F.N.G. / The Yard

THE LAST DROP (UK)
Line-Up: Tony Inskip (vocals / guitar), Danny Unet (guitar), Phil Brough (bass), Roderick Vyse (drums)

Stoner Rock from Stoke On Trent previously operating as SHALLOW. Under their former title the band signed to Lee Dorrian's Rise Above imprint for the much praised '16 Sunsets In 24 Hours' album.

Upon discovery of an American act having previously registered the band title SHALLOW the group morphed into THE LAST DROP, subsequently releasing the 2002 album '...Where Were You Living A Year From Now?'

Albums:
WHERE WERE YOU LIVING ONE YEAR FROM NOW?, Rise Above (2002)
Echoes Of A Thousand Mountains / Pilgrim (Live) / The Cheese On Toast Experience / Cheese, Wine & Discussion / Mumrah / Sheer Dementia / Drummed Out Of The Brownies / Tree's Chilogy / The Talons Of Weng Chi'eng

LAVRA (FINLAND)
Line-Up: Jukka Sillanpää (vocals / guitar), Joonas Sukanen (guitar / keyboards), Toni Rakkolainen (bass), Mikko Lappalainen (drums)

Prior to the 1995 album 'Bluenothing', an intriguing blend of ambient Doom, LAVRA were operational under the title SCEPTICAL SCHIZO issuing the single 'The Plight' and a string of demos.

LAVRA subsequently folded with frontman Jukka Sillanpää going on to AS DIVINE GRACE, his colleague drummer Mikko Lappälainen joining that same band in 2000. Sillanpää has also held down a term of office with THIS EMPTY FLOW.

Albums:

BLUENOTHING, Demonsound HAM007 (1995)

Strange Lands / To Elide Something / Yesterday It Was Silent / From The Suction Of Blue / E Minor / Never

LEADFOOT (Raleigh, CL, USA)

Line-Up: Karl Agell (vocals), Graham Fry (guitar), Ryan Culp Barringer (guitar), Phil Swisher (bass), Jon McClain (drums)

Renowned outfit created by former CORROSION OF CONFORMITY personnel vocalist Karl Agell, an expatriate Swede, and bass player Phil Swisher, both having appeared on the transitional 'Blind' album. The duo, in league with another CORROSION OF CONFORMITY refugee guitarist Woody Weatherman, united with guitarist Graham Fry from Jazz Fusion acts CLOUD NINE and OZONE QUARTET and drummer Jon McLain of Punk band PICASSO TRIGGER to found LOOSE CANNON in 1993. However, before long Weatherman opted to return to the CORROSION OF CONFORMITY stable. Pulling in ex-MOTHERLOAD rhythm guitarist Ryan Culp Barringer the band soon after switched the band name to LEADFOOT.

A demo session laid down in the Spring of 1995 secured a recording contract with the Roadrunner label. The debut album 'Bring It On' was issued in the Autumn of 1997 but only in Japan and Europe. Oddly the record missed out on a North American release much to the very vocal chagrin of the band. Sometime after drummer Jon McClain made way for Tim Haisman.

The 'Take A Look' album found Barringer substituted by new six stringer Scott Little. Guitarist Graham Fry bowed out in late 2001. Rumours would circulate during 2001 that Agell and Swisher had united with current BROWN and erstwhile CORROSION OF CONFORMITY drummer Reed Mullin on a studio project.

LEADFOOT signed to the Swedish Lunasound Recordings label for a 2002 studio album 'We Drink For Free'.

Albums:

BRING IT ON, Roadrunner (1997)

Bring it On / Soul Full Of Lies / High Time / Roll All Over You / Right Between the Eyes / Ripe / Sooner / Young Dumb Snake / Throwing Out The Baby / Under The Sun / Naked Light / Forgotten One

TAKE A LOOK, The Music Cartel (1999)

Redline / Loose Cannon / Unkind / Built In A Day / War Against You / Take A Look / Reapin' Existence / Drift / Curse The Gods / Old West F-Over / Certain To Be Wrong / Blowhole / Panic Attack

LEAFHOUND (UK)

Line-Up: Peter French (vocals), Mick Halls (guitar), Derek Brooks (guitar), Stuart Brooks (bass), Keith George-Young (drums)

The illustrious LEAFHOUND, cited by some Hard Rock experts as one of the greatest bands ever, offered up only one now highly sought after sophisticated Hard Rock album in the LED ZEPPELIN / FREE mould. Collectors can expect to pay in excess of £1,000 for a mint copy.

The band was founded in London during 1969 under their original title of BLACK CAT BONES. Vocalist PETER FRENCH had previously been with the BRUNNING SUNFLOWER BLUES BAND, recording the 'Bullen St. Blues' album and had been enlisted post BLACK CAT BONES 'Barbed Wire Sandwich' album replacing BRIAN SHORT. In the band's earliest incarnation were guitarist Paul Kossof and drummer Simon Kirke; although both were to leave to form FREE before recording.

As BLACK CAT BONES the band issued one album for Decca Records titled 'Barbed Wire Sandwich'. The line-up for this record being Short, guitarists Rod Price, Derek Brooks and Bob Weston, bassist Stuart Brooks and drummer Phil Lenoir.

Following the album release Price departed to form the successful FOGHAT in America and French pulled in his cousin and ex-SWITCH member Mick Halls.

BLACK CAT BONES evolved into LEAFHOUND, comprising French, Halls, the Brooks brothers and drummer Keith Young. The band toured Europe and Scandinavia, prompting the release of the German issued 'Drowned My Life In Fear' single, but by the time the 'Growers Of Mushroom' album saw a release French had already bailed out to join ATOMIC ROOSTER, performing on their 'In Hearing Of' album.

French was later to travel to America joining CACTUS for their 'Ot n' Sweaty' record and, upon returning to Britain, French was to unsuccessfully audition for both URIAH HEEP and DEEP PURPLE.

By 1977 French was fronting German outfit

233

RANDY PIE on their 'Fast Forward' album before, quite bizarrely, becoming Joseph Goebbels for the Rock-Opera 'Der Fuhrer'. The singer began working with THIN LIZZY guitarist Brian Robertson and ex-FACES / WHO drummer Kenny Jones and a solo album, 'Ducks In Flight', emerged in 1978. This prior to an appearance even stranger than that of the Nazi propaganda minister when French mimicked STATUS QUO's Francis Rossi for the hit spoof single 'Status Rock' by THE HEADBANGERS!

In 1997 Stuart Brooks returned on the scene putting together a band titled WISHING WELL with ex-QUIET RIOT / DOKKEN / GREG LEON INVASION guitarist Greg Leon and former SURVIVOR drummer Mark Droubay.

The LEAFHOUND album was reissued on CD in 1994 on the See For Miles label.

British Retro Doomsters British Retro Doomsters KHANG would record a rendition of 'Stagnant Pools' on their 1999 'Premeditated' album. The famed ORANGE GOBLIN cut a cover version of a track from LEAFHOUND for a split 7" single with ALABAMA THUNDER PUSSY in 2000.

Singles/EPs:
Drowned My Life In Fear / It's Gonna Get Better, Telefunken U56 154 (1971)

Albums:
GROWERS OF MUSHROOM, Decca SKL-R 5094 (1970)
Chauffeur / Death Valley Blues / Feelin' Good / Please Tell My Baby / Coming Back / Save My Love / Four Women / Sylvester's Blues / Good Lookin' Woman

LEECHMILK (Atlanta, GA, USA)
Line-Up: Dan (vocals), Chris Edmonds (guitar), Greg Hess (bass),Charr (drums)

Atlanta Sludgecore founded in 1996. LEECHMILK served up their 2001 album 'Guilty Of Sloth' as a split record with Ohio's SOFA KING KILLER. The band would also include three tracks on the Berserker compilation 'South Of Hell'.

Albums:
STARVATION OF LOCUSTS, Spare Change (2000)
GUILTY OF SLOTH, Tee Pee (2001) (Split album with SOFA KING KILLER)
Of Wall / Dirtclot / Saltlick / The Garrote / Pigsticker / Descending

LEFT HAND SOLUTION (SWEDEN)
Line-Up: Kicki Höijertz (vocals), Jocke Mårdstam (guitar), Peter Selin (bass), Erik

Barthold (drums)

A Slow grinding Metal band with female Doom vocals. LEFT HAND SOLUTION were created in 1991 citing a line-up of Jorgen Fahlberg on vocals and bass, Jocke Mårdstam on guitar and drummer Liljan, later pulling in Peter Selin of REMEDY on bass. The band's first available recordings came with two tracks on the 1993 compilation album 'Metal North'.

Following the six track mini-album 'Shadowdance', which featured Kicki Höijertz on lead vocals, LEFT HAND SOLUTION adopted a new female vocalist Mariana Holmberg and recorded a 1995 demo entitled 'The Wounds Of Bitterness', scoring a deal with the German Nuclear Blast label. The group also contributed two tracks , 'She' and 'Hybrid Moments' to the 1996 MISFITS tribute album 'Hell On Earth'. Another cover came with a rendition of MINE's 'Nowhere To Go' on a further tribute offering.

Following the second album 'Fevered' Jocke Mårdstam left the band, being replaced by Janne Wiklund of UNHOLY and THE KRISTET UTSEENDE. An exclusive track 'Worn Away' surfaced on the April 1998 Nuclear Blast compilation 'Call Of The Dark II'.

The band line-up for the 2001 Thomas Hedquist produced 'Light Shines Black' opus stood at Holmberg, new guitarist Janne Wiklund, bass player Peter Selin and ex-ASPHYXIA drummer Erik Barthold. The record included a cover version of THE EURYTHMICS 'Missionary Man'.

Albums:
SHADOWDANCE, Mass Productions MASS CDS 63 (1995)
Shroud / Infernal / Solitary Fallen Angel / Nightbloom / Final Withering / Shadowdance
FEVERED, Nuclear Blast NB 239-2 (1997)
Thorns / Fevered / The Wounds Of Bitterness / Illusion / Angels With The Last Plagues / Scorns Of Time / The Futile Passion / Memories (Of The Tragedienne) / The Bleeding / Scarred
LIGHT SHINES BLACK, Massprodukticon MASS CD-84 (2001)
Light Shines Black / Soiled Souls / Missionary Man / Lucid Dream Desire / The Crooked Smile / Raven Wings / Vision / Persistence Of Memory / Heart Laid Bare / Orient Nights / A Road To Nowhere

LEGENDA (FINLAND)
Line-Up: Sir Luttinen (vocals / guitar / drums), Niko Karpinnen (bass)

A Doom Gothic assemblage convened by IMPALED NAZARENE and THE BLACK LEAGUE figure Sir Luttinen. Known for his work as a drummer in IMPALED NAZARENE and a plethora of session and side ventures, such as BEHERIT, DIABLOS RISING and HYPNOS, Sir Luttinen first built up this act as GANDHARVA LEGENDA ('Half God'), taking on the extra roles of vocalist and guitarist. Luttinen broke away from IMPALED NAZARENE during the summer of 1995 and in 1996 the project name was trimmed down to simply LEGENDA. Niko Karppinen, of MAPLE CROSS and a session man for SENTENCED, was welcomed onboard as bass player for a demo session entitled 'Chronicles'. During this timeframe Luttinen would also be working up a further solo venture dubbed ISANMAA.

LEGENDA signed to the French Holy Records label for the 1997 'Autumnal' album. Following the 'Eclipse' record of 1998 Karppinen decamped leaving LEGENDA's future in doubt.

Karppinen was also involved in the PLAN E endeavour, a union that culminated with the 'E Is For Your Ears' release performing with the BELIAL / IMPALED NAZARENE rhythm section of bassist Jani Lehtosaari and drummer Reima Kellokoski as well as ex-BELIAL keyboard player Reetta Saisa.

Luttinen has since performed with CATAMENIA.

Albums:
AUTUMNAL, Holy HOLY25CD (1997)
All Flesh Is Glass / Bloodred Sunset / Legend / By The Moonlight / Wolves, Honey, Wolves / Kings / Luciette / Autumn / At Nightfalls / Jackallian Cry / Black Sky / All Love Is Gone / Winter Night
ECLIPSE, Holy (1998)
The Night Has Drawn Night / Where The Devils Dance / Rev. 66 / Shades And Shadows / Dead Red Roses / Melancholy / Cohorts Of Demons / Sister Shadow Sister (Blooddance mix) / The Fall Of Crow / Springrealm / The Heart Of The North / Eclipse

THE LEMMINGS (NJ, USA)
Line-Up: Jim LaPointe (vocals / guitar), Sha Zaidi (bass), Mike Scott (drums)

New Jersey Fuzz Rockers THE LEMMINGS, founded in 1993, issued one self-financed and highly rated album. The group subsequently morphed into SHOVELHEAD during 2000 issuing an eponymous album through Meteor City.

Albums:
THE MARCH OF PROVOCATION, (1998)
Blue Mountain / Nam Song / Red Road / Middle Man / World Collision / Speciesism / The Wreckage / Northern Lights / Holy Liar / Cemetery Trail

LEPROSY FART (SWITZERLAND)
Line-Up: Simon Steinemann (vocals), Roger Sommer (guitar), Heiko Muuss (guitar), Simon Bischoff (bass), Adrian Slemeniak (drums)

A tactlessly named Death Metal band from Switzerland, LEPROSY FART also betrayed more than a few Doom influences in their music.

Formed in Winterthur during 1994 by guitarist Roger Sommer and original vocalist Roger Fritschi, the group also consisted of drummer Daniel Schürch and bassist Simon Bischoff early on before Schürch was replaced by Adrian Slemeniak.

Singles/EPs:
Intro / Leprosy / I Can't Find My Way / R.I.P. / To The End Of Life, Leprosy Fart (1996) ('Leprosy Fart' EP)

LES FAIDITS (BELGIUM / HOLLAND)
Line-Up: Jurgen Cobbaut (vocals), Mark Jansen (vocals), Kristell Lowagie (vocals), Kris Scheerlinck (guitar), Ronny Tijssen (guitar), Ingrid Heijen (bass), Jonne Ziengs (keyboards), Stijn Bannier (keyboards), Ivar De Graaf (drums)

A 2002 project collaboration of the cream of low countries Doom and Gothic. LES FAIDITS was founded by ex-SENGIR members singer Jurgen Cobbaut and guitarist Kris Scheerlinck. Also involved would be SAHARA DUST and former AFTER FOREVER vocalist Mark Jansen, female vocalist Kristell Lowagie, CALLENISH CIRCLE guitarist Ronny Tijssen, MORNING keyboard player Stijn Bannier, THE WOUNDED keyboard player Jonne Ziengs (keys, ex-BLACK WISH bass player Ingrid Heijen and drummer Ivar De Graaf of WITHIN TEMPTATION.

LET ME DREAM (FINLAND)
Line-Up: Tuuka Koskinen (vocals), Jani Koskela (vocals / guitar), Juhana Stolt (guitar), Marko Tuominen (bass), Jari Koskela (keyboards), Marko Jokinen (drums)

A Finnish Doom / Death Metal act that also incorporate elements of Black Metal into their sound. The band date back to 1989 when vocalist / guitarist Jani Koskela and drummer

Janne Peltoranta forged CONGESTION. Teemu Peltoranta would join the duo on keyboards in 1991 and guitarist Marko Pitkanen would be installed but quickly departed. Around this timeframe the demo 'Third Dimension' was laid down after which Marko Tuominen was enrolled for bass duties and a further tape arrived 'Bed Of The Ancient River'. CONGESTION would also tackle their first live gigs during 1993 but Teemu Peltoranta was to depart, replaced by Jari Koskela for a Finnish tour guesting for Argentinean act VIBRION.

The band's demo had by this stage come to the attention of the French Adipocere label and, switching title to LET ME DREAM, the group issued their debut album 'My Dear Succubus' in 1995. Shortly after the album release LET ME DREAM pulled in guitarist Jarno Keskinen but this latest recruit would enjoy only a fleeting tenure.

LET ME DREAM took on a national support tour to TWO WITCHES before going back into the studio for two more demo recordings 'The Maze' and 'Medley Rain'. Their next move was to found their own label imprint, Succubus Records, releasing 'Medley Rain' as a mini-album. The vacant guitar spot was filled at this juncture by Juhana Stolt. Another round of Finnish dates found LET ME DREAM as part of a package billing with TWO WITCHES and British band MIDNIGHT CONFIGURATION.

As a deal for a second album was struck with Italian concern Nocturnal Music Jani Koskela relinquished the lead vocal mantle to Tuuka Koskinen. LET ME DREAM would then participate in their first foreign show, an appearance at 'Hells Gate 999' festival in Talinen, Estonia.

The 'Greyscale' album would be promoted by a Finnish support tour to ENSIFERUM and FINNTROLL capitalized on by a further batch of shows with ANCIENT RITES.

In March of 2001 Janne Peltoranta decamped and Marko Jokinen of SINSATIONAL duly stepped into the breech.

<u>Singles/EPs:</u>
The Maze / Into The Deep Blue Sea / My Dear Succubus (Live) / Wolfborn (Live), Succubus (1999) ('The Maze' EP)

<u>Albums:</u>
MY DEAR SUCCUBUS, Adipocere CDAR 027 (1995)
Centuries Of Longing / Throne Of Dominating Force / The Sight / Burnt Into My Mind / Once In These Misty Fields / When The Sun Rises In The South / Thousand Decades Ago... / Bed Of The Ancient River / In Agony Of My Soul / A Clear Line Of

Sanity / When I Ride To Beyond / My Dear Succubus / Outro: A Cold Wind Blows
GREYSCALE, Nocturnal Music NM014 (2000)
The Maze / City Of Snow / The Spear In Your Hand / Medley Rain / The Crown / Julia / Into The Deep Blue Sea / Love Street 13 / Wolfborn / Outro: Medley Rain (Keyboard version)

LETZTE INSTANZ (GERMANY)

<u>Albums:</u>
BRACHIALROMANTIK, (1998)
OuvertÜRe / Sinnfonie / Folkxweise / Herzdame / Egotrip / Kartenhaus / Schlaflos / Glockenrequiem / Nachtmusik / Schlangentanz / Pennywise / Rosengarten / Der GeigenschÜLer

LID (UK / USA)
Line-Up: Eric Wagner (vocals), Daniel Cavanagh (guitar)

Project union of TROUBLE vocalist Eric Wagner and guitarist Daniel Cavanagh from England's ANATHEMA.

<u>Albums:</u>
IN THE MUSHROOM, Music For Nations (1997)
LID / Mary Agnes / The Dream Is Over / In The Mushroom / Window Pain / Rx / You Are Here / Randy Scouse Git / Alive / For All My Life

LIFE BEYOND (Glenn Dale, MD, USA)
Line-Up: Danny Kenyon (vocals / guitar), Louis Strachan (bass), Gus Basilika (drums)

Maryland's Doom Groovers LIFE BEYOND's membership boasts former INDESTROY, GUT SOUP, DELIRIUM and WRETCHED drummer Gus Basilika, ex-IRON FIST, IMMORAL and CREEPSHOW bassist Louis Strachan and frontman Danny Kenyon, a veteran of INDESTROY, GUT SOUP and VORTEX OF INSANITY. This triumvirate came together in 1999.

Gaining favourable press for the self financed 'Ancient Worlds' mini-album LIFE BEYOND put in a short burst of touring in late September billed with PLACE OF SKULLS. The band set to work on a full-length Frank Marchand produced album 'Thousand Vision Mist' aiming for a 2002 release.

<u>Albums:</u>
ANCIENT WORLDS, (2000)
Never Dead / Sacred Life / Black Rainbow / Resistance

236

LONG WINTER'S STARE (USA)
Line-Up: Chris Listing (vocals / guitar), Madrigal (guitar), Scarab (keyboards), Greg Bull (drums)

An experimental Black fuelled symphonic Doom act. The band purvey an adventurous form of Black Metal interlaid with subdued piano parts and topped off with Death growls. Rhode Island's LONG WINTER STARE was created as MANTHING in 1996. Evolving into LONG WINTER'S STARE the band for a time employed second guitarist Dwarn.

The bands second album 'Before The Dawn, So Go The Shadows Of Humanity', which included a twisted version of the KANSAS AOR classic 'Carry On My Wayward Son', saw backing vocals courtesy of KRIEG's Lord Imperial. During 1999 mainman Chris Listing would also issue tracks from his AS ALL DIE side venture as a split album 'In The Vacuum Of Blackened Space' shared with VEINKE.

The 2000 album 'The Tears Of Odin's Fallen' saw the addition of new vocalist Dierdrie Faith. Guest vocals once again came courtesy of Lord Imperial of KRIEG. LONG WINTER'S STARE dissolved shortly after this release.

Albums:
COLD TALE ETERNAL, Pantheon (1998)
Enter / Timeless & Somber / Sigh / Eternal Slumber / Anastasia / Paranoid / Clawing Out
BEFORE THE DAWN, SO GO THE SHADOWS OF HUMANITY, Dragon Flight (1999)
Blood Of Nazarene / He Is Insane / War Epic / Carry On My Wayward Son / Into The Darkness / Hounds / Remain Life Eternal / Into The Sun
THE TEARS OF ODIN'S FALLEN, Dark Symphonies (2000)
In The Hall Of Odin / Blood Of Steel / Blood Of My Fathers / Neolyth / The Last Call / In Arms / The Unknown God

LORD (FRANCE)
Line-Up: Lord Charon (vocals/bass), Aragorn (guitar), Countess Hoggsogoth (keyboards), Tipthereth (drums)

A Corpsepainted Black Metal act from Hazebouck plying lethargic Doom riffs, LORD evolved as a duo of Lord Charon and keyboard player Countess Hoggsogoth during 1994, adding guitarist Kleudde and drummer Morgon before the year was out. Previous to LORD founder Lord Charon had been a member of Thrash band MEGATHRASH prior to founding Black Metal outfit THESPIAN FLOW. The man's next move was to become bass player for Deathsters SEPULCHARAL. A meeting with Countess Hoggsogoth led in turn to the formation of FUNERAL PYRE, later titled LORD.

The following year LORD issued a demo cassette, 'Shadows Of Massacre', after which the band once more trimmed down to the founding duo.

Prior to recording the debut album guitarist Aragorn and drummer Tipthereth brought the ranks up to strength, although both Kleudde and Morgon contributed to the album sessions.

By 2000 LORD's roster comprised Lord Charon, Countess Hoggsogoth, guitarists The Nazgûl and Samigina and drummer Armageddon.

Albums:
BEHIND THE CURTAIN OF DARKNESS, Eldethorn ELD002 (1998)
Intro / Live To Fight, Fight To Die / Into Hell's Well / Midnight In The Graveyard / When Funeral Pyres Ablaze The Black Moon Sky / Under The Spell Of The Diabolical Sorcerer / Shadows Of Massacre / Calling From The Deepest Darkness / Gates To The Blazing Kingdom

LORD (UK)

A Welsh band with grandiose style, LORD's self-financed album has some excellent songs. The band split in 1992, with guitarist Dave Morse relocating to Los Angeles to form EVE'S TATTOO.

Albums:
GODSQUAD, Terminal TERM001 (1991)

LORDS OF THE STONE (HOLLAND)
Line-Up: Andre Dijkstra (vocals), Martine van Loon (vocals), Roel Dijkstra (guitar), Sander de Wys (bass), Danny Servaes (keyboards), Wichard Visscher (drums)
LORDS OF THE STONE, noted for their debut album inclusion of ex-THE GATHERING female vocalist Martine Van Loon, were founded in 1992 releasing their first demo tape titled 'Rhymes Of Bitterness' the same year. The band line-up at this juncture comprised vocalists Inga de Haas and Andre Dijkstra, GOD DETHRONED guitarist Henri Sattler, bass player Evert Jepma and GOD DETHRONED drummer Ard de Weerd.

Martine van Loon was inducted as vocalist in 1994. Tracks on a compilation album followed quickly capitalized on by a further demo, 'Diamond In The Dust'. A track from these sessions, 'Fire In The Winter', was released by Displeased Records as one half of a split 7" single with CELESTIAL SEASON. The following year Arjan van der Logt took over bass duties and Henk Van-Barneveld became keyboard player.

In 1996 LORDS OF THE STONE cut a third demo, 'In An Eyelid's Fall', which led to an album deal with Massacre Records. A completely new look band had Dijkstra and van Loon fronting up a fresh cast of musicians comprising guitarist Roel Dijkstra, bassist Sandra De Wys, GOD DETHRONED keyboard player Danny Servaes and drummer Wichard Visscher.

Singles/EPs:
Fire In The Winter, Displeased (1994) (split 7" with CELESTIAL SEASON)

Albums:
NIGHT FLOWERS, Massacre MAS PC0108 (1997)
Unbound / The Oldest Dance / Serenity / Memories / Power Of The Wolf / Fire In The Winter / Wander / Drifting Leaves / Weep / Visions / Undeceived

THE LORD WEIRD SLOUGH FEG
(San Francisco, CA, USA)
Line-Up: Mike Scalzi (vocals / guitar), John Cobbett (guitar), Adrian Maestas (bass), Greg Haa (drums)

A strange monicker for an equally bizarre band. THE LORD WEIRD SLOUGH FEG, the name being taken from a Celtic mythological figure as chronicled in the Ta'in Bo Cuailgne stories, are an out and out Doom / Psych flavoured Heavy Metal band but with added avant-garde twists. The Irish historical theme permeates through all the band's releases. Oddly, the band's label Dragonheart claims the act is influenced by MANOWAR, MANILLA ROAD and CIRITH UNGOL, an assertion the band themselves officially deny! The San Francisco based group, founded by Pennsylvania native Mike Scalzi and drummer Greg Haa originally from Maryland, was founded in 1990 with the intention of offering 'honour Metal', inspired by the singer's interest in Celtic myth. This fascination crossed over into early live shows, the war painted band adorning their stages with torches and bones. The 1990 incarnation of the band saw Scalzi and Haa joined by guitarist Chris Haa and bassist Justin Phelps. A succession of line-up changes, including bass player Stu Kane in 1994, witnessed the group in a constant state of flux until recording of the debut album.

The second album 'Twilight Of The Idols' was initially issued by the Doomed Planet label in North America as a vinyl release in 1998. An exclusive track entitled 'The Room' surfaced on the Bad Posture 'Metal Injection' album the same year. The Italian Dragonheart concern picked the 'Twilight Of The Idols' album up for international CD release the following year adding two extra tracks 'We'll Meet Again' and 'Warpspasm'.

In 1999 THE LORD WEIRD SLOUGH FEG line-up was credited as frontman Mike Scalzi, guitarist John Cobbett, bass player Jim Mack and drummer Greg Haa.

Although the 2000 'Down Among The Deadman' album would see the inclusion of John Torres, erstwhile member of ANGELWITCH and LÄÄZ ROCKIT, on bass, guitarist John Cobbett brother Dan took over four string responsibilities upon the recording sessions conclusion.

THE LORD WEIRD SLOUGH FEG toured Europe with SOLSTICE and TWISTED TOWER DIRE during July 2000. This relationship with SOLSTICE would be cemented further as both bands contributed tracks to a MANOWAR cover versions single issued by Doomed Planet in 2001. THE LORD WEIRD SLOUGH FEG donated 'Fast Taker', marking the inauguration of new bassist Adrian Maestas.

John Cobbett and Mike Scalzi busied themselves with the extreme Metal side venture HAMMERS OF MISFORTUNE (previously heralded as UNHOLY CADAVER), releasing the album 'The Bastard'.

The British Miskatonic Foundations label would reissue the debut album clad in new artwork and with extra tracks during 2002. Germany's Metal Supremacy label would release the same album in vinyl format. In June the band paired up with TWISTED TOWER DIRE for a run of shows in Germany. A fresh studio album, provisionally billed as 'The Traveller', was scheduled for 2002 release.

Singles/EPs:
Fast Taker, Doomed Planet (2001) (Split single with SOLSTICE)

Albums:
THE LORD WEIRD SLOUGH FEG, (1997)
Shadows Of The Unborn / 20th Century Wretch / Blarney Stone / The Red Branch / Why Not / High Season III / High Season IV / Highway Corsair
TWILIGHT OF THE IDOLS, Dragonheart CHAOS 005CD (1999)
Funeral March / Highlander / High Season II / The Pangs Of Ulster / Brave Connor Mac /

The Wickerman / Slough Feg / The Great Ice Wars / Life In The Dark Age / Warpspasm / Bi-Polar Disorder / The Wizard's Vengeance / We'll Meet Again
DOWN AMONG THE DEADMEN, Dragonheart (2000)
Sky Chariots / Walls Of Shame / Warriors Dawn / Beast In The Broch / Heavy Metal Monk / Fergus Mac Roich / Cauldron Of Blood / Troll Pack / Traders And Gunboats / Psionic Illuminations / Marauder / High Season / Death Machine
THE LORD WEIRD SLOUGH FEG, Miskatonic Foundation (2002)
Shadows Of The Unborn / 20th Century Wretch / Blarney Stone / The Red Branch / Why Not / Highway Corsair / High Season III / High Season IV / Intro / The Mask / High Season I / High Season II / The Red Branch (Demo version) / The Room / Headhunter

LOST BREED (CA, USA)
Line-Up: Pat Lydon (vocals / guitar), Eric Baestlein (guitar), Vinny Augustine (bass), Jamie Silver (drums)

A Californian Doom band that demoed with Wino of THE OBSESSED during 1988. LOST BREED would issue two upbeat Doom Metal offerings for the cult German Hellhound label before disbanding. Former frontman Chris Roseberry would later work with LEGACY whilst guitarist Eric Baestlein founded THE VENGEANCE BROTHERS.

Singles/EPs:
Desert Fox / No Hope, Lost Breed (1989)

Albums:
THE EVIL IN YOU AND ME, Hellhound HELL 023CD (1993)
Rescind The Horde / King Of Electric / Another Victim / Coffin Cheater / The Postman / Soul Chariot / Lost Breed / The Devil In You And Me / Nation's Song / Say You Love Satan / Storm Comes Down
SAVE YOURSELF, Hellhound H 0033-2 (1994)
Circles / B.A.C. (What You Fear) / Gears / Going Strong / 472 C.I. Of Death / Lease On Life / Chop / Dragon Of Chaos / You Don't Need To Live / Tonga Slut / Simulator / Up The Hill

LOST CENTURY (GERMANY)
Line-Up: Andreas Lohse (vocals), Martin Bayer (guitar), Jens Schäfer (guitar), Rudi Görg (bass), Jason Kubke (drums)

Including ex-APOSTASY vocalist Andreas

Lohse and former members of RESEARCH. LOST CENTURY's first demo of 1990 ' Miserality' featured original guitarist Phillip who left prior to the second demo of 1992 entitled 'A Truth Beyond'. Guitar duties for this tape were handled by Stefan.
Stefan quit before recording of the debut album began and, after its release, the group toured Germany opening for POLTERGEIST and CORONER.
Lohse founded THOUGHTSPHERE releasing the 2000 album 'Vague Horizons'.

Albums:
NATURAL PROCESS OF PROGRESSION, DMP 021-93 (1993)
The End / Submit To Stagnation / Cling To The Unreal / Delivering The Sentence, Part I: Birth, Part II: Murder, Part III: Conviction And Death / Trivial (Towards Destination)
COMPLEX MICROCOSM - MOVEMENT IN NINE RITUALS, T&T-Noise TT11-2 (1994)
Descending / Silent Inside / Like The One Above / Fallen Star / Second Coming / Wind In The Willows / Life Itself / Traverse The Veil / Complex Microcosm
POETIC ATMOSPHERE OF SEASONS, T&T TT 0018-2 (1995)
Seal Of Thorns / Autumn's Gift / Unicorn / Breathing Underwater: Death / Last Days Of Spring / Winter Twilight / Kryogenic / Summer's Dishonest Apologies / Search / Owe Me Awe

LOST DREAMS (AUSTRIA)
Line-Up: Markus Wenael (vocals), Andreas Maierhofer (guitar), Herbert Sporacolle (guitar), Thomas Auer (bass), Philip Hoertnagel (keyboards), Marco Eller (drums)

Albums:
REFLECTIONS OF DARKNESS, Lost Dreams (1999)
Reflections Of Darkness / Obsessed / Allways Beside You / Burning Eyes / The Funeral Of God / Believe In Evil (Live)

LOST GOAT (USA)
Line-Up: Erika Stoltz (vocals / bass), Eric Peterson (guitar), Tina Gordon (drums)

San Francisco Stoner power trio fronted by erstwhile BLOOD LIBEL vocalist / bassist Erika Stolz, also of AMBER ASYLUM. Guitarist Eric Peterson was previously with Wisconsin act NATURAL CAUSE whilst drummer Tina Gordon has credits with T.N.T. The LOST GOAT triumvirate came together during 1994. A split album with GRINCH surfaced through the Misanthropic label and in 1996 the 'Trapped On Earth' album. Touring found LOST GOAT as far afield as Alaska as guests to 7 YEAR BITCH the following year. During 1999 LOST GOAT toured America with L7 and NEBULA promoting the 'Equator' album, released by Man's Ruin on CD and Tee Pee Records for vinyl format. Further dates saw the band on the road with HIGH ON FIRE. The band got more than they bargained for when touring with MEN OF PORN during 2000 as the headline act lost half their band contingent. In order to complete the dates Stoltz and LOST GOAT roadie John Michaels substituted on bass and drums respectively.

Erica Stolz would contribute guest vocals to Portland's WITCH MOUNTAIN 2001 album '...Come The Mountain' on the track 'A Power Greater'.

Singles/EPs:
Pillar Of Salt / Rising, (199-) ('Beware Of Chupacabras' EP)
October / Golem, Alternative Tentacles VIRUS 208 (1997)
White Dog, Poverty PVTY-0009 (1998) (Split single with TOWEL)

Albums:
LOST GOAT, Misanthropic (1995) (Split album with GRINCH)
Rising / Fool Proof / The Dirty Ones / The Offering
TRAPPED ON EARTH, Life Is Abuse (1996)
Pillar Of Salt / Wailing Wall Blues / Trapped On Earth / Television / Freeway / Hand Of Man / The Last One / Golem
EQUATOR, Man's Ruin (1999)
Doin' Time / Bitter Pill / Downbound Train / White Dog - Purple Pussy / The Dirty Ones / Poison / Hell In Ruin
THE DIRTY ONES, Tee Pee (2002)
Seattle Shakedown / Maiden Twisted / Cracked And Burned / The Drifter / The Hanging Tree / Line 'Em / Spark / Going Far Out / Coedine

LOST IN TEARS (FINLAND)
Line-Up: L.H. Sjöblom (vocals), M. Rajanen (guitar), H.C. Frondén (guitar), A. Bomberg (guitar), C.F. Sjöblom (bass), Liljeberg (drums)

LOST IN TEARS, describing themselves as "Melodic Martyr Metal", are a Gothic Doom Metal band founded in the summer of 1997. In

LOST GOAT
Photo : El Danno

the Spring of 1999 the band introduced a third guitar to their line-up, manouevering original bassist A. Bomberg to guitar and inducting new member C.F. Sjöblom into the four string position. A brace of self-financed EPs, including December 1999's 'Ad Mortem' which was distributed globally by the Canadian Frowz Productions label, led to a recording deal with the Spanish Locomotive Music label for the 2002 album 'Dialogue With Mirror And God'.

Singles/EPs:
Forever Alone / Why Waste Grace On Me / Crystal Madonna / Moon Of Mine, (1998) ('Forever Alone' EP)
Lost Treasure / Past Of Tomorrow / Theatre Of Misery / Angel / Moon Of Mine (Remastered) / Theatre Of Misery (Radio edit), (1999) ('Ad Mortem' EP)

Albums:
DIALOGUE WITH MIRROR AND GOD, Locomotive Music (2002)
Intro / Without You / Night Descends / Dialogue With Mirror And God / X76 / Terribly Concerned / The Bleeding / Beauty From The Past / Siren / Vanity / Soul In Flames / So Cold

LOST IN TWILIGHT (FINLAND)
Line-Up: Jyri Aarniva (vocals), Jarno Laakso (guitar), Sami Inkiläinen (guitar), Jukka Hoffren (bass), Jarno Hänninen (keyboards), Janne Hänninen (drums)

LOST IN TWILIGHT arrived during 1998 touting a seven track self-financed totally instrumental album 'Descending Mist'. The line-up of the band, founded some four years earlier, was billed as a quartet of guitarists Jarno Laakso and Sami Inkiläinen, keyboard player Jarno Hänninen and drummer Janne Hänninen.
The four track 'Forever Autumn' EP arrived in the Autumn of 1999 and would debut the band's new vocalist Jyri Aarniva. LOST IN TWILIGHT would add bassist Jukka Hoffren for the 'Planeteer' EP, issued by Sound Riot Records during 2000.
In 2002 LOST IN TWILIGHT switched titles to DEVICE then DEVERCIA and subsequently switched labels to the Dutch Hammerheart concern.

Singles/EPs:
Diamonds In The Dust / Forever Autumn / Winter's Son / To Forgive, (1999)
Planeteer / As Mists Descend / Lost Generation / Vaya Con Diablos, Sound Riot SRP 10 (2000) ('Planeteer' EP)

Albums:
DESCENDING MIST, (1998)
Twilights Call (Intro) / Fountain Of Dreams / As Mist Descends / Paralyzing Agony / Forest Of Frozen Time / Circle Of Eternal Sorrow / Tranquility Before The Storm

LOVE HISTORY (CZECH REPUBLIC)
Line-Up: Marek Dihel (vocals), Richard Chrobok (vocals / guitar), Pavel Herich (vocals / guitar), Tom Cieply (bass), Hanka Vanková (keyboards), Radim Chrobok (drums)

Gothic Metal band LOVE HISTORY began life during 1992 billed ETERNITY. The band number no less than three lead vocalists with Marek Dihel responsible for bass vocals and both guitar players Richard Chrobok and Pavel Herich delivering Death growls. Drummer Radim Chrobok also weighs in on occasion credited simply with "screams".
The band's initial formation found the Chrobok cousins guitarist Richard and drummer Radim joined by second guitarist Martin Dejovec and later vocalist Robert and bassist Roman. Before long Dejovec was usurped by former BIGOTRY six stringer Richard Minx and the band rounded off by Eva on vocals, keyboards and flute.
By the Autumn of 1993 the new title of LOVE HISTORY had been decided upon and a demo session entitled 'The Astral Silence Of Blooming Virgin Beauty' recorded. As 1994 drew in Minx made his exit, later turning up in DISSOLVING OF PRODIGY, and Bilos of MALIGNANT TUMOUR was enrolled. At this juncture Eva opted out but would remain on hand as a session performer.
A mini-album 'Desires', released in late 1995 by the Italian Northern Darkness label, would signal a series of radical line-up ructions. Indeed, only the Chrobok cousins survived the cull, these two regrouping with keyboard player Radek to record the inaugural full-length offering 'Gallileo, Figaro - Magnifico', laid down in December of 1996. Much to their dismay though the Northern Darkness label would hold onto the tapes until finally releasing the album in mid 2000. Some compensation was offered by the Czech Shindy Productions concern who made the record available on cassette format.
LOVE HISTORY signed to The End Records in late 1998 for new product. The Chrobok's completely rebuilding the band in the process enlisting vocalist Marek Dihel, guitarist Pavel Herich, bassist Tom Cieply and keyboard player Hanka Vanková. The 'Anasazi' album would boast a supporting cast of eclectic musicians such as soprano vocalist Lada Soukupova, narrator Mark Allen and flautists

Xenie Stehlikova and Petr Parizek.

Albums:
DESIRES, Northern Darkness (1996)
From Bohemians's Woods And Fields /
Labyrinth Of Love / Desires / In Passion /
Through The Shady History
GALILEO, FIGARO - MAGNIFICO, Northern
Darkness (2000)
Galileo, Figaro - Magnifico..... / Desires - Part
II / The Gleam Of Midnight Sky / Alone /
Smell Of Tears / Secrets Of Dreams And
Moon - Dedicated To Eva / Night's Escape /
Morning's Rain / Enigmatic Love / Epilogue
ANASAZI, The End (2001)
Lost / Angealism / Korbel / Sown / Spiritual /
The Mass / Phantomous / Voices / Lost

LOVE LIKE BLOOD (GERMANY)
Line-Up: Yorck Eysel (vocals), Stephan
Noschilla (guitar), Gunnar Eysel (bass), Joxx
Schmidt (drums)

Gothic Rockers LOVE LIKE BLOOD, titled
after the classic KILLING JOKE song, were
founded in 1988 with an initial line-up of
vocalist Gonzo, guitarist Peter Büchle, bassist
Gunnar Eysel and drummer Joxx Schmidt.
The following year Gonzo quit to be replaced
by Yorck Eysel in time for their debut self-
financed EP 'Sinister Dawn'.
1990 saw the departure of Büchle and in
came Stephen Noschilla. LOVE LIKE BLOOD
released their debut full-length album, 'Flags
Of Revolution' in 1992, preceded by another
EP in the form of 1991's 'Ecstasy'.
The album was the first fruits of a deal with
Rebel Records and LOVE LIKE BLOOD
supported THE RUBICON on their 1992
German tour in support of the record.
Guitarist Marc Wheeler was added, but
departed after the release of 1994's
'Odyssee' album. So, for 1995's 'Exposure'
album the band recruited guitarist Colin
Hughes.
The 1998 EP included a cover version of
KILLING JOKE's seminal 'Love Like Blood'
and included guest sessions from Esa
Holopainen of AMORPHIS, drummer A.C. of
LACRIMOSA and GOREFEST's Ed Warby.
The band's 'Snakekiller' album was produced
by Peter Tägtgren of HYPOCRISY.
Ex-LOVE LIKE BLOOD man Adrian Hates
founded DIARY OF DREAMS to issue the
2000 album 'One Of 18 Angels'.
The 2000 album 'Enslaved + Condemned'
was produced by Simon Efemey. For their
2001 offering LOVE LIKE BLOOD came up
with the novel idea of chronologically
cataloguing the history of Gothic Rock. The
record, 'Chronology Of A Love Affair', took the
listener through a cover version timescape
commencing with JOY DIVISION's 'Decades'
and closing with the MARILYN MANSON tune
'Great Big White World'. Along the way LOVE
LIKE BLOOD offered representations of
PARADISE LOST's 'True Belief', TYPE O
NEGATIVE's 'Black No. 1', TIAMAT's
'Whatever That Hurts' and CHRISTIAN
DEATH's 'Church Of No Return' among
others. Naturally KILLING JOKE's 'Love Like
Blood' would also be in evidence.

Singles/EPs:
Doomsday / Swordilly / Two And A Half
Years / Tragic Vaudeville, Deathwish Office
(1989) ('Sinister Dawn' EP)
Revelation / Injustice / Last Evil Emotions /
Angie / Dear Catherine, Deathwish Office
(1991) ('Ecstasy' EP)
Kiss And Tell / Salvation / Doomsday II
(New Arrangement) / Tragic Vaudeville (New
Arrangement), Rebel 055-45283 (1992)
An Irony Of Fate, Rebel 084-45321 (1992)
Walking In Demimondes / Psychedelic
Passion / Siberian Pandemonium (Inferno
Mix) / Walking In Demimondes (Underworld
Mix), Rebel 055-45333 (1992)
('Demimondes' EP)
Stormy Visions, Rebel 055-45493 (1993)
Pale Sky / Dawnland / This Empty Ocean,
Focusion (1997) ('Taste of Damacles'
Promotional release)
Pale Sky / Love Like Blood / Ylene / Kill The
Snake / Tomorrow, Hall Of Sermon HOS
7071 (1998) ('Love Like Blood' EP)

Albums:
FLAGS OF REVOLUTION, Rebel SPV 076-
45352 (1992)
Within The Realm Of A Dying Sun / Apathy
And Boredom / Mercy Killing / Children /
Tears Of Liberation / Johannesburg / Out Of
Sight / The Tribute Of Manilla
AN IRONY OF FATE, Rebel SPV 084-45322
(1992)
The Everlasting Dream / Walking In
Demimondes / In The Shadows Of The Sun /
Look Out / Kiss And Tell / Siberian
Pandemonium / More Than Salvation? /
Noxious Secrets / Awake In Desire
SINISTER DAWN/ ECSTASY, Rebel SPV
076-45362 (1992)
Doomsday / Swordilly / Two And A Half Years
/ Tragic Vaudeville / Revelation / Injustice /
Last Evil Emotions / Angie / Dear Catherine
ODYSSEE, Rebel 084-45552 (1994)
Odyssee / Feedback / High Tension / Don't
Leave Me / Fallacious World / Night Is Young
/ Lures / Sedative Shots / Paralysis / Stormy
Visions / Blood Trails / Epitaph / Within The
Realm Of A Dying Sun (Live) / Dear

242

Catherine (Live)
EXPOSURE, Rebel 085-45752 (1995)
Exposure / Painkilling Suicide / Lost / Shed
Your Skin / Colours Of Perversity / Life /
Lethal Radiation / Hide
SNAKEKILLER, Rebel SPV 085-45752
(1998)
Into The Snake Pit / Pale Sky / Phrases /
Liberation / Snakekiller / Whispering
Memories / Ylene / This Empty Ocean /
Dawnland / Lost Evidence / Brainchild
ENSLAVED + CONDEMNED, Hall Of
Sermon (2000)
Love Kills / Cry Out / Dying Nation / Slow
Motion / The River / 7 Seconds / The Silver
Shot / Passionate / Violation / Bleeding / Like
A Bird / Remember
CHRONOLOGY OF A LOVE AFFAIR, Hall
Of Sermon (2001)
Decades / She's In Parties / A Strange Day /
Lucretia My Reflection / Church Of No
Return / Wasteland / Rain / April Skies /
Love Under Will / Love Like Blood / True
Belief / Copycat / Black No.1 / Whatever That
Hurts / Great Big White World

LOWRIDER (SWEDEN)
Line-Up: Peder Bergstrand (vocals / bass),
Ola Hellqvist (guitar), Niclas Stalfors (guitar),
Andreas Eriksen (drums)

Unashamed Karlstad based Stoners
LOWRIDER evolved from the all instrumental
act BEEF, a band generated in late 1996.
Having lost their bass player the BEEF pairing
of vocalist / bassist Peder Bergstrand and
guitarist Olla Hellqvist pulled in Niclas Stalfors
on guitar and recorded a demo that, by
necessity, saw Bergstrand performing vocals,
guitar, bass and drums. Shortly after
drummer Andreas Eriksen was enrolled and
the name LOWRIDER was taken on, adopted
from the WAR song.
LOWRIDER shared their 1998 'Split' album
with the ex-KYUSS and FU MANCHU band
NEBULA. Of interest to collectors was that
CD and vinyl versions boasted exclusive
tracks, the CD including 'Lameneshma' whilst
the vinyl edition added 'Ol Mule Pepe'.
LOWRIDER's 2000 full length 'Ode To Io'
album, which came packaged in elaborate
silver sleeve artwork, was promoted in
Europe by mainland gigs alongside DOZER
in October and November.

Albums:
SPLIT, Meteor City MCY002 (1998) (Split
CD with NEBULA)
Lameneshma / The Gnome, The Serpent,
The Sun / Shivaree / Upon The Dune (Full
version)

ODE TO IO, Meteor City MCY-012 (2000)
Caravan / Flat Earth / Convoy V / Dust
Settlin' / Sun Devil / Anchor / Texas Pt I & II /
Riding Shotgun / Saguaro / Ode To Io

LOW VIBES (FRANCE)
Line-Up: Matt (vocals / bass), Esteban
(guitar), Nico (drums)

Stoner trio dating back to 1997. In August of
1998 the band cut their opening demo 'Put
The Gun Down... Sweetie!', a four track effort
later reissued on CD format by Water Dragon
Records re-billed as 'Low Vibes'. From the
April 1999 'In The Midst Of A Drama' release
a whole stream of EPs ensued including the
'Coming Down To Velvet Lodge' split affair
shared with SPACE PATROL.
LOW VIBES August 2000 'Psychic Travel' EP
would be reissued in July of the following year
with all new sleeve artwork and an extra track,
a live version of 'Change'.

Singles/EPs:
Orange Blackbox / Tears Away / Evermore,
Water Dragon (1998) ('In The Midst Of A
Drama' EP)
Gone / The Flow / In Ourselves, Deeper /
Failure, Water Dragon (1998) ('Low Vibes'
EP)
Start Over / Orange Blackbox / The Flow /
Connection, Water Dragon (1999) ('Low
Vibes' Promotion release)
Start Over / Anyway / Get Lost, Water
Dragon (1999) ('Coming Down To The Velvet
Lodge' Split EP with SPACE PATROL)
Soul Salvation / Connection / Shine /
Traveller Song, Water Dragon (2000)
('Psychic Travel' EP)
Soul Salvation / Connection / Shine /
Traveller Song / Change (Live), Water
Dragon (2001) ('Psychic Travel' EP)

LUCIFER'S HAMMER (Mason, MI, USA)
Line-Up: Todd Cushman (vocals), Mike
Seabrook (guitar / keyboards), Andy Smith
(bass), John Caldwell (drums)

An obscure but revered underground
Doomdeath act out of Michigan. LUCIFER'S
HAMMER issued three demo sessions,
1989's Descent Into Beyond', 1992's The
Burning Church' and 1995's 'Hymns To The
Moon' upfront of the debut album 'The Mists
Of Time'. The band date back to the mid '80s.
'The Mists Of Time' included a cover version
of BATHORY's 'Enter The Eternal Fire'.

Albums:
THE MISTS OF TIME, (1997)
The Mists Of Time / Woodland Realm / Sad

Bird Midst / Phantom Spirit / Ethereal Sea Of Forever / Celestial Vision / Sonatina / Enter The Eternal Fire

GHOSTS OF FALL, (2001)
Ancient Gods / Lacus Mortis / Ghosts Of Fall / Land Of Winds & Ghosts / Mystic Dawn / The Usurper / Dark Tower / Garden Of Solitude / Entrance To Gehenna / Widow's Lament / Dark Tower (Remix)

LUCYFIRE (SWEDEN)

TIAMAT frontman Johan Edlund struck out on a no frills Gothic Rock n' Roll direction with the 2001 solo side project LUCYFIRE. Scoring a deal with SPV Records LUCYFIRE issued 'This Dollar Saved My Life at Whitehorse'. The album, produced by Dirk Draeger who also contributed guitar, saw the utilization of session performers Bertram Engel on drums, Jan Kazder on bass, Marc Engelmann on keyboards and secondary vocals courtesy of Sille Lemke. Quite bizarrely the record included a cover version of ZZ TOP's 'Sharp Dressed Man'.

Edlund, billing himself as "Notorious PIG" for the LUCYFIRE endeavour also assembled a live band for an appearance at the 'Mera Luna' festival in Hildesheim, Germany. The live LUCYFIRE band saw Edlund in the esteemed company of KINGDOM COME guitarist Eric Förster, TIAMAT's Anders Iwers on guitar, Carlos Satanos on bass, DARK TRANQUILITY keyboard player Martin Brändström and CATASTROPHE BALLET drummer Alexander Sauerländer.

Albums:
THIS DOLLAR SAVED MY LIFE AT WHITEHORSE, SPV (2001)
Baby Come On (She's A Devil Of A Woman) / Thousand Million Dollars In The Fire / Mistress Of The Night / Over & Out / As Pure As S.I.N. / Automatic / Perfect Crime / U Can Have All My Love 2nite / Sharp Dressed Man / Annabel Lee / The Pain Song

LULLACRY (FINLAND)

Line-Up: Tanya (vocals), Sami Vauhkonen (guitar), Sauli Kivilahti (guitar), Heavy (bass), Jukka Outinen (drums)

LULLACRY guitarists Sami Vauhkonen, also a GANDALF member, and Sauli Kivilahti started life as members of COARSE making an initial impact with the 'Downwards' demo

LULLACRY

244

and a track inclusion on the 'Suomi Finland Perkele' compilation album.

The inaugural LULLACRY line-up would see a rhythm section of bassist Kimmo Aroluoma and drummer Nalle Österman. However, both Aroluoma and Österman would bid their farewells before going on to GANDALF. The bass player would later session with Rap Metal band SOUL ABOVE.

Bringing in the blonde siren Tanya on lead vocals, bassist 'Heavy' and AT WINTER'S END drummer Jukka Outinen the band switched titles to LULLACRY and issued the 'Weeper's Aeon' session. LULLACRY would make their presence felt at the 'Nummirock' and 'Tuska Metalfest' events, gaining extra publicity as tour support to THE GATHERING. The group debuted with the 'Sweet Desire' album released by the Heart, Trust & Respect label before ascending to the Spinefarm concern for 'Be My God'.

The band would be dealt a major blow in May of 2002 when Tanya, undoubtedly the focal point of the band up to that juncture, left the fold.

In something of a coincidence LULLACRY soon announced Tanya's replacement as being - Tanja Lainio. The new singer soon made her mark, adding backing vocals to Swedish Gothic Metal band MARBLE ARCH's album 'Another Sunday Bright'.

Albums:
SWEET DESIRE, Heart, Trust & Respect HTR1319-2 (1999)
For Evermore / Alone / All For Nothing / Sweet Desire / My Dear Skinwalker / Downwards / Whisper In The Chaos / I Will Make My Paradise / The Chant / Feardance / The Autumn
BE MY GOD, Spinefarm SPI 127CD (2001)
Embrace Me / Be My God / Without The Dreamer / Into Your Heart / Trust / Pain, Walk With Me / I Don't Mind / Damn You / Bonfires Of Time / Thorn Of The Rose / Firequeen

LUNATIC INVASION (GERMANY)
Line-Up: Ramlow (vocals / keyboards), Wulfert (guitar / keyboards), Hellbach (bass), Majewski (drums)

An atmospheric Doom / Death Metal group from Germany, LUNATIC INVASION also have a rather Gothic touch.

Albums:
TOTENTANZ, Invasion IR 015 (1995)
Titentanz / Haut / Deads Paradise / Sturm / Asche Zu Asche / Fallen Angel / Gathering Of Bones / Dance Macabre / Prozession /

The Haunted Palace / Dark Prayers / Blut Gott

LUNGBRUSH (Chicago, IL, USA)
Line-Up: Roach (vocals), Jeff Holmes (guitar), Jon Billman (bass), Ricardo Salinaas (drums)

Albums:
OLD SCHOOL, NEW SCHOOL, Pavement 32303-2 (1999)
Urban Tribes / Lost / Sometimes / Exit / Bound / For A Minute / Heroin Suicide / Hindsight / Corporate Bullsh#*t / Clozaril / Janie / Synthetic / I Quit / Soiled

MADDER MORTEM
(NORWAY)
Line-Up: Agnete M. Kirkevaag (vocals), BP M. Kirkevaag (guitar), Eirik Ulvo Langnes (guitar), Pål Mozart Bjørke (bass), Mads Solås (drums)

MADDER MORTEM's fare was epic-laden Doom initially but the group would drift into more experimental waters by the time of the 2001 'All Flesh Is Grass' album. The group had debuted during 1993 billed as MYSTERY TRIBE for the demo session 'Days In Sorrow' armed with a line-up comprising lead vocalist Agnete M. Kirkevaag, guitarists BP M. Kirkevaag and Christian Ruud, bass player Boye Nyberg and Sigurd Nielsen on drums.
MADDER MORTEM signed to the influential yet ill-fated Misanthropy label in Britain for the 'Mercury' album of 1998. However, with Misanthropy's demise the album was afforded little promotion. Beset by such problems in the Autumn of 1999 the band split in two but would soon regroup with the addition of three new members: guitarist Eirik Ulvo Langnes, bassist Pål Mozart Bjørke and drummer Mads Solås.
A new demo convinced the German Century Media concern of their worth and second album 'All Flesh Is Grass' duly arrived in 2001.

Singles/EPs:
Misty Sleep EP, (1997)

Albums:
MERCURY, Misanthropy (1998)
Undertow / Under Another Moon / He Who Longed For The Stars / These Mortal Sins / The Grinding Silence / Loss / Remnants / Misty Sleep / Conversion
ALL FLESH IS GRASS, Century Media (2001)
Breaker Of Worlds / To Kill And Kill Again / The Cluster Children / Ruby Red / Head On Pillow / Turn The War On / 4 Chambers / Ten Times Defeat / Traitor's Mark

MADRIGAL (SWEDEN)
Line-Up: Martin Karlsson (vocals / guitar), Kristoffer Sundberg (guitar), Lukas Gren (bass), Linda Emanuelsson (keyboards), Marcus Bergman (drums)

Gothic Metal band founded whilst still all teenagers in Gothenburg during 1998. The same year MADRIGAL offered the two track 'Enticed' demo CD. The band's big break came in 2000 when a support slot to famed Death Metal band IN FLAMES impressed the headline act's vocalist Anders Friden to such a degree he offered to produce the band's debut album. Friden would also be instrumental in landing MADRIGAL a deal with Germany's Nuclear Blast label.
'I Die, You Soar' duly arrived in September of 2001, supported by an opening slot to THERION's November Scandinavian dates.

Albums:
I DIE, YOU SOAR, Nuclear Blast NB 655 (2001)
Same Face / Languish / Taint Of Shame / Mind In Disguise / In Debris / Ashen Eyes / Enticed / Moulded Pain

MAEL MORDHA (IRELAND)
Line-Up: Rob (vocals), Gerry (guitar), Dave (bass), Dod (bass)

Self styled 'Ceol Breatha Gaelach' or Gaelic Doom. The Pictish war painted MAEL MORDHA started life billed as UAIGNEAS. The band self-financed the 1999 'The Path To Insanity' EP. The exclusive track 'Atlas Of Sorrow' appears on a double album of Irish metal acts entitled 'In Unison'

Singles/EPs:
Tá Mael Mórdha Ag Teacht / A Path To Glory / The Serpent And The Black Lake / Godless Commune Of Sodom / Realms Of Insanity, Deasmumhan (1999) ('The Path To Insanity' EP)

MAGNIFIED EYE (DENMARK)
Line-Up: Torben Egebjerg (vocals), Klaus D.H. Riis (guitar), Torben Ravn (bass), Frode Bjerkely (drums)

Danish Groove Fuzz Rockers MAGNIFIED EYE came into being during 1999. The duo of guitarist Klaus D.H. Riss and vocalist Torben Egebjerg were first inspired with drummer Frode 'Corfu' Bjerkely joining in November. A demo was cut in April of 2000 after which bassist Michael completed the band. However, by that June Torben Ravn had made the four string position his own.
MAGNIFIED EYE contributed the track 'Fuel To The Fire' to the This Dark Reign 'Doomed ' compilation.

Albums:
THE LAST SUN, Daredevil DD018 (2002)
On The Edge Of A Stone / Keep Distance / The Last Sun / Secret Mountain / No Big Deal / Alcoholic Haze / Diesel Breath / Speed Wagon Hippie Chick / Conundrum / Zero

MAHAVATAR (New York, NY, USA)
Line-Up: Lizza Hayson (vocals), Karla
Williams (guitar), Eddie Gasior (bass), Evan
Glantz (flute), Itamar Ben-Zakay (drums)

Although a relatively new force New York's
MAHAVATAR ('Mind Hypnotic Visions
Towards Revolution') have made a sizable
impact even before any commercial release.
Musically MAHAVATAR employ Psych-Doom
overlaid with Eastern tribal rhythms to present
a uniquely compelling sound.
Israeli dreadlocked vocalist Lizza Hayson was
previously with FORESIGHT. In keeping with
their eclecticism guitarist Karla Williams hails
from Jamaica whilst drummer Peter
Lobodzinski is Polish.
The bands original bassist Benjamin Serf was
replaced by Eddie Gasior. Later additions saw
Itamar Ben-Zakay taking the drum stool and
Evan Glantz contributing flute.

MAJESTY (FINLAND)

MAJESTY is a solo Doom venture
undertaken by one Marko 'Lord Gravehill'
Hautamaki who handles all vocals and
instrumentation on the 'Doomsday Machine'
album.
Hautamaki, besides being a member of TWO
WITCHES as a guitarist, has also sessioned
for Jyrki Witch of TWO WITCHES' Gothic
Industrial project band SINMASTER,
appearing on their 2000 EP 'Seducer'.
Hautamaki - donating his services as a
keyboard player, is a member of another of
Jyrki Witch's endeavours, the Gothic Rock act
LA VAMPIRE NUE.

Albums:
DOOMSDAY MACHINE, Atcom Music (2001)
Embraced By Dawn / Reptilian Temptation /
Realm Of Confusion / Deadwood / I Walk
Without A Sound / Doomsday Machine

MALOMBRA (ITALY)
Line-Up: Mercy (vocals), Fabio Carfagna
(guitar), Diego Banchero (bass), Franz Ekurn
(keyboards / piano), Francesco La Rosa
(drums)

Genoese Darkwave Progressive Goth act
MALOMBRA are led by vocalist Mercy, the
man also behind offshoots IL SEGNO DEL
COMANDO and HELDEN RUNE.
From the opening 1993 album onwards
MALOMBRA underwent radical line-up
changes which eventually saw only Mercy as
the sole surviving member. Decamping would
be guitarist Matteo Ricci, bass player Mario
Paglieri, keyboard player Fabio Casanova

and drummer Luca Brengio.
The 1996 opus 'Our Lady Of The Bones'
garnered the band cult appeal internationally.
During 2001 the band committed themselves
to both a DEATH SS tribute album, recording
their version of 'The Hanged Ballad', and a
BLACK WIDOW homage 'King Of The
Witches' with an interpretation of 'Tears &
Wine'.
The MALOMBRA 2002 album 'The
Dissolution Age' saw a completely revised
line-up of Mercy on vocals, Roberto Lucanato
on guitar, Diego Banchero on bass, Franz
Ekurn on piano and keyboards and drummer
Francesco La Rosa. Guest lead guitar came
courtesy of Regan Graves of ABYSMAL
GRIEF.

Albums:
MALOMBRA, Black Widow (1993)
The Witch Is Dead / In The Year's Shortest
Day / Still Life With Pendulum / Butcher's
Love Pains / After The Passing
OUR LADY OF THE BONES, Black Widow
(1996)
The Arrival / Magna Mater / D.D.D / Laventa
Quemada / A Song For Sylvia Plath / Our
Lady Of The Bones / Sinister Morning /
Oniria / Stonehenge / Requiem For The
Human / Lost In Time, Lost In Space And In
The Meaning
THE DISSOLUTION AGE, Black Widow
BWRCD 053-2 (2001)
Intro: The Useless Millennium / The
Dissolution Age / Unknown Superiors / The
Duncan Browne Song / Everybody
Afterwards / The Anti-Sex / Venice Lido 1901
/ A Spiritual Waste / Mortal Despise Song /
Misery Domine / El Centro / The Lost Father
/ The Dissolution Age (Reprise)

MALASANGRE (ITALY)
Line-Up: JN-18 (vocals), VP-33 (guitar), NC-
9.5 (bass), FH-37 (drums)

Albums:
A BAD TRIP TO..., Red Sun (2002)
Bad Acid / The Last Day / Cerebral Suicide /
Venus In Furs / Transvirus / Dream
Machine... Evil Machine / Sangre / The Holy
Cure

MAMMOTH VOLUME (SWEDEN)
Line-Up: Jorgen Andersson (vocals), Daniel
Gustafsson (guitar / keyboards), Kalle Berlin
(bass), Niklas Andersson (drums)

MAMMOTH VOLUME have been lumped in
with the Stoner camp although they display a
degree of diversity which should really place
them in the Psych-Progressive field. The

group was founded during 1996, citing a line-up of former FKASKET BRINNER vocalist Jorgen Andersson, guitarist and keyboard player Daniel Gustafsson, bass player Kalle Berlin and drummer Emir Horozic. MAMMOTH VOLUME issued two demo CDR's in 'Vol. 1' and 'Vol.2: Tour & Turtle' landing a deal with the American based Music Cartel label. With the latter's departure Niklas Andersson took the drum stool.

A succession of albums followed, peaking to date with the highly regarded 'A Single Book Of Songs' in 2001, which soon became a Stoner favourite.

Besides MAMMOTH VOLUME the Anderssons and Gustafsson appear as members of OMMADAWN. Berlin also operates with LAM CHAM and Punk act SCENSUR.

Albums:
MAMMOTH VOLUME, Music Cartel (1999)
Seagull / Morningsong / Her Hair / Dervishsong / Horizon / Closer To The Sun / Shindig / Family Tree / The Pinball Referee / Matthew 6:21 / Super Runner
NOARA DANCE, Music Cartel (2000)
Matador / Larrivee / Bighead / Seeds In Rocky Places / Railroad Rider / As Say The Pilgrims, So Say I / Bride Of Flawless
A SINGLE BOOK OF SONGS, Music Cartel (2001)
To Gloria / Vipera Berus / K / Aum / The So Called 4th Sect / What Happened In Antioch? (including Myriad Of Sounds) / Evening Streeted / Pleroma / Brave Manic Mover / Out Take / Noara Dance / What If / Instead Of Circles
THE EARLY YEARS, The Music Cartel (2002)
Frisco / Diablo / Recycled Cunt / Demonic / Candlelight Dinner / Crazy Luzy / Broadsword / Noname / II / Excerpt Vaudeville / Fourfinger And Fishpie / Trod Alot / Expander / Helly's Creek / Vino Train / Baby's Coming Home / Studio Improv

MANDRAGORA SCREAM (ITALY)
Line-Up: Morgan LaCroix (vocals), Terry Horn (guitar), John Peter Morris (guitar), Luigi Stefanini (keyboards)

Albums:
FAIRY TALES FROM HELL'S CAVES, Nuclear Blast (2001)

MAMMOTH VOLUME
Photo : El Danno

248

Fairy / The Time Of Spells / Five Tear Drops / Brain Storm / Cryin' Clouds / Angel Dust / Little Zombies / Child Of The Storm / Starquake / Fairytale From Hell's Cave

MANNHAI (FINLAND)
Line-Up: Joanitor Muurinen (vocals), Ilkka Laaksomaa (guitar), Oppu Laine (bass), Junior Pietnen (drums)

Doom act MANNHAI was formed in the end of 1999 by guitarist Ilkka Laaksomaa and erstwhile AMORPHIS bassist Oppu Laine. Shortly after forming they were accompanied by a young drummer, Junior Pietinen. The band's quick composing process led them to the studio only four months later, where they recorded three songs, which were still completely instrumental. With those three heavy tracks, Joanitor Muurinen, the ex-XYSMA frontman, was allured to the band.
By the end of 2000 MANNHAI signed a deal with the leading Finnish record company Spinefarm Records. On the 24th of January 2001 MANNHAI started to record their debut album, 'The Sons Of Yesterday's Black Grouse' at the Saewolf studios in Helsinki. The album was soon licensed to Nuclear Blast's subsidiary Revolution label for the European release in September 2001.
MANNHAI announced the arrival of a sophomore album, provisionally entitled 'Evil Under the Sun', for a late 2002 release through Spinefarm Records. It would include a cover version of 'A New Day Yesterday' originally by JETHRO TULL.

Albums:
THE SON'S OF YESTERDAY'S BLACK GROUSE, Spinefarm (2001)
Gazers Of The Red-Hot Stones / She's One Of A Kind / No Need To Follow / Only For The Sake Of Losing / Cloudberry Jam / Spender / Lowbrow / Inhuman Woman / So I Said / 100,000 Years

MARBLE ARCH (SWEDEN)

An atmospheric Gothic Metal band previously known as EVERCRY. Under their former title the group released two albums 'Demise The Crown' and 'Focus'. Upon re-billing themselves MARBLE ARCH a deal was struck with the German Century Media label for a September 2002 Anssi Kippo produced album 'Another Sunday Bright'. Backing vocals would be delivered courtesy of LULLACRY vocalist Tanja Lainio.

Albums:
ANOTHER SUNDAY BRIGHT, Century

Media (2002)
A Million Crises / Silent Dance / For Real / The Inmost / Not The Ones / Fellow Sinner / Dead Air / End Of Words / Sudden Showers / Last Day Ever

MASS (GERMANY)

Albums:
MASS, Man's Ruin MR162 (2000)
White Light Yellow Pt. One / Ghosts / Copter / Drown / White Light Yellow Pt. Two / Chiller / Mistake / Flower / Earthquake

MASSIVE DECAY (GERMANY)
Line-Up: Markus Bosch (vocals / guitar), Jochen Schmidt (guitar / keyboards), Cornelius Grandy (bass), Andreas Besel (drums)

MASSIVE DECAY operate in the Doom Gothic Power Metal sphere. Frontman Markus Bosch and drummer Andreas Besel were previously with the 1991 covers act MAIDSTONE.
MAIDSTONE added guitarist Michael Aue in October of that year but soon replaced him with keyboard player Johannes Stein. The following year MAIDSTONE evolved into ALTERED STATE. In their new guise ALTERED STATE opted to pursue original material in the Doom Gothic mould. By 1994 a further name change saw the band becoming MASSIVE DECAY.
December of 1994 witnessed Stein being supplanted by Jochen Schmidt for the act's debut demo followed shortly after by recording of the band's first album 'Black Eternity'.

Albums:
BLACK ETERNITY, Brickhouse 18-200-FCD (1995)
Inspirations / Black Eternity / Psycho Dying / Suffer My Pain / The Excruciating Betrayer / Coarse Designations / Unrestrained Living / The Union Of Spirits / Inhuman

MASTERS OF REALITY
(Los Angeles, CA, USA)
Line-Up: Chris Goss (vocals / guitar), Tim Harrington (guitar), Googe (bass), Vinnie Ludovico (drums)

MASTERS OF REALITY had first formed in Syracuse, New York in 1981. It wasn't until the quartet recorded a four or five song demo that fell into the hands of Def American supremo Rick Rubin that they gained the keen ear of a record label. Going for a distinctly natural retro vibe MASTERS OF REALITY debuted in

1989 with a Rick Rubin produced eponymous album. Despite being titled after a BLACK SABBATH album the band leant heavily on '70s sounds with a laid back Blues-groove feel. As such MASTERS OF REALITY are generally acknowledged to have established a precedent for the later wave of Stoner Rock outfits. MASTERS OF REALITY were somewhat out of step with the then prevailing Hard Rock trends but this influence has certainly been acknowledged by artists seeking out the services of frontman Chris Goss as a producer.

Surprisingly, Chris Goss walked out on the band in the midst of an American tour. The frontman took the band name with him and pulled in ex-SHRAPNEL / IGGY POP guitarist Daniel Ray and drummer Jon Leamy. Harrington and Lodovico meantime founded THE BOGEYMEN during 1991 releasing the 'There's No Such Thing As...' album.

Quite amazingly veteran Goss was able to crystallize his retro leanings as CREAM drummer Ginger Baker joined in September of 1990 MASTERS OF REALITY for 1993's 'Sunrise On The Sufferbus'. Despite critical acclaim for the album proposed tours were shelved when Baker departed.

Goss delved into the world of production, being heavily involved with the highly influential KYUSS, prior to pulling MASTERS OF REALITY back together again for a scarce live album 'How High The Moon - Live At The Viper Room'. New members were guitarist Brendan McNichol, drummer Victor Indrezzo and keyboard player Chris Johnson. Goss also scored a production credit on STONE TEMPLE PILOTS 'Tiny Music - Songs From The Vatican Gift Shop' album and with QUEENS OF THE STONE AGE.

MASTERS OF REALITY issued a new album 'Welcome To The Western Lodge' in 1999. A European tour found Goss backed by McNichol, Leamy, bassist Paul Powell and EARTHLINGS keyboard player Mathias Schneberger. However, this album would not surface in America until a belated release some years later by Spitfire Records, in different sleeve artwork, addressed the balance. Back in America Goss united with ex-CULT vocalist Ian Astbury for an acoustic set at the Tibetan Independence festival.

Goss continued his production work with recent credits including IAN ASTBURY's 2000 solo album, UNIDA, SOULWAX and SLOBURN. Promoting the new studio album 'Deep In The Hole' in the autumn of 2001 Goss put in an evening of solo music at the Los Angeles Knitting Factory venue. Guest musicians on the day would include Peter Perdichizzi of THE FLYS, Nick Lucero of THE FLYS and QUEENS OF THE STONE AGE,

Josh Homme, MARK LANEGAN, Brendon McNichol and Roxy Saint. MASTERS OF REALITY would cut a live album compiled from dates on their December 2001 European dates for September 2002 release entitled 'Flak And Flight'. The recording band saw Goss joined by drummer John Leamy, bassist Nick Oliveri and guitarist Josh Homme with a guest appearance by MARK LANEGAN on the track 'High Noon Amsterdam'.

The QUEENS OF THE STONE AGE connection was strengthened in 2002 when Goss was revealed to be accompanying the band on the road as touring guitarist. Somehow Goss made space to produce tracks for former HOLE and SMASHING PUMPKIN's bassist Melissa Auf Der Maur as well as Nick Oliveri's MONDO GENERATOR. Goss also unveiled plans for a solo album in the works, offering up a series of projected titles such as 'Baboon And McMusic' and 'Peanuts And Orange Juice'. McNichol would also be found to be working with ex-PRONG and present KILLING JOKE drummer Ted Parsons in Ambient duo DRONE.

Singles/EPs:
The Candy Song / Blue Garden / Kill The King, Def American DEFA 112 (1989)

Albums:
MASTERS OF REALITY, Def American (1989)
The Candy Song / Doraldina's Prophecies / John Brown / Getting' High / Magical Spell / Theme For The Scientist Of The Invisible / Domino / The Blue Garden / The Eyes Of Texas / Lookin' To Get Rite / Kill The King / Sleepwalkin'
THE BLUE GARDEN, Def American 8384742 (1989)
Theme For The Scientist Of The Invisible / Domino / Blue Garden / Gettin' High / Candy Song / Magical Spell / Eyes Of Texas / Sleep Walkin' / Lookin' To Get Rite / John Brown / Kill The King
SUNRISE ON THE SUFFERBUS, American 514947-2 (1993)
She Got Me (When She Got Her Dress On) / J.B. Witchdance / Jody Sings / Rolling Green / Ants In The Kitchen / V.H.V. / Bicycle / 100 Years (Of Fears In The Wind) / T.U.S.A. / Tilt A Whirl / Rabbit One / Madonna / Gimme Water / Moon In Your Pocket
HOW HIGH THE MOON - LIVE AT THE VIPER ROOM, Red Ant PRO5017-2 (1997) (Promotion release)
How High The Moon / The Blue Garden / Alder Smoke Blues / Daraldina's Prophecies / She Got Me (When She Got Her Dress On)

/ Jindalee Jindalie / John Brown / Tilt-A-Whirl - Swingeroo Joe / Ants In The Kitchen - Goin' Down / 100 Years (Of Tears In The Wind)
WELCOME TO THE WESTERN LODGE, Brownhouse (1999)
It's Shit / Moriah / The Great Spelunker / Time To Burn / Take A Shot At The Clown / Baby Mae / Why The Fly? / Ember Day / Annihilation Of The Spirit / Calling Dr. Carrion / Boymilk Waltz / Lover's Sky / Also Ran Song
DEEP IN THE HOLE, Brownhouse (2001)
Third Man On The Moon / A Wish For A Fish / Counting Horses / Major Lance / Scatagoria / High Noon Amsterdam
REALITY SHOW, Cargo (2001)
How High the Moon / The Blue Garden / Alder Smoke Blues / Doraldina's Prophecies / John Brown / Jindalee Jindalie / She Got Me (When She Got Her Dress On) / Tilt-A-Whirl / Swingeroo Joe / Ant's In The Kitchen - Goin' Down / 100 Years (Of Tears In The Wind)

MASTODON (USA)

Albums:
REMISSION (Relapse)
Crusher Destroyer / March Of The Fire Ants / Where Strides The Behemoth / Workhorse / Ole' Nessie / Burning Man / Trainwreck / Trampled Under Hoof / Trilobite / Mother Puncher / Elephant Man

MAYFAIR (AUSTRIA)
Line-Up: Mario (vocals), Rene (guitar), Mötle (bass), Little (drums)

MAYFAIR, created during 1989, quite miraculously for such a duration still boast the same line-up. The band's first demo, 'Find My Screams Behind This Gate', would become the focus of much praise in the German Rock media. The group would go on to play festivals on the same bill as the likes of BLIND GUARDIAN, the beer swilling TANKARD and American Power Metal band ICED EARTH prior to signing to Swiss label Witchhunt Records.
The band debuted with 1993's 'Behind' before switching labels to WMMS and subsequently releasing the follow up 'Die Flucht'. This album recognized MAYFAIR's new flair for Psych Rock persuasions and a liberal Gothic touch to their sound to boot.
The third MAYFAIR album, 'Fastest Trip To Cyber Town', was produced by Stewart Bruce and recorded in London in the summer of 1997. Presenting the record was issued through King Pest in 1998 a more

Psychedelic facet of the group, as MAYFAIR had broken ties with WMMS.

Albums:
BEHIND, Witchhunt GIT 002 SPV 84-96632 (1993)
Behind / Advanced In Years / Generation Isolated / Madame Pest / Schlaflos Müde / Ecstasy
DIE FLUCHT, Music Is Intelligence WMMS 101 (1995)
X Ray Fever (Intro) / Atomic Prayer / Hotel Hunger / Last Spring / Dir Flucht / Adam / One Night And A Dream / Dear Julia / Sunlight / L.O.V.E. (Outro)
FASTEST TRIP TO CYBER-TOWN, King Pest 90067120 (1998)
Things Will Be Better / BG How Was PG Pure / Trip / Waterproof / Wonderbra's Driver / Cyber Wanda / The 90's / Gold Coated Girls / Bye Bye "Mr. T"/ I Never Stripped In Public / Walking Different / Josie Loves Decibel

MEGAPTERA (SWEDEN)
Line-Up: Mikael Svensson, Peter Nyström

Renowned Electro-Industrial Doom act. MEGAPTERA know no boundaries when it comes to utilizing sounds to create their uniquely bleak form of music. Always experimental, the band and its myriad of offshoots employs movie narration and monologues across a broad catalogue of limited edition releases.
The group was conceived in 1991 by Magnus Petterson and Mikael Svensson, soon being joined by Peter Nyström of FIRST AID. Following a cassette release MEGAPTERA issued the 'Songs From The Massive Darkness' vinyl album in a limited run of just 200 copies. However, Magnus Petterson left the fold during this period leaving the act as a duo. Despite being a strictly underground release 'Songs From The Massive Darkness' made a sizable impact upon the scene prompting a slew of label offers. MEGAPTERA also donated tracks to compilations such as 'Death Odors' and 'From Sickness To Death'.
The first CD release, Beyond The Shadow', was delivered in 1994 but by the following year the departure of Svensson found MEGAPTERA operating solely as a Nyström solo venture.
In addition to MEGAPTERA the individual members pursued a plethora of other endeavours. Mikael Svensson embarked upon the "Death Terror" project DEAF MACHINE in 1992 resulting in the 'Transistor' demo and albums 'Death Odors' and 'In The

Butchers Backyard'. Peter Nyström and Mårten Kellerman issued the 1995 album 'Notes From A Holy War' from their venture EACH DAWN I DIE.

Nyström would also issue product as INSTANT COLD COMMANDO in the form of 1993's 'Command The Slaves' opus and with the Noise act NEGRU VODA a succession of releases commencing with the 'An Impulse To Fear' shared cassette with THIRD EYE in 1994. NEGRU VODA would still be operational post millennium offering a split 10" single shared with DES ESSEINTES and a limited edition 7" single 'From Liquid Steel To Frozen Metal' for Cold Meat Industry. As if this activity was not enough to keep him occupied Nyström had yet another musical concern, OBSCENE NOISE KORPORATION, releasing the 1998 record 'Primitive Terror Action' and collectors edition tapes 'Life After Fallout' and 'Baited Breath'.

Nyström announced in 2002 that MEGAPTERA was being laid to rest as he concentrated his efforts on NEGRU VODA.

Albums:
SONGS FROM THE MASSIVE DARKNESS, (1992) (Vinyl. Limited edition 200 copies)
Hydraulik Machinery / Sighatul-Marmatei (The Cellar Of Death) / Plague Spot / Sludgy Heads Found In A Handbag / Dysentry / Kristus Insana
BEYOND THE SHADOW, Kronotop KNT001 (1994)
Human Sacrifice / Distinkt Killing / The Offering / Lebensborn / Epileptic Hospital / Behind The Wall / Intellektual Decompression / Catacombs
DISEASE, Art Konkret ART 21 (1996)
(Limited edition 999 copies)
The Passage To Your Evil Dreams / Disoriented / Haunted By Demons / The Squire Goes Insane: Part 1 Warm And Relaxed, Part 2 Evil Thoughts Are Growing, Part 3 Going Berzerk And Hits His Wife With A Hammer, Part 4 Panic, Leads To Suicide
DEEP INSIDE, Slaughter Production (1997)
(Limited edition 500 copies)
Brainghost / Lurking Fear / Deep Inside
BEAUTIFUL CHAOS, Fever Pitch Music FP18 (1998)
Final Day (First Cut) / Massmurder Part II / Sleep / The Passage
LIVE IN ROSTOCK, Bastet (1998) (Limited edition 200 copies)
Intro: The Squire Goes Insane Part 1 – Warmer / Shadowland / Deep Inside / Breakfast At West's / The Passage
THE CURSE OF THE SCARECROW, Release Entertainment RR6979 (1998)
Disturbance / Cog Wheel Machinery / Don't Desecrate The Dead / The Curse Of The

Scarecrow / More Disturbance / Hear My Bowels / Kingdom Of Death / Skullfracture
ELECTRONIC UNDERGROUND, Slaughter Productions SPCD08 (2000)
Electronic Underground Part 1 / Electronic Underground Part 2 / Metal Blaster / Megaptera Theme / Hypnotic Fear / Someone's At The Door / Power Vibrations / Last Machinery
BEYOND THE MASSIVE DARKNESS, Cold Meat Industry CMI92 (2001)
Hydraulik Machinery / Sighatul-Marmatei (The Cellar Of Death) / Plague Spot / Sludgy Heads Found In A Handbag / Dysentry / Kristus Insana / Human Sacrifice / Distinkt Killing / The Offering / Lebensborn / Epileptic Hospital / Behind the Wall / Intellektual Decompression / Catacombs

THE MELVINS (Aberdeen, WA, USA)
Line-Up: Buzz Osbourne (vocals / guitar), Mark Deutrom (bass), Dale Crover (drums)

THE MELVINS inhabit the territory afforded to true cult acts. Crossing all musical boundaries with impunity THE MELVINS raid the coffers of Punk, Grunge, Stoner and Doom and far more besides to achieve an end result which has left critics in disarray. Notably revered by NIRVANA's Kurt Cobain the band would provide an obvious inspiration. Indeed, THE MELVINS' drummer Dale Crover performed on two tracks on NIRVANA's 1989 album 'Bleach'.

The band's debut album, featuring bassist Lori Black, was produced by Mark Deutrom and released on his own Alchemy label. Bassist Matt Lukin joined MUDHONEY following the 'Ozma' album and shared single with STEEL POLE BATH TUB. His place was taken by Tom Flynn for the 'Bullhead' album. THE MELVINS cut a version of LOU REED's 'Venus In Furs' for a split 7" single shared with NIRVANA.

Other releases saw THE MELVINS covering the KISS classic 'God Of Thunder' for a compilation album 'Hard To Believe'.

Joe Preston took over bass guitar for 1992 as the same year saw the trio all releasing separate solo EPs. King Buzzo collaborated with Dale Nixon for his record whilst Dale Crover would work with Debbi Shane. The drummer also released a further solo outing proper with the 'Forwards' / 'Backwards' 7" on Man's Ruin Records.

Preston's EP had guests from DENIAL FIEND and SALTY GREEN. Meantime the band was back together again for the 'Lysol' mini-album, a record that included two FLIPPER covers and a take on ALICE COOPER's 'The Ballad Of Dwight Fry'.

1993's 'Houdini' brought THE MELVINS to a

whole new audience due to the attention of co-producer and contributor Kurt Cobain of NIRVANA. Osbourne and Crover put down the bass guitar on the album despite a credit to 'Lomax'. 'Houdini' included another KISS cover 'Going Blind' alongside MC5's 'Sonic Reducer'. The band was later brought up to strength with the addition of CLOWN ALLEY's Mark Deutrom.

In 1994 THE MELVINS pulled in Deutrom into their ranks as bass player for the 'Stoner Witch' album, co-produced with Garth Richardson. The band also contributed 'Euthanasia' to the 'Dope, Guns n' Fucking In The Streets Volume Five' EP shared with GAS HUFFER, HELMET and the DWARVES. Touring to promote 1996's 'Stag', co-produced by FUDGE TUNNEL's Alex Newport, had the band out on the road supporting KISS in America and as part of the 'Lollapalooza' festivals.

Amphetamine Reptile issued a whole slew of 7" singles the same year. Included amongst the tracks being versions of FLIPPER's 'Way Of The World', WAYNE KRAMER's 'Poison', CLOWN ALLEY's 'Theme' and THE GERMS 'Lexicon Devil'.

Kevin Rutmanis took over bass guitar for 1999's 'The Maggot' album. The record included a customary cover, this time FLEETWOOD MAC's 'Green Manalishi (With The Two Pronged Crown)'. The same year Crover, acting as lead vocalist, unveiled his Stoner-Doom side outing ALTAMONT releasing an eponymous album for Man's Ruin, shared incidentally with his wife Lori S.'s retro infused ACID KING.

Osbourne founded the eclectic high profile side project FANTOMAS with ex-FAITH NO MORE & MR. BUNGLE front man Mike Patton and former SLAYER and GRIP INC. drummer DAVE LOMBARDO for live work in 2000.

The 'The Crybaby' album entirely comprised cover versions bolstered by a huge roll call of guests. NIRVANA's 'Smells Like Teen Spirit' was bizarrely cut with '70s Pop idol LEIF GARRETT, the JESUS LIZARD's 'Blockbuster' with David Yow, 'G.I. Joe' with FAITH NO MORE's Mike Patton, 'Spineless' with members of SKELETON KEY and TOOL in collaboration on their 'Divorced'. 'The Man With The Laughing Hand Is Dead' had PAIN TEENS' Bliss Blood and MOONLIGHTERS guitarist Henry Boglan on board.

Justin Broadrick of GODFLESH created THRONES in 2000 in collaboration with THE MELVINS and EARTH man Joe Preston.

Singles/EPs:
Oven / Revultion, Leopard Gecko (198-) Your Blessened, Slap A Ham (1989) (Flexi 7"

single)
Sweet Young Thing Ain't Sweet No More / , Tupelo (1990) (Split 7" single with STEEL POLE BATH TUB)
With Yo Heart, Not Yo Hands / Four Letter Woman / Anal Satan, Sympathy For The Record Industry (1990)
Wispy / Antioxidote / Hog Leg / Charmicarmicat, Tupelo TUP EP 31 (1991) ('Egg Nog' EP)
Venus In Furs / , Communion (1991) (Split 7" single with NIRVANA)
Son Of Bleeaargh, Slap A Ham (1991) Isabella / Porg / Annum / Skeeter, Tupelo TUP 39 (1992) ('King Buzzo' EP)
Hex Me / Dead Wipe / Respite / Hurter, Tupelo TUP 40 (1992) ('Dale Crover' EP) The Eagle Has Landed / Bricklebrit / Hands First Flower, Tupelo TUP 41 (1992) ('Joe Preston' EP)
Night Goat / Adolescent Wet Dream, Amphetamine Reptile SCALE 44 (1992)
Hooch / Sky Pup Detective, Rise (1992)
Queen / Sweet Willy Rollbar, Atlantic (1993) (Promotional release)
Someday / Love Canal, Slap A Ham SAH 13 (1995)
I Like Porn /, Amphetamine Reptile SCALE 74 (1995) (Split 7" single with GUVNOR)
Lexicon Devil / Pigtro, Amphetamine Reptile SCALE 82 (1996)
In The Rain / Spread Eagle Beagle (Special mix) / Prairie Sun, Amphetamine Reptile SCALE 83 (1996)
Leech (Live) / Queen (Special mix), Amphetamine Reptile SCALE 84 (1996)
Way Of The World / Theme, Amphetamine Reptile SCALE 85 (1996)
It's Shoved / Forgotten Principles (Live '83), Amphetamine Reptile SCALE 86 (1996)
G.G.I.I.B.B.Y.Y. (Out Take) / Thereza Screams, Amphetamine Reptile SCALE 87 (1996)
Poison / Double Troubled, Amphetamine Reptile SCALE 88 (1996)
Specimen (Out Take) / All At Once, Amphetamine Reptile SCALE 89 (1996)
Jacksonville (Live) / Dallas (Live), Amphetamine Reptile SCALE 90 (1996)
The Bloat (Demo) / Fast Forward, Amphetamine Reptile SCALE 91 (1996)
Nasty Dogs And Funky Kings / H.D.Y.F., Amphetamine Reptile SCALE 92 (1996)
How / Harry Lauders Walking Stick Tree (Mix) / Brutal Truth / Zodiac, Amphetamine Reptile SCALE 95 (1996)
Spit It Out, Amphetamine Reptile SCALE 100 (2000) (One Sided Gig 7" Single)

Albums:
GLUEY PORCH TREATMENTS, Alchemy VM 103 (1986)

Hairspray Queen / If You Must / Downer / Floyd The Barber / Paper Cuts / Spank Thru / Beeswax / Pen Cap Chew / Mexican Seafood / Aero Zeppelin
10 SONGS, CZ Records CZ002 (1986)
Easy As It Was / Now A Limo / Grinding Process / #2 Pencil / At A Crawl / Disinvite / Snake Appeal / Show Off Your Red Hands / Over From Underground / Crayfish
OZMA, Tupelo TUPLP 7 (1987)
Ozma / Oven / Let God Be Your Gardener / Creepy Smell / Koollegged / Green Honey / Agonizer / Raise A Paw / Love Thing / Ever Since My Accident / Revulsion - We Reach / Dead Dressed / Cranky Messiah / Claude / My Small Percent Shows Most / Candy O / Eye Flys / Echo Head - Don't Piece Me / Heater Moves And Eyes / Steve Instant Newman / Influence Of Atmosphere / Exact Paperbacks / Happy Grey Or Black / Leech / Glow God / Big As A Mountain / Heaviness Of The Load / Flex With You / Bitten Into Sympathy / Gluey Porch Treatments / Clipping Roses / As Was It / Over From Under The Excrement
BULLHEAD, Tupelo TUP CD 26 (1991)
Boris / Anaconda / Ligature / It's Shoved / Zodiac / If I Had An Exorcism / Your Blessed / Cow
YOUR CHOICE LIVE SERIES 012, Your Choice YCR 012 (1991)
Heather Moves And Eyes / At A Crawl / Anaconda / Eye Flys / Koollegged / Tanked / Let God Be Your Gardener / Revulsion
LYSOL, Tupelo TUP 42 (1992)
Hung Bunny / Roman Dog Bird / Sacrifice / Second Coming / The Ballad Of Dwight Fry / With Teeth /
HOUDINI, East West 7567 82532-2 (1993)
Hooch / Night Goat / Lizzy / Going Blind / Honey Bucket / Hag Me / Set Me Straight / Sky Pup Detective / Joan Of Arc / Teet / Copache / Pearl Bomb / Spread Eagle Beagle / Sonic Reducer
PRICK, Amphetamine Reptile ARR 58-333 (1994)
How About / Rickets / Pick It n' Flick It / Montreal / Chief Ten Beers / Underground / Chalk People / Pinch The Lion / Pure Digital Silence / Larry / Roll Another One
STONER WITCH, East West 7567827042 (1994)
Sweeties / Queen / Sweet Willy Rollbar / Revolve / Goose Freight Train / Roadbull / At The Stake / Magic Pig Detective / Sheril / June Bug / Lividity
STAG, Mammoth 7567 82878-2 (1996)
The Bit / Hide / Yacob's Lab / The Bloat / Tipping The Lion / Goggles / Soup / Captain Pungent / Berthas / Cotton Mouth
HONKY, Amphetamine Reptile AR 64 (1997)
They Must All Be Slaughtered / Mombius

Hibachi / Lovely Butterfly / Pitfalls In Serving Warrants / Air Breather Deep In The Arms Of Morphius / Laughing With Satan At Lucifer's Sideshow / How / Harry Lauder's Walking Stick tree / Grin / In The Freaktose The Bugs Are Dying
1996 SINGLES VOLUME 1-12, Amphetamine Reptile AR 63CD (1997)
Lexicon Devil / Pigtro (Special mix) / In The Rain / Spread Eagle / Prairie Sun / Leech (Live) / Queen / Way Of The World / Theme (Live) / It's Shoved / Forgotten Principles / G.G.I.I.B.B.Y.Y. (Out Take) / Theresa Screams / Poison / Double Troubled / Specimen / All At Once / Jacksonville (Live) / Dallas (Live) / Bloat (Demo) / Fast Forward / Nasty Dogs And Funky Kings / H.D.Y.F / How / Walking Stick Tree / Zodiac
ALIVE AT THE FUCKER CLUB, Amphetamine Reptile AM REP 072 (1998)
Boris / It's Shoved / Bar-X-The Rocking M / Antitoxidote / The Bloat / Lizzy / Mombius Hibachi
THE MAGGOT, Ipecac Recordings (1999)
Amazon / We All Love / Manky / The Green Manalishi (With The Two Pronged Crown) / The Horn Bearer / Judy / See How Pretty, See How Smart
THE BOOTLICKER, Ipacac Recordings (1999)
Toy / Let It All Be Judy / Black Santa / We We / Up The Dumper / Mary Lady Bobby Kins / Jew Boy Flower Head / Lone Rose Holding Now / Prig
THE CRYBABY, Ipacac Recordings (2000)
Smells Like Teen Spirit / Blockbuster / Ramblin' Man / G.I. Joe / Mine Is No Disgrace / Spineless / Tool / The Man With The Laughing Hand Is Dead / Oakie From Muskogee / Dry Drunk / Moon Pie
ELECTRORETARD, Man's Ruin MR2002 (2001)
Shit Storm / Youth Of America / Gluey Porch Treatments / Revolve / Missing / Lovely Butterflies / Tipping The Lion / Interstellar Overdrive

MEMENTO MORI (SWEDEN)
Line-Up: Messiah Marcolin (vocals), Michael Wead (guitar), Nickkey Argento (guitar), Marty Marteen (bass), Snowy Shaw (drums)

A band that comprised former CANDLEMASS vocalist Messiah Marcolin (real name Jan Alfredo Marcolin) and Michael Wead (real name Mikael Vikström), of former HEXENHAUS and KING DIAMOND infamy. MEMENTO MORI also included Snowy Shaw (who had been with both KING DIAMOND and MERCYFUL FATE) and bassist Marti Marteen (real name Mårten Sandberg) previously with NAGASAKI and

254

HEXENHAUS

The group debuted with the 'Rhymes Of Lunacy' album in 1993 before adding keyboard player Migeul Robaina in 1994. However, the enigmatic Marcolin quit following the release of the second album ('Life, Death And Other Morbid Tales') to join STILLBORN. Shaw then contributed to the re-formed MERCYFUL FATE, whilst Wead teamed up with ABSTRAKT ALGEBRA.

At first Marcolin was replaced by former NEOCORI vocalist Stefan Karlsson, although the third album, 'La Danse Macabre', featured ex-TAD MOROSE vocalist Kristian Andren. Drums were now handled by ex-PARASITE and HEXENHAUS man Johan Billerhag, after Helgesson left to join MERCYFUL FATE and ILL WILL. Robaina also upped and left in favour of Jocke Floke.

Kristian Andren was to make a guest showing on the 1997 STREET TALK album 'Collaboration'.

Marcolin was to rejoin the ranks for MEMENTO MORI's 1997 album 'Songs For The Apocalypse Vol. IV'.

Albums:
RHYMES OF LUNACY, Black Mark BMCD 32 (1993)
The Rhyme / The Seeds Of Hatred / Morbid Tear / The Caravan Of Souls / Lost Horizons / When Nothing Remain / Forbidden Dreams / Little Anne's Not An Angel / Fear Of God / The Riddle / The Monolith
LIFE, DEATH AND OTHER MORBID TALES, Black Mark BMCD51 (1994)
To Travel Within / The Passage... / A Passenger On Psycho's Path / Lam / Misery Song / Just Another Morbid Tune / My Secret Garden / Heathendoom
LA DANSE MACABRE, Black Mark BMCD 71 (1996)
Endlessly / Lost Worlds / Crown Of Thorns Part II, III & IV / La Danse Macabre / Morpheus (My Deadly Friend) / The Loser's Trail / Prelude / The Beggar's Waltz
SONGS FOR THE APOCALYPSE VOLUME IV, Black Mark BMCD 124 (1997)
The Things You See (And The Things You Don't) / Under My Blackened Sky / One Sign Too Many / Burned By Light / Memento Mori / I Prayed / Animal Magnetism / Out Of Darkness

MEMORIA (CZECH REPUBLIC)
Line-Up: Petr Stanek (vocals), Zdenek Pastorek (guitar), Rostislav Skacel (guitar), Filip Chud_ (bass), Petr Duba (keyboards), Iva Dokoupilova (viola), Pavel Fojtik (drums)

MEMORIA from Skalièka originally came together in June of 1988 as MYSTERY. The group was assembled by two former SILENT STREAM OF GODLESS ENERGY members guitarist Rostislav Skacel and Pavel Chud_ along with vocalist Honza _oc, Filip Chud_ on bass, Hanka Ry_ková on flute and Michal Hajda on drums. This union cut its teeth with the December 1998 demo 'Desire'.

During June of the following year Petr Duba was enrolled on keyboards but shortly after _oc and Ry_ková bailed out. As an interim measure Pavel Chud_ took on the lead vocal mantle and Zdenìk Pastorek came in to cover on guitar. The band's sound would be further augmented by violist Iva Dokoupilová.

MEMORIA set to work recording the debut album 'Children Of The Doom' for Leviathan Records. However, the fluctuations within the band had yet to cease, Hajda making way midway through the recording process for new drummer Pavel Fojtik in March of 2000.

Albums:
CHILDREN OF THE DOOM, Leviathan (2001)
Zero On Display / Change / Garden Of The Roses / Hellbound / Children Of The Doom / Nothing / May Face / Paradise?

MEMORIUM (SWEDEN)
Line-Up: Fredrik Strömqvist (vocals), Markus Görsch (guitar), Joel Görsch (bass), Daniel Andersson (keyboards)

MEMORIUM supply a combination of Gothic Rock and Heavy Metal.

Singles/EPs:
Black Roses / Gods Of Frozen Water / Dance With Death / A Girl, LHM 0220 (1994) ('Memorium' EP)

MEMORY GARDEN (SWEDEN)
Line-Up: Stefan Berglund (vocals), Anders Looström (guitar), Rick Gustafsson (guitar), Ken Johansson (bass), Tom Johansson (drums)

Kumla based Doom Metal band MEMORY GARDEN, led by noted vocalist Stefan Berglund were created during December 1992. The band was suitably named after the TROUBLE song 'Memory's Garden'.

A 1993 demo and a single, the 1994 'Badlands' outing produced by produced by the ever busy Dan Swanö of EDGE OF SANITY, prompted the Swedish Heathendoom label to secure a contract for the 1995 debut four track 'Forever' EP. A novel departure was the single 'Ta Nagon Hart I Muschen Sa Ger Vi Oss Av Till Tomteland', a

Christmas record featuring four festive favourites issued to fans. The single, which came complete with artwork depicting the MEMORY GARDEN logo topped with snow and a Santa Claus hat, is now extremely rare having only had 300 copies pressed.

Original drummer Tom Johansson would make way for the then 15 year old ex-TARGET drummer Tom Björn. In 1996 the band drafted erstwhile FIFTH REASON and ABSTRAKT ALGEBRA guitarist Simon Johansson in favour of previous incumbent Rick Gustaffson. A full-length effort, 'Tides', emerged the same year.

In 1997 Björn would find himself a member of two acts having taken onboard the role of drummer in MEMENTO MORI. He would later take on extra duties with HEMISFEAR.

MEMORY GARDEN's progress was such that their next port of call would be the Metal Blade label, bowing in for the American concern with 1998's 'Verdict Of Prosperity', overall a more groove orientated album. The album saw production duties handled by Mike Wead of MERCYFUL FATE. Touring in Scandinavia ensued to promote the release upfront of an appearance at the prestigious annual 'Wacken Open Air' festival in Germany. In 1999 MEMORY GARDEN contributed tracks to no less than three tribute albums. Donations were made to the QUEENSRYCHE 'Taking Hold Of The Flame' album with a rendition of 'The Needle Lies', a MERCYFUL FATE effort with 'Nightmare Be Thy Name' and also a take on BLACK SABBATH's 'Country Girl'.

The 2001 'Mirage' album, once more produced by Wead in his own Miseria recording studio, capitalized on previous efforts and returned the band to their Doom roots.

Singles/EPs:
Badlands / Blessed Are The Dead,
Megagrind IVR / MGREP 002 (1994)
Warlord / Inarticulo Mortis / Forever /
Autumn Anguish, Heathendoom Music HDM 001 (1995)
('Forever' EP)
Ta Nagon Hart I Muschen Sa Ger Vi Oss Av Till Tomteland, Megagrind IVR / MGREP 005 (1995)

Albums:
TIDES, Heathendoom Music HDMCD 003 (1996)
Genesis / Dream Horizons / The Rhyme Of The Elder / Trapped At The Pharoes / Judgement Day / The Innocent Sleep / AQ New Dawn / Blissfull
VERDICT OF PROSPERITY, Metal Blade

(1998)
Carved In Stone / Awkward Tale / Shadow Season / Tragic Kingdom / The Sum Of All Fear / Split Image / Outward Passage / Wasteland Foretold / Amen
MIRAGE, Metal Blade (2000)
Prologue / A Long Grey Day / Hallowed Soil / Shade / Navigate / Revelation / Yearning / River Of Sludge / My Pain / The Search

MEN OF PORN (USA)
Line-Up: Tim Moss (vocals / guitar / piano), Joe Goldring (guitar), Brian Hill (bass), Sean Taylor (drums)

MEN OF PORN
Photo : Alex Obleas

MEN OF PORN took the Stoner genre into uncharted waters by layering their own peculiar brand of Metal with washes of feedback and distorting everything to uncomfortable degrees. So extreme is the band's experimentation that MEN OF PORN have been dubbed 'Confusion Metal'.

For the 'Experiments In Feedback' album, issued by Small Stone Recordings in 2001, the band retitled themselves as PORN (THE MEN OF). The group now featured a line-up of erstwhile RITUAL DEVICE vocalist / guitarist Tim Roth, noted producer and member of the MELVINS and SPILTH bassist Billy Anderson and former SWANS and OUT IN WORSHIP drummer Joe Goldring. The record also cited a huge tally of Stoner royalty as studio guests including Guy Pinhas of THE OBSESSED, ACID KING and GOATSNAKE, Brian Hill of BUZZOV-EN and ACID KING, Joey Osbourne of ACID KING and ALTAMONT and Jon Weiss of HORSEY and the HELIOS CREED band.

Albums:
PORN AMERICAN STYLE, Man's Ruin

(1999)

Comin' Home (Smoking Pot On A Sunday Afternoon While UFO's Drone Overhead) / Dancing Black Ladies / Porch Song / Fat Trout / Teabaggin' / Ballad Of The Bulldyke / Pyleven / Ode To Theodore's / Highlife / Ballad Of The Bulldyke (Jam Jar Superstar Remix) / Double Don / End

EXPERIMENTS IN FEEDBACK, Small Stone Recordings (2001)

One Of These Days / Capp Street / Feedback II / Sister (Valium mix) / Feedback IV / Outta Site / Sister / Feedback VII / Sister (Nod Mix) / Loop

MENTAL HOME (RUSSIA)

Line-Up: Sergey Dmitriev (vocals / guitar), Denis Samusev (bass), Michael Smirnoff (keyboards), Igor Dmietriev (drums)

Moscow Death Metal act formed in November of 1993. The original MENTAL HOME line-up comprised the two Dmitriev siblings, vocalist / guitarist Sergey and drummer and keyboard player Igor. Also involved was lead guitarist Roman Povarov and bass player Denis Samusev. Taking an atmospheric Doom-laden Death Metal approach the quartet released their inaugural demo session 'Funeral Service' in January of 1994.

Shortly after, the MENTAL HOME returned to the studio and in July of the same year 'Mirrorland' was issued by the domestic Metal Agen concern, soon selling out of its initial 5,000 run.

A setback occurred when Povarov injured his hand in an accident. The guitarist shifted over to keyboards to accommodate his disability and MENTAL HOME drafted Sergey Kalachov for the 'Vale' outing. This album would see a release through Morbid Noizz. Quite spectacularly the album actually sold out after a few months and hit the number one position in the Russian Metal charts.

Despite this upward turn in the bands fortunes Povarov departed. Michael 'Maiden' Smirnoff took not only the vacant keyboard position but also became MENTAL HOME's business manager.

In March of 1997 the band retired to the studio completing the 'Black Art' album by June. With MENTAL HOME's profile riding high the first brace of albums were also reissued.

The bands progress had not gone unnoticed outside of Russia and American based The End Records engineered a deal with the band to release 'Vale' and 'Black Art'.

Albums:
FUNERAL SERVICE, (1994)

MIRROR LAND, (1995)
VALE, The End TE001 (1998)
Stranger Dove / Southern Calm Waters / Aevin's Cave / The Euphoria / The Vale / My Necklace / Christmas Mercy / Their Finest Voyage
BLACK ART, The End TE006 (1998)
Under The Wing / The Plague Omen / Into The Realms Of Marena / Silent Remembrance / In The Shades Of Inspiration / Pagan Freedom / Winter Art / On A Hand Of The Universe / Tides Of Time
UPON THE SHORES OF INNER SEAS, The End (2000)
Downstairs / Late To Revise / Eternal Moan / Bliss / Against My Will / Breakdown / Stained / Amidst The Waves '99

MERCY (SWEDEN)

Line-Up: Rick Wine (vocals), Andrija 'Witchking' Veljaca (guitar), Tom Mitchell (bass), Johan Norell (drums)

Swedish outfit MERCY, having evolved from Heavy Metal band TURBO in December of 1980, featured in their early days future CANDLEMASS vocalist Messiah Marcolin. In their relatively short history the band underwent numerous line-up shuffles.

The debut album, 'Swedish Metal', was recorded by Yugoslavian ex-HOROSCOPE guitarist Andrija Veljaca (sometimes going under the name of Yandriya Veechking or 'Witchking'), bassist Christian Karlsson (adopting the bizarre anglicized Christian C. Greenfood) and drummer Paul Gustavsson (as Paul G. Judas). Gustafsson later joined HIGH VOLTAGE then OVERHEAT, but by the self-financed 'Mercy' album only Veljaca remained alongside ex-ROUGH LIZZARDS vocalist Eddy Markulin (a.k.a. Messiah Marcolin) and guitarist Magnus Klinto.

Further ructions occurred as the band effectively split but reassembled, with new guitarist Jörgen Horst and bass player Ulf Croncell in tow. With this revised line-up MERCY cut the 'Witchburner' album, switching from their previous Power Metal persuasions to outright Doom. The group recorded a two track demo, 'Bangers of Destruction' and 'Black Death' for a Dutch label. When this proposed deal failed to materialize Marcolin bailed out to join the groundbreaking Stockholm act CANDLEMASS.

During 1987 MERCY, comprising Veljaca, along with Anders Strengberg on lead vocals, Roger Johansson on bass and Johan Norell, cut an album for a German label entitled 'Stormbringer'. However, these tapes would remain shelved for many years.

The line-up changed again for the self-

258

financed 'King Doom' with Veljaca now teamed with vocalist Rick Wine, bassist Tom Mitchell and drummer Peter Svensson. After recording the album Svensson left for OVERHEAT and made way for Johan Norell once again.

This record was later re-released in Germany as 'Black Magic', formatted with different versions of songs and extra tracks.

Albums:
SWEDISH METAL, Metal Shock MCI 111 (1982)
State Of Shock / Don't Stop Heavy Guitar / Heavy Sound / Lost In Time / Stranger From The Dark
MERCY, Fingerprint FINGLP 008 (1984)
Heavy Metal Warriors / Dirty Love / Metal Mania / Tyrant / Master Of Disaster / Spanish Eyes / Zombie
WITCHBURNER, Fingerprint FINGLP013 (1984)
KING DOOM, Mercy MCY112 (1988)
Death's Company / Tribulation / 1953-1988 / Black Magic / Evil Prepares / Memory / Heartbreak In Hell / Sorrows / Darkness
BLACK MAGIC, Imtrat (1989)
Death's Company / Tribulation / 1953-1988 / Black Magic / Evil Prepares / Memory / Heartbreak In Hell / Sorrows / Darkness / Mercy / Black Dead

MERMAID (SPAIN)

Albums:
HIGH DIMENSION IS THE DIRECTION, Safety Pin (2001)
Hypnotizer / Aguaverde Freeland / Walkin' The Tiger / Sweets / Rollergirl / Walk From Regio's / White Elevator Horses

MESZADA (GERMANY)
Line-Up: Markus Kurscheidt (vocals / keyboards), Stephan Kesselmeier (guitar), Kai-Philipp Scöllmann (guitar / keyboards), Roman Berndt (bass), Florian Sonnemann (drums)

A new group that has become well known to the Gothic crowd in their native Germany, MESZADA were voted best newcomers of 1995 by the influential 'Zillo' magazine.

Albums:
ANEPIGRAPHA, BluNoise 444015 (1995)
Anepigrapha / Secrecy / Aus Psyche Gebaut / Liquid Thinking / Dictator's Goodbye / Herzegowina / C'Est Arrive Pres De Chez Vous / Abschied
BLOSSOM, Alice In Wonderland AIW 070 (1997)

Euphorbia Helioscopia / Naked / Causeway / Shorn / Nuphar Lutea / Actress / Lilium Martagon / Betrayed / Hass / Exile / Anemone Nemorosa

MIDNIGHT CONFIGURATION (UK)

Industrial accented, Doom-laden Gothic Rockers from Nottingham. MIDNIGHT CONFIGURATION stray adventurously away from tried and trusted formulas, adding a genuine touch of malevolence to their music with an innovative use of film scores and electronica. Originally a solo project conceived by erstwhile EVERY NEW DEAD GHOST man and mentor of Nightbreed Records Trevor Bamford, as MIDNIGHT CONFIGURATION evolved guitarist Nick Hopkinson and vocalist Lisa Ross became permanent members.

Vocalist Lisa Ross left the band to concentrate on her other act BROTHER ORCHID, in union with husband Kneill Brown, whilst recording the 2000 album 'Dark Hours Of The Southern Cross'. However, Ross did record vocals for three tracks on the subsequent 'Redemption Of The Physical World' album of 2001.

Singles/EPs:
Nightmare Station / Dark Desires / The Fire Inside / Night Of The Soul, Nightbreed NIGHTMCD1 (1994) ('Gothtec' EP)
Spectral Dance, Nightbreed NIGHTMAXICD3 (1995)

Albums:
THE KISSING SKULL, Nightbreed (1995)
Night Invocation / Chaos Mind / The Chains Of Reason / Undead – Lifeforce / Dark Desires / No Real Mercy / The Kissing Skull / The Wake (More Souls For The Fire) / Darkside / Unearthly Twilight / No Real Mercy (Edit Mix) / Chains Of Reason (Darkwave Mix) / Chaos Mind (Exposure Mix) / Undead (Totentanz Mix) / The Kissing Skull (Apocalypse Now Mix)
FUNERAL NATION, Nightbreed NIGHTCD15 (1997)
Subterrania (Descent) / Transmission Soul / Sinister Sinister / Graveyard Eyes / Force / Mesmerize / Snowblind / A Gothic Lullaby / Funeral Nation / Sacred Cities / Unfolding The Wings Of Winter / Chaos Mind 2 (Resurrected) / Breaking The Spirit / Manifestation (Ascent)
DIGITAL INTERFERENCE, Nightbreed NIGHTCD19 (1998)
Spirit Anthem / Funeral Nation (Religion mix) / Sinister Sinister (Night Time) / Arabian Force / Funeral Nation (Toxic! Remix) /

MINOTAURI

Sacred Cities (Featuring Faithful Dawn) / Force (Featuring House Of Usher) / Kissing Skull (Guitar Edit) / Transmission Soul (Featuring Squid) / Mesmerize (Toxic! Remix) / Transmission Soul (Featuring Attrition) / Wings Of Winter (Bela Le Bamford Mix) / Graveyard Eyes (Braveheart) / Chaos Mind (Perennial) / Sinister Sinister (4am) / Darksize (23)
DARK HOURS OF THE SOUTHERN CROSS, Nightbreed NIGHTCD40 (2000)
Leviathan Call / Dancefloor Poison / Lord Of Darkness / Edge Of Harvest / Legion / City Of The Dead / Demonize / Dying Sea / Banshee Chimes / Decline And Fall / Walk Away / Castaway
REDEMPTION OF THE PHYSICAL WORLD, Nightbreed NIGHTCD46 (2001)
Necroscope / Devil Dance / Pandemonium / Kingdom Come / Arkham Fury / Aether Intro / Aether Ships / Falling Down (Sci Fi Version) / Faith Eternal / Darkness Be Thy Name / Phantom / Necronomicon

MINAS TIRITH (NORWAY)
Line-Up: Frode Forsmo (vocals), Stian Krabol (guitar), Gottskalk (bass), Tony Kirkemo (drums)

Avant-garde act founded in 1989 with Black persuasions combined with elements of Jazz, Doom and Death Metal. MINAS TIRITH bassist Gottskalk also has connections with

TULUS and OLD MAN'S CHILD.

Singles/EPs:
My Rotting Girl / Heartbeat / Chain Of Grief / Applewine, AR (1993) ('Mythology' EP)

Albums:
THE ART OF BECOMING, Art 196 (1996)
The Living Dead / The Colour Of Nothing / Sympathy From The Devil / The Art Of Becoming / In The Night I Walk / X = 666 / In Union We Die / A Child Is Born In Babylon / Holy Brother
DEMONS ARE FOREVER, Facefront (1999)

MIND FAILURE (New York, NY, USA)
Line-Up: Brian Thane Chaffee (vocals), Ken Jacobsen (guitar), Tony Spagone (bass), Jörg Michael (drums)

Albums:
MIND FAILURE, Amarok RTD 397.0028.2 (1997)
Gateway To Deadly Sins / Etude / What They Don't Know / Mindfailure / Thou Shalt Live / Cataclysm / Nefarious / Section Terminal

MINOTAURI (FINLAND)
Line-Up: Ari Honkonen (vocals / guitar), Tommi Dakarinen (bass), Viljami Kinnunen (drums)

MINOTAURI is the Doom Metal vehicle for vocalist / guitarist Ari Honkonen, member of the veteran act MORNINGSTAR. Although MINOTAURI, a venture formulated to deliver retro Doom with NWoBHM influences, was created in 1995 only rehearsal tapes surfaced until the first official demo session 'Devil Woman'. This was quickly followed up by the 'Life Is Pain' 7" single. Limited to 500 copies and released by the specialist German Iron Bonehead Productions, 'Life Is Pain' soon sold out.

MINOTAURI are featured on the Miskatonic Foundation compilation album 'At The Mountains Of Madness II' and also issued a four track 10" EP, 'Doom Metal Invasion', in 2002. MINOTAURI united with their Doom Brethren REVEREND BIZARRE and SPITUS MORTIS for a tour across Finland dubbed appropriately enough the 'Friends Of Hell' tour.

Honkonen, besides still retaining membership of MORNINGSTAR, operated PERKELE for a 1995 demo 'Pohjula', this latter act subsequently evolving into IRONBIRD, issuing a further demo 'In The Name Of Turisas'.

Singles/EPs:
Pain Of Life / Violence, Iron Bonehead Productions (2000) (7" single. Limited edition 500 copies)
Cemetery Shadows / Frustrated / Paid Love / You Will Learn…, Iron Bonehead Productions (2002) (10" 'Doom Metal Invasion' single)

MIRROR OF DECEPTION (GERMANY)
Line-Up: Markus Baumhauer (vocals), Michael Siffermann (guitar), Jochen Fopp (guitar), Klaus Schmidt (bass), Gunnar Drescher (drums)

Retro Doomsters forged in 1990 borrowing much from the pioneering Swedish style and proud of it. MIRROR OF DECEPTION was created in September of 1990 by guitarists Michael Siffermann and Jochen Fopp. However, it would be a full two years before the band was brought up to its full complement with vocalist Markus Baumhauer, bass player Rainer Hampel and drummer Ingo Häderle.

An eponymous demo arrived in 1993 capitalized on by 1994's 'Words Unspoken' and the 1996 session 'Veil Of Lead'. After this

MIRROR OF DECEPTION
Photo : Suzan Tesic

261

set of recordings Hampel took up an offer to join END OF GREEN and Häderle also disembarked. The new recruit on bass was Klaus Schmidt whilst Gunnar Drescher came in on loan from Power Metal band BEYOND THE DARK to make up the numbers.

In 1997 the 'Veil Of Lead' recordings were issued in a CD EP format by Sub Zero Recordings. MIRROR OF DECEPTION would return to the studio for a further demo workout 'The Float Sessions'. The same year the group would commence recording of their debut album 'Mirrorsoil' although this would not emerge until 2001. During the interim Fopp broke ranks but would make a return.

MIRROR OF DECEPTION played in the UK during February alongside SOLSTICE and WARNING. Christoph Semmelrodt of THE BLUE SEASON took Drescher's place on a temporary basis in March of 2001 for a string of German gigs opening for Austrian outfit JACK FROST. Further gigs with END OF GREEN took place during the Autumn.

MIRROR OF DECEPTION would donate their take on 'One Mind' to a 2001 ST. VITUS tribute album. Also issued was an album collection comprising the band's demos, EP and rehearsal tapes.

Singles/EPs:
Der Weg… / Be Kept In Suspense / Emptiness / Asylum / …Ewigkeit?, Sub Zero (1997) ('Veil Of Lead' EP)

Albums:
MIRRORSOIL, Miskatonic Foundation (2001) Asylum / Veil Of Lead / Weiss / Sole / Be Kept In Suspense / Dreams Of Misery / Cease / Float
PAST AND PRESENT 1993-2000, (2001)

MISDEMEANOR (SWEDEN)
Line-Up: Vera Olofsson (vocals), Jenny Möllberg (guitar), Sara Fredriksson (guitar), Jenny E Lindahl (bass), Mia Möllberg (drums)

All female Stoners formulated in 1992, originally citing a line-up of guitarist Jenny Möllberg, bass player Jenny E Lindahl, drummer Mia Möllberg and guitarist Cissi. This latter member drifted away sometime in 1994. Vera Olofsson was inducted as lead vocalist in Spring of that year and MISDEMEANOR debuted live during the September. Sara Fredriksson made up the numbers on second guitar shortly after.

MISDEMEANOR's inaugural demo tape, billed as 'Fountain Of Youth', was delivered in early 1995. Recordings for an EP were cut the same year but did not emerge until some time after, issued as 'The Misdemeanor EP',

pressed on violet vinyl by Nicke Andersson of THE HELLACOPTERS' label Psychout in May of 1997. On the live front the band put in some valuable supports to high profile visiting acts such as QUEENS OF THE STONE AGE, NEBULA and FU MANCHU.

Travelling to California in 1998 MISDEMEANOR laid down tracks for a Meteor City release. Issued in February of 1999 the record witnessed backing vocals from UNIDA's John Garcia and production handled by BRANT BJORK. Further sessions that year, produced by Chips of SATOR, resulted in the 7" single 'You're Nothing (And You Know It)'.

The group donated their rendition of 'Bastards Will Pay' to a TROUBLE tribute album but hit a snag when Mia Möllberg vacated the drum stool. MISDEMEANOR subsequently cut a cover version of the MISFITS 'Hybrid Moments' for a Freebird Records tribute album with Brad Davis sitting in as session sticksman. The band drafted Richard Ankers as new drummer in July of 2001. MISDEMEANOR's 2002 full-length eponymous debut, produced and mixed by the ENTOMBED duo of Alex Hellid and Nico Elgstrand, would surprisingly include Indian sitar legend TAJ MAHAL on the track 'Parashoot'. Touring to promote the album included UK gigs supporting RAGING SPEEDHORN. A video for the track 'Let Me Know' also scored heavy rotation on Swedish TV.

Singles/EPs:
Misdemeanor EP, Psycheout (1997)
Snowballing / Gizmo / Venom / Love Song, Meteor City (1999) ('5 Wheel Drive' EP)
You're Nothing (And You Know It) / Y.S.B.T., Freakscene (1999)

Albums:
MISDEMEANOR, Muse Entity (2002)
Let Me Know / Not the One / Annoying / Mastery / The Beer Hunter / Knowing / Parashoot / It's So Big / Trust / 6R12

MIS.DIVINE (GERMANY)
Line-up: Sven Neumann (vocals), Sandra Besoke (vocals), Matthias Keyser (guitar), Mirko Bunzel (guitar), Marc Engelberg (bass), Markus Langhans (drums)

An Industrial flavoured Gothic Rock act. Previously known as MISCARRIAGE under which title the band recorded a demo tape 'Heritage Of The Past' added vocalist Sven Neumann for a second demo and by the third effort 'The Difference Between' the band had drafted drummer Markus Langhans and second vocalist Sandra Besoke. After a fourth tape 'Blutsyndrom' the band opted for a name change to MIS.DIVINE.

MIS.DIVINE's debut album was produced by Andy Classen of HOLY MOSES. The band has supported the likes of DISHARMONIC ORCHESTRA, TORCHURE, ATROCITY and WARPATH to name a few.

Albums:
ANGSTTRIADEN, Rawk RTD 397.0026.2 (1997)
Mediaseele / Down In A Hole / Hybrid Angel / Black Thoughts / Placebo Effect / On Thorns We Lay / Störfaktor / Home / Architect Of Pain / Swallow / Ego Sunwalk

MISFITS (Lodi, NJ, USA)
Line-Up: Glenn Danzig (vocals), Doyle (guitar), Jerry Only (bass), Robo (drums)

An American institution. MISFITS came to the attention of the European Rock audience through METALLICA bassist Cliff Burton's seeming insistence on wearing MISFITS T-shirts most days! The band, complete with B movie horror facepaint, soon became a cult hit in the clubs with their merchandise being much sought after.

The MISFITS were created in 1977 by muscle-bound vocalist Glenn Anzalone (previously with cover acts WHODAT AND BOOJANG and TALUS), bassist Jerry Caiafa and drummer Manny. Caiafa soon changed his name to Jerry Only whilst Anzalone opted for a new surname of Danzig for the debut single 'Cough Cool' and sophomore release the 'Bullet' EP. Deliberately designed to shock the EP featured a photograph of President Kennedy on the sleeve with a bullet hole in the head.

As Manny departed joining this formidable duo were guitarist Franché Coma (real name Frank LaCita) and drummer Mr. Jim (real name Jim Catania), the latter a previous WHODAT AND BOOJANG member. Mr. Jim also operated his own act CONTINENTAL CRAWLER with another ex-WHODAT AND BOOJANG man guitarist Stevie Lin issuing a three track single in 1979.

The MISFITS lost Coma and in October of 1978 Rick Riley came in before his position was taken a few weeks later by ex-PAROTTOX / THE SMITHEREENS / THE WHORELORDS / SLASH and THE SKABS guitarist Bobby Steele. Mr. Jim also bailed out and in came drummer Joey Image also of THE WHORELORDS (real name Joey Poole). Mr. Jim and Riley created ACES AND EIGHTS.

A projected European tour, with Doyle Only taking over from Steele, who quit to join THE UNDEAD, guesting for THE DAMNED increased the band's notoriety when Danzig and Steele were jailed for assault. MISFITS in fact only performed one show (at Leicester De Montfort hall) before pulling out of the tour. Upon their return to America EERIE VON (real name Arthur Googy) replaced Image for the 'Three Hits From Hell' EP released in 1981.

Image joined ACES AND EIGHTS with Riley and renamed himself 'Bazooka Joey' much later to join HUMAN BUFFET.

Confusingly another New York act, fronted by Liz Davies, decided to release a single 'Mommi I'm A Misfit' billed as THE MISFITS the same year.

1983's live album 'Live Evil' has a guest appearance from BLACK FLAG man HENRY ROLLINS. The following year Eerie Von was out amid bitter acrimony, his place being taken by Todd Swally and then former BLACK FLAG man Robo.

Von would be back for his ROSEMARY'S BABIES band releasing 1983's 'Blood Lust' album. Reverting back to his real name of Googy the ex-MISFITS drummer founded the Hare Krishna band ANTIDOTE. Googy also became a devotee of Krishna and adopted the name 'Bliss'.

MISFITS suffered with an ever revolving door when it came to drummers with ex-GENOCIDE / VERBAL ABUSE man Brian 'Damage' Keats having a stint before the return of Swally. Keats stay was about as brief it could be. The drummer did not even last one gig, falling off his drum stool drunk after just one song! Immediately post MISFITS Keats travelled in rapid succession through HELLBENT, THE KRETINS, THE HELLHOUNDS and THE SKULLS. Keats would later clean up his act to figure in ANGELS IN VAIN, PRINCESS PANG, RAGING SLAB and DOPPLER.

The MISFITS filled the gap with former SARDONICA drummer Dr. Chud.

In 1987 METALLICA, fast rising to the peak of their global popularity, introduced a whole new legion of listeners to the MISFITS by covering 'Last Caress' and 'Green Hell' on their 'Garage Days' EP.

Upon the dissolving of the MISFITS some members united with ex-YNGWIE MALMSTEEN vocalist JEFF SCOTT SOTO to found the short-lived Rock band KRYST THE CONQUEROR. Chud issued a solo album under the titled SACRED TRASH in 1994.

Danzig meanwhile attempted to create a new act with members of MINOR THREAT / THE MEATMEN personnel Lyle Preslar and Brian Baker but instead created SAMHAIN reuniting with Eerie Von (now on bass guitar)

263

and Preslar. (Baker went on to DAG NASTY, JUNKYARD and BAD RELIGION). SAMHAIN, retaining the services of Von, eventually evolved into the internationally recognized DANZIG.

By 1995 a re-formed MISFITS comprised Only, vocalist Michael Graves, guitarist Doyle ('Wolfgang Von Frankenstein') and Dr. Chud, a man who wears a jacket made from a real cow's ribcage and spine covered in goat hair! The band got back into live action touring America on a package bill with ANTHRAX.

The MISFITS were honoured with the tribute album 'Violent World' which saw the likes of PRONG, THERAPY? and NOFX paying homage.

Steele now divides his time between MOURNING NOISE, the ZERO PROPHETS and TIMES SQUARE, the latter act with his girlfriend World Champion boxer Jill Matthews.

1999 saw the band's status being recognized with the release of two toy action figures of Jerry Only and Doyle Wolfgang Von Frankenstein.

Collectors should note that not only was there an alternative New York band titled THE MISFITS of 1981 but also two acts of the same name from the '60s from San Diego and Texas as well as a Scottish version. All issued one-off singles.

Ex members Michael Graves and Dr. Chud founded the suitably titled GRAVES in league with guitarist Tom Logan and former FAST TIMES bassist Graham Westfield.

Singles/EPs:
Cough Cool / She Blank, Plan 9 PL1001 (1977) (USA release)
Horror Business / Teenagers From Mars / Children In Heat, Plan 9 PL 1009 (1977) ('Bullet' EP)
Night Of The Living Dead / Where Eagles Dare / Rat Fink, Plan 9 PL1011 (1979) ('Night Of The Living Dead' EP)
London Dungeon / Horror Hotel / Ghoul's Night Out, Plan 9 PL1013 (1981) ('Three Hits From Hell' EP)
Beware EP, Cherry Red PLP9 (1981) Halloween / Halloween II, Plan 9 PL1017 (1981) (USA release)
Die Die My Darling, Plan 9 PL9-03 (1987)

Albums:
WALK AMONG US, Ruby 925756-1 (1982) 20 Eyes / I Turned Into A Martian / All Hell Breaks Loose / Vampira / Nike A Go Go / Hate Breeders / Mommy, Can I Go Out And Kill Tonight / Night Of The Living Dead / Skulls / Violent World / Devil's Whorehouse / Astro Zombies / Brain Eaters

EVIL LIVE, Aggressive Rock AG 023 (1983) (USA release)
20 Eyes / Night Of The Living Dead / Astro Zombies / Horror Business / London Dungeon / All Hell Breaks Loose / We Are 138
EARTH AD - WOLF'S BLOOD, Caroline PL9-CD 02/3 (1984)
Earth AD / Queen Wasp / Devilock / Death Comes Ripping / Green Hell / Mommy, Can I Go Out And Kill Tonight / Wolfs Blood / Demonomania / Bloodfeast / Hellhound / Die, Die My Darling / We Bite
LEGACY OF BRUTALITY, Plan 9 CD06 (1986)
Angelfuck / Who Killed Marilyn? / Where Eagles Dare / She / Halloween / American Nightmare / Static Age / TV Casualty / Hybrid Moments / Spinal Remains / Come Back / Some Kinda Hate / Theme For A Jackal
BEST OF THE MISFITS, Revolver REVLP 74 (1986)
THE MISFITS COLLECTION, Plan 9 PL9CD (1988)
THE MISFITS COLLECTION VOLUME 2, Caroline CAROL 7515-2 (1995)
AMERICAN PSYCHO, Geffen GEFSD 25126 (1997)
Abominable Dr. Phibes / American Psycho / Speak Of The Devil / Walk Among Us / The Hunger / From Hell they Came / Dig Up Her Bones / Blacklight / Resurrection / This Island Earth / Crimson Ghost / Day Of The Dead / The Haunting / Mars Attacks / Hate The Living, Love The Dead / Shining / Don't Open 'Til Doomsday
STATIC AGE, Caroline CAROL 7520-2 (1997)
Static Age / TV Casualty / Some Kinda Hate / Last Caress / Return Of The Fly / Hybrid Moments / We Are 138 / Teenagers From Mars / Come Back / Angelfuck / Hollywood Babylon / Attitude / Bullet / Theme For A Jackal / She / Spinal Remains / In The Doorway
FAMOUS MONSTERS, Roadrunner (1999)
Kong At The Gates / The Forbidden Zone / Lost In Space / Dust To Dust / Crawling Eye / Witch Hunt / Scream! / Saturday Night / Pumpkin Head / Scarecrow Man / Die Monster Die / Living Hell / Descending Angel / Them / Fiend Club / Hurting Humans / Helena / Kong Is Unleashed
CUTS FROM THE CRYPT, Roadrunner 618467 (2001)
Dead Kings Rise (Demo) / Blacklight (Demo) / The Haunting (Demo) / The Hunger (Demo) / Dr. Phibes Rises Again (Demo) / I Got A Right / Monster Mash / I Wanna Be A NY Ranger / Scream (Demo) / 1,000,000 Years B.C. / Helena 2 / Devil Doll / Fiend Without A

Face / Bruiser / No More Moments / Rise Above

THE MISSION (UK)
Line-Up: Wayne Hussey (vocals / guitar), Simon Hinkler (guitar), Craig Adams (bass), Mick Brown (drums)

Leading Gothic Rock act out of Leeds, famously founded by erstwhile SISTERS OF MERCY personnel vocalist / guitarist Wayne Hussey and bassist Craig Adams. Hussey had also served an early '80s term with Pop acts DEAD OR ALIVE and previously THE WALKIE TALKIES. Hussey would only perform a handful of gigs with DEAD OR ALIVE, leaving that band in 1984 and apparently having briefly been involved in the genesis of the even more controversial FRANKIE GOES TO HOLLYWOOD.

With Hussey and Adam's acrimonious departure from the SISTERS OF MERCY a band unit was created controversially dubbed THE SISTERHOOD, also by no coincidence the name given to the SISTERS OF MERCY fan club. With SISTERS OF MERCY mentor Andrew Eldritch swift issuing of product under the SISTERHOOD name, the 1986 album 'Gift', Hussey's band became THE MISSION. Reports at the time suggested that even this revised moniker was a swipe at Eldritch, the supposed provisional title of the next SISTERS OF MERCY album having been forecast as 'On A Mission To Rise And Reverberate'. Paradoxically, although never gaining the cult kudos afforded Eldritch's band, THE MISSION would go on to outsell them both in terms of records and concert tickets.

The first formation of THE MISSION included former RED LORRY YELLOW LORRY drummer Mick Brown and ex-ARTERY and PULP guitarist Simon Hinkler. The interest provoked by the SISTERS OF MERCY connection would place the debut single, 'Serpent's Kiss' released in May of 1986, into the lower reaches of the charts. From that point on THE MISSION steadily built up a fan base all of their own. Signing to major label Mercury Records the group made an immediate impact with the 1986 album 'God's Own Medicine'. The record saw backing vocals contributed by ALL ABOUT EVE's Julianne Regan, a trend which would continue for successive releases.

Undoubtedly THE MISSION's finest statement came with the March 1988 album 'Children'. Nearly topping the UK album charts 'Children', produced by ex-LED ZEPPELIN bassist JOHN PAUL JONES, was preceded by the eight minute hit single 'Tower Of Strength', a song fittingly of grandiose LED

ZEPPELIN-esque proportions with a trademark Eastern aura to match.

1989 conjured up the odd spectre of a spoof Glam Heavy Metal band THE METAL GURUS - actually a union of SLADE frontman Noddy Holder, "Hipster Looney" (Wayne Hussey), "Slink" (Simon Hinkler), "Lucky Mick" (Mick Brown) and "Rick Spangle" (Craig Adams).

1990 was ushered in with the Tim Palmer produced 'Carved In Sand' album preceded by a further hit single 'Butterfly On A Wheel'. A second single, 'Deliverance' released in March promoted the UK 'Deliverance' tour. Supported by THE WONDERSTUFF the band would add another former RED LORRY, YELLOW LORRY man Dave Wolfendon on second guitar.

Bearing in mind that it was a compilation of out-takes, the October 1990 album 'Grains Of Sand' testified to the strength of THE MISSION's UK fan base by charting at no. 28. The 'Grains Of Sand' material had been recorded during the productive 'Carved In Sand' sessions but was unused at the time. The CD format of the record also added a further two additional tracks in 'Tower Of Strength (Casbah mix)' and 'Butterfly On A Wheel (Troubadour mix)'.

1990 would prove a pivotal year for the band with members dealing with not only fame but also an acknowledged drug dependency. Wayne Hussey was famously bodily removed from a live TV show in Britain, 'The James Whale Show', the singer plainly drunk. An American tour was postponed with Hinkler reportedly suffering from a rheumatic problem. During gigs in Canada Hinkler walked out, leaving THE MISSION mid tour without a guitarist. ALL ABOUT EVE's Tim Brecheno plugged the gap on a temporary basis.

The single 'Hands Across The Ocean' was recorded by THE MISSION as a trio, Wayne Hussey handling the main guitar parts.

The group would regroup with Hinkler for a mammoth show at Finsbury Park the following year, oddly utilizing an onstage saxophone player much to fans bemusement, but it was not to last. Craig Adams opted out but soon found himself back in the limelight as bass player for THE CULT. The Electro sounds of the 1992 'Masque' album backfired. These sessions saw the introduction of SPEAR OF DESTINY guitarist Mark 'Gemini' Thwaite, JESUS AND MARY CHAIN bass player Matthew Parkin and PENDRAGON and HEARTLAND keyboard player Rik Carter. For touring Andy Cousins of ALL ABOUT EVE supplanted Parkin.

Vertigo issued the retrospective 'Sum And Substance' compilation album in January 1994, notable for its inclusion of two new tracks in 'Sour Puss' and 'Afterglow'. The double vinyl album edition would add three extra tracks namely 'Serpents Kiss', 'Like A Hurricane' and 'Garden Of Delight'. Members of the band's fan club would be treated to a restricted release flexi disc of THE MISSION blasting through a exceptionally heavy rendition of THE OSMONDS 'Crazy Horses'. The group also found itself back in the charts and on 'Top Of The Pops' once more backing up 'Tower Of Strength' yet again courtesy of a remix from KILLING JOKE man Youth.

THE MISSION, only retaining Hussey and Brown from the previous line-up, returned in 1995 with the 'Neverland' album. Released on the band's own Equator imprint with distribution through major label Sony the album charted in the UK illustrating the fans durability and loyalty. The main track from the album, 'Raising Cain' had familiar echoes, deliberately reusing a speeded up loop track from the band's biggest hit 'Tower Of Strength'. An unlikely hit was scored in South Africa with 'Lose Myself In You' attaining major radio play backed by a quick burst of unplugged gigs.

In August of 1996, on THE MISSION's tenth anniversary, Wayne Hussey called it a day. Following completion of tour work to promote the 'Blue' album the band bowed out with a performance to over 60,000 fans in Johannesburg.

Hussey relocated to California whilst Andy Cousins created a fresh venture LUCYNATION, later re'joining ALL ABOUT EVE. Rik Carter busied himself with THE VEGASTONES and would join Cousins in ALL ABOUT EVE.

THE MISSION reactivated themselves in 1999, putting in co-headline dates in North America alongside GENE LOVES JEZEBEL to accompany a compilation album 'Resurrection'. Renewed interest in the band took THE MISSION to such previously unvisited countries as Mexico, Brazil, Argentina. A new studio album 'Aura' was delivered in November of 2001, the band now citing a line-up of Hussey, Adams, Thwaite and drummer Scott Garrett of THE CULT and GOD LIVES UNDERWATER. Post recording Thwaite was forced to bow out due to prior touring commitments with TRICKY.

The March 2002 single 'Shine Like A Star' included a cover version of DEPECHE MODE's 'Never Let Me Down'. Once again line-up problems reared up, this time in the midst of South American dates in May. Having completed four successful Brazilian gigs Craig Adams bailed out. With further shows booked throughout Chile, Peru and Argentina a compromise was reached whereby Hussey would perform songs of THE MISSION with

local musicians before closing with solo material. However, as it turned out most gigs were still confusingly billed as THE MISSION. The mid 2002 version of THE MISSION comprised Hussey, guitarist Rob Holliday, bass player Richard Vernon and drummer Scott Garrett. However, gigs in July would be without the services of Garrett who had damaged ligaments in his hand. Whilst Garrett undertook an enforced period of recuperation Richard Beesley from the GARY NUMAN band would sit in for festival shows in Europe. With these gigs wrapped up WAYNE HUSSEY embarked upon a string of solo shows in the UK during August.

The September 2002 release 'Aural Delights' comprised outtakes, B sides, demos and acoustic renditions of recent material and was made available only through the band's official website. A North American headline tour would coincide with the album release after which WAYNE HUSSEY visited Poland and Portugal for a further series of solo shows.

Singles/EPs:
Serpent's Kiss / Wake (R.S.V.), Chapter CHAP 6 (1986) **70 UK**
Serpent's Kiss / Wake (R.S.V.) / Naked And Savage, Chapter 22 12 CHAP 6 (1986) (12" single)
Garden Of Delight / Like A Hurricane, Chapter 22 CHAP 7 (1986) **50 UK**
Garden Of Delight / Like A Hurricane / Over The Hills And Far Away / The Crystal Ocean, Chapter 22 12 CHAP 7 (1986) (12" single)
Garden Of Delight / Like A Hurricane / Dancing Barefoot / The Crystal Ocean, Chapter 22 L12 CHAP 7 (1986) (12" single)
Stay With Me / Blood Brother, Mercury MYTH 1 (1986) **30 UK**
Stay With Me / Blood Brother / Islands In A Stream, Mercury MYTHX 1 (1986) (12" single)
Wasteland / Shelter From The Storm, Mercury MYTH 2 (1987) **11 UK**
Wasteland / Shelter From The Storm / 1969 (Live) / Serpent's Kiss (Live), Mercury (1987)
Wasteland / Shelter From The Storm / Dancing Barefoot (Live), Mercury MYTHX 2 (1987) (12" single)
Wasteland / Shelter From The Storm / 1969 (Live) / Wake (Live), Mercury (1987) (12" single)
Severina / Tomorrow Never Knows, Mercury MYTH 3 (1987) **25 UK**
Severina / Tomorrow Never Knows / Wishing Well, Mercury MYTHX 3 (1987) (12" single)
Tower Of Strength / Fabienne, Mercury MYTH 4 (1988) **12 UK**
Tower Of Strength / Fabienne / Dream On / Breathe (Instrumental), Mercury MYTHX 4

(1988) (12" single)

Beyond The Pale / Tadeusz (1912-1988), Mercury MYTH 6 (1988) **32 UK**

Beyond The Pale / Tadeusz (1912-1988) / **Love Me To Death** / For Ever More, Mercury MYTHX 6 (1988) (12" single)

Kingdom Come / Child's Play (Live), Mercury MYTH 7 (1988)

Kingdom Come / Child's Play (Live) / The Crystal Ocean, Mercury (1988) (12" single)

Kingdom Come / Child's Play (Live) / Garden Of Delight (Live), Mercury (1988) (CD single)

Amelia (Live) / Amelia (Album version) / Stay With Me (Demo) / Tower Of Strength (Casbah mix), Mercury (1990) (USA release)

Butterfly On A Wheel / The Grip Of Disease, Mercury MYTH 8 (1990) **12 UK**

Butterfly On A Wheel (The Magnificent Octopus mix) / The Grip Of Disease / Kingdom Come (Forever And Again), Mercury (1990) (12" single)

Butterfly On A Wheel (Magnum Opus mix) / Kingdom Come (Forever And Again) / Kingdom Come (Heavenly mix), Mercury (1990) (10" single)

Deliverance / Mr. Pleasant, Mercury MYTH 9 (1990) **27 UK**

Deliverance / Mr. Pleasant / Heaven Sends Us, Mercury (1990) (12" single)

Deliverance (Sorcerer's mix) / Blockbuster (Live) / Metal Guru (Live) / Mama We're All Crazee Now (Live), Mercury (1990) (12" single)

Deliverance / Heaven Sends You / Mr. Pleasant / Virginia Plain (Live), Mercury (1990) (10" single)

Into The Blue / Bird Of Paradise, Mercury MYTH 10 (1990) **32 UK**

Into The Blue / Bird Of Paradise / Divided We Fall, Mercury MYTHX10 (1990) (12" single)

Hands Across The Ocean / Amelia / Love, Vertigo (1990) **29 UK**

Hands Across The Ocean / Amelia / Love / Amelia (Live) / Tower Of Strength (Mix) / Mercenary, Vertigo (1990) (12" single)

Hands Across The Ocean / Amelia / Love / Amelia (Live) / Stay With Me / Mercenary, Vertigo (1990) (12" single)

Never Again / Beautiful Chaos, Vertigo (1992) **34 UK**

Never Again / Beautiful Chaos / Never Again (F1 mix) / Never Again (Zero G mix), Vertigo (1992) (12" single)

Like A Child Again / All Tangled Up In You, Vertigo (1992) **30 UK**

Like A Child Again / Hush A Bye Baby (Child Again) (Joe Gibbs remix) / Like A Child Again (Mark Saunders remix) / All Tangled Up In You, Vertigo (1992) (12" single)

Like A Child Again (Extended version) / Like A Child Again (Remix) / All Tangled Up In You, Vertigo (1992) (10" single)

Like A Child Again (Remix) / Like A Child Again (Extended version) / All Tangled Up In You / Hush-a-Bye Baby (Child Again), Vertigo (1992) (CD single)

Shades Of Green / You Make Me Breathe, Vertigo (1992) **49 UK**

Shades Of Green / Sticks And Stones / Trail Of Scarlet / Spider And The Fly, Vertigo (1992) (CD single)

Tower Of Strength (East India Cairo mix edit) / Wasteland (Musketeer mix), (1994) **33 UK**

Tower Of Strength (East India Trans Cairo mix) / Wasteland (Musketeer mix) / Serpents Kiss (Slaughter mix), (1994) (12" single)

Tower Of Strength (East India Cairo mix edit) / Tower Of Strength (East India Cairo mix) / Deliverance (Sorcerer's mix), (1994) (CD single)

Tower Of Strength (Tribal Mantra mix) / Tower Of Strength (Bombay mix) / Tower Of Strength (Lysergic dub) / Tower Of Strength (Zen Acoustic mix), (1994) (CD single)

Tower Of Strength (East India Trans Cairo mix edit) / Wasteland (Musketeer mix) / Tower Of Strength (Lysergic dub), (1994) (CD single)

Afterglow (Edit Olympic mix) / Sour Puss (Glamour Puss mix), (1994) **53 UK**

Afterglow (Full Length Olympic mix) / Cold As Ice / Valentine / Sour Puss (Glamour Puss mix), (1994) (12" single)

Afterglow (Edit Olympic mix) / Sour Puss (Glamour Puss mix) / Cold As Ice / Valentine, (1994) (CD single)

Afterglow (Full Length Olympic mix) / Afterglow (Reso Central mix) / Afterglow (San Marino Score Against England In 7 Seconds mix) / Afterglow (Snow On The Ground mix), (1994) (CD single)

Raising Cain / Sway / Neverland, (1994) Swoon (Over The Moon edit) / Swoon (Over The Moon mix) / Swoon (Bubble Wrap mix) / Swoon (Full Balloon mix), (1995) (CD single)

Swoon (Full Balloon edit) / Whore / Wasting Away / Swoon (Resurrection mix), (1995) (10" single)

Swoon (Full Balloon edit) / Whore / Wasting Away, (1995) **73 UK**

Lose Myself In You (Radio edit) / Instant Karma / Pictures Of Matchstick Men / Lose Myself In You (Album version), (1995)

Heaven Knows (Live) / Sway (Live) / Swoon (Live) / Raising Cain (Live), (1995) ('Live' EP. German promotion release)

Coming Home / Perfect Sunrise / Coming Home (Godlike version), (1996)

Evangeline / Anyone But You / Melt / Swoon (Resurrection mix), Playground Recordings

PNGCD001 (2001)
Shine Like A Star / Never Let Me Down / Spider & The Fly (In The Ointment) / **Sorry…**, Playground Recordings PGNDCD 003 (2002)

Albums:
GOD'S OWN MEDICINE, Mercury MERH 102 (1986) **14 UK**
Wasteland / Bridges Burning / Garden Of Delight / Stay With Me / Let Sleeping Dogs Lie / Sacrilege / Dance On Glass / And The Dance Goes On / Severina / Love Me To Death
THE FIRST CHAPTER, Mercury MISH 1 (1987) **35 UK**
Over The Hills And Far Away / Serpent's Kiss / The Crystal Ocean / Dancing Barefoot / Like A Hurricane (Extended version) / Tomorrow Never Knows / Wishing Well
CHILDREN, Mercury 834 263-2 (1988) **2 UK**
Beyond The Pale / Wing And A Prayer / Heaven On Earth / Tower Of Strength / Kingdom Come / Breathe / Shamara Kye / Black Mountain Mist / Heat / Hymn (For America)
CARVED IN SAND, Mercury 842 251-2 (1990) **34 NEW ZEALAND, 7 UK**
Amelia / Into The Blue / Butterfly On A Wheel / Sea Of Love / Deliverance / Grapes Of Wrath / Belief / Paradise (Will Shine Like The Moon) / Hungry As The Hunter / Lovely
GRAINS OF SAND, Mercury 846 937-2 (1990) **28 UK**
Hands Across The Ocean / The Grip Of Disease / Divided We Fall / Mercenary / Mr. Pleasant / Kingdom Come (Forever And Again) / Heaven Sends You / Sweet Smile Of Mystery / Love / Bird Of Passage
MASQUE, Vertigo 512 121-2 (1992) **23 UK**
Never Again / Shades Of Green (Part II) / Even You May Shine / Trail Of Scarlet / Spider And The Fly / She Conjures Me Wings / Sticks And Stones / Like A Child Again / Who Will Love Me Tomorrow? / You Make Me Breathe / From One Jesus To Another / Until There's Another Sunrise
NO SNOW, NO SHOW: FOR THE ESKIMO, Windsong WINCD035 (1993)
Amelia / Wasteland / Serpent's Kiss / Belief / Severina / Butterfly On A Wheel / Into The Blue / Kingdom Come / Deliverance / Tower Of Strength / Crystal Ocean
SALAD DAZE, Nighttracks CDNT005 (1994)
Like A Hurricane / Severina / And The Dance Goes On / Wasteland / Tomorrow Never Knows / Wishing Well / Shelter From The Storm / Deliverance / Grip Of Disease / Belief / Kingdom Come / Butterfly On A Wheel / Bird Of Passage
SUM AND SUBSTANCE, Vertigo CD 518 447-2 (1994) **49 UK**

Wasteland / Severina / Stay With Me / Tower Of Strength / Beyond The Pale (Armageddon Mix) / Butterfly On A Wheel / Deliverance / Into The Blue / Amelia / Hands Across The Ocean / Never Again / Like A Child Again (Remix) / Shades Of Green (Part 2) / Sour Puss / Afterglow
NEVERLAND, Equator SMEECD001 (1995) **58 UK**
Raising Cain / Sway / Lose Myself In You / Afterglow (Reprise) / Stars Don't Shine Without You / Celebration / Cry Like A Baby / Heaven Knows / Swim With The Dolphins / Neverland (Vocal) / Daddy's Going To Heaven Now / Bates Motel
BLUE, Equator SMEECD002 (1996) **73 UK**
Coming Home / Get Back To You / Drown In Blue / Damaged / More Than This / That Tears Shall Drown The Wind / Black & Blue / Bang Bang / Alpha Man / Cannibal / Dying Room / Evermore & Again
RESURRECTION, Cleopatra CD CLP0756-2 (1999)
Prelude: Anniversary / Wasteland / Severina / Love Me To Death / Interlude: Never Forever / Beyond The Pale / Deliverance / Without You / Like A Child Again / Sacrilege / You Make Me Breathe / Crystal Ocean / Interlude: Suffer The Children / Butterfly On A Wheel / Interlude: Infection / Hands Across The Ocean / 1969 / Resurrection
EVERAFTER, Receiver RRCD-294-Z (2000)
Beyond The Pale / Hands Across The Ocean / Into the Blue / Butterfly On A Wheel / Raising Cain / Heaven Knows / Sway / Sacrilege / Swoon / Tower Of Strength / Deliverance / Like A Child Again / Can't Help Falling In Love / Like a Hurricane / 1969 / Crazy Horses (Studio version)
AURA, Playground Recordings PGNDCD002 (2001)
Evangeline / Shine Like The Stars / (Slave To) Lust / Mesmerized / The Light That Pours From You / Dragonfly / Happy / To Die By Your Hand / Trophy / It Never Rains… / Burlesque / Lay Your Hands On Me / Cocoon / In Denial
AURAL DELIGHT, Playground Recordings PGNDCD 004X (2002)
Amelia / Even You May Shine / Spider & The Fly (In The Ointment) / Sorry… / Anyone But You / Never Let Me Down / Never Again / Melt / Mesmerized (Reprise) / Swoon (Reprise) / Dragonfly (Demo) / Can't Help Falling In Love / Dragonfly (Acoustic) / Never Let Me Down (Acoustic) / Happy (Acoustic) / Burlesque (Acoustic)

MISSISSIPPI SLUDGE (USA)
Line-Up: Adam Elliot (vocals), Jeff Mohr (guitar), Tracey Scott (bass), A.J. Cavalier (drums)

Southern Sludge. Both drummer A.J.Cavalier and guitarist Jeff Mohr are former WORLD IN PAIN members. Cavalier also has credits fronting DIESEL MACHINE.

Albums:
BISCUITS AND SLAVERY, Record Heaven (2001)
Biscuits n' Slavery / Dirty Boy / (Untitled) / Family Cabin / Somethin' Gotta Give / Make Amends / Back To Back / Porchlight Blind / Sultry Lady

MISTRALTH (FINLAND)

A Helsinki based Gothic Doom partnership (and marriage) of multi-instrumentalist J.S. and vocalist Morsus-Ranae.

Albums:
DIARY OF DESPAIR, (2001)

MISTRESS (UK)
Line-Up: Dave Cunt (vocals), Misery (guitar), Dirty (bass), Migg (drums)

"Necro-Doom" out of Birmingham. MISTRESS are not only noted for their individual brand of Doom but for their membership's myriad of other project bands of diverse styles such as SALLY, ANAAL NATHRAKH, FROST, DEADSUNRISING, FROG and FUKPIG.
The group was founded in late 1999 as a trio of guitarist Misery, drummer Migg and a singer known in polite company as Dave Cunt. This trio cut the quaintly titled 'Fuck Off' demo, adding bassist Earl from Hardcore merchants AKBAR in April of 2000. Drunken from CREEP then took the bass mantle before the four string position for a sophomore demo 'Lord Worm' was handed over to Dirty, better known as drummer for Stoners SALLY.
A sizable contingent of MISTRESS perform with "89 style" Grindcore act FUKPIG. Migg is drummer for Black Metal band FROST and also operates the experimental project PROFESSOR FATE. The drummer also plies his trade with ABOYRM and DISGUST.

Albums:
MISTRESS, Rage Of Achilles (2002)
Bludgeon / God Of Rock / Goatboy / Necronaut / Stunt Cock / 5th In Line / D.V.D.A / Rebecca / Lord Worm

MITTERNACHT (ARGENTINA)

A one man keyboard symphonic ambient Black-Doom endeavour of Friedrich Curwenius.

Albums:
THE DESOLATION OF BLENDENSTEIN, Furias 0400 (2002)
The Desolation Of Blendenstein / The Pain Of Uncertainty / The Crushing Of Blendenstein / Mist Of Ravens / A Tribute To The Void / The Unveiling / The Dawn Of Uprising / War Against The Void / Last Battle in The Fields Of Blendenstein / The Desert Beside Blendenstein

MODERN FUNERAL ART (FRANCE)
Line-Up: Arnaud Spitz (vocals / bass), Benoît Sangoï (drums)

The MODERN FUNERAL ART Doom duo of vocalist / bassist Arnaud Spitz and drummer Benoît Sangoï also operate the Dark Wave project EVENLORE.

Albums:
HELL FIRE, Mono-Emotional 01072001-03 (2000)
The Hell-Fire Festival / Like Lucretia's Paramour / Under A Yew / Lovecraft Was A Liar / There Is No Death / Crosses / A Sepulchre By The Sea / The Hell-Fire Festival (Part 2) / The Pale Plutonian Shore / Gateways Of Slumber / The Astronomer / Almost Angels (Part 2)

MOLEHILL (Birmingham, AL, USA)
Line-Up: Shane (vocals), Andrew (guitar), Jeremy (guitar), Matt (bass), Billy (drums)

Alabama Sludge-Doom act rooted in a previous incarnation as SLIT. When SLIT introduced vocalist Shane the band morphed into MOLEHILL. Although the debut album 'Comfort Measured In Razor Lines' scored healthy press commendations the band found the going tough. For tour work Sonny came in on bass to supplant Matt but MOLEHILL folded sometime in 2000. Vocalist Shane and drummer Billy founded BLUE EYED BOY MISTER DEATH whilst Billy also held down the drummer position with LONG COLD STARE. Both guitarist Andrew and bassist Matt featured in RESIDUE.

Albums:
COMFORT MEASURED IN RAZOR LINES, Rage Of Achilles ILIAD001 (2000)
Dying Like Sisters / Balrac / Sleeping Through My Funeral / Graying Whore / Eye On / 24 Hour Mercy Plea

MONDO GENERATOR (USA)

Another in the long line of Stoner Rock royalty side projects. MONDO GENERATOR is the vehicle for bassist Nick Oliveri (aka 'Rex Everything') to vent his spleen. Oliveri's credits include QUEENS OF THE STONE AGE, KYUSS and DWARVES. Joining him on this endeavour were QUEENS OF THE STONE AGE / KYUSS man Josh Homme, Brent 'Burnt Mattress' Malkus, KYUSS / FU MANCHU drummer Brant Bjork and KARMA TO BURN's Rob 'Up n' Syder' Oswald.

The 2000 album 'Cocaine Rodeo' was of great curiosity to QUEENS OF THE STONE AGE FANS, including in its grooves '13th Floor' and 'Simple Exploding Man', both having been performed live by the former band on many an occasion. Indeed, '13th Floor' would be recorded by QUEENS OF THE STONE AGE on their rated 'R' album under the revised title 'Another Tension Head'.

Albums:
COCAINE RODEO, Southern Lord 18857-2 (2000)
13th Floor / Shawnette / Uncle Tommy / Miss Mary Gets A Boob Job / Unless I Can Kill / PigMan

MONSTER MAGNET
(New York, NY, USA)
Line-Up: Dave Wyndorf (vocals), John McBain (guitar), Joe Calendra (bass), Jon Kleinman (drums)

Although cited by more than one rock journalist as "The future of music" New York's MONSTER MAGNET have had difficulty in breaking away from their cult status, finally breaking through in 1999. The band's 'Spine Of God' album has an almost reverential status amongst the Stoner community although, in truth, MONSTER MAGNET's sound is as much reliant on '60s Garage and Psychedelia as it is '70s Doom. The band was forged in 1989 and went through numerous tags such as HEROIN MULE, NIPPLE TANK, WORLD OF PILLS and GRINNING GIBBON before settling on the name of a 1960's toy MONSTER MAGNET. Vocalist Dave Wyndorf had previously fronted SHRAPNEL, an act that had released a 1984 mini-album for Elektra.

Previous to MONSTER MAGNET the individual band members had paid their dues with a succession of ad hoc Stoner-Psych bands. Original vocalist Tim Cronin had operated in the '80s with acts such as THE SMOKING PETS and SKY LAB before founding DOGS OF MYSTERY in union with guitarist John McBain, previously with bands with such unlikely titles as EXISTENSIAL MOPED and (apparently) STEAMING RECTAL MUCUS. Prior to DOGS OF MYSTERY the Cronib / McBain axis had a formative 1987 band, in league with EXISTENTIAL MOPED bassist Tom Diello, entitled PINQUE PHLOID. This act, wherein Cronin took on the stagename 'Trash Twister', issued one demo tape 'A Fat Dick Named Charlie' before evolving into DOGS OF MYSTERY.

With DOGS OF MYSTERY McBain and Cronin released two tapes. 'And Therin Lies The Rub' and 'Metal Head Of Robeson'. The band line-up was fluid, especially for live gigs, at which Cronin took command of the drums and which sometimes found a local drunk by the name of Pocko utilizing a bullhorn for lead vocals. Jim Norton of THE SHOCK MUMMIES and Hardcore act CRUCIAL YOUTH was one of DOGS OF MYSTERY's many bassists and through his connections landed the band a gig supporting JANE'S ADDICTION. The group had recently enrolled guitarist Dave Wyndorf, their newest recruit having declined an offer to manage the band and suggesting a musical union instead. As such, DOGS OF MYSTERY opened for JANE'S ADDICTION citing a line-up of Wyndorf and McBain on guitar, Norton on bass and Cronin on drums.

Pre-DOGS OF MYSTERY Wyndorf had been running a comic store and demoing on a 4-track recorder as LOVE MONSTER during 1988. He would also fronted a Punk band PIGS IN SPACE which featured Jon Kleiman on the drums.

The Wyndorf, McBain and Cronin trio also became involved with both ACID REICH and Metal band RIPPING CORPSE at this juncture. An early ACID REICH recording, the instrumental 'Needlefreak' would later be credited as a MONSTER MAGNET tune when it appeared on the 'Sugarcube Caravan' compilation tape. DOGS OF MYSTERY morphed into a covers band KING FUZZ for a brief time before becoming MONSTER MAGNET.

The initial incarnation of MONSTER MAGNET was a trio with both Cronin and Wyndorf sharing lead vocals. A brace of demos was recorded and surfaced in the form of 'Forget About Life, I'm High On Dope' and 'I'm High, What Are You Going To Do About It?' From these sessions the 7" singles 'Freakship USA' and 'Murder' also emerged. MONSTER MAGNET's first impressions on the international Rock scene came with the delivery of a five track EP for the Glitterhouse label. In order to build a unit capable of performing live the band duly became a five piece with the addition of bassist Joe Calendra and drummer Jon Kleiman, both just having left THE SHOCK MUMMIES.

As a quintet the group recorded the 'Tab' album but this release would be shelved. It was only when 'Spine Of God' was released and MONSTER MAGNET's profile suddenly escalated that 'Tab' found a release. With an increase in live work Cronin decided that he was struggling on stage and so opted out. Wyndorf took over lead vocal duties as Cronin stayed with the group supervising lighting and special effects.

McBain departed after a nationwide tour guesting for SOUNDGARDEN and prior to 1993's 'Superjudge'. He would later figure in the Seattle acts HATER with SOUNDGARDEN's Ben Shepard and Matt Cameron and DEVILHEAD, again with Shepard. In 1997 McBain forged a new act WELL WATER CONSPIRACY issuing a debut self-titled album the same year that boasted cameo appearances from former Shepard and Cameron. MONSTER MAGNET filled the gap with ex-DAISYCUTTER man Ed Mundell. The following year MONSTER MAGNET contributed their version of 'Black Celebration' to a DEPECHE MODE tribute album. A side project comprising Mundell, Kleiman and Calendra would also be instigated in June of 1998 with John Garcia of KYUSS repute adding lead vocals. These tapes have yet to transpire. SADDAR BAZAAR covered 'Longhair' in 1999 as a single.

MONSTER MAGNET added guitarist Phil Caivano (previously bass player for SHRAPNEL) for live work to promote the commercial breakthrough 'Powertrip'. 'Powertrip' truly elevated the group from the status of a cult underground act to major status. With the 'Space Lord' single breaking out all over radio the band toured heavily, acting as openers to such heavyweights as METALLICA, MEGADETH and AEROSMITH. Caivano was announced as a full-time band member prior to recording the 2000 album. The same year Caivano produced New Jersey Punks ELECTRIC FRANKENSTEIN's 'Don't Touch Me, I'm Electric!' album. MONSTER MAGNET toured Europe in late 2000 as guests to QUEENS OF THE STONE AGE.

Mundell also operates the high profile side project THE ATOMIC BITCHWAX. Drummer Jon Kleiman bowed in with his own Rockabilly Garage venture THE RIBEYE BROTHERS, in league with Tim Cronin on the 2002 Meteor City album 'If I Had A Horse'. To top it all fans learned of a MONSTER MAGNET inspired 'supergroup' on the horizon billed as GALLERY OF MITES and cutting an album for Meteor City. Alongside MONSTER

MAGNET personnel Jon Kleiman, Ed Mundell & Tim Cronin, GALLERY OF MITES boasted a nine man strong line-up including Tommy Southard of SOLACE, Dwayne from BLACK NASA, Stu of HALFWAY TO GONE and Mike and Jim from LORD STERLING.

In 2001 an eponymous album emerged credited to LOVE MONSTER. The album was in actuality MONSTER MAGNET demos culled from a 1988 session. The band would also contribute 'Silver Future' to the 'Heavy Metal II' film soundtrack. MONSTER MAGNET, breaking a lengthy period of silence, would also have new material featured on the March 2002 'WWF Forceable Entry' compilation issued by Columbia Records, donating 'Live For The Moment'. The group would also figure on the BLACK SABBATH tribute 'Nativity In Black II', donating a rendition of 'Into The Void'. The band would also "celebrate" their departure from A&M Records with a month long trek of the States billed as the 'We're Free' tour.

Singles/EPs:
Freakshop USA / Lizard Johnny, (1989)
Murder / Tractor, (1989)
Evil / Elephant Bell / Spine Of God (Live), Glitterhouse GR204 (1993)
Twin Earth / Nod Scene, A&M 580281-7 (1993) **67 UK**
Twin Earth / Nod Scene / Medicine, A&M 580281-2 (1993) (12" single)
Negasonic Teenage Warhead / Blow 'Em Off, A&M (1995) **49 UK**
Negasonic Teenage Warhead / Blow 'Em Off / Eclipse This / Third Alternative / Look Into Your Orb For The Warning, A&M (1995) (CD single)
Negasonic Teenage Warhead / Blow 'Em Off / Murder (Live) / Superjudge (Live), A&M (1995) (CD single)
Dopes To Infinity / I'm Five Years Ahead Of My Time, A&M 581 032-7 (1995) **58 UK**
Dopes To Infinity / I'm Five Years Ahead Of My Time / Dinosaur Vacuum / Theme From 'Masterburner', A&M 581 032-2 (1995) (CD single)
Dopes To Infinity / I'm Five Years Ahead Of My Time / Looking To The Orb For A Warning, A&M 581 033-2 (1995) (CD single)
Dead Christmas / Blow 'Em Off, A&M 44098 (1995) ('I Talk To Planets' EP)
See You In Hell, A&M (1999)
Heads Explode / 1970 / Leapin' Lizards (Non album version) / Heads Explode (Video), A&M (2000)

Albums:
MONSTER MAGNET, Primo Scree EFA 08123-90 (1990)

271

Snake Dance / Tractor / Nod Scene / Freak Shop USA / Lizard Johnny
SPINE OF GOD, Glitterhouse GR017-2 (1992)
Pill Shovel / Medicine / Nod Scene / Black Mastermind / Zodiac Lung / Spine Of God / Snake Dance / Sin's A Good Man's Brother / Ozium
TAB, Caroline 1471 (1993)
Tab… / 25 / Longhair / Lord 13
SUPERJUDGE, A&M (1993)
Cyclops Revolution / Twin Earth / Superjudge / Cage Around The Sun / Elephant Bell / Dinosaur Vacuum / Evil / Stadium / Face Down / Brainstorm / Black Balloon
DOPES TO INFINITY, A&M 540 315-2 (1995) **51 UK**
Dopes To Infinity / Negasonic Teenage Warhead / Look To Your Orb For The Warning / All Friends And Kingdom Come / Ego, The Living Planet / Blow 'Em Off / Third Alternative / I Control, I Fly / King Of Mars / Dead Christmas / Theme from 'Masterburner' / Vertigo
POWERTRIP, A&M (1998) **29 SWEDEN**
Crop Circle / Powertrip / Space Lord / Temple Of Your Dreams / Bummer / Baby Gotterdammerung / 19 Witches / 3rd Eye Landscape / See You In Hell / Tractor / Atomic Clock / Goliath And The Vampires / Your Lies Become You
POWERTRIP - JAPANESE TOUR EDITION, A&M (1999)
Crop Circle / Powertrip / Space Lord / Temple Of Your Dreams / Bummer / Baby Gotterdammerung / 19 Witches / 3rd Eye Landscape / See You In Hell / Tractor / Atomic Clock / Goliath And The Vampires / Your Lies Become You / Big God / Kick Out The Jams / The Game / Temple Of Your Dreams (Live) / Dinosaur Vacuum (Live) / Baby Götterdämmerung (Live) / Cage Around The Sun (Live) / Bummer (Live) / Space Lord (Live)
GOD SAYS NO, Motor Music (2000)
17 GERMANY, 17 SWEDEN
Melt / Heads Explode / Doomsday / God Says No / Kiss Of The Scorpion / All Shook Out / Gravity Well / My Little Friend / Queen Of You / Down In The Jungle / Cry / Take It / Silver Future / I Want More

THE MONSTROUS BLUES
(AUSTRALIA)
Line-Up: Jason Betschwar (vocals / guitar), Paul Hausmeister (guitar), Simon Dalla Pozza (bass), Steve O'Brien (drums)

Wollongong Riff Rockers. THE MONSTROUS BLUES membership were all at one time in THE UNHEARD. Guitarist Paul Hausmeister and drummer Steve O'Brien were also with TUMBLEWEED.

Singles/EPs:
Being King / Octane / Group No 6 / Bring It Down / Drive, High Beam (2001) ('High Octane' EP)

MONUMENTUM (ITALY)
Line-Up: Andrea Zanetti (vocals), Francesca Nicoli (vocals), Roberto Mammarella (guitar / bass / keyboards), Mox Christadoro (drums)

MONUMENTUM came together in mid 1987 with a line-up of vocalist Mark Westfall, guitarist Roberto Mammarella, bassist Anthony and drummer Mox Christadoro. They released a 1989 demo, entitled 'Musaeum Hermeticum', and two tracks from this tape - 'Nostalgia Of The Infinite' and 'Nephtali' - were released on a split EP in 1991 shared with ROTTING CHRIST.
MONUMENTUM effectively split following the demo release, but increased recording offers saw the band sign to Norway's DSP label. Unfortunately, before a release could be made, DSP's mentor Euryonymous was murdered. Finally seeing the light of day on Misanthropy Records, the debut album 'In Absenti Christi' utilizes the talents of two vocalists in ICONOCLAST's Andrea Zanetti and ATARAXIA's Francesca Nicoli. With MONUMENTUM reaping praise on the underground Metal scene the split EP with ROTTING CHRIST would bear witness to a picture disc reissue during 1996.
Following three years of absence MONUMENTUM's silence was broken with the inclusion of the new track 'The Color Of Compassion' included on a Misanthropy sampler entitled 'Presumed Guilty'. The recording line-up for this track comprised Mammarella, Christadoro, Federico Simonetta on bass and Daniele Bovo on keyboards.
Utilizing the session services of SOLEFALD's Cornelius Brastad MONUMENTUM delivered their rendition of the DEATH SS tune 'Black And Violet' to an Italian tribute album in 1999. In 2001 Mammarella pulled together a new team under the MONUMENTUM title to record the 'Ad Nauseum' album. Featured would be keyboard players Andrea Belluci and Daniele Bovo, vocalists Andrea Stefanelli of NUVOLA NESHUA and Alis Francesca Bos, bass player Diego Danelli and drummer Elisa Carrera. The latter would be unexpectedly forced out of the sessions when she fell pregnant.
Drummer Mox Christadoro has since worked

with numerous Italian bands including CRASH BOX, LAS CRUS and CARNIVAL OF FOOLS.
Roberto Mammarella also operates a Gothic Doom side project CULTUS SANGUINE and, with Andrea Belucci, TWO SOULS.

Singles/EPs:
Nostalgia Of The Infinite / Nephtali, Obscure Plasma (1991) (Split single with ROTTING CHRIST)

Albums:
IN ABSENTIA CHRISTI, Misanthropy (1995)
Battesimo: Nero Opaco / A Thousand Breathing Crosses / Consuming Jerusalem / Fade To Grey / On Perspective Of Spiritual Catharsis / SeluhS AggeloS / From These Wounds / Terra Mater Orfanorumj / Nephtali / La Noia
AD NAUSEUM, Tatra (2002)
Last Call For Life / Anger Vacui / Distance / Under Monochrome Rainbow / Perche Il Mio Amore / I Stand (Nowhere) / Numana / A Tainted Retrospective / No Redemption / Reaping For Abel

MOOD (HUNGARY)
Line-Up: Gábor Holdampf (vocals), Sándor Fuleki (guitar), Kolos Hegyi (guitar) Ferenc Marek (bass), Tamás Koltay (drums)

MOOD brought in bassist Ferenc Marek in April of 1997. During 1998 Sony Music in Hungary organized a tribute concert to BLACK SABBATH to celebrate the release of the 'Reunion' album, enlisting MOOD to perform a set of classic BLACK SABBATH songs. Improved distribution and healthy reviews for 'Wombocosmic', which closed with a cover version of TROUBLE's "Scuse Me', succeeded in bringing the MOOD name to areas outside of Eastern Europe. MOOD's fourth album 'The Fourth Ride Of The Doomanoids', produced by Greg Hemming, included a bonus disc with the 1996 'Burning Slow' demo tracks and a cover version of BLACK SABBATH's 'Lonely Is The Word'. MOOD appear to have folded in late 2001.

Albums:
VOLUME 1, Hammer HMRCD008 (1996)
The Shell / Demons From The Inside Pocket / Plastic Man / Four Winds Are Blowing / Nameless (Guitar Feedback) / Children Of The Dew / Take Me Away / Sleep Time / Moonbath / Bleeding To The Bliss / Burning Slow / Brainshuttle - Dragging Myself Alone / Out Of Date / Stardrifter / Soulcrusher
SLOW DOWN, Vida DDRCDS-003 (1997)
WOMBOCOSMIC, Hammer HMRCD004

(1999)
Intro / I The Bloodstained Embyro / The Untold / Circles / Dislocated / 11000 Days Below Zero / Wombocosmic / Down Under / Glow Burn Scream / Feed To Rise / Blindseeing / Breathe The Air / Someday / "Scuse Me
THE FOURTH RIDE OF THE DOOMANOIDS, Hammer (2000)

MOONLESS NIGHT (ITALY)
Line-Up: Fabio (vocals), Malcus (guitar), Davide (guitar), Mirko The Unbeliever (bass), Alabarda (drums)

Doom outfit MOONLESS NIGHT issued a self-financed eponymous album in 1999. The band drafted second guitarist Davide, from Savona Metal band LAST RITES, in April 2001.

Albums:
MOONLESS NIGHT, Moonless Night (1999)
Cruel Darkness / Truppo Tardi / Sorrow n' Death / Paranoia / The Final Kiss

MOONLYGHT (CANADA)
Line-Up: Sébastien Robitaille (vocals / guitar), Vince (guitar), Davey (bass), Thierry Nadeau-Cossette (keyboards), Guillaume Côté (drums)

Gothic Doom outfit out of Quebec. MOONLYGHT evolved during 1995 with an initial line-up comprising vocalist / guitarist Sébastien Robitaille and guitarist Vince. By April of 1996 this pair had drafted bass player Christian Jacques along with drummer / keyboard player Luc Gaulin. As this quartet MOONLYGHT cut the opening demo session 'Midwinter Melodies' that same year. Shortly after keyboardist Guillaume Tremblay was added to the ranks, however by the close of 1997 this newest recruit had left. Worse was to come the following year when both Gaulin and Jacques decamped, the latter to concentrate on his own band NO TURN AROUND.
The band was effectively reborn in 2000. Guillaume Côté was inducted as new drummer whilst Davey became bassist and Thierry Nadeau-Cossette took on the mantle of keyboard player. With this version of the band MOONLYGHT recorded the debut album 'Progressive Darkness', released by Metal Disk Records.

Albums:
PROGRESSIVE DARKNESS, Metal Disk (2002)
Fantasy / The Sceptic Traveller / Ride On Ice

Storm / A Tale From A Fantastic Kingdom /
The Autumn's Freezing Harmony / From
Honour To Nothingness / Progressive
Darkness

MOONSPELL (PORTUGAL)

Line-Up: Langsuyar (vocals), Tanngrisnir
(guitar), Mantus (guitar), Tetragrammaton
(bass), Neophytus (keyboards), Nisroth
(drums)

MOONSPELL are the band that put Portugal
on the Metal map. Having been founded in the
early '80s as MORBID GOD and gaining a
deal with French label Adipocere via their
'Anno Satanae' demo, MOONSPELL have
quickly made inroads into the European Rock
market.
Having made themselves almost instantly the
frontrunners in the Portuguese Metal scene
MOONSPELL were quick to accept an offer
from major German independent label
Century Media. The resulting 1995 album,
'Wolfheart', produced by GRIP INC. guitarist
Waldemar Sorychta, garnered much
favourable press.
MOONSPELL toured Europe as support act
to TIAMAT and MORBID ANGEL in 1995

before returning to studio work in order to
cook up the second album 'Irreligious'.
Promoting 'Irreligious', MOONSPELL
conducted two European tours, as their
stature grew rapidly from a guest slot with
SAMAEL to a much higher profile jaunt with
TYPE O NEGATIVE.
1997 would witness the 'Second Skin Live'
album before the group hit back in 1998 with
the brand new studio effort 'Sin-Pecado'. The
album displayed a far more adventurous style
than previous efforts and the band's move
away from Metal forced bassist Ares to
depart. MOONSPELL persevered, putting in
shows during 1997 supporting heavyweights
such as KISS and MANOWAR. Ares
meantime created DEEPSKIN for the 'Judas'
album.
MOONSPELL toured Germany in early 2000
supported by veterans KREATOR and
KATATONIA.
Their 2001 album 'Darkness And Hope'
scored a no. 79 placing on the German album
charts. Bravely the band took on a cover
version of the OZZY OSBOURNE classic 'Mr.
Crowley'. The band began a headline
American tour, supported by LACUNA COIL,
on December 5th at the Trocadero venue in

MOONSPELL
Photo : Paulo Moreira

Philadelphia. MOONSPELL would be back on a further major European string of dates in March of 2002, co-billed with label mates TIAMAT and FLOWING TEARS.

Singles/EPs:
Goat On Fire, Molon Lave (1994) (7" single)
Wolves From The Fog, Molon Lave (1994) (7" single)
Opium (Radio Edit) / Raven Claws / Ruin And Misery / Opium (Album Version), Century Media 77140-2 (1996)
Second Skin/ An Erotic Alchemy (Remix) / Sacred / Second Skin (Video Edit), Century Media 77189-3 (1997) ('Second Skin' EP CD1)

Albums:
UNDER THE MOONSPELL, Adipocere AR 021 (1994)
Allah Akbar! La Allah Ella Allah! / Tenebrarum Oratorium / Opus Diabolicum / Chorai Lusitania!
WOLFHEART, Century Media CD77097-2 (1995)
Introduction / Wolfshade (A Werewolf Masquerade) / Love Crimes / ...Of Dream And Drama (Midnight Ride) / Lua D'Inverno / Trebraruna / Vampiria / En Erotic Alchemy / Alma Mater
IRRELIGIOUS, Century Media 77123-2 (1996)
Perverse... Almost Religious / Opium / Awake / For A Taste Of Eternity / Ruin And Misery / A Poisoned Gift / Subversion / Raven Claws / Mephisto / Herr Spiegelmann / Full Moon Madness
2ECOND SKIN, Century Media 77189-2 (1997)
2econd Skin / Erotik Alchemy (Per Version) / Sacred / 2econd Skin (Video Edit) / Opium (Live) / Awake (Live) / Herr Spiegelmann (Live) / Of Dream And Drama (Midnight Ride) (Live) / Ruin And Misery (Live) / Mephisto (Live) / Alma Mater (Live)
SIN- PECADO, Century Media CD 77190-2 (1998)
Slow Down! / Handmade God / Second Skin / Abysmo / Flesh / Magdalene / VC (Gloria Domini) / Eurotic A / Mute / Dekadance / Let The Children Cum To Me... / The Hanged Man / 13!
THE BUTTERFLY EFFECT, Century Media (1999)
Soulsick / Butterfly FX / Can't Bee / Lustmord / Selfabuse / I Am The Eternal Spectator / Soulitary Vice / Disappear Here / Adapables / Angelizer / Tired
DARKNESS AND HOPE, Century Media 8090-2 (2001)
Darkness And Hope / Firewalking / Nocturna

/ Heartshaped Abyss / Devilred / Ghostsong / Rapacious / Made Of Storm / How We Became Fire / Than The Serpents In My Hands / Mr. Crowley

MORENDOES (NORWAY)
Line-Up: Østen Bergøy (vocals), Jon Arve Jøssang (vocals / guitar), Frankie Bø (guitar), Sveinung Eie (bass), Jon Eirik Steinstø (keyboards)

Stavanger's MORENDOES place themselves squarely in Gothic Rock territory, adding a touch of uniqueness with an almost Industrial electronic edge. Beginning their career path billed as WAKE in the early '90s a demo surfaced under that former title. Discovering other musical outfits of the same name the group adopted the new title of MORENDOES for a self-financed album in 1994 'There Is No Salvation'. The group line-up at this time stood at lead vocalist Jan Kenneth Barkved, guitarists Tommy Olsson and Jon Arve Jøssang, bass player Sveinung Eie, keyboard player Jon Eirik Steinstø and Lars Bjørnar Jøssang on drums.
A period of turbulence then ensued, sparked off as Barkved was replaced by Østen Bergøy. Losing their drummer MORENDOES solved the problem by relying on a drum machine. More significant a loss was the departure of founder member Tommy Olsson, the guitarist joining the high profile act THEATRE OF TRAGEDY. His vacancy was filled by Frankie Bø. Yet further fluxes had Østen Bergøy leaving the band in 1998 and Jon Arve Jøssang taking over as vocalist. In this incarnation MORENDOES cut the promotion single 'Jump Of Existence' but shortly after Bergøy, who had sessioned for TRISTANIA, was reinstated.
Former members Tommy Olsson and Jan Kenneth Barkved created a new band ELUSIVE, this act also including MORENDOES keyboard player Jon Eirik Steinstø.

Albums:
THERE IS NO SALVATION, (1994)
Shadow Dance / Louise / Lost In The Shades / This Is Blindness / Fall Of Heaven / Sackloth And Ashes / Soulscape

MORGION (Orange County, CA, USA)
Line-Up: Jeremy Peto (vocals / bass), Gary Griffith (guitar), Dwayne Boardman (guitar), Ed Morgan (keyboards), Rhett Davies (drums)

Atmospheric Doom mongers MORGION convened during 1990, issuing a demo, which secured a contract with the Wild Rags concern for the 'Rabid Decay' mini-album. A few years later saw a label switch to Relapse and the band released another title in 1996 called 'Among Majestic Ruin'. Despite the anti-Metal climate of the time, the band, which had been slogging in the underground for several years, received some degree of critical acclaim for this offering. The recordings for the 'Among Majestic Ruin' album hark back as far as 1994. Keyboard player Ed Morgan had departed prior to the album release and MORGION subsequently added ex-NEPENTHE guitarist Gary Griffith. Further activities saw MORGION contributing a cover version of IRON MAIDEN's 'To Tame A Land', produced by the esteemed Bill Metoyer, to a tribute album and a version of CELTIC FROST's seminal 'Procreation (Of The Wicked' to a 1996 Dwell homage entitled 'In Memory Of Celtic Frost'.

Bolstered by this albeit small success, the band re-entered the studio to work on their first true full-length release for Relapse. Originally, billed as 'A Raven In Scarlet Night', the full-length album emerged in 1999, featuring a returning Ed Morgan and simply titled 'Solanari'. Recordings had been initially delayed when frontman Jeremy Peto suffered a severe injury after being stabbed in the neck. 'Solanari' featured the production services of Schneebi who had previously worked with ST. VITUS and THE OBSESSED. Both Pet and drummer Rhett Davis also operate the Black Metal band CRIMSON RELIC in alliance with erstwhile DIVINE EVE man Xanthorvaar and Greg Anderson of THORR'S HAMMER.

In early 1999 MORGION keyboard player Brandon Livingston died unexpectedly.

The band commenced work on a new studio album, 'Cloaked By Ages, Crowned In Earth', with producer Matthias Scheeberger during mid 2002. These recordings marked the inauguration of new personnel bassist Justin Christian, keyboard player Peter Surowski and former MINDROT vocalist Adrian Leroux. Jeremy Peto would join the ranks of the resurrected veteran Thrash act DARK ANGEL during August of 2002.

Singles/EPs:
Travesty, (199-)

Albums:
AMONG MAJESTIC RUIN, Relapse RR 6924 (1996)
Relic Of A Darkened Past / In Ashen Tears (Thus I Cry) / Travesty / Basking Under A Blacksun Dawning / Invalid Prodigy
SOLINARI, Relapse RR 6415 (1999)

The Serpentine Scrolls-Descent To Arawn / Canticle / Solinari / Nightfall Infernal / All The Glory... / ...All the Loss / Blight / ...The Last Sunrise

MORNINGRISE (ITALY)
Line-Up: Diego Balbo (vocals), Luigi Alberio (vocals), Roberto Fazari (guitar), Alessandro Monopoli (guitar), Maurizio Galazzi (bass), Micheler Ercolano (drums)

A Black Doom act that included former AGARTHI drummer Michele Ercolano. The band was founded by guitarists Roberto Fazari and Gabriele Castelnuous, bassist Maurizio Gallazzi and singer Diego Balbo. MORNINGRISE later pulled in Ercolano on drums and second vocalist Luigi Alberio whose clean vocals supplanted Balbo's growls and grunts.

In 2000 Castelnuous departed to be replaced by former ACRON man Mirko Placido. However, within months he in turn had been ousted by ETHEREAL guitarist Alessandro Monopoli.

Albums:
DRAGONS OF THE SUN, (1998)

MORPHIA (HOLLAND)
Line-Up: Jasper Pieterson (vocals), Roger Koedoot (guitar), Martin Koedoot (guitar), Erik van Tulder (bass), Peter van Tulder (keyboards), Bert Bonestroo (sound engineer), Ernst-Jan Lemmen (drums)

A Dutch Symphonic Doom band unusual in crediting their sound engineer Bert Bonestroo as an official group member and also in boasting the sibling guitar spearhead of the Koedoot brothers Martin and Roger. MORPHIA started life in 1995, making the transition from Death Metal to Doom with the 1997 demo tape 'Poison Minded'. The debut 'Unfulfilled Dreams' album arrived a year later.

In April of 2001 Erik van Tulder and vocalist Jasper Pieterson were brought into the ranks to replace the departed Werner Wensink.

Albums:
UNFULFILLED DREAMS, (1998)
Unfulfilled Dreams / Ab Inscientia Depositus Sum (A.I.D.S) / How I Feel / My Endless Death / Thor's Symphony / Desire / The Day I Died / Ithiniëlle
FROZEN DUST, Fear Dark FD006 (2002)
Flashback / The Sun / The Forest / Wicklow Mountains / Frozen Dust / When Silence Fell / Again / Long Lost / Forced To Obey / Emptiness

MORTAL (USA)
Line-Up: Jerome, Jyro

The MORTAL album features guest sessions from THE CRUCIFIED / STAVESACRE men vocalist Mark Salomon and bassist Jeff Bellew.

Albums:
FATHOM, Intense FLD9425 (1993)
Alive And Awake / Neplusultra / Rift / Jil Sent Me / Ex-Nihilo / Above And Beyond / Rainlight / Bright Wings / Xix / Promulgate / Electrify / Godspeed

MORTIIS (NORWAY)

A solo project from Haavard Ellefsen, previously bassist of premier Black Metal act EMPEROR, MORTIIS specialize in ambient electronic Doom music. Mortiis also conducted another electronic band, VOND, in order to give vent to more "negative" music!
The album 'Crypt Of The Wizard' was also issued as separate set of five 12" singles. Early MORTIIS releases were issued in limited edition coloured vinyl only serving to increase the mystique surrounding the man. Signing to British label Earache Records for 'The Stargate' album, featuring CRADLE OF FILTH vocalist Sarah Jezebel Deva, brought the enigmatic figure to a wider audience.
MORTIIS employed a seven man band for a chaotic tour of America during 1999, which saw the act banned from many venues.
Mortiis, who always appears in public with fake elf ears and crooked nose, has also written a book titled 'Secrets Of My Kingdom' for future publication. Mortiis also operates FATA MORGANA and the vampyristic CINTECELE DIAVOLUI.

Singles/EPs:
Blood And Thunder, (199-) (7" single)
Ferden Og Kullet, Dark Dungeon Music (1996) (12" single)
En Sirkel Av Kosmisk Kaos, Dark Dungeon Music (1996) (12" single)
Vandreren's Sang, Dark Dungeon Music (1996) (12' single)
Stjernetödt, Dark Dungeon Music (1996) (12' single)
I Mörkret Drömmende, Dark Dungeon Music (1996) (12' single)

Albums:
FØDT TIL Å HERSKE, Malicious MA003CD (1995)
Født Til Å Herske Part I / Født Til Å Herske Part II
ANDEN SOM GJORDE OPPROE (THE REBELLIOUS SPIRIT), Cold Meat Industries CMI 31 (1995)
Det Var En Gang Et Menneske / Over Odermark / Opp Under Fjellet Toner En Sang / Tiden Er En Stenlagt Grar / Fra Fjelltronen / En Mork Horisont / Visioner Av En Eldgammel Frertid
KEISERN AV EN DIMENSION UKJENT (EMPEROR OF A DIMENSION UNKNOWN), Cold Meat Industry (1996)
Reisene Til Grotter Of Ødemarker / Keiser Av En Dimension Ukject
CRYPT OF THE WIZARD, Dark Dungeon Music (1996)
Ferden Og Kullet / Da Vibygde Tårnet / Under Tårnet's Skygge / En Sirkel Av Kosmisk Kaos / Vandreren's Sang / Den Bortdrevne Regnbuen / Trollmannen's Krypt / Stjernefødt / I Mørket Drømmende / Fanget I Krystal
THE STARGATE, Earache (1996)
Child Of Curiosity And The Old Man Of Knowledge / I Am The World / World Essence / Across The World Of Wonders / (Passing By) And Old And Raped Village / Towards The Gates Of The Stars / Spirit Of Conquest - The Warfare / Army Of Conquest - The Warfare (Ever Onwards)

MOTHERCAKE (SWEDEN)
Line-Up: Martin Ohlsson (vocals), Petter Englund (guitar), Patrik Berglin (guitar), Henrik Paulsson (bass), Thomas Jönsson (drums)

Singles/EPs:
Fists Of Fury / Bag Lady, (2001)
('Mothercake Vs. Half Man' EP)

MOTHER SUPERIOR (SWEDEN)
Line-Up: David Berlin (vocals / guitar), Sölvi Blöndal (guitar), Per Ellverson (guitar / keyboards), Fredrik Cronsten (bass), Anders Stub (drums)

Uppsala based Garage Stoners not to be confused with the Los Angeles act of the same name that has acted as backing band for HENRY ROLLINS.
MOTHER SUPERIOR are rooted in the mid '80s Punk band THE APPLEKARTERS, comprising vocalist David Berlin, bass guitarist Sölvi "Silver" Blöndal alongside Jesper Hammarström and Jonas Meshesha. This act journeyed to London in 1991 switching the title of the band to THY STEAMROLLER. A further change in 1993 resulted in the name tag MOTHER SUPERIOR. Drummer Anders Stub is an erstwhile member of BIG FISH. The sticksman also operates as guitarist for 454.

The debut album 'The Mothership Has Landed', released in August of 1996 in Sweden - where it was nominated for a Grammy award - and in April of the following year on mainland Europe. A second album, 'The Mothership Movements', was recorded in September of 1997 but after many delays finally surfaced in early 1999. The band adopted a new tack after this release with guitarist Fredrik Cronsten and bassist Blöndal switching instruments.

Guitarist Per Ellverson has latterly become a kind of unofficial member of Punk act THE MAGGOTS.

Singles/EPs:
Have You Seen My Cat / You Gotta Gotta / Good Is Good, Bad Affro (2001) ('Brothers And Sisters' EP)

Albums:
THE MOTHERSHIP HAS LANDED, (1997)
Yeah Baby / Velocity City / Breakin' It Down / C'Mon / Too Bad (Freddie's Song) / Down The Straight And Narrow / Radically Cool / Keep On Movin' / Love Gone Bad / Reach Out
THE MOTHERSHIP MOVEMENT,

Loudsprecher LSD024 (1998)
Wreck My Mind / El Salvatore / Everything Goes When You're Gone / Revolconfusion / Psychedelic Clone / Save My Soul / Constant Reminder / The Big Bad Ass Mama Jama Conspiracy / Revolutions In All Directions / Keep On Keepin' On / I've Got Soul / Redeem / Love Can Tame The Wild

MOURNFUL BELOVETH (IRELAND)
Line-Up: Darren (vocals), Frank (guitar), Brian (guitar), Aidrian (bass), Dermod Smyth (keyboards), Tim (drums)

Much vaunted Irish Doom act MOURNFUL BELOVETH would come to note supporting CATHEDRAL on their debut Irish dates. A demo, 'Autumnal Fires' preceded the 2001 debut album 'Dust', which garnered positive reviews throughout the Metal underground.

The band had been created in 1992, morphing from the Death Metal band TRAUMATISED. This act, which held within it's ranks vocalist Darren, guitarist Frank and drummer Tim had released two demos and held the honour of supporting CRADLE OF FILTH in Dublin. Darren, Tim and second guitarist Brian were also involved with

MOURNFUL BELOVETH

278

PATHOS. Both Frank and Brian also cite past membership of HEMLOCK.

MOURNFUL BELOVETH's Adrian also subs for ARCANE SUN and has also been involved with Black Doom act KINGDOM. In outside activities vocalist Darren also pursued the Death Metal band KARYNANA for a time.

MOURNFUL BELOVETH were planning a follow up album with a projected title of 'The Sullen Sulcus'.

Albums:
DUST, (2001)
The Mountains Are Mine / In Mourning My Days / Dust / Autumnal Fires / All Hope Is Pleading / Sinistra

MOURNFUL CONGREGATION
(AUSTRALIA)

An exercise in depression and dirgeful malevolence exercised by the mysterious duo of Damon and Ben. MOURNFUL CONGREGATION was first conceived in 1993 with the 'Weeping' tape following in 1994. Further sessions resulted in 1995's 'An Epic Dream Of Desire' prior to a period of inactivity.

The band re-emerged in 1999 touting the 'Tears From A Grieving Heart' promotional cassette. A split 7" single in alliance with French act DOOMCULT WORSHIP finally saw MOURNFUL CONGREGATION committed to a commercial release in 2000. 'The Dawning Of Mournful Hymns' is a collection of previous demos.

Singles/EPs:
The Epitome Of Gods And Men Alike, Impaler Of Trendies Productions (2000) (7" split single with DOOMCULT WORSHIP)

Albums:
THE DAWNING OF MOURNFUL HYMNS, Weird Truth Productions (2002)

MOURNING NOISE (NJ, USA)
Line-Up: Mike Mansfield (vocals), Tommy Koprowski (guitar), Chris Morance (bass), Steve Zing (drums)

Punk act with horror overtones, MOURNING NOISE featured a pre-SAMHAIN drummer Steve Zing. The debut 1981 line-up of the band comprised Zing, IMPLOSION lead vocalist Mike Mansfield, guitarist Tommy Koprowski and bass player Chris Morance. An early demo, 'Underground Noise', surfaced on the cassette compilation 'Meathouse 1'. Jon Carcich would be added on second guitar during June of 1983 and

Pete Marshall took over bass the following year. MOURNING NOISE debuted with the 1983 EP 'Dawn Of The Dead'. Limited to 1,000 copies 'Dawn Of The Dead' had cover art designed by none other than GLENN DANZIG. A further release found two live tracks 'Progress For The People' and 'Radical' included on the 'Hardcore Takes Over' compilation EP.

MOURNING NOISE introduced Joe 'Jay' Olivetti as their new frontman in 1984 but in another switch Mike Mansfield resumed the position shortly after in an all new look band which found Ashley Morance on guitar and Chris Morance on bass. The 1986 single 'Runaway', a cover of the DEL SHANNON '60s hit and credited to STEVE ZING as a solo artist, would become a sought after rarity, having been pressed in a run of just 100 copies. Oddly a 'Chris Marino' credited on the recording is actually Chris Morance. Finally Tommy Koprowski returned to MOURNING NOISE ousting Ashley Morance. With the break up of MOURNING NOISE Mansfield teamed up with CHYNA. Pete Marshall would follow Zing into the ranks of SAMHAIN, acting as touring bassist.

Singles/EPs:
Dawn Of The Dead / Fighting Chance / Laser Lights / Demon Eyes / Addiction, Nightlatche (1983) ('Dawn Of The Dead' EP)
Demon Eyes / Crimson Carrie / Progress For The People, Radcore RAD002 (1990) ('Live Nightmares' Split EP with THE PARASITES)

Albums:
DEATH TRIP DELIVERY, Grand Theft Audio GTA033CD (1998)
Nestle Baby Killer / Death In A White Cloud / Crimson Carrie / Mr. Surveillance / Progress For The People / Monster Madness / Murder Machine / Empty Grave / Monster Madness / Vincent's Theme / Underground Zero / Barbarian Hunt / Dawn Of The Dead / Fighting Chance / Laser Lights / Demon Eyes / Addiction / Monster Madness / Vincent's Theme / Underground Zero / Foolish Grief / Progress For The People (Live) / Fighting Chance (Live) / Vincent's Theme (Live) / Laser Lights (Live) / Sergio (Live) / Addiction (Live) / Demon Eyes (Live) / Radical (Live) / Crimson Carrie (Live) / Dawn Of The Dead (Live) / Monster Madness (Live) / Batman

MR. PLOW (Houston, TX, USA)
Line-Up: Jeremy Plow (vocals / guitar), Justin Plow (guitar), Greg Plow (bass), Dave Plow (drums)

Albums:
HEAD ON, (2000)
Right On / Mexican Smoke / The Gauntlet /
Travis Bickle / Beat Down / Truck Stop /
Lovin' Molly

M-SQUAD (Brooklyn, NY, USA)
Line-Up: Eli Brown (vocals), Mike Nichols
(guitar), Matt Holt (bass), Mike Jett (drums)

Previously known as BLOOD FARMERS,
having released a now highly sought after
eponymous Doom classic on the illustrious
Hellhound label in 1995 under that title.
Replacing original guitarist Dave Depraved
with Mike Nichols M-SQUAD entered spaced
out, Stoner realms for their debut.

Albums:
M-SQUAD, Primate 980515 (1999)
Catapult / Tractor / Rust / Hoedown Jam /
Meant For Dying / DVMF / Vagabond / I'm
Gone
SMOKE, Primate (2002)

MUDHOLE (SWEDEN)
Line-Up: Janne Miller (vocals / guitar), Johan
Norehag (guitar), Micke Gällnegård (bass),
Jan-Åke Olofsson (drums)

Sabbath inspired Rockers out of Klövsjö in
Jämtland, northern Sweden. MUDHOLE
delivered a demo 'Stuck In A Snowdrift
Volume 1'.

THE MUSHROOM RIVER BAND
(SWEDEN)
Line-Up: Spice (vocals), Anders Linusson
(guitar), Saso (bass), Robert Hansson
(drums)

A Stoner-Doom based outfit out of Varnamo
that attracted early attention due to the
inclusion of SPIRITUAL BEGGARS vocalist
Spice, first as a guesting member than as full-
time frontman. The band unit came together
initially as a trio of guitarist Anders Linusson,
bass player Alexander 'Saso' Sekulovski and
drummer Andreas Grafenauer. This team had
actually decided to fold when Grafenauer
close to pack in the drums, but thought it best
to go out with a posthumous demo for which
Spice (real name Christian Stöstrand and an
erstwhile member of AEON) agreed to
commit lead vocals. As the recordings got
underway the title of THE MUSHROOM
RIVER BAND was conceived.
Linusson, Spice and Saso re-forged the
group in March of 1997, enrolling the then 16
year old drummer Chris Rockstrom. In
October of the same year THE MUSHROOM

RIVER BAND put in their inaugural live gig. A
second gig shortly after found Linusson
taking command of lead vocal duties as Spice
was unable to participate being ridden with
influenza. The following year recordings were
undertaken which surfaced as the
'Rocketcrash' demo. A further tape, dubbed
'No Quarter' after the name of the recording
studio, prompted interest from various labels.
Under their own steam the band issued the
previous 'Rocketcrash' sessions as limited run
of 500 10" vinyl EPs on their own Tea Pot
label.
The band's negotiations finally resolved
themselves in the summer of 2000 as THE
MUSHROOM RIVER BAND signed to the
American Stoner specialists Meteor City. The
agreement had proven complicated as Spice
was contracted through the SPIRITUAL
BEGGARS to Music For Nations. Hopeful of a
positive outcome the group had already
commenced recording the debut album
'Music For The World Beyond' in April. The
album, licensed to JVC Victor in Japan with
an extra bonus track 'Loser's Blues', received
exemplary reviews globally but the band's
promotional activities were curbed by Spice's
commitments to SPIRITUAL BEGGARS. The
band managed only two gigs, one at the
Stockholm Volcanic Rock club and the other
at the Swedish 'Tullarock' festival.
During April and May of 2001 the band finally
managed to engage in a full European tour
billed alongside HØEK, THE AWESOME
MACHINE and PAWNSHOP. With Spice's two
bands on ever conflicting schedules the
singer announced in October that he was to
exit from SPIRITUAL BEGGARS to fully
concentrate his efforts on THE MUSHROOM
RIVER BAND.
The group drafted a new drummer, Robert
Hansson, in March of 2002. A second album,
'Simsalabim', arrived in March of 2002 in
Europe through the German Century Media
label and in Japan via JVC Victor. THE
MUSHROOM RIVER BAND would figure on
the Small Stone '70s era tribute 'Sucking In
The 70s' donating a rendition of 'Walk Away'
by the JAMES GANG.

Singles/EPs:
Twin Lyrics No. 1 / Super Insomnia / B.M. /
Loser's Blues, Tea Pot (1999) ('Rocketcrash'
10" single. Limited edition of 500)

Albums:
MUSIC FOR THE WORLD BEYOND, Meteor
City MCY-013 (2000)
To The World Beyond / Mud-Crusher /
Racing / Way To Go / 29' 2_" (Into Thin Air) /
The Mushroom River / More Beer (Pelekas

Part I) / Addicted / Sir B's Tune / A Sad Story / Nurse / Free
SIMSALABIM, Meteor City MCY-024 (2002)
Simsalabim / Bugs / Make It Happen / Change It / My Vote Is Blank / Tree Of No Hope / Proud Of Being Cool / Time-Laps / The Big Sick Machine / Run, Run, Run

MUSTASCH (SWEDEN)
Line-Up: Ralf Gyllenhammar (vocals / guitar), Hannes Hansson (guitar), Mats Stam Johansson (bass), Mats Dojan Hansson (drums)

MUSTACH was created in 1998 comprising B-THONG vocalist / guitarist Ralf Gyllenhammar, guitarist Hannes Hansson, bass player Mats Stam Johansson and drummer Mats Dojan Hansson.
The band had a demo of 'Homophobic-Alcoholic' included on the 1999 compilation 'Molten Universe Volume One'. MUSTACH also featured on the 2000 compilation albums 'Burn Down To Zero', with a demo version of the track 'Taunus' and UNDERDOGMA'S 'Judge Not' with another demo, 'Coomber'. The 2002 orange vinyl 'Down In Black' single was restricted to just 350 copies.

Singles/EPs:
Homophobic-Alchoholic / The Wave / Serpent - The Zodiac (Bazaar) / Fabian's World Taunus / Coomber, Majesty (2001) ('The True Sound Of The New West' EP)
I Hunt Alone / Kill You For Nothing, Majesty (2002)
Down In Black / Coomber (Live), Majesty (2002)

Albums:
ABOVE ALL, Majesty (2002)
Down In Black / I Hunt Alone / Into The Arena / Muddy Waters / Ocean Song - Orust / Sympathy For Destruction / Teenage Pacifier / Insanity Walls / White Magic / The Dagger

MY DYING BRIDE (UK)
Line-Up: Aaron (vocals), Calvin (guitar), Andrew (guitar), Ade (bass), Martin (violin / keyboards), Rick (drums)

MY DYING BRIDE are at the forefront of the British Doom Metal movement that includes such bands as label mates ANATHEMA. Relentlessly slow, thick, heavy chords allied with remarkably morose lyrics make MY DYING BRIDE a unique proposition and certainly a challenge to the listener.
Formed in June 1990, the band released the 'Towards The Sinister' demo (noted for it's

complete absence of bass) shortly after, followed by the 'God Is Alone' single on the French Listenable label. The band signed to Peaceville Records to release the 'Symphonaire Infernus Et Spera Empyrum' EP, debuting new bassist Ade in the process. MY DYING BRIDE's first full-length album, 'As The Flower Withers', established the band among press and fans alike and provided the opportunity for their first tour of Europe. The progress gained by another EP, 'The Thrash Of Naked Limbs', was marred by drummer Rick badly damaging his hand, thus cancelling a projected tour with G.G.F.H.
Prior to the groundbreaking 'Turn Loose The Swans' album (which came in three different sleeves) the band added violinist / keyboardist Martin to the band and toured Europe once more. Another EP, 'I Am The Bloody Earth', kept the momentum going.
MY DYING BRIDE toured as support to IRON MAIDEN across Europe in late 1995. However, drummer Rick departed in 1997 and for their projected 1998 album MY DYING BRIDE pulled in the services of YEAR ZERO and VALLE CRUSIS drummer Mike Unsworth in order to fill the gap.
1998 saw MY DYING BRIDE issuing the experimental '34.788%... Complete' album with yet another new drummer ex-DOMINION man Bill Law. The band remained strangely inactive on the touring front though as guitarist Calvin Robertshaw departed. He would swiftly be replaced by erstwhile SOLSTICE, SERENITY and KHANG member Lee Baines.
For touring commitments in 1999 the band pulled in BAL SAGOTH's Jonny Maudling for live keyboards. The band's more permanent line-up was completed with the addition of ex-ANATHEMA and SOLSTICE drummer Sean Steels and former SOLSTICE guitarist

MY DYING BRIDE
Photo : Simon Mooney

281

Hamish Glencross.
An ex-MY DYING BRIDE keyboard player Mark Newby Robson joined CRADLE OF FILTH rebilling himself Mark De Sade. MY DYING BRIDE themselves witnessed a change of keyboard players in April 2002 when Sarah Stanton took over from Yasmin Ahmed. MY DYING BRIDE also announced the release of their first live album, 'Voice Of The Wretched', the same month.

Singles/EPs:
God Is Alone / De Sade Soliloquy, Listenable (1991)
Symphonaire Infernus Et Spera Empyrium / God Is Alone / De Sade Soliloquy, Peaceville VILE 27T (1992)
The Thrash Of Naked Limbs / Le Cerf Malade / Gather Me Up Forever, Peaceville VILE 37T (1993)
I Am The Bloody Earth / Transcending (Into The Exquisite) / Crown Of Sympathy (Remix), Peaceville VILE 44T (1994)
Sexuality Of Bereavement / Crown Of Sympathy, Peaceville Collectors CC5 (1994)

Albums:
AS THE FLOWER WITHERS, Peaceville VILE 32 (1992)
Silent Dance / Sear Me / The Forever People / The Bitterness And The Bereavement / Vast Choirs / The Return Of The Beautiful / Erotic Literature
TURN LOOSE THE SWANS, Peaceville VILE (1993)
Sear Me MCMXC III / Your River / The Songless Bird / The Snow In My Hand / The Crown Of Sympathy / Turn Loose The Swans / Black God
THE STORIES, Peaceville VILE 45 (1994) (EP Box Set)
Symphonaire Infernus Et Spera Empyrium / God Is Alone / De Sade Soliloquay / The Thrash Of Naked Limbs / Le Cerf Malade / Gather Me Up Forever / I Am The Bloody Earth / Transcending (Into The Exquisite) / Crown Of Sympathy
TRINITY, Peaceville VILE 46 (1995)
I Am The Bloody Earth / Transcending / Crown Of Sympathy / The Thrash Of Naked Limbs / Le Cerf Malade / Gather Me Up Forever / Symphonaire Infernus Et Spera Empyrium / God Is Alone / De Sade Soliloquy / Sexuality Of Bereavement
THE ANGEL AND THE DARK RIVER, Peaceville CDVILE50 (1995)
The Cry Of Mankind / From Darkest Skies / Black Vote / A Sea To Suffer In / Two Winters Only / Your Shameful Heaven
LIKE GODS OF THE SUN, Peaceville VILE65 (1996)

Like Gods Of The Sun / Dark Caress / Grace Unhearing / A Kiss To Remember / All Swept Away / For You / It Will Come / Here In The Throat / For My Fallen Angel
34.788%... COMPLETE, Peaceville CDVILE 74 (1998)
The Whore, The Cook And The Mother / The Stance Of Evander Sinque / Der Uberlebende / Heroin Chic / Apocalypse Woman / Base Level Erotica / Under Your Wings And Into Your Arms
THE LIGHT AT THE END OF THE WORLD, Peaceville CDVILE 79 (1999)
She Is The Dark / Edenbeast / The Night He Died / The Light At The End Of The World / The Fever Sea / Into The Lake Of Ghosts / The Isis Script / Christliar / Sear Me III
MEISTERWERK I, Peaceville CDVILE 81 (2000)
Symphonaire Infernus Et Spera Empyrium (Demo) / Crown Of Sympathy / The Grief Of Age (Demo) / A Kiss To Remember / Grace Unhearing (Portishell) / For You / Unreleased Bitterness / Sear Me 3 / Cry Of Mankind (Video)
MEISTERWERK II, Peaceville CDVILE 85 (2001)
Sear Me MCMXCIII / Follower / Vast Choirs (Demo) / She Is The Dark / Catching Feathers (Demo) / Two Winters Only / Your River / Some Velvet Morning / Roads
THE DREADFUL HOURS, Peaceville CDVILE 90 (2001)
The Dreadful Hours / The Raven And The Rose / Le Figlie Della Tempesta / Black Heart Romance / A Cruel Taste Of Winter / My Hope The Destroyer / The Deepest Of All Hearts / The Return To The Beautiful
THE VOICE OF THE WRETCHED, Peaceville (2002)
She Is The Dark / The Snow In My Hand / The Cry Of Mankind / Turn Loose The Swans / A Cruel Taste Of Winter / Under Your Wings And Into Your Arms / A Kiss To Remember / Your River / The Fever Sea / Symphonaire Infernus Et Spera Empyrium

MY GARDEN (TURKEY)
Line-Up: Emir Agar (vocals), Alper T. Dagli (guitar), Gökhan Baykal (guitar), Can Karkin (bass), Burcú Karli (keyboards), Serhat Bektas (drums)

A Turkish Doom Metal band blessed (!) with a Death Metal favouring vocalist, MY GARDEN formed in 1990 and released their first demo, 'Neon Lights', at the end of 1994.
Following their signing to Arctic Serenades, MY GARDEN released the same tracks from the tape (albeit re-recorded) for their debut EP.

Singles/ EPs:
Neon Lights / I Wondered Lonely As A
Cloud / Captive Hands / Lost In Blue
Aegean, Arctic Serenades SERE006 (1996)
('Neon Lights' EP)

MYRIADS (NORWAY)
Line-Up: Mona Undheim Skottene (vocals /
keyboards), Alexander Twiss (vocals / guitar),
J.P. (guitar), Mikael Stokdal (keyboards), Rudi
Junger (drums)

MYRIADS

Stavanger based Gothic Metal outfit. The
band fuse Black, Death, Gothic, Folk and
Industrial elements to achieve an eclectic
sound all of their own. MYRIADS was created
during September of 1997 comprising ex-
OVERFLOATER and TWIN OBSCENITY
member Alexander Twiss handling both clean
and Death vocals as well as guitars, Mikael
Stokdal with keyboard and Black vocals,
erstwhile TWIN OBSCENITY vocalist and
keyboard player Mona Undheim Skottene,
guitarist J.P. and drummer Rudi Jünger.
MYRIADS marked their arrival with the
Øyvind Grødem produced demo 'In Spheres
Of Time' recorded during July of 1998. This
session, which saw Knud Kleppe handling
bass guitar in the studio, led in turn to a deal
with the Napalm label, the debut album,
released in November of 1999, also bearing
the same title as the previous demo. Bass
was once more delegated to Knud Kleppe
and also Torp. The band had only just
performed live for the first time a matter of

days beforehand at a gig in Trondheim.
Successive dates found the band on tour in
Norway as guests to ATROX.
Having released the 2002 'Introspection'
album MYRIADS would still be on the search
for a bass player.

Albums:
IN SPHERES WITHOUT TIME, Napalm
NPR074 (1999)
Fragments Of The Hereafter / The Day Of
Wrath / Spheres Without Time / Seductive
Hate / Dreams Of Reality
INTROSPECTION, Napalm NPR099 (2002)
Enigmatic Colours Of The Night / Miserere Mei
/ Inside / The Sanctum Of My Soul / Portal To
The Mind / Falling In The Equinox / Flickering
Thoughts / Encapsulated / The Ascent

MYSTIC CHARM (HOLLAND)
Line-Up: Rini Lipman (vocals), Herwig
Schuiling (guitar), Gerlach Timmer (bass),
Gerard van Assen (drums)

MYSTIC CHARM operate in traditional '70s
influenced no-frills Doom but are distinctive in
employing the growling female vocals of Reni
Lipman. The band started life in December of
1989 with an initial line-up comprising
Lipman, guitarist Herwig Schuiling, bass
player Luis Gonzalez and Mark van de
Bovenkamp on drums. MYSTIC CHARM then
underwent line-up changes with bassist
Gerlach Timmer and drummer Gerard van
Assen taking over the rhythm section.
A demo tape in 1992, dubbed 'Endless
Sickness' pre-empted the 1993 'Lost Empire'
7" EP for the Belgian Shiver label. A full-
length album, 'Shadows Of The Unknown',
arrived in May of 1994. By August of that year
Marc van der Bend had taken over the drum
stool but before long the band broke up.
MYSTIC CHARM reunited in 2000, Schuiling
and Timmer forging a fresh alliance with
vocalist Rein of SERAPHIQUE and TO
ELYSIUM, second vocalist Egbert of
PHILOSOPHER and DEAD HEAD drummer
Hans Spijker. This latter member was soon
forced out to concentrate on his priority act
and MYSTIC CHARM's original drumming
candidate Mark van de Bovenkamp resumed
his position.
Herwig Schuiling also operates SLEEPLESS,
issuing the mini-album 'Voices Of Doom'.

Singles/EPs:
Lost Empire / Endless Sickness, Shiver
SHR004 (1993)

Albums:
SHADOW OF THE UNKNOWN, Shiver

283

(1994)
Shadows Of The Unknown / Mystic Charms / Window Of Reality / Deadly Embrace / Saved Soul / Lost Empire / Beyond Darkness / Crushed Virginity / Endless Sickness
HELL DID FREEZE OVER, (2001)

THE MYSTICK KREWE OF CLEARLIGHT (New Orleans, LA, USA)
Line-Up: Jimmy Bower (guitar), Paul Webb (guitar), Andy Shepherd (bass), Ross Karpelman (keyboards), Joey La Caze (drums)

The intriguing and entirely instrumental, keyboard laden Psych-Rock of THE MYSTICK KREWE OF CLEARLIGHT is laid down by members of DOWN, EYEHATEGOD and CROWBAR. The project was conceived in 1996 as a Blues Rock improvisational jam session.
Guitarist Jimmy Bower, a seasoned veteran of EYEHATEGOD, SUPERJOINT RITUAL, DOWN and CROWBAR, had been jamming with organ player Ross Karpelman and EYEHATEGOD vocalist Mike Williams in the 1990 band SISTER MORPHINE, later entitled DRIP. As EYEHATEGOD's career took off Karpelman became the band's tour manager and would later gain credits for keyboards on PANTERA's 'The Great Southern Trendkill' album.
THE MYSTICK KREWE OF CLEARLIGHT was a resurrection of those formative jam sessions. Although an instrumental endeavour in the main, CORROSION OF CONFORMITY's Pepper Keenan did add vocals to early demos. The CORROSION OF CONFORMITY connection would be strengthened when Bower stepped into the band, not as guitarist, but temporary drummer for live work.
THE MYSTICK KREWE OF CLEARLIGHT would also share a split release with ACID KING dubbed 'The Father, The Son And The Holy Smoke', pulling off the coup of having Doom Godfather Scott 'Wino' Weinrich of SAINT VITUS and THE OBSESSED lending lead vocals.

Singles/EPs:
Buzzard Hill (My Backyard) / Veiled, Man's Ruin (2001) ('The Father, The Son And The Holy Smoke' split EP with ACID KING)

Albums:
THE MYSTICK KREWE OF CLEARLIGHT, Tee Pee (2000)
Swamp Jam / Electrode / Ride Out / Trapeze / A Fool's Outfit / El Niño Brown

MYTHIC (OH, USA)
Line-Up: Dana Duffey (vocals / guitar), Mary Bielich (bass), Terri Heggen (drums)

Although MYTHIC's career was fleeting they certainly left their mark on the Metal scene. Far from being a typical girl Rock group MYTHIC employed the trademark guttural growls of Dana Duffey with guitars tuned way down making them probably the most well known of all female Death-Doom Metal acts.
In early 1991, guitarist Dana Duffey contacted the all female Death Metal band DERKETA after seeing them in an underground fanzine to see if they were interested in adding a fourth member. At that time, the Pittsburgh based DERKETA had actually broken up, unbeknownst to Dana who was living in Toledo, Ohio at the time. Dana decided to visit Pittsburgh to meet with the remaining members of DERKETA, former WORMHOLE and MASTER MECHANIC bassist Mary Bielich and drummer Terri Heggen. All seemed to go well so Dana relocated to Pittsburgh and the trio began writing music. It was decided that Dana would also be the vocalist and main lyricist for the band. The name MYTHIC was chosen and the band was officially born.
Within a month a three song rehearsal tape was recorded on a 4-track recorder to spread the word throughout the underground scene. The tracks were 'The Destroyer', 'Scarred For Life' and 'Grande Grimoire'. MYTHIC than played several shows on the East coast including in Rhode Island, Cleveland, Detroit, and Pittsburgh.
Later that same year they recorded an official, live recorded demo entitled 'The Immortal Realm'. Tracks were 'Thy Future Forecast', 'The Destroyer', 'The Oracle', 'Taste of the Grave', 'Grande Grimoire' and 'Lament Configuration'. This six song tape received heavy promotion, proving MYTHIC to be substantially more than an "all girl" novelty. Within a year of forming they were offered a MCD from Relapse Records. Again, MYTHIC were eager to record and entered the studio immediately. The three song release entitled 'Mourning In The Winter Solstice' was released in 1992 on MCD, 7" record (both traditional black and limited blue vinyl) and cassette. Soon after this release, MYTHIC parted ways with Terri Heggen and a session drummer was used for what would be the final performance at the legendary 'Milwaukee Metalfest VI'.
After the festival, MYTHIC strangely disbanded. Dana promptly formed Black Metal band DARK MOON and later her more prominent act DEMONIC CHRIST. Bielich

went on to join the Doom band
NOVEMBER'S DOOM, Brian Griffin of
BROKEN HOPE's side project EM SINFONIA
and by 2001 was a member of PENANCE.

<u>Singles/EPs:</u>
Winter Solstice / Lament Configuration /
Spawn Of Absu, Relapse (1992) ('Mourning
In The Winter Solstice' EP)

MYTHOLOGICAL COLD TOWERS
(BRAZIL)
Line-Up: Samej (vocals), Flagellum (guitar),
Nechron (guitar), Leonard (bass), Akenaton
(keyboards), Hamon (drums)

Brazilian epic Doom Death with Portuguese
lyrics. The band would lose keyboard player
Akenaton for the second album, 2000's more
Gothic influenced 'Remoti Meridiani Hymni -
Towards The Magnificent Realm Of The Sun'
released by Somber Music.

<u>Albums:</u>
**SPHERE OF NEBADDON: THE DAWN OF
A DYING TYFFERETH**. Sound Riot
Productions (1996)
In The Forgotten Melancholic Waves Of The
Eternal Sea / Celestial Dimensions Into
Silence / The Vastness Of A Desolated Glory
/ Slaves In The Imaginary Abyssal Line /
Exotic Voluptuousness Of A Lost Feeling Of
Life / Golden Bells From The Eternal Frost /
Mythological Cold Towers / Of Inexistancy /
A Portal To My Darkest Soul / Sphere Of
Nebaddon
**REMOTI MERIDIANI HYMNI - TOWARDS
THE MAGNIFICENT REALM OF THE SUN**,
Somber Music (2000)
The Lost Tribes Of Amazon: A Glimpse In
The Maze Of Forest (Prologue) / Glorious
Traces Of The Fall Of Tahuantinsuyu /
Remoti Meridiani Hymni / Opulence Of The
Signals / Colossal Megalithic Monument /
Contemplating The Brandish Of The Torches
/ Tiwanako: A Gateway To Kalasasaya
(Epilogue)

NAEVUS (GERMANY)
Line-Up: Uwe Groebel (vocals/ guitar), Oli Grosshans (guitar), Sven Heimerdinger (bass), Mathias Straub (drums)

Young Doom Rockers founded in Beitingheim during 1991. At first NAEVUS concentrated on down-tuned Sludge Metal approach but by the 1996 demo 'Autumn Sun' their style had shifted to a more intense Stoner Doom sound.
NAEVUS issued a single for the British label Flashpoint Records followed up by a further track on a split EP shared alongside MOOD, Americans REVELATION, Japan's CHURCH OF MISERY.
In 1999 frontman Uwe Groebel founded Doom act VOODOO SHOCK, working in alliance with the former END OF GREEN rhythm section of bass player Oliver Merkle and drummer Mathias Sifferman.

<u>Singles/EPs:</u>
Gallery Of Fantasy / Skydiver, Flashpoint (1997)

<u>Albums:</u>
SUN MEDITATION, Rise Above RISE 16 (1998)
One In Two (Forest) / Sun Meditation / Skydiver / Dreamrider / Mirrordancer / Gallery Of Fantasy / Dreamworld Wizard - The Sleeping / The Third Sun / Intense Perception / Palace Of The Winds / The Art To Love

NASHVILLE PUSSY (Atlanta, GA, USA)
Line-Up: Blaine Cartwright (vocals / guitars), Ruyter Suys (guitar), Corey Parks (bass), Jeremy Thompson (drums)

Propagators of "Southern discomfort". NASHVILLE PUSSY have risen above their initial shock Rock impact to a well deserved status of highly respected road dogs boasting the very real rarity of a genuine female guitar hero Ruyter Suys. Founded by ex-NINE POUND HAMMER founder and guitarist Blaine Cartwight NASHVILLE PUSSY toured America relentlessly prior to landing a major deal with Mercury Records. The group had originally been conceived as HELL'S HALF ACRE during the mid '90s with Cartwright, his wife Ruyter Suys on guitar and drummer Adam Neal. Although based in Georgia, extolling Southern roots and having named the band after an infamous quote from Detroit Motor City Madman TED NUGENT's 'Double Live Gonzo' opus, NASHVILLE PUSSY's guitarist Ruyter Suys is in fact a Canadian.

With the addition of the towering bassist Corey Parks, the sister of NBA star Cherokee Parks and famed for her onstage fire breathing routine, the group debuted in 1988 with the succinctly titled album 'Let Them Eat Pussy'. Produced by FASTBACKS guitarist Kurt Bloch and delivered through the independent Amphetamine Reptile label, such was the furore created that Mercury swiftly picked the album up for a re-release. The track 'Fried Chicken And Coffee' even landed the honour of a Grammy nomination for 'Best Heavy Metal Performance'. Touring had NASHVILLE PUSSY opening up for MARILYN MANSON.
The 2000 album 'High As Hell' was once again produced by Kurt Bloch. Parks was replaced by Tracey Almazon, guitarist with HELLDORADO and drummer for THE WIVES, in September 2000 as NASHVILLE PUSSY recorded a version of MOLLY HATCHET's 'Flirtin' With Disaster' for the 'Run Ronnie Run' movie soundtrack. The following year their take on TURBONEGRO's 'Age Of Pamparius' appeared as the lead track on the 'Alpha' tribute album.
This same track would subsequently appear on the August 2002 Sanctuary compilation album 'Mad Mike Jones Presents: Mototrax 1'. Meantime Parks reportedly received an offer to join the high profile HOLE but turned the offer down. These rumours of links with Courtney Love would persist with supposed plans between the pair for a brand new act although Parks would eventually emerge with a separate entity entitled THE LIZZIES.
In the summer of 2001 NASHVILLE PUSSY's take on TWISTED SISTER's 'The Kids Are Back' featured on a tribute album 'Twisted And Strange'. Japanese versions of NASHVILLE PUSSY's 2002 album 'Say Something Nasty', issued on the JVC Victor label, added three extra tracks in 'Beat Me Senseless', 'Can't Get Rid Of It' and 'Rock And Roll Hoochie Koo'. By this stage the band included Katie Lynn Campbell, formerly with FAMOUS MONSTERS.

<u>Singles/EPs:</u>
Go Motherfucker Go / Milk Cow Blues, Get Hip GH210 (1999)

<u>Albums:</u>
LET THEM EAT PUSSY, Amphetamine Reptile (1998)
Snake Eyes / You're Goin' Down / Go Motherfucker Go / I'm The Man / All Fucked Up / Johnny Hotrod / 5 Minutes To Live / Somebody Shoot Me / Blowin' Smoke / First I Look At The Purse / Eat My Dust / Fried Chicken And Coffee

286

HIGH AS HELL, TVT (2000)
Struttin' Cock / Shoot First Run Like Hell / She's Got The Drugs / Wrong Side Of The Gun / Piece Of Ass / High As Hell / You Aint Right / Go To Hell / Rock And Roll Outlaw / Lets Ride / Blowjob From A Rattle Snake / Drive

SAY SOMETHING NASTY, Artemis (2002)
Words Of Wisdom / Say Something Nasty / Gonna Hitchhike Down To Cincinnati And Kick The Shit Outta Your Drunk Daddy / You Give Drugs A Bad Name / The Bitch Just Kicked Me Out / Keep On Fuckin' / Jack Shack / Keep Them Things Away From Me / Here's To Your Destruction / Let's Get The Hell Outta Here / Slow Movin' Train / Beat Me Senseless / Can't Get Rid Of It / Rock n' Roll Hoochie Coo / Outro

NATAS (ARGENTINA)

Line-Up: Sergio Chotsourian (vocals / guitar), Claudio Filadoro Rilec (bass), Walter Briode (drums)

NATAS ('The Creams'), sometimes credited as LOS NATAS or THE NATAS on record sleeves, are generally acknowledged to be among the elite of the South American Stoner contingent. Founded in 1993 the trio emerged with a 1995 cassette 'En Busca De La Especia' crediting a line-up of vocalist / guitarist Sergio Chotsourian, bassist 'El Mono' and drummer Walter Briode. The 'Delmar' tape followed in 1996, now with bass delegated to 'Maitor'. A further cassette release 'Rutation' came in 1998 and that year the cult Man's Ruin label of Frank Kozik picked 'Delmar' up for North American release adding two extra tracks on the CD format. 1999's 'Unreleased Dopes' collected together the early releases on CD for the Western market adding outtakes from the 'Delmar' sessions.

A brand new studio album 'Ciudad De Brahman', which included a guest Hawaiian guitar spot from producer Dale Crover of the MELVINS, came courtesy of Man's Ruin in 1999. NATAS conducted their debut North American live dates paired up with GAMMERA for a run of shows throughout September of 2000. Bassist Miguel Fernández would be replaced by Claudio 'Pastor' Filadoro Rilec, also operational in side projects GALLOS DE RINA and SANDIABLO.

The 2002 'Corsario Negro' album for the

NATAS
Photo : El Danno

287

Small Stone Recording label, which saw Gonzalo 'Crudo' Villagra on bass guitar, was recorded and produced in Argentina by the highly respected figure of Billy Anderson. Vinyl versions were issued by the Italian Vinyl Magic company.

NATAS personnel guitarist Sergio Chotsourian and drummer Walter Briode also feature in Stoner act SANTORO.

Singles/EPs:
El Gobernador I / El Gobernador II, Orbital (1999) (Split EP with VIAJE A 800. 10" vinyl)
Xanadu / El Pappo / Tiempos Violentos / Bodokentorten / El Convoy, Vinyl Magic (2000) ('Livin' La Weeda Loca' EP. 10" vinyl Italian release)
El Gobernador I / El Gobernador II / Polvaredo No Es Nada / Soma, Cargo (2001) (German release)
El Cono Del Encono, Black Juju (2002) (Split EP with DOZER)

Albums:
DELMAR, Man's Ruin (1998)
Samurai / 1980 / Trilogia / I Love You / Soma / Muxcortoi / Delmar / Negro / Alberto Migre
CIUDAD DE BRAHMAN, Man's Ruin (1999)
Carl Sagan / Meteoro 2028 / Tufi Meme / La Ciudad De Brahman / Silvetle / Brista Del Desierto / Paradise / Alohawaii / Adolescentes / 999 / El Resplendor / Rutation / Palvaredo / Nada
UNRELEASED DOPES, Beard Of Stars (1999)
Meteoro 2028 / Correindo En La Montania / Highway Sun / Brisa Del Desierto / Asteroides / Division Miami / Viento Dorado / El Resplandor / Alohawaii
NATAS, Icarus (2000) (Split album with DRAGONAUTA)
Xanadu / El Pappo / El Convoy / Tiempes Violentos / Bodokentorten
CORSARIO NEGRO, Small Stone Recordings SS 028 (2002)
2002 / Planeta Solitario / Patasdeelefante / El Conodelencono / Lei Motive / Hey Jimmy / Contemplandolaniebla / Bumburi / Americano / El Gouchito / Corsario Negro

NEBULA (USA)

Line-Up: Eddie Glass (vocals / guitar), Ian Ross (guitar), Mark Abshire (bass), Ruben Romano (drums)

Upon their exile from Stoner Rockers FU MANCHU frontman Eddie Glass, bassist Mark Abshire and drummer Ruben Romano forged a liaison with ex-KYUSS / THE OBSESSED bassist Scott Reeder. The latter was to depart prior to recording of the first album though and another FU MANCHU refugee, Mark Abshire plugged the gap for recording. The band would make their presence felt on the live front in 1998 embarking on US tours with SIXTY WATT SHAMEN and MUDHONEY.

NEBULA debuted with a split four track EP shared with Sweden's LOWRIDER. Originally issued in November of 1998 in aquamarine coloured vinyl format, a further issue came in February of the following year on CD. An EP for the Man's Ruin label 'Sun Creature' also emerged, the CD variant including an additional fourth track 'Fly On'.

The Jack Endino produced 1999 album 'To The Center' saw a cover of THE STOOGES 'I Need Somebody' with guest vocals from MUDHONEY's Mark Arm. NEBULA would prove their staying power on the live circuit on the road with NASHVILLE PUSSY throughout the Spring in America before hopping over to Germany for co-headline gigs with UNIDA. By September the band was back on European soil packaged with THE AWESOME MACHINE and later ORANGE GOBLIN. US gigs, commencing in October, paired NEBULA with THE ATOMIC BITCHWAX and CORE for an exhaustive set of dates running through until late November.

Live activity in 2000 had NEBULA and LOST GOAT partaking of US West Coast gigs in February before NEBULA formed a package billing with ZEN GUERILLA and THE GO for a lengthy series of nationwide gigs. In May touring partners ROADSAW journeyed with the band across the UK and into Europe. NEBULA would return the favour to ROADSAW inviting them over for a short batch of American gigs in November. That same month NEBULA graced Australian shores, supported by ROLLERBALL, before making a return trip to the UK for two high profile gigs with the HELLACOPTERS.

During 2001 NEBULA set about an extensive global road campaign. Californian gigs with MUDHONEY opened up the proceedings and then in early February the band added ROADSAW guitarist Ian Ross to the ranks. With this revised line-up NEBULA joined a US tour package of CORROSION OF CONFORMITY, CLUTCH and THE MYSTICK KREWE OF CLEARLIGHT. Gigs into March witnessed a union with ZEKE upfront of shows in the UK in alliance with ORANGE GOBLIN. An extensive series of shows in Scandinavia and Europe saw ON TRIAL as openers and by May the band was back into America paired with CHERRY VALLANCE. NEBULA also scored valuable slots on the UK's premier 'Leeds' and 'Reading' festival events and put in an appearance at the 'Popkomm' music industry convention in

NEBULA
Photo : El Danno

Cologne. Whilst in the UK the band also cut a radio session for the John Peel show, these recordings swiftly transferring over to the bootleg market. Spreading their net globally NEBULA put in live shows in Australia in September followed by gigs in Brazil and Argentina the following month.

Relapse Records reissued the debut 'Let It Burn' in 1999 with extra tracks. As NEBULA geared up for a bout of American touring toward the close of May 2002 with NASHVILLE PUSSY, Meteor City Records would compile all of the early EP tracks together with new tracks 'Rocket', 'Long Day' and 'Bardo Airways' as the album collection 'Dos EPs'.

Singles/EPs:

Anything From You / Full Throttle / Back To The Dawn / Fall Of Icarus, Meteor City MCY-004 (1998) (Split EP with LOWRIDER)
Rollin' My Way To Freedom / Sun Creature / Smokin' Woman / Fly On, Man's Ruin MR-133 (1998) ('Sun Creature' CD single)
Rollin' My Way To Freedom / Sun Creature / Smokin' Woman, Man's Ruin MR-133 (1998) ('Sun Creature' 10" single)
Clearlight / Humbucker / Full Throttle (Live), Sweet Nothing (1999)
Do It Now / Cosmic Egg / Untitled, Sweet Nothing (2001)

Albums:

LET IT BURN, Tee Pee TP-010 (1998)
Elevation / Down The Highway / Let It Burn / Vulcan Bomber / Dragon Eye / Raga In The Bloodshot / Pyramid
TO THE CENTER, Sub Pop SPCD 493 (1999)
To The Center / Come Down / Whatcha Lookin' For / Clearlight / Freedom / Antigone / I Need Somebody / So Low / Synthetic Dream / Fields Of Psilocybin / Between Time / You Mean Nothin'
CHARGED, Sub Pop SPCD 535 (2001)
Do It Now / Beyond / Giant / Travellin' Man's Blues / Instant Gratification / This One / Ignition / Shaker / Goodbye Yesterday / All The Way
DOS EPS, Meteor City (2002)
Rocket / Long Day / Bardo Airways / Anything From You / Rollin' My Way To Freedom / Fall Of Icarus / Smokin' Woman / Fly On / Full Throttle / Sun Creature / Back To The Dawn

NECARE (Newport, VA, USA)
Line-Up: Erin Vernon (vocals), Ryan Henry (guitar / bass / keyboards), April Leightty (violin), Greer Cawthon (drums)

Virginian Doom Metal originally founded as a duo of versatile multi-instrumentalist Ryan Henry and drummer Greer Cawthon. Adding singer Erin Vernon and violinist April Leightty, the four track 'Ophelia' EP was recorded under the pseudonym of 'Nihilist'.

Henry operates Black Metal band MALICE in association with guitarist 'Schizo', better known as Chris Molinarco of DIVINE SILENCE.

NECARE's 2001 album includes poems from EVOKEN and FUNEBRARUM man Nick Orlando set to music.

Singles/EPs:
Azrael / Misericordian / Juliet Consigned To Flames Of Woe / Ophelia, Necare (1999) ('Ophelia' EP)

NECROMANDUS (UK)
Line-Up: Bill Branch (vocals), Barry Dunnery (guitar), Dennis McCarten (bass), Frank Hall (drums)

Cumbrian Progressive Doom Metal band managed by OZZY OSBOURNE's personal assistant David Tangye and produced by BLACK SABBATH guitarist TONY IOMMI. Created under the original name of HOT SPRING WATER the quartet comprised vocalist Bill Branch, guitarist Barry Dunnery, bass player Dennis McCarten and drummer Frank Hall. A name change to HEAVY HAND led eventually to NECROMANDUS, a union of Nostradamus and Necromancy.

The band was spotted playing in the Lake District by Iommi on one of BLACK SABBATH's early tours. NECROMANDUS, upon Iommi's instigation, scored a deal with major label Vertigo with the BLACK SABBATH man producing and lending guitar to the title track 'Orexis Of Death'.

Intended for release in 1972 the album was shelved at the time due to Dunnery's departure from the band and was only issued many decades later.

Dunnery, McCarten and Hall would attempt to create a band with OZZY OSBOURNE in 1976 upon the singer's first split from BLACK SABBATH. This unit, the first incarnation of BLIZZARD OF OZZ, actually worked up a full album's worth of material. Due to the chaotic circumstances prevailing at the time this project floundered and Osbourne drifted back to his former act for his swansong 'Never Say Die' album.

Hall and Dunnery re-formed NERVES and Dunnery would later to be found in the ELECTRIC LIGHT ORCHESTRA offshoot VIOLINSKI. Hall's recent work includes the Jazz Rock act THE CHILDREN and his own band THE BINMEN, led by former SWEET vocalist Malcolm McNulty.

Albums:
OREXIS OF DEATH, Audio Archives (1999)
Mogidisimo / Nightjar / A Black Solitude / Homicidal Psychopath / Still Born Beauty / Gypsy Dancer / Orexis Of Death / Mogididimo

THE NEFILIM (UK)
Line-Up: Carl McCoy (vocals), Paul Miles (guitar), Cian Houchin (bass), Simon Rippin (drums)

As the main protagonist behind the sombre Gothic veterans FIELDS OF THE NEPHILIM, vocalist Carl McCoy set up THE NEFILIM after his departure from the aforementioned group in October 1991 and took a radically heavier direction.

McCoy resurrected FIELDS OF THE NEPHILIM in 2000.

Singles/ EPs:
Xodus / Shine / Melt (The Catching Of The Butterfly), Beggars Banquet NUM.XIII.33 (1995)
Penetration, Beggars Banquet 005-45853 (1995)

Albums:
ZOON, Rebel 085-45862 (1995)
Still Life / Xodus / Shine / Penetration / Melt (The Catching Of The Butterfly) / Venus / Pazuzu (Black Rain) / Zoon (Part I & II: Saturation) / Zoon (Part III: Wake World) / Coma

NEGATIVE REACTION
(New York, NY, USA)
Line-Up: Ken E. Bones (vocals / guitar), Damon Limpy (bass), Glenn Smog (drums)

A New York Sludge-Doom outfit born out of Hardcore roots in 1990. The band debuted commercially with the track 'Poisoned Friendship' shared with WHATSOEVER on a split 7" single through the band's custom imprint Rot n' Roll Records. Further split singles ensued allied with SOUNDBITE HOUSE and Punk act VIOLENT SOCIETY. NEGATIVE REACTION also included two rare tracks, 'Deathbed' and 'NFG' on the compilation album 'More Lies from the Underground'. The debut album, 'Endofyourerror' crediting a rhythm section of Mark Skunk on bass and drummer Brian Alien, arrived in 1996. This record, although still carrying trademark Hardcore elements, witnessed the band's uncompromising plunge into Doom.

NEGATIVE REACTION's 'The Orion Chronicles' album, released by the Colorado

NEGATIVE REACTION
Photo : Rob Witt

Game Two concern, featured the jaw dropping 38 minute 'The Moon Song'. The record, comprising just three tracks, closes with an unaccredited take on HAWKWIND's 'Lords Of Light'. Following recording Damon Limpy took over the bass role.

Singles/EPs:
Poisoned Friendship / Simply Stupid, Rot n' Roll (1993) (Split single with WHATSOEVER)
We Got Problems / I'll Have Another, Rot n' Roll (1994) (Split single with SOUNDBITE HOUSE)
Noise Junkie / Hot Clam Chowder / Mercy Killing, Rot n' Roll (1995) (Split single with VIOLENT SOCIETY)
Slight Abrasion Of The Cornea / Dianoga, Game Two GT-11 (1998) ('The Orbit' EP)

Albums:
ENDOFYOURERROR, (1996)
NFG / Kevorkian's Innocence / Sludge / Nebula And The Two Toed Sloth / Reserved / Plutonium Ryborg / Dethbed / When The Rose Dies / Us / Ten Souls Gather
THE ORION CHRONICLES, Game Two GT-19 (2001)
The Moon Song / Hypothermia / Lords Of Light

NEMA (MI, USA)

Albums:
BRING OUR CURSES HORN, Pollute 044 CD (1999)

NEMESIS (SWEDEN)
Line-Up: Leif Edling (vocals / bass), Christian Weyherd (guitar), Anders Wallin (guitar), Anders Waltersson (drums)

NEMESIS are best remembered for ultimately evolving into CANDLEMASS following their only record.
The fledgling group that recorded the debut mini-album in 1984 comprised vocalist / bassist Leif Edling, guitarist Anders Wallin, guitarist Christian Weberyd and drummer Anders Waltersson.
'Day Of Retribution' was later re-released through Active at the height of CANDLEMASS' fame with the addition of bonus tracks 'Blackstone Wielder' and 'Demons Gate'. These songs featured on the very first CANDLEMASS demo recorded in 1985 featuring a line-up of band leader Edling, ex-ATC guitarist Mats Björkman, second guitarist Klas Bergwall and drummer Matz Ekström.

Albums:
DAY OF RETRIBUTION, Fingerprint MLP003 (1984)

Black Messiah / In God We Trust / Theme Of The Guardians / The King Is Dead / Goodnight
DAY OF RETRIBUTION, Active ATVCD 15 (1990)
Black Messiah / In God We Trust / Theme Of The Guardians / The King Is Dead / Goodnight / Blacknight / Blackstone Wielder / Demons Gate

NEOCORI (SWEDEN)
Line-Up: Stefan Karlsson (vocals), Magnus Ludvigsson (guitar), Michael Christmasson (guitar), Mikael Höglund (bass), Stefan Suomalanen (drums)

NEOCORI trade in grandiose Doom Metal. Interestingly, bassist Mikael Höglund has been a member of the influential GREAT KING RAT as well as Brit Rockers THUNDER. Indeed, he was still a member of the latter group when he recorded with NEOCORI.
The same year as the single release found NEOCORI gaining greater exposure with the inclusion of the track 'Into The Flesh' on the American sampler album 'Best Unsigned European Bands' on the Showcase label.
Vocalist Stefan Karlsson was later to join MEMENTO MORI for a tour in 1995.

Singles/EPs:
Purgatory Dreams / Invite Reality / Feet Of The Liar / Into The Flesh, Evil EVIL007 (1994)

NEUROSIS (Oakland, CA, USA)
Line-Up: Scott Kelly (vocals / guitar), Steve Von Till (vocals / guitar), Dave Edwardson (bass), Jason Roeder (drums)

Described as groundbreaking Death Metal, avant-garde Hardcore, the ever challenging NEUROSIS have doggedly refused to be compartmentalized. The band has made an indelible mark on the Rock scene with eclectic Alt Rock which blends a myriad of styles including even Gothic and Medieval overlaid with spiritually infused lyrical content laden with endtime prophecies. As such NEUROSIS are one of the very few bands to truly set themselves apart from the pack. The teenage NEUROSIS started as a trio in the mid '80s of vocalist / guitarist Scott Kelly, bassist Dave Edwardson and drummer Jason Roeder. Their first burst of energy would be delivered in the form of 1987's 'Pain Of Mind', a vicious, no holds barred Hardcore assault. Adding guitarist Steve Von Till for 1989's transitional 'Word As Law' album NEUROSIS began to display elements of eccentricity that would see song concepts stretching into

uncharted realms. The band added ex-CHRIST ON PARADE keyboard Player Noah to their line-up for live work.
NEUROSIS signed to the Alternative Tentacles label for the supreme 'Souls At Zero' album, confounding critics with a record that borrowed from Grunge, Gothic and Metal interspersed with string and woodwind as well as narrative passages from celluloid sources such as 'Triumph Of The Will' and 'Star Wars'. The next career step was planned as an EP but 'Enemy Of The Sun' duly arrived as a full album.
Their 1996 Billy Anderson produced 'Through Silver In Blood' album, complete with an opening twelve minute title track, would land the group deserved accolades and opened up the NEUROSIS catalogue to the mainstream Rock public. The 1999 'Times Of Grace' album was produced by the renowned Steve Albini. NEUROSIS toured America with TODAY IS THE DAY and UNSANE.
The band members also operate a conceptual side project titled TRIBES OF NEUROT under which guise they released the split 'Static Migration' CD together with WALKING TIME BOMBS in 1998. Edwardson sessioned for NOISEGATE on their 1999 album.
The band reissued the debut 'Pain Of Mind' in November of 2000, restoring the original artwork and adding a bonus disc of early live and demo material.

Singles/EPs:
Nonsense / Pollution (Demo) / Self Doubt, Alternative Tentacles (1988) ('Aberration' EP)
Prayer / An Offering / Flood / Sovereign, Tribes Of Neurot (2000) ('Sovereign' EP)

Albums:
PAIN OF MIND, Alchemy VM 105 (1987)
Pain Of Mind / Self Taught Infection / Reasons To Hide / Black / Training / Progress / Stalemate / Bury What's Dead / Geneticide / Ingrown / United Sheep / Dominoes Fall / Life On Your Knees / Grey
THE WORD AS LAW, Lookout LOOKOUT CD 21 (1989)
Double Edged Sword / The Choice / Obsequious Obsolescence / To What End? / Tomorrow's Reality / Common Inconsistencies / Insensitivity / Blisters / Life On Your Knees / Pain Of Mind / Grey / United Sheep / Pollution / Day Of The Lords
EMPTY, Alternative Tentacles (1990)
SOULS AT ZERO, Alternative Tentacles VIRUS 109 (1992)
To Crawl Under One's Skin / Souls At Zero / Zero / Flight / The Web / Sterile Vision / A Chronological For Survival / Stripped /

Takehnase / Empty
ENEMY OF THE SUN, Alternative Tentacles
VIRUS 134 (1993)
Lost / Raze The Stray / Burning Flesh In The
Year Of The Pig / Cold Ascending / Lexicon /
Enemy Of The Sun / The Time Of The
Beasts / Cleanse
THROUGH SILVER IN BLOOD, Relapse RR
6938 (1996)
Through Silver In Blood / Rehumanize / Eye
/ Purify / Locust Star / Strength Of Fates /
Become The Ocean / Aeon / Enclosure In
Flame
TIMES OF GRACE, Relapse RR 6419 (1999)
Suspended In Light / The Doorway / Under
The Surface / The Last You'll Know / Belief /
Exist / End Of The Harvest / Descent / Away
/ Times Of Grace / The Road To Sovereignty
A SUN THAT NEVER SETS, Relapse (2001)
Erode / The Tide / From The Hill / A Sun
That Never Sets / Falling Unknown / From
Where Its Roots Run / Crawl Back In /
Watchfire / Resound / Stones From The Sky
PAIN OF MIND, Neurot (2000)
Pain Of Mind / Self Taught Infection /
Reasons To Hide / Black / Training /
Progress / Stalemate / Bury What's Dead /
Geneticide / Ingrown / United Sheep /
Dominoes Fall / Life On Your Knees / Grey /
Stalemate (Live) / Black (Live) / Instrumental
(Live) / Grey (Live WFMU demo) / Pollution
(Demo) / Life On Your Knees (Demo) /
Reasons To Hide (Demo) / Ingrown (Demo) /
Pain of Mind (Demo) / Dominoes Fall
(Demo)

NEW TESTAMENT (RUSSIA)
Line-Up: V. Gorbachev (vocals), V. Volkov
(guitar), S. Skripnikov (bass), V. Kozimenko
(drums)

A Russian Christian Doom Metal band!

Albums:
HALLELUJA, (1991)
EXORCIST, (1992)

NIGHTFALL (GREECE)
Line-Up: Efthims Karadimas (vocals / bass),
Mike Galiatsos (guitar), Chris Adamou
(guitar), George Aspiotis (keyboards),
Costas Savidas (drums)

NIGHTFALL first came to prominence with
their 1991 demo 'Vanity', immediately
prompting a deal from Holy Records.
Promoting the debut album, 'Parade Into
Centuries', NIGHTFALL supported
PARADISE LOST in Athens during 1992.
The band would add keyboard player George
Aspiotis in early 1993 to increase the depth of

NIGHTFALL
Photo : Nico Wobben

their music. In June of that year NIGHTFALL
released a limited edition, red vinyl single
titled 'Oh Black Queen, You're Mine'. All 1,500
copies quickly sold out.
The impact made by their first album enabled
NIGHTFALL to line-up an extensive European
tour during 1994 to promote their new
'Macabre sunsets' album and NIGHTFALL
claimed a first by being the only Greek band
to date to headline a European tour. Fellow
Holy Records acts MISANTHROPE,
CELESTIAL SEASON and SADNESS
supported.
Having released 'Eons Aura' and 'Athenian
Echoes' during 1995 NIGHTFALL would
return in 1997 with the provocatively titled
'Lesbian Show'.

Singles/EPs:
Oh Black Queen, You're Mine / As Your
God Is Failing Once Again / Enormous (The
Anthem Of Death), Holy (1993)

Albums:
PARADE INTO CENTURIES, Holy HOLY01
(1992)
Thoughts / Domestication Of Wildness /
Vanity / The Passage / In God They Trust /
For My Soul, When The Dark Falls Into... /
Immaculate (Enslaved By Need) / Birth /
Crying Out The Fear Within / Domestication
Of Wildness (Long Version)

MACABRE SUNSETS, Holy HOLY04 (1994)
H POLID C EALW / Precious (All My Love Is
Lost) / As Your God Is Failing Once Again /
Macabre Sunsets / Bitterness Leads Me To
My Saviour Death / Mother Of All Gods,
Mother Of Mine / Poetry Of Death /
Enormous (The Anthem Of Death) / As Your
God Is Failing Once Again (Original Version)
EONS AURA, Holy HOLY (1995)
Eroding / Ardour I Was / Until The Day God
Helps Us All / Thor
ATHENIAN ECHOES, Holy HOLY14 (1995)
Aye Azure / Armada / Ishtar (Celebrate Your
Beauty) / The Vineyard / I'm A Daemond /
Iris (And The Burning Aureole) / My Red,
Red Moon (Emma O) / Monuments Of Its
Own Magnificence
LESBIAN SHOW, Holy HOLY 28 CD (1997)
Lesbian Show / Aenon / Dead Woman,
Adieu / The Secret Admirer / My Own Troy /
The Fleshmaker / Death Star / Cold Bloody
Killer / Lashed August Reign
DIVA FUTURA, Holy (199-)
Master, Faster, Sweet Disaster / Sin / The
Sheer Misfit / Diva / Licked One's Iced Lips /
Picture Me / Some Deaths Take For Ever /
Lowve / Ceaseless / My Traitor's Kiss /
Pleasure

NIGHTINGALE (SWEDEN)
Line-Up: Dan Swanö (vocals / guitar /
keyboards / drums), Tom Nouga (guitar), Erik
Oskarsson (bass)

Yet another in the multitude of side projects of
UNICORN and EDGE OF SANITY's Dan
Swanö, NIGHTINGALE is his Doom,
Progressive venture. The man played all the
instruments bar bass on the debut 'The
Breathing Shadow' as well as producing the
affair. Overall NIGHTINGALE's sound is a
heady mixture of '80s New Wave with epic
Rock and Gothic vibes.
The subsequent 'The Closing Chronicles...'
album was co-produced by Tom Nouga who
led Swanö through his self-created musical
jungle. The second outing turned out to be a
bleak even melancholic affair. Now there's a
surprise.
Both Dan Swanö and bassist Erik Oskarsson
would feature as session players with
GODSEND.

Albums:
THE BREATHING SHADOW, Black Mark
BMCD 66 (1995)
Nightfall Overture / Sleep... / The
Dreamreacher / Higher Than The Sky /
Recovery Grub / The Return To Dreamland /
Gypsy Eyes / Alone? / A Lesson In Evil /
Eye For An Eye

**THE CLOSING CHRONICLES (THE
BREATHING SHADOWS PART II)**, Black
Mark BM CD 90 (1996)
Deep Inside Of Nowhere / Revival /
Thoughts From A Stolen Soul / So Long (Still
I Wonder) / Steal The Moon / Intermezzo /
Alive Again: I) The Release, II) Shadowland
Revisited, III) Breathless / The End.
I, Black Mark (2000)
Scarred For Life / Still In The Dark / The
Game / Game Over / Remorse And Regret /
Alonely / I Return / Drowning In Sadness /
Dead Or Alive / The Journey's End /
Breathing

NIGHTLY GALE (POLAND)
Line-Up: Waldemar Sagen (vocals), Jaroslaw
Toifl (guitar / bass / keyboards), Slawomir
Pyrzyk (guitar / keyboards / drums)

Exceptionally depressing Doom. NIGHTLY
GALE released a batch of demos
commencing with 1996's 'Dream Of The Dark
Hour' followed by 1998's 'The Bleeding Art'
and finally 1999's 'Erotica' before signing to
Pagan Records for the debut album.

Albums:
...AND JESUS WEPT, Pagan MOONCD
027 (2001)
I'm The Only Way / In Despair Of Solitude /
And If I Say That You Died / Cutting God's
Throat / Place Where You Are

NIGHTMARE VISION (UK)

An obscure Doom Metal act.

Albums:
SUFFERING FROM ECHOES, (198-)

NIGHTSTICK (Weymouth, MA, USA)
Line-Up: Alex Smith (vocals / bass), Cotie
Cowgill (guitar), Robert Williams (drums)

Infamous purveyors of disharmonic, abrasive
Doom. The 'Blotter' album ambitiously, yet
successfully, tackled PINK FLOYD's epic 'Set
The Controls For The Heart Of The Sun' and
still had appetite enough to take on a LYDIA
LUNCH cover too.
1998's 'Ultimatum' was a war themed concept
outing hinged upon just one laborious riff that
would be periodically revisited throughout the
entire piece overlain with the conflicting
sounds of battle and Berlioz.

Singles/EPs:
In Dahmer's Room, Relapse (1996)

Albums:
BLOTTER, (1995)
Workers Of The World Unite!! / Some Boys /
Set The Controls For The Heart Of The Sun /
Mommy, What's A Funkadellic / 5/21/93 /
Blotter / Fellating The Dying Christ
ULTIMATUM, Relapse (1998)
Ultimatum: "Cut It Off, Then Kill It" / United
Snakes / The Pentagon / Pig In Shit / 4 More
Years / August 6, 1945: a) Flight; b) Fright /
Dream Of The Witch's Sabbath - Massacre
Of Innocence (Air Attack) / Ultimatum: "He...
Is... Dead... Wrong" (4-track version) /
Ultimatum (Live @ Mama Kin's)
DEATH TO MUSIC, Relapse (1999)
Babykiller / Jarhead / Young Man, Old Man /
(Won't You Take Me To) Junkytown / The
American Way / Free Man / In Dahmer's
Room / Boot Party Theme / Egghead: i) I Am
Egghead, ii) Naked Came The Egg, iii)
Egghead Is Dead

NIGHTWISH (FINLAND)

Line-Up: Tarja Turunen (vocals), Erno
Vuorinen (guitar), Sami Väskä (bass),
Tuomas Holopainen (keyboards), Jukka
Nevalainen (drums)

A grandiose, keyboard driven Metal band that
has risen to huge successes in mainland
Europe and South America. NIGHTWISH was
originally conceived as a side project of
NATTVINDENS GRÅT members keyboard
player Tuomas Holopainen and bassist Sami
Vänskä with female vocals. NIGHTWISH
started life as a Folk band but decided that
the only genre of music that could ably cope
with the power of vocalist Tarja Turunen was
Heavy Metal.
NIGHTWISH's 1997 demo was a strictly
acoustic affair but a second tape the same
year introduced electric guitars and drums.
NIGHTWISH also drafted the services of a
permanent drummer Jukka Nevalainen.
Hugely successful in their native Finland with
regular chart appearances, NIGHTWISH's
debut 1997 single entered the Finnish charts
at number 8 and by January 1999 the band
had no less than two singles in the top three
and a top ten album 'Oceanborn'. Japanese
variants of the album came complete with an
exclusive extra track 'Nightquest'.
Despite this obvious progress the band
remained strangely inactive with Turunen and
Holopainen concentrating on studying with
the other band members conducting national
service in the Finnish army. During 2000
NIGHTWISH would repeat earlier successes
with the 'Wishmaster' album. Once again the
Japanese market benefited from an extra
track in 'Sleepwalker'.
With interest in NIGHTWISH rising rapidly

Spinefarm issued a lavish limited edition set
entitled 'Golden Wishes'. Comprising the
band's first three albums plus a disc of rarities
all in picture disc format.
The band, following on from previous chart
entries 'The Carpenter', 'Sacrament Of
Wilderness' and 'Walking In The Air', scored
their fourth consecutive gold status single in
Finland during the summer of 2001 when
'Over the Hills and Far Away' charted high.
Tarja Turunen would guest on the 2001 debut
album from Argentinean Symphonic Metal
band BETO VASQUEZ INFINITY, a group that
had supported NIGHTWISH at their 2000
show in the Argentine capitol Buenos Aires.
Bassist Sami Vänskä was replaced by Marco
Hietala of TAROT and SINERGY during
October of 2001. During March of 2002
keyboard player Tuomas Holopainen was
announced as part of the formation of a
Finnish 'Gothic Metal supergroup' dubbed
FOR MY PAIN. Joining him in this endeavour
would be the ETERNAL TEARS OF
SORROW triumvirate of bassist Altti
Veteläinen, guitarist Olli-Pekka Törrö and
drummer Petri Sankala, guitarist Lauri
Tuohimaa of EMBRAZE and fronted by
REFLECTION vocalist Juha Kylmänen.
NIGHTWISH's 'Century Child' album opened
the floodgates for the band on the global
scene. It would debut on the Finnish charts at
the no. 1 position, soon achieving platinum
status for having broken the 30,000 units sold
mark, and at no. 5 in Germany. The album
was preceded in their homeland by a record
breaking no. 1 single 'Ever Dream' which
occupied the top position for a five week run.
Before long 'Century Child' had made its mark
on most of the European charts and took just
24 hours to sell out of its first pressing when
issued in Brazil. The band would tour Brazil,
Chile and Argentina to capacity audiences. A
second single, 'Bless The Child', which came
complete with the previously unreleased
'Lagoon' track', maintained the momentum
throughout August.

Singles/EPs:
The Carpenter, Spinefarm (1997)
Sacrament Of Wilderness, Spinefarm
(1998)
Walking In The Air / Nightquest /
Tutankhamen, Spinefarm (1999)
Sleeping Sun / Walking In The Air /
Swanheart / Angels Fall First, Spinefarm
(1999)
Deep Silent Complete / Sleepwalker,
Spinefarm (2000)
Everdream, Spinefarm SPI 148 (2002)
Bless The Child / Lagoon / Wayfarer,
Drakkar (2002)
Bless The Child / Over The Hills And Far

NIGHTWISH

Away (Video) / Bless The Child (Video) / (Video interview), Drakkar (2002)

Albums:
ANGELS FALL FIRST, Spinefarm SPI 47 CD (1998)
Elvenpath / Beauty And The Beast / The Carpenter / Astral Romance / Angels Fall First / Tutankhamen / Nymphomaniac Fantasia / Know Why The Nightingale Sings / Lappi
OCEANBORN, Spinefarm SPI 67SP (1999)
Stargazers / Gethsemane / Devil The Deep Dark Ocean / Sacrament Of Wilderness / Passion And The Opera / Swanheart / Moondance / The Riddler / The Pharaoh Sails To Orion / Walking In The Air
WISHMASTER, Spinefarm SPI 87CD (2000)
She Is My Sin / The Kinslayer / Come Cover Me / Wanderlust / Two For Tragedy / Wishmaster / Bare Grace Misery / Crownless / Deep Silent Complete / Dead Boy's Poem / FantasMic
WISHMASTOUR, XIII Bis (2000) (Limited edition)
Wishmaster / Sleepwalker / Passion And The Opera / Nightquest / A Return To The Sea / Once Upon A Troubadour / Sleeping Sun / Sacrament Of Wilderness
GOLDEN WISHES, Spinefarm (2001) (4 disc vinyl picture disc set. Limited edition 1,000)
Elvenpath / Beauty and the Beast / The Carpenter / Astral Romance / Angels Fall First / Tutankhamen / Nymphomaniac Fantasia / Know Why The Nightingales Sings / Lappi / Stargazers / Gethsemane / Devil & The Deep Dark Ocean / Sacrament Of Wilderness / Passion And The Opera / Swanheart / Moondance / The Riddler / The Pharaoh Sails To Orion / Walking In The Air / She Is My Sin / The Kinslayer / Come Cover Me / Wanderlust / Two For Tragedy / Wishmaster / Bare Grace Misery / Crownless / Deep Silent Complete / Dead Boy's Poem / Fantasmic / Sleepwalker (Heavy version) / Walking In The Air (edit) / Nightquest / The Carpenter (Single version) / Sacrament Of Wilderness (Single version) / Tutankhamen (Single version)
FROM WISHES TO ETERNITY, Spinefarm SPI 100CD (2001) **7 FINLAND**
The Kinslayer / She is My Sin / Deep Silent Complete / The Pharaoh Sails To Orion / Come Cover Me / Wanderlust / Crimson Tide-Deep Blue Sea / Swanheart / Elvenpath / FantasMic, Part III / Dead Boy's Poem / Sacrament Of Wilderness / Walking In The Air / Beauty And The Beast / Wishmaster
OVER THE HILLS AND FAR AWAY, Spinefarm (2001) **139 FRANCE, 85 GERMANY**
Over The Hill And Far Away / 10th Man

Down / Away / Astral Romance / The Kinslayer (Live) / She Is My Sin (Live) / Sacrament Of Wilderness (Live) / Walking In The Air (Live) / Wishmaster (Live) / Deep Silent Complete (Live)
CENTURY CHILD, Spinefarm SPI 149CD (2002) **1 FINLAND, 15 AUSTRIA, 32 FRANCE, 5 GERMANY, 53 SWEDEN, 50 SWITZERLAND**
Bless The Child / End Of All Hope / Dead To The World / Ever Dream / Slaying The Dreamer / Forever Yours / Ocean Soul / Feel For You / The Phantom Of The Opera / Beauty Of The Beast

NORTHWINDS (FRANCE)
Line-Up: Sylvian Auve (vocals), Vincent Niclas (guitar), Marco (keyboards), Benjamin LeClere (drums)

Classic Doom from the unlikely source of Paris. NORTHWINDS began life as far back as 1987, then entitled R.I.P. In the band's formative years R.I.P. operated mainly as a covers act tackling songs by the likes of BLACK SABBATH, WITCHFINDER GENERAL and the NWoBHM movement. Initially Sebastian Thuriez occupied the lead guitar role and Remi Rateau bass. Thuriez would relocate to Japan and his position was duly taken by David Marcos. However, Marcos too would decamp.
A demo secured a deal with the Italian Black Widow label. The newly titled NORTHWINDS would contribute cover versions to various tribute compilations including takes on ST. VITUS 'Clear Window Pane' to a Ravenmoon Records collection, 'Night Of The Witch' by DEATH SS and an inclusion on a BLACK WIDOW tribute.
The 1998 album 'Great God Pan' included a cover of BLACK SABBATH's 'A National Acrobat'. NORTHWINDS 2001 album, 'Masters Of Magic', would include both new and old material as well as an intro and outro composed and recorded by none other than famed Italian Horror Metal act DEATH SS. The bass parts for the album would be recorded by Thomas Bastide, Sebastien Thuriez, Benjamin Leclere and Vincent Niclas.

Albums:
GREAT GOD PAN, Black Widow BWRCD 021-2 (1998)
Great God Pan / The Pain / A National Acrobat / The Forest Of Koncoret / Mother And Son / Northwinds
MASTERS OF MAGIC, Black Widow BWRCD 040-2 (2001)
The Great Ancient / Over The Mountain /

NORTHWINDS

Lost Paradise / Entre Chien Et Loup / Violet Rainbow / Broceliande / King Of A Green Mountain / Dancing In Moonlight / The Book Of Thoth

NOSFERATU (UK)
Line-Up: Dominic LaVey (vocals), Damien Deville (guitar), Stefan Diablo (bass), Rat Scabies (drums)

NOSFERATU are rated as one of the most commercially successful UK based Gothic Rock acts. The group, comprising pivotal member guitarist Damien DeVille, a former member of SISTER MIDNIGHT, vocalist Louis DeWray and bass player Vlad Janiczek, debuted with the inclusion of the track 'Bloodlust' on the Nightbreed 'New Alternatives' compilation album released in June of 1990. Their first tour would come in October of the same year sharing British stages with EVERY NEW DEAD GHOST. An inaugural six track EP, entitled 'The Hellhound', was cut in May of the following year, subsequently being released by the band's own newly established label Possession Records that same September. With strong reviews 'The Hellhound' soon sold out of two pressings. Live work witnessed December gigs with openers CHILDREN OF STUN and a support to the re-formed SEX GANG CHILDREN at London's Camden Underworld.

A brace of singles, 'Vampyres Cry' and the red vinyl 'Diva' pre-empted a further opening slot to the SEX GANG CHILDREN in 1992. Signing to the Cleopatra label NOSFERATU released the single 'Inside The Devil', a song which broke into the singles charts albeit at a lowly no. 131, backed up by a 13 date UK tour in April of 1993. In May the debut album 'Rise' arrived, proceeding to sell some 20,000 copies. However, after recording vocalist Louis DeWray made way for a new frontman Niall Murphy. With this revised line-up NOSFERATU ventured into Europe for gigs in October prior to yet more British gigs the following month to bolster recognition for the single 'Savage Kiss'. With NOSFERATU's star ascending the Cleopatra label weighed in with the compilation album 'Legend'.
Early 1994 would be spent fostering a fan base on mainland Europe, NOSFERATU taking in gigs in Belgium, Holland and Germany. 'The Prophecy' album was delivered in November and fared well on the independent charts. American editions of the album added a bonus track in 'Sucker For Love'. Unfortunately momentum was stalled as the band fractured just as a British tour got underway leaving DeVille as the sole surviving member. DeWray subsequently went on to DITZTY MICRO.
NOSFERATU regrouped with the recruitment of vocalist Dominic LaVey and bass guitarist Dante Savarelle. Prior to fronting

298

NOSFERATU LaVey had already garnered an impressive track record of Gothic inclined acts such as ADREAM, RETURN TO KHAF'JI, DISCIPLES OF THE WATCH, CANDEELA VERVAIN and THE LANGUAGE OF FLOWERS.

Having dissolved the Possession imprint NOSFERATU agreed terms with the Hades label to record a single 'The Haunting', the B side of which scored a version of ALICE COOPER's 'Nothing's Free'. A run of UK and French gigs preceded recording of the 'Prince Of Darkness' album, issued in August of 1996. The group would also donate their version of '100 Years' to a CURE tribute album.

Live drums would be employed on the 1997 'Lord Of The Flies' album for the first time, sessioned by none other the notable figure of Rat Scabies from THE DAMNED. Indeed, album cover artwork even went so far as to include the title NOSFERATU (FEATURING RAT SCABIES). Bass would be in the hands of Doc Milton but for road work in 1998 NOSFERATU would be joined by four stringer Stefan Diablo, a veteran of RAINSTONES and Ska Pop act BAD MANNERS. The Scabies / Diablo rhythm axis remained intact for the 'Revamped' album of 1999. A further cover version, this time THE DOORS 'People Are Strange', was included on a Cleopatra tribute offering as well as scoring a track for use as a soundtrack to the 'Vampyre Masquerade' role playing game. Back on European soil NOSFERATU appeared at the prestigious German 'Gotik Wave Treffen' festival, the line-up featuring Tony Woods on bass for this occasion.

NOSFERATU's first live album, 'Reflections Through A Darker Glass' emerged in March of 2000. In early 2002 the band, now seeing Matt Cherry as live drummer, returned to British stages.

Singles/EPs:
Siren (Hellfire mix) / Lament (The Last Chapter) / Dark Angel (Edit) / Crysania (Believe In Me), Possession (1991) ('The Hellhound' EP)
Vampyres Cry / Vampyres Cry (Rosary mix) / Abominations / Crystal Ring, Possession (1992)
Diva / Diva (Scarlet mix) / The Wiccaman / Her Heaven (Angelic mix), Possession (1992)
Inside The Devil / Inside The Devil (Remix / Away, Possession (1993) (12" single)
Inside The Devil / Away / Inside The Devil (Remix / Crystal Ring, Possession (1993) (CD single)
Savage Kiss / Savage Kiss (Brutal mix) / Time Of Legends, Possession (1993) (CD single)
Savage Kiss / Time Of Legends / The Keeper's Call, Possession (1993) (12" single)
The Haunting / Nothing's Free / The Haunting (Swamp mix), (1995)

Albums:
RISE, Possession (1993)
The Gathering / Rise / Dark Angel / Her Heaven / Lucy Is Red / Lament / Alone / Vampyres Cry / Crysania / Siren / Away / Close
LEGEND, Cleopatra (1994)
The Wiccaman / Abominations (Assylum mix) / Dark Angel (Daemon mix) / Arabian Heat / The Crystal Ring / Diva (Scarlet mix) / Siren (Hellfire mix) / Pictures of Betrayal / Vampyres Cry (Rosary mix) / Inside The Devil (Remix)
PROPHECY, Possession POSSTX008 (1994)
Requiem / Farewell My Little Earth / Fever / The Keeper's Call / Thrill Killer / Time Of Legends / Shadowmaker / Savage Kiss / Grave Desires / Soul Trader / The Enchanted Tower
PRINCE OF DARKNESS, Hades (1996)
Eye Of The Watcher / Ravage / Uninvited Guest / The Haunting (Main mix) / Into The Night / The Passing / Graveyard Shift / The Haunting (Swamp mix) / The Hunger / Invocation
LORD OF THE FLIES, Hades (1998)
Torturous / Ascension / The Tempest / Witching Hour / The Gauntlet / Six Feet Below / Darkness Brings / Lord Of The Flies
REVAMPED, (1999)
Darkness Brings (Aphelion edit) / Uninvited Guest (No Other Medicine) / The Gauntlet (Demon Seed remix) / Graveyard Shift (Hunchback edit) / Heaven (Version 1.2) / Into The Night (Pre-Raphaelite Repro) / Ravage (Bloodstone Version 1.1) / Witching Hour (Midnight Derangement) / Blind Faith
REFLECTIONS THROUGH A DARKER GLASS, (2000)
Inside The Devil / Happy Ending / Rise / Wiccaman / Alone / Dark Angel / Graveyard Shift / Savage Kiss / Keeper's Call / Abominations / Witching Hour / Siren
THE BEST OF NOSFERATU VOLUME I : THE HADES YEARS, (2001)
The Witching Hour / Torturous / The Night Is Young (Manic mix) / Lucifer Rising (Part 2) / Darkness Brings / Ascension / Uninvited Guest (No Other Medicine) / The Gauntlet (Demon Seed mix) / Graveyard Shift / Invocation / The Haunting (Video)

NOVADRIVER (Detroit, MI, USA)
Line-Up: Mark Miers (vocals), Billy Reedy

(guitar), James B. Anders (bass), Eric Miller (drums)

Detroit's NOVADRIVER trade in '70s US Rock laced with plenty of British themed Psychedelia. Following the 'Void' album, which featured a cover version of AEROSMITH's 'Season Of Wither', NOVADRIVER recruited Kenny Tudrick on lead vocals, a dexterous veteran of the Detroit scene as guitarist with both BIG BLOCK and THE NUMBERS as well as acting as drummer for the DETROIT COBRAS.
The 2002 FIVE HORSE JOHNSON album 'The No. 6 Dance' witnessed guest sessions from both guitarist Billy Reedy and ex-singer Mark Miers on piano.

Albums:
VOID, Small Stone Recordings SS-022 (2001)
Satellite Night / Rocket Superstar / Spinning Into No Future / End Of The Universe / Sleep / Shoot The Sky / Void / Sixty Seven / Particle Explosion / Seasons Of Wither

NOVEMBER'S DOOM (Chicago, IL, USA)
Line-Up: Paul Kuhr III (vocals), Larry Roberts (guitar), Eric Burnley (guitar), Brian Whited (bass), Joe Nunez (drums)

NOVEMBER'S DOOM

An illustrious name on the American Doom circuit. Chicago's NOVEMBER'S DOOM arrived in 1991 making an immediate impact with their combination of both male and female lead vocals and monolithic slabs of dirge driven Metal. NOVEMBER'S DOOM have supported the likes of OPETH, MOONSPELL, AMORPHIS, OBITUARY and LACUNA COIL as well as putting in numerous headline status gigs.
The band, coming together in 1989, had previously operated as Thrash Metal merchants LACERATION with a line-up of

vocalist Paul Kuhr III, former FULL METAL ELVIS guitarist Steve Nicholson, second vocalist Cathy Joh Henja and drummer Jim Dobleski. As LACERATION the band issued the opening demo 'The Way Of All Flesh', adopting a Death / Doom approach for a second demo session 'Scabs' and the subsequent 'Ripping Avulsion' 7" single. In 1991 the band adopted the title of NOVEMBER'S DOOM and set a strictly Doom course from that point on.
A deal with the Italian Regress label led in turn to the debut 1995 album 'Amid Its Hallowed Mirth' recorded for Avantgarde Music. At this stage NOVEMBER'S DOOM replaced Dobleski with new drummer Joe Hernandez.
NOVEMBER'S DOOM would attract a glut of press by drafting the sultry Mary Bielich on bass, a veteran of MASTER MECHANIC, Dana Duffey's MYTHIC, WORMHOLE and DERKETA. With this revised line-up NOVEMBER'S DOOM, retaining just Kuhr and Hejna from the debut, weighed in with the 1997 three track EP 'For Every Leafe That Falls'. Newly onboard would be guitarist Eric Burnley alongside Abbas Jaffary of EMBER manning the drum stool and additional guest guitar courtesy of Erik Kikke of AVERNUS.
Both Kuhr and Bielich would also participate in BROKEN HOPE guitarist Brian Griffin's side act EM SINFONIA.
Griffin would produce the 1998 outing 'Of Sculptured Ivy And Stone Flowers'. Session drums for this release were handled by Sascha Horn. Erik Kikke would also contribute his talents once more. Post release NOVEMBER'S DOOM enrolled ex-DEAD SERENADE guitarist Larry Roberts and drummer Joe Nunez. The latter was previously with NEUROTOXIN. The drummer was also involved with DEBRIS, the "Super-Doom" project of TROUBLE's Ron Holzner and ST. VITUS' Dave Chandler.
The 2000 roster of NOVEMBER'S DOOM for the album 'The Knowing', co-produced by the band and Chris Djuricec, saw the line-up stabilizing around Kuhr, Burnley, Roberts, Bielich and Nunez. Burnley would also involve himself as part of the spoof Black Metal band THOTH.
In April 2001 NOVEMBER'S DOOM put in a showing at the New England 'Hardcore & Metal' festival. Bielich would decamp though to join Pennsylvania Stoners PENANCE.
The debut 'Amid Its Hallowed Wrath' would be re-released through the Dark Symphonies label complete with extra tracks. Studio recordings later that year for the 2002 album 'To Welcome The Fade' issued by Dark Symphonies, with highly respected producer Neil Kernon at the helm, would see bass

duties in the capable hands of session recruits Brian Gordon of ION VEIN and famed TROUBLE four stringer Ron Holzner. The NOVEMBER'S DOOM line-up for 2002 stood at Paul Kuhr on vocals, guitarists Eric Burnley and Larry Roberts, AVERNUS and EVE OF MOURNING man Brian Whited on bass with Joe Nunez on drums.

Albums:
AMID ITS HALLOWED MIRTH, Avantgarde (1995)
Aurora's Garden / Amour Of The Harp / Tears Of The Beautiful / My Agony, My Extasy / Best Of My Desire / Chorus Of Jasmine / Dance Of The Laises / Sadness Rain
FOR EVERY LEAF THAT FALLS, (1997)
For Every Leaf That Falls / The Jealous Sun / Dawn Breaks
OF SCULPTURED IVY AND STONE FLOWERS, Martyr Music Group (1998)
With Rue And Fire / The Jealous Sun / Suffer The Red Dream / All The Beauty Twice Again / Reaping Forest Calm / For Every Leaf That Falls / Serenity Forgotten / Forever With Unopened Eye / Dawn Breaks
THE KNOWING, Dark Symphonies (2000)
Awaken / Harmony Divine / Shadows Of Light / Intervene / Silent Tomorrow / In Faith / Searching The Betrayal / Last God / In Memories Past / The Day I Return / Aura Blue / Silent Tomorrow (Dark edit)
TO WELCOME THE FADE, Dark Symphonies (2002)
Broken / Torn / Not The Strong / Dark Fields For Brilliance / If Forever / The Spirit Seed / The Lifeless Silhouette / Within My Flesh / Lost In A Day

Instrumentalisierung / Why I Need The Light / From Sorrow To Sun / Totentanz Im Blut / Wired Notes / Have You Ever Seen / Free Like Never Before

NOX MORTIS (GERMANY)

Founded in 1993 NOX MORTIS released the 'Epitaph' and 'Wald Der Angst' demos before recording their 1996 debut album.
A mixture of Darkwave and Metal, Prophecy Records were the label who showed the greatest interest in snapping up the group - whose keyboard player has been a church organist for eight years - for their album deal.

Albums:
IM SCHATTEN DES HASSES, Prophecy Productions PRO 002 (1996)
Intro / Im Schatten Des Hasses / Lost In Selfhate / Horizon Of Shadows / Castle Of Eternity / Choirs In Trance / Outro
7 LIES, Prophecy Productions PRO 014 (1999)
I`m Floating / Thoughts / In The Grey Of The Clouds / 3:31 pm / Parabel Chiflrierter

301

THE OBSESSED

(Washington DC, USA)
Line-Up: Wino (vocals / guitar),
Mark Laue (bass), Ed Gulli
(drums)

Cult Doom outfit centred upon the renowned figure of Wino (real name Scott Weinrich). THE OBSESSED, originally titled WARHORSE, were created in the early '80s. Formative live shows fronted by singer Vance Bokis, which had the band glammed up with make up and high heels, demonstrated the group's blend of influences well with covers of artists such as THE BEATLES and the SEX PISTOLS often being aired.

With Wino being joined by bassist Mark Laue and drummer Ed Gulli, replacing former sticksman Dave Williams, this unit released the now rare 'Sodden Jackyl' EP before Wino jumped ship to front SAINT VITUS replacing Scott Reagers. Wino would also anonymously perform bass duties for THE MENTORS in 1987. With Wino onboard SAINT VITUS released a series of classic Doom efforts such as 'Born Too Late' and 'Mournful Cries', finally bowing out with the 'Live' album.

German Doom label Hellhound issued a collection of archive tracks in 1990 prompting a re-formation of the band with Wino now being joined by ACID CLOWN bass player Danny Hood and ex-POISON 13, SCRATCH ACID and ACID CLOWN drummer Greg Rogers for 1992's 'Lunar Womb'. This record was cut for the German Doom aficionados Hellhound Music. Sadly Hood would later die in a motorbike accident. Subsequent European touring saw Hood replaced by ACROSS THE RIVER and DARKSIDE bassist Scott Reeder.

Such was the impact of the 'Lunar Womb' album THE OBSESSED were now recognized influence on the scene and the band were signed up to major label Columbia. Reeder decamped to Stoners KYUSS and his place was taken by former BEAVER, SCREAM and B.A.L.L. man Guy Pinhas for the 1994 'The Church Within' album. Promotion was accelerated for this release with support dates to WHITE ZOMBIE, an appearance at the 'Dynamo Open Air' festival in Holland and even video airings on MTV.

Wino featured in the ad hoc BULLRING BRUMMIES act that included BLACK SABBATH's bassist Geezer Butler and JUDAS PRIEST's vocalist Rob Halford contributing a track to the 'Nativity In Black' BLACK SABBATH tribute album.

With Columbia dropping the band THE OBSESSED struck out into indie territory once again, issuing the 'Altamont Nation' EP through Bongload Custom Records. Included in the grooves would be a rendition of GRAND FUNK RAILROAD's 'Inside Looking Out'. However, somewhat inevitably the band folded once again in 1995. Wino created SHINE, an act that soon evolved into SPIRIT CARAVAN with ex-WRETCHED bassist Dave Sherman and former IRON MAN and PENTAGRAM drummer Gary Isom. SPIRIT CARAVAN debuted in 1999 with the 'Dreamwheel' EP and full-length 'Jug Fulla Sun' album.

Pinhas and Rogers forged GOATSNAKE with erstwhile KID ENGINE guitarist Greg Anderson. Pinhas left this act (his temporary replacement being Scott Reeder!) to join ACID KING and FIREBALL MINISTRY, the latter act with former MEGADETH drummer Nick Menza.

The appropriately named Doom Records would keep hardcore fans of the band happy during the mid to late '90s with a welcome series of re-releases and rare archive recordings. 1999's 'Incarnate' album, issued by Southern Lord, is a collection of early demos and rare material. Included were an unreleased lead track 'Yen Sleep' and cover versions of GRAND FUNK RAILROAD's 'Inside Looking Out' and LYNYRD SKYNYRD's 'On The Hunt', the latter track featuring Dale Crover of THE MELVINS on drums.

The FOO FIGHTERS covered 'Iron & Stone' as a B side to their 2000 single 'Breakout'.

Singles/EPs:
Iron And Stone, Invictus (1983) ('Sodden Jackyl' EP)

Albums:
THE OBSESSED, Hellhound HELLCD 008 (1990)
Tombstone Highway / Way She Fly / Forever Midnight / Ground Out / Fear Child / Freedom / Red Disaster / Inner Turmoil / River Of Soul
LUNAR WOMB, Hellhound H 0015-2 (1992)
Brother Blue Steel / Bardo / Hiding Mask / Spew / Kachina / Jaded / Back To Zero / No Blame / No Mas / Endless Circles / Lunar Womb / Embryo
THE CHURCH WITHIN, Columbia 476504-2 (1994)
To Protect And To Serve / Field Of Hours / Streamlined / Blind Lightning / Neatz Brigade / World Apart / Skybone / Streetside / Climate Of Despair / Mourning / Touch Of Everything / Decimation / Living Rain
INCARNATE, Southern Lord (1999)
Yen Sleep / Concrete Cancer / Peckerwood Stomp / Inside Looking Out / Mental Kingdom / Sodden Jackal / Iron & Stone /

Indestroy / Streetside / Mourning / Spirit Caravan / Skybone / On The Hunt

OFFENSE (SPAIN)
Line-Up: Mariano (vocals / bass), Javi (guitar), Loren (guitar), Wensho (drums)

Spanish Death / Doom band OFFENSE were formed in 1990 by the trio of Javi, Loren and Wensho. They were soon joined by bassist Fede and vocalist Murgui and this line-up recorded the demos 'Basic' and 'The Cry'. 'Basic' went on to sell more than 1,200 copies.

Tragically, Fede perished in a cycling accident on the 14th December 1990 and this event not only prevented OFFENSE from rehearsing but led to the departure of Murgui. Once over the grief of losing their band mate OFFENSE recruited vocalist / bassist Mariano and the group later signed to Abstract Emotions and issued the 7" 'Shining Down' EP in 1995. An album was to follow

Singles/EPs:
Shining Down EP, Abstract Emotions (1995)

Albums:

ASIDE, Abstract Emotions AE 003 (1995)
Seating On Distress / Why? / The Defect / Law Of Life / Shining Dawn / Aside / Basic

OFFICIUM TRISTE (HOLLAND)
Line-Up: Pim (vocals), Gerard (guitar), Johan (guitar), Lawrence (bass), Martin (drums / keyboards)

Rotterdam's OFFICIUM TRISTE deal in labouring Gothic Doom. Drummer Martin and guitarist Johan had previously been members of RECRIMINATED, an act that dissolved in 1994. Founding OFFICIUM TRISTE with lead singer Pim and bass player Maarten the new grouping issued a three track demo the same year which attracted the attention of Fuck You Records. The band retired to the studio cutting tracks for a proposed release but nothing further was heard from Fuck You. Undaunted Pim set up his own label Weeping Willow and promptly issued the three track red vinyl EP 'Mountains Of Depressiveness' limited to just 500 copies.

Bass player Maarten would break ranks in 1995 being supplanted by Johan as OFFICIUM TRISTE signed to the Teutonic Existence label for their debut album 'Ne

OFFICIUM TRISTE

Vivam' issued in April 1997. OFFICIUM TRISTE would then forge an alliance with Californian Doom mongers COLD MOURNING, sharing a split single. Despite this practical progress the band collapsed in 1998. A farewell offering was made with the 'Roses On My Grave' release, the B side of which featured a rendition of 'Headstone' originally by British band CHORUS OF RUIN. Endeavouring to strive forward Martin, Johan and Pim created XI:LIX (11:59) enrolling Johan on guitar. This unit soon succumbed to a full OFFICIUM TRISTE reunion with new guitarist Johan originally involved. He would leave in April 2000 and the band reshuffled to accommodate new bass player Lawrence, a multi-talented individual who has credits as drummer with Black Metal band LIAR OF GOLGOTHA and as guitarist with Death Metal act DEATH SENTENCE.

2000 saw a re-release of debut 'Ne Vivam' on vinyl format by the Dutch Badger label. Meantime OFFICIUM TRISTE signed to Displeased Records for a new album.

Singles/EPs:
Officium Triste Part II / Mountains Of Depresiveness / Dreams Of Sorrow, Weeping Willow (1996) (7" red vinyl single. 500 copies)
Fading Like A Dying Candle / Downfall: Through Veils Of Grey, Weeping Willow (1998) (Split single with COLD MOURNING)
Roses On My Grave / Headstone, Weeping Willow (1998) (7" single)
Roses On My Grave / Pathway Of Broken Glass / Divinity, (2000) ('Promo 2000 CD single)

Albums:
NE VIVAM, Teutonic Existence (1997)
Frozen Tears / Lonesome / A Journey Through Woodlands Green / One With The Sea / Dreams Of Sorrow / Stardust / Psyche Nullification / The Happy Forest
THE PATHWAY, Displeased D00090 (2002)
Roses On My Grave / Pathway (Of Broken Glass) / Foul Play / Camouflage / Divinity / Deep Down / This Is Goodbye

OJM (ITALY)

Albums:
HEAVY, Beard Of Stars (2002)
The Sleeper / Revelations / You Come / T.V. Eye / Mix Up! / As I Know / Strange Dreams / Follow My Leader / Theorem

OLD MAN GLOOM (USA)
Line-Up: Aaron Turner (vocals / guitar), Nate Newton (guitar), Caleb Scofield (bass)

OLD MAN GLOOM include CONVERGE bassist Nate Newton on guitar, Caleb Scofield of CAVE IN on bass and ISIS frontman and owner of Doom specialist label Hydra Head Aaron Turner on vocals and guitar. The project arrived with a January 2000 record 'Meditations In B'. The two 2001 albums 'Seminar II: The Holy Rites of Primitivism Regressionism' and 'Seminar III: Zozobra', a single mammoth 27 minute track, were issued at the same time.

OLD MAN GLOOM debuted live in March of 2001 drafting sampler Luke Scarola for the occasion.

Albums:
MEDITATIONS IN B, Tortuga TR008 (1999)
Afraid Of / Flood I / Simian Alien Technology: Message Received / Sonic Wave Of Bees / Sonar Enlightenment Program / Rotten Primate / The Exploder Whale / Poisoner / An Evening At The Gentleman's Club For Apes / Vipers / Test Result: Alien Ape Distress Signal / Flood II / Resolving the De-Evolution Conflict
SEMINAR II: THE HOLY RITES OF PRIMITIVISM REGRESSIONISM, Tortuga TR013 (2001)
Brain Returns To Initial State / Bells Dark Above Our Heads / Branch Breaker / Radio Crackles Spill Down My Face / Hot Salvation / Breath Drops Out In Ice and Glass / Rape Athena / Roar Of The Forest Rose To Thunder / Clenched Tight In The Fist Of God / . . .Only Dogs Hear (Here) / Jaws Of The Lion / Smoke Out Loud / Deserts In Your Eyes / Meditation In B Parts V & VI / Cinders Of The Simian Psyche / Three Ring Ocean Sideshow
SEMINAR III: ZOZOBRA, Tortuga TR014 (2001)
Zozobra

ON THORNS I LAY (GREECE)
Line-Up: Steven (vocals), Chris (guitar / keyboards), Jim (bass), Fotis (drums)

Previously known as PHLEBOTOMY (and originally a trio with Steven handling drums as well as lead vocals) during this time they released the demo 'Beyond The Chaos' in March 1992 and the limited edition EP 'Dawn Of Grief'.

The band adopted the new title of ON THORNS I LAY at the same time they added drummer Fotis in February 1992. In early 1994, the group recorded the 'Voluptuous' demo, inciting interest from Holy Records. A deal would follow.

The sophomore effort 'Orama' was a concept album based on the legend of Atlantis.

Following a run of commendable albums for Holy Records ON THORNS I LAY switched to the Greek Black Lotus concern for the 'Angeldust' album.

Albums:

SOUNDS OF BEAUTIFUL EXPERIENCE, Holy HOLY12CD (1995)
Voluptuous Simplicity Of The Line / All Is Silent / A Sparrow Dances / Cleopatra / A Dreamer Can Touch The Sky / Rainy Days / Sunrise Of A New Age / One Thousand Times / Taxidi Nostalgias
ORAMA, Holy HOLY29CD (1997)
Atlantis I / The Songs Of The Sea / Oceans / In Heaven's Island / Atlantis II / Atlantis III / If I Could Fly / Aura / The Blue Dream
CRYSTAL TEARS, Holy (1999)
Crystal Tears / My Angel / Obsession / Crystal Tears II / Ophelia / Eden / Enigma / Midnight Falling / All Is Silent / Feelings
FUTURE NARCOTIC, Holy (2000)
Infinity / Future Narcotic / The Threat Of Seduction / Feel Her Lust / Love Can Be A Wave / Ethereal Blue / Heaven's Passenger / Desire / Back To That Enigma / The K Song
ANGELDUST, Black Lotus BLRCD 028 (2001)

Sick Screams / A Light In Paradise / Deep Thoughts / Angeldust / Moving Cities / Black Cold Nights / Independence / Neverending Hope

ON TRIAL (DENMARK)
Line-Up: Guf, Nikolaj, Morten (guitar), Henrik (guitar), Nikolaj (bass), Bo

Copenhagen Acid Rockers ON TRIAL, founded during the mid '80s, include personnel from BABY WOODROSE. Musically the band has been described as 'Psych-Stoner'. A Hard Rock album 'Like This…' for the Snogrock label was delivered in 1988 but is now discounted by the band as unrepresentative. The official debut album, 1995's 'S.K.U.N.K.' ('70 Kilometers Of Underwater Nothingness, Kaptain!'), was limited to just 500 copies.
Just upfront of the 2000 'New Day Rising' album a 10" EP of cover versions arrived which found ON TRAIL honouring their Acid Rock forefathers with renditions of the pre PENTAGRAM act MACABRE's 'Be Forewarned', THIRD BARDO's 'Five Years Ahead Of My Time, ROKY ERICKSON's 'I've Always Been Here Before', LOVE's 'Signed

OPERATOR GENERATOR
Photo : El Danno

305

DC' and 'Slip Inside This House' by the 13th FLOOR ELEVATORS.

Singles/EPs:
Be Forewarned / Five Years Ahead Of My Time / I've Always Been Here Before / Signed DC / Slip Inside This House, Delirium (2000) ('Head' EP)
Higher / That's Right, Bad Afro (2002)

Albums:
LIKE THIS..., Snogrock (1988)
70 KILOMETERS OF UNDERWATER NOTHINGNESS, KAPTAIN!, Omnium (1995)
HEAD ENTRANCE, (1997)
Indict Me / Lovecraft / Blood Butterfly / Slip Inside This House / Five Senses / Into The Void / Reasons - Outside The Door # 2
NEW DAY RISING, Delirium CD071 (2000)
Flashin' Ghast / As If / Pot Of Gold / Long Time Gone / Doubt / Cast It Aside / Sleeper / Do You See Her? / New Day Rising / Outside The Door
PSYCHEDELIK FREAKOUT PARTY, (2001)

OPERATOR GENERATOR (CA, USA)
Line-Up: Mitchell French (vocals), Thomas Choi (guitar), Joe Tucci (bass), Jon Mercer (drums)

Californian Stoners OPERATOR GENERATOR are fronted by MITCHELL FROOM, a man citing credits previously as bassist for IMPERIAL SPACE POD, DEAR DECEASED and CATS FROM CHAOS. Guitarist Thomas Choi was formerly with the pre-SLEEP act ASBESTOS DEATH.
The original incarnation of the band saw Anthony Lopez on drums and Froom handling bass until Joe Tucci took over the role. Following the 12th Planet eponymous three track EP Lopez was replaced by Michael Parkinson. A later addition to the drum stool found Jon Mercer occupying the position. OPERATOR GENERATOR undertook an extensive American tour alongside MEN OF PORN in the fall of 2001.
In May of 2002 Froom announced the formation of a side project TORCH THE VILLAGE in league with bassist Anthony Buhagiar of CANYON CREEP and a guitarist from WOODSHED.

Singles/EPs:
Arctic Quest / Infinite Loop / Equinox Planetarium, 12th Planet (2000) ('Operator Generator' EP)

Albums:
POLAR FLEET, Man's Ruin (2001)
Equinox Planetarium / Polar Fleet /

Museum's Flight / Atmosphere Insect - The Launch / Quaintance Of Natherack / Arctic Quest / Infinite Loop / Soil Of Lavamore

OPETH (SWEDEN)
Line-Up: Mikael Åkerfelt (vocals / guitar), Peter Lindgren (guitar), Martin Mendez (bass), Martin Lopez (drums)

Another in the long list of albums produced by EDGE OF SANITY's Dan Swanö. Vocalist / guitarist Mikael Åkerfelt and drummer Anders Nordin are ex-ERUPTION. Starting life influenced by the rawer Black Thrash acts OPETH have steadily matured into more melancholic landscapes with each successive release.
The late '80s act ERUPTION had featured Åkerfeldt, Nordin, guitarist Nick Döring and bassist Stephan Claesberg. When singer David Isberg's previous band OPET had floundered when the main mass of members split off to create CROWLEY the two parties combined to reforge the act subtly re-titled OPETH.
Second guitarist Andreas Dimeo was recruited for OPETH's debut gig supporting THERION. However, shortly after both Dimeo and Döring decamped quickly after. The former CRIMSON CAT duo of Kim Pettersson and Johan De Farfalla plugged the gap for a second show but the pair would also drift off and more significantly Isberg left for pastures new in LIERS IN WAIT.
Åkerfeldt took the lead vocal role as he rebuilt the band with Nordin and bassist Stephan Guteklint. Securing a deal with the British Candlelight Records label the debut album 'Orchid' was cut using previous member De Farfalla on session bass. Gigs followed including a British show alongside VED BUENS ENDE, HECATE ENTHRONED and IMPALED NAZARENE.
OPETH's second album was promoted with a support slot to MORBID ANGEL in the UK and to CRADLE OF FILTH in Europe. Following these dates both Nordin and De Farfalla made their exit
Akerfeldt teamed up with Swanö, KATATONIA's Blackheim and Jonas Renske to create side project BLOOD BATH in 2000. OPETH toured the UK in May of 2002 supported by ARCH ENEMY. Later that year the group revealed they were planning not one but two new Fredrik Nordström produced studio albums, a 'heavy' album to be mixed by erstwhile SABBAT guitarist Andy Sneap and a 'mellow' record mixed by PORCUPINE TREE frontman Steve Wilson.

Albums:

ORCHID, Candlelight CANDLE 010CD
(1995)
In Mist She Was Standing / Under The
Weeping Moon / Silhouette / Forest Of
October / The Twilight Is My Robe / Requiem
/ The Apostle In Triumph
MORNING RISE, Candlelight CANDLE 015
(1996)
Advert / The Night And The Silent Winter /
Nectar / Black Rose Immortal / To Bid You
Farewell
MY ARMS, YOUR HEARSE, Candlelight
CANDLE 025CD (1998)
Prologue / April Ethereal / When / Madrigal /
The Amen Corner / Demon Of The Fall /
Credence / Karma / Epilogue
STILL LIFE, Peaceville (1999)
The Moon / Godhands Lament / Benighted /
Moonlapse Vertigo / Face Of Melinda /
Serenity Painted Death / White Cluster
BLACKWATER PARK, Peaceville (2001)
The Leper Affinity / Bleak / Harvest / The
Drapery Falls / Dirge For November /
Funeral Portrait / Patterns In The Sky /
Blackwater Park

OPHTHALAMIA (SWEDEN)
Line-Up: Legion (vocals), It (guitar), Night
(bass), Winter (drums)

Black Doom. Formed by It (real name Tony
Särkää) in 1989 under the name of
LEVIATHAN, It was later to create
ABRUPTUM and VONDUR. Originally the
band was fronted by All but he would depart
prior to recording. The first album 'A Journey
In Darkness' would benefit from the
production skills of EDGE OF SANITY mentor
Dan Swanö and had guest lead vocals from
Shadow, in reality DISSECTION vocalist Jon
Nödtveidt.
Bass for OPTHALAMIA's 'Via Dolorosa'
album was supplied by Mourning (real name
Robert Ivarsson).
OPHTHALAMIA drummer Winter (real name
Benny Larsson) is also a member of EDGE
OF SANITY, GODSEND and PAN-THY-
MONIUM. Bassist Night (real name Emil
Nödtveidt) now plays with SWORDMASTER.
OPHTHALAMIA vocalist All - who also fronts
VONDUR - replaced Legion (real name Erik
Hagstedt) who quit to front premier Black
Metal Thrashers MARDUK. The new man on
the drums would be Bone, another member of
DISSECTION whilst Night took over bass but
would later shift to second guitar, allowing
Mist to cover the four string position.
With the apparent disappearance of It and the
jailing for murder of Shadow it seemed
OPHTHALAMIA's career was over but the
band re-emerged in 1998 for the 'Dominion'
album, a concept affair based on

Shakespeare's 'Macbeth'!
The other 1998 release 'A Long Journey' is in
fact a re-recording of the debut album with
extra tracks including a VENOM cover.

Albums:
A JOURNEY INTO DARKNESS, Avantgarde
AV003 (1994)
A Cry From The Halls Of Blood - Empire Of
Lost Dreams / Enter The Darkest Thoughts
Of The Chosen - Agonys Silent Paradise /
Journey In Darkness - Entering The Forest /
Shores Of Kaa-Ta-Nu - The Eternal Walk Pt
II / A Lonely Soul - Hymn To A Dream / Little
Child Of Light - Degradation Of Holyness /
Castle Of No Repair - Lies From A
Blackened Heart / This Is The Pain Called
Sorrow - To The Memory Of Me / I Summon
Thee Oh Father - Death Embrace Me
VIA DOLOROSA, Avantgarde AVR013
(1995)
Intro - Under Ophthalamian Skies / To The
Benighted / Black As Sin, Pale As Death /
Autumn Whispers / After A Releasing Death
/ Castle Of No Repair (Part II) / Slowly
Passing The Frostlands / A Winterlands Tear
/ Via Dolorosa / My Springnights Sacrifice /
Ophthalamia / The Eternal Walk (Part III) /
Nightfall Of Mother Earth / Summer Distress
/ Outro - Message To Those After Me /
Death Embrace Me (Part II) / A Lonely
Ceremony / The Eternal Walk / Deathcrush
TO ELISHA, Necroplis NR013 (1997)
A Cry From The Halls Of Blood - Empire Of
Lost Dreams (1991 demo) / A Lonely
Ceremony - The Eternal Walk (1990
rehearsal) / Journey In Darkness - Entering
The Forest (Rehearsal) / Castle Of No
Repair - From A Blackened Heart (1991
demo) / Shores Of Kaa Tu Nu - The Eternal
Walk Part II (1991 demo) / Nightfall Of
Mother Earth - Summer Distress (1994
rehearsal) / Enter The Darkest Thoughts Of
The Chosen - Agony's Silent Paradise (1992
version) / Deathcrush (Rehearsal) / Sacrifice
(Rehearsal) / I Summon Thee Father - Death
Embrace Me (1991 demo)
A LONG JOURNEY, Necropolis (1998)
A Cry From The Halls Of Blood - Empire Of
Lost Dreams / Enter The Darkest Thoughts
Of The Chosen - Agony's Silent Paradise /
Journey In Darkness - Entering The Forest /
Shores Of Kaa-Ta-Nu - The Eternal Walk
(Part II) / A Lonely Soul - Hymn To A Dream
/ Little Child Of Light - Degradation Of
Holyness / Castle Of No Repair - Lies From
A Blackened Heart / This Is The Pain Called
Sorrow - To The Memory Of Me / I Summon
Thee, Oh Father - Death Embrace Me
DOMINION, No Fashion NFR024 (1998)
Elishias Mistresses Gather / Time For War /
Final Hour Of Joy / Great Are The Deeds Of

Death / Eclipse Of Life (The Eternal Walk IV) / A Black Rainbow Rising (Castle Of No Repair III) / Dominion / Legacy Of The True (Death Embrace Me II)

ORANGE GOBLIN (UK)

Line-Up: Ben Ward (vocals), Joe Hoari (guitar), Pete O'Mally (guitar), Martin Millard (bass), Chris Turner (drums)

Supremely heavy to the point of inducing numbness, ORANGE GOBLIN have trod the path of the cult Stoner underground elite since their inception. Whilst going under the title of OUR HAUNTED KINGDOM, and featuring erstwhile Hardcore FABRIC drummer Chris Turner, this quintet of London based Psychedelic '70s inspired Doomsters were offered a deal by CATHEDRAL's Lee Dorrian to sign to his label Rise Above Records. Lee had caught just the one gig at the Devil's Church venue billed alongside ELECTRIC WIZARD and MOURN but it was enough to convince him of ORANGE GOBLIN's potential. The band duly debuted with a now extremely scarce split 7" single 'The Aquatic Fanatic' shared with ELECTRIC WIZARD. Various delays found the debut album 'Frequencies From Planet Ten' finally seeing a release in late 1997.

Drummer Chris Turner teamed up with ex-IRON MONKEY guitarist Dean Berry and ACRIMONY guitarist Stuart O'Hara for live gigs titled THE DUKES OF NOTHING.

During 1999 ORANGE GOBLIN committed their take on 'Black Shapes Of Doom' to the TROUBLE tribute album released by Freedom Records.

ORANGE GOBLIN would also cut a cover version of a track from the influential early '70s act LEAFHOUND for a split 7" single with ALABAMA THUNDER PUSSY in 2000. The band gained the prestigious opening slot to the May 2001 British ALICE COOPER / DIO dates.

ORANGE GOBLIN cut their 'Coup De Grace' album for a March 2002 release. It was produced by Scott Reeder of KYUSS and included a guest appearance from KYUSS / UNIDA vocalist John Garcia. For the album ORANGE GOBLIN cut a cover of the MISFITS 'We Bite'. Japanese variants came with the traditional extra track in 'Bad Blues' The video for the track 'Monkey Panic' was directed by ENTOMBED's Alex Hellid.

ORANGE GOBLIN arranged European tour dates in cahoots with ROADSAW commencing late February.

ORANGE GOBLIN would be confirmed for another round of American tour dates in May of 2002, acting as openers to old comrades ALABAMA THUNDER PUSSY. Guitarist Pete

O'Malley left the band in August, apparently to pursue a career in art.

Singles/EPs:
Freelance Fiend, Eccentric Man (2001) (Split single with ALABAMA THUNDERPUSSY)

Albums:
FREQUENCIES FROM PLANET TEN, Rise Above RISE 15 (1997)
The Astral Project (Class A) / Magic Carpet / Saruman's Wish / Song Of The Purple Mushroom Fish / Aquatic Fanatic / Lothlorian / Land Of Secret Dreams / Orange Goblin / Star Shaped Cloud
TIME TRAVELLING BLUES, Rise Above CDRISE 18 (1999)
Blue Snow / Solarisphere / Shine / The Man Who Invented Time / Diesel (Phunt) / Snail Hook / Nulear Guru / Lunarville 7, Airlock 3 / Time Travelling Blues
THE BIG BLACK, Rise Above CDRISE 25 (2000)
Scorpionica / Quincy The Pigboy / Hot Magic Red Planet / Cozmo Bozo / 298kg / Turbo Effalunt (Elephant) / King Of The Hornets / You'll Never Get To The Moon In That / Alco Fuel / The Big Black
COUP DE GRACE, The Music Cartel (2002)
Your World Will Hate This / Monkey Panic / Rage Of Angels / Made Of Rats / Whiskey Leech / Getting High On The Bad Times / Graviton / Red Web / Born With Big Hands / Jesus Beater / We Bite / Stinkin' O' Gin

ORA PRO NOBIS (RUSSIA)

Line-Up: Dmitry Grigoriev (vocals / guitar), Alexander Guljaev (guitar) Andrey Zimenkov (bass), Evgeniy Trefilov (drums)

St. Petersburg Progressive Doom. The band unit came together during 1994 and would adopt the title of ORA PRO NOBIS (Latin 'Pray For Us') a year later. The opening demo tape 'Doomed' would be very much in the Gothic-Doom style with violin provided by Anastasija Ivanova but by the 'Dedication' album the band had adopted a more basic approach.

Former AWESOME guitarist Pavel Botov sessioned on 'Dedication' whilst Natalia Pilipenko delivered backing vocals.

ORA PRO NOBIS, whilst centred upon frontman Dmitry Grigoriev, have been blighted by a series of line-up shuffles with guitarists Alexander Guljaev and Alexey Koscheev, violinist Anastasija Ivanova, bassist Andrey Zimenkov and keyboard player Andrey Konstantinov all being cited as erstwhile members.

Following the 1998 album 'Dreams Of The

Eternal' ORA PRO NOBIS underwent another radical overhaul of their line-up, inducting a new rhythm section of DEMARCH bassist Max Kuznetsov and drummer Ilya Safronov of Thrash band MOR.

Trefilov subsequently joined AZEROTH.

Albums:
DEDICATION, Metal Agen (1996)
DREAMS OF THE ETERNAL, Metal Agen (1998)

ORDEAL (ITALY)
Line-Up: Maurizio, Gabriele Santamaria (guitar)

ORDEAL is the guitar based venture of experimentalist dark Ambient duo Maurizio and guitarist Gabriele Santamaria. The pair also operate the ambient strains of ABIURA FATIMA and the Electronic act I BURN.

Albums:
MA/AN, Eibon ORD033 (2002)
An Xtraordinary Popular Delusion / Ma|an / 0 Number Needed To Treat / Graduale / One Haiku In Halfsleep / Waiting: One Empty Dish And A Dead Clock / Just The Same

Logic Aside / Season 2 / Amazon Phalanx 2.0

ORPHANAGE (HOLLAND)
Line-Up: Lex Vogelaar (vocals / guitar), Rosan van der Aa (vocals), George Oosthoek (vocals), Eric Hoogendoorn (bass), Guus Eikens (keyboards), Erwin Poldermann (drums)

Dutch outfit ORPHANAGE's driving force is guitarist/vocalist Lex Vogelaaar, a former member of TARGET. He initially recorded a trial demo with keyboard player Guus Eikens titled 'Morph', which led to the formation of ORPHANAGE.

This initial recording also utilized the services of CELESTIAL SEASON vocalists Jason Kohnen and Stefan Ruiters, together with PARALYSIS drummer Stephan van Haestregt.

As the project evolved into a permanent band ORPHANAGE added bassist Eric Hoogendoorn and vocalist Martine van Loon, although at the time she was still fronting THE GATHERING. In 1994 this line-up recorded the demo 'Druid', a tape that also featured the talents of THE GATHERING keyboardist

ORPHANAGE

Frank Boeijen.

Enrolling yet another vocalist in George Oosthek, ORPHANAGE contributed two tracks to the DFSA Records compilation album 'Paradise Of The Underground' prior to the departure of van Haestregt. A temporary replacement was found in GOREFEST's Ed Warby.

Drummer Erwin Polderman was recruited in time for the debut album 'Oblivion'. Vocalist Rosan van der Aa was eventually replaced by Martine van Loon.

Following the groundbreaking 1996 album 'By Time Alone' (a heady mix of Metal and Gregorian choirs) ORPHANAGE issued the 'At The Mountains Of Madness' EP co-produced by former VENGEANCE man Oscar Holleman. ORPHANAGE also put in a showing at the Dynamo festival in 1997.

In 1996 both Hoogendoorn and Poldermann founded a side project SILICON HEAD together with PLEURISY guitarist Axel Becker. SILICON HEAD's debut album 'Bash' was produced by Vogelaar.

Singles/EPs:
At The Mountains Of Madness (Video mix) / Five Crystals (Oscar mix) / The Crumbling Of My Denial (Live) / Sea Of Dreams (Live), Displeased DSFA 1008 (1997)

Albums:
OBLIVION, Displeased DSFA 1001 (1995) Chameleon / Weltschmerz / The Case Of Charles Dexter Ward / In The Garden Of Eden / Journey Into The Unknown / Druid / Veils of Blood / Sea Of Dreams / The Collector / Victim Of Fear
BY TIME ALONE, Displeased DSFA 1004 P (1996) At The Mountains Of Madness / Five Crystals / The Dark Side / Deceiver / Cliffs Of Moher / By Time Alone / Ancient Rhymes / Odyssey / Requiem / Leafless / Deliverance
INSIDE, Nuclear Blast NB 510-2 (2000) Grip / Twisted Games / Inside / The Stain / Pain / Deal With The Real / Behold / Weakness Of Flesh / Kick / Drag You Down / From The Cradle To The Grave

ORPHANED LAND (ISRAEL)

Line-Up: Kobi Farhi (vocals), Yossi Sassi (guitar), Matti Svatitzki (guitar), Uri Zelcha (bass), Sami Bachar (drums)

ORPHANED LAND purvey their own brand of what has been dubbed "Oriental Metal". The group was founded in 1991 under the original title of RESURRECTION switching to ORPHANED LAND the following year. The band line-up stood at vocalist Kobi Farhi, guitarists Yossi Sassi and Matti Svatitzki, bassist Uri Zelcha and drummer Sami Bachar.

As such the band guested for visiting international artists such as TIAMAT and CATHEDRAL. In 1993 the debut demo 'The Beloveds Cry' was issued immediately creating a media stir. So much so that Greek label Metal Invader would re-release the tape on CD format shortly after. The demo was reissued by Holy Records in 1994 and yet again by the MDMA label in 1999, giving the band the odd historical quirk of having their demo reissued three times by three labels!

ORPHANED LAND struck a deal with the French Holy Records organization for two albums opening proceedings with 1994's 'Sahara' which included reworkings of all four demo tracks. The lyrics of 'Sahara' dealt almost exclusively with religious based themes and/or adaptations of writing from various holy scriptures. The 1996 album 'El Norra Alila' also sold well across Europe prompting a fresh deal with the German Century Media label.

The band would also donate their version of 'Mercy' to the PARADISE LOST tribute 'As We Die For Paradise Lost'. In later years ORPHANED LAND underwent line-up fluctuations citing a roster of Farhi, Sassi, Zelcha, female vocalist Shlomit Levy and keyboard player Itzik Levy.

Albums:
SAHARA, Holy (1994) Sahara: The Sahara's Storm / Sahara: Blessed Be Thy Hate / Sahara: Ornaments Of Gold / Sahara: Aldiar Al Mukadisa - The Holy Land Of Israel / Seasons Unite / The Beloveds Cry / My Requiem / Orphaned Land - The Storm Still Rages Inside...
EL NORA ALILA, Holy HOLY18CD (1996) Find Your Self, Discover God / Like Fire To Water / The Truth Within / The Path Ahead, A Never Ending Way: The Path Ahead / The Path Ahead, A Never Ending Way: A Never Ending Way / Takasim / Thee By The Father I Pray / Flawless Belief / Joy / Whisper My Name When You Dream / Shir Hama'A lot / El Meod Na'Ala / Of Temptation Born / The Evil Urge / Shir Hashirim
THE BELOVED'S CRY, Raven Music (2000) Seasons Unite / Above You All / Pits Of Despair / The Beloved's Cry / My Requiem / Orphaned Land - The Storm Still Rages Inside

ORQUESTA DEL DESERTO (USA)

A somewhat mellow Desert Rock outing

iissued by a combination of Stoner elite. ORQUESTA DEL DESERTO, an intriguing mixture of Rock, Blues and Latin sounds - including the San Jacinto horn section, was led by Alfredo Hernandez of KYUSS, CHÉ and QUEENS OF THE STONE AGE infamy. Joining him would be GOATSNAKE and WOOL man Pete Stahl and Mario Lalli of FATSO JETSON and the DESERT SESSIONS.

Albums:
ORQUESTA DEL DESERTO, Meteor City (2002)
Shadow Stealing / After Blue / Waiting For That Star To Fall / Make Fun / Globalist Dreams / Mary Strange / From This View / Smooth Slim / Scorned Liver / Alicia's Song

OVERSOUL (Shaurea, OK, USA)
Line-Up: Dennis Cornelius (vocals / guitar), Chris Greenway (guitar), David Arnett (bass), Patric Barrett (drums)

Doom-laden OVERSOUL is the brainchild of veteran guitarist Dennis Cornelius, a man who has laid down a dirgeful delivery for acts such as MORTICIOUS, DARKOFAGUS, King Fowley of DECEASED's spoof Satanic Metallers DOOMSTONE and more reverentially REVELATION. Cornelius joined the Baltimore act in time for their third album '...Yet So Far' and participated in a legendary European tour in alliance with ST. VITUS and SOLITUDE AETURNUS.
With the break up of REVELATION Cornelius relocated to Oklahoma, soon forging a friendship with drummer Patric Barrett. The duo created COR issuing the 1998 'Memory Driven' demo. An album deal was secured with Brainticket Records after a name switch to OVERSOUL. However, the band's attempts at drafting a female bassist named Julie, who had never played bass before and was learning the songs at the rate of one a month, failed when it was decided the studio bass sound was so bad it necessitated a full re-recording.
SUBSANITY man David Arnett was enrolled to the four string position and shortly after his SUBSANITY band mate guitarist Chris Greenway boosted OVERSOUL to a quartet.

Albums:
SEVEN DAYS IN NOVEMBER, Brainticket (2000)
Games / Bee Sting / Forgive Me / Matters Of The Soul / Inner Dilemma / Sphere Of Unhappiness: i) Withdrawing From The World, ii) Fathernature, iii) Feel, iv) Sphere

OXIPLEGATZ (SWEDEN)

A one man Sci-Fi infused "Cyber Doom" undertaking by ex-AT THE GATES man Alf Svensson, contributing vocalists to the project included Uno Bjurling (vocalist with Svensson's Punk outfit ORAL), Håkan Bjurgvist and Sara Svensson.
Alf Svensson had originally formed GROTESQUE with Tomas Lindberg, Kristian Wahlin and Thomas Eriksson. The quartet released an EP entitled 'Incantation' before splitting due to personal differences.
While Wahlin proceeded to form LIERS IN WAIT, Svensson and Lindberg put AT THE GATES together, although Alf Svensson would ultimately choose to leave the group in order to pursue his other musical avenues.
The 1997 release, 'Worlds And Worlds', includes a track entitled 'Graveyard Dream' that was originally written in 1990 for GROTESQUE.

Albums:
FAIRYTALES, Fairytale FTCD 001 (1995)
Starseed / Fairytale / Northern Stars / His Time Has Come / I See It Now... / Dark Millenium (There Shall Never Be Another Dawn) / Conclusion / Lust For Life / Numb / Departure / Vision / Adrift / Oh No...
WORLDS AND WORLDS, Adipocere FTCD003 (1997)
Battle Of Species / First Contact - Conflict / Aftermath / Quest / Graveyard Dream / Usurpers / The End Is Nigh / Abandon Earth / Journey
SIDEREAL JOURNEY, (1999)
A Black Hole Is Swallowing The Sun / They Learned Of Its Existence / For Persistence / Bringer Of Obliteration / Into Nowhere / For Persistence / So It's Our Final Hour / The Light From The Perishing Sun / Ahead - The Universe! / No Longer Will We Be The Meek Ones / How Could We Ever Know / Head For That Star / As One Surveys This Ocean / The Londrive A Silent Vibration / Several Planet In Orbit / Enemies!? / Once More Proven - We Are Not Alone / Lightspeed - Flung Into Hyperspace / No Clue To Where This Jump Is Taking Them / Breathless / Turning Up The Power, Accelerating Again / This Time Passage Was Violent / Rings, Spread Like Rippled Water / They Stare Unblinking / Eternal Night / How Many Worlds / These Beings Failed And Perished / Ahead Once More / This Journey Has Taken Us / The Moon Was Land In Orbit / Can This Be What We Hope For / Teraform - Alter The Environment / And So One Day The Sleepers Awaken

PALE DIVINE
(Glen Mills, PA, USA)
Line-Up: Greg Diener (vocals / guitar), Jim Corl (bass), Darin McCloskey (drums)

PALE DIVINE combine traditional Metal, Psychedelia and a self-confessed reverence for Doom pioneers PENTAGRAM. The group first made their mark with a 1997 five track demo 'Crimson Tears'. A second session was recorded the following year but withheld after original bass player Jay Purnell decamped. PALE DIVINE inducted Jim Corl as substitute for live work before he too was to leave. Larry Stout of DOGMA HOLLOW was drawn into the fold for an appearance at the 'Stoner Hands Of Doom' festival this latest four stringer then relinquished his position. The return of Corl to the ranks brought some much needed stability.

Plans to issue a 7" single of PENTAGRAM's '20 Buck Spin' through Game Two Records evolved into a full-blown album deal. As it transpired PENTAGRAM's own Bobby Liebling was impressed enough to guest on the '20 Buck Spin' track. Liebling got so involved he even scores lyric credits and vocals to the previously instrumental close out track 'Dark Knight'.

PALE DIVINE

Albums:
THUNDER PERFECT MIND, Game Two GT-21 (2002)
Amplified / Magic Potion / Judas Wheel /

Pale Divine / Gods, Monsters & Men / Dream Flower / Star Child / Devil's Mark / 20 Buck Spin / Dark Knight

PALE FOREST (NORWAY)
Line-Up: Kristin Fjellseth (vocals), Tony Jørgensen (guitar), Jarle Hagen (guitar), Lars Magnus Jenssen (bass), Eyvind Brox (keyboards), Bernhard (drums)

A genre defying "dark Pop" band founded as PANGAEA during 1996 by guitarist Tony Jørgensen and bassist Lars Magnus Jenssen. As a drummer Jørgensen cited credits as a veteran of Punk act GOD SHAVE THE QUEEN, Industrial Metal band HYBRID MISSING and, MARY JANE and switching to guitar, Indie Rockers act FRUIT. Jenssen meantime had paid his dues with Death Metal band DEWY FIELD. Joining the duo would be former DISTORTION, MARY JANE and UNCLE MEAT guitarist Jarle Hagen, keyboard player Jan Petter Ringvold, ex-DEWY FIELD drummer Bernhard and finally vocalist Kristin Fjellseth.

Shortly after completion of the line-up PANGAEA evolved into PALE FOREST. Anders Byfuglkien temporarily took over the keyboard role until the teenage Eyvind Brox took the role in 1997. A subsequent demo soon landed a deal with the Voices Of Wonder label and PALE FOREST debuted with the 'Layer One' mini-album and follow up 'Transformation Hymns' album, both in 1998. Fjellseth would become involved with the Black Metal band CREST OF DARKNESS in 1999, appearing on 'The Ogress' album and 2000's 'Project Regeneration'. PALE FOREST themselves would issue their third product, the 'Of Machines And Men' album in February 2000.

The band would switch labels to the French Listenable concern for the 2001 opus 'Exit Mould'. The album would be licensed to North America through The End Records. Touring in Europe during early 2002 would see PALE FOREST as special guests of THE GATHERING.

Albums:
LAYER ONE, Voices Of Wonder VOW065 (1998)
Inside The Violence / Mother Cocoon / Pictureframe / Hurt Me
TRANSFORMATION HYMNS, Voices Of Wonder VOW066 (1998)
Once Again / Karma Violins / Puny Minds / Asylum Pyre / Nothing Left / Bedlam Friends / Layer One / Transformation Hymns / Remnant Song / Fading / Butterfly Clan
OF MACHINES AND MEN, Voices Of

PALE FOREST

Wonder VOW073CD (2000)
A Second Opinion / Part II / Prom Queen /
Redrum / Mooncycle / Becoming One /
Tristesse / Taller, Yet Smaller / Sound Of The
Machine / Mentally Deranged / We Have
Died
EXIT MOULD, Listenable (2001)
Stigmata / Exit Mould / Urban Walls / Orphan
Heart / Nine-Eight / Spiral / Revelation / A
Perspective On Certain Matters According To
X / The Pale Suit Of Drunkenness / Mr.
Trenchcoat / These Old Rags / Holy Summer
/ Mistaken Identity

PARADIGMA (NORWAY)
Line-Up: Tom Kvålsvoll (bass vocals / guitar),
Chris Eidskrem (tenor vocals / bass), Zilla
(soprano vocals / keyboards), Kjetil Hektoen
(drums)

A Norwegian Doom Metal band that debuted
with the 1993 demo 'As Autumn Dies'.
PARADIGMA's 'Skadi' EP includes a version
of the RUSH classic 'Witch Hunt'. Tom
Kvålsvoll, who also cites credits with
NOCTURNAL BREED (billed under the alias
'Tom Bombakill'), would add guest vocals to
noted British act ESOTERIC's
'Metaporphogenesis' EP and to the HAGALZ'
RUNEDANCE 'Volven' album.
Frontman Tom Erik Evensen would leave the
fold leaving Tom Kvålsvoll to assume the role.
Chris Eidskrem would switch over to guitar

with the bass position being taken over by
FUNERAL's Einar Fredriksen in 1997. K.V.
Lervag's place on drums would be taken by
Kjetil Hektoen. During October of 2001
keyboard player and soprano vocalist Zilla
would accompany Pagan Folk artist HAGALZ'
RUNEDANCE on their German tour
supporting SUBWAY TO SALLY.
Tom Kvålsvoll, would join DHG under the
stage name 'Thrawn' during March of 2002,
replacing Jens Ryland.

Singles/EPs:
Best Regards (Astral Version) / Half /
Witch Hunt / Agonized / Come Winter (The
Skadi Interpretation), Head Not Found HNF
021 (1996) ('Skadi' EP)

Albums:
MARE VERIS, Head Not Found HNF 008
(1995)
Come Winter / Best Regards / Inner
Chanting / One Away From Paradise / Sleep
/ The Shadow / Terra Mater / Journey's End /
When The Storm Comes Down

PARADISE LOST (UK)
Line-Up: Nick Holmes (vocals), Gregor
Mackintosh (guitar), Aaron Aedy (guitar),
Stephan Edmondson (bass), Lee Morris
(drums)

A Halifax Heavy Metal band in the traditional

313

PARADISE LOST
Photo : Paul Medlock

mould - although replete with Gothic overtones - PARADISE LOST started life as a Death Metal act and, since their inception in 1988, the group have gained a huge reputation in Europe, where all of their albums have sold strongly.

The band's first gig was secured by their debut demo given to Bradford's Frog and Toad pub. Proceeds from their second demo were used to finance their first two European gigs in Holland. Having debuted with 'Lost Paradise' on Peaceville Records in February of 1990 the group found themselves as part of the much vaunted "big three" new wave of Gothic Death Metal bands. As such PARADISE LOST led the charge ahead of rivals ANATHEMA and MY DYING BRIDE, both of which were also part of the Peaceville stable. March 1991's 'Gothic' album, also on Peaceville Records, secured the band chart placings across Europe - in particular Germany - before switching labels to Music For Nations.

With a new deal PARADISE LOST released the 'Shades Of God' album in 1992. Produced by Simon Effemy and including keyboards from Robert John Godfrey of THE ENID, it was a record which, by blending acoustic passages in with the more familiar harsh "deathness" of earlier works, was to pull the band out of the underground and into the realms of commercial success.

In 1993 undertook their first tour of America supporting MORBID ANGEL and KREATOR. In May 1994 the group appeared at the AEROSMITH headlined 'Rock Am Ring' festival in Germany to over 80,000 people. The 'Seals The Sense' interim EP, promoted by touring with SEPULTURA, maintained the band's momentum. By mid 1994 PARADISE LOST were outselling METALLICA in Germany, surely helped by the popularity of the 'Harmony Breaks' video, which secured a number 19 position in the national German video charts.

Having released the 'Icon' album in June of that year by the end of 1994 PARADISE LOST were already working on the follow-up, although they would part company with drummer Matt Archer. By Christmas, ex-MARSHALL LAW and LIFE man Lee Morris found himself on the drum stool.

The group performed British warm up dates in early 1995 under the guise of THE PAINLESS and would tour hard promoting the new record 'Draconian Times' putting in Australian dates and a headlining appearance at the Dynamo Festival in Holland for good measure. The album charted high in the UK and reinforced their reputation in Europe establishing PARADISE LOST as a major act. 'Draconian Times' would go on to sell an unprecedented amount for the band's genre, eclipsing the million sales mark.

PARADISE LOST would re-emerge in 1997 with a newly shorn look and a quite different

314

new album in 'One Second' that, despite notwithstanding any drop in heaviness, drew heavily on more diverse artists in the Gothic mould. Ironically, the album turned out to be the band's groundbreaking release.

Subsequent touring found the band concentrating on the European market, but British dates were slotted in during January 1998.

PARADISE LOST returned with the John Fryer produced 'Believe In Nothing' album in February of 2001. Japanese versions of the album, issued on the Toshiba EMI label, came complete with no less than three extra tracks namely 'Sway', 'Gone' and 'Waiting For God'. The band would tour Germany, where once more the band had achieved a high chart placing, co-headlining with Gothic veterans SISTERS OF MERCY. The same year noted German Gothic Rock act LOVE LIKE BLOOD covered 'True Belief' for their covers album 'Chronology Of A Love Affair'. In band downtime Lee Morris hooked up with his former MARSHALL LAW comrade vocalist Andy Pyke, EXCALIBUR and HARDWARE guitarist Paul Solynskyj and ex-SLAMMER guitarist Milo Zavenic, touting a METALLICA tribute band DAMAGE INC. for a tour of Holland.

PARADISE LOST announced the signature of a new label contract with the G.U.N. label in May of 2002, setting to work on a new record, provisionally entitled 'Deus' (subsequently switched to 'Symbol Of Life'), with producer Rhys Fulber. Early reports revealed the band had demoed cover versions of BRONSKI BEAT's Small Town Boy' (one in a long line of Gothic bands to have covered this track) and DEAD CAN DANCE's 'Xavier'.

Singles/EPs:
In Dub, Peaceville VILE19T (1990)
As I Die / Rape Of Virtue / Death Walks Behind You / Eternal (Live), Music For Nations KUT 150 (1993)
Ember's Fire / Sweetness / True Belief / Your Hand In Mine (Live), Music For Nations KUT 157 (1994) ('Seals The Sense' EP)
Gothic / Rotting Misery / Breeding Fear / The Painless, Peaceville VILE 41 (1994)
The Last Time / Walk Away / Masters Of Misrule / Laid To Waste, Music For Nations KUT 165 (1995) **60 UK**
Forever Failure / Another Desire / The Fear, Music For Nations KUT 169 (1995) **66 UK**
Just Say Words / How Soon Is Now? / Just Say Words (Album mix) / Cruel One, Music For Nations 12KUT 174 (1997) (12" single) **53 UK**
Just Say Words / Soul Courageous / Just Say Words (Album mix) / Cruel One, Music

For Nations CDKUT 174 (1997) (CD single)
Just Say Words / How Soon Is Now? / Just Say Words (Album mix) / Albino Flogged Black, Music For Nations CDXKUT 174 (1997) (CD single)
One Second / The Hour / Slave / One Second (Remix), Music For Nations (1998)

Albums:
LOST PARADISE, Peaceville VILE17 (1990)
Intro / Deadly Inner Sense / Paradise Lost / Our Saviour / Rotting Misery / Frozen Illusion / Breeding Fear / Lost Paradise
GOTHIC, Peaceville VILE26 (1991)
Gothic / Dead Emotion / Shattered / Rapture / Eternal / Falling Forever / Angel Tears / Silent / The Painless / Desolate
SHADES OF GOD, Music For Nations MFN 135(1992)
Mortals Watch The Day / Crying For Eternity / Embraced / Daylight Torn / Pity The Sadness / No Forgiveness / Your Hand In Mine / The Word Made Flesh / As I Die
ICON, Music For Nations MFN 152 (1994)
Embers Fire / Remembrance / Forging Sympathy / Joys Of The Emptiness / Dying Freedom / Widow / Colossal Rains / Weeping Words / Poison / True Belief / Shallow Seasons / Christendom / Deus Misereateur
DRACONIAN TIMES, Music For Nations MFN184 (1995) **16 UK**
Enchantment / Hallowed Land / The Last Time / Forever Failure / Once Solemn / Shadowkings / Elusive Cure / Yearn For Change / Shades Of God / Hands Of Reason / I See Your Face / Jaded
ONE SECOND, Music For Nations CDMFN 222 (1997) **21 FRANCE, 5 SWEDEN, 31 UK**
One Second/ Just Say Words/ Lydia/ Mercy / Soul Courageous / Another Day / The Sufferer / This Cold Life / Blood Of Another / Disappear / Sane / Take Me Down
REFLECTIONS, Music For Nations (1998)
Say Just Words / Hallowed Land / True Belief / Pity The Sadness / Eternal / Forever Failure (Remix) / Gothic / One Second / Rotting Misery (Remix) / Last Time / Mercy / Widow / Embers Fire / As I Die / Soul Courageous (Live) / Blood Of Another (Live) / As I Die (Live)
HOST, EMI (1999) **67 FRANCE, 19 SWEDEN, 61 UK**
So Much Is Lost / Nothing Sacred / In All Honesty / Harbour / Ordinary Days / It's Too Late / Permanent Solution / Behind The Grey / Wreck / Made The Same / Deep / Year Of Summer / Host
BELIEVE IN NOTHING, EMI (2001)
18 FINLAND, 49 FRANCE, 10 GERMANY, 43 SWEDEN

315

I Am Nothing / Mouth / Fader / Look At Me Now / Illumination / Something Real / Divided / Sell It To The World / Never Again / Control / No Reason / World Pretending

PARAGON OF BEAUTY (GERMANY)
Line-Up: Markus B. Monesol (vocals), Andreas Schuler (guitar), Oliver (guitar), Taisha (bass), Sol (drums)

Atmospheric ambient Darkwave Metal band PARAGON OF BEAUTY was created in May of 1994, completing the line-up in August of that year with the induction of female bassist Taisha. The band issued the 1996 demos 'Starwoven' and 'Snowfall Summerdream' upfront of a 1997 EP 'Wundenozean'.
PARAGON OF BEAUTY toured Europe alongside KATATONIA in 1998. The sophomore album 'Seraphine - Far Gone Gleam' closed with a cover version of the FISH track 'The Company'.
PARAGON OF BEAUTY folded during 2002, vocalist Markus B. Moesol and bassist Taisha founding SHIVERTRIP whilst other members subsequently creating a fresh band unit SOLIDLY SINGULAR.

Albums:
THE SPRING, Prophecy Productions PRO 009 (1998)
Wundenozean / Oh Dear Beloved Marblequeen / Among The Midnight Kings / Snowfall Summerdream / A Cosmos For A Lovestarved Child / Where The Nights Still Dance / Godbirds / Sunset Funeral
SERAPHINE - FAR GONE GLEAM, Prophecy Productions (2000)
To My Unfading Sorrow / After Vapours Have Oppressed Our Plains / Narrenjagd / Wie Ein Zartes Blatt Im Morgenwind / The Company / Lonesome
COMFORT ME INFINITY, Prophecy Productions (2001)
This Impossible Moment / One Step Into Nothingness / Yonder Thy Primrose Path, My Shuddered Face / Comfort Me, Infinity / A Drowning Day / About Glum Naiades And Idle Gods / How Futile It Seems To Sow / I Wished You Wouldn't Fall Silent

PARAMAECIUM (AUSTRALIA)
Line-Up: Andrew Tompkins (vocals / bass), Jason De Ron (guitar)

Highly respected Australian outfit PARAMAECIUM's first rumblings upon the international Doom scene came with the Death styled 'Silent Carnage' demo. PARAMAECIUM's 1994 debut, 'Exhumed Of The Earth' issued by the R.E.X. label was explicit in its lyrical narrative telling of the exploits of Christ leaving no doubt as to the band's spiritual bent. The line-up for this recording comprised Andrew Tompkins on vocals, guitarist Jason De Ron and MORTIFICATION drummer Jayson Sherlock. The evangelical theme carried over into the group's sophomore effort 'Within The Ancient Forest', this time the album theme being Tompkins' conversion to his faith. By this juncture Chris Burton had augmented PARAMAECIUM on second guitar.
A stopgap EP, 'Repentance', comprised tracks from the 'Silent Carnage' demo plus 1994 outtakes.
The 1999 album 'A Time To Mourn' features PARAMAECIUM as a trio of Tompkins, Mark Orr on drums and a guesting Ian Arkley of ASHEN MORTALITY and SEVENTH ANGEL. After a six year absence guitarist Jason De Ron rejoined the band in mid 2002.

Singles/EPs:
Repentance EP, (1997)

Albums:
EXHUMED OF THE EARTH, R.E.X. (1994)
The Birth And The Massacre Of The Innocents / Injudicial / The Killing / Untombed / The Voyage Of The Severed / Haemorrhage Of Hatred / Removed Of The Grave
WITHIN THE ANCIENT FOREST, (1995)
In Exordium / Song Of The Ancient / I Am Not Alive / The Grave, My Soul / Gone Is My Former Resolve / Of My Darkest Hour / Darkness Dies
A TIME TO MOURN, (1999)
A Moment / I'm Not To Blame / My Thoughts / Betrayed Again / Enter In Time / Live For The Day / Even The Walls / Unceasing

PARRACIDE (GERMANY)
Line-Up: Dirk Widmann (vocals), Patrick Hagmann (guitar), Oliver Irgang (guitar), Mario Bayer (bass), Michael Zeissl (keyboards), Marc Werner (drums)

A German, Gothic Death Metal act. The split album with EVEREVE had only 500 copies manufactured.

Albums:
PARRACIDE / EVEREVE, Parracide-Evereve (1995) (Split album with EVEREVE)
Depression / Lost / Absorbed Mind / TB / Endpoint

PAWNSHOP (NORWAY)
Line-Up: Kjell Undheim (vocals), B.K. Saestad (guitar), Gaute Tengesdal (bass), John Skatoy (drums)

Stavanger Stoners created by guitarist B.K. Aestad and bassist Gaute Tengesdal, both erstwhile members of TONES.

PENANCE (New Kensington, PA, USA)
Line-Up: Brian 'Butch' Balich (vocals), Terry Weston (guitar), Matt Tuite (guitar), Mary Bielich (bass), Mike Smail (drums)

Pennsylvania's PENANCE arrived on the scene with the 1990 'Living Truth' demo session. A Doom band of high repute PENANCE would nonetheless undergo a series of both line-up and label changes throughout their career. Debut album, 1992's 'The Road Less Travelled' was issued by Lee Dorrian of CATHEDRAL's Rise Above Records. At this juncture PENANCE comprised vocalist / guitarist Brian Lawrence Goodbread, guitar player Terry Weston, bassist Rich Freund and drummer Mick Smail. All four were previously with Thrash outfit DREAM DEATH. PENANCE would embark on European touring as guests to CATHEDRAL and SLEEP. Smail had also contributed drums for the CATHEDRAL album 'Forests Of Equilibrium'.

Lee Smith replaced Brian Lawrence and Frank Miller came in on bass guitar for the 'Parallel Corners' album, released by German label Century Media, in 1994.

A promotional EP recorded in 1998 'Bridges To Burn', which saw Brian L. Goodbread contributing session bass guitar, preceded 1999's self-financed 'Proving Ground', that witnessed addition of the band's third career vocalist Brian 'Butch' Balich and yet another bassist in Ron Leard. Lee Smith meantime

PENANCE
Photo : Derek Anderson

went on to join SALLY.

PENANCE kept up the recorded output with a very limited private pressing 'Turn For The Worse' EP. By September 2000 Weston, Smail and Balich had been joined by erstwhile MYTHIC, NOVEMBERS DOOM, WORMHOLE, MASTER MECHANIC, SUBMACHINE and EM SINFONIA bassist Mary Bielich and former WICKERMAN and MUSTACHE member Matt Tuite. This line-up cut the Chris Koslowski produced 'Alpha And Omega' record for Martyr Music Group. Ron Leard would later turn up in HUMBUCKER, debuting with the 'Mondo Electro' album.

Singles/EPs:
Bitter / Dead Already / Never Lost / Bleed You, Penance (1998) ('Bridges To Burn' EP)

Albums:
THE ROAD LESS TRAVELLED, Rise Above (1992)
The Unseen / A Wayfarer's Tale / If They Would Cut My Throat Out... / Misgivings / Soulrot / Not What It Seems / Penance
PARALLEL CORNERS, Century Media CD77077-2 (1994)
Words Not Deeds / Born to Suffer / Words To Live By / Destroyed By One / Crosses / Visions / Reflections / Monster I've Become
PROVING GROUND, Penance (1999)
Proving Ground / Cloudless / Transcending / Dead Already / Bitter / Pain / Never Lost / Cast In Grey / Bleed You / Circle #9 / Slipping...
ALPHA AND OMEGA, Martyr Music Group (2001)
Wizards Of Mind / New Machine / See The Light / Reaching / Eden Fallen

PENITENT (NORWAY)
Line-Up: Bernt Sunde (vocals), Karsten Hamre (keyboards)

Stavanger's PENITENT is centred on multi-instrumentalist and poet Beastus Rex (real name Karsten Hamre). Musically PENITENT roams the landscapes of Doom, Death and Black Metal threaded together with a unique strain of self-styled "theatrical madness". Drums are supplied by Azgoth, otherwise known as Asbjørn Log. The PENITENT project debuted with an eponymous 1995 demo upfront of the 'Melancholia' album, issued the following year by Cold Meat Industry. Such was the impact of 'Melancholia' that it was subsequently re-issued as both a vinyl picture disc and CD, the latter adding three bonus demo tracks.

In August of 1996 PENITENT signed to the Austrian Draenor Productions, this relationship bearing February 1997's 'The Beauty Of Pain' and the following year's 'As Life Fades Away', the latter heavily Baroque influenced work now minus Asbjørn Log leaving PENITENT effectively a solo venture. 1999's 'Roses By Chaos Spawned' featured guest session vocalists Ellen White and Mark Andrew Goldfine. A homage to Beethoven, 'Maestro Beethoven', led to PENITENT, now utilizing members of the band NOISEBOX, contributing a musical interpretation of William Blake's poem 'On Another's Sorrow' to a specially commissioned album.

Bernt Sunde, also known for his employment as keyboard player with FORLORN, was taken onboard as PENITENT lead vocalist during early 2000.

The compilation album 'Reflections Of Past Memories' was released by the Bulgarian Counter Attack Productions. PENITENT signed to the German Ars Metalli label for a projected 2001 release of the 'Songs Of Despair' album. However, after lengthy delays the band switched labels to the Italian Beyond Productions imprint, finally seeing 'Songs Of Despair' released in June of 2002. During this hiatus Bernt Sunde opted out of PENITENT during the December of 2001 to concentrate on his COGNOSCENTI endeavour and his membership of FORLORN.

Hamre also has concerns with side projects ARCANE ART, in alliance with Bernt E. Egeland, and VEILED ALLUSIONS.

Albums:
MELANCHOLIA, Cold Meat Industry CMI 39 (1996)
I Det Uendelige / Stille / Veien / The Dance Of Demons / The Undertaker / Possessive Thought / Det Sorte Tjern
THE BEAUTY OF PAIN, Draenor Productions DRP001 (1997)
Autumn Is The Beauty Of Pain / Black Is The Sun Shining / Into The Great Inferno / A Mournful Bridge Over A River Of Tears / Necropolis / My Secret Garden
AS LIFE FADES AWAY, Draenor Productions DPR003 (1998)
Entering The Gate / The Birth Of My Funeral / I Die And Become / The Shadow Of Sorrow / Into The Vast Eternity / A Last Temptation
ROSES BY CHAOS SPAWNED, Memento Mori (1999)
Voices In The Night / A Bleeding Heart Of Desire / In Mortal Fear (Life & Death Part I) / The Arcane Epitaph / Ancient Despair / In Mortal Darkness (Life & Death Part II) / The Endless Spheres
MAESTRO BEETHOVEN, Memento Mori (2000)
Moonlight Sonata / Für Elise / Coriolan Overture / Ode To Joy / Consecration of The

House / Symphony in E / The Creatures of Prometheus / Egmont Overture / Sonata in F Major

REFLECTIONS OF PAST MEMORIES, Counter Attack Productions (2000)
Fragments of My Past / The Black Lake / A Mournful Bridge Over A River of Tears / Into The Great Inferno / Necropolis / A Last Temptation / Entering The Gate / Into The Vast Eternity / Necropolis (OMS remix) / A Mournful Bridge Over A River Of Tears (Fragments mix) / Black Is The Sun Shining (Red Moon Instrumental Deconstruction)
SONGS OF DESPAIR, Beyond Productions (2002)
Despair / God And Country / The Test Of Time / Phantoms Of Lost Existence / A Gate To Past Times / Manifesto / Ancient Wisdom Of The Forest / At Feasts Full Of Warm Blood

PENTAGRAM (VA, USA)
Line-Up: Bobby Liebling (vocals), Victor Griffin (guitar), Martin Swaney (bass), Stuart Rose (drums)

One of the forerunners of Doom Metal PENTAGRAM, for so long an obscure cult act, were brought to attention by the new wave of Doom bands such as CATHEDRAL, many citing PENTAGRAM as a direct influence. The band, dating back to the early '70s, have been through numerous line-ups and many break ups. Notwithstanding this they have built up an enviable following.

The group, known as MACABRE at this time, released their first single, 'Be Forewarned', in 1972. The band included mainman Bobby Liebling, guitarist Vince McAllister, bassist Greg Mayne and drummer Geoff O'Keefe. Pre-PENTAGRAM both O'Keefe and Mayne had been operational in the band SPACE MEAT. This act enrolled Liebling as lead vocalist and re-billed themselves STONEBUNNY. With Liebling's departure the band reverted back to SPACE MEAT. Subsequently O'Keefe and Liebling would lay the foundation of PENTAGRAM.

This inaugural PENTAGRAM line-up also cut the 'Hurricane' single in 1973 and had added second guitarist Randy Palmer to the ranks in time to cut a promotional single in 1974 featuring a cover of the ROLLING STONES 'Under My Thumb'. Prior to Palmer officially joining the ranks of PENTAGRAM, circa 1973, he and PENTAGRAM's drummer Geoff

PENTAGRAM

319

O'Keefe and vocalist Bobby Liebling, together with mutual friend Mike Matthews committed some of Randy's compositions to tape. The project was billed as BEDEMON after a mispronunciation of two earlier title suggestions 'Behemoth' and 'Demon'. These initial sessions resulted in a three song demo comprising 'Child Of Darkness', 'Serpent Venom' and 'Frozen Fear'. The enthusiasm engendered by these tracks fired off further sessions which culminated in a whole album's worth of material. Two of these BEDEMON songs, 'Starlady' and 'Touch The Sky' would subsequently be utilized by PENTAGRAM.

Fate nearly intervened when, according to Liebling, KISS main men GENE SIMMONS and PAUL STANLEY, attended a rehearsal and offered to buy two PENTAGRAM compositions 'Hurricane' and 'Star Lady' for $10,000 each - provided they could be re-credited to Simmons / Stanley! Liebling apparently turned the offer down.

By 1976 Palmer had been replaced by Marty Iverson. Following Palmer's departure from PENTAGRAM he would reconvene with O'Keefe, Matthews and Liebling to cut further BEDEMON material during 1979. BEDEMON would evolve to find PENTAGRAM and GALACTIC 5 bassist Greg Mayne taking over from Matthews. BEDEMON, now with Palmer, O'Keefe, Mayne and guitarist Norman Lawson of SEX II, would still be recording material as late as 1986.

With the release of the 1978 'Livin' In A Ram's Head' single PENTAGRAM had undergone a drastic change with Liebling now joined by guitarists Richard Kueht and Paul Trowbridge, bassist Marty Swaney and drummer Joe Hasselvander.

However, PENTAGRAM split following the release of the single, although the band would become active again in 1981 (by pure coincidence on Halloween) when Liebling teamed up with Hasselvander again in DEATHROW, a band featuring guitarist Victor Griffin and erstwhile PENTAGRAM bassist Marty Swaney. By 1984, under pressure from fans, DEATHROW became PENTAGRAM. line-up recorded the band's first full-length album but Hasselvander (who recorded a solo album entitled 'Lady Killer' for Dutch East departed prior to its release) joined SIMMONDS, the band assembled by SAVOY BROWN man Kim Simmonds, in 1985. The drummer sessioned for BURNING STARR, then teamed up with British athletic rockers RAVEN. Hasselvander also appeared under the pseudonym of 'Matthew Hopkins' on the Thrash by DEVIL CHILDE which included members of VIRGIN STEELE.

Undeterred the band pulled in drummer Stuart Rose for recording of second album

'Day Of Reckoning'. After a series of live dates PENTAGRAM folded yet again in the summer of 1988. The band did resurface in 1989 but predictably folded shortly after. However, interest was renewed when English label Peaceville Records re-released both albums. Hasselvander was persuaded to opt out of RAVEN and Griffin and Swaney also returned.

Griffin had relocated to California founding PISTONHEAD with the illustrious Scott 'Wino' Weinrich of THE OBSSESSED and SAINT VITUS. Hasselvander was persuaded to opt out of RAVEN and Griffin and Swaney also returned.

Griffin and Hasselvander were lured to an arrangement with CATHEDRAL for European live work, lending a great degree of both interest and credibility to the British band at that juncture, but returned to resurrect PENTAGRAM to record the 'Be Forewarned' album which incidentally saw a reworking of PISTONHEAD's 'Too Late'. Dates in America saw headliners and supports to ACE FREHLEY.

During 1988 the independent Peace label issued a compilation of rare and unreleased PENTAGRAM material from the '70s, including tracks recorded with Marty Iverson on guitar. Griffin would break ranks again indulging in a self-confessed drink and drugs binge brought on by the deaths of family members. When he emerged from the other side of this purgatory Griffin had become a Christian, later creating the spiritually based Doom act PLACE OF SKULLS with ex-DEATHROW bassist Lee Abney.

1999 saw a return of the band for the 'Review Your Choices' album on the Italian Black Widow label. In a renewed period of activity PENTAGRAM, now featuring Dale Russell as live drummer, also laid down tracks for BLUE CHEER and CAPTAIN BEYOND tribute albums.

PENTAGRAM undertook reunion dates with Liebling, Griffin, Hasselvander and Lee Abney from PLACE OF SKULLS on bass.

Upon hearing of Doomsters PALE DIVINE's plans to cut a cover of '20 Buck Spin' for their debut 'Thunder Perfect Mind' album Bobby Liebling was impressed enough to guest on the track. Liebling got so involved he even scores lyric credits and vocals to the previously instrumental close out track 'Dark Knight'.

Singles/EPs:
Be Forewarned / Lazy Lady, Intermedia (1972) (As MACABRE)
Hurricane / Earth Flight, Buffo Socko (1973)
Under My Thumb / When The Screams Come, Test, Gemini (1973) (Band

Promotion)
Livin' In A Ram's Head / When The Screams Come, High Voltage (1979)
Relentless / Day Of Reckoning, Peaceville Collectors CC1 (1992)

Albums:
PENTAGRAM, Pentagram (1985)
Relentless / Sign Of The Wolf (Pentagram) / All Your Sins / Run My Course / Death Row / Dying World / The Ghoul / You're Lost, I'm Free / The Deist / Sinister / 20 Buck Spin
THE DAY OF RECKONING, Napalm (1987)
Day Of Reckoning / Broken Vows / Madman / When The Screams Come / Burning Saviour / Evil Seed / Wartime
PENTAGRAM, Peace PCE 005 (1988)
Hurricane / Be Forewarned / Under My Thumb / Earth Flight / Wheel Of Fortune / Walk In The Blue Light / Smokescreen / Star Lady / Little Games / Much Too Young To Know / Livin' In A Ram's Head
RELENTLESS, Peaceville (1993)
Death Row / All Your Sins / Sign Of The Wolf / The Ghoul / Relentless / Run My Course / Sinister / The Deist / You're Lost, I'm Free / Dying World / 20 Buck Spin
BE FOREWARNED, Peaceville VILE42CD (1994)
Live Free And Burn / Too Late / Ask No More / The World Will Love Again / Vampyre Love / Life Blood / Wolf's Blood / Frustration / Bride Of Evil / Nightmare Gown / Petrified / A Timeless Heart / Be Forewarned
HUMAN HURRICANE, Downtime Recordings (1998)
Forever My Queen / The Bees / Out Of Luck / Goddess / Target / Devil Child / Much Too Young To Know / If The Winds Would Change / The Diver / Rape / Livin' In A Ram's Head / Buzzsaw / Starlady / Show 'Em How / Downhill Slope / Hurricane / Burning Rays
REVIEW YOUR CHOICES, Black Widow BWRCD 031 (1999)
Burning Rays / Change Of Heart / Living In A Ram's Head / Gorgon's Slave / Review Your Choices / The Diver / The Bees / I Am Vengeance / Forever My Queen / Mow You Down / Downhill Slope / Megalomania / Gilla?
SUB BASEMENT, Black Widow (2001)
Blood Lust / Buzz Saw / Drive Me To The Grave / Sub Intro / Sub-Basement / Goin' In Circles "Reaching For An End" / Mad Dog / After The Last / Tidal Wave / Out Of Luck / Target
FIRST DAZE HERE (THE VINTAGE COLLECTION), Relapse RLP 6521 (2002)
Forever My Queen / When The Screams Come / Walk In The Blue Light / Starlady / Lazylady / Review Your Choices / Hurricane /

Livin' In A Ram's Head / Earth Flight / 20 Buck Spin / Be Forewarned / Last Days Here

PENUMBRA (FRANCE)
Line-Up: Krysten (vocals), Ohra (vocals), Jarlaath (vocals / oboe) / Neo (guitar), Dorian (guitar), Agon (bass), Zoltan (keyboards), Garlic (drums)

A Gothic Metal act out of France founded in 1996. PENUMBRA was created by vocalist / oboist Maxime (aka 'Jarlaath') and guitarist Michel (aka 'Dorian'), building the band up to a septet for a debut 1999 album 'Emanate' for the Serenades label. Previously the band, initially known as IMPERATORIA, had issued a 1997 demo which soon sold out of its 1,000 pressing. Band members were listed as Jarlaath, Dorian, second guitarist 'Neo' (real name Michel), keyboard player 'Zoltan' (Xavier), bassist 'Aldric' (Cedric), drummer 'Hekchen' (Gregory) and vocalists Medusa, Aramis and Scyllia. Despite healthy sales PENUMBRA would suffer a severe split in the ranks and would also break away from their label.
PENUMBRA rebuilt the band for a new deal with the Season Of Mist label and the April 2002 'The Last Bewitchment' album. New faces alongside surviving personnel Jarlaath, Dorian, Neo and Zoltan would include vocalists Krysten and Ohra, bassist Agon and a drummer named Garlic! The band would tour Holland alongside DYING TEARS upfront of French shows in April with WITHIN TEMPTATION.
The band parted ways with vocalist Ohra in late April of 2002.

Albums:
EMANATE, Serenades (1999)
Intro / Lycanthrope / New Scaring Senses / Bloody Experience / Falling Into My Soul / Turn Them Off / Doppelganger / Underwater Dream
THE LAST BEWITCHMENT, Season Of Mist SOM 062 (2002)
Neutral / Priestess Of My Dreams / The Last Bewitchment / Moaning On Earth / Insurrection / Testament / The Young Martyr / A Torrent Of Fears / Pie Jesu

PERSECUTION (GERMANY)
Line-Up: Stellen (vocals / bass), Sascha (guitar), Sebastian (guitar), Volker (keyboards), Flecky (drums)

Oelsnitz based Gothic Death Metal act founded in 1995. To date PERSECUTION have released three demo sessions, 1995's 'Wozu noch Lieden', 1998's 'First Vision' and

321

'Nightfall In Mind' in October 2000.

Drummer 'Flecky' also operates with another Gothic Metal outfit BLACK SWAN whilst keyboard player Volker also shares duties with ESCAPE FROM DIASPAR.

PHLEGETHON (FINLAND)
Line-Up: Jussi Nyblom (vocals / bass), Teemu Hannonen (guitar), Juha Tykkyläinen (guitar), Lasse Pyykkö (drums)

A Finnish Doom / Death Metal band. Drummer Lasse Pyykkö was later to be found as a member of SARNATH.

Albums:
FRESCO LUNGS, Witchunt WIHU 9208 (1992)
Stone Me / Without Tea Waters / 0-520 / Encapsulation Of The Ark Of The Covenant / Ornaments / The Golden Face

PILOTOS (SWEDEN)
Line-Up: Ivan (vocals / guitar), Nico (guitar), Jeppe (bass), Pek (drums)

Stoner "Riff Rock" band out of Gothenburg. Formed in 1999 PILOTOS include the former DE DEVIL members vocalist / guitarist Ivan and bassist Jeppe. PILOTOS debuted in December of 2000 with the self-financed 'Going To Hell' EP and subsequently featured a track on the 'Sacred Groove' compilation issued by the Mexican Monstruo De Gila label. A second four track EP, 'Pilotos', followed in July of 2001.

Singles/EPs:
One Two Vs. The Treatment / Crossfire / The New Deal / Going To Hell, Pilotos (2000) ('Going To Hell' EP)
Saved A Seat For You / It's Gonna Be OK / Be With You / Dead Serious Woman, Pilotos (2001) ('Pilotos' EP)

PLACE OF SKULLS (Knoxville, TN, SA)
Line-Up: Victor Griffin (vocals / guitar), Lee Abney (bass), Tim Tomaselli (drums)

PLACE OF SKULLS, named after the Biblical reference to Golgotha, are the spiritually motivated Doom act of the esteemed Victor Griffin, veteran of PENTAGRAM, CATHEDRAL and DEATHROW.

Griffin had broken away from PENTAGRAM in sad circumstances indulging in a self-imposed purgatory of drink and drugs after the shock of the death of family members. When he had finally got through this ordeal the guitarist, a newly found Christian, created PLACE OF SKULLS in early 2000. Bass player Lee Abney was a former colleague from DEATHROW days whilst drummer Tom Tomaselli was located after auditions.

PLACE OF SKULLS issued a three track demo to secure a deal with Man's Ruin Records. In July of 2002 the band would be joined on second guitar by the almost reverential figure of Scott Weinrich, better known as THE OBSESSED, ST. VITUS and SPIRIT CARAVAN frontman Wino. By August the 'Doom elite' quota of the band had been elevated even further with the addition of erstwhile TROUBLE bassist Ron Holzner.

Albums:
NAILED, Southern Lord (2002)
The Fall / Never Die / Don't Let Me Be Misunderstood / Feeling Of Dread... / ... / Love She Gave / Return / Song Of Solomon

PLASTER (USA)

Albums:
LONG WAY FROM EARTH, Lucid Haze (1999)
Jupiter's Moon / Bottom Of The Bag / Last Real Thing Alive / Forest Of Never / Friends Of The Toad / Colour From Outer Space / Tomorrow's Yesterday / Funky Car / Inside The Sky / Mushroom Flower
13013, Lucid Haze (2001)
Sympathy Generator / Haunted Sleep / You Were Wrong / The Mongrel / End Of The Line / Hallucination Orbit / Belly Of Mars / Waiting / Plastered Haunted Sleep / Out Of Mind / Hedgehog / F.P.U.O.

PLUTONIUM ORANGE (FINLAND)
Line-Up: Samuli Liekkinen (vocals / guitar), Juha Raivio (guitar), Antti Sjöblom (bass), Pasi Pasanen (drums)

Jyväskylä based, Metallic edged Stoners PLUTONIUM ORANGE were forged in early 2000 debuting with the 'Fruit Of The Doom' demo the same year. Previously drummer Pasiu Pasanen had been involved with Black Metal unit MORNINGSTAR and Death Metal band MURDER IN ART. Pasanen and guitarist Juha Raivio, another former MURDER IN ART man and previous to that with WATERFRONT WEIRDOS, also operate a Doom Metal band side venture. Raivio also features in EMBRAZE.

Singles/EPs:
Bring Out Your Dead / 13 Minutes Of Agony / Fruit Of The Doom, (2001) ('Volume' EP)

POD PEOPLE (AUSTRALIA)
Line-Up: Brad Nicholson (vocals), JJ (guitar),

POD PEOPLE

Mel Walker (guitar), DD (bass), Maggs (drums)

Unashamed Doomsters out of Canberra. The group's first recording line-up comprised vocalist Brad Nicholson, guitarists Paul and Ivan, bass player Dunc and drummer Adrian. POD PEOPLE would self-finance an opening 1995 EP before undergoing a traumatic upheaval which resulted in sole founding member Nicholson surviving to carry on the name. A new look Stoner-Doom band unit was formulated upon guitarist Mel Walker of PAGAN BABIES, second guitarist Josh, bassist Dave and ex-SLUG and PRECURSOR drummer Maggot 'Maggs' McFly.

This darker and heavier variant of POD PEOPLE offered up the 1998 EP 'Swinging Beef'. The media coverage afforded this release aided in gaining valuable support slots to visiting international acts such as ENTOMBED, BRUTAL TRUTH and CATHEDRAL. The group would also gain the honours of appearing at the 'Metal For The Brain' festival four years consecutively. Their spirit of self-industry was marked in 1999 with the issue of a further EP 'Soil', the opening track of which 'Goin' South' was selected for the 'Full Metal Racket' compilation album released by Triple J.

The band remained strangely quiet during 2001 for two reasons at the opposite end of the luck spectrum, drummer Maggs spending much of the year ill and undergoing surgery whilst Nicholson jetted around the world having won a globetrotting holiday as a competition prize. POD PEOPLE signed to High Beam Music for the inaugural full-length album 'Doom Saloon'.

Brad Nicholson and DD also operate as drummer and guitarist respectively for LOG. Josh is a full time member of the infamous BLOOD DUSTER and sessions on the ALCHEMIST 'Eve Of The War' album.

Singles/EPs:
Close / Naughty / Today / Dog / In My Way, (1995) ('Pod People' EP)
Woolly Mammoth / Modah / Sneaky / Spark / Lupton Swayles, (1998) ('Swinging Beef' EP)
Goin' South / Pommygranite / The Way / Rewind / Karmageddon / Swing, (1999) ('Soil' EP)

Albums:
DOOM SALOON, High Beam Music HBM012 (2002)
Filling The Void / The Missed / Roadblock / Hoovin' / Subterranean / Look Beneath / Ascend To Glamstonia / Testing The Waters / King Tide / Non Prophet

POEMA ARCANUS (CHILE)
Line-Up: Claudio Carrasco (vocals), Igor

Leiva (guitar), Claudio Botarro (bass), Michel (keyboards), Luis Moya (drums)

A Doom band out of Santiago forged during 1990 as a quartet of vocalist Claudio Carrasco, guitarist Igor Leiva, bassist Italo and drummer Alonso. POEMA ARCANUS would lose the original rhythm section over time with Claudio Botarro taking the bass position and Eduardo enrolling on drums. The band's first product was the 1995 'Underdeveloped' demo capitalized on by 'Innocent Shades' the following year. A live tape, featuring keyboard player and backing vocalist Roxanna, 'Southern Winds' emerged in 1998 upfront of the debut album for Picoroco Records 'Arcane XIII'. Assistance came in the recording studio from CRIMINAL guitarist Rodrigo Contreras.
In 1999 Luis Moya of fellow Doomsters ASEIDAD took over the drum mantle and Michel came in on keyboards.

Albums:
ARCANE XIII, Picoroco (1998)
Nocturnal Blossom / Latent Eclipse / Conummatum Est / Vastness / Essence / Female Poison / Timeless Sands / R'lyeh / Ensonacion / Isolation / Winds Of July / Desde El Umbral

POETRY (SPAIN)
Line-Up: Jaime (vocals), Begona (guitar), Julio (guitar), Javi (bass), Angel (drums)

Doom Metal band from Barcelona forged in 1995.

Albums:
CATHARSIS, Arise ARISE010 (1998)
De Onthology (Intro) / Enjoy This Moment / The Eagle Of The Reason / Decadence / The Other Edge / The Troubadour Of Sophia / Both Sides Of The Coin / Inspiration Are You / Expire

POTHEAD (Seattle, WA, USA)
Line-Up: Brad (vocals / guitar), Jeff Dope (bass), Sebastian Meyer (drums)

The native Seattle Stoner duo of vocalist / guitarist Brad and bassist Jeff Dope would wind up based in Berlin, Germany more out of luck than planning. The pair had intended to seek refuge in Amsterdam's more liberal European climes for their pot smoking Rock n' Roll habits but, by way of France and Spain, ended up in the old German capital.
The 1993 'USA!' album collected together formative demos, cut with the aid of a drum machine. POTHEAD had previously debuted

live in October of 1991. The pair would later add drummer Sebastian Meyer, embarking upon an industrious series of retro Rock n' Roll favoured albums. By the millennium POTHEAD had established their own Janitor label.

Albums:
USA!, (1993)
Mr. America / Penalize Me / Smokin' Hope / We Were Young / Planet Of The Apes / Diamond Love / Indecision / Burned / Mission Impossible / Garlic-Tipped Bullet / Tyrant / Naught / Angry Son / Rot / Gravel Road Woman / Salo / Child / Double Black
RUMELY OIL PULL TRACTOR, (1995)
New Horizon / The Ugly Duckling / Law Man / Dead Poet' s Society / Allison / Threshing Bee / Black War / Promised Land / Soon / My Religion / Fire / Hidden Fields / Idle Bellingham / Blue Nitrogen
DESSICATED SOUP, Goldrush (1995)
Desiccated Soup / I'm A Sinner Too / Never Want It Like That / Burnin' Blue Like Alcohol / Round & Round / Narcissus / Wild Mustang / I'll Confess / Funkenbus / Waiting For Luck / Could Not Deal / The Trouble With Pothood / Wanderers / Hurry
LEARN TO HYPNOTIZE, Slipdisc (1997)
Indian Song / The Magic lantern / Twisted Tomato / Learn To Hypnotize! / Saul / Stop / You Should Talk / Kite / Henry And Mabel / Madness / All Those Memories / Life To Death / Little Magnus / Weird Bird / Y-Road / Miracle
FAIRGROUND, Goldrush (1999)
Fairground / Spiritual Need / Police State / Brothers And Sisters / Chess / Music / Ichobad / Mary Jane / If You Wonder / No Nothin' / A King An Inch / California Day / Standing Alone / Understand
POT OF GOLD, Goldrush (2000)
Appreciate / The Man Won't Tell / Catch 22 / Year Of The Rat / We Know / Lose Your Mind / Lull Of Winter
BURNING BRIDGES, (2000)
The Neighbor / Valley Of Fire / My Own Shadow / Broken Glass / Fifty Years / Everlasting Gobstopper / Burning Bridges / Trillions / Like Of Men / Run
GRASSROOTS, Janitor (2001)
Let's Complete / Tiagiato / Rock The Border / New Chapter / Satisfied / Wild Weed / Deliverance / Damnation / Rose Garden / Dope Says Nope / Diamond / Rut / 2nd Fret / 4-3-Eighty-Two / Put It Inside / Victim / I Thought You Would / Someday / Festung

PROMETHEUS (SWEDEN)
Line-Up: Sharon Lind (vocals), Roger Johansson (vocals / guitar), Mattias Karlsson

(guitar), Joachim Forsberg (bass), Erik Nykvist (keyboards), Henrik Langmark (drums)

A Gothic Doom act founded by erstwhile NIGHTSHADE members vocalist bassist Joacim Forsberg, guitarists Andreas and Roger Johannson and drummer Henrik Langmark with the addition of female lead vocalist Jenny. The band took on the title of PROMETHEUS, so named after the Greek god that brought fire to mankind. With this line-up PROMETHEUS recorded an opening demo 'The Visionaire Extreme' during June of 2001. Line-up changes would then blight the band as Andreas decamped. In October keyboard player Erik Nykvist was inaugurated but by the following month Jenny had quit. The band added second guitarist Mattias Karlsson of SOUL DECAY in January of 2002 and a new singer, Sharon Lind, in March for recording of a second demo 'Angel Lies'.

Bassist Joachim Forsberg is also a member of OVERLORD whilst Roger Johansson operates with Black Speed Metal act MORTHIRIM. Langmark can be also found in the ranks of MORPHEUS.

PRONG (New York, NY, USA)
Line-Up: Tommy Victor (vocals / guitar), Mike Kirkland (bass), Ted Parsons (drums)

With their arrival New York's PRONG prompted much well deserved praise due to their avant-garde Hardcore approach. Founded by guitarist Tommy Victor, sound engineer for the legendary New York CBGB's club, ex-DAMAGE bassist Mike Kirkland and former SWANS drummer Ted Parsons.

The 'Prove You Wrong' album was produced by Mark Dodson although apparently not to the band's liking. Subsequent releases came with a Terry Date production credit. Following the album's release the band pulled in former FLOTSAM & JETSAM man Troy Gregory on bass. He would later decamp to found Psychedelic Rockers THE WITCHES.

The album of remixes 'Whose Fist Is It Anway' saw PRONG being joined by KILLING JOKE / MURDER INC. bassist Paul Raven and FOETUS man Jim Thirlwell.

PRONG gained the valuable opening position for PANTERA's 'Far Beyond Driven' American tour. The band even had time to form a makeshift pseudo-Death metal spoof band with PANTERA vocalist Phil Anselmo under the title of YETI.

The band drafted former SUFFER / DROWN bassist Rob Nicholson. However, PRONG folded when Victor joined DANZIG in 1996. Parsons teamed up with GODFLESH. Nicholson also teamed up with DANZIG in

1997 then journeyed onto WHITE ZOMBIE under the new guise of 'Blasko'. For live work PRONG pulled in STEEL PROPHET bassist Vince De Juan Dennis who returned to his parent act upon completion of touring.

Erstwhile PRONG members would announce a whole slew of activities during late 2001. Tommy Victor assembled a band project in alliance with drummer Dan Laudo and HALFORD and DIESEL MACHINE guitarist Pat Lachman. The rhythm section of Paul Raven and Ted Parsons spread their net wide touring as members of GODFLESH, recording with Parsons' former SWANS colleagues Norman Westberg and Algis Kizys as well as forming part of the reconstituted KILLING JOKE.

Not content with all this activity the bass player would also found a Los Angeles based side endeavour SOCIETY ONE in union with ex-WHITE ZOMBIE drummer Ivan DePrume. Parsons also had other cards up his sleeves, working with ex-MASTERS OF REALITY guitarist Brendan McNichol in Ambient duo DRONE and with the New York act TELEDUBGNOSIS.

PRONG re-formed in early 2002 for a short burst of American touring citing a line-up of Victor, DIESEL MACHINE guitarist Rich Gonzales, bass player Brian Perry and drummer Dan Laudo. However, Gonzales's conflicting schedules saw PRONG heading out onto the road as a trio before the swift induction of replacement Monte Pittman, an erstwhile live guitarist for MADONNA's 'Drowned World' tour. PRONG then cut a four track demo, making the track 'Initiation', written by HALFORD and DIESEL MACHINE guitarist Pat Lachman, available for internet download.

Meantime ex-drummer Ted Parsons, whilst announcing news of his own new ventures, would be vociferous in his condemnation of the revised version of PRONG. The ex-drummer revealed he was collaborating with former GODFLESH man Justin Broadrick in a venture entitled JESU and participating in new KILLING JOKE recordings. Further endeavours transpired as two projected albums credited to TELEDUBGNOSIS, one of remixes and the other of new material. Live dates for TELEDUBGNOSIS would see Parsons joined by Scotty Hard on guitar and Tony Maimone on bass.

The rejuvenated PRONG would guest for DANZIG on their summer American dates, supplanting Swedish Black Metal band MARDUK, denied access due to immigration problems. However, reports that PRONG themselves had been ejected from the tour before the Cincinnati, Ohio date, replaced by CHIMARIA, proved unfounded as the band later resumed their position.

During August PRONG signed to the Spanish Locomotive Music label. Their touring schedule for August would take in a one-off UK show at London's Camden Underworld and a showing at Belgium's 'Pukkelpop' festival upfront of launching a three week American headline tour commencing October 16th. PRONG would then return to European shores for a month's worth of gigs beginning on November 12th

Singles/EPs:
Third From The Sun (Extended version) / Third From The Sun / Mind The Gap, Spigot SPT 3 (1989)
Defiant / Decay / Senseless Abuse / In My View, Strange Fruit SFPSCD 078 (1990) ('Peel sessions' EP)
Snap Your Fingers, Snap Your Neck / Another Worldly Device / Prove You Wrong / Beg To Differ, Dragnet DRA 660062 (1994)

Albums:
PRIMITIVE ORIGINS, Spigot SPT1 (1986)
Disbelief / Watching / Cling To Life / Denial / Dreams Like That / In My Veins / Climate Control / Persecution
FORCE FED, Spigot SPT 2 (1988)
Freezer Burn / Forgery / Senseless Abuse / Primitive Origins / Aggravated Condition / The Coliseum / Decay / It's Been Decided / Force Fed / The Taming / Look Up At The Sun / Drainpipe / Third From The Sun / Mind Gap
BEG TO DIFFER, Epic 4663751 (1990)
For Dear Life / Steady Decline / Beg To Differ / Lost And Found / Your Fear / Take It In Hand / Intermenstrual D.S.B. / Right To Nothing / Prime Cut / Just The Same / Third From The Sun (Live)
PROVE YOU WRONG, Epic 4689452 (1991)
Irrelevant Thoughts / Unconditional / Positively Blind / Prove You Wrong / Hell If I Could / Pointless / Contradictions / Torn Between / Brainwave / Territorial Rites / Get A Grip (On Yourself) / Shouldn't Have Bothered / No Way To Deny It
WHOSE FIST IS IT ANYWAY, Epic 658000-2 (1992) **58 UK**
Prove You wrong (Fuzzbuster mix) / Hell If I Could / Get A Grip On Yourself / Irrelevant Thoughts (Safety mix) / Talk Talk (Xanax mix)
CLEANSING, Epic 474796-2 (1994) **71 UK**
Another Worldly Device / Whose Fist Is This Anyway / Snap Your Fingers, Snap Your Neck / Cut-Rate / Broken Peace / One Outnumbered / Out Of This Misery / No Question / Not Of This Earth / Home Rule / Sublime / Test

RUDE AWAKENING, Epic 483651-2 (1996)
Controller / Caprice / Unfortunately / Face Value / Avenue Of The Finest / Slicing / Without Hope / Mansruin / Innocence Gone / Dark Signs / Close The Door / Proud Division

THE PROPHECY (UK)
Line-Up: Matt Lawson (vocals), Greg O'Shea (guitar), Christian (guitar), Carlos (bass), John Bennett (drums)

A Northern 'Renaissance Doom' act that debuted with the demo 'Her Embrace, My Ruin'. Early members guitarist Will Castledine and bassist Berrin Bison Casey would decamp in 2001. THE PROPHECY made significant headway with their four track, self-financed EP 'To End All Hope'. Recording line up for this recording was vocalist Matt Lawson, Greg O'Shea handling guitar, bass and keyboards and drummer John Bennett. Violins would be delivered courtesy of Karen McCloud. After the EP's release THE PROPHECY added second guitarist Christian and former SEER'S TEAR bassist Carlos.

Singles/EPs:
To End All Hope EP, (2001)

PROPHET (FINLAND)
Line-Up: Aleksi Ahokas (vocals), Sami Koikkalainen (guitar), Seppo Nummela (guitar), Jape Nummenpaa (bass), Tea Dickman (keyboards), Pete Raatikainen (drums)

Gothic Metal band PROPHET is centred upon the diverse talents of Aleksi Ahokas, also known for his work with a multitude of bands such as DIABLERIE, RAPTURE, EXCELSIOR and SNOWGARDEN. The group emerged brandishing a 1997 demo tape 'The Sky Takes You Away' followed by a three track session 'Gone' in 1998. A single 'Miles Away' was delivered in 1999 upfront of a further promotion effort 'Death Becomes You' in 2000. A second single, the four track 'Broken Promise', paved the way for a fourth demo entitled 'Dirty' in 2001.

The February 2002 album 'Fragile Prologue' would, besides PROPHET band members guitarist Sami Koikkalainen and drummer Pete Raatikainen, also include a number of notable guests. Henri Urponpoika Sorvali aka 'Trollhorn' of FINNTROLL and MOONSORROW would donate keyboards, DENIGRATE guitarist Seppo Nummela added an "eighties style" guitar solo whilst DIABLERIE and TRIONES frontman Henri Villberg weighed in with "growl" vocals.

The band would later adopt the new title of FRAGILE HOLLOW so as to avoid confusion with the global plethora of acts all laying claim to the title PROPHET.

Both Ahokas and Koikkalainen, billed simply as 'Mr. A' and 'Mr. K' respectively, forged a fresh project with DENIGRATE's 'Mr. T' in mid 2002 entitled RAIN PAINT. This union signed to My Kingdom Music for a debut album provisionally billed as 'Nihil Nisi Mors'.

Albums:
FRAGILE PROLOGUE, Irond (2002)
2001: Broken Promise - I Don't Believe In Love / 2001: Broken Promise - Are We Through? / 2001: Broken Promise - I Kiss And Let You Die / 2001: Broken Promise - Broken Promise / 2000: Death Becomes You - Death Becomes You / 2000: Death Becomes You - Is Lust What We Are? / 2000: Death Becomes You - I Tried / 1999: Miles Away - Now I Die / 1999: Miles Away - As I Prove You My Lies / 1999: Miles Away - Gone / 1999: Miles Away - Miles Away

PSICORRAGIA (PERU)
Line-Up: Mario Romanet Rivas (vocals / bass), Marco Borra Ramírez (guitar), Alick González Mujica (guitar), Antonio Duncan Pérez (keyboards), Manuel Saavedra Chamolí (drums)

Melancholic and experimental Death Doom outfit established by vocalist / bassist Mario Romanet and dating to 1994. After numerous line-up shuffles, which featured guitarist Frame Milón along the way, the introduction of guitarist Alick González Mujica and pianist Antonio Duncan Pérez in 1997 afforded some stability, resulting in the 1998 six track demo session 'Otoño' ('Autumn') to which Víctor Degollar donated his skills on violin. Degollar would break away from the band and Erick Reynaga took over the role. However, when Reynaga also decamped PSICORRAGIA opted to forgo this instrument indefinitely and remain a quintet.

American Line Productions subsequently signed PSICORRAGIA for the 'La Pasión De Lo Mortal' album. Former member Victor Degollar aided on string parts for the recording.

Albums:
LA PASION DE LO MORTAL, American Line Recordings (2001)
Vagitus / Padecer Solamente / Otono / Nuestro Rio De Recuerdos / Estrofas A La Muerte / Amen / La Misma Historia / Aspid

PUDDY (CANADA)
Line-Up: Paulo Rizzo (vocals / guitar), Ronaldo Falasca (guitar), Ron Vaillancourt (guitar), Richard Frost (drums)

Albums:
SWEETSPOT, Puddy (2000)
I Gave You My Love, You Gave Me The Clap / Was It Nothing? / Silicones / Derek's Song / Potsie Doesn't Live Here Anymore / Down / Did You Drop Something? / J. Vs. The Dumptruck / Suck Test / Jaded / Scum / The Tale Of The Sleepy Air Traffic Controller / Barricade

PUNY HUMAN (USA)
Line-Up: Jim Starace (vocals), Josh Diamond (guitar), Jason Diamond (bass), Iann Robinson (drums)

PUNY HUMAN include erstwhile GREY members guitarist Josh Diamond and bassist Jason Diamond. Frontman Jim Starace was previously with SERE and NORMAN BATES & THE SHOWERHEADS. Drummer Iann Robinson is known for his VJ role on MTV.

Albums:
REVENGE IS EASY, Small Stone Recordings (2000)
Raze The Leghorn Bar / Goddess Of The Metal / Eating Cigarettes / Lefty Among The Leeches / Jesus Has My Leg / Stink Of Two Men / Spatial Interpolation / Jimbo The Hutt / Way Of The Intercepting Fist / Damone

PYOGENESIS (GERMANY)
Line-Up: Flo Schwarz (vocals / guitar), Tim Ellermann (guitar), Roman Schönsee (bass), Wolle (drums)

PYOGENESIS have evolved from their inception in 1990 as a basic Thrash outfit IMMORTAL HATE into an incarnation of the more creative extreme Doom-Death Metal bands before landing latterly into the realms of bleak Pop. Their first demo led to a deal with a Colombian record company on which label two EPs were released. Not satisfied with this arrangement, PYOGENESIS signed to French Black Metal label Osmose to release the 'Ignis Creatio' album, but found themselves lumped in with the predominantly Satanic acts on Osmose. Original drummer Pit was asked to leave following the album's release and was replaced by Wolle.

PYOGENESIS opened for ANATHEMA on their February 1994 European tour. Bassist Joe Proell was superseded by ex-DYSTROPHY man Roman Schönsee in early 1995.

PYOGENESIS made a clean break from their Metal roots in 1996, crossing over to more of an Indie Pop stance signalled by their 'Love Nation Sugarhead' mini-album. The record featured SKYCLAD vocalist Martin Walkyier on the track 'Female Drugthing'. The group toured Europe as support to Americans SOCIAL DISTORTION in early 1997.

Schönsee created THE DREAMSIDE then THE BLOODLINE for the 2000 album 'Opium Hearts'. Members of PYOGENESIS also operate the extreme Grindcore act GUT.

Schönsee would act as producer for the eponymous EP issued by Gothic Punks THE NERVES during 2002.

Singles/EPs:
Still Burn In Fire / Like Tears (In The Dust) / On Soulwings / Underneath Orion's Sword / Ignis Creatio, Osmose Productions OPCD013 (1993) ('Ignis Creatio' EP)
Through The Flames / In The End / Down / Lost In Revery, Nuclear Blast NB 106-2 (1993) ('Waves Of Erotasia' EP)
Silver Experience / Love Nation Sugarhead 3. Female Drugthing / So Called Sensation / The Zentury / Clones, Nuclear Blast NB 27361 62052 (1996) ('Love Nation Sugarhead' EP)
She Makes Me Wish I Had A Gun, Hamburg (2002)
I Feel Sexy / Every Day / Angels Welcome Us / You And Your Band / Punk Rock Is Her Life (Unplugged), Nuclear Blast (2002) ('I Feel Sexy Everyday' EP)

Albums:
SWEET X RATED NOTHINGS, Nuclear Blast NB113-2 (1994)
Intro / Fade Away / Sweet X Rated Nothings / It's On Me / I'll Search / Skykiss / These Roads / Golden Sins / Masquerade / Through The Flames / Extasis / Coming Home
TWINALEBLOOD, Nuclear Blast NB135 (1995)
Undead / Twinaleblood / Weeping Sun / Every Single Day / Abstract Life / Empty Space / Sinfeast / Those Churning Seas / Snakehole / Addiction Hole / God Complex / Supavenus / Bar Infernale / I'm Coming
UNPOP, Nuclear Blast (1996)
Blue Smiley's Plan / Get Up / Love Nation Sugarhead / Alternative Girl / Rhapsodie In E / Junkie On A Cloud / To Me / Cheapo Speakers / All The Pills / Silver Experience / My Style / Ton-Recycling / XXL Ego King / Lower All Your High Standards / Sehnsucht
MONO, OR WILL IT EVER BE THE WAY IT USED TO BE, Nuclear Blast (1999)
Fake It / Drive Me Down / She's The Bomb / You Push Me / Will It Ever Be / I Thought / Just Ironic / Would You Take / The Needs / My Saline Eyes / I Remember / I Spite Of It / Africa
(P) DIFFERENT SONGS IN DIFFERENT SOUNDS, Nuclear Blast (2000)
Empty Space / Every Single Day / These Roads / I Remember / Blue Smiley´s Plan / Rhapsodie In E / Just Ironic / Will It Ever Be / Silver Experience / Twinaleblood And Steel / Fade Away / Would You Take (DAB) / Would You Take (March 1999) / Son Of Fate / Love Nation Sugahead
SHE MAKES ME WISH I HAD A GUN, Hamburg (2002)
Intro / I Don't Know / Don't You Say Maybe / I Feel Sexy / Separate The Boys From Men / Everyday / She Cries / Lunacy / Punk Rock Is Her Life / The Pain Of Heartache / Sleep All Day - Rock The Night / Empathy / As You Wish / A Cross To Wear

QUEENS OF THE STONE AGE (USA)

Line-Up: Josh Homme (vocals / guitar), Nick Oliveri (bass), Alfredo Hernandez (drums)

Stoner Rock outfit assembled by members of the highly influential KYUSS. Founded by ex-KYUSS guitarist Josh Homme all members have also contributed to the 'Desert Sessions' albums, a collusion with members of FU MANCHU drummer Brant Bjork (another ex-KYUSS man) and ex-MONSTER MAGNET man John McBain.

Homme took time out in early 2000 to tour as guitarist for THE SCREAMING TREES.

The 2000 EP 'Feel Good Hits Of The Summer' featured cover versions of THE KINKS 'Everybody's Gonna Be Happy' and 'Who'll Be The Next In Line' with ROMEO VOID's 'Never Say Never'. The DESERT SESSIONS track 'Monster In My Parasol', co-written by Josh Homme and FATSO JETSON's Mario Lalli - originally found on 'Desert Sessions Volume IV: Hard Walls And Little Trips', would reappear in a new guise recorded by the QUEENS OF THE STONE AGE for their 2000 album 'Rated R'. Limited edition European versions, re-dubbed 'Rated X', boasted new cover art and a bonus track 'Clarissa'.

The Group toured Europe in late 2000 with support acts MONSTER MAGNET and SNAKE RIVER CONSPIRACY. For the band's 2001 European dates they were joined by erstwhile SCREAMING TREES man MARK LANEGAN. Originally intended as a short term liaison it appeared that Lanagen had joined the band on a semi-permanent basis.

The band cut a new album 'Songs For The Deaf' throughout the fall of 2001 utilizing the talents of NIRVANA and FOO FIGHTERS man Dave Grohl as a session drummer. However, they would be joined by FU MANCHU's BRANT BJORK, another KYUSS campaigner, by that November. Also sitting in on the album sessions would be A PERFECT CIRCLE bassist Paz Lenchantin and WEEN's Gene Ween. Dave Grohl would be back in the picture too, performing on drums at a one-off show at The Troubadour in West Hollywood on March 7th.

During early 2002 the QUEENS OF THE STONE AGE pairing of Josh Homme and Nick Oliveri in union with AMEN's Casey

QUEENS OF THE STONE AGE
Photo : El Danno

329

QUEENS OF THE STONE AGE
Photo : Michael Schmelling

Chaos and Shannon Larkin embarked on a less than expected diversion with the band project THE EAGLES OF DEATH METAL. Initially titled HEAD BAND upon initial press releases, this unit would issue the album 'Peace Love And Death Metal' through Homme's own Rekords label. Oliveri was also discovered to be working on a new album with another project, MONDO GENERATOR.

QUEENS OF THE STONE AGE commenced touring to promote 'Songs For The Deaf' in Atlanta on May 27th. The touring line-up saw Dave Grohl on drums although both parties were stressing the temporary nature of this arrangement, the FOO FIGHTERS man's last show being July 28th at the Fuji Rock Festival in Nigata, Japan. Another high profile figure, A PERFECT CIRCLE's Troy Van Leeuwen would later be added to the live line up. UK shows brought about a strange twist when an organized group booking of deaf people, confused by posters advertised with the current album title, turned up to a concert in Hull. The band would resume headlining dates in North America in Washington DC on August 30th apparently utilizing the services of drummer Kelli Scott of BLINKER THE STAR and SPOOKEY RUBEN. However, within days of this announcement it transpired that it would in actual fact be former DANZIG drummer Joey Castillo who had landed the position. QUEENS OF THE STONE AGE would be supported by AND YOU WILL KNOW US BY THE TRAIL OF THE DEAD for this run of shows.

Homme and Oliveri would also make time, working with RAGE AGAINST THE MACHINE drummer Brad Wilk, to pen five songs for use in the movie soundtrack to the Jodie Foster film 'The Dangerous Lives Of Altar Boys'. Nick Oliveri made his presence felt on the HENRY ROLLINS assembled 'West Memphis Three' benefit album 'Rise Above', lending lead vocals to a version of BLACK FLAG's 'Jealous Again'.

Singles/EPs:
The Lost Art Of Keeping A Secret, (2000)
Feel Good Hits Of The Summer / You're So Vague / Never Say Never / Who'll Be Next In Line / Feel Good Hit Of The Summer (Video), Interscope (2000)

Albums:
QUEENS OF THE STONE AGE, Man's Ruin MR151 (1998)
Regular John / Avon / If Only / Walkin' On The Sidewalks / You Would Know / How To Handle A Rope / Mexicola / Hispanic Impressions / You Can't Quit Me Baby / Give The Mule What He Wants / I Was A Teenage Hand Model
RATED R, Motor Music (2000)
Feel Good Hit Of The Summer / The Lost Art Of Keeping A Secret / Leg Of Lamb / Auto Pilot / Better Living Through Chemistry /

Monsters In The Parasol / Quick And To The Pointless / In The Fade / Tension Head / Lightning Song / I Think I Lost My Headache
SONGS FOR THE DEAF, Interscope (2002)
Six Shooter / No One Knows / First It Giveth / Song For The Dead / Sky Is Falling / Millionaire / Hanging Tree / Go With The Flow / I'm Gonna Leave You / Do It Again / God Is Radio / Mosquito Song / Song For The Deaf

THE QUILL (SWEDEN)

Line-Up: Magnus Ekvall (vocals), Christian Carlsson (guitar), Roger Nilsson (bass), George Atlagic (drums)

Beginning life as QUIL this Swedish, Blues based Stoner infused Rock outfit was created in the early '90s with a line-up of lead vocalist Magnus Ekwall, guitarist Christian Carlsson, keyboard player Anders Haglund, drummer George Atlagic and original bassist Peter Holm. With Holm's departure Roger Nilsson stepped in as new bassist toward the close of 1993. THE QUILL then got to grips with recording a debut album, laid down in a three week session at Berno Studios in Malmo. The record was picked up by Dave Constable's Megarock concern for release in March of 1995, promoted with a video shot for the lead track 'Jet Of Water'. Live work included a round of domestic dates with ABSTRAKT ALGEBRA and a showing at the BLACK SABBATH headlined Karlshamm festival.

German dates were booked but then pulled and following further Swedish festival dates THE QUILL busied themselves on a new album. However, in June of 1997 Haglund opted out, THE QUILL deciding to persevere minus a keyboard player.

Initial recording sessions, utilizing the same studio as the debut, would be capitalized on by a second period in which extra tracks were recorded. Amongst these would be versions of TROUBLE's 'A Sinner's Fame' and BLACK SABBATH's 'Fairies Wear Boots'. The former appeared on the tribute album 'Bastards Will Pay' whilst the latter is included on the 1999 'Evermore' EP. 1998 would be rounded off by Scandinavian dates sharing stages with BULLHORN.

The following year THE QUILL appeared at the prestigious 'Sweden Rocks' festival as part of a billing which included DIO, DEEP PURPLE, CAPTAIN BEYOND and MOTÖRHEAD. Roger Nilsson loaned himself out to prestigious Thrash act ARCH ENEMY for North American tour dates in January of 2000.

The 2000 reissued version of the eponymous debut album, licensed for Meteor City for the North American market and clad in all new artwork, added a cover version of the mighty TROUBLE's 'A Sinner's Fame'. THE QUILL drummer George Atlagic would stand in as a temporary replacement on FIREBIRD's 2001 European tour. Roger Nilsson would get in on the extracurricular action too contributing in the studio to a new SPIRITUAL BEGARS album.

Japanese variants of the 2002 'Voodoo Caravan' album, released by the JVC Victor label, added two exclusive tracks in 'Gather Round The Sun' and 'Thousand Years'. June found THE QUILL embarking upon a short headline tour of Holland.

THE QUILL have made numerous contributions to various tribute albums. Included amongst these are 'Where Eagles Dare' donated to Meteor City's 'Slave To The Power' IRON MAIDEN homage, 'Frozen Over' on the CAPTAIN BEYOND 'A Thousand Days Of Yesterday' tribute, 'S.O.S.' to Small Stone Recording's 'Right In The Nuts' AEROSMITH collection and NOVEMBER's 'Mount Everest' on the 'Power From The North' Swedish Metal album. An unreleased track from the 'Silver Haze' album sessions 'Unbroken' is included on the Underdogma compilation 'Judge Not'.

In June of 2002 both Nilsson and Atlagic would team up with FIREBIRD.

Singles/EPs:
Evermore / Fairies Wear Boots / Sparrow / Silver Haze, (1999) ('Evermore' EP)

Albums:
THE QUILL, Megarock MRRCD023 (1995)
Jet Of Water / Dry / Lodestar / Homespun / From Where I Am / The Flood / In My Shed / Gleam / Not A Single Soul / In The Sunlight I Drown / I Lost A World Today / Sweetly
SILVER HAZE, RX 9651-2 (1999)
Evermore / Grand Canyon / Freedom Mountain / Under A Wow / Stirring Times Ahead / Mercury / Into The Volcano (I Fly) / Universal Treehouse / Who's Cryin' / Aeroplane / Rockets Collide
THE QUILL, Meteor City MCY 008 (2000) (USA release)
Dry / Homespun / Lodestar / From Where I Am / The Flood / In My Shed / A Sinner's Fame / Not A Single Soul / In the Sunlight I Drown / I Lost A World Today / Sweetly
VOODOO CARAVAN, SPV 085-72572 (2002)
Voodoo Caravan / Sell No Soul / Shapes of Afterlife / Until Earth Is Bitter Gone / (Wade Across) The Mighty River / Save Me / Hole in My Head / Overlord / Travel Without Moving / Drifting / Virgo

QUINTAINE AMERICANA
(Boston, MA, USA)
Line-Up: Robert E. Dixon (vocals / guitar),
Marc Upton Schleicher (bass), Jason
Beaugard King (drums)

Bottom end, bellicose Boston "Heavy
Southern" trio QUINTAINE AMERICANA
made an initial impact with the Bill Miller
produced June 1996 debut 'Needles'. Bassist
Marc Upton Schleicher cites credits with
GRIND, KEV-O-MATIC and CRACKTORCH
whilst drummer Jason Beaugard King has
featured in Industrial Sludgers KINGS OF
FEEDBACK.
QUINTAINE AMERICAN added guitarist
Peter Wendell Valle for the September 2002
offering 'Dark Thirty', produced by the
esteemed pairing of Andrew Schneider and
Mudrock.

Albums:
NEEDLES, Cherry Disc (1996)
Aunt Ruth / Waitress At Bills / Retarded
Whore / Round 'Em Up / Sioux City / The
Rifleman / I'm Sorry / Caught Fly / Sioux City
/ The Faces Don't Look Right
DECADE OF THE BRAIN, (1998)
Black Car / ...And They Were Drinkin' /
Lucky Town, You Are No Longer Safe / Old
Tricks Again / This Ain't No Saturday Night /
Jean's Greens / Shakes / Swan Dive Into A
Lake Of Fire / Burn / Feeling Good Mentally,
A Little Shaky Physically
THE DEVIL WENT DOWN TO MISSISSIPPI,
Curve Of The Earth (2000)
Hogs / Set Me On Fire / Wash / (Scott Kahn
Owes Me) $350 / I Don't Love Nothin' / Delta
Blue
DARK THIRTY, (2002)

QUITTER (Boston, MA, USA)
Line-Up: Hari Hassin (vocals), Ian Ross
(guitar), Bob Maloney (bass), Craig Riggs
(drums)

Boston's QUITTER comprise three refugees
from the esteemed ROADSAW with former
drummer Hari Hassin taking on lead vocals
and ROADSAW's frontman Craig Riggs
stepping behind the drum kit. Bass player Bob
Maloney is known as guitarist for MILLIGRAM
and NEBULA.

Albums:
QUITTER, Tortuga Recordings (2002)
Intro / Black Box / Tear You Down / Blind /
Midtro / Fool's Gold / Mobity Mosely /
Whiskey Chixx (Demo)

RAGING SLAB (USA)
Line-Up: Greg 'Jagory Slab' Strzempka (vocals / guitar), Elyse Steinman (guitar), Mark Middleton (guitar), Alec Morton (bass), Bob Pantella (drums)

RAGING SLAB were one of the very first acts unafraid to blend Southern Boogie with Punk and Metal. RAGING SLAB were formed in 1983 by vocalist / guitarist Greg Strzempka after he moved to New York's lower East side from Washington D.C., although he was originally from Western Pennsylvania.

The initial RAGING SLAB formation found Strzempka joined by slide guitarist Elyse Steinman, second guitarist Dimitri Brill (better known as DJ Dimitri from Pop act DEEE-LITE) and drummer Kory Clarke. The latter of course would subsequently go onto to famously front WARRIOR SOUL. This first version of the band cut their teeth with an inaugural gig at the renowned Lower East Side venue 8-BC.

RAGING SLAB debuted in 1986 with the 'Slabbage' album. The 'Assmaster' album on Buy Our Records followed. The album came complete with a comic book penned by Marvel Comics artist Pat Redding detailing the exploits of the band-created 'Assmaster' character. At this point the group, having been through a succession of line-up changes, were a four-piece comprising Jagory Slab, Elyse Steinman, bassist Alec Morton and drummer Tim Finefrock.

Since their inception RAGING SLAB have been through a succession of drummers, including Kenny Kness on the 'True Death' mini-album (who also played with a later line-up of the former RCA signed AVIATOR), former WHIPLASH / SLAYER man T.J. Scaglione and SAVATAGE's Steve Wacholz on 1989's eponymous effort for RCA Records. Bob Pantella took their place for live work.

The self-titled 1989 album also saw the introduction of guitarist Mark Middleton and included two tracks previously on the 'True Death' EP, namely 'Get Off My Jollies' and 'Shiny Mama'. Guests included BADLANDS and former BLACK SABBATH vocalist RAY GILLEN. RAGING SLAB had initially been signed to RCA purely on a demo deal in December 1988 but as the project progressed the label offered the band a an album deal

RAGING SLAB
Photo : El Danno

333

that immediately led to them being placed in the studio. The album, produced by SHRAPNEL guitarist Daniel Rey, fared well on the sales front with exposure to the band being boosted by heavy MTV rotation of the video 'Don't Dog Me'.

In 1989 RAGING SLAB were joined by former GENOCIDE, MISFITS, ANGELS IN VAIN and PRINCESS PANG drummer Brain 'Damage' Keats. The journeyman drummer would later join DOPPLER, THE FUZZTONES and TRAMDRIVER. During 1990 the band toured heavily supporting a diverse range of acts such as WARRANT, RED HOT CHILI PEPPERS, MOLLY HATCHET and the RAMONES. With live work completed the band purchased a farmstead in Pennsylvania, equipping it with a home studio and set to work on the follow up album with producer Alex Perialis. Intended to be entitled 'From A Southern Space' the resulting album was blocked by RCA Records as unsatisfactory and tapes were shelved.

RAGING SLAB maintained momentum by guesting for GUNS N' ROSES before a return to the studio. These sessions culminated in the album 'Freeburden', overseen by producer Michael Bienhorn. Drums for this set of recordings were handled by Jack Irons of RED HOT CHILI PEPPERS and PEARL JAM repute. The band would be left reeling when RCA once again rejected the material and refused to release it.

Rick Rubin's Def Jam label weighed in during 1992 to buy the band out of their RCA deal, swiftly ensconcing the band in the studio once again. The 'Dynamite Monster Boogie Concert' saw production from the esteemed Brendan O'Brien and benefited from string arrangements courtesy of JOHN PAUL JONES of LED ZEPPELIN. Issued in 1993 the album made a sizable impact with a video for the track 'Anywhere But Here' being debuted on MTV's spoof cartoon show 'Beavis & Butthead'.

By 1994 Paul Sheehan was on the drum stool as RAGING SLAB toured Europe as support to Pop Rockers TEXAS. Other shows had the band acting as openers to MONSTER MAGNET and LENNY KRAVITZ. However, during British shows RAGING SLAB's misfortune when it came to drummers reared its head again when Sheehan suffered an extreme knee injury which put him out of action. Greg Strzempka would aid fellow Southern Stoners FIVE HORSE JOHNSON, acting as producer for their 'Double Down' album.

1995 would be another trying year for the band. In a repeat of their RCA experience a projected album 'Black Belt In Boogie' was shelved by Rick Rubin. Disillusioned guitarist Mark Middleton decamped. RAGING SLAB cut another album, 'Sing Monkey Sing', which was released with little fanfare during 1996. Rubin's record label wound up operations and RAGING SLAB were left high and dry once more, unable to release new product until the year 2000 due to the nature of their contract with their former label.

In 1999 the group set to work on a fresh studio album, initially employing drummer Phil Ondich. Their latest recruit would opt out to join BLACK LABEL SOCIETY and Dale Crover of the MELVINS stepped in. Although Crover performed some live dates with RAGING SLAB he too would make an exit, the band finally settling on TIDY and MONO PUFF sticksman Rob Cournoyer. As soon as the contractual chains were lifted RAGING SLAB set to work affirming their continued existence. The band donated a cover of MOUNTAIN's 'Mississippi Queen' for the 'In The Groove' tribute album, AEROSMITH's 'Bone To Bone' for the Small Stone Recordings' 'Right In The Nuts' collection and 'Pole Cat Woman' to the Underdogma label's 'Judge Not.' compilation.

Signing to Stoner indie label Tee Pee Records RAGING SLAB issued 'The Dealer', soon embarking upon North American gigs dubbed the 'Rulin' The Roost' tour. The band's projected 2001 European tour would fall victim to the September terrorist attacks, the band's original scheduled flight due to leave from Pittsburgh to Holland on September 11th.

RAGING SLAB would be back in September 2002 with a new album, the wryly entitled 'Raging Slab (Pronounced 'Eat Shit')'. Included would be the track 'Ruby' in dedication to the late, great RUBY STARR. The album would be promoted with a lengthy series of European, UK and Scandinavian dates.

Singles/EPs:
Mr. Lucky / Rocks Off Is Rocks Off, Buy Our Records BOR 12011 (1987)
Bent For Silver, RCA 9177 (1989)
Take A Hold / Move That Thang / Weatherman, American 858 437-2 (1994)

Albums:
SLABBAGE, (1986)
ASSMASTER, Buy Our Records BOR-12-011 (1987)
Feel To Much / Bitch To Kill / Mr. Lucky / Miracles / Rocks Off Is Rocks Off / Alpha Jerk / King Pompadour / Shiny Mama / The Shield / Assmaster
TRUE DEATH, Buy Our Records (1988)
Get Off My Jollies / Shrivel / Thunder

Chucker / I Heard The Owl
RAGING SLAB, RCA PD 90396 (1989)
Don't Dog Me / Joy Ride / Sorry's All I Got /
Waiting For The Potion / Get Off On My
Jollies / Shiny Mama / Geronimo / Bent For
Silver / When Love Comes Loose / Dig A
Hole / San Loco
**DYNAMITE MONSTER BOOGIE
CONCERT**, Def American 74321 28759-2
(1993)
But Her / Weatherman / Pearly / So Help Me
/ What Have You Done? / Take A Hold /
Laughin' And Cryin' / Don't Worry About The
Bomb / Lynne / Lord Have Mercy / National
Dust / Ain't Ugly None
SING MONKEY SING, American 943 079 2
(1996)
Should'a Known / Econoliner / Never Comin'
Down / Nobodies / Lay Down / Gracious /
C'mon 'n' On / She Like Ta / Better / Wrong /
Gravity / Checkyard Demon / The Skull's
Ending
THE DEALER, Tee Pee (2001)
Here Lies / "Sir Lord Ford - When Electricity
Came To Arkansas" / Doublewide / Real
Good Time / Too Bad / Chasin The Dragon /
Flap Your Boogie Flap / That's Alright / The
Ballad Of Truly Mae / Bit The Lightning / I
Don't Know You / Roadless Rider / (What I)
See Through You / I Saw The Light / That
Aint What I Meant / Good Mornin Lil'
Schoolboy
**RAGING SLAB (PRONOUNCED 'EAT
SHIT')**, Tee Pee (2002)
Little Red Lights / Boogalooser / Ruby / Miss
Delicious / Dry Your Eyes / Hell Yawns
Before Me / Black Bell / Chrome Won't Get
You Home / Shake What You Can / Never
Never Know / When The Cock Crows / Bury
Me Deep / For What You're Worth

RAINCARNATION (POLAND)
Line-Up: Adam Tuchowski (vocals), Dariusz
Szermanowicz (guitar), Mariusz Machnicki
(bass), Monika Piasecka (keyboards / violin),
Remigiusz Nowicki (drums)

Albums:
AT THE BOTTOMLESS LAKE, Morbid
Noizz (2001)
At The Bottomless Lake (Part I) / Judas /
Northern Song / Lsar / Hatred / The Planets
/ Dance Macabre / Dialogue / Saimaa / The
Master Of Rings / Svart / Spring Execution /
At The Bottomless Lake (Part II) / Spring
Execution - Nothingness / Spring Execution-
Dreams Impression

RAIN FELL WITHIN (USA)
Line-Up: Dawn (vocals), Laurie (vocals),
Kevin (guitar), Jason Wood (guitar), Charles

(bass), John (keyboards), Tim Miller (drums)

A Northern Virginian genre defying Metal
band, RAIN FELL WITHIN are hailed as
among the very elite of underground Doom /
Gothic acts. The group, initially entitled IN
MEDIA RES, was conceived during October
of 1996, the initial formation citing a line-up of
flame haired vocalist Dawn, guitarist Kevin,
fretless bassist Charles, guitarist William
Rucker and drummer John 'Sardonius'
Brown. A four track live demo session
surfaced in 1997 followed by the
professionally recorded 1998 tape 'Solemn
Days'.
During November of the same year both
Rucker and Brown made their exit. Tim Miller
of PSYCHOPHANCY filled the drum vacancy
in the December. The following year RAIN
FELL WITHIN debuted commercially with the
'Believe' album, produced by the AURORA
BOREALIS duo of Ron Vento and Jason Ian-
Vaugh Eckert. The latter's services were
utilised in the live arena in 1999 before Owen
Davis of GARDEN OF SHADOWS and
FORTY DAYS LONGING joined the fold.
Released in January of 2000 by the Dark
Symphonies label 'Believe' captured the
imagination of the Metal underground
receiving enthusiastic reviews and going on
to sell over 7,000 copies. Live work saw RAIN
FELL WITHIN putting in festival performances
at the 'New England Metal & Hardcore', 'New
Jersey Metal Meltdown' and 'Milwaukee
Metalfest' events. Jen of AUTUMN TEARS
would be on hand for backing vocals these
gigs.
January of 2001 signalled the departure of
Owen. Temporarily RAIN FELL WITHIN took
onboard Eric Sayenga of WITCHUNT but
within a month he was out of the picture.
Jason Ian-Vaugh Eckert would also deputise
on the live front on a short term basis. The
band set about recording a new album
'Refuge' and drafted two new members,
vocalist Laurie and guitarist Jason Wood,
toward the end of these sessions.

Albums:
BELIEVE, Dark Symphonies (2000)
A False Reality / Alone / Believe / Sorrow
Becomes Me / The Sun In My Wound
REFUGE, Dark Symphonies (2002)
Torn Apart / In The Knowing Of You / The
Child Beneath / In My Dreams / Save Your
Soul / Winter's Embrace / Into The Tower /
Sirens / Burned Away / Passing Time

RAIN PAINT (FINLAND)

Exceptionally sombre Metal act. The

335

formation credits itself simply as Mr. A (Aleksi Ahokas), Mr. T and Mr. K (Sami Koikkalainen), actually personnel with a wealth of experience from acts such as FRAGILE HOLLOW, DENIGRATE, RAPTURE, SNOWGARDEN and DIABLERIE.

<u>Albums:</u>
NIHIL NISI MORS, My Kingdom Music (2002)
Death, Drive & Fear / Forbidden Love / Freezes Day / Loose And Over / To Miss Spring / Rain Paint / Raven Nevermore / Sleeping Beauty / Outro

RAJNA (FRANCE)
Line-Up: Jeanne Lefebvre (vocals), Fabrice Lefebvre (strings / percussion)

RAJNA take Gothic, ethereal Darkwave into the realms of the truly adventurous employing such diverse ethnic instrumentation from India, Tibet and Nepal as bamboo flutes, kora, sanza, udu, djembe, harp loma, ramkie, santoor, bendir and derbouka. The band first made their mark in 1997 citing a line-up of the operatically trained vocalist Jeanne, Fabrice Lefebvre on strings and percussion and Gerard Chambellant, the latter tackling obscure instruments such as the yang t'chin. The groundbreaking 'Yahili' record was recorded within the unique confines of a Tibetan monastery. 2001 found Chambellant leaving after the heavily mystic influenced 'The Heady Wine Of Praise' album. This album would include a cover version of DEAD CAN DANCE's 'Cantara'.

<u>Albums:</u>
ISHATI, Projekt PRO00113 (1999)
Kahar / Yak / Silnen Kempur / Rajna / Sanctuary / Ophelia / Bilaki / Nomineum / Lahul Nati / Sién / Nundré / Traghodhia / Sharanghi
YAHILI, Holy HOL00052 (2000)
Road To Kandahar / Traöma / Diakri / Shalai / Adjah / Diwali / Shandailö / Dies Irae / Gansha Gaurab / Ham Shallam / Malia Vali / Yihillish
THE HEADY WINE OF PRAISE, Holy HOL00065 (2001)
The Passage / Sunyata / Marian / Cantara / Syrta / Mysterious Lanka / Kalos Irtes / Elizian Dance / Surya / Pearl Of Ashes / Black Star / Lullaby / OM Mani Padme Hum / Kezh
THE DOOR OF SERENITY, Holy HOL00074 (2002)
Djalambo / Belorbai / Tore Sensuous / The Door Of Serenity / Elisia / Whirling Souls / Masati / Dervishing / Into The Dream / Shalim Dhar / Djalambo (Epilogue)

RAS ALGETHI (ITALY)
Line-Up: Mauro Berchi (vocals / guitar), Matteo (guitar), Huldus (guitar), Luca (keyboards), Silvio (drums)

Without question Italy's most distinguished Doom act, despite their legacy of just one commercially released album. The band debuted with a 1994 demo CD 'Oblita Divinitas' of which a handful of copies were distributed.
Although RAS ALGETHI made a huge impact with the 'Onericon - The White Hypnotic' album internal disputes tore the band apart. Frontman Mauro Berchi and guitarist Matteo created the more Gothically inclined CANAAN for a 1996 debut 'Blue Fire'.

<u>Albums:</u>
ONEIRICON - THE WHITE HYPNOTIC, Wounded Love (1995)
Aldebaran Crossing / The Bride Eternal / When Fire Is Father / Keys Of Urtam (A Translucent Vision) / With An Halo Of Flames / Symbols (In Luce Obliqua) / Nubes Obscura / In White Hypnotic

RED AIM (GERMANY)
Line-Up: Dr. Don Rasmussen-Rogers (vocals), Benjamin Buss Foxworth (guitar), El Davide (bass), Ray Kitzler (keyboards), Mitch Buchanen (drums)

Metal Stoners RED AIM arrived on the scene during the mid '90s, debuting with the eclectic 1996 'Sinai Jam' album, the band being unafraid to employ a whole variety of ethnic instruments such as sitars and didgeroidoos. At this juncture the band comprised vocalist Pascal Flach, guitarist Benjamin Buss Foxworth, bassist Patrick Schappert and drummer Thore Huppert. In 1998 RED AIM inducted a new lead singer, Dr. Don Rasmussen-Rogers. By the 2000 album 'Call Me Tiger' Stefan Gemballa had taken over on drums. That year RED AIM would also cover IRON MAIDEN's 'The Trooper' for inclusion on a tribute album.
RED AIM split from the People Like You label following the critically acclaimed 'Saartanic Cluttydogs' opus, the album title a tongue in cheek reference to the band's native Saarland. Touring to promote the record saw RED AIM linking up with 7 ZUMA 7, although with Foxworth unable to commit to these dates Christian Theisinger of SHARD temporarily took the position for live work.
Signing to major independent Metal Blade the group revised its line-up as bassist Thorsten Erbel was supplanted by EL NINO's El Davide. Adding keyboard player Ray Kitzler to

the line-up RED AIM would promote the May 2002 'Flesh For Fantasy' album, which included a surreal cover of the SCORPIONS staple 'Rock You Like A Hurricane', with appearances at two prestigious German festivals at the 'Wacken Open Air' and 'Summerbreeze' events.

Both guitarist Benjamin Buss and drummer Stefan Gemballa have also made names for themselves operating the highly rated Gothic Rock outfit FLOWING TEARS.

<u>Singles/EPs:</u>
Aprilfuckers / Tombola / Supertrooper, People Like You (2000) ('The Aprilfuckers' EP)

<u>Albums:</u>
SINAI JAM, QREC 03 (1996)
Monastir / Wombar / Wombat / Desert Spoon / Sinai Jam / Nadi
ORANGE, (1998)
CALL ME TIGER, People Like You (2000)
Em Zabbebabba Sai Bou / Beach Polyp / Bupp, The Tasmanian Devil / Haiti Poison / Krumbernkamatran / Ez Pasa, No Pasar / Phoenicopterus / Call Me Tiger
SAARTANIC CLUTTYDOGS, People Like You (2001)

Sandokan / My Jonaise / Lumo Law (Low Lighter Yaw) / Walter / Torso Tiger / Till Z. Palladin / Electrobazaaride / Gorilla Cunt / Kung Fu Fighting / Double Crackfrog Blues
FLESH FOR FANTASY, Metal Blade (2002)
The Golden Nonstop / El Gonzo Mondial / My Lovely Mr. Singingclub / Highway Crucifix / Aroma / Goodbye Sam, Hello Samantha / Snokeshooter / Tombola / Kneel Down And Blow For Forgiveness / Rock You Like A Hurricane / Aprilfuckers

RED GIANT (Cleveland, OH, USA)
Line-Up: Alex (vocals / guitar), Damien (guitar), Brian (bass), Chris (drums)

<u>Albums:</u>
PSYCHOBLASTER AND MISUSE OF POWER, Cambodia (1995)
Ironlung / Galaxy Headway / Millennium Falcon 27th Dimension / Fast Orange / Cydonia / Sonic Mind Shrine / Rooms Of Shord / Solar Lord / Welders Are Heroes
ULTRA MAGNETIC GLOWING SOUND, Tee Pee TP1015-2 (1999)
1960 Starchief / Blue-White Supergiant / Saturn Missile Battery / Pervert / .865 (The Battle For Longitude) / Ring Of The Acid

RED GIANT
Photo : El Danno

337

Pope / Devils Of The Fall / Floor Girl / When Sirius Rises / Thread / Kill The Condors / Another Dying Admiral

REIGN (UK)
Line-Up: John Cook (vocals / bass), Mick Sturrie (guitar), Ronnie McClean (drums)

REIGN debuted with the well received demo 'The Silent Nation'. REIGN gained valuable exposure on the British 'Underground Titans' tour alongside GOMORRAH, INCARCERATED and DECOMPOSED. Toured Europe with MORTIFICATION in 1994.

Albums:
EMBRACE, Mausoleum 904016-2 (1995)
Ad Extremum / Forlorn Existence / Wings Of Sorrow / Erosion / A Sombre Tale / Obscured / Infinity Within / Never Forever / Lacuna / Colour Circus
EXIT CLAUSE, Mausoleum 71278-60015-2 (1995)
Freakshow / In Isolation / Alles Im Arsch / Dei Gratia / Abolition (My Release) / Violate / Chemical Rebirth / Exit Clause

RENAISSANCE (BELGIUM)
Line-Up: Santiago Janssens (vocals), Chriss Ions (guitar / keyboards), Dirk Vollon (bass)

RENAISSANCE are a Doom-Death act founded in November of 1991. Throughout the course of their career and through successive works the part has steadily drifted into a Gothic tinged Progressive Metal sound. The original formation of the band numbered vocalist Santiago Janssens, guitarist Domingo Smets, ex-CHRONIC DEATH guitarist / keyboard player Chriss Ons, bass player Dirk Vollon, keyboard player Veronique Aerts and drummer Jürgen De Wispelare. This unit recorded an opening demo dubbed 'Archway', released in 1992 but would then be wrought by line-up changes with De Wispelare, Aerts and Smets making their exit. Smets would subsequently feature in AGATHOCLES and ANCIENT RITES.
A split EP for the After Dark label shared with Black Metal band ANCIENT RITES arrived in January of 1993 swiftly followed by single through the Shiver label, splitting the 13 minute epic 'Tired Blood- Vaudeville' over two sides of vinyl.
Despite the departure of Dirk Vollon RENAISSANCE cut the conceptual first album 'The Death Of Art'. For a time the band also operated under the revised title of RINASCIMENTO in an effort to avoid confusion with the noted UK Folk act. Under this title a limited edition album, 'Rinascimento Demos 1995-1998', emerged. The RENAISSANCE triumvirate of Chriss Ons, Santiago Janssens and Dirk Vollon would reunite in 2000 but little progress was made. By 2001 Vollon had broke away to join SHADOWDANCE and bassist Kris Trappeniers had joined the fold.
Future product will not be issued under the RENAISSANCE name.

Singles/EPs:
Windows, After Dark (1993) (Split single with ANCIENT RITES)
Tired Blood / Vaudeville, Shiver (1993)

Albums:
THE DEATH OF ART, (1994)
The Death Of Art / Archway

REVELATION (Baltimore, MD, USA)
Line-Up: Dennis Cornelius (vocals / guitar), Jim Hunter (bass), Steve Branagan (drums)

A revered name in Doom circles. REVELATION, a title lending equal credence of thought to the Bible and the first song on the debut TROUBLE album, have issued three hard to get hold of albums to date. The band began life in May of 1986 centred upon the duo of vocalist / guitarist John Brenner and drummer Steve Branagan. A whole stream of demo recordings would be ignited with the arrival in January of 1987 with the 'Face Reality' session. Before the close of the year two further tapes, 'Terminal Destiny' in June and 'Images Of Darkness' in November, had been issued. A fourth attempt, 'Illusion Of Progress', which debuted new bass player Bert Hall Jr. and displayed a more ambitious almost Progressive approach, was delivered in March of 1989. The exposure afforded to their inclusion on the Doom Metal sampler 'Dark Passages' in 1990 sparked REVELATION's commercial debut for Lee Dorrian of CATHEDRAL's specialist Doom imprint Rise Above with the 'Salvations Answer' album. However, not content to rest on their laurels the band swiftly made available the 'The Unbearable Vision' cassette in the summer of 1991. Before the year was out Josh Hart had taken the position of bass player.
REVELATION switched to the German based Hellhound concern for the sophomore album 'Never Comes Silence' in 1993. Once again REVELATION reaped critical acclaim for this record, amongst whose grooves was contained the sprawling 18 minute title track. The band would be rocked though at this juncture when both Brenner and Hart

decamped. Long-standing fan of the band Dennis Cornelius, a veteran of MORTICIOUS, DARKOFAGUS and King Fowley of DECEASED's spoof Black Metal act DOOMSTONE, duly stepped up to the breech as the new REVELATION frontman. The revised version of the band made their entrance with the 'Mourning Son' promo. Jim Hunter of OCTOBER 31 came on board in the Spring of 1994 as permanent bassist and a third album, 'Yet So Far', would also emerge via Hellhound solidifying their burgeoning reputation. Finally their work ethic paid off as the band put in a bout of European touring alongside the elite of American Doom ST. VITUS and SOLITUDE AETURNUS.

In late 1996 the four track 'Frozen Masque' tape was distributed but would also act as a marker for the first chapter in the REVELATION saga. Jim Hunter would re-surface on the OCTOBER 31 album 'Fire Awaits You'. Cornelius would relocate to Oklahoma there founding COR which after demo submissions evolved into OVERSOUL for the 2000 album 'Seven Days In November'.

In mid 2002 REVELATION re-formed citing a line-up of vocalist / guitarist Dennis Cornelius, bass player Jim Hunter and Steve Branagan on drums. Joining the classic trio would be ex-OVERSOUL guitarist Chris Greenway. With the announcement of the band's return REVELATION also confirmed an appearance at the 'Doom Shall Rise' European two-day Doom metal festival to be held in Crailsheim, Germany in February 2003.

Albums:
SALVATIONS ANSWER, Rise Above (1991)
Lost Innocence / Salvations Answer / Infinite Nothingness / Paradox / Images Of Darkness / Long After Midnight / Poets And Paupers / Waiting… For The End
NEVER COMES SILENCE, Hellhound (1993)
Against Nature / Ashes / The Unbearable Vision / Frustration / One Lame Step / Spectre / Wounds Which Do Not Heal / Unreal / Never Comes Silence
…YET SO FAR, Hellhound (1995)
Soul Barer / Eternal Search / Little Faith / Grasping The Nettle / Mourning Son / Fallen / Alone / Natural Steps / …Yet So Far

REVENANT (NJ, USA)
Line-Up: Henry Veggian (vocals / guitar), Dave Jengo (guitar), Tim Scott (bass), Will Corcoran (drums)

Singles/EPs:
Distant Eyes / Degeneration, Thrash (1989)

Albums:
PROPHECIES OF A DYING WORLD,
Nuclear Blast (1991)
Prophecy Of A Dying World / Spawn / Ancestral Shadows / The Unearthly / Asphyxiated Time / Distant Eyes / Valedictions

REVEREND BIZARRE (FINLAND)
Line-Up: Magister Albert (vocals / bass), Peter Vicar (guitar), Earl Of Void (drums)

Dealing in Sabbathian, all enveloping, quagmire Doom REVEREND BIZARRE not so much burst, but dragged themselves into the Metal arena with their debut album 'In The Rectory Of The Bizarre Reverend'. The band had originally convened in the small Southern Finnish town of Lohja with a line-up of vocalist / bassist Magister Albert, guitarist Peter Vicar and drummer Juippi during 1994. However, with Vicar's relocation to Turku in 1997 REVEREND BIZARRE folded.

In 1998 Magister Albert also moved to Turku and the group was duly resurrected. Coming in on drums would be Earl Of Void, having been just released from prison. This trio weighed in with the demo tape 'Slice Of Doom'.

The band has figured on the ST. VITUS tribute 'A Timeless Tale' issued by Raven Moon Records and on the compilations 'Not Of This Earth' released by the Italian Black Widow concern and Myskatonic's 'At The Mountains Of Madness Vol. II'.

REVEREND BIZARRE's debut album, 'In The Rectory Of The Bizarre Reverend' released by the Mastervox subsidiary Sinister Figure, proved to be so enormously, ponderously heavy as to almost defy description. The closing track 'Cirith Ungol' weighed in at a gargantuan 21 minutes duration.

Albums:
IN THE RECTORY OF THE BIZARRE REVEREND, Sinister Figure SFGCD10 (2002)
Burn In Hell! / In The Rectory / The Hour Of Death / Sodoma Sunrise / Doomsower / Cirith Ungol

THE RIBEYE BROTHERS (USA)

THE RIBEYE BROTHERS was a union of the MONSTER MAGNET duo of drummer Jon Kleiman and former frontman Tim Cronin.

Albums:
IF I HAD A HORSE, Meteor City (2002)
If I Had A Horse... / Mister Ray Charles / Bootful Of Piss / D.W.I. / How Does It Feel /

Drinkin' And Stinkin' / Last Place Champs /
Mr. Ray Charles / Steakhat / Swagger Turns
To Stagger / Don't Pass Me By / Love
Theme / To Find Out / Girl

RICKSHAW (SWEDEN)
Line-Up: Bobby Dawn (vocals / guitar), Jocke
(guitar), Carlos Satanos (bass), Mackahbuzz
(drums)

Gothenburg's RICKSHAW aim to blend Punk
with a healthy injection of classic Rock &
Metal. RICKSHAW came into being during
1998, founded by vocalist / guitarist 'Bobby
Dawn' (Robert Nilsson) and guitarist Jocke.
RICKSHAW frontman Bobby Dawn previously
operated as guitarist for DORIAN GRAY,
HIGH TV and PEEKABOO STREET as well
as serving time on the drums with LORELEI.
Bassist Carlos Satanos was formerly with
Hard Rockers ABANDON. The group
underwent a series of line-up changes, losing
early members such as keyboard player
Andreas 'Andy Bebop' Östberg, drummer
Magnus Timmeras and bass player Henrik
Antonsson.
The band's debut EP 'The Electric
Showdown' for the HDP label swiftly sold out
of the initial pressing of 300 with a second
run, again of just 300 but manufactured in red
vinyl, soon selling out too. Their next effort in
2000, a combined single with TRIGGER,
would be restricted to 500 white vinyl copies.
In 2002 RICKSHAW embarked upon a whole
slew of varied endeavours including a version
of the KENNY ROGERS / DOLLY PARTON
Country & Western hit 'Islands In The Stream'
for a Country tribute, a take on the KISS
ballad 'Beth' for Nosebleeder Records,
TANK's 'Don't Walk Away' for yet another
tribute collection and a split single with THE
AWESOME MACHINE.
A split single was delivered in collaboration
with American Punks THE STRAP ONS for
the Bootleg Blooze label. A further shared
effort, an album with TRIGGER entitled
'Action...Go!' surfaced in September of 2002.

Singles/EPs:
Electric Showdown / A.Y.G.T.K. / Superfly /
Fuel, HDP (1999) ('Electric Showdown' EP)
One Dollar / Going Down To Hell / Get It
On, HDP (2000) ('One Dollar' EP. Split EP
with TRIGGER)
Nothing To Lose, HDP (2001) (Split single
with ADAM WEST) (Limited edition 500
copies)
Numbing Fuel / Kick It, Bootleg Blooze
BOOZE 003 (2002) (Split EP with NOISE
REALITY)
Hang Tough - Stiff Neck / Bad Breath Baby,

Bootleg Blooze BOOZE 006 (2002) (Split EP
with THE STRAP ONS)

Albums:
TENDER SONGS OF LOVE, Beluga
BELUGALP010 (1999)
Rifle Ticket / Dog Faced Boy / Selfabuse /
One Dollar / Got Me Going / Hey Man! (I´m
Elvis) / Superfly / Electric Showdown / Settle
For Silver / Sukker / Don´t Get Mad (Get
Evil) / Left Handed Suzy
DOUBLE DELUXE, Daredevil DD014 (2001)
(Split album with HATEBALL)
Buckle Up! / She Used To Dance / Tribute To
Punk Rock / Life In Hypercolor / Fukk Shitt
Upp / Only My Soul / Pockets Full Of
Sunshine (Loose It)
ACTION... GO!, Devil's Shitburner (2002)
(Split album with TRIGGER)
Action... Go! / Satellite Soul / Temple Of Your
Choice / That's Bullshit - This Sucks /
Enough Is Enough / Perfect Crime / Bikerboy

RIDGE (SWEDEN)
Line-Up: Andreas Bergstrom (vocals / guitar),
Johannes Svensson (guitar), Jonas Jonsson
(bass), Johan Olsson (drums)

Swedish Stoners. Consistently blighted by
unfavourable comparisons to FU MANCHU
the band decided to call it quits.

Albums:
**A COUNTRYDELIC AND FUZZED
EXPERIENCE IN A COLOMBIAN
SUPREMO**, Molten Universe MOLTEN 012
(2001)
Afro / No Way Near / Rancho Relaxo / Como
Un Toro / Avalanche / Cayuga 240 / Fuelle /
Zeb / Godspeed / Silver Dragon

RITE (FINLAND)
Line-Up: Jarkko Laatikainen (vocals), Sami
Lintunen (guitar), Janne Savolainen (guitar),
Manu Kuitunen (bass), Juha Kivikanto
(drums)

Mikkeli based '70s themed Stoner-Doom act
RITE was conceived during 1994, citing an
original line-up of vocalist Jarkko Laatikainen,
guitarist Sami Lintunen, bass player Harri
Valkonen and drummer Juha Kivikanto. A
further member, second guitarist Tero
Pantsar, was added the following year and an
opening 1995 tape led onto the following
years 'Galaktus' demo. 1997's 'Blackflash'
session would then land RITE with a deal for
the 'Goddamn' EP issued through the Water
Dragon label. However, by 1998 Valkonen had
opted out to pursue a career as a tourist
guide and RITE welcomed onboard Manu

Kuitunen.

In March of 2002 RITE pulled in second guitarist Janne Savolainen. This revised line-up cut the TANK track 'Just Like Something From Hell' for the Bad Reputation 'Tanked – A Tribute To The Filth Hounds' tribute album. The first full-length album 'Shoot Skull For Jackpot' was delivered in June.

Singles/EPs:
Comet Cruiser / Volume / Witch (The Wicked Bitch) / Evilride, Water Dragon (2000) ('Goddamn' EP)

Albums:
SHOOT SKULL FOR JACKPOT, Water Dragon (2002)
Bastard Song / One Hell Of A Mess / Surmanajo / Climbin' The Blacklist / Human Fuse / Das Vegas / Sharpshooter / Doomsday Machine / One Man Revolution / Damned If I Do

ROACHPOWDER (SWEDEN)
Line-Up: Francisco Rencoret (vocals), George Bravo (guitar), Hogge Calmroth (bass), Masen Persson (drums)

Although based in Sweden the heavy Stoner unit ROACHPOWDER, titled after the poison cum drug in William S. Burroughs 'Naked Lunch', is fronted up by the Chilean exiles vocalist Francisco Rencoret and guitarist George Bravo. The band started life billed as ERRATIC TALE, later becoming the Grunge orientated SKINTRADE with the initial line-up featuring former GLORY drummer Jonas Östman.. Under this title, and joined by former WESTERN FRONT, BAM BAM BOYS and JAGGED EDGE singer Matti Alfonzetti and guitarist Stefan Bergström, two albums were released; 1993's 'Skintrade' and 1995's 'Roachpowder'. With the departure of Alfonzetti the remaining members opted to persevere as ROACHPOWDER.

Following the 'Viejo Diablo' album the group added the high profile figure of bassist Lasse Rosenberg, a man whose credit list included ENTOMBED, THERION, MONASTRY and CARBONISED amongst others.

George Bravo would gain production credits on female Stoners MISDEMEANOR's version of the MISFITS 'Hybrid Moments' in mid 2002.

Albums:
VIEJO DIABLO, The Music Cartel (1998)
Get Out Of My Way / Galactic Blues / Viejo Diablo / Black Stone / Cosmic Emperor / The Sun / New Orleans / See You Burn / Demon Bitch / King Of The Hill, Part 1 / King Of The Hill, Part 2 / Super Galactic Gargel Blazter

ATOMIC CHURCH, The Music Cartel (2001)
House Of The Wicked / Purgatorio Amoroso / All Hail And Kneel Before Me / To Ebola With Love / Balls Of The Sun / Harp / No Reasons / Bullets Of Creation / Oceans Red / Into The Center

ROADSAW (Boston, MA, USA)
Line-Up: Craig Riggs (vocals), Ian Ross (guitar), Tim Catz (bass), Hari Hassin (drums)

Boston hard edged Stoners. ROADSAW make no pretences and proudly announce their music as being Metal first and foremost. The group is centred upon bassist Tim Catz, a veteran of the Boston Rock scene first making an impression with Heavy Metal band SEKA. This unit saw Catz alongside vocalist / guitarist Stu Shoaps, guitarist Billy O'Malley and drummer Tim Jordan. This group, adding future GODSMACK man Erna Sully, switched titles to STRIP MIND in 1993, apparently after legal action brought down on them by Porn actress Seka. Catz would also find time to become 'Ozzy' as frontman for club BLACK SABBATH covers band BLACK SALAD. By 1994 STRIP MIND had dissolved and ROADSAW, pulling in ex- JOE and X-15 vocalist Craig Mills, had reared up in its place. ROADSAW, comprising Riggs, Catz, guitarist Darryl Shepherd, a man who cited credits with SLAPSHOT, SUPAHEAD, SLAUGHTER SHACK and DESLOCK, and drummer Hari Hassia, debuted with the 1994 'Fancy Pants' single, released by the local Boston label Curve Of The Earth. This relationship also bore the albums '$1,000,000' and 'Nationwide', both impressing fans and critics alike with their marked heaviness. Signing to the MIA label ROADSAW cut the 'Not Today' album. However, with promotion copies already released to press and radio, MIA went under leaving the band with no commercial release.

Guitarist Darryl Shepherd bailed out, founding MILLIGRAM, and former RUMFORD bass player Ian Ross switched instruments to take over the lead guitar vacancy.

The 1999 'Takin' Out The Trash' album of rarities, demos and outtakes would include cover versions of VAN HALEN's 'Outta Love Again', CROSBY, STILLS, NASH & YOUNG's 'Almost Cut My Hair' and THE BAGS 'I Smell A Rat'. The band would contribute their version of 'Toys In The Attic' to the 2000 Small Stone Recordings AEROSMITH tribute 'Right In The Nuts'. The band also shared a split EP with Nottingham's BLACKROCK.

ROADSAW guitarist Ian Ross would loan himself out to NEBULA for 2001 tour work.

The band would sign to the Swedish Lunasound label for the 2002 offering 'Rawk n' Roll'. Tortuga Recordings issued a lavish double vinyl gatefold edition of 'Rawk n' Roll' with differing sleeve artwork. Tortuga also incited collectors further with a restricted run of just 100 on glorious purple vinyl. Ross made a return to ROADSAW in time for European tour dates in alliance with ORANGE GOBLIN commencing late February 2002.

Tim Catz has been known to operate in various side ventures including BLOODSHOT and HONEYGLAZED. Riggs, Ross and Hassia, with MILLIGRAM and NEBULA man Bob Maloney on bass guitar, now operate QUITTER. This new act, seeing Hassia take on the role of lead vocalist, issued an eponymous album for Tortuga Recordings.

Singles/EPs:
Fancy Pants / Handed You Your Ass, Curve Of The Earth (1994)
Sickest Ride, Shot From A Cannon Music (1995)
Not Today / Interplanetary Love Song, Man's Ruin (1996) ('American Dream' EP)
Busted Monk / Where Is My Mind, Underdogma (2001) (Split EP with BLACKROCK)

Albums:
$1,000,000, Curve Of The Earth (1996)
Gotta / Fell Off The Earth / Non-Phenomenal / Sickest Ride / Fancy Pants / Rotted Out / Theme From 'Hassle' / Random / Handed You Your Ass / Starcock
NATIONWIDE, Curve Of The Earth COTE 049 (1997)
Untitled / Keep On Sailing / Not Today / In Threes / Satellite / Black Flower / Ratted Out / Thanks For Nothing / Top Koms / Signal / Overspill / Van-O-Rama / Motorcaster / All Shrivelled Up / Untitled
NOT TODAY, MIA (1998) (Promotion release)
TAKING OUT THE TRASH, Shot From A Cannon Music (1999)
Outta Love Again / Interplanetary Love Song / Fancy Pants / Handed You Your Ass / Unintentional Instrumental (WMBR Live) / Bummer (Live demo) / Forever Today (Demo) / Gone / Arlen / Come Around / Freaks (Demo) / Starcock (Demo) / I Smell a Rat (WMBR Live) / Almost Cut My Hair
RAWK N' ROLL, Lunasound LUNA008CD (2002)
Right On Through / Bad Ass Rising / Disconnected / Scorpion Bowl / Foot / Your Own Private Slice Of Hell / The Finger / That's Mr. Motherfucker To You / Buried Alive

/ Blackout Driver / Burnout / Hoof

ROLLERBALL (AUSTRALIA)

Brisbane based 'Retro-Futuristic' band ROLLERBALL employ enough '70s van associated imagery to place them fairly and squarely in the Stoner camp.

The group came into being when LOAD members Dave Talon and Beeswax pooled their talents with VANGUARD vocalist Tenpin, this trio drawing in Fingers McLaughlin to forge ROLLERBALL.

ROLLERBALL added new drummer Cracker Roach in time for recording of the 2000 EP 'Let Your Hair Hang Down'. Subsequent tour dates across Australia saw ROLLERBALL headlining the 'Stonerphonic' package billing over THUMLOCK and BOBSLEDGE. The band would also act as openers to NEBULA, QUEENS OF THE STONE AGE and ROLLINS BAND.

2002 had the band supporting FU MANCHU. In mid 2002 bassist Guvnor bowed out, with Junior soon taking his place for recording of a studio album provisionally billed as 'Super Structure'.

Singles/EPs:
Jonothan E. / Lost In Space / Dragon / Eye Of The Storm / Lowly Sublime / Lake Of Life, Rhythm Ace RA101 (1999) ('Lost In Space' EP)
Evie Part One (Let Your Hair Hang Down) / Classical Stimuli / Knockin' The Top Off / 24 Hours / Lake Of Life (Live), Rhythm Ace RA102 (2000) ('Let Your Hair Hang Down' EP)

Albums:
ROLLERBALL, Water Dragon (2002)
Jonothan E. / Classical Stimuli / Knockin The Top Off / Lost In Space / Lowly Sublime / Eye Of The Storm / 24 Hours / Evie (Part One) / Main Frame / Dragon / Reflections / Believe In The Breeze / Lake Of Life (Live) / Theme From Odyssey

RONDELLUS (ESTONIA)

Line-Up: Maria Staak (vocals / hurdy gurdy / organistrum), Veikko Kiiver (vocals / organistrum), Miriam Andersen (vocals / harp), Tonu Joesaar (fiddle), Robert Staak (lute / frame drum)

A quite unique proposition amongst Metal circles. The Tallinn based Estonian medieval choral folk act RONDELLUS, founded in 1993, would create a stir with their 2002 release 'Sabbatum'. Incredibly these classically trained musicians took on the might of BLACK SABBATH delivering an

RONDELLUS

album entirely composed of classic BLACK SABBATH tracks recorded as if laid down originally in the 14th century. Not only were guitars, bass and drums replaced by hurdy gurdy, harp, lute, fiddle and even bagpipes but all the lyrics were translated and sung in Latin! In a huge contrast of styles, Ozzy Osbourne's trademark wails had been replaced by the Gregorian chants of Veikko Kiiver and the exquisite medieval harmonies of Maria Staak and Miriam Andersen whilst Tony Iommi's crushing riffs had been transformed into delicate harp and fiddle passages.

The album, no doubt due to its originality of concept and the superb vocal and musical performances, proved to be a major hit in the Metal community. It was suitably recorded at the Tallinn Merchant Guild, home of the Estonian history museum.

Prior to delving into the world of Heavy Metal RONDELLUS had three 'early music' albums to their credit 'Secular Music In France From The XIVth-XVth Century' and 'Sanctum Rosarium', both in 1995 and 1998's 'Carmina Sanctorium'.

Albums:
SABBATUM, Beg The Bug 211200-002 (2002)
Verres Militares (War Pigs) / Oculi Filioli (Junior's Eyes) / Funambulus Domesticus (A National Acrobat) / Symptoma Mundi (Symptom Of The Universe) / Post Murum Somnii (Behind The Walls Of Sleep) / Post Aeternitatem (After Forever) / Magus (The Wizard) / Solitudo (Solitude) / Rotae Confusionis (Wheels Of Confusion) / Planetarum Vagatio (Planet Caravan) / Via Gravis (A Hard Road) / Architectus Urbis Caelestis (Spiral Architect)

ROSEMARY'S BABIES (USA)
Line-Up: J.R. (vocals), C.A. Richie (guitar), Post Mortem (bass), Eerie Von (drums)

Shock Horror act ROSEMARY'S BABIES formed by former MISFITS / ANTIDOTE drummer EERIE VON. In 1983 bassist Post Mortem departed to be replaced by the strangely titled Big Ones.

Von and Mortem would unite briefly in the studio for the I'M AFRAID project.

Both Von and guitarist C.A. Richie joined GLENN DANZIG in the formative SAMHAIN. Von would switch to bass guitar for SAMHAIN and DANZIG and would also issue solo product in the '90s.

Albums:
BLOOD LUST, Ghastly RB0001 (1983)

Blood Lust / I'm Gonna Be Sick / Happy Song / Inferior / Small Minds, Think Small / Talking To The Dead / Sanctioned Violence / Let's Molest 10 Year Olds / One Dead Low Life / That's Alright, That's OK

ROTOR (GERMANY)
Line-Up: Tim (guitar), Marco (bass), Milan (drums)

Albums:
ROTOR, Monster Zero (2002)
Windkanal / Neoplan / Orange Onion Orbit / Homogene / Magma Planet / A Madrugada

THE RUBES (OH, USA)
Line-Up: Mace (vocals / bass), Brent Beaver (guitar), Greg Fee (drums)

An Ohio Retro Rock trio. Drummer Greg Fee and bassist Brent Beaver were previously a member of '80s Metal band EPITAPH.

Albums:
HOKUM, Underdogma (2002)
Snake Oil / Wonder Why / 20 Three / Change My Mind / Smoke And Mirrors / Disguise / Take Your Time (Hiding In A Cloud) / To The Next Step / Interlude / The Ballad Of Sisyphus Mac Duff

RUBICON (UK)
Line-Up: Andy Delany (vocals), Paul Wright (guitar), Peter Yates (guitar / keyboards), Tony Pettitt (bass), Nod Wright (drums / keyboards)

Gothic Rockers RUBICON are actually FIELDS OF THE NEPHILIM minus vocalist Carl McCoy. The charismatic frontman had split the band in order to create NEFILIM and his erstwhile colleagues soldiered on, for a while even known as RUBICON aka FIELDS OF THE NEPHILIM.

RUBICON opened for FISH on his 1993 tour of Germany.

Singles/EPs:
Watch Without Pain / Watch Without Pain (Full Version) / Killing Time (Demo Version), SPV 056-48653/L (1992)
Crazed / Chains Are Gone / Brave Hearts (Cellar Tape), Beggar's Banquet (1992)
Before My Eyes / Standing Alone / On Your Side / Hard For You, Beggar's Banquet (1993)
Insatiable / Bury My Gold / Prime, Beggar's Banquet (1995)

Albums:
WHAT STARTS ENDS, SPV 084-48742 (1992)

Before My Eyes / Crazed / Watch Without
Pain / Brave Hearts / Killing Time / Inside
Your Heard / Unspoken / Hard For You /
Rivers / What Starts Ends
ROOM 101, Beggar's Banquet (1995)
Ageless / Rest A While / Doubt All /
Insatiable / Cut Down / On Your Side / This
Drenching Night / Bury My Gold / Empty
Hands / Eat With Me

RUIN (NEW ZEALAND)
Line-Up: Phil (vocals / guitar), Julian Smith
(guitar), Matt Bulldozer (bass), Dane (drums)

Hamilton Doomsters rooted in the esteemed
Death Metal band MASOCHRIST. As
MASOCHRIST the band issued a total of four
releases including the 'Nothing is Forever'
album. Pre MASOCHRIST guitarist Julian
Baddies had journeyed through such acts as
THUNDER MONKEY, SWAMP GOBLIN,
DEEP SIX, THE BADDIES and HELL TO PAY.
Vocalist / guitarist Phil and drummer Dane
had also partnered Baddies in HELL TO PAY,
Phil also tracing a band lineage as a guitarist
through THE CROWBAR EFFECT and
CHURCHBURNER whilst the drummer's
musical heritage included DEEP SIX and, as

vocalist / bassist a slew of acts including
F.I.C., SINFEEDER, ENSHRINE, AZAZEL,
ANIMOSITY and GORE GLORY.
Following the 2001 MASOCHRIST album
'Last Disaster', and opting for a Doom
direction, and enlisting Matt Bulldozer on
bass, RUIN was founded in late 2001 soon
issuing the EP 'Extreme Volume Demanded'.
Despite the rawness of the recording RUIN
weighed in with an exemplary slab of high
grade Doom Metal.
Both Baddies and frontman Phil operate the
'Lo-Fi' side venture SOUL ECLIPSE in union
with Issacha, Dane and Dolf De Borst of THE
DATSUNS. Other extracurricular endeavours
include Baddies, Phil & Dane in Punk band
THE NIGHTMARES, the Grindcore union
NAGASAKI MANTRA featuring Baddies, Phil
and Dane and the experimental acoustic
tones of ANGELS ABLAZE, a project of
Baddies and Claire Vincent. Dane also wields
the drumsticks in 3 MAN WALL.

Singles/EPs:
None Of The Bells & Whistles / Scared Out
Of Life / Blow Down The Town / Vertical
Spark / ...Warning Us, Black 13 (2001)
THE SABIANS

RUIN

S

(Oakland, CA, USA)
Line-Up: Justin Marler (vocals / guitar), Patrick Huerta (guitar), Rachel Fisher (bass), Chris Hakius (drums)

An intriguing reunion of singer songwriter Justin Marler and drummer Chris Hakius, both previously with the Arcadian and venerated Doom act SLEEP. Marler had actually come out of a self-imposed sabbatical to found THE SABIANS. Following the impact afforded by the titanic SLEEP debut 'Volume One' released by the Earache label in 1992 Marler had actually been, by his own confession, near to suicide and had been self-mutilating. Marler's response to his illness was to enter a Russian Orthodox monastery, the St. Herman of Alaska Brotherhood, and to live the life of a monk for several years. Whilst under religious orders Marler penned a book 'Youth Of The Apocalypse And The Last True Rebellion' and recorded an acoustic album 'Lamentations'.

THE SABIANS, which also included guitarist Patrick Huerta and bass player Jake Daley, put out the 'Empty Your Heart' demo. Rachel Fisher took the bass position before releasing the 'Beauty For Ashes' album produced by FUDGE TUNNEL man Alex Newport. The album retains the heaviness implied by the musicians' tradition allied to spirituality, chanting passages and even Punk overtones.

Albums:
BEAUTY FOR ASHES, Music Cartel (2002)
Via Dolorosa / Breathe / Beauty For Ashes / Restoration / Black Lie / Downcast / Lull

SACRAMENT (PA, USA)
Line-Up: Rob Wolfe (vocals), Brian Toy (guitar), Erik Ney (bass), Paul Graham (drums)

A Christian Metal band. SACRAMENT's 1990 album 'Testimony For Apocalypse' featured vocalist Mike Torane and guitarist Mike DiDonato. The latter would depart and Torane was replaced by Rob Wolfe.
DiDonato joined forces with SACRAMENT bassist Erik Ney and BELIEVER drummer Joe Daub to create FOUNTAIN OF TEARS.

Albums:
TESTIMONY OF APOCALYPSE, R.E.X. (1990)
Testimony Of Apocalypse / Slave To Sin / Hellfire Denied / Repentance / Valley Of Dry Bones / Mortal Agony / Conquer Death / Absence Of Fear / The Risen / Blood Bath
HAUNTING OF VIOLENCE, R.E.X. (1992)

Haunts Of Violence / Carry The Corpse / Destructive Heresies / The Wicked Will Rot / Supplication Of The Destitute / Souls In Torment / Separate From / Iniquity / Seared Consciences / Under Threat Of Death / Portraits Of Decay

SACRILEGE (UK)
Line-Up: Lynda 'Tam' Simpson (vocals), Damien Thompson (guitar), Tony May (bass), Spikey T. Smith (drums).

Birmingham Thrash metal band SACRILEGE date back to 1984 fronted by female vocalist Tam. The group's debut product, 'Behind The Realms Of Madness', shifted a respectable 7,000 copies, although soon after recording the first album original guitarist Mitch and bassist Tony May left the band to pursue more Hardcore projects. SACRILEGE were then approached by FM Revolver Records, but this ultimately led nowhere.
Undeterred, the band again recorded, this time with the assistance of Rob Bruce at Birmingham's famous Rich Bitch studios. Recording was completed for 'Within The Prophecy', with producer Mike Ivory in January 1987, when Music For Nations subsidiary Under One Flag stepped in with a deal.
At this juncture the band recruited new bassist Paul Morrisey and second guitarist Frank Healey, although in late 1987 drummer Andrew Baker was replaced by Paul Brookes. The third album, 'Turn Back Trilobite', saw SACRILEGE moving away from mainstream Thrash and starting to explore slower, more Doom orientated material with a bit of Folk thrown in for good measure. At this point the band's line-up consisted of Tam, Thompson, Frank Healey on bass and Spikey T. Smith on drums.
Regrettably, the band turned in very few live appearances, which resulted in a fairly stagnant career, despite the obvious maturity and increased sales on successive albums.
Post SACRILEGE both Healy and Baker founded CEREBRAL FIX and Healy later went on to BENEDICTION. Brookes joined BENEDICTION then Power Metal band MARSHALL LAW in 1999.

Albums:
BEHIND THE REALMS OF MADNESS,
Children Of The Revolution GURT 4 (1985)
Life Line / Shadow From Mordor / At Death's Door / A Violation Of Something Sacred / The Closing Irony / Out Of Sight Out Of Mind
WITHIN THE PROPHECY, Under One Flag FLAG 15 (1987)
Sight Of The Wise / The Fear Within / Winds

Of Vengeance / The Captive / Spirit Cry /
Flight Of The Nazgul / Insurrection / Search
Eternal
TURN BACK TRILOBITE, Under One Flag
FLAG 29 (1989)
Father Time (Beneath The Gaze) / Silent
Dark / Soul Search / Awaken
(Suryanamaskar) / Key To Nirvana / Into The
Sea Of Tranquility / Equinox

SACRIVERSUM (POLAND)
Line-Up: Kate (vocals), Mario (guitar),
Sunrise (guitar), Remo (vocals / bass),
Bürger (keyboards), Zombie Attack (Drums)

SACRIVERSUM are noted for ambitiously
attempting a Gothic Metal homage to Irish
poet and playwright Samuel Beckett with
2000's 'Beckettia'.
The band dates to 1992 paying their dues
with the demos 'Dreams Of Destiny' and 'The
Shadow Of The Golden Fire', the latter
featuring female vocalist Alexandra.
SACRIVERSUM's transition from their early
Death Metal to more melancholic Gothic
sounds had become apparent by their debut
album 'Soteria'.
New vocalist Kate and drummer Zombie
Attack were added prior to the 'Beckettia'
album.

Albums:
SOTERIA, Morbid Noizz (1997)
Majesty Is Blind / Meditates / Sacred
Betrayal / Soteria / Overwhelming
Monuments / Paradise / Hybris / Hamartia
BECKETTIA, Serenades SR 023 (2000)
Intro / Waiting For Godot / Vision / The
Krapp's Last Tape / Happy Days / Spectral
Trio / An Act Without Words / Lullaby / Not
Me / Nacht Und Träume
**THE SHADOWS OF THE GOLDEN FIRE -
EARLY DAYS**, Conquer CRD057 (2001)
Across The Dust / Whispers / Pure Evil / In
Emotional Garden / Never Give Up / From
Your Blood / Tears / Wounded Flames /
Revenger / Defended Land / Dreams Of
Destiny / Taste Of Defeat / Defended Land
(New version) / Taste Of Defeat (New
version)

SADNESS (SWITZERLAND)
Line-Up: Steff (vocals / guitar), Chiva (guitar
/ keyboards), Erik (bass), Gradel (drums)

Following the first SADNESS demo, merely
titled 'Y', in 1990 bassist Erik departed to join
ALASTIS. His place was taken by Andy and a
further demo, 'Eodipus', was released.
SADNESS signed to the Polish label Mystic
Records for the 'Evangelion' album and

toured Poland alongside BEHEMOTH,
ASGARD, COLD PASSION and LIMBONIC
ART.
'Danteferno' was produced by former CELTIC
FROST bass player Martin E. Ain.
In 1997 Chiva debuted his side project act
CHIVA with the 'Oracle Morte' album.

Albums:
AMES DE MABRE, Witchunt WIHU 9313
(1994)
Ames De Marbre / Lueurs / Tristessa / Opal
Vault / Tears Of Sorrow / Red Script /
Antofagasta
DANTE FERNO, Godhead GOD020 (1996)
Danteferno / The Mark Of The Eldest Son /
Tribal / Delia / Below The Shadows /
Shaman / Aphrodites Thorns / Talisman
EVANGELION, Mystic Radio 99 (1998)
Mr. Faust / Heretic / Dias De Las Muertes /
Nosfera / Tears Of Sorrow (remastered) /
Danteferno (remastered) / Red Script (demo
version 1990)

SAD WHISPERINGS (HOLLAND)
Line-Up: J.A. van Leeuwen, E.R. Veniga, M.
Schrikkema, W.W.B. Wolda

A melodic Doom / Death Metal act.

Albums:
SENSITIVE TO AUTUMN, Foundations 2000
SDN 2007 (1993)
The Tombstone / Vale Of Tears / Free As The
Wind / Fear Glanced Eyes / Tears On My
Pillow / Timeless Grief / The Last Day Of
April / Leaving Me Behind / Sparks In The
Dust / Sensitive To Autumn

SAINT VITUS (Los Angeles, CA, USA)
Line-Up: Scott Reagers (vocals), Dave
Chandler (guitar), Mark Adams (bass),
Armando Acosta (drums)

Highly influential cult Doom outfit whose
records are now highly sought after. Although
SAINT VITUS is now hailed as a pioneering
act the band battled apathy for much of their
career. The Los Angeles based group
originally formed as TYRANT in 1979 by
vocalist Scott Reagers, guitarist Dave
Chandler, bassist Mark Adams, and drummer
Armando Acosta.
Delivering a quagmire of subterranean,
slothful Doom SAINT VITUS left many critics
reeling with their eponymous 1984 debut
record released on S.S.T. Records, the label
owned by BLACK FLAG guitarist Greg Ginn.
Reagers left the fold after recording 1985's
'Hallow's Victim' but was to return from the
wilderness in the mid '90s. SAINT VITUS

were fronted by THE OBSESSED's Scott 'Wino' Weinrich from the 1986 'Born Too Late' record. For this album vocal takes already laid down by Reager had to be recorded over by Wino. Promoting the 1988 'Mournful Cries' outing SAINT VITUS toured Europe extensively, later putting in a rare UK showing with AGNOSTIC FRONT. Wino would also aid LOST BREED for demo recordings during this time frame. The 1990 live album was recorded at Gammelsdorf in Germany during 1989.

Touring Europe once more in 1990 the band were supported by Swedes COUNT RAVEN. Wino then opted out to reform THE OBSESSED. After THE OBSESSED came to grief in 1995 Wino re-established himself with SHINE. After a solitary single SHINE evolved into SPIRIT CARAVAN.

With Wino's departure Christian Linderson of former opening act COUNT RAVEN assumed the vocal mantle as 'Lord Chritus' for 1991's 'Heavier Than Thou'.

DON DOKKEN produced the 1992 'C.O.D.' album but the band would fold. SAINT VITUS re-formed with Scott Reagers for the 1994 'Die Healing' opus, recorded in Berlin and produced by Harris Johns, but would soon fracture once more.

Linderson re-emerged with a new act TERRA FIRMA created with ex-UNLEASHED guitarist Fredrik Lindgren. SAINT VITUS reformed with Scott Reagers for the 1994 'Die Healing' opus, recorded in Berlin and produced by Harris Johns, but would soon fracture once more.

Guitarist Dave Chandler has since created DEBRIS INC. with another Doom veteran, Ron Holzner of TROUBLE.

Singles/EPs:
Darkness / White Stallions / The Walking Dead, S.S.T. SST042 (1985)
War Is Our Destiny, S.S.T. (1985) (American promo 12")
The End Of The End / Thirsty And Miserable / Look Behind You, S.S.T. SST119 (1989)

Albums:
SAINT VITUS, S.S.T. SST 022 (1984)
Saint Vitus / White Magic, Black Magic / Zombie Hunger / The Psychopath / Burial At Sea
HALLOW'S VICTIM, S.S.T. SST 052(1985)
War Is Our Destiny / White Stallions / Mystic Lady / Hallow's Victim / The Sadist / Just Friends (Empty Love) / Prayer For The (M)Asses
BORN TOO LATE, S.S.T. SST 082CD (1986)

Born Too Late / Clear Windowpane / Dying Inside / H.A.A.G. / The Lost Feeling / The War Starter
MOURNFUL CRIES, S.S.T. SST 161CD (1988)
Intro / The Creeps / Dragon Time / Shooting Gallery / Intro / Bitter Truth / The Troll / Looking Glass
V, Hellhound H-0005-2 (1990)
Living Backwards / I Bleed Black / When Emotion Dies / Patra (Petra) / Ice Monkey / Jack Frost / Angry Man / Mind-Food
LIVE, Hellhound 8468732 (1990)
Living Backwards / Born Too Late / The War Starter / Mind-Food / Looking Glass / White Stallions / Dying Inside / War Is Our Destiny / Mystic Lady / Clear Windowpane
HEAVIER THAN THOU, S.S.T. SST 266CD (1991)
Clear Windowpane / Born Too Late / Look Behind You / Thirsty And Miserable / Dying Inside / The Lost Feeling / H.A.A.G. / Shooting Gallery / Bitter Truth / Dragon Time / War Is Our Destiny / White Stallions / White Magic, Black Magic / Saint Vitus
C.O.D., Hellhound HELLCD017 (1992)
Intro / Children Of Doom / Planet Of Judgement / Shadow Of A Skeleton / (I Am) The Screaming Banshee / Plague Of Man / Imagination Man / Fear
DIE HEALING, Noise N0035UX (1994)
Dark World / Let The End Begin / Trail Of Pestilence / Sloth / Return Of The Zombie / In The Asylum / Just Another Notch

SALEM (ISRAEL)

Line-Up: Ze'eb Tanaboim (vocals), Lior Mizrachi (guitar), Giora Hirsch (guitar), Michael Goldstein (bass), Amir Neubach (drums)

An Israeli Black Doom Metal band that trace their history back to the very roots of Black Metal in the mid '80s. Frontman Ze'eb Tanaboim was in correspondence with the late MAYHEM mentor Euronymous in regards to releasing a SALEM record on his Deathlike Silence label. Tanaboim was also in communication with Euronymous's arch-rival and eventual murderer Varg Vikernes of BURZUM although on less salubrious terms. Allegedly Vikernes posted a nail bomb to Tanaboim after the SALEM man had offered to shoot him for derogatory comments against Jews.

The corpse paint bedecked SALEM, with new drummer Amir Neubach, emerged once more with the 1992 demo 'Millions Slaughtered'. Other founder members included Tanaboim, guitarists Lior Mizrach and Giora Hirsch with bass player Mikael Goldstein. These tapes were included as part of the band's first release for Morbid Records 'Creating Our Sins'.

SALEM's third release, the Colin Richardson produced 'Moment Of Silence', saw a drift into Gothic territory and the loss of Hirsch and Neubach. The album included an ambitious version of PINK FLOYD's 'Set The Controls For The Heart Of The Sun'. Niv Nakov was their new drummer.

Albums:
CREATING OUR SINS, Morbid (1994)
Masquerade In Claustrophobia / Creating Our Sins / Old Wounds / Millions Slaughtered / Children Don't Fight / Execution / Necromancy / Fields Of Death / Voices From Hell / Fucking Maniac / Old Wounds / Emotional Demands / Slow Death / Children Don't Fight / Fields Of Death
KADDISH, Morbid (1995)
The Fading / Above The Ground / Eyes To Match A Sul / Kaddish / Fear Of The Future / Dying Embers / Desert Prayer / The Edge Of The Void / Ha'ayana Bo'eret / The One That No One Knows
MOMENT IN SILENCE, BNE (1998)
Moment In Silence / Winter's Tear / Hour Glass / Flames / Set The Controls For The Heart Of The Sun / In Another Dimension / The Worst To Come / An Unwanted Guest / Symbiosis / Eyes To Match A Soul / Who Will Comfort Me Now?

SALLY (UK)
Line-Up: Lee Smith (vocals), Andrew Parker (guitar), Nigel Baker (guitar), Peter Brown (bass), Darren Donovan (drums)

Birmingham Doom band, named after 'Texas Chainsaw Massacre' heroine Sally Hardisty, led by ex-ELECTRIC WIZARD and PENANCE frontman Lee Smith. The group came together in 1996 as a trio of Darren 'Dirty' Donovan on drums and lead vocals, guitarist Andrew 'Godboy' Parker and bassist Peter 'Browny' Brown. During 1997 guitarist Nigel Baker augmented the line-up and SALLY cut two demo tapes, subsequently scoring a record deal with Lee Dorrian of CATHEDRAL's Rise Above label. Shortly before recording SALLY inducted Lee Smith on vocals.

SALLY have supported KARMA TO BURN, ORANGE GOBLIN and ELECTRIC WIZARD. Baker decamped in 1999 and SALLY opted to persevere as a quartet. Drummer Darren Donovan also operates as bassist with 'Necro-Doom' merchants MISTRESS.

A Billy Anderson produced sophomore album is expected during 2002.
Albums:

SALLY, Rise Above (2000)
Lord Of The Trees / Monolick / Uno / Four Twelve / Rolling Thunder / Monkey Steals The Peach / Kentucky Fried Motherfucker / Sonic Mountain

SAMAEL (SWITZERLAND)
Line-up: Vorphalack (Vocals / guitar), Masmisiem (bass), Xytraguptor (drums)

Proud to be recognized as one of the gloomiest bands in Europe. Over a series of finely crafted albums SAMAEL have built up an enviable reputation for quality Metal with a unique touch. 1999's 'Eternal' was widely acknowledged to be a classic of the genre.

SAMAEL heralded their arrival with the 1987 demo recording titled 'Into The Infernal Storm Of Evil'. SAMAEL's 1989's 'Medieval Prophecy' mini-album featured a cover of HELLHAMMER's 'The Third Of The Storm'. SAMAEL's next release in 1990 was the demo tape 'From Dark To Black'.

The 'Rebellion' mini-album boasted a cover of ALICE COOPER's 'I Love The Dead'.

The group added keyboard player Rudolphe H. for live dates in 1995 with SENTENCED and for the recording of 1996's 'Passage' all drum parts were programmed and Xytraguptor (later simply 'Xytra' then 'Xy') assumed a new role as keyboard player. A second guitarist, Khaos from French Death Metallers GORGON, was also brought in for recording and live dates. SAMAEL's relationship to SENTENCED was strengthened as Vorphalack added backing vocals to the Finn's 'Down' outing.

SAMAEL's 'Worship Him' album went on to sell over 10,000 copies in Europe. The follow up 'Blood Ritual' was produced by GRIP INC.'s Waldemar Sorychta.

For 'Ceremony Of Opposites', produced by Sorychta once again, SAMAEL added keyboard player Rudolphe H.

SAMAEL's 1996 album 'Passage' would be re-released two years later with ambient Classical remixes of all tracks by Xy. The man's skills in the studio would be recognized outside of SAMAEL, gaining production credits on two albums , 'Sleep of the Angels' and 'A Dead Poem' by Greek Black Metal veterans ROTTING CHRIST. Xy also operates his own label Parallel Union Records in collaboration with War D. of ALASTIS.

Upfront of schedule European summer festival performances guitarist Kaos announced his departure in mid 2002.

Singles/EPs:
Medieval Prophecy, Necrosound (1989)

349

Rebellion / After The Sepulture / Into The Pentagram / I Love The Dead / Static Journey, Century Media 77099-2 (1995) ('Rebellion' EP)

Albums:
WORSHIP HIM, Osmose Productions OPCD001 (1991)
Sleep Of Death / Worship Him / Knowledge Of the Ancient Kingdom / Morbid Metal / Rite Of Cthulhu / The Black Face / Into The Pentagram / Messengers Of The Light / Last Benediction / The Dark
BLOOD RITUAL, Century Media CM97372 (1992)
Epilogue / Beyond The Nothingness / Poison Infiltration / After The Sepulture / Macabre Operetta / Blood Ritual / Since The Creation / With The Gleam Of Torches / Total Consecration / Bestial Devotion / Until The Chaos
SAMAEL 1987-1992, Century Media 77085-2 (1993)
Epilogue/ Beyond The Nothingness / Poison Infiltration / After The Sepulture / Macabre Operetta / Blood Ritual / Since The Creation / With The Gleam Of Torches / Total Consecration / Bestial Devotion / ...Until The Chaos / Sleep Of Death / Worship Him / Knowledge Of The Ancient Kingdom / Morbid Metal / Rite Of Cthulhu / The Black Face / Into The Pentagram / Messengers Of The Light / Last Benediction / The Dark
CEREMONY OF OPPOSITES, Century Media CD 77064-2 (1994)
Black Trip / Celebration Of The Fourth / Son Of Earth / 'Til We Meet Again / Mask Of The Red Death / Baphomet's Throne / Flagellation / Crown / To Our Martyrs / Ceremony Of Opposites
PASSAGE, Century Media 77127-2 (1996)
Rain / Shining Kingdom / Angel's Decay / My Saviour / Jupiterian Vibe / The Ones / Liquid Souls / Moonskin / Born Under Saturn / Chosen Race / A Man In Your Head
EXODUS, Century Media 77210-2 (1998)
Exodus / Tribes Of Cain / Son Of Earth / Winter Solstice / Ceremony Of The Opposites / From Malkuth To Kether
PASSAGE/XYSTRA, Century Media (1998)
Rain / Shining Kingdom / Angel's Decay / My Saviour / Jupiterian Vibe / The Ones / Liquid Souls / Moonskin / Born Under Saturn / Chosen Race / A Man In Your Head / Regen / Glanzednes Königreich / Des Engels Untergang / Jupiterianische Schwingungen / Die Volter Kamen / Der Stamm Kains / Mondhaut / Mein Retter / Wintersonnenwerde / Ein Mensch Im Kopf
ETERNAL, Century Media (1999)
Year Zero / Ailleurs / Together / Ways / The Cross / Us / Supra Karma / I / Nautilus And Zeppelin / Infra Galaxia / Berg / Radiant Star

SAMHAIN (USA)

Line-Up: Glenn Danzig (vocals), Peter Marshall (guitar), Eerie Von (bass), Steve Zing (drums)

Although hampered by low budget production SAMHAIN were the breeding ground from which GLENN DANZIG, having excised himself from Punk outrage merchants MISFITS, cultured their dark brooding rock style that would evolve into DANZIG.

Early members included Lyle Preslar of MINOR THREAT and THE REPTILE HOUSE / THE MEATMEN drummer London May.

Danzig recruited another MISFITS refugee drummer EERIE VON to assume the bass role. Von had been post MISFITS a member of ROSEMARY'S BABIES releasing the 'Blood Lust' album before enrolling in Hare Krishna Hardcore mongers ANTIDOTE where he adopted the spiritual stage name of 'Bliss'. Immediately prior to joining SAMHAIN Von was operating a studio project I'M AFRAID with ex-MOURNING NOISE guitarist Chris Morance and erstwhile ROSEMARY'S BABIES bassist Post Mortem.

Guitarist Pete Marshall's pedigree includes GENOCIDE (where he went under the name Pistol Pete) and MOURNING NOISE. Drummer Steve Zing is also ex-MOURNING NOISE.

1990's 'Final Descent' saw the inclusion of guitarist JOHN CHRIST later of DANZIG. Marshall joined BRAIN EATERS and DITCH WITCH. Zing created Punk band CHYNA reuniting with erstwhile MOURNING NOISE colleagues.

May founded LUNCHBOX in 1987 for the 'Jesus, Judas And Me' album then DEAD, WHITE AND BLUE in 1991 for a string of singles before DISTORTED PONY for the Steve Albini produced 'Punishment Room' album. During 1997 May was a member of THE AMAZING CHAN CLAN issuing the 'Meteor Shower' single.

EERIE VON issued a joint album credited to EERIE VON/MIKE MORANCE called 'Uneasy Listening' in 1996 and a solo album 'The Blood And The Body' in 1998.

SAMHAIN, with bassist London May replacing Eerie Von, reformed in 1999 for live work supporting DANZIG! Glenn Danzig performing two shows each night.

October of 2001 witnessed a double 7" vinyl tribute to SAMHAIN. Limited to just 500 copies 'The Rebirthing', issued by Spastmathic Records, crammed in no less than 10 bands paying homage.

Albums:

INITIUM, Plan 9 (1984)
Initium-Samhain / Black Dream / All Murder, All Guts, All Fun / Macabre / He-Who-Can-Not-Be-Named / Horror Biz / The Shift / The Howl / Archangel / Unholy Passion
UNHOLY PASSION, Plan 9 (1985)
Unholy Passion / All Hell / Moribund / The Hungry End / I Am Misery
NOVEMBER COMING FIRE, Revolver REVLP 82 (1986)
Diabolos '88 / In My Grip / Mother Of Mercy / Birthright / To Walk The Night / Let The Day Begin / Halloween II / November's Fire / Kiss Of Steel / Unbridled / Human Pony Girl
FINAL DESCENT, Plan 9 (1990)
Night Chill / Descent / Death... In It's Arms / Lords Of The Left Hand / The Birthing / Unholy Passion / All Hell / Moribund / The Hungry End / Misery Tomb / I Am Misery
SAMHAIN LIVE 86-86, E-Magine 1064 (2002)
All Hell / Samhain / The Shift / The Howl / Unholy Passion / All Murder, All Guts, All Fun / I Am Misery / The Hungry End / Horror Biz / He-Who-Can-Not-Be-Named / Black Dream / Death Comes Ripping / Mother Of Mercy / To Walk The Night / Halloween II / In My Grip / London Dungeon / Archangel

SANCTUS (Los Angeles, CA, USA)
Line-Up: Jason McCrarey (vocals), Royce Hsu (guitar), Mike O' Meara (guitar), Brent Gobson (bass), Adrian Ross (keyboards), Michael Chi (drums)

California act SANCTUS were created in 1998 under the name of PANTHEON, issuing a demo under this name. Scoring a deal with Metal Blade Records the band duly adopted the new title of SANCTUS for the 2000 'Aeon Sky' album. Bassist Brent Gibson would depart in March of 2002.

Albums:
AEON SKY, Metal Blade (2000)
Empyreal / If We Fall... / Odyssey / November / Tired Of The Pain / Thought I Saw Your Wings / Thy Desolation / Remnants

SANDIABLO (ARGENTINA)
Line-Up: Gabriel Raimondo (vocals), Claudio Filadoro (guitar), Hernan Espejo (guitar), Adrián Corrales (bass), Martín Cipriano (drums)

Buenos Aires Stoners SANDIABLO is another arm of the NATAS and GALLOS DE RINA bassist 'Pastor' Claudio Filadoro. The band initially comprised Filadoro on guitar and drummer Martín Cipriano joined by vocalist Gabriel Raimondo, guitarist Hernan Espejo and bass player Adrián Corrales.
By June of 2001 Filadoro had assumed the role of vocalist / bassist fronting a quartet of Espejo and second guitarist Mariano Rojo with Cipriano retained on drums.
To date SANDIABLO have appeared on a tribute album to N.D.I. and the compilation 'Tiempos Violentos'.

SANTORO (ARGENTINA)
Line-Up: Jose (vocals), Sergio (guitar), Gonzalo (bass), Gonzalo (drums)

Buenos Aires Stoners SANTORO, fronted by former MASSACRE singer Jose, ex-CARNE GUACHA bassist Gonzalo and erstwhile RAIZ drummer Gonzalo, debuted with an eponymous 1999 demo tape. The 2001 SANTORO album, released by the German People Like You label, features Sergio of NATAS on vocals and guitar.
Following the album release Walter Broide of NATAS took over on drums and Caesar De Cabezones became the band's new frontman.

Albums:
SANTORO, People Like You (2001)
Yo No Hay / Germinal / Turbolorna / Me Sangra / Cain Y Abel / Tutankamon / Hay Market / Astraliano / Aquavulva / Marlon Brandon / Un Vaso / Super8Volante

THE SATELLITE CIRCLE (SWEDEN)
Line-Up: Jonas Ericson (vocals), Jonas Nordin (guitar), Fredrik Holmgren (bass), Rolf Bergqvist (keyboards), Henke Frohm (drums)

THE SATELLITE CIRCLE fuse Doom with healthy portions of '70s Psych-Southern influenced Hard Rock. Based in Umea the band came together during 1997 as a trio of Jonas Ericson handling both lead vocals and drums, guitarist Jonas Nordin and bass player Fredrik Holmgren. A deal was soon secured with the British Rage Of Achilles label for the November 2000 mini-album 'Way Beyond The Portal Of The Bone White Rubber Sun'.
The eponymous album arrived in June of 2001. THE SATELLITE CIRCLE added two new members for live work and recording of a 2002 album in Hammond organ player Rolf Bergqvist and drummer Henke Frohm.
In keeping with their retro stance the members of THE SATELLITE CIRCLE travel to gigs in a 1962 Volvo PV544. Indeed, the band has stated it will only ever use vintage Volvos as official transport!

351

Albums:
WAY BEYOND THE PORTAL OF THE BONE WHITE RUBBER SUN, Rage Of Achilles ILIAD006 (2000)
Kick You Right Back / At The End Of The Day / Reconcile / The More I Drink / From Where You Stand
THE SATELLITE CIRCLE, Rage Of Achilles ILIAD014 (2001)
You Were Never The King / Remedy / Black Mountainside / Slow Descent / The Thin White Line Between Happiness And Sanity / Simplicity / The Beginning Of The End Of The World / I Need To Keep This To Myself / The Beginning Of The End Of The World - Part 2

SATURNUS (DENMARK)
Line-Up: A.G. Jensen (vocals), Kim Larsen (guitar), Brian Hansen (bass), Anders Ro Nielsen (keyboards), Jesper Saltoft (drums / keyboards)

A Danish Doom / Death band initially titled ASSESINO. The band can trace it's history back to the 1991 union of vocalist Thomas A.G. Jenson, guitarists Kim Sindahl and Christian Brenner, bass player Brian Hansen and drummer Pouli Choir as ASSESINO.
The band actually split but reunited with fresh recruit Jesper Saltoft. A period of flux ensued with Sindahl decamping and guitarist Michael Andersen and keyboard player Anders Ro Nielsen being drafted. At this stage the unit opted for the new title of SATURNUS.
1994 saw the inclusion of guitarist Kim Larsen and the following year the exit of Andersen. A support gig to Britain's Doom mongers MY DYING BRIDE made a weighty impression on the band who acknowledge their shift in style to a gloomy, melancholic style from this juncture.
SATURNUS cut their debut album 'Paradise Belongs To You' for the Euphonious label which included new drummer Morten Skrubbeltrang. Promoting the album SATURNUS ambitiously employed an 8 piece choir for live gigs.
After a mini-album 'For The Loveless Lonely Nights' a switch in drummers had Peter Poulsen joining in time for the Flemming Rasmussen produced 'Martyre' album.
SATURNUS suffered further internal strife in 1999 with new enlistees being drummer Morten Plenge, guitarist Tais Pedersen and bassist Peter Heede.
Both Larsen and Nielsen sessioned on BLAZING ETERNITY's debut album of 2000.

Albums:
PARADISE BELONGS TO YOU, Euphonious

PHONI 005 (1996)
Paradise Belongs To You / Christ Goodbye / As We Dance The Path Of Fire And Solace / Pilgrimage Of Sorrow / The Fall Of Nakkiel (Nakkiel Has Fallen) / Astral Dawn / I Love Thee / The Underworld / Lament For This Treacherous World
FOR THE LOVELESS LONELY NIGHT, Euphonious (1998)
Starres / For Your Demons / Thou Art Free / Christ Goodbye (Live) / Rise Of Nakkiel (Live) / Consecration
MARTYRE, Euphonious (2000)
Inflame Thy Heart / Empty Handed / Noir / A Poem (Written In Moonlight) / Softly On The Path You Fade / Thou Art Free / Drown My Sorrow / Lost My War / Loss (In Memorium) / Thus My Heart Weepeth For Thee / In Your Shining Eyes

SAVIOUR MACHINE (CA, USA)
Line-Up: Eric Clayton (vocals), Jeff Clayton (guitar), Charles Cooper (bass), Nathan Van Hala (keyboards), Jayson Heart (drums)

Theatric Gothic infused Metal with an apocalyptic Christian message spearheaded by the bald jewel headed visionary Eric Clayton. SAVIOUR MACHINE was created in Southern California during 1989 by the Clayton siblings, vocalist Eric and guitarist Jeff, in alliance with bass player Dean Forsyth and drummer Chris Fee. An eponymous demo the following year secured a deal with Frontline Records. However, following an appearance at a 1992 Christian Rock festival in Irvine Fee made his exit as Samuel West took over.
Things did not run as smoothly with Frontline Records as had been hoped. SAVIOUR MACHINE toured as openers to DELIVERANCE but would find themselves ejected before the close of the tour as promoters apparently misjudged their Christian beliefs. During recording of the sophomore album the band, now complemented by keyboard player Nathan Van Hala and yet another new drummer Jayson Heart, broke free of their contract. Frontline would only press up 1,000 copies of this record. SAVIOUR MACHINE signed to the German Metal label Massacre Records signalling a relationship, which would result in the fostering of a large German fan base. The band's first taste of European roadwork came with tour of Germany in 1994 capitalized on by a return visit, including Dutch dates, in May of 1995. The first brace of albums would also find themselves remastered and re-released by Massacre.
Touring in Europe garnered the band a wealth of media coverage with Eric Clayton's image

allied to the bands ministerial message making quite an impact. Shows from these dates would later be issued as the 1995 'Live In Deutschland' album.

With demand high the band headlined once more in Germany in March 1996. SAVIOUR MACHINE would then embark on the ambitious 'Legend' concept. Spanning three albums with over five hours of music this "Unofficial soundtrack to the end of the world" rendered the Book of Revelation into a no holds barred Rock opera format. The debut 'Legend' chapter arrived in 1997 with 'Legend II' ensuing the following year.

Guitarist Carljohan Grimmark of Swedish Christian Metal band NARNIA would join SAVIOUR MACHINE for their 2001 'Legend III:I' installment.

The band would return to Germany for their first live European performance in three years taking the stage on the December 9th 2001 at the 'Christmas Rock Night' In Ennepetal.

Eric Clayton strengthened the relationship with NARNIA by acting as session vocalist for the Swedes 'The Great Fall' album.

Singles/EPs:
Behold a Pale Horse (Legend II version) / Behold a Pale Horse (Ego Mix) / Behold a Pale Horse (Classical Mix) / New World Order, Massacre (1998)

Albums:
SAVIOUR MACHINE I, Frontline (1993)
Carnival of Souls / Force of the Entity / Legion / Ludicrous Smiles / Wicked Windows / Son of the Rain / Killer / The Widow and the Bride / Christians and Lunatics / The Mask / A World Alone / Jesus Christ
SAVIOUR MACHINE II, Massacre (1994)
Saviour Machine I / The Gates / Enter the Idol / The Hunger Circle / Child in Silence / Ascension of Heroes / Paradox / The Stand / American Babylon / Ceremony / Overture / Love Never Dies / Saviour Machine II
LIVE IN DEUTSCHLAND, Massacre (1995)
Introduction / Killer / Carnival of Souls / Enter the Idol / The Wicked Window / Legion / Paradox / The Stand / A World Alone / Jesus Christ / Overture / Love Never Dies / Saviour Machine II
LEGEND I, Massacre (1997)
Overture / A Prophecy / I Am / Legend 1:1 / The Lamb / The Eyes of the Storm / The Birth Pangs / The Woman / The Night / The Sword of Islam / Gog: Kings of the North / The Invasion of Israel / World War III - The Final Conflict I / Ten - The Empire / Legend 1:11 / The Beast / Antichrist I
LEGEND II, Massacre (1998)
The Convenant / New World Order / The

Whore of Babylon / Legend 11:1 / The False Prophet / Mark of the Beast / Antichrist II: The Balance of Power / World War III - The Final Conflict II / Behold a Pale Horse / The Martyrs Cry / The Promise / The Sixth Seal / Legend 11:11 / The Holy Spirit / The Bride of Christ / Rapture: The Seventh Seal / War in Heaven - The Second Fall
SYNOPSIS, Massacre MAS CD0292 (2001)
Saviour Machine I / Carnival Of Souls / American Babylon / Ludicrous Smiles / Legend I:I / The Lamb / Ascension Of Heroes / Legion / Behold A Pale Horse / A World Alone / Legend II:II

SCENE KILLER (NJ, USA)

Not so much a band as an assemblage of the finest of New Jersey's underground Rock talent pulled together by Jim Hogan of SOLARIZED and including material dating back to January of 1999. The SCENE KILLER album brought together elements of THE ATOMIC BITCHWAX, MONSTER MAGNET, CORE, DAISYCUTTER, SIX SIGMA, ROTGUT, BURNOUT KING, THE LEMMINGS, SOLACE, SOLARIZED, DRAG PACK and HALFWAY TO GONE. Contributing musicians included ETERNAL ELYSIUM's Yukito Okazaki, IRON MAN's Alfred Morris III as well as members of GIANT SLOTH. The record was mixed by Jack Endino.

Albums:
SCENE KILLER, Meteor City MCY-017 (2001)
Intro / Island Zero / Pit Of The Soul / You Know / Aurora / Interlude / Back Of My Mind / Midnight Snack / Psychic Down / Wasteland / Found / Buckshot / As You Look

SCHALIACH (NORWAY)
Line-Up: Peter Dalbekk (vocals / guitar), Ole Børud (guitar / bass / drums)

Despite the typically Black Metal logo and undoubted extremities of their music SCHALIACH are not all they seem. Founded by Ole Børud of EXTOL the band is in fact a Christian self-styled "Unblack" Doom styled Metal band.

Albums:
SONRISE, Pleitegeier PGD 7970 (1997)
The Last Creed / You Maintain / In Memorium / A Fathers Mourning / A Whisper From Heaven / On A Different Day / Coming Of The Dawn / Sonrise

SCISSORFIGHT (Portsmouth, NH, USA)
Line-Up: Ironlung (vocals), Geezum H. Crow

(guitar), Jarvis (bass), Kevin J. Strongbow (drums)

Although native to New Hampshire SCISSORFIGHT, titled after the interlocking legs position favoured by porn stars, delivered deep South, detuned subterranean rumblings embellished by Ironlung's narrative lyrics and local slang. First known of in 1995 SCISSORFIGHT comprised the heavily bearded figure of vocalist Ironlung, so called after his resilience to a hacking cough, guitarist Geezum H. Crow (aka Jay Fortin), bassist Jarvis, and drummer Joel Muzzey. The drum position would shortly after be filled by Ironlung's brother Kevin J. Strongbow.

The band opened proceedings for local label Wonderdrug with the April 1998 Ken Cmar produced album 'Guaranteed Kill'. Music critics, unable to compartmentalize SCISSORFIGHT, conveniently labelled the band as 'Redneck'. Ken Cmar would be at the helm for the follow up 'Ball's Deep' in June of the following year before the band moved on to Tortuga Recordings, debuting for their new label with the patriotically titled 'New Hampshire', produced by Andrew Schneider. The 2001 'Piscataqua' album would include the novel 'Fuck' trilogy, a triptych of cover versions by the likes of the DEAD KENNEDYS, THE DWARVES and G.G. ALLIN. Also included would be a rendition of AEROSMITH's 'Lick And A Promise'. MTV VJ Iann Robinson would pick up on the band at this juncture plugging SCISSORFIGHT mercilessly.

Promoting the 'Mantrapping For Sport And Profit' album SCISSORFIGHT embarked upon US touring as opening act on CANDIRIA, BIOHAZARD and CLUTCH shows. The 'American Cloven Hoof Blues' album consists of new and re-recorded material specifically for the British market.

Touring North America in May of 2002 had SCISSORFIGHT packaged with SHADOW'S FALL, UNEARTH and LAMB OF GOD.

Albums:
GUARANTEED KILL, Wonderdrug 2 (1998)
American Cloven Hoof Blues / Supervirgin VS. Death Machine / Helicopter Killing Cottonmouth / Fine Me / Chocorua Mountain Woman / Moosilaukie Rot / 1893 / Build More Prisons / Mulekick / Tempest Of Skulls / Harvest Of Horror / Joke / Planet Of Ass / Mjolnir In The Valley Of The Hags
BALL'S DEEP, Wonderdrug 1700 (1999)
Drunken Hangman / Human Head / The Gibbetted Captain Kidd / Scarecrow Season / Curse Of The Returned Astronaut / Quantrill's Raiders / Stove By A Whale / Balls Deep / Kancamagus Mangler / Cramp /

Scream Of The Wendigo
NEW HAMPSHIRE, Tortuga TR06 (2000)
Granite State Destroyer / The Ballad Of Jacco Macacco / Injection Site / Billy Jack Attack / Lamprey River / Cycloptic Skull / Roman Boxing Glove / The Gruesome Death Of Edward Teach / Musk Ox / Mountain Man Boogie / Dead Thunderbird
PISCATAQUA, Tortuga TR09 (2001)
Outmotherfucker The Man / Shewolf / Too Drunk To Fuck / Fuck 'em All / Drink Fight And Fuck / Lick And A Promise / Just Head
MANTRAPPING FOR SPORT AND PROFIT, Tortuga TR019 (2001)
Acid For Blood / New Hampshire's All Right If You Like Fighting / Rats U.S.A. / Deliver The Yankee Coffin / The Most Dangerous Animal Is Me / Hazard To Navigation / Hammerdown / Blizzards, Buzzards, Bastards / Mantrap / Death In The Wilderness / Candy Clark / Go Cave! / Cram It Clown
AMERICAN CLOVEN HOOF BLUES, Eccentric Man ECC002CD (2001) (UK release)
Helicopter Killing Cotton Mouth / Tempest Of Skulls / New Hampshire's Alright If You Like Fighting / Proving Grounds / Cadaver Recovery Man / The Complete Outlaw / 1893 / Mud & Guts / Cult Extraction / Up In The Country / Riot On The Village Green / Planet Of Ass

SCULPTURED (Portland, OR, USA)
Line-Up: Brian Yager (vocals), Don Anderson (vocals / guitar / keyboards), Jason Walton (bass), Clint Idsinga (trombone), Burke Harris (trumpet), John Schlegel (drums)

Mentored by AGALLOCH's Don Anderson Portland's SCULPTURED attempt to take Death Metal into uncharted waters. Anderson provides gruff vocals and the bulk of the instrumentation whilst Brian Yager contributes clean vocals. Bass guitar comes courtesy of AGALLOCH and ESPECIALLY LIKELY SLOTH man Jason Walton. The sombreness of SCULPTURED's musical landscape was enhanced by the novel use of a horn section. John Haughm of AGALLOCH took over on drums for the 2000 'Apollo Ends' album.

Albums:
THE SPEAR OF THE LILY IS AUREOLED, The End TE004 (1999)
Together With The Seasons / Almond Beauty / Lit By The Light Of Morning / Fashioned By Blood And Tears / Fulfillment In Tragedy For Cello And Flute / Her Silence / Our Illuminated Tomb
APOLLO ENDS, The End TE010 (2000)

354

Washing My Hands Of It / Above The 60th Parallel / Snow Covers All / Betweeen Goldberg / Apollo Destroys, Apollo Creates / Song To Fall On Deaf Ears / Summary

SEA OF GREEN (CANADA)
Line-Up: Travis Cardinal (vocals / guitar), Eric Kuthe (bass), Matt Dowd (drums)

Smooth, laid back Stoner trio out of Toronto. SEA OF GREEN are distinctive in their chosen field for purveying relatively upbeat music tinged with a retro acid edge. The group gelled in July of 1999 with the assimilation of ex-SEEDS OF DISCORD frontman Travis 'Jesus' Cardinal and former KUTHE personnel bassist Eric Kuthe and drummer Chris Bender. Signing to the Music Cartel SEA OF GREEN debuted with the Nick Blagona produced EP 'Northern Lights'.
The 2001 album 'Time To Fly' maintained the Blagona connection and includes a cover version of PINK FLOYD's 'Breathe'. The record was licensed to Rise Above Records for UK release.
Original drummer Chris Bender would later make way for Matt Dowd. SEA OF GREEN put in a joint headline tour of the UK during March of 2002 alongside MARSHAN. Preparations would be made during the summer for a fresh studio album provisionally billed as 'Karmic Mirror'.

Singles/EPs:
Move The Mountains / Look To The Sky / If You Want My Soul / Time & Space / Change With Me / In The Sun, Music Cartel (2000) ('Northern Lights' EP)

Albums:
TIME TO FLY, Music Cartel (2001)
Annihilation / Women Today / Ever After / Come On Down / Deep Inside / Orion's Belt / People Of The Earth / Long Time Coming / End Of Eternity / Breathe / Red Haired Dreams / Dune

SEAR BLISS (HUNGARY)
Line-Up: Andras Nagy (vocals / bass), Janos Barbarics (guitar), Csaba Csejtei (guitar), Winter (keyboards), Gergely Szücs (keyboards), Zoltan Csejtei (drums)

Szombathely based SEAR BLISS are a Gothic infused Black Metal band.
SEAR BLISS first arrived on the Metal scene

SEA OF GREEN
Photo : El Danno

355

with their 'Pagan Winter' demo tape of April 1995, leading directly to a record contract with Two Moons Records.

During early 1997 SEAR BLISS promoted the subsequent 'Phantoms' album with shows in Europe opening for MARDUK and TSATTHOGGA.

With SEAR BLISS making serious strides Two Moons re-released the 'Pagan Winter' demo on CD adding bonus tracks to make up the 1997 release. However, subsequent touring highlighted divisions within the band unit and keyboard player Winter departed to give more concentration to his solo projects ARUD and FOREST SILENCE.

SEAR BLISS also pulled in new members guitarist Viktor Max Scheer and drummer Zoltan Schönberger.

Albums:
PHANTOMS, Two Moons TM1201-2 (1996)
Far Above The Trees / Aeons Of Desolation / 1100 Years Ago / As The Bliss Is Burning / Land Of The Phantoms / Beyond The Darkness / With Mournful Eyes
THE PAGAN WINTER - IN THE SHADOW OF ANOTHER WORLD, Two Moons TM 1202 2 (1997)
Ancient / The Pagan Winter / ...Where Darkness Always Reigned / Twilight / In The Shadow Of Another World
THE HAUNTING, Two Moons TM 1205 2 (1998)
Tunnels Of Vision / Hell Within / Land Of Silence / Unholy Dance / Soulless / The Haunting / Left In The Dark

SEASONS OF THE WOLF

(Sarasota, FL, USA)
Line-Up: Wes Waddell (vocals), Barry Waddell (guitar), Dennis Ristow (keyboards), Phaedra Rubio (bass), Wayne Hoefle (drums)

A Florida based Gothic flavoured Progressive Metal band with a spiritual edge that has seen the SEASONS OF THE WOLF dubbed 'New Age Metal'. The group, founded in 1988 by ex-EQUINOX vocalist Wes Waddell and keyboard player Dennis Ristow, debuted with two demo tapes prior to founder member bassist Clay Yeagley being replaced by DANGEROUS CURVES female four stringer Phaedra Rubio. A six track, self-titled CD would be contracted but this deal subsequently fell through. The tapes finally arrived in 1996 via the band's own Earth Mother Music imprint. In 1998 Rubio lost his position to Chris Whitford.

Momentum accelerated with the issue of the 1999 'Lost In Hell' album, after which

SEASONS OF THE WOLF surfaced on tribute albums to artists such as QUEEN, IRON MAIDEN, with 'Flash Of The Blade' and BLACK SABBATH.

'Nocturnal Revelation' was delivered in 2001.

Albums:
SEASONS OF THE WOLF, Earth Mother Music (1996)
Victim Of Darkness / October Moon / Misty Shades Of Green / Electric Dimension / Long Cold Winter / 10,000-10,000 / Quiet Earth
LOST IN HELL, Adrenaline (1999)
Lost In Hell / S.O.S. / Interstellar / Voo Doo Master / Initiation / One Land One King / Abandoned City / Communion / Witchfinder / A Face In The Mist / Vengeance / Land Of The Dead (Live)
NOCTURNAL REVELATION, Earth Mother Music (2001)
New Age Revolution / Dead Zone / Quilex / Nocturnal Revolution / Dance Of A Thousand Veils / Liar / Magnetic Star / Skulls / Dark And Lonely Depths / Storm Of The Century / Starstruck / NR3 / Transmission

SECRET DISCOVERY (GERMANY)

Line-Up: Kai Hoffmann (vocals / keyboards), Falk Hoffmann (guitar), Michael Gusky (guitar), Mathias Glathe (bass), Tom Thues (drums)

Gothic Metal band SECRET DISCOVERY were formed in 1989. The band's 1996 album provided the breakthrough for SECRET DISCOVERY outselling its predecessors fourfold.

The band toured Europe as part of the 'Out Of The Dark' festivals sharing billing with MOONSPELL, THE GATHERING and CREMATORY. Further high profile gigs in Germany ensued as guests to RAMMSTEIN. A projected tour with NEFILIM was cancelled due to illness in the headlining act's camp.

SECRET DISCOVERY broadened their horizons with the EP 'Philharmic Diseases' by the inclusion of Classical influences. The band delved further into experimentation with the 'Slave' album.

1997 had SECRET DISCOVERY back on the road with LACRIMOSA and once again as part of the 'Out Of The Dark' festivals with MY DYING BRIDE, DARK and SENTENCED.

An interesting promotional release not made available to the public would be an album of 'Follow Me' remixes commissioned from club DJs across Germany.

Despite building up a solid fan base SECRET DISCOVERY called it a day. The band bowed out with a self-released live album recorded at the Zeche venue in Bochum during May 0f 1999. The record would be restricted to just 444 hand numbered copies.

Singles/EPs:
Cage Of Desire (Single version) / Down From Hell (Live) / Try To Live (Live) / Cage Of Desire (Rattle mix), Sound Factory (1994)
Colour My Life / Hello Goodbye / Ask Your God / Just For You (Again) / War, G.U.N. GUN 083 BMG (1995) ('Secret Discovery' EP, Promotional release)
Hello Goodbye (Single Edit) / Small World / Hello Goodbye (Long Version), G.U.N. GUN 084 BMG 74321 34410-2 (1995)
Colour My Life / One Good Reason / War, G.U.N. Gun 094 BMG 74321 37579-2 (1995)
A Question Of Time / Hello Goodbye / When Does It End / Again, G.U.N. GUN 108 BMG 74321 41954-2 (1996) ('Philharmonic Disease' EP)
Slave To The Rhythm (Single mix) / Slave To The Rhythm (Prince P.A.L. Club mix), G.U.N. (1997) (Promotion release)
Slave To The Rhythm (Single Edit) / Slave To The Rhythm (Rhythm Mix) / Slave To The Rhythm (Fat Beats) / Slave To The Rhythm (Raven & Pervert Biomechanical Mix), G.U.N. (1997)
Follow Me (Album version) / How Can I Learn / In My Dreams / Follow Me (E-Mix) / Follow Me (Norrim Radd-Mix), G.U.N. (1998)
You Spin Me Round / American Lifestyle / Hello Goodbye / One Good Reason, G.U.N. (1999)

Albums:
WAY OF SALVATION, (1991)
Endless Grey / Way To Salvation II / Down From Hell / Alien / Try To Live / Zerstörer / Way To Salvation I
DARKLINE, Rough Trade RTD 362 0005 2 41 (1992)
Dark Line (Theme) / Another Life / Dream Retailer / Flower In The Dust / Daily Nightmare / Friday 13th / Evil Feeling / The Other Side / Killed By Words / Feel The Time / Last Try
INTO THE VOID, Rough Trade RTD 362 0009 2 42 (1994)
Introduction / Time Has Come / Western World / Execution Day / Despair / Part Of Me / I Left The Real / Let Me Always / Salvation / into The Void
WASTED DREAMS, Sound Factory 359.0038.2 42 (1994)
Intro / Si Dangereux / My Rules / Meaningless / Cage Of Desire / Outlaw / Beyond The Past / When Does It End / The Signs / Just For Living
A QUESTION OF TIME, G.U.N. GUN 083

BMG 74321 34411-2 (1996)
Colour My Life / One Good Reason / Hello Goodbye / Just For You (Again) / A Question Of Time / Ask Your God / War / Think About / Wrapped In Black / What A Light / Society
SLAVE, G.U.N. GUN 126 BMG 7 4321 46532 2 (1997)
I Don't Care / Follow Me / Slave To The Rhythm / A Simple Impression / American Lifestyle / Night Falls / Seductive Angel / New Generation / Your Own / Serious Days / Kill Me
THE FINAL CHAPTER, G.U.N. (1999)
Mystery Land / You Spin Me Round / Wake Me With A Kiss / American Lifestyle / Hello Goodbye / Slave To The Rhythm / Love Kills / Colour My Life / One Good Reason / Follow Me / Si Dangereux / Cage Of Desire / When Does It End / In My Dreams / How Can I Learn / Small World
LIVE AT ZECHE BOCUM 02/05/99, (2000)
I Don´t Care / Colour My Life / Feel The Time / You Spin Me Round / Another Life / Love Kills / Slave To The Rhythm / Serious Days / New Generation / In My Dreams / Execution Day / Your Own / When Does It End

SEMLAH (SWEDEN)
Line-Up: Joleni (vocals), Tommy Eriksson (guitar), Thomas Johnson (bass), Johannes Bergh (drums)

A Doom unit founded during 2001 by erstwhile COUNT RAVEN guitarist Tommy 'Wilbur' Eriksson. Joining forces with Thomas Johnson SEMLAH, named after a seasonal pastry or an ancient siege ladder depending upon which story you are led to believe, would be created, locating a drummer in Johannes Bergh and ex-STRONGHOLD vocalist Joleni. SEMLAH released the 'Ruin' demo in 2002 and would be invited to perform at the 'Doom Shall Rise' European two-day Doom metal festival to be held in Crailsheim, Germany in February 2003.

SENTENCED (FINLAND)
Line-Up: Ville Laihiala (vocals / bass), Miika Tenkula (guitar), Sami Lopakka (guitar), Sami Kukkohovi (bass), Vesa Ranta (drums)

An Oulu based Death Metal band that leaned more towards the classic NWoBHM sound as each album progressed until later works centred upon a Doom-Death direction. Indeed, the band's classic British Rock influences were so evident the 1994 EP even went so far as to cover IRON MAIDEN's 'The Trooper'.
SENTENCED was created during 1989 by

357

the trio of guitarists Miika Tenkalu and Sami Lopakka along with drummer Vesa Ranta. In this incarnation the band cut their inaugural demo sessions the following year dubbed 'When Death Joins Us'. After recording SENTENCED's numbers were brought up to full-strength with the addition of vocalist / bassist Taneli Jarwa as they scored a deal with the French Thrash label for the 1991 debut album 'Shadows Of The Past'. This effort garnered the band praiseworthy media coverage internationally prompting a fresh deal with the domestic Spinefarm label. 1993's sophomore outing 'North From Here' would see the band adding a greater degree of melody to their work whilst retaining the technical edge.

'The Trooper' EP, for new label Century Media, kept the faithful happy until the arrival of 'Amok'. This album succeeding in selling 30,000 units.

SENTENCED toured Europe with TIAMAT and SAMAEL as Century Media re-released the bands first brace of albums to a wider audience.

Ever eager to experiment the 1995 EP 'Love And Death' included a version of BILLY IDOL's 'White Wedding'.

Jarwa often toured as bassist for IMPALED NAZARENE when the SENTENCED schedule allowed. Jarwa had departed following the 'Love And Death' EP.

Jarwa's place was filled by former BREED man Ville Laihiala for the 1996 Waldemar Sorychta produced 'Down' album. Backing vocals came courtesy of Vorphalack of SAMAEL. The bands new lead vocalist brought another new dimension the SENTENCED sound as Laihiala opted for a clean vocal style more suited to the more recent, doomier outings. Global touring had SENTENCED hitting their stride with dates in Europe, America and Japan. SENTENCED also formed part of the billing for the December 1996 'Dark Winter Nights' touring festival alongside DEPRESSIVE AGE, LACRIMOSA, THE GATHERING and DREAMS OF SANITY.

The 1998 opus 'Frozen', which found bassist Sami Kukkohovi of BREED and MYTHOS added to the roster, would once again be produced by Sorychta.

The 2000 'Crimson' album would lend recognition to SENTENCED's status as it reached the coveted number 1 position in the Finnish album charts. Later in the same year the album would be relaunched in picture disc vinyl format.

Meantime erstwhile frontman Jarwa resurfaced fronting THE BLACK LEAGUE the same year.

In February of 2001 Century Media repackaged the 'Amok' and 'Love & Death' records on a single CD re-release. Laihiala was also to be revealed as in collaboration with Jesper Stromblad of IN FLAMES on an extracurricular band project.

SENTENCED bounced back in style during May of 2002 with the Hiili Hiilesmaa produced album 'The Cold White Light', their 'No One There' single charting at the number 2 position in Finland. Shortly after the album itself hit the top spot in its first week of release. The band shortly after unveiled an extensive European tour schedule for October, supported by LACUNA COIL. North American shows had SENTENCED combining forces with LACUNA COIL, IN FLAMES and DARK TRANQUILITY.

Singles/EPs:
The Trooper / Desert By Night / In Memoriam / Awaiting The Winter Frost, Spinefarm SPI 015 (1993) ('The Trooper' EP)
The Way I Wanna Go / Obsession / Dreamlands / White Wedding / Love And Death, Century Media 77101-2 (1995) ('Love And Death' EP)
Killing Me, Killing You / Dead Moon Rising, Century Media (1999)

Albums:
SHADOWS OF THE PAST, Thrash THR015-NR340 (1992)
When The Moment Of Death Arrives Rot To Dead / Disengagement / Rotting Ways To Misery / The Truth / Suffocated Beginning Of Life / Beyond The Distant Valleys / Under The Suffer / Descending Curtain of Death
NORTH FROM HERE, Spinefarm SPI13CD (1993)
My Sky Is Darker Than Thine / Wings / Fields Of Blood / Harvester Of Hate / Capture Of Fire / Awaiting The Winter Frost / Beyond The Wall Of Sleep / Northern Lights / Epic
AMOK, Century Media CD77076-2 (1994)
The War Ain't Over! / Phoenix / New Age Messiah / Forever Lost / Funeral Spring / Nepenthe / Dance On The Graves (Lil 'Siztah') / Moon Magick / The Golden Stream Of Lapland
DOWN, Century Media 77146-2 (1996)
Intro - The Gate / Noose / Shadegrown / Bleed / Keep My Grave Open / Crumbling Down (Give Up Hope) / Sun Won't Shine / Ode To The End / 0132 / Warrior Of Life (Reaper Reedemer) / I'll Throw The First Rock
STORY - GREATEST KILLS, Spinefarm SPI44CD (1997)
Noose / Nepenthe / Sun Won't Shine / Dance On The Graves / The Way I Wanna

Go / White Wedding / My Sky Is Darker Than Thine / The Trooper / Desert By Night / In Memorium / Awaiting The Winter Frost / The Truth
CRIMSON, Century Media 77346-2 (2000) **1 FINLAND**
Bleed In My Arms / Home In Despair / Fragile / No More Beating As One / Broken / Killing Me, Killing You / Dead Moon Rising / The River / One More Day / With Bitterness And Joy / My Slowing Heart
AMOK / LOVE & DEATH, Century Media (2001)
The War Ain't Over! / Phoenix / New Age Messiah / Forever Lost / Funeral Spring / Nepenthe / Dance On The Graves (Lil 'Siztah') / Moon Magick / The Golden Stream Of Lapland / The Way I Wanna Go / Obsession / Dreamlands / White Wedding / Love And Death
THE COLD WHITE LIGHT, Century Media 8146-2 (2002) **1 FINLAND, 45 GERMANY, 5 SWEDEN**
Konevitsan Kirkonkellot / Cross My Heart And Hope To Die / Brief Is The Light / Neverlasting / Aika Multaa Muistot (Everything Is Nothing) / Excuse Me While I Kill Myself / Blood & Tears / You Are The One / Guilt And Regret / The Luxury Of A Grave / No One There

SERENADE (UK)

Line-Up: John Alexander (vocals), Fraser McGartland (guitar), Gerry Magee (guitar), Stephen Mitchell (bass), Graeme McGartland (drums)

A Glasgow rooted Doom Metal band forged during March of 1994. Previous to this the bulk of the band members had operated in IMMORTAL RITES. As SERENADE they heralded their arrival with the demo tape 'Let Loose The Beauty Within'. This release would subsequently be reissued as an official cassette EP by Deviation Records. Later still these sessions would be allied to material from HARMONY for a split CD release on Arctic Serenades.
SERENADE's first full-length opus, 'The 28th Parallel' issued by Deviation, would prove to be a conceptual piece based upon the discoveries of Christopher Columbus. The album generated laudatory reviews but SERENADE's gig schedule was spartan. The sophomore outing, 1998's 'The Chaos They Create' took the concept theme into an obscurer destination, the story line this time regarding the struggles of a Celtic farming family.
At this juncture SERENADE split away from Deviation Records and also suffered major internal turbulence. Guitarist Gerry Magee

broke away and bass player Stephen Mitchell relocated to Aberdeen.
For the 'Plague Of Time' EP release, distributed by the group's own label Golden Lake Productions, SERENADE trimmed down to a trio with guitarist Fraser McGartland taking on bass duties for recording.
A latter day band line-up saw the induction of new personnel MITHRAS vocalist Raynor Coss and guitarist Adam Chapman.
SERENADE members are also committed to the Stoner side venture MONGOOSE III.

Singles/EPs:
Where The River Flows End / Let Loose The Beauty Within / Born Into Sorrow / Casting The Flash, Arctic Serenades SERE 008 (1995) ('Let Loose The Beauty Within' EP, Split CD with HARMONY)
Depth Of The Bleeding Angel / Plague Of Time / Casting The Flesh - Say Hello To Hell, Golden Lake Productions (2001) ('Plague Of Time' EP)

Albums:
THE 28TH PARALLEL, Deviation (1996)
Introduction: 1492 / Daring To Dream / The Hearing / Ocean Of Despair / Beyond The Mist / Arrival / San Salvador / The Encounter / Homeward / Eden / To Face The Glory / Eden After The All / This Was Their World / Eternal Dream
THE CHAOS THEY CREATE, Deviation (1998)
The Raptures Of The Moribund / Blue Empyreans / Embracing Weave Of Wheat / Sundown Angels / Flames Dance / Woeful Third Season / Chaos... / The Hermit And The Wolves / Rains Wash Away (Parts 1 To 3)
THE SERPENT'S DANCE, Golden Lake Productions GOLD007CD (2002)
Into The Serpents Dance / Slaves Of Chaos / Dying Light / March Of Darkness / Betrayal Of Faith / Armageddon Comes / Evenslaughter / Nevermore

SERENITY (UK)

Line-Up: Daniel Savage (vocals), Lee Baines (guitar), Richard Savage (guitar), Brendan Dawson (bass), Gary Riley (drums)

SERENITY were borne from a split in the ranks of SOLSTICE during 1994. Guitarist Lee Baines, bass player Brendan Dawson and drummer Gary Riley left SOLSTICE and added vocalist Daniel Savage to form SERENITY. The band recorded their debut recordings in the form of a three track demo featuring 'Black Tears', 'Then Came Silence' and 'Spirituality' in July 1994.

Shortly after the demo Daniel's brother Richard joined on rhythm guitar. Meanwhile the tape had bagged the band a deal with France's Holy Records. Prior to their first album SERENITY undertook their first ever gig supporting MY DYING BRIDE in September.

Savage quit in early 1997, resulting in the cancellation of a British tour. As SERENITY collapsed, Baines, Riley and Rich Savage opted to carry on as a unit founding a further heavyweight outfit KHANG. This new formation, which also included vocalist Bryan Outlaw, ex-DOOM bassist Bri and former MY DYING BRIDE drummer Rick Miah, debuted with the 1999 album 'Premeditated'.

Lee Baines would later join the ranks of MY DYING BRIDE.

Albums:
THEN CAME SILENCE, Holy HOLY 10 (1995)
Black Tears / Change / Then Came Silence / The Darkest Things / Spirituality / One For The Red Sky / I Am With You
BREATHING DEMONS, Holy HOLY 20 (1996)
So? / Darker With My Eyes Open / 10 Snakes / The River / The Way I Bleed / Breathing Demons / Frustrate / Inside Of I

SERPENT (SWEDEN)
Line-Up: Piotr Wawrzeniuk (vocals), Johan Lundell (guitar), Lars Rosenberg (bass), Per Karlsson (drums)

SERPENT date back to 1993 when the band were formed as a side project by then ENTOMBED bassist Lars Rosenberg and CONCRETE SLEEP / THERION's bassist Andreas Wahl. The band soon enlisted THERION drummer Piotr Wawrzeniuk on vocals and drums before completing the line up with guitarist Johan Lundell.

Wahl departed in 1994 and was replaced by Ulf Samuelsson of SUFFER. Drummer Per Karlsson, another former SUFFER compatriot, joined SERPENT following recording of the debut album.

Unsatisfied with the reception to the debut album, SERPENT split from Radiation Records before undergoing an even more traumatic event when Rosenberg left the fold. Ironically, his swift replacement was none other than Wahl. This line-up soon got back into action by donating a fresh recording, a song titled 'The Fog', to a couple of compilation albums prompting a deal with Heathendoom Music.

Karlsson joined T.A.R. in January of 1997.

Albums:
IN THE GARDEN OF SERPENT, Radiation RAD006 (1996)
Fly With The Flow / Save From Ourselves / The Order / Stoned The Dawn / Magic / Lost Dreams / Frozen Cosmos / In Memorium / Drown / Corpse City
AUTUMN RIDE, Heathendoom HDMCD005 (1997)
Prologue / Dimension Zero / The Shot / Chasing The Dragon / Autumn Ride / The Fog / Mars's Boogie / Live Through This

SEVENCHURCH (UK)
Line-Up: Martin Spear (vocals), Dave Smart (guitar), Dave Capel (guitar), Paul Oliver (bass), Grahame Bastable (drums)

An Oxford Doom Metal act formed in 1989, vocalist Martin Spear was added in 1991 after his former group MADAM ADAM had split.

SEVEN CHURCH's demo, 'Nefarious', featured as one of the more successful entries in Radio One's 'Rock War' competition and, in 1992, the band signed to Noise and eventually released the debut album 'Black Insight'.

Albums:
BLEAK INSIGHT, Noise NO222-2 (1993)
Perceptions / Low / Surreal Wheel / Crawl Line / Sanctum / Autobituary

SEVEN FOOT SPLEEN
(Granite Falls, NC, USA)

North Carolina Hardcore edged Sludge. A 7" split single was issued in alliance with GACY'S PLACE. Ex-members founded STONE OF ABEL.

Albums:
ENTER THERAPY, Tee Pee TP1010-2 (2000)
Fetchin' Boy / Free Crutch Rental / Big Rig Blues / It Smells / Leech Eater / Joy Of The Worm / Clean Catch Urine Specimen / Without Thumbs / Rag Acne / Power / Jerky

SHADOW DANCERS (NORWAY)
Line-Up: Stian Johansen (vocals), Rym (guitar), Sanders (guitar), Joy B. (bass), Jontho Pantera (drums)

Although SHADOW DANCERS are Gothic Rock in style the band membership is firmly entrenched in Black Metal folklore led as they are by vocalist Stian Johansen, better known as Occultus of MAYHEM.

Johansen, a member of THY ABHORRENT, had been editor of 'Sepulcharal Noise' fanzine and an employee of the late Euronymous at his infamous 'Helvete' store when he bravely filled the awning chasm in the MAYHEM ranks left after the suicide of Dead. Johansen's stay was short and after a matter of weeks he exited to found PERDITION HEARSE.

SHADOW DANCERS was founded in collusion with RAGNAROK members guitarist Rym (Øyvind Trindborg) and drummer Jontho Pantera (John Thomas Bratland) along with second guitarist Sanders and bassist Joy B. Besides RAGNAROK both Rym and Jontho also operate with CROWHEAD.

Albums:
EQUILIBRIO, (1999)
In The Heart Of America / Tears From Heaven / Son Of Aequilibrium / The Wasp / The Island / Sherwood Life / The Glum Comedy / Revelation / My Fate / When It's All Over / Beyond Death

SHADOW PROJECT (USA)
Line-Up: Rozz Williams (vocals / guitar), Eva O (vocals / guitar), Jill Emery (bass), Paris (keyboards), Pete Tomlinson (drums)

A Satanic Gothic offshoot of CHRISTIAN DEATH led by the late Rozz Williams and wife Eva O.

Albums:
DREAMS FOR THE DYING, Fire Music (1992)
Static Jesus / Days Of Glory / Funeral Rites / Zaned People / Thy Kingdom Stalker / Holding You Close / Lord Of The Flies / The Circle And The Cross

SHALLOW (UK)
Line-Up: Tony Inskip (vocals / guitar), Danny Unet (guitar), Phil Brough (bass), Roderick Vyse (drums)

Stoner Rock from Stoke On Trent. SHALLOW was created during 1994 by ex-INTEGRITY drummer Roderick Vyse as a trio. The band was boosted to a quartet with the addition of Rod's erstwhile INTEGRITY colleague and guitarist Danny Unet in March of 1996. A split 7" single was delivered in collaboration with JAYNE DOE prior to hooking up with the Undergroove label for the four track EP 'Live At Heimi Hendersons', actually recorded at Nottingham's Square Dance studios in a single 12 hour session and produced by the esteemed Dave Chang.

SHALLOW had the track 'Sugar Glider' included on the Rise Above label compilation 'Rise 13' prior to signing to Lee Dorrian's imprint for the much praised '16 Sunsets In 24 Hours' album. Initially the record was recorded for Rise Above with a minimal budget at a band member's house but parent label Music For Nations insisted on higher quality. '16 Sunsets In 24 Hours' was duly re-recorded, the second version adding newer material.

A version of 'Moon Child' was donated to an IRON MAIDEN tribute album issued by the Meteor City label.

Upon discovery of an American act having previously registered the band title SHALLOW the group morphed into THE LAST DROP, subsequently releasing the 2002 album '...Where Were You Living A Year From Now?'

Singles/EPs:
Eight Minutes To The Sun / Neon Tee Pee / Something Unusual / Sugar Glider, Undergroove (1998) ('Live At Heimi Hendersons' EP)

Albums:
16 SUNSETS IN 24 HOURS, Rise Above RISE28CD (2000)
Anatomy Of A Giant / Liquid Cosh / Tartu (The Mystery Man Of The Balkans) / Rise Of Clocks - Motion In Reverse / The Bard / Titanic / God Module / Loaded But Empty? / Cake Ape

SHAMEN'S RIDE (AUSTRALIA)
Line-Up: Gareth (vocals), Damon (guitar), Alf, Perry

Sydney Grunge style Stoners forged in 2000. SHAMEN'S RIDE first delivered a three track CD entitled 'Waves' in January of 2002 before releasing the 'Roll Out The Red' album.

Singles/EPs:
Waves / Oceans Of The Mind / Worldly Wise Man, Highbeam Music HBM004 (2001)

Albums:
ROLL OUT THE RED, Highbeam Music HBM024 (2000)
Boneyard / Parachute / The Lane / Nowheresville / Roll Out The Red / Making The Wheel / Fly / Pulling The Crowd / Jaded / Mother Of Loads / Eyes Of The Blind

SHAPE OF DESPAIR (FINLAND)
Line-Up: Azhemin (vocals), N.S. (vocals), Jarno Salomaa (guitar), Tomi Ullgren (bass)

SHAPE OF DESPAIR is a Doom infused Death Metal act assembled by members of THY SERPENT and BARATHRUM. The band, originally assembled in 1995, was initially titled RAVEN issuing the 1998 demo tape 'Alive In The Mist'.

The act became SHAPE OF DESPAIR in 1999 with the addition of THY SERPENT man Azhemin and female singer N.S.

Bassist Tomi Ullgren and guitarist Jarno Salomaa also act as guitar players in RAPTURE.

Albums:

SHADES OF..., Spikefarm NAULA 005 (2000)
...In The Mist / Woundheir / Shadowed Dreams / Down Into The Stream / Sylvan Night
ANGELS OF DISTRESS, Spikfarm NAULA 018 (2001)
Fallen / Angels Of Distress / Quiet These Paintings Are / ...To Live For My Death... / Night's Dew

SHARD (GERMANY)

Albums:

KINCH VS. SHARD, Daredevil DD007 (2000) (Split album with KINCH)
I'll Take You Higher / Medicine Man / My Sad Machine / Wake Me Up

SHEAVY (CANADA)

Line-Up: Steve Hennessey (vocals), Dan Moore (guitar), Keith Foley (bass), Ren Squires (drums)

Class Stoner act SHEAVY was formulated St. John's, Newfoundland during the summer of 1993, originally billed as GREEN MACHINE in honour of the KYUSS track and initially intended to be a non-career side venture. The inaugural line-up of GREEN MACHINE cited vocalist Steve Hennessy, guitarists Dan Moore and Sterling Robertson, bass player Paul Grouchy and drummer Ren Squires. Moore at this juncture was operational with another act AFTER FOREVER, a band Squires had auditioned for.

The group, now minus Robertson, made their entrance with the 1993 'Reproduction' demo, this eight track affair being made up of five studio cuts and three live tracks amongst which were included covers of KYUSS tunes 'Green Machine' and 'Thumb'. Press reaction was enthusiastic and swift, many critics pointing out the obvious tonal similarities of Hennessy with a certain OZZY OSBOURNE. After release an American act was discovered going under the name GREEN MACHINE necessitating a name switch to SHEAVY.

An enforced lull in activities, caused by Hennessy's studies, put the band on ice for nearly a year before, regrouping, the ten track

'Slaves To Fashion' promotion cassette followed in 1994. Even though Grouchy performed live with the band, his college studies prevented commitment to studio sessions and therefore Moore added bass duties to his role in laying down 'Slaves To Fashion'. Limited to 300 tapes the demo novelly was distinguished by warrant of every individual copy having different sound effects and dialogue making each one unique.

A subsequent 1995 single, 'Dalas Tar' which closed with a homage to BLACK SABBATH's 'Tomorrow's Dream', was issued by the Montreal based Mag Wheel imprint in a 1,000 run pressing, half in regular black vinyl with the remainder manufactured in clear vinyl. Of the two original compositions on the single one cut was culled from the earlier demo with the other, appropriately billed 'Untitled', was an unfinished attempt at a new track.

SHEAVY's album debut came with the self-financed 'Blue Sky Mind' album issued through the band's own Dallas Tar label. Restricted to 1,200 copies 'Blue Sky Mind' combined new tracks with the 'Slaves To Fashion' demo sessions. Hennessey's Ozz-like vocal style then reaped unexpected results as none other than TONY IOMMI of BLACK SABBATH invited the singer down to Los Angeles to work up songs for a proposed solo album from the veteran guitarist. Unfortunately the tapes were shelved when Iommi embroiled himself in the BLACK SABBATH re-formation.

Grouchy decamped and SHEAVY soldiered on with a succession of temporary four stringers to fulfil gig commitments until Keith Foley was inducted in January of 1996. Another cassette then ensued, 'Live At The Loft' being a 300 copy run shared as a split release with AFTER FOREVER. A previously unheard live take on 'Electric Sleep' would be donated to the 'Peace-A-Chord '96' compilation album, issued in the summer of 1997 by Kansas Kahn Records.

SHEAVY would share vinyl space with arch Japanese Doomsters CHURCH OF MISERY for the June 1998 split album 'Born Too Late'. Clad in a sleeve mimicking BLACK SABBATH's 'Born Again' album the SHEAVY contributions comprised a re-work of 'Destiny's Rainbow', live tracks and a live in the studio version of BLACK SABBATH's infamous 'War Pigs'. Only 1,000 of these split albums would be pressed initially. That same month SHEAVY's inaugural full-length commercial album release, 'Electric Sleep', emerged through Lee Dorrian of CATHEDRAL's specialist label Rise Above. Intriguingly the original version of the album title track would exclusively appear nestled in the grooves of Meteor City's 'Welcome To

Meteor City' compilation that same month. SHEAVY had also been approached by the Man's Ruin label and consequently offered a rendition of LYNYRD SKYNYRD's 'Saturday Night Special' for use on a proposed 10" single. This would not materialize.

The 'Dalas Tar' single saw a re-pressing of just 100 copies in January of 1999. Meantime 'The Electric Sleep' was granted a North American release in March through Music Cartel, US versions being augmented by a bonus track 'The Last Parade'. Further exclusives came in the form of a version of 'Face In The Mirror', formed part of the Meteor City 'In The Groove' collection and an unreleased take of 'Pictures Of You' used on the UK 'Rise 13' album.

In early 2000 Moore, Squire and former bassist Paul Grouchy assembled an ad hoc project band billed as THE MARILYNS in order to record a MISFITS cover song for the Freebird tribute album 'Graven Images'.

The 'Celestial Hi-Fi' album surfaced on Rise Above in March of 2000 and would be issued in North America by Music Cartel just over a month later. Japanese variants on the JVC Victor label added two bonus tracks in 'El Camino' and 'Nine December'.

SHEAVY recorded a brand new Mike Butcher produced studio album 'Synchronized' in Belgium toward the close of 2001. However, by August of 2002 this record had still to be released.

Singles/EPs:
Dalas Tar / Untitled / Tomorrow's Dream, Mag Wheel (1995)
Dalas Tar / Untitled / Tomorrow's Dream, Mag Wheel (1999) (Limited edition 100 copies)

Albums:
BLUE SKY MIND, Dallas Tar (1996)
Mountains Of Madness / Blue Sky Mind / Domelight / Cosmic Overdrive / Sea Of Tomorrow / Supa-Hero / The Gun it Jam / Psycho Universe (Live) / First / Shining Path / Dalas Tar / The Everlasting / Dreamer's Mind / Lonely & Me / Crock / Month Of Sundays
BORN TOO LATE, Game Two (1998) (Split CD with CHURCH OF MISERY)
Destiny's Rainbow '96 / Suitcase Blues (Live) / Mountains Of Madness (Live) / Blue Sky Mind (Live) / Domelight (Live) / War Pigs (Live in studio)
THE ELECTRIC SLEEP, Rise Above (1998)
Virtual Machine / Velvet / Destiny's Rainbow / Face In The Mirror / Born In A Daze / Pictures Of You / Automaton / Savannah / The Electric Sleep / Last Parade / Saving Me

From Myself / Oracle / Stardust
CELESTIAL HI-FI, Rise Above (2000)
Hyper Faster / What's Up Mr. Zero? / Stingray - Part II / Solarsphere / Strange Gods, Strange Altars / Celestial Hi-Fi / Mountains Of Madness / Persona / A Utopian Interlude / Gemini (The Twins) / Tales From The Afterburner
SYNCHRONIZED, (2002)
Last Of The V8 Interceptors / Kill Queens Go Disco / Ultraglide / Next Exit To Vertigo / Part Of The Machine ... / Synchronized / AFX ....Thrown For A Loop / Invasion Of The Micronauts / Set Phasers To Stun / Firebird 350

SHINE (Washington DC, USA)
Line-Up: Wino (vocals / guitar), Dave Sherman (bass), Gary Isom (drums)

Stoner Rock outfit created by the revered figure of ex-SAINT VITUS and THE OBSESSED frontman Scott 'Wino' Weinrich. SHINE announced their arrival with the 'Powershine' demo. The 1998 single is released on Tolotta Records, the label owned by FUGAZI's J.O. Lally. Joining Wino in this venture would be ex-HEAVY SOUL and WRETCHED bassist Dave Sherman and drummer Gary Isom. The latter boasted an illustrious career path stretching into the annals of pedigree Doom with such acts as HEAVY SOUL, IRON MAN, UNORTHODOX, WRETCHED and PENTAGRAM.

SHINE soon switched titles to SPIRIT CARAVAN under threat of legal action from another act that had previously registered the title. The band's debut album 'Jug Fulla Sun' had at that stage already been recorded but luckily not manufactured. As SPIRIT CARAVAN the band released two highly regarded albums before folding in May of 2002.

Singles/EPs:
Lost Sun Dance / Courage, Tollota (1998)

SHOVELHEAD (NJ, USA)
Line-Up: Jim LaPointe (vocals / guitar), Sha Zaidi (bass), Mike Scott (drums)

A Fuzz Rock power trio out of central New Jersey. The axis of frontman Jim LaPointe, bassist Sha Zaidi and drummer Mike Scott had been operational since 1993 as THE LEMMINGS, having released a 1998 album 'The March Of Provocation' under that title. The band became SHOVELHEAD in 2000.

Albums:
SHOVELHEAD, Meteor City (2001)

Purity / Shovelhead / Total Freedom / Sleeper / Born To Lose / Cities Of The Red Night

SHRAPNEL (USA)
Line-Up: Dave Wyndorf (vocals), Dave Vogt (guitar), Daniel Rey (guitar), Phil Caivano (bass), Dan Clayton (drums)

SHRAPNEL guitarist Daniel Rey would become a much in-demand producer by the late '80s, working with the RAMONES, CIRCUS OF POWER and WHITE ZOMBIE to name but a few. He also recorded with MANITOBA'S WILD KINGDOM.
In 1997 Rey formed part of a unit including Joey Ramone and Jerry Only and Dr. Chud of the MISFITS, cutting a track for the IGGY POP tribute album 'We Will Fail'.
Vocalist Dave Wyndorf would found Stoner Rock institution MONSTER MAGNET and would later be joined by bassist Phil Caivano.

Albums:
SHRAPNEL, Elektra (1984)
Didn't Know I Loved You ('Til I Saw You Rock n' Roll) / Nations / Master Of My Destiny / Hope For Us All / It's A Crime

SIDEBURN (SWEDEN)
Line-Up: Jani Kataja (vocals / bass), Morgan Zocek (guitar), Tor Penten (drums)

Sabbath laden Swedish power trio SIDEBURN came together in 1998. Although being distinctly Metal SIDEBURN's debut record 'Trying To Burn The Sun' does amble into Psych-Stoner, modern Goth and even Latino balladry to provide an intriguing mix.

Albums:
TRYING TO BURN THE SUN, Beard Of Stars (2002)
Planet Of Doom / Doin' Fine / Revolution / Ceremony / Trying To Burn The Sun / Rainmaker Burn / Sweet Love Of Youth / Today / Sideburn / Moongarden / Pornomaniac

SILENT CRY (BRAZIL)
Line-Up: Ana Marcia (vocals), Dilpho Castro (vocals / guitar), Roberto Freitas (bass), Bruno Selmer (keyboards)

Doom act SILENT CRY was established by guitarist Dilpho Castro in 1993, initially with a line up including bassist Cristiano Jarbos, keyboard player Antonio Mattos and drummer Jefferson Guimaraes. The bass position soon switched hands to Jaderson Vitorino as SILENT CRY cut a debut demo 'Tanatolilo Opulate, Plenilunio', During 1995 female

vocalist Suelly Riberio joined as did BETSAIDA guitarist Cassio Brandi and the group issued a further cassette 'Tears Of Serenity' in 1997.
Mattos would depart in 1998 to be replaced by Bruno Selmer. Former DEAD BRAIN drummer Ricardo Meirelles would join the fold too, Guimaraes having relocated to America to found another Doom band ANGELIC GRIEF. In this incarnation SILENT CRY signed to the domestic Demise label issuing their first album 'Remembrance' in 1999. 'Goddess Of Tears' followed in 2000, a record which witnessed another line-up change with Roberto Freitas coming in on bass.
In early 2001 Riberio then Brandi opted out. SILENT CRY enrolled Ana Marcia as their new lead vocalist and set to work on a new album.

Albums:
REMEMBANCE, Demise (1999)
Forgotten Dreams / Tragic Memory / Celestial Tears / Ages / My Last Pain / The Death Invites To Dance / Innocence / Remembrance
GODDESS OF TEARS, Demise (2000)
Desire Of Dreams / Last Visions / Tears Of Serenity / Eclipse / Crying Violins / Illusions Of Perfection / The End Of The Innocence / Good-bye In The Silence

SILENTIUM (FINLAND)
Line-Up: Matti Aikio (vocals), Tiina Lehvonen (vocals), Juha Lehtioksa (guitar), Toni Lahtinen (guitar), Sami Boman (keyboards), Jani Laaksonen (violin), Janne Ojala (drums)

Mournful Doom septet SILENTIUM was borne out of the mid '90s band FUNERAL. Line up changes within FUNERAL, which saw vocalist Matti Aikio and keyboard player Sami Boman joined by violinist Jani Laaksonen, prompting a radical shift in musical direction for the band. With the further augmentation of guitarists Toni Lahtinen and Juha Lehtioksa, as well as drummer Jaro Ojala - former members of ENSLAVEMENT and SKIRMISH, the band had evolved to such a degree a switch in titles to SILENTIUM was adopted in February of 1996.
Newly billed SILENTIUM debuted with the 'I Llacrimo' demo. General reaction was positive and tracks would spread further afield courtesy of inclusion on the 'Sometimes Death Is Better' compilation put out by the Belgian Shiver label.
In August of 1998 a follow up session, 'Camere Misera' ensued. These tapes would witness the enrollment of female vocalist Tiina Lehvonen. Shortly afterward Ojal departed

and was duly replaced by Janne Ojala, a DEHYDRATED and ex-FUNERAL member. SILENTIUM's rise had been observed by the Finnish Spikefarm label that would commission the band for the 'Infinita Plango Vulnera' album. Released in August 1999 the record broke the Finnish national top 100 charts. A second album, 'Altum', arrived in March 2001 followed up by the four track EP 'SI.VM.ET.A.V.VM.'

During October of 2001 Ojala would deputize for GLOOMY GRIM on their European tour dates.

Singles/EPs:
Apart / Grievous Beauty / I Bleed For... / Lament, Spikefarm NAULA015 (2001) ('SI.VM.ET.A.V.VM.' EP)

Albums:
INFINITA PLANGO VULNERA, Spikefarm NAULA001 (1999) 91 FINLAND
Solicitude / Forever Sleep / Redemption / Autumn Heart / Whatever The Pain / Maiden Of The Forest / Requiem / With Blood Adorned / At The Dawn I Wept / Solicitude
ALTUM, Spikefarm NAULA019 (2001)
Revangelis / Blasphemer / To My Beloved One / Painless /...Repent... / Into The Arms Of The Night / The Lusticon / The Sinful / The Propheter Of The Unthroned

SILENT STREAM OF GODLESS ELEGY (CZECH REPUBLIC)

Line-Up: Petr Stanek (vocals / guitar), Michal Hajda (guitar), Kiril Chlebnikov (bass), Zuzana Zamazalova (violin), Pavla Lukasova (violin cello), Radek Hajda (drums)

A Doom band laced with Pagan imagery and adventurous enough to include violins and cellos alongside the expected modern day arsenal. The act was founded by the Hajda brothers guitarist Michal and drummer Radek along with bassist Filip Chudy, frontman Petr Stanek and violinist Zuzana Zamazalova in 1995. SILENT STREAM OF GODLESS ELEGY debuted with the promotional tape 'Apotheosis' capitalized on by 1996's 'Amber Sun'. A second violinist Ski was added after the debut album 'Iron'.

Following the sophomore 'Behold The Shadows' outing Chudy lost his place to Kiril Chlebnikov and the 16 year old Pavla Lukasova took Ski's position. The erstwhile members guitarist Rostislav Skacel and Pavel Chud_ would subsequently found MYSTERY, a band that evolved into MEMORIA for the 'Children Of The Doom' album.

SILENT STREAM OF GODLESS ENERGY guitarist Radek Hajda would later join Austrian Death Metal band DARKSIDE. Zuzana Zamazalova would feature as a guest on the 2002 outing 'Ocean Of The Lost' from Austrian Gothic Rockers FLOODLAND.

Albums:
IRON, Leviathan (1996)
Ugly Jewel / Passion And Desire / Iron Mask / Last... / Desolated Remains / Only Stream / Crying Haven / Burned By Love To Christ / Bittery Sweet / Naked Susan / Amber Sea / Apotheosis
BEHOLD THE SHADOWS, Redblack (1998)
Wizard / Garden / The Last Place / Old Woman's Dance / When Sun Rises For The Last Time / Summoning Of The Muse / Ghost / Embrace Beyond / Black Tunnel / Shadow / Cantara / I Come And Stand At Every Door
THEMES, Redblack (2000)
Lovin' On The Earth / We Shall Go / My Friend... / Theme I / In Bone Frames / Theme II / Flowers Fade Away / Eternal Cry Of Glory / Theme III / Il Tsohg / Winter Queen / Hrob (The Grave)

SIN ILUSIONES (ARGENTINA)

Line-Up: Nicolas (vocals / guitar), Martin (bass), Gustavo (drums)

Buenos Aires Garage Stoner band founded in 1997 by ex-members of DESPERAR. The 1999 debut 'Uno' was issued by Mexican label Smogless.

Albums:
UNO, Smogless (1999)
Tuve Miedo / Llorar / Ser / Crepita / Vencida / Perdoname / Desierto / Quizas / Miedo / Girasol / Golpes
JUGANDO EN EL PARAISO, Progreso (2000)
Hombre Sagrado / Jugando En El Paraiso / Te Envuelve / Infierno / Hoy Voy A Caer / Aixa / Instrumental / Tu Amor / Lagrimas / Alguna Vez / Vencida / Crepita / Verdad / Espera

SINMASTER (FINLAND)

SINMASTER is the Gothic / Industrial crossover side endeavour of Jyrki Witch of TWO WITCHES, LA VAMPIRE NUE and GODLIKE. Joining him on this endeavour for the four track 'Sinmaster' EP, released by Atcom Music and limited to 500 copies, would be a whole host of Finnish Gothic and Doom Metal names.

Included were ANCIENT RITES man Jan 'Örkki' Yrlund, also an erstwhile member of both PRESTIGE and LACRIMOSA, former

LOVE LIKE BLOOD and present day LA VAMPIRE NUE and TWO WITCHES guitarist Toby and second guitarist Timv of TWO WITCHES, SHADE FACTORY, GODLIKE and DEI SIX. Also on hand would be guest contributions from MAJESTY and SHADE FACTORY's Marko 'Gravehill' Hautamaki, Karina Eames of BELTANE and SEPULCRUM MENTIS, EXEDRA and LA VAMPIRE NUE guitarist Marty Kasprzak.

Besides SINMASTER Jyrki Witch also operates LA VAMPIRE NUE alongside Kasprzak, Hautamaki and Toby, GODLIKE and the covers bands FIXED FRAME (totally devoted to honouring DEPECHE MODE) and WITCH.

Singles/EPs:
Seducer (Manipulation mix) / Hungry For Sin (Distortion JTW mix) / Seducer (Godlike remix), / Naughty (Again) (JTW mix)

SINOATH (ITALY)
Line-Up: Cucinotta, Messina, Correnti

An Italian Doom Metal band.

Singles/EPs:
Forefather Of Human Faults / The Raising Stillness / Sinoath, (1995) ('Still In The Grey Dying' EP)

Albums:
RESEARCH, Polyphemus POLYPH 003 (1995)
Faith Ways / All My Thoughts / Lucifer's Shapes / ...On My Skin / Luxuria / Ascension / Gloomily Dressed / No Truth

SIR HEDGEHOG (CANADA)
Line-Up: Jonas Fairley (vocals), Paul Slater (guitar), Brendy Marklinger (bass), Steve Oliver (drums)

Vancouver Doom aficionados SIR HEDGEHOG came into being in 1995 comprising vocalist Jonas Fairley, guitar player Paul Slater, bassist Simon Oliver and drummer Steve Oliver.

This version of the band recorded the demo 'The Legend Of Sir Hedgehog', issued in 1997

In late 1998 these sessions were compiled with other demo recordings for a limited run CD. The following year Simon Oliver made his exit and Brendy Marklinger assumed the bass role.

The eponymous album became a talking point on the Stoner underground scene for its portrayal of Zeppesque nostalgia. Oddly many reviewers failed to note the inclusion of

an extra unaccredited track dubbed 'Blonde Sabbath', a somewhat bizarre amalgamation of BLACK SABBATH's 'Children Of The Grave' and BLONDIE's 'Call Me'.

Albums:
SIR HEDGEHOG, (2001)
Otherside / Magic Garden / Mountain Of Attention / Freedom Guild United / Chu De Phat / Gimme The Bone / Bitchlord / The Cleavage And The Clamp / Olympus Mons / Blonde Sabbath

THE SISTERS OF MERCY (UK)
Line-Up: Andrew Eldritch (vocals), Adam Pearson (guitar), Mike Varjak (guitar), Simon Denbigh (nurse to the doctor), Dr. Avalanche (drums)

Andrew Eldritch's vehicle that delivered a fan reverence that translated into hard album sales. THE SISTERS OF MERCY, engineered by a series of seemingly ruthless line-up culls and a mystique enhanced by imagery and obtuse lyrics, managed to retain their cult status in spite of mainstream success.

Always frontrunners in the Gothic Rock field the band actually plied hard driving Rock lent a sombre edge by Eldritch's maudlin vocal style. Since the early '90s the band has been locked into an unyielding dispute with the record label making THE SISTERS OF MERCY's standing as a major act even more remarkable.

THE SISTERS OF MERCY had been formulated in Leeds during the late '70s with an initial line-up of Andrew 'Eldritch' Taylor on vocals, guitarist Gary Marx and a drum machine (credited as 'Dr. Avalanche'). In this guise the band issued the 1980 'Damage Done' single, having just 1,000 copies pressed up on their own Merciful Release imprint. Craig Adams, previously with THE EXPELAIRES, got involved on bass which helped define their by now unique sound. THE SISTERS OF MERCY put in their first live appearance in February of 1981 and shortly after second guitarist Ben Gunn augmented the band roster.

A series of single releases throughout 1982 and 1983, with 'Body Electric' being voted 'Single of the week' by the influential Melody Maker magazine, rapidly built up an underground following. A tour of the UK as opening act to THE PSYCHEDELIC FURS paved the way for the single 'Alice'. Despite being hailed by the Gothic Rock crowd as almost messiah-like the band continued to inject both a sense of humour and traditional Rock n' Roll spirit into their live performances peppering live sets with oblique cover versions of HOT CHOCOLATE's 'Emma' and DOLLY PARTON's 'Jolene'. The 'Alice' single was granted a North American release in 12" format and the group duly crossed the Atlantic for their first US shows.

The band put out the atmospheric 'The Reptile House' EP in May of 1983 after which Wayne Hussey, already a veteran of THE WALKIE TALKIES, DEAD OR ALIVE and HAMBI & THE DANCE, supplanted Gunn. Hussey's enrollment in April of 1984 brought a new element of acoustic based songwriting into the band.

With this version of the band Eldritch first made an impression on the national charts, the June 1984 single 'Body And Soul' making it to number 46, albeit oddly billed at this juncture simply as THE SISTERS. The group had struck a distribution deal with the major WEA label for this and future outings. Internationally their star would be rising too. THE SISTERS OF MERCY travelled to New York for two sell out gigs before launching into their 'Black October' tour of the UK and Europe.

'Walk Away' followed its predecessor into the lower reaches of the singles charts paving the way for the debut album, 'First And Last And Always', launched in March of 1985 and making the top twenty. Although the band held solid for a UK headline tour dubbed as the 'Tune In, Turn On, Burn Out' dates, Marx quit upon the eve of the album release. Much to fans consternation THE SISTERS OF MERCY then split, bowing out unexpectedly and without warning with a show at London's Royal Albert Hall.

Marx founded GHOST DANCE whilst Hussey and Adams forged THE SISTERHOOD, this band's title was also the name of THE SISTERS OF MERCY fan club. A bitter war of words between Eldritch and Hussey erupted in the Rock media. To counter Hussey's plans Eldritch, now based in Berlin, quickly formulated his own band billed as THE SISTERHOOD, rush releasing a Dance based single and issuing the 1986 album 'The Gift'. Many at the time missed the significance of the political machinations behind the scenes, Eldritch blatantly detailing the sum of an RCA publishing advance in song lyrics and cleverly lending his album with a double barrelled meaning, 'Gift' being German for 'Poison'. Hussey and Adams retitled their act THE MISSION and subsequently built a career to rival Eldritch's own.

A new look THE SISTERS OF MERCY comprised guitarist James Ray, erstwhile GUN CLUB and FUR BIBLE bassist Patricia Morrison, ex-SUICIDE keyboard player Alan Vega and drummer Lucas Fox.

When the dust had settled Eldritch legally owned THE SISTERS OF MERCY title but by now had whittled the official line-up down to just himself, Morrison and a drum machine. Nevertheless the next THE SISTERS OF MERCY album 'Floodland' proved a major album, going top ten in the UK boosted by the hit single 'This Corrosion'. Both 'Dominion', featuring the massed vocals of the New York choral society and backed by a lavish video shot in the ancient Jordanian city of Petra, and 'Lucretia My Reflection', made a significant impression, this forward momentum prompting the enlistment of a fresh band unit in early 1990.

Dispensing with Morrison's services the SISTERS OF MERCY duly enlisted SIGUE SIGUE SPUTNIK and GENERATION X bass player Tony James in her stead. Guitars came courtesy of Andreas Bruhn and ALL ABOUT EVE's Tim Bricheno. The media would have a field day when Morrison and Eldritch started trading bitter jibes with Eldritch claiming Morrison did not actually perform on 'Floodland'. The ousted bassist issued an album 'Reflect On This' with her own PATRICIA MORRISON BAND then joined Punk veterans THE DAMNED.

October 1990's 'Vision Thing' built upon the progress of 'Floodland', once again engendering a healthy crop of hit singles with the epic 'More' and 'Doctor Jeep'. Overall THE SISTERS OF MERCY had developed a Hard Rock edge to their sound for this release which many critics viewed as an attempt to crack the North American market. What had actually transpired in the studio was that finished, finely polished mixes, had been scrapped in favour of initial rough recordings to give the album its abrasive tone. MAGGIE REILLY would add her distinctive tones on backing vocals.

By now the band was big enough to play two consecutive shows at Wembley Arena, warming up for these gigs with dates in Brazil. In March of 1991 THE SISTERS OF MERCY embarked upon North American gigs commencing in Canada. The world tour would then wend its way through the former Eastern Bloc territories before a massive arena tour of Germany where the band was now of superstar status. A return to America had the band headlining an eclectic package bill comprising GANG OF FOUR, WARRIOR SOUL and Rappers PUBLIC ENEMY. A series of festival events, such as the huge German 'Rock Am Ring' show and the UK's prestigious 'Reading Festival' wrapped up live work.

1992's retrospective album 'Some Girls Wander By Mistake' charted even higher, reaching number 5 in the UK. The single

'Temple Of Love', re-recorded with the late Ofra Haza on vocals, also fared well peaking at number 3. More European summer festivals ensued as well as a mammoth show at the Birmingham NEC. On a less grander scale, but probably more awe inspiring, a fan club member got to witness the band perform in their living room as a warm up gig in Oberhausen. As the band entered 1993 they would hook up with another set of alternative heroes, DEPECHE MODE, for a further rash of European mainland gigs.

The 'Greatest Hits Volume 1- A Slight Case Of Overbombing' album would signal a new recording 'Under The Gun', cut with new guitarist Adam Pearson and with vocal embellishment from TERRI NUNN of BERLIN fame. Pearson, having contributed to acts such as 3000 REVS, HEARTS ON FIRE, JOHNNY THUNDERS and RED LORRY, YELLOW LORRY would add a degree of much need stability to the band and would retain his position until the present day.

A return to Germany found THE RAMONES as support act. A spate of British gigs in London and at the Birmingham NEC once again closed the year.

1994 would be taken up by behind the scenes manouevering between the band and their label, a situation which would continue for many years to come. Eldritch would also embroil himself in remixing tracks for German Industrialists DIE KRUPPS.

Second guitarist Chris Sheehan, a New Zealander who cited prior experience with BABYLON ZOO and had a parallel solo career as CHRIS STARLING, enrolled in 1996 and one 'Ravey Davey' was assigned to look after the Dr. Avalanche drum computer. That year the group performed an unannounced club gig in Leeds during June under the handle NEAR METH EXPERIENCE. With the band's self-imposed ban on activity now reaching the three year marker fans would be relieved to learn that THE SISTERS OF MERCY were scheduled to act as special guests to the reformed SEX PISTOLS 'Helter Skelter' festival tour of Germany. Three gigs were scheduled but only two took place.

To fulfil contractual obligation Eldritch would apparently give East West a Techno album credited to SSV, an album still as yet unreleased.

THE SISTERS OF MERCY live line-up for 1997's 'Distance Over Time' tour, pre-empted by a further Leeds NEAR METH EXPERIENCE gig, had the Yugoslavian Mike Varjak taking Sheehan's role as the latter was undertaking tour duties with Australian Pop act THE MUTTON BIRDS. Another addition would be Simon 'Sigh' Denbigh, previously with the BATFISH BOYS, MARCH VIOLETS and D-ROK. These dates officially kicked off in Eastern Germany at the 'Woodhenge' festival. A Philadelphia gig soon became famous in fan folklore for Eldritch's onstage quip that THE SISTERS OF MERCY were "A Rock n' Roll band". On a more serious note reports stated that Eldritch had vetoed three support bands originally scheduled to perform, apparently because of their 'Gothic' associations.

1998 had the band industrious on the live front with sell out gigs in the UK, Europe and North America dubbed the 'Event Horizon' tour. The band would re-visit the USA the following year on the 'To The Planet Edge' dates.

THE SISTERS OF MERCY were active in 2000, bringing back Chris Sheehan and Simon Denbigh for their 'Trip The Light Fantastic' gigs. Advance promotion for this run of dates notably used the truncated band name SISTERS. Varjak meantime was busy with his project JACKIE ON ASSID.

2001 had the band out on the road on the 'Exxile In Euphoria' tour celebrating the ten year anniversary of their last studio album. German gigs saw PARADISE LOST as special guests.

In 2002 THE SISTERS OF MERCY were still operational, headlining a number of German festivals with Adam Pearson back in the ranks. Guitarist Chris Sheehan issued a solo album 'Planet Painkiller'.

Singles/EPs:
Damage Done / Watch / Home Of The Hitman, Merciful Release (1980)
Body Electric / Adrenochrome, C.N.T. (1982)
Alice / Floorshow, Merciful Release (1982)
Anaconda / Phantom, Merciful Release (1983)
Alice / Floorshow / 1969 / Phantom, Merciful Release (1983)
Kiss The Carpet / Lights / Valentine / Burn / Fix, Merciful Release (1983) ('The Reptile House' EP)
Temple Of Love / Heartland, Merciful Release (1983)
Temple Of Love / Heartland / Gimme Shelter, Merciful Release (1983) (12" single)
Body And Soul / Train, Merciful Release (1984) **46 UK**
Body And Soul / Train / After Hours / Body Electric, Merciful Release (1984) (12" single)
Walk Away / Poison Door, Merciful Release (1984) **45 UK**
Walk Away / Poison Door / On The Wire, Merciful Release (1984) (12" single)
No Time To Cry / Blood Money, Merciful Release (1985)

369

No Time To Cry / Blood Money / Bury Me Deep, Merciful Release (1985) (12" single)
This Corrosion / Torch, Merciful Release (1987) **7 UK**
This Corrosion / Torch / Colours, Merciful Release (1987) (12" single)
Dominion / Sandstorm / Untitled, Merciful Release (1988) **13 UK**
Dominion / Sandstorm / Untitled / Emma, Merciful Release (1988) (12" single)
Dominion / Sandstorm / Untitled / Ozy-Mandias, Merciful Release (1988) (CD single)
Lucretia My Reflection / Long Train, Merciful Release (1988) **20 UK**
More / You Could Be The One, Merciful Release (1990) **21 UK**
Doctor Jeep / Knockin' On Heaven's Door (Live), Merciful Release (1990) **37 UK**
When You Don't See Me / Ribbons (Live) / Something Fast (Live), Merciful Release (1991) (German release)
Temple Of Love 1992 / I Was Wrong (American fade), East West (1992) **3 UK**
Under The Gun / Alice (1993), East West (1993) **19 UK**

Albums:
FIRST AND LAST AND ALWAYS, Merciful Release (1985) **14 UK**
Some Kind Of Stranger / No Time To Cry / Amphetamine Logic / Marian / First And Last And Always / Nine While Nine / Black Planet / A Rock And A Hard Place
FLOODLAND, Merciful Release (1987) **9 UK**
Dominion / Mother Russia / Flood I / Lucretia My Reflection / 1959 / This Corrosion / Flood II / Driven Like The Snow / Neverland / Torch / Colours
VISION THING, Merciful Release (1990) **11 UK**
Vision Thing / Ribbons / Detonation Boulevard / Something Fast / When You Don't See Me / Doctor Jeep / More / I Was Wrong
SOME GIRLS WANDER BY MISTAKE, East West (1992) **5 UK**
Alice / Floorshow / Phantom / 1969 / Kiss The Carpet / Lights / Valentine / Fix / Buirn / Kiss The Carpet (Reprise) / Temple Of Love / Heartland / Gimme Shelter / Damage Done / Watch / Home Of The Hitmen / Body Electric Adrenochrome / Anaconda
GREATEST HITS VOLUME 1 - A SLIGHT CASE OF OVERBOMBING, East West (1993) **14 UK**
Under The Gun / Temple Of Love 1992 / Vision Thing / Detonation Boulevard / Doctor Jeep / More / Lucretia My Reflection / Dominion - Mother Russia / This Corrosion / No Time To Cry / Walk Away / Body And

Soul

THE 69 EYES (FINLAND)
Line-Up: Jyrki (vocals), Bazie (guitar), Timo Timo (guitar), Archzie (bass), Jussi 69 (drums)

Garage fuelled Gothic Rockers THE 69 EYES emerged in 1992 with the 'Bump n' Grind' album. THE 69 EYES 1994 EP included a cover of the KISS track 'Deuce'. This track would also be included on the album 'Motorcity Resurrection', only issued in Japan the following year.
On THE 69 EYES' 'Savage Garden' album, produced by Timo Tolkki of STRATOVARIUS, ex-HANOI ROCKS guitarist Andy McCoy contributed to the track 'Wild Talk'.
1996 would find the band paying homage to their musical heroes by appearing on no less than three tribute albums namely 'I Wanna Be The Stooges' on the French Revenge label, the 'D.F.F.D.' tribute to THE DICTATORS on the Spanish Roto imprint and also a MISFITS album 'Hell On Earth' issued in Sweden. The following year the NEW YORK DOLLS would be honoured with THE 69 EYES donating a track to the 'Stranded In The Doll's House' Japanese compilation on Hurtin' Records.
1999's 'Wasting The Dawn' album, which saw ENTOMBED's Lars G. Petrov and Alex Hellid as session guests, would garner the band more widespread popularity internationally. The September 2000 Johnny Lee Michaels produced release 'Blessed Be' proved to be a spectacular success for the band reaching number 4 in the national Finnish album charts. The leading single 'Gothic Girl' would also chart as did it's successors 'Brandon Lee' and 'The Chair', the latter reaching number 2.
THE 69 EYES toured Germany in May of 2001 as guests to PARADISE LOST. The band's December single 'Dance D'Amour', which topped the Finnish charts, would come complete with a B side take on THE DOORS' 'You're Lost Little Girl'. THE 69 EYES' success would continue into 2002 with the 'Paris Kills' album being certified a gold release in their native Finland.

Singles/EPs:
Barbarella, Gaga Goodies (1991)
Music For Tattooed Ladies And Motorcycle Mamas Volume One, Gaga Goodies (1994)
Tang / Velvet Touch / 69 Eye / Motor Mouth, Gaga Goodies (1995)
Wasting The Dawn / Wasting The Dawn (Edit) / You Ain't The Reason, Roadrunner (1999)
Gothic Girl / Velvet Touch, Roadrunner

(2000)
Brandon Lee (Radio mix) / Brandon Lee / Brandon Lee (Video), Roadrunner (2000)
The Chair / Heaven/Hell / The Chair (Club mix), Roadrunner (2001) **2 FINLAND**
Stolen Season / The Chair (Video), Roadrunner (2001)
Dance D'Amour / You're Lost Little Girl, Roadrunner (2001) **1 FINLAND**

Albums:
BUMP N' GRIND, (1992)
Voodoo Queen / Juicy Lucy / Alive / House By The Cemetery / Hot Butterfly / Sugarman / Dream Master / Too Sick For You / No Hesitation / Blind For Love / The Hills Have Eyes / Barbarella / Burning Love
SAVAGE GARDEN, Gaga Goodies (1995)
Wild Talk / Tang / Smashed n' Trashed / Velvet Touch / Mr. Pain / Lady Luck / Motor City Resurrection / Ghettoway Car / Get It Off / Always / Demolition Derby
MOTORCITY RESURRECTION, (1995)
(Japanese release)
Discipline / Deuce / Mrs. Sleazy / Hot Butterfly / Sugarman / Stop Bitching! / Barbarella / Gimme Some Skin / Juicy Lucy / The Hills Have Eyes / Too Itching For Action / No Hesitation / Alive! / Gimme Some Head
WRAP YOUR TROUBLES IN DREAMS, Gaga Goodies GOOD 38 (1997)
Call Me / D.I.D. / Broken Man / Get Around / Too Much To Lose / Sore Loser / Skanky Man / Wrap Your Troubles In Dreams / Hellcity 1999 / Turbo Bitch / L8R S8N
WASTING THE DAWN, Roadrunner (1999)
Truck On / Lay Down Your Arms, Girl / Wasting The Dawn / You Ain't The Reason / Lazarus Heart / Who's Gonna Pay The Bail? / All-American Dream / Be My Speed / Hand Of God / Next Stop Paradise / Starshine
BLESSED BE, Roadrunner (2000)
4 FINLAND
Framed In Blood / Gothic Girl / The Chair / Brandon Lee / Velvet Touch / Sleeping With Lions / Angel On My Shoulder / Stolen Season / Wages Of Sin / Graveland
PARIS KILLS, Roadrunner (2002)
1 FINLAND
Crashing High / Dance D'Amour / Betty Blue / Grey / Radical / Don't Turn Your Back On Fear / Stigmata / Forever More / Still Waters Run Deep / Dawn's Highway"

SIXTY WATT SHAMAN (Baltimore, USA)
Line-Up: Daniel Kerzwick (vocals / guitar), Joe Selby (guitar), Reverend James Robert Forrester (bass), C.J. Dukehart III (drums)

Maryland Stoner merchants SIXTY WATT SHAMAN evolved out of SUPERCREEP, a side project of then APPROACH members bassist Joe Selby and drummer Chuck 'C.J.' Dukehart III. SUPERCREEP would morph into SIXTY WATT SHAMAN with Selby assuming the lead guitar role, the Reverend James Robert Forrester, a professional body piercer and real life ordained minister of the California Universal Life church, taking bass and Daniel Kerzwick on vocals. Prior to APPROACH Selby had operated as bassist for ANASAZI and CLOCKSHOP.
The band debuted with the April 1998 album 'Ultra Electric'. A split 7" single 'Stone's Throw Away' in collaboration with SPIRIT CARAVAN arrived the following year via Tee Pee Records.
The group signed with the Spitfire label for the sophomore J.P. Gaster produced 'Seeds Of Decades' album. The band would also contribute the track 'Southern Gentleman' to the Spitfire 'Inhale 420: The Stoner Rock Compilation' album, this version being an album out-take. SIXTY WATT SHAMAN toured America in 2000 as support to CROWBAR and Zakk Wylde's BLACK LABEL SOCIETY 'Penchant For Violence' dates prior to jumping onboard the CORROSION OF CONFORMITY / CLUTCH tour.
During January of 2001 long-standing member Dukehart III bowed out in favour of Kenny Wagner. Dukehart would unite with former SOLARIZED personnel in New Jersey Stoners HALFWAY TO GONE. However, come May Wagner had been usurped by former HANDOVER man 'Minnesota Pete' Campbell. This latest recruit could claim session credits with major acts such as BLUE OYSTER CULT and TED NUGENT. SIXTY WATT SHAMAN toured the UK and Europe in November. (Paradoxically Dukehart would later leave HALFWAY TO GONE duly being replaced by... Kenny Wagner!)
The band's third album, 'Reason To Live' scheduled for a September 2002 release, would be produced by none other than the esteemed figure of KYUSS, UNIDA and THE OBSESSED bassist Scott Reeder.

Singles/EPs:
Stone's Throw Away / , Tee Pee (1999) (Split 7" single with SPIRIT CARAVAN)
Fear Death By Water / New Trip / One More Time, Spitfire (2000) (Promotion release)
Seeds Of Decades / Roll The Stone, Spitfire (2000)

Albums:
ULTRA ELECTRIC, Game Two (1999)
Rumor Den / Burn Baby Burn / Southern Gentleman / Beverly / Where You Been / Permethrin / Interplanetary Pit Stop /

Supercreep / Cactus Mexicali / New Trip / Bemis Manifesto / Pull The Strings
SEED OF DECADES, Spitfire (2000)
Fear Death By Water / Seed Of Decades / Poor Robert Henry / Devil In The Details (Part 1) / Devil In The Details (Part 2) / Low Earth Orbit / One More Time / Roll The Stone / Red Colony / Rumor Den / Stone's Throw Away / Busy Dying / New Trip / I've Been Down
REASON TO LIVE, Spitfire (2002)
Nomad / Reason To Live / Blind By Morning / Horse You Rode In On / Our Name Is War / The Mill Wheel / Long Hard Road / The Evil Behavior Of Ordinary People / My Ruin / Breathe Again / One Good Leg And A Bottle Of Booze / All My Love / Distance / When The Morning Comes / When I'm Alone / All Things Come To Pass

SKEPTICISM (FINLAND)
Line-Up: Jani, Eero

A Finnish experimental and virtually anonymous Doom act. Following a debut 7" single in 1992, a year after SKEPTICISM's formation, the group released the four track 'Aeothe Kaear' demo session. Acknowledging the loss of a bass player in 1993 SKEPTICISM subsequently ceased all live activities. The acclaimed 'Stormcrowfleet' album followed in 1995.
SKEPTICISM did return to the live forum with a gig in Turku during January of 2001. They would repeat the feat in December of the same year as a launch for the two track 'The Process Of Farmakon' release.
The band's guitarist and drummer also operate with THROMDARR whilst J. Korpihere is employed on session bass guitar. The 1999 'Aes' release consisted solely of one 28 minute track.

Singles/EPs:
Skepticism, (1992) (7" single)
The Process Of Farmakon, Red Stream RSR-0155 (2002)

Albums:
STORMCROW FLEET, Red Stream (1995)
Sign Of A Storm / Pouring / By Silent Wings / The Rising Of The Flames / The Gallant Crow / The Everdarkgreen
ETHERE, Red Stream (1997)
The March And The Stream / Aether / Chorale
LEAD AND AETHER, Red Stream RSR-0120 (1998)
The Organium / The March And The Stream / The Falls / Forge / -Edges- / Aether
AES, Red Stream RSR-0129 (1999)
Aes

SKYWISE (ITALY)
Line-Up: Francesco Esposito (vocals / bass), Emiliano Giardulli (guitar), Ennio Cecaro (guitar), Emiliano Lembo (keyboards), Francesco Buoniconti (drums)

SKYWISE are a heavy Psych flavoured Doom outfit out of Rome, founded in the summer of 1998 as a trio of vocalist / bassist Francesco Esposito, guitarist Emiliano Giardulli and drummer Marcello. The group's members boast heritage through such underground bands as DESASTER, SUPERFETAZIONE, AIWAZ and GOLDEN CIRCLE.
A basic four track demo incited a degree of interest before Lorenzo took over the role of drummer for a further recording, simply titled 'Demo 1999'. This tape garnered favourable reviews in 'Metal Hammer' and 'Metal Shock' magazines. SKYWISE would enlist the services of Ennio Cecaro to provide Moog layers on the track 'Rise From The Ashes' on the demo and subsequently Cecaro would be inducted into the SKYWISE fold as second guitarist.
A third demo was pitched at record labels, after which Francesco Buoniconti became SKYWISE's latest drummer in December of 2000. The band had secured a deal with the Yperano record label but then withdrew, signing to the German Daredevil label. SKYWISE pulled in Emiliano Lembo as keyboard player for recording of the debut album 'Morning Star', issued in December 2001.

Albums:
MORNING STAR, Daredevil DD 0013 (2001)
Rise From The Ashes / Mountains Of The Moon / The Darkest Hour (Morning Star) / My Rotten Kingdom / Hellgate / Beyond Redemption / Earth 2012 / The Ghastly Workshop Of Hiram Kyram / Farewell Blues (Live)

SLEEP (San Jose, CA, USA)
Line-Up: Al Cisneros (vocals / bass), Matt Pike (guitar), Chris Hakius (drums)

Celebrated proto-Doom Sabbathian Rock act that since their demise have entered the hallowed annals of Stoner folklore. SLEEP, unafraid to display their influences, emerged with the 1991 'Volume One' album for Tupulo. The band comprised vocalist / bassist Al Cisneros, guitarists Matt Pike and Justin Marler and drummer Chris Hakius. SLEEP had evolved from a Punk inclined band entitled ASBESTOS DEATH established by Cisneros, Hakius and guitarist Tom Choi.

SLEEP

ASBESTOS DEATH would graduate to a quartet with the introduction of Matt Pike on guitar and, as their music laboured into a more Doom fulfilled role with the singles 'Dejection' for Profane Existence and the self-released 'Unclean', Choi departed - eventually founding OPERATOR GENERATOR. Meantime ASBESTOS DEATH recruited Justin Marler as replacement and switched the band title to SLEEP.

After the SLEEP debut, exposure in Europe would be gained with a signature to the British extreme Metal label Earache for the 'Sleep's Holy Mountain' album of 1992, by this stage Marler having vacated the picture. The erstwhile guitarist had actually been, by his own confession, near to suicide and had been self-mutilating. Marler's response to his illness was to enter a Russian Orthodox monastery to live the life of a monk for several years.

The impact made by the 'Sleep's Holy Mountain' record upon the underground scene generated waves big enough to catch the interest of the major labels and SLEEP duly signed to London Records for a follow up. Announced in the press as 'Dopesmoker' the album, already recorded prior to the London deal, never emerged. It transpired the band had opted to completely rewrite and re-record the lyrics. The project, initially scheduled for a 1995 release date, finally

transpired as one mammoth 52 minute long leviathan of a track dubbed 'Jerusalem'. London baulked and dropped the band. SLEEP would dissolve in 1997.

With 'Jerusalem' now the stuff of legend trading on the bootleg market was rampant. Eventually Lee Dorrian's Rise Above label secured official rights to the album for UK license whilst in North America a release was negotiated through the Music Cartel.

Pike set about formulating a fresh act, emerging with HIGH ON FIRE in 1999 and issuing an eponymous three track EP followed by the 'Art Of Self Defense' album in 2000. Marler, no longer residing in the monastery, together with Hakius, would surface with a fresh project entitled THE SABIANS. This band, including guitarist Patrick Huerta and bass player Rachel Fisher, put out the 'Empty Your Heart' demo before releasing the 'Beauty For Ashes' album produced by FUDGE TUNNEL man Alex

Albums:
VOLUME ONE, Tupelo TUP CD 034 (1992)
Stillborn / The Suffering / Numb / Anguish / Catatonic / Nebuchadnezzar's Dream / The Wall Of Yawn / Prey
SLEEP'S HOLY MOUNTAIN, Earache MOSH 079CD (1993)
Dragonaut / Druid / Evil Gypsy / Some Grass / Aquarian / Holy Mountain / Inside The Sun / From Beyond / Nain's Baptism

JERUSALEM, Rise Above (1999)
Jerusalem

SLEEPING GODS (GERMANY)
Line-Up: Anja Henning (vocals), Tim Siebrecht (vocals / guitar / bass), Anja Henning (vocals), Markus Stephan (guitar), Lars Pristl (drums)

A Gothic charged Death Metal band out of Kassel, SLEEPING GODS were formed in 1993 and would record their debut album 'Above And Beyond' some two years later. Session bass guitar on the debut album was supplied courtesy of producer Andy Classen of HOLY MOSES repute.

Albums:
ABOVE AND BEYOND, AFM 34326-422 (1995)
Scene Of Emptiness / The Die Is Cast / Blood Is Thicker Than Water / Vivianes Lamentation / Through The Timeless / Extreme Unction / Sleeping Goddess / Threats Of Providence
REGENERATED, AFM CD 37584-422 (1997)
The Wingless / Regenerated / Dead Calls / Just A Blue Blackness / None To Soon / Vastness / Some Far Beyond / Dreaming / Reflection Of Soul

SLO BURN (Palm Springs, CA, USA)
Line-Up: John Garcia (vocals), Chris Hale (guitar), Damon Garrison (bass), Brady Houghton (drums)

Renowned for having featured former KYUSS vocalist John Garcia. Initially Garcia returned to a career working at a veterinary surgery after the final collapse of his previous act in 1995, but soon returned to his roots and set about establishing a fresh band unit, drafting members of WOLF guitarist Chris Hale, bassist Damon Garrison and drummer Brady Houghton. An opening demo was made up of three tracks 'Wheel Fall', 'Cactus Jumper' and 'Positiva'. With SLO BURN underway Garcia also busied himself with other endeavours including a mooted collaboration with members of Chicago's revered TROUBLE and a Desert Rock act 13.
SLO BURN would only issue a solitary EP, 'Amusing The Amazing', released by Malicious Vinyl in 1996. The band landed valuable mass exposure as invites to the BLACK SABBATH led 'Ozzfest' tour but a further run of North American dates in alliance with MASTERS OF REALITY scheduled for August would be curtailed when their parent record label went into liquidation. SLO BURN folded in September of 1997. John Garcia was found fronting KARMA TO BURN later that year although his employment with the West Virginians lasted a mere twelve gigs. The singer came back to prominence with UNIDA.
The SLO BURN 1996 demos would turn up on the KYUSS 'Black Jeweler' bootleg.

Singles/EPs:
July / Muezli / Pilot The Dune / Prizefighter, Malicious Vinyl MV-5003-2 (1996) ('Amusing The Amazing' EP)

SLOTH (UK)
Line-Up: Gaz (vocals), Roland (guitar), Will (bass), Vince (drums)

Doom merchants SLOTH were created during August 1999 by ex-members of GODZILLA. Bassist Will Palmer is a veteran of cult Doomsters MOURN. By September the newly formed act had debuted live as support to SPIRIT CARAVAN in London. An opening demo session was cut in January of the following year with production handled by Dave Chang.
Japanese versions of the 2000 album 'The Voice Of God' on the JVC Victor label came with an exclusive track 'The Sadist'.

Albums:
VOICE OF GOD, Eccentric Man EC001CD (2000)
Wishman / Lord Of The Gallows / Geminian / Into The Sun / Green Magick / The Voice Of God / Casting The Circle

SLOW HORSE (New York, NY, USA)
Line-Up: Dan Bukszpan (vocals / guitar), Ernest Anderson (bass), Scott Sanfratello (drums)

The dreary anaesthetized Doom styled SLOW HORSE, founded in November of 1996, debuted with an eponymous outing through the Dutch Freebird label in 1998. It would feature a novel cover version of CHRIS ISAAK's 'Wicked Game'. The band was convened in November of 1996 by vocalist / guitarist Dan Bukszpan, a veteran of the Massachusetts 1989 Hardcore act MISTER SOFTEE, Speed Metal band VOMITORIUM and, until 1996, NECRODESTRUCTION.
Following the debut SLOW HORSE fractured down to just Bukszpan before the trio was brought back up to strength with the addition of bassist Ernest Anderson and drummer Mike Gandia. The second SLOW HORSE release, issued by Berserker Records and produced by Martin Bisi, was curiously also

SLOW HORSE
Photo : El Danno

375

SLUDGEPLOW
Photo : El Danno

simply titled 'Slow Horse' but generally referred to as 'Slow Horse II'. The band had pulled in HIGHER OCTANE drummer Scott Sanfrantello in time for recording. Anderson departed on October of 2001, eventually being replaced by D. Levine.

SLOW HORSE would tour America with German Doom act CALUMUS and also solidify this relationship with a split 7" single through Berserker Records.

Albums:
SLOW HORSE, Freebird (1998)
Lick My Wounds / All Good Intentions / Wicked Game / When Are You Coming Home? / No One Wants You When You're Down / What's The Use
SLOW HORSE II, Berserker (2000)
I'm Nothing, I'm No One / The Games You Play / Stay / Let It Slide / Coming Unhinged / Nameless / Untitled / The Last / No. 9

SLUDGEPLOW (USA)
Line-Up: Jeff Cornell (vocals / guitar), Chad Hartgrave (bass), Steve Driscoll (drums)

As the name implies, SLUDGEPLOW trade in morose, sluggish Rock. The group came into being in Iowa during January of 1991 presenting an initial line-up of vocalist / guitarist Jeff Cornell, bass player Chad Hartgrave and drummer Pete Prentice. This trio cut the demo session 'Turned Earth'. Live

work followed but in May of 1992 Prentice made his exit. It would signal the first of many changes of face on the drum stool.

An extensive eight month nationwide touring schedule saw the introduction of Bill Coney on drums but later dates found Bob Hall at the kit, maintaining his position for a second tape 'Everything'. Coincidentally both Coney and Hall had prior experience with the same bands, SCORCHED EARTH POLICY and IOWA BEEF EXPERIENCE. Hall made a return to the latter act and Eric Kranz took over drum duties. Tapes recorded at this juncture would subsequently emerge as the 'Coleslaw' album.

1995 heralded a momentous move for the band as the core SLUDGEPLOW pairing of Cornell and Hartgrave relocated the band to Seattle. There they teamed up with former VOODOO GEARSHIFT drummer Mark Bruggerman. Despite this step SLUDGEPLOW remained inactive for a number of years as members pursued alternative careers as tattoo artists. The group was finally reinvigorated when ex-BLACK CALVIN and STUNT MUMMIES man Scott Driscoll became the band's eighth drummer. The 'Hash' album saw light of day in 1999. A split single 'Passion Fruit' shared with SCRID was issued by the Ismista label in October.

Singles/EPs:
Passion Fruit, Ismista SI 0057 (1999) (Split

376

single with SCRID)

Albums:
COLESLAW, Sludgeplow (1999)
Crayons / Subdued / Reactionary / Lady / Fred / Feed Me / Creature - Grimoire
HASH, Sludgeplow (1999)
Instinct / Winston / Passion Fruit / Assgrinder / Apathetic Dysentery / The Captain, The Crew And The Eternal Search For Truth

SMOKE (Los Angeles, CA, USA)

Line-Up: Marc Star (vocals / guitar), Stephan Michael Newman (bass), Danny Foronda (drums)

SMOKE include former THUNDERFUCK 69 man Marc Star. The 2002 album 'Smoke Follows Beauty' was produced by Martin Schneeberger.

Albums:
SMOKE FOLLOWS BEAUTY, Kozmik (2002)
Opening Track / Here It Comes / Splitfire / Devil Down / Hallucination / The Mark of Brahm / Black Bat / Mina's Song / Caveman / Redux

SMOKE BLOW (GERMANY)

Line-Up: Jack Letten (vocals), Kentucky (guitar), J.R.(guitar), Burn Hellhammer (bass), Fabrizio (drums)

Kiel based Garage Stoner. SMOKE BLOW describe their sound as 'Plutonium fuelled Stoner Punk' or, more intriguingly, 'Anal Doom'.

Singles/EPs:
Altamont Speedway Massacre EP, Zillion (1999) (10" single)
Mexico, Burning Harbour (2000) ('The Real Deal From Kiel' split EP with BONEHOUSE)
Junkie Killer / Pissbottlman, Radio Blast Recordings (2001) ('The Story Of Uncle Goddamn' EP)

Albums:
SMOKE'S A BLOWIN' BLACK AS COAL, Cargo (1999)
Nexus Starride / Satan's Highway / Monsterrock / Vex Me No More / Girls, Bombs And Booze / Electric Mud / 1-0-3-5- Speedy Surprise / Phantom 308 / Microphoneheads And Psychotic Flys / Ride / Oak (Solar Breeze)
777 BLOODROCK, Cargo CAR 006 (2000)
777 Bloodrock / Ugly Germ Trash / Beelzebubba Walk / Bozena / Canyon Pool Punks / 99th Floor Higher Elevation / West Virginia / Blacula (Deadlier Than Dracula) / Senorita Spitfire / Masterblast No. 1 / Pulp Fiction Nazis / Must Die Le Mans
PUNKADELIC - THE GODFATHER OF SOUL, Loudsprecher (2001)
Dschingis / White Powder - Black Smoke / Outta Jail / TV Show / Sweetwater / Thermometer Voice / Commander Of Doom / Mexico / Invisible Boy / Damaged / Getting Over / Bruce Lee Coverband (The Great Commercial Fuck-Up)

SOILENT GREEN
(New Orleans, LA, USA)
Line-Up: Ben Falgoust II (vocals), Brian Patton (guitar), Donovan Punch (guitar), Scott Williams), Tommy Buckley (drums)

New Orleans SOILENT GREEN, somewhat akin to the famous Sci-Fi food substitute the band is named after, blend an unspeakable mix of influences ranging through Grindcore, Sludge and Blues based Southern Rock. The band's discordant style of galloping Grindcore juxtaposed with quagmire like viscosity has both confounded critics and generated admiration from the extreme Metal scene. SOILENT GREEN guitarist Brian Patton is also a member of EYEHATEGOD.
SOILENT GREEN gelled together in 1988 comprising erstwhile NUCLEAR CRUCIFIXION guitar players Donovan Punch and Brian Patton with drummer Tommy Buckley. NUCLEAR CRUCIFIXION operated with Punch and Patton involved with vocalist Glenn Rambo, bassist David Moran and drummer Darren Schallenburg. This unit put out the demo sessions 'Killing Ourselves To Live' and 'Torture Of Humanity' prior to Punch, Patton and Rambo founding SOILENT GREEN.
The band's line-up would prove fluid and momentum was slowed when Patton took up position in the more active EYEHATEGOD.
The group stabilized with the introduction of bassist Scott Williams in 1992, lead singer Louis Benjamin Falgoust II of PARALYSIS being inducted the following year. This version of the band cut the opening album, 'Pussysoul', for Dwell Records during 1995. Promotion on the road in North America witnessed gigs with EXTREME NOISE TERROR.
The group also recorded tracks for what transpired to be a split 10" single with GRIEF, and made an appearance on the 'Cry Now, Cry Later' double 7" single compilation, both of these releases issued by Pessimiser/Theologian Records.
Patton's schedule with EYEHATEGOD resulted in a fallow year for SOILENT GREEN in 1996 but 1997 opened in style, the band

acting as guests to PANTERA and CLUTCH on a string of Texan dates. Tracks would be laid down with engineer Keith Falgoust before further road activity in union with CRISIS, ANAL CUNT and CHOKE, prior to hooking up in December with PANTERA, ANTHRAX and COAL CHAMBER in Florida and Mississippi. SOILENT GREEN switched labels to the Relapse concern for the February 1998 'A String Of Lies' EP swiftly capitalized on by the full length 'Sewn Mouth Secrets'. Between these releases the group put in live dates with BRUTAL TRUTH upfront of a showing at the 'Milwaukee Metalfest'. Another two month round of gigs resumed as part of the 'Nawleans Swamp Tour' in alliance with CROWBAR and EYEHATEGOD.

SOILENT GREEN paid respect to the originators of Doom BLACK SABBATH in unique fashion by donating a track billed as 'Lord Of The Southern Priest', actually a medley of 'Lord Of This World', 'The Sign Of The Southern Cross' and 'Disturbing The Priest', to the Hydrahead tribute compilation 'In These Black Days - Volume 6'.

In downtime Patton resumed activities with EYEHATEGOD whilst Falgoust formed an unholy alliance with CROWBAR guitarist Sammy Duet to found GOATWHORE for 2000's 'The Eclipse Of Ages Into Black' album.

Donovan bowed out in 1999 and Falgoust's colleague in GOATWHORE Ben Stout maneuvered over to fill the SOILENT GREEN guitar vacancy. A third album was recorded, provisionally entitled 'The Devil Wears A Lamb's Skin', eventually emerging as 'A Deleted Symphony For The Beaten Down' in 2001.

US dates had SOILENT GREEN navigating the country as part of the 'Extreme Music For Extreme People' tour.

The band announced another bout of North American touring, commencing January 16th 2002, in alliance with headliners GWAR and GOD FORBID. In December of 2001 however, the band would be involved in a road accident while travelling in the Washington area. Their van skidded on black ice, leaving guitarist Brian Patton and bassist Scott Williams with broken bones. As a result SOILENT GREEN cancelled all shows.

Quite bizarrely Scott Williams sustained another injury to his as yet unhealed shoulder in another auto accident. With dates in Japan scheduled in league with EYEHATEGOD the band rapidly drafted fill-in bassist Jonny Modell.

After a due period of recuperation the band jumped back onboard the GWAR tour but in a quite surreal turn of events the band was involved in a second van accident on the 11th of April that injured vocalist Ben Falgoust and stand-in tour bassist Jonny Modell. Falgoust had been forced to avoid an out of control car and the band's vehicle smashed into the back of an 18 wheel truck. The singer came off worst breaking two legs but Modell received a broken collar bone. None too surprisingly SOILENT GREEN was forced off the tour yet again.

Amidst all of SOILENT GREEN's trouble one ray of light emerged with the announcement that Ben Falgoust and Jay Branch of SKINCRAWL's new label Incision Records were gearing up for a debut release, a limited edition split 7" affair between SOILENT GREEN and none other than EYEHATEGOD. Restricted to just 2,000 pieces the record was made even more collectable by the fact that 500 of these would be in either clear or coloured swirl vinyl.

In mid 2002 Relapse reissued 'A Deleted Symphony for the Beaten Down' in a limited run of 1,000 gatefold packaged vinyl pressings. 900 of these rarities came in clear green vinyl with an even scarcer 100 copies manufactured in clear vinyl.

In August Tommy Buckley would session for JONES LOUNGE, the new band of former EXHORDER vocalist Kyle Thomas.

Singles/EPs:
Sewn Mouth Secrets / Cat With Nine Claws / Felt Nothing, Relapse RR6985 (1998) ('A String Of Lies' EP)

Albums:
PUSSYSOUL, Dwell (1995)
Thirteen Days A Week / Slapfuck / Falling From A 65 Storey Building / Lips As So Of Blood / The Wrong Of Way / Needlescrape / Zebra Zombies / Keep Crawling / Twitch Of An Eye / Golfers Just Love Punishment / Love None / Branding Of Thieves
SEWN MOUTH SECRETS, Relapse RR 6405 (1998)
It Was Just An Accident / So Hatred / Build Fear / Looking Through Nails / Breed In Weakness / Cold-Steel Kiss / Openless / Her Unsober Ways / Sewn Mouth Secrets / Walk A Year In My Mind / Gagged Whore / Emptiness Found / Sticks And Stones
A DELETED SYMPHONY FOR THE BEATEN DOWN, Relapse RLP6481 (2001)
Hand Me Downs / A Grown Man / Swallowhole / Afterthought Of A Genius / An Addicts' Lover / Later Days / Clockwork Of Innocence / Daydreaming The Color Of Blood / Last One In The Noose / She Cheated On You Twice

SOLACE (USA)
Line-Up: Jason (vocals), Tommy Southard (guitar), Rob Hulz (bass), Matt Gunverdahl (drums)

SOLACE were founded by ex-PRUNELLA SCALES and GODSPEED guitarist Tommy Southard alongside his GODSPEED colleague bassist Rob Hulz. Immediately post GODSPEED Southard had been a member of SUGARTOOTH but then would found SLAP ROCKET in union with NUDESWIRL vocalist Shane Green, former GODSPEED bass player Chris Kosnik and drummer Keith Ackerman. SLAP ROCKET would only get to contribute one song, 'Holy Mother Sunshine', to a compilation album before Kosnik and Ackerman's commitments to their main act ATOMIC BITCHWAX drew them away. Southard duly created SOLACE enlisting old comrade Rob Hulz and GLUE NECK vocalist Jason. For the initial SOLACE demos Ackerman sat in on drums.
The debut album, 'Destined For Reality' with Jason Silverio on drums, was a split affair with fellow New Jersey Rockers SOLARIZED. Following this release Matt Gunverdahl of Punk act HOGAN'S HEROES took the drum stool.
A double gatefold vinyl edition of the 'Further' album would add 'Another Life' from an IRON MAIDEN tribute album and a version of THE MISFITS 'We Bite'.
Southard would be announced as part of the MONSTER MAGNET inspired 'supergroup' billed as GALLERY OF MITES, cutting a 2002 album for Meteor City. Alongside MONSTER MAGNET personnel Jon, Ed & Tim GALLERY OF MITES boasted a nine man strong line-up including Dwayne from BLACK NASA, Stu of HALFWAY TO GONE and Mike and Jim from LORD STERLING.

Singles/EPs:
Burn / Red 5 (Failing Through), Warpburner (1999) ('Solace' EP)

Albums:
JERSEY DEVILS, Freebird Meteor City FMC001 (1998) (Split CD with SOLARIZED) Heavy Bitch - 2 Fisted / Dirt / Try / Funk No. 49
FURTHER, Meteor City MCY-010 (2001) Mandog / Black Unholy Ground / Followed / Whistle Pig / Hungry Mother / Angel's Dreaming / Suspicious Tower / Heavy Birth - Two Fisted

SOLAR ANUS (JAPAN)
Line-Up: Tenkotu Kawaho (vocals / bass), Maki Takahasi (vocals), Wataru Isiko (guitar),

Takahiro Seki (drums), Ten Watanabe (Japanese drums)

Legendary Cosmic Doom act mentored since inception in 1996 by Tenkotu Kawaho. The debut SOLAR ANUS album 'On', clad in elaborate Psychedelic artwork executed by Kawaho, arrived on the band's own Gyokumon label.
For the sophomore 'Trance!!' effort SOLAR ANUS inducted a female lead vocalist Maki Takahasi. Promoting this record the band toured France in the summer of 1999.
Mirai of SIGH contributed keyboards to the 2000 album 'Next World News'.
All SOLAR ANUS track titles are in the Japanese language.

Albums:
ON, Gyokumon GYO 001 (1997)
TRANCE!!, Gyokumon GYO 002 (1999)
NEXT WORLD NEWS, Gyokumon GYO-003 (2000)

SOLARIZED (Eatontown, NJ, USA)
Line-Up: Jim Hogan (vocals / guitar), Dave Topolenski (guitar), Mike Fiore (bass), Reg Satana (drums)

A premier Stoner act out of central New Jersey. SOLARIZED was borne out of DAISYCUTTER, a band that splintered when members Ed Mundell and Tim Cronin quit to join MONSTER MAGNET. Vocalist / guitarist Jim Hogan and female drummer Regina Satanas duly founded SOLARIZED pulling in Lou Gorra on bass.
The debut 'Neanderthal Speedway' album, issued by Man's Ruin, cited a line-up of Hogan, Gorra, Satana and guitarist Pete Hauschild, the latter joining mid term into the recording process. Guesting would be erstwhile compatriots Ed Mundell and Tim Cronin.
The 'Jersey Devils' album was a split affair, pitching SOLARIZED's 'Eight Ways To Sunday' EP with fellow New Jersey band SOLACE. A further track from these sessions surfaced on a Rise Above compilation album. During the summer of 1999 Hauschild opted out and SOLARIZED drafted SOUL PREACHER guitarist Lee Stuart to fill in for touring in North America. However, with the close of these dates both Gorra and Stuart made their exit, creating HALFWAY TO GONE in league with SIXTY WATT SHAMAN man Chris Dukehart. SOLARIZED regrouped by inducting ex-DRAG PACK six stringer Dave Topolenski and former HORSCACK '77 bassist Mike Fiore for the 'Driven' album, issued in 2001 through Meteor City. The

album included a cover version of THE DAMNED's Stab Yor Back',

Hogan achieved the mammoth feat of assembling a cast of New Jersey's underground Rock's finest for the Jack Endino mixed SCENE KILLER project album. Featured would be members of acts such as MONSTER MAGNET, ETERNAL ELYSIUM, SIX SIGMA, CORE, BURNOUT KING, IRON MAN, ROTGUT, DRAG PACK, THE CLONE OBEY, SOLACE, THE LEMMINGS, GIANT SLOTH, THE ATOMIC BITCHWAX, THE RIBEYE BROS., SHOVELHEAD and HALFWAY TO GONE.

Topolenski and Satanas also proved industrious outside of the SOLARIZED camp, recording material for a project dubbed CRATERMAKER.

Mike Fiore decamped in March of 2002.

Albums:
EIGHT WAYS TO SUNDAY, Freebird Meteor City FMC 001 (1998) (Split CD with SOLACE)
Slide / Drifter / Crucible / Sugar Bag
NEANDERTHAL SPEEDWAY, Man's Ruin MR076 (1999)
Nebula Mask / Aftermath / Fire Breather / Psyclone Tread / Iron Hide / February Sixth (Anti Life Equation) / Solar Fang / Black Light Swill / Cloud King / Shifter / Gravity Well / Monolith
DRIVEN, Meteor City (2001)
Intro / Dig The Ride / Born Of Fire / Chrome Shop / Meanspirit / Angel / Stab Yor Back / Firefight / Box Full Of Dirt / Southbound / Conspiracy / World Without End

SOLITUDE (Delaware, USA)
Line-Up: Keith Saulsbury (vocals / guitar), Dan Martinez (guitar), Rodney Cope (bass), Mike Hostler (drums)

Delaware's SOLITUDE, forged in 1985, made an impact on the tape trading scene with their 'Focus Of Terror' demo in 1987 and the following year's 'Sickness' recording. A final demo 'Fall Of Creation' led directly to a deal with Red Light Records and a license with a subsequent England's Music For Nations label.

SOLITUDE have toured alongside CELTIC FROST, DEATH ANGEL and SACRED REICH.

Albums:
FROM WITHIN, Bulletproof CDVEST 18 (1994)
Twisted / No Future / Tipping The Balance / Alter The Red / Mind Pollution / From Within / The Afterlife / A Loss Of Blood / The Empty / Poisoned Population / In This Life / Side Winder

SOLITUDE AETURNUS
(Arlington, TX, USA)
Line-Up: Robert Lowe (vocals), John Perez (guitar), Edgar Riviera (guitar), Count Lyle Steadham (bass), John 'Wolf' Covington (drums)

STEVE MOSLEY of SOLITUDE AETURNUS
Photo : Nico Wobben

Ultra Doom Heavy Metal act SOLITUDE AETURNUS were created in 1987 by erstwhile ROTTING CORPSE Thrash Metal guitarist John Perez as SOLITUDE.

SOLITUDE put out a 1988 demo prior to altering their name so as not to be confused with the Delaware act of the same name. The band's line-up at this juncture was Perez, vocalist Kristoff Gabehart, guitarist Tom Martinez, bassist Chris Hardin and drummer Brad Kane.

The band, with only Perez remaining from the original incarnation, soon separated themselves from the Thrash pack with the launch of their 'Into The Depths Of Sorrow' album in 1991 which displayed SOLITUDE AETURNUS' obvious homage to BLACK SABBATH and epic, if sluggish, workouts.

The group had originally signed to King Classic Records and the album had been ready for release in 1990, but due to problems with the label it didn't see the light of day until the following year. By this time the group had

380

ROBERT LOWE of SOLITUDE AETURNUS
Photo : Nico Wobben

been snapped up by Roadrunner Records, releasing the 'Beyond The Crimson Horizon' sophomore effort in 1992.

In 1992 Perez took on a side venture hooking up with erstwhile GAMMACIDE man Rick Perry founded the Industrial flavoured PUNCTURE in league with POST MORTEM STATEMENT sampler Per Nilsson and drummer Larry Moses of Punk acts WHY AM I? And DAYS OF DECISION. Perez made his exit from PUNCTURE the following year in order to concentrate fully on his priority act.

After touring in America with KILLERS, SOLITUDE AETURNUS switched to Pavement Records for 1994's 'Through The Darkest Hour' (issued in Britain on Bulletproof), supporting its release with American tours opening for MERCYFUL FATE and European dates with REVELATION.

The group was disappointed with the ensuing 'Downfall' album from a production angle and, more to the point, by the fact that it was not pushed in America or Europe for the group to make any further significant headway. The album cover for 'Downfall' was changed for the European version without the band's knowledge because the record company deemed it to be "too dark".

Nevertheless, the Texan group was able to pick up some dates with MORGANA LEFAY in 1997 and gained a new deal with the German Massacre label. However, bassist Count Lyle Steadham departed to be replaced by Steve Mosley.

1998's 'Adagio' album was recorded at Rhythm Studios in Bidford, England and co-produced by the band and Paul Johnston. A bonus track, a cover of BLACK SABBATH's 'Heaven And Hell', was included for good measure. SOLITUDE AETURNUS also covered OZZY OSBOURNE's 'No More tears' for the 'Legend Of A Madman' tribute album.

SOLITUDE AETURNUS would plan on a sixth studio album for issue sometime in 2002 through the Massacre label. Meantime vocalist Robert Lowe gigged with side project CONCEPT OF GOD. Former SOLITUDE AETURNUS bassist Lyle Steadham debuted his new act GHOULTOWN with the album 'Give 'Em Enough Rope' backed up by a lengthy North American tour schedule.

Albums:
INTO THE DEPTHS OF SORROW,
Roadracer RO 92652 (1991)
Dawn Of Antiquity / Opaque Divinity / Transcending Sentinels / Dream Of Immortality / Destiny Falls To Ruin / White Ship / Mirror Of Sorrow / Where Angels Dare To Tread
BEYOND THE CRIMSON HORIZON,

Roadracer RO 91682 (1992)
Seeds Of The Desolate / Black Castle / The Final Sin / It Came Upon One Night / The Hourglass / Beneath The Fading Sun / Plague Of procession / Beyond...
THROUGH THE DARKEST HOUR,
Bulletproof CDVEST35 (1994)
Falling / Haunting The Obscure / The 8th Day / Mourning / The 9th Day / Awakening / Pain / Pawns Of Anger / Eternal (Dreams Part II) / Perfect Insanity / Shattered My Spirit
DOWNFALL, IRS IRSCD 993.022 (1996)
Phantoms / Only This (And Nothing More) / Midnight Dreams / Together And Wither / Elysium / Deathwish / These Are The Nameless / Chapel Of Burning / Concern
ADAGIO, Massacre MAS CD0161 (1998)
My Endtime / Days Of Prayer / Believe / Never / Idis / Personal God / Mental Pictures / The Fall / Insanity's Circles / Lament / Empty Faith / Spiral Descent / Heaven And Hell

SOLSTICE (UK)

Line-Up: Morris Ingram (vocals), Richard M. Walker (guitar), Lee Netherwood (bass), Rick Budby (drums)

British Doom act SOLSTICE debuted with the 1991 demo tape 'Lamentations', following this with a 1992 effort 'MCMXCII'. Throughout the band's formative years Lennaert Roomer held the drum position but by 1994 SOLSTICE had added former SHIP OF FOOLS guitarist John Piras and vocalist Simon Matravers, previous singer Mark Stojsavljevic having left in August of 1993 to found SEER'S TEAR.

The band toured with YEAR ZERO, ANATHEMA and Swedes COUNT RAVEN throughout 1994 promoting the 'Lamentations' album. Ex-IRONSIDE drummer Sean Steals joined the band in early 1995. Matravers was replaced in August 1995 by American singer Tom Phillips of WHILE HEAVEN WEPT and TWISTED TOWER DIRE repute. Phillips would return to America in 1996, resurrecting WHILE HEAVEN WEPT and also becoming involved with ARISE FROM THORNS and BRAVE.

Confusion reigned in the SOLSTICE camp during 1997 as their 'Halycon' album, originally recorded for Stormstrike Records, was sold to the Italian Godhead label, for a CD issue, and then to Black Tears for release in 10" vinyl format. Meantime Steals joined ANATHEMA the same year. By the 1998 album 'New Dark Age' SOLSTICE were fronted by Morris Ingram joining the ranks of bassist Chaz Netherwood, guitarists Rich Walker and Hamish Glencross and drummer Rick Budby.

Former SOLSTICE men drummer Sean

Steals and guitarist Hamish Glencross joined the ranks of MY DYING BRIDE in 1999. Back in America, Phillips issued the debut WHILE HEAVEN WEPT album 'Sorrow Of The Angels' in 1999. Guitarist John Piras went on to greater recognition in premier Black Metal act CRADLE OF FILTH renaming himself Gian Pyres.

Touring in July of 2000 in Europe had the band packaged with American acts TWISTED TOWER DIRE and THE LORD WEIRD SLOUGH FEG. The band cemented a relationship with the latter act by contributing a version of MANOWAR's 'Gloves Of Metal' to a joint SOLSTICE / THE LORD WEIRD SLOUGH FEG tribute single released by the specialist Doomed Planet label.

The band inducted new guitarist Rob Mendes for recording of the 'Englander' EP although Walker announced the dissolution of SOLSTICE in April of 2002. The guitarist and lynchpin of the band intended to devote more time to his record label Miskatonic Foundation. Walker, together with vocalist Anthony and former WARRIOR, STORMWATCH and WITCHFYNDE man Dave Hewitt would create a fresh Metal band billed as TYRANT. Meantime other erstwhile SOLSTICE members Lee Netherwood and Morris Ingram founded FIREBLADE.

Singles/EPs:
Gloves Of Metal, Doomed Planet (2001) (Split single with THE LORD WEIRD SLOUGH FEG)

Albums:
LAMENTATIONS, Candlelight 007 (1994)
Neither Time Nor Tide / Only The Strong / Absolution In Extremis / These Forever Bleak Path / Last Wish / Winter Moon Rapture / The Man Who Lost The Sun
HALYCON, Godhead (1996)
The Ravenmaster / To Ride With Tyr / Graven Deep / Halycon / Gloves Of Metal / Only The Strong / Winter Moon Rapture
NEW DARK AGE, Misanthropy (1999)
New Dark Age / The Sleeping Tyrant / Cimmerian Codex / Alchemiculte / Hammer Of Damnation / The Anguine Rose / Blackthorne / The Keep / Cromlech / New Dark Age II / Legion XIII

SOMNUS (Cleveland, OH, USA)
Line-Up: Scott Hilberg (vocals / guitar), Dennis Downey (guitar), Steve Rolf (bass), Rhiannon (keyboards / vocals), Chris Stolle (drums

A dark, Gothic inclined Pagan Metal act out of Cleveland. The SOMNUS concept was borne during 1995 by ex-ODIOUS SANCTION man vocalist / guitarist Scott Hilberg, guitarist Erik Rueschman and shortly thereafter, bass player Lou Spencer. The following year saw the completion of the line-up as vocalist / keyboard player Rhiannon, a former member of Thrashers ATOMIC WARFARE and known for her role as a session member of AVERNUS, and drummer Scott Shetler made up the numbers. This union marked their arrival with the 1997 demo tape 'To Return The Crimson Skies'.

Engaging in live activity SOMNUS set about honing their craft on the gig circuit, including appearances at the 'World Series Of Metal' festival in Cleveland (in actual fact performing at this event annually from 1996 to 2001) as well as the Michigan 'International Death Fest'. Ex-THANATOPSIS man Chris Stolle supplanted Shetler as the band's new drummer in late 1997 for a further demo recording. The following year SOMNUS donated the song 'Silent Reverence' exclusively to a Lost Disciples compilation album entitled 'Visionaries Of The Macabre Vol. 1'. The band would gain further exposure by having their rendition of 'Seasons In The Abyss' included on the 1999 Dwell Records SLAYER tribute album 'Gateway To Hell'. Unceasing live work would find SOMNUS regularly on the stages at the 'Milwaukee Metalfest' and 'March Metal Meltdown' shows. Additionally, the band got in valuable opening slots to visiting international artists such as DIMMU BORGIR, EMPEROR, MY DYING BRIDE, OPETH, AMORPHIS and MOONSPELL among many others.

In March of 2000, the SOMNUS debut CD 'Awakening The Crown' was issued through Root of All Evil Records. After release Rueschman decamped and in early 2001 Spencer also made his exit, the bassist opting to concentrate his efforts on his other act MANTICORE. Initially Dave Ingram of BLOOD COVEN was brought in as substitute on lead guitar but this liaison was brief. SOMNUS was brought back up to full compliment with the inauguration of SANCTORUM members guitarist Dennis Downey and bassist Steve Rolf.

SOMNUS featured on a limited edition 7" single as a split venture with label mates THEATRE OF THE MACABRE in 2001. Offering up the previously unavailable composition 'The Deceiver' the record, pressed in green vinyl, would be restricted to a pressing run of 666 copies.

Singles/EPs:
The Deceiver, Root Of All Evil (2001) (Split single with THEATRE OF THE MACABRE)

Albums:

AWAKENING THE CROWN, Root Of All Evil (2001)
Unfulfilled Prophecy / A Calling Of Arms / The Alchemist / Forever The Serpent / Beyond The Shores / Envy Of The Seraph / Lair Of The Wendol / Within / Fulfilling The Throne / The New Beginning
THROUGH CREATION'S END, Root Of All Evil ROE 032 (2002)
The Gate Of Wolves / Warlock's Feast / Dawn Of Spirits / Tribunal Of Woe / The Deceiver / Lament For Winter's Passing / Creation's End / Unfulfilled Prophecy (Live)

SONS OF OTIS (CANADA)
Line-Up: Ken Baluke (vocals / guitar), Frank Sargeant (bass), Ryan Aubin (drums)

Canadian low end Psych-Rockers founded in Toronto in late 1992 by the trio's Detroit born founder and guitarist / vocalist Ken Baluke. Originally simply entitled OTIS, in deference to the character from the cult movie 'Henry: Portrait Of A Serial Killer', the band added the 'Sons Of' appendage due to threat of legal action from a US act of the same title. However, in 1994, and still billed OTIS, the group released a 6 track EP 'Paid To Suffer'.
It was with the debut full-length album recording 'SpaceJumboFudge' for Hypnotic Records the band first became known as SONS OF OTIS. Despite this forward step SONS OF OTIS encountered problems with Hypnotic, which forced a parting of the ways. Quite incredibly the band, acknowledged to have gone through at least ten drummers during this period and finally resorting to a drum machine, remained in self-seclusion for three years writing new material.
The renowned Frank Kozik of Man's Ruin Records snapped the band up in 1998. The resulting 'Templeball' album, the title a reference to a opiate hash blend, was promoted with a European tour in allegiance with ELECTRIC WIZARD, the live band now including drummer Emilio Mammone. Shortly after Tony Jacome of SHALLOW NORTH DAKOTA temporarily took the drum stool. Man's Ruin would also reissue the 'SpaceJumboFudge' record, albeit minus the three tracks the band had recently re-recorded for 'Templeball'. With the collapse of Man's Ruin SONS OF OTIS would then sign to The Music Cartel for the September 2001 album 'Songs For Worship', within its Psychedelic grooves would rest a fuzzed out version of JIMI HENDRIX's 'In From The Storm'. SONS OF OTIS would also settle on a new drummer in Ryan Aubin.
SONS OF OTIS issued a 10" picture disc single in 2002, the A side being a cover of

STEPPENWOLF's 'The Pusher'. Originally slated for release through Germany's Monster Zero label 'The Pusher' would finally be delivered by Music Cartel.
Ken Baluke also operated the 'Ambient Drone' side endeavour OX.

Singles/EPs:
Relapse / Nothing / Windows / Pain / Beware / Drone, (1994) ('Paid To Suffer' EP)
The Pusher / Dark Sun, Music Cartel (2002) (10" single)

Albums:
SPACEJUMBOFUDGE, Hypnotic HYPSD1043 (1996)
Super Typhoon / You're Nothing / The Truth / Sidebar / Clowns / Big Muff / World / Theme / Anti-Nauseant / Windows (Paid To Suffer version)
TEMPLEBALL, Man's Ruin MR159 (1999)
Mile High / Nothing / Vitus / Windows Jam / Super Typhoon / Down / Mississippi Queen / New Mole / Steamroller / Diesel
SONGS FOR WORSHIP, Music Cartel TMC51 CD (2001)
The Hunted / Losin' It / I'm Gone / The Other Side / Cold City Blues / In From The Storm / Tankard II

SORCEROR (SWEDEN)
Line-Up: Anders Engberg (vocals), Peter Furulid (guitar), Mats Leidholm (guitar), Johnny Hagel (bass), Richard Evensand (drums)

A renowned Stockhom Doom band founded during 1994 by guitarist Peter Furulid and bass player Johnny Hagel. SORCEROR, who also had a track inclusion on a 'Rockbox' compilation album, issued two of the most in demand demos in the annals Swedish Metal. The SORCEROR American album release is actually a combination of two demos from 1989 and 1992's 'The Inquisition'. The second demo features drummer Tommy Karlsson. The Brain Ticket label was the creation of John Perez of Texan Doomsters, SOLITUDE AETURNUS who wanted to establish Doom acts in North America. SORCERER had the honour of being the first release on the Perez label. The reissue of the demos included a remixing of the second demo, and three unreleased tracks entitled 'Wisdom', 'Northern Seas', and 'At Dawn'. The second demo also had a cover of the RAINBOW tune, 'Stargazer'.
With the departure of vocalist Anders Engberg in 1993 SORCEROR folded. Naturally the various members of SORCEROR went on to greater things.

384

Engberg now fronts the highly regarded Pomp Power Metal act LION'S SHARE as well as APHASIA. Bassist Johnny Hagel carved a reputation with TIAMAT before joining SUNDOWN and busying himself with his solo venture CINNAMON SPIRAL, whilst drummer Rickard 'Richard' Evensand went to a succession of high profile and diverse acts including Funksters IT'S ALIVE, SOUTHPAW, EYEBALL, Death Metal band EBONY TEARS and DOG FACED GODS.

Interestingly, SORCEROR have recently re-formed.

Albums:
SORCEROR, Brainticket B001 (1995)
Premonition / The Sorcerer / Northern Seas / Queen In Black / Inquisition / Wisdom / Stargazer / At Dawn / Anno 1503 / Born With Fear / Dark Ages / The Battle / Visions

SORROW (New York, NY, USA)
Line-Up: Andy Marchione (vocals / bass), Brett Clarin (guitar), Billy Rogan (guitar), Mike Hymson (drums)

A Doom fuelled, lethargic Death Metal act with a political edge to their lyrics. The band was previously known as APPARITION under which title two demo sessions and a 7" single for the Relapse label were released.

For a short period Andy Marchione's position as lead singer was temporarily filled by guitarist Billy Rogan. In a tragic accident Marchione had suffered carbon monoxide poisoning in a car. Marchione went into a coma from which he eventually recovered but unfortunately the girl who was with him died. After two albums Roadrunner dropped the band which promptly folded. Following the collapse of SORROW ex-members founded Ambient Doomsters JOURNEY INTO DARKNESS.

Drummer Mike Hymson would go on to DYSTOPIA before founding Nu-edged Metal act WEHATEJULIA in alliance with PSYCHO's Larry Forman.

Albums:
FORGOTTEN SUNRISE, Roadrunner (1991)
Awaiting The Savior / Eternally Forgotten / Curse The Sunrise / A Waste Cry For Hope
HATRED AND DISGUST, Roadrunner (1992)
Insatiable / Forced Repression / Illusion Of Freedom / Human Error / Separative Adjectives / Unjustified Reluctance

SOULDIVIDER (SWEDEN)
Line-Up: Jonas Gustafson (vocals), Martin Henricsson (guitar), Andreas Hahne (guitar),

Mattias Nilsson (bass), Claes Lysen (drums)

SOULDIVIDER bassist Mattias Nilsson assembled the side project THE SATANIC ALL STARS during 2002 comprising vocalist Sick Royale, GODEATGOD guitarist Scott Myers and HIBERNUS MORTIS drummer Caesar Placeres.

Singles/EPs:
A Need To Escape / Anymore / Strange Feeling 4 AM / Inhale Your Destination / Second Ride, (2001) ('The Big Relax' EP)

Albums:
SUPERSOUND CITY, 12th Planet Music (2002)
Time To Reflect / Supersound City / Suburban Sin Club / A Long Way / Things Undone / Dead Set Now / Confusion / Soulshaker Queen / An Even Side Of The Stone / Tension & Relief / Buckshot / The Rift

SOULPREACHER (Raleigh, NC, USA)
Line-Up: Anthony Staton (vocals), Mike Avery (guitar), Robb Hewlett (bass), Mark Drums)

Southern fried Stoner merchants SOULPREACHER deal in the most mournful lyrics delivered atop slothful detuned slabs of riffing.

The band is rooted in a prior act FORSAKEN comprising vocalist Anthony Staton, guitarist Mike Avery, bassist Robb Hewlett and drummer Mark Schindler. Switching title to SOULPREACHER and substituting Schindler for new Sticksman Brian Watson the band issued the 'Worship' EP through Man's Ruin. 'When The Black Sunn Rises' followed the same year.

Singles/EPs:
Alibaster I / Alibaster II (The Sleep) / Salvation / Blues For A Blackened World / Thirteen, (2000) ('Worship' EP)
When The Black Sunn Rises... The Holy Men Burn / Kingdom / Last Prayer / Something To Slow You Down / Deadnothingspace, Berserker (2000) ('When The Black Sunn Rises' EP)

SOULSEARCH (AUSTRIA)
Line-Up: T.K. (vocals / guitar), K.P. (guitar), S.B. (bass), E.O. (drums)

An Anonymous Salzburg based Doom band that have progressed, according to the band, from 1991 Gothic Doomsters through Folk-Doom with the 1994 'Die Essenz' EP, which featured Wolfgang Schrammel on keyboards, to an amalgam of epic Doom

385

Metal and ambience. SOULSEARCH, fronted by Thom Kirchbirger, themselves style their brand of music as "Norikum Doom", after the ancient European Celtic homelands.

Female bassist Clara augmented the line-up for the 1998 album 'Abred Vs. Anwyn – Behind The Archaic Alliance', SOULSEARCH's first record to be issued by an outside label.

The band would claim that the three track 2000 'Iherno' EP would be their last recorded output. An exceptionally limited run of 100 vinyl pieces made 'Iherno' hugely collectable. Both vocalist / guitarist Kirchberger and drummer Jurgen perform outside of SOULSEARCH in Death Metal Band FEYNDHAMMER. Keyboard player Hajot also cites membership of THELEMA.

Singles/EPs:
Untapped Horizons / In Earth / Star Chamber / Fruit Of The Doom, Soulsearch (1994) ('Die Essenz' EP)
Heervater / Narbenvolk / Hymne, Soulsearch (2000) ('Iherno' EP)

Albums:
NATURE FALLS ASLEEP, Dream Machine Productions (1992)
GWYNEDD, Serenades SR012 (1997)
Neumondblut (The Principle Of Womanhood) / Feldfeuer (Fires Of The Womb) / Ahnenstahl (The Synonym For The Godly Mystery) / Schwarze Erde (The Guilt Of Blood) / Ährenschuld (Breathing The Land) / Kundgebung / Rabenhorst (Last Days Of A Bloodless Land)
ABRED VS. ANWYN - BEHIND THE ARCHAIC ALLIANCE, Serenades SR020 (1998)
The Sidh / Dazzling Niam / Owl Aided / Aeds Traces / Golden Torques / Achard Forcha / Seals Of Gessa / Cythraw / Archaic Alliance

SOULSEARCH (Seattle, WA, USA)
Line-Up: Chris Cornell (vocals / guitar), Kim Thayil (guitar), Ben Shepard (bass), Matt Cameron (drums)

SOUNDGARDEN deal in stark, brooding, hewn to the bone minimalist metal, much of it tethered to unrelenting bass riffs. Vocalist Chris Cornell has made his mark in the rock annals by defining a genre of pain-laden wails that accompanied the huge riffs perfectly. Of all the acts to benefit from the Grunge torrent SOUNDGARDEN are perhaps the act with the closest ties to a traditional rock sound with hints of the '70s greats.

Coming together in 1984 SOUNDGARDEN comprised vocalist Chris Cornell (who at this point also played drums onstage), guitarist Kim Thayil and bassist Hiro Yamamoto. The band added erstwhile FEEDBACK and SKIN YARD drummer Matt Cameron in 1986 and signed to influential label Sub Pop, the record company owing a debt of honour to Thayil as he had brought together founders Jonathon Poneman and Bruce Pavitt.

SOUNDGARDEN made their first steps with the 'Hunted Down' single. The 7" version coming in blue vinyl whilst the 12" EP being offered in a garish orange.

Before signing to major A&M Records, the first of Sub Pop's roster to do so, SOUNDGARDEN's last Sub Pop single was to be a bastardized variant of the OHIO PLAYERS 'Fopp', the EP also containing a reworking of THE RAMONES 'I Can't Give You Anything'.

In mid 1990 Yamamoto was supplanted by erstwhile NIRVANA bassist Jason Everman. Yamamoto would turn up some five years later with TRULY, an act conceived with SCREAMING TREES man Mark Pickerel. This line-up of SOUNDGARDEN cut only one track, a take on the BEATLES 'Come Together' prior to Everman making way for Ben Shepard. The band's new bassist had previously been a member of 600 SCHOOL, MARCH OF CRIMES (alongside PEARL JAM guitarist Stone Gossard) and EPISODE. Everman was to journey through SKUNK, NIRVANA and onto New York's MINDFUNK. (and then the army!).

Splinter group TEMPLE OF THE DOG created a useful diversion in 1991 as Cornell and Shepard united with their rehearsal studio friends Stone Gossard and Jeff Ament, both ex-MOTHER LOVE BONE and future PEARL JAM frontman Eddie Vedder. As grunge grew the collective talent involved in TEMPLE OF THE DOG was enough to chalk up double platinum status for the album.

Cornell was also to co-produce the SCREAMING TREES album 'Uncle Anesthesia' the same year.

'Badmotorfinger' propelled the band into the American charts and with an invaluable support slot to GUNS N' ROSES 'Illusion' touring extravaganza SOUNDGARDEN were on their way, a headlining jaunt to Britain proving a sell out.

The first single from 'Badmotorfinger' was 'Jesus Christ Pose', a controversial title featuring an instrumental version of BLACK SABBATH's 'Into The Void' as a B side.

The follow up 'Rusty Cage' single boasted a somewhat bizarre choice of cover versions on the B side of spoof act SPINAL TAP's 'Big Bottom' and legendary loons CHEECH & CHONG's 'Earache My Eye'.

Third single 'Outshined' carried on the obtuse

B side tradition capturing a version of British metallers BUDGIE's 'Homicidal Suicide', Punk merchants FEAR's 'I Don't Care About You' and JIMI HENDRIX's 'Can't You See Me'. In October the band slotted in an appearance opening the California 'Day On The Green' festival in front of 50,000 Rock fans there to see headliners METALLICA, QUEENSRYCHE and FAITH NO MORE.

Cameron and Shepard created HATER in 1993 with ex-MONSTER MAGNET guitarist John McBain, erstwhile 600 SCHOOL / EPISODE bassist John Waterman and FIRE ANTS vocalist Brian Wood releasing an eponymous album on A&M Records the same year.

Cameron and Cornell also united with PEARL JAM men bassist Jeff Ament and guitarist Mike McReady to forge M.A.C.C. the same year.

'Superunknown' was recorded at HEART's Bad Animals studio in Seattle and produced by Michael Beinhorn. As the American rock public fully embraced Grunge SOUNDGARDEN, after completing a headline slot on the Far East festival package dubbed a 'Big Day Out' with THE RAMONES and SMASHING PUMPKINS, were to find themselves in March 1994 with an uncompromising 70 minute no holds barred hard rock album, debuting at number 1 and going on to surpass the triple platinum sales mark.

By April SOUNDGARDEN were touring Britain once more but the media were quick to jump on the fact that the band seemed withdrawn and apathetic. A planned headline spot at the 'Reading Festival' was scrapped at the last minute the band citing reasons involving the recording schedule of their next album as rumours filtered through that SOUNDGARDEN were uninterested in touring.

1996's 'Down On The Upside' was recorded at PEARL JAM guitarist Stone Gossard's studio. A far more accessible affair it was to be the band's last record. Typically the album launched a succession of British hit singles with its parent easily breaking the platinum sales mark in America.

Sensationally the band was reported to have split after twelve years as a going concern. A statement issued by A&M on April 9 1997 gave the news that they had mutually and amicably decided to disband. Rumours abounded that tension within the group had been at an all time high with musical differences concerning the recording of 'Down And The Upside' playing a part. Shepherd had also been more interested in pursuing his side project, DEVILHEAD and the other solo offering, HATER, with Matt Cameron whose

second album was due to be released in mid 1997.

Both Shepard and Cameron put in performances on ex-MONSTER MAGNET guitarist John McBain's WELL WATER CONSPIRACY self titled '97 album. Shepard also put in further efforts on the 1998 DESERT SESSIONS album 'Volume I & II', an in the wilderness jam session convened by ex-KYUSS men guitarist Josh Homme and drummer Brant Bjork.

Cameron was to guest sporadically on live work for Homme's post KYUSS act QUEENS OF THE STONE AGE and in late 1997 was confirmed as session drummer for THE SMASHING PUMPKINS. The drummer also deputized for PEARL JAM on their 1998 tour when Jack Irons left the band and appeared on RUSH vocalist GEDDY LEE's 2000 solo album.

2000 found Thayil as a key member of NO WTO COMBO, an alternative 'supergroup' alliance together with DEAD KENNEDYS frontman Jello Biafra, ex-NIRVANA bassist Krist Novoselic and erstwhile SWEET 75 drummer Gina Mainwal for the album 'Live From The Battle In Seattle'.

Thayil would also unite with Novoselic, ALICE IN CHAINS drummer Sean Kinney and Country legend JOHNNY CASH to cut a rendition of 'Time Of The Preacher' for the WILLIE NELSON tribute album 'Twisted Willie'.

Rumours emerged in late 2000 that Cornell was tipped to replace the departed Zack De La Rocha in RAGE AGAINST THE MACHINE. Whilst many cited an obvious conflict of styles as well as record company contractual obligations as being prime reasons this purported union could not transpire, it was revealed by early summer 2001 the two parties had in fact been working in the studio for quite some time.

Much to the band members annoyance demo recordings, cut at the Seattle Bad Animals studio, were leaked and widely circulated on the internet. By early 2002 the union with Chris Cornell was announced officially as CIVILIAN, the band also being scheduled for an appearance on the U.S. leg of the 'Ozzfest' tour. These plans were subsequently scrapped but by the summer it looked as though the alliance, having smoothed over management beaurocracy, was back on the agenda.

Singles/EPs:
Hunted Down / Nothing To Say, Sub Pop SP 12A (1987) (USA release)
Hunted Down / Entering / Tears To Forget / Nothing To Say / Little Joe / Hand Of God, Sub Pop SP12B (1987) (USA release)

('Screaming Life' EP)
Fopp / Fopp (Dub) / Kingdom Of Come / Swallow My Pride, Sub Pop SP 17 (1988)
Flower / Head Injury / Toy Box, S.S.T. SST 231CD (1989)
Hands All Over / Come Together / Heretic / Big Dumb Sex, A&M AMCD560 (1990) (10" single)
Loud Love / Fresh Deadly Roses / Big Dumb Sex (dub) / Get On The Snake, A&M AMY 574 (1990) ('Loud Love' EP)
Room A Thousand Years Wide / HIV Baby, Sub Pop SP 83 (1990) (USA release)
Jesus Christ Pose / Stray Cat Blues, A&M AM 862 (1992) (7" single) **30 UK**
Jesus Christ Pose / Stray Cat Blues / Into The Void (Stealth), A&M AMCD 862 (1992) (CD single)
Rusty Cage / Touch Me, A&M AM 874 (1992) (7" single) **41 UK**
Rusty Cage / Touch Me / Show Me, A&M AMY 874 (1992) (12" single)
Rusty Cage / Touch Me / Big Bottom / Earache My Eye, A&M AMCD 874 (1992) (CD single)
Outshined / I Can't Give You Anything, A&M AM 0102 (1992) (7" single) **50 UK**
Outshined / I Can't Give You Anything /Homicidal Suicide, A&M AM 0102 T (1992) (12" single)
Outshined / I Can't Give You Anything / I Don't Care About You / Can't You See Me, A&M AM 0102CDX (1992) (CD single)
Spoonman / Fresh Tendrils, A&M 580539-7 (1994) (7" single) **20 UK**
Spoonman / Fresh Tendrils / Cold Bitch / Exit Stonehenge, A&M 580539-2 (1994) (CD single)
The Day I Tried To Live / Like Suicide (Acoustic), A&M 580595-7 (1994) (7" single) **42 UK**
The Day I Tried To Live / Like Suicide (Acoustic) / Kickstand (Live), A&M 580595-1 (1994) (12" single)
Black Hole Sun / Beyond The Wheel (Live) / Fell On Black Days (Live), A&M 580736-7 (1994) (7" single) **12 UK**
Black Hole Sun / Beyond The Wheel (Live) / Birth Ritual (Demo), A&M 580737-2 (1994) (CD single)
Black Hole Sun / My Wave (Live) / Jesus Christ Pose (Live) / Spoonman (Remix), A&M 580737-2 (1994) (CD single)
Fell On Black Days / Kyle Petty, Son Of Richard / Motorcycle Loop, A&M 580947-7 (1995) (7" single) **24 UK**
Fell On Black Days / Kyle Petty, Son Of Richard / Fell On Black Days (Video), A&M 580947-2 (1995) (CD single)
Fell On Black Days /Girl U Want / Fell On Black Days (Demo), A&M 580947-5 (1995) (CD single)

Pretty Noose / Jerry Garcia's Finger, A&M 581620-7 (1996) (7" red vinyl single) **14 UK**
Pretty Noose / Applebite / An Unkind (Interview With Eleven's Alain And Natasha), A&M 5816202 (1996) (CD single)
Burden In My Hand / Karaoke, A&M 581854-7 (1996) (7" single) **33 UK**
Burden In My Hand / Bleed Together / She's A politician / Chris Cornell Interview, A&M 581855-2 (1996) (CD single)
Blow Up The Outside World / Dusty, A&M 581986-7 (1996) (7" single) **38 UK**
Blow Up The Outside World / Dusty / Gun, A&M 581987-2 (1996) (CD single)
Blow Up The Outside World / Get On The Snake / Slice Of Spacejam, A&M 581986-2 (1996) (CD single)

Albums:
ULTRAMEGA OK, S.S.T. SST 201CD (1988)
Flower / All Your Lies / 665 / Beyond The Wheel / 667 / Mood For Trouble / Circle Of Power / He Didn't / Smokestack Lightning / Nazi Driver / Head Injury / Incessant Mace / One Minute Of Silence
LOUDER THAN LOVE, A&M CDA 5252 (1989)
Ugly Truth / Hands All Over / Gun / Power Trip / Get On The Snake / Full On Kevin's Mom / Loud Love / I Wake / No Wrong No Right / Uncovered / Big Dumb Sex
BAD MOTORFINGER, A&M 395374-2 (1991) **39 UK, 39 USA**
Rusty Cage / Outshined / Slaves And Bulldozers / Jesus Christ Pose / Face Pollution / Somewhere / Searching With My Good Eye Closed / Room A Thousand Years Wide / Mind Riot / Drawing Flies / Holy Water / New Damage
SUPERUNKNOWN, A&M 540 215-2 (1994) **4 UK, 1 USA**
Let Me Drown / My Wave / Fell On Black Days / Mailman / Superunknown / Head Down / Black Hole Sun / Spoonman / Limo Wreck / The Day I Tried To Live / Kickstand / Fresh Tendrils / 4th Of July / Half / Like Suicide / She Likes Surprises
DOWN ON THE UPSIDE, A&M 540 526-2 (1996) **7 UK, 2 USA**
Pretty Noose / Rhinosaur / Zero Chance / Dusty / Ty Cobb / Blow Up The Outside World / Burden In My Hand / Never Named / Applebite / Never The Machine Forever / Tighter And Tighter / No Attention / Switch Opens / Overfloater / An Unkind / Boot Camp
THE A-SIDES, A&M 540833-2 (1997) **63 USA**
Nothing To Say / Flower / Loud Love / Hands All Over / Get On The Snake / Jesus Christ Pose / Outshined / Rusty Cage / Spoonman

/ The Day I Tried To Live / Black Hole Sun / Fell On Black Days / Pretty Noose / Burden In My Hand / Blow Up The Outside World / Ty Cobb / Bleed Together

SOUR VEIN (New Orleans, FL, USA)
Line-Up: T-Roy (vocals / guitar), Liz (guitar), Josh (bass), Mike (drums)

SOUR VEIN are a Southern Doom outfit relocated from Cape Fear, North Carolina to New Orleans and conceived by former BUZZOVEN man vocalist / guitarist T-Roy. The band, originally known as SOUR VAIN (and on occasion $OUR VEIN), started life as a Punk band, entering the world of Doom in 1998 upon the induction of former 13 guitarist Liz. Prior to their dark and heavy days SOUR VEIN had issued a split 7" single with BUZZOVEN. T-Roy had formed part of BUZZOVEN's touring line-up during 1996.
SOUR VEIN debuted with four tracks produced by EYEHATEGOD's Jimmy Bower included on the Game Two compilation 'He Is No Good To Me Dead'. A full-length eponymous album surfaced on Game Two during 2000.
The band has also contributed their version of

LYNYRD SKYNYRD's 'Simple Man' to a Slowride tribute album and also donated a track to a Raven Moon ST. VITUS tribute collection.
The band has had a fluid rhythm section citing drummers Henry, Mike and Slim Spencer amongst the ranks. Latterly SOUR VEIN has signed to Southern Lord records.

Albums:
SOUR VEIN, Game Two GT-15 (2000)
Salvation / Dirty South / Uneasy / Gone / Snakerunn / Plead The Fifth / Burial / Intake

SOUTHERN GUN CULTURE (TX, USA)
Line-Up: Danny Grochow (vocals / guitar), Amber Dickerson (bass), Trent Parker (drums)

Texan Stoner trio SOUTHERN GUN CULTURE include the former FAMOUS CHRISTIANS and HROSSA rhythm section of bassist Amber Dickerson and drummer Trent Parker. Inducting ex-FRONT LAWN REVOLUTION and MAD TAXI frontman Danny Grochow SOUTHERN GUN CULTURE was created in September of 2000.

SOUR VEIN
Photo : El Danno

389

Albums:
ROOM 65, Monotremata (2002)
Broken Wing / Free / Hemi / Somethin' /
Salvation / Brave New World / Slow Heavy /
Art Of War - Pillars Of Hercules (RKF v.2.0)

SOUTHFORK (SWEDEN)
Line-Up: Gunnar Lööf (vocals / guitar), Henrik
Bergqvist (guitar), Anders Fästader (bass),
Sebastian Sippola (drums)

Blues based Stoners dating back to 1997.
SOUTHFORK came together with a union of
vocalist / guitarist Gunnar Lööf and drummer
Sebastian Sippola. By the summer of the
following year the band was rounded out with
the addition of guitarist Henrik Bergqvist and
bassist Anders Fästader, the latter having
already made a name for himself with GREAT
KING RAT, TITANIC TRUTH and with JOHN
NORUM's band. Following completion of the
'Straight Ahead' album Thomas Thorberg
supplanted Fästader.
Both Thorberg and Sippola would feature on
the debut PLANKTON album.

Albums:
SOUTHFORK, Black Mark (1999)
Space Revolution / Stray Dog / Superglue /
Walk New Worlds / Everything Must Go /
Man Made Of Stone / One Way Freeway /
Spitfire / Graceland Boogie / Far Beyond
STRAIGHT AHEAD, Black Mark (2001)
Blame It On Me / Overlord / Perfect / When
I'm Done / By Your Side / A Different Kind /
Ride Of Your Life / Nothing To Say /
Evocation Blues

SPACEBOY (Santa Cruz, CA, USA)
Line-Up: Clifford Dinsmore (vocals), John
Kaufman (guitar), Bill Blair (guitar), Adam
Cantwell (bass), Jade Dylan (drums)

Santa Cruz Doomsters SPACEBOY include
former BLAST! Vocalist Clifford Dinsmore and
bassist Adam Cantwell of THE FUCKING
CHAMPS. The band debuted with a 1994 7"
single issued through the Galaxia label.
Signing to Southern Lord SPACEBOY set to
work on a 2002 Billy Anderson produced
album. Originally with a projected title of 'The
Melting World' this opus arrived with the by
now trademark epic title of 'Searching The
Stone Library For The Green Page Illusion'.

Albums:
GETTING WARM ON THE TRAIL OF HEAT,
Frenetic FR005 (1998)
Planet Of Pot / Horses In Great Open
Spaces / Ancient Civilizations / Pink Domain
/ Return To Cannabis Island / Stoner Fort /

Emitic Translation Cathedral / Elf Song
**THE FORCE THAT HOLDS TOGETHER A
HEART TORN TO PIECES**, Howling Bull
Entertainment (2000)
Six Marshall Silver / The Maze / Strange
New Powers / Pot Hibernation
**SEARCHING THE STONE LIBRARY FOR
THE GREEN PAGE OF ILLUSION**,
Southern Lord SUNN18 (2002)
Searching The Stone Library For The Green
Page Of Illusion / The Melting World /
Spaceship / Eye Pillow / The Monsoon

SPACE PROBE TAURUS (SWEDEN)
Line-Up: Ola Sjöberg (vocals / guitar), Per
Boder (guitar), Magnus Eronen (bass), Erik
Sundler (drums)

Marking their arrival with a 1997 demo tape
'Low On Karma High On Speed' SPACE
PROBE TAURUS offered up prime grade
Swedish Fuzz Rock.
The band, initially entitled SNAKE MACHINE,
had been convened in 1992 by guitarist Per
Boder, previously vocalist for MACABRE END
and GOD MACABRE, and drummer Erik
Sundler. A few months after formation Ola
Sjöberg, another veteran of MACABRE END
and GOD MACABRE, enrolled on bass.
Unable to locate a suitable frontman Boder
and Sjöberg shared vocal responsibilities on
debut demo recordings in May of 1993
'Skinned Women And Mescaline'. These
recordings never made it as far as the public
domain.
Later that year a singer named Enberg was
drafted. Sjöberg switched instruments to
guitar upfront of a second recording session,
1994's 'Ride The Wildebeest'. Enberg
decamped and SNAKE MACHINE was put on
ice. In this lull Sundler joined up with
SUPERNOVA then in 1996 TAILPIPE. It
would not be until 1997 that the band, newly
billed SPACE PROBE TAURUS, fired up once
more.
The 'Low On Karma High On Speed' session
saw Sjöberg handling lead vocals. In 1998
two further cassettes, 'Hallucination
Generation' and 'Acid Worship' were
delivered. SPACE PROBE TAURUS
committed a remixed version of the demo cut
'Calling Cosmos' to the Meteor City 'I Am
Vengeance' Richard R. Anasky horror movie
soundtrack album that same year. SPACE
PROBE TAURUS would eventually end up
being filmed for the movie too.
The band contributed their rendition of
'Second Time Around' to the 1999 BLUE
CHEER tribute album 'Blue Explosion'
compiled by the Italian Black Widow label.
The early track 'Dancing Jupiter' surfaced on
the July SpeedBall Entertainment collection

390

'Vol. 2'.

Jonas Stålhammar, yet another erstwhile MACABRE END man joined the band on bass prior to recording the 'Insect City' EP for Game Two Records. However, in November of 2000 SPACE PROBE TAURUS would dump their latest recruit in favour of Magnus Eronen, an ex-member of MOANING WIND and comrade of Sundler's in TAILPIPE. With their new line-up the group laid down a new track 'Taurus Rising' for use on a Hellbilly compilation album.

Singles/EPs:
Insect City / Mescaline / Dirt Cult '72, Slow Ride SR-03 (2002)

SPANCER (GERMANY)
Line-Up: Markus (vocals), York (guitar), Kaptain (bass), Jan (drums)

Braunschweig retro Doomsters. The self-financed 'Countdown To Victory' EP drew heavy praise from the Doom community.

Singles/EPs:
Receive My Firestorm / Master File God / Asunder / The Beat Goes On, (2002) ('Countdown To Victory' EP)

SPARZANZA (SWEDEN)
Line-Up: Fredrik Weileby (vocals), David Johannesson (guitar), Calle Johannesson (guitar), Johan Carlsson (bass), Anders Åberg (drums)

Another in the tradition of Swedish Stoner acts. Karlstad's SPARZANZA was founded in 1996 by vocalist / bassist Peter Eriksson, the guitarist brothers David and Calle Johannesson with Anders Åberg on drums. At this formative stage the group was going under the title of SHALLOW, cutting an opening demo in this guise.

Shortly after recording Eriksson opted to concentrate solely on lead vocals and Andreas Kloss of THE HERMAPHRODITES took on bass duties. This version of the band, now called SPARZANZA, cut a single 'Wheeler Dealer'. Upon its release Kloss prioritized THE HERMAPHRODITES and duly decamped. Johan Carlsson of TAILPIPE and DAWN OF DECAY plugged the vacancy. In 1997 SPARZANZA issued a split 7" single 'Burnin' Boots' as a collaboration with LOWRIDER. Further exposure outside of Sweden was generated with the inclusion of 'Liquid Thoughts' on the Meteor City compilation 'Welcome To Meteor City' and 'Black Jack Vegas' on the 'A Fistful Of Freebird' release.

Eriksson was asked to leave in 1999, drafting Fredrik Weileby for recordings which surfaced on a further split release in league with SUPERDICE for Water Dragon Records.

Singles/EPs:
Bonanza Justice / Gorilla Circus / Wheeler Dealer, (1997)
Burnin' Boots, Meteor City Singles Club (1997) (Split single with LOWRIDER)
Angel Of Vengeance / Be Myself, Water Dragon (1999) (Split single with SUPERDICE)

Albums:
ANGELS OF VENGEANCE, Water Dragon WDSZZ015 (2002)
Velodrome Home / Amanda / The Sundancer / Black Velvet Syndrome / Logan´s Run / Crossroad Kingdom / Coming Home In A Bodybag / The Desert Son / Silverbullet

SPEEDEALER (Lubbock, TX, USA)
Line-Up: Jeff Hirschberg (vocals / guitar), Eric Schmidt (guitar), Rodney Skelton (bass), Harden Harrison (drums)

Volatile Punk, Sabbath driven Blues Rockers. Previously known wittily as REO SPEEDEALER upon their 1994 formation by frontman Jeff Hirshberg, guitarist Eric Schmidt, bassist Rodney Skelton and Harden Harrison on drums. 'Cocaine' Dave Woodward, a veteran of THE AGITATORS, HEAD SWIM and TRUCKERPUSSY, would front the band as lead vocalist in 1996 for REO SPEEDEALER's debut album at which time the remainder of the band line-up would be credited as guitarists Jewf and Chunkles, bassist Hot Rod and drummer TobyJuan. Dave opted out to deal with his drug dependency and, cleaning up, later joined BILLYCLUB. Before the somewhat inevitable threat of legal action from the veteran AOR act REO SPEEDWAGON the band had issued two albums under REO SPEEDEALER title.

June 1998's 'Here Comes Death', released by Royalty Records, was produced by Daniel Rey. However, Royalty soon collapsed and the album was subsequently picked up for re-release by the Palm Pictures imprint. SPEEDEALER toured as support to GWAR and THE MISFITS in America then as guests to MOTÖRHEAD during late 2000.

Meantime two erstwhile SPEEDEALER members, singer Dave Woodward and drummer Mark Baker, made it back into the spotlight with a new high profile Punk act THE HELLIONS in alliance with ex-RIGOR MORTIS and present day GWAR bassist

Casey Orr and erstwhile PUNCTURE guitarist Mike Todd.

Skelton would gain the honours of penning the lyrics to FU MANCHU's 'California Crossing' album title track.

2002's 'Second Sight' album was afforded the distinction and heightened media exposure of being produced by erstwhile METALLICA bass player Jason Newsted. Japanese versions added two extra tracks in 'A Quiet Desperation' and 'Idle Hands'. Touring in North America during June found SPEEDEALER packaged with SKINLAB and SUPERJOINT RITUAL. Latterly the band has added bassist Rich Mullins, previously with KARMA TO BURN, to the line-up. August gigs had SPEEDEALER as part of a strong package comprising BRAND NEW SIN and headliners FU MANCHU.

Albums:
HERE COMES DEATH, Royalty (1998)
Hit It And Run / CCCP (Cold War Blues) / You Lose, I Win / Nobody's Hell Like Mine / Cream/ #1 / Sasparilla / Death / Hate You Better / No More / Drink Me Dead / 1:50 AM / Washed Up / Absinthe / We Are Diseased / Dealer's Choice / Tweeked / California

Tumbles Into The Sea
SECOND SIGHT, Palm Pictures (2002)
Leave Me Alone / Second Sight / All The Things You'll Never Be / The Thin Air / Days Of Red / As Ever / Kill Myself Tonight / Blinded / Fractured / Slowly, Burning... Alive / Infinitesimal / Machinations

SPICKLE (New Orleans, LA, USA)
Line-Up: Paul Webb (guitar), Gregg Harney (guitar), Bret Dulac (bass), Kenney Sumera (drums)

An all instrumental Pscych-Stoner quartet. The band is rooted in the Southern styled Hardcore act DULAC SWADE, a formation forged in 1993 by guitarist Paul Webb and bass player Bret Dulac. Before long this duo would be augmented by drummer Fat Mike, a veteran of MISSION D.C. and DRUNKS AGAINST MAD MOTHERS, and erstwhile THERMAS vocalist Kenny Sumera. This latest recruit also had drumming skills, performing this role in the band COTTONMOUTH which also included Paul Webb. Sumera would also temp for HAWG JAW as guitarist. Two 7" singles followed promoted by extensive touring.

SPEEDEALER
Photo : El Danno

SPRIT CARAVAN
Photo : El Danno

DULAC SWADE members duly created SPICKLE and promptly organized a split DULAC SWADE / SPICKLE album.
The 2002 SPICKLE album 'The Right To Remain Silent' was produced by Chris George of NOLA and included guest sessions from members of HOSTILE APOSTLE and SUPLECS.

Albums:
SPICKLE, Berserker BER004 (2000)
Millennium Falcon / Fusion / Wood Good / Cucaracha / Two Shotta Sake / Shove-it / Room Rent / Appliance
THE RIGHT TO REMAIN SILENT, Berserker BER011 (2002)
Intro/Cottonmouth / Spastic Orion / It's A Nice Day To Die / Valve Cover / Backbreak / Bread Puddin'/ Psych / 2-3= -Fun / Spore Addict / C'Mon / Cadence / Gherkin...

SPIRIT CARAVAN (USA)
Line-Up: Scott Weinrich (vocals / guitar), Dave Sherman (bass), Gary Isom (drums)

Revered outfit assembled in the late '90s by the legendary Doom Rock personality of Scott 'Wino' Weinrich, former front man for two of the Doom movements most influential acts THE OBSESSED and ST. VITUS.
When THE OBSESSED folded in 1995, following the much lauded 'The Church Within' album, Wino, having taken time out to

rid himself of acknowledged addictions, travelled from California to his native Maryland to create SHINE. After a demo entitled 'Powershine' and a solitary 7" single release during 1997 SHINE duly evolved into SPIRIT CARAVAN with ex-HEAVY SOUL and WRETCHED bassist Dave Sherman and drummer Gary Isom. The latter boasted an illustrious career path stretching into the annals of pedigree Doom with such acts as HEAVY SOUL, IRON MAN, UNORTHODOX, WRETCHED and PENTAGRAM.
As SPIRIT CARAVAN the group debuted with a low-key 7" single shared with SIXTY WATT SHAMAN. The 'Dreamwheel' five track EP and full-length album 'Jug Fulla Sun' arrived in 1999, both reaping heavy praise from the Doom / Stoner community. February 2000 gigs across the USA were dubbed the 'Wretched determination' tour.
The 'So Mortal Be' 7" single was another typically underground release, only made available through mail order. After a run of dates throughout North America during April of 2002 in league with former PENTAGRAM guitarist Victor Griffin's new outfit PLACE OF SKULLS, Wino disbanded SPIRIT CARAVAN in May. By July he would be found in PLACE OF SKULLS, acting as second guitarist.

Singles/EPs:
Darkness And Longing, Tee Pee (1999)
(Split 7" single with SIXTY WATT SHAMAN)

393

Dreamwheel / Burnin' In / Re-Alignment - Higher Power / Sun Stoned / C, Yourself, Meteor City (1999) ('Dreamwheel' EP)
So Mortal Be / Undone Mind, Tolotta (2002)

Albums:
JUG FULLA SUN, Tolotta (1999)
Healing Tongue / Courage / Cosmic Artifact / Fear's Machine / Power Time / Dead Love - Jug Fulla Sun / Fang / Chaw / Melancholy Grey / Sea Legs / Kill Ugly Naked / Lost Sun Dance / No Hope Goat Farm
ELUSIVE TRUTH, Tolotta (2001)
Spirit Caravan / Black Flower / Retroman / Find It / Futility's Reasons / Cloudy Mirror / Elusive Truth / Darkness & Longing / Lifer City / Outlaw Wizard / The Departure

SPIRITU (USA)
Line-Up: Jadd Schickler (vocals),

Albums:
SPIRITU, Meteor City (2002)
Z (Noonday Demon) / Fat Man In Thailand / Glorywhore / Clean Livin' / Woman Tamer / Slump

SPIRITUAL BEGGARS (SWEDEN)
Line-Up: Christian Stöstrand (vocals / bass), Mike Amott (guitar), Ludwig Witt (drums)

The highly rated SPIRITUAL BEGGARS was originally formed as a side project to CARCASS by ex-CARNAGE and CARCASS guitarist Mike Amott. Amott also operates the equally successful Death Metal band ARCH ENEMY. Although the band's heritage was placed firmly in the extreme Metal spectrum SPIRITUAL BEGGARS offered up a distinct contrast with tripped out retro Riff Rock.
Amott united with ex-AEON man Christian Stöstrand, the band becoming a full-time venture following Amott's split from CARCASS after the 'Heartworks' album. Having released an early mini-album on Wrong Again with Pingo Sjöholm contributing session bass tracks, the fully-fledged 'Another Way To Shine' was originally intended to be released by Swedish label Megarock Records. However, a decision had been taken to fold the label in order to relaunch themselves as a production company, so the album was eventually issued by Music For Nations in a licensing deal.
Music For Nations showed enough faith in the band to issue the third album, 'Mantra III', in January 1998. Produced by Fredrik Nordström, the band continued to defy all trends by offering a tirade of '70s influenced heavy riffs. The band embellished their studio sound by utilizing the talents of MOJOBONE

organ player Per Wiberg and percussionist Stefan Isebring.
'Mantra III' found Stöstrand adopting the name 'Spice' and the inclusion of keyboard player Per Wiberg. Heavy touring saw support dates to FU MANCHU.
In 1999 SPIRITUAL BEGGARS contributed their version of 'Mr. White' to the TROUBLE tribute album issued on Freedom Records. Witt founded side project FIREBIRD in 2000 in alliance with CATHEDRAL's Leo Smee and ex-CARCASS guitarist Bill Steer.
Spice also figured as lead vocalist on the 'Music For The World Beyond' 2000 album by Stoners THE MUSHROOM RIVER BAND, a group he had been involved with dating back as far as 1997.
The Japanese JVC Victor label released the 'Ad Astra' album in March and included two bonus songs in the form of 'Let The Magic Talk' and 'It's Over'. In August that same year JVC Victor issued the archive 'Mantra III' and 'Another Way To Shine' albums. Three exclusive tracks would be added to the former in 'The Band Is Playing', 'Redwood Blues' and an alternate mix of 'Euphoria' whilst the 1996 record, clad in different sleeve artwork, was augmented by a demo version of 'Broken Morning'.
Rumours circulated during 2001 that Spice was set to leave the band. Although officially denied at first Spice did indeed decamp in October, committing to THE MUSHROOM RIVER BAND full-time. SPIRITUAL BEGGARS brought in GRAND MAGUS vocalist Janne Christoffersson and THE QUILL bassist Roger Nilson as replacements. In June of 2002 bassist Roger Nilsson too would join up with ex-NAPALM DEATH and CARCASS guitarist Bill Steer's FIREBIRD act.

Singles/EPs:
Euphoria / If You Should Leave / Mushroom Tea Girl (Mad Jam version), Froghouse (1998) ('Violet Karma' 10" EP)

Albums:
SPIRITUAL BEGGARS, Wrong Again (1994)
Yearly Dying / Pelekas / The Space Inbetween / If This Is All / Under Silence / Magnificent Obsession
ANOTHER WAY TO SHINE, Music For Nations CDMFN 198 (1996)
Magic Spell / Blind Mountain / Misty Valley / Picking From The Box / Nowhere To Go / Entering Into Peace / Sour Stains / Another Way To Shine / Past The Sound Of Whispers
MANTRA III, Music For Nations (1998)
Homage To The Betrayed / Monster

Astronauts / Euphoria / Broken Morning / Lack Of Prozac / Superbossanova / Bad Karma / Send Me A Smile / Cosmic Romance / Inside Charmer / Sad Queen Boogie / Mushroom Tea Girl
AD ASTRA, Music For Nations (2000) **76**
GERMANY
Left Brain Ambassadors / Wonderful World / Sedated / Angel Of Betrayal / Blessed / Per Aspera Ad Astra / Save Your Soul / Until The Morning / Escaping Fools / On Dark Rivers / The Goddess / Mantra
ON FIRE, Music For Nations (2002)
Street Fighting Saviours / Young Man - Old Soul / Killing Time / Fools Gold / Moog Intro - Black Feathers / Beneath The Skin / Fejee Mermaid / Dance Of The Dragon King / Tall Tales / Lunatic Fringe I / Lunatic Fringe II / Lunatic Fringe III / Look Back

SPIRITUS MORTIS (FINLAND)
Line-Up: Vesa Lampi (vocals), Jussi (guitar), V.P. (guitar), Teemu (bass), Veli-Matti Yli-Mäyry (drums)

SPIRITUS MORTIS
Photo : Marco Hamalainen

One of the founding fathers of the Finnish Doom genre. SPIRITUS MORTIS, originally entitled RIGOR MORTIS, came together during 1988 by the Maijala sibling duo of bassist / vocalist Teemu and guitarist Jussi. V.P. Rapo was intended initially as a temporary stand in drummer but his role would become permanent. Upon discovering the already established American Metal band RIGOR MORTIS a name switch to SPIRITUS MORTIS was duly adopted. The group bowed in with the 1990 promotional tape 'At The Halls Of Death'. A succession of demos ensued including December 1997's 'Ars Moriendi' session but, splintered by the military draft, the band nearly fizzled out in the late '90s.
Getting back into gear the band enrolled lead vocalist Tomi Murtomäki but soon enrolled

Vesa Lampi in early 2000 as a permanent frontman. Lampi had previously been vocalist / bassist for WORROAR as well as guitar player in KHARON. With this line-up SPIRITUS MORTIS created the simply billed 'Demo 2000'. A further change in personnel occurred when V.P., actually citing guitar as his instrument of first choice, opted to manouevre to the guitar role as the band roped in Veli-Matti Yli-Mäyry as their new drummer. This version of SPIRITUS MORTIS cut the 2001 demo tape 'Forward To The Battle'. The band are planning a debut album for 2002 release.
Lampi also busies himself as frontman for NORMAALIMÄKI.

SPIRIT WEB (Chicago, IL, USA)
Line-Up: Scott Hoffman (vocals), Paul Speredes (guitar), Brent Sullivan (bass), Tony Rios (drums)

Heavy Metal band forged from the union of erstwhile SYRIS members vocalist Scott Hoffman and guitarist Paul Speredes with the former WINTERKILL / SLAUTER XTROYES rhythm section of bassist Brent Sullivan and drummer Tony Rios.
The debut 'Spirit Web' album garnered enthusiastic reviews across Europe.

Albums:
SPIRIT WEB, Stentorian (2000)
Ghostly Chill / Seeping Shadows / Cut You Loose / Osiris Be Thy Judge / Foolish Hope / Once Beyond / Madness Creeps / Never Time / Days Of Nowhere / Undivine Intervention / Reflections And Sighs.

STINKING LIZAVETA
(Philadelphia, PA, USA)
Line-Up: Yanni Papadopoulos (guitar), Alexi Papadopoulos (bass), Cheshire Augusta (drums)

West Philadelphia Doom-Jazz combo STINKING LIZAVETA, founded in 1994, include Alexi Papadopoulos utilizing stand up bass and the skills of female drummer Cheshire Augusta.
STINKING LIZAVETA's 1996 debut album 'Hopelessness And Shame' was produced by the esteemed Steve Albini.

Albums:
HOPELESSNESS AND SHAME, (1996)
Some Go To Hell / Refinery / Wheaton / Father's Song / Schuylkill / P.K. Party / Work Zombie / Schute Lube / Peace Maker / Axitol / Vent / Temptation / Lbj
SLAUGHTERHOUSE, (1997)

Slaughterhouse / Vicious Circle / Sex
Emergency / Ultimate Ass Kicking / The
Drop / Front Window / Slower Beauty /
Running From The Enemy / Slide You Off
The Board / Bullet Park / Bell Song
III, Tolotta (2001)
War Of The Worlds / Revelationary / Stupid
MF Tenuous / Diana / The Sentence / Kira /
Davis / Shu Shu / The Hanged Man / Naked
And Alone / Eastern Sun

STONE IN EGYPT (HOLLAND)
Line-Up: Tjeerd de Jong (vocals / guitar),
Paul Knuivers (bass), Michel Janse (drums)

A self-styled Stoner cum Space Rock group
from Emmeloord, Holland. The initial line-up
comprised a trio of vocalist / guitarist Tjeerd
de Jong, bass player Han Schilder and
drummer Robert Koole. This unit recorded a
self-financed CD in 1999 entitled 'Swallowing
Stars... Spitting Up Stardust'.
In February of 2000 STONE IN EGYPT
recorded the promo session 'Katmandu
Dreampiece', resulting in a recording contract
with Cold Blood Industries. The band's debut
album, simply billed 'Stone In Egypt' was
issued in November 2000.
In mid 2002 STONE IN EGYPT underwent a
radical facelift inducting new personnel Paul
Knuivers on bass guitar and drummer Michel
Janse.

Albums:
STONE IN EGYPT, Cold Blood Industries
(2000)
Tomb Transmission / A French Suitcase /
Seeking Oblivion / Suicidal Surfing /
Dieselfreak / Snake Carrier / New Queen Of
Turbo Bass Sound / She's Water / Katmandu
Dreampiece / Nebula Sky

STONER KINGS (FINLAND)
Line-Up: Starbuck (vocals), Shank (guitar),
Wolf (guitar), Gonzo (bass), Crash (drums)

Although a relatively new on the scene Stoner
/ raw Rock n' Roll act the STONER KINGS
pseudonyms belie a strong pedigree on the
Finnish Metal scene.

Albums:
BRIMSTONE BLUES, Rebel Breed
Recordings BL001 (2002)
The Ebb And The Flow / Cosmic Dancer /
Cobblestone Road / Tragedy Man /
Stonehenge / Goner / Damn Delilah /
Limbonic Void / Journey's End / Postmortem
Blues

STONER KINGS
Photo : Esko Soini

STONERWITCH (ARGENTINA)
Line-Up: Fernando Gigliotti (vocals / guitar),
Santiago Urueña (bass), Sebastián Romani
(drums)

As the name implies, STONERWITCH,
founded in Buenos Aires during 1999,
operate on Stoner-Doom territory. The group
first evolved when vocalist / guitarist
Fernando Gigliotti placed ads for available
musicians to form a band, duly enrolling
drummer Sebastián Romani and bassist
Rodrigo Teixido. This trio soon after got down
to practicalities and recorded the debut album
'Ojos Del Salado', released in February of
2000, a true homegrown product being
recorded in Gigliotti and Romani's bedrooms.
A second album 'Yerba Del Diablo' was
delivered in 2001. A limited release of rarities,
'Besides' including a version of THE
BEATLES 'Tomorrow Never Knows', arrived in
May 2002.

Albums:
OJOS DEL SALADO, Stonerwitch (2000)
Introduzione / Perdita Durango / Stone
Flower / Aire Gris / Turboduster / Mordiendo
El Polvo / Combustión / Ojos Del Salado /
Sol Negro / Bs. As. UFO/ II / Ritual / Saeta
YERBA DEL DIABLO, Stonerwitch (2001)
El Chupacabras (ET Highway) / Oceano /
Black Sábato / Natalia Natalia / Soy Un Devil
/ Supertumba / Humo Y Ocio / Yerba Del

Diablo / S.E.T.I. / La Barranca / Ten Confianza, Estúpido / Todo Va Mejor Con Satán
BESIDES, Stonerwitch (2002)
Cocola Quest / Anfibio / Dale Al Mono Un Arma / Toro Muerto / Green Rhino / No Te Dejes Caer / Star All Dope / No Sabemos Porque / Tomorrow Never Knows

STRONGHOLD (NORWAY)

A Christian Death-Doom act. STRONGHOLD sole member Erik also operates in IMPLACABLE.

Albums:
PRAYERS FROM A YEARNING HEART, Nordic Mission NMCD02 (199-)
Prayer Of The Yearning / Praise / Tears / Lament / In Strongest Arms

SUB SECOND ROCKET (SWEDEN)
Line-Up: Peter Magnusson (vocals), Patric Ifverson (guitar), Daniel Melkersson (bass), Ola Sundström (drums)

Malmö Fuzz Rockers dating back to 1998. Shortly after forming SUB SECOND ROCKET inducted bassist Måns Tomsby and then drummer Viggo Haremst. With this line-up an opening demo was cut in January of 1999.
Ola Sundström took the drum position in April and that same year pulled in Daniel Melkersson on bass.

Albums:
HORSEPOWER, Darevil DD016 (2002)
Deff / Desert Pearl / Big Fat No / Blue Fox / Death Roll / Broken Jaw / Horsepower

SUBSTANCE FOR GOD (ISRAEL)
Line-Up: Alon Moradi (vocals), Micha Yossef (guitar), Asi Yacobovitch (guitar), Noam Roda (bass), Dor Caduri (drums)

Albums:
ASSEMBLY OF FLOWERS, Radiation (1996)
The Love I've Bereaved / The Swan Song / Memorial Prayer / Behind The Wreath / Verse Of Sorrow / Assembly Of Flowers / Crowned Seclusion / The Promise

SUBVERSION (GERMANY)
Line-Up: Mike (vocals), Sandro Uhlmann (guitar)

Albums:
RUST FORMATION, Daredevil DD006 (2000)

Hot Season / Earnester / Demon / Gasoline / In Dreams / Relax / Hell Is A Place On Earth / B.M.C. / Horror Vacui / Rust Formation
BEATIN' THE SHIT OUT OF IT, Daredevil DD015 (2002)
Scratch / JC On Welfare / A Losing Race / Subversion / Outta Here / Tons Of Tar

SUBWAY TO SALLY (GERMANY)
Line-Up: Eric Hecht (vocals / bagpipes), Bodenski (guitar), Simon (guitar), Ingo Kampf (guitar), Sugary (bass), Mr. T.W. (drums), Frau Schmidt (violin)

A Potsdam (Berlin) based Folk Metal band taking many influences from the pioneering SKYCLAD. SUBWAY TO SALLY appeared in 1991 and quickly established themselves as a prolific live act (including a festival appearance with FISCHER Z) until they were able to record their debut album at the close of 1993 for the Dutch owned Costbar label.
In 1994 SUBWAY TO SALLY made a distinct impression with a set at the annual 'Popkomm' music industry gathering in Cologne and quickly scored slots on several compilation albums prior to recording the second album, 'MCMXCV', with producer Sven Regner.
The group would be subsequently be as busy in the studio as on the live circuit as new albums appeared in both 1996 and 1997, the latest of which ('Bannkrieg') being found on new label BMG.
SUBWAY TO SALLY members guested on SKYCLAD's 'The Answer Machine' album.
The band's set at the 1999 annual 'Wacken' festival featured a genuine wedding as the band played along to two of their fans' marriage live onstage.

Albums:
SUBWAY TO SALLY, Subway To Sally (1994)
Cromdale / Rainman / Queen Of Argyll / Barleycorn / Elvis Lives / Planxtchen / An Der Zeit / Traum Vom Tod / Die Braut / The Keach / In The Creel / Bonnie Johnnie Lowrie, Down The Line / But We Don't Know / Where The Lucky?
MCMXCV, Vielklang EFA 03207-2 (1995)
Krähenfrass / Grabrede / Arche / Sommertag / Auf Der Flucht / Requiem / Erdbeermund / Banks Of Sicily / Der Bräutigam / Die Hexe / Die Jagd / Carrickfergus
FOPPT DEN DÄMON, Vielklang 74321 35966-2 (1996)
Kyrie / Der Sturm / Kain / Sag Dem Teufel / Der Hofnarr / Die Ratten / Abgesang / Herbstzeit /. Julia Und Die Räuber / Auf Der

Reise / Traum Und Tod / Der Vagabund /
Maria
BANNKRIES, BMG 74321 50091-2 (1997)
Alle, Psallite Cum Luya / Mephisto / Unterm
Galgen / Ein Baum / Das Rätsel / Kruzifix /
Sanctus / Zu Spät / Liebeszauber / Element
Des Verbrechens / Schlaflied / Syrah
DIE ROSE IM WASSER, Ariola (2000)
Alle, Psallite Cum Luya / Minne / Schlaflied /
Die Jagd / Maria / Erdbeermund / Syrah /
Abgesang / Sanctus / Element Des
Verbrechens / Die Rose Im Wasser / Traum
Vom Tod II / Ein Baum / Muede /
Henkersbraut / Ohne Liebe / Sag Dem Teufel
(Video)
HERZBLUT, Megalux (2001) 15 GERMANY
Die Schlacht / Veitstanz / Das Messer /
Herrin Des Feuers / Kleid Aus Rosen / Wenn
Engel Hassen / Krötenliebe / Accingite Vos /
So Rot / Drei Engel / Kleid Aus Rosen
(unplugged)

SUCCUBUS (SWITZERLAND)
Line-Up: Philipp Gloor (vocals), Judith
Leuenberger (vocals), Roman Kovalik
(guitar), Jan Liniger (guitar), Patrick Hersche
(bass), Lukas Schaerer (drums)

An orchestral based Gothic Metal act.
SUCCUBUS utilizes sweeping keyboard
landscapes with both Baroque and lyrical
romanticism to set themselves apart from the
pack. The band's live show sees the adoption
of candles, nebula, fire breathing and
pyrotechnics onstage to induce atmosphere.
Frontman Phillip Gloor, who paints one half of
his head black and the other white, has been
known to wear full chainmail and armour
onstage. The group, founded by vocalist
Gloor, guitar player Roman Kovalik and
drummer Lukas Schaerer experienced line-
up problems to begin with. This necessitated
the recruitment of Patrick Hersche, ex-
member of Death Metal band MESSIAH and
then with AMON, in order to lay down bass on
the debut 'Stripped Angels' EP. Following
these sessions Hersche decamped from
AMON to join up with SUCCUBUS on a full
time basis.
During September of 1999, Pia Lustenberger,
a classically educated singer and flautist,
augmented the SUCCUBUS line-up. became
a new member. Her heavenly voice and her
talented flute-playing brought new influences
and an enormous enrichment to
SUCCUBUS. A further addition came in April
of 2000 with the induction of female lead
guitarist Jan Liniger.
Lustenberger performed her last concert with
SUCCUBUS in December of 2001. Judith
Leuenberger, previously with SADUCED, duly
took over the role.

Singles/EPs:
Stripped Angels / Differences / Hymn To
The Past / Fly To The Sky, (1999)
Tears / Tears (Instrumental version) / Trianon
De Jerimas, (2000) (Promotion single)

SUFFER (SWEDEN)
Line-Up: Joakim Öhman (vocals), Ulf
Samuelsson (guitar), Patrik Andersson
(bass), Per Karlsson (drums)

Gloom ridden Deathsters SUFFER date to
1988, when the first line-up comprised
vocalist Joakim Öhman, bassist Patrik
Andersson and drummer Conny Granqvist.
The group added guitarist Ronny Eide in
1990, but a line-up shuffle saw Granqvist
depart in favour of ex-WORTOX and ALTAR
drummer Per Karlsson.
Following the release of the 'Structures'
album, SUFFER split. Andersson joined IN
BETWEEN DAYS.
Guitarist Ulf Samuelsson joined the
THERION offshoot band SERPENT for their
'In The Garden Of The Serpent' album. He
was joined by a further SUFFER member
drummer Per Karlsson in 1996. The following
year Karlsson joined T.A.R.
Öhman attempted a resurrection of SUFFER,
with erstwhile members of ABHOTH guitarist
Jörgen Kristensen and drummer Mats
Blyckert, but this has yet to bear fruit.

Singles/EPs:
On Sour Ground / My Grief, New Wave
NWR EP039 (1993)
Impressive Turns / Infectious / Global
Warning / Wrong Side Of Life, Napalm
NPRCD 002 (1993) ('Global Warning' EP)
Human Flesh (Live) / Wrong Side Of Life
(Live), Immortal Underground IUPEP001
(1993)

Albums:
STRUCTURES, Napalm NPRCD006 (1994)
Temporary Sane / Passionate Structures /
Lie Within / Selected Genes / A Frenetic
Mind / Maginary Homecoming / The Killing
Culture / Freedom Of Speech

SUMMONER (ITALY)
Line-Up: Paulo Cattaneo (vocals), Giorgio
Belltrami (guitar), Luca Cinsani (bass),
Stefano Magni (keyboards), Massimo
Corbani (drums)

SUMMONER are a Gothic infused Black /
Death Metal act convened in January of 2001
by former personnel from the recently
dissolved DEATH SEAGULL'S SCREAM,
guitarist Giorgio Belltrami, keyboard player

Stefano Magni and drummer Massimo Corbani. Initially SUMMONER was fronted by a female vocalist but this idea was abandoned as Paulo Cattaneo took the lead vocal role. The band was completed with the addition of bass player Luca Cinsani.

Valuable support slots to LACUNA COIL followed before SUMMONER issued the four track self-financed EP 'Summoner's Sign'. Second guitarist Igor would be added to the ranks shortly after.

Singles/EPs:
The Maskplague / Tears I've Shed / Summoner's Sign / Vicious Fruit, (2001) ('Summoner's Sign' EP)

SUNDOWN (SWEDEN)
Line-Up: Mathias Lodmalm (vocals / guitar), Andreas Johansson (guitar), Johnny Hagel (bass), Christian Silver (drums)

A maudlin Gothic Metal act convened by frontman Mathias Lodmalm following his break from CEMETARY. Joining Lodmalm for the 1997 'Design 19' album would be bassist Johnny Hagel of TIAMAT and SORCEROR notoriety, guitarist Andreas Johansson and drummer Christian Silver. SUNDOWN struggled on for a sophomore outing, 1999's 'Glimmer', but with a completely overhauled line-up. Ranked alongside Lodmalm and Silver would be guitarist Herman 'Manne' Engstrom and bass player Andreas Karlsson. Hagel made his exit to concentrate on his solo venture CINNAMON SPIRAL.

Lodmalm would also act as producer and keyboard player for the debut VASARIA album, his colleague Christian Silver providing session drums.

Following 'Glimmer' Lodmalm, together with Silver and Engstrom, resurrected CEMETARY of sorts with CEMETARY 1213 for 'The Beast Divine' album. By 2000 guitarist Andreas Johansson had joined Death Metal band AUBERON.

Albums:
DESIGN 19, Century Media (1997)
Aluminum / 19 / Judgement Ground / Voyager / Synergy / As Time Burns / Don't Like To Live Today / Slither / Emotional / 112 - Ghost In The Machine
GLIMMER, Century Media (1999)
Lifetime / Divine / Halo / Prey / Star / Glimmer / Stab / [22] / Wired / Silencer

SUNN O))) (USA)

Believed by many to be the heaviest band ever, simply by warrant of the deliberate use of such low end sound frequencies as to spontaneously trigger unwelcome bowel movements. SUNN O))), describing themselves as a musical homage to Drone godfathers EARTH, comprise Greg Anderson of GOATSNAKE and BURNING WITCH and BURNING WITCH's Stephen O'Malley. SUNN O))) more than made their presence felt with the subterranean rumblings of the 1999 demo session 'The Grimrobe Tapes'. The 200 album 'OO Void' issued by Rise Above and produced by the esteemed KYUSS veteran Scott Reeder, despite numbering only four tracks clocked in at nearly an hour of distorted bass reliant drone.

During 2000 guitarist Stephan O'Malley would join forces with bassist James Plotkin, a veteran of such esteemed acts as OLD, REGURGITATION, SCORN and ATOMSMASH, vocalist Alan Dubin of OLD and MANBYRD drummer Tim Wyskida to found KHANATE for an eponymous album.

The five track minimalist 'Flight Of The Behemoth' would be produced by Masami Akita, better known as the mentor of Japanese avant-garde Industrialists MERZBOW.

Both O'Malley and Anderson also operate THORR'S HAMMER.

Albums:
OO VOID, Rise Above (2000)
Richard / NN O))) / Rabbit's Revenge / Ra At Dusk
FLIGHT OF THE BEHEMOTH, Southern Lord (2002)
Mocking Solemnity / Death Becomes You / Sunn0))) BOW 1 (Merzbow remix) / Sunn0))) BOW 2 (Merzbow remix) / FWTBT: (I Dream Of Lars Ulrich Being Thrown Through The Bus Window Instead Of My Master Mystikall Kliff Burton)

SUNNSHINE (Richmond, VA, USA)
Line-Up: Joe Deleon (vocals), Jeff Srsic (guitar), Chris Mcpherson (guitar), Joshua Kayer (bass), Kevin White (drums)

Singles/EPs:
Aviator / Engender / Untrainedeye / Bound, Underdogma (2001) ('Engender' EP)

SUNRIDE (FINLAND)
Line-Up: Jani Peippo (vocals), Wille Naukkarinen (guitar), Mikko Rikala (guitar), Janne Julin (bass), Veli-Matti Suihkonen (drums)

Finns SUNRIDE, founded in Jyväskylä during 1996, offer up ultra heavy, Groove Riffrock. The band debuted commercially with the

'Magnetizer' EP for the Italian Boundless label in 1999. These recordings, clad in completely different artwork, saw a re-issue on 10" vinyl through the German People Like You label the following year. 2000 also had SUNRIDE donating their version of 'Children In Heat' to the 'Graven Images' MISFITS tribute album.

The album 'The Great Infiltration', recorded for People Like You, would arrive in February 2001. A limited edition variant in white marbled vinyl was restricted to just 500 copies. Bassist Janne Savolainen backed out in July 2001 as former four stringer Janne Julin reoccupied his position.

European touring in October 2002 had the band paired up with DOZER.

Singles/EPs:

Ascending The Throne / Long Goner / So Me / Demonshelter / Burn Me!, Boundless BLRMCD014 (1999) ('Magnetizer' EP)
False Independence / Under Control, World (2002) ('You Only Die Twice' EP)
The Earthmover / Jetride-A-Like, Popcity (2002)

Albums:

THE GREAT INFILTRATION, People Like You PRISON 025-2 (2001)
The Earthmover / Hello (Transparent You) / Sympathy Overdose / Palestine / The King Cloud / Inhuman Groover / The Great Infiltration / Sweet Reverie (Saving Grace) / Deadwrong Companion / Straightliner

SUPLECS (New Orleans, LA, USA)

Line-Up: Durel Yates (vocals / guitar), Danny Nick (bass), Andrew Preen (drums)

New Orleans Southern Doom forged by erstwhile MALIGNANT MINDS personnel vocalist / guitarist Durel Yates and bassist Danny Nick. SUPLECS started life in 1994, although Nick would seize the opportunity to join EYEHATEGOD in 1997, effectively putting SUPLECS on hold. Nick returned to the fold, the band issuing the first album 'Wrestlin' With My Lady Friend' through Man's Ruin in April of 2000. Road work saw the group criss-crossing North America with EYEHATEGOD and ALABAMA THUNDERPUSSY.

A second album, 'Sad Songs… Better Days', was also issued through Man's Ruin although just before the label famously went under. This Dark Reign picked the record up for a 2002 re-release with different sleeve art.

Albums:

WRESTLIN' WITH MY LADY FRIEND, Man's Ruin (2000)

Stalker / Dope Fu / Fish On A Highway / Moped / 2000 Leagues / Road To Nowhere / Eastwood / Into the Rut / Rampage / Pissin' In the Wind
SAD SONGS… BETTER DAYS, Man's Ruin MR2018 (2001)
White Devil / Rock Bottom / Control / Training Wheels / Blue Runner / Unstable / Lightning Lady / Out Of Town / Unexpected Trauma

SUPURATION (FRANCE)

Line-Up: Fabrice Loez (vocals / guitar), Ludovic Loez (guitar), Laurent Bessault (bass), Thierry Berger (drums)

A French Death Doom Metal band steeped in Gothic influences, SUPURATION released two albums (the second, 'Still In The Spheres', including a cover of TEARS FOR FEARS' 'Shout') before shortening the band name to SUP.

In 1995 a limited edition CD emerged (only 500 copies were pressed) entitled '9092' containing a number of tracks previously only released as singles or on compilation albums between 1990 and 1992.

The group would tour with Swiss outfit CORONER in early 1996.

Albums:

THE CUBE, Reincarnate SUP 07 CD (1993)
Prelude / The Elevation / Soul's Speculum / 1308. JP. 08 / The Cube / Through The Transparent / Partitions / Spherical Inner-Sides / The Accomplishment / 4TX. 31B / The Dim Light
STILL IN THE SPHERES, Reincarnate SUP 08 CD (1994)
The Crack / The Cleansing / Back From The Garden / Variation On Theme 4Tx.31B / Shout
9092, Pias (1995)
The Creeping Unknown / Isolated / In Remembrance Of A Coma / Sultry Obsession / 1308. JP. 08 / Sojourn In The Absurd / Ephemeral Paradise / Reveries Of A Bloated Cadaver / In Remembrance Of A Coma / 1308. JP. 08 / Half-Dead / Hypertrophy-Sordid & Outrageous Emanation / Sultry Obsession / Reveries Of A Bloated Cadaver
ANOMALY, Revelation REV 003 (1995)
Anomaly / Pain Injection / In Those Times / The Work / Ocean Of Faces / In The Deepest Silence / Dialogue (D-ÄN & T-ÖN) / D-ÄN'S Last Order / Reset / D-ÄN'SUP V 1.1
TRANSFER, Revelation REV 005 (1996)
Ocean Of Faces (D-Än Mix) / Ocean Of Faces (Acoustic Version) / Pain Injection (Limb Mix) / Ocean Of Faces (Cradle Mix) /

The Work (Acoustic) / Pain Injection (Demo Version) / In Those Times (Demo Version) / The Work (Demo Version)

SVARTSINN (SWEDEN)

Solo artist SVARTSINN delivers Dark soundscapes.

Albums:
DEVOURING CONSCIOUSNESS, Eibon SVA032 (2002)
Draped In Shadows / I Morkets Makt / Livredd / The Dark Covet / Reaching Desolation / Devouring Consciousness / Withering Visions / Skumringen Skjuler Skogens Sorg

SWEET DISEASE (SWITZERLAND)
Line-Up: Renaud (vocals), Yvan (guitar / programming), Florian (bass), Patrick (keyboards), Albert F. (drum programming)

A Gothic Metal band.

Albums:
NIHIL, Witchunt OPUS 001 (1993)
Adonis / I Miss Someone / A-Bis / Dead Sky / Pleasure / Prostitute Sky / I Wish I Could Be Endless / Joy (Why Do You Feel?) / Unreality / Buy Your Own Death / A Waltz / Thing
FAITH-ECTOMY, (1997)
A New Kind Of Slave / Faithectomy / Deviate / Faith (Hate-o Mix) / Dance Of The W*** / Faithectomy (Ditherized)
BREECHLOADER, XIII Bis (2000)
Egocaine / Focus / Sub / Product I / Neurogrinder / Disposed For Pain / Product II / End Of Noise / Hater / Diatribe / Product III / Rise / Re-Noise Mix

SWEET ROXX (USA)

BOULDER members delivering unashamed '80s Metal.

Singles/EPs:
(You Could Be Involved In A) Metal Massacre / Rock Stars On The Road, Shifty (2002)

SYMPHONY OF GRIEF (NJ, USA)

New Jersey Doom-Death act with distorted vocals. The group was previously known as CEREBUS. SYMPHONY OF GRIEF's 'The Infernal Creation' demo made waves on the underground scene, leading up to the 'Immortal Fluids' split 7" single in collaboration with MEMORIUM.

Singles/EPs:
Immortal Fluids, Grinding Peace (1994) (Split single with MEMORIUM)
Our Blessed Conqueror EP, Wild Rags (1995)

SYSTEM 13 (AUSTRALIA)
Line-Up: Matt (vocals / guitar), Kylie Lovejoy (bass),

Brisbane Cosmic Doom. The 2000 album 'The Mothership Has Landed... Release The Alien' closed with an unaccredited hidden track 'Macroscope'.

Albums:
THE MOTHERSHIP HAS LANDED... RELEASE THE ALIEN, Rhythm Ace (2000)
The Mothership Has Landed / Cosmic Dream / Voyager III / Red Rocket / Space Doctor (Moon Rocker) / Venus Tonight / Macroscope

TAINT (UK)
Line-Up: Jimbob (vocals / guitar), Stophe (bass), Chris (drums)

Grade A Hardcore edged Swansea Sludge. Convening in 1994, TAINT's inaugural live performance was as support to Death Metal band PARRICIDE in December of that year. TAINT emerged brandishing the June 1995 demo 'Bellydown'. A further cassette demo was delivered the following year with the '10 Times Better' session arriving in January of 1997. The debut album, recorded at Thumb Studios in Nottingham during November of 1999, includes a CLUTCH cover 'Impetus' buried within the closing track 'Release'. Stuart O'Hara of ACRIMONY and IRON MONKEY contributes guitar to the track 'Doom Control'.
Al Harries had taken over the drums by 2002 as TAINT issued a split album with BLACK EYE RIOT for the Black Phoenix label.
Bass player Stophe also operates with Hip Hop act MONKEY IN A WASHING MACHINE, SOMETHING IN THE WATER and has sessioned for THE HEADCASE LADZ.

Albums:
DIE DIE TRUTHSPEAKER, Household Name HAUS030 (2000)
Blackspot / Fatman Sedates Us Again / Only A Few / No-one's Saviour / Doom Control / Release (feat. 'Impetus')
TAINT, Black Phoenix BLPHCD 001 (2002) (Split album with BLACK EYE RIOT)

TCHORT (CANADA)
Line-Up: Eric Coucke (vocals / guitar), Les Godfrey (guitar), Nick Sewell (bass), Michael Borges (drums)

TCHORT (Russian for 'Devil') began life as a quirky Death Metal band, complete with violinist, but increasing elements of humour, old school Heavy Metal and Eric Coucke's uncanny vocal resemblance to Ozzy Osbourne has crept into the mix. The band's music has diversified enough to even be accepted into the realms of Doom and then as the band admitted to a fuzzier bent, the Stoner camp then beckoned.
TCHORT debuted their new Doom leanings with the four track 1995 'Aces Of Shroom' demo tape. These tracks combined with new material produced by Rob Sanzo subsequently made up the self-financed album 'Nightside Of Eden'. The band at this juncture comprised Coucke on vocals and guitar, second guitarist Les Godfrey, bassist

Nick Sewell and drummer Chris Gramlech. The 'Government Issue Rock n' Roll Volume II' album included a radicalized cover version of IRON MAIDEN's 'Number Of The Beast'. Their 'Love Metal' EP also contained a cover, more obliquely this time as the band laid waste to BONEY M's Disco hit 'Rasputin'. TCHORT would spend the summer of 2002 making ready a new Ian Blurton produced studio album 'No Shirt, No Shoes, No Salvation'.

Singles/EPs:
Rasputin / Storm Chaser / Love Metal / Love Metal (Radio edit), (2002) ('Love Metal' EP)

Albums:
NIGHTSIDE OF EDEN, Tchort TCH001 (1996)
Tantric Dream Fish / Satan Love Boogie / Fly Agaric / Dogstar / 20 Visions Of Eve / Wonderlamb War March / Godeater / Synesthesia / Ace Of Schrooms / The Rainbow Warlords
THE HEAVENS ARE SHOWING THE GLORY OF TCHORT, Sonic Unyon (1998)
5th Business In The Red Room / Building A Bomb For Tomorrow's Today / Ballad Of The Dirty Earth / Clopus Clan / The Great Beelzebub Pie Conspiracy / Lamba Sutra / Handsome Gruesome / Kama Lamba / Gorey Hallelujah (Let Us Prey) / Wonderlamb Gospel / Dragon Doll / Georgia Mountain High / The Next War
GOVERNMENT ISSUE ROCK N' ROLL, Ilimunatus (2001)
Soul Embargo / Obsessed / Virgin Forest / If At Faust You Don't Succeed / Sunday Morning Exorcism / The Curse Of Tchort (Live)
LOVE METAL, Illuminatus (2002)
Rasputin / Storm Chaser / Love Metal / Love Metal (Radio edit) / Soul Embargo / Obsessed / Virgin Forest / If At Faust You Don't Succeed / Sunday Morning Exorcism
GOVERNMENT ISSUE ROCK N' ROLL VOLUME II, Sonic Unyon (2002)
Midnight Deadline / Turbo Honky / Sir Lord Brubek / Find Your Way / Move On / The Number Of The Beast

TEETH OF LIONS RULE THE DIVINE (UK / USA)

TEETH OF LIONS RULE THE DIVINE, titled after the EARTH track, are a bona fide Stoner-Doom 'supergroup'. This 2001 combo featured the talents of CATHEDRAL mainman Lee Dorrian on vocals, BURNING WITCH, SUNN0))) and KHANATE member Steve

O'Malley, GOATSNAKE, SUNN0))) and THORR'S HAMMER man Greg Anderson and erstwhile IRON MONKEY and HARD TO SWALLOW member Justin Greaves.

The initial conception of the band gelled in 2000 when Stephen O'Malley and Justin Greaves started writing up material with Marvin of THE VARUKERS on bass guitar. Working in Greaves hometown of Nottingham, this proto instrumental version of the band actually put in a low key gig at the miniscule Old Angel pub.

The unrelentingly, stupefyingly heavy and trance-like April 2002 debut album, produced by Billy Anderson and comprising just three tracks clocking in at 55 minutes, is named after the infamous maximum security mental asylum. 'The Smiler' is a KILLDOZER cover version.

Albums:
RAMPTON, Rise Above (2002)
He Who Accepts All That Is Offered (Feel Bad Hit Of Winter) / New Pants And Shirt / The Smiler

TEFRA (UK)
Line-Up: Chris Tsotsos (vocals), Darren Parkinson (guitar), Gavin Parkinson (bass), Col Butler (drums)

TEFRA, Greek for 'Ashes Of The Dead', began life during late 1996 as a heavily Sabbath orientated Doom Metal band. Following a year and a half of stabilizing a line-up comprising Greek born vocalist Chris Tsotsos, guitarist Darren Parkinson, bass player Jonny Park and drummer Simon Gratton TEFRA cut an opening demo tape. A second session, dubbed 'Carved In Mind', drew in healthy praise from the worldwide Doom community.

In late 1999 the existing rhythm section broke away and the following year witnessed the induction of Gavin Parkinson on bass and Chris Mills on drums. However, Mills decamped early in 2001, TEFRA drafting Col Butler of Black Metal act THE BELONGING in his stead. This new unit laid down the '7/10ths To Madness' EP under the aegis's of producer Greg Chandler in 2002.

Singles/EPs:
The Clown / Out Of Balance / Stoned Revolution / Ashes Of The Dead / Crawling Fear, (1999) ('Carved In Mind' EP)
Carved In Mind / Apotefrosis / Anything Less / Goat Of Mendez / Epi Tas, (2002) ('7/10ths To Madness' EP)

TERRA FIRMA (SWEDEN)
Line-Up: Christian Lindersson (vocals), Fredrik Lindgren (guitar), Nico Moosebeach (bass), Izmo Ledderfejs (drums)

Stoner Metal fronted by ex-COUNT RAVEN and SAINT VITUS frontman Christian 'Lord Chritus' Lindersson and former UNLEASHED guitarist Fredrik Lindgren. Taking their name from the track 'Never Coming Back To Terra Firma' by the cult Swedish act WEREWOLVES ON WHEELS, the band was rounded out by ALBATROSS bassist Nico Moosebeach ('Putz Weck') and drummer Izmo Ledderfejs.

TERRA FIRMA emerged with a mid 1996 demo 'Rock n' Roll Splendour' comprising 'Rainbow Ride', 'In Orbit' and 'High Horses', two tracks of which would be soon reissued as a limited edition 7" single on Freedom Records. With this release under their belts TERRA FIRMA put in their first live showing at a gig with MURDER SQUAD at Stockholm's Café 44. A second six track demo session was cut in November of that year, a track from which, 'Fifth Wheel', was utilized for a split 7" single shared with GODSCENT through Clear Blue Sky Records. Although label offers were prompted TERRA FIRMA opted instead to craft a third five track demo in mid 1997.

In 1997 a TROUBLE cover version was duly donated to a tribute album and in December TERRA FIRMA recorded their first album. However, it would not see the light of day until 1999, issued by SPV in Europe and in North America through The Music Cartel. During the interim further TERRA FIRMA material surfaced with a Jazz Rock interpretation lent to MOTÖRHEAD's 'Bomber'. Promoting the album extensive tour work throughout Europe saw the band teamed up with ORANGE GOBLIN and CATHEDRAL. A second round of gigs, the September 'Rainbow Ride' tour, had LEADFOOT and ROADSAW as support, A picture disc single issued in March of 2000, limited to 1,000 copies, paired 'Spiral Guru' with a rendition of JETHRO TULL's 'For A Thousand Mothers'.

Fredrik Lindgren also operates in Punk act LOUD PIPES and Thrash band BORN OF FIRE, the latter a collaboration with the ENTOMBED duo of Peter Stjarnvind and Richard Cabeza in alliance with Dimman.

Singles/EPs:
Rainbow Ride / In Orbit, Freedom (1996)
Spiral Guru / For A Thousand Mothers, The Music Cartel (2000)

Albums:
TERRA   FIRMA,   SPV   80000175

404

(1999)Rainbow Ride / Goatburn / Good Stuff / And The 8th Seal Was Her`s / Separate Graves / Spiral Guru / Fifth Wheel / Nimbus / Troll Formula / Altered Beast
HARMS WAY, SPV (2001)
Freebassing / Groundman / Harms Way / Have Demon, Will Travel / Threefivenine / Dust Parade / Sway / Open Season / Steel Scale

THALARION (SLOVAKIA)
Line-Up: Nela Horvathova (vocals), Juraj Grezdo (vocals / keyboards), Juraj Schlosser (guitar), Peter Bartakovic (bass), Peter Schlosser (drums)

The Doom-laden THALARION made their entrance under the title of FATAL INFECTION with the 1991 cassette 'Black Raven'. Previously members had been going under the band name BASTARD, issuing a brace of demos but with the addition of ex-NAILED NAZARENE vocalist Juraj Grezdo and a shift in musical styles a new tag of FATAL INFECTION was decided upon. The 'Best Art' session would follow in 1993 and 'Behind The Door Of Sorrow' the following year before a name switch to THALARIAN was adopted.
A deal was struck with the American Wild Rags concern for a projected four track mini-album to be entitled 'Dominium Unfold' but after sending finished DATs the band heard no more from the label. Chalking this up to experience 'Towards The Obscure Slumberland' eventually arrived in 1996, issued as a cassette album by the Slovakian Hallelujah label. For the 1998 'Tales Of The Woods… Thus Was Written' record, released by Emancipation Records subsidiary Mighty Music, the band brought in female vocalist Nela Horvathova, previously a member of Slovakian Doom colleagues DYSANCHELY. Her placement would be made permanent for the 2000 album 'Four Elements Mysterium', sharing lead vocals with Juraj Grezdo.

Albums:
TOWARD THE OBSCURE SLUMBERLAND, Hallelujah (1996)
Lunatic's Third Eye / The Odyssey / Perverse Love To God / Thou, Who Walk To Eternity / As The Memories Of Slavs Awake / The Pyramid Of Sorrow / Towards The Obscure Slumberland / Unreal Delusions / A Lullaby Untold
TALES OF THE WOODS… THUS WAS WRITTEN, Mighty Music PMZ004-2 (1998)
…And Pain Silently Sings / Goddess Of Beauty And Wisdom Sleeps For Evermore (Mournful Ode To Lada) / Diva Leaves Me… (In My Loneliness) / Shadow-veiled Nayanna (She Reveals To Me Every Night) / …Through The Sleeping Nightland / Sonnet Of My Grief / Where The Twilight Dwells Forever… / Beyond The Incantations Of The White Queen / Perun's Thunder Of Revenge Will Storm Aloud / Kania (My Vampiric Bride)
FOUR ELEMENTS MYSTERIUM, Mighty Music PMZ011-2 (2000)
Cold Waters Of Turbulent Torrents / A Herald Of Sorrow & Wretchedness / A More Than Fiendish Malevolence / Icon Of Hopelessness / Almost Forgotten Empire / Where The Sloes Mature / Carnival / A Staircase To My Soul / In April We Wept

THAT'S ALL FOLKS (ITALY)
Line-Up: C.C. (vocals / guitar), L.S. (guitar), M.R. (bass), Nik (drums)

Groove based Acid Rock. The Bari based trio was formulated in the early '90s, operating initially as a covers band heavily reliant on ROLLING STONES material. THAT'S ALL FOLKS made a commercial debut with the 1992 7" single 'You Gotta Pay'. An EP, 'Reptile Soul', led up to a shared single with NEBULA, this release breaking the Italians into the global media. The band would then self-finance a four way split single through their own Lasers Eye Foundation label, sharing vinyl space with HOGWASH, VORTICE CREMISI and ACAJOU.
Frontman C.C. is also involved with HOGWASH personnel in COLT .38.

Singles/EPs:
You Gotta Pay / Smokle, El Borracho (1992)
Reptile Soul / My Moan / Winsome Underwear / The Sambuca Song / X-Posed Bosom, Toast (1996) ('Reptile Soul' EP)
Aquasphere, Last Scream (1998) (Split single with NEBULA)
March Of The Chameleons, Lasers Eye Foundation (1999) ('Cookery Course' four way split EP with ACAJOU, HOGWASH & VERTICE CREMISI)

Albums:
SOMA… 3RD WAY TO SION, Beard Of Stars (2000)
Ghosts & Echoes / Afterbite / Here Comes The Witchfinder / Buia Omega The Seed / Watchin' Collidin' Stars / Marigold / The Scavenger / The Unexpected Voyage Of Wounded Men / Soma… 3rd Way To Zion
PSYCHE AS ONE OF THE FINE ARTS, Beard Of Stars (2002)
Firesphere / Jumboo / The Plasma / Always Radiant And Fucked / Real Last Night / I'm Half-Sick Of You / Soul.Vent / Motormouse & Autocat / Dany / March Of The Chameleons

405

THEATRE OF TRAGEDY (NORWAY)

Line-Up: Raymond I. Rohonyi (vocals), Liv Kristine Espenaes (soprano vocals), Pal Bjastad (guitar), Tommy Lindal (guitar), Erik T. Saltro (bass), Lorents Aspen (keyboards), Hein Frode Hansen (drums)

Frontrunners in the field of Euro Gothic Metal THEATRE OF TRAGEDY made a big impression on the German Rock conscious led by the vocal delivery of guttural Death Metal growls of Raymond I. Rohonyi juxtaposed with the dynamic clarity of Liv Kristine. In more recent years THEATRE OF TRAGEDY has shed their Gothic skin and successfully transported their fan base into more industrial landscapes.

The band catalyst was drummer Hein Frode Hansen, previously a member of PHOBIA, an act that included pre-ENSLAVED personnel vocalist Grutle Kjellson and guitarist Ivar Bjornson.

Hansen together with vocalist Raymond I. Rohonyi, guitar players Pal Bjastad and Tommy Lindal, PAINTHEAD bassist Eirik T Saltrø and keyboard player Lorentz Aspen gelled together to create SUFFERING GRIEF in October of 1993. Although fronted by the Death Metal grunts of Rohonyi the band even at this formative stage were endeavouring to branch out into more atmospheric material. Evidence of this was displayed early on with Rohonyi's use of old English lyrical script. The band would operate as LE REINE NOIR for a matter of days before setting on the title THEATRE OF TRAGEDY in April of 1994.

The same year THEATRE OF TRAGEDY added female vocalist Liv Kristine and unleashed a debut demo tape that immediately scored a deal with the German Massacre label and soon found the group in Unisound Studios with EDGE OF SANITY's Dan Swanö.

The group debuted in 1995 with a self-titled album. THEATRE OF TRAGEDY hit the road with ATROCITY before working on their second record, 'Velvet Darkness They Fear', with Peter Coleman. The Moscow based Nedeltcho Boiadjiev string quartet play on four songs. The album promptly sold over 40,000 copies.

Unfortunately, following the completion of the record guitarist Tommy Lindal suffered a stroke. He was replaced for the ensuing European tour with a substitute. Touring to promote the record saw further dates with ATROCITY and inclusion on the billing of the September 1996 'Out Of The Dark' touring festival, alongside GOREFEST, SAMAEL and MOONSPELL.

The band undertook a further European tour in April 1997 with HEAVENWOOD and LAKE OF TEARS to promote the mini-album 'A Rose For The Dead'. The record contained a cover version of JOY DIVISION's 'Decades' and remixes by industrialists DAS ICH of 'And When He Falleth' and 'Black As The Devil Painteth'.

LIV KRISTINE issued solo work during a lull before 1998's 'Aegis' album. This opus would ambitiously find the band venturing into fresh musical territory. THEATRE OF TRAGEDY drafted new guitarist Frank Claussen for this album, which broke the band, scoring chart success in both Germany and Holland.

The band signed to major label East West for 2000's 'Musique' album, shedding two members in the process - guitarist Tommy Olsson and bassist Eirik T. Saltrø, a subsequent tour lending itself to the 'Closure: Live' opus. Olsson reunited with his former MORENDOES colleagues to create a new act dubbed ELUSIVE.

THEATRE OF TRAGEDY would spend the latter half of 2001 recording their 'Assembly' album, also cutting a version of the VANILLA FUDGE staple 'You Keep Me Hangin' On'. The band would also induct Vegard K. Thorsen on guitar. An EP entitled 'Let You Down', would be scheduled for solely Norwegian release in 2002 comprising of the title track, 'You Keep Me Hangin' On' and special remixes of 'Let You Down', 'Universal Race', and 'Envision'.

Singles/EPs:

Der Tanz Der Schatten (Club Mix) / Black As The Devil Painteth / A Hamlet For A Slothful Vassal / Der Tanz Der Schatten (Album Version), Massacre MASSCD0116 (1996)

A Rose For The Dead / Der Spiegel / As The Shadows Dance / And When He Falleth (Remix) / Black As The Devil Painteth (Remix) / Decades, Massacre (1997)

Cassandra (Cheap Wine edit) / Aœde (Edit) / Cassandra (Album version), Massacre (1998)

Der Tanz Der Schatten / Der Spiegel / Samantha / A Hamlet For A Slothful Vassal / Virago, Massacre (1999) (Limited edition shape picture disc)

Image / Machine / Fragment (Element remix) / Machine (VNV Nation remix), East West (2000)

Machine / Machine (VNV Nation remix) / Machine (Element remix) / Radio (Kallisti remix) / Reverie (Current Chill mix) / Image (French version) / Image (Video), East West (2001)

Albums:

THEATRE OF TRAGEDY

THEATRE OF TRAGEDY, Massacre CD063
(1995)
A Hamlet For A Slothful Vassal / Cheerful
Dirge / To These Words I Beheld No Tongue
/ Hollow Hearted, Heart Departed / ...A
Distance There Is... / Sweet Art Thou / Mire /
Dying - I Only Feel Apathy / Monotone
VELVET DARKNESS THEY FEAR,
Massacre MASSCD107 (1996)
Velvet Darkness They Fear / Fair And
'Guiling Copesmate Death / Bring Forth Ye
Shadow / Seraphic Deviltry / And When He
Falleth / Der Tanz Der Schatten / Black As
The Devil Painteth / On Whom The Moon
Doth Shine / The Masquerader And The
Phoenix
A ROSE FOR THE DEAD, Massacre MAS
CD0130 (1997)
A Rose For The Dead / Der Spiegel / As The
Shadows Dance / And When He Falleth
(DAS ICH remix) / Black As The Devil
Painteth (DAS ICH remix) / Decades
AEGIS, Massacre MAS CD0159 (1998)
40 GERMANY, 21 HOLLAND
Cassandra / Lorelei / Angelique / Aoede /
Siren / Venus / Poppea / Bacchante
MUSIQUE, East West (2000) **39 GERMANY**
Machine / City Of Light / Fragment / Musique
/ Commute / Radio / Image / Crash-Concrete
/ Retrospect / Reverie / Space Age / The
New Man
INPERSPECTIVE, Massacre DPO267
(2000)

Samantha / Virago / Lorelei (Icon Of Coil
Remix) / The Masquerader And Phoenix
(Phoenix Mix) / On Whom The Moon Doth
Shine (Unhum Mix) / Der Tanz Der Schatten
(Club Mix)
CLOSURE: LIVE, Massacre MAS CD0293
(2001)
Intro - And When He Falleth / Der Spiegel /
Cassandra / Venus / Black As The Devil
Painteth (RMX v2) / Siren / Poppæa /
Bacchante / A Distance there is / Der Tanz
Der Schatten / Cassandra (Video) / Der Tanz
Der Schatten (Video)
ASSEMBLY, East West (2002)
Automatic Lover / Universal Race / Episode /
Play / Superdrive / Let You Down / Starlit /
Envision / Flickerlight / Liquid Man / Motion

THE FROZEN AUTUMN (ITALY)

Electronic Gothic Rock act THE FROZEN
AUTUMN debuted with the 1994 'Oblivion'
tape. The band had been conceived a year
earlier by Diego Merlotto, shortly after adding
Claudio Brosio on guitar as a session player.
The 'Pale Awakening' debut album saw
release through a German label, picking up
valuable praise from the Gothic media in
Europe. The 1997 follow up 'Fragments Of
Memories' signalled a lengthy relationship
with the Italian Eibon label.
1998 saw Merlotto founding the 'Cold Wave'
endeavour STATIC MOVEMENT with

407

girlfriend Arianna for the 'Visionary Landscapes' record.

Eibon Records reissued the debut album in 2000, retitling it 'The Pale Collection' and adding 'This Time' and a cover version of 'Bio Vital' originally by DECODED FEEDBACK.

THE FROZEN AUTUMN would return in April of 2002 with the 'Emotional Screening Device' album, limited editions being made available in real leather packaging. The album included a cover version of CANAAN's 'Sperm Like Honey'.

Albums:
PALE AWAKENING, (1995)
Pale Awakening / Again / Winter / Another Tear / Onyria / This Time / In The Nightime / Wait For Nothing / Scent Of Innocence / When Dreams Became Memories
FRAGMENTS OF MEMORIES, Eibon (1997)
The Echoes Of My Lies / There's No Time To Recall / Dusk Is Like A Dagger / Winter (Reprise) / Don't Cry For Me (Version) / Chimney's Song / Painted Girls / Fragments Of Memories / I'm Coming From Nowhere / The Forgotten Frontiers
THE PALE COLLECTION, Eibon (2000)
Pale Awakening / Again / Winter / Another Tear / Onyria / This Time / Wait For Nothing / When Dreams Become Memories / This Time (Electro Mix) / Bio Vital
EMOTIONAL SCREENING DEVICE, Eibon FZA034 (2002)
Second Sight (D) / Silence Is Talking / When Are You Sad / Wintertag / Is Everything Real? / Precious Lives / Emotional Screening Device / Verdancy Price / Sperm Like Honey / Freon Heart, Fayence Mind / Second Sight (A)

THE GATHERING (HOLLAND)

Line-Up: Arneeke van Giersbergen (vocals), Jelmer Wiersma (guitar), Rene Rutten (guitar / flute), Hugo Prinsen Geerligs (bass), Frank Boeijen (keyboards), Hans Rutten (drums)

THE GATHERING have evolved from their 1989 Death Metal inception to more eclectic and diverse influences upon each successive release. THE GATHERING, bolstered by the striking looks of van Giersbergen, have established themselves as a major force on the European Rock scene and despite veering off into their own territory musically still hold legions of Rock fans as loyal supporters.

The band, hailing from the town of Oss, took their name from the 'Highlander' movie and cut their teeth performing covers by such artists as CELTIC FROST, POSSESSED and CARNIVORE. THE GATHERING's first impact came with the 1990 rehearsal demo session 'An Imaginary Symphony' in 1990. The original line-up of the band featured vocalist Bart Smits and guitarist Jelmer Wiersma. Bassist Hugo Prinsen Geerligs and keyboard player Frank Boeijen were added to the line-up prior to recording of the 1991 demo 'Moonlight Archer'.

THE GATHERING toured Holland as support to DEATH and MORBID ANGEL before signing to the Foundation 2000 label. Following the release of debut album 'Always' in 1992, Smits quit, founding WISH, to be replaced by two vocalists Martine van Loon and Niels Duffhues. The former would divide her duties with another Dutch Gothic inclined act ORPHANAGE, a spirit of comradeship existing between the two bands as THE GATHERING keyboard player Frank Boeijen sessioned on ORPHANAGE's 'Druid' demo.

Both van Loon and Duffhues departed after the second album 'Almost A Dance', van Loon going on to front LORDS OF THE STONE, and THE GATHERING added Anneke van Giersbergen for 'Mandylion'. Co- production on 'Mandylion' was credited to GRIP INC. guitarist Waldemar Sorychta. This album saw the band adventurously breaking away from the Gothic Doom fare of previous works. Their bravery in ditching heaviness in favour of varied sound textures worked in the band's favour as album and concert ticket sales rose sharply.

As a diversion Anneke Von Giersbergen featured as a guest vocalist for German 'Country' Metal band THE FARMER BOYS cover version of DEPECHE MODE's 'Never Let Me Down Again' during 1996. The 1997 'Nighttime Birds' album saw THE GATHERING opening up to Progressive elements and the act would find themselves listed as Holland's top Rock draw.

Ambitiously the group stretched their fans loyalty to the limit with the sprawling double album 'How To Measure A Planet?'. European headline shows in April of 1998 had THE GATHERING topping a bill over label mates LACUNA COIL and SIEGMEN. The experiment proved a resounding success and led in turn to the band's inaugural North American dates, including an appearance at the 1999 'Milwaukee Metal Fest'. Momentum was maintained with the 'Superheat' live album.

The band's early roots were explored on the 2001 retrospective release 'Downfall, The Early Years'. As well as archive material the album included rare live tracks from an early concert.

THE GATHERING would apparently part ways with Century Media in early 2002 to set

up their own Psychonaut imprint, also announcing future collaborations with ULVER's Trickster G. However, subsequent announcements from their record label revealed the band was still under contract. A projected album, 'Black Light District' was set to include guest contributions from Denis 'Piggy' D'Amour of esteemed Canadian avant-garde Thrashers VOIVOD.

Festival appearances for THE GATHERING in August included Belgium's 'Eurorock', the Budapest 'Sziget' event, 'M'Era Luna' and 'Summer Breeze' both in Germany, the Greek 'Stagazer' show and 'Long Live Rock n' Roll' in Moscow. Eagerly anticipated new material would be delivered the previous month in the form of the 'Black Light District' single. Clocking in at an epic sixteen minutes long the track featured guest backing vocals from Sarah Jezebel Diva, known for her work with CRADLE OF FILTH.

Singles/EPs:
Strange Machines (Single Edit) / Strange Machines / In Motion 1 (Live) / Leaves (Live), Century Media 77135-2 (1996)
Adrenaline / Leaves (Edit) / Third Chance / Leaves (Album Version), Century Media 77135-2 (1996)
Kevin´s Telescope / In Power We Entrust The Love Advocated / When The Sun Hits / Confusion (Demo Eroc mix), Century Media (1997)

The May Song (Radio edit) / The Earth Is My Witness (Edit) / Strange Machines (with the Metropol Orchestra) / The May Song, Century Media (1997)
Liberty Bell / Shrink / Frail (Live), Century Media (1998)
Rollercoaster (Radio edit) / Theme from 'The Cyclist' / Leaves (Live with the Metropol Orchestra) / Liberty Bell (Video), Century Media 77296-3 (2000)
Amity 'Radio mix) / Life Is What You Make It / Amity (Trip Pop Radio mix) / Amity (Timecode Audio Remix) / Amity (Extended Trip Remix) / Amity (Three People Remix) / Amity (Live) / Life Is What You Make It (Documentary video), Century Media (2001)
Black Light District / Debris / Broken Glass, Psychonaut PSYN003MCD (2002)

Albums:
ALWAYS..., Foundation 2000 FDN 2004CD (1992)
The Mirror Waters / Subzero / In Sickness And Heals / King For A Day / Second Sunrise / Stonegarden / Gaya's Dream
ALMOST A DANCE, Foundation 2000 (1993)
On A Wave / The Blue Vessel / Her Last Flight / The Sky People / Nobody Dares / Like Fountains / Proof / Heartbeat Amplifier / Passage To Desire
MANDYLION, Century Media 77098-2 (1995)

Strange Machines / Eleanor / In Motion / Leaves / Fear The Sea / Mandylion / Sand And Mercury / In Motion

NIGHTIMEBIRDS, Century Media 77168-2 (1997)
On Most Surfaces / Confusion / The May Song / The Earth Is My Witness / New Moon Different Day / Third Chance / Kevin's Telescope / Nighttime Birds / Shrink

HOW TO MEASURE A PLANET?, Century Media 77268-2 (1999)
Frail (You Might As Well Be Me) / Great Ocean Road / Rescue Me / Marooned / Travel / South American Ghost Ride / Illuminating / Locked Away / Probably Built In The Fifties / How To Measure A Planet? / My Electricity / Liberty Bell / Red Is A Slow Colour / The Big Sleep

SUPERHEAT LIVE, Century Media (1999)
The Big Sleep / On Most Surfaces / Probably Built In The Fifties / Liberty Bell / Marooned / Strange Machines / Nighttime Birds / My Electricity / Sand And Mercury

IF-THEN-ELSE, Century Media 77298-2 (2000)
Rollercoaster / Shot To Pieces / Amity / Bad Movie Scene / The Colorado Incident / Beautiful War / Analog Park / Herbal Movement / Saturnine / Morphia's Waltz / Pathfinder

DOWNFALL - THE EARLY YEARS, Hammerheart 720 2000 182 (2001)
In Sickness And Health / Gaya's Dream / Always... / Subzero / Anthology In Black / Second Sunrise / Downfall / In Sickness And Health / Second Sunrise / Six Dead, Three To Go / Downfall / Another Day / Share The Wisdom

THEMGOROTH (POLAND)
Line-Up: Asmodeus (vocals / guitar), Kiejstut (bass), Sammach (keyboards), Alkalon (drums)

An extreme outfit, Polish underground kings THEMGOROTH mix Black Metal and Gothic influences to fine effect. Founded in November of 1991 the group's first line-up comprised Miroslaw Dziadek on vocals, guitarist Piotr Dawid, bassist Piotr Deckert-Firla and Marek Herman on drums. By August of 1993 Mariusz Mrozek was inducted on keyboards. The band recruited guitarist Sammach in October of that year and debuted with a two track demo 'Gate To The Unknown' and 'Equilibrium' the following year. The debut 'Gate To The Unknown' album was recorded for the Czech Sheer label in 1995. Two years later THEMGOROTH expanded their sound with the addition of flautist Magda Wodniak. However, the band's momentum in recording a second album was stalled with the tragic death of Deckert-Fila, killed in a car crash in August. Only two months later both Wodniak and Mrozek decamped. By October THEMGOROTH had regrouped, pulling in bassist Darek Chmielowski and guitarist Dominik Gryzbon in 1998. The band also boosted their entourage with the addition of female lead vocalist Sylwia. Czapek and the roster would be finalized by enrolling Piotr Wojcik ('Smrtan') on keyboards. This radically revised version of the band cut the second album 'Highway Into Unknown' for Dagdy Music, issued in 1999.

Albums:
GATE TO THE UNKNOWN, Amber Otmar Nytra (1995)
The Initiate / Gate To The Unknown / Dead Valley / A Poet Inspired By Pain / In The Name Of...

HIGHWAY INTO THE UNKNOWN, Dagdy Music (1999)
Highway Into The Unknown / A Poet Inspired By Pain / Is This You, Maybe? / Gate To The Unknown / Dead Valley / In The Name Of...

THERGOTHON (FINLAND)
Line-Up: Niko Sirkiä (vocals), Mikko Ruotsaainen (guitar), Sami Kaveri (guitar), Jori Sjöroos (drums)

THERGOTHON are renowned for releasing one of the most melancholic and bleak Doom albums of all time. The band first emerged with the 1991 demo 'Ftaghn-Nagh Yog Sothtoth'. Various members of THERGOTHON later formed THIS EMPTY FLOW, releasing a 1996 album 'Magenta Skycode'.

Albums:
STREAM FROM THE HEAVENS, Avantgarde Music AV001 (1995)
Everlasting / Yet The Watchers Guard / The Unknown Kadath In The Cold Waste / Elemental / Who Rides The Astral Wings / Crying Blood + Crimson Snow

THERION (SWEDEN)
Line-Up: Christofer Johnsson (guitar / vocals), Peter Hansson (guitar), Erik Gustafsson (bass), Oskar Forss (drums)

Cited by many as the most adventurous Metal band at present. THERION present a sound swathed with huge operatic choirs and oriental orchestral arrangements. Although starting life as a run of the mill Death Metal band THERION have with each successive release wrung every ounce of adventurism

CHRISTOFER JOHNSSON of THERION
Photo : Nico Wobben

out of each record increasing their status in Europe along the way.

The roots of THERION lay in the late '80s Swedish band BLITSKRIEG, which featured bassist / vocalist Christofer Johnsson, guitarist Peter Hansson and drummer Oskar Fors.

Formed as MEGATHERION in 1988, with a line-up of Johnsson on vocals and guitar, guitarist Hansson, ex-CREMATORY bassist Johan Hansson and drummer Mika Tovalainen, shortly after the band shortened the name to THERION and replaced their rhythm section with bassist Erik Gustafsson and drummer Oskar Forss.

Initial demos in 1989 were completed with the temporary services of vocalist Matti Karki, now of DISMEMBER. This line-up, minus Karki, recorded THERION's first mini-album 'Time Shall Tell', which was initially released as a limited edition of 1,000. However, subsequent pressings have been made.

Bassist Oscar Gustaffson left following the 'Of Darkness' album. For the 'Symphony Masses' album (released through Megarock in 1993) only Johnsson remained, adding guitarist Magnus Barthelson, bassist Andreas Wahl and former CARBONIZED drummer Piotr Wawrzenuik.

Wahl and Wawrzeniuk, guitarist Johan Lundell and ENTOMBED bassist Lars Rosenberg forged a 1993 side project titled SERPENT. The industrious Wahl also operated another side band CONCRETE SLEEP.

The group toured Europe in 1995 as support to Canadians ANNIHILATOR and the group drafted in ENTOMBED / SERPENT bassist Lars Rosenberg on a temporary basis for the shows.

Having signed to German label Nuclear Blast, 1995's 'Lepaca Kliffoth' featured a cover of CELTIC FROST's 'Sorrows Of The Moon'. The album also saw vocalist Claudia Maria Mohri, who appeared on CELTIC FROST's 'Into The Pandemonium' album, and baritone Hans Groning.

THERION toured South America during 1995 during which Rosenberg opted to leave ENTOMBED and join THERION on a permanent basis.

In November the group added ex-UNANIMATED guitarist Jonas Mellberg together with former NECROPHOBIC keyboard player Tobbe Sidegard. Wawrzenuik and Rosenberg also released the debut SERPENT product 'In The Garden Of The Serpent' to round off 1995.

As 1996 began THERION contributed a track to a Japanese IRON MAIDEN cover album on the Toys Factory label and entered a new stage of their career with the 'Theli' release,

an ambitious amalgam of Metal and Middle Eastern influences all overlaid with choral vocals.

With the release of 'Theli' THERION undertook an extensive tour of Germany, supporting AMORPHIS. Further dates saw the band as part of the 'Out Of The Dark' festivals on a bill alongside MY DYING BRIDE and SENTENCED.

The 1997 album release, originally planned as an EP, featured versions of RUNNING WILD's 'Under Jolly Roger', JUDAS PRIEST's 'Here Come The Tears', SCORPIONS 'Fly To The Rainbow' and IRON MAIDEN's 'Children Of The Damned'. The band would indulge in yet more covers with the 1999 release 'Crowning Of Atlantis' with a guesting Ralf Scheepers of PRIMAL FEAR making his presence felt on the bands version of 'Crazy Nights', originally by Japanese Metal band LOUDNESS. Also included were takes of MANOWAR's 'Thor' and ACCEPT's 'Seawinds'.

In keeping with their left-field character, THERION contributed a version of 'Summer Night City' to a 2001 Death Metal ABBA tribute. The track would also turn up on their 'Secrets Of The Runes' album alongside a further cover - the SCORPIONS 1976 track 'Crying Days'. THERION bassist Fredrik Isaksson would form part of the reconvened GRAVE during September 2001.

THERION would part ways with drummer Sami Karppinen during March of 2002. The band cut a rendition of 'Fight Fire With Fire' for a Nuclear Blast METALLICA tribute collection.

Singles/EPs:
Time Will Tell / Dark Eternity / Asphyxiate With Fear / A Suburb To Hell, House Of Kicks (1990)
The Beauty In Black / Arrival Of The Darkest Queen / Evocation Of Vovin / The Veil Of Golden Spheres, Nuclear Blast NB125-2 (1995)
Siren Of The Woods (Single Version) / Cults Of The Shadow (Edit Version), Nuclear Blast NB 178-2/27361 61782 (1996)

Albums:
OF DARKNESS, Deaf DEAF 6 (1991)
The Return / Asphyxiate With Fear / Morbid Reality / Meglamaniac / A Suburb To Hell / Genocidal Raids / Time Shall Tell / Dark Eternity
BEYOND SANCTORIUM, Active ATV 23 (1992)
Future Consciousness / Pandemonic Outbreak / Cthulu / Symphony Of The Dead / Beyond Sanctum / Enter The Depths Of Eternal Darkness / Illusions Of Life / The

Way / Paths / Tyrants Of The Damned
SYMPHONY MASSES - HO DRAKON HO MEGAS, Megarock MRR 002 (1993)
Baal Reginon / Dark Princess Naamah / A Black Rose / Symphoni Drakonis Inferni / Dawn Of Perishness / The Eye Of Eclipse / The Ritual Dance Of The Yezidis / Powerdance / Procreation Of Eternity / Ho Dracon Ho Megas
LEPACA KLIFFOTH, Nuclear Blast NB 127 (1995)
The Wings Of The Hydra / Melez / Arrival Of The Darkest Queen / The Beauty In Black / Riders Of Theli / Black / Darkness Eve / Sorrows Of The Moon / Let The New Day Begin / Lepaca Kliffoth / Evocation Of Vovin
THELI, Nuclear Blast NB179 (1996)
Preludium / To Mega Therion / Cults Of The Shadow / In The Desert Of Set / Interludium / Nightside Of Eden / Opus Eclipse / Invocation Of Naamah / The Siren Of The Woods / Grand Finale - Postludium
A'RAB ZARAQ LUCID DREAMING, Nuclear Blast NB 249-2 (1997)
In Remembrance / Black Fairy / Fly To The Rainbow / Under Jolly Roger / Symphony Of The Dead / Here Come The Tears / Enter The Transcendental Sleep / The Quiet Desert / Down The Qliphothic / Tunnel / Up To Netzach - Floating Back / The Fall Into Eclipse
VOVIN, Nuclear Blast NB 27361 63172 (1998)
The Rise Of Sodom And Gomorrah / Birth Of Venus Illegitima / Wine Of Aluqah / Clavicula Mox / The Wild Hunt / Eye Of Shiva / Black Sun Draconian Trilogy / The Opening / Morning Star / Black Diamonds / Raven Of Dispersion
CROWNING OF ATLANTIS, Nuclear Blast (1999) **85 GERMANY**
The Crowning Of Atlantis / Mark Of Cain / Clavicula Nox (Remix) / Crazy Nights / From The Dionysian Days / Thor / Seawinds / To Mega Therion (Live) / The Wings Of The Hydra (Live) / Black Sun (Live)
DEGGIAL, Nuclear Blast NB 442-2 (2000) **43 GERMANY**
Seven Secrets Of The Sphinx / Eternal Return / Enter Vril-Ye / Ship Of Luna / The Invincible / Deggial / Emerald Crown / The Flight Of The Lord Of Flies / Flesh Of The Gods / Via Nocturna Part I, II / O Fortuna
SECRETS OF THE RUNES, Nuclear Blast (2001) **74 GERMANY**
Ginnungagap (Prologue) / Asgård / Midgård / Schwarzalbenheim (Svartalfheim) / Jotunheim / Ljusalfheim / Vanaheim / Nifelheim / Muspelheim / Helheim / Secret Of The Runes (Epilogue) / Crying Days (Remixed) / Summernight City (Remixed)

THE SINS OF THY BELOVED
(SWEDEN)
Line-Up: Glenn Morten Nordbø (vocals / guitar), Anita Auglend (vocals), Arild Christensen (vocals / guitar), Ola Aarrestad (bass), Anders Thue (keyboards), Ingfrid Stensland (keyboards), Stig Johansen (drums)

Symphonic Gothic Metal act THE SINS OF THY BELOVED was found in late 1996 initially entitled PURGATORY. A name switch was adopted prior to the release of the three track 'All Alone' EP released by the Italian Nocturnal Music label. Already with the sultry teenage Ingfrid Stensland on keyboards the band boosted their orchestration in September of 1997 by enlisting second keyboard player and pianist Anders Thue for a 1998 demo session 'Silent Pain'. These tapes would score a deal with the Napalm label for the debut 'Lack Of Sorrow'.
THE SINS OF THY BELOVED would have a track featured on the 1999 Hall Of Sermon label compilation 'Ladies, Queens & Sluts'. Touring in 2000 backing up the sophomore 'Perpetual Desolation' saw the group on the road with TRISTANIA.
In January of 2001 lead vocalist Anita Auglend curtailed her services and the band pulled in Hege-Marie Aanby from Stavenger. However, Aanby too was out of the picture by April.

Singles/EPs:
All Alone / Memories / Worthy Of You, Nocturnal Music (1997)

Albums:
LAKE OF SORROW, Napalm (1997)
My Love / The Kiss / Worthy Of You / Lake Of Sorrow / Until The Dark / All Alone / Silent Pain
PERPETUAL DESOLATION, Napalm NPR 079 (2000)
The Flame Of Wrath / Forever / Pandemonium / Partial Insanity / Perpetual Desolation / Nebula Queen / The Mournful Euphony / A Tormented Soul / The Thing That Should Not Be

THE TEMPTER (SPAIN)
Line-Up: Ivan (vocals), Carlos (guitar), Antonio Ruiz (guitar), Miguel (bass), Manuel (drums)

Madrid based Doom band. THE TEMPTER opened proceedings with the 1996 demo 'Evenfall', which included a cover version of WITCHFINDER GENERAL's 'Burning A Sinner' but was unfortunately blighted by an amateurish production. The 2000 'The Dark Sound Of The Doom' session, once again including a cover, this time of 'War Machine' by KISS, elicited a more positive response.

THE TEMPTER has appeared on a whole raft of tribute albums in homage to bands such as BLACK WIDOW's 'Conjuration', BLACK SABBATH's 'Falling Off The Edge Of The World', NECROMANDUS and DEATH SS.

THIS EMPTY FLOW (FINLAND)
Line-Up: Jori Sjöroos (vocals / instruments), Augustus Mattila (bass), Niko Sirkiä (keyboards)

The intensely dismal Doom-laden act THIS EMPTY FLOW feature ex-members of THERGOTHON Jori Sjöroos and Niko Sirkiä. In 1996 the band added guitarist, and producer of debut album 'Magenta Skycode', Jukka Sillanpää to the line-up.
Sirkiä then departed as in 1997 keyboard player Hanna Kalske made her presence felt. THIS EMPTY FLOW signed to Italian Doom specialists Eibon Records for February 2001's 'Nowafter' opus.

Albums:
MAGENTA SKYCODE, Avantgarde Music AV016 (1996)
Nowafter / Useless / Stream / Towards Distant / Snow Blind / Distress / (But I Am) Still / Sweet Bloom Of Night Time Flowers
THREE EMPTY BOYS, Plastic Passion (1999)
Blear / Drops / Dive Nothing / To Drink Atlantic Dry / Angels Playground / Playground Of The Angels / Hello Spaceboy / Rebuilt Passage / Hunger / Abell / This Empty Boy
USELESS AND EMPTY SONGS, Plastic Passion (2000)
Useless (Trip To Mäntyluoto version) / One Song About Solitude / Everything-Nothing / Dubby / Of Blossom And Decay
NOWAFTER, Eibon TEF025 (2001)
Je(n!)i Force / Marmite / Stilton / Shoreditch / And Also The Drops / Ashby-de-la-Zouch / One Song About Solitude / Dubby / Drops / Angels' Playground / Rebuilt Passage / Hunger / Of Blossom And Decay

THIS TANGLED WEB (AUSTRALIA)
Line-Up: Nick (vocals / guitar / bass / keyboards / drums), Garran (vocals / guitar / keyboards / drums)

Genre defying New South Wales act THIS TANGLED WEB blend enough laboured Doom and melancholic Gothicness into their undoubtedly Death Metal fuelled sound to confound most reviewers. The group was assembled during May of 1998 as a trio featuring lead vocalist Dave and multi-instrumentalists Nick and Garran. Although the band lost the services of Dave in 2000 the project continued, issuing a well received demo.
The November 2001 single 'Nothing To Hold You Here' featured former HEADLIFTER drummer Aram on a session basis.

Singles/EPs:
No Funeral / Recycle, (2001) ('Nothing To Hold You Here' EP)

THORNS OF THE CARRION
(Cincinnati, OH, USA)
Line-Up: Marquis Thomas (vocals / guitar), Allen Scott (guitar), Brad Howard (bass), Leslie Anderson (keyboards), Ash Thomas (drums)

Accomplished mournful, contemporary edged Doom Metal mongers dating back to late 1992. The act was convened as CARRION LORD by guitarist Allen Scott and vocalist Matt Chapman. Augmenting the band with the addition of guitarist Doug Nevel, keyboard player Marquis Thomas and drummer Tony Willwerth and as THORNS OF THE CARRION laid down a 1993 demo session 'The Ancient Life'.
Nevel would disembark upfront of a second cassette 'The Garden Of Dead Winter' and the group utilized Mark Haap for session lead guitar. Bass was handled in the studio by ESTUARY OF CALAMITY drummer Ash Thomas. These recordings, which took less than ten hours to complete start to finish, would also be issued on CD format by Wild Rags although not to the band's favour.
As 1995 broke Willwerth quit. Ash Thomas would take the vacancy. Jimmy Eldred moved in on bass guitar and in November of the same year Nevel returned to the rankings. With this revised line-up THORNS OF THE CARRION cut a further promotional tape 'The Willow Weeps For Me'. Before the year was out a further demo 'Darkness In The Elegy Season' had emerged. The group boosted their sound with the enlistment of third guitarist Adam Moses but it was a short-term gain as Nevel decamped for the second time. The numbers depleted further when Eldred left.
Opting for a complete new strategy for their debut 1996 album 'The Scarlet Tapestry' produced by Todd Buck by replacing the wayward members with Leslie Anderson on harp and flute. 1997 witnessed a heavy touring schedule to back up the album

release.
Moses would be the next in line to exit as ESTUARY OF CALAMITY guitarist Brad Howard filled the gap. In 1998 the band then adopted a radical reshuffle manouvering Marquis Thomas to guitar, Howard over to bass and Anderson to keyboards.
In July of 1999 founder member Matt Cameron finally threw in the towel necessitating Marquis Thomas to add lead vocals to his duties. THORNS OF THE CARRION in their new guise would contribute their rendition of 'The Jonah' to a Dwell Records KING DIAMOND tribute album.
In 2000 a five track self-financed EP 'Eve Songs' arrived.

Singles/EPs:
The Garden Of Dead Winter, Wild Rags (1996)
Naomi's Waters / Carmilla / Song For Lucretia / To Covet The Dancing Winds / Eve Of The Emerald Sun, (2000) ('Eve Songs' EP)

Albums:
THE SCARLET TAPESTRY, (1997)
Cry The Everstill Dream / Tears For The Raven Muse / The Tragedy Of Melpomene / Bleak Thorn Laurels / The Drifting Snow / Beautiful Thorns To Caress The Girl / By The Brilliance Of Candlelight / Memories Forever Unadorned / The Ashen Embrace

THORR'S HAMMER (USA)
Line-Up: Runhild Gammelsäeter (vocals), Stephen O'Malley (guitar), Greg Anderson (guitar), James Hale (bass), Jamie Sykes (drums)

Despite the Norwegian album title THORR'S HAMMER are in fact a project band led by BURNING WITCH's Stephen O'Malley and drummer Jamie Sykes (an expatriated Yorkshireman!) GOATSNAKE's Greg Anderson. Female lead vocals are handled by the striking figure Ihsahn of EMPEROR's girlfriend Runhild Gammelsäeter.
Both O'Malley and Anderson also busy themselves with SUNN0))). Sykes would return to the UK, joining THE ENCHANTED.

Albums:
DOMMEDAGSNATT, Southern Lord (2000)
Norge / Troll / Dommedagsnatt / Mellom Gadgeme

35007 (HOLLAND)
Line-Up: Euwot Baart (vocals), Bertus Fridael (guitar), Michel Boukhoudt (bass), Mark Sponsalee (keyboards), Sander Evers (drums)

A somewhat anonymous Eindhoven based Electro-Stoner act, 35007 do not credit individual musicians on their album covers. Initially entitled LOOSE the group subsequently adopted the Alabama zip code as their moniker. Bassist and main spokesman for the band Michel Boukhoudt also operates with the ALABAMA KIDS. Drummer Jacco van Roy was also an ALABAMA KIDS man, as well as citing credits with 7ZUMA7. Debuting in 1994 with the 'Especially For You' album, 35007 immediately staked their own ground by blending mammoth riffs with trance inducing electronica. The group's second eponymous album was released on October 14th 1997 to celebrate the anniversary of Chuck Yeager's successful attempt at breaking the sound barrier. A 10" single was cut for the Man's Ruin label after which drummer Sander Evers was enrolled, replacing Jacco van Roy. The completely instrumental 'Liquid' album comprised just 4 voluminous tracks.
For live work 35007 employ the services of VJ Luck to add visual enhancement to the band's "Cosmic groove".

Singles/EPs:
Von Braun / Artificial Intelligence / Sea Of Tranquillity, Stickman (2001) ('Sea Of Tranquility' EP)

Albums:
ESPECIALLY FOR YOU, Stickman (1994)
Zandbak / Cosmic Messenger / Basiculo Ad Cunnum / Suave / Bad Altitude / The Elephant Song / U-Mu-M'Nu- / Water
35007, (1997)
Herd / Soul Machine / Short Sharp Left / Undo / Big Bore / Vein / 66 / Powertruth / Locker - Zero 21
LIQUID, Stickman (2002)
Tsunami / Crystalline / Evaporate / Voyage Automatique

THROTTLEROD (Richmond, VA, USA)
Line-Up: Matt Whitehead (vocals / guitar), Bo Leslie (guitar), Chris Sundstrom (bass), Kevin White (drums)

Jagermeister sponsored Virginian Rockers THROTTLEROD describe themselves as "Heavy ass Southern Rock". The group was conceived in Columbia, South Carolina during July of 1999 first, impacting with the self-financed EP 'By The Horns'. THROTTLEROD's line-up at this juncture comprised the quartet vocalist / guitarist Matt Whitehead, guitarist Bo Leslie, bass player Travis Nicholson and drummer Jon McNabb. Following their signature to the Underdogma label for the 2000 album 'Eastbound And Down', THROTTLEROD toured North America aggressively on a non-stop campaign which saw them through until November of 2001. Dates during 2000 found THROTTLEROD hooked up with SIX SIGMA, ALABAMA THUNDERPUSSY, WEEDEATER, PUNY HUMAN and HALFWAY TO GONE amongst others. October of 2002 was taken up by sharing stages with QUINTANE AMERICA. With these dates completed the band relocated to Richmond, Virginia although they would lose the services of bassist Travis Nicholson, bringing In Chicago native Chris Sundstrom as substitute.

The band cut a version of LYNYRD SKYNYRD's 'Simple Man' for a tribute album the same year. Other airings included the inclusion of an early demo version of the track 'Wifebeater' on the Victory Records compilation 'A Fistful Of Rock Volume 8' and a take on RAM JAM's seminal 'Black Betty' for the Small Stone Recordings 'Sucking In The Seventies' compilation.

Added drummer Kevin White in mid 2002.

Albums:
EASTBOUND AND DOWN, Underdogma (2000)
Blue T-Top / On The Hunt / Dale / Little Wave / Three Rings / American Guadelupe / Hogwild / 1.8 / Alone On The Moon / Wifebeater / Swaller / The Platter / Somethin' Dirty

THULSA DOOM (NORWAY)
Line-Up: Papa Doom (vocals), Doom Perignon (guitar), Angelov Doom (bass), Fast Winston Doom (drums)

An Oslo based project forged in 1999 by producer 'El Doom', better known as Ole Petter Andreasson, renowned for his behind the desk contributions at his Caliban studios to acts such as GLUCIFER, HELLRIDE, his own "Bonerrock" side project THE CUMSHOTS and THE WONDERFOOLS amongst many others. THULSA DOOM was formulated comprising Papa Doom on vocals, THE REJECTS guitarist Doom Perignon and the RUMBOID rhythm section of Herman Doom on bass and Fast Winston Doom (Halvor Winsnes) on the drums. Although as yet untitled, the band conjured up a two track demo of 'She Fucks Me' and 'Cities After Cheese', securing a deal for an EP through the Spanish Safety Pin label. With Herman Doom opting out to concentrate on his other act REVEREND LOVEJOY new tracks would be laid down with Angelov Doom from Stoners BLACK DEBBETH. This revised

version of the band, now entitled THULSA DOOM, cut three new tracks 'Sins Of The Next Man', 'Birthday Pony' and 'Fatboys Head' for the EP, released in June of 2000.

Major label EMI Records would pick THULSA DOOM up for a full-length album for Norwegian release whilst Devil Doll subsidiary This Dark Reign Recordings took on the record for North America. Provisionally titled 'Keyboards Oh Lord Why Don't We' and subsequently 'Aim For Something Soft, Use Something Hard' the record finally emerged as 'The Seats Are Soft But The Helmet Is Way Too Tight'. Released in May of 2001 the regular format would be preceded a month earlier by a limited edition vinyl variant issued by the Big Dipper label.

The band spent the summer of 2002 working on a follow up album provisionally billed as '...And Then Take You To A Place Where Jars Are Kept'. El Doom would also assemble an Oslo 'Desert Rock' inspired recording project dubbed THE CALIBAN SESSIONS including musicians from acts such as THULSA DOOM, AMULET, JR. EWING, RUSSIAN POKER, THE CUMSHOTS, BRUT BOOGALOO, BORN ELECTRIC, INSENSE, PILEDRIVER, BLACK DEBBETH and the OLSO MOTHERFUCKERS.

Singles/EPs:
Sins Of The Next Man / Birthday Pony / Fatboys Head / Cities After Cheese / She Fucks Me, Safety Pin SPC008 (2000) ('She Fucks Me' 10" single)
City Of People / Sleep With Celebrity, Custom Heavy (2002)

Albums:
THE SEATS ARE SOFT BUT THE HELMET IS WAY TOO TIGHT, EMI 07243 532339 21 (2001)
Centerfold Blues / You Go First / Clean Your Plate / Ambulance Ride / Sins Of The Next Man / Definition Of What Made Me / Birthday Pony / 21st Century, Where Can I Get A Fuckable Little Grungette? / He's The Head / Way Too Tight

T.H.U.M.B. (ITALY)
Line-Up: Andrea Granzotto (vocals / guitar), Luca Cuzzolin (guitar), Paulo Girotto (bass), Lisa Cappellazzo (drums)

T.H.U.M.B., naturally titled after the KYUSS track, evolved in 1999, at first a covers band operating in Garage and Grunge territory. By the release of the 'Garaged' CD the band would be proud to label themselves as "Heavy Psych Stoner Trips". The initial formation of the band comprised vocalist /

guitarist Andrea 'Ganga' Granzotto, bass player Paulo 'Bokal' Girotto and drummer Lisa Cappellazzo. The drift into the realms of Stoner was triggered by the introduction of second guitarist Luca 'Nando' Cuzzolin, this new sound being captured on the six song self-financed EP 'Newz From The Topaz'.

Early gigs had T.H.U.M.B. acting as openers to Doom legend PAUL CHAIN. A limited edition live album, simply billed 'Alive' and including a cover version of 'El Rodeo' by KYUSS, 'Gardening At Night' by R.E.M. and BLUR's 'Song 2', was distributed among friends and local fans in September of 2001. The band soon after laid down the debut studio album 'Garaged', generating favourable worldwide press coverage. However, in April of 2002 Granzotto broke ranks. T.H.U.M.B. duly readjusted themselves, switching Cuzzolin and Girotto to the vocal role for a fresh EP 'New Day Rising'.

Singles/EPs:
Down On The Road / Like A Day / Fire Girl / The Alien's Ballad / Dancing Junkie / Space Trip (To The Seventh Sun), (2000) ('Newz From The Topaz' EP)
Devil Woman / Hate Song / Creation Process / Echoes And Daemons / Visions From Mars, (2002) ('New Day Rising' EP)

Albums:
ALIVE, (2001)
Intro / El Rodeo / Untitled / Alone / The Evil One / Last Day On Earth / Song 2 / Gardening At Night / Desert Sea / T.H.U.M.B.
GARAGED, (2001)
The Evil One / Alone / Tell Me / The Drunk Camel's Breakfast / Sheep / Psychodestroyer

THUMM (CANADA)
Line-Up: Steve Kennedy (vocals / guitar), Chris Peddle (guitar), Andrew Fisher (bass), Pete Hanlon (drums)

Mount Pearl "Heavy Groove Riff Rawk". THUMM was originated in late 1997 by rhythm guitarist Chris Peddle and vocalist / guitarist Steve Kennedy. Initially entitled THUMB, after the KYUSS track, a swift name change to THUMM became in order upon discovery of the Italian T.H.U.M.B. and Australian THUMB.

The group was rounded out with the attachment of a rhythm section comprising bassist Andrew Fisher and drummer Pete Hanlon. This quartet showed their hand with the 'Rule Of Thumb' demo, issued through the band's quaintly titled Thumb Up Your Ass label.

Steve Kennedy also performs with HARDLINER whilst Pete Hanlon holds down duties with HOWL.

Albums:
BLACK MOON SAND, (1999)
Yesterdayz Alibies / Sandbox / Blinded / Understand / Odd Man / Black Moon Sand / The Fall / For the Last Time

THUMLOCK (AUSTRALIA)
Line-Up: Ben Lough (vocals / guitar), Raff Lacurto (guitar), Wayne Stokes (bass), Greg Eshman (drums)

Wollongong Sci-Fi infused Rockers. THUMLOCK self-financed their 1997 debut 'Dripping Silver Heat' which drew the attention of the High Beam Music label, resulting in the 1999 'Lunar Mountain Sunrise' follow up. Beginning life as a trio of vocalist / guitarist Ben Lough, bassist Wayne Stokes and drummer Greg Eshman THUMLOCK introduced second guitarist Raff Lacurto into the fold for recording of 'Lunar Mountain Sunrise'.

2000's 'Liquid Emerald Odyssey' saw their music spreading further afield as Italian Stoner specialists Beard Of Stars took the band on for European distribution. Two singles were launched from the album and the band also cut a track 'Out Of Focus' for a BLUE CHEER tribute album. A collectors' single featuring the BLUE CHEER song plus two exclusive studio recordings of 'Moon Dragon' and 'Zygocact' was delivered in June of 2000 and limited to just 200 copies. Live promotion included opening slots to both HAWKWIND and the ROLLINS BAND.

The critically acclaimed 'Sojourns Lucid Magic' arrived in April of 2002, preceded by the single 'Modulator', the latter including a cover version of HAWKWIND's 'You Shouldn't Do That'.

Singles/EPs:
Tee Pee / Ludd / First Last / Opotiki / Whispering In Secret Rooms, (1997) ('Dripping Silver Heat' EP)
Moon Dragon / Out Of Focus / Zygocact, High Beam Music (2000) (Limited edition 200 copies)
Starquake, Daredevil (2000) (Four way split EP with ROLLERBALL, RIDGE & COCKBURN)
Rockin Course / Starquake / First Last, High Beam Music HBMS03 (2001) ('Rockin Course' EP)
Modulator / Taipan Eclipse / You Shouldn't Do That, High Beam Music HBMS06 (2002)

THUMLOCK
Photo : Paul Jones

Albums:
LUNAR MOUNTAIN SUNRISE, High Beam
Music HBM001 (1999)
Starquake / Dusky Afternoon / The
Ornithopter / Jaspers Brush / Summercloud /
Lunar Mountain Sunrise
EMERALD LIQUID ODYSSEY, High Beam
Music HBM005 (2000)
Rockin Course / Ethereal / Blue Water /
Tramp The Charger / Doom Lord Dying /
Emerald Liquid Odyssey / Zygocact /
Railroad The Sunset / Planet Neptune
SOJOURNS LUCID MAGIC, High Beam
Music HBM023 (2002)
Intro / Modulator / Time Machine / Bat Eyes /
Neo Trantor / Hot Ostrich / Mt. Andronicas /
Mantas Praying / Zathium Biker /
Moondragon / Flash The Marble To The West

THUNDERSTORM (ITALY)
Line-Up: Fabio 'Thunder' Bellan (vocals /
guitar), Sandro (guitar), Omar (bass),
Massimo Tironi (drums)

Doom-laden Italian Metal band forged in the
early '90s by frontman Fabio 'Thunder' Bellan.
THUNDERSTORM issued two demos,
'Thunderstorm' and 1994's 'Force Of Evil'
promoting these release with support slots to
ANATHEMA. 'Force Of Evil' would comprise
three studio recordings plus six live cuts
including a rendition of BLACK SABBATH's

'Symptom Of The Universe'. The
THUNDERSTORM membership for this
release would be credited to Bellan on
"Thunder voice and lightning riffs", bassist
Andrea Salvetti "The bottom end" and
drummer Marco Riva "Barbaric cannons of
destruction".
However, in 1998 Bellan folded the band and
launched SAD SYMPHONY in alliance with
drummer Massimo Tironi for an eponymous
cassette demo. As SAD SYMPHONY Bellan
and Torini would be joined by bassist Nicola
and keyboard player ("The electric wall") Ivan
'The Phantom' Fantoni.
This new unit would re-enlist Omar and re-title
itself THUNDERSTORM, scoring a deal with
the Northwinds label. Second guitarist Sandro
Mazzoleni would augment the line-up during
November 2000.
Tironi would decamp in January of 2002 to be
temporarily replaced for live work by Gabriele,
actually Tironi's drum tutor. An October 2002
album, originally entitled 'Glory And
Sadness', would emerge as 'Witchunter
Tales'. First editions would include an
exclusive bonus track, a cover of «BLACK
SABBATH's 'Electric Funeral'. Session drums
on the album would be laid down by
DRAKKAR's Christian Fiorani.

Albums:
SAD SYMPHONY, Northwinds (2001)
Ascension / Dark Knight / Time / The Rite /

THUNDERSTORM

Sphere Of Mine / Vision Of Death / The
Prophecy / Sad Symphony / Faded Memory
WITCHUNTER TALES, (2002)

THYESTEAN FEAST (FINLAND)
Line-Up: M. Häkkinen (vocals), J. Savimäki
(guitar), M. Saarinen (guitar), M. Saikkonen
(bass), Matti Pirttimäki (keyboards),
J. Raatikainen (drums)

Dark, Gothic fuelled symphonic Metal.
THYESTEAN FEAST's first step into the
commercial arena was with the 1999 demo
'Ophion's Messiah'. Unhappy with the
recording quality of this effort a further
session followed entitled 'The Fall Of
Astraea'. Keyboard player Matti Pirttimäki was
then inducted. Following the recording of the
'Cycles Of Worldburn' album drummer Toni
Sotikoff was replaced by J.Raatikainen.

Albums:
CYCLES OF WORLDBURN, Trisol (2001)
Cindemonium / White Widow / Order Of The
Elder Serpent / Oblivions Bliss / The Fall Of
Astraea / Unio Mystica / Cycles Of
Worldburn / Prophecy Of The Last Days /
Chimera Curse / Treason

THY SERPENT (FINLAND)
Line-Up: Luopio (vocals / bass / keyboards),
Azhemin (vocals / keyboards), Sami Tenetz
(guitar), Agathon Frosteus (drums)

A Doom Death Metal band, THY SERPENT
formed in 1992 as guitarist Sami Tenetz
began recording rehearsal tapes followed by
more professional sounding demos, including
1994's 'Frozen Memory'.
With interest from Spinefarm Records Tenetz

opted to recruit band members to a project he
had worked on single handedly up to that
point. After a number of changes a stable
group of musicians were found that enabled
recording of 1996's 'Forest Of Witchery'
meisterwerk to be commenced.
Oddly, Spinefarm has gone on record to state
that THY SERPENT will never play live.
Nevertheless, the 1998 album saw the
inclusion of CHILDREN OF BODOM guitarist
Alexi Laiho into the ranks.
Drummer Agathon Frosteus also operates
with GLOOMY GRIM, NOMICON,
BARATHRUM and SOULGRIND. Luopio
would session for SOULGRIND's 1998 record
'Whitsongs' whilst keyboard player Azhemin
would contribute to the 1999 SOULGRIND
album 'Kalma'. Members of the band involved
themselves with BARATHRUM for the 2000
side project act SHAPE OF DESPAIR issuing
the 'Shades of...' album.
THY SERPENT man Tomi Ullgren also
performs as guitarist with RAPTURE.

Singles/EPs:
Death EP, Spinefarm (2000)

Albums:
FOREST OF WITCHERY, Spinefarm SPI
36CD (1996)
Flowers Of Witchery Abloom / Of Darkness
And Light / Traveller Of Unknown Plains /
Only Dust Moves... / Like A Funeral Veil Of
Melancholy / Wine From Tears
LORDS OF TWILIGHT, Spinefarm (1997)
Prometheus Unbound / The Forest Of
Blåkulla / Ode To The Witches - Part IV / In
Blackened Dreams / As Mist Descends From
the Hills / Unknown / Epic Torment / In
Blackened Dreams / Ode To The Witches -
Part III
CHRISTCRUSHER, Nuclear Blast NB 327-2
(1998)
Chambers Of The Starwatchers / Curtain Of
Treachery / Thou Bade Nothingness / Go
Free The Wolves / Circles Of Pain /
Christcrusher / Crystalmoors / Calm Blinking
DEATH, Spinefarm SPI102CD (2000)
Deathbearer / Wounds Of Death / Sleep In
Oblivion / Parasites

TIAMAT (SWEDEN)
Line-Up: Johan Edlund (vocals / guitar),
Magnus Sahlgrem (guitar), Johnny Hagel
(bass), Lars Skold (drums)

Less tastefully known in their formative years
as TREBLINKA (during which time vocalist
Johan Edlund also pursued his side project
GENERAL SURGERY), the Swedish quartet
adopted the title of the Sumerian goddess of

chaos and mythical planet TIAMAT. The band has evolved from a derivative Speed Metal / Death act to a more substantial stance in offering aggression with adventurous Progressive variances.

As TREBLINKA the band consisted of vocalist/guitarist Johan "Hellslaughter" Hedlund, bassist Klas Wistedt, guitarist Stefan Lagergren and drummer Andreas Holmberg, but upon taking the TIAMAT moniker the Swedish group would be rocked with constant reshuffling of personnel.

TIAMAT toured Europe in 1991 with label mates UNLEASHED, although 1992's 'Astral Sleep' album saw both Lagergren and Holmberg depart for EXPULSION and the record was recorded by vocalist/guitarist Johan Edlund, guitarist Thomas Petersson, bassist Jörgen Thulberg and drummer Niklas Ekstrand.

The band's 1993 line-up comprised Edlund, keyboard player Kenneth Roos and drummer Ekstrand. Live gigs were performed with Edlund, Roos and guitarist Thomas Petersson.

Musical differences saw TIAMAT split following a 1993 tour of Europe to promote the 'Clouds' album with UNLEASHED and MORGOTH. Petersen and Roos departed, leaving Johan Edlund to carry on with a new line up that included ex-SORCEROR bassist Johnny Hagel.

The 'Sleeping Beauty - Live In Israel' was recorded in Tel Aviv in June 1993. Later shows found the band touring alongside PARADISE LOST and VOODOO CULT.

1994's Space Rock charged 'Wildhoney' album found keyboards contributed by GRIP INC. guitarist Waldemar Sorychta and the single choice, 'Gaia', included a cover version of PINK FLOYD's 'When You're In' as one of the additional tracks. Predictably the line-up fluxed yet again with Ekstrand and Petersson discharging themselves and drummer Lars Skold welcomed into the fold.

The band toured as support to TYPE O NEGATIVE in Europe during 1994 and TIAMAT successfully headlined the 1995 Dynamo Festival in Holland and toured Britain as support to BLACK SABBATH. The same year a limited edition album, 'A Musical History Of Tiamat', would give fans further live material in the form of an extra CD.

1997's 'A Deeper Kind Of Slumber' heralded another shift in TIAMAT's musical landscape as Edlund ventured into distinctly ambitious

TIAMAT
Photo : Harald Hoffmann

Progressive Rock territory. Naturally the ebb and flow of band members continued unabated too with CEMETERY's Anders Iwers enrolling on guitar as in a straight swap Johnny Hagel joined CEMETERY. The ex-TIAMAT man would later be found ensconced in SUNDOWN before pursuing his own CINNAMON SPIRAL and LITHIUM projects. Meanwhile further internal manoeveres in TIAMAT saw Iwers shifting to bass when Petersson rejoined later. Iwers would also find extracurricular activities deputizing for Italian act LACUNA COIL after both their guitarists pulled out of an October 1997 tour at short notice.

TIAMAT returned with the 2000 Gothic infused 'Skeleton Skeletron' outing. Petersson bailed out yet again. The band, complete once more with a yo-yo-ing Petersson bouncing back, got to grips with a November European package tour alongside running mates ANATHEMA and TRISTANIA.

Johan Edlund struck out on a no-frills Gothic Rock n' Roll direction with the 2001 solo side project LUCYFIRE. Scoring a deal with SPV Records LUCYFIRE issued 'This Dollar Saved My Life at Whitehorse'. Edlund, billing himself as "Notorious PIG" for the LUCYFIRE endeavour also assembled a live band for an appearance at the 'Mera Luna' festival in Hildesheim, Germany. The same year leading German Gothic Rock act LOVE LIKE BLOOD would cover 'Whatever That Hurts' for their covers album 'Chronology Of A Love Affair'.

The 2002 TIAMAT album 'Judas Christ', which once again garnered the band chart success in Sweden, would see American variants adding the bonus cut 'Cold Last Supper' plus a video clip of 'Vote For Love'. European summer festival appearances throughout July and August for the band included showings at the German 'Zillo' and 'Summer Breeze' events as well as Spain's 'Rock Machina' festival, the Czech 'Brutal Assault' open air gig and the Viennese 'Metalfest'.

TIAMAT would embark upon touring in mainland Europe as part of a co-billing with PAIN. Regular guitarist Thomas Petersson would be unable to participate, being replaced temporarily by SOUTHFORK's Henrik Bergqvist. DARK TRANQUILLITY's Martin Brändström would handle the keyboard duties.

Singles/EPs:
A Winter Shadow / Ancient Entity, CBR CBR-S 125 (1990)
Gaia (Video Edit) / The Ar (Radio Cut) /When You're In / Whatever That Hurts (Video Edit) / The Ar (Ind. Mix) / Visionaire (Remixes Longform Version), Century Media 77089-2 (1994) ('Tour Sampler' EP)

Cold Seed / Only In My Tears It Lasts (The Cat mix) / Three Leary Biscuits, Century Media CD 77 167-2 (1997)
Brighter Than The Sun (Radio edit) / Sympathy For The Devil / Children Of The Underworld / Brighter Than The Sun, Century Media (1999)
For Her Pleasure / Lucy (Demon mix) / Brighter Than The Sun (Bullsrun mix) / As Long As You Are Mine (Lodmalm mix), Century Media (2001)

Albums:
SUMERIAN CRY, Metalcore CORE 9 (1991)
Intro: Sumerian Cry Part I / In The Shrines Of The Kingly Dead / The Malicious Paradise / Necrophagous Shadows / Apotheosis Of Morbidity / Nocturnal Funeral / Altar Flame / Evilized / Where The Serpents Ever Dwell / Outro / Sumerian Cry Part II / The Sign Of The Pentagram
THE ASTRAL SLEEP, Century Media CM7722 (1992)
Neo Aeon / Lady Temptress / Mountain Of Doom / Dead Boys Quire / Sumerian Cry (Part III) / Ancient Entity / The Southernmost Voyage / Angels Far Beyond / I Am The King (Of Dreams) / A Winter Shadow / The Seal
CLOUDS, Century Media 84 9736-2 (1993)
In A Dream / Clouds / Smell Of Incense / A Caress Of Stars / The Sleeping Beauty / Forever Burning Flames / The Scapegoat / Undressed
THE SLEEPING BEAUTY - LIVE IN ISRAEL, Century Media 77065 (1994)
In A Dream / Ancient Entity / The Sleeping Beauty / Mountains Of Doom / Angels Far Beyond
WILDHONEY, Century Media CD770802 (1994)
Wildhoney / Whatever That Hurts / The Ar / 25th Floor / Gaia / Visionaire / Kaleidoscope / Do You Dream Of Me? / Planets / A Pocket Size Sun
A MUSICAL HISTORY OF TIAMAT, Century Media (1995)
Where The Serpents Ever Dwell / The Sign Of The Pentagram / Ancient Entity / Dead Boys Choir / The Southernmost Voyage / A Winter Shadow / Smell Of Incense / A Caress Of Stars / The Sleeping Beauty / When You're In / Visionaire / Do You Dream Of Me? / A Pocket Sized Sun / Whatever That Hurts (Live) / The Ar (Live) / In A Dream (Live) / 25th Floor (Live) / Gaia (Live) / Visionaire (Live) / Kaleidoscope (Live) / Do You Dream Of Me? (Live) / The Sleeping Beauty (Live) / A Pocket Sized Sun (Live)
A DEEPER KIND OF SLUMBER, Century Media 77180-2 (1997) **39 SWEDEN**
Cold Seed / Teonanacatl / Trillion Zillion Centipedes / The Desolate One / Atlantis As

421

A Lover / Alteration X / Four Leary Biscuits / Only In My Tears It Lasts / The Whores Of Babylon / Kite/ Phantasma / Mount Marilyn / A Deeper Kind Of Slumber

SKELETON SKELETRON, Century Media (2000) **56 SWEDEN**

Church Of Tiamat / Brighter Than The Sun / Dust Is Our Fare / To Have And Have Not / For Her Pleasure / Diyala / Sympathy For The Devil / Best Friend Money Can Buy / As Long As You're Mine / Lucy

JUDAS CHRIST, Century Media 8080-2 (2002) **52 SWEDEN**

The Return Of The Son Of Nothing / So Much For Suicide / Vote For Love / The Truth's For Sale / Fireflower / Sumer By Night / Love Is As Good As Soma / Angel Holograms / Spine / I Am In Love With Myself / Heaven Of High / Too Far Gone

TODAY IS THE DAY (Nashville, TN, USA)
Line-Up: Steve Austin (vocals / guitar), Bill Kelliher (bass), Chris Reeser (keyboards), Mike Hyde (drums)

TODAY IS THE DAY's forte is apocalyptic notions woven into a distinctly Satanic tapestry of Black Metal based around the turning of the millennium. Musically the band adventurously span all genres of the extreme music field with each album testing the mettle of their fan base to the limit. The band actually evolved through the Hardcore / Indie scene but would successively introduce new elements of sound including Grindcore, sampling, Metal and Psychedelia. Whichever musical landscapes the band choose to make their own during any given time TODAY IS THE DAY never deliver anything less than the absolute extreme.

Frontman Steve Austin forged the debut line-up in alliance with drummer Brad Elrod. The pair relocated from Detroit to Nashville, Tennessee, took onboard bass player Mike Herrell in 1992 and laid down the self-financed 'Supernova' EP. The band made a return to Detroit to cut further demo tracks, which were distributed, as a limited release cassette. These tracks would prompt the offer of a label deal from the Amphetamine Reptile label in February of 1993.

Further recordings emerged on a shared EP billed as 'Clusterfuck' shared with GUZZARD and CHOKEBONE. These three acts subsequently toured nationwide putting in over 40 shows and into Europe for a further 45 gigs as a package bill. Returning to North American shores TODAY IS THE DAY hooked up with HELMET and SICK OF IT ALL for a further run of shows.

Promoting 1994's 'Willpower' TODAY IS THE DAY road work would prove extensive, March

1995 U.S. dates allied to UNSANE, LOVE 666 and STEELPOLE BATHTUB giving way to a further leg in union with NEUROSIS and GROTUS in May then headliners throughout October.

Headline European gigs in early 1996 led to the invaluable spin off as the band scored a session on Radio One's John Peel show. Touring through March and April saw the band on the road with NEUROSIS, BARKMARKET, 7 YEAR BITCH and LOGICAL NONSENSE. In May the band allied themselves with GLAZED BABY and ZENI GEVA before closing the year with a further rash of headline shows.

Austin revamped the band completely by drafting bassist Chris Reeser and drummer Mike Hyde for the groundbreaking 'Temple Of The Morning Star' opus in 1997. The pivotal track around which the 'Temple Of The Morning Star' album revolves is actually a real Satanic ritual conducted by the Denver Temple Of The Morning Star cult overladen with music. The band took this extravaganza on the road in North America as part of a strong underground billing sharing stages with HELMET, EYEHATEGOD, COALESCE and the MELVINS. These dates extended into the next year adding gigs with UNSANE, BLOODLET and CONVERGE. By 1998 the band headquarters had shifted base yet again, this time to Clinton, MA.

In 1999 the trio morphed once more with new faces being bassist Bill Kelliher and drummer Brann Dailor, both previously members of Rochester Metal band LETHARGY. This revised line-up would be debuted at the 'Milwaukee Metalfest' and 'New England Hardcore Metal' festival. The album 'In The Eyes Of God' granted the group a wider international appeal. There would be no respite in live activity that year, commencing with shows billed with SKINLAB and NAPALM DEATH. Later gigs, heralded as the 'Contamination' tour had SOILENT GREEN, EXHUMED, NASUM and MORGION as road partners. European shows then ensued, the band tagged with VOIVOD and NEUROSIS.

Austin produced the debut album from BANE 'It All Comes Down To This' adding guest vocals too. Other acts to benefit from Austin's production talents include CONVERGE and BURN THE PRIEST Former TODAY IS THE DAY members Keliher and Dailor founded MASTADON in 2001. TODAY IS THE DAY would join MOTÖRHEAD and MORBID ANGEL's summer American 2002 'Hammered' tour as guests. The band line-up for the September 2002 record 'Sadness Will Prevail' stood at Austin, guitarist Mike Morton, bass player Chris Debari, drummer Michael Kilpatric along with the AMBER ASYLUM string section of violinist Kris Force and cellist Jackie Gratz.

Singles/EPs:
Clustefuck EP, Amphetamine Reptile (1994) (Split EP with GUZZARD and CHOKEBONE)
Invincible / Breadwinner, Trash Art (2001) (Split EP with 16)

Albums:
SUPERNOVA, Amphetamine Reptile 22 (1993)
Black Dahlia / 6 Dementia Satyr / Silver Tongue / Blind Man At Mystic Lake / Adult World / The Begging / The Kick Inside / Goose Is Cooked / Timeless / Rise / The Guilt Barber / Self Portrait / Untitled
WILLPOWER, Amphetamine Reptile 33 (1994)
Willpower / My First Knife / Nothing To Lose / Golden Calf / Sidewinder / Many Happy Returns / Simple Touch / Promised Land / Amazing Grace
TODAY IS THE DAY, Amphetamine Reptile 46 (1996)
Hai Piranha / Marked / Bugs Death March / A Man Of Science / Realization / Black Iron Prison / Mountain People / Ripped Off / The Tragedy / She Is In Fear Of Death / I Love My Woman / Dot Matrix
TEMPLE OF THE MORNING STAR, Relapse RR 6964 (1997)
Temple Of The Morning Star / The Man Who Loves To Hurt Himself / Blindspot / High As The Sky / Miracle / Kill Yourself / Mankind / Pinnacle / Crutch / Root Of All Evil / Satan Is Alive / Rabid Lassie / Friend For Life / My Life With You / I See You / Hermaphrodite / Temple Of The Morning Star - Sabbath Bloody Sabbath
IN THE EYES OF GOD, Relapse 6424 (1999)
In The Eyes Of God / Going To Hell / Spotting A Unicorn / Possession / The Color Of Psychic Power / Mayari / Soldier Of Fortune / Bionic Cock / Argali / Afterlife / Himself / Daddy / Who Is The Black Angel? / Martial Law / False Reality / The Russian Child Porn Ballet / The Cold Harshness Of Being Wrong Throughout Your Entire Life / Honor / Worn Out / There Is No End
LIVE TILL YOU DIE, Relapse 6457 (2000)
The Color Of Psychic Power / Pinnacle / Feel Like Makin' Love / Temple Of The Morning Star / Wicked Game / Crutch / Ripped Off (Acoustic) / High As The Sky / In The Eyes Of God / Users / Tda / Blindspot / Why Don't We Do It In The Street / Afterlife / The Man Who Loved To Hurt Himself
TODAY IS THE DAY, This Dark Reign 1002 (2000) (Split album with METATRON)

The Descent / The Nailing / Tabula Rasa
SADNESS WILL PREVAIL, Relapse 6532 (2002)
Maggots And Riots / Criminal / Distortion Of Nature / Crooked / Butterflies / Unearthed / The Descent / Death Requiem / Christianized Magick / Voice Of Reason: Vicious Barker / Face After The Shot / The Ivory Of Self-Hate / The Nailing / Mistake / Invincible / Aurora / Sadness Will Prevail Myriad / Spaceship / Flowers Made Of Flesh / Your Life Is Over / Control The Media / Vivicide / Miasma / Times Of Pain / Breadwinner / Friend / Never Answer The Phone / I Live To See You Smile / Sadness Will Prevail Theme 1

TO ELYSIUM (HOLLAND)
Line-Up: Esther (vocals), Rein (vocals), Andries, Manny, Ray, Sjoerd Visch (drums)

Gothic Metal with a self-confessed "down to earth Death Metal" approach albeit employing soprano vocalist Esther and Death grunter Rein. TO ELYSIUM was founded in 2000 by erstwhile members of ALTAR, BLACK OUT and SERAPHIQUE, issuing the opening 'Collision Course' shortly after formation.
Rein was previously with SERAPHIQUE and MYSTIC CHARM. Manny worked with OUT and VAN EAST and drummer Sjoerd Visch has credits with both ALTAR and MONOLITH.

Albums:
DEAREST VILE, Cold Blood Industries CBI 0203 (2002)
Harangue / He Rears His Head In Laughter / In Collision / Bug / The Devil Herself / Dana In Darkness / Chaos-Sun / Seas Of Starvation / Meridians Fall / To A Flame / Doomcraft

TOMMERMEN (NORWAY)
Line-Up: Geir Berntsen (vocals), Rune Henden (guitar), Fredrik Nyegaard (bass), Jörgen Honerud (drums)

Exceptionally high class Doom. TOMMERMEN, whose lyrics are all in native Norwegian, delivered an absolute classic of the genre in the catchy 'Sortemenn', a song about lumberjacks!

Singles/EPs:
Sortemenn / Fordi / Englebarn / Fri / Utakt / Hvis / Ild & Regn, Edgerunner EDGE005CD (2002)

TOTENNACHT (AUSTRIA)
Line-Up: Hagen (vocals), Said El Mahdi (guitar / keyboards), Cornelius Dix

(keyboards)

TOTENNACHT is the Doom / Gothic Metal side project of WERWOLF vocalist Hagen complete with German lyrics and programmed drums.

Albums:
DER SCHWARZE PRINZ, Serpent Qui Danse SQD 01 (1996)
Der Schwarze Prinz / Vampir Des Herzens / Flammentor / Romantisches Sterben / Der Freudige Tote / Schrei / Tod Ist Abstrakt / Der Komödiant / Von Zwergen Und Riesen / Die Neue Erde

TOTIMOSHI (Oakland, CA, USA)
Line-Up: Antonio Aguilar (vocals / guitar), Meg Castellanos (bass), Don Voss (drums)

Californian, Latino rooted "Head Metal" conjured up in November of 1997 by frontman Antonio Aguilar and his Cuban born wife and bassist Meg Castellanos. Their opening 1998 demo would benefit from the media exposure afforded to it by the use of Billy Anderson as producer. Picking up strong local reviews, TOTISMOSHI cut a self-financed album released in December of the following year. Road work and a burgeoning reputation led to a deal with the Berserker label, Alex Newport of FUDGE TUNNEL and NAILBOMB infamy handling production on the 'Mysteriosi' album of 2002.
Touring to promote the 'Mysteriosi' release saw the introduction of drummer Don Voss and included October gigs with THEORY OF RUIN.
Ex-drummer Johan Zamora would find favour with GREENHOUSE EFFECT and MEN OF PORN.

Albums:
TOTISMOSHI, (1999)
Early Riser / Whole / Tourniquet / Boar / Drag / God Sent / Horace Brown / Circles / 396
MYSTERIOSI, Berserker (2002)
Float / Screwed / Cellophane / The Bleed / Dirt Farmer / Vitreol-a / Oblivion / Horselaugh

TRAIL OF TEARS (NORWAY)
Line-Up: Ronni Thorsen (vocals), Helena Iren Michaeisen (vocals), Runar Hansen (guitar), Terje Heiseldal (guitar), Kjell Rune Hagen (bass), Frank Roald Hagen (keyboards),

Founded as NATT in 1994 TRAIL OF TEARS are an ambitious Black Metal act employing both male and female lead vocals. The band was wrought with perpetual line-up challenges on the path to the debut album for Dutch label DSFA Records.
Original female singer Ales Vik exited in favour of Helena Irena Michaelsen upfront of the demo 'When Silence Cries'. Further changes saw drummer Vidar Uleberg on his way out in favour of Jonathon Perez and the augmentation of keyboards to the band courtesy of Frank Roald Hagen.
Following the demo release guitarist Michael Krumis decamped and in came Runar Hansen. Supporting the promotion of the 'Disclosure In Red' album TRAIL OF TEARS toured with guests GAIL OF GOD prior to further dates alongside TRISTANIA. November 1999 found TRAIL OF TEARS on the road with CALLENISH CIRCLE.
The recording of the second album 'Profoundemonium' witnessed the acrimonious split with Michaelsen as TRAIL OF TEARS handed over the position of lead female vocals to Cathrine Paulsen.
TRAIL OF TEARS vocalist Ronni Thorsen also forms part of SCARIOT, the band project assembled by IN THE WOODS drummer Anders Kobros and ex-SATYRICON guitarist Daniel Olaisen. Thorsen would also lend his talents to TRISTANIA's 'World Of Glass' album as well as to BLOODRED THRONE.
TRAIL OF TEARS' third album would be set to include a cover version of FAITH NO MORE's 'Caffeine'.

Albums:
DISCLOSURE IN RED, DSFA DSFA1018 (1998)
When Silence Cries / The Daughters Of Innocence / The Day We Drowned / Mournful Pigeon / Swallowed Tears / Illusion? / Enigma Of The Absolute / Words Of The Fly / Temptress / The Burden
PROFUONDEMONIUM, Napalm NPR 084 (2000)
Countdown To Ruin / Driven (Through The Ruins) / Fragile Emotional Disorder / Profoundemonium / Sign Of The Shameless / In Frustration's Preludium / In Frustration's Web / Released At Last / Image Of Hope / Disappointment's True Face / The Haunted

TRAINING FOR UTOPIA (CA, USA)
Line-Up: Maven (vocals), Don Clark (guitar), Steve (bass), Morley (drums)

An uninhibited Northern California Christian Hardcore rooted Metal band centred upon the Clark brothers Don, formerly with OFFSET, and Ryan. Confusingly Ryan Clark adopted the stage name Maven leading many to believe Maven and Ryan were two different people. TRAINING FOR UTOPIA initially weighed in with chaotic and discordant noise-fests. By 2000's 'Throwing A Wrench Into The American Music Machine' had streamlined their sound with obtuse lyrical matter, eerie minimalist riffing and effects-laden pulsing electronica drawing appreciation from the Sludgecore crowd. Oddly the Christian music sector turned its back on the album effectively stifling distribution.

In 2001 it appeared that TRAINING FOR UTOPIA were no more, the Clark siblings having relocated to Seattle. They created side venture THE AMERICAN SPECTATOR in alliance with the COALESCE duo of vocalist Sean Ingram and drummer James Dewees alongside ZAO's Jesse Smith also on drums.

Singles/EPs:
The Falling Cycle / Dead Signal / Pretty Picture Of Lies / Thoughtless Reminders, Solid State ('The Falling Cycle' EP)
Modus Operandi / Police John, Police Red, Solid State (1998) ('Training For Utopia' Split EP with ZAO)

Albums:
PLASTIC SOUL IMPALEMENT, Solid State (1998)
Plastic Soul Impalement / A Good Feeling / Brother Hezakiah / Two Hands / Pretty Picture Of Lies / Black Forest / One Zero One / Burning Match In Hand / Human Shield / Single Handed Attempt At Revolution / A Gift To A Dying Friend
THROWING A WRENCH INTO THE AMERICAN MUSIC MACHINE, Solid State (2000)
50,000 Screaming TFU Fans Can't Be Wrong / White Boy's Burden / The State Of Wyoming Is Worthless / Burt Reynolds Vs. Godzilla / Tennessee Midget / Everything, Including The Stars, Is Falling (Baby) / New York City Is Overrated / Dead Signal 2000 / The Art Of Killing A Copy Machine / Seeing Eye Fruit Bat

TRANSONIC SCIENCE (GERMANY)
Line-Up: Erguen Aktuerk (vocals), Markus Bongard (guitar), Gerald Kirsch (bass), Peter Begerow (drums)

Cologne, Grunge influenced Stoners TRANSONIC SCIENCE were founded in 1997, issuing a six track demo cassette the following year. The track 'Granada', from their self-funded 1999 album 'Leapardo Lombardo', would prove a huge download hit on Napster.

Albums:
LEAPARDO LOMBARDO, (1999)

Leopardo Lombardo / Melody / Xenon / Post War Grizzly / Granada / Acrobat / Electric / Mephisto's Kitchen
SUNSHINE BABY HOME, (2000)
Solar Love / Yeah, She Said / Brand New Swallow Machine / Nidation / Sunshine Baby Home
DEVILLAC VS. TRANSONIC SCIENCE, Daredevil DD010 (2001) (Split album with DEVILLAC)
Blame The Mono / Yeah She Said / Solar Love / Sunshine Baby Home / Nidation / Brand New Swallow Machine

TRANSPORT LEAGUE (SWEDEN)
Line-Up: Tony Jelencovich (vocals / guitars / keyboards), Johan Reiven (bass), Lars Häglund (drums)

TRANSPORT LEAGUE was created by B-THONG vocalist Tony Jelencovich as a side project during 1994. However, by the time the 'Stallion Showcase' album found a release two years later the singer had split from his main act. TRANSPORT LEAGUE toured Scandinavia during late 1996 with a new line-up of Jelencovich, guitarist Peter Hunyadi, bassist Ken Sandin and drummer Mattias Starander. This line-up recorded the 1997 album 'Superevil'.

Bassist Johan Reiven became drummer for Rap Metal act LOK.

During November of 2001 both Peter Hunyadi and Patrik J. Sten made their exit. TRANSPORT LEAGUE regrouped around a revised line-up of Jelencovich, guitarist Adam M, DIA PSALMA bass player Stitch and MERCILESS drummer Stipe. The band would self-finance the 2002 release 'Grand Amputation' through their own Hoffa Communications label.

Albums:
STALLION SHOWCASE, Mascot M 7016-2 (1996)
Cosmical Satanical / Bolivian Dog / Hell n' Back / Blood Sucking Super Bitch / Amp-Shock / Heading Down / Want's You / Soul / Molotov / Jupiter / Ride Baby
SUPEREVIL, Mascot M 7027-2 (1997)
Lost In The Desert Of Habib / Proud Cuts / Jesus Came / Magnetric Star / High Riding Witch / Rotten Soil / Filthy Old Liars / Led Prison / Mantha / Bloodblinder / Superevil
SATANIC PANIC, Pavement (2000)
Hell Predicted / Plague Ship / Neck Draft / Shut To Drown / Man Sized Drain / Tar / Lord Of A Thousand / Psycho Connected / Un-Man Conquer / Last / Creep Provider
GRAND AMPUTATION, MNW (2002)

TRICKY WOO (CANADA)
Line-Up: Andrew Dickson (vocals / guitar),
Eric LaRock (bass), Phil Burns (keyboards),
Pat Conan (drums)

Mellow Montreal Stoner. Initially very much in
the '60s three chord Garage Rock mould of
the 1997 debut 'Rock n' Roll Music Part One'
would by the time of the laid back 'Sometimes
I Cry' album, produced by erstwhile CHANGE
OF HEART man Ian Blurton. A split from
original guitarist Adrian Popovitch resulted in
the subsequent induction of keyboard player
Phil Burns and TRICKY WOO toned down
their mood considerably.
The band was created in 1995, founder
member and drummer Sasha Roiz laying
down his sticks after second album 'The
Enemy Is Real' to become the band's
manager, with Pat Conan taking over the
percussive role. Conan would also hold down
drum duties in TINKER and SACKVILLE. For
the 2001 'Les Sables Magiques' record, which
witnessed diversions into '70s jam style
Boogie, TRICKY WOO had Ryan Marshall on
bass guitar. Touring across North America in
May had the band packaged with SIXTY
WATT SHAMAN and NASHVILLE PUSSY.
TRICKY WOO announced they were to fold in
March of 2002 but would then simply evolve
into SOFT CANYON. In June of that year
Conan teamed up with THE CARNATIONS.

Singles/EPs:
Magibus / Fool For Your Loving / Love
Narcosis / High On A Mountain, Magwheels
(2001) ('Tricky Woo' 10" EP)

Singles/EPs:
The Claw / Gas City / Hot Blood / Baby
Wants A Suicide, Magwheels (1996)
Ten Tons / Rock And Roll Versus The World
/ Lust For You / Pistol Generation, Grenadine
(1998)
Trouble / Rock n' Roll Gypsy, Estrus (2002)

Albums:
ROCK N' ROLL MUSIC PART ONE, SSG
(1997)
Hot Kitty / The Claw / Pussy Power / Get
Around / Crime / I Am The Leper / Tough
Shakes / Aladinspain / Kentucky Derby /
Wholesale / Duane Eddy / 16/17
THE ENEMY IS REAL, Sonic Unyon (1998)
On Thunder's Throne / Let Us Sing / Teach
Us American / Easy / Fever / Region 2 /
Nothin' But A Man / Pink Mountains / Blue
Flames / Ten Tons / Riot Time / Pleasure
Unit / I Own You / Lead Wings
SOMETIMES I CRY, Sonic Unyon (1999)
Altamont Raven / Fly The Orient / Born Due

/ Allright / Let The Goodtimes Roll / I Need
Love / Sad Eyed Woman / Hypnotic
Persuasion / Electric Orchard / Fell From A
Cloud / Tails Of A Sunray / Lady Of The
Wind
LES SABLES MAGIQUES, Tee Pee (2001)
Ring Sweet Mercy / 6 Cats And A Podium /
Lonesome Road / Lil-lay Bank Blues / Beau
Soleil / Don't Get The Music Worried / Szabo
Gabo / Les Sables Magiques / Liberty Drawl
/ Strange Meat / Winter

TRISTANIA (NORWAY)
Line-Up: Vibeke Stene (vocals), Morton
Veland (vocals / guitar), Anders H. Hidle
(guitar), Rune Osterhus (bass), Einar Moen
(keyboards), Kenneth Olsson (drums)

A much vaunted female fronted Darkwave
Gothic project TRISTANIA was created in late
1996. Keyboard player Einar Moen and
guitarist Morten Veland were both previously
with UZI SUICIDE. Debuting with the 'Widow's
Weeds' album in 1998 for the Austrian
Napalm label the band made a sizable
impression, their song-based approach
striking a positive chord with the Rock media.
Østen Bergøy of MORENDOES would lend
backing vocals to this and subsequent
recordings. Another significant session
contributor would be violinist Pete Johansen.
The band made a significant impact with their
2000 album 'World Of Glass'. Guest session
vocals for this recording came courtesy of
Ronny Thorsen of TRAIL OF TEARS and
SCARIOT. However, Veland subsequently left
the band during May of the same year. His
place would be taken by two vocalists, Kjetil
Ingebrethsen and Østen Bergøy. In this
incarnation TRISTANIA would tour Brazil and
Chile during January 2002.
Vibeke Stene created side project GREEN
CARNATION with EMPEROR's Tchort and
Mitgliedern from IN THE WOODS. Veland
would found SIRENIA for a 2002 debut
album. TRISTANIA undertook headline gigs in
Colombia and Mexico during August.

Singles/EPs:
Sirene / Midwintertears / Pale Enchantress /
Cease To Exist, Napalm NRR036 (1997)
('Tristania' EP)

Albums:
WIDOW'S WEEDS, Napalm NPR041 (1998)
Preludium / Evenfall / Pale Enchantress /
December Elegy / Midwintertears / Angellore
/ My Lost Lenore / Wasteland Caress /
Postludium
BEYOND THE VEIL, Holy (1999)
Beyond The Veil / Aphelion / A Sequel Of

Decay / Opus Relinque / Lethean River /
...Of Ruins And A Red Nightfall /
Simbelmyna / Angina / Heretique / Dementia
WORLD OF GLASS, (2001)
The Shining Path / Wormwood / Tender Trip
On Earth / Lost / Deadlocked / Selling Out /
Hatred Grows / World Of Glass / Crushed
Dreams / The Modern End

TRISTITIA (SWEDEN)
Line-Up: Thomas Karlsson (vocals), Luis
Beethoven Galvez (guitar / bass /
keyboards), Bruno Nilsson (drums)

Labeled as "Extreme dark Doom" TRISTITIA
evolved from a meeting in August 1992
between the half Chilean / half Swedish
guitarist ("All true axes of darkness, hatred
and madness") Luis Beethoven Galvez and
vocalist ("Chants of death") Thomas Karlsson.
Galvez was a former member of PAGAN
RITES along with Karlsson, although the
latter had also worked with AUTOPSY
TORMENT.
TRISITIA's first four track demo in 1993
featured 'Winds Of Sacrifice', 'Dancing Souls',
'Burn The Witch' and 'The Other Side'.
A second demo followed in 1994, once more
boasting four tracks (in this instance
'Reminiscences Of The Mourner', 'Envy The
Dead', 'Ashes Of The Witch' and 'Mark My
Words'. It was only at this point that the band
added drummer Bruno Nilsson and signed
with French label Holy Records.
Nilsson was not in the group for long as he
was to depart in favour of ex-PAGAN RITES
drummer Adrian Letelier.

Albums:
ONE WITH DARKNESS, Holy HOLY11CD
(1995)
Sorrow / Kiss The Cross / One With
Darkness / Winds Of Sacrifice / Burn The
Witch / Hymn Of Lunacy / Ashes Of The
Witch / Dancing Souls / Adagio 1809 /
Reminiscences Of The Mourner / Dance Of
The Selenites
CRUCIDICTION, Holy HOLY 21 CD (1996)
Ego Sum Resurrectio / Christianic
Indulgence / Crudiction / Wintergrief / Envy
The Dead / Lioness' Roar / Mark My Words /
Gardenia / Final Lament
THE LAST GRIEF, Holy (2000)
Once Upon A Dawn... / In The Light Of The
Moon / Slaughtery / Evolic / Golden
Goddess Of Fire / Tears And Tequila /
Angelwitch's Palace / Memory's Garden /
Instrumental Hollowcoast / MediEvil / Under
The Cross / Darknia: The Last Grief

TROUBLE (Chicago, IL, USA)
Line-Up: Eric Wagner (vocals), Rick Wartell
(guitar), Bruce Franklin (guitar), Sean
McAllister (bass), Jeff Olson (drums)

A Metal band heavily embroiled in '70s retro
Doom, sounding uncannily like Birmingham's
finest, TROUBLE debuted with a self-titled
album in 1984 on the Enigma label. Dating
back to their formation in Chicago during
1979 TROUBLE remained a cult act
throughout the greater portion of their career
and it is only with the Stoner Rock trend of the
mid '90s their legacy has been truly
recognized.
Drummer Jeff Olson quit in late 1985 entering
into the church.
1987's 'Run To The Light' saw TROUBLE with
a fresh rhythm section of bassist Ron Holzner
and drummer Dennis Lesh.
TROUBLE signed with Rick Rubin's Def
American label for the eponymous album
released in early 1990. At this point the band
had settled on a line-up comprising Eric
Wagner, Rick Wartell, Holzner and ex-
ZOETROPE drummer Barry Stern for the
eponymous 1990 album.
Fellow American Thrashers TOURNIQUET
covered the track 'The Tempter' on their 1991
album 'Psycho Surgery'. Lesh meantime had
teamed up with fellow Chicago Metal band
STYGIAN fronted by ex-WRATH singer Gary
Golwitzer for two EPs and an album.
Following 1992's 'Manic Frustration' Olsen
was welcomed back to the fold for their
swansong effort 'Plastic Green Head'. Stern
teamed up with British Doomsters
CATHEDRAL for live work in 1994. Guitarist
Rick Wartell founded WET ANIMAL. Wagner
forged the oddly titled LID for a 1997 album
with ANATHEMA's guitarist Daniel Cavanagh.
Later shows saw TROUBLE fronted by former
EXHORDER vocalist Kyle Thomas. The band
also operated for a short period with
CROWBAR drummer Craig Nunebacher
before Stern's return.
TROUBLE eventually added former
CATHEDRAL drummer Dave Hornyak as
replacement for Stern.
Olsen and Franklin united with KINGS X
frontman Doug Pinnick to create
SUPERSHINE in 1999. Lesh joined
CHASTAIN and also featured in the offshoot
project band SOUTHERN GENTLEMEN.
Meantime Holzer forged MUSTACHE then
DEBRIS INC., the latter act in union with
SAINT VITUS frontman Dave Chandler. The
band enrolled SKULLSICK NATION
frontwoman Karyn Crisis and guitarist Afzaal
Nasiruddeen for recording of a cover version
of X's 'Nausea'. Frontwoman Karyn Crisis
and guitarist Afzaal Nasiruddeen on a cover

of X's "Nausea" DEBRIS INC. would later see the addition of former TROUBLE and ZOETROPE drummer Barry Stern.

Wagner would contribute guest vocals to FOO FIGHTERS man Dave Grohl's Metal elite PROBOT project album of 2001. Meantime TROUBLE bassist Ron Holzner would lay down session bass tracks for NOVEMBER'S DOOM's 2001 album. By August of 2002 Holzner had teamed up with PLACE OF SKULLS, the high profile Doom act led by erstwhile PENTAGRAM guitarist Victor Griffin and SAINT VITUS and THE OBSESSED veteran Scott Weinrich.

Singles/EPs:
Assassin / Tales Of Brave Ulysses, Metal Blade (1984)

Albums:
TROUBLE, Metal Blade 47543 (1984)
The Tempter / Assassin / Victim Of The Incense / Revelation / Bastards Will Pay / The Fall Of Lucifer / Endtime / Psalm 9
THE SKULL, Metal Blade 47544 (1985)
Pray For The Dead / Fear No Evil / The Wish / The Truth Is, What Is / Wickedness Of Man / Gideon / The Skull
RUN TO THE LIGHT, Metal Blade CDZORRO74 (1987)
The Misery Shows / Thinking Of The Past / On Borrowed Time / Run To The Light / Peace Of Mind / Born In A Prison / Tuesday's Child / The Beginning
TROUBLE, American Recordings 8424212 (1990)
At The End Of The Daze / Wolf / Psychotic Reaction / Sinner's Fame / Misery Shows (Act III) / Rip / Black Shapes Of Doom / Heaven On My Mind / END / All Is Forgiven
MANIC FRUSTRATION, American Recordings 512 556-2 (1992)
Touch The Sky / 'Scuse Me / Sleeper / Fear / Rain / Tragedy Man / Memory's Garden / Plastic Green Card/ Hello Strawberry Skies / Mr. White / Breathe
PLASTIC GREEN HEAD, Bulletproof CDVEST 45 (1995)
Plastic Green Head / The Eye / Flowers / Porpoise Song / Opium Eater / Hear The Earth / Another Day / Requiem / Long Shadows Fall / Below Me / Tomorrow Never Knows

TUMMLER (Champaign, IL, USA)
Line-Up: Brad Buldak (vocals), Jay Vance, Steve Hill (bass), Jason Casanova

Sci-Fi orientated Doom named after the 'Gummo' movie character. This Illinois quartet titled their debut album 'Queen To Bishop IV'

after a line that features in both cult Science Fiction movies 'Bladerunner' and '2001: A Space Odyssey'. The group, which had started life as a jam band, debuted with a three track demo during 1999 comprising 'Armadillo', 'The Burning Of West Memphis' and 'Lost Sense Of The Cosmic'.

The various members of TUMMLER gained experience in a variety of acts, Jason Casanova with MARY CELESTE, bassist Steve 'Dr.' Hill with HAZZARD COUNTY MOLOKO RUNNERS, Jay Vance with CASTOR issuing two albums and Brad Buldak with MORGUE, featuring on their 1991 record.

TUMMLER, splitting with bassist Steve Hill, would record their first album for the Small Stone Recordings label, November 2002's 'Early Man', with producer Matt Talbott.

Albums:
QUEEN TO BISHOP IV, Man's Ruin (2000)
Intro / Armadillo / Soul Driver / Lifelike / Nitrous Girl / Blatant Disregard For The Untamed Void
EARLY MAN, Small Stone Recordings (2002)
Shooting Blanks / Arlo / Freightliner / Planet Moai / Here's To Your Destruction / Lost Sense Of The Cosmic

TWIN EARTH (SWEDEN)
Line-Up: Oscar Björklund (vocals / guitar), John Sjölin (guitar), Kristoffer Gottberg (bass), Daniel Halén (drums)

Stoners TWIN EARTH can track their lineage back to as far as junior school! The ambitious pre-teen formation of frontman Oscar Björklund, guitarist Makkan and drummer Dala first convened in 1991 as FORCE. Optimistically FORCE issued a demo the following year which included a cover of BLACK SABBATH's seminal 'Paranoid'.

The band evolved into the Swedish language Stoner outfit SOLITUDE. Under this new guise the band released an eponymous demo in 1994 and the 'Vili I Frid' effort in 1995. SOLITUDE would also donate a track to the compilation album 'At Last: Rockfocus Vol. I'. However, Makkan would depart in late 1995 to join SNAKES OF CHRIST (later VOYAGER) and John Sjölin took his place.

Another name switch found SOLITUDE morphing into TWIN EARTH and to commemorate a 1996 demo session 'Space Jam', with Sjölin handling bass, was issued. The year would prove to be cataclysmic for drummer Dala though as he was hospitalized for six months with a serious paralyzing illness. His road to recovery was slow but the sticksman vowed to carry on although he had lost the grip in his right hand. Dala had special drumsticks and gloves designed.

Four stringer Jocke Nauclér, ex-guitarist with DAMNED RIVER, would be pulled in for a series of gigs in 1997 culminating in the recording of a promotional cassette 'The Sunride Sessions'. Plans were laid for further recordings in late 1998 and, with Dala undergoing surgery, VOYAGER's Andreas Ohlson stepped into the breech for the 'Eroticon VI' tapes.

Ultimately Dala's valiant efforts were not enough and reluctantly in December of 1999 the drummer laid down his sticks. TWIN EARTH supplanted their ailing colleague with Daniel Halén, known from NOCTA and Black Metal outfit CRAFT. This new incarnation issued the 'Dig A Hole' demo which secured an album deal with Italian label Beard Of Stars for the debut release 'Black Stars In A Silvery Sky' in October 2000. The same year TWIN EARTH would feature on the Mexican compilation 'Sacred Groove' from Monsruo De Gila Records.

Nauclér would decamp to be replaced by Kristoffer Gottberg.

Albums:
BLACK STARS IN A SILVERY SKY, Beard Of Stars (2000)
Dig A Hole / Get My Soul Out / The End Of The Road / Blues / Close But Far Away / Handout / Obelix / Eroticon VI / Ask For Water

TYPE O NEGATIVE (Brooklyn, NY, USA)
Line-Up: Pete Steele (vocals / bass), Kenny Hickey (guitar), Josh Silver (keyboards), Johnny Kelly (drums)

Formed by the towering figure of ex-CARNIVORE frontman Pete Steele, TYPE O NEGATIVE premiered as a quartet in 1988. The band's Gothic influences and nihilistic experimental bent afforded onto their distinct brand of Metal has enabled TYPE O NEGATIVE to find their own unique placing in the Rock field. Steele is also unafraid to address deliberately provocative issues and record cover artwork featured a blurred close up of the vocalist's anus for 1992's 'Origin Of The Faeces'. This album also found the band taking self-degradation to the limits with live audience cat calls of 'You suck' mixed in. The band members photographs are tellingly obscured by excrement.

'Bloody Kisses' tamed the act as they prepared to muscle in on the mainstream. The album's commercial success prompting the re-release of its predecessor in less offensive packaging.

Steele earnt himself a following from both female and gay male fans when appearing in the January 1996 issue of 'Playgirl' magazine. This was followed by the release of the group's new studio album 'October Rust' soon afterwards.

TYPE O NEGATIVE were inactive during late 1997 Kelly kept his hand in stepping into the breach for PIST. ON drummer Jeff McManus. His colleague having suffered a serious respiratory illness in the midst of PIST. ON's American tour.

In 1998 Steele shared lead vocals on the track 'Finale' with Kat Bjelland of BABES IN TOYLAND as part of the Sci-Fi comic-breed series soundtrack album 'Songs Of The Witchblade'. Touring in February 2000 saw COAL CHAMBER as support.

The 2000 drolly titled compilation 'The Least Worst Of' included three new songs in 'It's Never Enough', 'Stay Out Of My dreams' and '12 Black Rainbows'.

During 2001 leading German Gothic Rock act LOVE LIKE BLOOD would cover 'Black No. 1' for their covers album 'Chronology Of A Love Affair'. TYPE O NEGATIVE themselves re-emerged in 2002 touting a version of the old DEEP PURPLE warhorse 'Highway Star' as their contribution to the NASCAR 'Crank It Up' album. Steele's presence would also be felt on the 2002 'Fight' opus of leading German Metal queen DORO, the TYPE O NEGATIVE frontman duetting with Ms. Pesch on the track 'Descent'.

Singles/EPs:
Christian Woman / Christian Woman (Remix) / Suspended In Dusk, Roadrunner RR 2378-3 (1994)
My Girlfriend's Girlfriend / Black Sabbath (From The Satanic Perspective) / Blood And Fire (Remix), Roadrunner (1996)
Love You To Death (Radio) / Summer Breeze (Rejected Radio) / Love You To Death, Roadrunner (1996) (Mail order only EP)
Cinnamon Girl (Depressed Mode mix) / Cinnamon Girl (US Radio mix) / Cinnamon Girl (Extended mix), Roadrunner RR 2270-3 (1997)
Everything Dies, Roadrunner (1999)

Albums:
SLOW, DEEP, HARD, Roadracer RO 9313-2 (1991)
Unsuccessfully Coping With The Natural Beauty Of Infidelity / Der Untermensch / Xero Tolerance / Prelude To agony / Glass Walls Of Limbo (Dance mix) / The Misinterpretation Of Silence And It's Disastrous Consequences / Gravitational Constant: G = 6.67 x 10-8 cm 3 gm sec. 2

ORIGIN OF THE FAECES, Roadrunner RR
9006-2 (1992)
I Know You're Fucking Someone Else / Are
You Afraid / Gravity / Pain / Kill You Tonight /
Hey Pete / Kill You Tonight (Reprise) /
Paranoid
BLOODY KISSES, Roadrunner RR 9100-2
(1993)
Machine Screw / Christian Woman / Black
No. 1 (Little Miss Scare-All) / Fay Wray
Come Out To Play / Kill All The White People
/ Summer Breeze / Set Me On Fire / Dark
Side Of The Womb / We Hate Everything /
Bloody Kisses (A Death In The Family) /
3.0.1.F. / Too Late: Frozen / Blood And Fire /
Can't Lose You
OCTOBER RUST, Roadrunner RR 8874-2
(1996) **8 AUSTRIA, 26 UK, 42 USA**
Bad Ground / Love You To Death / Be My
Druidess / Green Man / Red Water
(Christmas Mourning) / My Girlfriend's
Girlfriend / Die With Me / Burnt Flowers
Fallen / In Praise Of Bacchus / Cinnamon
Girl / The Glorious Liberation Of The
People's Technocratic Republic Of Vinnland
By The Combined Forces Of The United
Territories Of Europa / Wolf Moon (Including
Zoanthrobe Paranoia) / Haunted / ?
WORLD COMING DOWN, Roadrunner
(1999) **17 SWEDEN, 49 UK**
Skip It / White Slavery / Sinus / Everyone I
Love Is Dead / Who Will Save The Sane? /
Liver / World Coming Down / Creepy Green
Light / Everything Dies / Lung / Pyretta Blaze
/ All Hallows Eve / Day Tripper
THE LEAST WORST OF, Roadrunner
(2000) **50 GERMANY**
The Misinterpretation Of Silence And Its
Disastrous Consequences (Wombs And
Tombs mix) / Everyone I Love Is Dead /
Black No. 1 / It's Never Enough / Love You To
Death / Black Sabbath (From The Satanic
Perspective) / Christian Woman / 12 Black
Rainbows / My Girlfriend's Girlfriend
(Cheese Organ mix) / Hey Pete (Pete's Ego
Trip version) / Everything Dies / Cinnamon
Girl (Depressed Mode mix) / Unsuccessfully
Coping With The Natural Beauty Of Infidelity
/ Stay Out Of My Dreams

U

UFOMAMMUT (ITALY)
Line-Up: Urlo (vocals / bass),
Poia (guitar), Alien (keyboards),
Vita (drums)

A Psych 'Space-Doom' outfit out of Tortona. UFOMAMMUT cite their "four clergymen of the spacemonster" as vocalist / bassist Urlo, guitarist Poia, Korg player Alien and drummer Vita. The group debuted with the 1998 demo 'Malleus Malleficarum' followed by 1999's 'Satan' session.
UFO MAMMUT would also record their version of 'Peace Of Mind' for the BLUE CHEER tribute 'Blue Explosion' issued by the Black Widow label.

Albums:
GODLIKE SNAKE, Beard Of Stars (2000)
UFO pt. 1 / Satan / Oscillator / Snake / Zerosette / Smoke / Nowhere / Superjunkhead / Hozomeen (+ Mammut) / Where? (Video)

ULTRA (USA)
Line-Up: Don Evans (vocals), Galen Niles (guitar), Larry McGuffin (guitar), Scott Stevens (bass), Tom Schleuning (drums)

A Texan twin guitar act operational during the '70s. With the revival of Southern style Metal prompted by the late '90s Stoner movement many long lost independently released gems started to resurface, one of them being the eponymous ULTRA album resurrected by Monster Records.
ULTRA was born out of the act HOMER, a unit comprising vocalist / drummer Don Evans, guitarists Galen Niles, a former member of '60s outfit THE OUTCASTS, and Van Wilks with bassist Chet Himes. HOMER was to falter when VAN WILKS struck out on a solo career, issuing the 'Bombay Tears' album for major label Mercury, and Chet Himes opted to pursue a career on the other side of the recording console reaping subsequent credits on albums by artists such as TED NUGENT.
The duo of Evans and Niles hooked up with guitarist Larry McGuffin, bass player Scott Stevens and drummer Tom Schleuning to found a fresh act ULTRA. McGuffin had been a student of Niles post the HOMER period and had persuaded his mentor to kickstart another band.
The band toured hard but would fold in 1978, the tracks that make up the 2000 release having been recorded in 1976-77.

Albums:

ULTRA, Monster (2000)
Mutants / Android / Battery / Ten Years Since / Lamp Black, White Fight / Windjammer / Diggin' Deep / Circe / Seasons Pass / City On Ice / The Desert / Souled There With Care / Man On The Street / Get Away / Compass / Hot n' Cold

UMBRA ET IMAGO (GERMANY)
Line-Up: Mozart (vocals), Alex Perin (guitar), Lutz Demmler (bass), Nail (keyboards)

A Gothic Darkwave rock act formed in 1991, UMBRA ET IMAGO were the first German band to combine a live S&M show with their onstage act!
The band toured Germany during late 1997 supported by ENDLESS, on a trek dubbed the 'No God And No Love' tour.

Singles/EPs:
Kleine Schwester / Sex Statt Krieg / Kleine Schwester (Schwesterlein Mix) / Sex Statt Krieg (Love And Peace Mix) / Devotion, Spirit Production SON 0155-2 (1996) ('Sex Statt Krieg' EP)

Albums:
TRUÄUME, SEX UND TOD, Spirit Production (1992)
Never / Her Sleep / Rider In The Dain / Desiderium / Falling / Lost Dream / Erotica / Vision
INFANTILE SPIELE, Spirit Production (1993)
Away / Hash Dreams / Gothic Erotic / Parent Song / Endorphin / Vampir Song / Getühle Zerplatzt
REMEMBER DITO, Spirit Production (1994)
Remember Dito / Actions Speak Louder Than Words / Erotica / Session
GEDANKEN EINES VAMPIRS, Spirit Production DW 075-2 (1995)
Intro / Viva Lesbian / Genealogie Der Moral / Der Kliene Tod / Gedanken Eines Vampirs / Wake Up / Devotion / Sail Away / Nächste Ausfahrt / Wolfsfrau / Mit Dir (Swinging Session)
MYSTICA SEXUALIS, Spirit Production DW 0195-2 (1996)
Requiem Mit Dem Ich Meine Mitmenschen Um Verzeihung Bitten Möchte / Hörst Du Mein Rufen / Es War Einmal Eine 'O' / You Are Poison For Me / Kleine Schwester / Der Trieb / Hass / Black Waves/ Madeira / Wintertage
THE HARD YEARS - LIVE, Oblivion CD 085-61832 SPV (1997)
Intro / Sex Statt Krieg / Es War Einmal Eine O / You Are Poison For Me / Devotion / Kein Gott Und Keine Liebe / Kleine Schwester /

Gothic Erotic / Erotica
MACHINA MUNDI, SPV 085-62062 CD
(1998)
Ein Kleines Märchen (Intro) / Erwachet / Es
Brennt Die sehnsucht / Machina Mundi /
Oneway Love / Alles Schwarz / Milch / Der
Kampf Des Mannes / Gothic Ritual / Don't
Stop To Learn / Mein Herz Und Meine Seele
MEA CULPA, Oblivion (2000)
Intro / Lieber Gott / Schmerz / Mea Culpa /
Goth Music / Prinz Vogelfrei / Teutonenlied /
Jahr Und Tag / Aufrecht / Weinst Du / "1780"
/ Amadeus / Vater

UNDISH (POLAND)
Line-up: Ada Szarata (vocals), Michel
Christoph (guitar), Michal Branny (guitar),
Gracjan Jeran (guitar), Darak Was (bass),
Robert Baum (drums)

Gothic Metal band UNDISH employ some
remarkable female vocals courtesy of Ada
Szarata juxtaposed with the Death grunt
growls of drummer Robert Baum.
UNDISH toured Germany in August 1997
alongside SAVIOUR MACHINE and
THEATRE OF TRAGEDY.

Albums:
ACTA EST FABULA..., Massacre MAS
PCO126 (1997)
With Blood And Suffering / I Believe / Rose
In The Window / I'm Sorry / Someone... /
Reflection... Part One / Reflection... Part Two
/ With Blood And Suffering (Part Two)

UNEARTHLY TRANCE (USA)
Line-Up: Rion Lipynsky (vocals / guitar), Jay
Newman (bass), Darren Verni (drums)

Underground Doom. UNEARTHLY TRANCE
made their first impressions in 2000 with the
cassette 'Sonic Burial Hymns'. An EP release
arrived a year later. A second guitarist,
Jeremy Curles, decamped and the group
soldiered on as a trio issuing the 'Lord
Humanless Awakens' 7" single through
Southern Lord.
The members of UNEARTHLY TRANCE
described their activities as being Darren
Verni on "Drums of war, spirit of Mentu and
Vril", Jay Newman as "Subsonic current,
sadistic smoke ritualist" and Rion Lypinsky
with "6 string sonic frost, voice of the cult".
Both Lipynsky and Verni had previously been
members of CROOKED STICK. The drummer
also cites credits with VRIL, L.O.M.,
DRUGGED APE and MONGOLOID NUN.
Newman was with MASHED UP EAGLE.
UNEARTHLY TRANCE would spend May and
June of 2002 on the road in North America as

openers to ELECTRIC WIZARD and SONS
OF OTIS. A third single release, 'Hadit', swiftly
sold out of its limited run of just 200 copes.
UNEARTHLY TRANCE readied themselves
for a full-length album working with producer
Steven O'Malley of GOATSNAKE.
Lipynsky and Newman also serve with
THRALLDOM.

Singles/EPs:
Blackheart (Blacklung) / Moonsmoke /
Branches Of Anti-Gravity / Phoenix Undead /
Lord Humanless Awakens / Storm Of Infinity,
(2001)
Lord Humanless Awakens / Summoning
The Beast, Southern Lord (2001)
August Sun Of Midnight / Raised By The
Wolves / V.V.V.V. / Pyre, (2002) ('Hadit' EP.
Limited edition 200 copies)

UNHOLY (FINLAND)
Line-Up: Pasi Aijö (vocals / bass), Jarkko
Toivonen (guitar), Jade Muhli (guitar), Veer
Vanhala (keyboards), Jan Kuhahen (drums)

Originally titled HOLY HELL and formed by
vocalist / bassist Pasi and guitarist Jarkko in
1988, the group released the 'Kill Jesus'
demo prior to a name change to UNHOLY.
Initial live work in Finland adopting the de
rigeur Black Metal corpsepaint, but over time
this was dropped as UNHOLY's music
developed into more avant-garde and
melancholic realms.
The Finns' first recording under the new name
was the 1990 demo 'Procession Of Black
Doom' followed by a further tape, 'Demo
11.90'. The fourth demo, 'Trip To Depressive
Autumn', in 1991 scored the band a deal with
Lethal Records.
UNHOLY guitarist Jarkko Toivonen later
formed TIERMES, releasing a self-titled
album in 1997. However, the following year
UNHOLY, with new member Veera Muhli on
vocals and keyboards, was resurrected for
the 'Rapture' album. The band added second
guitarist Jade Vanhala in 1999 for live work.
UNHOLY announced they were to fold during
2002.

Singles/EPs:
Stench Of Ishtar / Autumn / Creative
Lunacy / The Trip Was Infra Green, Lethal
(1992) ('Trip To Depressive Autumn' EP)

Albums:
FROM THE SHADOWS, Lethal LRC003
(1993)
Alone / Gray Blow / Creative Lunacy /
Autumn / Stench Of Ishtar / Colossal Vision /
Time Has Gone / The Trip Was Infra Green /

Passe Tiemes
THE SECOND RING OF POWER,
Avantgarde AV005 (1995)
The Second Ring Of Power / Languish For
Bliss / Lady Babylon / Neverending Day /
Dreamside / Procession Of Black Doom /
Covetous Glance / Air / Serious Personality
Disturbance
RAPTURE, Avantgarde (1998)
Into Cold Light / Petrified Spirits / For The
Unknown One / Wunderwerck / After God /
Unzeitgeist / Deluge
GRACE FALLEN, Avantgarde (1999)
Of Tragedy / Immaculate / Daybreak / When
Truth Turns Its Head / Wanderer / Reek Of
The Night / Haoma / Seeker / Athene Noctua

UNIDA (USA)
Line-Up: John Garcia (vocals), Scott Reeder
(bass)

UNIDA were formed by ex-KYUSS and SLO
BURN vocalist and Stoner guru John Garcia.
Just previous to UNIDA Garcia had featured
as part of the JMJ project band, a
collaboration with Jason Burns and Mike
Riley that contributed to the 'Welcome To
Meteor City' compilation.
The initial band comprised of Garcia
alongside guitarist Arthur Seay, former NOT
ACTUAL SIZE and LAB bass player Dave
Dinsmore and drummer Miguel 'Mike'
Cancino.
The band debuted with a split album shared
with Swedish band DOZER, 'The Best Of
Wayne-Gro'. Following completion of the
debut Chris Goss produced 1999 album
'Coping With The Urban Coyote' Garcia's
erstwhile KYUSS colleague bassist Scott
Reeder joined UNIDA for live work. Lengthy
European tour schedule commenced in
Denmark during October, taking the band
through Europe and closing in England during
mid November.
2000 found UNIDA signing to the American
Recordings label. Strangely, in November of
2001 the band were then dumped just after
completion of an album recording. Having
been produced by George Drakoulias the
band later let it be known the album had cost
$350,000 to record.
In early 2002 Seay would also announce the
formation of a high profile side endeavour
dubbed DR. FUNGUS. Joining him on this
venture would be COAL CHAMBER bassist
Nadja Puelen, ADEMA drummer Kris Kohls
and former DRAIN STH drummer Martina
Axen. Garcia unveiled a further band project
dubbed HERMANO, the new outfit being
confirmed for a live European debut at the
2002 'Dynamo Open Air' festival.

Albums:
SPLIT, Meteor City MCY003CD (1999) (Split
CD with DOZER)
COPING WITH THE URBAN COYOTE,
Cargo (1999)
Thorn / Black Woman / Plastic / Human
Tornado / If Only Two / Nervous / Dwarf It /
You Wish

UNORTHODOX (USA)
Line-Up: Dale Flood (vocals / guitar), Josh
Hart (bass), Ronnie Kalimon (drums)

UNORTHODOX was a respected member of
the Maryland Doom family that was put into
the spotlight by the German Hellhound label.
Initially billed as ASYLUM the band cut the
debut 1993 'Asylum' album re-billed as
UNORTHODOX. Musicians for the first record
included frontman Dale Flood, former
INDESTROY bassist Jeff Parsons and
drummer Ronnie Kalimon, a veteran of
INTERNAL VOID and IRON MAN.
Parsons place would be taken by
REVELATION's Josh Hart for the 1994 follow
up 'Balance Of Power'. UNORTHODOX
reformed in the late '90s with Flood being
joined by Parsons, WRETCHED bassist
Johnny Wretched and ex-WRETCHED
drummer Mikey Phillips. Bassist Rob
Hampshire would be a later inductee.

Albums:
ASYLUM, Hellhound (1993)
Intro: The Open Door / Suicide King /
Unseen World / Realize A Dream / Asylum /
Cyclone / Feel Like You / Scorpio Rising /
Smoke 'n Joe / Forgotten Image /
Neanderthal / Harvest
BALANCE OF POWER, Hellhound (1994)
Junkie / To Kill A Monster / Peacemaker /
Well Aware / Lost In Tomorrow / Maimed And
Slaughtered / The Zombie Dance / Standstill
/ Price Of Life / The Gate / Motherless /
Unorthodox

VALHALL (NORWAY)
Line-up: Ronny Sorkness
(vocals), Geir Kolden (guitar),
Robin Olsen (guitar / keyboards),
Kenneth Sorkness (bass), Gribb
(drums)

Drums on the Norwegian Doom outfit VALHALL's second album are performed by the ubiquitous character Fenriz of DARKTHRONE under his pseudonym of Lee Bress.
Guitarist Frode Malm would depart following the 'Moonstoned' album. New recruit was Frank Wanberg on keyboards.

Albums:
MOONSTONED, Head Not Found HNF009 (1995)
Tidal Waves / Pagan Token / Doom / Dreamer / Infinite Grieve / Come Winter / Relief / Vulture Trace Time / Moonstoned / Soul Trip
HEADING FOR MARS, Head Not Found (1997)
Intro / Arctic / Mindblaster / Mountain / Ocean / Sleeper / Childhood Memories / Livets Soyle / Past Era / Darkness Between Two Shadows / The Dream Of A Jester / Outro

VENI DOMINE (SWEDEN)
Line-Up: Fredrik Ohlsson (vocals / guitar), Torbjörn Weinesjö (guitar), Magnus Thorman (bass), Thomas Weinesjö (drums)

High class Christian Metallers VENI DOMINE have established themselves with a brace of superb albums of orchestral Metal. Classical influences abound and the band are even unafraid to use chanting monks for effect! VENI DOMINE's first brace of albums were produced by HEAVY LOAD's Wahlqvist brothers Ragne and Styrbjörn. The band was rooted in an earlier act dubbed GLORIFY, a Sollentuna based union of ex-DISCIPLES guitarist Torbjörn Weinesjö, his sibling drummer Thomas, singer Fredrik Ohlsson and bass player Anders Olofsson. In 1988 Olofsson was supplanted by Magnus Thorman and the group adopted the revised title of SEVENTH SEAL, performing at the British Christian 'Greenbelt' festival under that name during 1990. This show resulted in a deal with the British based Kingsway label. However, due to a proliferation of acts titled SEVENTH SEAL the name VENI DOMINE was decided upon.
As VENI DOMINE the band debuted with the 'Fall Babylon Fall' album, oddly initially recorded in Eastbourne, England during the summer of the previous year. Unsatisfied with the result the band pulled in the Wahlqvist brothers to complete the job back in Sweden. Issued through the Christian R.E.X. label it would soon make an impression upon the regular Rock market. The cover artwork for 'Fall Babylon Fall' was executed by the highly rated fantasy artist Rodney Matthews.
VENI DOMINE toured Germany in 1996 on a bill with SAVIOUR MACHINE and SOUL CAGES to further promote the 'Material Sanctuary' album, once again clad in a superb Rodney Matthews sleeve design. Keyboards on the album were donated by Mats Lidbrandt. With renewed interest generated by the second record Massacre Records re-released debut 'Fall Babylon Fall' in 1997 complete with 'Visions' as a bonus track.
For the third album, 'Spiritual Wasteland', VENI DOMINE inducted new members bass player Gabriel Ingemarson and BISHOP GARDEN keyboard player Mattias Cederlund.
Vocalist Fredrik Ohlsson also fronts HOAX, an outfit featuring ex-CANDLEMASS guitarist Lasse Johansson. The singer was also involved with ZOIC with the guitarist and his CANDLEMASS colleagues guitarist Mats 'Mappe' Björkman and drummer Janne Lindh for a well received 1996 album 'Total Level Of Destruction'.
VENI DOMINE's 2002 line up stood at vocalist Fredrik Sjöholm (having changed his name from Ohlsson), guitarist Torbjörn Weinesjö, bass player Gabriel Ingemarson and Thomas Weinesjö on drums. A fourth album was being readied for late 2002 release.

Albums:
FALL BABYLON FALL, REX 7901 420057 (1992)
Face Of The Prosecutor / King Of The Jews / In The Day Of The Sentinel / Wisdom Calls / Armageddon / O Great City / The Chronicle Of The Seven Seals, Part I: The Scroll And The Lamb, Part II: The Seals, Part III: The Golden Censer
MATERIAL SANCTUARY, Massacre MASS CD074 (1995)
The Meeting / Eccesinstes / Material Sanctuary / Ritual Of The Sinner / The Mass / Behold The Signs / Wrath Of The Lion / Beyond The Doom / Baroque Moderne
SPIRITUAL WASTELAND, Thunderload (1998)
Dawn Of Time / Last Letter From Earth / If I Fall Asleep / Hysterical History / Riddle Of Eternity / The Temple / Someone's Knocking / Silent Lamb / 1st Of Ten / The Letter

VIAJE A 800 (SPAIN)
Line-Up: Jose 'Pot' (vocals / bass), Jose Angel (guitar), Chumbo (guitar), David (drums)

Southern Spanish 'Doom n' Rollers' VIAJE A 800 ('Trip to 800') were formulated in 1996. The band issued the 'Santa Agueda' demo and toured Algeria before breaking up, subsequently re-emerging shortly after for a shared a split 10" release in 1999 with Argentineans NATAS upfront of the debut album 'Diablo Roto De'.

Singles/EPs:
Higomon / Solo / Inmensa, Orbital Records (1999) (10" split single with NATAS)

Albums:
DIABLO ROTO DE, Custom Heavy (2001)
Roto Blues / Cardio Limite / Solo / Higomon 2 A / Largo Beso Recto / Higomon 2 B / Vuelo Inferno-After En Marte / Humo De Mota / Valiums

VIOLET VORTEX (GREECE)
Line-Up: St. Spirus (vocals / bass), Thomas G. (guitar), Alexander P. (guitar), Alex T. (drums)

Traditionally laced Doom. VIOLET VORTEX's first foray came with the 1999 cassette 'Rush Hour Of Lust', capitalized on by a second effort 'Indulge In Reverie' which arrived in 2000.

Albums:
LURE ELEGANT, Secret Port (2002)
Trouble / Luv / Bitter Love / Riding Forever Free / Ultraviolet Dreams / Marsyas, The Satyr / Blind Truth / Lure Of Vistage Elegant / Nunny Song (Live video)

VISCERAL EVISCERATION (AUSTRIA)
Line-Up: Hannes Wuggenig (vocals / guitar), Jürgen Hajek (guitar) (guitar), Dominik Lirsch (bass), Stephan Strnad (drums)

A disconcerting mixture of Sludge Doom, gore drenched lyrics and hyper speed bursts of Grindcore. VISCERAL EVISCERATION debuted with the 1994 cassette 'Savour Of Seething Meat'. After the Napalm Records album 'Incessant Desire For Palatable Flesh' album the group renamed themselves AS I LAY DYING and put out a further cassette, 'As I Lay Dying', delivered in 1995.

Albums:
INCESSANT DESIRE FOR PALATABLE FLESH, Napalm NPR004 (1994)
(I Am) Enamoured Of Dead Bodies / At The

Epicurean Gynaecologist / Muse Perverse / Knee Deep In Blood I Wade / Chewing Female Genital Parts / Tender Flesh... On The Bier / Gangling Menstrual Blood-Broth For Supper

VOID OF SILENCE (ITALY)
Line-Up: Malfeitor Fabban (vocals), Ivan Zara (guitar / bass), Riccardo Conforti (keyboards / drums)

VOID OF SILENCE specialize in morose, ambient Doom music. The duo of keyboard player and drummer Riccardo Conforti, also a member of SYRION and erstwhile drummer for OBLIVION, and guitarist / bassist Ivan Zara, ex-OBLIVION and MYSTICAL REALMS, convened the project during November of 1999.
Working on the EP 'Toward The Dusk' VOID OF SILENCE introduced ABORYM and FUNERAL ORATION bass player Malfeitor Fabban, acting as lead vocalist. After release of the February 2002 'Criteria Ov 666' album for the Code 666 label Conforti would session on recordings for an EPHEL DUATH album 'The Painter's Pallette'.
The band parted ways with vocalist Malfeitor Fabban during the summer of 2002.

Albums:
TOWARD THE DUSK, Nocturnal Music (2001)
A Mild From Hate / Elemental Pain / Deamons From My Imagination / Exstasy In The Spiral / My Private Hell / Nigredo: Panic Malediction
CRITERIA OV 666, Code 666 (2002)
Velocity. Electricity. TV Necro / With No Half Measure / Anthem For Doomed Youth / Anger / The Ultimate Supreme Intelligence / Nothing Immortal
Victory! / Universal Separation / XTC-Elevation-Trip

VOODOO SHOCK (GERMANY)
Line-Up: Uwe Groebel (vocals / guitar), Michi (bass), Späcky (drums)

VOODOO SHOCK are led by erstwhile NAEVUS man Uwe Groebel. The group was conceived in 1999, Groebel utilizing the services of END OF GREEN members bass player Oliver Merkle and drummer Mathias Sifferman for the initial line-up and a subsequent four track demo tape recorded in late 2000. A rendition of 'Petra' would also be cut for inclusion on a SAINT VITUS tribute album on Raven Moon Records.
Groebel pulled in Swiss musicians bassist Michi (Michael Greilinger) and drummer

Späcky for recording of a debut 2002 album which ambitiously attempts a Doom interpretation of the MOODY BLUES 'Nights In White Satin'.

VORTEX OF INSANITY (MD, USA)

Line-Up: Zak Campbell (vocals / bass), Steve Chapman (guitar), Danny Kenyon (guitar), Rob Brannigan (drums)

Maryland Doom act signed to the German Hellhound label. Both guitarist Danny Kenyon and drummer Rob 'Cougin' Brannigan are both erstwhile members of Thrashers INDESTROY. Kenyon would also spend time with DREADNOT in 1990.

Post VORTEX OF INSANITY Kenyon reunited with another former INDESTROY drummer Gus Basilica to create GUT SOUP. The pair would subsequently found LIFE BEYOND in 1999 with ex-CREEPSHOW frontman Louis Strachan.

Albums:
SOCIAL DECAY, Hellhound (1994)
The End Is Nigh / Social Decay / What You Get / Immoral Standing / C I A / The Zone / Shut Up / Thorazine / Assimilation / Misfit Of Society

THE WANT (USA)

Stoner-Doom band fronted by vocalist Kenneth Lear. The band split after the solitary 'Greatest Hits Volume 5' album.

Albums:
GREATEST HITS VOLUME 5, Southern Lord (2000)
Supertoker / Pass It On / Slight Of Hand / Star 69 / Groove / 4 Pictures / Ballroller / Silver Chord / Yeah-Yeah / Not A Word To The Soul / Goodbye

WARHEAD (ITALY)

Line-Up: Kevin Throath (vocals), Fabio Scipioni (guitar), Fausto Colasanti (guitar), Walter Vincenti (bass), Walter Sacripanti (drums)

WARHEAD has made the transition from Thrash Hardcore Crossover to Doom in a career spanning two decades. The group was founded as a Punk influenced Thrash act in 1982 by guitarists Fabio Scipioni and Faust Colasanti, debuting with a 1983 demo tape 'In Rock We Trust'. A self-financed mini-album, 'The Black Radio', arrived in 1986 and a seasonal 7" in 1987 'X-Mas Bop'. The B-side to this record was a raucous cover of Irving Berlin's famed 'White Christmas' that saw DEATH SS man Paul Chain acting as studio guest.
By 1991 the group members had opted for a Psychedelic Rock experiment dubbed MOONSHINER. In this incarnation they released a cassette but, with a fresh rhythm section, reactivated WARHEAD for club gigs and a further cassette release 'Ten Years On The Road'. Former REVENGE vocalist Kevin Throath was added, alongside studio musicians bass player Walter 'Winning' Vincenti and drummer Walter Sacripanti to record the 1998 Stoner-Doom flavoured 'Sand'son' album. The record was not only produced by Paul Chain but included some trademark guitar solos too.

Singles/EPs:
X-Mas Bop / White Christmas, Warhead (1987)
One More Time In Jail, Mosca (1989)

Albums:
THE BLACK RADIO, Warhead (1986)
SAND'SON, New LM NLM022 (1998)
The Downwinders / Black Out In Cell Block 10 / Foolkiller / Keep Inside / S And S.O.N. / Fire From Within / I Lose Control / Shootin'

Stars / In Mission For God

WARHORSE (Worcester, MA, USA)

Line-Up: Jerry Orne (vocals / bass), Todd Laskowski (guitar), Mike Hubbard (drums)

Ultra-ponderous Stoner Doom from Massachusetts not to be confused with Nick Simper's '70s post DEEP PURPLE act or indeed - closer to home: Wino's pre-OBSESSED band.
The band was born out of a power struggle that tore apart a prior act DESOLATE when one half of the band wished to pursue Black Metal and the other Death Metal. In defiance bassist Jerry Orne split away endeavouring to forge a Doom powered band. WARHORSE was created in the Spring of 1996 Orne on bass, ex-DAHLIA'S DEAD vocalist / guitarist Krista Van Guilder and drummer Mike Hubbard from Death Metal veterans INFESTATION. The original band also had on board a second guitarist, Brian, but he soon found himself surplus to requirements.
With a 'chick' upfront WARHORSE generated plenty of press but would deliberately play down the stereotyped image. With this line-up WARHORSE cut an eponymous six track album in 1998. However, in August of that year Van Guilder would make his exit and Matt Smith was drafted as substitute.
WARHORSE inaugurated their revised line-up with a 7" single 'The Lysergic Communion', an edited version of their previous 18 minute workout of the same track released on a previous demo. Touring to promote this outing saw invitations to appear at the Virginia 'Stoner Hands Of Doom' festival and the annual 'Hardcore & Metal Fest' prior to a run of club dates. These plans were scuppered when Smith bowed out unexpectedly citing the prospect of marital bliss as being preferable to a life of Doom.
WARHORSE quickly pulled in former DESOLATE guitarist Todd Laskowski as Orne took the lead vocal duties on board and WARHORSE were promptly added back on to the 'Hardcore & Metal Fest' show with the minimum of rehearsal time.
Laskowski cut his teeth on the 12" single 'The Priestess' released by Ellington Records on 'blood' red vinyl. The B side to this release comprised a cover version of WARGASM's 'Wasteland'.
The band signed to noted Doom promoters Southern Lord for the 2000 album 'As Heaven Turns To Ash'. WARHORSE would also grace the Meteor City Records IRON MAIDEN tribute with their take on 'Total Eclipse'.
During March and April of 2001 WARHORSE journeyed America as touring partners to premier UK Stoners ELECTRIC WIZARD.

Singles/EPs:
The Lysergic Communion - Hymn I: On Your Knees / The Lysergic Communion - Hymn II: Thy Cup Runneth Over, Burden Of Being (1999)
The Priestess Jam / Wasteland, Ellington (2000) ('The Priestess' 12" single)
I Am Dying / Horizons Burn Red, Southern Lord (2002)

Albums:
WARHORSE, Warhorse (1998)
AS HEAVEN TURNS TO ASH, Southern Lord SUNN009 (2000)
Dusk / Doom's Bride / Black Acid Prophecy / Amber Vial / Every Flower Dies No Matter The Thorns (Wither) / Lysergic Communion / Dawn / Scrape / And The Angels Begin To Weep

WARNING (UK)

Line-Up: Pat Walker (vocals / guitar), Marcus Hatfield (bass), Stuart Springthorpe (drums)

WARNING arrived on the British Metal landscape touting a 1997 demo 'Blessed Be The Sabbath', the title of which amply demonstrated the band's reverence for '70s style Doom. A track from these sessions, 'Cemetery Eyes', subsequently made its way onto the compilation album 'At The Mountains Of Madness'. WARNING had formed some two years earlier citing a line-up of frontman Pat Walker, who holds down a day job in an artificial limb factory, bass player Johnny Blade and drummer Stuart Springthorpe. This unit debuted in the live environment acting as openers to ORANGE GOBLIN and MOURN, subsequently cutting the opening February 1996 demo session 'Revelation Looms'. Further shows, pre-empting the 'Blessed Be The Sabbath' demo, saw WARNING guesting for acts such as IRON MONKEY, SOLSTICE and ELECTRIC WIZARD.

Johnny Blade made way for Marcus Hatfield as WARNING signed to the Miskatonic Foundation label for the Dave Chang produced 'The Strength To Dream' album.

Albums:
THE STRENGTH TO DREAM, Miskatonic Foundation (2001)
The Return / The Face That Never Dies / Something Hurts / How Can It Happen? / The Strength To Dream

WE (NORWAY)

Line-Up: Thomas Felberg (vocals), Don A. Dons (guitar), Geir A. Jensen (bass), Kristian Kirkvaag (drums)

A highly regarded act WE, who have built up a strong underground following of ardent supporters, defy categorization yet find their most vocal support in the Stoner field.

The debut 'In A Field Of Moose' album was at first issued on the band's own label Nun Music and distributed in Oslo through a network of friends. Voices Of Wonder subsequently picked the album up for national distribution shortly after. Just over a thousand copies of 'In A Field Of Moose' were manufactured. 1995 proved a slow year for the band with just a handful of gigs performed and a four track demo laid down. Nevertheless, enough interest was piqued to sign WE up to Voices Of Wonder, who had yet to see the band play live, for the follow up 'Violently Coloured Sneakers' album of September 1996. Reviews were complimentary and WE undertook not only gigs in Norway but also a short run of German dates.

The 1997 'Wooferwheels' album, recorded and mixed in just 8 days, would break WE onto the international market, the band's efforts being highly praised in particular by the Stoner community. A limited edition vinyl variant of 'Wooferwheels', restricted to just 500 copies, added the exclusive track 'Applestomps'. 'Wooferwheels' would be praised to the hilt by the Norwegian Rock magazine 'Scream' generating healthy sales. With the album making a significant impact in mainland Europe WE toured Germany, returned to Norway for gigs including shows supporting FU MANCHU and SPIRITUAL BEGGARS and then headed back to Germany for a further run of shows.

In promoting the 'Livin' The Lore' album WE would be personally invited by Chris Goss, enthused by a copy of 'Wooferwheels' given to him by the band in 1998, to act as openers for MASTER OF REALITY's European dates that year. To loosen up for these important gigs WE performed at an open air show in Oslo billed as THE SMUTPEDDLERS performing a set of cover versions, including MASTERS OF REALITY's 'She Got Me'.

The Drunken Maria label released a 10" EP 'From The Spaceways' in 2000, this outing featuring a take on THE GROUNDHOGS 'Cherry Red' and being manufactured in suitably Psychedelic marbled vinyl. The 'Care For Dominance' EP of the same year, with a version of BLUE OYSTER CULT's 'Dominance And Submission' as the flip side, would also excite collectors, only 500 being pressed in a variety of yellow, pink and standard black vinyl. The following year WE shared a split release with the renowned Danish Acid Rockers GAS GIANT.

WE broke away from the Voices Of Wonder

label to sign with Black Balloon for the 2002 album 'Dinosauric Futurobic'.

Singles/EPs:
Flyin' / Cherry Red / Boom Boom / Apes Family, Drunken Maria (2000) (10" 'From The Spaceways' EP)
Carefree / Dominance And Submission, Feedback Underground 002 (2000) ('Care For Dominance' EP)
Jinxed / Wooferwheels (Live), Black Balloon (2002) (10" single)

Albums:
IN A FIELD OF MOOSE, Nun Music NUN001CD (1994)
Being What It Could / Shame / Total Heaviousity / Fall / Cowsong / Another Occasion / In A Field Of Moose / Blown Odyssey / Wrecked / Days
VIOLENTLY COLOURED SNEAKERS, Voices Of Wonder VOW056 (1996)
The Tribe / Heat / Violently Coloured Sneakers / Hangaroundsounds / Good Afternoons / Turtlewalken / Go!
WOOFERWHEELS, Voices Of Wonder VOW063 (1997)
Wooferwheels / Out There / Last Argument Of Kings / Inbetween The Days / Stuks Of Khun De Prorok / Chase Vampire (Tribute) / Im Dschungel von Kraut
LIVIN' THE LORE, Voices Of Wonder VOW070 (1999)
Full Moon With A Label / I And I / Peddler / Red Morning / Shades We Wear
GAS GIANT VS. WE, Burnthehippie BHR005 (2001)
Last Stronghold Of The Freaks / Stronghold / The Trip
DINOSAURIC FUTUROBIC, Black Balloon (2002)
Galactic Racetrack / Carefree / Dinosauric Futurobic / Organic Room / Cosmic Bound / Toothgottago / Jinxed / Antidote / (Still Got The) Hats Off / From The Spaceways / 1971

WEEDEATER (Wilmington, NC, USA)
Line-Up: Dave Collins (vocals / bass), Shep (guitar), Keko (drums)

Fronted by Dave 'Dixie' Collins, WEEDEATER first came to prominence by way of Collins term of duty with the mayhemic BUZZOV-EN. When BUZZOV-EN ran out of steam in 1998 Collins was freed up to concentrate on WEEDEATER, an act that had actually been gigging for some five years previous.
Billy Anderson would produce the debut 'And Justice For Y'All' album for Game Two Records in 2000, included on which was a radical reworking of CROSBY, STILLS &

NASH's 'Southern Cross'.
The sophomore effort, once again produced by Billy Anderson and provisionally entitled 'Beezlebubba' but emerging as 'Sixteen Tons', was delivered in March of 2002.

Albums:
AND JUSTICE FOR Y'ALL, Game Two (2000)
Tuesday Night / Monkey Junction / Free / Hungry Jack / Shitfire / Calico / Truck Drivin Man / Southern Cross / #86
SIXTEEN TONS, Berserker (2002)
Bull / Potbelly / Wanted / Dummy / #3 / Woe's Me / Buzz / Riff / Lines / Kira Mae

WELLWATER CONSPIRACY (USA)
Line-Up: Ben Shepherd (vocals / bass), John McBain (guitar), Matt Cameron (drums)

WELLWATER CONSPIRACY comprise ex-MONSTER MAGNET guitarist John McBain and former PEARL JAM and SOUNDGARDEN man Matt Cameron. Both men were also involved with HATER. The band would be fronted by Ben Shepherd, another SOUNDGARDEN veteran. WELLWATER CONSPIRACY emerged with a set of low key 1993 7" singles whose sleeve credits identified John McBain as being joined by vocalist 'Zeb' and drummer 'Tad Dameron', both SOUNDGARDEN members having to remain anonymous due to contract. A free single dubbed 'A Metal Creep's Portico', a split release with Swedish band THE ROTS OF ECHO, would be issued with the September 1995 Ptolemaic Terrascope magazine.
The triumvirate opted for an almost mellowed out, Psychedelic direction on their 1997 debut 'A Declaration Of Conformity', even going so far as to cover SYD BARRETT's 'Lucy Leave' and THE SPIDERS 'Nati Bati Yi'.
Shepherd opted out by the time of the 'Brotherhood Of Electric' opus. The 1999 album saw Cameron taking the main vocal role with Josh Homme of KYUSS and QUEENS OF THE STONE AGE guesting alongside Glenn Slater of THE WALKABOUTS. Although still firmly planted in the '60s the record did please fans of the members' priority acts by including the Sabbathian riff factory of 'Van Vanishing'.
Cameron had re-joined PEARL JAM by the close of the millennium, however WELLWATER CONSPIRACY, complete with Ben Shepherd once again, did return for a third album 'The Scroll And Its Combinations'. The track 'C, Myself And Eye' featured a guesting Kim Thayil of SOUNDGARDEN donating a trademark guitar solo whilst

WEEDEATER
Photo : El Danno

'Felicity's Surprise' is embellished by the distinctive tomes of one 'Wes C. Addle' (Actually PEARL JAM's Eddie Vedder).

For live gigs the esteemed producer and ex-SKINYARD member Jack Endino would join the band on bass with Glen Slater on keyboards.

Singles/EPs:
Sandy / Nati Bati Yi, Superelectro (1993) (7" single)
Sleeveless / You Do You, Superelectro (1993) (7" single)
Trowerchord / Green Undertow, Superelectro (1994) (7" single)
Germanium / Telescopic / The Solar Know, Ptolemaic Terrascope POT-19 (1995) (Free split EP with THE ROTS OF ECHO)
Compellor / In Pursuit Of Gingerbread Man, Superelectro (1997)
Tidepool Telegraph / Now Invisibly / Far Side Of Your Moon (Live) / Of Dreams, Third Gear (2000)
Of Dreams / Hal McBlaine (Live), TVT (2001)

Albums:
A DECLARATION OF CONFORMITY, Third Gear 17 (1997)
Sleeveless / Shel Talmy / The Ending / Sandy / Far Side Of The Moon / Lucy Leave / Green Undertow / Enebrio / You Do You / Space Travel In The Blink Of An Eye / Nati Bati Yi / Declaration Of Conformity / Trowerchord / Palomar Observatory
BROTHERHOOD OF ELECTRIC, Timebomb 435232 (1999)
Destination 24 / Compellor / Teen Lambchop / Hal BcBlaine / Born With A Tail / Destination 7 / Red Light, Green Light / B.O.U. / Psycho Scrimm / Van Vanishing / Right Of Left Field / Ladder To The Moon / Dark Passage / Good Pushin' / Dr. Browne Dr. Greene / Jefferson Experiment
THE SCROLL AND ITS COMBINATIONS, TVT (2001)
Tidepool Telegraph / I Got Nightmares / C, Myself And Eye / Tick Tock 3 O'clock / What Becomes Of The Clock / Felicity's Surprise / Now, Invisibly / Of Dreams / Brotherhood Of Electric / The Scroll / Keppy's Lament

WELTSCHMERZ (ITALY)

A solo Darkwave project of former MONUMENTUM bassist Anthony Duman. WELTSCHMERZ arose in 1994 debuting with the 'Metaphysical Barocque' demo cassette the same year. This would be capitalized on by the inclusion of the track 'Understand' on the 'Apocalypse II' compilation issued by the Berlin based Abyss Records.

Signing to Doom specialists Eibon Records, WELTSCHMERZ released the full-length 'Symptomes De Ruine' in 1995. Further compilation inclusions led up to the release of November 2001's 'Capitale De La Douleur'. Duman would collaborate with CANAAN on their 'Walk Into My Open Womb' album.

Not to be confused with the Electronic Gothic act out of Prague that shares the same title.

Albums:
SYMPTOMES DE RUINE, Eibon LAD05 (1995)
CAPITALE DE LA DOULEUR, Eibon WEL031 (2001)
Jade Eclipse / Under Archons' Domain / Maha Pralaya / Downfall Bolero / Capitale De La Douleur / Colore Di Pioggia E Di Ferro / Inanna Incarnates / Omegadawn

WE, THE GODS (HOLLAND)

Line-Up: Rich (vocals), Matthijs (guitar), Elwin (guitar), Twan (bass), Michiel (keyboards), Raymond (drums)

WE, THE GODS is rooted in the early 1999 Death Metal act CANCER SUSPECTED AGENT, founded by ex-ARCANUM and BIOSFEAR drummer Raymond and former OBSTRUCTION bassist Arjan on guitar. With the addition of bass player Heidi alongside former PHILOSOPHER personnel Mario on guitar and vocalist Richard, previously also involved with NEMESIS and SAD REALITY, the band shifted emphasis over to a much darker, Doom style. With the change in style the band opted for a name switch to WE, THE GODS in August of the same year.

A mini-album 'Dark Embrace' was cut in June of 2000. Former CHRISTIAN DEATH man Wim Leydes contributed keyboards to this recording. A permanent keyboard player, ex-DARK RIVERS FLOW member Michiel joined the band in December.

Arjan made his exit in April of 2001, his place being taken by Elwin, also of DARK RIVERS FLOW. With this line-up WE, THE GODS undertook a gigging schedule billed with THE WOUNDED, OFFICIUM TRISTE, WHISPERING GALLERY and AFTER FOREVER.

Further membership changes witnessed the departure of both Mario and Heidi in January of 2002. Regrouping, WE, THE GODS inducted Matthijs on guitar and Twan of CLITINC on bass while Michiel took over Mario's vocal parts.

Prior to joining WE, THE GODS Matthijs had a history with acts such as PHLEGMATIC, LODESTAR and KRAVEN. The guitarist also divides his time with DARK RIVERS FLOW, SHAPELESS and IMAGO DEI.

Albums:
DARK EMBRACE, (2000)
Felting Beauty / Leaves / Effete God / See-ers / Forever Is Gone

WHILE HEAVEN WEPT
(Dale City, VA, USA)
Line-Up: Tom Phillips (vocals), Scott Loose (guitar), Jim Hunter (bass), Jake Bodnar (keyboards), Jason Gray (drums)

Almost a cult institution, WHILE HEAVEN WEPT, beset by constant line-up fluctuations, has nevertheless engendered an almost reverential status within the annals of Doom. Mentor Tom Phillips is known for his associations with such diverse acts as PARASITIC INFESTATION, GRAND BELIAL'S KEY, TWISTED TOWER DIRE, BRAVE and ARISE FROM THORNS.

The origins of WHILE HEAVEN WEPT lay in the act DREAM WYTCH, forged in November of 1989 by erstwhile POLARIS guitarists Chris Galvan and Tom Phillips. The duo intended to bring to life an act that would incorporate elements of Doom, Progressive Rock and classical influences but with a marked atmosphere of "utter despair". However, between 1990 and 1993 DREAM WYTCH was afflicted by unceasing line-up changes culminating in Tom Phillips remaining as sole founder member. This pivotal moment of change within the band was to coincide with a number of personal tragedies in the musician's life and so a new band title of WHILE HEAVEN WEPT was adopted.

In late 1993 bass player Gabe Funston and drummer Jon Paquin were enrolled and in January of the following year recording sessions took place which yielded the limited edition 'Into The Wells Of Sorrow' 7" single for the Open Eye label, material for a split single with Californians COLD MOURNING and an EP 'Lovesongs Of The Foresaken'. Despite this very tangible solid progress Funston decamped in April of 1995. WHILE HEAVEN WEPT regrouped by drawing in former GREY DIVISION BLUE musicians guitarist Kevin Hufnagel, also having credits with THE FIFTH SEASON, along with viola and bass player D. Clayton 'Varsalin' Ingerson.

This revised version of the band retired to Neptune Studios in the Autumn of 1995, home of the band's previous sessions, to record the album 'Sorrow Of The Angels'. Unfortunately these tracks were left unfinished as the band were reportedly frustrated at being unable to achieve the sound they desired. With WHILE HEAVEN WEPT on temporary hiatus Phillips kept active, lending guest vocals to demos for TWISTED TOWER DIRE and joining the British underground Doom band SOLSTICE as frontman. Meantime Hufnagel embarked upon solo work issuing the cassette 'While I Wait' and involving himself with Clayton Ingerson in a band project DSYRYTHMIA.

With Phillip's return to North America in 1996 the 'Sorrow Of The Angels' endeavour would be resurrected, the singer working with Ingerson and Paquin. It would be a full year before actual recording commenced in August of 1997, finally seeing the light of day courtesy of the Italian Eibon label in late 1998. The record, comprising three nine minute dirgeful protestations, saw Phillips handling vocals, guitar and keyboards. In order to perform the material in the live arena WHILE HEAVEN WEPT was reconstructed with Phillips and Paquin enlisting aid of TWISTED TOWER DIRE's guitarist Scott Waldrop and bass player Jim Murad. However, with TWISTED TOWER DIRE's career path accelerating this latest incarnation of WHILE HEAVEN WEPT lasted a little over three months before priorities necessitated the withdrawal of Waldrop and Murad. Jim Hunter, of OCTOBER 31 and previously with REVELATION, became the band's new bassist with guitar duties delegated to the sibling duo of Scott and Michelle Loose, both of ARISE FROM THORNS. Scott Loose had in fact been an early member of WHILE HEAVEN WEPT back in 1993. With a concrete line-up the group put in extensive road work promoting the album across North America sharing stages with acts such as REVELATION, SPIRIT CARAVAN, INTERNAL VOID and PALE DIVINE amongst many others.

Citing "internal tensions" the group was to fracture. Phillips had become involved with ARISE FROM THORNS as a studio consultant during recording of their 'Before An Audience Of Stars' album and subsequently joining the band as second guitarist. With WHILE HEAVEN WEPT on hold Phillips allied himself with Scott and Michelle Loose to found Progressive Rock band BRAVE, a band unit which undertook over a hundred live performances over a two year period and released the 4 track EP 'Waist Deep In Dark Waters'. With Phillips combating a major illness added to internal frustrations within BRAVE this latest venture was to flounder.

Phillips reactivated WHILE HEAVEN WEPT, severing ties with BRAVE in April 2001. Joining him would be Scott Loose on guitar,

Jim Hunter on bass and a series of drummers starting with BRAVE's Trevor Schrotz. Former comrade Jon Paquin took on the position briefly before Phil Bloxom, veteran of '80s Heavy Metal band HELLION, took the drum stool. The following candidate would be Jason Gray of Death-Doom act FORTY DAYS LONGING and shortly after WHILE HEAVEN WEPT's sound would be embellished further with the addition of keyboards from OVERDOSE man Jake Bodnar. This union crafted the 'Of Empires Forlorn' album.

The German Metal Supremacy label weighed in with a retrospective release 'Chapter One: 1989-1999'. A new studio album, 'Vast Oceans Lachrymose' is targeted for release through the band's own imprint Vast Music Lachrymose Productions.

Singles/EPs:
Into The Well Of Sorrow EP, Open Eye (1994)
In Aeturnum / La Mort D'mour / Sorrow Of The Angels, Sinistrari (1995) ('Lovesongs Of The Forsaken' EP)
Split, Game Two (1998) (7" split single with COLD MOURNING)
The Drowning Years EP, Maniacal (2002)

Albums:
SORROW OF THE ANGELS, Eibon (1998)
Thus With A Kiss I Die / Into The Wells Of Sorrow / The Death Of Love / September
CHAPTER ONE: 1989-1999, Metal Supremacy MS009 (2002)
OF EMPIRES FORLORN, Eibon (2001)

WHISPERING FOREST (ESTONIA)
Line-Up: Mart (vocals), Katrin (vocals / keyboards), Tönis (guitar), Heijo (guitar), Raino (bass), Ranno (drums)

Baltic Doom employing both male and female lead vocals. WHISPERING FOREST was formed in October 1995 with a line-up of guitarists Tömis and Heijo, vocalist / bassist Alan, drummer Jaanus and female lead singer Kai. By 1996 Kai had been supplanted by Katrin, who also augmented keyboards to the bands sound, and bass player Anders had been drafted as the group issued two demos 'Old Fortress' and 'Last Sunset'.

The following year Raino took the four string position for the demo session 'Darkest Side' as WHISPERING FOREST struck a deal with American label Pantheon Records for a proposed split album with NINGIZZIA. New man Anders took the vocals for recording as Vambola ousted Jaanus. However, after only one gig WHISPERING FOREST saw Vambola vacate the drum stool.

1999 saw the band add two more new members in singer Mart and drummer Ranno.

Singles/EPs:
Black Orchid / Darkest Side, Whispering Forest (1998) ('...So Begins The End' Promotional CD single)

Albums:
OF SHADOWS AND PALE LIGHT, Whispering Forest (1998)
Curse / On These Endless Autumn Nights / Last Sunset / Winterbird / Shine Of Lethe / Black Orchid / Twined As One / Tulesõnad (Words Of Fire) / Darkest Side / Of Shadows And Pale Light;

WHISPERING GALLERY (HOLLAND)
Line-Up: Reiner Vreeswijk (vocals), Barry van Trigt (guitar), Hubert ter Muelen (bass), Fred Provoost (keyboards), Jurian ver Baar (drums)

Sombre Doom with Death grunt vocals courtesy of Reiner Vreeswijk. WHISPERING GALLERY was created in 1995 releasing the 'Gallery Of Dreams' demo two years later. 1998 saw their signatures applied to a deal with Killerwhale Records for the four track EP 'Poems From A Forgotten Dream'. The same year two demo songs surfaced on the Skull Crusher Records compilation 'Crushed Skull Vol. 1'.

WHISPERING GALLERY's debut full length album 'Like A Dream Of Never Ending Beauty Love Never Dies' saw an internal switch in personnel with guitarist Hubert Ter Muelen manouevering to bass and previous four stringer Barry van Trigt relocating to guitar
In January of 2001 former drummer Pascal made way for Jurian Ver Baar.

Singles/EPs:
The Lord Of The Enchanted Forest / My Final Hour On Earth / Tragedies Of A Darkened Soul / Into The Valley Of Loneliness, Killerwhale (1998) ('Poems From A Forgotten Dream' EP)

Albums:
LIKE A DREAM OF NEVER ENDING BEAUTY... LOVE NEVER DIES, Killerwhale (2000)
Intro / A World Of Immortality / Uriel In Requiem / Soul Sacrifice / An Eternity Of Mourning / My Heavenly Escape / Daydream / Quest For Kingdom / Maid Of Orleans / Your Shapeless Body

WHITE ZOMBIE (USA)
Line-Up: Rob Zombie (vocals), Jay Yuenger

(guitar), Sean Yseult (bass), Ivan DePrume (drums)

New York's theatrical Horror Rockers WHITE ZOMBIE, fronted by the imposing figure of Rob Zombie (real name Rob Straker) progressed through a clutch of independent releases before assaulting the American consciousness with their 1992 album 'La Sexorcisto'.

A mere month after their formation in October of 1985 the group committed themselves to vinyl with the four track 7" EP 'Gods On Voodoo Moon'. Limited to just 300 copies this now exceptionally scarce item witnessed a band line-up credited to vocalist Rob Straker, guitarist Ena Kostabi, bass player Sean Yseult and drummer Peter Landau. Their next effort, the 1986 single 'Pig Heaven' revealed a band already in flux with Straker and Yseult now joined by guitarist Tim Jeffs and drummer Ivan DePrume. 'Pig Heaven' was initially issued in a black and white artwork cover and restricted to 500 copies. A second pressing of a further 500 came clad in a full colour sleeve.

WHITE ZOMBIE self-financed their first batch of mini-albums beginning with May 1987's 'Psycho Head Blowout'. The band's line-up at this time included guitarist Tom Guay who was to have made way for John Ricci by the Bill Laswell produced 'Make Them Die Slowly' album recorded in November of 1988. Shortly after the record's release Jay Yeunger took the guitarist's position.

The group faced the threat of legal action over the use of KISS bassist GENE SIMMONS' copyrighted make-up design depicted on the cover of the 'God Of Thunder' EP during the first few months of 1990.

DePrume was ousted in favour of a new drummer Philo. However, Philo's tenure was short and in early 1995 former EXODUS / TESTAMENT man John Tempesta was behind the kit.

As concerns grew as to the permanent status of the band an album of dance remixes 'Supersexy Swingin' Sounds' was issued in 1996 giving the band a further American hit.

A Japanese tour found DAMN THE MACHINE / MUMBO'S BRAIN man Mark Poland on the drums. Another new recruit was former SUFFER / PRONG / DANZIG bassist Rob Nicholson, although for WHITE ZOMBIE he was retitled Blasko. Yseult meantime created FAMOUS MONSTERS for the album 'In The Night!!'.

ROB ZOMBIE released his first solo album, 'Hellibilly Deluxe' through Geffen in August 1998. The record was cut with the help of Tempesta, NINE INCH NAILS men Charlie Clouser and Danny Lohner plus MÖTLEY CRÜE drummer Tommy Lee.

Singles/EPs:
King Of Souls / Gentlemen Junk / Tales From The ScareCrow Man / Cat's Eye Resurrection, (1985) ('Gods On Voodoo Moon' EP. Limited edition 300 copies)
Pig Heaven / Slaughter The Gray (1986)
God Of Thunder / Love Razor / Disaster Blaster 2, Caroline CLNT 1 (1989)
More Human Than Human / Blood Milk And Sky (Kero Kero Keropfi And The Smooth Operator) / More Human Than Human (Jeddark Of The Tharks Super Mix), Geffen GFST 92 (1995) (10" single) **51 UK**
Electric Head Part 2 (The Ecstasy) / El Phantasmo And The Chicken Run Blast-O-Rama / Super Charger Heaven / More Human Than Human (The Warlords Off Mars megamix), Geffen GFST 22140 (1996) (12" single) **31 UK**
Electric Head Part 2 (The Ecstasy) / El Phantasmo And The Chicken Run Blast-O-Rama / More Human Than Human (Princess Of Helium Ultra) / Blood, Milk & Sky (Im Ho Tep 3,700 Year Old Boogie mix), Geffen GFSTD 22140 (1996) (CD single)
Electric Head Part 2 (The Ecstasy) / More Human Than Human (Princess Of Helium Ultra) / Blood, Milk & Sky (Im Ho Tep 3,700 Year Old Boogie mix) / Thunder Kiss '65 (Swinging Lovers extended remix), Geffen GFSXD 22140 (1996) (CD single)

Albums:
PSYCHOHEAD BLOWOUT, Silent Explosion SILENT 001 (1987)
Eighty-Eight / Fast Jungle / Gun Crazy / Kick / Memphis / Magdalene / True Crime
SOULCRUSHER, Silent Explosion SILENT 002 (1988)
Ratmouth / Shack Of Hate / Crow 2 / Drowning The Colossus / Die Zombie Die / Skin / Truck On Fire / Future Shock / Scum Kill / Diamond Ass
MAKE THEM DIE SLOWLY, Caroline CARCD 3 (1989)
Demonspeed / Disaster Blaster / Murderworld / Revenge / Acid Flesh / Power Hungry / Godslayer
LA SEXORCISTO: DEVIL MUSIC VOL. 1, Geffen GEFD 24460 (1992) **26 USA**
Welcome To Planet Motherfucker / Psychedelic Slag / Knuckle Duster (Radio L.A.) / Thunder Kiss '65 / Black Sunshine / Soul Crusher / Cosmic Monsters Inc. / Spiderbaby (Yeah, Yeah, Yeah) / Knuckle Duster (Radio 2 B) / Thrust! / One Big Crunch / Grindhouse (A Go Go) / Starface / Warp Asylum
ASTROCREEP 2000: SONGS OF LOVE,

DESTRUCTION AND OTHER SYNTHETIC ILLUSIONS OF THE ELECTRICHEAD, Geffen GED 24806 (1995) **25 UK, 6 USA**
Electric Head Part One (The Agony) / Super Charger Heaven / Real Solution No. 9 / Creature Of The Wheel / Electric Head Part Two (The Ecstasy) / Grease Paint And Monkey Brains / I, Zombie / More Human Than Human / El Phantasmo And The Chicken Run Blast-O-Rama / Blur The Technicolor / Blood, Milk And Sky / The Sidewalk Ends Where The Parade Begins
SUPERSEXY SWINGIN' SOUNDS, Geffen GED 24976 (1996) **17 USA**
Phantasmo / Blood, Milk & Sky / Real Solution / Electronic Head Part 1 / I'm Your Boogie Man / Electronic Head Part 2 / More Human Than Human / I, Zombie / Grease Paint And Monkey Brains / Blur The Technicolour / Super Charger Heaven

WIND OF THE BLACK MOUNTAINS
(USA)

WIND OF THE BLACK MOUNTAINS is a one man project from MASOCHIST founder member Tchort. Ejected from MASOCHIST (as that band evolved into SUMMON) Thchort endeavoured with his highly praised Doomy Black Metal venture.
A bass player intended to become a member of the band was to fall out with Tchort and subsequently created the solo venture BURNING WINDS.

Singles/EPs:
Force Fed Into Blasphemy / The Rise Of Darkness, Moribund)

Albums:
SING THOU UNHOLY SERVANTS, Moribund (1998)
Force Fed Into Blasphemy / An Autumn Evening / Black Goat / Beautiful Sorrow / Adversary / The Rite Of Darkness / The Shadow / Thou Shalt Not Mourn

WINGS OF FURY (HOLLAND)
Line-Up: Miriam Dammers (vocals), Wilburt Beurskens (guitar), Tim Oehlen (guitar), Aryan Wever (bass), Marc Wassen (keyboards), Pascal Wilbers (drums)

A relatively young Gothic Metal band founded as THE FACULTY in 1999. Initially guitarist Wilburt Beurskens and keyboard player Marc Wassen formulated the idea for a band and with the addition of second guitarist Tim Oehlen and soprano vocalist Miriam Dammers this unit became THE FACULTY. In January of 2000 the band was brought up to strength with a rhythm section of bass player Aryan Wever and drummer Pascal Wilbers and subsequently switched titles to become WINGS OF FURY.
The band debuted with the self-financed 'Enigma Of Life' demo EP.

Singles/EPs:
The Poem Of Truth (Intro) / Hogmanay Night / Shattered Paradise / The Last Words / Drowning Visions, Wings Of Life (2000) ('Enigma Of Life' EP)

WINTER (USA)
Line-Up: John Alman (vocals / bass), Stephen Flam (guitar), Joe Conclaves (drums)

A truly underground Doom act. WINTER's releases are highly sought after gems of depression. Guitarist Stephen Flam later turned up as a member of THORN.

Albums:
INTO DARKNESS, Future Shock (1991)
Oppression Freedom Oppression (Reprise) / Servants Of The Warsmen / Goden / Power And Might / Destiny / Eternal Frost / Into Darkness
ETERNAL FROST, Nuclear Blast (1994)

WISH (HOLLAND)
Line-Up: Bart Smith (vocals), Alwin Roes, Micha v.d. Ven

Industrial Dance / Gothic Metal act WISH were created in 1993 by ex-THE GATHERING vocalist Bart Smits and former Doom Metallers Alwin and Micha, both ex-DEAD END. Initially the band employed two bassists but dispensed with one to inaugurate guitarist Xander van Aart for debut album 'Monochrome'. Following an EP 'Jane Doe' and the demo tape 'Eve Of Self Destruction' van Aart departed and was replaced by Bas van der Kar.
WISH bounced back in 1999 with an EP release upfront of the 2000 mini album 'Ground Zero Heaven'.

Singles/EPs:
Bitch / Fetish / Feather / The Miracle Gun, Sound Riot SRP.09 (2000) ('Ground Zero Heaven' EP)

Albums:
MONOCHROME, Moon Light MOON 001 (1995)
Balance / Ten Bridges Burning / Rain / Thelena / Elsewhen / Judas Kiss / Gentle Nova / Monument

445

WITCHFINDER GENERAL (UK)

Line-Up: Zeeb (vocals), Phil Cope (guitars), Rod Hawks (bass), Graham Ditchfield (drums)

Wolverhampton NWOBHM tongue in cheek occult based Metal band formed in 1979 by vocalist Zeeb and guitarist Phil Cope. Original members included bassist Toss McReady and drummer Steve Kinsell. WITCHFINDER GENERAL's Doom driven style was heavily reminiscent of prime time BLACK SABBATH indeed the band were often dismissed by critics who ventured the comparison was too derivative.

The band signed to Heavy Metal Records in 1980 and released the poorly produced 'Burning A Sinner' single. The debut album was handled by producer Pete Hinton. WITCHFINDER GENERAL split with their rhythm section whilst in the studio and quickly added bassist Rod Hawks and drummer Graham Ditchfield.

The debut album attracted publicity as the sleeve featured Page Three model Joanne Latham being ritually 'executed' on a gravestone. The second album sleeve rather too predictably followed up on this theme.

Oddly, in spite of achieving little during the band's lifetime, in recent times WITCHFINDER GENERAL have enjoyed posthumous respect from numerous Death Metal and Doom bands.

A later WITCHFINDER GENERAL member bassist Zakk Bajjon created BAJJON, later joined Steve Grimmett's LIONSHEART and would gain kudos by producing CRADLE OF FILTH.

With the resurgence of interest in NWoBHM across Europe it looked as though the WITCHFINDER GENERAL albums would unfortunately be never reissued as Heavy Metal Records label boss Paul Birch is now a born again Christian and objects to the band's lyrical stance. However, after much pressure 'Death Penalty' finally saw a 1996 CD release. By 2000 Bajjon was a member of RAINMAKER 888.

Singles/EPs:
Burning A Sinner / Satan's Children, Heavy Metal HEAVY 6 (1981)
Soviet Invasion / Rabies / R.I.P., Heavy Metal HM 17 (1982)
Music / Last Chance, Heavy Metal HMPD 21 (1983)

Albums:
DEATH PENALTY, Heavy Metal HMRLP 7 (1982)
Invisible Hate / Free Country / Death Penalty / No Stayer / Witchfinder General / Burning A Sinner / RIP
FRIENDS OF HELL, Heavy Metal HMRLP 13 (1983)
Love On Smack / Last Chance / Music / Friends Of Hell / Requiem For Youth / Shadowed Images / I Lost You / Quietus Reprise

WITCH MOUNTAIN (Portland, OR, USA)

Line-Up: Rob Wrong (vocals / guitar), Johnny Beluzzi (guitar), David Noopaugh (bass), Nathan Carson (drums)

A Portland Psychedelia infused Doom band of high repute. WITCH MOUNTAIN was founded by a union of vocalist / guitarist Rob Wrong, an erstwhile member of IOMMI STUBBS and M99 and drummer Nate Carson of BRONZE and BISHOP OF BATTLE. The group went through a succession of bass players until Kip Larson's position was taken by David Noopaugh, another former IOMMI STUBBS man.

Recordings intended for demos would be released by the Rage Of Achilles label as the 1999 mini-album 'Homegrown Doom' The follow up full-length album '...Come The Mountain' would be recorded in August of 2000 and co-produced by Mike Lastra of SMEGMA. Erica Stolz of LOST GOAT contributes guest vocals to the track 'A Power Greater'.

'...Come The Mountain' would be reissued by the Mountastic label during 2002 with added extra tracks. WITCH MOUNTAIN would act as headliners at the Arizona 'Stoner Hands Of Doom' festival in November.

Albums:
HOMEGROWN DOOM, Rage Of Achilles ILIAD003 (1999)
Indian Passage / Foxy Mule / Victim Of Chord Changes / Iron Long (Part I) / Iron Long (Part II)
...COME THE MOUNTAIN, Rage Of Achilles ILIAD011 (2001)
Rock On / Indian Passage / Victim Of Chord Changes / Foxy Mule / A Power Greater / Iron Long (Pt. 1) / Iron Long (Pt. 2) / Rocaine / Iron Long (Pt. 3) / The Scientist's

WITHERING SPRING

(Newton, MA, USA)
Line-Up: Max Kovalsky (vocals / guitar), Eugene Tikh (guitar / keyboards), John Leighton (bass), Dylan Campbell (drums)

Doom Black-Death act WITHERING SPRING issued a brace of demos, 1995's 'Seasons Past' and the 1997 'Forsaken Future' tape.

WITCH MOUNTAIN
Photo : El Danno

WITHIN TEARS (Brooklyn, NY, USA)

WITHIN TEARS is the "one man musical journey into pain and misery" of Anthony Lauer. The band's original formation in 1999 had been that of a duo with vocalist / guitarist / keyboard player Lauer working in alliance with vocalist Sal Sgroi, both former members of Hardcore outfit SUBJECTION. Session personnel employed at this time included vocalist Barbara Nolan and drummer Andrew K. This unit recorded the 2001 album 'Moments Of Life… Chapter One' self-financed album which included a cover version of the CANDLEMASS track 'Solitude'. A second album 'A Soul Frozen In Sorrow' was projected for 2002 release.

WITHIN TEMPATION (HOLLAND)
Line-Up: Sharon Janny den Adel (vocals), Robert Westerholt (guitar), Michiel Papenhove (guitar), Jeroen van Veen (bass), David Martien Westerholt (keyboards), Ivar de Graaf (drums)

Doom Metal act WITHIN TEMPTATION have made serious headway into the European market with a series of adventurous releases. The band, founded during 1996, is fronted by the striking figure of vocalist Sharon Janny den Adel. Former THE CIRCLE and VOYAGE guitarist Robert Westerholt convened the act, drafting his girlfriend den Adel and erstwhile band colleagues bassist Jeroen van Veen and guitar player Michiel Papenhove. NEMESIS man Dennis Leeflang would occupy the drum stool and Roberts brother David Martijn took over the keyboard role.

This line-up recorded the 'Enter' demos and within a few months had various record company offers to choose from. Signing to the DSFA label WITHIN TEMPTATION would also at this juncture manouevere Ivar de Graaf onto the drum stool. Leeflang subsequently joined forces with TIME MACHINE and SUN CAGED.

The inaugural 'Enter' album was released in April 1997. An appearance at the 'Dynamo' festival led to a two week tour throughout Europe. However, by the close of the year de Graaf had made his exit. His replacement was Ciro Palma.

WITHIN TEMPTATION would perform at the 'Dynamo' festival once more the following year, this time promoted to the main stage, and would also appear at the 'Noorderslag' event. A mini-album 'The Dance' would be released to capitalize on this exposure.

In 1999 de Graaf made his return. WITHIN TEMPTATION would completely dispense with the Death Metal vocal style for the Oscar Holleman produced 'Mother Earth' album relying solely on den Adel's majestic vocal ability. The move would garner a whole new fan base for the band. Meanwhile, outside activities for den Adel would see the vocalist acting in a guest capacity for AYREON and on the AFTER FOREVER 'Prison Of Desire' album.

Guitar player Michiel Papenhove would depart in mid 2001. For live work during August Ruud Jolie of BROTHERHOOD FOUNDATION filled in prior to Jelle Bakker, a member of FROZEN SUN, taking the position permanently.

During November WITHIN TEMPTATION announced a rather unique show performed with the Broerekerk Church in Zwolle complete with full choir and Opera singer. Fans received the news with such enthusiasm a second show had to be added to satisfy demand.

WITHIN TEMPTATION members van Veen, de Graaf and Papenhove also operate the avant-garde Rock outfit J.I.M. GENERATOR. By mid 2002 Ivar de Graaf was also ensconced in the Dutch / Belgian Doom 'Supergroup' LES FAIDITS assembled by ex-SENGIR members singer Jurgen Cobbaut and guitarist Kris Scheerlinck.

Singles/EPs:
Restless / Pearls Of Light / Restless (Classical version), DSFA (1997)
Our Farewell (Radio version) / Dark Wings / Our Farewell (Album version) / Our Farewell (Acoustic version), DSFA (2001)
Ice Queen (Radio version) / Mother Earth (Live - Leidse Kade) / Caged (Live - Leidse Kade) / Ice Queen (Live - Leidse Kade) / Ice Queen (August 2000 Demo) / Caged (August 2000 Demo), DSFA (2001)

Albums:
ENTER, DSFA (1997)
Restless / Enter / Pearls Of Light / Deep Within / Gatekeeper / Grace / Blooded / Candles / Restless (Classical version)
THE DANCE, DSFA (1999)
The Dance / Another Day / The Other Half (Of Me) / Pearls Of Light (Remix) / Restless (Remix)
MOTHER EARTH, DSFA (2001)
Mother Earth / Ice Queen / Our Farewell / Caged / The Promise / Never-ending Story / Deceiver Of Fools / Intro / Dark Wings / Perfect Harmony

WITHOUT FACE (HUNGARY)
Line-Up: Juliette (vocals), Andras (vocals), Roomy (guitar), Akos (bass), Sazsa (keyboards), Peter (drums)

Progressive Gothic act WITHOUT FACE, founded in 1997, marked their arrival with a demo the following year. The band, which employs both female lead vocals of Juliette and male lead of Andras, issued a debut album 'Deep Inside' through Hammer Music Productions in June of 2000. This would subsequently see an American license through Dark Symphonies in December of 2001.

WITHOUT FACE signed to Earache subsidiary Elitist Records for the 2002 effort 'Astonomicon'.

Albums:
DEEP INSIDE, Hammer Music Productions (2000)
Caledioscope / Sands Of Time / I And I / Hymn To The Night / Screaming Heartbeat / Deepression / The Picture

WOOLY MAMMOTH
(Washington D.C, USA)
Line-Up: Zac Eller (vocals / guitar), Jason Dale Stevens (guitar), Aaron Claxton (bass), Phil Adler (drums)

Singles/EPs:
Ten Ton Baby / Crying Dog / Six Hundred Pounds Of Stolen Trucker Speed / Elm Hall, Underdogma (2002) ('Ten Ton Baby' EP)

WORSHIP (FRANCE / GERMANY)
Line-Up: Mad Max (vocals / drums), Daniel The Doomonger (guitar)

Truly bleak, moroseful Doom. WORSHIP exemplifies life becoming art as, according to reports frontman 'Mad Max' would commit suicide by jumping off a bridge. The group was centred on Frenchman Mad Max, also known as editor of the 'Ocean Morphique' fanzine and German guitarist Daniel The Doomonger, known for his previous endeavours with SOMBER SERENITY.

WORSHIP debuted with a 1999 cassette 'Last Tape Before Doomsday', the band making a statement with their self-styled "trend krushing" Doom, dismissing all Gothic pretensions. A split 7" EP release shared with Belgians AGATHOCLES then arrived on the Impaler Of Trendies label and a further 10" split release in union with STABAT MATER for Pianiac.

Max recorded his parts for the debut album 'Last Vinyl Before Doomsday' before journeying to Canada. Upon his return, and after a reported heavy drinking session in July of 2001, he ended his life.

Albums:
LAST VINYL BEFORE DOOMSDAY,
Pianiac (2001)
Whispering Gloom / Solicide And The Dawning Of The Moonkult / Eclipse Of Sorrow / Worship

THE WOUNDED (HOLLAND)
Line-Up: Marco van der Velde (vocals / guitar), Edwin Pol (guitar), Andy Haandrikrnan (bass), Jonne Ziemgs (keyboards), Ralph de Vries (drums)

THE WOUNDED are a melancholic Dark Wave outfit that layer classical Progressive elements atop their Gothically charged Rock. Quite incredibly bravely for a Hard Rock act THE WOUNDED took on a cover of BRONSKI BEAT's 'Smalltown Boy' for their album 'The Art Of Grief', although the band did introduce not only an unhitherto missing heaviness but the very un-Jimmy Sommerville-like line of 'Stay the fuck away'! The band began life in 1999, founded by vocalist / guitarist Marco van der Velde, bassist Andy Haandrikmaan and guitarist Erwin Pol. The group debuted with a demo tape 'Starpeople' and for a time employed the services of bassist Nick Brockman. Upon the latter's enrollment in the SALACIOUS GODS Haandrikmaan resumed his position.

Pol made his exit in the Spring of 2001, being replaced by Erwin de Jong. THE WOUNDED came back with a second album for Cold Blood Industries in 2002 'Monument'. The band would induct drummer Alwin Schnoing in early June.

By mid 2002 Jonne Ziengs was also ensconced in the Dutch / Belgian Doom 'Supergroup' LES FAIDITS assembled by ex-SENGIR members singer Jurgen Cobbaut and guitarist Kris Scheerlinck.

Albums:
THE ART OF GRIEF, Coldblood Industries (2000)
Your Roses Will Burn / Smalltown Boy / We Pass Our Bridal Days / The Art Of Grief / Frailty Thy Name Is Woman / (Where Are You Now) / Against All Gods / Billet Doux / In Silence...

THE WOUNDED

WRENCH (AUSTRALIA)
Line-Up: Nigel (vocals), Craig (guitar), Jon (bass), Chris (drums)

Albums:
OSCILLATOR BLUES, High Beam HBM003 (2001)
Gravitron / Humanoid / Twenty Times / Oscillator Blues / Free Ride / Drive On / Aloha Mama / Sleepy John / Avalanche / Headlight / Lights Came Down / Green Mars

WRETCHED (Washington D.C.,USA)
Line-Up: Dave Sherman (vocals), Jeff Parsons (guitar), Johnny Wretched (bass), Gus Basilika (drums)

A riff based Doom act that rode the renaissance wave of U.S. Doom propagated by the German Hellhound label. The debut 1993 album witnessed a line-up of former HEAVY SOUL man Dave Sherman on vocals, guitarist Jeff Parsons, bassist Johnny Wretched and drummer Gus Basilika. Mike Phillips took over the drum stool for the final album, 1995's 'Center Of The Universe'.
During 1996 the WRETCHED line-up comprised Sherman, Parsons, Wretched and drummer Gary Isom, the latter a veteran of such underground acts as UNORTHODOX, IRON MAN and HEAVY SOUL. With WRETCHED's demise Isom teamed up with famed Doomsters PENTAGRAM.
Vocalist Dave Sherman later came to prominence as a member of SPIRIT CARAVAN and EARTHRIDE. Jeff Parsons journeyed through UNORTHODOX and INDESTROY whilst Gus Basilika was also prominent in INDESTROY, GUTSOUP and LIFE BEYOND.

Albums:
LIFE OUT THERE, Hellhound (1993)
Endless Morning / Verbal Suicide / The One I Seek / Standing Down / Unknown Soul / No Stopping / Living In Dread / See Your Face / Life Out There / The Fight
PSYCHOSOMATIC MEDICINE, Hellhound (1994)
Golden Child / Blind Commitment / Peace Run / Still Life / Define Why / What Will Become / Watch And See
CENTER OF THE UNIVERSE, Hellhound (1995)
Losing World / Realm Of Freedom / Centre Of The Universe / Unveiled / Suspended Animation / Kingpin / Doom Jesus / Day In Day Out / Snakebite

WYTCHCRAFT (GERMANY)
Line-Up: Kai Tubbesing (vocals), Patrice Kestner (guitar), Daniel Westheide (guitar), Eric Asmussen (bass), Fabian Regmann (drums)

The inception of German Doom band WYTCHCRAFT was instigated in 1998 after founder members Patrice Kestner, ex-SATANIZED, and Daniel Westheide, a veteran of HALLOWED SINS and VOX DEORUM, had just indulged in a heavy CANDLEMASS album listening session. Thoroughly inspired the duo set to work, although it would be a year and a half before any solid progress was made. An initial self-financed EP of May 1999, recorded with the aid of a drum machine, found Kestner handling vocals. The opening track 'Beyond' subsequently appeared on two compilation albums 'Eternal Malice' and the Twilight magazine offering 'Into The Dark Season'. WYTCHCRAFT even scored radio play in far flung Argentina.
During the summer of 2000 SHATTERED LIFE, OPION and DEAD SVAN DARK man vocalist Kai Tubbesing joined the fold and the following year TWILIGHT PICTURES bassist Eric Asmussen also entered the picture. Drummer Fabian Regmann completed the line-up.
Patrice Kestner also operates Death Metal band HUMAN TARGET.

Albums:
TO DIE IN THE ARMS OF WINTER, (2002)
To Die In The Arms Of Winter / Questions / Under The Surface (Live) / Entities From An Unknown Plane (Live) / Beyond (Live)

YEARNING (FINLAND)
Line-Up: Juhani Palomäki
(vocals / guitar / keyboards),
Tero Kalliomäki (guitar), Petri
Salo (bass), Toni Kostiainen
(drums)

Sombre Metal act created in 1994 under an original title of FLEGETON. First product was the demo 'Through The Desolate Lands' prior to a title switch to YEARNING and a further four track tape billed as 'The Temple Of Sagal'. Inaugural outing for the French Holy label was the inclusion of the track 'Autumn Funeral' on the 'Holy Bible' compilation. The debut album 'With Tragedies Adorned' was recorded at Tico Tico studios in September 1996 and released in February of the following year.

'With Tragedies Adorned' saw YEARNING citing a line-up comprising Juhani Palomäki on vocals, guitars and keyboards, guitarist Tero Kalliomäki, bass player 'Mr. Woodland' (Petri Salo) and drummer T. Kristian. Later that year the group also cut their version of PARADISE LOST's 'Eternal' for donation to a tribute album. This band formation held solid for the follow up 'Plaintive Scenes' but by the time of the third album 'Frore Meadow' YEARNING was down to an official duo of Juhani Palomäki and T. Kristian.

Drummer Toni Kostiainen would fill in on a live session basis for THYRANE during 2001. YEARNING themselves toured Europe in October of 2001 alongside label mates MISANTHROPE and GLOOMY GRIM enlisting guitarist Matti S., bassist Loikas and keyboard player Jouni J.N. for these dates.

Albums:
WITH TRAGEDIES ADORNED, Holy (1997)
Remnants Of The Only Delight / Bleeding For Sinful Crown / Flown Away / Haze Of Despair / The Temple Of Sagal / Release / In The Hands Of Storm / Canticum
PLAINTIVE SCENES, Holy (1999)
Naaveta / Unwritten / Grey / Soliloquy / Plaintive Scenes / Soliloquy II / Eyes Of The Black Flame / Nameless
FRORE MEADOW, Holy (2001)
Bleak / Solitary / Autumn / The Fall / Years Of Pain / Forsaken / Frore Meadow / The Race / Elegy Of Blood / In Strange Slowfooted Fever / Disappearance

YEAR ZERO (UK)
Line-Up: Russ McAteer (vocals), Mark Griffiths (guitar), Murray Geddes (bass), Mike Unsworth (drums)

Formed by guitarist Mark Griffiths following

his departure from CATHEDRAL at the close of their 1992 American tour. Opened for COUNT RAVEN in 1994. Griffiths would later join the post CARCASS act BLACKSTAR.

Albums:
NIHIL'S FLAME, Hellhound H0027-2 (1994)
Prefall / Planetfall / Headache Station / Harsh Believing / Civilization Dreaming / Wishing Horse / Year Zero / Evergreen (Fool's Throne) / Shining Violet / Invention Of God / Eternal Dawn
CREATION, Hellhound H0038-2 (1995)
Solar Creation / Inches Deep / The Savage Wound / Zeal For War / Mirror Spirit / Kingdom Pain / Mainline Inertia / Delirium Bound / Chaos Cage

YETI (TX, USA)
Line-Up: Eric Harris (guitar), Tommy Atkins (bass), Doug Ferguson (keyboards), Jon Teague (drums)

YETI issued a Progressive, sombre instrumental album 'Things To Come' which reaped immediate underground praise. The band had been created during the Autumn of 1998 as a merger between two acts, the already existing YETI and EST MORT. Sadly keyboard player Doug Ferguson died of pancreatitis shortly after release. He was just 32 years old.

Albums:
THINGS TO COME, Two Ohm Hop (2000)
Two Fingers / Interstellar Biplane / Go Like This / Est Mort

YOB (Portland, OR, USA)
Line-Up: Mike Scheidt (vocals / guitar), Isamu Satu (bass), Gabe Morley (drums)

Supremely heavy Doom mongers. YOB was brought into being by vocalist / guitarist Mike Scheidt during the mid '90s. Previous to founding YOB Scheidt had operated as a drummer with Hardcore acts CHEMIKILL and DIRTY SANCHEZ and held down bass duties in H.C. MINDS. The original incarnation of YOB featured Scheidt alongside bassist Lowell Iles and drummer Greg Ocon. However, by the time of recording the 2001 album 'Elaboration's Of Carbon' Yob comprised Scheidt, bassist Isamu Satu, previously with Death Metal act THROMBUS and former LIGHTWEIGHT drummer Gabe Morley.
Satu also operates H.C. MINDS whilst Morley divides his time with FINGERTRAP.
YOB signed to the Swedish Lunasound label for an October 2002 album 'Catharsis'.

Albums:
ELABORATIONS OF CARBON, 12th
Records (2001)
Universe Throb / All The Children Forgotten /
Clear Seeing / Revolution / Pain Of J /
Asleepin Samsara

ZARAZA (CANADA)
Line-Up: Jacek The Doomhammer (vocals / keyboards / samples), Grzegorz Haus Ov Doom (vocals / keyboards)

A 1993 founded experimentation in Doom. Originally intending on a Grindcore direction the duo of Jacek The Doomhammer and Grzegorz Haus Ov Doom subsequently shifted tack into electronic Doom. A demo 'Life Is Death Postponed' preceded the 1997 album 'Slavic Blasphemy'. A further album 'No Paradise To Lose' was cut in 1999 but the band members dissatisfaction with the finished result saw its postponement.
ZARAZA debuted live in May of 1999 as opening act to MERZBOW. For this performance TRONDANT vocalist Chloe joined them. The 'No Paradise To Lose' recordings, complete with an intended bonus disc of three LAIBACH covers, was made available in MP3 format.

Albums:
SLAVIC BLASPHEMY, Musicus Phycus (1997)
24 Hours / Zakazany / Every Day Is A Funeral / Necessary / Cell Of Skin / Zaraza

ZEBULON (SWEDEN)
Line-Up: Klas Morberg (guitar / vocals), Hakan Morberg (guitars), Jojje Bohlin (bass), Thomas Johnson (drums)

ZEBULON is rooted in the Stockholm Death Metal act DESULTORY, an act that issued a series of commendable albums, 'Forever Gone' in 1992, 'Into Eternity' in 1993, 'Bitterness' in 1994 and the final effort 'Swallow The Snake' during 1996, the last three for Metal Blade Records.
Pulling in bass player Jojje Bohlin during 1997 the act switched musical direction, becoming ZEBULON in the process. A February 1998 demo session secured a label deal with the German Century Media label and the band entered the studios with DISMEMBER's Fred Estby to record tracks for an intended EP release. These songs would eventually emerge on the 'Cape Canaria' EP, released by the small German specialists People Like You.
ZEBULON would debut live as openers for ENTOMBED during December of 1999.

Singles/EPs:
Overflown / The Day / Burning Fuel / Goddamned, People Like You (2000) ('Cape Canaria' EP)

Albums:
VOLUME 1, People Like You (2001)
Funeral Trip / Burning Fuel / Follow The Blind / Demonic / Blood And Her Sisters / Tempo Gigante / Overflown / A Beautiful War / Down-Out / Whips And Robots

ZEROCHARISMA (FINLAND)
Line-Up: Manne Ikonen (vocals), Tommi Kiviniemi (guitar), Ville Liekkinen (guitar), Mikko Paavilainen (bass), Aki Parviainen (drums)

Detuned Riff Rockers ZEROCHARISMA started out in the mid '90s. Lead vocalist Manne Ikonen would be added following recording of the debut 2000 'Flip The Man' EP, issued by the German Monster Zero label.
ZEROCHARISMA would donate the previously unheard track 'Undertakeaway' to a 2002 People Like You compilation album 'The Mighty Desert Rock Evengers' in mid 2002.

Singles/EPs:
Oracle Ridin' / Astro Caliphornia / Space Probe / Flip The Man, Monster Zero MZR003 (2000) ('Flip The Man' EP)
Voodoo Science / Liftin' Phoenix, World WORLD001 (2001)

ZOIC (SWEDEN)
Line-Up: Fredric Olsson (vocals), Lasse Johansson (guitar), Mappe Björkman (guitar), Peter Edwards (bass), Janne Lindh (drums)

ZOIC was forged by former CANDLEMASS guitarist Lasse Johansson with the services of his CANDLEMASS colleagues Mats 'Mappe' Bjorkmann, also a former member of ATC, and drummer Janne Lindh. Also joining in were VENI DOMINE's vocalist Fredric Olsson and bassist Peter Edwards.
Former CRIMSON GLORY frontman Midnight was originally slated to perform vocals on the album but financial constraints rendered this idea redundant.
Fredric Olsson later contributed backing vocals for GODGORY. Guitarist Mappe Bjorkman would be operating CRANK during 2001.

Albums:
TOTAL LEVEL OF DESTRUCTION, Powerline PLRCD01 (1996)
Intro / No Time / What Do You Believe In / Madmen / Warlords / Lost My Faith / Raven's Death (Instrumental) / Words Was Spoken / Never Be The Same / St. Dilon (Instrumental)

ROB ZOMBIE (USA)

WHITE ZOMBIE main man Rob Zombie released his debut solo album, 'Hellbilly Deluxe', in August 1998. The album was recorded with WHITE ZOMBIE / ex-TESTAMENT guitarist John Tempesta, NINE INCH NAILS duo Charlie Clouser and Danny Lohner and MÖTLEY CRÜE drummer TOMMY LEE. For live work Zombie employed the services of Blasko, in reality ex-SUFFER / DROWN and DANZIG man Rob Nicholson.

The 1999 'Words & Music Of Frankenstein' album is Zombie's homage soundtrack to the classic '30s horror movies. A 2000 album of remixes saw tracks mixed by Clouser and German Art-Industrialists RAMMSTEIN. Behind the scenes Zombie would be working on a $7 million horror movie 'House Of 1000 Corpses' for a June 2001 release through Universal. However, Universal deemed the film's content too graphic and backed out.

The November 2001 release 'The Sinister Urge' would see none other than OZZY OSBOURNE as a high profile guest vocalist. When launched into the public domain the album would sell just under 150,000 copies in its debut week in America landing a number 8 chart placing. The album track 'Never Gonna Stop' would also turn up as part of the soundtrack to 2002's 'Rollerball', a remake of the cult '70s Sci-fi horror movie. Zombie would also have new material featured on the March 2002 'WWF Forcible Entry' compilation issued by Columbia Records donating 'Never Gonna Stop' (Edge's Theme).

For ROB ZOMBIE's early 2002 American headline dates British Punk veterans THE DAMNED were announced as support act. However, within a few shows THE DAMNED had pulled themselves from the tour, reportedly disappointed at the lukewarm crowd reaction. Later shows had Zombie stepping up to headline the second stage for the 'Ozzfest' tour.

Further studio activity found Zombie working alongside Joey Ramone on a genuine all star cast tribute album 'We're A Happy Family'. The pair brought in the expected names of the current Rock / Punk world but also such heavyweights as U2, KISS, THE PRETENDERS and METALLICA. Zombie himself donated his take on 'Blitzkrieg Bop'. It would also be learnt that Zombie was still engaged in production of his horror flick 'House Of 1000 Corpses', taking the independent route since the project was dropped by Universal. The movie would subsequently be picked up by Lions Gate Films.

Albums:
HELLBILLY DELUXE, Geffen (1998)
19 NEW ZEALAND, 45 SWEDEN, 37 UK
Call Of The Zombie / Superbeast / Dragula / Living Dead Girl / Perversion / Demonoid Phenomenon / Spookshow Baby / How To Make A Monster / Meet The Creeper / The Ballad Of Resurrection Joe And Rosa Whore / What Lurks On Channel X? / Return Of The Phantom Stranger / The Beginning Of The End
THE WORDS & THE MUSIC OF FRANKENSTEIN, Zombie A Go Go (1999)
A Word Of Friendly Warning / Frankenstein - Main Title / The Moon's Rising / You Shall Have Your Proof / Look! It's Moving! / Come Away, Fritz / He Hated Fritz / Search Every Ravine / Bring Him To The Village / A Toast / Grand Appassionato / The Bride Of Frankenstein / Prologue / I'm Glad To See The Monster Roasted / Monster Entrance / The Monster! It's Alive! / Processional March / Forget? If Only I Forget / A Strange Apparition - Pretrus Entrance / You'll Need A Coat / Pastorale / Chase Music - Crucifixion - Monster Breaks Out / We Beter Get Away From These Parts / The Hermit's Fiddle (Ave Maria) / Alone-Bad, Friend-Good / The Music Of Friends (Ave Maria) / This Is The Fiend / Fire In The Hut - The Graveyard / Dance Macabre- Female Monster Music / Monster Enters - Monster Theme / In The Tower Part 1 / In The Tower Part 2 / Creation Part 1 / Creation Part 2 - Female Monster Music / Creation Part 2 / She Hate Me... Like Others / Explosion Part 1 / Explosion Part 2 / The Son Of Frankenstein - Main Title / It Wasn't My Father's Fault / The Message / The General / The Discovery / The Examination / Has He Asked You To Rob Any Graves? / The Result Of The Examination / The Giant-Looking For A Monster / The Evil Flute (Flute Solo 1) / I Scare Him To Death / The Evil Flute (Flute Solo 2) / Don't Touch Him, Frankenstein / The Death Of Ygor / There's A Monster Afoot / The Monster Appears - The Monster's Lament / Monster On A Rampage - The Menace Destroyed / Herewith I Deed To You
AMERICAN MADE MUSIC TO STRIP BY, Geffen 490349-2 (2000)
Dragula (Si Non Oscillas, Noli Tintinnare mix) / Living Dead Girl (Subliminal Seduction mix) / Superbeast (Girl On A Motorcycle mix) / Meet The Creeper (Pink Pussy mix) / How To Make A Monster (Kitty's Purrrrformance mix) / Spookshow Baby (Black Leather Cat Suit mix) 7. What Lurks On Channel X? (XXX mix) / Demonoid Phenomenon (Sin Lives mix) / Return Of The Phantom Stranger (Tuesday Night At The Chop Shop mix) / The Ballad Of Resurrection Joe And

Rosa Whore (Ilsa She-Wolf Of Hollywood
mix)
THE SINISTER URGE, Geffen 493147
(2001) **38 FINLAND, 8 USA, 12 CANADA**
Sinners Inc. / Demon Speeding / Dead Girl
Superstar / Never Gonna Stop (The Red,
Red Kroovy) / Iron Head / (Go To) California
/ Feel So Numb / Transylvania Transmissions
(Part 1) / Bring Her Down (To Crippletown) /
Sum Of The Earth / House Of 1,000
Corpses

Also available from

CHERRY RED BOOKS

Rockdetector
A-Z of
BLACK METAL
Garry Sharpe-Young

ISBN 1-901447-30-8

Throughout the history of Rock no other genre has pushed the boundaries of aural extremity and social rebellion quite like Black Metal. Many of the bands in this book operate way beyond the parameters of the established Rock scene carving their own left hand path in the darkest depths of true underground music.

Over a decade Black Metal has spawned legions of bands making up a truly global rebellion. For the first time ever this ultimate authority documents detailed biographies, line-ups and full discographies with track listings of over 1,000 groups.

Included are in-depth treatises on the major artists such as CRADLE OF FILTH, DIMMU BORGIR, EMPEROR, MAYHEM, IMMORTAL and MARDUK as well as spanning out to include sub-genres such as Viking Metal, the Black Ambient scene and even the ultimate irony of Christian Black Metal. Also chronicled are the originators such as VENOM, WITCHFYNDE, BATHORY and MERCYFUL FATE.

Paper covers, 416 pages, £14.99 in UK

www.cherryred.co.uk

Rockdetector
A-Z of
DEATH METAL
Garry Sharpe-Young

ISBN 1-901447-35-9

Reviled and revered in equal measure since its inception over a decade ago the phenomenon known as Death Metal has pushed Hard Rock music to the very edge of acceptability and way beyond. Born out of the Thrash Metal eruption, Death Metal took vocals to the realms of the unintelligibly insane, drove the blastbeats harder and pushed guitar riffs into a swarming blur. The familiar mythical subject matter of its parent Heavy Metal, and its bastard offspring Grindcore, has become the pariah of the music world as much as the depths of the underground scene has fostered and nurtured its steady growth to this day with each band striving to achieve renewed goals of sickness.

From the founding fathers such as NAPALM DEATH, CARCASS, DEATH, INCANTATION, IMPETIGO and MORBID ANGEL to the rise of Swedish Death Metal legends IN FLAMES, CARNAGE and AT THE GATES, the Death Metal of MARDUK, the Christian Death Metal of MORTIFICATION and the politically charged Noisecore of AGATHOCLES. All genres old and new are analyzed in depth with full career histories and detailed discographies.

No area of the globe has provided a safe haven and this book documents the burgeoning uprise of Death Metal bands in the Far East, Eastern Europe and South America.

Be warned - even though some of the band names are not for the faint-hearted the song titles will leave you reeling.

Paper covers, 416 pages, £14.99 in UK

Rockdetector
A-Z of
POWER METAL
Garry Sharpe-Young

ISBN 1-901447-13-8

Power Metal is Heavy Metal taken to the absolute, surgically precise, limit. When the major Metal institutions staked their claim they engendered a whole legion of followers in their wake. These up and coming acts were not simply content to match the volume levels of their forefathers though. Riffs evolved into complex, labyrinthine proportions, vocals scorched higher altitudes and, yes, they even managed to crank out some more volume as part of the formula. Power Metal had been born.

The acceleration of aggression afforded by the Thrash Metal movement helped boost the rise of Power Metal. As the first wave of Thrash waned, a ready audience of Metal fans lay waiting for something just as heavy but with sophistication. The British guard such as IRON MAIDEN and JUDAS PRIEST had opened the door, now a whole flood of American Metal flooded through ATTACKER, JAG PANZER, ICED EARTH, SAVATAGE and QUEENSRYCHE. In Europe bands rooted in Thrash matured at an alarming rate with HELLOWEEN, GAMMA RAY, BLIND GUARDIAN, RUNNING WILD and GRAVE DIGGER establishing lengthy careers. In latter years Power Metal itself has branched off on its own evolutionary trail spawning Symphonic Metal and Progressive Metal. A recent upsurge in the fortunes of bands such as SONATA ARTICA from Finland, ANGRA from Brazil and RHAPSODY from Italy illustrates just how global the reach of Power Metal has become. Cult acts from the 80s have been reforming at an alarming rate in order to cope with demand.

This book documents the full scope of the world-wide Power Metal phenomenon, tracing the lineage of the bands that paved the way, the first 80s wave of bands, the stoic survivors, the new breed and the myriad spider web like side projects. All with exhaustive, unique histories and detailed discographies.

Paper covers, approx 450 pages £14.99 in UK

Rockdetector
A-Z of
THRASH METAL
Garry Sharpe-Young

ISBN 1–901447–09–X

THRASH METAL. At first mocked by the Rock traditionalists Thrash would swamp the hard 'n' heavy world propelling one of it's own - METALLICA, to the very pinnacle of Rock's elite.

In the early 80s Thrash breathed new life into the Rock scene providing older acts with a much needed kick. This new force opened the floodgates to armies of teens armed with flying Vs, bullet belts and a sense of purpose that would fuel genres such as THRASHCORE, CROSSOVER and TECHNICAL SPEED METAL. Without Thrash there would be no DEATH METAL, no BLACK METAL. That explosion of aggression has seen subsequent afterblasts, most recently in Europe and South America where there has been a genuine renaissance of Thrash Metal.

Without doubt Thrash Metal continues to make its mark in the biggest possible way. The 'big four' METALLICA, MEGADETH, ANTHRAX and SLAYER are all documented here in the greatest possible detail with full, up to the minute histories, exclusive photographs and global discographies. No stone is left unturned in pursuit of knowledge of ex-members, rare recordings and career milestones. The author has interviewed all these major acts. Indeed, he was the last journalist to interview Metallica's late Cliff Burton. The early days of Megadeth are straight from the mouth of Dave Mustaine.

Also covered are the legion of groundbreaking Bay Area acts such as METAL CHURCH, TESTAMENT, EXODUS, DEATH ANGEL and HIRAX. The European Thrash explosion of KREATOR, RAGE, DESTRUCTION, SODOM, GRAVE DIGGER and HELLOWEEN is also covered in frightening detail. The PAGAN THRASH of SABBAT, the avant garde eccentricity of CELTIC FROST and the FUNK THRASH of MORDED - it's all here. The second wave of Thrash with major artists such as SEPULTURA, PANTERA and MACHINE HEAD takes the genre right up to the new breed of Thrashers, now a truly world-wide phenomenon. All examined in depth.

Thrash Metal is not only alive, it is thriving. If you thought this rawest form of Heavy Metal was consigned to the past, this book will deliver a rude awakening! Read the book, buy the records and bang that head!!

Paper covers, 464 pages £14.99 in UK

www.cherryred.co.uk

Rockdetector
OZZY OSBOURNE
THE STORY OF THE OZZY OSBOURNE BAND
(AN UNOFFICIAL PUBLICATION)
Garry Sharpe-Young

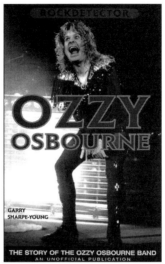

ISBN 1-901447-08-1

Until 1978 THE original and definitive Heavy Metal band BLACK SABBATH was fronted by the irrepressible Ozzy Osbourne. With Osbourne at the helm BLACK SABBATH sold tens of millions of albums. When he finally broke away to fly solo Ozzy would achieve the unthinkable. Not only would he deliver one of the seminal Rock records ever crafted to mark his resurrection but he also used it as a career-making catalyst that would see him trounce his former band mates and evolve into a cult icon.

Along the way Ozzy displayed an enviable knack of choosing a series of groundbreaking guitarists such as Randy Rhoads, Jake E. Lee and Zakk Wylde. There would also be the unsung heroes such as songwriter extraordinaire Bob Daisley and a series of world renowned bassists, drummers and keyboard players.

This then is the story of the Ozzy Osbourne band - in their own words and detailed exclusively here for the first time.

Chronicled with first-hand interviews, this is the real story of the first prototype Blizzard of Ozz band, how Ozzy met Randy Rhoads, the painful saga of Rhoads' replacement Bernie Tormé and the torturous audition processes for successive guitarists and drummers told by both successful and unsuccessful candidates.

The Ozzy Osbourne story - as told by Bob Daisley, Lee Kerslake, Tommy Aldridge, Bernie Tormé, Brad Gillis, Steve Vai, Phil Soussan, Carmine Appice and many, many more.

Garry Sharpe-Young has interviewed more than twenty Ozzy band members and associates solely for this work thus making it the most detailed account of Ozzy's career so far.

"Ozzy Osbourne's solo career would prove spectacular, bizarre and extremely lucrative…" ROUGH GUIDE TO ROCK

Paper covers 368 pages £14.99 in UK

www.cherryred.co.uk

Rockdetector
BLACK SABBATH
Garry Sharpe-Young

FORTHCOMING EARLY 2003

ISBN 1-901447-16-2

Over a full decade Black Sabbath had dominated Heavy Metal. As much as Led Zeppelin scorned the term, Black Sabbath embraced it. In an age of bona fide super-groups Sabbath were unquestionably the heaviest thing stalking the planet and quite remarkably had remained a solid unit where others around them suffered ongoing membership fall-outs and line-up re-incarnations. Tony Iommi, Geezer Butler, Ozzy Osbourne and Bill Ward had weathered internal storms just as ferocious as every other band out on the circuit but had remained resolute. They had conquered the globe, sold close to 50 million albums and without concession had not pulled back one iota from delivering absolute, pure Heavy Metal.

In 1977 the unthinkable happened. Ozzy Osbourne decamped. He would be lured back for one last album "Never Say Die", before flying solo, rapidly building a band unit that would equal the repute of the mothership. The Iommi / Butler / Ward triumvirate at first bounced back in quite spectacular fashion by re-inventing themselves courtesy of their new frontman, the highly gifted Ronnie James Dio. Two classic albums followed but then the picture shattered. For the next two decades Black Sabbath faltered on a rocky path between all too brief moments of genius and fallow desperation. Only Tony Iommi stuck to his guns, the lynchpin amidst a tangled web of chaos. A succession of vocalists took up the challenge- Ian Gillan, Jeff Fenholt, David Donato, Glenn Hughes, Ray Gillen, Tony Martin and Ronnie James Dio once again. Harried by the press at every turn, Tony Iommi nevertheless succeeded in breathing new life into Black Sabbath time and time again. With the band's back catalogue still in heavy demand, those albums crafted in these times of adversity are now recognised as some of Sabbath's finest moments and the huge array of players that travelled through the ranks is now a constant source of fascination and rumours for Sabbath fanatics. Here, for the very first time with exclusive interviews conducted for this book including ones with the late Ray Gillen and Cozy Powell as well as the highly controversial figure of Jeff Fenholt and mysterious Dave Donato, is the definitive account of those years. The auditioning, song writing and recording processes of albums such as "Born Again", "Eternal Idol" and "Seventh Star" are examined in depth making this the definitive account. Author Garry Sharpe-Young is editor in chief at www.rockdetector.com the world's biggest Rock devoted database.

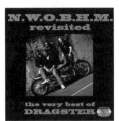

DRAGSTER
N.W.O.B.H.M. Revisited – The Very Best Of Dragster
So This Is England / Destiny / Heartbeat / Bite The Bullet / Ambitions / Mirror Image / Running / Here Comes The Weekend / You Win Again / Running (Version 2) / Bite The Bullet (Version 2) / Ambitions (Volume 2) / Running With The Pack / Until The Morning / Showtime / Action / I Didn't Know I Loved You / Hot legs / Hellraiser

A first time CD release for New Wave of British Heavy Metal legends Dragster. This 19 track compilation features all their fans favourites including "Bite The Bullet", "Running" and "Ambitions".

CDMETAL 17

GASKIN
End Of The World / No Way Out
Sweet Dream Maker / Victim Of The City / Despiser / Burning Alive / The Day Thou Gavest Lord Hath Ended / End Of The World / On My Way / Lonely Man / I'm No Fool / Handful Of Reasons / Dirty Money / Free Man / Just Like A Movie Star / Say Your Last Word / Broken Up / Ready For Love / Come Back To Me / High Crime Zone / Queen Of Flames / No Way Out

Gaskin were one of the most influential N.W.O.B.H.M. bands, to this day bands cite them as a major influence. In 1991 Lars Urich of Metallica included Gaskin on the "NWOBHM '79 Revisited" compilation he released. This double album on one CD features two extremely rare and collectable albums from the band. The original artwork is re-produced, with a full discography.

CDMETAL 6

THE HANDSOME BEASTS
Beastiality
Sweeties / David's Song / Breaker / One In A Crowd / Local Heroes / Another Day / Tearing Me Apart / High Speed / BONUS TRACKS: The Mark Of A Beast / All Riot Now / Sweeties (Single Version) / You're On Your Own

First time on CD for this legendary LP, originally issued as the first release by Wolverhampton based Heavy Metal Records. The original 9 track album has now been joined by four bonus cuts including the singles "All Riot Now" and "Sweeties" to give the definitive Handsome Beasts collection.

CDMETAL 5

MYTHRA
The Death & Destiny LP
Paradise / England / Warrior Of Time / Vicious Bastard / Heaven Lies Above / At Least They Tried / The Death Of A Loved One / The Age Of Machine / Death & Destiny / Killer / Overlord / UFO / Blue Acid

In their short-lived career at the start of the 1980's Mythra managed to gain themselves a reputation that now sees them as one of Britains Heavy Metal treasures. Cited as a 'revolutionary record' by Iron Pages' Matthias Mader this album includes tracks never released on CD format before.

CDMETAL 16

SAVAGE
Hyperactive
We Got The Edge / Eye For An Eye / Hard On Your Heels / Blind Hunger / Gonna Tear Your Heart Out / Stevies Vengeance / Cardiac / All Set To Sting / Keep It On Ice / BONUS TRACKS Runnin' Scared / She Didn't Need You / We Got The Edge (Single Version)

Savage are one of the leading cult bands of the whole New Wave Of British Heavy Metal movement that happened in the early eighties. This seminal album also includes the Mansfield based band's ultra rare three track 12" "We Got The Edge" as a bonus.

CDMETAL 10

WITCHFYNDE
The Best Of Witchfynde

Give 'Em Hell / Unto The Ages Of The Ages / Ready To Roll / Leaving Nadir / Getting' Heavy / Pay Now/ Love Later / Stage Fright / Wake Up Screaming / Moon Magic / In The Stars / The Devil's Playground / I'd Rather Go Wild / Cloak And Dagger / Cry Wolf / Stay Away / Fra Diabolo

Witchfynde was part of the New Wave Of British Heavy Metal of the early 80's that spawned the likes of Iron Maiden, Def Leppard and Judas Priest. Witchfynde still have a great significance on the later generations of Heavy Metal artists, Metallica and Paradise Lost regularly state the band as an influence. This CD includes 16 prime cuts that include the singles, "Give Em Hell", "In The Stars" and "I'd Rather Go Wild" as well as the best tracks from their rare LP's Give Em Hell, Stagefright and Cloak And Dagger. Iron Page's journalist Matthias Mader, an expert in the field has written the liner notes for this release.

CDMETAL 1

HEAVY METAL RECORDS
Singles Collection Vol. 1: Various Artists

THE HANDSOME BEASTS *All Riot Now / The Mark Of The Beast / Breaker / Crazy / One In A Crowd /* BUFFALO *Battle Torn Heroes / Women Of The Night /* DRAGSTER *Ambitions / Won't Bring You Back /* LAST FLIGHT *Dance To The Music / I'm Ready /* SPLIT BEAVER *Savage / Hound Of Hell /* SATANIC RITES *Live To Ride / Hit And Run*

This is a fifteen track round-up of the first batch of singles released by Heavy Metal Records, the legendary Metal label of the early 80's. Again a highly collectable and expensive package when originally released, with rare and collectable tracks from Buffalo, Dragster, Last Flight, Split Beaver, Satanic Rites and Handsome Beasts. This release appears on CD for the first time, with a full colour booklet that contains a full discography, detailed liner notes and pictures of each of the sleeves.

CDMETAL 3

NEW ELECTRIC WARRIORS
Various Artists

TURBO *Running /* BUFFALO *Battle Torn Heroes /* STREETFIGHTER *She's No Angel /* STORM TROOPER *Grind And Heat /* TAROT *Feel The Power /* BASTILLE *Hard Man /* OXYM *Hot Rain /* DAWN WATCHER *Firing On All Eight /* VARDIS *If I Were King /* SILVERWING *Rock And Roll Are Four Letter Words /* RHABSTALLION *Chain Reaction /* COLOSSUS *Holding Back Your Love /* JEDEDIAH STRUT *Workin' Nights /* WARRIOR *Still On The Outside / KOSH *The Hit /* RACE AGAINST TIME *Bedtime*

This was the first compilation album to feature bands from the N.W.O.B.H.M. Originally released 17 years ago, the album is now available for the first time on CD. Contributing bands include, Silverwing, Oxym, Buffalo and Streetfighter which was the first band to feature John Sykes of future Thin Lizzy- Whitesnake fame.

CDMETAL 13

N.W.O.B.H.M. METAL RARITIES VOL. 3
Various Artists

GIRLSCHOOL *Take It All Away / It Could Be Better* TWISTED ACE *I Won't Surrender / Firebird* SOLDIER *Sheraleer / Force* JAGUAR *Back Street Woman / Chasing The Dragon* DENIGH *No Way / Running* STATIC *Voice On The Line / Stealin'* SEVENTH SON *Metal To The Moon / Sound & Fury* WHITE LIGHTNING *This Poison Fountain / Hypocrite* DRAGONSLAYER *I Want Your Life / Satan Is Free / Broken Hearts*

The latest in the British Steel series, collecting many ultra rare single releases from the late 70's/ early 80's New Wave Of British Heavy Metal movement, most of which have never appeared on CD before. Vol. 3 includes bands such as Twisted Ace, Soldier and Jaguar, plus the very first single by Girlschool.

CDMETAL 14

ROXCALIBUR
Various Artists

BLACK ROSE *No Point Runnin'/ Ridin' High* BRANDS HATCH *Brands Hatch/ No Return* BATTLEAXE *Burn This Town/ Battleaxe* SATAN *Oppression/ The Executioner* MARAUDER *Battlefield/ Woman Of The Night* UNTER DEN LINDEN *Wings Of Night/ Man At The Bottom* SKITZOFRENIK *Exodus/ Keep Right On.*

Originally issued via Guardian Records in 1982, all fourteen cuts are unique to this album which gathered together some of the New Wave of British Heavy Metal scenes rising stars and includes contributions from Black Rose, Marauder, Battleaxe and Skitzofrenik.

CDMETAL 15

CHERRY RED BOOKS

We are always looking for interesting books to publish.
They can be either new manuscripts or re-issues of deleted books.
If you have any good ideas then please
get in touch with us.

CHERRY RED BOOKS
a division of Cherry Red Records Ltd.
Unit 17, Elysium Gate West,
126-128 New King's Road
London SW6 4LZ

E-mail: iain@cherryred.co.uk

Web: www.cherryred.co.uk

NOTES

NOTES

NOTES

NOTES